Wellington's Men Remembered

Wellington's Men Remembered

A Register Of Memorials To Soldiers
Who Served In The Peninsular War
And At Waterloo 1808 – 1815

Volume II

M – Z

Janet and David Bromley

Foreword By His Grace The Duke Of Wellington

First published in Great Britain in 2015 by
The Praetorian Press
an imprint of
Pen & Sword Books Ltd
47 Church Street
Barnsley
South Yorkshire
S70 2AS

ISBN 978 1 84884 750 7

A CIP catalogue record for this book is
available from the British Library

Typeset in Sabon by
Malcolm Bates, Auldgirth, Dumfriesshire

Printed and bound in Malta by
Gutenberg Press Ltd

Pen & Sword Books Ltd incorporates the Imprints of Pen & Sword Aviation, Pen & Sword Family History, Pen & Sword Maritime, Pen & Sword Military, Pen & Sword Discovery, Wharncliffe Local History, Wharncliffe True Crime, Wharncliffe Transport, Pen & Sword Select, Pen & Sword Military Classics, Leo Cooper, The Praetorian Press, Remember When, Seaforth Publishing and Frontline Publishing

For a complete list of Pen & Sword titles please contact
PEN & SWORD BOOKS LIMITED
47 Church Street, Barnsley, South Yorkshire, S70 2AS, England
E-mail: enquiries@pen-and-sword.co.uk
Website: www.pen-and-sword.co.uk

Contents

FOREWORD BY

HIS GRACE THE DUKE OF WELLINGTON
KG., LVO., OBE., MC., DL

Some twelve years or so ago the Association of Friends of the Waterloo Committee conceived the idea of a "Register of Memorials" to record the existence of over 3000 memorials to British and Allied Soldiers who fought in the Peninsular War and at Waterloo. These exist in no less than 24 countries in the world. The concept was originally initiated by Bob Elmer of Australia but was taken over by Janet and David Bromley ten years ago.

Many memorials are now lost due to the closure of churches, decay, age and the removal of headstones to ensure ease of maintenance for churchyards and cemeteries. "Wellington's Men Remembered" will provide a permanent record of the memorials to so many men who served in the defeat of Napoleon two hundred years ago.

I commend the huge amount of time and effort dedicated to the research by Janet and David Bromley and also more than 400 contributors who have helped with the project for so many years.

Wellington

6th April 2011

"How sleep the brave, who sink to rest,
By all their country's wishes blest"

William Collins, *Ode written in 1796*

Dedicated To All The
Peninsular And Waterloo Men
Who Lie In
Unmarked Graves

Introduction

Publication of Vol. II of *Wellington's Men Remembered* completes the research recording memorials to over 3,150 men who served in the Peninsular War and at Waterloo together with 150 regimental and battlefield memorials in 28 countries worldwide, many supported with photographs. Some men are represented by multiple memorials in different geographical locations.

Most have been found on site visits. Others which have not yet been found or are no longer extant have been traced by means of documentary research in libraries and archives and have been recorded from published memorial inscriptions. Many of the latter represent memorials that have long been lost, others still remain to be visited and recorded. Some men have been entered into the Register on the strength of church burial records.

Entries are recorded following the rules laid out in the Introduction to Vol. I. Officers and men are listed under the name, rank and regiment they held in 1815 or earlier if they served in the Peninsula but were not at Waterloo. In Vol. II. Two the names with the prefix Mac Mc and M[c] are filed in the name sequence as if they are all written as *Mac, so McNair comes after Macnab*. As the illustrations file is computer generated this arrangement is not possible. Here all the Macs come first and the Mcs follow after Maxwell, McCreagh comes after Maxwell.

Ranks and details of service are recorded from various sources, including the *Challis Index*, the *Army List*, *Hart's Army List*, regimental histories and the *London Gazette*. Comparison of data from these various sources reveals that records of dates of service and appointments vary slightly. Every effort has been made to ensure accuracy, but in a minority of cases it has been difficult to reconcile conflicting records. This applies particularly to ranks from the eighteenth century.

Full inscriptions of memorials are recorded, compacted to reduce space and set in capitals for consistency of presentation. The actual layout of style can normally be seen in the photograph. Locations of memorials are included in the heading to Church, Cemetery, Town, County and Country for overseas records. In the case of memorials to families, on which the soldier is mentioned together with other family members, only an extract of the relevant part is normally included. Omissions are identified by (..............) and refer to other members of the family or unrelated detail. These can be seen from the photograph.

Family relationships between men are recorded, with reference to the rank that they held at the time of Waterloo or at the end of their Peninsular service if they did not serve at Waterloo, in the same way as ranks are recorded in the heading. Memorials to wives which refer to their husband are not included unless the memorial includes a specific note of her husband's service record in addition to his rank and regiment.

Each entry comprises:

Full name
Rank and Regiment
Location of memorial and indication of a photograph in the DVD
Ranks and dates of appointment
Service in the Peninsula and at Waterloo
Other service records before 1808 and after 1815
Honours medal and awards
Family links
Bibliographical references

Where a memorial inscription has been recorded from a published source and the grave has not been found, the details are included in the form in the published list of memorial inscriptions, and indicated by the abbreviation (M.I.). These are shown within "........". Such memorial inscriptions are sometimes abstracts of the full memorial record as they were produced mainly for genealogical research.

A small number of memorials which indicate presence in the Peninsular War and Waterloo have been omitted if it has not been possible to authenticate the claims made on the memorial inscription. These will be subject to further research and incorporated into a Supplement contained within Volume Two.

The technical description of memorials has follows a simplified version of the classification in *Recording and Analysing Graveyards* by Harold Mytum published in 2000. The following broad classification has been adopted:

Altar Box/Chest tomb	Brass memorial tablet	Column
Cross	Headstone	Ledger stone
Low monument	Mausoleum	Memorial tablet
Monument	Obelisk	Pedestal tomb
Sarcophagus	Statue	Table tomb

If a search failed to locate a memorial which has been traced from a memorial inscription it is marked as 'No longer extant'. It is always possible that a search has failed to reveal the memorial or it was not found because it is seriously eroded or buried beneath dense and impenetrable undergrowth. Other memorials have been destroyed as a result of war damage, the clearance of churchyards, or decay caused by weathering and vandalism. Some headstones have been arranged around cemetery walls or used as paving stones in order to ease ground maintenance.

Generally a memorial tablet will be found inside a church, while graves and headstones will obviously be located in the churchyard or cemetery. Many memorials, particularly gravestones carved in soft stone such as sandstone, have deteriorated over the years, and it has not always been possible to identify the entire inscription. Where this is the case, all the words identifiable have been included, and missing words or letters marked ********.

Where there is documentary evidence of the precise location of the burial place of a man, but no evidence of the existence of a grave or memorial, an entry is occasionally made in the form of 'buried at' and the grave number recorded. In some cases monumental masons have made errors of spelling, and these have been reproduced as they appear on the memorial.

Photographs of memorials appear on a DVD inserted into each volume and are noted after the location of the memorial. In the case of regimental and battlefield memorials, photographs will appear on the DVD in Volume Two.

Unfortunately it has not been possible to obtain permission to take photographs or receive permission to reproduce a photograph for copyright reasons in a small number of cases.

Over the period of the survey, the quality of cameras has improved significantly. The photographic skills of contributors and their equipment has also improved over the years. Consequently the photographs reproduced in the illustrations database vary widely in quality from high-definition digital images to poor quality camera images taken on less sophisticated equipment. All have been included as representing the best available image of the memorial. Where better images become available, they will be added to the ongoing database.

Bibliographical references are included for each man where they have been found, including monographs, biographies from the *Dictionary of National Biography* and other national biographies, *Royal Military Calendar*, *Household Brigade Journal*, *United Service Journal* (later *United Service Magazine*), *Gentleman's Magazine*, *Annual Register*, and regimental histories. Occasionally obituaries published in newspapers are noted. Bibliographical references of a more general nature which are not specific to an individual will appear in the Bibliography in Volume Two.

The Place Index records memorials under the name of the county in England and Scotland, as found in contemporary published gazetteers of the mid-nineteenth century. The exception is Cumbria, which includes places previously in Lancashire, Cumberland and Westmoreland. *Fullerton's Parliamentary Gazetteer - 1845* is used as the definitive source for English and Welsh place names. In Scotland, Fullerton's *Topographical and Historical Gazetteer of Scotland* 1842 and for Ireland, *Fullerton's Parliamentary Gazetteer 1844-45* have been used for verification. Many towns have been transferred from county to county over the years. For instance, Slough, now in Berkshire, was previously in Buckinghamshire, and there are many examples of this kind. If in doubt, it is recommended to check adjacent counties.

A Supplement contains records of men with surnames A – L which have been obtained since Volume One was published. The Addenda contains additional information for some of the entries in A – L received since publication of Vol. I. Two new sections record Battlefield memorials arranged alphabetically under place and Regimental Memorials arranged under the regimental name.

Another section is devoted to the King's German Legion which incorporates KGL entries in Vols I and II including all names on the memorial at La Haye Sainte. Memorials to men who survived the war and are buried in Germany and regimental memorials to those who died in battle have been supplied by Georg Baumann of Hanover who has researched the Royal Hanoverian Army and the King's German Legion for many years. German names have been recorded under the German variation of the name, although anglicised versions of their names also appear on other memorials such as the regimental memorials in Biarritz.

The editors acknowledge that there are inevitably inconsistencies in the text caused by transcription and typing errors, and the problem of transcribing contributions from many diverse sources and information supplied in photographic form in various levels of quality.

We are grateful for all the help and encouragement that we have received from family and friends and the many members of the Waterloo Association and others who have given so much of their time to locate and photograph memorials for us.

Janet and David Bromley

Abbreviations

AAG	Assistant Adjutant General
Asst	Assistant
ADC	Aide de Camp
Adjt	Adjutant
AG	Adjutant General
Bart	Baronet
Bt	Brevet
AQMG	Assistant Quartermaster General
CB	Companion of the Order of the Bath
CMG	Companion of the Order of St Michael and St George
CO	Commanding Officer
Com	Commissary
DAAG	Deputy Assistant Adjutant General
DAG	Deputy Adjutant General
DAQMG	Deputy Assistant Quartermaster General
DQMG	Deputy Quartermaster General
EOPS	Engaged on a Particular Service
GCB	Knight Grand Cross of the Order of the Bath
GCH	Knight Grand Cross of Hanover
GCMG	Knight Grand Cross of the Order of St Michael and St George
GCMM	Grand Cross of the Royal Order of Military Merit of France
GCSI	Knight Grand Commander of the Star of India
GOC	General Officer Commanding
KB	Knight Companion of the Order of the Bath (pre-1815)
KC	Knight of the Crescent
KCB	Knight Commander of the Order of the Bath
KCH	Knight Commander of the Royal Hanoverian Guelphic Order
KG	Knight of the Garter
KGL	King's German Legion
KH	Knight of the Royal Hanoverian Guelphic Order
KMB	Knight of Maximilian of Bavaria
KMM	Military Order of Merit of Prussia
KMT	Knight of Maria Theresa of Austria
KOYLI	King's Own Yorkshire Light Infantry
KP	Knight of the Order of St Patrick
KSA	Knight of St Anne of Russia
KSF	Knight of St Ferdinand
KSG	Knight of St George of Russia
KTS	Knight of the Tower and Sword of Portugal
KW	Knight of William of Holland
MGS	Military General Service medal
MI	Memorial inscription
MKW	Military Knight of Windsor
NCO	Non Commissioned Officer
NGS	Naval General Service medal
Obit	Obituary
OC	Officer Commanding
PC	Privy Councillor
QMG	Quartermaster General
RA	Royal Artillery
RE	Royal Engineers
RHA	Royal Horse Artillery
RHG	Royal Horse Guards
RN	Royal Navy

Acknowledgements

His Grace the Duke of Wellington, Jack Abernethy, Henry and Catherine Adams, Marmaduke Alderson, Kerrie Alexander, Robert Allard, Charles Anderson, Rachel Andrews, Roger Ansell, Peter Applebee (Adelaide Northern Districts Family History Group), José Manuel Ariza, Garry Ashby, C. E. John Ashton, Wendy Atkin, Linda Attrell, Australian Cemetery Index, Terry Babbage, John Backhouse, Ken A. Baddeley, Diane and Keith Baines, Derek Baker, Joe Baker, Mrs M. Baker, D. and M. Ball, Derek Barber, R. W. Barber, the Revd Lee Bastion, Georg Baumann, Cynthia and Roger Bayliss, Bedfordshire Libraries, Eva Beech, Christopher Bell, Phil Bendall, Marcus de la Poer Beresford, Alice Berkeley, Paul J. Bennett, Stephen Best, Tony Bibby, Tony and Jill Birch, Gillian Blake, Peter Blakebrough, Frank Bland, Allan Boldero, Michael Bond, Alison Boreham, Chris Bray, Brian Bridges, Michael Broadhouse, Australian Cemeteries Index, Derek Broadhurst, Stephen Bromley, Brompton Cemetery, Brookwood Cemetery Society, Peter and Audrey Brown, Kathleen Brown, Freda Browne, Andrew Browning, Suzanne Brunt, Norman H. Brunyee, Paul F. Brunyee, Philip Brunyee, Michael Bryant, Brenda J. Buchanan, Buckinghamshire Libraries, D. and M. Buckley, Father Ian Bullock, Alan Bullwinkle, George Burley, Ron Burrows, Stephen Callaghan, Barbara Capel, Count Emo Capodilista, Barry Cargill, Carlisle Reference Library, David Carpenter, Jo Carter, Frances Carver, Peter Catley, R. Gordon Champ, Barrie and Margaret Chapman, Alain Chappet, John Checketts, John A. Christie, Rupert Clark, Sidney J. Clark, Frank A. O. Clarke, John Clarke, Clash-of-Steel.com, John Clements, Bridget Clifford, Delphine Coleman, William Colfer, Rosemary Collins, Reg W. Connor, Tim Cooke, Graeme Cooper, William and Jenifer Cordeaux, Robin E. Cousins, Lynn Craig, Malcolm Craig, Bruce Cripps, J. Barry Crisp, Jonathan Crook, Allen Crosbie, Michael Crumplin, Des Cummins, Raymond Cusick, Stephen Daglish, Margaret Daniel, John Darwent, Bruce Davies, Eddy Davis, Catherine Delahunty, Margaret Denton, Elizabeth Deverell, Elizabeth Dineley, Carole and John Divall, Nimrod Dix, Peter Donnelly, Jean Downer, John Downham, Robert Dows-Miller, Derek Drake, E. J. Draper, Andrew Driver, Duke of Wellington's Regimental Museum and Archives, Robin Dunbar, Dundee Library and Information Services, Michael B. Dunn, Craig Durham, Paddy Earp, Stuart Eastwood, Gabrielle and Han Ebke, Steven Ede-Borrett, Dudley Edwards, Roger Edwards, John Ellis, Bob Elmer, Otto Ludwig Engelbrecht, Michael and Wendy Ethelston, George Evelyn, Stuart Fagan, Jean Fanthorpe, Gary Farmer, Susan M. Farrington, Leo Favret, Dick Ferguson. Dan FitzGerald, Scott Flaving, Ian Fletcher, the Revd Stephen and Will Fletcher, Andrew Floyd, Peter Foden, John Foreman, S. L. Forster, Charles Freemantle, Friends of Highgate Cemetery, Friends of Kensal Green Cemetery, Friends of Nunhead Cemetery, Friends of Sheffield General Cemetery, Friends of Southampton Old Cemetery, Friends of York Cemetery, Patricia Frykberg, Tom Fulton, Jane Furlong, Gail Fynes, Ted Gale, Basil Garratt, Steve Geary, Caroline Gerard, Lucien Gerke, William Gervais, Alan Gibb, John Gierke, Derek Glen, Gareth Glover, J. Godley, Richard Goodridge, Kevin Gorman, Lou Gotfreund, Mary Gough, Russell Granger, Jim Grant, Peter Gratton, the Revd Alastair Gray, Ken Gray, Barry Greenwood, Barry Gregson, John Grehan, Ieuan Griffiths, Anne Grimshaw, Colette Grosjean, Guards Museum, Joan and Prodip Guha, Richard and Trisha Gunn, Rosemary Hales, Halifax Public Library Nova Scotia, Roger Hall, Sandy and Elizabeth Hall, Yvonne Hall, David Hallewell, William Hallewell, Nick Hallidie, Clive Hamilton, David Hammersley, Peter Hammersley, William Hanna, Clare Harding, Malcolm Harper, David and Hilary Harris, Hank Harris, Mrs Hattrell, Shirley M. Hay, Frank Haylett, Philip Haythornthwaite, Peter Helmore, Dave Hemingway, Rod Henley, Andrew Hepworth, George Hewitt, Dennis Hill, Malcolm Hill, Richard Hill, Derek Hindle, Peter Hoare, Alan and Natasha Holliday, Ellie and Chris Hollings, Henning Homann, David Hooper, David Horn, Ben Hughes (author of *Conquer or Die*), John R. Hughes, Merrion Hughes, Ed Humphreys, Katie Hyde, Mike Hyde, Imperial War Museum, Dennis and Denise Ireland, Cheryl and Michel Itthurraide, Alan Jackson, Janice Jackson, Jocelyn Jackson, Judith Jackson, Dr Gordon James, R. H. James, Jarrold Publishing, Canon Johnson, Mrs B. Johnson, Jane

Johnson, Janice Johnson, Bruce Jones, Colin Jones, Derek and Jean Jones, Jane Jones, Louise Jones, S. Jones, Sean Jones, Trevor Jones, Ronald Kay, Andrew Kemel, Kensal Green Cemetery staff, Keswick Computer Services, Mrs Ketley, Glen Kilday, J. Bishop King, Robin and Sarah King, E. L. Kirby, Chris Kirk, Manfred Knigge, Alan Lagden, Elizabeth and Jim Laidlaw, Paul Lanagan, Gordon Lane, Victoria Lendrum, Larry Leone, Last Post Fund Montreal, Rose La Terriere, Bernard Lavell, Edgar Lawrence, Jim Lees, Miss D. G. Le Faye, Leona Lefoley, Victoria Lendrum, John Lester, M. I. Lindley, Nick Lipscombe, Bill Little, Duncan Lodge, Bob Longden, Francisco José Martinez López, Santiago López, Patricia Luxford, Maurice McCabe, Alison McCall, Terry McCabe, Joanne McCarthy, Craig McCauley, J. M. McClaren, Jean McCulloch, Anthony McIntosh, David McKinna, Michael MacMahon, Michael Maguire, John Macro, Elizabeth Manneke, Roger Manning, J. David Markham, Angela Martin, Miguel Angel Largo Martin, Robin Martin, Helen Meddings, Gloria Miles, Brian Milhench, Richard Miller, Sir Stephen Miller, Suzi Millar, Bob Millward, Colin Milne, David and Maureen Milner, Richard Milsom, Yves Moerman, Brian Money, Judith Monk, John Montgomery (RUSI), Mike Moody, John Morewood, William Morison, Tony Morisset, Alan Morley, Clive Morris, Dorothy and Ron Morris, Brenda Morrison, Bob Moulder, Maria Murphy, Norman Murphy, Gerald Napier, National Trust of Australia, Tony Negus, Niagara Historical Society and Museum, Ontario Canada, Dean and Chapter of Newcastle upon Tyne Cathedral, Alistair Nichols, Bob Nicholls, Thomas Nielsen, Bill Norman, North Staffordshire Victorian Military History and Research Society, John O'Brien, John Ogden, Keith Oliver, Orders & Medals Society, Oxfordshire and Buckinghamshire Light Infantry Museum, Julia Page, Jane and Gary Parker, Michael Parroy, Steven Payne, Anne Pealing, Johanna Peebes, Pen and Sword Ltd, Dennis Perriam, Perth and Kinross Heritage Trust, Doug Peters, Audrey Phillips, Ben Phillips, Gill Picken, Ron Pigram, C. A. Pirie, Fulvio Poli, David Poole, Portsmouth Napoleonic Society, Victor Powell, Terry Pratt, Isobel Pridmore, Andrew Prince, John Provan Christine Pullen, Emma, Guy, James and Katharine Purchon, Queen's Lancashire Regimental Museum, Frances Radley, Mrs V. H. Ramage, Helen and John Ratcliffe, Frederick and Joyce Ratcliffe, George and Susan Ratcliffe, Ken Ray, Dinah Read, Redcoats website, Tony Redsell, Wilson Reid, Arie Rens, Fiona Reynoldson, Nettie Rice, Colin Richardson, Charles Robinson, Mr and Mrs Ryder-Richardson, Paul Ridgley, Cynthia and Derek Ringrose, Charles Robinson, Hilary Robinson, Mark Robinson, Michael Robinson, Peter Robinson, Peter Robson, David Rogers, Ken A. Rowley, K. Rowley-Brecon, Elizabeth Roy, Royal Green Jackets Museum, John Rumsby, Ailsa Rushbrooke, His Grace the Duke of Rutland, Trevor Rutter, Charles Sale, Salford Local History Library, Waltraud von Salzen, Chris Sanham, Mrs E. Saunders, Tanya Schmoller, Scots Guards Archives, Valerie Scott, Ken Sears, Bill Sidgwick, Terry Senior, John Sewell, T. Sewell, Chris Shaw, George Shaw, Matthew Shaw (Brompton Cemetery), Maya Sheridan, R. J. M. Sinnett, Geoffrey Skeet, Anne Slack, Iain Small, Ken Smallwood, Nicol Smith, Peter Smith, Bryan Somers, Alan Sorenson (Libraries Northern Ireland), John and Jeremy Spikens, Barry Stephenson, the Revd Brian H. Stevens, Peter and Judith Stevens, Theo Steward, F. H. Stirling, Klaus Stolze, Alison J. Stratton, Beverley and Gordon Stroud, Klaus Stüber, Duncan Sutton (Surrey History Centre), G. Symes, Michael Symington, Clive Symons, Lawrence Taylor, Patricia A. Taylor, Liz Teall, Richard Tennant, Ron and Margaret Thompson, Peter G. Thompson, Ray Thorburn, Carys Thorn, Peter Thorn, Dominique Timmermans, Alan Tod, Thelma Todd (Institute of Directors), Malcolm Toes, Gabor Toth (Wellington City Library, New Zealand), Robert Tripp, Paul Tritton, C. L. Tweedale, Claude Van Hoorebeeck, David Verran, Waltraud von Salzen, Mr and Mrs Waddelow, Martin Wade, Alan Walker, Valerie M. Walker, Douglas Walshe, John Walters, Karen Walton, P. W. Ward, Helen, Philip, Nicholas and Edmund Wareham, Robert Wareham, William Warre, Winifred Waterall, Dr A. W. Webb, Sir Evelyn Webb-Carter, Lady Jane Wellesley, Westminster Abbey Dean and Chapter, John White, Stephen White, Betty Whitehouse, Mr and Mrs D. A. Whitehouse, Libby and Rob Whitethread, the Revd David Whiteman, Ruth Whittle, Mark Whyman, Wikimedia Commons, Peter Wigan, Stuart Wilkinson, Tony Wilks, Sheila and Martin Wills, Doug Wilson, Edward and Primrose Wilson, Jennifer Wilson, Tom Winks, C. John Wood, Ron Woollacott, C. S. Worthington, Ken Wray, Christine Wright, Evan Wright, Philip Wright, Paul and Ann Wylie, Alan, Ian and Jane Yonge, Colin Yorke, Frank and Joan Young, Geoffrey Young.

Register of Names

ALL NAMES BEGINNING MAC ARE INTERFILED WITH NAMES BEGINNING MC

MACANDREW, John

Assistant Surgeon. 9th Regiment of Light Dragoons.
Tomb in partly railed enclosure: Ryde Cemetery, Isle of Wight. Old Cemetery Section B Plot 85–87. (Photograph)

IN MEMORY OF / SIR JOHN MACGREGOR MD KCB / DIED JAN 13TH 1866 AGED 71 YEARS.

Hospital Mate 27 Jun 1809 – Feb 1810. Asst Surgeon 9th Lt Dragoons 15 Feb 1810. Half pay 1 Jun 1818. Asst Surgeon 1st Foot 28 Sep 1826. Surgeon 14th Foot 30 Apr 1829. Surgeon 78th Foot 15 Feb 1833. Surgeon 40th Foot 29 Jul 1836. Staff Surgeon 7 Jul 1846. Deputy Inspector General 21 Oct 1853. Inspector General 28 Nov 1856.

Served in the Peninsula Jul 1811 – Apr 1813. Present at Alba de Tormes. Also served at Walcheren 1809, India 1839 (present in the Afghanistan expedition 1841–1842), Gwalior 1843 (present at Maharajapore), Ceylon 1848 (present at the Matale Rebellion) and India 1857 (present in the the Indian Mutiny at Delhi and Lucknow). Retired 31 Dec 1858. CB 1858. KCB 1859. Honorary Physician to the Queen 1859. Received award for distinguished and meritorious service 1859. Changed his name by Royal Licence from Macandrew to MacGregor 1863.

MACARA, Sir Robert

Lieutenant Colonel. 42nd (Royal Highland) Regiment of Foot.
Memorial monument: Waterloo Cairn, Kinrara Estate, Torr Alvie Hill, Invernesshire, Scotland. (On private land). (Photograph)

TO / THE MEMORY OF / SIR ROBERT MACARA / OF / THE 42ND REGIMENT, OR, ROYAL HIGHLANDERS, / COLONEL JOHN CAMERON / OF / THE 92ND REGIMENT, OR, GORDON HIGHLANDERS / AND / THEIR BRAVE COUNTRYMEN / WHO GLORIOUSLY FELL AT THE BATTLE OF / WATERLOO / IN JUNE 1815 / ERECTED BY / THE MOST NOBLE MARQUIS OF HUNTLY / AUGUST 16TH 1815.

Capt 42nd Foot 1802. Major 14 Nov 1805. Bt Lt Colonel 1 Jan 1812. Lt Colonel 16 Apr 1812.

Served in the Peninsula Apr 1812 – Apr 1814. Present at Salamanca, Burgos, Pyrenees, Nivelle, Nive, Orthes and Toulouse where he was severely wounded. The regiment lost 84 officers and men killed and 349 wounded. Gold Cross for Pyrenees, Nivelle, Nive, Orthes and Toulouse. KCB 2 Jan 1815. Present at Quatre Bras where he commanded the 42nd Foot. During the battle the 42nd Foot and the 44th Foot were attacked by French cavalry, Macara gave the order to form square but the French Lancers were on them before the rear file had closed up. Macara was left outside the square but he gave the order to fire and was wounded by his own men. As he was being carried off the field he was attacked again by the Lancers and killed. Macara had trained to be a surgeon and qualified for the post with the East India Company. From 1782–1802 he was in India employed as a surgeon in native wars. He preferred the life of a soldier and in 1802 purchased a Captaincy in the 42nd Foot with the money he had saved in India. In 1808 the 2nd Battalion of the 42nd was sent to the Peninsula and the 1st Battalion was sent to Walcheren but Macara was left behind in Ireland. Not until Apr 1812 did he go on active service at the advanced age of 53.

McARTHUR, Charles
Lieutenant. 79th (Cameron Highlanders) Regiment of Foot.
Ledger stone: Chapel Yard Cemetery, Inverness, Scotland. (M.I.)

"TO THE MEMORY OF LIEU^{T} CHARLES MCARTHUR, LATE OF THE 79TH REG^{T} OF FOOT, WATERLOO OFFICER, WHO DIED 25TH NOV^{R} 1846, AGED 70. THIS TRIBUTE OF AFFECTIONATE REMEMBRANCE IS PLACED HERE BY HIS WIDOW ELIZABETH CAMPBELL, WHO DIED ON THE 20TH FEBRUARY 1867, AGED 84; ...."

Volunteer 79th Foot. Ensign 9 Nov 1809. Lt 17 Oct 1811. Lt 2nd Royal Veteran Battalion 24 Feb 1820.
Served in the Peninsula Sep 1813 – Apr 1814. Present at Nivelle, Nive and Toulouse (wounded). Present at Quatre Bras where he was severely wounded. Also served at Walcheren 1809 as a Volunteer with the 79th Foot. Retired in 1821.

MACARTHUR, Edward
Lieutenant. 39th (Dorsetshire) Regiment of Foot.
Obelisk: Brompton Cemetery, London. (Grave number BR 66467). (Photograph)

LIEUTENANT GENERAL / SIR EDWARD MACARTHUR / KCB / COLONEL 100TH FOOT / DIED 4TH JANUARY 1872 / AGED 83. / WAS PRESENT AT / CORUNNA / VITTORIA NIVELLE / THE PYRENEES NIVE / ORTHES / AND TOULOUSE.

Bust: St John's Churchyard, Parramatta, Australia. (Photograph)

IN MEMORY OF/ LIEU^{T} GENERAL SIR EDWARD MACARTHUR K.C.B. / ELDEST SON OF / JOHN MACARTHUR ESQUIRE / OF / CAMDEN & PARRAMATTA / DIED 4TH JAN^{RY} 1872 / ERECTED BY HIS / WIDOW

Ensign 60th Foot 27 Oct 1808. Lt 39th Foot 6 Jul 1809. Capt 19th Foot 8 Feb 1821. Major 10 Jun 1826. Bt Lt Colonel 23 Nov 1841. Bt Colonel 20 Jun 1854. Major General 26 Oct 1858. Lt General 14 Jan 1866.
Served in the Peninsula with $2/60^{th}$ Oct 1808 – Jan 1809 and $1/39^{th}$ Nov 1811 – Apr 1814. Present at Corunna, Vittoria, Pyrenees, Nivelle, Nive, Garris, Orthes, Aire and Toulouse. Served with the Army of Occupation 1815. CB. Also served in North America 1814, Australia 1824 (his proposals for establishing a colonial militia were rejected by the Governor). On his return to England he always advocated Australian affairs. His early childhood was spent in Australia as his parents emigrated there in 1790. Served in Ireland 1837 (AAG). Returned to Australia 1851 (Deputy Adjutant General in Sydney). Went with Major General Nickle, the Commander-in-Chief to the Eureka stockade to diffuse the miners' rebellion. On death of Nickle became Commander of Forces in Australia 1855. Returned to England 1860. MGS medal for Corunna, Vittoria, Pyrenees, Nivelle, Nive, Orthes and Toulouse. KCB. Colonel 100th Foot 28 Sep 1862. Wrote two books on emigration to Australia, *Colonial Policy of 1840 and 1841 as illustrated by the Governor's Despatches,* 1841 and *Brief Remarks on Colonization,* 1846.
REFERENCE: Dictionary of National Biography. Dictionary of Australian Biography.

MACAWAN, James see MACOWEN, James

McBARNETT, William
Lieutenant. 79th (Cameron Highlanders) Regiment of Foot.
Named on the Memorial: St Andrew's Church (now Musée Historique), Biarritz, France. (Photograph)

Promoted from the ranks. Ensign 24 Apr 1805. Lt 1 Jan 1807. Captain 19 May 1813.

Served in the Peninsula Aug 1808 – Jan 1809 and Jan 1810 – Apr 1814. Present at Corunna, Cadiz, Busaco, Foz d'Arouce, Fuentes d'Onoro, Salamanca, Burgos, Nivelle, Nive and Toulouse where he was severely wounded 10 Apr 1814 and died from his wounds 17 Apr 1814. Also served in Sweden 1808 and Walcheren 1809.

MACBEAN, Alexander
Lieutenant. 2nd Battalion Light Infantry, King's German Legion.
Headstone: Rothiemurchus Churchyard, Speyside, Invernesshire, Scotland. (Photograph)

IN LOVING MEMORY OF / ALEXANDER McBEAN, LIEUT 2ND BATTALION LIGHT INFANTRY / K.G.L. DIED AT AUCHTERBLAIR, 24TH AUGT 1850, AGED 64 YEARS.

Ensign 28 Apr 1813. Lt 27 Nov 1813.
Served in the Peninsula Nov 1813 – Apr 1814. Present at Nivelle, Nive (wounded 9 Dec 1813), St Etienne and Bayonne. Also served in the Netherlands 1814–1815.

MACBEAN, Forbes
2nd Captain. Royal Artillery.
Headstone: St Cuthbert's Churchyard, Kirkleatham, Yorkshire. (Plot No 326). (Photograph)

IN MEMORY OF / COLONEL FORBES MACBEAN, / ROYAL ARTILLERY / WHO DIED AT KIRKLEATHAM ON THE / 10TH JUNE 1853, / AGED 64 YEARS. / ....

Memorial tablet: St Cuthbert's Church, Kirkleatham, Yorkshire. (Photograph)

SACRED / TO THE MEMORY / OF / COLONEL FORBES MACBEAN / ROYAL ARTILLERY / WHO DIED AT KIRKLEATHAM / ON 10TH JUNE 1853 / AGED 64 YEARS. / ....

2nd Lt 15 Sep 1804. 1st Lt 20 May 1805. 2nd Capt 20 Dec 1814. Capt 22 Mar 1829. Bt Major 10 Jan 1837. Bt Lt Colonel 16 Aug 1839. Lt Colonel 23 Nov 1841. Bt Colonel 11 Nov 1851.
Served in the Peninsula Aug 1808 – Jan 1809. Present at Corunna. Present at Waterloo in Captain J. Sinclair's Brigade. Also served at Copenhagen 1807, Sweden 1808 and Walcheren 1809 (present at the siege of Flushing) and Canada (present in the Canadian uprising of 1837–1838, he served at St Eustache and Prescott, receiving the thanks of the Lieutenant Governor and was awarded a Bt Lieutenant Colonelcy). MGS medal for Corunna. Retired on full pay 1 Apr 1844. Brother of 1st Lt Archibald MacBean Royal Artillery, Capt Frederick MacBean 6th Foot and Major William MacBean Staff Appointment in Spain and Portugal.

MACBEAN, William
Major. Staff Appointment in Spain and Portugal not holding a Regimental Commission.
Named on the Memorial tablet: Badajoz Wall, British Cemetery, Elvas, Portugal. (Photograph)

Ensign 6th Foot Feb 1796. Lt Oct 1796. Capt 25 Oct 1804. Bt Major 16 Feb 1809. Bt Lt Colonel 30 May 1811. Lt Colonel 100th Foot Dec 1815. Bt Colonel 19 Jul 1821. Major General 22 Jul 1830. Lt General 23 Nov 1841. Portuguese Army: Lt Colonel 19th Line 25 Mar 1809. Colonel 24th Line 5 Feb 1812.
Served in the Peninsula with 6th Foot Aug 1808 – Jan 1809. With Portuguese Army Mar 1809 – Feb 1813 and May 1813 – Apr 1814 (O/c 9 Portuguese Brigade Oct 1813 – Apr 1814). One of the officers chosen to train the Portuguese Army. Present at Rolica, Vimeiro, Corunna, Busaco, Lamego (severely wounded 30 Dec 1810), Salamanca, San Sebastian (Mentioned in Beresford's Despatches), Bidassoa, Nivelle, Nive (Mentioned in Beresford's Despatches), Adour and Bayonne (severely wounded). Also served in Holland 1794 (as a Volunteer) and in the Irish Rebellion 1798 (present at Vinegar Hill). Gold Cross for

Busaco, Salamanca, San Sebastian and Nive. MGS medal for Rolica, Vimeiro, Corunna and Nivelle. KCB 1830. KTS. Colonel 92nd Foot 31 May 1843. Brother of 2nd Capt Forbes MacBean Royal Artillery, Capt Frederick MacBean 6th Foot and 1st Lt Archibald MacBean Royal Artillery.
REFERENCE: *Royal Military Calendar, Vol. 4, pp. 345–6. Gentleman's Magazine, Jul 1855, pp. 93–4. Annual Register 1855, Appx. p. 275.*

McCABE, John
Captain. 51st (2nd Yorkshire West Riding) Light Infantry.
Named on the Regimental Memorial: KOYLI Chapel, York Minster, Yorkshire. (Photograph)

Ensign 81st Foot Apr 1802. Lt 13 May 1802. Lt 51st Foot 12 Aug 1803. Capt 7 Dec 1809.
Served in the Peninsula Feb 1811 – Nov 1812. Present at Fuentes d'Onoro, second siege of Badajoz, Moriscos, Salamanca, Burgos and San Munos where he was killed during the retreat from Burgos Nov 1812. Also served in Ceylon 1803 (present in the first Kandian War).

McCARTHY, Owen
Sergeant. 51st (2nd Yorkshire West Riding) Light Infantry.
Named on the Regimental Memorial: KOYLI Chapel, York Minster, Yorkshire. (Photograph)
Served in the Peninsula where he was killed.

McCLINTOCK, James
Ensign. 88th (Connaught Rangers) Regiment of Foot.
Table tomb: Derry Cathedral Burial Ground, Londonderry, Northern Ireland. (M.I.)

"................. ALSO TO THE MEMORY OF CAPTAIN JAMES McCLINTOCK 88TH REGT, LATE ADJUTANT LONDONDERRY MILITIA. HE DIED THE 15TH APRIL 1850, AGED 56 YEARS."

Ensign 12 May 1812. Lt 25th Nov 1815.
Served in the Peninsula Apr 1814. Half pay 25 Feb 1816. Became Captain and Adjutant Londonderry Militia.

McCREAGH, Michael
Major. Staff Appointment in Spain and Portugal not holding a Regimental Commission.
Memorial tablet: Holy Trinity Church, Leeds, Yorkshire. (South wall). (Photograph)

TO THE MEMORY OF / COLONEL SIR MICHAEL M'CREAGH / C.B. K.C.H. K.C.T.S. & & & / WHOSE DISTINGUISHED SERVICES ARE RECORDED / IN THE ANNALS OF HIS COUNTRY. / HE DEPARTED THIS LIFE ON THE 31ST OF AUGUST 1834 / IN THE 49TH YEAR OF HIS AGE. / (VERSE)

Stall plate: Westminster Abbey, London. (Photograph)

MICHAEL M'CREAGH ESQUIRE., / LIEUTENANT COLONEL IN THE ARMY AND / MAJOR IN THE PORTUGUESE SERVICE / COMPANION OF THE MOST HONOURABLE / MILITARY ORDER OF THE BATH / NOMINATED 4TH JUNE 1815.

Named on the Memorial tablet to Portuguese Commanders at Albuera: Albuera Wall, British Cemetery, Elvas, Portugal. (Photograph)

Ensign 39th Foot 1 Feb 1797. Lt 25 Jun 1802. Lt 37th Foot 27 Aug 1803. Capt 7th West India Regt 14 Sep 1804. Capt 1st Foot 14 Oct 1807. Bt Major 27 Apr 1809. Bt Lt Colonel 3 Oct 1811. Lt Colonel 13th Foot

4 Oct 1821. Bt Colonel 27 May 1825. Portuguese Army: Major 7th Line 10 Jul 1809. Lt Colonel 26 Aug 1809. Lt Colonel 5th Caçadores 3 Nov 1810. Colonel 3rd Line 10 Jul 1813.

Served in the Peninsula with Portuguese Army Jul 1809 – Feb 1814. Present at Busaco (Mentioned in Beresford's Despatches), Albuera, Salamanca, Burgos, Vittoria, San Sebastian (Mentioned in Beresford's Despatches 31 Aug 1813, Nive (Mentioned in Beresford's Despatches), Bidassoa and Bayonne. Gold Cross for Albuera, Salamanca, Vittoria, San Sebastian and Nive. CB. KCH. KCTS. At the start of the Peninsular War certain British officers were selected to go to Portugal to organise the Portuguese Army and McCreagh was chosen to be one of these. On his arrival in Portugal, Beresford asked him to form the 7th Portuguese Regiment of Infantry and he became the Lt Colonel. He turned it into an efficient fighting force which served well at Busaco and the retreat to Torres Vedras. He was next given the 5th Caçadores regiment and again transformed it into a well-disciplined force. Also served in the West Indies 1802 (present at Demerara and Antigua). Exchanged to the 37th Foot so that he could stay in the West Indies 1803 (present at Trinidad). He then commanded a company in the 7th West India Regt and it was here that he showed his skill at organising and disciplining a regiment, to prove so useful later with the Portuguese Army. Went to India with 13th Foot 1823 (present in the Ava campaign in command of the 1st Bengal division of the Army, but suffered a stroke and had to return home). Inspecting Field Officer of the Northern Recruiting District 1832 until his death in 1834. Sir Michael was, apart from his military talents, a classical scholar, poet and linguist.
Reference: United Service Journal, Oct 1834, pp. 286–8. Gentleman's Magazine, Jan 1835, p. 94.

McCRIMMON, Donald

Ensign. 42nd (Royal Highland) Regiment of Foot.
Named on the Memorial: St Andrew's Church (now Musée Historique), Biarritz, France. (Photograph)

Volunteer 42nd Foot. Ensign 5 Jan 1814.

Served in the Peninsula Oct 1813 – Apr 1814. Present at Nivelle, Nive, Orthes and Toulouse where he was killed 10 Apr 1814.

McCULLOCH, William

2nd Captain. Royal Engineers.
Memorial: St Mary's Church, Athlone, County Westmeath, Ireland. (M.I.) (No longer extant). (Graveyard has been redeveloped and graves removed to another church in Athlone, where most headstones are stacked)

"SACRED TO THE MEMORY OF CAPTAIN WILLIAM McCULLOCH OF THE CORPS OF ROYAL ENGINEERS WHO DEPARTED THIS LIFE ON THE 10TH OF FEBRUARY 1814 IN THE 35TH YEAR OF HIS AGE. THIS OFFICER SERVED IN SPAIN UNDER THE DUKE OF WELLINGTON AND PARTICULARLY AT THE SEIGE OF CIUDAD RODRIJO."

2nd Lt 1 Aug 1805. 1st Lt 1 Dec 1805. 2nd Capt 1 May 1811.

Served in the Peninsula Jun 1811 – Jun 1812. Present at the siege of Ciudad Rodrigo where he was severely wounded 16 Jan 1812. Returned home and died of his wounds in Athlone 10 Feb 1814.

McCURDY, Thomas

Assistant Surgeon. 47th (Lancashire) Regiment of Foot.
Ledger stone: Donaghmore Parish Churchyard, Donaghmore, County Donegal, Ireland. (Photograph)

HERE LYETH THE BODY OF THOS. / MCCURDY OF MAUGHREKELLAGHAN / LATE SURGEON OF THE 47TH REGT. OF / FOOT WHO DEPARTED THIS LIFE ON / THE 12TH DAY OF NOVEMBER 1826. / AGED 35 YEARS. / ....

Hospital Mate 12 May 1810. Asst Surgeon 47th Foot 23 Jul 1812.

Served in the Peninsula Mar 1812 – Apr 1814. Present at Cadiz, Seville, Puente Largo, Vittoria, San Sebastian, Bidassoa, Nivelle, Nive and Bayonne.

MACDERMID, John
Captain. 95th Regiment of Foot.
Low monument: East Preston Street Burial Ground, Edinburgh, Scotland. (Photograph)

ERECTED / BY THE MANAGERS / OF THE ROYAL INFIRMARY / OF EDINBURGH / OVER THE REMAINS OF / CAPTAIN JOHN MACDERMID, / RIFLE BRIGADE. / WHO DIED 29TH OCTOBER 1845 / HE BEQUEATHED SIX THOUSAND AND FIVE HUNDRED POUNDS TO THE ROYAL INFIRMARY / AND FIVE HUNDRED POUNDS TO THE DESTITUTE SICK SOCIETY.

Ensign 7th West India Regt 2 Feb 1804. 2nd Lt 95th Foot 30 Mar 1804. 1st Lt 28 Mar 1805. Capt 21 Aug 1810.

Served in the Peninsula with 1/95th Aug 1808 – Jan 1809 and Jul 1809 – Aug 1812. Present at Cacabellos, Corunna, Coa, Busaco, Pombal, Redinha, Casal Nova, Foz d'Arouce, Sabugal, Fuentes d'Onoro, Ciudad Rodrigo, Badajoz (wounded) and Salamanca. Half pay 23 Apr 1818.

McDERMOTT, Henry
Captain. 88th (Connaught Rangers) Regiment of Foot.
Named on the Memorial: St Andrew's Church (now Musée Historique), Biarritz, France. (Photograph)

Ensign Dillon's Regiment of the Irish Brigade 31 Dec 1795. Ensign Cape Regiment 26 Jun 1801. Ensign 70th Foot 27 Sep 1803. Lt 9th Reserve Battalion 27 Dec 1803. Lt 88th Foot 7 Aug 1804. Capt 13 Jul 1809. Portuguese Army: Capt 13th Line 2 Apr 1809. Retired 3 Nov 1809.

Served in the Peninsula with 88th Foot Jun 1809 – Jun 1811 and Sep 1812 – Feb 1814. With Portuguese Army Apr – May 1809. Present at Talavera (wounded), Busaco (wounded), Sabugal, Fuentes d'Onoro, Vittoria (wounded) and Orthes where he was killed 27 Feb 1814. Also served in South America 1807 (present at Buenos Ayres).

McDERMOTT, Thomas
Lieutenant. Staff Corps of Cavalry.
Buried in St George's Chapel, Windsor, Berkshire. (Burial record)

Cornet 25 Feb 1805. Lt 21st Lt Dragoons 21 May 1807. Lt Staff Corps of Cavalry 13 May 1813.

Served in the Peninsula Aug 1813 – Apr 1814 (attached to HQ Apr 1814). Present in the Pyrenees, Orthes and Toulouse. Also served in Ireland (present in the Irish Rebellion 1798) and the Cape of Good Hope 1806. MGS medal for Pyrenees, Orthes and Toulouse. Military Knight of Windsor 12 Dec 1838. Died 25 Apr 1862 aged 89 years.

MACDONALD, Alexander
Lieutenant Colonel. Royal Artillery.
Memorial tablet: All Saints' Parish Church, Leamington Spa, Warwickshire. (In recess of north transept). (Photograph)

SACRED / TO THE MEMORY OF THE LATE MAJOR GENERAL ALEXANDER / MACDONALD, C.B. AND K.S.A., ROYAL ARTILLERY, WHO DIED / AT LEAMINGTON ON THE 21ST MAY 1840, AGED 63, OF WHICH / HE HAD BEEN 46 YEARS AN OFFICER IN THE SERVICE. / GEN. MACDONALD WAS OF THE FAMILY OF GLENCOE, THE ELDEST / SON OF AN OFFICER DISTINGUISHED FOR HIS BRAVERY AND GOOD / CONDUCT; HAD BEEN ON ACTIVE SERVICE IN THE WEST INDIES, IN / EGYPT, WALCHEREN, THE FALL OF DANTZIG AND BATTLE OF

WATERLOO. / WAS A COMPANION OF THE BATH AND A KNIGHT OF THE RUSSIAN ORDER / OF ST ANNE. / THIS TRIBUTE TO HIS MEMORY IS RECORDED BY HIS / SURVIVING BROTHER AND SISTERS.

Headstone: Warriston Cemetery, Edinburgh, Scotland. (Section A2 Grave number 576). (Photograph)

SACRED / TO THE MEMORY OF / CHARLOTTE MACDONALD / .... / AND SISTER OF / MAJ^R^ GEN^L^ A. MACDONALD C. B. & K. ST. A. / ROYAL ARTILLERY

2nd Lt 1 Jan 1794. 1st Lt 14 Aug 1794. Capt-Lt 2 Oct 1799. Capt 13 Sep 1803. Bt Major 4 Jun 1811. Bt Lt Colonel 2 Jan 1814. Colonel 29 Aug 1825. Major General 10 Jan 1837.

Served in the Peninsula 1811–1813 in command of a troop of Horse Artillery. Present at Ciudad Rodrigo, Salamanca and Majalahonda. Present at Waterloo where he commanded six troops of Horse Artillery attached to the Cavalry. Awarded pension of £300 per annum for wounds at Waterloo. Also served at Ferrol 1800 and Walcheren 1809 (present at the siege of Flushing). CB and Order of St Anne (2nd class).

MCDONALD, Allan

Lieutenant. 92nd Regiment of Foot.
Named on the Memorial: St Andrew's Church, (now Musée Historique), Biarritz, France. (Photograph)

Ensign 30 May 1811. Lt 5 Aug 1813.

Served in the Peninsula May – Dec 1813. Present at Vittoria, Pyrenees, Nivelle and Nive where he was killed 13 Dec 1813.

MACDONALD, Archibald

Major. 1st Garrison Battalion.
Headstone: Mirzapur Cemetery, India. (M.I.)

"SACRED TO THE MEMORY OF LIEUTENANT COLONEL ARCHIBALD MACDONALD, KCB, LATE ADJUTANT GENERAL OF HIS MAJESTY'S FORCES IN INDIA, WHO DIED ON THE 19TH NOVEMBER 1827."

Capt 45th Foot 13 Oct 1808. Major 1st West India Regt 27 Jun 1811. Major 3rd Garrison Battalion 21 Jan 1813 (in March 1815 this became the 1st Garrison Battalion). Bt Lt Colonel 25 Nov 1813.

Served in the Peninsula Jun – Aug 1809 (ADC to Major General Erskine) and Sep 1810 – Apr 1811 (DAAG to 2nd Division Cavalry). Present at Usagre, Aldea de Ponte and Arroyo dos Molinos. Also served at Walcheren 1809, the Netherlands 1814 (DAG), Inspecting Field Officer of London Recruiting District 1818 (AAG) and India 1826 (Adjutant General of Bengal Division of the Forces in India) where he died 1827. KCB.

MACDONALD, Donald

Major. 92nd Regiment of Foot.
Headstone: New Calton Burial Ground, Edinburgh, Scotland. (Photograph)

ERECTED BY / ELIZABETH MCDONALD / WIFE OF THE LATE / LIEU^T^ COLONEL DONALD MCDONALD / OF THE / 92ND REG^T^ OF GORDON HIGHLANDERS / WHO DIED ON THE 19TH JUNE 1829 / IN THE 56 YEAR OF HIS AGE. / IN HIM HIS COUNTRY LOST / ONE OF ITS BEST AND BRAVEST DEFENDERS / AND THOSE WHOM HE HONOURED WITH HIS FRIENDSHIP / A FRIEND MOST HONOURED AND BELOVED.

Ensign Edinburgh Royal Volunteers 10 Mar 1797. Lt 31 Aug 1797. Ensign 81st Foot 22 Feb 1799. Lt 92nd Foot 20 Mar 1799. Capt 8 Jul 1803. Major 26 Nov 1812. Bt Lt Colonel 18 Jun 1815.

Served in the Peninsula Aug 1808 – Jan 1809 and Oct 1810 – Mar 1812. Present at Corunna, Fuentes d'Onoro and Arroyo dos Molinos (severely wounded and awarded pension of £300 per annum). Present at Quatre Bras (wounded) where he had taken command after Lt Colonel Mitchell was wounded and Waterloo where he commanded the 92nd Foot and on the advance to Paris. CB and Bt Lt Colonelcy. Also served at the Helder 1799 (present at Alkmaar where he was wounded), Egypt 1801 (present at Alexandria where he was wounded), Copenhagen 1807 (present at Kiöge), Sweden 1808 and Walcheren 1809. Order of 4th Class of St Vladimir of Russia.

Reference: Royal Military Calendar, Vol. 5, pp. 94–5.

MACDONALD, Donald

Captain. 42nd (Royal Highland) Regiment of Foot.

Headstone in the shape of a Celtic Cross: St Michael's Churchyard, Inveresk, Midlothian, Scotland. (Photograph)

IN MEMORY OF / DONALD MACDONALD / CAPTAIN 42 ROYAL HIGHLANDERS / WHO DIED AT MUSSELBURGH / 24TH SEPTEMBER 1865 AGED 84 / ....

Ensign 8 Apr 1801. Lt 9 Jul 1803. Capt 25 Jan 1810.

Served in the Peninsula Aug 1808 – Jan 1809, Jul 1810 – May 1812 and Mar – Apr 1814. Present at Corunna, Busaco, Fuentes d'Onoro (severely wounded) and Ciudad Rodrigo. MGS medal for Corunna, Busaco, Fuentes d'Onoro and Ciudad Rodrigo. Present at Quatre Bras (wounded) and Waterloo. Half pay 27 May 1819.

McDONALD, Donald

Captain. 91st Regiment of Foot.

Named on the Memorial tablets: Badajoz Wall and Albuera Wall, British Cemetery, Elvas, Portugal. (Photograph)

Capt 31 Mar 1803. Bt Major 25 Apr 1808. Portuguese Army: Lt Colonel 11th Line 26 Aug 1809.

Served in the Peninsula with 91st Foot Aug 1808 – Jan 1809 and Portuguese Army Aug 1809 – Apr 1812. Present at Rolica, Vimeiro, Cacabellos, Corunna, Busaco, Redinha, Albuera, second siege of Badajoz and Badajoz. One of the officers chosen in 1809 to take charge of units in the Portuguese Army. He led the 11th Line of Infantry until Apr 1812 when he was killed at the siege of Badajoz. Gold Medal for Albuera and Badajoz.

McDONALD, Donald

2nd Captain. Royal Engineers.

Named on the Regimental Memorial: Rochester Cathedral, Rochester, Kent. (Photograph)

2nd Lt 12 Sep 1808. Lt 24 Jun 1809. 2nd Capt 20 Oct 1813.

Served in the Peninsula Jul 1813 – Apr 1814. Present at Cadiz. Served with the Army of Occupation in France 1815–1818. Also served at Walcheren 1809 and the Netherlands 1814–1815. Permanent half pay 28 Sep 1824. Died at Upper Norwood 17 Oct 1872.

McDONALD, Duncan see McDONNELL, Duncan

McDONALD, Edward

Private. 12th (Prince of Wales's) Regiment of Light Dragoons.

Named on the Regimental Memorial: St Joseph's Church, Waterloo. (Photograph)
Present at Waterloo where he was killed.

MACDONALD, George

Lieutenant. 27th (Inniskilling) Regiment of Foot.
Low monument: Torquay Churchyard, Devon. (Photograph)

ALSO SACRED / TO THE MEMORY OF / GENERAL GEORGE MACDONALD / WHO WAS BORN ON THE 10TH OCTOBER 1784 / AND DEPARTED THIS LIFE ON THURSDAY / THE 1ST MARCH 1883. / (VERSE)

Ensign 5 Sep 1805. Lt 25 Jul 1806. Capt 17 Aug 1815. Major 31 Aug 1830. Bt Lt Colonel 10 Jan 1837. Bt Colonel 16 Nov 1851. Major General 31 Aug 1855. Lt General 29 Jan 1863. General 25 Oct 1871.

Served in the Peninsula with 1/27th Nov 1812 – Apr 1814. Present at Castalla, Tarragona and Barcelona. Present at Waterloo where he was wounded three times. Also served at Hanover 1805, Sicily 1806–1810, Ishchia and Procida 1810 and North America 1814 (present at Plattsburgh). Half pay 19 Jun 1841. Governor of Sierra Leone 1841–1845. Colonel 96th Foot 27 Dec 1860. Colonel 16th Foot 12 Feb 1863. Later became 'Father of the British Army'.

McDONALD, George

Sergeant. 48th (Northamptonshire) Regiment of Foot.
Ledger stone: St John's Churchyard, Parramatta, Australia. (Section 1, Row E, Grave 12). (Photograph)

SACRED TO THE MEMORY OF GEORGE McDONALD QUARTER MASTER SERGEANT OF HIS MAJESTY'S 48TH REGIMENT OF FOOT WHO SERVED HIS KING AND COUNTRY 32 YEARS AND FOUGHT IN THE DIFFERENT ENGAGEMENTS OF TALAVERA, ALBUERA, RODRIGO, SALAMANCA, BADAJOS, VITTORIA, PYRENEES, ORTHES, TOULOUSE AND NIVELLE. ENDED HIS MORTAL CAREER ON THE 28 JULY 1834 AGED 60 YEARS.

Served in the Peninsula Jul 1809 – Apr 1814. Present at Talavera, Albuera, Ciudad Rodrigo, Badajoz, Salamanca, Vittoria, Pyrenees, Nivelle, Orthes and Toulouse. Also served in Australia 1817–1824.

McDONALD, Hon. James

Captain and Lieutenant Colonel. 1st Regiment of Foot Guards.
Named on Memorial Panel VI for Bergen-op-Zoom: Royal Military Chapel, Wellington Barracks, London. (M.I.) (Destroyed by a Flying Bomb 1944)

Ensign 29 Dec 1799. Lt and Capt 25 Feb 1804. Capt and Lt Col 7 Apr 1813.

Served in the Peninsula with 3rd Battalion Oct 1808 – Jan 1809 and Jul 1811 – May 1813. (ADC to Major General Lambert Feb – May 1812). Present at Corunna, Cadiz, and Seville. Also served in Sicily 1806, the Netherlands 1814 (present at Bergen-op-Zoom where he was killed 8 Mar 1814).

MACDONALD, John

Major. 43rd (Monmouthshire) Light Infantry Regiment of Foot.
Monument: Kensal Green Cemetery, London. (8891/84/RS). (Photograph)

THE GRAVE OF / LIEUT-GENERAL SIR JOHN MACDONALD / KNIGHT GRAND CROSS / OF THE MOST HONOURABLE ORDER OF THE BATH / ADJUTANT GENERAL OF THE FORCES / AND COLONEL OF / THE 42ND ROYAL HIGHLAND REGIMENT. / THROUGH A SERVICE OF 55 YEARS / IN AN ARMY OF WHICH HE WAS JUSTLY PROUD / HE SUSTAINED / WITH AN UNDEVIATING CONSISTENCY / THE CHARACTER OF A BRITISH SOLDIER. / IN WAR HE SHARED WITH

OTHERS / THE DANGERS OF BATTLES. / IN PEACE HE ADMINISTERED / WITH A FIRM YET GENTLE HAND / THE DUTIES / OF THE HIGH AND RESPONSIBLE OFFICE / OF ADJUTANT GENERAL / FOR A PERIOD OF 20 YEARS / MANY A SOLDIER FEELS THAT HE HAS LOST A FRIEND / THERE ARE OTHERS WHO FEEL THEIR LOSS TO BE / IRREPARABLE / BORN IN THE HIGHLANDS OF SCOTLAND 1774 / HE DIED IN LONDON ON THE 28TH MARCH 1850.

Brass Memorial tablet: Royal Garrison Church, Portsmouth, Hampshire. (Back of a choir stall).

GENERAL SIR JOHN MC / DONALD G.C.B., COLONEL / 42ND (ROYAL HIGHLAND) REGT / BORN 1776 DIED 1850 / DD: LIEUT GENERAL / THE HON SIR JAMES / YORKE SCARLETT G.C.B.

Ensign 89th Foot 15 Apr 1795. Lt 2 Feb 1796. Capt 22 Oct 1802. Major 43rd Foot 20 Feb 1806. Lt Colonel 1st Garrison Battalion 17 Mar 1808. Bt Colonel 4 Jun 1814. Major General 27 May 1825. Lt General 28 Jun 1838.

Served in the Peninsula 1811 and 1813 – Apr 1814 (Deputy Adjutant General). Present at Cadiz, Barrosa (Mentioned in Despatches), Nive and Bayonne. Gold Medal for Barrosa and Nive. MGS medal for Egypt. CB. Also served in Ireland 1798 (present in the Irish Rebellion at Ross and Vinegar Hill), Malta 1800, Egypt 1801 (present at Alexandria), Copenhagen 1807, Sweden 1808 (Military Secretary to Lord Cathcart), Walcheren 1809 (DAG to Sir John Hope) and Ireland 1812 (again Military Secretary to Sir John Hope). At Bayonne Hope was wounded and taken prisoner and Macdonald was allowed to go into the Citadel to nurse his friend. Deputy Assistant General at Horse Guards 14 Aug 1818. Adjutant General 1830–1850. He proved to be an efficient Adjutant General, always courageous and sincere. A clear writer of minutes and orders which was very important as he was responsible for military discipline in the cavalry and infantry. KCB 1827. GCB 1847. Colonel 67th Regiment 25th Aug 1828 and Colonel 42nd Regiment 15th March 1844.

REFERENCE: *Dictionary of National Biography. Gentleman's Magazine, May 1850, p. 533. Annual Register, 1850, Appx, p. 215.*

McDONALD, John

Captain. 88th (Connaught Rangers) Regiment of Foot.

Memorial window: All Saints' Episcopal Church, Kinloch Rannoch, Perthshire, Scotland. (East window). (Photograph)

ERECTED BY ADRIANA MCDONALD IN MEMORY OF HER HUSBAND GENERAL SIR JOHN MCDONALD OF DALCHOSNIE. COL 92ND HIGHLANDERS WHO DEPARTED THIS LIFE JUN 24TH 1866 AGE 76.

Buried in the family mausoleum: All Saints' Episcopal Church, Kinloch Rannoch, Perthshire, Scotland. (East end of church). (Photograph of exterior and interior)

Ensign 17 Dec 1803. Lt 21 Mar 1805. Capt 7 Sep 1809. Bt Major 26 Aug 1813. Bt Lt Colonel 4 Sep 1817. Major 91st Foot 29 Nov 1821. Lt Colonel 23 Sep 1824. Lt Colonel 92nd Foot 21 Nov 1828. Bt Colonel 10 Jan 1837. Major General 9 Nov 1846. Lt General 20 Jun 1854. General 7 Mar 1862. Portuguese Army: Major 2nd Line Apr 1809. Lt Colonel 14th Line 14 Apr 1812.

Served in the Peninsula with Portuguese Army Apr 1809 – Apr 1814. Present at Busaco, Redinha, Pombal, Campo Mayor, first siege of Badajoz, Albuera, Badajoz, Alba de Tormes, Vittoria, Pyrenees Mentioned in Despatches, (wounded, and awarded pension of £300 per annum) and Toulouse. Also served in South America 1807 (present at Buenos Ayres with 88th Foot where he was wounded) and Ireland 1848 (commanded forces sent to suppress the insurrection and commanded the Kilkenny District 1848–1849). Gold Medal for Vittoria and Pyrenees (commanded 14th Portuguese Line). Commanded 92nd Foot 1828–1846. MGS medal for Busaco, Albuera, Badajoz and Toulouse. Portuguese Gold Medal and Cross.

KCB 4 Feb 1856. Colonel 53rd Foot 8 May 1854. Col 92nd Foot 25 May 1855. After he retired he devoted himself to improving his Scottish estates. Magistrate for the County of Perth.
Reference: Gentleman's Magazine, Aug 1866, p. 273.

McDONALD, John
Captain. 50th (West Kent) Regiment of Foot.
Table stone: Cill Chriosd Churchyard, near Broadford, Isle of Skye, Scotland. (Photograph)

SACRED / TO THE MEMORY OF / CAPTAIN JOHN McDONALD / OF HIS MAJESTY'S 50TH REGIMENT / WHO DIED 8TH NOVEMBER 1823 / AGED 45 YEARS. / THIS STONE HAS BEEN PLACED / BY HIS AFFLICTED WIDOW / FLORA McLEAN, / AS A SMALL TOKEN OF HER GREAT / AFFECTION, AND OF THE ********* / ********** TO THE SINCERE AND HONOURABLE / FRIEND, THE BRAVE SOLDIER / AND THE HONEST MAN.

Ensign 1804. Lt 19 Dec 1805. Capt 25 Jun 1812.
Served in the Peninsula Aug 1808 – Jan 1809 and Jun 1810 – Mar 1813. Present at Vimeiro, Corunna (wounded), Fuentes d'Onoro and Arroyo dos Molinos. Also present at Walcheren 1809. Half pay 1814.

MACDONALD, Ronald
Captain. 92nd Regiment of Foot.
Low monument: Cille Choirill Graveyard, Brae Lochaber, Invernesshire, Scotland. (Photograph)

RAONULL MACALASDAIR, / OICHEAR A MHACHA, / MAC RAONULL IC IAIN OPERARDAIR / AGUS AIR A MHNAOI / HANNAH STIUBHART / RANALD MACDONALD, / CAPT 92 REGIMENT, / BORN AT MOY OCTOBER 24 17** DIED AT THE FORT OCTOBER 15 18** / . ...

Lt Jan 1800. Capt 23 May 1805.
Served in the Peninsula Oct 1810 – Mar 1814. Present at Fuentes d'Onoro, Arroyo dos Molinos, Alba de Tormes, Vittoria, Pyrenees (wounded), Nivelle and Nive (wounded and awarded pension of £100 per annum). Also served in Egypt 1801 (present at Alexandria where he was wounded).

MACDONALD, Stephen
Lieutenant. 1st Light Battalion, King's German Legion.
Grave: Cheriton Churchyard, Sandgate, Kent. (No Longer extant). (M.I.)

"STEPHEN MACDONALD / LIEUTENANT OF THE LATE 1st LT BN KING'S GERMAN LEGION SUBSEQUENTLY ADJUTANT OF THE HANOVERIAN JAGER GARDE / DIED AT SANDGATE NOV 13 1871 AGED 78"

Lt Pembroke Militia 1810. Ensign 1st Lt Battalion King's German Legion 22 Dec 1812. Lt 5 Apr 1814.
Present at Waterloo and with the Army of Occupation. Also served in North Germany 1813–1814 (wounded at Sehestadt 10 Dec 1813) and the Netherlands 1814–1815. After Waterloo the regiment was disbanded and he joined the Hanoverian Jaeger Garde as Adjutant until 1820, when he returned to England. Became the first Registrar of Births, Marriages and Deaths at Folkestone 1837.
Reference: Stephen MacDonald: service in the KGL. Waterloo Journal, Aug 1981, pp. 12– 4.

McDONNELL, Duncan
Lieutenant. 50th (West Kent) Regiment of Foot.
Named on the Memorial: St Andrew's Church (now Musée Historique), Biarritz, France. (Photograph)

Lt 29 Dec 1807.

Served in the Peninsula Sep 1810 – Mar 1814. Present at Fuentes d'Onoro, Arroyo dos Molinos, Almarez, Alba de Tormes, Vittoria, Pyrenees (wounded), Nivelle, Nive, Garris, Orthes and Aire where he was killed 2 Mar 1814. Also served at Walcheren 1809. Also known as McDonald.

MACDONELL, James

Captain and Lieutenant Colonel. Coldstream Regiment of Foot Guards.
Interred in Catacomb B (v107 c2 13849) Kensal Green Cemetery, London.
Memorial: Royal Military Chapel, Wellington Barracks, London. (M.I.) (Destroyed by a Flying Bomb 1944)

"IN MEMORY OF / GENERAL SIR JAMES MACDONELL, G.C.B. K.C.H. / COLONEL 71ST HIGHLAND LT INFANTRY. BORN JANUARY, 1780; DIED 15TH MAY, 1857. COLDSTREAM GUARDS, FROM 1811 TO 1830. HE WAS PRESENT WITH THE 78TH REGIMENT AT THE BATTLE OF MAIDA, AND WHEN IN THE COLDSTREAM GUARDS AT THE BATTLES OF SALAMANCA AND VITTORIA, AND THE PASSAGE OF THE NIVE AND THE NIVELLE. HE FOUGHT AT QUATRE BRAS AND AT WATERLOO, WHEN HE COMMANDED THE LT COMPANIES OF THE 2ND BRIGADE OF GUARDS AT HOUGOUMONT, AND BY HIS DISTINGUISHED AND GALLANT CONDUCT GAINED THE PARTICULAR APPROVAL OF THE DUKE OF WELLINGTON. / PLACED BY HIS NIECE, MRS. STUART FORBES."

Ensign Independent Company 25 Oct 1793. Lt 78th Foot 4 Jan 1794. Capt 17th Lt Dragoons 13 Oct 1794. Major 1 Jul 1802. Major 78th Foot 17 Apr 1804. Lt Colonel 17 Sep 1809. Lt Colonel 2nd Garrison Battalion 21 Feb 1811. Capt and Lt Colonel Coldstream Guards 8 Aug 1811. Bt Colonel 12 Aug 1819. Lt Colonel 27 May 1825. Major General 22 Jul 1830. Lt General 23 Nov 1841. General 20 Jun 1854. Portuguese Army: Lt Colonel 12th Line 26 Aug 1809.

Served in the Peninsula with Portuguese Army 26 Aug 1809 – 21 Aug 1810 and with Coldstream Guards May 1812 – Jan 1814. Present at Salamanca, Burgos, Vittoria, Bidassoa, Nivelle and Nive. Present at Waterloo in command of the Lt Company of the 2nd Battalion Coldstream Guards. Present at Hougoumont (wounded) in command of all troops inside Hougoumont and closed the gate with several officers and men. Chosen by the Duke of Wellington for the legacy left to the 'bravest man in England'. Macdonell shared it with Sgt Graham, one of those who helped him close the gate. KCB. KCH. Knight of Maria Theresa. Knight of St Vladimier 4th Class. Gold Medal for Maida. MGS medal for Salamanca, Vittoria, Nivelle and Nive. Also served at Sicily 1806 (present at Maida), Egypt 1807 (present at Rosetta and siege of Alexandria), Ireland 1831–1838 and Canada 1838–1842 (present in the Rebellion). Colonel 79th Foot 14 Jul 1842 and Colonel 71st Foot 8 Feb 1849. Died 15 May 1857.

Reference: Dictionary of National Biography. Dictionary of Canadian Biography. Gentleman's Magazine, Jun 1857, p. 733. Annual Register, 1857, Appx, p. 309.

MACDOUGALL, Sir Duncan

Captain. 85th (Buckinghamshire Volunteers) Light Infantry Regiment of Foot.
Memorial tablet: St Paul's Cathedral, London. (Crypt south side). (Photograph)

ERECTED / TO THE MEMORY OF / COLONEL SIR DUNCAN MACDOUGALL, K. C. S. F. / OF SOROBA, ARGYLLSHIRE / BY THOSE FRIENDS AND COMRADES TO WHOM HIS PUBLIC SERVICES AND HIS PRIVATE WORTH / WERE BEST KNOWN / HE SERVED WITH THE 53RD AND 85TH REGIMENTS AT THE CAPE, IN THE PENINSULAR, AND IN FRANCE / AT THE SIEGES OF BADAJOZ, BURGOS AND ST SEBASTIAN / AT BAYONNE, AND AT THE BATTLE OF SALAMANCA / WHERE, THOUGH WOUNDED, HE GALLANTLY SAVED THE COLOURS OF HIS REGIMENT / IN AMERICA, HE WAS AT THE BATTLES OF BLADENSBURG, BALTIMORE, AND NEW ORLEANS / ALSO AT THE CAPTURE OF WASHINGTON / HE FINALLY COMMANDED THE 79TH HIGHLANDERS, UNTIL HE RETIRED FROM THE BRITISH ARMY / TO JOIN THE BRITISH

AUXILIARY LEGION IN SPAIN / AS QUARTERMASTER GENERAL UNDER HIS FRIEND SIR DE LACEY EVANS / AND RECEIVED THE ORDER OF ST FERDINAND FROM QUEEN ISABELLA II, / IN HIS LATER YEARS HE RAISED THE LANCASHIRE ARTILLERY MILITIA, / AND WAS AMONG THE FIRST TO PROMOTE THE VOLUNTEER MOVEMENT. / HE WAS A CHIVALROUS SOLDIER, AND A WARM HEARTED FRIEND. / HE DIED ON THE 10TH DECEMBER 1862 / IN THE 76TH YEAR OF HIS AGE.

Ensign 71st Foot 6 Apr 1804. Lt 23 Apr 1805. Capt Cape Regiment 19 Jun 1806. Capt 53rd Foot 6 Feb 1812. Capt 85th 25 Jan 1813. Bt Major 20 Oct 1814. Bt Lt Colonel 21 Apr 1825. Major 79th Foot 16 Jul 1830. Lt Col 10 Sep 1833.

Served in the Peninsula with the 53rd Foot at Salamanca where he was severely wounded but managed to save the colours. From Jan 1813 he served with the 85th Foot. Present at Badajoz, Burgos, San Sebastian, Nivelle, Nive and Bayonne. MGS medal for Salamanca, San Sebastian, Nivelle and Nive. Also served in North American 1814–1815 (present at Bladensburg, Capture of Washington, Baltimore, where he was ADC to General Robert Ross, and at New Orleans where he was ADC to Major General Pakenham and Fort Bowyer). Later appointed Colonel of the 9th Regiment of the British Legion in Spain (QMG under Sir de Lacey Evans with whom he had been at the battle of New Orleans in 1815). Retired from the Legion 1836. Awarded the medal for the British Legion of Spain. Knight Commander of St Ferdinand. Retired 1838. He was an advocate of Volunteer Corps. Raised Royal Lancashire Artillery 1853. Wrote *Hints to Volunteers on Various Subjects,* 1860 and *History of the Volunteer Movement,* 1861.

REFERENCE: *Dictionary of National Biography. Gentleman's Magazine, Jan 1863, p. 133. Annual Register, 1862, Appx, pp. 371–2.*

McELROY, Peter

Corporal. 13th Regiment of Light Dragoons.

Gravestone: Ranipet Cemetery, North Arcot District, Madras, India. (M.I.)

"SERGEANT PETER MCELROY / TRUMPET MAJOR, 13TH LT DRAGOONS / AGED 35 YEARS / DIED 1ST AUG 1819. / HE, WHO SINCERELY REGRETS THE LOSS OF A / FAITHFUL COMRADE AS THE LAST TRIBUTE / OF RESPECT, ERECT THIS TOMB; / T. BENNET SERGEANT SADDLER."

Sgt Jul 1815.

Present at Waterloo with his friend Sgt Thomas Bennet. After Waterloo promoted to Sergeant and Trumpet Major. Also served in India 1819 where he died 1 Aug 1819.

MACFARLANE, Andrew Angus

Captain. 91st Regiment of Foot.

Memorial: Arrochar Churchyard, Dumbartonshire, Scotland. (Broken in two and lying on side against wall). (Photograph)

SACRED TO THE MEMORY OF / CAPN ANDREW MCFARLANE / OF THE 91ST ARGYLLSHIRE REGIMENT, / WHO DIED 4TH JANY 1859, AGED 80 YEARS. / ....

Lt 26 Oct 1804. Capt 10 Sep 1812.

Served in the Peninsula Aug 1808 – Jan 1809 and Oct 1812 – May 1813. Present at Rolica, Vimeiro, Cacabellos and Corunna. Also served at Hanover 1805, Walcheren 1809 and the Netherlands 1814. MGS medal for Rolica, Vimeiro and Corunna. Half pay 25th Feb 1816.

MACFARLANE, John

Private. 12th (Prince of Wales's) Regiment of Light Dragoons.

Named on the Regimental Memorial: St Joseph's Church, Waterloo. (Photograph)

Present at Waterloo where he was killed.

McGILLIWIE, James
Lieutenant and Adjutant. 85th (Buckinghamshire Volunteers) Light Infantry Regiment of Foot.
Headstone: Sandpits Cemetery, Gibraltar. (M.I.)

"JAMES MCGILLIWIE, LIEUT. AND ADJT., / 85TH REG., D. 12 AP., 1827, A. 44."

Ensign and Adjutant 18 Feb 1813. Lt 14 Oct 1814.

Served in the Peninsula Aug 1813 – Apr 1814. Present at Nivelle, Nive and Bayonne. Also served in North America 1814–1815 (present at Bladensburg, Baltimore, New Orleans and Fort Bowyer), Malta and Gibraltar 1821 where he died 12 Apr 1827.

McGLASHAN, James Edwin
Lieutenant. 2nd Battalion Light Infantry, King's German Legion.
Ledger stone: British Garrison Cemetery, Kandy, Sri Lanka (Ceylon). (Photograph)

HERE LIES THE BODY / OF / CAPT JAMES M^{C}GLASHAN / OF HM'S XIXTH REG^{T} / WHO DIED ON 2ND OF DEC, 1817 / AGED 26 YEARS. / HE DISTINGUISHED HIMSELF AT THE BATTLES / OF BUZACO AND ALBUERA. / HE SERVED IN GERMANY, WHERE HE WAS APPOINTED / A COMPANION OF THE GUELPHIC ORDER OF KNIGHTHOOD. / AND HE OBTAINED THE MEDAL / BESTOWED BY THIS GRATEFUL COUNTRY / ON ALL WHO FOUGHT AT WATERLOO. / IN HIS LAST ILLNESS HE RECEIVED THE HOLY SACRAMENT / WITH EXEMPLARY DEVOTION / AND UNDER THE LINGERING APPROACH OF A PAINFUL DEATH / HE WAS SUSTAINED BY MANLY FORTITUDE / AND CHRISTIAN HOPE.

Ensign 9 Nov 1809. Lt 24 Apr 1811. Capt 22 Aug 1815.

Served in the Peninsula Sep 1810 and Mar 1811 – Sep 1812. Present at Busaco, Albuera, second siege of Badajoz, siege of Salamanca Forts and Moriscos (severely wounded). Present at Waterloo (ADC to Major General Sir James Lyon). After the war he was promoted Captain and served in Germany for a time. Exchanged into the 1st Ceylon Regt 16 Sep 1817, but shortly afterwards succumbed to an attack of fever and died 2 Dec 1817.
Reference: Lewis, J. Penry, List of inscriptions on tombstones and monuments in Ceylon, 1913, reprint 1994, pp. 296–7.

McGLASHAN, John
Private. 42nd (Royal Highland) Regiment of Foot.
Buried in Methven Churchyard, Perthshire, Scotland.

Pte 1812.

Served in the Peninsula Apr 1812 – Apr 1814. Present at Salamanca, Pyrenees, Nivelle, Nive, Orthes and Toulouse. Present at Waterloo and the Occupation of Paris. MGS medal for Salamanca, Pyrenees, Nivelle, Nive, Orthes and Toulouse. Died 22 Sep 1869 aged 82.
Reference: Obit. Perthshire Advertiser, No. 3086, 23 Sep 1869.

MACGLASHAN, Neil
Captain. 42nd (Royal Highland) Regiment of Foot.
Pedestal tomb: St George's Cemetery, Lisbon, Portugal. (Grave number D1 13). (Photograph)

SACRED / TO THE MEMORY OF / CAPT NEIL MACGLASHAN / OF THE / 42ND (OR) ROYAL

HIGHLANDERS. / WHO DIED AT / LISBON 9 JULY 1811. / AGED 22 YEARS. / HIS BROTHER OFFICERS / HAVE ERECTED THIS / STONE / TO HIS MEMORY / IN TESTIMONY OF / THEIR ESTEEM.

Lt 27 Nov 1806. Capt 17 May 1810.

Served in the Peninsula with 2/42nd Jul 1809 – Jul 1811. Present at Busaco and Fuentes d'Onoro.

MCGOWAN, William

Drummer. 27th (Inniskilling) Regiment of Foot.
Buried in Donnybrook Cemetery, Dublin, Ireland. (Burial record)

Drummer 27th Foot Mar 1809 (aged 12). Drummer 94th Foot 7 Jun 1817. Pte 59th Foot 30 Dec 1818. Cpl 25 Nov 1820. Sgt 25 Aug 1822. Quartermaster Sgt 14 Sep 1828.

Served in the Peninsula with 3/27th Mar 1809 – Apr 1814. Present at Badajoz, Vittoria, Pyrenees, Nivelle, Nive and Toulouse. Also served in North America 1814–1815 (present at Plattsburgh), India 1818–1827 (present at Bhurtpore – commanded a company, assaulted the breach when his commander was severely wounded and awarded Army of India medal), Gibraltar 1834–1836 and Malta 1846. MGS medal for Badajoz, Vittoria, Pyrenees, Nivelle, Orthes and Toulouse, Army of India and Army Long Service and Good Conduct MedalS (LSGC) 1835 and Army Meritorius Service Medal (MSM) 1862 – only the second such medal awarded in the 59th Foot. Served for 26 years and 206 days. Discharged 11 Apr 1837. Died 4 Oct 1887.

Reference: McInnes, Ian, Orders and Medals Research Society Journal, Mar 2009, pp. 44–5.

MACGREGOR, Duncan

Assistant Surgeon. 4th (King's Own) Regiment of Foot.
Obelisk: Agram Cemetery, Bangalore, Mysore, India. (M.I.)

"TO COMMEMORATE THE DEATH OF MAJOR JOSEPH DOHERTY 13TH DRAGOONS 12TH JUNE 1820 / LT JOHN POTTS 31ST JANUARY 1822 / LT W. A. BROWN 4TH NOVEMBER 1822 / CAPTAIN F. GROVE 6TH MAY 1827 / D. MACGREGOR ASST SURGEON 13TH DRAGOONS 16TH SEPTEMBER 1822 / AND MAJOR EDWARD TAYLOR GILLESPIE 26TH NOVEMBER 1836."

Hospital Mate General Service 18 May 1812. Asst Surgeon 2/4th Foot 5 Nov 1812. Asst Surgeon 56th Foot 7 Dec 1815. Asst Surgeon 5th Dragoon Guards 10 Jul 1817. Asst Surgeon 22nd Lt Dragoons 5 Feb 1818. Asst Surgeon 13th Lt Dragoons 25 Dec 1818.

Served in the Peninsula 1812–1813. Also served in India 1819 where he died at Bangalore 16 Sep 1822.

MACGREGOR, George

Lieutenant Colonel. 59th (2nd Nottinghamshire) Regiment of Foot.
Memorial: Royal Garrison Church Graveyard, Portsmouth, Hampshire. (M.I.)

"SACRED / TO THE MEMORY OF / LT COL GEORGE MACGREGOR CB / OF H.M. 59TH REGIMENT / OBIIT 7 AUG 1828 / AETAT 48."

Capt 3 Apr 1797. Major 30 May 1805. Bt Lt Colonel 1 Jan 1812. Lt Colonel 4 Jun 1813.

Served in the Peninsula Sep 1808 – Jan 1809. Present at Corunna where he was wounded. CB. Also served in the Cape of Good Hope 1792–1795, India 1797–1798, Walcheren 1809 (present at the siege of Flushing), East Indies 1811 (present in Java), Macassar in Celebes Islands 1814 and India 1824–1826 (present at Bhurtpore). Brother of Capt James McGregor 59th Foot.

McGREGOR, Hugh

Captain. 91st Regiment of Foot.
Memorial: Portobello Old Parish Churchyard, Portobello, Midlothian, Scotland. (M.I.)

"JOHN M^{C}GREGOR, ESQUIRE DIED AT RANNOCH / .... / ALSO HIS SON COLONEL HUGH OF THE 63RD REGIMENT DIED HERE ON 31ST MAY 1851 / AGED 73 / SERVED IN THE PENINSULA / CAPTAIN 79TH HIGHLANDERS / SALAMANCA BATTLE MEDAL."

Ensign Clan Alpine Fencibles 1 Mar 1799. Ensign 79th Foot 9 Feb 1804. Lt 25 Mar 1805. Capt 17 Aug 1806. Capt 91st Foot 2 Jul 1812. Bt Major 12 Aug 1819. Capt 63rd Foot 4 May 1820. Bt Lt Colonel 10 Jan 1837.

Served in the Peninsula May – Aug 1812. Present at Salamanca. MGS medal for Salamanca. Also served in the Netherlands 1814–1815 with 91st Foot. Half pay 25 Dec 1821.

McGREGOR, James

Captain. 59th (2nd Nottinghamshire) Regiment of Foot.
Named on the Regimental Memorial monument: Christ Church Churchyard, Tramore, County Waterford, Ireland. (Photograph)

Ensign 1807. Lt 3 Jun 1808. Capt 25 Sep 1813.

Served in the Peninsula Sep 1808 – Jan 1809 and Sept 1812 – Apr 1814. Present at Corunna, Cadiz, Vittoria (severely wounded), Nivelle, Nive and Bayonne. Present at Waterloo in reserve at Hal, storming of Cambrai and with the Army of Occupation. Also served at Walcheren 1809. Lost in the *Sea Horse* shipwreck off the coast of Ireland, 30 Jan 1816. Brother of Lt Colonel George McGregor who was in command of 1/59 serving in India during the Peninsular War.
REFERENCE: *Gentleman's Magazine, Mar 1816, p. 278.*

MACGREGOR, Malcolm

Captain. 78th (Highland) Regiment of Foot.
Buried at St Andrew's Church, Plymouth, Devon.
Memorial tablet: St Cuthbert's Church, Edinburgh, Scotland. (M.I.)

"SACRED / TO THE MEMORY OF LIEUT COLONEL MALCOLM MACGREGOR / 78TH HIGHLANDERS / WHO DIED AT PLYMOUTH 4TH JANUARY 1847 AGED 67 YEARS"

Ensign 24 Jun 1802. Lt 24 Jun 1804. Capt 7 Aug 1811. Bt Major 22 Jul 1830. Bt Lt Colonel 9 Nov 1846.

Served in the Netherlands 1814–1815 (present at Merxem and Antwerp). Also served in Sicily 1806 (present at Maida), Egypt 1807 (present at Alexandria, Rosetta and El Hamet. Taken prisoner of war in Cairo for four months). Served in the army for 45 years. Died in 1847 after a fall from his horse.

McGRIGOR, Sir James

Director General. Army Medical Department.
Obelisk: Kensal Green Cemetery, London. (9797/84/RS). (Photograph)

SIR JAMES MCGRIGOR BAR^{T} / KCB MD FRS &C. / DIRECTOR GENERAL OF / THE ARMY MEDICAL DEPARTMENT / THREE TIMES LORD RECTOR / OF MARISCHAL COLLEGE ABERDEEN / BORN 9TH APRIL 1771, / DIED 2ND APRIL 1858. / HE SERVED IN HOLLAND / THE WEST AND EAST INDIES, / CROSSED THE DESERT AS CHIEF OF / THE MEDICAL STAFF / IN THE EXPEDITION TO EGYPT / UNDER SIR DAVID BAIRD, / WAS CHIEF OF THE MEDICAL DEPARTMENT / OF THE ARMY IN THE PENINSULA / WHERE HIS ADMINISTRATIVE ABILITY / WON FROM THE DUKE OF WELLINGTON, / THIS MARKED DISTINCTION. / 'HE WAS ONE

OF THE MOST ABLE AND / SUCCESSFUL OF PUBLIC SERVANTS'

Statue: Royal Military College, Sandhurst, Berkshire. (Photograph)

SIR JAMES / M^C^GRIGOR BAR^T^ M. D. KCB KC KCTS / FRS / DIRECTOR GENERAL / OF THE ARMY / MEDICAL DEPARTMENT / 1815–1851 / BORN 1771 DIED 1858 / SERVED WITH THE BRITISH ARMIES / IN / HOLLAND – THE WEST INDIES / EGYPT – WALCHEREN / THE PENINSULA / ONE OF THE MOST / INDUSTRIOUS ABLE AND SUCCESSFUL / PUBLIC SERVANTS / I HAVE EVER MET WITH. / DUKE OF WELLINGTON / ERECTED BY / PUBLIC SUBSCRIPTION / THE CHIEF CONTRIBUTORS BEING / MEDICAL OFFICERS OF THE ARMY

The statue originally stood at Atterbury Street, Millbank, London in front of the Royal Military Medical College until 2003 when it was moved to Sandhurst.

Obelisk: Duthie Park, Aberdeen, Aberdeenshire, Scotland. (Photograph)

THIS OBELISK / IS ERECTED TO THE MEMORY OF / SIR JAMES MCGRIGOR, BART M.D. K.C.B. F.R.S. &C. / FOR THIRTY-SIX YEARS DIRECTOR-GENERAL OF THE ARMY MEDICAL / DEPARTMENT, AND SEVERAL TIMES LORD RECTOR OF / MARISCHAL COLLEGE, ABERDEEN. / HE WAS BORN IN STRATHSPEY, NORTH BRITAIN, ON THE / 9TH OF APRIL A.D. 1771. / HE ENTERED THE ARMY AS SURGEON OF THE CONNAUGHT / RANGERS IN 1793, AND SERVED THE TWO FOLLOWING YEARS IN / THE CAMPAIGN OF HOLLAND. / HE WAS AFTERWARDS MEDICAL CHIEF IN THE EXPEDITION / AGAINST THE ISLAND OF GRENADA; IN THE EXPEDITION UNDER SIR / DAVID BAIRD. FROM BOMBAY THROUGH THE DESERTS OF THEBES AND / SUEZ TO ALEXANDRIA, AND ALSO IN THE WALCHEREN EXPEDITION. / HE WAS CHIEF OF THE MEDICAL DEPARTMENT OF THE ARMY / UNDER THE DUKE OF WELLINGTON IN THE PENINSULAR WAR, / FROM THE SIEGE OF CIUDAD RODRIGO, IN THE YEAR 1811, TO THE / FINAL BATTLE OF TOULOUSE IN 1814. / HE WAS FAVOURABLY MENTIONED IN THE DESPATCHES OF ALL / THE GENERALS UNDER WHOM HE HELD THESE RESPONSIBLE / POSTS, AND WAS REPEATEDLY NOTICED IN THOSE OF THE DUKE / OF WELLINGTON, WHO, ON 26TH OF JULY, 1814, REFERRING / TO THE MANNER IN WHICH MR MCGRIGOR HAD CONDUCTED / THE DEPARTMENT UNDER HIS DIRECTION. WROTE THUS: – / "I CONSIDER HIM ONE OF THE MOST INDUSTRIOUS, ABLE, AND / SUCCESSFUL PUBLIC SERVANTS I HAVE EVER MET WITH." / IN THE COURSE OF FIFTY-SEVEN YEARS OF ACTIVE SERVICE / HE WAS EXPOSED TO THE VICISSITUDES OF WAR AND CLIMATE / BESIDES ENCOUNTERING SHIPWRECK AND OTHER DANGERS AT SEA. / YET HE LIVED TO OBTAIN A TRANQUIL AND HAPPY OLD AGE. / HE DIED IN LONDON ON THE 2ND OF APRIL, A.D. 1858. / THIS MEMORIAL / IS ERECTED NEAR THE PLACE OF HIS EDUCATION AND THE / SCENES OF HIS YOUTH. / THIS OBELISK, ERECTED IN 1860 IN THE QUADRANGLE OF MARISCHAL COLLEGE BY THE WIDOW AND / NEAR RELATIVES OF SIR JAMES M^C^GRIGOR, WAS REMOVED TO THE PRESENT SITE WITH THE FULL / CONSENT OF HIS REPRESENTATIVES WHEN THE UNIVERSITY BUILDINGS WERE EXTENDED

Brass Memorial tablet: Royal Garrison Church, Portsmouth, Hampshire. (Back of a choir stall)

SIR JAMES M^C^GRIGOR / BARONET K.C.B., M.D / DIRECTOR GENERAL ARMY / MEDICAL DEPARTMENT / DIED 1858 AGE 87 / DD: THE OFFICERS ARMY MEDICAL DEPT.

Surgeon 88th Foot 25 Sep 1793. Surgeon Royal Horse Guards 9 Feb 1804. Deputy Inspector of Hospitals 27 Jun 1805. Inspector General 25 Aug 1809. Director General of Army Medical Department 13 Jun 1815–1851.

Served in the Peninsula Jan 1812 – Apr 1814 (Principal Medical Officer attached to HQ from Jul 1812). Present at Badajoz, Burgos and the retreat, Vittoria, Pyrenees (Mentioned in Despatches) and Toulouse. MGS medal for Egypt, Badajoz, Vittoria, Pyrenees and Toulouse. KCB. Also served in Flanders 1794–1795, West Indies 1796, Ceylon and India 1800, Egypt 1801, Portsmouth 1809 (treating the sick and wounded from Corunna) and Walcheren 1809. MD 1804. KTS. KCB. FRS 1816. Greatly improved the medical services to the army. Renowned for his administrative ability, courage and ability to take responsibility, he began the system of medical reports and returns from all military stations. Married Mary, the sister of Lt Colquhoun Grant, one of Wellington's Intelligence officers on 23 Jun 1810. Author of several works including *Memoirs on the Health of the 88th and other regiments*, Bombay, 1801, *Medical sketches of the Expedition to Egypt from India,* 1804, *Memoir on the Health of the Army in the Peninsula,* 1810. In July 1812 Wellington was writing to Lord Bathurst 'by the attention of Dr McGrigor, one of the officers of the department, the wounded had been well attended to with a hope, thereby founded, that many of these valuable men would be saved to the service.' Founded the Natural History and Anatomy Museum at Fort Pitt in Chatham.

REFERENCE: *Dictionary of National Biography. Gentleman's Magazine, May 1858, pp. 553–6. Annual Register, 1858, Appx, pp. 398–401. Blanco, Richard L., Wellington's Surgeon General: Sir James McGrigor, 1974. McGrigor, Mary, Sir James McGrigor, a biography, 2000. McGrigor, Mary, editor, Sir James McGrigor, the scalpel and the sword: the autobiography of the father of army medicine, 2000. McGrigor, Sir James, The autobiography of Sir James McGrigor, late Director General of the Army Medical Department, 1861. Kaufman, M.H., Post Peninsular War activities of Sir James McGrigor (1771–1858), Wellington's Director-General of the Army Medical Department, Journal of Medical Biography, Vol. 14, No. 1, 2006, pp. 23–9.*

MACGREGOR, Sir James see MACANDREW, John

MACHELL, John Thomas

Lieutenant. 18th Regiment of Light Dragoons.

Memorial tablet in floor: Beverley Minster, Beverley, Yorkshire. (North Transept). (Photograph)

.... / JOHN THOMAS MACHELL, / SON OF THE ABOVE / WHO DIED THE 13TH OCTR 1853; / AGED 58. / HE WAS PRESENT AT THE SIEGE OF BADAJOS / AND SERVED IN THE 18TH HUSSARS / AT WATERLOO.

Ensign 12th Foot 12 Aug 1813. Lt 18th Lt Dragoons 24 Feb 1814. Half pay 10 Nov 1821.

Served in the Peninsula as a Volunteer. Present at Waterloo. Brother of Lt Lancelot Machell Royal Engineers, killed at San Sebastian.

MACHELL, Lancelot

Lieutenant. Royal Engineers.

Memorial tablet: Beverley Minster, Beverley, Yorkshire. (North Transept). (Photograph)

TO THE MEMORY OF / LANCELOT MACHELL, / LIEUT. IN THE ROYAL ENGINEERS, / THE THIRD SON OF / CHRISTOPHER AND ANN MACHELL; / HE WAS KILLED IN THE TRENCHES / AT ST SEBASTIAN IN SPAIN, AFTER / THE UNSUCCESSFUL ATTACK UPON THAT PLACE, / ON THE 28TH JULY 1813, / IN THE 21ST YEAR OF HIS AGE: / ESTEEMED AND RESPECTED / IN HIS PUBLIC AND PRIVATE CHARACTER. / "THE THREE OFFICERS OF THE ENGINEERS EMPLOYED / TO CONDUCT THE DIFFERENT PARTS OF THE COLUMNS / OF ATTACK, BEHAVED ADMIRABLY, BUT SUFFER'D SEVERELY / CAPTN. LEWIS LOST HIS LEG. LIEUT. JONES WAS WOUNDED / AND TAKEN, AND LIEUT MACHELL ON HIS RETURN WAS / KILLED IN THE TRENCHES." / LIEUT. GENL. SR T. GRAHAM'S / REPORT 26TH JULY.

Named on the Regimental Memorial: Rochester Cathedral, Rochester, Kent. (Photograph)

Named on the Monument to Fletcher, Rhodes, Collyer and Machell: San Sebastian, Spain. (Photograph)

TO FLETCHER, RHODES, COLLYER AND MACHELL

2nd Lt 21 Jul 1810. Lt 1 May 1811.

Served in the Peninsula Dec 1812 – Jul 1813. Present at the first siege of San Sebastian on the first attack on 18 Jul. On the 25 Jul 1813 he was leading a column to the assault and was killed in the trenches on return. Brother of Lt John Thomas Machell 18th Lt Dragoons.

McINNES, Alexander
Cornet. 2nd Life Guards.
Ledger Stone: Kensal Green Cemetery, London. (16973/84/PS). Inscription illegible. (Photograph)

Cornet 2nd Life Guards 7 Jun 1809. Lt 10 Mar 1810. Capt 1 Mar 1813. Resigned commission 1813. Rejoined as Cornet and Sub Lt 16 Jun 1814. Lt 25 Nov 1818.

Served in the Peninsula Nov 1812 – Jul 1813. Present at Vittoria. Resigned shortly after Vittoria but rejoined in 1814. Present at Waterloo as a Cornet. MGS medal for Vittoria. Changed his name to Nicholson in 1821 and retired from the army as Lieutenant Alexander Nicholson 21 Jun 1822. Died 9 Feb 1862.

Reference: McKannand, A., Captain Alexander McInnes, or Nicholson, 2nd Life Guards, c. 1822. Journal of the Society for Army Historical Research, Vol. 47, No. 192, Winter 1969, pp. 222–4.

MACINTOSH, Alexander Fisher
Lieutenant. 3rd (Prince of Wales's) Dragoon Guards.
Memorial tablet: Glasgow Cathedral Churchyard, Glasgow, Lanarkshire, Scotland. (On monument to Anderson of Douhills in iron railings). (M.I.)

"GENERAL ALEXANDER FISHER MACKINTOSH KH / COL 93 SUTHERLAND HIGHLANDERS / B 13TH JAN 1795 / DIED 28 AUG 1868."

Cornet 14th Lt Dragoons 31 Oct 1811. Lt 3rd Dragoon Guards 11 Jul 1812. Capt 60th Foot 9 Jun 1816. Capt 79th Foot 19 Jul 1819. Capt 11th Foot 6 Feb 1823. Major 93rd Foot 18 Sep 1823. Major 15th Foot 9 Jul 1825. Lt Colonel 15 Dec 1825. Bt Colonel 28 Jun 1838. Major General 11 Nov 1851. Lt General 2 Aug 1858. General 27 Dec 1864.

Served in the Peninsula Jul 1812 – Apr 1814. Present at Alba de Tormes, San Munos, Hormanza, Vittoria, Tarbes, St Gaudens and Toulouse. Also served in Canada 1827 in command of 15th Foot (suppressed riots in Montreal in 1832 where he was wounded by the rioters). Returned home 1833, awarded KH and commended for his actions. MGS medal for Vittoria and Toulouse. Colonel 15th Foot 1825–1834. Colonel 90th Foot 4 Mar 1857. Colonel 93rd Foot 3 Jun 1862.

McINTOSH, Hugh
Captain. 101st (Duke of York's Irish) Regiment of Foot.
Memorial tablet: St Mary the Virgin's Church, Carisbrooke, Isle of Wight. (North wall). (Photograph)

IN MEMORY OF CAPT. HUGH McINTOSH LATE 16TH / LIGHT DRAGOONS AND 101ST FOOT DIED 1832. / ....

Grave: St Mary the Virgin Churchyard, Carisbrooke, Isle of Wight. (M.I.)

" CAPTAIN HUGH McINTOSH, HALF PAY 101ST REGT AND 16TH LIGHT DRAGOONS, DIED 2 SEPTEMBER 1832, AGED 65 YEARS."

Promoted from the ranks. Lt 16th Light Dragoons 1 Aug 1804. Capt 11 Jul 1811. Capt 101st Foot 6 May 1813.

Served in the Peninsula Oct 1811 – Nov 1812. Present at Llerena, Castrejon and Salamanca. Returned to England on sick leave Nov 1812.

MACINTYRE, David

Captain. 91st Regiment of Foot.

Named on the Memorial: St Andrew's Church (now Musée Historique), Biarritz, France. (Photograph)

Ensign 79th Foot 3 Sep 1805. Lieutenant 91st Foot 20 Mar 1806. Captain 9 Mar 1809.

Served in the Peninsula Aug 1808 – Jan 1809 and Oct 1812 – Nov 1813. Present at Rolica, Vimeiro, Corunna, Pyrenees and Nivelle where he was killed Nov 1813.

MACKAY, George

Captain. 48th (Northamptonshire) Regiment of Foot.

Ledger stone shared with Lt John Campbell: Pioneer Memorial Park, Bunnerong, Sydney, New South Wales, Australia. (Photograph)

.... / HERE ALSO IS DEPOSITED / THE BODY OF / CAPTAIN GEORGE MACKAY / OF / HIS MAJESTY'S 48 REGT / WHO DIED ON THE 2ND DECR 1823 / AGED 37 YEARS.

Ensign 6 Oct 1803. Lt 4 Jan 1805. Capt 13 May 1812.

Served in the Peninsula Jul 1809 – Apr 1814. Present at Talavera where he was taken prisoner until Apr 1814. Also served in Australia in the Garrison at Sydney 1817–1823 where he died.

MACKAY, Honeyman

Lieutenant. 68th (Durham) Regiment of Foot.

Headstone with Cross on top: Locksbrook Cemetery, Bath, Somerset. (Photograph)

COLONEL HONEYMAN MACKAY / BORN DECR 19TH 1791 / DIED MARCH 23RD 1875 / WALCHEREN / AND / PENINSULA.

Ensign 96th Foot 8 Aug 1807. Lt 68th Foot 18 May 1809. Capt 5th West India Regt 30 May 1816. Capt 90th Foot 10 Oct 1816. Major 22 Jul 1830. Bt Lt Colonel 9 Nov 1846. Bt Colonel 20 Jun 1854.

Served in the Peninsula Jun 1811 – Apr 1814. Present at the siege of Salamanca Forts, Moriscos, Salamanca, Burgos and retreat from Burgos, Vittoria (wounded), Pyrenees, San Marcial, Nivelle, Adour and Orthes. Also served at Walcheren 1809 (present at the siege of Flushing) and the Mediterraanean 1820–1824 and 1826–1829. MGS medal for Salamanca, Vittoria, Pyrenees, Nivelle and Orthes. Half pay 27 May 1835.

MACKAY, John

Private. 42nd (Royal Highland) Regiment of Foot.

Ledger stone: St Margaret's Churchyard, Rothesay, Isle of Bute, Scotland. (Photograph)

ERECTED BY / BENJAMIN MACKAY / IN MEMORY OF / HIS FATHER / JOHN MACKAY / WHO WAS PRESENT AT THE / BATTLES OF QUATRE BRAS / AND WATERLOO 1815 / DIED 4TH JANUARY 1861 / AGED 67 YEARS / ....

Pte 25 Feb 1810. Cpl 30 Apr 1829.

Present at Quatre Bras, Waterloo and at the Capture of Paris. Also served in Gibraltar 1826–1832, Malta 1832–1834 and the Ionian Islands 1834–1836. Returned to England and discharged 22 Nov 1837 after serving 26 years. He joined at 15 years of age so his first three years were under age and did not count in the total.

MACKAY, Joseph

Ensign. 1st (Royal Scots) Regiment of Foot.
Chest tomb: Reay Old Burial Ground, Reay, Caithness, Scotland. (Photograph)

TO THE MEMORY OF / ENSIGN JOSEPH MACKAY / 1ST ROYALS / WHO DIED AT RAIGBEGG INVERNESSHIRE / ON THE 27TH OF AUGUST 1848 / AGED 68 YEARS / HIS REMAINS ARE INTERRED IN THE / CHAPEL YARD BURYING GROUND INVERNESS / ....

Chest tomb: Chapel Yard Cemetery, Inverness, Scotland. (Photograph)

ERECTED / TO THE MEMORY / OF / ENSIGN JOSEPH MACKAY OF REAY, / LATE OF THE ROYALS, WHO HAD BEEN FOR MANY / YEARS CATECHIST IN THE PARISHES OF MOY, / DALAROSSIE AND DUTHIL AND DIED UPON / THE 27TH AUGUST 1848 AT THE SCHOOLHOUSE / OF RAIGBEG IN THE 68TH YEAR OF HIS AGE. / HE WAS A LOVING HUSBAND AND AN AFFECTIONATE / FATHER. FEW COULD VIE WITH HIM IN HIS WONDERFUL / TALENTS, SPIRITUAL EXPERIENCE AND BROTHERLY / LOVE WITH THE OTHER GRACES WHICH ADORN THE / CHRISTIAN LIFE. IN PRIVATE HE EXHIBITED THE EFFECTS / OF THE DOCTRINES HE INCULCATED IN / PUBLIC BY A CLOSE WALK WITH GOD AND BY A / KIND, AFFABLE AND HUMBLE DEPORTMENT / TOWARDS ALL, LOVING HIS VERY ENEMIES. / NO INSINUATION OR PERSUASION COULD INDUCE / HIM TO FORSAKE THE GOOD OLD PRINCIPLES OF THE / CHURCH OF SCOTLAND, THOUGH GREATLY / PERSECUTED FOR HIS STEADY ADHERENCE. / HE WAS A FAITHFUL WITNESS UNTO DEATH / AND UPON SUCH HE HAS PROMISED TO BESTOW THE CROWN OF LIFE. / (VERSE)

Sgt Reay Fencibles (disbanded in 1814). Ensign 1st Foot 6 Oct 1814.

Present at Waterloo where he was wounded. Half pay 1 Aug 1816. Returned home to Reay where he lived for 40 years.

MACKAY, Robert Faror

Private. 42nd (Royal Highland) Regiment of Foot.
Tablestone: Reay Old Burial Ground, Reay, Caithness, Scotland. (Photograph)

REST SOLDIER / REST / SACRED TO THE / MEMORY OF THE LAMENTED / ROBERT FAROR MACKAY / WHO DIED AT / KENSARY WATTEN / JANUARY 25TH 1874 / AGED 82. / THE DECEASED SERVED IN THE / 42ND ROYAL HIGHLANDERS, / OR BLACK WATCH, / DURING THE PENINSULAR WAR, / AND THE CLOSING VICTORY / OF WATERLOO. / THIS MEMORIAL STONE IS ERECTED / BY HIS SONS, AUGUST 1875.

Pte 25 Nov 1810.

Served in the Peninsula Apr 1812 – Apr 1814. Present at Pyrenees, Nivelle, Nive, Orthes and Toulouse. Present at Waterloo in Lt Colonel John Campbell's Company where he was wounded at Quatre Bras, his left leg broken. Discharged unfit for further service 24 Dec 1815. MGS medal for Pyrenees, Nivelle, Nive, Orthes and Toulouse.

MACKAY, William

Captain. 68th (Durham) Regiment of Foot.
Mural wall plaque. Mackay enclosure, Chapel Yard Cemetery, Inverness, Scotland. (Photograph)

HERE / ARE / DEPOSITED / THE / MORTAL REMAINS / OF / LIEUT COL WILLIAM MACKAY, / LATE OF / THE 68TH REGT OF LT INFANTRY, / WHO DIED AT HEDGEFIELD / NEAR INVERNESS 2ND MARCH 1845. / COLONEL MACKAY / SERVED IN THE WEST INDIES, / HOLLAND AND THE PENINSULA / AND IN NORTH AMERICA. / IN ACTION NEAR SALAMANCA / HE RECEIVED / TWENTY TWO BAYONET WOUNDS / FROM THE EFFECT OF WHICH / HE NEVER ENTIRELY RECOVERED. / THIS STONE / IS ERECTED BY HIS WIDOW, / WHO DESIRES TO RECORD THE WORTH / OF ONE WHOSE ESTIMATE OF HIMSELF, / RENDERED HIM PARTICULARLY / UNOSTENTATIOUS, WHILE HIS / READY KINDNESS, GENEROSITY AND / UPRIGHTNESS OF CHARACTER CAUSED HIM / TO BE BELOVED AND ESTEEMED / WHEREVER HE WAS KNOWN.

Ensign 24 Nov 1803. Lt 25 May 1804. Capt 9 Jan 1812. Bt Major 21 Jan 1819. Bt Lt Colonel 10 Jan 1837.

Served in the Peninsula Jun 1811 – Sep 1812. Present at the siege of Salamanca Forts, Moriscos (severely wounded, received 22 bayonet wounds 21 Jun 1812. He was taken prisoner but was so ill that when the French left Moriscos he was left behind. Awarded pension of £100 per annun). Also served in the West Indies, Walcheren 1809 and Canada 1819. Discharged in Canada as a consequence of the climate affecting his wounds. Half pay 12 Apr 1821.

MACKENZIE, Alexander

Captain. 42nd (Royal Highland) Regiment of Foot.
Interred in Catacomb B (10186 / Cat B v126 c4) Kensal Green Cemetery, London.

Ensign 7 Feb 1804. Lt 16 May 1805. Capt 6 Jan 1814.

Served in the Peninsula Aug 1808 – Jan 1809 and May 1812 – Apr 181. Present at Corunna, Salamnca, Burgos, Pyrenees, Nivelle, Nive, Orthes and Toulouse where he was severely wounded. Also served at Walcheren 1809. Half pay 1814. Died Apr 1852 aged 80.

McKENZIE, Donald

Sergeant. 79th (Cameron Highlanders) Regiment of Foot.
Headstone: Inverness Cemetery, Inverness, Invernesshire, Scotland. (Photograph)

SACRED / TO THE MEMORY OF / SERGT DONALD MCKENZIE / OF THE 79TH REGT / WHO DIED ON THE 12TH JANUARY / 1867 / AGED 86 YEARS. / ....

Served in the Peninsula 1808 – Jan 1809 and 1810 – Apr 1814. Present at Corunna, Busaco, Fuentes d'Onoro, Salamanca, Burgos (wounded), Pyrenees, Nivelle, Nive and Toulouse. Present at Waterloo. MGS medal for Corunna, Busaco, Fuentes d'Onoro, Salamanca, Pyrenees, Nivelle, Nive and Toulouse.

McKENZIE, George Davis

Captain. 5th (Northumberland) Regiment of Foot.
Ledger stone: Holy Trinity Churchyard, Ilfracombe, Devon. (North West corner. Seriously eroded). (Photograph)

HERE RESTS THE REMAINS / OF / GEORGE DAVIS McKENZIE / LATE CAPTAIN OF THE 5TH REGIMENT OF FOOT WHO / DIED AT ILFRACOMBE AUGUST 1826 AGED 35 / ELDEST SON OF LIEUT. COL. McKENZIE OF THE / 5TH REGIMENT OF FOOT WHO FELL AT THE BATTLE OF / CORUNNA IN WHICH ENGAGEMENT AND / WITH MUCH OTHER HARD SERVICE BOTH HIS

SONS / CAPT MCKENZIE AND LIEUT HOLLAND / McKENZIE OF THE SAME REGIMENT WHO DIED AT / MONTSERRAT.

Ensign 85th Foot 15 Oct 1802. Lt 5th Foot 5 Aug 1804. Capt 30 Aug 1809.

Served in the Peninsula with 1/5th Jul 1808 – Jan 1809, 2/5th Feb 1812 – Feb 1813 and 1/5th Aug 1813 – Apr 1814. Present at Rolica, Vimeiro, Corunna, Salamanca, Nivelle, Nive, Adour, Orthes, Vic Bigorre and Toulouse. Served with the Army of Occupation until 1818. Also served at Walcheren 1809 and North America 1814–1815. His father was Lt Colonel John Mackenzie, Commanding Officer of 5th Foot at Rolica, Vimeiro and Corunna where he was killed. His brother Lt John Holland Mackenzie 5th Foot was also at these battles and died later in the West Indies at Montserrat.

MACKENZIE, Hugh

Captain and Paymaster. 71st (Highland Light Infantry) Regiment of Foot.
Gravestone: St Ninian's Old Churchyard, Stirling, Stirlingshire. Scotland. (No longer extant)

Pte 1780. Paymaster 8 Nov 1798.

Served in the Peninsula Aug 1808 – Jan 1809 and Sep 1810 – Apr 1814. Present at Rolica, Vimeiro, Corunna, Sobral, Fuentes d'Onoro, Arroyo dos Molinos, Almarez, Alba de Tormes, Vittoria, Pyrenees, Nive, Garris, Orthes, Aire, Tarbes and Toulouse. Present at Waterloo and with the Army of Occupation until 1818. Also served in Gibraltar 1782 (present at the siege), India 1790–1791 (present at the seige of Pondicherry), Cape of Good Hope 1806, South America 1807 (present at Buenos Ayres) and Canada 1819. Half pay 16 Aug 1824 after serving for 44 years. MGS medal for Rolica, Vimeiro, Corunna, Fuentes d'Onoro, Vittoria, Pyrenees, Nive, Orthes and Toulouse. Died in Stirling 25 Jun 1854.

McKENZIE, John

Lieutenant Colonel. 5th (Northumberland) Regiment of Foot.
Named on the Memorial tablet to the Peninsular War, San Vicente, Elvina, Corunna, Spain. (Photograph)

ROLICA BUSSACO TALAVERA LA ALBUERA / VIMEIRO FUENTES DE O ORO BADAJOZ PIRINEOS / SAHAGUN ALMAREZ SALAMANCA ORTHEZ / CORUNA CIUDAD RODRIGO VICTORIA TOULOUSE / PENINSULAR WAR 1808–1814 / IN MEMORY / OF BRIGADIER GENERAL ROBERT ANSTRUTHER, WHO FORMED PART / OF THE RESERVE UNDER GENERAL SIR JOHN MOORE, / AND DIED IN CORUNNA ON 14 JANUARY 1809, / AND LIEUTENANT COLONEL JOHN MACKENZIE, 5TH FOOT / WHO DIED IN PALAVEA DE ABAIXO, CORUNNA, ON 15 JANUARY 1809. / 200TH ANNIVERSARY OF THE BATTLE OF CORUNNA 1809–2009 EXCMO. AYUNTAMIENTO DE A CORUNA ASSOCIATI N HIST RICO CULTURAL "THE ROYAL GREEN JACKETS" / EMBAJADA DE S. M. BRITANICA EN ESPANA. ASSOCIACI N NAP LEONICA ESPA OLA.

Capt 103rd Foot 30 Jun 1795. Capt 85th Foot 11 Nov 1795. Major 28 Aug 1801. Major 5th Foot 1 Aug 1804. Lt Colonel 5th Foot 5 May 1806.

Served in the Peninsula with 1/5th Jul 1808 – Jan 1809. Present at Rolica, Vimeiro and Corunna. Wounded in a skirmish to capture a French battery on the evening of 14 Jan 1809 and died from his wounds on 15 Jan 1809. Buried on the left-hand side of Sir John Moore. Gold Medal for Rolica and Vimeiro. Both his sons, Capt George Davis McKenzie and Lt John Holland Mckenzie, were with him at Rolica, Vimeiro and Corunna in 5th Foot.

McKENZIE, John Holland

Lieutenant. 5th (Northumberland) Regiment of Foot.
Named on the Ledger stone to his brother: Holy Trinity Churchyard, Ilfracombe, Devon. (North West corner. Seriously eroded). (Photograph)

Buried in Montserrat, West Indies.

Ensign May 1807. Lt 5th Foot 21 Apr 1808.

Served in the Peninsula with 1/5th Jul 1808 – Jan 1809 and 2/5th Jul 1809 – Jun 1812. Present at Rolica, Vimeiro, Corunna, Redinha, Casal Nova, Foz d'Arouce, Sabugal, Fuentes d'Onoro, second siege of Badajoz, El Bodon and Ciudad Rodrigo where he was severely wounded 19 Jan 1812. Served with the Army of Occupation until 1818. Also served in North America 1814–1815 and the West Indies 1819–1826 where he died of fever in Montserrat. His father was Lt Colonel John Mackenzie Commanding Officer of 5th Foot at Rolica, Vimeiro and Corunna where he was killed. His brother, Capt George Davis McKenzie 5th Foot was also with him at these battles.

MACKENZIE, John Randoll

Colonel. 78th (Highland) Regiment of Foot.
Memorial: St Paul's Cathedral, London. (North transept). (Joint memorial with Major General Langwerth). (Photograph)

NATIONAL MONUMENT / TO MAJOR GENERAL / J. R. MACKENZIE, / AND BRIGADIER GENERAL / E. LANGWERTH, / WHO FELL AT / TALAVERA, / JULY 28TH / MDCCCIX.

Lt Royal Marines 1788. Capt 78th Foot 1793. Major Feb 1794. Lt Colonel 27 Feb 1796. Bt Colonel 1 Jan 1801. Major General 25 Apr 1808.

Served in the Peninsula Dec 1808 – Jul 1809 (O/c 2 Brigade, Apr – Jun 1809 O/c 3 Division Jun – Jul 1809). Present at Talavera where he was killed, Mentioned in Despatches and awarded Gold Medal. Commanded a brigade at Talavera consisting of the 2/24th, 2/31st and 1/45th. This was 3,000 men to face 10,000 French soldiers, and Mackenzie was killed in the ensuing battle. With the aid of the 14th Lt Dragoons and the Guards (1st Battalion Coldstream Guards and 1st Battalion Third Regiment of Foot Guards) the French were driven back. Also served in the Cape of Good Hope 1794, India 1801–1802, Sicily 1806 (commanded 78th Foot at Maida), and Egypt 1807 (present at El Hamet). MP for Boroughs and Sutherland.

Reference: Gentleman's Magazine, Aug 1809, p. 780.

MACKENZIE, Kenneth

Lieutenant Colonel. 52nd (Oxfordshire) Light Infantry Regiment of Foot.
Altar tomb: Hythe Churchyard, Hythe, Kent. (South side of church). (M.I.)

"IN THE VAULT ARE DEPOSITED THE REMAINS OF LIEUTENANT GENERAL SIR KENNETH DOUGLAS BARONET OF GLENBERRIE COLONEL OF THE 58TH REGIMENT ELDEST SON OF KENNETH MACKENZIE ESQUIRE OF KILCOY CASTLE ROSSHIVE. HE ENTERED THE ARMY AT THE AGE OF 13 AND SERVED HIS KING AND COUNTRY WHENEVER CALLED UNTIL HIS DEATH WHICH TOOK PLACE IN LONDON NOVEMBER 22ND 1833 AGED 79 YEARS. HE ASSUMED THE NAME AND ARMS OF DOUGLAS BY SIGN MANUAL ON THE 19TH OCTOBER 1831 IN MEMORY OF HIS UNCLE SIR ALEXANDER DOUGLAS OF GLENBERRIE. HE MARRIED ON THE 18TH DECEMBER 1804 (WHEN LIEUTENANT COLONEL MACKENZIE OF THE 52ND REGIMENT) RACHEL ONLY DAUGHTER OF ROBERT ANDREWS ESQUIRE OF THIS TOWN AND PORT BY WHOM HE HAD NINE CHILDREN AND LEFT SURVIVING SIX VIZ: ROBERT ANDREWS, ALEXANDER DOUGLAS, EDWARD, RACHEL, LYNEDOCH AND DONALD. KENNETH AND WILLIAM DIED IN THEIR INFANCY AND KENNETH HIS THIRD SON DIED IN CEYLON."

Memorial window: Sir John Moore Library, Shorncliffe, Kent. (Photograph)

KENNETH MACKENZIE

Ensign 33rd Foot 26 Aug 1767. Lt 1775. Lt 14th Foot 1783. Capt 13 May 1794. Major 90th Foot May 1794. Bt Lt Colonel 4 Jun 1799. Lt Colonel 52nd Foot 24 Feb 1802. Bt Colonel 25 Apr 1808. Major General 4 Jun 1811. Lt General 19 Jul 1821.

Served in the Peninsula 1810. Present at Cadiz, but returned home because the heat affected his injuries. Also served in Guernsey 1767–1783, West Indies 1783–1793, Flanders 1793–1794 (present at Valenciennes and Dunkirk where he was wounded), Gibraltar 1795–1796, Egypt 1801 (commanded 90th Foot when Lt Colonel Hill was wounded). Returned to England in command of 44th Foot. Joined 52nd Lt Infantry and proceeded to help Sir John Moore train the Light troops at Shorncliffe but had to retire on half pay due to a fall from his horse causing concussion of the brain. Later served in the Netherlands 1813–1814 (joined staff of Lord Lynedoch and remained in command of the troops in Antwerp when the expedition returned home). Colonel 58th Foot 1 Mar 1828. Changed surname to Douglas Oct 1831.

REFERENCE: Dictionary of National Biography.

MACKENZIE, Maxwell

Major. 71st (Highland Light Infantry) Regiment of Foot.
Named on the Memorial: St Andrew's Church (now Musée Historique), Biarritz, France. (Photograph)

Ensign 87th Foot 6 May 1797. Ensign 53rd Foot 2 Oct 1798. Lt 71st Foot 6 Oct 1798. Capt 25 Jun 1803. Bt Major 30 May 1811. Major 4 Jun 1813. Bt Lt Colonel 21 Jun 1813.

Served in the Peninsula Aug 1808 – Jan 1809 and May 1811 – Dec 1813. Present at Rolica, Vimeiro (wounded), Corunna, Arroyo dos Molinos, Almarez, Alba de Tormes, Vittoria, Pyrenees (severely wounded), Nivelle and Nive where he was killed Dec 1813. Gold Medal for Vittoria and Pyrenees. Also served at Walcheren 1809.

McKENZIE, Roderick

Private. 42nd (Royal Highland) Regiment of Foot.
Headstone: Dumbarton Cemetery, Dumbarton, Dumbartonshire, Scotland. (M.I.)

"RODERICK MCKENZIE – AN OLD DISCIPLE, SERVED IN PENINSULAR WAR AND AT WATERLOO / DIED 2 APRIL 1865 / AGED 82."

Served in the Peninsula Jul 1809 – Apr 1814. Present at Busaco, Fuentes d'Onoro, Ciudad Rodrigo, Salamanca, Pyrenees, Nivelle, Nive, Orthes and Toulouse. MGS medal for Busaco, Fuentes d'Onoro, Ciudad Rodrigo, Salamanca, Pyrenees, Nivelle, Nive, Orthes and Toulouse.

MACKINNON, Daniel

Captain and Lieutenant Colonel. Coldstream Regiment of Foot Guards.
Interred in Catacomb B (v37 d72), Kensal Green Cemetery, London. (Re-interred from Battersea Church 1856)

Ensign 16 Jun 1804. Lt and Capt 25 Mar 1808. Capt and Lt Colonel 25 Jul 1814. Major 22 Jun 1826. Bt Colonel 22 Jun 1826. Lt Colonel 22 Jul 1830.

Served in the Peninsula Mar 1809 – Aug 1811 and Jun – Sep 1812 (ADC to Major General Stopford Jun – Aug 1811). Present at Douro, Talavera, Busaco, Fuentes d'Onoro and Ciudad Rodrigo. Present at Waterloo where he commanded the Grenadier Company of the Coldstream Guards at Hougoumont (severely wounded in the knee before he moved to Hougoumont). Also served at Hanover 1805, Copenhagen 1807 and the Netherlands 1814. After Sep 1812 Mackinnon was employed on recruiting services in England until Apr 1814. He was well liked by his fellow officers and his men, was extremely brave in facing the enemy which gave encouragement to the men. He loved to play practical jokes on his fellow officers. Commanded Coldstream Guards 1830–1836. Nephew of Major General Henry

Mackinnon who was killed at the siege of Ciudad Rodrigo. Author of *Origins and history of the Coldstream Guards*, 2 vols, 1832. Died in London 22 Jun 1836.
Reference: Dictionary of National Biography. United Service Journal, Sep 1836, pp. 94–6. Gentleman's Magazine, Aug 1836, pp. 208–9.

MACKINNON, Henry
Colonel. Coldstream Regiment of Foot Guards.
Memorial monument: St Paul's Cathedral, London. (North transept). The memorial is shared with Robert Craufurd. (Photograph).

ERECTED BY THE NATION / TO MAJOR-GENERAL ROBERT CRAUFORD, / AND MAJOR-GENERAL HENRY MACKINNON / WHO FELL AT CIUDAD RODRIGO JAN^{RY} 19TH 1812

Memorial: Royal Military Chapel, Wellington Barracks, London. (M.I.) (Destroyed by a Flying Bomb 1944)

"IN MEMORY OF MAJOR-GENERAL HENRY MACKINNON, ... OF THE COLDSTREAM GUARDS. MAJOR-GENERAL H. MACKINNON FELL AT THE SIEGE OF CIUDAD RODRIGO ON THE 19TH JANUARY, 1812. PLACED BY THEIR SURVIVING RELATIVES."

Also named on Memorial Panel VII for Ciudad Rodrigo: Royal Military Chapel, Wellington Barracks, London. (M.I.) (Destroyed by a Flying Bomb 1944)

Ensign 43rd Foot 31 May 1790. Lt 30 Nov 1792. Capt of an Independent Company 11 Apr 1793. Lt and Capt Coldstream Guards 9 Oct 1793. Capt and Lt Colonel 18 Oct 1799. Bt Colonel 25 Oct 1809. Major General 1 Jan 1812.

Served in the Peninsula Mar – Dec 1809 (O/c 2 Brigade 3rd Division), Dec 1809 – Feb 1810 (O/c 1 Brigade 3rd Division. Feb 1810 – Jul 1811 and Nov 1811 – Jan 1812. Present at Douro, Salamonde, Talavera, Busaco (Mentioned in Despatches), Fuentes d'Onoro (Mentioned in Despatches), and Ciudad Rodrigo (Mentioned in Despatches). Gold Medal for Busaco, Fuentes d'Onoro and Ciudad Rodrigo. Killed at the siege of Ciudad Rodrigo, 19 Jan 1812 when a magazine exploded killing 108 men. His nephew Daniel Mackinnon had his body buried at Espeja. Also served in Flanders 1794, Ireland 1798 (Brigade Major to Major General George Nugent), the Helder 1799, Egypt 1801, Hanover 1805 and Copenhagen 1807. Uncle of Capt and Lt Colonel Daniel Mackinnon Coldstream Guards.
Reference: Mackinnon, Henry, Journal of the campaign in Portugal and Spain from the year 1809 to 1812, 1812, reprint 1999. Dictionary of National Biography. Gentleman's Magazine, Feb 1812, p. 190.

MACKRELL, Thomas
Captain. 44th (East Essex) Regiment of Foot.
Memorial tablet: Afghan Memorial Church, St John the Evangelist, Colaba, Bombay, India. (Photograph)

XLIV / FOOT / LIEU^{T} COL^{L} / T. MACKRELL

Named on the Afghanistan War Memorial, Regimental Chapel of the Essex Regiment and the Royal Anglian Regiment, Warley, Essex. (Photograph)

The memorial was originally erected in St Mary's Church, Alverstoke, Hampshire, and moved to Warley in 1926 together with the regimental colours.

"SACRED TO THE MEMORY OF COLONEL T. MACKRELL ADC TO HER MAJESTY ……………….."

Ensign 19 Sep 1804. Lt 25 May 1807. Capt 1 Oct 1812. Major 12 Nov 1825. Lt Colonel 25 Jun 1830.

Served in the Peninsula Aug 1813 – Apr 1814 on the East Coast of Spain (present at Tarragona). Also served in Malta 1806–1807, Sicily 1808 (went to the Bay of Naples 1809 to capture Ischia and Procida), North America 1814–1815 (present at Bladensburg, Capture of Washington and New Orleans), India 1822 (present in the first Burmese War) and Afghanistan 1839–1841 (led the storming party on 10 Nov 1841 to capture the Rika-Bashee Fort in Kabul which was opposite the Mission compound and was killed in the attempt.

MACKWORTH, Digby
Captain. 7th (Royal Fusiliers) Regiment of Foot.
Chest tomb: St John the Baptist Churchyard, Llanhennock, Monmouthshire, Wales. (Photograph)

COL SIR DIGBY MACKWORTH BART / WHO DECEASED SEPTEMBER 22 1852 / AGED 63 YEARS.

Lt 9 Jul 1807. Capt 16 Jul 1812. Capt 13th Lt Dragoons 31 Dec 1818. Bt Major 21 Jan 1819. Major 13 Aug 1830. Bt Lt Colonel 10 Jan 1837.

Served in the Peninsula with 2/7th Apr 1809 – May 1811 and 1/7th May 1811 – Apr 1814. Present at Douro, Talavera, Busaco, Olivencia, Albuera, second siege of Badajoz, Badajoz, Nivelle, Nive, Orthes and Toulouse. Appointed ADC to Lord Hill after Albuera. Present at Waterloo (ADC to Lord Hill). Also served in India 1818 (present at Madras with 13th Lt Dragoons). ADC to Lord Hill when Lord Hill was appointed Commander of Forces in Great Britain 1828. MGS medal for Talavera, Busaco, Albuera, Badajoz, Nivelle, Nive, Orthes and Toulouse. KH for his work in putting down the riots in the Forest of Dean 1830 and Bristol 1831. Half pay 13 Aug 1830. Educated at Westminster. Deputy Lieutenant of Monmouthshire.
Reference: Gentleman's Magazine, Nov 1852, pp. 524–6. Annual Register, 1852, Appx, pp. 312–13.

MACLAGAN, David
Staff Surgeon. Medical Department.
Mural wall monument: Dean Cemetery, Edinburgh, Scotland. (Section PW 2098). (Photograph)

DAVID MACLAGAN, M. D. F. R .S. E. / PHYSICIAN TO THE FORCES / SURGEON IN SCOTLAND TO THE QUEEN / BORN 8TH FEBRUARY 1785 / HE SERVED WITH THE 91ST REGIMENT / IN WALCHEREN 1809 / AND ON THE MEDICAL STAFF IN THE PENINSULA / 1811 TO 1814 / WAS PRESENT AT THE BATTLES OF / SALAMANCA, VITTORIA, BADAJOZ / PYRENEES, NIVELLE AND NIVE. / SETTLED IN CIVIL PRACTICE IN 1816 / AND WAS SUCCESSIVELY PRESIDENT / BOTH OF THE ROYAL COLLEGE OF SURGEONS / AND OF THE ROYAL COLLEGE OF PHYSICIANS / OF EDINBURGH / DIED 6TH JUNE 1885

Asst Surgeon 91st Foot 10 Sep 1807. Staff Surgeon with Portuguese Army 10 Oct 1811. Physician and Assistant Inspector of Hospitals 26 May 1814.

Served in the Peninsula with Portuguese Army Dec 1811 – Apr 1814. Present at Badajoz, Salamanca, Vittoria, Pyrenees, Nivelle (Mentioned in Beresford's Despatches) and Nive. Also served with the 91st Foot at Walcheren. MD Edinburgh 1805. FRCP 1811. Retired 13 Oct 1814. MGS medal for Badajoz, Salamanca, Vittoria, Pyrenees, Nivelle and Nive.

MACLAINE, Archibald
Lieutenant Colonel. 7th West India Regiment of Foot.
Low monument: Highgate Cemetery, London. (Photograph)

"TO THE MEMORY OF / GENERAL SIR ARCHIBALD MACLAINE, KCB, / CELEBRATED FOR HIS BRAVERY AT THE BATTLES OF / MALLAVELLY, SERINGAPATAM, ASSIERGUR, / AND AT THE CAPTURE OF SEVILLE, FOR HIS UNPRECEDENTED / DEFENCE OF FORT MATAGORDA, / FOR FIFTY-FIVE DAYS WITH ONLY ONE HUNDRED AND FIFTY-FIVE MEN, / AGAINST MARSHAL SOULT, WHO HAD A FORCE OF EIGHT / THOUSAND MEN. HE RECEIVED THE HONOUR / OF KNIGHTHOOD, KCB, ALSO THE ORDER OF / CHARLES THE 3RD OF SPAIN IN 1816. / BECAME COLONEL OF THE 52ND FOOT IN 1847, AND GENERAL / OF THE ARMY IN 1855. / HE DEPARTED THIS LIFE 9TH MARCH, 1861, IN HIS 89TH YEAR. / THIS TOMB / IS ERECTED BY / HIS AFFECTIONATE WIFE.

Named on the Family Memorial Cross: Warriston Cemetery, Edinburgh, Scotland. (Section N Grave number 46 South side). (Photograph – see John Maclaine)

Ensign 94th Foot 16 Apr 1794. Lt 29 Apr 1795. Capt 22 Dec 1804. Major 87th Foot 4 Oct 1810. Lt Colonel 7th West India Regt 25 Jan 1813. Bt Colonel 22 Jul 1830. Major General 23 Nov 1841. Lt General 11 Nov 1851. General 5 Jun 1855.

Served in the Peninsula Feb – Nov 1810, Dec 1810 – Jul 1811 and Jan – Sep 1812. Present at Cadiz (Mentioned in Despatches), Barrosa (severely wounded and awarded pension of £200) and Seville (Mentioned in Despatches). At Cadiz, during the defence of Fort Matagorda, Maclaine and his small force were heavily outnumbered by the French. He held the Fort from 22 Feb until 22 Apr 1810 until ordered to evacuate by Lt General Thomas Graham. MGS medal for Barrosa. Knight of Charles III of Spain. Also served in India 1799 (present at Malavelly, Seringapatam where he was so severely wounded that he was in hospital for a year), the Polygar War 1801 (wounded), Mahratta Wars 1802–1804 (present at Julnaghur, Gawilghur, Asseerghur where he was wounded and Argaum). Ordered home 1804 because of numerous wounds sustained between 1789 and 1804. KCB 1852. Colonel 52nd Foot 8 Feb 1847. Brother of Capt Hector Maclaine 57th Foot, Major John Maclaine 73rd Foot killed at Waterloo and Capt Murdoch Maclaine 20th Foot killed at Maida 1806.

Reference: Gentleman's Magazine, Apr 1861, p. 459. Annual Register, 1861, Appx, p. 467.

MACLAINE, Hector

Captain. 57th (West Middlesex) Regiment of Foot.

Memorial tablet: St Mary the Virgin's Church, Thornbury, Gloucestershire. (North Aisle). (Photograph)

.... / ALSO THE REMAINS OF THE ABOVE NAMED / COLONEL HECTOR MACLAINE, YOUNGEST SON / OF GILLEAN MACLAINE ESQR OF SCALLASDALE, / ISLE OF MULL. HE SERVED IN THE 64TH REGT / IN THE WEST INDIES AND SURINAM, JOINED / THE 57TH REGT IN PORTUGAL IN 1811 AS CAPTAIN, / AND WAS PRESENT EVERYWHERE WITH LORD / HILL'S DIVISION. HE FOUGHT AT VITTORIA, / RONCESVALLES, THE PYRENEES, IN FRONT / OF PAMPLUNA, AT NIVELLE, TARBES, ORTHES / AND TOULOUSE, BESIDES CONSTANT SKIR- / MISHING, AS HE WAS ATTACHED TO AND FRE- / QUENTLY COMMANDED THE LIGHT COMPANIES / OF GEN: BYNG'S BRIGADE. HE WAS WOUNDED / AND RECEIVED A MEDAL FOR HIS DISTIN- / GUISHED CONDUCT AT NIVELLE. HE SERVED / AFTERWARDS IN NORTH AMERICA, AND FRANCE. / AFTER THE WAR HE RESIDED MANY YEARS AT / KINGTON IN THIS PARISH AND DEPARTED THIS / LIFE THE 15TH JANUARY 1847 AGED 62. REGRETTED / BY HIS FRIENDS, THAT IS BY ALL WHO KNEW HIM.

Named on the Family Memorial Cross: Warriston Cemetery, Edinburgh, Scotland. (Section N Grave number 46 South side). (Photograph – see John Maclaine)

Ensign 64th Foot 1803. Lt 46th Foot 25 Sep 1804. Capt 57th Foot 1 Dec 1806. Major 14 May 1819. Lt Colonel 9 Sep 1824. Bt Colonel 28 Jun 1838.

Served in the Peninsula Aug 1811 – Apr 1814. Present at Vittoria, Pyrenees, Nivelle (severely wounded), Aire and Vic Bigorre, Tarbes, Orthes and Toulouse. Served with the Army of Occupation until 1818. Gold Medal for Nivelle. Also served in the West Indies (present at the Capture of Surinam 1804), Gibraltar 1806 and North America 1814–1815. Brother of Lt Colonel Archibald Maclaine 7th West India Regt, Major John Maclaine 73rd Foot killed at Waterloo and Capt Murdoch Maclaine 20th Foot killed at Maida 1806.
REFERENCE: Gentleman's Magazine, Mar 1847, p. 310.

MACLAINE, John

Major. 73rd (Highland) Regiment of Foot.
Memorial: Inside Mausoleum, Evere Cemetery, Brussels, Belgium. (Photograph)

MAJOR / JOHN / McLAINE / 73RD REGIMENT

Family memorial Cross on pedestal base: Warriston Cemetery, Edinburgh, Scotland. (Section N Grave number 46 South side). (Photograph)

.... / JOHN / FOURTH SON OF GILLIAM AND MARIE MACLAINE / FELL MORTALLY WOUNDED AT WATERLOO A MAJOR IN THE 73RD REGT / HE WAS A BRAVE SOLDIER AND HAD SEEN MUCH SERVICE IN INDIA, / WAS VERY PARTICULARLY DISTINGUISHED / AT THE STORMINGS OF SERINGAPATAM AND TURNAGUL.

Ensign 7 Feb 1794. Lt 30 Aug 1796. Capt 25 Dec 1804. Major 28 May 1812.

Present at Waterloo (severely wounded and died later in Brussels). Also served in India 1798–1814 with 1/73rd (present at Seringapatam 1799 and Turnagel 1802). Left the 1st Battalion on their arrival in Australia in 1814 and joined the 2nd Battalion enabling him to take part at Waterloo. Very well liked by his men as he treated them fairly. He suggested to his Colonel that the practice of flogging should cease in the regiment. One of the select band of soldiers buried in the Mausoleum at Evere. Brother of Capt Hector Maclaine 57th Foot, Lt Colonel Archibald Maclaine 7th West India Regt and Capt Murdoch Maclaine 20th Foot killed at Maida 1806.
REFERENCE: Lagden and Sly, The 2/73rd at Waterloo, 2nd edition, 1988, pp. 146–50.

McLASHER, James

Private. 12th (Prince of Wales's) Regiment of Light Dragoons.
Named on the Regimental Memorial: St Joseph's Church, Waterloo. (Photograph)

Present at Waterloo where he was killed.

McLEAN, Donald

Private. 42nd (Royal Highland) Regiment of Foot.
Headstone: Old Parish Churchyard, Largs, Ayrshire, Scotland. (Photograph)

DONALD McLEAN / LATE OF THE 42ND REGT / DIED / JULY 3RD 1819 / AGED 52 YEARS.

Present at Waterloo in Captain James Stirling's Company.

MACLEAN, George

Treasury Clerk. Commissariat Department.
Interred in Catacomb B (v86 c18), Kensal Green Cemetery, London.

Treasury Clerk Jul 1812. Dep Asst Comm General 22 Oct 1816. Asst Com General 24 May 1834. Com General 29 Dec 1849.

Served in the Peninsula 1813 – Apr 1814. Present at Orthes and Toulouse. Also served in Cape of Good Hope (present in the Kaffir War 1851–1853). Knighted on return from the Cape. Served in the Crimea as Chief of Commissariat with the Army in the East (present at the siege of Sebastopol). MGS medal for Orthes, Toulouse. Medal and clasp for the Crimea. KCB. Died in 1861.

MACLEAN, John Leyburn
Lieutenant. 43rd (Monmouthshire) Light Infantry Regiment of Foot.
Grave: Old Churchyard, Spital, Windsor, Berkshire. (Grave number: O 129)

Ensign 23 Mar 1810. Lt 27 Mar 1811. Capt 7 Apr 1825.

Served in the Peninsula Apr 1813 – Apr 1814. Present at Vittoria, Pyrenees, Bidassoa, Nivelle, Nive, Tarbes and Toulouse. Also served in North America (present at New Orleans). MGS medal for Vittoria, Pyrenees, Nivelle, Nive and Toulouse. Appointed to Her Majesty's Honourable Corps of Gentlemen at Arms Apr 1847. Military Knight of Windsor 11 Jul 1864. Died 4 Jul 1873.

MACLEOD, Alexander
Lieutenant. 61st (South Gloucestershire) Regiment of Foot.
Tombstone: City Cemetery, Peshawar, India. Inscription illegible. (M.I.)
Headstone: Bellie Cemetery, Bellie, Morayshire, Scotland. (East central part of Cemetery) (Photograph)

SACRED / TO THE MEMORY / OF / WILLIAM MACLEOD / LATE CAPTN IN THE 13TH ROYAL / VETERAN BATTALION / WHO DIED AT LIFFORD / ON THE 8TH OF JULY 1833 / AGED 72 / AND HIS ONLY SON / ALEXANDER BRIGADIER / LIEU. COLONEL 61ST REG. CB / WHO DIED IN INDIA 18TH AUGUST / 1849 AGED 57 YEARS

Ensign 3 Aug 1809. Lt 12 Dec 1811. Capt 31 Dec 1825. Bt Major 28 Jun 1838. Major 7 Jan 1842. Lt Colonel 26 Jul 1844.

Served in the Peninsula Mar 1810 – Sep 1812. Present at Busaco, Torres Vedras and covering the siege of Ciudad Rodrigo. Also served in Ireland 1812–1816, Jamaica 1816–1822, Ceylon 1828–1839, India 1845 (in command of the 61st Regiment), the Punjab campaign 1848–1849 (present at Sadulapur, Chillianwalla and Gujarat 1849 – appointed Brigadier and commanded the 7th Brigade of Infantry). At the end of the war he resumed command of the 61st Foot at Peshawar where he died 18 Aug 1849. MGS medal for Busaco and Medal with two clasps for the Wars in the Punjab. CB. Son of Capt William Macleod 13th Royal Veteran Battalion. Both father and son served together in the 61st Foot at the battle of Busaco.

MACLEOD, Charles
Lieutenant Colonel. 43rd (Monmouthshire) Light Infantry Regiment of Foot.
Memorial tablet: Westminster Abbey, London. (Chapel of John the Baptist). (Photograph)

TO THE MEMORY OF / LIEUT COL. CHARLES MACLEOD / WHO FELL AT THE SIEGE OF BADAJOS, / AGED 26 YEARS. / THIS MONUMENT IS ERECTED BY HIS BROTHER OFFICERS. / "IN LIEUT COL. MACLEOD OF THE 43RD REGT / WHO WAS KILLED IN THE BREACH: HIS MAJESTY HAS SUSTAINED / THE LOSS OF AN OFFICER, WHO WAS AN ORNAMENT TO HIS PROFESSION / AND WAS CAPABLE OF RENDERING THE MOST IMPORTANT SERVICES / TO HIS COUNTRY". / VIDE. MARQUIS WELLINGTON'S DISPATCH. 8TH OF APRIL 1812.

Ensign 71st Foot 5 Sep 1799. Lt 62nd Foot 21 Mar 1800. Capt 3rd West India Regt 22 Apr 1802. Capt 13th Foot 25 May 1803. Major 4th Garrison Battalion 26 Nov 1806. Major 43rd Foot 28 May 1807. Lt Colonel 16 Aug 1810.

Served in the Peninsula with 1/43rd Oct 1808 – Jan 1809, Jul 1809 – Dec 1810 and May 1811 – Apr 1812. Present at Vigo, Coa, Busaco, Ciudad Rodrigo (Mentioned in Despatches) and Badajoz (where he

was killed and Mentioned in Despatches). Gold Medal for Busaco, Ciudad Rodrigo and Badajoz. Also served in India 1805 (ADC to Lord Cornwallis) and Copenhagen 1807. He was buried in a cornfield overlooking the regimental camp. His brother James who was in the Royal Artillery, was present together with six officers of the 43rd – the only ones who were not wounded. He was mourned by the whole regiment and especially by his best friend William Napier. One of Maitland's men, Sgt Thomas Blood said "There was not a man in that corps but would have stood between him and the fatal ball that struck his head, so esteemed was he by all, and only twenty seven years of age." Brother of 2nd Captain James Alexander Macleod Royal Artillery who died in the battle for Rangoon 1824 and Captain Henry George Macleod. 35th Foot.
Reference: Oxfordshire Light Infantry Chronicle, 1895, pp. 97–115.

MACLEOD, Donald

Staff Surgeon. Medical Department.
Tombstone: Scotch Cemetery, Calcutta, India. (M.I.)

"TO THE MEMORY OF DONALD MACLEOD M. D. / INSPECTOR-GENERAL OF H. M. HOSPITALS IN INDIA / WHO IN VARIOUS PARTS OF THE WORLD / HAD LONG SERVED HIS COUNTRY / THIS TRIBUTE OF FILIAL LOVE AND REVERENCE IS / DEDICATED BY HIS AFFLICTED DAUGHTER / BORN AT BERNISDALE INVERNESSHIRE N. B: / DIED AT CALCUTTA 12 NOV 1840."

Memorial tablet: St Andrew's Kirk, Calcutta, India. (Photograph)

DONALD MACLEOD M. D. / INSPECTOR GENERAL OF H. M. HOSPITALS / IN INDIA. / BORN AT BERNISDALE, INVERNESSHIRE / DIED AT CALCUTTA 12 NOV 1840

Ensign and Regimental Mate Breadalbane Fencible Infantry 22 Mar 1798. Hospital Mate 10 Sep 1799. Asst Surgeon 82nd Foot 30 Jan 1800. Surgeon 38th Foot 24 Nov 1803. Staff Surgeon 9 Sep 1813. Deputy Inspector of Hospitals in India 27 Nov 1828. Inspector General 1 Jun 1837.

Served in the Peninsula with 1/38th Aug 1808 – Jan 1809, Jun 1812 – Oct 1813 and with Staff Oct 1813 – Apr 1814. Present at Rolica, Vimeiro, Corunna, Castrejon, Salamanca, Burgos, the retreat from Burgos (present at Villa Muriel), Osma, Vittoria, San Sebastian and Orthes. Also served at the Helder 1799, Cape of Good Hope 1806, South America 1807, Minorca 1808, Walcheren 1809 and North America 1814 (present at Plattsburgh). Died in Calcutta 12 Nov 1840 aged 61.

MACLEOD, George Francis

Captain. Royal Engineers.
Headstone: Christ Churchyard, Penrith, Cumbria. (West wall of Churchyard). (Photograph)

SACRED / TO / THE MEMORY OF / LIEUT COLONEL / GEORGE FRANCIS MACLEOD, C. B / ROYAL ENGINEERS. / WHO WAS BORN AT SHOOTERS HILL / IN THE COUNTY OF KENT / AND DIED AT HIS RESIDENCE IN THIS PARISH / ON THE 26TH OF JULY A. D. 1851. / IN THE 66TH YEAR OF HIS AGE. / BLESSED ARE THE DEAD WHICH DIE IN THE LORD. REV. CH 4 VER 21

Lt 1 Jul 1801. 2nd Capt 1 Jul 1806. Capt 1 May 1811. Bt Major 6 Feb 1812. Bt Lt Colonel 21 Jun 1817. Lt Colonel 23 Mar 1825.

Served in the Peninsula 1811–1812. Present at first siege of Badajoz, second siege of Badajoz, Ciudad Rodrigo (Mentioned in Despatches) and Badajoz where he was severely wounded. Also served in Sicily 1806–1809 (present at Maida), Walcheren 1809 and the Netherlands 1814–1815. MGS medal for Maida, Ciudad Rodrigo and Badajoz. CB. In 1829 he sold out but was allowed to retain the rank without pay or promotion.

MACLEOD, Henry George
Captain. 35th (Sussex) Regiment of Foot.
Memorial: Old Windsor Churchyard, Windsor, Berkshire. (M.I.)

"SACRED TO THE MEMORY OF / COLONEL / SIR HENRY GEORGE MACLEOD / KNIGHT OF THE HANOVERIAN ORDER OF / THE GUELPH AND ST VLADIMIR / AND LATE GOVERNOR OF / THE ISLAND OF TRINIDAD / SON OF LIEUTENANT GENERAL / SIR JOHN MACLEOD, G.C. AND OF / LADY EMILY DAUGHTER OF WILLIAM / .... MARQUESS OF LOTHIAN / .... BORN AUGUST 1791 / DIED 20TH OF AUGUST 1847 / ...."

2nd Lt Royal Artillery 3 Nov 1807. 1st Lt 15 Jul 1808. Capt 4th Garrison Battalion 29 Sep 1813. Capt 35th Foot 10 Dec 1813. Bt Major 21 Jun 1817. Lt Colonel 18 Aug 1825. Bt Colonel 28 Jun 1838.

Served in the Peninsula with Royal Artillery 1809 – Feb 1811. Present at Douro, Talavera and Busaco. Present at Waterloo on Staff as DAQMG (wounded). Also served in Dantzig 1813 and Canada 1817 (ADC to the Duke of Richmond). Knighted 1837 when appointed Governor of St Christopher. Lieutenant Governor of Trinidad 1842. Governor of Trinidad 1843. MGS medal for Talavera and Busaco. KH. Order of St Vladimir of Russia 4th Class for services at the siege of Dantzig 1813. Brother of Lt Colonel Charles Macleod 43rd Foot who was killed at Badajoz and 2nd Captain James Macleod who was killed at the battle of Rangoon 1824.
Reference: Gentleman's Magazine, Nov 1847 pp. 540–1. Annual Register, 1847, Appx pp. 248–9.

McLEOD, Swinton
Surgeon. 42nd (Royal Highland) Regiment of Foot.
Interred in Catacomb B (Pub v31 tier 3), Kensal Green Cemetery.

Asst Surgeon Staff 8 Sep 1797. Surgeon 42nd Foot 3 Jul 1803. Deputy Inspector General of Hospitals 5 Nov 1829.

Served in the Peninsula Jul 1809 – May 1812 and May 1813 – Apr 1814. Present at Busaco, Fuentes d'Onoro, Ciudad Rodrigo, Pyrenees, Nivelle, Nive, Orthes and Toulouse. Present at Quatre Bras and Waterloo. Also served in Egypt 1801. Half pay 1829. Died 27 Dec 1847.

MACLEOD, William
Captain. 13th Royal Veteran Battalion.
Headstone: Bellie Cemetery, Bellie, Morayshire, Scotland. (East central part of Cemetery). (Photograph)

SACRED / TO THE MEMORY / OF / WILLIAM MACLEOD / LATE CAPTN IN THE 13TH ROYAL / VETERAN BATTALION / WHO DIED AT LIFFORD / ON THE 8TH OF JULY 1833 / AGED 72 / AND OF HIS ONLY SON / ALEXANDER, BRIGADIER / LIEUT. COLONEL 61ST REGT. CB / WHO DIED IN INDIA 18TH AUGUST / 1849 AGED 57 YEARS

Ensign 24th Foot 24 Jun 1796. Lt 61st Foot 5 Mar 1797. Capt 11 Sep 1806. Capt 13th Royal Veteran Battalion 25 Jan 1813. Capt 6th Royal Veteran Battalion Dec 1819. Capt 2nd Royal Veteran Battalion Dec 1821.

Served in the Peninsula Nov 1809 – Mar 1813, Apr – Jul 1813 and Nov 1813 – Apr 1814. Present at Busaco, siege of Salamanca Forts and Salamanca (severely wounded). Father of Lt Alexander Macleod. 61st Foot. Both father and son served together in the 61st Foot at the battle of Busaco.

McMAHON, Thomas
Lieutenant Colonel. 17th (Leicestershire) Regiment of Foot.
Low monument in railed enclosure: Kensal Green Cemetery, London. (15884/100–113/PS). (Photograph)

GENERAL THOMAS McMAHON BARONET / KNIGHT GRAND CROSS OF THE BATH / AND COLONEL OF THE 10TH REGIMENT OF FOOT / BORN 27TH DECEMBER 1779 DIED 10TH APRIL 1860

Ensign 22nd Foot 2 Feb 1797. Lt 40th Foot 24 Oct 1799. Lt 32nd Foot 9 Jul 1802. Capt 16th Battalion of Reserve 8 Oct 1803. Capt 82nd Foot 14 Aug 1804. Major 15th Foot 6 Nov 1806. Major 2nd West India Regt 20 Apr 1809. Bt Lt Colonel 4 May 1809. Lt Colonel 17th Foot 20 Jun 1811. Bt Colonel 4 Jun 1814. Major General 27 May 1825. Lt General 28 Jun 1838. General 20 Jun 1854. Portuguese Army: Bt Lt Colonel 1809. Brigadier 1811. Colonel 15th Line 1811.

Served in the Peninsula with Portuguese Army May 1808 – Feb 1812. Present at Fuentes d'Onoro. Also served in the Irish Rebellion 1798, Ferrol 1800, Malta 1800, India (Adjutant General to the Forces 1813. Present in Nepal 1814 and the Mahratta Wars 1817–1818) and India 1839–1847 (Commander of the Forces in Bombay). Lt Governor of Portsmouth 1834. Colonel 94th Foot 28 Mar 1838. Colonel 10th Foot 28th Sep 1847. KCB.

Reference: Annual Register, 1860, Appx, p. 461.

MACMAHON, William O'Bryen

Captain. 96th Regiment of Foot.
Memorial: St John's Church, Hampstead Road, London. (M.I.)

"HERE LIETH THE BODY OF WILLIAM O'BRYEN MACMAHON ESQ LATE A CAPTAIN IN HIS MAJESTIES 73RD REG OF FOOT WHO DIED 15TH OCT 1826 AGED 42. HE WAS A BRAVE SOLDIER PRESENT IN NEARLY ALL THE GLORIOUS BATTLES FOUGHT IN THE PENINSULA WHERE HE WAS WOUNDED / AND SERVING HIS COUNTRY DURING THE LATE WARS IN MOST PARTS OF THE WORLD HE DISPLAYED A ZEAL AND INTREPITUDE WHICH SECURED HIM THE APPROBATION OF HIS COMMANDER AND ENTITLED HIM TO BE REMEMBERED AMONGST THOSE VALIANT MEN THROUGH WHOSE EXERTIONS THE AMBITIOUS PROJECTS OF FRANCE WERE DEFEATED AND THE PEACE OF EUROPE RESTORED. HE LEFT AN ONLY SON WILLIAM MACMAHON"

Ensign 91st Foot 28 Aug 1804. Lt 10 Apr 1806. Capt 96th Foot 9 Sep 1813. Portuguese Army: Capt 1 Caçadores 23 May 1812. Retired 23 Jun 1814.

Served in the Peninsula with 91st Foot Aug 1808 – Jan 1809 and with Portuguese Army May 1812 – Apr 1814. Present at Rolica, Vimeiro, Corunna, Salamanca, Vittoria, Pyrenees, Bidassoa, Nivelle, Orthes and Toulouse. Also served at Hanover 1805 and Walcheren 1809.

McMILLAN, William

Troop Sergeant Major. 2nd (Royal North British) Regiment of Dragoons.
Memorial: Mochrum Old Kirkyard, Mochrum, Dumfriesshire, Scotland. (M.I.)

"ERECTED BY WILLIAM MCMILLAN, TENANT IN BOGHOUSE IN MEMORY OF .... ALSO OF THE ABOVE NAMED WILLIAM MCMILLAN, FORMERLY SERGEANT IN THE SCOTCH GREYS, AND PRESENT WITH HIS REGIMENT AT THE BATTLE OF WATERLOO, WHO DIED AT BOGHOUSE ON THE 7TH OF DECEMBER 1867, AGED 91."

Pte Lanark and Dumbarton Fencible Cavalry 15 Jun 1795 – 17 May 1800. Pte 2nd Lt Dragoons 12 Jan 1801. Cpl 1805. Sgt 1810. Troop Sgt Major 1813.

Present at Waterloo in Capt Vernor's Troop (severely wounded in the head and wrist during the cavalry charge) and with the Army of Occupation. Discharged 18 Nov 1818.

MACNAB, Alexander
Captain. 30th (Cambridgeshire) Regiment of Foot.
Memorial tablet: St Paul's Cathedral, London. (Crypt). (Photograph)

SACRED / TO / THE MEMORY OF / CAPTAIN ALEXANDER MACNAB 30TH REGT / AIDE – DE – CAMP TO LIEUT GENERAL / SIR THOMAS PICTON WHO WAS WITH HIM / SLAIN AT WATERLOO / HIS BODY LIES ON THE FIELD OF BATTLE / IN THE HOPE OF A BLESSED RESURRECTION. / THIS TABLET IS ERECTED BY / HIS NEPHEWS THE REV A MACNAB D.D. / AND REV A. W. MACNAB BOTH OF / CANADA SEPT 1876

Named on the Regimental Memorial: St Joseph's Church, Waterloo. (Photograph)

Ensign Queen's Rangers (in Canada) 1800. Ensign 26th Foot 1803. Lt 30th Foot 16 Jan 1804. Capt 11 May 1809.

Served in the Peninsula Apr – May 1809 and Jun 1810 – Jun 1813. Present at Sabugal, Fuentes d'Onoro, Ciudad Rodrigo, Badajoz, Salamanca, Burgos and the retreat from Burgos (present at Villa Muriel). Present at Quatre Bras and Waterloo where he was killed (ADC to Sir Thomas Picton). Also served in Ireland 1804–1809 and the Netherlands 1814–1815.

McNAB, Allan
Lieutenant. 92nd Regiment of Foot.
Memorial tablet: Innis Bhuidhe, Killin, Perthshire, Scotland. (Photograph)

IN MEMORY / OF / ALLAN / IN HONOUR OF HIS COUSIN / LIEU^{T}: ALLAN M^{C}NAB, / 92^{D} REG^{T} / WHO, AFTER SERVING HIS COUNTRY / IN HOLLAND, PORTUGAL & SPAIN / AT LAST / ON THE FIELD OF ALMEIDA / GLORIOUSLY FELL: / 5 MAY 1811. / THIS STONE / HAS BEEN ERECTED / BY / HIS AFFECTIONATE COUSIN / ARCHIBALD M^{C}NAB / ....

Ensign Jul 1805. Lt 11 Dec 1806.

Served in the Peninsula Aug 1808 – Jan 1809 and Oct 1810 – May 1811. Present at Corunna and Fuentes d'Onoro, where he was severely wounded 5th May and died of his wounds 9 May 1811. Both arms were injured, his right arm from its socket and left arm in splinters 'has proved himself of the genuine old Highland stamp by an exhibition of fortitude barely human and which has attracted the admiration of the whole army here.' (Colonel Cameron). Also served at Walcheren 1809.

MACNAB, John
Lieutenant. 94th Regiment of Foot.
Memorial in railed enclosure: St Fillan's Churchyard, Dundurn, Comrie, Perthshire, Scotland. (Photograph)

"CAPTAIN JOHN MC NAB / 94TH REGT OF FOOT DIED 26 JUNE 1854"

Ensign 4 Jul 1811. Lt 16 Feb 1815.

Served in the Peninsula Mar – Apr 1814. Present at Vic Bigorre and Toulouse. Half pay 25 Dec 1818 on the disbanding of the regiment. MGS medal for Toulouse.

McNAIR, James
Captain. 52nd (Oxfordshire) Light Infantry Regiment of Foot.
Family Memorial: Glasgow Necropolis, Glasgow, Scotland. (Photograph)

SACRED TO THE MEMORY OF / LIEU^{T}. COL. JAMES MCNAIR KH. / OF GREENFIELD NEAR GLASGOW, / LATE OF HM 73RD REG^{T} / WHO SERVED DURING THE PENINSULAR WAR / AND

AT WATERLOO. / IN THE 52ND LIGHT INFANTRY. / AND DIED AT GREENFIELD, 11TH MAY 1836. / AGED 48 YEARS. / ....

Ensign 14 Mar 1805. Lt 30 Jun 1805. Capt 11 May 1812. Major 25 Apr 1822. Lt Colonel 73rd Foot 3 Aug 1830.

Served in the Peninsula with 1/52nd Aug 1808 – Jan 1809 and Jul 1809 – Sep 1812. Present at Corunna, Coa, Busaco, Pombal, Redinha, Casal Nova, Foz d'Arouce, Sabugal, Fuentes d'Onoro, Badajoz (where he was a volunteer in the storming party and was severely wounded) and Salamanca. Present at Waterloo and with the Army of Occupation. Also served in Sicily Sep 1806, Sweden May 1808, the Netherlands 1814 and North America 1823–1826. KH.

McNEIL, Roderick
Captain. 23rd Regiment of Light Dragoons.
Pedestal tomb: Old Common Cemetery, Southampton, Hampshire. (K69 007). (Photograph)

SACRED TO THE MEMORY OF / RODERICK MCNEIL / OF THAT ILK AND BARRA INVERNESSHIRE / LAST CHIEF OF THAT ANCIENT LINE. / GENERAL IN THE ARMY, / COLONEL 78TH HIGHLANDERS / DIED 22ND OCTOBER 1863. / ENTERED THE ARMY 1808 / WAS AT CORUNNA AND WATERLOO. / COMMANDED A DIVISION OF THE MADRAS ARMY FOR 3 YEARS. / MARRIED 1ST ISABELLA CAROLINE DAUGHTER OF THE LATE / CHARLES BROWNLOW ESQ. OF LURGAN IRELAND, / SECOND ELIZA WIDOW OF J. MIDDLETON ESQ. OF MIDANBURY HOUSE / SOUTHAMPTON. AND DAUGHTER OF THE LATE GENERAL GEORGE CARPENTER. / ....

Ensign 52nd Foot 17 Mar 1808. Lt 9 May 1809. Lt 91st Foot 19 Jul 1810. Capt 60th Foot 1 Dec 1814. Capt 23rd Lt Dragoons 19 Jan 1815. Major 2nd Life Guards 9 Aug 1821. Bt Lt Colonel 17 Jan 1822. Bt Colonel 10 Jan 1837. Major General 9 Nov 1846. Lt General 20 Jan 1854. General 21 Dec 1862.

Served in the Peninsula with 2/52nd Aug 1808 – Jan 1809. Present in the Corunna campaign. Present at Waterloo with 23rd Lt Dragoons. Also served at Walcheren 1809, Swedish Pomerania 1813, the Netherlands 1814 (present at Bergen-op-Zoom) and India with 78th Foot 1846–1851 (on Staff commanding a division of the Army in the Madras Presidency). Colonel 8th Foot 18 Mar 1855. Col 78th Foot 3 Jun 1860.
Reference: Gentleman's Magazine, Dec 1863, pp. 806–7. Branigan, Keith, Last of the Clans: General Macneil of Barra, 41st Chief of the Clan Macneil, 2010.

MACNEILL, Archibald
Captain. 91st Regiment of Foot.
Memorial tablet: Rosehill Cemetery, Montrose, Angus, Scotland. (M.I.)

"COLONEL ARCHIBALD MACNEILL, LATE CAPT. H. M. 91ST REGIMENT, DIED HERE 2.8.1867 AGED 82 ...."

Ensign 18 Aug 1804. Lt 15 Aug 1805. Adjt 15 Jun 1809–1813. Capt 25 Nov 1813.

Served in the Peninsula Aug 1808 – Jan 1809 and Oct 1812 – Apr 1814. Present at Rolica, Vimeiro, Cacabellos, Corunna, Pyrenees, Nivelle, Nive, Orthes, Aire and Toulouse. Half pay 25 Feb 1816. Later served in the Forfar Militia. MGS medal for Rolica, Vimeiro, Corunna, Pyrenees, Nivelle, Nive, Orthes and Toulouse.

McNEILL, Donald

Major. 91st Regiment of Foot.

Family Mural tablet: St John the Evangelist's Churchyard, Edinburgh, Scotland. (Left-hand side in the second bay below the church near Lothian Road). (Photograph)

.... / ALSO OF THEIR UNCLE, / COLONEL DONALD MCNEILL / OF THE 91ST REGIMENT, / WHO DIED 9TH NOVEMBER 1846 / ....

Lt Apr 18 1794. Capt 11 Dec 1804. Major 1 Aug Aug 1811. Bt Lt Colonel 26 Aug 1813. Lt Colonel 3 Sep 1818.

Served in the Peninsula Aug 1808 – Jan 1809 (Brigade Major to General Anstruther) and Sep 1812 – Oct 1813. Present at Rolica, Vimeiro, Corunna and Pyrenees (severely wounded at Sorauren when in command of the Light Companies of the Highland Brigade). Awarded Gold Medal, Bt Lt Colonelcy and a pension of £300 a year for his wounds. Also served in the Cape of Good Hope 1795, Hanover 1805 and Walcheren 1809. CB. One of the four officers in the regiment selected to raise a certain number of men in 1804 for which he received promotion. Retired in 1824.

Note: Name also recorded as McNeal.

MACNISH, William

Surgeon. 63rd (West Suffolk) Regiment of Foot.

Memorial: Warriston Cemetery, Edinburgh, Scotland. (Section P1. Grave number 108). (Photograph)

TO THE MEMORY OF / WILLIAM MACNISH, MD., / LATE SURGEON H.M. 63RD REGT. / WHO DIED 16 FEB 1866

Asst Surgeon 5th Foot 4 Aug 1804. Surgeon 63rd Foot 6 Jul 1809.

Served in the Peninsula with 1/5th Jul 1808 – Jan 1809 and 2nd Battalion of Detachments Feb 1809. Present at Rolica and Vimeiro. Did not go to Corunna with the regiment as he was left in Lisbon with the wounded. Also served at Hanover 1805 (wrecked on coast of Holland on way to Hanover and taken prisoner by the Dutch), South America 1807 and Walcheren 1809. MD Glasgow 1815. MGS medal for Rolica and Vimeiro. Half pay 20 May 1824.

McNIVEN, Thomas William Ogilvy

Lieutenant. 42nd (Royal Highland) Regiment of Foot.

Obelisk: St Michael's Churchyard, Inveresk, Midlothian, Scotland. (Photograph)

AN / FREACADAN / DUBH / TO THE MEMORY / OF / LIEUT COLONEL / T. W. OGILVY / MCNIVEN / WHO DIED / AT HIS RESIDENCE / TUSCULUM, / MUSSELBURGH / ON THE 21 NOVEMBER 1870, / IN THE 77TH YEAR / OF HIS AGE. / HE SERVED IN THE / 42ND ROYAL HIGHLANDERS, / THE BLACK WATCH / IN THE PENINSULA AND THE / SOUTH OF FRANCE, / AND WAS / SEVERELY WOUNDED / WHILE CARRYING / THE REGIMENTAL COLOURS / AT THE BATTLE OF / TOULOUSE / ON THE / 10TH OF APRIL / 1814. / ERECTED BY / THE OFFICERS OF THE 42ND / SERVING AND RETIRED / TO THE MEMORY OF / A GALLANT SOLDIER.

Ensign 23 Jul 1812. Lt 31 Mar 1814. Lt 26th Foot Feb 1818. Capt 80th Foot 29 Oct 1825. Major 24 May 1833. Bt Lt Colonel 11 Nov 1851.

Served in the Peninsula Dec 1813 – Apr 1814. Present at Bayonne, Orthes, Aire and Toulouse (severely wounded carrying the regimental colours and awarded pension of £70 per annum). Also served in Gibraltar 1818–1822, Malta and Corfu 1826–1829 and Syria 1840 (AAG on a 'Particular Service'). Half pay 24 May 1833. MGS medal for Orthes and Toulouse.

McNULTY, John
Private. 88th (Connaught Rangers) Regiment of Foot.
Buried in Ruthin Road Cemetery, Wrexham, Wales. (Burial record)

Pte 88th Foot 25 Aug 1806 – 24 Jan 1815. Pte 68th Foot 19 Feb 1817. Cpl 1818.

Served in the Peninsula with 88th Foot. Present at Badajoz where he was wounded. Also served in Canada with 68th Foot. Discharged 3 Jun 1823 owing to an accident in Albany Barracks in Canada. Returned to Ireland in 1840s and later moved to Wrexham where he was known as the Irish Attorney General as he would represent Irish people brought before the local court. Died 16 Aug 1870.

MACOWEN, James
Private. 42nd (Royal Highland) Regiment of Foot.
Mural memorial tablet: St Bean's Churchyard, Trinity Gask, Kinkell, Perthshire, Scotland. (The churchyard is adjacent to, and behind the garden of Kirk House. The church is a ruin that fell into disuse about 1639). (Photograph)

ERECTED BY / WILLIAM MACOWEN OF LONDON / IN MEMORY OF HIS GRANDFATHER / PETER MACOWEN .... / HIS GRANDMOTHER CATHARINE DRUMMOND .... / THEIR SONS JOSHUA AND JAMES / WHO FOUGHT BRAVELY AT THE BATTLE OF WATERLOO / WITH THE 42ND HIGHLANDERS (THE BLACK WATCH). / JAMES SURVIVED HIS WOUND AFTER A FEW YEARS ONLY. / JOSHUA DIED ABROAD WITH HIS REGIMENT / ON THE NEAR COMPLETION OF HIS FULL TERM OF SERVICE. /...................

Present at Waterloo in Capt James Stirling's Company where he was wounded and died a few years later from his wounds. His brother Joshua also served at Waterloo.
Note: Named as Macawen in regimental records.

McPHERSON, Alexander
Lieutenant. 92nd Regiment of Foot.
Memorial tablet in wall of railed enclosure. Burial ground (on A86 near Balgowan), Laggan, Invernesshire, Scotland. (Photograph)

IN MEMORY OF / LIEUTT ALEXANDER MCPHERSON, / LATE OF THE 92 REGT / WHO DIED AT RUTHVEN ON THE 30TH SEPT 1853. / AGED 62. / ....

Ensign 15 Dec 1808. Lt 22 Oct 1812.

Served in the Peninsula Oct 1810 – Apr 1813. Present at Fuentes d'Onoro, Arroyo dos Molinos, Almarez and Alba de Tormes. Present at Quatre Bras where he was severely wounded. Half pay 25 Mar 1817. MGS medal for Fuentes d'Onoro.

McPHERSON, Daniel
Captain. Glengarry Light Infantry Fencibles.
Obelisk: Warriston Cemetery, Edinburgh, Scotland. (Section E. Number 51). (Photograph)

IN MEMORY OF / MAJOR DANIEL MCPHERSON / LATE OF THE 2ND ROYAL VETERAN BATTALION / HE WAS BORN IN THE PARISH OF LAGGAN, / IN THE LORDSHIP OF BADANACH, / AND COUNTY OF INVERNESS, / AND DIED AT EDINBURGH 15TH JUNE 1856 / IN THE 77TH YEAR OF HIS AGE. / HE ALSO SERVED IN THE 8TH OR KING'S REGIMENT / AND GLENGARRY LIGHT INFANTRY / AND WAS PRESENT AT THE SIEGE OF / COPENHAGEN / AND ATTACK ON SACKETTS HARBOUR CANADA / WHERE HE WAS SEVERELY WOUNDED, / AND RECEIVED THE WAR MEDAL / WITH A CLASP FOR / MARTINIQUE.

Ensign 8th Foot 26 Jun 1806. Lt 18 Jun 1808. Capt Glengarry Light Infantry Fencibles 6 Feb 1812. Capt 2nd Royal Veteran Battalion 1813.

Present at Copenhagen with 8th Foot 1807. Also served at Martinique 1809 (present at the siege of Fort Bourbon), Canada 1813 (present at attack on Sackett's Harbour, the American naval base 20 May 1813, where he was severely wounded and awarded pension of £100 per annum). MGS medal for Martinique.

MACPHERSON, Donald

Captain. 39th (Dorsetshire) Regiment of Foot.

Memorial tablet: Parish Church, Laggan, Invernesshire, Scotland. (Photograph)

IN MEMORY OF / COL. DONALD MACPHERSON, K.H. / 39TH REGT / WHOSE REMAINS ARE INTERRED / IN THE VAULT OF HIS ANCESTORS, / IN THE OLD CHURCH OF LAGGAN. / HE DIED AT BURGIE HOUSE / ON THE 28TH DECEMBER 1851, AGED 77. / HE WAS ENGAGED IN ACTIVE SERVICE, / SHARING IN THE GLORIES, AND DANGERS / OF THE PENINSULAR WAR; / HE WAS HONOURED AND BELOVED BY HIS / COMPANIONS IN ARMS: / AND IN PRIVATE LIFE HE NO LESS ENJOYED / THE RESPECT, AND ATTACHMENT / OF ALL WHO KNEW HIM. / AS A MEMORIAL OF HER LOSS, AND AFFECTIONS / THIS TABLET IS ERECTED BY HIS WIDOW.

Ensign 8 Apr 1796. Lt 22 Jul 1797. Capt 5 Jan 1805. Bt Major 12 Aug 1819. Major 12 Aug 1824. Lt Colonel 1 Apr 1832.

Served in the Peninsula with 2/39th Jul 1808 – Dec 1811 and 1/39th Jan 1812 – Apr 1814. Present at Busaco, first siege of Badajoz, Albuera, Arroyo dos Molinos, Vittoria, Pyrenees, Nivelle, Nive, Orthes, Aire and Toulouse. Also served in North America 1814–1815. MGS medal for Busaco, Albuera, Vittoria, Pyrenees, Nivelle, Nive, Orthes and Toulouse. KH. Retired 10 Feb 1837. Cousin of Major John Macpherson 92nd Foot who died of wounds from Nive Jan 1814.

MACPHERSON, Duncan

Lieutenant. 79th (Cameron Highlanders) Regiment of Foot.

Named on the Regimental Memorial: St Joseph's Church, Waterloo. (Photograph)

Ensign 8 Oct 1807. Lt 19 Jul 1810.

Served in the Peninsula Aug 1808 – Jan 1809 and Jan 1810 – Apr 1814. Present at Corunna, Coa, Foz d'Arouce, Fuentes d'Onoro, Salamanca, Burgos, Pyrenees, Nivelle, Nive and Toulouse (severely wounded). Present at Quatre Bras and Waterloo where he was killed 18 Jun. Also served in Sweden 1808 and Walcheren 1809.

McPHERSON, Duncan

Lieutenant. 92nd Regiment of Foot.

Named on the Memorial: St Andrew's Church (now Musée Historique), Biarritz, France. (Photograph)

Ensign 15 Oct 1807. Lt 15 Dec 1808.

Served in the Peninsula Aug 1808 – Jan 1809 and May – Dec 1813. Present at Corunna, Vittoria, Pyrenees, Nivelle and Nive where he was killed 13 Dec 1813.

MACPHERSON, Evan

Ensign. 36th (Herefordshire) Regiment of Foot.

Buried in Dalry Cemetery, Edinburgh, Scotland. (Grave number 376). (M.I.)

"LIEUT EVAN MACPHERSON DIED 5 DEC 1859"

Ensign 6 Sep 1812. Lt and Adjt 1 Apr 1819.

Served in the Peninsula Jan 1813 – Apr 1814. Present at Pyrenees, Bidassoa, Nivelle, Nive, Vic Bigorre, Tarbes and Toulouse. Awarded pension of £50 for loss of one eye at Foraish 1813.

McPHERSON, John

Major. 92nd Regiment of Foot.
Named on the Memorial: St Andrew's Church (now Musée Historique), Biarritz, France. (Photograph)

Lt 26 Feb 1798. Capt 24 Nov 1803. Major 5 Apr 1813. Bt Lt Colonel 26 Aug 1813.

Served in the Peninsula Aug 1808 – Jan 1809 and Oct 1810 – Jan 1814. Present at Corunna, Fuentes d'Onoro, Arroyo dos Molinos (severely wounded), Almarez, Alba de Tormes, Vittoria, Pyrenees (wounded 25 July and severely wounded 31 July 1813) and Nive (severely wounded 13 Dec and died of his wounds 1 Jan 1814). Gold Medal for Vittoria and Pyrenees. Also served at Walcheren 1809. Cousin of Capt Donald Macpherson 39th Foot.

McPHERSON, Philip

Lieutenant. 43rd (Monmouthshire) Light Infantry Regiment of Foot.
Headstone: York Cemetery, York, Yorkshire. (Grave number Z/15/13). (Photograph)

SACRED TO THE MEMORY OF / MATILDA, / WIFE OF / COLONEL P. McPHERSON, C.B. / INSPECTING FIELD OFFICER / OF THE YORK DISTRICT / WHO DEPARTED THIS LIFE / ON THE 19TH DECR 1858. / AGED 58. / PHILIP McPHERSON C.B. / MAJOR GENERAL / DIED FEB 2ND 1864 / AGED 73

Volunteer 52nd Foot May 1809. Ensign 43rd Foot 2 Nov 1809. Lt 13 Nov 1811. Lt 30th Foot 25 Apr 1816. Lt 46th Foot 19 May 1825. Lt 35th Foot 12 Oct 1826. Capt (unattached) 13 Mar 1827. Capt 17th Foot 26 Nov 1841. Major 1 Aug 1844. Bt Lt Colonel 4 Jul 1843. Bt Colonel 20 Jun 1854. Major General 24 Dec 1858.

Served in the Peninsula with 52nd Foot Jul 1809 – Nov 1809 and 43rd Foot Nov 1809 – Dec 1812 and Nov 1813 – Apr 1814. Present at Coa, Busaco, Pombal, Redinha, Casal Nova, Foz d'Arouce, Sabugal, Fuentes d'Onoro, Ciudad Rodrigo, Badajoz (wounded), Castrejon, Salamanca, San Munos, Nivelle, Nive, Tarbes and Toulouse. Also served in India 1843 as ADC to Sir Charles Napier (present at Scinde, Meeanee, and Hyderabad, awarded medal and twice Mentioned in Despatches. CB), Crimea 1854 – Jun 1855 in command of 1st Brigade 4th Division (present on the heights above Sebastopol but had to leave owing to ill health). Knight of Legion of Honour 4th class of the Medjidee and Turkish medal. MGS medal for Busaco, Fuentes d'Onoro, Ciudad Rodrigo, Badajoz, Salamanca, Nivelle, Nive and Toulouse. Colonel 13th Foot 15 Aug 1863. Inspecting Field Officer of the York District. Died 2 Feb 1864 aged 73.
Reference: Gentleman's Magazine, May 1864, pp. 660–1. Oxfordshire Lt Infantry Chronicle, 1897, pp. 120–1.

MACQUEEN, John Donald

Captain. 74th (Highland) Regiment of Foot.
Gravestone: Old Churchyard, Spital, Windsor, Berkshire. Inscription not recorded. (Grave number O 107).

Ensign 14 Jul 1800. Lt 25 Jun 1803. Capt 26 Apr 1810. Major 20 Oct 1830.

Served in the Peninsula 1810 – Apr 1814. Present at Busaco, retreat to the lines of Torres Vedras, Pombal, Redinha, Casal Nova, Foz d'Arouce, Sabugal, Fuentes d'Onoro (severely wounded), Salamanca, Capture of Madrid and Retiro, retreat to Portugal, Vittoria (wounded three times), Pyrenees, Nivelle, Nive, Orthes, Tarbes and Toulouse (severely wounded and left for dead on the battlefield, but was rescued by his foster brother John Gillanders. Gillanders carried him to a house which was full of officers and called for a bed for his Captain. A wounded officer lay on the bed and when he saw how badly injured McQueen was he got up and made room for him. This officer was Sir Thomas Brisbane. Awarded pension of £100 per annum). Also served in North America 1818–1824 and 1825–1828 and Bermuda 1828–1829. MGS medal for Busaco, Fuentes d'Onoro, Salamanca, Vittoria, Pyrenees, Nivelle, Nive, Orthes and Toulouse. Barrack master at Dundee and Perth. Retired in 1834. KH 1835. Military Knight of Windsor. Died in 1866 aged 80.

MACREADY, Edward Nevil

Ensign. 30th (Cambridgeshire) Regiment of Foot.
Headstone and Cross on low monument: St Peter's Churchyard, Leckhampton, Gloucestershire. (Photograph)

SACRED / TO / THE MEMORY / OF / EDWARD NEVIL MACREADY, / MAJOR UNATTACHED LATE 30TH REGT / WHO DIED SUDDENLY / AT CLEVEDON, SOMERSET, / ON THE 4TH DAY OF NOV 1848, / AGED 50 YEARS. / (VERSE) / ....

Memorial tablet: St Peter's Church, Leckhampton, Gloucestershire. (Photograph)

HOLLAND. / QUATRE BRAS. / WATERLOO. / ASSEERGHUR. / TO THE / BELOVED AND REVERED MEMORY / OF / EDWARD NEVIL MACREADY, / MAJOR IN HER MAJESTY'S SERVICE, / LATE OF THE 30TH REGIMENT. / THIS TABLET IS DEDICATED / BY / HER WHOM HE HAS LEFT TO MOURN / THRO' LIFE HIS IRREPARABLE LOSS. / SOLDIER GO HOME: WITH THEE THE FIGHT IS WON.

Volunteer 30th Regt 1 Mar 1814. Ensign 8 Sep 1814. Lt 20 Jul 1815. Capt 16 Jul 1829. Major 22 Nov 1839.

Present at Quatre Bras and Waterloo. Still only an Ensign, Macready had to lead his company at Waterloo as he was the only surviving officer. At the end of the day he and 16 men were the only survivors of his Lt Company, out of 3 officers and 51 men. He was promoted to Lieutenant for his gallantry after the battle. Present at the Capture of Paris and with the Army of Occupation. Also served in the Netherlands 1814–1815, India 1818 (present in the Mahratta Wars 1819, including the siege of Asseerghur), Ceylon (Military Secretary to General Sir John Wilson) and Ionian Islands (ADC to Mr Stewart Mackenzie, Lord High Commissioner). Half pay 1839. His brother William Charles Macready, the famous Shakespearian actor, purchased Edward Macready's commission 30 September 1814. Macready kept a diary giving a full account of his service and especially of the Waterloo campaign.

McWHAN, Samuel

Corporal. 95th Regiment of Foot.
Headstone: Girthon Cemetery, Gatehouse of Fleet, Dumfriesshire, Scotland. (Photograph)

ERECTED / BY / JAMES OSWALD / IN MEMORY OF / HIS GRANDFATHER SAMUEL McWHAN / CORPORAL 95 REGIMENT OF FOOT WHO DIED IN / THE GENERAL HOSPITAL VITTORIA / 1 SEPTEMBER 1813 / ....

Served in the Peninsula until Jun 1813. Present at Vittoria where he was severely wounded and died of his wounds Sep 1813.

MADDEN, Edward Marcell

Lieutenant. 95th Regiment of Foot.
Memorial tablet: Chichester Cathedral, Sussex. (North Nave Aisle, North Wall). (Photograph)

TO THE MEMORY OF EDWARD MADDEN, / OF THE RIFLE BRIGADE, / WHO DIED ON THE 22ND DAY OF MARCH 1819, / AGED 23 YEARS; / THIS TABLET IS ERECTED / BY HIS BROTHER

OFFICERS, / TO MARK THEIR DEEP REGRET FOR HIS LOSS, / AND AS A TESTIMONY OF THEIR HIGH AND LASTING SENSE / OF HIS VIRTUES, SOCIAL AND MILITARY, / HIS MANLY AND LIBERAL PRINCIPLES, / HIS FRANK AND GENEROUS TEMPER, / HIS UNSULLIED HONOR, / AND HIS TRIED AND CONSPICUOUS / GALLANTRY, / IN THE FACE OF THE ENEMIES / OF HIS COUNTRY.

Family tombstone: Chichester Cathedral Churchyard, Sussex. (South-east corner). (No longer extant). (M.I.)

"................... / OF EDWARD MADDEN / (HIS YOUNGER SON) WHO LIES BURIED UNDERNEATH, / LATE A LIEUTENANT IN THE RIFLE BRIGADE, / WHO DIED OF CONSUMPTION / BROUGHT ON BY THE HARDSHIPS OF SERVICE / ON THE 22ND OF MARCH 1819, / AGED 23 YEARS. / ...."

2nd Lt 2 May 1811. 1st Lt 13 May 1813.

Served in the Peninsula with 2/95th Jan 1813 – Mar 1814. Present at San Millan, Vittoria, Pyrenees, Vera, Bidassoa (wounded) and Nivelle. Present at Waterloo. Half pay Dec 1818 on reduction of the 3rd Battalion, but died of consumption three months later. Brother of Capt William Sterling Madden 52nd Foot who was killed at Badajoz, and Lt Wyndham Carlyon Madden 43rd Foot and step brother of Lt Colonel Henry Ridewood 45th Foot.

MADDEN, George Allan

Major. 12th (Prince of Wales's) Regiment of Light Dragoons.

Memorial tablet: English Heritage store, Fort Brockhurst, Gosport, Hampshire. (Removed from south wall of nave of the Royal Garrison Chapel). (Reference number: 83100127). (Photograph)

TO THE MEMORY OF / MAJOR-GENERAL SIR GEORGE ALLAN MADDEN / KNT. C.B. AND COMMANDER OF THE ORDER / OF THE TOWER AND SWORD / BORN JANUARY 3RD 1771. DIED DECEMBER 8TH 1828 / AGED 57 YEARS. / HIS EARLIER SERVICES WERE IN CORSICA / AND EGYPT AND SUBSEQUENTLY HE / DISTINGUISHED HIMSELF IN THE WAR OF / THE PENINSULA, PARTICULARLY NEAR / FUENTE DE CANTOS IN ESTREMADURA / WHERE, AT THE HEAD OF THE BRIGADE / OF PORTUGUESE CAVALRY, UNDER HIS / ORDERS, HE GALLANTLY CHARGED AND / REPULSED THE FRENCH ARMY OF ANDALUSIA / ON THE 15TH SEPTEMBER 1810 COMMANDED / BY MARSHALL MORTIER AND BY THIS / BRILLIANT EXPLOIT WAS THE MEANS OF / SAVING THE SPANISH ARMY UNDER THE / MARQUIS DE LA ROMANA FROM DESTRUCTION.

Cornet 14th Lt Dragoons 14 Mar 1789. Lt 12th Lt Dragoons 12 Jul 1791. Capt 29 Jun 1793. Major 25 Dec 1800. Bt Lt Colonel 4 Jul 1805. Bt Colonel 4 Jun 1813. Major General 12 Aug 1819. Portuguese Army: Brigadier Cavalry 24 Sep 1809. Brigadier 7th Portuguese Brigade 4 Oct 1812.

Served in the Peninsula with Portuguese Army Sep 1809 – Apr 1812 and Aug 1812 – Apr 1814. Present at Fuentes de Cantos (Mentioned in Beresford's Despatches 15 Sep 1810), Usagre and Pyrenees (Mentioned in Beresford's Despatches). Gold Medal for Pyrenees. CB. Knighted 1817. Also served in Corsica 1795, Portugal 1797–1800 (Under Lt General Sir C. Stuart), Egypt 1801 (present at Alexandria and Rahmanie). A court martial took place in the regiment in 1801 when Madden alleged that his Lt Colonel had perjured himself. This resulted in Madden being tried and dismissed from the service. He had influential friends and was allowed to retire. When the Yeomanry was called out in 1805 he became Inspecting Field Officer of the Midland District. This proved to be good experience for his next appointment when Beresford appointed him Commandant of a Brigade of Cavalry on the re-organisation of the Portuguese Army in 1809. When Wellington inspected the Portuguese cavalry he was much impressed with Madden's work. Even more so when he heard of the affair at Fuentes de Cantos. The Spanish army had almost been destroyed at Carrera and only Madden's Portuguese cavalry stopped the French advance. Retired from the Portuguese Army 13 Oct 1814.

Reference: *Dictionary of National Biography. Royal Military Calendar, Vol. 4, pp. 48–117. Gentleman's Magazine, Mar 1829, pp. 277–9. Thompson, J., The services of General Sir George Madden, 1999.*

MADDEN, William Sterling

Captain. 52nd (Oxfordshire) Light Infantry Regiment of Foot.
Memorial tablet: Chichester Cathedral, Chichester, Sussex. (M.I.)

"WILLIAM STERLING MADDEN ON 6TH APRIL 1812, / AGED 24, KILLED ON BREACH AT BADAJOS."

Family tombstone: Chichester Cathedral Churchyard, Sussex. (South-east corner). (M.I.)

"SACRED / TO THE MEMORY OF / WILLIAM STERLING MADDEN / (SON OF MAJOR MADDEN, BARRACK-MASTER OF / THIS PLACE), LATE A CAPTAIN OF THE 52ND REGT OF LT. INFANTRY / WHO WAS KILLED ON THE BREACH OF BADAJOZ IN / SPAIN ON THE NIGHT OF THE 6TH OF APRIL, 1812, / AGED 24 YEARS. / …………………"

Ensign 72nd Foot 21 Jul 1798. Lt 35th Foot 21 Dec 1799. Lt 52nd Foot 18 Feb 1800. Captain 10 Jul 1805.

Served in the Peninsula with 2/52nd Aug 1808 – Jan 1809 and 1/52nd Jul 1809 – Apr 1812. Present at Vimeiro, Vigo, Coa, Busaco, Pombal, Redinha, Casal Nova, Foz d'Arouce, Fuentes d'Onoro, Ciudad Rodrigo and Badajoz where he volunteered for the storming party at the siege of Badajoz and was killed 6 Apr 1812. Brother of Lt Edward Marcell Madden 95th Foot and Lt Wyndham Carlyon 43rd Foot and step brother of Lt Colonel Henry Ridewood 45th Foot.

MADDEN, Wyndham Carlyon

Lieutenant. 43rd (Monmouthshire) Light Infantry Regiment of Foot.
Altar tomb: St Peter and St Paul's Churchyard, Bergh Apton, Norfolk. (Near southern boundary of graveyard). (Photograph)

IN MEMORY OF / THE REVD WYNDHAM CARLYON / MADDEN M. A. / RECTOR OF THIS PARISH / WHO DIED 13TH MAY 1864, / AGED 70 YEARS. / ALSO OF / WILLIAM AND EDWARD / CHILDREN OF THE ABOVE / REVD W. C. MADDEN / AND CHARLOTTE HIS WIFE / WHO DIED IN THEIR INFANCY / ALSO OF HENRIETTA RIDEWOOD / NIECE OF THE ABOVE / AND ONLY CHILD OF THE LATE / COLONEL RIDEWOOD / OF THE 45TH REG / AND CHARLOTTE HIS WIFE / WHO DIED FEB 3RD 1865.

Ensign 18 Feb 1808. Lt 3 May 1809. Capt 92nd Foot 10 Feb 1820.

Served in the Peninsula with 2/43rd Aug 1808 – Jan 1809 and 1/43rd Jul 1811 – Jun 1812 and Oct 1813 – Apr 1814. Present at Vimeiro (wounded), Ciudad Rodrigo, Badajoz (severely wounded and awarded pension of £70 per annum), Bidassoa, Nivelle (severely wounded), Tarbes and Toulouse. Also served in North America 1814–1815 (present at New Orleans). Half pay 1821. MGS medal for Vimeiro, Ciudad Rodrigo, Badajoz, Nivelle and Toulouse. Retired 1825, and entered the church, becoming Rector of St Peter and Paul, Bergh Apton. Brother of Lt Edward Marcell Madden 95th Foot and Capt William Sterling Madden 52nd Foot and step brother of Lt Colonel Henry Ridewood 45th Foot.

MADIN, George

Corporal. 33rd (1st Yorkshire West Riding) Regiment of Foot.
Headstone: Nottingham Cemetery, Nottingham, Nottinghamshire. (near to Friend's Meeting House). (Photograph)

IN / AFFECTIONATE / REMEMBRANCE OF / GEORGE MADIN, / WHO DIED DEC^R 28TH, 1874, / AGED 84 YEARS. / FORMERLY SERGEANT IN THE 33RD REGT. OF FOOT / (OR WELLINGTON'S OWN). / HE SERVED IN THE ACTIONS OF / QUATRE BRAS AND WATERLOO / ....

Pte 1 Apr 1811.

Present at Quatre Bras and Waterloo (blinded in left eye). Also served in the Netherlands 1814 (present at Bergen-op-Zoom where he was wounded). Discharged 1817. Later served in the Nottinghamshire Militia.

MADOX, Henry

Captain. 6th (Inniskilling) Regiment of Dragoons.
Low monument: Abbey Cemetery, Bath, Somerset. (Photograph)

SACRED / TO THE MEMORY OF / COLONEL HENRY MADOX K.H. / LATE LIEUT COLONEL OF THE / 6TH OR INNISKILLING DRAGOONS / IN WHICH REGIMENT HE SERVED / MORE THAN THIRTY YEARS. / IN THE CAMPAIGN OF 1815 / HE WAS SENIOR CAPTAIN / AND AS SUCH COMMANDED THE / REGIMENT DURING A GREAT PART / OF THE BATTLE OF WATERLOO, / ON THE 18TH OF JUNE 1815 / BROUGHT IT OUT OF ACTION / CONTINUED IN COMMAND / AT THE CAPTURE OF PARIS / AND WITH A SHORT INTERVAL / TILL ITS RETURN TO ENGLAND. / HE WAS BORN / ON THE 9TH OF FEBRUARY 1782 / AND DIED / ON THE 18TH OF MARCH 1865

Memorial window: Bath Abbey, Bath, Somerset. (Photograph)

COLONEL HENRY MADOX K.H. BORN FEBRUARY 9TH 1789. DIED 18TH MARCH 1865.

THE ABOVE WINDOW AND THIS TABLET ARE PLACED BY / ROSE MADOX. SACRED TO THE MEMORY, AND IN LOVING / REMEMBRANCE OF HER HUSBAND COLONEL HENRY MADOX K.H. / LATE OF THE 6TH OR INNISKILLING DRAGOONS, IN WHICH REGIMENT HE SERVED / THIRTY YEARS. IN THE CAMPAIGN OF 1815 HE WAS SENIOR CAPTAIN AND AS / SUCH COMMANDED IT DURING A GREAT PART OF THE BATTLE OF WATERLOO ON THE / 18TH OF JUNE 1815, BROUGHT IT OUT OF ACTION, CONTINUED IN COMMAND AT THE / CAPITULATION OF PARIS, AND WITH A SHORT INTERVAL TILL ITS RETURN TO ENGLAND. / A BRAVE AND ABLE SOLDIER, JUST, TRUE, AND KIND, A SINCERE CHRISTIAN HE CLOSED HIS LONG / AND HONOURABLE LIFE ON 18TH OF MARCH 1865. HE WAS BORN ON THE 3RD FEBRUARY 1782. (VERSE)

Cornet 14 Mar 1800. Lt 23 Jul 1803. Capt 19 Dec 1805. Bt Major 18 Jun 1815. Major 15 May 1817. Lt Colonel 18 Jan 1833. Bt Colonel 28 Jun 1838.

Present at Waterloo. After Quatre Bras he was ordered with three troops of cavalry to Genappe to help carry the wounded infantry back to Brussels. On 18th June he commanded the right squadron of the Inniskillings in the charge, and during the last stages of the battle took command of the regiment owing to the death and wounds of senior officers. Awarded Bt Majority for Waterloo. Half pay 1825, but returned to full pay in 1833. KH.

Reference: Gentleman's Magazine, Apr 1865, p. 534. Morley, Alan, Colonel Henry Madox KH, Bath Abbey Annual Report, 2012. (Text and photographs of the memorial in Bath Abbey).

MAGENIS, Henry Arthur
Lieutenant. 7th (Royal Fusiliers) Regiment of Foot.
Low monument with hipped top: Kensal Green Cemetery, London. (10508/118/2). (Photograph)

IN MEMORY OF / HENRY ARTHUR MAGENIS / LT COL. LATE COMMANDING THE 87TH AND 27TH REGIMENTS / AND INSPECTING FIELD OFFICER OF THE YORK RECRUITING DISTRICTS. / DIED AT YORK THE 14TH OF NOVEMBER 1852. AGED 58. / WAS PRESENT AT THE BATTLES OF / NIVELLE, ORTHES, TOULOUSE & NEW ORLEANS.

Cornet Royal Horse Guards 1 Oct 1812. Lt 7th Foot 4 Mar 1813. Capt 37th Foot 9 Sep 1819. Capt 28th Foot 19 Oct 1820. Capt 82nd Foot 30 Sep 1824. Major 20 Nov 1827. Major 93rd Foot 22 Feb 1831. Major 87th 25 Feb 1831. Bt Lt Colonel 23 Nov 1841. Lt Colonel 18 Apr 1845. Lt Colonel 27th Regt 23 Mar 1849.

Served in the Peninsula with 1/7th Nov 1813 – Apr 1814. Present at Nivelle, Orthes, Bordeaux and Toulouse. Also served in North America 1814 (present at New Orleans), Mauritius and Cape of Good Hope 1823–1830 (on staff of Sir Galbraith Lowry Cole). MGS medal for Nivelle, Orthes and Toulouse. Colonel 87th Foot 1845–1849. Colonel 27th Foot 1849–1852. Inspecting Field Officer of York Recruiting District 1 Apr 1852 where he died a few months later.

MAHER, Philip
Private. 51st (2nd Yorkshire West Riding) Light Infantry.
Headstone: Ross Burial Ground, Ross, Tasmania, Australia. (Photograph)

SACRED / TO THE MEMORY / OF / PHILIP MAHER / WHO DEPARTED THIS LIFE / ON THE 31ST MARCH A.D. 1845 / AND SERVED AS QUARTER MASTER SERGEANT / IN THE 51ST K. O. Y. L. . I. / DURING A LONG CAMPAIGN IN THE / PENINSULA AND WATERLOO / AND LATE BARRACK SERGEANT / AT ROSS / AGED 56 YEARS.

Pte 21 Jun 1811. Cpl 29 Jun 1823. Sgt 25 Jul 1825. Quartermaster Sgt 22 Mar 1827.

Served in the Peninsula 1812–1814. Present at Burgos, retreat from Burgos, San Munos, Vittoria, Pyrenees, Nivelle and Orthes. Present at Waterloo in Capt Peter Smellie's Company. Also served in the Netherlands 1814–1815 and in Australia (Barrack Sergeant in Ross, Tasmania). Discharged 27 Jan 1844.

MAHON, Luke
Lieutenant and Captain. 3rd Regiment of Foot Guards.
Memorial stone and low monument: Guards Cemetery, St Etienne, Bayonne, France. (Photograph)

TO THE MEMORY / OF / CAPTAIN MAHON / THIRD GUARDS / WHO DIED OF WOUNDS RECEIVED / IN ACTION BEFORE BAYONNE / ON THE 14 APRIL / 1814

Memorial tablet: St Nicholas's Church, Tuxford, Nottinghamshire. (Photograph)

THE DESIGN ABOVE REPRESENTS THE BURIAL PLACE OF CAPTN WHITE AND THREE OF / HIS BROTHER OFFICERS. I. B. SHIFFNER FRANCIS R. HOLBURNE AND LUKE MAHON. / CAPTS WHITE AND SHIFFNER WERE BURIED TOGETHER IN THE GRAVE MARKED WITH THEIR / INITIALS, THE CROSS WAS FORMED OF A LARGE TREE AS IT GREW THE TOP BEING CUT OFF / AND PLACED ACROSS, ABOVE WHICH IT HAD BEEN PENETRATED BY A 24LB SHOT WHICH / REMAINED IN THE TREE AS REPRESENTED. – WITH THE DRUMS AND COLOURS AS PLACED / AT THE FUNERALS IN A VALLEY ABOUT A MILE FROM BAYONNE. / THERE WERE AFTER-WARDS STONES PLACED AT THE HEAD OF EACH GRAVE BY THE / SURVIVING OFFICERS OF THE REGIMENT / ....

(Remainder of this memorial refers exclusively to Lt and Capt Charles Lawrence White)

Named on the Memorial: St Andrew's Church (now Musée Historique), Biarritz, France. (Photograph)

Named on Memorial Panel VII for the Sortie from Bayonne: Royal Military Chapel, Wellington Barracks, London. (M.I.) (Destroyed by a Flying Bomb 1944)

Ensign 6 Feb 1806. Lt and Capt 27 Jun 1811.

Served in the Peninsula Apr 1809 – Aug 1811 and Apr 1814. Present at Douro, Talavera, Busaco, Fuentes d'Onoro and Bayonne where he was severely wounded at the Sortie from Bayonne 14 Apr 1814 and died of his wounds 15 Apr 1814.

MAINWARING, John Montague

Lieutenant Colonel. 51st (2nd Yorkshire West Riding) Light Infantry.
Buried in St Mary's Churchyard, Cowes, Isle of Wight. (Burial register)

Ensign 67th Foot 31 May 1784. Lt 11 Nov 1789. Capt 8 Oct 1794. Major 22 Jun 1801. Lt Colonel 90th Foot 23 Nov 1804. Lt Colonel 51st Foot 21 Apr 1808. Bt Colonel 4 Jun 1813. Major General 12 Aug 1819. Lt General 10 Jan 1837.

Served in the Peninsula Oct 1808 – Jan 1809 and Feb – Aug 1811. Present at Lugo, Corunna, Fuentes d'Onoro, second siege of Badajoz (wounded in the trenches and went back to Lisbon and then to England). Also served in the West Indies 1785–1794 (present in Grenada and Martinique), Ireland, Guernsey and Jersey 1808, Walcheren 1809 (present at the siege of Flushing) and West Indies 1819 (on Staff at Antigua). Commandant of Hilsea Barracks Portsmouth 1812. Commandant of Albany Barracks Isle of Wight 1814. Died 11 Jan 1842 aged 80.

Reference: Royal Military Calendar, Vol. 4, pp. 12–14. Gentleman's Magazine, Sep 1842, pp. 321–2.

MAIR, John Hastings

Captain. 7th (Royal Fusiliers) Regiment of Foot.
Memorial: St George's Anglican Church, Grenada, West Indies. (Buried in the precincts). (Photograph)

2nd Lt 21st (Royal North British) Fusiliers 27 Sep 1805. Lt 7th Foot 19 Feb 1806. Capt 17 Jul 1811. Bt Major 7 Jan 1819. Major 30 Dec 1824. Lt Colonel (unattached) 19 Dec 1826.

Served in the Peninsula with 1/7th Aug 1810 – Oct 1812. Present at Busaco (severely wounded), Pombal, Condeixa, Olivencia, first siege of Badajoz, Albuera, Aldea de Ponte, Ciudad Rodrigo and Badajoz (commanded storming party of the 4th Division on the Trinidad Bastion where he was severely wounded and awarded pension of £100 per annum). Gold Medal for Badajoz. Served with the Army of Occupation 1815–1818. Also served in Copenhagen 1807, Martinique 1809, Ireland 1818, Corfu 1825 (in command of the 7th Foot) and Portugal 1826 (Judge Advocate in Sir William Clinton's expedition), KH. KTS. On his return to England was employed in quelling disturbances in rural areas and also the riots in London. He drew up for the government a plan for rural police to stop the burning of property and hayricks in isolated areas. Formed a constabulary force in the west of England 1830. Verified records of service of men in the army. Governor of Dominica 1835. Governor of Grenada 1836 where he died 21 Mar 1836 after an illness of only five days.

Reference:Gentlman's Magazine, Oct 1836, p. 430. United Service Journal, Jul 1836, pp. 387–8.

MAISTER, John

Lieutenant Colonel. 34th (Cumberland) Regiment of Foot.
Memorial tablet: Ripon Cathedral, Yorkshire. (Photograph)

SACRED TO THE MEMORY OF / GENERAL JOHN MAISTER / OF LITTLETHORPE, / COLONEL

86TH REGIMENT. / BORN 7TH MAY 1778. DIED 18TH MAY 1852. / ....

Ensign 54th Foot 13 Nov 1793. Lt Independent Company 14 Jun 1794. Lt 61st Foot 9 Apr 1794. Capt 117th Foot 30 Mar 1795. Capt 20th Foot 3 Sep 1795. Major 20 Jun 1801. Lt Colonel 34th Foot 20 Aug 1807. Bt Colonel 4 Jun 1814. Major General 19 Jul 1821. Lt General 10 Jan 1837. General 11 Nov 1851.

Served in the Peninsula Jul 1809 – Jun 1810. Present at Olivencia. Also served at the Helder 1799 (wounded four times on 6 Oct 1799) and Malta. Later appointed Commandant of Troops in the Windward and Leeward Islands. Colonel 86th Foot 25 Aug 1843.

MAITLAND, Frederick

Colonel. 1st Ceylon Regiment.

Memorial tablet: St Mary the Virgin Church, Hartfield, Sussex. (South wall of chancel). (Photograph)

SACRED / TO THE MEMORY OF / GENERAL FREDERICK MAITLAND, / COLONEL OF HER MAJESTY'S 58TH REGT OF FOOT: / WHOSE REMAINS ARE DEPOSITED IN A VAULT BENEATH. / BORN 3RD SEPTR 1763. / DIED AT TONBRIDGE WELLS, 27TH JANY 1848. / HE WAS THE YOUNGEST SON OF / GENERAL / THE HONBLE SIR ALEXANDER MAITLAND BART. / AFTER A LONG CAREER / OF ACTIVE AND DISTINGUISHED SERVICE / MARKED BY SPOTLESS INTEGRITY / HE RETIRED TO HOLLYWYCH IN THIS PARISH / HIS AMIABLE AND GENEROUS NATURE CAUSE / HIM TO BE / MOST DEEPLY LAMENTED / BY A SORROWING FAMILY.

Ensign 14th Foot 1 Sep 1779. Lt 19 Sep 1782. Lt 30th Foot 20 Oct 1784. Capt 60th Foot 2 Dec 1789. Bt Major 21 Aug 1793. Bt Lt Colonel 2 Jul 1794. Major 9th Foot 2 Oct 1794. Lt Colonel 1 Sep 1795. Lt Colonel 27th Foot 17 Nov 1796. Bt Colonel 1 Jan 1800. Lt Colonel 29th Foot 4 Aug 1804. Major General 30 Oct 1805. Colonel 1st Ceylon Regt 22 Feb 1810. Lt General 1 Jan 1812. General 27 May 1825.

Served in the Peninsula Jul – Oct 1812. Commanded the British Army in the Mediterranean 1811 until arrival of Lord W. Bentinck. On his arrival Maitland took a force of 7,000 men from Sicily to the East coast of Spain. Also served as a Marine on HMS *Union* (present at the siege of Gibraltar 1781), the West Indies 1787 (AQMG and Military Secretary to Sir Ralph Abercrombie), Tobago 1793, Martinique, St Lucia and Guadeloupe 1794, the Helder 1799, West Indies 1800 (QMG), Surinam 1804 and Martinique 1809. Gold Medal for Martinique. He served for 20 years in the West Indies which affected his health so much that he had to leave the Peninula in 1812. Governor of Grenada 1805–1812. Lt Governor of Dominica 13 Jan 1813. Colonel 58th Foot 11 Dec 1833.

REFERENCE: Gentleman's Magazine, Apr 1848, pp. 437–8. Annual Register, 1848, Appx, pp. 209–10.

MAITLAND, Peregrine

Captain and Lieutenant Colonel. 1st Regiment of Foot Guards.

Interred in Catacomb B (v48 c7 & 8), Kensal Green Cemetery, London. Removed to Tongham, near Farnham, Surrey, 4 Oct 1873 on the death of his wife.

Celtic cross: St Paul's Churchyard, Tongham, Surrey. (Photograph)

IN MEMORY OF / PEREGRINE MAITLAND / KNIGHT / GRAND CROSS OF THE ORDER / OF THE BATH. / GENERAL IN HER MAJESTY'S SERVICE. / BORN 1777. DIED 1854. / AND OF SARAH HIS WIFE / DAUGHTER OF / CHARLES 4TH DUKE OF RICHMOND. / BORN 1792. DIED 1873.

Memorial: Royal Military Chapel, Wellington Barracks, London. (M.I.) (Destroyed by a Flying Bomb 1944)

"IN MEMORY OF SIR PEREGRINE MAITLAND, G.C.B., GENERAL IN HER MAJESTY'S SERVICE. BORN 6TH JULY, 1777; DIED 30TH MAY, 1854. HE SERVED IN THE FIRST GUARDS FROM 25TH

JULY, 1792, TO 14TH JUNE. 1814, AND TOOK PART IN THE CAMPAIGN OF 1794 IN FLANDERS; IN THE CAMPAIGN OF 1808–9 IN SPAIN, UNDER GENERAL SIR JOHN MOORE, K.B., INCLUDING THE BATTLE OF CORUNNA; IN THE EXPEDITION TO THE SCHELDT OF 1809, AND WAS SECOND IN COMMAND AT THE CAPTURE OF SEVILLE IN 1812. HE COMMANDED THE 1ST BRIGADE OF GUARDS IN FRANCE FROM AUG 1813, TILL THE PEACE IN 1814; AND IN THE FOLLOWING YEAR AT QUATRE BRAS AND AT WATERLOO, WHERE THAT BRIGADE DEFEATED THE FINAL ATTACK OF THE FRENCH, MADE BY THE GRENADIERS OF THE IMPERIAL GUARD, FOR WHICH SERVICE THE NAME OF GRENADIERS WAS CONFERRED UPON THE FIRST GUARDS. HE REMAINED IN COMMAND TILL 1818. PLACED BY LIEUT. GENERAL C. L. B. MAITLAND, C.B., LATE GRENADIER GUARDS, AND HIS OTHER SURVIVING CHILDREN".

Ensign 1st Foot Guards 25 Jul 1792. Lt and Capt 30 Apr 1794. Capt and Lt Colonel 25 Jun 1803. Bt Colonel 1 Jan 1812. Major General 4 Jun 1814. Lt General 22 Jul 1830. General 9 Nov 1846.

Served in the Peninsula with 3rd Battalion Oct 1808 – Jan 1809 and 2nd Battalion Jul 1811 – Feb 1813 and May 1813 – Apr 1814 (O/c 1 Brigade 1st Division from Jul 1813). Present at Lugo, Corunna, Cadiz, Seville (Mentioned in Despatches), Bidassoa, Nive (commanded 1st Brigade of Guards), Adour and Bayonne. Present at Quatre Bras and Waterloo (commanded 1 British Brigade of the 1st Division. These were the troops who later in the day were to defeat the charge made by Napoleon's Guard and thus turned the tide of battle). KCB 22 Jun 1815. Knight 3rd Class of St Wladimir of Russia. 3rd Class of Wilhelm of the Netherlands. Gold Medal for Nive. MGS medal for Corunna. Also served in Flanders 1794, Ostend 1798 and Walcheren 1809. After Waterloo married as his second wife Lady Sarah Lennox, daughter of the Duke of Richmond. When the Duke was appointed Governor General of Canada in 1818 Maitland was appointed Lt Governor of Upper Canada. Unfortunately for Maitland the Duke died in 1820 and he did not find life easy under Lord Dalhousie the new Governor General. He was appointed Lt Governor of Nova Scotia 1828–1834 but there was general relief when he left Canada as he lacked diplomatic skills after such a long period as an army officer. Appointed Commander in Chief of Forces in Madras 1836, and then Governor and Commander in Chief in the Cape of Good Hope 1843. Colonel 76th Foot 19 Jul 1834. Colonel 17th Foot 2 Jan 1843. GCB 1852. He played first class cricket for the MCC from 1798–1808.
Reference: Dictionary of National Biography. Dictionary of Canadian Biography. Royal Military Calendar, Vol. 3, pp. 370–1. Gentleman's Magazine, Sep 1854, pp. 300–1. Annual Register, 1854, Appx, pp. 306–7. Picken, Gill, A Knight in Tongham churchyard, St Paul in Tongham Parish News, Apr 2004, pp. 14–18 and May 2004, pp. 10–14.

MALCOLM, John
Lieutenant. 42nd (Royal Highland) Regiment of Foot.
Family Memorial tablet: Glasgow Necropolis, Glasgow, Scotland. (Photograph)

……………… / JOHN MALCOLM, HIS BROTHER / MAJOR IN THE 42ND ROYAL HIGHLANDERS. / BORN NOV. 1790, DIED 14 NOV 1829. / ………………

Ensign 19 Feb 1807. Lt 14 Dec 1809. Capt 7 Apr 1825. Bt Major 25 Dec 1828.

Served in the Peninsula Jul 1809 – Jun 1813. Present at Busaco, Fuentes d'Onoro, Ciudad Rodrigo, Salamanca and Burgos. Present at Waterloo.
Reference: Malcolm, John, Reminiscences of a campaign in the Pyrenees and South of France in 1814, 1826, reprint 1999.

MALKIN, William
Corporal. 45th (Nottinghamshire) Regiment of Foot.
Headstone: Borough Cemetery, Leek, Staffordshire. (Photograph)

SACRED / TO THE MEMORY OF / WILLIAM MALKIN / LATE OF HER MAJESTY'S 45TH REGIMENT / WHO DIED 26TH APRIL 1865 / AGED 82 YEARS. / HE WAS PRESENT / AT THE BATTLES OF / VIMIERA VITTORIA / TALAVERA PYRENEES / BUSACO NIVELLE / SALAMANCA ORTHES / TOULOUSE

Served in the Peninsula Aug 1808 – Jan 1809 and 1810 – Apr 1814. Present at Vimeiro, Talavera, Busaco, second siege of Badajoz (severely wounded), Salamanca, Vittoria, Pyrenees, Nivelle, Orthes and Toulouse. MGS medal for Vimeiro, Talavera, Busaco, Ciudad Rodrigo, Salamanca, Vittoria, Pyrenees, Nivelle, Nive and Toulouse.

MALLOCK, John McGrigor

Assistant Surgeon. 16th (Queen's) Regiment of Light Dragoons.
Tombstone: Old Lancer Lines Cemetery, Secunderabad, India. (M.I.)

"SACRED TO THE MEMORY OF SURGEON JOHN MCGRIGOR MALLOCK MD, H.M.'S 46TH REGT. WHO DEPARTED THIS LIFE ON THE 2ND JUNE 1832. AGED 45 YEARS."

Hospital Mate 28 Sep 1809. Asst Surgeon 16th Lt Dragoons 16 Apr 1812. Surgeon 46th Foot 2 Feb 1826.

Served in the Peninsula Oct – Dec 1812 and Sep 1813 – Apr 1814. Present at Nivelle, Nive and Bayonne. Present at Waterloo. Also served at Walcheren 1809 and India 1826.

MANCOR, Andrew

Captain. 59th (2nd Nottinghamshire) Regiment of Foot.
Grave: The Howff Cemetery, Dundee, Angus, Scotland. (Photograph)

ERECTED / BY / CAPTAIN ANDREW MANCOR, 59TH REGT / .... / THE ABOVE / CAPTAIN ANDREW MANCOR / DIED 6TH MAY 1856, AGED 89. / HIS LIFE WAS DEVOTED TO HIS COUNTRY / FOR A PERIOD OF 30 YEARS ON ACTIVE SERVICE, / HAVING ENTERED THE BRITISH ARMY 1785 / AND RETIRED 1816. / HIS MEMORY LIVES IN HIS MERITS.

Pte 3rd Foot Guards 1785. Promoted from the ranks while Sgt Major. Ensign and Adjutant 59th Foot 6 Oct 1804. Lt 16 Jun 1807. Capt 3 Sep 1812.

Served in the Peninsula Sep 1808 – Jan 1809 and Sep – Dec 1812. Present at Corunna and Cadiz. Also served at Walcheren 1809. Half pay 1 Aug 1816. MGS medal for Corunna. Served in the army for 30 years.

MANDILHON, Philip

Lieutenant. 54th (West Norfolk) Regiment of Foot.
Memorial: St John's Church Cemetery, Trichinopoly, India. (M.I.)

"CAPT. PHILIP MANDILHON, H.M.'S 54TH REGT. WHO DIED 30 JUNE 1836, AGED 45 YEARS. THIS MONUMENT WAS ERECTED BY BROTHER OFFICERS AS A LAST TRIBUTE OF THEIR ESTEEM AND REGARD."

Ensign 1 Nov 1809. Lt 7 Nov 1811. Capt 30 Jan 1823.

Present at Waterloo in reserve at Hal, siege of Cambrai, Capture of Paris and with the Army of Occupation. Also served in North Germany 1813 (present at Stralsund), Cape of Good Hope 1819 and in India (present in the first Burmese War 1824–1825).

MANLEY, John

Sergeant. 14th (Buckinghamshire) Regiment of Foot.
Headstone: St Michael and All Angels, Heavitree, Exeter, Devon. (Photograph)

IN MEMORY OF / COLOUR SERGEANT JOHN MANLEY / LATE OF THE 14TH REGT OF FOOT / AND 1ST DEVON MILITIA / WHO WAS PRESENT AT THE BATTLE OF WATERLOO / HE DIED 26TH APRIL 1872 / AGED 85 YEARS.

Present at Waterloo in Capt George Bolton's Company. Later Colour Sergeant. Chelsea Out-Pensioner 14 Oct 1856. Awarded pension of ten pence per day.

MANNERS, Charles
1st Lieutenant. Royal Artillery.
Gravestone: New Cemetery, Cheltenham, Gloucestershire. Inscription not recorded.

2nd Lt 3 Nov 1807. 1st Lt 24 Sep 1808. 2nd Capt 6 Nov 1827. Capt 10 Jun 1837. Bt Major 28 Nov 1854.
Served in the Peninsula Feb 1810 – Dec 1813. Present at Barrosa (wounded), siege of Tarifa and siege of Cadiz. MGS medal for Barrosa. Also served in the West Indies 1822–1832 and Ionian Islands 1838–1840. Retired on full pay Aug 1840. Died in Cheltenham 23 Oct 1874.

MANNERS, Lord Charles Somerset
Lieutenant Colonel. 3rd (King's Own) Regiment of Dragoons.
Memorial tablet: Mausoleum, Belvoir Castle, Rutland. (Photograph)

GENERAL LORD CHAS SOMERSET / MANNERS, K.C.B. / SECOND SON OF / CHARLES, (FOURTH) DUKE OF RUTLAND, / BORN 1780. / DIED 1855.

Cornet 10th Lt Dragoons 7 Feb 1798. Lt 1 Jun 1799. Capt 21 Aug 1800. Major 13 Oct 1808. Lt Colonel 23rd Lt Dragoons 1 Aug 1811. Lt Colonel 3rd Dragoons 2 Jul 1812. Bt Colonel 6 Nov 1817. Major General 27 May 1825. Lt General 28 Jun 1838. General 20 Jun 1854.
Served in the Peninsula Oct 1808 – Jan 1809, Jun 1811 – Jul 1812 and Aug 1812 – Apr 1814. (ADC to Lord Wellington Jun 1811 – Jul 1812). Present at Sahagun, Benevente, Salamanca, Vittoria and Toulouse. Not present at Waterloo, but with the 3rd Dragoons in the Army of Occupation. Also served at Walcheren 1809 (ADC to Lord Chatham). ADC to the Prince Regent 1817. Gold Medal for Salamanca, Vittoria and Toulouse. KCB. MGS medal for Sahagun and Benevente. MP for Cambridgeshire 1802–1830. On the death of his brother Robert in 1835 became MP for Leicestershire until 1852. Colonel 11th Lt Dragoons 22 Jun 1839. Colonel 3rd Lt Dragoons 8 Nov 1839. Brother of Lt Colonel Lord Robert Manners 10th Lt Dragoons.

MANNERS, Robert
Lieutenant. Royal Artillery.
Named on the Regimental Memorial: St Joseph's Church, Waterloo. (Photograph)

2nd Lt 1 Oct 1808. 1st Lt 13 Mar 1811.
Served in the Peninsula Jul 1810 – Aug 1811 and Mar 1813 – Apr 1814. Present at Cadiz and second siege of San Sebastian. Present at Waterloo where he was present at the Battle of Ligny 16 Jun, attached to Captain Cleeve's German Battery (wounded). On 18 Jun at Waterloo he was with Major Roger's brigade and was severely wounded. He died in a wagon between Waterloo and Brussels as the result of these two wounds. Also served at Walcheren 1809.

MANNERS, Hon. Lord Robert William
Lieutenant Colonel. 10th (Prince of Wales's Own Royal) Regiment of Light Dragoons.
Memorial tablet: Mausoleum, Belvoir Castle, Rutland. (Photograph)

THE RIGHT HONBLE LORD / ROBERT WILLIAM MANNERS. / THIRD SON OF / CHARLES

(FOURTH) DUKE OF RUTLAND, / BORN 1781. / DIED 1835.

Cornet 29 Nov 1798. Lt 23 Jan 1800. Capt 5 Nov 1803. Major 3 May 1810. Lt Colonel 2nd Foot 2 May 1811. Lt Colonel 23rd Lt Dragoons 2 Jul 1812. Lt Colonel 10th Lt Dragoons 12 Nov 1814. Bt Colonel 19 Jul 1821. Lt Colonel 3rd Dragoons 2 Jun 1825. Major General 22 Jul 1830.

Served in the Peninsula Nov 1808 – Jan 1809 and Jul 1811 – Sep 1812 (Extra ADC to Lord Wellington). Present at Sahagun, Benevente, Ciudad Rodrigo, Badajoz, siege of Salamanca Forts and Salamanca. Present at Waterloo where he took command of 10th Lt Dragoons early in the day when Colonel Quentin was wounded. CB. Also served at Walcheren 1809 (present at the siege of Flushing. ADC to Lt General Earl of Chatham) Half pay 1819. MP for Scarborough 1802–1806 and Leicestershire 1806–1835. Keen sportsman. Brother of Lt Colonel Lord Charles Manners 3rd Dragoons.

MANNERS, Russell
Major. 74th (Highland) Regiment of Foot.
Grave: St James's Churchyard, Shirley, Southampton, Hampshire. (M.I.)

"RUSSELL MANNERS CB. LATE 74TH REGIMENT. 25TH JANUARY 1850, AGE 71."

Ensign 74th Foot 1791. Lt 9 Jun 1794. Capt 3 May 1801. Major 11 Mar 1808. Bt Lt Colonel 6 Feb 1812.

Served in the Peninsula Feb 1810 – Feb 1813 and Jan – Apr 1814. Present at Busaco, Foz d'Arouce, Sabugal, Fuentes d'Onoro (Mentioned in Despatches), second siege of Badajoz, El Bodon, Ciudad Rodrigo (Mentioned in Despatches), Badajoz (Mentioned in Despatches), Salamanca, Orthes, Vic Bigorre, Tarbes and Toulouse. Gold Cross for Fuentes d'Onoro, Ciudad Rodrigo, Badajoz and Orthes. MGS medal for Busaco, Salamanca and Toulouse. CB. Also served in India 1795 in the 2nd Mysore War (present at Seringapatam and siege of Pondicherry).
Reference: Gentleman's Magazine, Mar 1850, p. 336.

MANNINGHAM, Coote
Colonel. 95th Regiment of Foot.
Chest tomb: All Saints' Churchyard, Little Bookham, Leatherhead, Surrey. (Photograph)

IN THIS VAULT ARE DEPOSITED THE REMAINS OF / MAJOR-GENERAL COOTE MANNINGHAM, EQUERRY TO THE KING, / AND COLONEL OF THE 95TH, OR RIFLE REGIMENT OF FOOT: / THIS CORPS HE ORIGINALLY RAISED AND FORMED, / AND BY HIS UNWEARIED ZEAL AND EXERTION, / AS WELL AS EXCELLENT DISCIPLINE AND GOOD EXAMPLE, BROUGHT / TO THE HIGHEST STATE OF MILITARY REPUTATION AND DISTINCTION. / HE DIED AT MAIDSTONE ON THE 26TH DAY OF AUGUST 1809, / IN THE 44TH YEAR OF HIS AGE, / AN EARLY VICTIM TO THE FATIGUES OF THE CAMPAIGN IN SPAIN / OPERATING ON A CONSTITUTION ALREADY ENFEEBLED / BY LONG SERVICE IN THE WEST INDIES / AND HONOURABLE WOUNDS RECEIVED IN THAT CLIMATE

Reverse side of tomb: (Photograph)

IN THE YEAR 1933 THIS TOMB WAS RECONSTRUCTED BY COLONEL SIR / MERVYN MANNINGHAM BULLER, BARONET, LATE RIFLE BRIGADE, AND THE / OFFICERS OF THAT REGIMENT. IN THE YEAR 1816 THE 95TH OR RIFLE / REGIMENT WAS RENAMED THE RIFLE BRIGADE. THE TABLET BEARING THE / EARLY ARMS AND EQUIPMENT OF THE REGIMENT IS DEPOSITED IN THE / REGIMENTAL MUSEUM IN WINCHESTER.

Note: The tomb was restored in 1933 and at the same time the superstructure was removed and taken to the Royal Green Jackets Regimental Museum at Winchester where it remains. (Photograph)

Memorial tablet: Westminster Abbey, London. (Photograph)

SACRED TO THE MEMORY OF / MAJOR GENERAL COOTE MANNINGHAM, / COLONEL OF THE 95TH OR RIFLE REGIMENT OF INFANTRY, / AND EQUERRY TO THE KING. / IN TESTAMENT TO A FRIENDSHIP, WHICH COMMENCED IN EARLY YOUTH, / WAS CONFIRMED AND MATURED BY TIME, REMAINS UNCHILLED BY DEATH, / AND HUMBLY LOOKS FOR A REUNION IN ETERNITY. / THE DISTINGUISHED SOLDIER, / TO WHOM FRIENDSHIP ERECTS THIS INADEQUATE MEMORIAL, / BEGAN HIS CAREER OF MILITARY ACTION AT THE SIEGE OF GIBRALTAR, / AND CONCLUDED IT AT THE VICTORY OF CORUNNA / TO WHICH HIS SKILL AND GALLANTRY CONSPICUOUSLY CONTRIBUTED, / HE FELL AN EARLY VICTIM / TO THE VICISSITUDES OF CLIMATE AND THE SEVERITIES OF WAR; / AND DIED THE 26TH AUGUST 1809, AGED 44. / YET, READER, / REGARD NOT HIS FATE AS PREMATURE, SINCE HIS CUP OF GLORY WAS FULL, / AND HE WAS NOT SUMMONED / TILL HIS VIRTUE AND PATRIOTISM HAD ACHIEVED, EVEN HERE, / A BRILLIANT RECOMPENSE; / FOR HIS NAME IS ENGRAVEN ON THE ANNALS OF HIS COUNTRY. / IN HIM, THE MAN AND THE CHRISTIAN TEMPERED THE WARRIOR / AND ENGLAND MIGHT PROUDLY PRESENT HIM TO THE WORLD, / THE MODEL OF A BRITISH SOLDIER!

Named on the Rifle Brigade Memorial: Winchester Cathedral, Winchester, Hampshire. (Photograph)

Ensign 39th Foot 5 Jun 1782. Lt 71st Foot 16 Dec 1783. Lt 39th Foot 14 Jan 1784. Capt 16 Dec 1785. Major 45th Foot 23 Feb 1791. Lt Colonel 105th Foot 18 Apr 1794. Lt Colonel 41st Foot 1 Sep 1795. Colonel 1 Jan 1798. Colonel 95th Foot 25 Apr 1800. Major General 1 Jan 1805.

Served in the Peninsula Nov 1808 – Jan 1809 (O/c 3 Brigade 1st Division). Present at Corunna. Gold Medal for Corunna. Also served in Gibraltar 1782 (present during the siege), West Indies 1791 (present at Martinique, St Lucia and Guadeloupe), San Domingo 1795 (Adjutant General, severely wounded). Returned to England and in 1799 with Colonel William Stewart wrote the memorandum which resulted in the Rifle Corps being raised in 1800. During 1800–1801 Stewart set out to organise the new regiment. The Standing Orders were issued under Coote Manningham's name but drawn up by Stewart. The Experimental Corps was organised by Apr 1800. Manningham served on the staff at home until 1808 when he went to the Peninsula. After Corunna he did not serve again. His health was suffering from wounds received in his long service in the West Indies and he died in Maidstone 26 Aug 1809 aged 44. The tablet in Westminster Abbey refers to him as 'the model of a British soldier.' The men in the regiment sang this song at Waterloo:

Colonel Manningham he was the man,
For he invented a capital plan,
He raised the Corps of Rifle Men,
To fight for England's Glory.

Reference: Manningham, Coote, Regulations for the Rifle Corps formed at Blatchington barracks, 1801. Military lectures delivered to Officers of the 95th (Rifle) Regiment at Shorncliff Barracks, Kent, during the Spring of 1803, by Coote Manningham, Colonel of the 95th (Rifle) Regiment, 1803.

MANSEL, John

Major. 53rd (Shropshire) Regiment of Foot.

Low monument in railed enclosure: St Nicholas of Myra's Churchyard, Kimmeridge, Dorset. Inscription not recorded. (Photograph)

Memorial window: St Nicholas of Myra Church, Kimmeridge, Dorset. (Photograph)

TO THE MEMORY OF LIEUTENANT COLONEL / JOHN MANSEL C.B. OF SMEDMORE WHO

DIED / JANY 29TH 1863 AND OF LOUISA MANSEL

Ensign Mar 1795. Lt 3 Sep 1795. Capt 4 Apr 1800. Major 22 Aug 1805. Bt Lt Colonel 1 Jan 1812.

Served in the Peninsula Aug 1811 – Oct 1812 (in command of Light Companies of 6th Division) and Apr 1814. Present at Carpio, siege of Salamanca Forts, Salamanca and siege of Burgos. Returned home with a fever and did not go back until Apr 1814 in time for Toulouse. Gold Medal for Salamanca and Toulouse. CB. Also served in the West Indies 1795–1806 (present in Charib War), St Lucia, St Vincent, Capture of Trinidad and Porto Rico (present at the siege of Mori Castle 1797), India 1807–1811 (present in Bengal instructing sepoys in light infantry training) and St Helena 1815 (in command of the island during part of Napoleon's captivity). Returned home in 1817. Deputy Lieutenant of Dorset. Died 29 Jan 1863 aged 86. Brother of Capt Robert Christopher Mansel 53rd Foot.

Reference: Royal Military Calendar, Vol. 4, pp. 391–3. Gentleman's Magazine, Mar 1863, p. 395.

MANSEL, Robert Christopher

Captain. 53rd (Shropshire) Regiment of Foot.

Low monument with cross on hipped top: St Martin's Churchyard, Cheriton, Kent. (Photograph)

LT GENERAL ROBERT CHRISTOPHER MANSEL K.H. / COLONEL H.M. 68TH LIGHT INFANTRY / DIED APRIL 8 1864 AGED 75

Ensign 10th Foot 29 Jan 1807. Lt 25 Jan 1808. Capt 4th West India Regt 4 Feb 1813. Capt 53rd Foot 8 Jul 1813. Capt 93rd Foot 6 Jan 1820. Bt Major 5 Jul 1821. Major 96th Foot 9 Jun 1825. Bt Lt Colonel 10 Jun 1826. Bt Colonel 23 Nov 1841. Major General 11 Nov 1851. Lt General 26 Oct 1858.

Served in the Peninsula with 53rd Foot Mar – Apr 1814. Present at Toulouse where he was severely wounded and awarded pension of £100 per annum. Also served in the Mediterranean with 10th Foot, Ireland (present in the Rebellion 1848 and responsible for transferring criminals from prison to ships for convict settlements abroad). Originator of the military prison system. MGS medal for Toulouse. KH. Colonel 68th Foot 4 Jun 1857. Brother of Major John Mansel 53rd Foot.

Reference: Gentleman's Magazine, May 1864, p. 677.

MANUEL, John

Private. 79th (Cameron Highlanders) Regiment of Foot.

Headstone: St Michael's Churchyard, Trefeglwys, Montgomeryshire, Wales. (Corner of churchyard near road, below yew trees). (Photograph)

ER / COF / AM JOHN MANUEL / LLAWR-Y-GLYN / YMUNODD A'R FYDDIN GYDA'R 79 / GATRAWD, YR Y FBLWYDDYN 1800, / CAFODD EI GLWYFO YN WATERLOO; / BU FARW RHAGFYR 5 FED. 1871, / YN 89 MLWYDD OED. / HEFYD AM SARAH, EI WRAIG, / A FUR FARW CHWEFROR 25 AIN. / 1832, / YN 39 MLWYDD OED.

English translation:

IN LOVING MEMORY OF JOHN MANUEL, LLAWR-Y-GLYN. JOINED THE ARMY IN THE 79TH REGIMENT IN 1800. WAS INJURED IN THE BATTLE OF WATERLOO. DIED THE 5TH DECEMBER 1871 AGED 89 YEARS. ALSO HIS WIFE SARA, DIED 25 FEB 1832 AGED 39 YEARS.

Private 1800.

Served in the Peninsula. Present in the Pyrenees. Present at Waterloo in Capt Peter Innes's Company where he was wounded. Also served in Egypt 1801. MGS medal for Egypt and Pyrenees.

MARCH, Charles Lennox, Earl of (5th Duke of Richmond)
Captain. 52nd (Oxfordshire) Light Infantry Regiment of Foot.
Memorial tablet: Chichester Cathedral, Sussex. (Photograph)

TO THE MEMORY OF / CHARLES 5TH DUKE OF RICHMOND, KG. / LORD LIEUTENANT OF SUSSEX, COLONEL IN CHIEF OF THE MILITIA OF THE COUNTY / AND AIDE DE CAMP TO THE QUEEN. / HE WAS APPOINTED AT AN EARLY AGE AS A LIEUTENANT IN THE 13TH LIGHT DRAGOONS / AND ON THE 10TH JULY 1810 ENTERED THE SEAT OF CONFLICT / AS AIDE DE CAMP AND ASSISTANT MILITARY SECRETARY TO THE DUKE OF WELLINGTON / WITH WHOM HE REMAINED UNTIL THE CLOSE OF THE WAR IN 1814. / HE WAS ENGAGED IN ALL THE SKIRMISHES, AFFAIRS, GENERAL ACTIONS AND SIEGES / WHICH TOOK PLACE DURING THAT PERIOD. / IN JANUARY 1814 HE LEFT THE HEADQUARTERS STAFF TEMPORARILY / TO TAKE COMMAND OF HIS COMPANY IN THE 1ST BATTALION 52ND LIGHT INFANTRY / THEN FORMING PART OF THE CELEBRATED LT DIVISION / AND ON THE 27TH FEBRUARY WAS PRESENT WITH THAT REGIMENT AT THE BATTLE OF ORTHES / WHERE HE WAS SEVERELY WOUNDED. / FOR THESE SERVICES HE RECEIVED THE WAR MEDAL WITH EIGHT CLASPS. / AT THE END OF 1814 HE WAS APPOINTED AIDE DE CAMP TO THE PRINCE OF ORANGE / WHOM HE ATTENDED AT QUATRE BRAS AND WATERLOO. / WHETHER SERVING ON THE STAFF OF THE ARMY, DOING DUTY WITH THE REGIMENT / HE WAS EQUALLY DISTINGUISHED FOR HIS BRAVERY AND ZEAL. / WHEN PEACE WAS RESTORED HE RETIRED FROM THE MORE ACTIVE DUTIES OF THE PROFESSION / AND UNDERTOOK THE COMMAND OF THE MILITIA OF HIS COUNTY. / IN THE YEAR 1842, HE AGAIN RESPONDED TO THE CALL OF HIS QUEEN AND COUNTRY / AND UNDERTOOK THE MOST ACTIVE PART IN RE-ESTABLISHING / THE CONSTITUTIONAL FORCE OF THE KINGDOM / EVINCING ALL THE ENERGY OF HIS EARLY DAYS / IN ORGANISING AND BRINGING TO A PERFECT STATE OF DISCIPLINE, / THE REGIMENT OF WHICH HE WAS THE HONOURED CHIEF FOR THE LONG TERM OF FIFTY-ONE YEARS / AND TO WHICH HE CONTINUED TO DEVOTE HIS UNWEARIED PERSONAL ATTENTION / TO THE LATEST HOUR OF HIS LIFE. / BORN 3RD AUGUST 1791. DIED 21ST OCTOBER 1860. / THIS TABLET IS ERECTED / BY THE OFFICERS AND NON-COMMISSIONED OFFICERS / WHO SERVED UNDER HIM IN THE ROYAL SUSSEX LT INFANTRY MILITIA / AS A HUMBLE TRIBUTE OF ADMIRATION AND ESTEEM / AND AS A MARK OF THE DEEP AFFECTION HIS GENEROUS NATURE INSPIRED.

Statue: Huntly, Aberdeenshire, Scotland. (Photograph)

ERECTED / AS A MEMORIAL OF / CHARLES GORDON LENNOX / FIFTH DUKE OF RICHMOND / BY / THE TENANTRY OF / THE LORDSHIP OF HUNTLY / 1862

Ensign 8th Garrison Battalion 8 Jun 1809. Lt 13th Lt Dragoons 21 Jun 1810. Capt 92nd Foot 9 Jul 1812. Capt 52nd Foot 3 Apr 1813. Bt Major 15 Jun 1815. Lt Colonel 25 Jul 1816.

Served in the Peninsula Jul 1810 – Apr 1814 (ADC to Lord Wellington). Feb 1814 (with 52nd Foot at Orthes). Present at Busaco, Fuentes d'Onoro, Ciudad Rodrigo, Badajoz, Salamanca, Vittoria, first siege of San Sebastian, Pyrenees, Bidassoa, Lezaca (Mentioned in Despatches Oct 1813) and Orthes with 52nd Foot where he was severely wounded. Sent home with Despatches for Salamanca and Pyrenees. At the siege of Ciudad Rodrigo he volunteered for the storming party and entered the breach with the Prince of Orange and Lord Fitzroy Somerset. Next day all three were reprimanded by Wellington as he did not like his staff officers risking their lives. Present at Waterloo as ADC to the Prince of Orange. Also served in Ireland 1809 (ADC to his father). Half pay 25 Jul 1816. MGS medal for Busaco, Fuentes d'Onoro, Ciudad Rodrigo, Badajoz, Salamanca, Vittoria, Pyrenees and Orthes. Became the 5th Duke of Richmond in 1819. Colonel of the Royal Sussex Light Infantry Militia. His influence and support were major factors in establishing the MGS medal for all ranks in 1848, as before this only Waterloo medals had been issued to other

ranks.
Reference: Gentleman's Magazine, Dec 1810, pp. 665–9 (Under Richmond). Annual Register, 1860, Appx, p. 483. (Under Richmond).

MARENHOLZ, Wilhelm von
Lieutenant. 8th Line Battalion, King's German Legion.
Named on the Regimental Memorial: La Haye Sainte, Waterloo. (Photograph)

Lt 15 Jan 1808.
Served in the Peninsula Aug 1812 – Apr 1813. Present at Castalla. Present at Waterloo where he was killed. Also served in the Baltic 1807, Mediterranean 1808–1814 and the Netherlands 1814.

MARLAY, George
Captain. 14th (Buckinghamshire) Regiment of Foot.
Memorial: Highgate Cemetery, London. (M.I.)

"HERE LIES IN PEACE AWAITING THE RESURRECTION / THAT WHICH IS MORTAL OF LIEUT: COL: GEORGE MARLAY, CB. / NATUS 1791. OBIT 8 JUNE 1830."

Named on the Family Box tomb: Holly Road Burial Ground, Twickenham, London. Seriously eroded and inscription recorded from memorial inscription. (Photograph)

"HERE LIE INTERRED THE REMAINS OF / LADY CATHERINE MARLAY, / ……………… / THEIR BELOVED AND ONLY SON / LIEUTENANT COLONEL GEORGE MARLAY, / COMPANION OF THE ORDER OF THE BATH, / WHO DIED DEEPLY LAMENTED ON DECLINE IN LONDON / ON THE 8TH DAY OF JUNE 1830, AGED 39. / ………………"

Ensign 9th Foot 4 Aug 1802. Lt 4 Sep 1802. Lt 28th Foot 19 Jul 1803. Capt 8th Battalion of Reserve 27 Oct 1804. Capt 2nd Garrison Battalion 25 Feb 1805. Capt 14th Foot 4 Jun 1810. Bt Major 21 Jun 1813. Bt Lt Colonel 21 Jun 1817.
Served in the Peninsula Sep 1808 – Jan 1809, May – Jun 1909 (on Staff as ADC to General E. Paget) and 1813 – Apr 1814 (AAG). Present at Corunna, Nivelle, Nive, Orthes and Toulouse. Gold Cross for Nivelle, Nive, Orthes and Toulouse. Present at Waterloo. CB. Also served at Hanover 1805 and Sweden 1808. Half pay March 1816. Died 8 Jun 1830.

MARR, Earl of see ERSKINE, JOHN FRANCIS MILLER in Supplement

MARSCHALCK, Heinrich von
Captain. 1st Light Infantry, King's German Legion.
Named on the Regimental Memorial: La Haye Sainte, Waterloo. (Photograph)

Ensign 23 Mar 1805. Lt 17 Jul 1809. Capt 4 Apr 1814.
Served in the Peninsula Aug 1808 – Jan 1809 and Mar 1811 – Apr 1814. Present at Vigo, Albuera, siege of Salamanca Forts, Moriscos, Salamanca, Venta del Poza, San Millan, Vittoria, Tolosa, Bidassoa, Nivelle, Nive, Bayonne and St Etienne. Present at Waterloo where he was killed. Also served at Hanover 1805, the Baltic 1807–1808, Walcheren 1809 and the Netherlands 1814.

MARSH, William
Corporal. 12th (Prince of Wales's) Regiment of Light Dragoons.
Named on the Regimental Memorial: St Joseph's Church, Waterloo. (Photograph)

Present at Waterloo where he was killed.

MARSHALL, Anthony
2nd Captain. Royal Engineers.
Named on the Regimental Memorial: Rochester Cathedral, Rochester, Kent. (Photograph)

2nd Lt 1 Oct 1808. Lt 1 Aug 1809. 2nd Capt 28 Feb 1814. Capt 29 Jul 1825. Bt Major 10 Jan 1837. Lt Colonel 19 Feb 1841. Bt Colonel 11 Nov 1851. Major General 30 May 1856. Lt General 20 Apr 1861.

Served in the Peninsula Mar 1811 – Oct 1813. Present at second siege of Badajoz, Ciudad Rodrigo (wounded), Vittoria, San Sebastian (severely wounded). Served with the Army of Occupation 1815–1818. Retired on full pay 12 Jul 1845. MGS medal for Ciudad Rodrigo, Vittoria and San Sebastian. Died at Plymouth 25 May 1865.

MARSHALL, George
Captain. 82nd (Prince of Wales's Volunteers) Regiment of Foot.
Box tomb: New Burial Ground, Up Park Camp, St Andrew's Parish, Kingston, Jamaica, West Indies. (Photograph)

SACRED / TO THE MEMORY OF / GEORGE MARSHALL, K. H. / LATE LT-COLONEL. COMMANDING / H. M.'S 82ND REGIMENT / OF FOOT / WHO, AFTER 42 YEARS MERITORIOUS SERVICE, / DIED OF FEVER, / 2ND JUNE, 1841, / AT U. P. C., AGED 58.

Ensign 6 Dec 1799. Lt 15 Aug 1804. Capt 27 Oct 1808. Bt Major 27 May 1825. Major 23 Oct 1835. Bt Lt Colonel 28 Jun1838. Lt Colonel 21 Jun 1839.

Served in the Peninsula Aug 1808 – Jan 1809 and Oct 1812 – Apr 1814. Present at Rolica, Vimeiro, Corunna, Burgos, Vittoria, Pyrenees (wounded at Maya), San Marcial, Nivelle (severely wounded) and Orthes. Also served in Minorca 1800–1802, Copenhagen 1807, North America 1814–1815 (wounded at Niagara), Mauritius 1819–1829, Gibraltar 1837–1839 and Jamaica 1840 where he died in a yellow fever epidemic in command of the regiment. KH.

MARSHALL, George
Lieutenant. 92nd Regiment of Foot.
Family Memorial stone: St Andrew's Churchyard, Bellie, Lochaber, Morayshire, Scotland. (East centre of Cemetery). (Photograph)

ERECTED BY / LIEUT COL WILLIAM MARSHALL / TO THE MEMORY OF A REVERED PARENT. / 1857 / THIS STONE WAS ORIGINALLY PLACED BY / WILLIAM MARSHALL OVER THE GRAVES / IN MEMORY OF HIS SON MAJOR / ALEXANDER MARSHALL WHO DIED / AT KEITHMORE ON 31ST DAY OF / JANUARY 1807 IN THE 33RD YEAR OF HIS / AGE. AND OF HIS SPOUSE JEAN GILES / WHO DIED AT NEWFIELD COTTAGE / DANDALEITH ON THE 13TH DAY OF / DECEMBER 1821 IN THE 85TH YEAR OF HER AGE. / BOTH WHOSE REMAINS ARE HERE INTERRED. / HERE ALSO LIE THE REMAINS OF / WILLIAM MARSHALL ESQ. HUSBAND / OF THE ABOVE JEAN GILES A MAN OF / VIRTUE AND INTEGRITY. FROM A HUMBLE / STATION IN LIFE HE ROSE TO DISTINCTION / BY THE INDUSTRIOUS CULTIVATION OF A / NATURAL TALENT EVENTUALLY BECAME / FACTOR ON THE ESTATE OF ALEXANDER / DUKE OF GORDON AN OFFICE WHICH HE / HELD FOR MANY YEARS PERFORMING HIS / DUTIES WITH FIDELITY AND COMPLETE SATISFAC / TION OF HIS EMPLOYER AND THE TENANTARY. / ALTHOUGH SELF TAUGHT HE MADE CONSIDERABLE / PROGRESS IN MECHANICS AND OTHER / BRANCHES OF NATURAL SCIENCE IN WHICH / HIS LEISURE HOURS WERE FREQUENTLY / DEVOTED. BUT HE WAS CHIEFLY NOTED FOR HIS / SKILL AND FINE TASTE IN MUSIC THE / SCOTTISH AIRS AND MELODIES COMPOSED / BY HIM BEING WIDELY

KNOWN AND / APPRECIATED. HE DIED UNIVERSALLY ES / TEEMED AT NEWFIELD COTTAGE, DANDALEITH / ON THE 29TH DAY OF MAY 1833 IN THE / 85TH YEAR OF HIS AGE. / OF A FAMILY OF SIX CHILDREN BESIDES / THE ABOVE NAME ALEXANDER. / FRANCIS A JEWELLER DIED IN LONDON. / JOHN A $CAPT^{N}$ IN THE ARMY DIED IN INDIA / AND GEORGE A LIEUT IN THE ARMY DIED / IN SPAIN. JANE AN ONLY DAUGHTER / WIDOW OF JOHN MCINNES ESQ / DANDALEITH AND WILLIAM A RETIRED / LIEUT. COL. OF THE ARMY BEING THE SOLE / PRESENT SURVIVORS. HERE ALSO LIE / INTERRED THE REMAINS OF THE ABOVE NAMED / LIEUT. COL. WILLIAM MARSHALL OF THE / 79TH CAMERON HIGHLANDERS WHO AFTER A LONG / PERIOD OF ACTIVE AND ARDUOUS SERVICE WITH / HIS REGIMENT AND THE LOSS OF HIS RIGHT / ARM AT QUATRE BRAS RETIRED TO NEWFIELD / COTTAGE, DANDALEITH WHERE HE SPENT THE / LAST 30 YEARS OF HIS LIFE ESTEEMED BY ALL / WHO KNEW HIM FOR HIS SINCERE PIETY AND / UNOSTENTATIOUS CHARITY. HE DIED / 29TH AUGUST 1870 IN THE 91ST YEAR / OF HIS AGE. / ....

Ensign Jan 1806. Lt 8 Feb 1808.

Served in the Peninsula Jan 1811 – Aug 1812. Present at Fuentes d'Onoro, Arroyo dos Molinos and Almarez. Also served at Walcheren 1809. Died 27 Aug 1812 from fatigue and possible effects of Walcheren fever. Brother of Lt John Marshall 26th Foot and Capt William Marshall 79th Foot.

MARSHALL, John
Lieutenant. 26th (Cameronian) Regiment of Foot.
Buried in St Mary's Cemetery, Madras, India. (Burial Register)

Family Memorial stone: St Andrew's Churchyard, Bellie, Lochaber, Morayshire, Scotland. (East centre of Cemetery). (Photograph)

See full Family Inscription under George Marshall 92nd Foot above.

.... / JOHN A $CAPT^{N}$ IN THE ARMY DIED IN INDIA

Ensign 29th Foot 11 Feb 1808. Lt 26th Foot 11 Aug 1808. Capt 31 Dec 1827.

Served in the Peninsula Sep 1811 – Jun 1812. Present at the Coa (but the regiment was removed from the Peninsula as so many were sick with Walchern fever). Also served at Walcheren 1809, Gibraltar 1812–1822 and India 1828 where he died of cholera in Madras 13 Mar 1829. Brother of Capt William Marshall 79th Foot and Lt George Marshall 92nd Foot.

MARSHALL, John
Lieutenant. 91st Regiment of Foot.
Interred in Catacomb B (v77 c13), Kensal Green Cemetery, London.

Ensign 14 May 1808. Lt 23 Nov 1809. Capt 20 Feb 1823. Bt Major 28 Jun 1838. Bt Lt Colonel 28 Nov 1854.

Served in the Peninsula Aug 1808 – Jan 1809 and Apr 1813 – Apr 1814. Present at Rolica, Vimeiro, Cacabellos, Corunna, Vittoria, Pyrenees (wounded), Pamplona (wounded), Nivelle, Nive and Orthes (severely wounded). Also served at Walcheren 1809. Half pay 16 Feb 1838. MGS medal for Rolica, Vimeiro, Corunna, Pyrenees, Nivelle, Nive and Orthes. Died in London 1859.

MARSHALL, William
Captain. 79th (Cameron Highlanders) Regiment of Foot.
Family Memorial stone: St Andrew's Church, Bellie, Lochaber, Morayshire, Scotland. (East centre of Cemetery). (Photograph)

See full Family inscription under George Marshall above

.... / HERE ALSO LIE / INTERRED THE REMAINS OF THE ABOVE NAMED / LIEUT. COL. WILLIAM MARSHALL OF THE / 79TH CAMERON HIGHLANDERS WHO AFTER A LONG / PERIOD OF ACTIVE AND ARDUOUS SERVICE WITH / HIS REGIMENT AND THE LOSS OF HIS RIGHT / ARM AT QUATRE BRAS RETIRED TO NEWFIELD / COTTAGE, DANDALEITH WHERE HE SPENT THE / LAST 30 YEARS OF HIS LIFE ESTEEMED BY ALL / WHO KNEW HIM FOR HIS SINCERE PIETY AND / UNOSTENTATIOUS CHARITY. HE DIED / 29TH AUGUST 1870 IN THE 91ST YEAR / OF HIS AGE.

Ensign 10 Nov 1799. Lt 79th Foot 25 Jun 1803. Capt 19 Jul 1810. Major 29 Jul 1824. Bt Lt Colonel 16 Jul 1830. Lt Colonel 1 Jan 1838.

Served in the Peninsula Aug 1808 – Jan 1809 and Jan 1810 – Apr 1814. Present at Corunna, Cadiz, Busaco, Foz d'Arouce, Fuentes d'Onoro, Salamanca, Burgos (present at Capture of the Horn Work where he was wounded and Mentioned in Despatches), Nivelle, Nive and Toulouse (severely wounded). Present at Waterloo (severely wounded at Quatre Bras where his right arm was amputated and awarded pension of £100 per annum) and with the Army of Occupation until 1818. Also served at Ferrol 1800, Egypt 1801 (present at Mandora, Alexandria, Rahmanie and awarded Gold Medal from the Sultan), Copenhagen 1807, Sweden 1808 and Walcheren 1809 (present at the siege of Flushing), Ireland and Canada 1830 (Inspecting Field Officer of Militia in Nova Scotia. Present in the Canadian Rebellion 1837–1838). MGS medal for Egypt, Corunna, Busaco, Fuentes d'Onoro, Salamanca, Nivelle, Nive and Toulouse. Retired 1838. Died 29 Aug 1870 aged 91 at Craigellachie. Brother of Lt John Marshall 26th Foot and Lt George Marshall 79th Foot.

MARSLAND, Henry

Sergeant. 51st (2nd Yorkshire West Riding) Light Infantry.

Named on the Regimental Memorial: KOYLI Chapel, York Minster, Yorkshire. (Photograph)

Served in the Peninsula. Present at Nivelle Nov 1813 where he was severely wounded and died of his wounds.

MARTEN, Thomas

Cornet: 2nd Life Guards.

Low monument in railed enclosure: St Mary's Churchyard, Beverley, Yorkshire. (Old restored Cemetery). (Photograph)

SACRED TO THE MEMORY OF / LIEUT GENERAL THOMAS MARTEN, K.H., COLONEL 6TH (INNISKILLING) DRAGOONS / WHOSE MORTAL REMAINS ARE INTERRED IN THE VAULT BENEATH THIS TOMB / BORN AT WINCHELSEA 29TH DECEMBER 1797 DIED AT BEVERLEY 22ND NOVEMBER 1868 / (VERSE)

Cornet 22 Nov 1813. Lt 23 Jun 1817. Capt 4 May 1822. Major 12 Dec 1826. Lt Colonel 1st Dragoons 29 May 1835. Bt Colonel 9 Nov 1846. Major General 20 Jun 1854. Lt General 16 Feb 1862.

Served in the Peninsula Mar – Apr 1814. Present at Toulouse. Present at Waterloo and the Capture of Paris. MGS medal for Toulouse. KH. Colonel 6th Light Dragoons 12 Nov 1860 until his death in 22 Nov 1868.

MARTIN, Donald N.

1st Lieutenant. Royal Artillery.
Grave: St Nicholas's Churchyard, Plumstead, Kent. (No longer extant. Destroyed by a flying bomb in the Second World War). (M.I.)
Named on the Regimental Memorial: St Nicholas's Church, Plumstead, Kent. (No longer extant. Destroyed by a flying bomb in the Second World War)

2nd Lt 5 Jun 1809. 1st Lt 28 Aug 1812.

Served in the Peninsula 1811 – Apr 1814. Present at Fuentes D'Onoro (wounded), Cadiz and Carthagena. Died at Woolwich 8 Dec 1815.

MARTIN, John

Captain. 23rd Regiment of Light Dragoons.
Family chest tomb: St Andrew's Churchyard, Enfield, London. (Photograph)

MAJOR GENERAL / JOHN MARTIN / SON OF / THE LATE THOMAS MARTIN ESQ, / DIED THE 27TH DAY OF MAY / 1852 / IN THE 68TH YEAR OF HIS AGE. / ....

Family Memorial tablet: St Andrew's Church, Enfield, London. (High on south wall of nave). (Photograph)

IN THE FAMILY VAULT NEAR THIS CHURCH / ARE DEPOSITED THE MORTAL REMAINS OF / MAJOR-GENERAL JOHN MARTIN, / ELDEST SON OF THOMAS MARTIN, ESQR., OF ENFIELD, MIDDLESEX. / HE WAS BORN THE 25TH OF NOVEMBER 1788, / AND ENTERED THE ARMY THE 30TH OF JULY 1807. / HE SERVED WITH THE 23RD LT DRAGOONS AT THE BATTLE OF TALAVERA, / ON THE 22ND, 27TH AND 28TH OF JULY 1809. / ALSO IN THE CAMPAIGN OF 1815, / INCLUDING THE BATTLE OF QUATRE-BRAS, RETREAT ON THE FOLLOWING DAY, / AND THE BATTLE OF WATERLOO. / HE DIED UNMARRIED THE 27TH MAY 1852. / THIS UNPRETENDING TABLET, AS A SMALL TRIBUTE OF / AFFECTION AND GRATITUDE, / IS ERECTED BY HIS GODSON AND HEIR, / ALFRED PLANTAGENET FREDERICK CHARLES SOMERSET.

Cornet 30 Jul 1807. Lt 16 May 1809. Capt 8 Feb 1813. Major 93rd Foot 10 Jan 1822. Lt Colonel 12 Jun 1823. Bt Colonel 28 Jun 1838. Major General 11 Nov 1851.

Served in the Peninsula Jun – Dec 1809. Present at Talavera. Present at Quatre Bras covering the retreat of the infantry and Waterloo. Half pay 12 Jun 1823. MGS medal for Talavera.

MARTIN, Samuel Coote

Lieutenant Colonel. 1st Regiment of Foot Guards.
Memorial stone in railed enclosure: Garden of the former Mayor's House, Bidart, France. (Photograph)

CI GÎT / LE LIEU COLONEL / S. C. MARTIN / LES CAPITAINES / THOMSON ET WATSON, / DE LA GARDE ROYALE / DE S M BRITTANIQUE / TUE SUR LE CHAMP DE / BATAILLE LE 14 / DÉCEMBRE 1813.

Named on the Memorial: St Andrew's Church (now Musée Historique), Biarritz, France. (Photograph)

Named on Memorial Panel VII for Nive: Royal Military Chapel, Wellington Barracks, London. (M.I.) (Destroyed by a Flying Bomb 1944)

Ensign 6 Nov 1798. Lt and Capt 25 Nov 1799. Bt Major 4 Jun 1811. Capt and Lt Colonel 30 Jul 1812.

Served in the Peninsula with 1st Battalion Oct 1808 – Jan 1809, Oct 1810 – Jun 1811 (ADC to Major General Disney) and May – Dec 1813 again with 1st Battalion. Present at Corunna, Cadiz, Bidassoa, Nivelle and Nive where he was killed 12 Dec 1813. Educated at Eton. The three officers of the 1st Foot Guards were all buried in the same grave – Lt Colonel Samuel C. Martin, Capt Henry R. Watson and Capt Charles W. Thompson. The house where they are buried was the headquarters of General John Hope from Dec 1813 to Jan 1814.

MASCHECK, C.
Captain. 4th Dragoons, Dutch Cavalry.
Named on the Memorial to Dutch officers killed at Waterloo: St Joseph's Church, Waterloo. (Photograph)

MASSIE, Thomas
Ensign. 52nd (Oxfordshire) Light Infantry Regiment of Foot.
Named on the Regimental Memorial: St Michael's Cathedral, Bridgetown, Barbados, West Indies. (M.I.)

Ensign 52nd Foot 8 Dec 1813. Lt 28 Sep 1815. Lt 2nd Foot 6 Jun 1816.

Present at Waterloo. Transferred to 2nd Foot and went with the regiment to the West Indies in 1816. Died during a yellow fever epidemic in Barbados Dec 1816.

MASTER, William Chester
Captain and Lieutenant Colonel. 3rd Regiment of Foot Guards.
Memorial tablet: St Mary's Church, Almondsbury, Gloucestershire. (Photograph)

IN MEMORY OF / WILLIAM CHESTER MASTER, / BORN JANUARY 4TH 1785. DIED NOVEMBER 20TH 1868. / SON OF MAJOR RICHARD MASTER, BY ISABELLA FRANCES EGERTON. / HE SUCCEEDED ON THE DEATH OF HIS UNCLE THOMAS MASTER 1823 / TO KNOLE PARK AND THE REST OF THE CHESTER ESTATES, / AND TO THE ABBEY CIRENCESTER AND THE REST OF THE MASTER ESTATES, / ON THE DEATH OF HIS COUSIN LADY CARTARET 1863, / HE ENTERED THE SCOTS FUSILIER GUARDS 1801 AT THE AGE OF 16, / SERVED THROUGH THE PENINSULAR WAR, TAKING PART IN THE / BATTLES OF VITTORIA, BADAJOZ, FUENTES D'ONOR AND TALAVERA / AND BECAME LT COLONEL. / FOR 60 YEARS HE WAS GENTLEMAN USHER OF THE PRIVY CHAMBER / TO GEORGE 3RD GEORGE 4TH WILLIAM 4TH AND VICTORIA, / COLONEL MASTER MARRIED 1814, ISABELLA MARGARET, / DAUGHTER OF COLONEL THE HONBLE STEPHEN DIGBY, / AND HAD ISSUE 7 SONS AND 3 DAUGHTERS. / HIS REMAINS WERE THE LAST TO BE INTERRED IN THE VAULT BENEATH.

Ensign 5 Feb 1801. Lt and Capt 25 Jul 1805. Capt and Lt Colonel 9 Dec 1813.

Served in the Peninsula Mar 1809 – Jan 1814 (ADC to Major General Sir E. Stopford), Oct 1811 – Apr 1812 and Nov 1812–1814. Present at Douro, Talavera, Fuentes d' Onoro, Badajoz and Vittoria. MGS medal for Talavera, Fuentes d'Onoro, Badajoz and Vittoria. CB. Retired in 1820.
Reference: Household Brigade Journal, 1868, p. 328.

MATHEWS, Thomas
Private. 16th (Queen's) Regiment of Light Dragoons.
Headstone: Malpas Churchyard, Malpas, Cheshire. (Photograph)

IN MEMORY OF / THOMAS MATHEWS / (OF MALPAS) / WHO DIED OCT 22ND 1872, / AGED 78 YEARS. / HE SERVED IN THE 16TH LANCERS AT WATERLOO / AND BHURTPORE. / ....

Present at Waterloo in Capt King's Troop. Also served in India 1822 (present at the siege of Bhurtpore 1824–1826). Died 22 Oct 1872 aged 78.

MATHIAS, George
Lieutenant. 1st (Royal Scots) Regiment of Foot.
Brass Memorial tablet: Royal Hospital, Chelsea, London. (Photograph)

TO THE GLORY OF GOD / AND IN MEMORY OF / REVEREND GEORGE MATHIAS M.A. / CHAPLAIN OF THE / ROYAL HOSPITAL, 1846 TO 1869, / AND CHAPLAIN IN ORDINARY TO / HER MAJESTY QUEEN VICTORIA 1857 / WHO, AFTER SERVING WITH THE 1ST ROYALS, / AND LATER WITH THE 79TH HIGHLANDERS / FROM 1812 TO 1834: IN CANADA DURING / THE AMERICAN WAR 1812–1814, IN THE / MARCH TO PARIS 1815, IN INDIA AND / AGAIN IN CANADA, FINALLY LEFT THE / ARMY WHEN A CAPTAIN AND / ENTERED INTO HOLY ORDERS. / BORN 21 SEP. 1796. / DIED 10 MARCH 1884.

Ensign 1 Aug 1813. Lt 22 Sep 1814. Capt (unattached) 19 Nov 1825. Capt 79th Foot 8 Jun 1826.

Served with the Army of Occupation 1815. Also served in Canada during the American War 1812–1814, India 1817 and Canada 1825–1832. Retired 10 Oct 1834 and entered the church. Chaplain to Royal Hospital Chelsea 15 Aug 1846–1869. Chaplain-in-Ordinary to Queen Victoria 1857. Died 10 Mar 1884.

MATHISON, John Augustus
Lieutenant. 77th (East Middlesex) Regiment of Foot.
Grave: St James's (Anglican) Church Cemetery, Hudson, Quebec, Canada. (M.I.)

"SACRED TO THE MEMORY OF JOHN AUGUSTUS MATHISON LIEUT. OF H. M. 77 FOOT AND CAPTN. OF THE 17 PORTUGUESE GRENADIERS BORN IN LONDON, ENGLAND DEC 25TH 1781. DIED IN HUDSON, CANADA NOV 5TH 1868 AGED 87 YEARS. ...."

Midshipman Royal Navy 1796. Ensign 77th Foot 8 May 1811. Lt 12 Aug 1813. Portuguese Army: Lt 17th Line 29 Mar 1813.

Served in the Peninsula with 77th Foot Jul 1811 – Mar 1813. With Portuguese Army Mar 1813 – Apr 1814. Present at El Bodon, Ciudad Rodrigo, Badajoz (wounded), Vittoria, Pyrenees (wounded), Bidassoa (wounded), Nive, Orthes and Toulouse. Also served in the Royal Navy 1796 and served on HMS *Temeraire* at Trafalgar. Resigned from the navy in 1806. MGS medal for Ciudad Rodrigo, Badajoz, Vittoria, Pyrenees, Nive, Orthes and Toulouse. Half pay 1817. Later appointed Captain and Lieutenant Colonel in the Canadian Militia.

MATSON, Edward
Lieutenant. Royal Engineers.
Interred in Catacomb B (v151 c 3&4), Kensal Green Cemetery, London.

2nd Lt 7 May 1810. 1st Lt 1 May 1811. Capt 9 Jan 1821. Major 10 Jan 1837. Lt Col 1 Apr 1846. Colonel 20 Jun 1854. Major General 10 Sep 1856.

Served in the Peninsula Dec 1812 – Dec 1813 and Mar – Apr 1814. Present at San Millan, Vittoria, Pamplona, San Sebastian, Bidassoa, Nivelle and Bayonne. Served with the Army of Occupation until Nov 1818. Also served in North America 1814–1815 (present at New Orleans and Fort Bowyer). MGS medal for Vittoria, San Sebastian and Nivelle. Brigade Major of Royal Sappers and Miners 1831. Died 3 Sep 1873.
Reference: Annual Register, 1873, Appx, pp. 150–1.

MATTHEWSON, Robert
Private. 12th (Prince of Wales's) Regiment of Light Dragoons.
Named on the Regimental Memorial: St Joseph's Church, Waterloo. (Photograph)

Present at Waterloo where he was killed.

MAULE, George Silvester
1st Lieutenant. Royal Artillery.
Grave: St Luke's Churchyard, Charlton, Kent. (Grave number 242). (No longer extant). (M.I.)

"HERE ARE DEPOSITED THE REMAINS OF CAPTN GEORGE SILVESTER MAULE, OF THE ROYAL REGIMENT OF ARTILLERY, WHO DIED 18 OCT, 1839, AGED 46 YEARS."

2nd Lt 4 Jun 1810. 1st Lt 14 Feb 1814. 2nd Capt 31 Jul 1832.

Served in the Peninsula Nov 1812 – Apr 1813. Present at Castalla, Tarragona and Villa Franca (in support of the cavalry). Present at Quatre Bras and Waterloo. Also served on gun boats in the Adriatic in 1812.

MAUNSELL, Frederick
Lieutenant. 85th (Buckinghamshire Volunteers) Light Infantry Regiment of Foot.
Buried in the Family Vault: St John's Churchyard, Limerick, Ireland.
Memorial tablet: St Mary's Cathedral, Limerick, Ireland. (Photograph)

TO / THE MEMORY / OF / GENERAL FREDERICK / MAUNSELL, / COL. 85TH THE KING'S LIGHT INFANTRY REGT, / WHO SERVED IN THIS REGIMENT WITH DISTINCTION, / IN THE PENINSULAR AND AMERICAN WARS, / HE DIED AT BRAY, CO WICKLOW, / ON OCTOBER 18TH 1875, AGED 82 YEARS. / HIS REMAINS LIE IN THE FAMILY VAULT / ST JOHN'S CHURCHYARD. / THIS TABLET IS ERECTED IN LOVING MEMORY / BY HIS SORROWING WIDOW AND SON. / (VERSE)

Ensign 18th Foot 16 Apr 1812. Lt 28 Jan 1813. Lt 85th Foot 18 Mar 1813. Capt 24 Jun 1819. Major 14 Aug 1827. Lt Colonel 23 May 1836. Bt Colonel 9 Nov 1846. Major General 20 Jun 1854. Lt General 1 Jun 1862.

Served in the Peninsula Aug 1813 – Apr 1814. Present at San Sebastian, Bidassoa, Nivelle, Nive and Bayonne. Also served in North America 1814–1815 (present at Bladensberg (wounded), New Orleans (severely wounded) and Capture of Fort Bowyer), Malta and Gibraltar 1821–1832 and North America 1835–1842 (served in Canada during the Rebellion 1838–1839). Inspecting Field Officer Cork Recruiting District 19 Jun 1846. Colonel 85th Light Infantry 2 Apr 1865 until his death at Bray, County Wicklow on 18 Oct 1875 aged 82. The last survivor of the regiment who served in the Peninsula and America. Brother of Capt George Maunsell 3rd Dragoon Guards.

MAUNSELL, George
Captain. 3rd (Prince of Wales's) Regiment of Dragoon Guards.
Memorial tablet: St Mary's Cathedral, Limerick, Ireland. (Photograph)

SACRED / TO THE MEMORY OF / LIEUT COLONEL GEORGE MAUNSELL / 3D OR PRINCE OF WALES'S DRAGOON GUARDS / WHICH REGIMENT HE COMMANDED FOR MANY YEARS. SERVED WITH / IT THROUGHOUT THE WHOLE PENINSULA WAR AND RECEIVED MEDALS / FOR THE BATTLE OF TALAVERA ALBUERA VITTORIA AND TOULOUSE. / HE WAS BELOVED BY HIS BROTHER SOLDIERS / AND RESPECTED BY THE ENEMIES OF HIS COUNTRY. / THE ALMIGHTY, WHO PROTECTED HIM IN THE DAY OF BATTLE / SUFFERED HIM TO DEPART THIS LIFE IN PEACE. / SINCERE. HONORABLE. GENTLE AND BRAVE / HIS SURVIVING RELATIVES HAVE ERECTED THIS TESTIMONIAL / IN COMMEMORATION OF HIS WORTH / DIED SEPTR 4TH 1849. / SOLDIER REST THE WARFARE O'ER / SLEEP THE SLEEP THAT KNOWS NOT BREAKING; / DREAM OF BATTLED FIELDS NO MORE / DAYS OF DANGER NIGHTS OF

WAKING.

Cornet 13 Mar 1806. Lt 25 Dec 1806. Capt 18 Jul 1811. Major 21 Nov 1828. Lt Colonel 15 Sep 1838.

Served in the Peninsula Apr 1809 – Apr 1814. Present at Talavera, Albuera, Usagre, Aldea de Ponte, Maguilla, Vittoria and Toulouse. MGS medal for Talavera, Albuera, Vittoria and Toulouse. Died 4 Sep 1849. Brother of Lt Frederick Maunsell 85th Foot.

MAUNSELL, John Edward
1st Lieutenant. Royal Artillery.
Low monument: Kensal Green Cemetery, London. (18897/92/RS). (Photograph)

………………. / ALSO OF THE ABOVE NAMED JOHN EDWARD MAUNSELL / LATE OF ROYAL HORSE ARTILLERY / BORN 8TH DAY OF / DECEMBER 1787. DIED 20TH DAY OF JANUARY 1869

2nd Lt 14 Jun 1805. 1st Lt 1 Jun 1806. 2nd Capt 24 Mar 1817.

Present at Waterloo in Major Beane's Troop, Royal Horse Artillery. Half pay 14 Nov 1826.

MAXWELL, Archibald Montgomery
2nd Captain. Royal Artillery.
Obelisk: Jesmond Cemetery, Newcastle upon Tyne, Northumberland. (M.I.)

"HERE LIES THE REMAINS OF COLONEL ARCHIBALD MONTGOMERY MAXWELL KH. LIEUTENANT COLONEL 36TH REGIMENT. AGED 58 YEARS. DIED 21ST MAY 1845. HE SERVED HIS COUNTRY FOR FORTY-FIVE YEARS WITH CREDIT AND DISTINCTION. THIS MONUMENT WAS ERECTED BY GENERAL SIR ROGER SCHEAFFE BART AND THE OFFICERS OF THE 36TH REGIMENT AS A TESTIMONY OF THEIR RESPECT. HE DIED AT NEWCASTLE BARRACKS."

2nd Lt 1 Jul 1801. 1st Lt 17 May 1803. 2nd Capt 1 Feb 1808. Capt 12 Feb 1825. Bt Major 27 May 1825. Major 95th Foot 24 Jan 1828. Bt Lt Colonel 25 Nov 1828. Lt Colonel 36th Foot 22 Aug 1834. Bt Colonel 23 Nov 1841.

Served in the Peninsula May – Sep 1813. Present on the East coast of Spain at two sieges on the fortress of Tarragona and in the Italian campaigns under Sir William Bentinck (Brigade Major to the artillery at the Capture of Genoa 1814). KH. Also served in Calabria 1806–1807 (present at Scylla Castle). Commanded 36th Foot from 1834 until his death 21 May 1845.
Reference: Maxwell, Montgomery, My adventures, 2 vols, 1845.

MAXWELL, Hamilton
Captain. 42nd (Royal Highland) Regiment of Foot.
Mural memorial tablet: St Mary's Churchyard, Dumfries, Dumfriesshire, Scotland. (Photograph)

TO THE MEMORY OF / MAJOR HAMILTON MAXWELL / SECOND SON OF SIR WILLIAM MAXWELL / OF MONCRIEFF, BARONET, WHO DIED AT / FRIARS CORSE, 14TH DEC 1850 / IN THE 64TH YEAR OF HIS AGE. / ……………….

Ensign 26th Foot 30 Jan 1806. Lt 7 May 1807. Capt 42nd Foot 14 May 1812.

Served in the Peninsula Oct 1808 – Jan 1809 and Sep 1811 – Jun 1812. Present at Corunna. MGS medal for Corunna. Also served at Walcheren 1809. Late became Major in the Dumfriesshire Militia.

MAXWELL, Robert
Lieutenant. 74th (Highland) Regiment of Foot.
Named on the Regimental Memorial: St Giles's Cathedral, Edinburgh, Scotland. (Photograph)

Lt 1 May 1804. Capt 17th Line Portuguese Army 24 Mar 1810.

Served in the Peninsula with Portuguese Army Mar 1810 – Jun 1811. Present at first siege of Badajoz (wounded) and second siege of Badajoz where he was wounded 5 Jun 1811 and died of his wounds 11 Jun 1811.

MAXWELL, William

Sergeant. 74th (Highland) Regiment of Foot.
Pedestal tomb: Dean Cemetery, Edinburgh, Scotland. (Section F). (Photograph)

HERE ARE DEPOSITED THE REMAINS OF / WILLIAM MAXWELL / WHO DIED JULY 10TH 1856 AGED 70 YEARS. / HE SERVED THROUGHOUT THE WHOLE OF THE LATE PENINSULAR WAR / AS A NON COMMISSIONED OFFICER IN THE 74TH HIGHLANDERS / AND WAS MUCH RESPECTED BY THE OFFICERS / AND BELOVED BY HIS COMRADES. / HE WAS APPOINTED SUPERINTENDENT OF THE UNITED INDUSTRIAL / SCHOOLS IN THIS CITY AT THEIR INSTITUTION IN 1847 / AND MOST ZEALOUSLY PERFORMED HIS DUTIES UNTIL HIS DEATH. / THE CHILDREN UNDER HIS CHARGE LOVED HIM / AS IF HE HAD BEEN THEIR FATHER / AND HE TREATED THEM WITH ALL THE AFFECTION OF A PARENT. / THIS MONUMENT HAS BEEN ERECTED / AS A TESTIMONY OF REGARD BY HIS FRIENDS IN THE ARMY / AND THOSE CONNECTED WITH THE SCHOOLS.

Pte 9 Oct 1807. Cpl 25 Jun 1810. Sgt 25 May 1812. Quartermaster Sgt 12 Jul 1829.

Served in the Peninsula Feb 1810 – Apr 1814. Present at Badajoz, Salamanca, Vittoria, Pyrenees, Nivelle, Nive, Orthes and Toulouse. Also served in North America 1818–1825. Discharged 8 Jun 1833. MGS medal for Badajoz, Salamanca, Vittoria, Pyrenees, Nivelle, Nive, Orthes and Toulouse. Awarded the Regimental medal for six actions, Army Long Service medal and Good Conduct medal. From 1847 until his death in 1856 he was Superintendent of the United Industrial Schools in Edinburgh.

MAY, Sir John

Captain. Royal Artillery.
Grave: St Nicholas's Churchyard, Plumstead, Kent. (No longer extant. Destroyed by a flying bomb in the Second World War). (M.I.)
Named on the Regimental Memorial: St Nicholas's Church, Plumstead, Kent. (No longer extant. Destroyed by a flying bomb in the Second World War)

2nd Lt 6 Mar 1795. 1st Lt 7 Oct 1795. Capt-Lt 18 Apr 1803. Capt 1 Jun 1806. Bt Major 6 Feb 1812. Bt Lt Colonel 27 Apr 1812. Major 2 Mar 1825. Lt Colonel 29 Jul 1825. Bt Colonel 22 Jun 1830. Colonel 10 Jan 1837. Major General 28 Jun 1838.

Served in the Peninsula Mar – Jun 1809, Jul 1809 – Mar 1812 (Brigade Major of Artillery) and Apr 1812 – Apr 1814 (AAG Royal Artillery). Present at Douro, Talavera, Busaco, Fuentes d'Onoro, Ciudad Rodrigo (Mentioned in Despatches), Badajoz (Mentioned in Despatches), siege of Salamanca Forts (wounded and Mentioned in Despatches), Salamanca, Vittoria (wounded), San Sebastian (Mentioned in Despatches), Bidassoa, Nivelle, Nive, Adour and Toulouse. Present at Quatre Bras, Waterloo and the Capture of Paris (AAG Royal Artillery). Also served on bomb vessels 1797–1801 and Copenhagen 1807. Gold Cross for Badajoz, Salamanca, Vittoria, San Sebastian, Nivelle, Nive and Toulouse. KCB. KCH. KTS. Died in London 8 May 1847.
Reference: Annual Register, 1847, Appx, p. 228.

MEAD, Charles

2nd Lieutenant Commissary. Royal Artillery Drivers.
Headstone: All Saints' Churchyard, Westbere, Canterbury, Kent. (Photograph)

………………. / LIEUTENANT CHARLES MEAD / ROYAL ARTILLERY / HUSBAND OF THE ABOVE ELIZABETH MEAD / WHO DIED APRIL 21ST 1873 / IN THE 88TH YEAR OF HIS AGE

2nd Lt Commissary 1 May 1813.

Served in the Peninsula Mar – Apr 1814. Also served in France with the Army of Occupation 1815. Retired from the army 1 Aug 1816. The Corps of Royal Artillery Drivers were gradually reduced after 1814. Four troops were disbanded 1 Jan 1813, two on 1 Jul 1816 and two on 1 Aug 1816. The officers being placed on half pay. In 1817 the remaining troops were placed under the command of RA officers. Charles Mead later moved to Fordwich becoming Mayor from 1834–1848 and Magistrate.

MEAKIN, Joseph

Private. 1st (King's) Dragoon Guards.
Buried in St Lawrence's Churchyard, Heanor, Derbyshire. (Burial register)

"JOSEPH MEAKIN OF LANGLEY BURIED 18TH JUNE 1882, AGED 94 YEARS. AN OLD WATERLOO SOLDIER BURIED ON THE 67TH ANNIVERSARY OF THE BATTLE."

Present at Waterloo.

MEALLING, Thomas

Sergeant. 1st (Royal) Regiment of Dragoons.
Ledger stone: St Andrew's Churchyard, Shifnal, Shropshire. (Photograph)

THOMAS MEALLING. / (LATE SEARJENT IN / HER MAJESTY'S 1ST ROYAL DRAGOONS) / WHO DEPARTED THIS LIFE OCT 28TH 1859 / AGED 86 YEARS. / HE SERVED HIS COUNTRY 27 YEARS; / FOUGHT IN THE PENINSULAR WAR AND / WAS WOUNDED AT FUENTES D'ONOR. / ………………. / (REMAINDER OF INSCRIPTION ILLEGIBLE)

Bronze Memorial tablet on concrete plinth: St Andrew's Churchyard, Shifnal, Shropshire. (Photograph)

SERGEANT / THOMAS MEALLING / 1ST ROYAL DRAGOONS / WHO SERVED HIS COUNTRY FOR 27 YEARS / AND FOUGHT IN THE PENINSULAR WAR / BORN 1776 IN DORSET / DIED 28TH OCTOBER 1859 / WHOSE REMAINS ARE BURIED CLOSE BY

Private 25 Sep 1797. Corporal 1805. Sergeant 1808.

Served in the Peninsula. Present at Fuentes D'Onoro (wounded). MGS medal for Fuentes d'Onoro. Served for 27 years. Discharged 6 Feb 1825 aged 50.
Note: The original ledger stone has been relocated near to the War Memorial and a new bronze memorial tablet erected by the Shropshire War Memorial Association 15 Oct 2011.

MEARES, Richard Goldsmith

Lieutenant. 2nd Life Guards.
Headstone: St John's Cemetery, York, Western Australia, Australia. (Photograph)

PENINSULA / WATERLOO / SACRED / TO THE MEMORY OF / RICHARD GOLDSMITH MEARES / LATE GOVERNMENT RESIDENT OF THE YORK / DISTRICT AND CAPTAIN IN THE SECOND / REGIMENT OF LIFE GUARDS / WHO DIED ON THE 9TH JANUARY 1862 / AGED 82 YEARS / ……………….

Lt North Yorkshire Militia 1 Jan 1804. Lt 7th Foot 10 Mar 1808. Cornet 2nd Life Guards 4 Jul 1809. Lt 23rd Sep 1812. Capt 24 Mar 1817.

Served in the Peninsula with 2nd Life Guards, Nov 1812 – Apr 1814. Present at Vittoria and Toulouse. Present at Waterloo. Half pay 12 Dec 1818. Retired Jul 1829 and sailed for Western Australia with his family of eight children. Found life in Australia hard as he had no land, £500 of the money from the sale of his commission had been given to a man to buy land for him but he lost his money. By 1837 he was a Magistrate and by 1840–1841 Government Resident in Murray District. Moved to York in 1842 and among his many responsibilities helped to found York Race Club and started importing English thoroughbreds. Early Director of Western Australian Agricultural Society. MGS medal for Vittoria and Toulouse.
Reference: Dictionary of Australian Biography.

MEE, John

Lieutenant. 5th Garrison Battalion.
Headstone within kerbed enclosure: Old Common Cemetery, Southampton, Hampshire. (G045 011). Headstone severely damaged, laid flat and inscription largely illegible. (Photograph)

CAPT. JOHN MEE / LATE OF 24TH REGT / DEPARTED THIS LIFE / OCTOBER 29TH 1865 / IN HIS 85TH YEAR / ....

Lt 24th Foot 16 Feb 1808. Lt 5th Garrison Battalion 7 Jan 1813.
Served in the Peninsula Apr 1809 – Jan 1811. Present at Talavera and Busaco. 5th Garrison Battalion was disbanded in 1814. Half pay 6 Feb 1815. MGS medal for Talavera and Busaco. Served 40 years as a Magistrate for the County of Dublin. Died in Southampton 29 Oct 1865 aged 85.
Reference: Gentleman's Magazine, Dec 1865, p. 799.

MEEK, Jacob

Lieutenant. 14th (Buckinghamshire) Regiment of Foot.
Low monument: St Wilfred's Churchyard, Mobberley, Cheshire. (Photograph)

TO THE MEMORY OF / LT COLONEL JACOB MEEK / WHO DIED AT MOBBERLEY ON 15TH DEC 1857 AGED 70 / HE WAS AN EXCELLENT OFFICER AND HIS RELIGIOUS AND MORAL / PRINCIPLES WERE UNCOMPROMISING / HE WAS GREATLY ESTEEMED BY A LARGE CIRCLE OF ACQUAINTANCES / AND MUCH LOVED WHERE INFINITELY KNOWN

Ensign York Chasseurs 21 Mar 1810. Ensign 14th Foot 24 May 1810. Lt 22 Oct 1812. Capt (unattached) 23 Jun 1825. Capt 94th Foot 18 Aug 1825.
Served on the East coast of Spain, Malta, Sicily, in Sir William Bentinck's expedition to Genoa 1814 and with Sir Hudson Lowe in the Mediterranean May 1815. Retired 26 Apr 1834. Friend of Capt John Blakiston 27th Foot and died while on a visit to his friend at Mobberley Hall 15 Dec 1857. They both lie in the same churchyard.

MEIGHAN, Michael William

Lieutenant. 32nd (Cornwall) Regiment of Foot.
Headstone: St Mary's Churchyard, Dublin, Ireland. (M.I.) (Church deconsecrated and is now a restaurant. Churchyard opened as a public space. Gravestones were removed and placed in three rows along a wall to the rear of the open space. Some slabs form part of the pavement, but this memorial not visible)

"SACRED TO THE MEMORY OF / MICHAEL WILLIAM MEIGHAN / LATE CAPTAIN IN HIS MAJESTY'S 32ND REGT OF FOOT. / HE WAS A DISTINGUISHED OFFICER / AND WAS SEVERELY WOUNDED AT THE BATTLE OF WATERLOO. / HE DEPARTED THIS LIFE ON THE 8TH SEPTEMBER 1833 / IN THE 52ND YEAR OF HIS AGE. THIS MONUMENT WAS ERECTED / BY HIS AFFECTIONATE WIDOW."

Ensign 17 Dec 1805. Lt 9 Nov 1807. Capt 30 Sep 1819.

Served in the Peninsula Jul 1811 – Apr 1814. Present at the siege of Salamanca Forts, Salamanca, Burgos and retreat from Burgos. Present at Waterloo where he was severely wounded. Also served at Walcheren 1809. Half pay 25 Oct 1822.

MEIN, John Alexander

Major. 74th (Highland) Regiment of Foot.
Chest tomb: Msida Bastion Garden of Rest Floriana, Malta. (Photograph)

JOHN ALEXANDER MEIN / BORN TANJORE, INDIA 1786 / DIED MALTA 1841. / COLONEL COMMANDING THE 74TH / HIGHLAND REGIMENT OF FOOT / 1823–1841

Ensign 14 Nov 1799. Lt 5 Apr 1801. Capt 29 Feb 1804. Major 11 Nov 1813. Lt Colonel 20 Mar 1823. Bt Colonel 28 Jun 1838.

Served in the Peninsula Feb 1810 – Jun 1811 and Jan – May 1812. Present at Busaco and siege of Badajoz. Also served in India Nov 1799 – Feb 1806 (present at Ahmednuggar, Assaye (wounded, where all officers of the 74th Foot were either killed or wounded with one exception), Argaum, Gawilghur, Chandore and Jaulnah), Walcheren 1809, Canada 1818 and West Indies 1834. Held a commission in the regiment for 41 years with hardly any leave of absence. Commanded the 74th Foot from 1823–1841, dying in command in Malta on 9 Nov 1841 from the effects of a fever contracted in the West Indies. Brother of Major Nicol Alexander Mein 43rd Foot and Major William Mein 52nd Foot

Reference: Duckers, Peter, On service in India: the Mein photographs 1870–1901, 2000. Gentleman's Magazine, Feb 1842, p. 230.

MEIN, Nicol Alexander

Major. 43rd (Monmouthshire) Light Infantry Regiment of Foot.
Memorial tablet on family Mausoleum: Canonbie Churchyard, Dumfriesshire, Scotland. (Photograph)

IN MEMORY OF / NICOL ALEXANDER MEIN ESQUIRE, / LATE LIEUTENANT COLONEL OF THE 43RD REGIMENT, / DEPUTY LIEUTENANT AND MAGISTRATE / FOR THE COUNTY, / WHO DIED AT MARSH HOUSE / ON THE 8TH DAY OF JUNE, 1847, / AGED 70 YEARS.

Ensign 52nd Foot 13 May 1797. Ensign 74th Foot 13 Jun 1798. Lt 27 Mar 1799. Capt 85th Foot 4 Jun 1801. Major 21 Sep 1809. Major 43rd Foot 25 Jan 1813. Bt Lt Colonel 4 Jun 1814.

Served in the Peninsula with 43rd Dec 1813 – Apr 1814. Present at Tarbes and Toulouse. Served in France with 1/43rd at the Capture of Paris and with the Army of Occupation. Also served in India 1797–1801 (present at Malavelly, siege of Seringapatam – awarded a medal by the East India Company for his gallantry), West Indies 1801–1802, Walcheren 1809 (present at the siege of Flushing) and North America 1814–1815 (present at New Orleans where he was Mentioned in Despatches). Deputy Lieutenant and Magistrate for Dumfriesshire. Retired 9 Sep 1819. Brother of Major John Alexander Mein 74th Foot and Major William Mein 52nd Foot.

Reference: Carlisle Journal, 26 Jun 1847.

MEIN, William

Major. 52nd (Oxfordshire) Light Infantry Regiment of Foot.
Memorial tablet on family Mausoleum: Canonbie Churchyard, Dumfriesshire, Scotland. (Photograph)

IN MEMORY OF / WILLIAM MEIN CB / LATE LIEUTENANT & COMMANDER / OF THE 52ND REGIMENT / DEPUTY LIEUTENANT AND MP FOR THE COUNTY / WHO DIED AT MARSH HOUSE CANONBIE / ON JANUARY 18 1836 / PROUDLY ERECTED IN HIS HONOUR / BY HIS AUSTRALIAN DESCENDENTS JULY 2010

Ensign 74th Foot 20 Sep 1797. Ensign 52nd Foot Jan 1798. Lt Nov 1799. Capt 14 Aug 1804. Bt Major 6 Feb 1812. Bt Lt Colonel 7 Oct 1813. Major 52nd Foot 11 Nov 1813.

Served in the Peninsula Aug 1808 – Jan 1809 and Jul 1809 – Dec 1813. Present at Corunna, Coa, Busaco, Pombal, Redinha, Casal Nova (wounded), Foz d'Arouce, Sabugal, Fuentes d'Onoro, Ciudad Rodrigo (first to enter Fort St Francisco, severely wounded and awarded Brevet Majority), Badajoz (severely wounded), Salamanca, San Millan, Vittoria, Pyrenees, Vera (wounded), Bidassoa (severely wounded, Mentioned in Despatches and awarded Brevet Colonelcy), Nivelle and Nive (commanded regiment, was severely wounded and awarded pension of £300 per annum). Gold Medal for Nive. Had to return to England to recover. His wounds did not allow him to rejoin the 52nd at Waterloo but he joined the Army of Occupation until Mar 1817. Retired on half pay 16 Jul 1818 as a consequence of his Peninsular wounds. CB. Also served at Ferrol 1800, Sicily 1806–1807 and the Baltic 1808. MP for Dumfriesshire. Deputy Lieutenant and Magistrate for Dumfriesshire. Brother of Major Nicol Mein 43rd Foot and Major John Alexander Mein 74th Foot.

REFERENCE: Gentleman's Magazine, Jun 1836, p. 662.

MELHUISH, Samuel Camplin

2nd Captain. Royal Engineers.

Named on the Regimental Memorial: Rochester Cathedral, Rochester, Kent. (Photograph)

2nd Lt 25 Apr 1809. Lt 28 May 1810. 2nd Capt 20 Dec 1814. Capt 24 Feb 1829. Major 28 Nov 1854.

Served in the Peninsula Jun 1811 – Apr 1814. Present at Badajoz (wounded leading the 5th Division to the assault), Adour and Bayonne (wounded). Also served in the Netherlands and France 1815. Retired Jul 1836. MGS medal for Badajoz. Died at Taunton 30 Mar 1856.

MELVILLE, David

Lieutenant. Royal Engineers.

Named on the Regimental Memorial: Rochester Cathedral, Rochester, Kent. (Photograph)

2nd Lt 12 Jul 1809. Lt 1 May 1811.

Served in the Peninsula 22 Mar 1811 – 10 May 1811. Present at first siege of Badajoz 24 April. He was wounded 9 May and 10 May was killed in the attack on San Christobal after 49 days service in the Peninsula.

MELVILLE, Robert

Captain. 68th (Durham) Regiment of Foot.

Grave: St Mary's Cemetery, Niagara, Canada. (M.I.)

"ROBERT MELVILLE, CAPT HM 68TH REGT DIED 1848"

Ensign 25 Oct 1804. Lt 20 Jul 1805. Capt 19 Aug 1813.

Served in the Peninsula Jun 1811 – Apr 1814. Present at the siege of Salamanca Forts, Moriscos, Salamanca, Burgos, Vittoria, Pyrenees, San Marcial, Nivelle, Adour and Orthes. Also served at Walcheren 1809, Ionian Islands 1822 and Canada 1824. MGS medal for Salamanca, Vittoria, Pyrenees, Nivelle and Orthes. Retired 1829.

MENCE, Haffey

Lieutenant. 44th (East Essex) Regiment of Foot.

Interred in Kensal Green Cemetery, London. (11637/170/4). (No longer extant)

Ensign 13 Aug 1812. Lt 27 Apr 1814.

Served in the Peninsula Aug 1813 – Apr 1814. Present at Tarragona. Also served in North America

1814 (present at Bladensburg, Washington, Baltimore, New Orleans and Fort Bowyer). Half pay 25 Mar 1817. Died Jul 1854.

MENZIES, William
Corporal. Royal Artillery.
Headstone laid flat: Old Parish Churchyard, Blairgowrie, Perthshire, Scotland. (Photograph)

………………. / WILLIAM MENZIES LATE QUARTERMASTER SERGEANT / WHO DIED 11TH JULY 1856 AGED 67 YEARS. / ……………….

Pte 1 Jan 1808. Cpl 1812. Sgt 1822. Quartermaster Sgt 1827.

Served in the Peninsula 1808 – Jan 1809. Present at Corunna. MGS medal for Corunna. Discharged 30 Sep 1830 due to ill health from long service. Awarded pension of two shillings and one halfpenny a day.

MERCER, Alexander Cavalié
2nd Captain. Royal Artillery.
Low monument: St David's Churchyard, Exeter, Devon. (Photograph)

SACRED TO THE MEMORY OF GENERAL ALEXANDER CAVALIE MERCER COLONEL COMMANDANT R. A. / WHO DEPARTED THIS LIFE THE 9TH NOVEMBER 1868 AGED 85

Memorial stone marking position of Mercer's Troop at Waterloo, Waterloo, Belgium. (Photograph)

THIS STONE MARKS THE LAST POSITION / OF G TROOP ROYAL HORSE ARTILLERY / COMMANDED BY CAPTAIN A. C. MERCER / DURING THE BATTLE OF WATERLOO / 18 JUNE 1815. FROM HERE THE TROOP / TOOK A CONSPICUOUS PART IN DEFEATING / THE ATTACKS OF THE FRENCH CAVALRY

2nd Lt 20 Dec 1797. 1st Lt 1 Dec 1801. 2nd Capt 3 Dec 1806. Capt 20 Jun 1815. Bt Major 12 Aug 1819. Lt Colonel 5 Jun 1835. Colonel 1 Apr 1846. Major General 20 Jun 1854. Lt General 29 Aug 1857. General 9 Feb 1865.

Present at Quatre Bras and Waterloo (commanding 'G' Troop of the Royal Horse Artillery who suffered great losses of men and horses. After the battle he commanded 'D' Troop replacing Major Beane who was killed). Also served in South America 1807–1808, the Netherlands and France 1815–1816, Canada 1823–1829 and North America 1837–1862. Commanded the Garrison at Dover Castle 1863. Colonel Commandant 9th Brigade Royal Artillery 1859. His later life was dominated by the lack of recognition for his service at Waterloo. Son of General Mercer Royal Engineers.
Reference: Mercer, Cavalié, Journal of the Waterloo campaign, Cavalié Mercer, reprint 2003. Glover, Gareth, ed., Reminiscences of Waterloo: the correspondence between Henry Leathes and Alexander Mercer of G Troop RHA, 2004. Dictionary of Canadian Biography.

MERCER, Cavalie Shorthose
Captain. Royal Engineers.
Table Sarcophagus: St Peter's Church, St George, Bermuda, West Indies. (M.I.)

"IN MEMORY OF / CAVALIE S. MERCER / CAPTAIN ROYAL ENGINEERS / WHO DEPARTED THIS LIFE / AUGUST 25TH 1819 / AGED 30 YEARS."

2nd Lt 1 Jul 1804. 1st Lt 1 Mar 1805. 2nd Capt 23 Apr 1810. Capt 20 Oct 1813.

Served in the Peninsula Aug 1808 – Jan 1809. Present at Rolica and Vimeiro. Also served in the West

Indies where he died in Bermuda 1819.

MERCER, Charles Wilkinson
Captain. 51st (2nd Yorkshire West Riding) Light Infantry.
Named on the Regimental Memorial: KOYLI Chapel, York Minster, Yorkshire. (Photograph)

Ensign 71st Foot 6 Mar 1796. Lt 51st Foot 12 Jul 1798. Capt 2 Mar 1805.
Served in the Peninsula Oct 1808 – Jan 1809. Present at Corunna. Also served as a Marine with the fleet under Sir John Jervis in 1796, with the 51st Regiment in Ceylon (present in the first Kandian War 1803) and Walcheren where he died of a fever in the summer of 1809.

MERCER, Douglas
Captain and Lieutenant Colonel. 3rd Regiment of Foot Guards.
Grave: Protestant Cemetery, Naples, Italy. (M.I.)

"LIEUT-GENERAL DOUGLAS MERCER HENDERSON, / OF FORDELL, FIFE, COLONEL 68TH REGT., OB 21 MAR., / 1854, A. 69"

Memorial: Royal Military Chapel, Wellington Barracks, London. (M.I.) (Destroyed by a Flying Bomb 1944)

"THIS WINDOW IS GIVEN BY G. WM. MERCER HENDERSON, OF FORDELL, LATE CAPTAIN SCOTS FUSILIER GUARDS, IN MEMORY OF HIS FATHER, LIEUT.-GENERAL DOUGLAS MERCER HENDERSON, C.B., OF FORDELL, FIFE, COLONEL 68TH REGIMENT, 3RD GUARDS, 1803–37. SERVED IN HANOVER, AT WALCHEREN; WOUNDED AT SOBRAL AND BARROSA, WHEN AIDE-DE-CAMP; CIUDAD RODRIGO, SALAMANCA, MADRID, BURGOS, THE BIDASSOA, THE NIVE, THE NIVELLE, QUATRE BRAS, AND WATERLOO, WHERE HE COMMANDED THE 2ND BATTALION AT THE CLOSE OF THE ACTION."

Ensign 24 Mar 1803. Lt and Capt 20 Mar 1806. Capt and Lt Colonel 20 Dec 1813. Bt Colonel 22 Jun 1830. Major General 23 Nov 1841. Lt General 11 Nov 1851.
Served in the Peninsula Apr 1810 – Apr 1811 (ADC to Major General Dilkes) and Sep 1811 – Feb 1814. Present at Cadiz, Barrosa (wounded), Sobral (wounded), El Bodon, Ciudad Rodrigo, Salamanca, Burgos, Bidassoa, Nivelle and Nive. Present at Quatre Bras, Waterloo and the Capture of Paris. At Waterloo he commanded the 2nd Battalion towards the end of the day. CB. Also served at Hanover 1805 and Walcheren 1809. MGS medal for Barrosa, Ciudad Rodrigo, Salamanca, Nivelle and Nive. Colonel 3rd Foot Guards 1837–1841. Colonel 68th Foot 31 Jan 1850. Later assumed the surname of Mercer Henderson. Died in Naples 21 Mar 1854.
Reference: Gentleman's Magazine, Aug 1854, p. 191. Annual Register, 1854, Appx, pp. 281–2. (Under Henderson).

MERCER, James
1st Lieutenant. 95th Regiment of Foot.
Memorial tablet in wall of family mausoleum: Caterline, Kincardineshire, Scotland. (Photograph)

.... / THEIR SON / JAMES MERCER. LIEUTENANT IN THE RIFLE BRIGADE / WAS KILLED WHEN ON PIQUET AT BARBA-DEL-PUERCO IN PORTUGAL / ON THE 19TH MARCH 1810 IN THE 26TH YEAR OF HIS AGE.

2nd Lt 13 Mar 1806. 1st Lt 3 Mar 1808.
Served in the Peninsula with 2/95th Oct 1808 – Jan 1809 and 1/95th Jul 1809 – Mar 1810. Present at

Vigo and Barba del Puerco where he was killed 19 Mar 1810.

MERCER, Robert

Captain and Lieutenant Colonel. 3rd Regiment of Foot Guards.
Named on Memorial Panel VIII for Bergen op Zoom: Royal Military Chapel, Wellington Barracks, London. (M.I.) (Destroyed by a Flying Bomb 1944)

Ensign 10 Dec 1799. Lt and Capt 3 Sep 1801. Capt and Lt Colonel 5 Mar 1812.

Served in the Peninsula Mar 1809 – Jul 1812 (DAQMG 1st Division Jun 1809 – Apr 1811 and DAQMG 7th Division Apr 1811 – Jun 1812). Present at Douro, Talavera and Fuentes d'Onoro. Also served in the Netherlands 1814 (present at Bergen-op-Zoom where he was killed 8 Mar 1814).
Reference: Gentleman's Magazine, May 1814, p. 525.

MERLEN, J. B. van

Major General. Staff, Dutch Cavalry.
Memorial tablet: St Joseph's Church, Waterloo. (Photograph)

D. O. M. / A LA MÉMOIRE DU GÉNÉRAL-MAJOR / BARON VAN MERLEN / TUÉ AU CHAMP D'HONNEUR, LE 18 JUIN 1815 / À LA BATAILLE DE WATERLOO / À LA TÊTE DE LA BRIGADE DE CAVALERIE NO 1. / DANS CE CHAMP BELLIQUEUX / OU SA VALEUR SUCCOMBE, SA GLOIRE ET NOS REGRETS / ACCOMPAGNENT SA TOMBE / RIP

Named on the Regimental Memorial to officers of the Dutch 6th Regiment of Hussars killed at Waterloo, St Joseph's Church, Waterloo, Belgium. (Photograph)
Named on the Memorial to Dutch officers killed at Waterloo: St Joseph's Church, Waterloo. (Photograph)

METCALFE, Henry

Ensign. 32nd (Cornwall) Regiment of Foot.
Family Memorial: Kirkbride Churchyard, Cumbria. Inscription not recorded.

Ensign 18 Mar 1813. Lt 27 Jul 1815.

Served in the Peninsula Apr 1814. Present at Waterloo (severely wounded). Half pay 25 Mar 1817. Died 1828. Third son of the Rector of Kirkbride.

METCALFE, John

Lieutenant. 45th (Nottinghamshire) Regiment of Foot.
Named on the Memorial: St Andrew's Church (now Musée Historique), Biarritz, France. (Photograph)

Ensign Feb 1807. Lt 16 Jun 1808.

Served in the Peninsula Sep 1811 – Dec 1812 and Nov 1813 – Feb 1814. Present at Ciudad Rodrigo, (in command of men from 45th, 74th and 88th Foot engineering the sap for the siege where he was Mentioned in Despatches), Badajoz (wounded 24 and 26 Mar and severely wounded 6 Apr 1812) and Orthes where he was killed 27 Feb 1814.

METHOLD, Edward

1st Lieutenant. 23rd (Royal Welch Fusiliers) Regiment of Foot.
Ledger stone: Kensal Green Cemetery, London. (24500/22–27/IR). (Photograph)

SACRED / TO THE MEMORY OF / MAJOR EDWARD METHOLD / LATE OF THE COUNTY OF DURHAM / DIED AT KENSINGTON JULY 14TH 1877 / IN HIS 81ST YEAR / ………………

Memorial window: St Mary Abbots Church, Kensington, London. (East window). (Photograph)

THIS WINDOW WAS DEDICATED IN REMEMBRANCE OF MAJOR EDWARD METHOLD, BORN MARCH 29TH 1797, AT BEAMISH PARK, DURHAM, DIED AT 11, ALBERT PLACE, JULY 14TH 1877.

2nd Lt 17 Sep 1812. 1st Lt 23 Mar 1815. Lt 19th Lt Dragoons 1 Jun 1820. Capt 3rd Dragoon Guards 11 Oct 1821. Bt Major 10 Jan 1837.

Present at Waterloo with the 23rd Foot. Half pay 1821. Retired in 1837.

MEYER, Friedrich Ludwig

Lieutenant Colonel. 3rd Regiment of Hussars, King's German Legion.
Named on the Regimental Memorial: La Haye Sainte, Waterloo. (Photograph)
Named on the Waterloo Column, Hanover, Germany. (Photograph)

Capt 10 Oct 1803. Major 1st Hussars 25 Oct 1810. Lt Col 3rd Hussars 10 Oct 1813.

Served in the Peninsula Aug 1808 – Jan 1809 and Feb 1811 – Jun 1812. Present at Pombal, Sabugal, Fuentes d'Onoro (wounded) and El Bodon. Present at Waterloo where he was severely wounded and died of his wounds 6 Jul 1815. Also served in the Baltic 1808–1808 and the Netherlands 1814.

MEYER, Johann

Lieutenant. 5th Line Battalion, King's German Legion.
Named on the Memorial: St Andrew's Church (now Musée Historique), Biarritz, France. (Photograph)

Ensign 10 Jul 1806. Lt 6 Sep 1809.

Served in the Peninsula Sep 1808 – Apr 1814. Present at Douro, Talavera, Busaco, Fuentes d'Onoro, Ciudad Rodrigo, Salamanca, Burgos, Vittoria, San Sebastian, Bidassoa, Nivelle, Nive, St Etienne and Bayonne where he was killed Apr 1814. Also served at Hanover 1805 and the Baltic 1807–1808.

MEYRICKE, John Chabbert

Lieutenant. 43rd (Monmouthshire) Light Infantry Regiment of Foot.
Family Memorial brass tablet: St Laurence's Church, Ludlow, Shropshire. (Photograph)

………………. / ALSO OF / LIEUT. JOHN CHABBERT MEYRICKE, / 43RD REGT. BORN 1792. / KILLED AT THE SIEGE / OF NEW ORLEANS, 1815.

Ensign Shropshire Militia 29 Aug 1804. Ensign 43rd Foot 4 May 1809. Lt 29 Aug 1810.

Served in the Peninsula with 1/43rd Aug 1812 – Apr 1814. Present at San Munos, Vittoria, Pyrenees, Vera, Bidassoa, Nivelle (wounded), Nive, Tarbes and Toulouse. Also served in North America 1814–1815 where he was killed at New Orleans 8 Jan 1815.

MIDDLEDITCH, William Martin

Sergeant. 1st Regiment of Foot Guards.
Headstone: Great Churchyard, Bury St Edmunds, Suffolk. (Photograph)
New replica headstone erected by the Suffolk branch of the Grenadier Guards Association Commemorating the 350th Anniversary of the Regiment 2006. (Photograph]

SACRED / TO THE MEMORY OF / WILLIAM MIDDLEDITCH. / LATE SERGEANT MAJOR OF THE GRENADIER GUARDS. / WHO DIED NOVBR. 13TH 1834 / AGED 53 YEARS. / A HUSBAND, FATHER, COMRADE FRIEND SINCERE. / A BRITISH SOLDIER LIES BURIED HERE. / IN SPAIN AND FLUSHING AND AT WATERLOO, / HE FOUGHT TO GUARD OUR COUNTRY FROM THE FOE; / HIS COMRADES BRITONS, WHO SURVIVE HIM SAY, / HE ACTED NOBLY ON THAT

GLORIOUS DAY. / THIS INSCRIPTION IS A REPLICA OF THE ORIGINAL FACE / RESTORED BY THE SUFFOLK BRANCH OF THE / GRENADIER GUARDS ASSOCIATION / COMMEMORATING THE 350TH / ANNIVERSARY OF THE REGIMENT 2006.

Pte 21 Sep 1800. Cpl 22 Jun 1803. Sgt 15 Sep 1806. Sgt Major 29 Sep 1816.

Served in the Peninsula Oct 1808 – Jan 1809 and Apr 1811 – Apr 1814. Present at Corunna, Cadiz, San Sebastian, Nivelle, Nive and Bayonne. Present at Waterloo in Lt Colonel Jones's Company and with the Army of Occupation until Sep 1818. Also served in Sicily 1807, Walcheren 1809 (present at the siege of Flushing) and Ireland 1819. Discharged from the army 7 Feb 1821 owing to ill health and became landlord of the *Ram Inn* in Bury St Edmunds.

REFERENCE: Clark, Frank A. O., Borne to the grave by heroes. Grenadier Guards Association, 1994.

MIDDLEMORE, George

Major. 48th (Northamptonshire) Regiment of Foot.

Low monument and slate tablet: Trinity Cemetery, Tunbridge Wells, Kent. (Photograph)

SACRED TO THE MEMORY OF / LIEUT GENERAL MIDDLEMORE C.B. / COLONEL OF H. M. 48 REGT OF FOOT. / DEPARTED THIS LIFE 18 NOVEMBER 1850 / IN THE 81 YEAR OF HIS AGE.

At the head of the grave is a slate tablet erected in 1907 by the 1st Northamptonshire Regiment, (formerly 48th Foot), commemorating the battle of Talavera. Now badly flaked the inscription is not readable, but the inscription has been recorded from a memorial inscription:

"TALAVERA / IT WAS ON THE ADVANCE OF THE BATTALION TO THE RESCUE OF THE GUARDS THAT COL. DONELLAN WAS STRUCK AND PAINFUL AS MUST HAVE BEEN THE WOUND, HIS COUNTENANCE NOT ONLY DID NOT BETRAY HIS SUFFERING BUT PRESERVED HIS USUAL EXPRESSION. CALLING MAJOR MIDDLEMORE THE NEXT SENIOR OFFICER, COL DONELLAN SEATED ERECT IN HIS SADDLE, TOOK OFF HIS HAT, BOWED, AND SAID, MAJOR MIDDLEMORE, YOU WILL HAVE THE HONOUR OF LEADING THE 48TH TO THE CHARGE. THE BATTALION CHARGED AND RESCUED THE GUARDS, WHILST COL. DONELLAN WAS CONDUCTED TO THE REAR AND DIED AT TALAVERA. / GRAVE RESTORED AND THIS TABLET ERECTED BY THE OFFICERS OF THE 1ST NORTHAMPTONSHIRE REGIMENT IN 1907."

Ensign 86th Foot 16 Jan 1793. Lt Independent Company 5 Apr 1793. Capt 86th Foot 15 Oct 1794. Major 48th Foot 14 Sep 1804. Bt Lt Colonel 2 Nov 1809. Colonel 12 Aug 1819. Major General 22 Jul 1830. Lt General 23 Nov 1841.

Served in the Peninsula Jul 1809 – Apr 1810. Present at Talavera (commanded the 48th Foot after Lt Colonel Charles Donellan was fatally wounded). Gold Medal for Talavera. Also served as a marine on board HMS *Brunswick,* India 1799 (present at Seringapatam), Egypt 1801, India 1803 (present in the Mahratta Wars), Malta 1804, Gibraltar 1804–1809. Returned home 1811 due to ill health and appointed AQMG on staff of Severn District 1813, West Indies 1830 and St Helena 1836 (Governor 1836–1841). MGS medal for Egypt. CB. Colonel 76th Foot 2 Jan 1843. Colonel 48th Foot 31 May 1843.

REFERENCE: Dictionary of National Biography. Gentleman's Magazine, Jan 1851, pp. 95–6. Annual Register, 1850, Appx, p. 281.

MIDDLETON, John

1st Lieutenant. 95th Regiment of Foot.

Mural memorial tablet: Dean Cemetery, Edinburgh, Scotland. (Grave number 2159). (Photograph)

TO THE MEMORY OF / JAMES MIDDLETON, ESQ. / OF WALTHAM LODGE, MURRAY FIELD, / DIED 20TH NOV. 1854 AGED 84. / ALSO HIS BROTHER / MAJOR JOHN MIDDLETON, / LATE

OF THE SECOND BATTALION / RIFLE BRIGADE, / WHO DIED AT WALTHAM LODGE / 20TH DECEMBER 1867, AGED 86.

Ensign 75th Foot 10 Mar 1808. Ensign 91st Foot 5 Jan 1809. 1st Lt 95th Foot 4 Oct 1809. Capt 7 Apr 1825. Paymaster 2/95th Foot 25 Nov 1826.

Served in the Peninsula with 3/95th Mar 1810 – Apr 1814. Present at Cadiz (serving as Assistant Engineer), Barrosa, Ciudad Rodrigo (member of the storming party), Badajoz, Salamanca, San Millan, Vittoria, Pyrenees, Vera, Bidassoa, Nivelle, Nive, Orthes, Tarbes and Toulouse. Paymaster Cork Recruiting District 12 Jul 1844. Paymaster Edinburgh District Sep 1844. Retired on half pay with honorary rank of Major 1 Jul 1856. MGS medal for Barrosa, Ciudad Rodrigo, Badajoz, Salamanca, Vittoria, Pyrenees, Nivelle, Nive, Orthes and Toulouse.

MIDDLETON, William

Captain. 42nd (Royal Highland) Regiment of Foot.

Memorial: Glasgow Cathedral Churchyard, Glasgow, Lanarkshire, Scotland. (M.I.)

"MAJOR WILLIAM MIDDLETON DIED 13 APR 1859 BORN 15 MAR 1787".

Ensign 7th West India Regt 18 Jan 1802. Ensign 42nd Foot 9 Jul 1803. Lt 23 Jun 1804. Capt 10 May 1812. Half pay 24 Oct 1814. Capt 42nd Foot 19 May 1819. Major 15 Aug 1826.

Served in the Peninsula Aug 1808 – Jan 1809 and Apr – Jul 1812. Present at Corunna (severely wounded) and Salamanca. Also served in Gibraltar 1805, Walcheren 1809 (suffered a severe attack of fever), Gibraltar 1825–1829, Malta 1831–1834 and Cape of Good Hope 1834–1836. Retired 23 Aug 1839.

MILL, Charles

Major. 27th (Inniskilling) Regiment of Foot.

Memorial tablet: St Mary's Church, Fort St George, Madras, India. (M.I.)

"TO THE MEMORY OF LIEUTENANT-COLONEL CHARLES MILL, HIS MAJESTY'S 55TH REGIMENT, KILLED ON THE 3RD OF APRIL 1834 WHILST GALLANTLY LEADING ON HIS REGIMENT TO THE ATTACK AGAINST THE STOCKADE OF SOMARPETT, IN THE TERRITORY OF HIS HIGHNESS THE RAJAH OF COORG. EMINENTLY DISTINGUISHED AS A SOLDIER THROUGH A PERIOD OF NEARLY 40 YEARS, HE SERVED WITH THE BRITISH ARMY DURING ITS MOST EVENTFUL EPOCHS: AND HIS EXAMPLE OF COURAGE AND GALLANTRY INSPIRED HIS FOLLOWERS ON ALL OCCASION WITH THAT BRAVERY AND FORTITUDE SO CONSPICUOUS AT THE ASSAULT IN WHICH HE FELL. IN PRIVATE LIFE HE WAS UNIVERSALLY ESTEEMED. DEVOTED TO THE INTERESTS OF HIS REGIMENT AND THE HAPPINESS OF THOSE WHO SERVED UNDER HIM, HIS MEMORY WILL LONG BE CHERISHED WITH SENTIMENT OF THE HIGHEST RESPECT, AND THE PREMATURE DEATH CONTINUE A SOURCE OF THE DEEPEST REGRET TO ALL MORE PARTICULARLY HIS BROTHER OFFICERS WHO HAVE IN HIM LOST A BRAVE LEADER AND A KIND FRIEND, AND WHO HAVE ERECTED THIS TABLET IN TRIBUTE TO HIS WORTH. ÆTAT. 54."

Ensign 5 Oct 1795. Lt 1 Sep 1796. Capt 4 Aug 1804. Major 10 Nov 1813. Major 55th Foot 11 Jan 1821. Lt Colonel 10 Aug 1826.

Served in the Peninsula with 2/27th Jul – Oct 1813 and with Staff Dec 1813 – Apr 1814 (Brigade Major to General Haviland Smith). Present at Castalla, Tarragona and Ordal (severely wounded). Also served in the West Indies 1796 (present at the Capture of St Lucia and quelling of the riots in Grenada), the Helder 1799, Ferrol 1800, Egypt 1801 (present at Alexandria), Malta 1804, North America 1814 (present at Plattsburgh), Cape of Good Hope 1826 and India 1830 where he was present at the storming of

Kissenhully 2 Apr 1834 and led the attack on the stockade at Somarpett in Coorg 3 Apr 1834 where he was killed. In this action 100 men of the 55th Foot were killed or wounded.
Reference: United Service Journal, Sep 1835, p. 143.

MILL, James
Lieutenant. 40th (2nd Somersetshire) Regiment of Foot.
Memorial: Royal Garrison Church Graveyard, Portsmouth, Hampshire. (M.I.)

"SACRED / TO THE MEMORY OF / JAMES MILL ESQ / LATE OF THE 40TH REGIMENT / DIED MAY 7TH 1847 AGED 60."

Ensign 12 Apr 1809. Lt 18 Sep 1811. Capt 78th Foot 24 Mar 1816. Bt Major 8 Apr 1826.

Served in the Peninsula Jul – Sep 1811 and Feb 1813 – Apr 1814. Present at Vittoria, Pyrenees, Bidassoa, Nivelle, Nive, Orthes and Toulouse. Present at Waterloo where he was wounded in his right eye which was damaged for life. Half pay 7 May 1829.

MILLAR, Henry
Lieutenant. 40th (2nd Somersetshire) Regiment of Foot.
Grave: Cornelian Bay Cemetery, Hobart, Tasmania, Australia. (Section X, Plot 10, reference 14365). (Originally in the Campbell Street Cemetery, refurbished about 1923 and relocated to Cornelian Bay in 1940)

SACRED / TO THE MEMORY OF / CAPT HENRY MILLAR / H.M. 40TH REGT / DIED JANUARY 10TH 1866, / AGED 82 YEARS. / ....

Ensign 88th Foot 22 Nov 1798. Lt 19 Apr 1800. Lt King's German Legion 20 Aug 1805. Ensign 40th Foot 31 Mar 1808. Lt 5 Sep 1810. Capt 25 Jun 1827.

Served in the Peninsula Jan 1810 – Jun 1812. Present at Busaco, Redinha, first siege of Badajoz, Ciudad Rodrigo and Badajoz (severely wounded). Present at Waterloo and with the Army of Occupation until 1818. Also served in Australia 1823–1829 (Commandant at Moreton Bay convict settlement in Queensland). Remained in Australia when the 40th Foot left for India in 1829. Joined the Commissariat Department in Hobart where he died 10 Jan 1866. MGS medal for Busaco, Ciudad Rodrigo and Badajoz.

MILLAR, John
Hospital Assistant. Medical Department.
Buried in Sighthill Cemetery, Glasgow, Scotland.
Memorial: St Nicholas Old Churchyard, Carrickfergus, Northern Ireland. (Photograph)

TO THE MEMORY OF / STAFF SURGEON / JOHN MILLAR / WHO DIED AT GLASGOW / MAY 3RD 1850 / AGED 55 YEARS. / IN AFFECTIONATE REMEMBRANCE / THE OFFICERS WHO SERVED WITH HIM / IN THE 43RD LIGHT INFANTRY OF WHICH / REGT HE WAS SURGEON / FOR 18 YEARS / HAVE ERECTED THIS MONUMENT, / HIS REMAINS REST IN / LIGHTHILL CEMETERY AT GLASGOW.

Hospital Asst 19 Jul 1813. Asst Surgeon Staff 8 Feb 1821. Surgeon 43rd Foot 5 Nov 1829. Staff Surgeon 16 Dec 1845.

Served in the Peninsula Jul 1813 – Apr 1814. Present at Pyrenees, Nivelle, Nive and Orthes. Also served in North America 1814 (present at New Orleans), the Netherlands 1815 and Canada 1835 (present in the Rebellion 1837–1838). He made the march with the regiment across the Portage of the Madawaska to Quebec, a distance of 370 miles in 18 days with temperatures of minus 24 degrees. Wellington said of this:

'One of the greatest feats ever performed amd the only military achievement by British officers that he really envied'. Half pay from 1815–1821. MGS medal for Pyrenees, Nivelle, Nive and Orthes.

MILLER, Arthur

Major. 6th (1st Warwickshire) Regiment of Foot.
Ledger stone: St Munna's Churchyard, Taghmon, County Wexford, Ireland. (M.I.)

"HERE LIETH THE BODY / OF / ARTHUR MILLER ESQ; LATE MAJOR OF THE / 6TH REGIMENT OF FOOT / WHO DEPARTED THIS LIFE / MARCH 23RD 1827 IN HIS 61ST YEAR"

Ensign 53rd Foot 17 Apr 1790. Lt 11 Feb 1792. Capt 3 Sep 1795. Major 6th Foot 28 Sep 1804.

Served in the Peninsula Aug 1808 – Jan 1809. Present at Rolica, Vimeiro and Corunna. Retired 1809.

MILLER, Fiennes Sanderson

Major. 6th (Inniskilling) Regiment of Dragoons.
Low monument in Family enclosure: Old Churchyard, West End, Radway, Warwickshire. (Photograph)

IN MEMORY OF / FIENNES SANDERSON MILLER. LIEUT COL. 6TH INNISKILLING DRAGOONS. C.B. / BORN MAY 16TH 1783. DIED SEPT 12TH 1862.

Obelisk: Edgehill, Warwickshire. (Photograph)

THIS OBELISK WAS ERECTED BY / CHARLES CHAMBERS ESQRE R. N. / IN 1834 TO COMMEMORATE THE / BATTLE OF WATERLOO, / WHERE THE VITH INNISKILLING DRAGOONS / WERE COMMANDED BY / LIEUT. COL. F. S. MILLER / WHO, FOR HIS GALLANT CONDUCT / DURING THE ACTION IN WHICH HE WAS / VERY SEVERELY WOUNDED, / WAS MADE A COMPANION OF THE MOST / HONORABLE ORDER OF THE BATH.

Cornet 28 Dec 1799. Lt 9 Aug 1803. Capt 5 Oct 1804. Major 25 May 1809. Bt Lt Colonel 4 Jun 1814.

Present at Waterloo with Lt Colonel Joseph Muter (later Stratton) in command. After the death of Sir William Ponsonby the command of the Union Brigade was taken by Colonel Muter and Fiennes Miller took command of the 6th Dragoons. About 6.30pm he was severely wounded and had to be carried off the field. Awarded a pension of £300 per annum. CB. Retired in 1818 succeeding to his father's estate in Warwickshire. Magistrate and Deputy Lieutenant for Warwickshire.

MILLER, George

Captain. 95th Regiment of Foot.
Named on the Rifle Brigade Memorial: Winchester Cathedral, Winchester, Hampshire. (Photograph)

2nd Lt 18 Jul 1804. 1st Lt 8 May 1805. Capt 21 Jan 1808. Bt Major 3 Mar 1814. Bt Lt Colonel 18 Jun 1815. Major 23 Dec 1819. Lt Colonel (unattached) 25 May 1826. Bt Colonel 10 Jan 1837.

Served in the Peninsula with 1/95th Nov 1808 – Jan 1809 and 2/95th Mar 1810 – Jul 1811 and Sep 1813 – Apr 1814. Present at Cacabellos, Corunna, Cadiz, Malaga, Fuengirola (taken prisoner but escaped), Barrosa, first siege of Badajoz, San Sebastian, Bidassoa, Nivelle, Nive, Orthes and Tarbes. Present at Waterloo with 2/95th where he was wounded and awarded Bt Lt Colonelcy and CB. Gold Medal for Nivelle. Also served in South America 1807 (present at Buenos Ayres where he was taken prisoner) and Walcheren 1809. Half Pay 26 May 1826. Died 20 Nov 1843.

MILLER, James

Captain. 68th (Durham) Regiment of Foot.

Memorial tablet: St Kentigern's Churchyard, Lanark, Lanarkshire, Scotland. (In low walled enclosure). (Photograph)

SACRED TO THE MEMORY OF / WILLIAM LOCKHART ESQ OF BARONALD / .... / ALSO TO THE MEMORY OF / CAMILLA, THEIR ONLY CHILD / WHO DIED 20TH JANUARY 1848 / AND OF HER HUSBAND / BREVET MAJOR JAMES MILLER, / 68TH REGIMENT OF FOOT, / WHO DIED IN SPAIN OF WOUNDS RECEIVED / AT THE BATTLE OF SALAMANCA.

Capt 9th Royal Veteran Battalion 20 Jun 1798. Capt 68th Foot 18 Jan 1810. Bt Major 25 Jul 1810.

Served in the Peninsula Jun 1811 – Aug 1812. Present at the siege of Salamanca Forts, Moriscos and Salamanca where he was severely wounded and died of his wounds on 13 Aug 1812.

MILLER, William

Captain and Lieutenant Colonel. 1st Regiment of Foot Guards.

Headstone: Evere Cemetery, Brussels, Belgium. (Grave number 17 Way, Number 859). (Photograph)

THE REMAINS OF / LT COL. MILLER / OF THE 1ST REG. BRITISH FOOT GUARD / OF GLENLEE BORN NEAR EDINBURGH SCOTLAND / MORTALLY WOUNDED AT THE AGE OF 31 YEARS / IN THE ACTION WITH THE FRENCH ARMY / AT LES QUATRE BRAS 16TH JUNE 1815 / DIED AT BRUSSELS ON THE FOLLOWING / DAY – ARE DEPOSITED HERE. / MANY BRITISH GENTLEMEN FELL WITH HIM, / DOING THEIR DUTY NONE, OF A MORE SPOTLESS LIFE, / OR WHO HAD GIVEN FAIRER PROMISE OF RISING / TO EMINENCE IN HIS PROFESSION. / .... / THE REMAINS OF LT COL MILLER / WHICH HAD REPOSED IN THE PROTESTANT CEMETERY / BEYOND THE PORTE DE LOUVAIN AT BRUSSELS SINCE / THE BATTLE OF WATERLOO / WERE IN CONSEQUENCE OF THE EXTENSION OF THE CITY / NECESSITATING THE BREAKING UP OF THE GROUND / REMOVED AND RE-DEPOSITED HERE 14 APRIL 1886 / AND THE MONUMENT BEARING THE ABOVE / EPITAPH RAISED BY HIS BROTHER OFFICERS / REMOVED TO SCOTLAND.

Relocated memorial from Brussels: Stair Church, Stair, Ayrshire, Scotland. (In church mounted on North wall). (Photograph)

MANENT OPTIMA CAELO / THE REMAINS OF LT. COL. MILLER / OF THE FIRST REGT OF BRITISH FOOT GUARDS / OF GLENLEE. BORN NEAR / EDINBURGH IN SCOTLAND, AND MORTALLY / WOUNDED AT THE AGE OF 31 YEARS IN / THE ACTION WITH THE FRENCH ARMY / AT LES QUATRE BRAS, 16TH JUNE 1815 / DIED AT BRUXELLES ON FOLLOWING / DAY ARE DEPOSITED HERE. / MANY BRITISH GENTLEMEN FELL / WITH HIM DOING THEIR DUTY. NONE / OF A MORE SPOTLESS LIFE, OR WHO HAD / GIVEN FAIRER PROMISE OF RISING TO / EMINENCE IN HIS PROFESSION. / "SAW'ST GALLANT MILLER'S FAILING EYE / STILL BENT WHERE ALBION'S BANNERS FLY" / SCOTT / THE REMAINS OF LIEUT COLONEL WILLIAM MILLER, SECOND SON OF WILLIAM MILLER OF GLENLEE BARONET, (LORD GLENLEE) WHICH HAD REPOSED IN THE PROTESTANT CEMETERY BEYOND THE PORTE DE LOUVAIN AT BRUSSELS SINCE THE BATTLE OF WATERLOO, WERE, IN CONSEQUENCE OF THE EXTENSION OF THE CITY NECESSITATING THE BREAKING-UP OF THE GROUND, REMOVED AND RE-DEPOSITED THERE, IN THE NEW CEMETERY OF EVERE; AND THE ABOVE MONUMENT, RAISED BY HIS BROTHER OFFICERS, REMOVED TO AND ERECTED IN THE CHURCH OF STAIR, XX NOVEMBER MDCCCLXXXVI

Named on the Regimental Memorial: St Joseph's Church, Waterloo. (Photograph)

Named on Memorial Panel VIII for Quatre Bras: Royal Military Chapel, Wellington Barracks, London. (M.I.) (Destroyed by a Flying Bomb 1944)

Ensign 24 Sep 1803. Lt and Capt 31 Jul 1806. Adjutant 2 Oct 1806. Capt and Lt Colonel 3 Mar 1814.

Served in the Peninsula Aug 1808 – Jan 1809 (DAAG on Staff), with 3rd Battalion Jul 1811 – Mar 1814 (Brigade Major in Major General Sir John Lambert's Brigade Dec 1811 – Sep 1812) and Nov 1812 – Mar 1814 (Brigade Major in 1 Brigade 1st Division). Present at Corunna, Cadiz, Bidassoa, Nivelle, Nive, Adour and Bayonne. Present at Quatre Bras where he was severely wounded 16 Jun. As he lay dying he asked his friend Capt and Lt Colonel Charles Thomas if he could see the regimental colours once more. They were brought and waved around him which gave him great satisfaction. He was carried off the field but died in Brussels the next day. On 18 Jun his friend Charles Thomas was killed and was also buried with him.

Reference: Dictionary of National Biography.

MILLER, William

1st Lieutenant. Royal Artillery.

Memorial: Royal Garrison Church Graveyard, Portsmouth, Hampshire. (M.I.)

"SACRED / TO THE MEMORY OF / LIEUT WILLIAM MILLER / ROYAL ARTILLERY / WHO DIED ON HIS PASSAGE HOME FROM / FLUSHING SEPT 28TH 1809 / AGED 23."

2nd Lt 8 Sep 1803. 1st Lt 13 Sep 1803.

Served at Walcheren 1809 (present at the siege of Flushing). Died on his return to England 28 Sep 1809.

MILLER, William

Deputy Assistant Commissary General. Commissariat Department.

Family monument: Glasgow Necropolis, Glasgow, Lanarkshire, Scotland. (Photograph)

.... / WILLIAM MILLER CB, / COMMISSARY GENERAL, / DIED 10TH JULY 1858

Dep Asst Comm General 5 Aug 1811. Asst Com General 22 Oct 1816. Dep Com General 26 Jan 1837. Com General 29 Dec 1849.

Served in the Peninsula Mar 1812 – Apr 1814. Attached to the KGL Cavalry May 1812 – Jul 1813 and Cavalry 6 Brigade Jul 1813 – Apr 1814. Present at Salamanca, Vittoria and Toulouse. CB. MGS medal for Salamanca, Vittoria and Toulouse.

MILLER, William

Deputy Assistant Commissary General. Field Train, Department of Ordnance.

Buried in the English Cemetery, Bella Vista, Lima, Peru. In 1926 his body was transferred to the Panteon de los Proceres where the heroes of the War of Independence were buried.

Memorial tablet: St Mary the Virgin, Wingham, Kent. (Photograph)

IN HONOUR OF / GENERAL WILLIAM MILLER / GRAND MARSHAL OF PERU / A HERO OF PERUVIAN INDEPENDENCE / WINGHAM 1795 – CALLEO 1861 / PRESENTED BY THE / GOVERNMENT OF PERU / 2006

Dep Asst Comm General 5 Aug 1811. In Peruvian Army: Major 1818. General 1823. Grand Marshal 1834.

Served in the Peninsula Mar 1811 – Apr 1814. Present at Ciudad Rodrigo, Badajoz, San Sebastian and Bayonne. Also served in North America 1814–1815 (present at New Orleans). After the war travelled to

South America and like many retired soldiers offered his services to the various countries who were trying to achieve independence. In 1823 helped General San Martin to defeat the Spaniards in Peru and was made a General. Became a close friend of Simon Bolivar who made him Commander in Chief of his cavalry. He fought in all the major battles to secure independence for Chile and Peru, being wounded many times. The final battle was the Battle of Ayacuclo 9 Jul 1824. Consul General for Islands in the Pacific 1843. Died 31 Oct 1861 on board a British ship in Callao harbour in Peru as he wished to die under a British flag.
REFERENCE: *Miller, John, Memoirs of General Miller: in the service of the Republic of Peru, 1828–1829, reprint 1973. Hudson, Thomas N., Honourable Warrior, the Career of General William Miller, 2001. Dictionary of National Biography. Gentleman's Magazine, Feb 1862, pp. 236–7.*

MILLIGAN, Robert
Lieutenant. 11th Regiment of Light Dragoons.
Cross on stepped pedestal base: Ryde Cemetery, Ryde, Isle of Wight. (Old Cemetery, Section A, Plot 72 and 73). (Photograph)

IN MEMORY OF / ROBERT MILLIGAN / WHO DIED BELOVED AND REVERED / DECEMBER 21ST 1875 / AGED 88 YEARS / HE WAS SEVERELY WOUNDED AT THE / BATTLE OF WATERLOO / WHEN A LIEUTENANT IN THE 11TH LIGHT DRAGOONS / AND AFTERWARDS ENTERED AS A CAPTAIN / THE 2ND LIFE GUARDS / (VERSE)

Memorial tablet: Above front door of Convalescent Home, West Street, Ryde, Isle of Wight. (Photograph)

CONVALESCENT HOME / IN LOVING MEMORY OF / ROBERT AND ELIZABETH MILLIGAN / THIS BUILDING IS ERECTED BY / THEIR DAUGHTER, SOPHIA MILLIGAN / AD 1880.

Cornet 14 May 1812. Lt 22 Dec 1814. Capt 24 Apr 1816. Capt 2nd Life Guards 10 Oct 1816.

Present at Waterloo where he was severely wounded. Retired 1822. Robert Milligan's only daughter Sophia donated the money to build a convalescent home at the Ryde Royal Infirmary in memory of her parents. The memorial tablet above the front door of the Convalescent Home in West Street remains. His father was the founder of the West India Docks in London.

MILLIUS, Charles
Captain. Chasseurs Britanniques.
Named on the Memorial: St Andrew's Church (now Musée Historique), Biarritz, France. (Photograph)

Lt 1 May 1801. Capt 20 Feb 1811.

Served in the Peninsula Dec 1810 – Feb 1814. Present at Fuentes d'Onoro, second siege of Badajoz, Salamanca, Burgos, Vittoria (severely wounded), Nivelle and Orthes where he was killed Feb 1814.

MILLS, John
Lieutenant and Captain. Coldstream Regiment of Foot Guards.
Memorial tablet: St Paul's Church, Bisterne, near Ringwood, Hampshire. (Photograph)

IN / MEMORY OF / JOHN MILLS. / ELDEST SON OF / WILLIAM MILLS, ESQR / OF BISTERNE. / BORN AUG 11, 1789. / DIED FEB 28, 1871. / SERVED WITH THE COLDSTREAM GUARDS / IN THE PENINSULA AND IN HOLLAND / 1811–1814. / TALAVERA FUENTES D'ONORO / CIUDAD RODRIGO BADAJOZ / SALAMANCA BURGOS / HIS REMAINS REST / IN THE VAULT BENEATH THIS CHURCH / OF WHICH HE WAS THE FOUNDER

Ensign 21 Dec 1809. Lt and Capt 10 Jan 1814.

Served in the Peninsula Jan 1811 – Jan 1813. Present at Fuentes d'Onoro, Ciudad Rodrigo, Salamanca

and Burgos. Also served in the Netherlands 1813–1814. Resigned 31 Aug 1814. MGS medal for Fuentes d'Onoro, Ciudad Rodrigo and Salamanca.
Reference: Fletcher, Ian, ed., For King and country: letters and diaries of John Mills, Coldstream Guards, 1811–1814, 1995.

MILLS, John
Lieutenant. 2nd (Royal North British) Regiment of Dragoons.
Memorial tablet: All Saints' Church, Trull, Taunton, Somerset. (Photograph)

SACRED TO THE MEMORY OF / LIEUT. COLONEL JOHN MILLS, / LATE OF THE ROYAL SCOTS GREYS, IN WHICH REGIMENT / HE SERVED UPWARDS OF 20 YEARS AND WAS / ONE OF THE LAST SURVIVING OFFICERS OF THAT CORPS / WHO WAS PRESENT AT THE BATTLE OF WATERLOO. / DIED OCTOBER 17TH 1837 AGED 53. / HE LIVED BELOVED AND DIED LAMENTED.

Cornet 16 Dec 1806. Lt 5 May 1808. Capt 19 Jul 1815. Bt Major 15 Aug 1822. Bt Lt Col 10 Jun 1826.
Present at Waterloo in Capt R. Verner's Troop. Covered the retreat from Quatre Bras. On 18 Jun was part of Ponsonby's Brigade of Cavalry, and was wounded in one of the cavalry charges. One of the last survivors from the Scots Greys who fought at Waterloo.

MILLS, John
Lieutenant and Quartermaster. 51st (2nd Yorkshire West Riding) Light Infantry.
Named on the Regimental Memorial: KOYLI Chapel, York Minster, Yorkshire. (Photograph)

Quartermaster 8 Feb 1810.
Served in the Peninsula Feb 1811 – 11 Oct 1812. Present at Fuentes d'Onoro, second siege of Badajoz, Moriscos, Salamanca and siege of Burgos where he was killed 11 Oct 1812.

MILMAN, Francis Miles
Captain and Lieutenant Colonel. Coldstream Regiment of Foot Guards.
Hatchment: St Michael's and All Angels Church, Lower Machen, Monmouthshire, Wales. (Photograph)

GENERAL MILMAN. DIED 1856 AGED 73

Memorial: Royal Military Chapel, Wellington Barracks, London. (M.I.) (Destroyed by a Flying Bomb 1944)

"PLACED BY MAJOR-GENERAL GEORGE BRYAN MILMAN, C.B., IN MEMORY OF HIS FATHER, / LIEUT.-GENERAL. FRANCIS MILES MILMAN, / BORN, 1783; DIED, 1856. / HE SERVED IN THE COLDSTREAM GUARDS FROM 1800–37, AND COMMANDED THE REGIMENT IN THE PENINSULA, WHERE HE WAS PRESENT AT THE BATTLES OF ROLIÇA, VIMIERO, CORUNNA, TALAVERA. COLONEL OF THE 82ND REGIMENT, 1850."

Ensign 3 Dec 1800. Lt and Capt 28 Apr 1804. Capt and Lt Colonel 25 Dec 1813. Bt Colonel 22 Jul 1830. Major General 23 Nov 1841. Lt General 11 Nov 1851.
Served in the Peninsula Aug 1808 – Jan 1809 and Mar 1809 – Apr 1814 (ADC to Major General Caitlin Craufurd). Present at Rolica, Vimeiro, Lugo, Corunna, Douro and Talavera where he was severely wounded and nearly burnt alive on the battle field like so many others when the grass caught fire from the ammunition. He was saved by being pulled away from the flames by a private in the Coldstream Guards. Taken prisoner and remained in captivity until Apr 1814. MGS medal for Rolica, Vimeiro, Corunna and Talavera. Colonel 82nd Foot 25 Nov 1850.
Reference: Gentleman's Magazine, Feb 1857, pp. 238–9. Annual Register, 1856, Appx, p. 287.

MILNE, Alexander
Private. 92nd Regiment of Foot.
Memorial: Parish Churchyard, Hatton of Fintray, Aberdeenshire. (M.I.)

"ERECTED BY ALEXANDER MILNE IN MEMORY OF HIS FATHER ALEXANDER MILNE, LATE 92ND HIGHLANDERS, DIED LOWESHILL, 7 FEB 1871, AGED 83."

Pte 29 Apr 1805. Cpl 1822.

Served in the Peninsula 1808 – Jan 1809 and Oct 1810 – Apr 1814. Present at Corunna, Fuentes, d'Onoro, Arroyo dos Molinos, Alba de Tormes, Vittoria, Maya, Nivelle, Nive, Bayonne, Orthes and Toulouse. Present at Quatre Bras and Waterloo in Capt R. McDonald's Company. Also served at Copenhagen 1807 (present at Kiöge). Discharged 17 Oct 1826. MGS medal for Corunna, Fuentes d'Onoro, Vittoria and Pyrenees.

MILNES, William Henry
Captain and Lieutenant Colonel. 1st Regiment of Foot Guards.
Named on the Regimental Memorial: St Joseph's Church, Waterloo. (Photograph)
Memorial tablet: Inside Mausoleum, Evere Cemetery, Brussels, Belgium. (Photograph)

LIEUTENANT COLONEL / WILLIAM HENRY / MILNES / 1ST FOOT GUARDS

Named on Memorial Panel VIII for Waterloo: Royal Military Chapel, Wellington Barracks, London. (M.I.) (Destroyed by a Flying Bomb 1944)

Ensign 5 Jan 1804. Lt and Capt 4 May 1809. Capt and Lt Colonel 25 Jul 1814.

Served in the Peninsula Oct 1808 – Jan 1809 and Mar 1810 – May 1811 (ADC to Lt General William Bentinck) and Jun – Sep 1813. Present at Cadiz, Barrosa and East coast of Spain. Present at Waterloo where he was severely wounded and died of his wounds 20 Jun 1815. One of the select band of soldiers buried in the Mausoleum at Evere.

MILTON, Daniel
Private. 95th Regiment of Foot.
Headstone: General Cemetery, Halifax, Yorkshire. (Grave number 4200). (Photograph)

HERE LIES / DANIEL MILTON, / 95TH RIFLES / WHO FOUGHT AT / WATERLOO, / 18TH JUNE 1815. / HE DIED AT HALIFAX / 9TH APRIL 1856, AGED 80. / WE ALSO REMEMBER THE / 29 OTHERS BURIED HERE. / THIS STONE WAS PLACED / IN MEMORY OF ADRIAN SMITH / 18TH FEB 1943 / 18TH AUG 2012, / WHO LOVED THIS CEMETERY.

Pte Prince of Wales's Fencibles 24 Jun 1799. Pte 95th Foot 13 Mar 1801.

Served in the Peninsula 1808 – Jan 1809 and 1810 – Apr 1814. Present at Vimeiro, Corunna, Salamanca, Vittoria, Orthes and Toulouse. Present at Waterloo in Capt F. Le Blanc's Company. Also served at Walcheren. Discharged 15 Sep 1818. MGS medal for Vimeiro, Corunna, Salamanca, Vittoria, Orthes and Toulouse. Died 9 Apr 1856.
Note: Daniel Milton was burid in an unmarked grave, but a headstone was erected for him in 2013.

MINCHIN, Francis
Lieutenant. 51st (2nd Yorkshire West Riding) Light Infantry.
Buried in St George's Chapel, Windsor, Berkshire. (Burial record)

Ensign 30 Aug 1807. Lt 12 Jul 1809. Capt 22 Jun 1815.

Served in the Peninsula Oct 1808 – Jan 1809 and Apr 1811 – Oct 1813. Present at Corunna, Fuentes d'Onoro, second siege of Badajoz, Moriscos, Salamanca, Burgos, retreat from Burgos, Monasterio, San Munos, Vittoria, Pyrenees and San Marcial (severely wounded). Present at Waterloo, the siege of Cambrai and at the Capture of Paris. Also served at Walcheren 1809 (present at the siege of Flushing). MGS medal for Corunna, Fuentes d'Onoro, Salamanca and Pyrenees. Military Knight of Windsor 8 Jul 1862. Died at Windsor 5 Mar 1865.

MINCHIN, John Paul
Captain. 38th (1st Staffordshire) Regiment of Foot.
Headstone: St Augustine's Churchyard, Penarth, Glamorgan, Wales. (M.I.)

"JOHN PAUL MINCHIN, CAPTAIN 38TH REGIMENT OF FOOT DIED 1854 AGED 64."

Ensign 21 Aug 1804. Lt 8 Oct 1806. Capt 26 Nov 1812.
Served in the Peninsula with 1/38th Aug 1808 – Jan 1809, Jun – Dec 1812 and 2/38th Jan 1813. Present at Rolica, Vimeiro, Corunna, Castrejon, Salamanca and Burgos. Also served in the Cape of Good Hope 1806, South America 1807 and Walcheren 1809. MGS medal for Rolica, Vimeiro, Corunna and Salamanca. Half pay 6 Apr 1820.

MINSKIULL, John
Sergeant. 51st (2nd Yorkshire) West Riding Light Infantry.
Named on the Regimental Memorial: KOYLI Chapel, York Minster, Yorkshire. (Photograph)

Served in the Peninsula where he was killed.

MITCHELL, Andrew
Captain. 50th (West Kent) Regiment of Foot.
Headstone: Eglish Churchyard, Fivealley, County Offaly, Ireland. (Photograph)

HERE LIETH THE REMAINS OF CAPTN. / ANDREW MITCHELL LATE OF THE 7TH / ROYAL VOLN BATTALION FORMERLY OF / 50TH REGT WHO DIED AT PARSONSTOWN / 11TH SEPT 1847, AGED 61 YEARS / ....

Ensign 20 Mar 1804. Lt 9 May 1805. Capt 27 Jun 1811.
Served in the Peninsula Aug 1808 – Jan 1809, Sep 1810 – Jul 1811 and Mar – Apr 1814. Present at Vimeiro, Corunna, Fuentes d'Onoro, Tarbes and Toulouse. Also served at Walcheren 1809. MGS medal for Vimeiro, Corunna, Fuentes d'Onoro and Toulouse.

MITCHELL, Hugh Henry
Lieutenant Colonel. 51st (2nd Yorkshire West Riding) Light Infantry.
Memorial tablet: St Marylebone Church, London. (Photograph)

SACRED TO THE MEMORY OF / COLONEL HUGH HENRY MITCHELL / OF THE 51ST REGIMENT OF FOOT, / WHO SERVED WITH GREAT GALLANTRY AND DISTINCTION / SEVERAL CAMPAIGNS UNDER / THE DUKE OF WELLINGTON / IN SPAIN, PORTUGAL, AND FRANCE. / HE WAS THE SON OF / HUGH HENRY MITCHELL ESQR / OF THE COUNTY OF CORK. / MARRIED 3RD JULY 1804, / LADY HARRIET, ISABELLA, ELIZABETH, SOMERSET / DAUGHTER OF HENRY 5TH DUKE OF BEAUFORT, / AND DEPARTED THIS LIFE APRIL 20TH 1817, / IN THE 47TH YEAR OF HIS AGE. / SINCERELY BELOVED AND REGRETTED / BY HIS FAMILY AND FRIENDS.

Ensign 101st Foot 2 Jan 1782. Lt 14 Jun 1783. Lt 26th Foot 23 May 1786. Captain 2 Sep 1795. Major 17 Mar 1804. Lt Colonel 12 Dec 1805. Lt Colonel 51st Foot 13 Jun 1811. Bt Colonel 4 Jun 1813.

Served in the Peninsula Nov 1811 – Mar 1813 and Aug 1813 – Apr 1814. Present at Moriscos, Salamanca, Burgos, San Munos, San Marcial (Mentioned in Despatches), Nivelle and Orthes. Gold Medal for Salamanca and Orthes. Present at Waterloo (O/c 4 British Brigade). CB. Order of St Vladimir of Russia 3rd Class. Also served in India 1783, Canada 1786–1796 and Egypt 1801 (present at Alexandria).

MITCHELL, James

Lieutenant Colonel. 92nd Regiment of Foot.

Memorial: Kilmonivaig Churchyard, Spean Bridge, Invernesshire, Scotland. (Photograph)

IN MEMORY OF / LIEUTENANT COLONEL / JAMES MITCHELL, C.B. / OF THE XCII REGIMENT OF / GORDON HIGHLANDERS. / THIS TOMB IS ERECTED TO / PERPETUATE HIS GENTLEMANLY VIRTUE / AND HIS GALLANTRY AS A SOLDIER. / FROM 1794 TO 1815 HE WAS IN ACTIVE SERVICE / DURING ALL THE CAMPAIGNS / OF THAT MEMORABLE PERIOD. / HIS MILITARY CAREER TERMINATED WITH / THE BATTLE OF / WATERLOO. / BORN LOCHABER 1770 / DIED THERE 8TH JAN 1847 / AGED 77 YRS.

Ensign 100th Foot 24 Jun 1794. Lt 19 Sep 1797. Capt 92nd Foot 25 Jun 1803. Major 30 Mar 1809. Bt Lt Colonel 3 Mar 1814.

Served in the Peninsula Aug 1808 – Jan 1809, Oct – Nov 1811 and Jul 1813 – Apr 1814. Present at Corunna, Arroyo dos Molinos, Pyrenees, Maya (wounded), Nivelle, Nive, Garris, Orthes, Aire, Tarbes and Toulouse. Present at Quatre Bras, taking command of the regiment when John Cameron was killed, but he himself was wounded. Commanded the regiment at Waterloo and until 1819 when he retired. Also served in Gibraltar 1797, Ireland 1798 (present in the Rebellion), the Helder 1799 and Copenhagen 1807 (present at Kiöge). Gold Medal for Orthes. CB. Order of St Anne of Austria. Served with the regiment for 23 years.

MITCHELL, James

Hospital Assistant. Medical Department.

Headstone in railed enclosure: Rookwood Cemetery, Sydney, New South Wales, Australia. (Photograph)

SACRED / TO THE MEMORY OF / JAMES MITCHELL / WHO DIED / 1ST FEBRUARY 1871 / AND OF / AUGUSTA MARIA / HIS WIFE / WHO DIED 11TH JUNE 1871 / ALSO / DAVID SCOTT / MITCHELL / SON OF THE ABOVE / BORN 19TH MARCH 1836 / DIED 24TH JULY 1907 / FOUNDER & BENEFACTOR OF / THE MITCHELL LIBRARY / SYDNEY.

Memorial window: Garrison Church, Sydney, New South Wales, Australia. (Photograph)

IN MEMORY OF JAMES MITCHELL ESQ

Hospital Asst 7 Jun 1813. Asst Surgeon 48th Foot 29 Jun 1820.

Served in the Peninsula Jul 1813 – Apr 1814. During the Waterloo campaign he was in Brussels looking after the wounded. Also served in North America 1814 (present at New Orleans). Transferred to the 48th Regiment in 1820 as Asst Surgeon and went with them to Australia in 1821 where he retired on half pay 24 Jul 1822 and joined the Colonial Medical Department in 1823. Half pay 13 Sep 1833. He started in private practice and was dismissed from the Colonial Medical Department in 1837 after disciplinary action had been taken against him but was reinstated later for one day and allowed to resign. Afterwards becoming a landowner and industrialist – owning smelting works, tweed factories and was also the orig-

inal owner of the Hunter River Railway Company. His wealth was put to good use, as his son became the founder and benefactor of the Mitchell Library in Sydney.
Reference: Australian Dictionary of Biography.

MITCHELL, John

Captain. 25th (King's Own Borderers) Regiment of Foot.
Mural Memorial tablet: Canongate Burial Ground, Edinburgh, Scotland. (Photograph)

TO THE MEMORY OF / .... / JOHN MITCHELL, MAJOR GENERAL IN THE BRITISH ARMY, / BORN 11TH JUNE 1786, DIED 9TH JULY 1858 / ....

Ensign 57th Foot 9 Jul 1803. Lt 1st Foot 5 Dec 1804. Capt 1 Oct 1807. Capt 25th Foot 14 May 1812. Capt 92nd Foot 25 May 1820. Capt 49th Foot 2 Nov 1820. Capt 95th Foot 1 Dec 1823. Capt 79th Foot 8 Apr 1825. Bt Major 19 Jul 1821. Major (unattached) 1 Jun 1826. Bt Lt Colonel 10 Jan 1837. Bt Colonel 11 Nov 1851. Major General 31 Aug 1855.

Served in the Peninsula Apr 1810 – Oct 1811. Present at Busaco, Fuentes d'Onoro and Sabugal. Present at Waterloo as DAQMG (wounded) and with the Army of Occupation. Also served in the West Indies 1804, Walcheren 1809 (present at the siege of Flushing), Stralsund 1813 (DAQMG) and the Netherlands 1814–1815 (DAQMG). Half pay 1 Jun 1826. MGS medal for Busaco and Fuentes d'Onoro. His father had been in the diplomatic service and had taken his son with him overseas. He insisted that his son learnt several foreign languages and it proved useful to Wellington to have another linguist on his staff when dealing with correspondence to foreign powers. In later life Mitchell devoted himself to writing. He contributed to several magazines including the *United Service Journal* and *Fraser's Magazine* where in 1846 he wrote a series of articles on Napoleon's early campaigns. Published *The Fall of Napoleon*, 3 vols, 1845.

MITCHELL, Robert

Captain. 60th (Royal American) Regiment of Foot.
Headstone: St Saviour's Churchyard, St Helier, Jersey, Channel Islands. (Photograph)

SACRED / TO THE MEMORY OF / CAPT ROBERT MITCHELL / LATE OF THE 5TH BATT 60TH REGIMENT / WHO DIED ON THE 22ND OF JUNE 1829 / AGED 52 YEARS. / DEEPLY AND DESERVEDLY REGRETTED BY / ALL HIS ACQUAINTANCES. A MAN WHOSE / PRINCIPLES WERE HONOURABLE AND HIS CHA- / RACTER AS A SOLDIER WAS UNIMPEACHABLE. / ....

Lt 20 Sep 1808. Capt 18 Jan 1815.

Served in the Peninsula Apr 1809 – Apr 1814. Present at Talavera where he was severely wounded, taken prisoner, and remained in prison until Apr 1814.

MITCHELL, Samuel

Major. 95th Regiment of Foot.
Named on the Rifle Brigade Memorial: Winchester Cathedral, Winchester, Hampshire. (Photograph)

Lt Argyle Fencibles. Ensign 71st Foot 21 Jul 1800. 2nd Lt 95th Foot 9 Nov 1800. 1st Lt 10 Jul 1801. Capt 9 May 1805. Bt Major 21 Jun 1813. Major 2 Sep 1813. Bt Lt Colonel 21 Jan 1819. Lt Colonel 31st Foot 24 Dec 1827. Lt Colonel 3rd Foot 22 Jul 1830. Portuguese Army: Major 6th Caçadores 21 Apr 1812

Served in the Peninsula with 1/95th Jul 1809 – Dec 1810, 2/95th Jan 1811 – Feb 1812 and Portuguese Army Apr 1812 – Nov 1813. Present at Coa (wounded), Cadiz, Barba del Puerco, Pombal, Redinha, Foz d' Arouce, Sabugal, Fuentes d'Onoro, Ciudad Rodrigo (wounded taking part in the storming party), Almarez, Vittoria and Pyrenees (commanded the 6th Caçadores, wounded and Mentioned in Despatches).

Gold Medal for Vittoria and Pyrenees. CB. Also served in South America 1807, North America 1814–1815 (present at New Orleans) and India 1829 where he died at Berhampore 3 Jun 1833.

MITCHELL, Thomas

Lieutenant. 92nd Regiment of Foot.
Named on the Memorial: St Andrew's Church (now Musée Historique), Biarritz, France. (Photograph)

Ensign 28 Jun 1810. Lt 28 Jul 1813.

Served in the Peninsula May – Dec 1813. Present at Vittoria, Pyreneees, Maya (wounded Jul 1813), Nivelle and Nive where he was killed 13 Dec 1813.

MITCHELL, Thomas Livingstone

1st Lieutenant. 95th Regiment of Foot.
Low monument in railed enclosure: Camperdown Cemetery, Newtown, Sydney, Australia. (Photograph)

COLONEL SIR THOMAS LIVINGSTONE MITCHELL KT DCL / SURVEYOR GENERAL OF NEW SOUTH WALES / WHO DIED 5TH OCTOBER 1855 / IN HIS 64TH YEAR

Family Memorial tablet on railed enclosure: Camperdown Cemetery, Newtown, Sydney, Australia. (Photograph)

THIS PLAQUE COMMEMORATES THE RESTORATION OF THE GRAVE / OF / SIR THOMAS LIVINGSTON MITCHELL / SURVEYOR GENERAL OF NEW SOUTH WALES 1828–1855 / BY / THE INSTITUTION OF SURVEYORS NSW INC / IN ASSOCIATION WITH THE CAMPERDOWN CEMETERY TRUST / UNVEILED 24 MARCH 1966 / BY / HIS EXCELLENCY / THE HONOURABLE GORDON SAMUELS, AC / GOVERNOR OF NEW SOUTH WALES / …………………

Memorial tablet: Camperdown, Newtown, Sydney, Australia. (Photograph)

IN MEMORY OF / COLONEL SIR THOMAS LIVINGSTONE MITCHELL KT. D.C.L / SURVEYOR GENERAL OF NEW SOUTH WALES / WHO DIED 5TH OCTOBER 1855. / IN HIS 64TH YEAR. / ……………… / THIS PLAQUE WAS PLACED BY THE INSTITUTION OF SURVEYORS, NSW INC. / N.S.W. DIVISION OF THE INSTITUTION OF SURVEYORS AUSTRALIA, / AND THE LAND INFORMATION CENTRE, TO PAY RESPECTS TO SIR THOMAS MITCHELL / A GREAT PIONEER SURVEYOR / AND TO COMMEMORATE THE INSTITUTION OF SURVEYORS, N.S.W. DIVISION / CENTENARY YEAR, 1991 / …………………

2nd Lt 24 Jul 1811. 1st Lt 16 Sep 1813. Capt 54th Foot 5 Oct 1822. Bt Major 22 Jul 1826. Bt Lt Colonel 20 Jun 1854.

Served in the Peninsula with 1/95th Jan 1812 – Apr 1814 (attached to the QMG's department May – Oct 1812 and Apr 1813 – Apr 1814). Present at Ciudad Rodrigo, Badajoz, Salamanca, Pyrenees and San Sebastian. While in the QMG's department he studied surveying. After the end of the war in April 1814 Mitchell was asked to make models of all the main battlefields in the Peninsula. MGS medal for Ciudad Rodrigo, Badajoz, Salamanca, Pyrenees and San Sebastian. Instructor in topography at the Royal Military College 1819. Deputy Surveyor General of New South Wales 1827. Surveyor General 1828. Improved the accuracy of surveying and map making in the department which was important as vast tracts of land were being sold to new settlers. From 1831–1847 explored south-eastern Australia with great success and opened up vast areas of the country. Responsible for road making as well as surveying. He had all the passes made through the mountains to the interior of the continent and laid out towns and villages on the way. Known as the 'Cook of the Australian interior'. His experiences in the Peninsula gave him the knowledge to become an excellent Surveyor General, needed when the country was expanding rapidly. Knighted

in 1839. Wrote extensively including *Three expeditions in the Interior of Eastern Australia*, 2 vols, 1839, *Journal of an expedition into the Interior of Tropical Australia*, 1848 and *Outline of a System of surveying for Geographical and Military Purposes*, 1827. Died 5 Oct 1855.
REFERENCE: *Dictionary of Australian Biography. Gentleman's Magazine, Mar 1856, pp. 301–2. Journal of the Army Historical Research Society, Vol. 34, No. 138, Jun 1956, pp. 89–90. Cumpston, J. H. L., Thomas Mitchell: Surveyor and Explorer. Foster, William C., Sir Thomas Livingston Mitchell and his World 1792–1855: Surveyor General of New South Wales 1828–1855, 1985. Obit. Maitland Mercury and Hunter River General Advertiser, 10 October 1855.*

MITCHELL, William
Paymaster. 2nd Regiment of Hussars, King's German Legion.
Headstone: Nunhead Cemetery, London. Inscription not recorded. (Grave number 1115 Square 81)

Asst Paymaster 20th Lt Dragoons 27 Jun 1805. Paymaster 2nd Hussars King's German Legion 13 Aug 1812. Paymaster 1st Foot 3 Jul 1828.

Served in the Peninsula with 20th Lt Dragoons Feb – Sep 1809 and 2nd Hussars Sep 1810 – Jun 1813. Present at Cadiz and Barrosa. Also served in the Netherlands 1814–1815. Died 10 Apr 1848.

MOFFAT, William
Assistant Surgeon. 48th (Northamptonshire) Regiment of Foot.
Headstone: St Mungo's Burial Ground, Glasgow, Lanarkshire. (M.I.)

"TO THE MEMORY OF WILLIAM MOFFAT, ASSISTANT SURGEON 48TH REGT. 1808–1815, DIED 12TH AUGT 1857, AGED 74."

Hospital Mate 16 Apr 1808. Asst Surgeon 48th Foot 4 Jan 1810.

Served in the Peninsula with 48th Foot Jan 1810 – Jul 1811 and Apr 1812 – Apr 1814. Present at Talavera, Albuera, Badajoz, Salamanca, Vittoria, Pyrenees, Nivelle, Orthes and Toulouse. Half pay 25 Oct 1814. MGS medal for Talavera, Albuera, Badajoz, Salamanca, Vittoria, Pyrenees, Nivelle, Orthes and Toulouse.

MOLLOY, John
1st Lieutenant 95th Regiment of Foot.
Headstone: St Mary's Anglican Church Cemetery, Busselton, Western Australia. (Photograph)

SACRED / TO THE MEMORY / OF / JOHN MOLLOY / A LIEUTENANT COLONEL / IN HER MAJESTY'S ARMY / WHO DIED ON THE 8TH OCTOBER 1867, / AGED 87 YEARS. / HE WAS WITH SIR JOHN MOORE'S ARMY FROM / SALAMANCA TO VIGO, AND UNDER WELLINGTON / FOUGHT AT ROLICA, VIMIERA, SALAMANCA, / VITTORIA, THE PYRENEES, THE NIVELLE, NIVE, / TOULOUSE AND WATERLOO. IN THE 95TH / REGIMENT. HE WAS AMONG THE FIRST / SETTLERS OF THIS COLONY AND DIED AS / HE HAD LIVED A CHRISTIAN GENTLEMAN. / I HAVE FOUGHT A GOOD FIGHT / I HAVE FINISHED MY COURSE / I HAVE KEPT THE FAITH

2nd Lt 17 Dec 1807. 1st Lt 5 Jun 1809. Capt 5 Aug 1824. Bt Major 28 Jun 1838. Bt Lt Colonel 11 Nov 1851.

Served in the Peninsula with 2/95th Aug 1808 – Jan 1809 and with 1/95th Jun 1809 – Apr 1810 and Jul 1812 – Apr 1814. Present at Rolica, Vimeiro, Vigo, Salamanca, San Millan, Vittoria, Pyrenees, Vera, Bidassoa, Nivelle, Nive, Tarbes and Toulouse. Present at Waterloo with 1/95th (severely wounded). MGS medal for Rolica, Vimeiro, Salamanca, Vittoria, Pyrenees, Nivelle, Nive, and Toulouse. Half pay 28 May 1829 and emigrated to Australia. Settled in Augusta in Western Australia where he was appointed resident magistrate and Justice of the Peace in 1830. He was granted 12,813 acres of land and in 1839 moved

to Vasse, relocating his grant of land and building his house "Fairlawn". His wife, Georgiana, was an amateur botanist and sent many collections of wildflower specimens back to England.
Reference: Dictionary of Australian Biography. Cornhill Magazine, Dec 1897.

MOLYNEUX, Thomas
Lieutenant. 14th (Duchess of York's Own) Regiment of Light Dragoons.
Monument: Woodbury Park Cemetery, Tunbridge Wells, Kent. (Photograph)

IN LOVING MEMORY OF / LIEUT GEN. / MOLYNEUX WILLIAMS. K.H. / DIED MAY 19 1871. / ERECTED BY HIS WIDOW.

Midshipman Royal Navy 1806. Ensign 4th Foot 14 Feb 1811. Lt 77th Foot 28 Feb 1812. Lt 14th Lt Dragoons 7 Dec 1814. Capt 16 Sep 1819. Major 19 Sep 1826. Bt Lt Colonel 23 Nov 1841. Bt Colonel 20 Jun 1854. Major General 26 Oct 1858. Lt General 31 Mar 1866.

Served in the Peninsula with 4th Foot Jan – Mar 1812 and 77th Foot Apr 1812 – Apr 1814. Present at Badajoz, Bidassoa, Adour, St Jean de Luz, Bidart, siege of Bayonne and repulse of the Sortie. MGS medal for Badajoz. Also served as a Midshipman in the Royal Navy. Present at the attack on the French fleet by Admiral Cornwallis Aug 1805. Present at the disembarkation of troops in Portugal Aug 1808 and embarkation at Corunna Jan 1809. Served at Walcheren 1809 (in squadron of gunboats in the River Scheldt and at the bombardment of Ter Vere, Ramakins and the siege of Flushing). Landed on the Island of South Beveland (present at the taking of Fort Batz). Present at the evacuation of troops 1810. KH. Half pay 1826. Later assumed the surname of Williams.
Reference: Annual Register, 1871, Appx, pp. 152–3. (Under Williams).

MONCKTON, Hon. Carleton Thomas
Lieutenant. 16th (Queen's) Regiment of Light Dragoons.
Buried in St John Street Cemetery, Quebec, Canada.
Memorial tablet: Quebec Cathedral, Canada. (South gallery). (M.I)

" .... / SACRED TO THE MEMORY OF / THE HONORABLE CARLETON THOMAS MONCKTON, / FIFTH SON OF ROBERT ARUNDEL, FOURTH VISCOUNT GALWAY. / BY HIS WIFE ELIZABETH, DAUGHTER OF DANIEL MATTHEW, ESQ., OF FELIX HALL, / ESSEX, AND GREAT NEPHEW OF THE HONORABLE BRIGADIER GENERAL MONCKTON, / WHO SUCCEEDED TO THE COMMAND OF THE BRITISH ARMY, / UPON THE DEATH OF GENERAL WOLFE AT THE SPLENDID VICTORY / ACHIEVED ON THE HEIGHTS OF ABRAHAM, 13TH SEPTEMBER, A.D., 1759. / AT THE AGE OF FIFTEEN, HE ENTERED THE ARMY AND SERVED IN SPAIN, / AND AT THE BATTLE OF WATERLOO WAS A LIEUTENANT. / HE FOR SOME YEARS AFTERWARDS BECAME A CAPTAIN / IN THE 24TH REGIMENT OF INFANTRY WHICH HE ACCOMPANIED TO CANADA, / AND DIED AFTER A SHORT ILLNESS AT QUEBEC ON THE 10TH MAY, 1830, / IN THE 34TH YEAR OF HIS AGE, BELOVED BY HIS BROTHER OFFICERS / AND SINCERELY LAMENTED BY ALL WHO KNEW HIM. / THIS TABLET WAS ERECTED BY HIS SORROWING BROTHER AND SISTERS, / AS A TESTIMONY OF THEIR FOND AFFECTION TO ONE / MOST JUSTLY DEAR TO THEM. / AND IN THE HUMBLE HOPE THAT THROUGH FAITH IN CHRIST JESUS, / THE ONLY SAVIOUR, THEY TOGETHER WITH HIM, / MAY BE BLESSED AS ARE THOSE THAT DIE IN THE LORD"

Cornet 17 Sep 1812. Lt 8 Jul 1813. Lt 1st Life Guards 1 May 1816. Lt 18th Lt Dragoons 1 Apr 1819. Lt 85th Foot 24 May 1821. Lt 38th Foot 26 May 1822. Capt Cape Corps 27 Mar 1823. Capt 24th Foot 18 Mar 1824.

Served in the Peninsula Sep 1813 – Apr 1814. Present at Nivelle, Nive and Bayonne. Present at Waterloo. Later served in Canada where he died in Quebec 10 May 1830.

MONCUR, William
Sergeant. 71st (Highland Light Infantry) Regiment of Foot.
Headstone: Parish Church of Fetteresso, Stonehaven, Aberdeenshire, Scotland. (M.I.)

"IN MEMORY OF WILLIAM MONCUR, LATE SERGEANT IN THE 71ST REGIMENT OF FOOT, WHO, AFTER SUFFERING THE FATIGUE AND CALAMITY OF WAR, VIZ. IN SPAIN AND AT WATERLOO, DIED IN PEACE AT TOADSTOCK IN FETTERESSO, THE 24TH OCT 1816 AGED 32 YEARS".

Served in the Peninsula Aug 1808 – Jan 1809 and Sept 1810 – Apr 1814. Present at Rolica, Vimeiro, Corunna, Fuentes d'Onoro, Arroyo dos Molinos, Almarez, Vittoria, Pyrenees, Nivelle, Nive, Orthes, Aire, Tarbes and Toulouse. Present at Waterloo in Captain C. Johnston's Company.

MONEY, Archibald
Major. 11th Regiment of Light Dragoons.
Chest tomb: St Andrew's Churchyard, Trowse, Norfolk. (Against east wall of church). (Photograph)

LIEUT GENERAL ARCHIBALD MONEY C.B. K. C. / COLONEL OF H. M. 2ND (ROYAL NORTH BRITISH) DRAGOONS / DIED 25TH AUGUST 1858 / AGED 80 YEARS.

Cornet Apr 1794. Lt 13 May 1794. Capt-Lieut and Capt Jul 1800. Major 14 Dec 1809. Bt Lt Colonel 4 Jun 1814. Bt Colonel 10 Jan 1837. Major General 9 Nov 1846. Lt General 20 Jun 1854.

Served in the Peninsula Jun 1811 – Jun 1813. Present at El Bodon, Castrejon, Salamanca and Venta del Pozo. Present at Waterloo where he commanded the regiment towards the end of the day and at the Capture of Paris. CB for Waterloo. Also served in Flanders 1794–1795 (present at Cateau, Tournai, Roubaix and Lannoy), the Helder 1799 (present at Bergen and Egmont-op-Zee), Cadiz 1800 and Egypt 1801 (present at Grand Cairo and Alexandria. KC.). MGS medal for Egypt and Salamanca. Colonel 2nd (Royal North British) Dragoons 24 May 1852.
Reference: Gentleman's Magazine, Oct 1858, p. 416. Annual Register, 1858, Appx, pp. 428–9.

MONTAGU, Frederick Augustus Courtenay
Captain. 23rd (Royal Welch Fusiliers) Regiment of Foot.
Memorial tablet: St Cyriac's Church, Lacock, Wiltshire. (Photograph)

TO FREDERICK AUGUSTUS COURTENAY MONTAGU / CAPTN OF THE 23RD REGIMENT OR ROYAL WELCH FUSILIERS / AND MAJOR IN THE PORTUGUESE SERVICE / ADORNED WITH THE CHOICEST GIFTS OF HEAVEN / NATURE HAD WREATHED THE OLIVE BRANCH / THAT SO CONSPICUOUSLY FLOURISHED ON HIS BROW / AS EMBLEMATIC OF HIS AMIABLE AND AFFECTIONATE MIND / PATRIOTISM AND LOYALTY / THAT ROUSED HIM TO SEEK MARTIAL GLORY, / LED HIM TO VOLUNTEER HIS SERVICE / IN HIS COUNTRY'S CAUSE AT THE EARLY AGE OF 16 / AND AFTER DISPLAYING UNDAUNTED COURAGE IN HOLLAND, / IN MARTINIQUE IN THE EXPULSION OF THE FRENCH / FROM PORTUGAL / AND LASTLY AT THE AGE OF 26 / AT THE MEMORABLE BATTLE OF ALBUERA IN SPAIN / FOUGHT ON THE 16TH OF MAY IN THE YEAR 1811 / HE FINISHED HIS MORTAL CAREER / PIERCED THROUGH THE HEART BY A MUSKET BALL / WHILST GALLANTLY LEADING HIS MEN TO A CHARGE / HE NOBLY FELL / LEAVING THE LAURELS SO GLORIOUSLY ACQUIRED / TO BE ENTWINED AROUND THE HEARTS OF / HIS AFFLICTED PARENTS / WHO / IN COMMEMORATION OF THEIR DEAR DEPARTED SON / ERECTED THIS MONUMENT.

Ensign 22nd Foot 14 Jan 1797. Lt 4th Foot 6 Dec 1800. Lt 81st Foot 19 Oct 1803. Capt 23rd Foot 21 Mar 1805.

Served in the Peninsula with 1/23rd Dec 1810 – May 1811. Present at Redinha, Olivencia, first siege of Badajoz and Albuera where he was killed 16 May 1811. Also served in Hanover 1805, Copenhagen 1807 and Martinique 1809.

MONTAGU, Hon. Henry Robinson

Ensign. 3rd Regiment of Foot Guards.
Headstone: Clewer Churchyard, Windsor, Berkshire. Inscription not recorded.

Ensign 21 Apr 1814. Lt and Capt 12 Jun 1823. Capt and Lt Colonel 21 Sep 1832. Bt Colonel 9 Nov 1846. Major 28 Jun 1850. Lt Colonel 17 Feb 1854. Major General 20 Jun 1854. Lt General 20 Sep 1861. General 8 Mar 1869.

Present at Quatre Bras and Waterloo. Also served in the Crimea 1855 in command of 1st Division (present at the siege and fall of Sebastopol – medal). Commander of Legion of Honour, Sardinian Medal, Turkish Medal and 3rd Class of Medjidie. Became 6th Lord Rokeby 7 Apr 1847. KCB 3 May 1856. Colonel 77th Foot 13 Feb 1861. Colonel Scots Guards 13 May 1875. GCB 29 May 1875. Died 25 May 1883 aged 85.
REFERENCE: *Dictionary of National Biography.*

MONTAGU, Willoughby

1st Lieutenant. Royal Artillery.
Memorial tablet: St Paul's Church, Clapham, London. (North wall). (M.I.)

"MAJOR WILLOUGHBY MONTAGU, R. A. BORN 15 MAY 1791 DIED 2 FEB 1873. NEPHEW TO FRANCES, FIRST LADY NEAVE OF DAGENHAM PARK, ROMFORD, ESSEX. KNIGHT OF RUSSIAN ORDER OF ST WLADIMER FOR THE SIEGE OF DANTZICK IN 1813–14. AT WATERLOO, 18 JUNE 1815. AN ADJUTANT AND STAFF OFFICER IN TWO DISTRICTS."

2nd Lt 26 Nov 1808. 1st Lt 11 Aug 1811. 2nd Capt 6 Nov 1827. Major 23 Nov 1841.

Present at Waterloo in Major W. Unett's Brigade and at the siege of Cambrai. Also served at the siege of Dantzig 1813. Knight of St Vladimir of Russia. Half pay Nov 1827.

MONTAGUE, John

Ensign. 52nd (Oxfordshire) Light Infantry Regiment of Foot.
Ledger stone: Brompton Cemetery, Brompton, London. (BR7498. Compartment F:63x11.3). (Photograph)

SACRED / TO THE MEMORY OF / JOHN MONTAGUE / SECRETARY TO GOVERNMENT, / CAPE OF GOOD HOPE / BORN AUG 21 1797 / DIED NOV 4 1853 / CURA ET AMORE / ROBERTI EPISCOPI CAPETONIENSIS

Ensign 10 Feb 1814. Lt 9 Nov 1815. Capt 64th Foot 7 Nov 1822. Capt 40th Foot 7 Aug 1823.

Present at Waterloo. Joined 40th Foot who were then embarking for Australia in 1823. This ensured that he could become the Private Secreary to his wife's uncle, Lt Governor George Arthur. When the 40th Foot left Australia in 1830 for India Montagu sold his commission and returned to Van Diemen's Land, taking charge of the Treasury. Appointed Colonial Secretary in 1835. In 1837 disagreed with the Governor Sir John Franklin over convicts, dismissal of certain officials and siting of Christ's College. Montague refused to work with him and he was suspended in 1842. He was so successful in bringing his case to Lord Stanley, Secretary of State for the Colonies that Franklin was recalled and Montague was sent to the Cape of Good Hope as Colonial Secretary. He improved roads and encouraged immigration. During the governorship of Sir Peregrine Maitland, Montague successfully administered the finances so that there was enough money for the Cape Frontier Wars in 1852. He was overworked and suffering from ill health returned to England in 1852 where he died in London 4 Nov 1853.
REFERENCE: *Dictionary of National Biography.*

MONTGOMERY, Henry
Captain. 50th (West Kent) Regiment of Foot.
Gravestone: Disused Graveyard, Up Park Camp, Kingston, Jamaica, West Indies. (M.I.)

"BT MAJOR MONTGOMERY, DIED 11 AUGT, 1819, AGED 35".

Lt 20 Aug 1803. Capt 5 Jan 1809. Bt Major 26 Dec 1813.

Served in the Peninsula Aug 1808 – Jan 1809 and Dec 1811 – Apr 1814. (DAQMG Oct 1812 – Feb 1814. AQMG Mar – Apr 1814). Present at Vimeiro, Corunna and Badajoz. Also present at Walcheren 1809 and the West Indies 1819 where he died in a yellow fever epidemic in Jamaica in Aug 1819 at the same time as his father Paymaster John Montgomery 50th Foot and his brother-in-law Capt Benjamin Rowe also of the 50th Foot.

MONTGOMERY, Hugh Bernard
Lieutenant and Captain. 3rd Regiment of Foot Guards.
Buried in St James's Churchyard, Westminster, London.
Memorial: Royal Military Chapel, Wellington Barracks, London. (M.I.) (Destroyed by a Flying Bomb 1944)

"CAPTAIN HUGH BERNARD MONTGOMERY. / 3RD GUARDS. ENTERED THE REGIMENT MARCH 28, 1811, AND SERVED IN THE PENINSULA CAMPAIGN OF 1813, AND TILL THE END OF THE WAR. HE WAS SEVERELY WOUNDED AT BARROUILHET, DURING THE OPERATIONS OF THE NIVE, DECEMBER 12, 1813. HE WAS ALSO WOUNDED AT WATERLOO, IN THE DEFENCE OF THE CHÂTEAU OF HOUGOUMONT, JUNE 18, 1815. HE WAS BORN AT GREY ABBEY, IN THE COUNTY OF DOWN, IRELAND, AUGUST 28, 1790; DIED IN LONDON, MAY 2, 1817, AND LIES BURIED IN THE CEMETERY OF THE PARISH OF ST JAMES'S, WESTMINSTER. / THIS TABLET IS DEDICATED TO HIS MEMORY BY HIS BROTHER, COLONEL OCTAVIUS / MONTGOMERY, A.D. 1879."

Ensign 28 Mar 1811. Lt and Capt 9 Jun 1814.

Served in the Peninsula Apr 1813 – Apr 1814. Present at Vittoria, Bidassoa, Nivelle, Nive (severely wounded) and Bayonne. Present at Waterloo where he was severely wounded in the defence of Hougoumont. These wounds caused his death in 1817.

MONTGOMERY, John
Paymaster. 50th (West Kent) Regiment of Foot.
Gravestone: Disused Graveyard, Up Park Camp, Kingston, Jamaica, West Indies. (M.I.)

"JOHN MONTGOMERY, PAYMR. 50TH REGT. DIED 19TH AUG 1819. AGED 64."

Paymaster 17 Oct 1799.

Served in the Peninsula Aug 1808 – Jan 1809, Sep 1810 – Nov 1812 and May 1813 – Apr 1814. Present at Vimeiro, Corunna, Fuentes d'Onoro, Almarez, Alba de Tormes, Vittoria, Pyrenees, Nivelle, Nive, Garris, Orthes, Aire and Toulouse. Also served at Walcheren 1809 and the West Indies 1819 where he died in a yellow fever epidemic. His son Capt Henry Montgomery 50th Foot, and son-in-law Major Benjamin Rowe 50th Foot also died in the same epidemic.

MONTGOMERY, Knox
Lieutenant. 81st Regiment of Foot.
Table tomb: Kilbarron Churchyard, Ballyshannon Town, County Donegal, Ireland. (Photograph)

SACRED TO THE MEMORY / OF / CAP^{TN} KNOX MONTGOMERY / WHO DEP^{D} THIS LIFE / OCT 27TH 1837 AGED 50 YEARS

Ensign 1806. Lt 17 Mar 1808. Capt 18 Sep 1823.

Served in the Peninsula Nov 1808 – Jan 1809 and May 1813 – Apr 1814. Present at Corunna and Eastern Spain. Also served at Walcheren 1809 (present at the siege of Flushing where he was wounded). Half pay 24 Jul 1828.

MONYPENNY, Thomas Gybbon

Lieutenant. 30th (Cambridgeshire) Regiment of Foot.

Memorial tablet: Church of St Mary the Virgin, Rolvenden, Kent. (Barkan Chapel). (Photograph)

IN MEMORY OF/ LIEUT COL^{L} THOMAS GYBBON MONYPENNY, / OF HOLE HOUSE, IN THIS PARISH, / DIED 15TH OF JANUARY 1854, / ....

Ensign 13th Foot 22 Apr 1813. Lt 30th Foot 23 Mar 1815.

Present at Waterloo where he was wounded. Half pay 25 Mar 1817. Lt Colonel of the West Kent Militia. MP for Rye 1837–1841. Magistrate and Deputy Lieutenant of Kent.

REFERENCE: Gentleman's Magazine, May 1854, pp. 533–4.

MOORE, Charles

Captain. 67th (South Hampshire) Regiment of Foot.

Memorial tablet: St George's Chapel, Windsor, Berkshire. (West side wall of Deanery Cloisters). (Photograph)

.... / ALSO IN MEMORY OF / MAJOR CHARLES MOORE, HER HUSBAND, / WHO DIED AT WINDSOR ON THE 19TH OF MARCH 1865, AGED 89 YEARS. / HAVING FILLED THE POST OF GOVERNOR / OF THE MILITARY KNIGHTS OF WINDSOR FOR 22 YEARS

Cornet 5th Dragoon Guards 3 May 1800. Lt 13 Oct 1801. Capt 67th Foot 25 Apr 1811. Bt Major 22 Jul 1830. Capt 32nd Foot 29 Sep 1843.

Served in the Peninsula Aug 1811 – Dec 1812. Present at the siege of Cadiz and the East coast of Spain. Employed both on sea and shore in the suppression of the African slave trade. Military Knight of Windsor 6 Feb 1844 and became Governor of the Military Knights in the same year. Died 19 Mar 1865 aged 89.

MOORE, Edward

Lieutenant. 18th Regiment of Light Dragoons.

Headstone: St George's Cemetery, Lisbon, Portugal. (Grave number A5 50). (Photograph)

HERE LIES THE BODY / OF / EDWARD MOORE ESQ, / LIEUTENANT IN THE 18TH REGIMENT / OF / BRITISH LIGHT DRAGOONS. / WHO / DEPARTED THIS LIFE / ON THE 1ST DEC 1808 / AGED 25.

Cornet 19 Oct 1799. Lt 24 Apr 1801.

Served in the Peninsula Sep – Dec 1808. Brigade Major to Major General Charles Stewart. Died in Lisbon 1 Dec 1808.

MOORE, Francis

Private. 1st Regiment of Foot Guards.

Headstone: Glasgow Southern Necropolis, Glasgow, Lanarkshire, Scotland. (Photograph).

ERECTED / BY / JEANNE, / IN MEMORY OF HER FATHER / FRANCIS MOORE, / (LATE OF THE GRENADIER GUARDS / AND WAS IN THEIR RANKS / AT WATERLOO:) / WHO DIED AT GLASGOW, 4TH JUNE, 1875, / AGED 88 YEARS. / ....

Pte 20 Jun 1811.

Served in the Peninsula Jun 1811 – Apr 1814. Present at Nivelle, Nive and Bayonne where he was wounded. Present at Waterloo (wounded) in Lt Colonel Edward Stable's Company. MGS medal for Nivelle and Nive. Discharged 20 Jun 1818.

MOORE, George A.

1st Lieutenant. Royal Artillery.

Named on the Memorial: St Andrew's Church (now Musée Historique), Biarritz, France. (Photograph)

2nd Lt 1 Mar 1808. 1st Lt 24 Mar 1809.

Served in the Peninsula Feb 1813 – Feb 1814. Present at Garris where he was killed at the Passage of the Gave d'Oleron in France 15 Feb 1814. Also served at Walcheren 1809.

MOORE, Sir John

Colonel. 52nd (Oxfordshire) Light Infantry Regiment of Foot.

Sarcophagus in railed enclosure: San Carlos, Corunna, Spain. (Photograph)

IN MEMORY OF GENERAL SIR JOHN MOORE / WHO FELL AT THE BATTLE OF ELVINA WHILE COVERING / THE EMBARKMENT OF THE BRITISH TROOPS / 16TH JANUARY 1809. / TO THE GLORY / OF THE ENGLISH GENERAL MOORE, / AND HIS VALIANT COUNTRYMEN, / THE GRATITUDE OF SPAIN. / IN MEMORY OF THE ACTION OF / 16TH JANUARY 1809

Memorial tablet: St Paul's Cathedral, London. (South transept west side). (Photograph)

SACRED TO THE MEMORY OF / LIEUTENANT-GENERAL SIR JOHN MOORE, K. B. / WHO WAS BORN AT GLASGOW IN THE YEAR 1761. / HE FOUGHT FOR HIS COUNTRY / IN AMERICA, IN CORSICA, IN THE WEST INDIES, / IN HOLLAND, EGYPT, AND SPAIN; / AND ON THE 16TH OF JANUARY 1809, / WAS SLAIN BY A CANNON BALL, / AT CORUNNA.

Statue: Glasgow.

TO COMMEMORATE / THE MILITARY SERVICES OF / LIEUTENANT GENERAL SIR JOHN MOORE, KCB. / NATIVE OF GLASGOW, / HIS FELLOW CITIZENS / HAVE ERECTED / THIS MONUMENT. / 1819

Memorial monument: Esplanade, Sandgate, Kent. (Photograph)

THIS MEMORIAL WAS ERECTED IN 1909 TO / COMMEMORATE THE INSPIRING EXAMPLE OF THE / MANLY AND PATRIOTIC LIFE OF / LIEUTENANT- GENERAL SIR JOHN MOORE, K.B. / WHO FELL IN ACTION AT THE BATTLE OF CORUNNA / JANUARY 16TH 1809 / "REGARDLESS OF PERSONAL CONSIDERATIONS HE ESTEEMED / THAT TO WHICH HIS COUNTRY CALLED HIM THE POST OF HONOUR / AND BY HIS UNDAUNTED SPIRIT AND UNCONQUERABLE / PERSEVERANCE HE POINTED THE WAY TO VICTORY" / GENERAL ORDERS FEBRUARY 1ST 1809 / SIR JOHN MOORE RESIDED CLOSE TO THE SITE OF THIS / MEMORIAL WHEN IN COMMAND OF SHORNCLIFFE CAMP 1803–1804.

Memorial window: Former Sir John Moore Library, Shorncliffe, Kent. (Photograph)

TRIA JUNCTA IN UNA / JOHN MOORE

Statue: Gardens of the former Sir John Moore Library, Shorncliffe, Kent. (Photograph)

MOORE / 1761 – 1809

Statue: Sir John Moore Barracks, Army Training Regiment, Andover, Hampshire. (Photograph)

THIS PLAQUE / COMMEMORATES / THE OFFICIAL OPENING OF / SIR JOHN MOORE BARRACKS / THE HOME OF / THE L^{T} INFANTRY / BY / HER MAJESTY THE QUEEN / ON 27TH NOVEMBER 1986

Brass Memorial tablet: Royal Garrison Church, Portsmouth, Hampshire. (Back of a choir stall). (Photograph)

LIEUT: GENERAL SIR / JOHN MOORE, K.C.B. / KILLED AT CORUNNA / JAN 16 1809. AGED 47.

Statue: Bothwell, Lanarkshire, Scotland. (Notes and Queries, 3 Mar 1913, p. 343).

In one of the glens on the Orbiston estate is a statue of Sir John Moore by an unknown sculptor. The figure is 9ft high and is placed on a low pedestal. The General is represented standing in deep thought. There is a story to the effect that Sir John was a suitor for the hand of the then Lady Douglas, who erected this statue to commemorate her grief for his untimely death.

Shield: Mansion House, York, Yorkshire. (Photograph)

TRIA JUNCTA UNO / DURIS NON FRANGO / TO HONOUR THE MEMORY OF LIEU^{T} GEN SIR JOHN MOORE AND TO MARK HIS FALL, THIS SHIELD OF THE ARMS OF HIS FAMILY IS RAISED BY THE GENTLEMEN OF THE YORK SUBSCRIPTION COFFEE ROOM / MDCCIX

On the Roundel above the Regimental Memorial: KOYLI Chapel, York Minster, Yorkshire.

51ST REG^{T} / ENSIGN 2 MAR 1776 / MAJOR 1 OCT 1788 / L^{T} COL 30 NOV 1790 / TO 1 NOV 1795

Monument: Corunna, Spain. (Photograph)

AQUI CAYÓ JOHN MOORE, GENERAL EN JEFE / DEL ENÉRCITO INGLÉS, EN LA BATALLA DEL 16 / DE ENERO DE 1809, CONTRA LOS FRANCESES / DIRIGIDOS POR EL DUQUE DE DALMACIA / ICI EST TOMBÉ JOHN MOORE, CHIEF D'ARMÉE, / DANS LA BATTAILLE DU 16 JANVIER 1809. / CONTRE LES FRANÇAIS COMMANDÉS PAR LE / DUC DE DALMATIE. / MONOLITO INAUGURADO POR EL EMBAJADOR / DE FRANCIA, EXCMO. M. PATRICK LECERCO, / ELÀCALDE DE LA CORUNA, EXCMO. SR. / D FRANCISCO VÀZQUEZ VÀZQUEZ, / EL RECTOR DE LA UNIVERSIDAD DE LA CORU A. / EXCMO. SR. D. JOSE LUIS MAILAN GIL, / LA ASOCIATION "THE ROYAL GREEN JACKETS" / Y LA ORDEN DE CALBALLEROS DE MARIA PITA. / EL 16 ENERO DE 1998.

Memorial bust: San Carlos, Corunna, Spain. (Photograph)

SIR / JOHN MOORE / 1761–1809

Memorial Cross: On wall of San Carlos, Corunna, Spain. (Photograph)
Memorial tablet: BNP Bank, Waterfront, Corunna, Spain. (Photograph)

IN ESTA CASA / MURIO EL VALEROSA GENERAL INGLES / SIR JOHN MOORE / EL 16 DE ENERO

DE 1809, / A CONSECUENCIA DE LAS HERIDAS / OUE RECIBIO EL MISMO DIA / LUCHANDO HEROICAMENTE EN DEFENSA / DE LA INDEPENDENCIA ESPANOLA, / PRIMER CENRENARIO. / 1909

Memorial tablet: Via Zapatiera, Corunna, Spain. (Photograph)

XVI JANUARI MDCCCIX / XIX JANUARI MCMXXXI / JOANNES MOORE / EXERCYTUS BRYTANNYCY DUX

Memorial tablet: Via Zapatiera, Corunna, Spain. (Photograph)

TO THE MEMORY OF GENERAL / SIR JOHN MOORE / MORTALLY WOUNDED / IN THE FIELD OF BATTLE / AT ELVINA / 16TH JANUARY 1809 / LEST WE FORGET / CORUNNA 16TH JANUARY 1997

Memorial tablet: Via Zapatiera, Corunna, Spain. (Photograph)

NOT A DRUM WAS HEARD, NOT A FUNERAL NOTE, / AS HIS CORSE TO THE RAMPART WE HURRIED: / NOT A SOLDIER DISCHARGED HIS FAREWELL SHOT / OE'R THE GRAVE WHERE OUR HERO WE BURIED. / WE BURIED HIM DARKLY AT DEAD OF NIGHT, / THE SODS WITH OUR BAYONETS TURNING, / BY THE STRUGGLING MOONBEAM'S MISTY LIGHT / AND THE LANTERN DIMLY BURNING. / NO USELESS COFFIN ENCLOSED HIS BREAST, / NOR IN SHEET NOR IN SHROUD WE WOUND HIM; / BUT HE LAY LIKE A WARRIOR TAKING HIS REST / WITH HIS MARTIAL CLOAK AROUND HIM. / FEW AND SHORT WERE THE PRAYERS WE SAID, / AND WE SPOKE NOT A WORD OF SORROW; / BUT WE STEADFASTLY GAZ'D ON THE FACE OF THE DEAD, / AND WE BITTERLY THOUGHT OF THE MORROW. / SLOWLY AND SADLY WE LAID HIM DOWN, / FROM THE FIELD OF HIS FAME FRESH AND GORY; / WE CARV'D NOT A LINE, AND WE RAISED NOT A STONE, / BUT WE LEFT HIM ALONE WITH HIS GLORY / CHARLES WOLFE

Note: First four and eighth verses of the poem 'The Burial of Sir John Moore after Corunna' by Charles Wolfe.

Ensign 51st Foot 2 Mar 1776. Capt 82nd Foot 10 Jan 1778. Major 102nd Foot 23 Nov 1785. Major 60th Foot 16 Jan 1788. Major 51st Foot 1 Oct 1788. Lt Colonel 30 Nov 1790. Bt Colonel 21 Aug 1795. Major General 18 Jun 1798. Lt General 30 Oct 1805.

Served in the Peninsula Sep 1808 – Jan 1809 (GOC in Spain where he took over command after the Convention of Cintra). Present at the retreat to Corunna and Battle of Corunna where he was severely wounded and died hours later 16 Jan 1809. Gold Medal for Corunna. Also served in Minorca 1776, North America 1779, Corsica 1794, West Indies 1796–1797 (present at St Lucia in Sir Ralph Abercrombie's expedition who said 'Moore's conduct was the admiration of the whole army'), Ireland 1798 (present in the Rebellion), the Helder 1799 (present at Egmont-op-Zee where he was wounded), Minorca 1800, Egypt 1801 (present at Alexandria where he was wounded), Sicily 1806–1807 and Sweden 1808. KB. As a young man Moore travelled abroad with his father who was the tutor to the young Duke of Hamilton. On the Grand Tour Moore acquired several languages but his heart was set on a military career. One of his greatest achievements was when he was selected in 1803 to instruct Light Infantry regiments in an improved system of drill at Shorncliffe Barracks. His Light Infantry regiments became the Light Division, always relied upon in the Peninsula. Very popular with his officers. Colbourne said of him 'my friend he was a noble fellow'. Colonel 9th West India Regt 6 Sep 1798. Colonel 52nd Foot 8 May 1801. Brother of Admiral Sir Graham Moore (Memorial at St Andrew's Church, Cobham, Surrey) and uncle of Lt and Capt William George Moore 1st Foot Guards.

REFERENCE: Dictionary of National Biography. Moore, James, The life of Lieutenant General Sir John Moore, 2 vols, 1833. Moore, James Carrick, A narrative of the campaign of the British army in Spain, commanded by His Excellency Lieut.-General Sir John Moore, K.B. &c. &c. &c. &c. authenticated by official papers and original letters, 1809. Brownrigg, Beatrice, Life and letters of Sir John Moore, 1923. Maurice, John Frederick, Diary of Sir John Moore, 2 vols, 1904. Oman, Carola, Sir John Moore, 1953. Parkinson, R., Moore of Corunna, 1976. Day, R., The life of Sir John Moore, 2001. Fuller, J. F. C. Sir John Moore's system of training, 1924. Gentleman's Magazine, Feb 1809, pp. 177–9. Cole, John William, Memoirs of British Generals, Vol. 1, 1856, pp. 1–60. The Sir John Moore Memorial at Shorncliffe, Oxfordshire and Buckinghamshire Light Infantry Chronicle, 1923, pp. 131–7.

MOORE, Richard

Captain. 4th (King's Own) Regiment of Foot.
Memorial: St Mary's Churchyard, Cheltenham, Gloucestershire. (M.I.)

"SACRED TO THE MEMORY OF RICHARD MOORE ESQ (OF RATHDOWNEY, QUEEN'S COUNTY) LATE MAJOR IN THE 45TH REGIMENT WHO DEPARTED THIS LIFE ON THE 24TH OF SEPTEMBER 1844 AGED 67 YEARS. ...."

Ensign 16 May 1801. Lt 16 Dec 1803. Capt 16 Aug 1810. Capt 45th Foot 20 Apr 1820. Bt Major 22 May 1830.

Served in the Peninsula with 1/4th Aug 1808 – Jan 1809, Nov 1810 – Jun 1812, with 2/4th Jul 1812 – Jan 1813 and 1/4th Sep 1813 – Apr 1814. Present at Corunna, Fuentes d'Onoro, Badajoz, Salamanca, retreat from Burgos (present at Villa Muriel), Bidassoa, Nivelle, Nive and Bayonne. Also served at Walcheren 1809 and North America 1814.

MOORE, Samuel

Lieutenant. 28th (North Gloucestershire) Regiment of Foot.
Cross on pedestal base. Liverpool Pioneer Cemetery, New South Wales, Australia. (Photograph)

IN MEMORY OF / CAPT. SAMUEL MOORE / LATE OF H. M. 28TH REGT. / DIED APRIL 16TH, 1866 AGED 72. / ....

Ensign 31 Mar 1808. Lt 28 Jan 1810. Capt 14 Dec 1826.

Served in the Peninsula with the 1/28th Apr 1810 – Apr 1811 and Mar 1812 – Apr 1814. Present at Tarifa, Barrosa (wounded), Cadiz, retreat from Burgos and Vittoria (severely wounded). Present at Waterloo and with the Army of Occupation. Also served in Malta 1817, Ionian Islands 1818–1826 and Australia 1835, retired in 1839 and settled near Liverpool, New South Wales, Australia. MGS medal for Barrosa and Vittoria.

MOORE, William George

Lieutenant and Captain. 1st Regiment of Foot Guards.
Family Chest tomb: St Peter's Churchyard, Petersham, Surrey. (Photograph)
Memorial tablet: St Peter's Church, Petersham, Surrey. (Photograph)

IN MEMORY / OF / LIEUTENANT GENERAL / SIR WILLIAM MOORE, K.C.B., / WHO DIED / AT MONTROSE HOUSE, PETERSHAM, / OCTOBER 21ST 1862, / AGED 66 YEARS.

Ensign 52nd Foot 18 Apr 1811. Lt 10 Sep 1812. Lt and Capt 1st Foot Guards 29 Sep 1814. Bt Major 21 Jan 1819. Bt Lt Colonel 12 Feb 1824. Bt Colonel 28 Jun 1838. Major General 11 Nov 1851. Lt General 5 Jun 1855.

Served in the Peninsula Dec 1811 – Apr 1814 (ADC to Lt General Graham Apr – Sep 1813 and ADC

to Lt General Hope Oct 1813 – Apr 1814). Present at Ciudad Rodrigo, Badajoz, Salamanca, San Millan, Vittoria, San Sebastian, Nivelle, Nive, Adour and Bayonne (wounded and taken prisoner 14 Apr 1814 with Sir John Hope). Present at Waterloo as DAQMG. MGS medal for Ciudad Rodrigo, Badajoz, Salamanca, Vittoria, San Sebastian, Nive and Nive. KCB. Colonel Commandant 60th Rifles 26 Jan 1856. Educated at Harrow. Died 23 Oct 1862. Nephew of Sir John Moore.
Reference: Gentleman's Magazine, Dec 1862, p. 783. Annual Register, 1862, Appx, pp. 378–9.

MOORHOUSE, Joseph William

Lieutenant and Captain. 3rd Regiment of Foot Guards.
Tombstone: Colaba Cemetery, Bombay, India. (M.I.)

"HERE IS INTERRED THE BODY OF CAPTAIN WILLIAM JOSEPH MOORHOUSE OF H. M. 65TH REGT. WHO DIED ON THE 4TH MAY 1821 AGED 30 YEARS."

Ensign 30 Apr 1807. Lt and Capt 23 Apr 1812. Capt 65th Foot 18 Nov 1819.

Served in the Peninsula Apr – Jul 1810 and Nov 1811 – Jun 1812. Present at Cadiz and Ciudad Rodrigo. Present at Waterloo. Also served in India 1819 with the 65th Foot, where he died 4 May 1821 aged 30.

MORANT, Edward

Ensign. 1st Regiment of Foot Guards.
Named on Memorial Panel VI for the Scheldt: Royal Military Chapel, Wellington Barracks, London. (M.I.)
(Destroyed by a Flying Bomb 1944)

Ensign 9 Jun 1808.

Served at Walcheren 1809 and died 15 Sep 1809.

MORETON, Hon. Augustus John Francis

Captain and Lieutenant Colonel. 1st Regiment of Foot Guards.
Memorial tablet: Holy Trinity Church, Bembridge, Isle of Wight. (Photograph)

SACRED TO THE MEMORY / OF / THE HONORABLE / AUGUSTUS JOHN FRANCIS MORETON, / SECOND SON OF FRANCIS, / THIRD LORD DUCIE: / FORMERLY LIEUT. COLONEL / IN THE 1ST REGT OF FOOT GUARDS, / OF EAST CLIFF LODGE / IN THIS PARISH. / BORN JULY 10TH 1777, / DIED JULY 15TH 1854.

Cornet 25th Lt Dragoons. Lt and Capt 1st Foot Guards 2 Feb 1796. Capt and Lt Colonel 4 Apr 1805.

Served in the Peninsula with 3rd Battalion Oct 1808 – Jan 1809. Present at Corunna. Retired 4 May 1809. MGS medal for Corunna.

MORETON, William

Private. Royal Artillery.
Buried in St Mary's Churchyard, Sheffield, Yorkshire. (Burial register)

Pte Royal Artillery 1797.

Served in the Peninsula 1810 – Mar 1814. Present at Busaco, Fuentes d'Onoro, Ciudad Rodrigo, Badajoz, Salamanca, Vittoria, Pyrenees, Nivelle, Nive and Orthes. Present at Waterloo in Lt Colonel Ross's 'A' Troop. He received no wounds in all these encounters. Discharged 31 Jan 1819 on reduction in the army with a pension of one shilling a day. MGS medal for Busaco, Fuentes d'Onoro, Ciudad Rodrigo, Badajoz, Salamanca, Vittoria, Pyrenees, Nivelle, Nive and Orthes. After his discharge became a shoemaker and lived to be 100 years old. Died Jun 1862.

MOREWOOD, George Alexander
Physician. Medical Department.
Ledger stone: Walcot Cemetery, Bath, Somerset. (Area 4 Row B). (Photograph)

GEORGE ALEXANDER MOREWOOD. DIED 21 SEPT 1859.

Physician 7 Sep 1807.
Served in the Peninsula Nov 1808 – Jan 1809 and Mar – Jul 1812. Present at Corunna. Also served at Walcheren 1809 and North America 1813. MGS medal for Corunna. MA Glasgow 1802, MD 1806. Half pay 25 Dec 1814.

MORGAN, David
Assistant Surgeon. 50th (West Kent) Regiment of Foot.
Memorial tablet: St Woolos's Cathedral, Newport, Gwent, Wales. (Photograph)

THIS TABLET IS ERECTED IN MEMORY OF / DAVID MORGAN / (SON OF THE LATE DAVID NECK MORGAN, / OF ABERGAVENNY). / ASSISTANT SURGEON TO THE 50TH REGT FOOT, / WHO DEPARTED THIS LIFE 1ST JANY 1813, IN SPAIN / WHILST ASSIDUOUSLY EMPLOYED IN THE DUTIES OF / HIS PROFESSION, / JANUARY 1ST 1813 AET 35 YEARS. / WHERE HIS REMAINS ARE DEPOSITED UNTIL THE / RESURRECTION OF THE JUST / ....

Hospital Mate 1806. Asst Surgeon 50th Foot 17 Dec 1807.
Served in the Peninsula Sep 1810 – Dec 1812. Present at Arroyo dos Molinos and Almarez. Also served at Walcheren 1809. Died of disease in Coria 31 Jan 1813.

MORGAN, Hugh
1st Lieutenant. Royal Artillery.
Low monument: St Mary's Churchyard, Prestbury, Gloucestershire. (Photograph)

IN MEMORY OF / MAJOR HUGH MORGAN / OF THE ROYAL ARTILLERY / WHO DIED ON THE 25TH OF JUNE 1860, AGED 69.

2nd Lt Dec 21 Dec 1808. 1st Lt 7 Feb 1812. 2nd Capt 30 Jun 1830. Capt 13 May 1840. Bt Major 28 Nov 1854.
Served in the Peninsula May 1812 – Apr 1814. Present at the siege of Cadiz, Pyrenees, second siege of San Sebastian (severely wounded) and Toulouse. Present at the Capture of Paris and with the Army of Occupation until 1816. Also served at Walcheren 1809 (present at the siege of Flushing), Canada 1820–1824, Jamaica 1835–1839 and West Indies 1841–1842. Retired on full pay in Apr 1843. MGS medal for Pyrenees, San Sebastian and Toulouse.

MORGAN, John
Private. 11th Regiment of Light Dragoons.
Headstone: St Peter's Churchyard, Frampton-Cotterell, Gloucestershire. (Photograph)

SACRED / TO THE MEMORY OF / JOHN MORGAN CODRINGTON / OF THIS PARISH: / LATE OF HIS MAJESTY'S / XITH HUZZARS: / WHO FOUGHT / IN THE BATTLE OF / SALAMANCA, / WATERLOO & BHURTPOOR. / HE DIED OCTOBER 16TH 1873. / AGED 82 YEARS. / ....

Served in the Peninsula Jun 1811 – Jun 1813. Present at Castrejon, Salamanca and Venta del Pozo. Present at Waterloo in Capt J. A. Schreiber's Troop. Also served in India 1819 (present at the siege and Capture of Bhurtpore 1826). Army of India medal. MGS medal for Salamanca. Afterwards assumed the name of Codrington.

MORGAN, Reese
Private. 23rd (Royal Welch Fusiliers) Regiment of Foot.
Headstone: St Michael's Churchyard, Trefeglwys, near Aberystwyth, Powys, Wales. (Photograph)

IN MEMORY OF / REESE MORGAN / LATE OF PANT-Y-GLYN NEAR THIS VILLAGE / WHO DIED OCTOBER 8TH 1856 / AGED 61 YEARS. / (VERSE) / ....

Montgomery Volunteers. Pte 23rd Foot 6 Apr 1814.

Present at Waterloo in Capt Farmers No. 7 Troop where he was severely wounded and his right arm amputated. Discharged 3 Mar 1816 with a pension of one shilling per day aged 21 years.

MORIARTY, James
Lieutenant. 88th (Connaught Rangers) Regiment of Foot.
Named on the Memorial: St Andrew's Church (now Musée Historique), Biarritz, France. (Photograph)

Ensign 8 Mar 1810. Lt 13 May 1812.

Served in the Peninsula with 2/88th Dec 1810 – Jan 1811 and 1/88th Jun 1811 – Feb 1814. Present at Sabugal, Fuentes d'Onoro, El Bodon, Ciudad Rodrigo, Badajoz, Salamanca where he carried the colours and Orthes where he was killed 27 Feb 1814.

MORICE, Charles
Lieutenant Colonel. 69th (South Lincolnshire) Regiment of Foot.
Memorial tablet: St Mary's Church, Langley, Slough, Buckinghamshire. (Photograph)

TO THE MEMORY OF / COLONEL CHARLES MORICE, / OF HIS MAJESTY'S 69TH REGIMENT, / WHO AFTER TWENTY-ONE YEARS / OF CONSTANT AND ACTIVE SERVICE, / FELL MOST HONORABLY / IN THE SIGNAL BATTLE OF WATERLOO, / ON THE 18TH OF JUNE, 1815, / AND IN THE 40TH YEAR OF HIS AGE.

Ensign 15th Foot 11 Jun 1793. Lt 6 Dec 1794. Capt-Lt 27 Aug 1799. Capt 10 Nov 1800. Major 17 Jul 1802. Major Colonel Ramsay's Regiment 21 May 1803 Major Colonel Baille's Regiment 9 Aug 1806. Major 3 Ceylon Regt 31 Jul 1806. Lt Colonel 7 Jan 1808. Lt Colonel 69th Foot 4 Jun 1813. Bt Colonel 4 Jun 1814.

Present at Waterloo where he was killed at Quatre Bras, due to the inexperience of the Prince of Orange who insisted that they did not form square before the French Cavalry charged. Also served in the Netherlands 1814 (present at Bergen-op-Zoom where he was wounded). Educated at Eton.

MORISSET, James Thomas
Captain. 48th (Northamptonshire) Regiment of Foot.
Family Chest tomb in railed enclosure: Pioneer Cemetery, Holy Trinity Churchyard, Kelso, New South Wales, Australia. (Photograph)

TO THEIR MEMORY / SACRED / HERE LIETH / PAULINE CAROLINE / DAUGHTER OF COLONEL & EMILY MORISSET / DIED MAY 31 1849 / AGED 2 YEARS 8 MONTHS / OF SUCH IS THE KINGDOM OF HEAVEN / ALSO LIEUT. COL. / JAMES THOs. MORISSET / WHO DEPARTED THIS LIFE / 17TH AUG. 1852 / AGED 73 YEARS. / THIS PLAQUE WAS ERECTED BY / THE GG & GGG GRANDSON OF LT COL J. T. MORISSET / ANTHONY J. MORISSET / RONALD E. THOMPSON / DATE, 2004.

Memorial plaque: Attached to a tree in the town of Morisset, New South Wales, Australia. (Photograph)

UNVEILED BY MR CHRISTOPHER MORISSET / GREAT GRANDSON OF MAJOR J. T. MORISSET / ON THE 28TH OCTOBER 1978 / THIS MARKS THE SPOT WHERE / MAJOR J. T. MORISSET AND HIS / COMPANY CAMPED ON THE FIRST JOURNEY / OVER LAND FROM NEWCASTLE TO SYDNEY / IN APRIL 1825. / KINDLY DONATED BY ALD. FENNELL ON BEHALF / OF THE FENNELL AND FROST FAMILY.

Ensign 80th Foot 1 Feb 1798. Lt 8 Nov 1800. Capt 48th Foot 26 Dec 1805. Bt Major 12 Aug 1819. Major 8 Jun 1825. Bt Lt Colonel 19 Dec 1826.

Served in the Peninsula Apr 1809 – Jan 1812, Apr – Jul 1813 and Dec 1813 – Apr 1814 (ADC to Major General Inglis). Present at Douro, Talavera, Busaco, Albuera (wounded by a sabre cut to his face which disfigured him for life and awarded a pension of £100 per annum), Aldea de Ponte, Vittoria, Nive, Orthes and Toulouse. Morisset went with the 48th Foot to Australia in 1817 to garrison the colony. Commandant of Newcastle Penal Colony 1818–1823 where he organised the construction of roads and public buildings. Commandant at Bathurst 1823. Returned to England and wrote a report on convict control in New South Wales 1825. Commandant of Norfolk Island Penal settlement 1829–1834. Resigned owing to ill health. Police Magistrate in Bathurst 1838. MGS medal for Talavera, Busaco, Albuera, Vittoria, Nive, Orthes and Toulouse.

Reference: Australian Dictionary of Biography. Obit. Bathurst Free Press 21 Aug and 9 Oct 1852.

MORPHETT, Mars

Ensign 53rd (Shropshire) Regiment of Foot.

Memorial tablet: St Thomas's Church, San Thomé, Madras, India. (Photograph)

IN MEMORY OF / CAPTAIN MARS MORPHETT, / LATE OF H. M. 57TH REGIMENT OF FOOT, WHO DEPARTED THIS LIFE, / ON THE 4TH DAY OF OCTOBER 1860, IN THE 68TH YEAR OF HIS AGE. / CAPTAIN MORPHETT ENTERED THE BRITISH ARMY IN YEAR 1812, / AS A VOLUNTEER IN THE 2ND BATTALION 53RD REGIMENT, THEN / ON SERVICE IN THE PENINSULA, WHERE HE WAS THREE TIMES WOUNDED. / AFTER MORE THAN 30 YEARS OF HONOURABLE AND ZEALOUS SERVICE, IN / THE COURSE OF WHICH HE SEVERAL TIMES FOUGHT AND BLED IN HIS COUNTRY'S CAUSE, / HE LEFT THE ARMY, AND HELD THE OFFICE OF DEPUTY POST MASTER / GENERAL OF MADRAS, OF WHICH TOWN HE WAS ALSO HIGH SHERIFF. / A FEW YEARS SINCE COMPELLED BY LOSS OF SIGHT, HE RETIRED FROM PUBLIC / LIFE AND PASSED THE REMAINDER OF HIS DAYS SURROUNDED BY HIS / FAMILY, OF WHICH HE WAS EVER THE HONOURED AND BELOVED HEAD. / (VERSE) / THIS TABLET IS ERECTED BY A FEW FRIENDS / AS A MARK OF THEIR AFFECTIONATE ESTEEM AND REGARD.

Volunteer 53rd Foot Jul 1812. Ensign 36th Foot 22 Jul 1812. Ensign 53rd Foot 1 Oct 1812. Lt 29 Jun 1815. Lt 87th Foot 25 Sep 1823. Lt 48th Foot 28 Mar 1824. Lt 63rd Foot 17 Sep 1833. Capt 40th Foot 29 Jan 1836. Capt 57th Foot 22 Aug 1836.

Served in the Peninsula Jun 1812 – Apr 1813. Present at Salamanca (severely wounded). MGS medal for Salamanca. Also served in India 1814–1829. Awarded Army of India medal for Nepal (present at Fort Jeytuck). Retired 10 Dec 1842.

MORRIS, Samuel

Captain. 28th (North Gloucestershire) Regiment of Foot.

Family table tomb: Newcastle Church of Ireland, Newcastle, County Wicklow, Ireland. (Photograph)

………………. / SACRED TO THE MEMORY OF / SAMUEL MORRIS / LATE CAPT IN HER MAJESTY'S 28TH REGIMENT OF FOOT / WHO DIED THE 8TH OF JULY 1865. AGED 79. / INTERRED AT TORQUAY.

Ensign 31 Jan 1805. Lt 2 Apr 1806. Capt 25 Nov 1813.

Served in the Peninsula with 2/28th Jul 1809 – Jul 1810 and 1/28th Dec 1810 – Apr 1811 and Jul 1811 – Apr 1814. Present at Barrosa, Arroyo dos Molinos, Almarez, retreat from Burgos, Vittoria (wounded), Nivelle, Nive, Garris, Orthes, Aire and Toulouse. Half pay 25 Dec 1814. MGS medal for Barrosa, Vittoria, Nivelle, Nive, Orthes and Toulouse.

MORRIS, Thomas

Private. 23rd (Royal Welch Fusiliers) Regiment of Foot.
Headstone: St Fraid's Churchyard, Llansantffraid-ym-Mechain, Powys. (Photograph)

IN LOVING MEMORY OF / THOMAS MORRIS / WHO FOUGHT AT WATERLOO / DIED DECEMBER 5TH / 1874 AGED 82 YEARS / ....

Pte 9 Feb 1805.

Served in the Peninsula where he was wounded at San Sebastian. Present at Waterloo in Capt William Campbell's Company. Discharged 26 Oct 1816.

MORRISON, William

Captain. Royal Artillery.
Grave: St Peter's Churchyard, Wolverhampton, Staffordshire. (Burial record). (The churchyard is no longer extant and is now under the Wolverhampton University Harrison Learning Centre)

2nd Lt 1 Jan 1795. 1st Lt 28 Sep 1797. Capt-Lt 6 Dec 1803. Capt 1 Feb 1808. Bt Major 21 Sep 1813. Major 22 Apr 1826. Lt Colonel 6 Nov 1827.

Served in the Peninsula Aug 1808 – Jan 1809 and Oct 1812 – Apr 1814. Present at Rolica, Vimeiro, Corunna campaign, first and second sieges of San Sebastian (commanded a battery of six 18 pounders, Mentioned in Despatches 8 Sep 1813 and awarded Bt Majority), Bidassoa, Nivelle, and Adour (served on gun boats). Gold Medal for Vimeiro where he was in command of a brigade of artillery attached to Brigadier General Fane's brigade. Marched to Paris with a brigade of artillery after Waterloo, returning to England Feb 1816. Also served at the Helder 1799, Gibraltar 1804–1808 and the Netherlands 1815. Retired 25 Nov 1828. Died in Wolverhampton 30 Oct 1835 aged 55.
Reference: Royal Military Calendar, Vol. 5, p. 232.

MORTON, Harcourt

Captain. 14th (Buckinghamshire) Regiment of Foot.
Headstone: St Mary the Virgin's Churchyard, Masham, Yorkshire. (Photograph)

SACRED TO THE MEMORY OF / MAJOR HARCOURT MORTON, / WHO DIED ON THE 4TH OF JUNE 1854, / AGED 68 YEARS. / ....

Ensign 85th Foot 21 Apr 1808. Lt 10 Nov 1808. Lt 49th Foot 25 Jan 1813. Capt 14th Foot 12 Jan 1814. Bt Major 10 Jan 1837.

Served in the Peninsula Mar – Oct 1811. Present at Fuentes d'Onoro and the second siege of Badajoz (wounded 9 Jun 1811). Also served at Walcheren 1809. Transferred to the 49th Foot in 1813 and went to America (present at the Battle of Chrystler's Farm in Upper Canada Nov 1813 where he was wounded). MGS medal for Fuentes d'Onoro and Chrystler's Farm. Retired on half pay in 1816.

MOSS, John Irving

Lieutenant. 13th Regiment of Light Dragoons.
Gravestone: Church of England Cemetery, Bellary District, India. (M.I.)

"CAPT. JOHN IRVING MOSS, H.M.'S 48TH REGT, AGED 40 YEARS, DIED 27 APRIL 1831."

Cornet 27 Aug 1803. Lt 7 Mar 1805. Capt 31 Aug 1815. Capt 48th Foot 26 Feb 1828.

Served in the Peninsula Apr 1810 – Apr 1814. Present at Cadiz, Campo Mayor and Olivencia where he was taken prisoner 7 Apr 1811 and remained in prison until the end of the war. The 13th Lt Dragoons were on outpost flank duty at the crossing of Guadiana when they were attacked by French cavalry – two officers, one of them Lt Moss, and 50 men were captured. The fault lay with an officer of the QMG's department who had placed the men in the wrong position. Present at Waterloo. Half pay 1816. Joined 48th Foot 1828 and went to India where he died 1831.

MOULDER, Patrick William

Sergeant. 15th (King's) Regiment of Light Dragoons.
Chest tomb: St Mary the Virgin's Churchyard, Witney, Oxfordshire. (Photograph)

TO THE MEMORY OF / PATRICK WILLIAM MOULDER / LATE OF THIS PLACE: / AND REGIMENTAL SERJEANT MAJOR / OF THE 1ST OR QUEEN'S OWN CAVALRY REGIMENT OF / OXFORDSHIRE YEOMANRY CAVALRY. / DIED DEC 12 1836 AGED 51. / HE SERVED HIS COUNTRY FOR MORE THAN 15 YEARS IN THE / 15TH OR KING'S OWN REGIMENT OF HUSSARS, / IN WHICH HE WAS MANY YEARS A SERJEANT, AND FOUGHT AT WATERLOO. / IN 1817 HE JOINED THE OXFORDSHIRE YEOMANRY AS A REGIMENTAL SERGEANT MAJOR: / AND CONTINUED IN THE SAME REGIMENT UNTIL HIS DEATH. / HIS LOSS IS DEEPLY REGRETTED BY ALL THOSE WHO KNEW HIM / AND PARTICULARLY BY HIS COMMANDING OFFICER / WHO, ON MANY OCCASIONS OF VARIOUS SERVICE HAD FELT THE BENEFITS OF / HIS GREAT ZEAL, HIS EXTRAORDINARY ACTIVITY, / AND HIS UNQUESTIONED INTEGRITY; / AND WHO HAS CAUSED THE STONE TO BE RAISED / TO COMMEMORATE HIS RECORD.

Pte 2 Sep 1801. Cpl 25 Feb 1805. Sgt 18 Sep 1807.

Served in the Peninsula 1808 – Jan 1809 and 1813 – Apr 1814. Present at Sahagun (wounded), Cacabellos, Morales, Vittoria, Orthes and Toulouse. Present at Waterloo. Discharged 24 Apr 1817. Joined the Oxfordshire Yeomanry Cavalry as Regimental Sergeant Major. For many years was landlord of the Cross Keys Inn at Witney and it was there in Dec 1838 that he committed suicide. He was under the delusion that his Commanding Officer thought he had acted dishonestly with the regimental funds. This was not true. 3,000 people attended his funeral when he was buried with full military honours. Brother of Pte Robert Moulder 15th Lt Dragoons.

MOULDER, Robert

Private. 15th (King's) Regiment of Light Dragoons.
Headstone: St Mary the Virgin's Churchyard, Witney, Oxfordshire. Seriously eroded and inscription not recorded. (Photograph)

Enlisted 3 Jul 1801 at the age of 12. Trumpeter 25 Aug 1804. Pte 3 Jul 1810.

Served in the Peninsula 1808 – Jan 1809 and 1813 – Apr 1814. Present at Sahagun, Cacabellos, Morales, Vittoria, Orthes and Toulouse. Had a stroke in June 1814 and was discharged 8 Aug 1814. He had served for 13 years, but 6 years service was taken from his record as he was under age when he enlisted. Chelsea Out-pensioner with a pension of one shilling a day. He never recovered from the stroke, died March 1816 and was buried in his father's grave. Brother of Sgt Patrick Moulder 15th Lt Dragoons.

MOULSON, Edward

Ensign 89th Regiment of Foot.
Memorial: Tangacherry Cemetery, Malabar District, India. (M.I.)

"20TH JAN 1820 / LT EDWARD MOULSON / OF THE 89TH REGT"

Ensign 22 Dec 1808. Lt 24 Jun 1812.

Served in the Peninsula in Oct 1810. Present at Fuengirola where he was taken prisoner. Remained a prisoner until Apr 1814. Also served in India 1816 (present in the Pindari War 1817–1818) and died there in 1820.

MOUNTGARRETT, William

Lieutenant. 87th (Prince of Wales's Own) Irish Regiment of Foot.
Memorial: Military Burial Ground, Bhowanipore, India. (M I.)

"SACRED TO THE MEMORY OF / CAPTAIN WILLIAM MOUNTGARRETT, / OF H. M. 87TH REGIMENT, WHO DEPARTED THIS LIFE / ON THE 22ND OF AUG 1825, AGED 40 YEARS. / THIS IS ERECTED BY THOSE BROTHER OFFICERS WHO HAD / LONG KNOWN HIS WORTH AS A SOLDIER AND AS A FRIEND."

Ensign 38th Foot 19 Sep 1807. Lt 87th Foot 6 Oct 1808. Capt 19 May 1822.

Served in the Peninsula Mar 1809 – Apr 1814. Present at Douro, Talavera (captured and was a prisoner of war from Aug – Nov 1809), Cadiz, Barrosa, Vittoria (severely wounded), Nivelle and Orthes (severely wounded). Also served in Egypt 1807 (wounded) and India 1816 (present in the Pindari War 1817–1818). Awarded pension of £70 per annum for wounds received in Egypt, Vittoria and Orthes. Died in India 22 Aug 1825.

MOUNTSTEVEN, William Thomas Blewitt

Ensign. 28th (North Gloucestershire) Regiment of Foot.
Memorial: St Petrox's Churchyard, Dartmouth Castle, Dartmouth, Devon. (Photograph)

SACRED TO THE MEMORY OF / MAJOR GENERAL / WILLIAM T. B. MOUNTSTEVEN / LATE OF THE 28TH / AND 79TH REGIMENTS / WHO DIED ON THE 16TH DECEMBER 1871 / AGED 74 / TRUE CHRISTIAN SOLDIER. / ....

Ensign 28th Foot 25 Nov 1813. Lt 25 Oct 1820. Capt (unattached) 8 May 1835. Paymaster 79th Foot 10 Jun 1836. Bt Major 9 Nov 1846. Bt Lt Colonel 20 Jun 1854. Bt Colonel 1 May 1859. Major General 20 Jul 1866.

Present at Quatre Bras and Waterloo where he was severely wounded. Also served in Ireland (narrowly escaped assassination in command of a patrol) and in Gibraltar 1841. Half pay 1 Jan 1847 and was appointed Staff Officer of Pensioners at Plymouth 1 May 1859. Died 16 Dec 1871 while on duty in this post.

MUDGE, Richard Zachary

2nd Captain. Royal Engineers.
Named on the Regimental Memorial: Rochester Cathedral, Rochester, Kent. (Photograph)

2nd Lt 4 May 1807. Lt 14 Jul 1807. 2nd Capt 21 Jul 1813. Capt 23 Mar 1825. Lt Colonel 10 Jan 1837. Bt Colonel 11 Nov 1851.

Served in the Peninsula Jun 1809 – Jun 1810. Present at Douro and Talavera. Retired on full pay 7 Sep 1840. MGS medal for Talavera. Died at Teignmouth 24 Sep 1854.

MUDIE, Charles

Ensign. 1st (Royal Scots) Regiment of Foot.
Ledger stone: Kensal Green Cemetery, London. (3093/169/2). Inscription illegible. (Photograph)

Ensign 4 Nov 1813. Lt 48th Foot 4 Oct 1815.
Served in the Peninsula Mar – Apr 1814. Present at Waterloo. Half pay Mar 1817. Died 1841.

MULCASTER, Edmund R.
2nd Captain. Royal Engineers.
Named on the Regimental Memorial: Rochester Cathedral, Rochester, Kent. (Photograph)

2nd Lt 1 Mar 1804. Lt 1 Mar 1805. Adjutant 3 Aug 1808. 2nd Capt 24 Jun 1809.
Served in the Peninsula Aug 1808 – Jan 1809 and May 1809 – Mar 1812. Present at Rolica, Vimeiro, Corunna, Torres Vedras, first and second sieges of Badajoz, Ciudad Rodrigo (wounded 15 Jan 1812) and Badajoz where he was killed 25 Mar 1812. Also served in Sicily 1807–1808.

MÜLLER, Heinrich
Captain. 2nd Line Battalion, King's German Legion.
Named on the Memorial: St Andrew's Church (now Musée Historique), Biarritz, France. (Photograph)

Lt 20 Aug 1805. Capt 12 Mar 1812.
Served in the Peninsula Sep 1808 – May 1812 and Nov 1813 – Apr 1814. Present at Douro, Busaco, Fuentes d'Onoro, Ciudad Rodrigo, Nivelle, Nive, St Etienne and Bayonne where he was killed in the Sortie from Bayonne 14 Apr 1814. Also served at Hanover 1805, Mediterranean 1806–1807 and the Baltic 1807–1808.

MUNRO, Charles
Lieutenant. 45th (Nottinghamshire) Regiment of Foot.
Ledger stone: Southport Cemetery, Lancashire. (Section B Grave 646). (Photograph)

SACRED / TO THE MEMORY OF / SIR CHARLES MUNRO, BARONET / OF FOULIS, ROSS-SHIRE / DIED AT SOUTHPORT / JULY 12TH 1886 / AGED 92. / ....

Ensign 6 Apr 1810. Lt 5 Mar 1812.
Served in the Peninsula Sep 1811 – Dec 1812 and Nov 1813 – Apr 1814. Present at Ciudad Rodrigo, Badajoz (wounded), Salamanca, Nive, Orthes and Toulouse. Also served in North America 1814–1815. After the war went to South America and commanded a division of the Columbian Army under Bolivar (present at Agnotmar). MGS medal for Ciudad Rodrigo, Badajoz, Salamanca, Nive, Orthes and Toulouse. When he died on 13 Jul 1886 at the age of 92, he was one of the last few surviving veterans of the Peninsular War. Became 9th Baronet of Foulis.
REFERENCE: Obit. Southport Visiter, 17 Jul 1886.

MUNRO, David
Captain. 94th Regiment of Foot.
Low monument: Warriston Cemetery, Edinburgh, Scotland. (Section T Grave number 18). (Photograph)

IN MEMORY OF / MAJOR DAVID MUNRO / LATE OF THE OLD 94TH REGT OR SCOTTISH BRIGADE / WHO DIED AT EDINBURGH 10TH NOVEMBER 1863. / THE MEDAL WHICH HE RECEIVED FROM HIS SOVEREIGN / BEARS THE FOLLOWING NAMES: / FUENTES D'ONOR, CIUDAD RODRIGO, / BADAJOZ, SALAMANCA, VITTORIA, / PYRENEES, NIVELLE, NIVE, ORTHES & TOULOUSE.

Ensign 59th Foot 1807. Lt 94th Foot 1 Jun 1807. Capt 10 Feb 1814. Major 9 Dec 1828.
Served in the Peninsula Feb 1810 – Apr 1814. Present at Cadiz, Redinha, Casal Nova, Foz d'Arouce, Sabugal, Fuentes d'Onoro, second siege of Badajoz, Ciudad Rodrigo, Badajoz (wounded), Salamanca,

Vittoria, Pyrenees, Nivelle, Nive, Orthes, Vic Bigorre and Toulouse. Half pay 25 Dec 1818. Re-appointed on full pay 1 Dec 1828. Retired 23 Aug 1831. MGS medal for Fuentes d'Onoro, Ciudad Rodrigo, Badajoz, Salamanca, Vittoria, Pyrenees, Nivelle, Nive, Orthes and Toulouse. Died 10 Nov 1863 aged 79.

MUNRO, John

Private. 42nd (Royal Highland) Regiment of Foot.
Ledger stone: Old Hall Cemetery, Dunn, Caithness, Scotland. (Plot 14, west side adjacent to the old ruined church). (M.I.)

"IN MEMORY OF BROTHER JOHN MUNRO, DIED STEMSTER, 6 MAY 1868 AGE 21, / GRANDFATHER JOHN MUNRO PENINSULAR WAR, 42 ROYAL HIGHLANDERS, DIED DUNN 24 AUG 1837 AGE 56. / WIFE ANNIE MACDONALD SHARED HIS CAMPAIGNS, DIED DUNN 1 DEC 1856 AGED 69."

Pte 27 Jul 1806.

Served in the Peninsula 1808–1809 and Apr 1812 – Apr 1814. Present at Corunna, Salamanca, Burgos, Pyrenees, Nivelle, Nive, Orthes and Toulouse where he was wounded. Present at Waterloo. Discharged 16 Oct 1822 as unfit for service due to his wounds. His wife Annie was present with him on his campaigns.

MUNRO, William

Surgeon. 78th (Highland) Regiment of Foot.
Table tomb: Suddie burial ground, Black Isle, Avoch, Ross and Cromarty, Scotland. (M.I.)

"TO THE MEMORY OF WILLIAM MUNRO ESQ., LATE SURGEON OF THE 78TH HIGHLANDERS WHO DIED IN TAIN 15TH MARCH 1839, MUCH AND JUSTLY REGRETTED BY ALL HIS FRIENDS AND ACQUAINTANCES."

Hospital Mate 8 Apr 1805. Asst Surgeon 78th Foot 25 Apr 1805. Surgeon 3 Jun 1813.

Served in Sicily 1806 (present at Maida), Egypt 1807, Walcheren 1809 and Java 1811. Half pay 25 Apr 1816.

MUNRO, William

Private. Royal Artillery.
Curved family stone: Avoch Churchyard, Avoch, Black Isle, Ross and Cromarty, Scotland. (M.I.)

"IN MEMORY OF ANDREW MUNRO .... AND OF THEIR SON WILLIAM LATE OF THE ROYAL ARTILLERY WHO DIED 24TH APRIL 1856 AGED 76 YEARS."

Served in the Peninsula. Present at Vittoria. MGS medal for Vittoria.

MUNSTER, Earl of see FITZCLARENCE, George

MURCHISON, Robert P.

Captain. 43rd (Monmouthshire) Light Infantry Regiment of Foot.
Named on the Memorial: St Andrew's Church (now Musée Historique), Biarritz, France. (Photograph)

Ensign 57th Foot 23 Jul 1803. Lt 43rd Foot 5 Jun 1804. Adjutant 4 Dec 1806. Capt 8 Mar 1809.

Served in the Peninsula with the 1st Battalion Oct – Dec 1808 and Aug 1812 – Nov 1813. Present at San Millan, Vittoria, Pyrenees, Bidassoa and Nivelle where he was severely wounded and died of wounds 11 Nov 1813. Also served at Copenhagen 1807.

MURCHISON, Roderick Impey

Captain. 36th (Herefordshire) Regiment of Foot.

Chest tomb: Brompton Cemetery, London. (Compartment 5 185.0f x 6.3f). (Photograph)

TO THE MEMORY OF / SIR RODERICK IMPEY MURCHISON / BART. KCB. FRS. DCL. LLD., &C. / DIRECTOR GENERAL OF THE GEOLOGICAL SURVEY, / FOREIGN MEMBER OF THE INSTITUTE OF FRANCE, / MEMBER OF THE IMPERIAL ACADEMY OF SCIENCE OF ST PETERSBURG / AND OF MANY OTHER SCIENTIFIC SOCIETIES. / KNIGHT GRAND CROSS OF THE IMPERIAL ORDER OF / ST ANNE AND ST STANISLAUS OF RUSSIA &C &C. / AUTHOR OF THE SILURIAN SYSTEM OF ROCKS / AND OF RUSSIA AND THE URAL MOUNTAINS. / BORN AT TARADALE ROSS-SHIRE, 19TH FEBRY 1792 / DIED IN LONDON 22ND OCTOBER 1871.

Memorial in family railed enclosure St Clement's Churchyard, Dingwall, Caithness, Scotland. (Enclosure seriously overgrown and inscription recorded from memorial inscription). (Photograph)

"TO THE MEMORY OF SIR RODERICK MURCHISON BART., KCB. FRS. DCL. LLD. ETC. ONE OF THE FOUNDERS OF MODERN GEOLOGY. SON OF KENNETH MURCHISON OF FAIRBURN. BORN AT TARADALE FEB 19 1792, DIED IN LONDON OCT 22 1871. SERVED IN THE 36TH REGT OF FOOT AND 6TH INNISKILLING DRAGOONS. WAS PRESENT AT ROLEIA, VIMIERO, CARRYING THE COLOURS OF HIS REGIMENT, AND CORUNNA. ALSO PRESENT AT THE SIEGE OF CADIZ. GENEROUS, CHIVALROUS, MAGNANIMOUS, IN DUTY FEARLESS, A FAITHFUL PERFECT FRIEND. HIS HEART EVER REMAINED TRUE TO THE LAND OF HIS FOREBEARS."

Memorial: School Number 9, Ekaterinburg, Perm, Russia. (Photograph)

Stone and cast-iron plaque features the tooth whorl of a Permain shark called the *Helicoprion.* Erected by the Ural-Scottish Society in 2009.

English translation:

"TO RODERICK IMPEY MURCHISON, SCOTTISH GEOLOGIST, EXPLORER OF PERM KRAI, WHO GIVES TO THE LAST PERIOD OF PALEOZOIC ERA THE NAME OF PERM"

Blue plaque: 21, Calgate, Barnard Castle, County Durham. (Photograph)

FORMERLY / THE RESIDENCE OF / SIR RODERICK MURCHISON, / TWICE PRESIDENT OF THE ROYAL / GEOGRAPHICAL SOCIETY, HE DIED / IN 1871, AGED 79, A GREAT / GEOLOGIST AND EXPLORER, A TOWN / IN NEW ZEALAND, FALLS ON THE NILE, / A MOUNTAIN RANGE AND RIVER IN / AUSTRALIA AND A SOUND IN / GREEN LAND ARE ALL NAMED / AFTER HIM.

Ensign 12 May 1807. Lt 15 Dec 1808. Capt 13 Aug 1812.

Served in the Peninsula Aug 1808 – Jan 1809. Present at Rolica, Vimeiro and Corunna. Also served in Sicily 1808–1811 (ADC to his uncle General Sir Alexander Mackenzie) and Ireland 1812. Retired Aug 1815. MGS medal for Rolica, Vimeiro and Corunna. By 1825 he became interested in geology and eventually became the founder of modern geology. He surveyed the border between Wales, Shropshire and Herefordshire extensively in 1830 and found a different system of rocks which he called Siluria after the ancient inhabitants of that part of Britain called Silures. Traced similar deposits all over Europe and his research was published in a volume called *Siluria* in 1854. He was in Russia in 1840 and the results of his survey were published as *Geology of Russia and the Ural Mountains* in 1845. Was the first to discover gold deposits in Australia in 1841 by comparing rocks from the Ural mountains with those from Australia but he was not believed until Australian settlers started to discover gold in 1851. Responsible for planning much of the overseas research between 1850–1870. Director General of the Geological Survey 1855.

President of the Royal Geological Society for 16 years. KCB 1863. Baronet 1866. Helped to found the British Association.
Reference: Dictionary of National Biography. Annual Register, 1871, Appx, p. 162. Geike, A., Life of Sir Roderick I. Murchison, 2 vols, 1875.

MURDOCH, James Campbell
Captain. 91st Regiment of Foot.
Obelisk: Kilmadock Churchyard, Kilmadock, Perthshire, Scotland. (Photograph)

SACRED / TO THE MEMORY / OF / JAMES C. MURDOCH / WHO DIED AT BRIDGE OF TEITH, / SON JAMES LATE CAPT IN THE 91ST REGT / OR ARGYLLSHIRE HIGHLANDERS, / HE SERVED HIS COUNTRY AT WALCHEREN, / IN SPAIN AND PORTUGAL, / PYRENEES, FRANCE / AND WATERLOO. / HE DIED AT EDINBURGH / 30TH MARCH 1833, / AGED 49. / ERECTED BY HIS SISTER SARAH OF GARTINCABER."

Ensign 18 Jun 1806. Lt 28 May 1807. Capt 29 Nov 1810.
Served in the Peninsula Jan – Oct 1813. Present in the Pyrenees. Present in the Waterloo Campaign where he was present at Hal, the siege of Cambrai and with the Army of Occupation. Also served at Walcheren 1809.

MURPHY, Daniel
Private. 12th (Prince of Wales's) Regiment of Light Dragoons.
Named on the Regimental Memorial: St Joseph's Church, Waterloo. (Photograph)

Present at Waterloo where he was killed.

MURPHY, Philip
Private. 12th (Prince of Wales's) Regiment of Light Dragoons.
Named on the Regimental Memorial: St Joseph's Church, Waterloo. (Photograph)

Present at Waterloo where he was killed.

MURRAY, Sir Archibald John
Lieutenant and Captain. 3rd Regiment of Foot Guards.
Ledger stone: Brompton Cemetery, London. (Grave number BR 24218 Compartment M:15x118). (Photograph)

IN MEMORIAM / LIEUT. COLONEL / SIR ARCHIBALD J. MURRAY, / OF BLACKBARONY. BART. / DIED MAY 22 1860 / AGED 69. / ....

Ensign 21 Apr 1808. Lt and Capt 10 Dec 1812. Adjt 12 May 1814. Capt and Lt Colonel 20 Dec 1820.
Served in the Peninsula Apr 1810 – May 1811 and Jul 1811 – Jan 1813. Present at Cadiz, Barrosa, Ciudad Rodrigo, Salamanca and Burgos. MGS medal for Barrosa, Ciudad Rodrigo and Salamanca.

MURRAY, Donald
Sergeant. 59th (2nd Nottinghamshire) Regiment of Foot.
Ledger stone: St Andrew's Churchyard, Bolton, Lancashire. (Photograph)

SACRED / TO THE MEMORY OF / DONALD MURRAY, / NATIVE OF DORNOCH, NORTH / OF SCOTLAND, WHO DEPARTED / THIS LIFE JANUARY 2ND 1865 / IN THE 81ST YEAR OF HIS AGE.

Rossshire Miltia. Pte 59th Foot 20 Dec 1807. Cpl 1808. Sgt 28 Jun 1809.

Served in the Peninsula Sep 1808 – Jan 1809 and Sep 1812 – Apr 1814. Present at Corunna, Cadiz, Vittoria and San Sebastian where he was wounded. MGS medal for Corunna, Vittoria and San Sebastian. Discharged 1814.

MURRAY, Sir George

Colonel Commandant. 60th (Royal American) Regiment of Foot.
Interred in Catacomb B (v93 c4), Kensal Green Cemetery, London.
Memorial: Royal Military Chapel, Sandhurst, Berkshire. (Photograph)

IN MEMORY OF / GENERAL THE RIGHT HON. / SIR GEORGE MURRAY / G.C.B. G.C.H. / COLONEL 1ST ROYAL REGT OF FOOT / DIED 28TH JULY 1846 AGED 74. / HE SERVED IN HOLLAND EGYPT SYRIA THE WEST INDIES / DENMARK AND SWEDEN WAS Q. M. G. IN THE PENINSULA / COMMANDER IN CHIEF CANADA / CHIEF OF THE STAFF OF THE ARMY OF OCCUPATION IN FRANCE / COMMANDER OF THE FORCES IN IRELAND / AND TWICE MASTER GENERAL OF THE ORDNANCE / HE WAS GOVERNOR OF THIS COLLEGE / FROM 1819 TO 1824

Memorial: Royal Military Chapel, Wellington Barracks, London. (M.I.) (Destroyed by a Flying Bomb 1944)

"PLACED BY HIS GREAT-NEPHEW, SIR PATRICK KEITH-MURRAY, BART., LATE GRENADIER GUARDS IN MEMORY OF / GENERAL THE RIGHT HON. SIR GEORGE MURRAY, G.C.B., G.C.H., / COLONEL OF THE 42ND OR ROYAL HIGHLAND REGIMENT. / BORN, 1772; DIED, 1849. / 3RD GUARDS, FROM 1790 TO 1813. HE SERVED IN THE CAMPAIGNS OF 1793 AND 1794 IN FLANDERS. AFTER HOLDING VARIOUS APPOINTMENTS ON THE STAFF, HE WAS APPOINTED TO THE QUARTERMASTER-GENERAL'S DEPARTMENT, AND SERVED IN THE EXPEDITION TO HOLLAND, 1799, WHERE HE WAS WOUNDED IN THE ACTION AT THE HELDER; IN THE CAMPAIGN IN EGYPT, 1801; THE EXPEDITIONS TO HANOVER, 1805; AND TO COPENHAGEN, 1807. HE WAS QUARTERMASTER-GENERAL TO THE FORCES UNDER GENERAL SIR JOHN MOORE, K.B., IN SWEDEN AND IN PORTUGAL, AND TO THE ARMY OF THE GREAT DUKE OF WELLINGTON FROM 1809 TILL THE PEACE IN 1814".

Note: Royal Military Chapel inscription incorrectly gives date of death as 1849.

Memorial window: Church of the Ascension, Southam, Gloucestershire. (Photograph)

GENERAL THE RIGHT HONOURABLE SIR GEORGE MURRAY GCB 1846

Ensign 71st Foot 12 Mar 1789. Ensign 34th Foot 6 Jun 1789. Ensign 3rd Foot Guards 7 Jul 1790. Lt and Capt 16 Jan 1794. Capt and Lt Colonel 5 Aug 1799. Bt Colonel 9 Mar 1809. Colonel 60th Foot 9 Aug 1813. Major General 1 Jan 1812. Lt General 27 May 1825. General 23 Nov 1841.

Served in the Peninsula as QMG Aug 1808 – Jan 1809, May 1809 – Dec 1811 and Mar 1813 – Apr 1814. Present at Vimeiro, Corunna (Mentioned in Despatches), Douro, Talavera, Busaco, Massena's retreat (Mentioned in Despatches), Sabugal, Fuentes d'Onoro, Vittoria (Mentioned in Despatches), Pyrenees (Mentioned in Despatches), Nivelle (Mentioned in Despatches), Nive (Mentioned in Despatches), Orthes and Toulouse. Gold Cross for Corunna, Talavera, Busaco, Fuentes d'Onoro, Vittoria, Pyrenees, Nivelle, Nive, Orthes and Toulouse. Served with the Army of Occupation 1815–1818. Quartermaster General in Ireland Jan 1812 – Feb 1813 and returned to the Peninsula Mar 1813. Wellington wrote in 1812 that he had fresh reason every day to regret Murray's departure so was very pleased when Murray returned in March 1813. Murray was able to work well with Wellington and interpret his wishes. He was tactful in handling officers in his department and under him the Quartermaster General's Department ran smoothly.

Also served in Flanders 1793–1795 (present at St Amand, Famars, Valenciennes, Lincelles, Dunkirk and Lannoy), the Irish Rebellion 1798 (ADC to General Campbell), the Helder 1799 (wounded), Egypt 1801 (present at Rosetta, Rhamanie, Cairo and Alexandria), Hanover 1805, Sweden 1808 (QMG), Ireland 1812 – Feb 1813 (QMG), North America 1814–1815 (QMG). Governor of the Royal Military College, Sandhurst 1819–1824. Lt General of Ordnance Mar 1824. GCB 2 Jan 1815. GCH 1816. Grand Cross of Leopold, Grand Cross of St Alexander Newski and Grand Cross of the Red Eagle. Knight Commander of the Tower and Sword. Knight Commander of Maximillian Joseph. Knight Commander of St Henry and 2nd Class of the Crescent. Colonel 72nd Foot 24 Feb 1819. Colonel 42nd Foot 6 Sep 1823. Colonel 1st Foot 29 Dec 1843. MP for Perthshire 1824–1832 and 1834. Secretary of State for the Colonies 1828–1830 during Wellington's Premiership. Governor of Fort George 7 Sep 1829. Master General of Ordnance 1834–1835 and 1841–1846. Colonel Royal Artillery and Colonel Royal Engineers 1842–1846. Died 28 Jul 1846. Author of *Speech on the Roman Catholic Disabilities Relief Bill*, 1829, *Special Instructions for the Officer of the Quartermaster General's Department*. Editor of *Letters and dispatches of John Churchill, 1st Duke of Marlborough from 1702–1712*, 5 vols, 1845.

REFERENCE: *Dictionary of National Biography. Dictionary of Canadian Biography. Dictionary of Australian Biography. Ward, S. P. G., General Sir George Murray, Journal of the Society for Army Historical Research. Vol. 58, No. 236, Winter 1980, pp. 191–208. Royal Military Calendar, Vol. 4, pp. 182–3. Gentleman's Magazine, Oct 1846, pp. 424–6. Annual Register, 1846, Appx, pp. 270–2.*

MURRAY, George Home

Major. 16th (Queen's) Regiment of Light Dragoons.
Memorial monument: Burial Ground, Cawnpore, India. (M.I.)

"THIS MONUMENT IS ERECTED BY THE OFFICERS OF / H. M. 16TH LANCERS, AS A TOKEN OF RESPECT AND / REGARD, TO THE MEMORY OF / BRIGADIER GEORGE HOME MURRAY, C. B. / LIEUTENANT COLONEL OF H. M. 16TH LANCERS / IN WHICH CORPS HE SERVED WITH THE UTMOST / GALLANTRY AND DISTINCTION FOR A PERIOD OF NEARLY / FORTY YEARS. DIED IN COMMAND OF THE CAWNPORE / STATION, THE 15TH DEC 1834, AGED 59 YEARS."

Asst Surgeon 16th Lt Dragoons 1 Feb 1797. Ensign 92nd Foot 2 Oct 1800. Lt 53rd Foot 11 Oct 1800. Lt 16th Lt Dragoons 13 Nov 1802. Capt 6 Nov 1806. Major 18 Feb 1813. Bt Lt Colonel 18 Jun 1815. Lieutenant Colonel 25 May 1822.

Served in the Peninsula Apr 1809 – Aug 1811 and Dec 1811 – Apr 1814. Present at Douro, Talavera, Busaco (wounded), Redinha, Casal Nova, Foz d'Arouce, Sabugal, Llerena (wounded and Mentioned in Despatches), Castrejon, Salamanca, Venta del Pozo (wounded), Vittoria, Nivelle, Adour and Bayonne. Gold medal for Salamanca. CB. Present at Waterloo. Also served in India 1822 in command of the regiment. Present in the Bhurtpoore campaign 1824–1826 where he commanded the cavalry. This was the first action in which the lance was used by a British regiment. He commanded the Cawnpore brigade until his death from cholera 15 Dec 1834.

MURRAY, Hon. Henry

Lieutenant Colonel. 18th Regiment of Light Dragoons.
Memorial tablet: St Mary the Virgin's Church, Wimbledon, London. (Centre of gallery on south side). (Photograph)

SACRED / TO THE HONOURED AND BELOVED MEMORY OF / GENERAL THE HONBLE SIR HENRY / MURRAY K. C. B. / FOURTH SON OF DAVID SECOND EARL OF MANSFIELD BY THE HONBLE LOUISA CATHCART / BORN AUGUST 1784. / SERVED IN NAPLES, SICILY AND CALABRIA IN 1806 – 7 / AND WAS PRESENT AS A. D. C. TO THE HONBLE. GENERAL MEADE /

AT THE ATTACK ON ALEXANDRIA: SIEGE AND STORMING OF ROSETTA, / AND ON EVERY OTHER OCCASION WHEN OUR TROOPS WERE ENGAGED. / SERVED IN WALCHEREN IN 1809 AT THE LANDING, THE SIEGE AND SURRENDER OF FLUSHING, / REMAINING TILL THE ISLAND WAS EVACUATED BY THE BRITISH ARMY. / WENT IN COMMAND OF THE 18TH HUSSARS TO THE PENINSULA JANUARY 1813. / WAS DISABLED WHILE CROSSING THE ESLAR BY HIS HORSE FALLING WITH HIM, / AFTER WHICH HE COMMANDED THE REGIMENT AT THE ACTION OF MORALES DE TORO. / WAS COMPELLED TO BE SOME TIME IN HOSPITAL AT PALENCIA FROM AN ABSCESS ON HIS KNEE, / SERVED IN THE CAMPAIGN OF 1815, INCLUDING THE BATTLE OF QUATRE BRAS, / COMMANDED THE REAR REGIMENT OF THE COLUMN ON THE RETREAT DURING THE FOLLOWING DAY / AND AT THE BATTLE OF WATERLOO, HE LED THE 18TH. HUSSARS IN THE BRILLIANT CHARGE / OF SIR HUSSEY VIVIAN'S BRIGADE AT THE CONCLUSION OF THE ACTION. / COMMANDED THE WESTERN DISTRICT TEN YEARS, HE WAS SIXTY YEARS IN SERVICE. / AFTER A LONG AND SEVERE ILLNESS / BORN WITH THE MOST CHRISTIAN RESIGNATION AND FORTITUDE / HE DIED AT WIMBLEDON ON THE 29TH JULY 1860, DEEPLY LAMENTED BY HIS FAMILY AND / BY ALL THOSE WHO HAD KNOWN HIS EXCELLENT QUALITIES. / THE ABOVE INSCRIPTION IS ON A TABLET MADE BY SPECIAL PERMISSION / IN THE GARRISON CHAPEL OF THE CITADEL IN PLYMOUTH, / NEAR THE MONUMENT OF HIS DISTINGUISHED AND BELOVED SON / CAPTAIN ARTHUR STORMONT MURRAY, / RIFLE BRIGADE, / WHO WAS MORTALLY WOUNDED / WHILST GALLANTLY LEADING HIS COMPANY AGAINST THE WARLIKE BOERS / AT BLOEM PLAATS AT THE CAPE OF GOOD HOPE AUGUST 1848, AGED 28 YEARS. / TO WHOSE MEMORY ALSO THIS IS INSCRIBED BY HIS AFFECTIONATE MOTHER / AUGUST 1862.

The same tablet is also in the Garrison Church of the Citadel of Plymouth, Devon.

Cornet 16th Lt Dragoons 16 May 1800. Lt 40th Foot 11 Jun 1801. Capt 20th Lt Dragoons 24 May 1802. Major 26th Foot 26 Mar 1807. Major 18th Lt Dragoons 2 Aug 1810. Lt Colonel 2 Jan 1812. Bt Colonel 26 Jul 1830. Major General 23 Jun 1838. Lt General 11 Nov 1851. General 6 Feb 1858.

Served in the Peninsula Feb – Aug 1813 and Apr 1814. Present at Morales (severely wounded while in command of the 18th Lt Dragoons). Present at Quatre Bras and Waterloo where he led his regiment in the final charge at the end of the battle. KCB 1860. Also present in Ireland 1805, Sicily 1806, Egypt 1807 (present at Alexandria and Rosetta. ADC to General Meade), Walcheren 1809 (present at the siege of Flushing), Ireland 1842 (in command at Limerick) and Plymouth 1850. Commissioner of the Royal Hospital Chelsea and Royal Military College Sandhurst. Colonel 7th Dragoon Guards 18 Dec 1847. Colonel 14th Lt Dragoons 18 Mar 1853. Served in the army for 60 years.

Reference: Gentleman's Magazine, Sep 1860, p. 329. Annual Register, 1860, Appx, pp. 464–5.

MURRAY, James

Lieutenant. 20th (East Devonshire) Regiment of Foot.

Family Memorial tablet in walled enclosure: Lauder Churchyard, Lauder, Berwickshire, Scotland. (Photograph)

IN MEMORY / OF / JOHN MURRAY OF WOOPLAW / .... / JAMES THEIR ELDEST SON LIEUT 20TH REGT / OF FOOT WHO WAS WOUNDED AT THE BATTLE / OF ORTHES IN FRANCE 27 FEBY/ AND DIED THERE 7 MARCH 1814, / AGED 20 YEARS / ....

Memorial: St Andrew's Church (now Musée Historique), Biarritz, France. (Photograph)

Ensign 19 Dec 1811. Lt 20 Jan 1814.

Served in the Peninsula Nov 1812 – Mar 1814. Present at Vittoria, Pyrenees, Nivelle, Nive and Orthes where he was severely wounded 27 Feb and died of his wounds 7 Mar 1814.

MURRAY James
Sergeant. 61st (South Gloucestershire) Regiment of Foot.
Headstone: Golf Road Cemetery, Dornoch, Sutherland, Scotland. (Photograph)

ERECTED / IN MEMORY OF / JAMES MURRAY LATE OF THE / 61ST REG. WHO DIED AT DORNOCH 30TH MARCH / 1853 AGED 79.

Pte 19 Aug 1803. Cpl 1805. Sgt 1808.
Served in the Peninsula. Present at Toulouse. Discharged 28 Sep 1819. MGS medal for Toulouse.

MURRAY, Sir John
Colonel. 3rd West India Regiment of Foot.
Memorial tablet: St John's Church, St John's Wood, London. (West side of altar). (Photograph). Inscription recorded from memorial inscription.

"IN A VAULT BENEATH THIS CHAPEL / ARE DEPOSITED THE REMAINS OF / LT GEN SIR JOHN MURRAY / OF HILL HEAD N. BRITAIN, BARONET, KNIGHT COMMANDER. / CROSS OF THE GUELPHIC ORDER OF HANOVER / KNIGHT GRAND CROSS OF THE ORDER OF ST JANUARIUS / AND COLONEL OF THE 56TH REGT OF FOOT / WHO DIED AT FRANC FORT-ON-THE MYNE THE 13TH OCT 1827 AGE 59 YEARS. / ………………."

Ensign 3rd Foot Guards 24 Oct 1788. Lt and Capt 25 Apr 1793. Lt Colonel 84th Foot 15 Nov 1794. Bt Colonel 1 Jan 1800. Colonel Royal Regiment of Malta 23 Feb 1808. Major General 30 Oct 1805. Colonel 3rd West India Regt 27 May 1809. Lt General 1 Jan 1812. General 27 May 1825.
Served in the Peninsula Sep 1808 – Jun 1809 and Feb – Jun 1813 (GOC Eastern Spain). Present at Douro, Castalla and Tarragona. KCB and KCH. Also served in Flanders 1793–1794 (present at Valenciennes, Famars, Dunkirk, Maubege and Tournai), Cape of Good Hope 1796, Egypt 1801 (QMG) and India 1803–1805 (present in the Mahratta Wars where he fought against Holkar without much success). Wellesley recommended that Murray should be removed from command. He found him inefficient, lacking in self confidence and not enterprising enough. Murray returned home on notification of his rank of Major General. Also served in Sweden 1808 where he commanded the KGL with Sir John Moore. He served in the Peninsula in 1809 but was again indecisive in his actions and when Beresford was promoted over him he returned to England. Returned to the Peninsula again to the East coast of Spain 1813 and was instructed by Wellington to recapture Tarragona. He failed in the attempt and Wellington recommended a court martial for disobeying his orders. At the subsequent court martial in Jan 1815 Murray blamed the Spaniards for his failure. The prosecution failed to bring a good case against Murray and his lies were believed. He was acquitted on all charges except losing the guns and stores. The Prince Regent awarded Murray a GCH, for it was alleged that he was under his protection. Wellington said of him 'He always appeared to me to want what is better than abilities viz sound sense'. Colonel 56th Foot 31 Mar 1818. MP for Weymouth and Melcombe Regis 1811–1817. Educated at Westminster.
REFERENCE: Dictionary of National Biography. Royal Military Calendar, Vol. 2, pp. 227–9. Trial of Lieutenant General Sir John Murray by a Court Martial held at Winchester …, 1815.

MURRAY, John
Major. 20th (East Devonshire) Regiment of Foot.
Pedestal tomb: Jedburgh Abbey, Roxburghshire, Scotland. (Grave number 189). (Photograph)

TO THE MEMORY / OF MAJOR JOHN MURRAY / OF THE XXTH REGIMENT OF FOOT / WHO DIED ON THE 1ST OF JUNE 1818 / AGED 37 YEARS. / HE COMMENCED HIS MILITARY CAREER / IN HOLLAND IN THE YEAR 1797. / SHARED THE DANGERS AND GLORY / OF THE BRITISH ARMIES IN EGYPT. ITALY, / HOLLAND, PORTUGAL, SPAIN AND FRANCE. / FOUGHT IN THE

BATTLES OF MAIDA, / VIMIERA, CORUNNA, VITTORIA, THE PYRENEES, / NIVELLE AND OTHER BATTLES / AND WAS WOUNDED IN FOUR OF THESE ACTIONS. / HE HAD THE HONOUR OF COMMANDING / THE BRAVE VOLUNTEERS OF THE 4TH DIVISION / AT THE STORMING OF ST SEBASTIAN. / DISTINGUISHED FOR BRAVERY IN THE FIELD / MILD, AFFABLE AND KIND IN PRIVATE LIFE, / HE WAS ESTEEMED BY ALL WITH WHOM HE / SERVED, AND BELOVED BY ALL TO WHOM / HE WAS KNOWN.

Ensign 25th Foot 18 Oct 1797. Lt 20th Foot 12 Nov 1799. Capt 31 Oct 1806. Bt Major 21 Sep 1813. Major 30 Mar 1814.

Served in the Peninsula Aug 1808 – Jan 1809 and Nov 1812 – Apr 1814. Present at Vimeiro, Corunna, Vittoria, Pyrenees, Sorauren (wounded), San Sebastian (wounded leading the storming party, awarded Gold Medal and Bt Majority), Nivelle, Nive, and Orthes (severely wounded and awarded pension of £200 per annum). Also served at the Helder 1799, Egypt 1801, Sicily 1806 (present at Maida) and Walcheren 1809. His early death in 1818 was due to the severe wounds he sustained at Orthes.

MURRAY, John

Commissary General.
Memorial tablet: Ardeley Parish Church, Ardeley, Hertfordshire. (M.I.)

"JOHN MURRAY, COMMISSARY GENERAL TO H. M. FORCES, WHO DIED 30TH NOV 1834, AGED 69."

Comm General 2 Nov 1808.

Served in the Peninsula May 1809 – Jun 1810.

MURRAY, John

Private. 31st (Huntingdonshire) Regiment of Foot.
Tombstone: Cemetery No. 2, Dinapore, India. (M.I.)

"GLORIA IN EXCELSIS DEO / SACRED / TO THE / MEMORY OF JOHN MURRAY PRIVATE IN Hs Ms 31ST / REGT. A NATIVE OF WOODFORD IN THE / COUNTY OF GALWAY IRELAND / WHO AFTER A FAITHFUL PERFORMANCE OF HIS DUTY FOR A PERIOD OF 29 YEARS IN / THE ABOVE REGT WITH WHICH HE SERVED / DURING THE MEMORABLE WAR ON THE PENINSULA DEPARTED THIS LIFE / AT DINAPORE ON THE 15TH DAY OF NOVEMBER / 1836 IN THE 53RD YEAR OF HIS AGE. / DEEPLY REGRETTED BY HIS FRIENDS AND / ACQUAINTANCES AND LEAVING AN AFFECTIONATE WIFE AND SON TO DEPLORE THEIR LOSS. / THIS MONUMENT IS ERECTED BY A FEW / FRIENDS AS A MARK OF THEIR ESTEEM / REQUIESCANT IN PACE. AMEN."

Pte 1807.

Served in the Peninsula 1809 – Apr 1814.
Present at Talavera, Busaco, first siege of Badajoz, Albuera, Vittoria, Pyrenees, Nivelle, Nive, Garris, Orthes, Aire and Toulouse. Also served in India 1824 until his death in Nov 1836. Served for 29 years in the regiment.

MURRAY, Thomas

Lieutenant. 91st Regiment of Foot.
Headstone: St Mary the Virgin's Churchyard, Carisbrooke, Isle of Wight. (Section B. Grave number 274). Seriously eroded and inscription recorded from memorial inscription. (Photograph)

"FRANCES MURRAY .... ALSO CAPT THOMAS MURRAY OF THE 91ST REGT,

HUSBAND OF THE ABOVE, DIED ON FOREIGN SERVICE IN JAMAICA, 5 JAN 1826, AGED 46 YEARS."

Ensign 15 May 1808. Lt 11 Jul 1811. Capt 30 Nov 1824.

Served in the Peninsula Oct 1812 – Apr 1814. Present at Pyrenees, Nivelle, Nive, Orthes and Toulouse. Present at Waterloo in reserve at Hal, the siege of Cambri and with the Army of Occupation. Also served in the West Indies where he died in Jamaica in 1826.

MURRAY, William

Private. 92nd (Highland) Regiment of Foot.
Family monument: Marnoch Old Kirkyard, near Auchintoul, Aberdeenshire, Scotland. (Photograph)

.... / ALSO IN MEMORY OF / HIS PARENTS / WILLIAM MURRAY / OF THE 92ND GORDON HIGHLANDERS / WHO FOUGHT ALL THROUGH / THE PENINSULAR WAR / AGED 87 YEARS. / ALSO OF HIS WIFE / MARGARET WHITE / WHO WAS WITH HIM ALL THE TIME / AND WHO DIED AT AUCHINGOUL / AGED 96 YEARS.

Pte 1796.

Served in the Peninsula with 92nd Foot Aug 1808 – Jan 1809 and Oct 1810 – Apr 1814. Present at Corunna and Fuentes d'Onoro. Also served in Egypt 1801. MGS medal for Egypt, Corunna and Fuentes d'Onoro. Accompanied by his wife Margaret who survived all the hardships of the campaigns and lived to be 96. Discharged 18 Aug 1815 aged 46 years after 19 years in the army he was unfit for further service.

MUTER, Joseph

Lieutenant Colonel. 6th (Inniskilling) Regiment of Dragoons.
Family monument: Nether Kirkyard, St Cyrus, near Montrose, Kincardineshire, Scotland. (Kirkyard is located at foot of the cliffs along the shoreline of the St Cyrus Nature Reserve). (Photograph)

SACRED TO THE MEMORY / OF / SIR JOSEPH STRATON OF KIRKSIDE / COMPANION OF THE BATH / KNIGHT GUELPHIC ORDER OF HANOVER, AND OF THE ORDER OF ST VLADIMIR OF RUSSIA. / LIEUT.-GENERAL IN THE BRITISH ARMY / YOUNGEST SON OF / WILLIAM MUTER, ESQ., OF ANNFIELD, FIFESHIRE, AND MRS. JANET STRATON / OF KIRKSIDE, KINCARDINESHIRE. / THIS BRAVE AND ACCOMPLISHED OFFICER ENTERED THE ARMY IN EARLY LIFE / AND SERVED WITH DISTINGUISHED HONOUR DURING THE PENINSULAR WAR / AND AT WATERLOO, UNDER FIELD MARSHAL / THE DUKE OF WELLINGTON. / HE COMMANDED HIS OWN REGIMENT OF THE 6TH DRAGOONS UNTIL THE FALL OF THE GALLANT PONSONBY, / TO WHOSE BRIGADE HE BELONGED, / WHEN THE COMMAND OF THE BRIGADE DEVOLVED UPON HIM. / TOWARDS THE CLOSE OF THE ACTION SIR JOSEPH STRATON WAS WOUNDED / AND UPON THE TERMINATION OF THE WAR, AS A REWARD OF HIS SERVICES / HE HAD VARIOUS MILITARY HONOURS CONFERRED UPON HIM. / HE DIED COLONEL OF THE ENNISKILLEN DRAGOONS, / AT LONDON, 23D OCT., MDCCCXL, IN THE LXIII YEAR OF HIS AGE, / AND IS INTERRED HERE BY HIS OWN DESIRE.

Cornet 2nd Dragoon Guards Dec 1794. Lt 2 Dec 1795. Capt 13th Lt Dragoons 2 Mar 1797. Major 14 Aug 1801. Bt Lt Colonel 25 Apr 1808. Lt Colonel 6th Lt Dragoons 4 Jun 1813. Bt Colonel 4 Jun 1814. Major General 27 May 1825. Lt General 28 Jun 1838.

Served in the Peninsula with the 13th Lt Dragoons Apr 1810 – Sep 1812. Present at Campo Mayor, Albuera, Usagre, Arroyo dos Molinos and Alba de Tormes. Present at Waterloo in command of the Inniskillings where he was wounded. When Sir William Ponsonby was killed, Joseph Muter took command of the Union Brigade (1st, 2nd and 6th Dragoons). CB, KCH and Order of St Vladimir of Russia. Also served in Ireland 1819. Colonel 8th Lt Dragoons 24 Aug 1839. Colonel 6th Lt Dragoons 30 Apr 1840. Took the

name of Straton in 1810 after inheriting the property of his aunt, Miss Straton of Kirkside, Montrose. On his death 23 Oct 1840 he left £70,000 to Edinburgh University.
REFERENCE: *Gentleman's Magazine, May 1841, p. 537. (Under Straton). Annual Register, 1841, Appx, p. 173. (Under Straton)*

MUTTLEBURY, George
Major. 69th (South Lincolnshire) Regiment of Foot.
Ledger stone: Kensal Green Cemetery, London. (11245/49/3). Inscription illegible. (Photograph)

Ensign 55th Foot Jan 1795. Lt 3 Sep 1795. Capt 21 Feb 1798. Capt 69th Foot 5 Dec 1802. Bt Major 25 Jul 1810. Major 69th Foot 28 Nov 1811. Bt Lt Colonel 17 Mar 1814. Lt Colonel 10 Aug 1815.

Present at Quatre Bras and Waterloo. When Colonel Morice was killed at Quatre Bras with many of his men, George Muttlebury took command of the rest of the regiment. They fought at Waterloo with the depleted ranks of the 33rd Foot. CB for Waterloo. Re-appointed Lt Colonel of the 69th Foot in 1817. Also served in Flanders 1794–1795 (present at Nimwegen), West Indies 1796 (present at the Capture of St Lucia), the Helder 1799, West Indies 1800 (present at Dominica), India 1804–1806, the Netherlands 1813–1814 (present at Antwerp, Bergen-op-Zoom where he was Mentioned in General Graham's Despatch and awarded a Bt Lt Colonelcy) and India 1818–1821 where he was present in Madras with the 69th Foot (in command of the provinces of Malabar and Canara, but ill health forced him home in 1821). Retired in 1826. Died 16 Jan 1854.
REFERENCE: *United Service Magazine, Feb 1854, pp. 315–16. Annual Register, 1854, Appx, pp. 261–2.*

MYDDLETON, Richard Wharton
Lieutenant. 12th (East Suffolk) Regiment of Foot.
Obelisk: In a garden in Rookery Lane, Leasingham, Lincolnshire. (Formerly part of the grounds of Leasingham Hall). (Photograph)

RICHARD WHARTON / MYDDLETON / BORN 29 JANUARY 1795 / DIED OCTOBER 7TH 1885

IN MEMORY OF / RICHARD WHARTON MYDDLETON / AND HIS WIFE / FRANCES PENELOPE / MARRIED 15 DECEMBER 1823 / ………………..

Lt 12th Foot 18 Nov 1813. Capt 71st Foot 31 Dec 1818. Major 28 Dec 1832.

Served with the Army of Occupation until 1818. Also served in Canada 1825–1832 and Bermuda 1832–1834.
Note: An obelisk by the front door of Leasingham Hall commemorates some box wood trees said to have been brought back from Hougoumont.
REFERENCE: *Myddleton, Mrs Wharton, Reminiscences of a military life, Sleaford, 1879, privately printed.*

MYERS, Arthur
Lieutenant and Adjutant. 7th (Queen's Own) Regiment of Light Dragoons.
Named on the Regimental Memorial: St Joseph's Church, Waterloo. (Photograph)
Memorial tablet: St Joseph's Church, Waterloo. (Photograph)

SACRED / TO THE MEMORY / OF / MAJOR EDWARD HODGE / AND LIEUT. ARTHUR MYERS / OF THE / 7TH REGIMENT OF HUSSARS / WHO / WERE KILLED ON THE 17TH OF JUNE 1815. / THIS MONUMENT IS ERECTED / BY THEIR BROTHER OFFICERS / AS A TOKEN OF THEIR RESPECT / AND ESTEEM.

Cornet 29 Sep 1808. Adjutant 28 Mar 1809. Lt 24 May 1810.

Served in the Peninsula Aug 1813 – Apr 1814. Present at Orthes and Toulouse. Present at Waterloo where he was killed in the cavalry action at Genappe, 17 Jun 1815.

MYERS, John

Lieutenant. 57th (West Middlesex) Regiment of Foot.
Named on the Memorial: St Andrew's Church (now Musée Historique), Biarritz, France. (Photograph)

Ensign 13 Oct 1808. Lt 24 May 1811.

Served in the Peninsula Apr 1810 – Aug 1811 and Apr 1812 – Dec 1813. Present at the first siege of Badajoz, Albuera (wounded), Vittoria, Pyrenees, Nivelle and Nive where he was severely wounded 13 Dec 1813 and died of his wounds 23 Jan 1814.

MYERS, Sir William James

Lieutenant Colonel. 7th (Royal Fusiliers) Regiment of Foot.
Memorial tablet: St Mary's Church, Cheltenham, Gloucestershire. (Photograph)

ALBUERA / .... / HIS AFFLICTED FAMILY FOUND THEIR ONLY CONSOLATION FOR HIS LOSS / IN THE OPENING VIRTUES OF HIS SON / LIEUTENANT COLONEL SIR WILLIAM MYERS BARONET; / BUT OF HIM ALSO, / IT PLEASED THE ALMIGHTY TO DEPRIVE THEM, ON THE 16TH OF MAY 1811: / HE FELL WHEN LEADING ON / THE BRITISH FUSILEER BRIGADE AT THE BATTLE OF ALBUERA. / IN THE 27TH YEAR OF HIS AGE; / AND WITH HIM EXPIRED THE LAST HOPE OF HIS FAMILY, / WHOSE PRIDE AND AFFECTION WERE EQUALLY GRATIFIED BY HIS / SHORT BUT BRILLIANT CAREER. / THIS MONUMENT IS ERECTED BY A MOTHER, WHOM HIS DEATH HAS / BEREFT OF ALL EARTHLY CONSOLATION: / AND BY A SISTER, WHO THUS DEPRIVED OF HER GUIDE PROTECTOR, & FRIEND / AWAITS WITH ANXIOUS HOPE AND RESIGNATION / THE MOMENT OF THEIR ETERNAL REUNION.

Memorial: St Paul's, London. (North transept). (Photograph)

ERECTED AT THE PUBLIC EXPENSE TO THE MEMORY OF / LIEUTENANT COLONEL SIR WILLIAM MYERS, BART / WHO FELL GLORIOUSLY IN THE BATTLE OF ALBUERA, MAY 16TH 1811, / AGED 27 YEARS. / HIS ILLUSTRIOUS COMMANDER, THE DUKE OF WELLINGTON, BORE THIS HONORABLE TESTIMONY / TO HIS SERVICES AND ABILITIES, / IN A LETTER TO LADY MYERS, WRITTEN FROM ELVAS, MAY 20TH 1811. / "IT WILL BE SOME CONSOLATION TO YOU TO KNOW THAT YOUR SON FELL IN ACTION," / "IN WHICH, IF POSSIBLE, THE BRITISH TROOPS SURPASSED ALL THEIR FORMER DEEDS, AND AT" / "THE HEAD OF THE FUSILEER BRIGADE, TO WHICH A GREAT PART OF THE FINAL SUCCESS" / "OF THE DAY WAS TO BE ATTRIBUTED. AS AN OFFICER HE HAD ALREADY BEEN HIGHLY" / "DISTINGUISHED; AND, IF PROVIDENCE HAD PROLONGED HIS LIFE, HE PROMISED TO BECOME" / "ONE OF THE BRIGHTEST ORNAMENTS TO HIS PROFESSION, AND AN HONOUR TO HIS COUNTRY."

Capt Independent Company 18 Dec 1794. Lt and Capt Coldstream Guards 11 Jan 1800. Major 15th Foot 6 May 1802. Bt Lt Colonel 14 May 1802. Lt Colonel 62nd Foot 10 Jul 1802. Lt Colonel 7th Foot 15 Aug 1804.

Served in the Peninsula with 2/7th Apr 1809 – Oct 1810 and 1/7th Nov 1810 – Feb 1811. O/c 1 Brigade 4th Division Jul 1808 – Jan 1810 and 2 Brigade 4th Division Jan – May 1811. Present at Douro, Talavera (Mentioned in Despatches), Busaco, Torres Vedras, Pombal, Condeixa, Olivencia and Albuera where he commanded the Fusilier Brigade comprising the 7th and 23rd Regiments. Severely wounded 16 May and died 17 May 1811 at Valverde. Gold Medal for Talavera and Albuera. Also served in Egypt 1801 with the Coldstream Guards (wounded at Aboukir Bay).
Reference: Gentleman's Magazine, Jul 1811, p. 88.

MYLES, John
Lieutenant and Adjutant. 50th (West Kent) Regiment of Foot.
Named on the Memorial: St Andrew's Church (now Musée Historique), Biarritz, France. (Photograph)

Ensign and Adjt 17 Dec 1807. Lt 3 May 1809.

Served in the Peninsula Sep 1810 – Mar 1814. Present at Fuentes d'Onoro, Arroyo dos Molinos, Almarez, Alba de Tormes, Vittoria, Pyrenees (wounded 30 Jul 1813). Nivelle, Nive and Garris where he was severely wounded 13 Feb and died from his wounds 16 Mar 1814.

NANTES, Richard
Lieutenant. 7th (Royal Fusiliers) Regiment of Foot.
Buried in St George's Chapel, Windsor, Berkshire.

Lt 19 Oct 1809.

Served in the Peninsula with 1/7th Sep 1811 – Sep 1812 and Nov 1813 – Apr 1814. Present at Ciudad Rodrigo, Castrejon (wounded), Salamanca (severely wounded), Nive (wounded accidently by one of his own men), Orthes (wounded) and Toulouse. Half pay Dec 1814. MGS medal for Ciudad Rodrigo, Salamanca, Nive, Orthes and Toulouse. Military Knight of Windsor 5 Oct 1844. Died at Windsor 4 Apr 1871.

NAPIER, Hon. Charles
Lieutenant. 71st (Highland Light Infantry) Regiment of Foot.
Low monument: St George's Churchyard, Ruishton, near Taunton, Somerset. (Photograph)

SACRED TO THE MEMORY OF / MAJOR THE HONOURABLE CHARLES NAPIER / OF WOODLANDS IN THIS PARISH / THIRD SON OF FRANCIS SEVENTH LORD NAPIER. / HE SERVED HIS COUNTRY IN THE PENINSULAR WAR / AND WAS PRESENT AT THE BATTLES OF VITTORIA, NIVELLE AND NIVE. / THIS MEMORIAL IS ERECTED BY HIS WIFE AND CHILDREN / IN LOVING DEVOTION TO HIS MEMORY / BORN 24TH OCTOBER 1794 / DIED 15TH DECEMBER 1874

Ensign 16 Jan 1812. Lt 24 Jun 1813. Lt 73rd Foot 21 Mar 1816. Lt 88th Foot 20 May 1819. Capt 22 Feb 1821. Bt Major 17 Jun 1826.

Served in the Peninsula Apr 1813 – Mar 1814. Present at Vittoria, Nivelle and Nive. Half pay 17 Jun 1826. MGS medal for Vittoria, Nivelle and Nive. Cousin of Lt Colonel Charles James Napier 50th Foot, Capt and Lt Colonel George Thomas Napier 3rd Foot Guards and Major William Francis Patrick Napier 43rd Foot.

NAPIER, Charles James
Lieutenant Colonel. 50th (West Kent) Regiment of Foot.
Low monument. Royal Garrison Church Graveyard, Portsmouth, Hampshire. (Outside west entrance). (Photograph)

CHARLES JAMES NAPIER / BORN AUGUST 1782 / HYDERABAD / MEEANEE / CORUNNA / PENINSULA / DIED 29TH AUGUST 1853.

Brass Memorial tablet (1): Royal Garrison Church, Portsmouth, Hampshire. (Photograph)

BENEATH THIS TABLET / LIES THE BODY OF / GENERAL SIR CHARLES NAPIER, G.C.B. / 1782–1853 / CONQUEROR OF SCINDE.

Brass Memorial tablet (2): Royal Garrison Church, Portsmouth, Hampshire. (Back of a choir stall). (Photograph)

LIEUT GEN SIR CHARLES / JAMES NAPIER G.C.B. / DIED AUGUST 29TH 1853 / AGED 71 DD HIS / WIDOW AND NEPHEW / MAJ GEN W.C.E. NAPIER.

Statue: St Paul's Cathedral, London. (South side of Nelson's tomb). (Photograph)

CHARLES JAMES NAPIER, / A PRESCIENT GENERAL / A BENEFICENT GOVERNOR / A JUST MAN / BORN 1782 DIED 1853

Statue: Trafalgar Square, London. (Photograph)

CHARLES JAMES NAPIER / GENERAL / BORN / MDCCLXXXII / DIED / MDCCCLIII / ERECTED BY PUBLIC SUBSCRIPTION / THE MOST NUMEROUS CONTRIBUTORS / BEING PRIVATE SOLDIERS

Studded leather shield above an engraved brass plate: Church of the Ascension, Southam, near Cheltenham, Gloucestershire. (Photograph)

IN MEMORY OF GENERAL / SIR CHARLES NAPIER

Ensign 33rd Foot 31 Jan 1794. Lt 89th Foot 8 May 1794. Lt 68th Foot 1 Mar 1800. Lt 95th Foot 25 Dec 1800. Capt Royal Staff Corps 12 Dec 1803. Major Cape Regt 29 May 1806. Major 50th Foot 6 Nov 1806. Lt Colonel 102nd Foot 27 Jun 1811. Lt Colonel 50th Foot 2 Sep 1813. Bt Colonel 27 May 1825. Major General 10 Jan 1837. Lt General 9 Nov 1846.

Served in the Peninsula Sep 1808 – Mar 1809 and Aug 1809 – Jul 1811. Present at Corunna (severely wounded), Coa (ADC to Robert Crauford), Busaco (severely wounded), Fuentes d'Onoro and second siege of Badajoz. Severely wounded at Corunna and was prisoner of war until March 1809 when he was set free on condition that he did not fight again until an exchange had taken place. While he was in England waiting to fight again he wrote several books including *Military Law*, *Colonies* and *An Essay on the State of Ireland*. It was not until 1810 that he volunteered for the Light Brigade in which his brothers were serving – William in the 43rd and George in the 52nd. Awarded pension of £300 per annum for wounds from Corunna and Busaco. Gold Medal for Corunna. MGS medal for Busaco and Fuentes d'Onoro. Did not serve at Waterloo but was present at the siege of Cambrai and the Capture of Paris as a Volunteer. Also served in Ireland 1798 (present in the Irish Rebellion, ADC to Sir James Duff), North America 1813, Ionian Islands (Inspecting Field Officer 30 Jul 1818–1830) and India (Commander of the Army at Bombay 1841). After the disaster in Afghanistan 1841–1842 the Amirs in Scinde Province thought they could defeat the British. Napier, despite being heavily outnumbered, 2,800 men against 22,000 was victorious at Meeanee and Hyderabad and eventually controlled the whole province of Scinde. Governor of Scinde 1843. His administration of the Province was very successful but the East India Company did not like his methods and for four years Napier and the Board of Directors argued with each other. Returned to England in 1847. Wellington asked him to return in 1848 but when he got there the Sikh War was over and he finally returned to England in 1851. Was extremely popular with all ranks in the army. One of the first Generals to mention other ranks for their bravery as well as officers in his despatches. The statue in Trafalgar Square was erected mainly from contributions by private soldiers. KCB 1838. Colonel 22nd Foot 21 Nov 1843. GCB. Brother of Capt and Lt Colonel George Thomas Napier 3rd Foot Guards, Major William Francis Patrick Napier 43rd Foot and cousin of Lt the Hon. Charles Napier 71st Foot.

Reference: Dictionary of National Biography. Napier, William F. P., Life and Opinions of General Sir Charles James Napier, 2nd edn 1857, 4 vols, reprint 2011. Napier, William Francis Patrick, Conquest of

Scinde, with some introductory passages on the life of Major General Sir Charles James Napier, 1845, 2nd edn 1857. Gentleman's Magazine, Oct 1853, pp. 410–16. Annual Register, 1853, Appx, pp. 249–52.

NAPIER, George Thomas

Captain and Lieutenant Colonel. 3rd Regiment of Foot Guards.

Memorial tablet: Holy Trinity Church, Geneva, Switzerland. (East wall of south transept). (Photograph)

SACRED / TO THE MEMORY OF / GENERAL / SIR GEORGE THOMAS NAPIER, / KNIGHT COMMANDER OF THE BATH. / COLONEL / 1ST WEST INDIA REGIMENT. / BORN JUNE 30TH 1784. / DIED AT GENEVA, / SEPTEMBER 8TH 1855. / ERECTED / BY HIS SORROWING FAMILY.

Brass Memorial tablet: Royal Garrison Church, Portsmouth, Hampshire. (Photograph)

LIEUT. GENERAL SIR / GEORGE T. NAPIER K:C:B. / DIED SEP 8 1855. AGED 71 / D.D. HIS CHILDREN.

Cornet 24th Dragoons 25 Jan 1800. Lt 46th Foot 18 Jun 1800. Lt 52nd Foot 1 Dec 1802. Capt 5 Jan 1804. Bt Major 30 May 1811. Major 52nd Foot 27 Jun 1811. Bt Lt Colonel 6 Feb 1812. Lt Colonel 71st Foot 24 Mar 1814. Capt and Lt Colonel 3rd Foot Guards 25 Jul 1814. Bt Colonel 27 May 1825. Major General 10 Jan 1837. Lt General 9 Nov 1846. General 20 Jun 1854.

Served in the Peninsula Aug 1808 – Jan 1809 (ADC to Sir John Moore Nov 1808 – Jan 1809), Jul 1809 – Apr 1812 and Jan – Apr 1814. Present at Lugo, Corunna, Coa, Busaco (wounded), Pombal, Redinha, Casal Nova (severely wounded – arm broken and awarded Bt Majority), Ciudad Rodrigo (wounded in the same arm in the trenches and when he led a storming party at the assault was so severely wounded that his arm had to be amputated. Mentioned in Despatches, awarded Bt Lt Colonelcy and pension of £200 per annum). Returned home because of the wound but went back to the Peninsula in Jan 1814 and was present at Orthes, Tarbes and Toulouse (in command of 71st Foot). Also served in Sicily 1806–1807, the Baltic 1808 and Martinique Feb 1809. Gold Medal for Ciudad Rodrigo. MGS medal for Corunna, Martinique, Busaco, Orthes and Toulouse. KCB. Retired on half pay 19 Apr 1821. Governor of the Cape of Good Hope 1837–1844 where he improved conditions by introducing a new system of district schools, local government, abolition of internal taxes, enforced abolition of slavery, road improvements, opened up the country to trade and commerce by various public works which ensured employment. These improvements took place as there were no wars with the Kaffirs for the seven years of his Governorship. Lived in Europe, mainly in Nice from 1844 until his death in Geneva in 1855. Brother of Lt Colonel Charles James Napier 50th Foot, Major William Francis Patrick Napier 43rd Foot and cousin of Lt the Hon. Charles Napier 71st Foot.

REFERENCE: *Napier, George T., Passages in the early military life of General Sir George T. Napier, KCB., written by himself, 1884. Dictionary of National Biography. Gentleman's Magazine, Oct 1855, pp. 429–30. Annual Register, 1855, Appx, p. 306. United Service Magazine, Oct 1855, pp. 330–1.*

NAPIER, William Francis Patrick

Major 43rd (Monmouthshire) Light Infantry Regiment of Foot.

Low monument: West Norwood Cemetery, London. Inscription not recorded. (Photograph)

Memorial statue: St Paul's Cathedral, London. (Crypt south side). (Photograph)

GENERAL / WILLIAM FRANCIS PATRICK / NAPIER / HISTORIAN OF THE / PENINSULAR WAR / BORN 1785 DIED 1860

Brass Memorial tablet: Royal Garrison Church, Portsmouth, Hampshire. (Back of a choir stall). (Photograph)

GENERAL SIR WILLIAM / F. P. NAPIER K.C.B. / DIED FEB 12 1860 / AGED 74. DD HIS / FOUR DAUGHTERS.

Ensign Royal Irish Artillery 14 Jun 1800. Lt 62nd Foot 18 Apr 1801. Cornet Royal Regiment of Horse Guards 23 Aug 1803. Lt 52nd Foot 24 Dec 1803. Capt 43rd Foot 11 Aug 1804. Bt Major 30 May 1811. Major 14 May 1812. Bt Lt Colonel 22 Nov 1813. Bt Colonel 22 Jul 1830. Major General 23 Nov 1841. Lt General 11 Nov 1851. General 17 Oct 1859.

Served in the Peninsula with 1/43rd Oct 1808 – Jan 1809, Jul 1809 – Aug 1811, Apr 1812 – Feb 1813 and Aug 1813 – Mar 1814 (Brigade Major 1 Brigade Light Division Mar – Aug 1811). Present at Vigo, Coa (severely wounded), Busaco, Pombal, Redinha, Casal Nova (severely wounded), Foz d'Arouce, Fuentes d'Onoro, Salamanca, San Munos, Vera, Bidassoa, Nivelle, Nive (wounded at Arcangues) and Orthes. Served with the Army of Occupation 1815. Also served at Copenhagen 1807 (present at Kiöge). Gold Medal for Salamanca, Nivelle and Nive. MGS medal for Busaco, Fuentes d'Onoro and Orthes. KCB. Colonel 27th Foot 5 Jul 1848. Colonel 22nd Foot 18 Sep 1853. Half pay 17 Jun 1819 and devoted his life to writing and to his family. Lt Governor of Guernsey Feb 1842. Wrote: *History of the War in the Peninsula and in the south of France from the year 1807 to the year 1814, 6 volumes, 1828–1840* and *Conquest of Scinde, 1845*. This book was written in reply to criticism of his brother Charles's actions in Scinde province. Died 10 Feb 1860. Brother of Lt Colonel Charles James Napier 50th Foot, Capt and Lt Colonel George Thomas Napier 3rd Foot Guards and cousin of Lt the Hon. Charles Napier 71st Foot.

REFERENCE: Dictionary of National Biography. Bruce, H. A., ed., Life of General Sir William Napier, 2 vols, 1864. Gentleman's Magazine, Apr 1860, pp. 404–5. Annual Register, 1860, Appx, pp. 465–70.

NAPPER, Alexander

Lieutenant. 81st Regiment of Foot.
Memorial tablet: St Mary's Church, New Ross, County Wexford, Ireland. (Photograph)

LIEUTENANT ALEXANDER NAPPER / LATE OF H. M. 81ST REGIMENT / DEPARTED THIS LIFE ON THE 3RD OF JUNE 1843 / AGED 54 YEARS. / THIS TABLET WAS ERECTED BY / LIEUT ROBERT ALEXANDER NAPPER, / OF THE 55TH REGT BENGAL NATIVE INFANTRY, / AS A TRIBUTE TO THE MEMORY OF / AN AFFECTIONATE FATHER. / (VERSE)

Wexford Militia. Ensign 87th Foot 26 Oct 1807. Lt 16 Mar 1809. Lt 81st Foot 24 Jan 1811.

Served in the Peninsula Jun 1809 – Oct 1810. Present at Talavera and Cadiz. Half pay 11 Jul 1816.

NAPPER, George

Assistant Surgeon. Royal Artillery.
Named on the Regimental Memorial: St Nicholas's Church, Plumstead, Kent. (No longer extant. Destroyed by a Flying Bomb in the Second World War)

2nd Asst Surgeon 18 Feb 1807. Asst Surgeon 11 Nov 1811.

Served in the Peninsula Feb 1813 – Apr 1814 with 'F' Troop R.H.A. Present at Vittoria, San Sebastian, Bidassoa, Nivelle, Nive, Adour and Bayonne. Died at Woolwich 4 Oct 1823.

NASH, James

Captain. 26th (Cameronian) Regiment of Foot.
Memorial: St John's Church, Forfar, Angus, Scotland. (M.I.)

"CAPT JAMES NASH LATE 26TH REGIMENT OF FOOT. DIED 11 MAY 1836."

Ensign 14 May 1804. Lt 31 Jul 1805. Adjutant 14 May 1806. Capt 2 Jan 1812.

Served in the Peninsula Oct 1808 – Jan 1809 and Jul 1811 – Jun 1812. Present at Corunna. Also served at Walcheren 1809 and Gibraltar Jun 1812 – Apr 1814. There were so many sick in the regiment from Walcheren fever that the regiment was removed from the Peninsula so that they did not infect the other regiments. Half pay 1814.

NAYLOR, James Franklin
Captain. 1st (Kings) Dragoon Guards.
Ledger stone: Kensal Green Cemetery, London. (11607/74/2). Inscription illegible. (Photograph)

Ensign Essex Militia 16 Jun 1797. Lt 26 May 1798. Ensign 62nd Foot 27 Aug 1799. Cornet 1st Dragoon Guards 19 Oct 1799. Lt 4 Jun 1803. Capt 15 May 1806. Bt Major 1819.

Present at Quatre Bras where he covered the retreat of the infantry and at Waterloo (wounded). Toward evening when so many officers of the regiment had been killed or severely wounded, the command of the Household Brigade in the field fell on Naylor as the most senior officer, but at 7pm Naylor himself was wounded and had to leave the field. Served with the Army of Occupation until May 1816. Retired in 1826. Published *Sketch book of Sword positions,* 1814. Died 1854.
REFERENCE: *Glover, Gareth, ed., The Waterloo Diary of Captain James Naylor 1st Dragoon Guards, 1815–16, 2008.*

NEAL, William
Private. 95th Regiment of Foot.
Memorial Tablet: St James's Church, Pulloxhill, Bedfordshire. (Photograph)

IN MEMORY OF GEORGE GUDGIN, / DIED 25 APRIL 1841, AGED 47 AND / WILLIAM NEAL, DIED 25TH JANRY 1858, / AGED 63 WHO FOUGHT AT WATERLOO WHERE / THE LATTER WAS SEVERELY WOUNDED. / THEIR BODIES LIE IN THIS CHURCHYARD.

Pte 1 Apr 1813.

Served in the Peninsula 1813 – Apr 1814. Present at Nivelle, Nive, Orthes and Toulouse. Present at Waterloo (severely wounded) and with the Army of Occupation. Also served in Malta and the Ionian Islands. Discharged 14 Nov 1832. MGS medal for Nivelle, Nive, Orthes and Toulouse.

NEILLEY, William
Lieutenant. 40th (2nd Somersetshire) Regiment of Foot.
Headstone above Square Slab: Windermere Cemetery, Rostella, Tasmania, Australia. (Photograph)

SACRED TO THE MEMORY OF / WILLIAM NEILLEY ESQ J. P. FORMERLY CAPTAIN OF / H. M. XLTH & LX 3RD REGIMENTS WHO DEPARTED THIS / LIFE AT ROSTELLA 5TH FEB 1864 A. D. AGED 74 / YEARS / ....

Ensign 20 Apr 1809. Lt 26 Sep 1811. Adjt 5 Dec 1821. Capt 63rd Foot 26 Nov 1828.

Served in the Peninsula Jul 1811 – Apr 1814. Present at Ciudad Rodrigo, Badajoz, Castrejon, Salamanca, Vittoria, Pyrenees, Nivelle, Nive, Orthes and Toulouse. Present at Waterloo. Also served in Australia 1824–1828 (in command of the guard on a convict ship). Left the 63rd Foot 1833 and settled in Australia. MGS medal for Ciudad Rodrigo, Badajoz, Salamanca, Vittoria, Pyrenees, Nivelle, Nive, Orthes and Toulouse.
REFERENCE: *Doring, Margaret J., Notes on Captain Neilley of the 40th Regiment of Foot (1791–1864) and his book on military field exercises, 2006.*

NELSON, Robert
Sergeant Major. 12th (Prince of Wales's) Regiment of Light Dragoons.
Named on the Regimental Memorial: St Joseph's Church, Waterloo. (Photograph)

Present at Waterloo where he was killed.

NESHAM, Matthew
Sergeant. 43rd (Monmouthshire) Light Infantry Regiment of Foot.
Headstone: Staindrop Cemetery, County Durham. (Photograph)

IN / MEMORY OF / MATTHEW NESHAM, OF THIS PARISH / OF STAINDROP, WHO DEPARTED THIS LIFE / ON THE 21ST DAY OF MARCH 1871. / AGED 76 YEARS. / HE WAS FORMERLY SERGEANT IN THE 43RD REGT. / OF LIGHT INFANTRY, IN WHICH HE SERVED FOR / NEARLY SIXTEEN YEARS IN THE PENINSULA, / IN FRANCE, AND IN NORTH AMERICA. HE WAS / AT THE BATTLE OF TOULOUSE, AND AT THE / ATTACK ON NEW ORLEANS, ALSO / AT THE CAPTURE OF PARIS IN 1815.

Served in the Peninsula 1808 – Apr 1814. Present at Toulouse, the Capture of Paris 1815 and with the Army of Occupation. Also served in North America 1814–1815 (present at New Orleans). Died 21 Mar 1871 aged 76.
REFERENCE: *Oxfordshire and Buckinghamshire Light Infantry Chronicle, 1898, p. 284.*

NEVILLE, Park Percy
Lieutenant. 30th (Cambridgeshire) Regiment of Foot.
Buried in St George's Chapel, Windsor, Berkshire. (Burial record)

Ensign 29 Mar 1810. Lt 17 Jul 1811. Lt 13th Lt Dragoons 9 Nov 1826. Lt 26th Foot 14 Oct 1830. Capt 63rd Foot 27 Nov 1835. Major 16 Jul 1841. Bt Lt Colonel 11 Nov 1851.

Served in the Peninsula Jul 1810 – May 1813. Present at Cadiz, Sabugal, Fuentes d'Onoro, Barba del Puerco, Ciudad Rodrigo (as Assistant Engineer), Badajoz (wounded), Salamanca and Burgos (again as Assistant Engineer where he was severely wounded 4 Oct 1812). Present in the Waterloo campaign, where owing to his previous engineering exploits he was sent on special duty to the French frontier. Also served in the Netherlands 1814–1815 (present at Antwerp and Bergen-op-Zoom) and India during the Mahratta Wars 1817–1818 (present at Maheidpore and siege of Asseerghur). Decorated by the Nizam for the capture of a band of Pindarries. Served in India for 22 years and for part of the time commanded the left wing of the 63rd Foot. During his time in India he volunteered for the appointment of acting engineer. MGS medal for Fuentes d'Onoro, Ciudad Rodrigo, Badajoz and Salamanca. Army of India medal for Maheidpore and Asseerghur. Granted Freedom of the City of Dublin, his birthplace. Legion of Honour for services rendered in French ship *Bergalia* on passage from India to Europe 1831 where he restored order when the crew panicked. Half pay 19 Nov 1844. Appointed to Her Majesty's Honourable Corps of Gentlemen at Arms 1 Apr 1847. Military Knight of Windsor 30 Sep 1862. Died 6 Feb 1865.
REFERENCE: *Some recollections of the life of Lieut. Colonel P. P. Nevill, late major 63rd Regiment, 1864.*

NEWLAND, Robert
2nd Captain. Royal Artillery.
Ledger stone: All Saints's Churchyard, Hastings, Sussex. (Photograph)

IN MEMORY OF / ROBERT NEWLAND ESQ/ OF KEMPSTON HOUSE, BEDFORDSHIRE. / DIED AT HASTINGS JULY 12TH 1858 / AGED 70 YEARS / …………

2nd Lt 13 Sep 1804. 1st Lt 2 Jul 1805. 2nd Capt 20 Dec 1814.

Served in the Peninsula Sep 1811 – Apr 1814 with 'E' Troop, Royal Horse Artillery. Present at Llerena, siege of Salamanca Forts, Salamanca, Majalahonda, Morales, San Munos, Vittoria, Orthes and Toulouse. Present at Waterloo in Captain Mercer's Troop. Half pay 1820 and retired on the sale of his commission in 1831. MGS medal for Salamanca, Vittoria, Orthes and Toulouse.

NEWMARCH, William

Private. 1st Royal Veteran Battalion.
Headstone: St Helena Gardens, Sculcoates Lane Cemetery, Hull, Yorkshire. Seriously eroded. (Photograph)

ERECTED AS A TRIBUTE / OF FILIAL AFFECTION / IN MEMORY OF / WILLIAM NEWMARCH / OF THIS TOWN, / WHO DEVOTED 21 YEARS / OF HIS EARLY LIFE / IN THE DEFENCE OF / HIS COUNTRY, / UNTIL THE CLOSE OF THE / PENINSULA WAR. / AFTER A LONG LIFE OF / INDUSTRY / DEPARTED THIS LIFE / THE 25TH OF JUNE / 1854, AGED 83 YEARS. / .... / MAIDA. LANDYKE. BERGEN-OP-ZOOM, SANDHILLS. WILHELMSTADT. / EGYPT. VIMIERO. CORUNNA. / WALCHEREN. PYRENEES. BADAJOZ. / ALEXANDRIA.

Pte 20th Foot 17 Jul 1799 – 24 May 1812. Pte 1st Royal Veteran Battalion 25 May 1812.

Served in the Peninsula Aug 1808 – Jan 1809 and 1812–1814. Present at Vimeiro, Corunna and Pyrenees. Also served in Egypt 1801 (present at Alexandria), Sicily 1806 (present at Maida), Walcheren 1809 and the Netherlands 1814 (present at Bergen-op-Zoom). MGS medal for Egypt, Maida, Vimeiro and Corunna. Discharged 13 Jul 1814 owing to the loss of his left eye from opthalmia and poor vision in his right eye due to Walcheren fever. The 1st Royal Veteran Battalion was disbanded in 1814.

NEWTON, Hibbert

Lieutenant. 32nd (Cornwall) Regiment of Foot.
Table tomb: Church of Ireland Churchyard, Preban, County Wicklow, Ireland. (Photograph)

IN MEMORY OF HIBBERT NEWTON / ESQ. J.P. FOR CO. WICKLOW AND LATE / LIEUTENANT IN THE 32ND FOOT / WHO DIED AT BALLINGLEN THE 12TH DAY / OF FEBRUARY 1861 AGED 70 YEARS.

Ensign 27 Jul 1809. Lt 13 Apr 1813.

Served in the Peninsula Jul 1811 – Sep 1812. Present at the siege of Salamanca Forts (Mentioned in Despatches) and Salamanca (severely wounded). Half pay 1817. MGS medal for Salamanca. Magistrate for County Wicklow.
Note: The regiment also contained another officer of this name who became an Ensign Apr 1809 and later a Lieutenant serving at Salamanca where he was killed.

NICHOLAS, William

Captain. Royal Engineers.
Named on the Regimental Memorial: Rochester Cathedral, Rochester, Kent. (Photograph)

2nd Lt 21 Dec 1801. Lt 1 Jul 1802. 2nd Capt 28 Aug 1806. Capt 10 Jan 1812. Bt Major 27 Apr 1812 (posthumous award).

Served in the Peninsula Mar 1810 – May 1812. Present at Cadiz (commanded the Engineers on the death of Major Lefebre at Matagorda), Barrosa (Mentioned in Despatches) and Badajoz. In the third siege of Badajoz, he led the 4th Division to the assault on Trinidad breach, was severely wounded and died of his wounds 14 May 1812. Also served in Sicily 1805–1807, Egypt 1807 (present at Alexandria and Rosetta where he rescued General Meade who was severely wounded) and Sicily 1807–1809 (present at the defence of Scylla, AQMG and Mentioned in Despatches). Sir Thomas Graham wrote that 'no soldier ever distin-

guished himself more and his heroic conduct could never be forgotten'. Sir Richard Fletcher placed a monumental stone over his grave.
Reference: Dictionary of National Biography. Royal Military Calendar, Vol. 3, pp. 369–70.

NICHOLL, Edward
Captain. 84th (York and Lancaster) Regiment of Foot.
Family low monument: St John the Baptist's Churchyard, Llanblethian, Glamorgan, Wales. (Photograph)

………………… / AND OF LIEUTENANT COLONEL EDWARD NICHOLL OF H. M. 84TH REGIMENT OF FOOT / SON OF THE ABOVE EDWARD & CATHERINE NICHOLL / WHO DIED THE 28TH DAY OF JUNE 1847 AGED 70 YEARS. / …………………

Ensign 23 May 1800. Lt 13 Sep 1802. Adjutant 28 Jun 1804. Capt 14 Sep 1809. Bt Major 22 Jul 1819. Lt Colonel 17 Jan 1835.

Served in the Peninsula 1813 – Apr 1814. Present at Bidassoa, Nive and Bayonne. Also served at Walcheren 1809 (present at the siege of Flushing) and India (present in the Pindari War 1817–1818). Commanded 84th Foot from 1835–1838. Retired 2 Nov 1838 by sale of his commission. Lord Lieutenant of Glamorgan 28 Apr 1832.

NICHOLLS, George
Captain. 66th (Berkshire) Regiment of Foot.
Gravestone: St Mary's Cemetery, Cheltenham, Gloucestershire. (No longer extant). (M.I.)

"UNDER THIS STONE ARE LAID THE REMAINS OF MAJOR-GENERAL GEORGE NICHOLLS, FORMERLY OF H. M. SIXTY SIXTH REGIMENT WHO SERVED FIFTY EIGHT YEARS IN EACH QUARTER OF THE GLOBE. AT VITTORIA HE WAS SEVERELY WOUNDED. IN ST HELENA HE WAS ORDERLY OFFICER TO NAPOLEON. HE DIED AT (RODNEY TERRACE) CHELTENHAM (MARCH 11 1857 AGED 81) A CHILDLESS WIDOWER, BUT HE HAD FRIENDS WHO LOVED HIM MDCCCLVII"

Ensign 26 Jun 1799. Lt 25 May 1803. Capt 23 Feb 1809. Bt Major 5 Jul 1821. Bt Lt Colonel 10 Jan 1837. Bt Colonel 11 Nov 1851. Major General 31 Aug 1855.

Served in the Peninsula Jan 1812 – Sep 1813. Present at Vittoria (severely wounded and awarded pension of £100 per annum). MGS medal for Vittoria. Also served at St Helena as Orderly Officer to Napoleon and was in charge of the Longwood Establishment for 17 months. Served in the army for 58 years.

NICHOLS, Samuel
Corporal. (12th Prince of Wales's) Regiment of Light Dragoons.
Named on the Regimental Memorial: St Joseph's Church, Waterloo. (Photograph)

Present at Waterloo where he was killed.

NICHOLS, William
Captain. 3rd (East Kent) Regiment of Foot.
Ledger stone: Old Mortuary Chapel of St Mary's Graveyard, Henrietta Street, Bath, Somerset. (Photograph)

SACRED TO THE MEMORY / OF CAPTAIN / WILLIAM NICHOLS, / 2ND R. V. B., / FORMERLY OF THE 3RD REGT / OF FOOT OR BUFFS, / WHO DIED IN THIS CITY OCTOBER 14TH 1847, / AGED 75 YEARS.

Ensign 4 Aug 1804. Lt 11 Jul 1805. Capt 27 Jan 1814.

Served in the Peninsula Sep 1808 – Apr 1814. Present at Douro (wounded), Busaco, Vittoria, Pyrenees, Nivelle, Nive, Garris, Orthes, Aire and Toulouse. Also served in North America 1814–1815. Retired on full pay as Captain in 2nd Veteran Battalion 1832. MGS medal for Busaco, Pyrenees, Nivelle, Nive, Orthes and Toulouse.

NICHOLSON, Alexander see McINNES, Alexander

NICHOLSON, Benjamin Walter

Lieutenant. 30th (Cambridgeshire) Regiment of Foot.

Pedestal tomb with cross: Glasnevin Cemetery, Dublin, Ireland. (Photograph)

SACRED / TO THE MEMORY OF / MARIA / THE AFFECTIONATE WIFE OF / CAP^{T}. B.W. NICHOLSON, / LATE 30TH REG^{T} WHO DIED MAY 5TH / 1855 AGED 74 YEARS. / SHE ACCOMPANIED HIM IN HIS / CAMPAIGNS TO THE EAST INDIES / CAPE OF GOOD HOPE ST HELENA AND / WAS IN ANTWERP DURING THE THREE / DAYS OF WATERLOO WHERE HER HUSBAND HAD BEEN ENGAGED. / MAY SHE REST IN PEACE.

Ensign 13th Foot 20 Jul 1805. Lt 30th Foot 15 Apr 1806. Capt 20 Jul 1815.

Present at Waterloo. Also served in the Cape of Good Hope 1806, India 1807–1814 and the Netherlands Sep 1814. Half pay 25 Jun 1817.

NICHOLSON, Edward

Gunner. Royal Artillery.

Memorial: St Laurence's Churchyard, Morland, Cumbria. (M.I.)

"EDWARD NICHOLSON DIED JULY 15TH 1869 AT MORLAND LOW FIELD AGED 79"

Pte 12 Jan 1805.

Served in the Peninsula 1809 – Apr 1814. Present at Talavera, Busaco, Fuentes d'Onoro, Albuera, Badajoz (one of 30 Artillerymen who volunteered to join the Forlorn Hope in order to spike the guns when they were taken), Pyrenees and Toulouse. Present at Waterloo (wounded in Capt Napier's Company) and with the Army of Occupation. Also served in the West Indies. His wife Mary accompanied him throughout the Peninsula and was at Waterloo. Discharged 30 Jun 1826 with a pension of 1 shilling per day.

NICHOLSON, Huntly

Lieutenant. 42nd (Royal Highland) Regiment of Foot.

Headstone in railed enclosure: Officers' Graveyard, Royal Hospital, Kilmainham, Dublin, Ireland. (Photograph)

IN MEMORY OF / HUNTLY NICHOLSON / LATE CAPTAIN / 42 ROYAL REGIMENT / AND / ROYAL HOSPITAL / HE SERVED / IN THE PENINSULAR / AND / 1ST BURMESE WAR / FOR WHICH HE OBTAINED / TWO MEDALS. / HE DIED THE 18TH NOV. 1870 / AGED 77 YEARS / (VERSE)

Ensign 10 Oct 1811. Lt 5 Aug 1813. Capt 24 Mar 1838.

Served in the Peninsula Sep 1813 – Apr 1814. Present at Nivelle, Nive, Orthes and Toulouse. Also served in India 1824 (present at the quelling of the mutiny at Barrackpore) and the Burmese Campaign 1825–1826 (present at Prome). Awarded Army of India Medal for Ava. MGS medal for Nivelle, Nive, Orthes and Toulouse. Half pay 17 Sep 1839.

NICHOLSON, Thomas

Private. 1st (King's) Dragoon Guards.

Headstone: York Cemetery, York, Yorkshire. (Grave number O/11/28 – Inscription illegible and recorded from memorial inscription). (Photograph)

"TO THE MEMORY OF / THOMAS NICHOLSON / LATE TROOP SGT MAJOR 1ST / KINGS DRAGOON / GUARDS / WHO DEPARTED THIS LIFE / SEP 28TH 1850, AGED 60 YEARS / …………………"

Pte 24 Apr 1809. Cpl 17 Sep 1818. Sgt 25 Jul 1823. Sgt 25 Jul 1829. Troop Sgt Major 1 Sep 1831.

Present at Waterloo. Received seven sabre wounds through his body when charging with his regiment. Discharged 30 Dec 1841. Went to York and kept the 'Light Horseman' public house in the Fulford Road.

NICHOLSON, William

Corporal. 26th (Cameronian) Regiment of Foot.

Tablestone: St Michael's Churchyard, Dumfries, Scotland. (Photograph)

WILLIAM NICHOLSON / 26TH REGIMENT OF FOOT / DIED MAY 1857 AGED 72.

Served in the Peninsula 1808–1814. Present on the retreat to Corunna where he was taken prisoner until Apr 1814. Died in Dumfries in May 1857 aged 72. MGS medal for Corunna.

NICKLE, Robert

Captain. 88th (Connaught Rangers) Regiment of Foot.

Obelisk: Carlton Cemetery, Melbourne, Australia. (Photograph)

SACRED / TO THE MEMORY OF / MAJOR GENERAL SIR ROBERT NICKLE / K.H. / COMMANDER OF HER MAJESTY'S FORCES / WITHIN THE AUSTRALIAN COMMAND / OBIT 26TH MAY 1855 / ÆTAT 72 YEARS

Ensign Fencible Regt 22 Jan 1801. Lt 15th Foot 26 Jan 1802. Lt 88th Foot 4 Aug 1804. Capt 1 Jun 1809. Bt Major 21 Jan 1819. Major 28 Nov 1822. Lt Colonel 36th Foot 30 Jun 1825. Bt Colonel 28 Jun 1838. Major General 11 Nov 1851.

Served in the Peninsula Mar 1809 – Jul 1811 and Oct 1812 – Apr 1814. Present at Douro, Talavera, Busaco, second siege of Badajoz, Vittoria, Pyrenees, Nivelle, Nive (wounded), Orthes, Vic Bigorre, Tarbes and Toulouse (severely wounded). Served with the Army of Occupation 1815–1818. Also served in Ireland 1798 (present in the Irish Rebellion), South America 1807 (present at Buenos Ayres where he was severely wounded), North America 1814–1815 (present at Plattsburgh, passage of the Savannah and Sarinac River), West Indies 1831 (Governor of St Kitts), Canada 1837–1838 (present in the Rebellion) and Australia 1853–1855 (Commander of Forces in Australia). KH and KCB. Gold Medal for Nivelle. MGS medal for Talavera, Busaco, Vittoria, Pyrenees, Nive, Orthes and Toulouse. Died in Australia 26 May 1855 as a result of exposure to the heat during the riots of the gold miners at the Eureka stockade at Ballarat Dec 1854. Nickle went by himself on horseback in full uniform to diffuse the situation and calmed the miners down.

Reference: Dictionary of National Biography. Dictionary of Australian Biography.

NICOLAY, William

Lieutenant Colonel. Royal Staff Corps.

Memorial tablet: St Philip and St James's Church, Leckhampton, Cheltenham, Gloucestershire. (North transept). (Photograph)

TO THE MEMORY OF / LIEUT GENERAL SIR WILLIAM NICOLAY K.C.B: AND K.C.H, / COLONEL OF THE 1ST WEST INDIAN REGIMENT, / BORN 14TH APRIL 1771 DIED 3RD MAY 1842, / HE SERVED HIS SOVEREIGN AND COUNTRY WITH HONOR AND DISTINCTION / FOR A PERIOD OF 32 YEARS, / IN INDIA WITH THE ROYAL ARTILLERY: / IN THE WEST INDIES WITH THE ROYAL ENGINEERS; / IN THE PENINSULAR AND AT WATERLOO. / IN COMMAND OF THE ROYAL STAFF CORPS. / ALSO AS GOVERNOR AND COMMANDER IN CHIEF / OF THE FOLLOWING COLONIES: OF DOMINICA FROM 1824 TO 1831: / OF ST CHRISTOPHER, NEVIS, ANGUILLA AND THE VIRGIN ISLANDS IN 1832: / OF MAURITIUS AND ITS DEPENDENCIES FROM 1833 TO 1840. / HIS MORTAL REMAINS LIE ENTOMBED BENEATH THIS CHURCH. / ....

2nd Lt Royal Artillery 28 May 1790. 1st Lt 15 Aug 1793. 1st Lt Royal Engineers 15 Nov 1793. Capt 29 Aug 1798. Major Royal Staff Corps 26 Jun 1801. Lt Colonel 4 Apr 1805. Bt Colonel 4 Jun 1813. Major General 12 Aug 1819. Lt General 10 Jan 1837.

Served in the Peninsula 1808 – Jan 1809 attached to the Quarter Master General's department. Present at Corunna. Present at Waterloo (wounded), the Capture of Paris and with the Army of Occupation until 1818. The formation of the Royal Staff Corps in 1801 was to incorporate the engineer's functions into the Quartermaster General's Department in order for it to be under Horse Guards rather than Ordnance. William Nicolay became Major and was largely responsible for the organisation of the new Corps in June 1801. Also served in India 1791–1793 with the Royal Artillery (present at the sieges of Seringapatam and Pondicherry), and the West Indies with the Royal Engineers (present at the Capture of St Lucia 1796, where he was Commanding Engineer under Sir John Moore). Governor and Commander of troops in Dominica 1824 and St Kitts and Nevis 1831. Governor of Mauritius 1833 (responsible for the emancipation of slaves and the increase in trade and prosperity). Colonel 1st West India Regt 30 Nov 1839. KCB and KCH.

REFERENCE: Dictionary of National Biography. Royal Military Calendar, Vol. 4, p. 43. Gentleman's Magazine, Aug 1842, pp. 205–6. United Service Magazine, Jul 1842, pp. 385–9.

NICOLLS, Jasper

Lieutenant Colonel. 14th (Buckinghamshire) Regiment of Foot.
Memorial tablet: Holy Trinity Cathedral, Chichester, Sussex. (In Cloisters). (Photograph)

TO THE MEMORY OF / LIEUTENANT GENERAL / SIR JASPER NICOLLS, K.C.B. / WHO DIED AT SHINFIELD, BERKS, / ON THE 3RD MAY 1849 / IN THE 71ST YEAR OF HIS AGE. / HIS MILITARY SERVICES / WERE BEST KNOWN AT / BUENOS AYRES, CORUNNA, WALCHEREN, / ALMORAH, AND BHURTPORE / AND HE CLOSED HIS MILITARY CAREER, / IN INDIA, IN 1844, / AFTER BEING COMMANDER IN CHIEF THERE, / FOR THREE YEARS AND EIGHT MONTHS. / (VERSE)

Ensign 45th Foot 24 May 1793. Lt 25 Nov 1794. Capt 12 Sep 1799. Major 6 Jul 1804. Lt Colonel York Rangers 29 Oct 1807. Lt Colonel 14th Foot 31 Mar 1808. Bt Colonel 4 Jun 1814. Major General 19 Jul 1821. Lt General 10 Jan 1837.

Served in the Peninsula Nov 1808 – Jan 1809. Present at Corunna (Mentioned in Despatches and awarded Gold Medal). Also served in the West Indies 1797–1802, India 1803 (present at Argaum and Gawilghur, Military Secretary and ADC to Major General Oliver Nicolls), Hanover 1805, South America 1807 (present at Buenos Ayres and Mentioned in Despatches), Walcheren 1809 (present at the siege of Flushing and Mentioned in Despatches), Ireland 1812 (DAG), India 1815 (served in the Nepaul War where he was present at Almorah, QMG, Mentioned in Despatches and awarded CB), India 1816 (present in the Pindari and Mahratta Wars), India 1825 (commanded 2nd Division at siege of Bhurtpore). KCB. Returned to England 1831. Commander in Chief in India 13 Aug 1839 until Jan 1843 when he finally returned to England. Colonel 93rd Foot 31 May 1833. Colonel 38th Foot 15 Jun 1840. Colonel 5th Foot 4 Apr 1843. Died 3 May 1849.
REFERENCE: United Service Magazine, Jun 1849, p. 319. Royal Military Calendar, Vol. 4, pp. 184–6.

NICOLLS, William Dann
Captain. Royal Artillery.
Memorial: Grennan Churchyard, Parish of Thomastown, County Kilkenny. (No longer extant). (Photograph of churchyard). Inscription recorded from memorial inscription.

"SACRED TO THE MEMORY OF / LIEUTENANT COLONEL WILLIAM DANN NICOLLS, ROYAL ARTILLERY / WHO DIED AT SEA 10TH NOVEMBER 1839 / ……………….."

2nd Lt 1 Apr 1799. 1st Lt 3 Dec 1800. 2nd Capt 1 Jun 1806. Capt 20 Dec 1814. Bt Major 12 Aug 1819. Lt Colonel 21 Nov 1833.

Served at Walcheren 1809 (present at the siege of Flushing). Also served in Egypt 1801 (present at Alexandria), South America 1807 (present at Buenos Ayres where he was Mentioned in Despatches), Jamaica 1821–1823 and 1836–1839. Gold Medal for Egypt. Died on his way home from Jamaica.

NIGHTINGALL, Sir Miles
Lieutenant Colonel. 69th (South Lincolnshire) Regiment of Foot.
Memorial slab: Gloucester Cathedral, Gloucestershire. (In floor of Cloisters). (Photograph)

LIEUT GEN SIR MILES NIGHTINGALL KCB / COLL 49TH REGT, MP FOR EYE CO. SUFFOLK / DIED IN THIS CITY 17TH SEPTEMBER 1829 AGED 61 / HIS BODY RESTETH IN THE VAULT BELOW

Memorial window: Gloucester Cathedral, Gloucestershire. (Photograph)

……………….. / LIEUT GEN SIR MILES NIGHTINGALL / COLONEL 49TH REGT. MP. HE DIED 17TH / OF SEPTEMBER 1829. HIS BODY LYETH IN / THE CLOISTER / ………………..

Ensign 52nd Foot 4 Apr 1787. Lt 12 Nov 1789. Capt 125th Foot 5 Sep 1794. Major 121st Foot 28 Feb 1795. Lt Colonel 115th Foot 9 Sep 1795. Lt Colonel 38th Foot 28 Oct 1795. Lt Colonel 51st Foot 23 Jul 1802. Bt Colonel 25 Sep 1803. Lt Colonel 69th Foot 8 May 1806. Major General 25 Jul 1810. Lt General 4 Jun 1814.

Served in the Peninsula Aug – Nov 1808 (O/c 3 Brigade) and Jan – Jun 1811 (O/c 2 Brigade 1st Division). Present at Rolica (Mentioned in Despatches), Vimeiro (Mentioned in Despatches), Casal Nova, Miranda de Corvo, Foz D'Arouce (wounded and Mentioned in Despatches) and Fuentes d'Onoro (wounded). Left the Peninsula in July 1811 to take command of a Division in India but was sent to Java instead. Also served in India 1788–1797 (present at Dindegul 1790), Mysore War 1791 (present at Bangalore, Savandroog, operations before Seringapatam and Capture of Pondicherry 1793) Returned to England due to ill health Jan 1795 but in October of that year went to the West Indies (present at the Capture of Trinidad 1797. (AAG at St Domingo), the Helder 1799, Quiberon Bay 1800, India 1803 (present at Capture of Agra and battle of Lasswaree). QMG in India until 1807 when he returned to England, Java Oct 1813 – Nov 1815 (Commander-in-Chief and present at the action at the island of Celebes), India 1816–1819 (Commander-in-Chief at Bombay). Returned home and became MP for Eye in Suffolk 1819. Gold Medal for Rolica and Vimeiro. KCB 4 Jan 1815. Colonel 6th West India Regiment 20 Mar 1815. Colonel 49th Foot 19 Feb 1820.
Reference: Dictionary of National Biography. Royal Military Calendar, Vol. 2, pp. 379–85. United Service Journal, 1830, Part 1, pp. 195–6. Gentleman's Magazine, Nov 1829, pp. 463–5.

NISBET, Robert
Lieutenant. 13th Regiment of Light Dragoons.
Wall mural memorial: Eccles Churchyard, Eccles, Berwickshire, Scotland. (In Nisbet enclosure). (Photograph)

IN MEMORY / OF / ROBERT NISBET OF MERSINGTON ESQ. / LIEUT-COL IN THE ARMY, AND

/ FORMERLY CAPTAIN IN THE 13TH LIGHT / DRAGOONS, IN WHICH REGIMENT HE SERVED / THROUGHOUT THE PENINSULAR WAR / AND AT WATERLOO. / HE DIED JULY 25, 1865, AGED 75 YEARS. / ....

Cornet 7th Dragoon Guards 30 Nov 1809. Lt 13th Light Dragoons 26 Dec 1811. Capt 20th Light Dragoons 19 Nov 1818. Bt Major 10 Jan 1837. Bt Lt Colonel 11 Nov 1851.

Served in the Peninsula Dec 1812 – Apr 1814. Present at Nivelle, Nive, Garris, Orthes (wounded) and Toulouse. Present at Waterloo. MGS medal for Nivelle, Nive, Orthes and Toulouse. Half pay 19 Nov 1818.

NIXON, Edward

Assistant Surgeon. Coldstream Regiment of Foot Guards.
Blue plaque: King Street, Bishop Auckland, Durham. (Photograph)

FORMER RESIDENCE / OF SURGEON / EDWARD NIXON, SURGEON / FOR NEARLY 50 YEARS TO / THE DURHAM MILITIA / (LATER 4TH DURHAM LIGHT / INFANTRY). HE FIRST SERVED IN / THE COLDSTREAM GUARDS / UNDER THE / DUKE OF WELLINGTON IN / THE PENINSULAR WAR.

Hospital Mate Jan 1809. Ensign Nottingham Militia 25 May 1809. Asst Surgeon Jun 1809. Asst Surgeon Coldstream Guards 25 Oct 1810. Asst Surgeon 80th Foot 6 Aug 1818. Surgeon Durham Militia 24 Sep 1821.

Served in the Peninsula Mar 1811 – Mar 1813. Present at Fuentes d'Onoro and Salamanca. Resigned 27 Apr 1813. Later became Surgeon to the Durham Militia for nearly 50 years. MGS medal for Fuentes d'Onoro and Salamanca. Died 1869 aged 82.

NIXSON, Philip

Private. Royal Artillery.
Family Headstone: St Michael's Churchyard, Dalston, Cumbria. (M.I.)

" .... ALSO OF PHILIP, THEIR SON OF THE ROYAL ARTILLERY, WHO DIED ON HIS RETURN FROM CORUNNA AND WAS BURIED AT CANTERBURY FEB 18 1809 AGED 33."

Served in the Peninsula 1808–1809. Present at Corunna.

NOOTH, John Mervin

Lieutenant Colonel. 7th (Royal Fusiliers) Regiment of Foot.
Gravestone: Officers Cemetery, Military Burial Ground, Demerara, British Guinea, West Indies. (M.I.)

"JOHN MERVIN NOOTH, LT-COLONEL, ROYAL NORTH BRITISH FUZILIERS, C.B., DIED 23RD AUGUST, 1821, AGED 38."

Memorial: Bath Abbey, Bath, Somerset. (South-west porch). (Photograph)

LIEUTENANT COLONEL / JOHN MERVIN NOOTH C.B. / A LIEUT: COL: OF THE / XXI REGT OF FOOT, / DEPARTED THIS LIFE / AT DEMERARA / AUGUST XXIII MDCCCXXI / AGED XXXVIII YEARS. / TO EVINCE THE ESTEEM SO GENERALLY FELT FOR HIS TALENTS / TO HAND DOWN TO POSTERITY / THEIR VENERATION FOR HIS MANY VIRTUES / AND RECORD THEIR ADMIRATION FOR HIS CHARACTER / AS A GENTLEMAN AND A SOLDIER, / THE OFFICERS NON COMMISSIONED OFFICERS DRUMMERS AND PRIVATES / OF THE XXI OR ROYAL NORTH BRITISH REGIMENT OF FUSILIERS / HAVE ERECTED THIS TABLET TO HIS MEMORY. / HE WAS

A MAN / FRANK IN HIS MANNERS AND OF INFLEXIBLE RESOLUTION / SUSCEPTIBLE OF THE WARMEST ATTACHMENT / AND EVER THE TRUE SOLDIER'S STEDFAST FRIEND.

Lt 6 Jul 1796. Capt 6 Sep 1798. Major 30 Dec 1806. Bt Lt Colonel 20 Jun 1811. Lt Colonel 2 Jan 1812. Lt Colonel 21st Foot 6 Jun 1816.

Served in the Peninsula with 1/7th Aug 1810 – Jul 1811. Present at Busaco, Pombal, Condeixa, Olivencia, first siege of Badajoz and Albuera where he commanded the regiment. CB. Gold Medal for Martinique and Albuera. Also served at Halifax, Canada 1796–1802, West Indies 1802–1804, the Capture of Martinique 1809 and again in the West Indies 1819 where he died in Demerara 23 Aug 1821.

NORBERT, J. C.

1st Lieutenant. 1st Carabineers Regiment, Dutch Cavalry.
Named on the Memorial to Dutch officers killed at Waterloo: St Joseph's Church, Waterloo. (Photograph)

NORCLIFFE, Norcliffe

Lieutenant. 4th (Queen's Own) Regiment of Dragoons.
Pedestal tomb: Kensal Green Cemetery, London. (8155/102/PS). (Photograph)

HERE ALSO REST IN HOPE / THE MORTAL REMAINS OF / MAJOR GENERAL / NORCLIFFE NORCLIFFE, KH / OF LANGTON HALL, YORKSHIRE, / WHO DIED IN LONDON 8TH FEBRUARY / 1862, / AGED 70 YEARS

Cornet 5 Feb 1807. Lt 28 Apr 1808. Capt 29 Feb 1816. Bt Major 9 Aug 1821. Bt Lt Colonel 10 Jan 1837. Bt Colonel 11 Nov 1851. Major General 31 Aug 1855.

Served in the Peninsula Apr 1809 – Nov 1812. Present at Talavera, Busaco, Albuera, Usagre and Salamanca (severely wounded, nearly left for dead on the battlefield but with the surgeon's aid and the care given to him by his cousin Mrs Dalbiac, wife of the Commanding Officer he recovered). Half pay 22 May 1823. MGS medal for Talavera, Busaco, Albuera and Salamanca .
Reference: Transaction of the East Riding Antiquarian Society (1904), pp. 11–12. Gentleman's Magazine, Apr 1862, pp. 501–2. Annual Register, 1862, Appx, p. 383.

NORCOTT, Amos Godsil Robert

Major. 95th Regiment of Foot.
Memorial tablet: St Finbarr's Cathedral, Cork, County Cork, Ireland. (Photograph)

SACRED TO THE MEMORY OF / MAJOR GENERAL SIR AMOS NORCOTT, / (A GALLANT AND DISTINGUISHED OFFICER) / C.B. K.C.H. K.M.J. K.S.A. & & / WHO DIED AT MARYSBORO' HOUSE UPPER GLANMIRE / ON THE 8TH DAY OF JANUARY 1838, / AGED 60 YEARS. / HE SERVED IN THE CAMPAIGNS OF 1794–95 IN HOLLAND / AND WAS EMPLOYED IN THE EAST AND WEST INDIES / AND IN NORTH AND SOUTH AMERICA. / HE WAS WITH SIR JOHN MOORE / IN SWEDEN, PORTUGAL AND SPAIN / AND SUBSEQUENTLY SERVED UNDER / HIS GRACE FIELD MARSHAL / THE DUKE OF WELLINGTON / THROUGHOUT THE WHOLE OF / THE PENINSULAR WAR. / HE WAS SEVERELY WOUNDED AT TARBES, / AND ON THE 18TH JUNE AT THE MEMORABLE BATTLE OF / WATERLOO. / HE HAD BUT RECENTLY RETURNED / FROM THE ISLAND OF JAMAICA, / WHERE HE SERVED / AS LIEUTENANT GOVERNOR AND COMMANDER IN CHIEF / AND TERMINATED HIS BRILLIANT CAREER / IN COMMAND OF THE DISTRICT IN WHICH / HE FIRST COMMENCED HIS LONG CAREER. / ....

Named on the Rifle Brigade Memorial: Winchester Cathedral, Winchester, Hampshire. (Photograph)

Ensign Corps of Invalids 14 Feb 1793. Lt in Capt Clarke's Independent Company 18 Jun 1793. Lt 33rd Foot

20 Sep 1793. Capt 28 Feb 1794. Capt 95th Foot 22 Apr 1802. Bt Major 25 Sep 1803. Major 22 Dec 1808. Bt Lt Colonel 25 Jul 1810. Bt Colonel 12 Aug 1819. Lt Colonel 9 Sep 1819. Major General 22 Jul 1830.

Served in the Peninsula with 1/95th Aug 1808 – Jan 1809, with 2/95th Aug 1810 – Feb 1813 and Nov 1813 – Apr 1814. Present at Rolica, Vimeiro, Cacabellos, Corunna, Cadiz, Barrosa (Mentioned in Despatches), Seville, Nive, Orthes and Tarbes (severely wounded). Present at Waterloo where he was wounded in command of the 2nd Battalion and with the Army of Occupation. Awarded pension of £250 per annum for wounds at Tarbes and Waterloo. Gold Medal for Barrosa and Nive. CB 22 Jun 1815. KCH. Knight of St Anne of Russia, Knight of Maximilian and Joseph (Bavaria). Also served in Flanders 1794–1795 (present at Boxtel, Geldermalsen and Bureu), Cape of Good Hope 1796 (present at the Capture of the Dutch fleet at Saldanha Bay), Manila 1797, India 1798–1799 (present at Seringapatam), South America 1807 (present at Buenos Ayres where he was taken prisoner), Sweden 1808 and Walcheren 1809 (present at the siege of Flushing). Lieutenant Commander and Governor of Jamaica 1833. Commander of Southern district of Ireland Mar 1837. KCB 1831.

Reference: Gentleman's Magazine, Apr 1838, p. 430.

NORMAN, John Ballantine

Lieutenant. 2nd (Queen's Royal) Regiment of Foot.

Named on the Regimental Memorial, St Michael's Cathedral, Bridgetown, Barbados, West Indies. (Photograph)

Ensign Ayr Militia. Ensign 2nd Foot 6 Aug 1809. Lt 26 Apr 1810.

Served in the Peninsula Mar 1811 – Dec 1812. Present at Almeida, siege of Salamanca Forts, Salamanca, Burgos and retreat from Burgos. Also served at Walcheren 1809 and the West Indies 1815 where he died at Barbados during a yellow fever epidemic 19 Dec 1816.

NORRIS, George

Lieutenant. 47th (Lancashire) Regiment of Foot.

Family Memorial tablet: St Margaret's Church, Stanfield, Norfolk. (Photograph)

………… / AND OF LIEUT: GEORGE NORRIS, THEIR ELDEST SON / WHO FELL AT THE SIEGE OF / SAINT SEBASTIAN IN SPAIN, / AUGUST 31ST, 1813 / AGED 22 YEARS. / …………

Ensign 4 Sep 1809. Lt 30 Apr 1812.

Served in the Peninsula 1810 – Aug 1813. Present at Cadiz, Vittoria and San Sebastian where he was killed 31 Aug 1813 aged 22 years.

NORTH, William

Captain. 68th (Durham) Regiment of Foot.

Pedestal tomb: St Paul's Cemetery, Ipswich, Queensland, Australia. (Photograph)

IN MEMORY OF / WILLIAM NORTH / LATE MAJOR H. M. 68TH / LT INFANTRY / WHO DEPARTED THIS LIFE ON THE / 19TH JULY 1872 / AGED 90 YEARS / ………………..

Ensign 82nd Foot 21 May 1801. Lt 68th Foot 21 Dec 1803. Capt 8 Nov 1809. Major 8 Oct 1830.

Served in the Peninsula Jun 1811 – Dec 1812 and Jan – Apr 1814. Present at the siege of Salamanca Forts, Moriscos and Salamanca (wounded). MGS medal for Salamanca. Also served in Minorca 1801, West Indies 1804, Canada 1818–1823 and 1826–1829. Retired in 1833 and went to Australia where his son Joseph was serving in the 68th Foot.

NORTHERN, Lewis

Captain. 82nd (Prince of Wales's Volunteers) Regiment of Foot.
Headstone: Trafalgar Cemetery, Gibraltar. (Tomb number 89). (Photograph)

TO THE MEMORY / OF / LEWIS NORTHERN ESQ / LATE CAPTAIN IN THE 82D REGT / WHO DIED 11TH JULY 1810 / AGED 37 YEARS

Ensign 26 Oct 1794. Lt 73rd Foot 1798. Capt 82nd Foot 31 Oct 1804.

Served in the Peninsula Aug 1808 – Jan 1809 and Jun – Jul 1810. Present at Rolica, Vimeiro, Corunna and Tarifa where he died 17 Jul 1810.

NORTHEY, Edward Richard

Lieutenant. 52nd (Oxfordshire) Light Infantry Regiment of Foot.
Fallen Cross in kerbed border: Epsom Cemetery, Surrey. (Photograph)

.... EDWARD RICHARD NORTHEY 24 DECEMBER 1878 AGED 83 YEARS.

Memorial: Royal Military Chapel, Wellington Barracks, London. (M.I.) (Destroyed by a Flying Bomb 1944)

"CAPTAIN EDWARD RICHARD NORTHEY / 3RD GUARDS, 1822–26. SERVED IN 52ND LIGHT INFANTRY, 1811–19. / D.D. HIS BROTHER LIEUT.-COLONEL WILLIAM BROOK NORTHEY, LATE COLDSTREAM GUARDS."

Ensign 52nd Foot 11 Jul 1811. Lt 1 Oct 1812. Capt York Rangers 24 Jun 1819. Capt 52nd Foot 10 Aug 1820. Lt and Capt 3rd Foot Guards 26 Sep 1822. Capt 25th Foot 13 Apr 1826.

Served in the Peninsula Oct 1812 – Apr 1814. Present at San Millan, Vittoria (wounded), Pyrenees, Vera, Bidassoa, Nivelle, Nive, Orthes, Tarbes and Toulouse. Present at Waterloo. MGS medal for Vittoria, Pyrenees, Nivelle, Nive, Orthes and Toulouse. Half pay 13 Apr 1826. Deputy Sherrif of Surrey 1856 and High Sheriff 1878. Died 24 Dec 1878. Brother of Lt Colonel Lewis Augustus Northey Quarter Master General's Department.

NORTHEY, Lewis Augustus

Lieutenant Colonel. Permanent Assistant Quartermaster General.
Buried in Kensal Green Cemetery, London. (Grave number 14185 Sq 31).

Ensign 29th Foot 11 May 1793. Lt 1 Mar 1794. Capt 5 Dec 1799. Bt Major Permanent AQMG 30 Nov 1807. Lt Colonel 4 Jun 1813.

Served in the Peninsula on Staff Dec 1808 – Jan 1809 and Apr 1813 – Apr 1814. Present at Corunna. Also served for three years as a Marine with the 29th Foot in action fought by Lord Howe 1 Jun 1794 (awarded NGSM for this action and action with Lord Hotham in 1795), Ireland 1798 (present in the Rebellion) and the Helder 1799. Brother of Lt Edward Richard Northey 52nd Foot. Died Nov 1857.

NUGENT, John

Private. 12th (Prince of Wales's) Regiment of Light Dragoons.
Named on the Regimental Memorial: St Joseph's Church, Waterloo. (Photograph)

Present at Waterloo where he was killed.

NUNN, Loftus
Lieutenant. 31st (Huntingdonshire) Regiment of Foot.
Memorial: Church of the Holy Evangelist, Carmoney, Newtownabbey, County Antrim, Northern Irleand. (Grave number EO15). (Photograph)

TO THE MEMORY OF / CAPT. LOFTUS NUNN, / LATE OF H. M. 31ST REGIMENT, / WHO DIED ON THE 11TH OF FEBRUARY / 1834: AGED 47 YEARS.

Ensign 24 Aug 1809. Lt 15 Jan 1812. Capt 16 Jun 1825.
Served in the Peninsula Jan 1810 – Aug 1813. Present at Busaco, Alba de Tormes, Salamanca (wounded and awarded pension of £70 per annum). Half pay 13 Feb 1828.

NUTTER, Robert
Private. Royal Regiment of Horse Guards.
Family memorial: Lister Lane Cemetery, Halifax, Yorkshire. (Photograph)

.... / ROBERT NUTTER / WHO DIED FEBY 23RD 1867, / AGED 74 YEARS / ....

Present at Waterloo in Capt Clement Hill's Troop.

OAKLEY, Richard Cater
Lieutenant. 20th (East Devonshire) Regiment of Foot.
Memorial tablet: St Petroc's Church, Bodmin, Cornwall. (Photograph)

THIS TABLET IS ERECTED / BY THE OFFICERS, / NON-COMMISSIONED OFFICERS, AND PRIVATES / OF THE XXTH REGIMENT OF FOOT, / TO THE MEMORY OF / CAPTAIN RICHARD CATER OAKLEY, / WHO DIED AT BELGAUM IN THE EAST INDIES / ON THE 2ND OF JUNE 1835. / TO REMAIN IN TESTAMENT OF THEIR ESTEEM / MOREOVER, SORROW.

Ensign 7 Mar 1811. Lt 21 Oct 1813. Capt 27 Dec 1827.
Served in the Peninsula Nov 1812 – Apr 1814. Present at Vittoria, Pyrenees (wounded at Roncesvalles 25 Jul 1813), Nive, Orthes (wounded) and Toulouse. Also served at St Helena and India 1819–1826. Returned to India 1828 where he died at Belgaum 2 Jun 1835. He exerted a good influence on his men. Taught in the day and Sunday schools. The respect that all ranks had for him was shown by the memorial that they had erected in his local church in England.

OBINS, Hamlet
Captain. 20th (East Devonshire) Regiment of Foot.
Ledger stone: St Mary's Churchyard, Prestbury, Gloucestershire. (Photograph)

HAMLET OBINS / LIEUT COL / IN HER MAJESTY'S SERVICE / FORMERLY / OF THE XXTH REGIMENT / DIED / THE 6TH DAY OF AUGUST / IN THE YEAR OF OUR LORD / 1848. / AGED 72 YEARS.

Ensign 27th Foot 21 Aug 1804. Ensign 68th Foot 3 Nov 1804. Lt 70th Foot 13 Apr 1805. Lt 57th Foot 10 Dec 1805. Capt Cape Regt 22 Dec 1808. Capt 20th Foot 19 Dec 1811. Bt Major 12 Apr 1814. Bt Lt Colonel 22 Jul 1830.
Served in the Peninsula with 20th Foot Dec 1812 – Jun 1813 and Jul 1813 – Apr 1814 (on staff as Brigade Major to the Division). Present at Vittoria, Pyrenees, Nivelle, Nive, Orthes and Toulouse (wounded and awarded Bt Majority). Half pay 29 Mar 1821. MGS medal for Vittoria, Pyrenees, Nivelle, Nive, Orthes and Toulouse.

O'CALLAGHAN, Hon. Sir Robert William

Lieutenant Colonel. 39th (Dorsetshire) Regiment of Foot.
Buried in the Family Vault: Lismore, County Waterford, Ireland. (Burial Register)

Ensign 28th Foot 29 Nov 1794. Lt 30th Lt Dragoons 6 Dec 1794. Capt 31 Jan 1795. Capt 22nd Lt Dragoons 19 Apr 1796. Capt 18th Lt Dragoons 3 Dec 1802. Major 40th Foot 17 Feb 1803. Lt Colonel 39th Foot 16 Jul 1803. Bt Colonel 1 Jan 1812. Major General 4 Jun 1814. Lt General 22 Jul 1830.

Served in the Peninsula Oct 1811 – Apr 1814 (O/C 3 Brigade 2nd Division Jan – Jul 1813 and Feb – Apr 1814). Present at Vittoria (Mentioned in Despatches for his defence of the village of Subijana), Pyrenees, Nivelle, Nive, Garris (wounded) and Orthes. Served with the Army of Occupation until 1818. Gold Medal for Maida, Vittoria, Pyrenees, Nivelle, Nive and Orthes. KCB. Also served in Sicily (present at Maida 1806), Scotland 1825–1830, India 1830 where he was Commander of Forces in Madras (present in the Coorg Wars). Returned to England 1836. GCB. Colonel 97th Foot 7 Sep 1829. Colonel 39th Foot 4 Mar 1833. Died in London 9 Jun 1840. Cousin of Lt Colonel Sir William Ponsonby 5th Dragoon Guards.
REFERENCE: Gentleman's Magazine, Oct 1840, pp. 425–6.

O'CONNELL, Richard

Lieutenant. 43rd (Monmouthshire) Light Infantry Regiment of Foot.
Sarcophagus: Mount Street Cemetery, Wellington, New Zealand. (Grave number GT 2). Inscription illegible and recorded from Mount Street Cemetery Inventory. (Photograph)

"CAPTAIN RICHARD O'CONNELL, 65TH REGIMENT. DIED 18TH AUGUST 1850. ERECTED BY HIS BROTHER OFFICERS"

Volunteer 43rd Foot 3 Apr 1812. Ensign 12 May 1812. Lt 15 Jul 1813. Lt 65th Foot 21 Aug 1828. Capt 16 Jul 1841.

Served in the Peninsula Mar 1812 – Apr 1814. Present at Badajoz as a volunteer (severely wounded in the storming party), Salamanca, retreat from Madrid, San Munos, Vittoria, Pyrenees (present at Lesaca and Vera) and Bidassoa. Half pay May 1816. Also served in Australia and New Zealand 1846 with the 65th Foot (present in the Maori Wars at the operations against Rangihaeata in the Horokiwi valley). MGS medal for Badajoz, Salamanca and Vittoria. Died 18 Aug 1850 aged 56.
REFERENCE: Obit. New Zealand Spectator and Cook's Strait Guardian, 21 Aug 1850.

O'CONNOR, Ogle Nesbit

Lieutenant. 79th (Cameron Highlanders) Regiment of Foot.
Chest tomb: Clonrush Churchyard, Whitegate, County Clare, Ireland. (Photograph)

SACRED / TO THE / MEMORY OF / OGLE NESBIT O'CONNOR 79TH REGT / .... / ERECTED 1841 / BY / THE SURVIVING / SHEWBRIDGE CONNOR MD., / CARLOW.

Ensign 15 Oct 1812. Lt 21 May 1814.

Served in the Peninsula Feb 1813 – Apr 1814. Present at the Pyrenees, Nivelle, Nive and Toulouse. Half pay 1818. Drowned whilst bathing in the River Shannon 1820.

O'DELL, Henry Edward

Lieutenant. 5th (Northumberland) Regiment of Foot.
Pedestal tomb: St John the Baptist's Churchyard, Clontarf, Dublin, Ireland. (Photograph)

SACRED / TO THE MEMORY OF / MAJOR HENRY E. O'DELL. / WHO DEPARTED THIS LIFE AT CLONTARF / DIED 18TH SEPTEMBER 1864 AGED 74 YEARS. / HE SERVED WITH THE 5TH REGIMENT OF FOOT / IN THE PENINSULAR WAR, / AND RECEIVED THE WAR MEDAL / AND NINE

CLASPS / FOR THE FOLLOWING BATTLES & SIEGES. / BUSACO SALAMANCA / FUENTES D'ONOR VITTORIA / CUIDAD RODRIGO PYRENEES / BADAJOZ NIVELLE / NIVE. / THIS MONUMENT IS ERECTED / BY HIS YOUNGEST DAUGHTER AND HER HUSBAND, / THE REV. J. PRATT, RECTOR OF CLONTARF. / HE LIVED DISTINGUISHED AS A SOLDIER / LOVED AS A PARENT, VALUED AS A FRIEND. / DIED LAMENTED BY ALL WHO KNEW HIM. / BLESSED ARE THE DEAD WHO DIE IN THE LORD.

Ensign 8 Jul 1806. Lt 25 Feb 1808. Capt 9 Jan 1822. Bt Major 10 Jan 1837.

Served in the Peninsula with 2/5th Jul 1809 – Aug 1812 and 1/5th Sep 1812 – Apr 1814. Present at Busaco, Redinha, Casal Nova, Foz d'Arouce, Sabugal, Fuentes d'Onoro, second siege of Badajoz, El Bodon, Ciudad Rodrigo, Badajoz, Salamanca (wounded), Vittoria, Pyrenees, Nivelle and Nive. Also served in South America 1807, North America 1814–1815, West Indies 1820–1826 and Mediterranean 1836–1839. MGS medal for Busaco, Fuentes d'Onoro, Ciudad Rodrigo, Badajoz, Pyrenees, Vittoria, Nivelle and Nive. Half pay 20 Sep 1839.

O'DONNELL, William

Lieutenant. 20th (East Devonshire) Regiment of Foot.
Headstone: St Mary's Churchyard, Cockhill, Buncara, County Donegal, Ireland. (Photograph)

HERE ALSO REPOSE THE MORTAL REMAINS OF / THE REV WILLIAM O'DONNELL, P.P. / CLONMANY / BROTHER TO / REV CHARLES & REV DENIS O'DONNELL / HE ENTERED MAYNOOTH COLLEGE IN 1802, / AND AFTER COMPLETING / HIS THEOLOGICAL STUDIES SUCCESSFULLY, / HE ADOPTED THE MILITARY PROFESSION; / HE WAS ENSIGN IN THE 7TH VETERAN BATTALION, / AND AFTERWARDS LIEUTENANT OF THE 20TH FOOT, / AND SIGNALLY DISTINGUISHED HIMSELF IN / SEVERAL SEVERE AND BLOODY BATTLES, IN THE / PENINSULAR WAR, IN ALL OF WHICH / GOD MIRACULOUSLY PRESERVED HIM. UPON THE DEMISE / OF HIS BROTHERS, BE EMBRACED HOLY ORDERS, AND / AFTER SPENDING A LONG LIFE CHARACTERISED BY / INCESSANT PAROCHIAL LABOURS, PATRIOTISM, / ZEAL, AND UNAFFECTED PIETY, / HE DEPARTED THIS LIFE THE 10TH FEB. 1856 / IN THE 77TH YEAR OF HIS AGE. / (VERSE)

Ensign 7th Veteran Battalion 19 Oct 1809. Ensign 20th Foot 28 Mar 1811. Lt 18 Nov 1813.

Served in the Peninsula Nov 1812 – Apr 1814. Present at Vittoria and Pyrenees. Half pay 1818 and entered the church. MGS medal for Vittoria and Pyrenees.
Reference: Doherty, Richard, The Waterloo Priest: the Reverend William O'Donnell, formerly Ensign William O'Donnell, XXth (East Devonshire) Foot, Waterloo Journal, Summer 2010, pp. 16–20.

OFFENEY, William

Lieutenant Colonel. 7th Line Battalion, King's German Legion.
Pedestal tomb: St George's Cemetery, Lisbon. (Grave number E11). (Photograph)
Inscription on four sides of memorial.

UNDERNEATH LIE THE REMAINS / OF / LIEU. COLONEL WILLIAM OFFENEY / OF THE / KING'S GERMAN LEGION. / ASSISTANT QUARTER MASTER GENERAL / TO THE CORPS OF THE BRITISH ARMY / UNDER / LT. GENERAL SIR R. HILL K.B. / WHO DIED AT BELEM / ON THE 12TH OF AUGUST 1812 / AT THE AGE OF 45 / THIS TOMB IS ERECTED TO HIS MEMORY / BY ONE WHO HAD THE GOOD FORTUNE / TO SERVE EARLY UNDER HIS AUSPICES / AND TO WHOM HE WAS NEARLY RELATED / AND PARTICULARLY DEAR. / HIS DISTINGUISHED CHARACTER AS AN OFFICER / STANDS ESTABLISHED IN THE DISPATCHES OF / THE DIFFERENT GENERALS UNDER WHOM HE / SERVED AND IN PRIVATE SOCIETY HIS AMIABLE / QUALITIES WERE NO LESS CONSPICUOUS. / THIRTY THREE YEARS OF HIS SHORT LIFE / WERE DEVOTED TO HIS

PROFESSION / ALMOST ENTIRELY SPENT ON ACTIVE SERVICE / IN THE EAST INDIES, HOLLAND, FLANDERS, / HANOVER, DENMARK, WALCHEREN / AND THE PENINSULA.

Bt Major 17 Nov 1803. Lt Colonel 2nd Line King's German Legion 9 Feb 1805. Lt Colonel 7th Line King's German Legion 29 Nov 1810.

Served in the Peninsula Aug 1808 – Jan 1809 (AQMG) and Apr 1811 – Aug 1812 (AQMG 2nd Division). Present at Vigo, Fuentes d'Onoro, Arroyo dos Molinos (wounded and Mentioned in Despatches) and Almarez. Gold Medal for Fuentes d'Onoro. Also served in Flanders 1794–1795, India, the Helder 1799, Hanover 1805, Copenhagen 1807 and Walcheren 1809. Died in the military hospital at Belem 17 Aug 1812 aged 45.

OFFLEY, Francis Needham
Major. 23rd (Royal Welch Fusiliers) Regiment of Foot.
Memorial tablet: St James's Church, Waresley, Huntingdon. (North aisle). (Photograph)

TO THE MEMORY OF / MAJOR / FRANCIS NEEDHAM OFFLEY, / WHO WAS KILLED / AT THE BATTLE OF SALAMANCA; / IN COMMAND OF THE 23RD / OR WELSH FUZILEER REGT / AGED 32 YEARS.

Lt 87th Foot 12 Aug 1795. 1st Lt 23rd Foot 5 Mar 1798. Capt Lieut and Capt 5 Apr 1801. Capt 26 May 1803. Major 23rd Foot 18 May 1806. With Portuguese Army: Lt Colonel Loyal Luisitanian Legion 29 Dec 1810. Lt Colonel 8th Caçadores Jan 1811.

Served in the Peninsula with Portuguese Army Jan – Jun 1811 and with 1/23rd Jul 1811 – Jul 1812. Present at Aldea de Ponte and Salamanca where he was killed 22 Jul 1812. Gold Medal for Salamanca. Also served at Martinique 1809.

OGLANDER, Henry
Major. 40th (2nd Somersetshire) Regiment of Foot.
Buried on Buffalo Island, Tinghae, Chusan, China.

Ensign 43rd Foot 28 Aug 1806. Lt 8 Sep 1808. Capt 47th Foot 2 Apr 1812. Bt Major 14 Oct 1813. Major 1st Garrison Battalion 27 Oct 1814. Major 40th Foot 30 Mar 1815. Lt Colonel De Watteville's Regt 14 Dec 1815. Lt Colonel 26th Foot 23 Oct 1817. Bt Colonel 10 Jan 1837.

Served in the Peninsula with 1/43rd Foot Jan 1809, Jul 1810 – June 1812 and with 47th Foot Feb 1813 – Apr 1814. Present at Vigo, Coa, Almeida, Busaco, Redinha, Casal Nova, Foz d'Arouce, Sabugal, Fuentes d'Onoro, Ciudad Rodrigo, Badajoz (severely wounded, his left arm amputated and severe wounds to body. Awarded pension of £300 per annum), Vittoria, San Sebastian (severely wounded, lost finger in his remaining hand and wounds to his body. Awarded pension of £150 per annum) and Bayonne. Gold Medal for San Sebastian where he commanded 47th Foot. CB. Also served at Copenhagen 1807 (present at Kiöge), Walcheren 1809 (present at the siege of Flushing), Gibraltar 1820, Ireland 1822 and India 1828. Commanded 26th Foot from March 1818 until his death in 1840. The regiment was ordered to China for the first Opium War in 1840 and Oglander went with them although on sick leave. He died on board the *Rohamany* on arrival at Chusan 26 Jun 1840. He was well liked and respected by his men. He maintained good order and discipline 'without which an army is but an armed mob'. Believed in reasoning with the men rather than punishing them. Was an advocate to remove flogging from the army. At all times he tried to improve the daily life of a soldier.
REFERENCE: Oxfordshire and Buckinghamshire Light Infantry Chronicle, 1901, p. 179, 1930, pp. 200–15

OGLE, James Gordon
Lieutenant. 33rd (1st Yorkshire West Riding) Regiment of Foot.
Gravestone: Trinity Churchyard, Hull, Yorkshire. (M.I.)

TO THE MEMORY OF / LIEUT JAMES GORDON / OGLE OF THE 33RD REGIMENT WHO DIED / SEP[TR] 12TH 1817. / THIS STONE IS ERECTED BY HIS BROTHER OFFICERS.

Ensign 3rd West Yorkshire Light Infantry. 8 Apr 1808. Lt 5 May 1809. Ensign 33rd Foot May 1811. Lieutenant 12 Sep 1814.

Present at Waterloo where he was wounded. Died at Hull 1817 aged 26.

O'GRADY, John Thomas

Lieutenant. 11th Regiment of Light Dragoons.

Memorial tablet: Knockainey Churchyard, County Limerick, Ireland. (Photograph)

SACRED / TO THE MEMORY OF / JOHN THOMAS O'GRADY / OF KILBALLYOWEN. / LIEUT 11TH DRAGOONS / WHO, HEIR TO AN AMPLE FORTUNE / AND EMINENTLY POSSESSING / THE RESPECT AND LOVE / OF HIS RELATIVES AND FRIENDS / SOUGHT HONOR IN THE FIELD / AND DIED IN HIS COUNTRY'S / SERVICE / AT ST MIGUEL'S IN SPAIN / ON THE 8TH OCTOBER 1811.

Cornet 13 Jul 1809. Lt 1 Jul 1811.

Served in the Peninsula Jun – Oct 1811. Present at El Bodon. Died of fever 8 Oct 1811.

O'GRADY, Standish

Lieutenant. 7th (Queen's Own) Regiment of Light Dragoons.

Memorial tablet: Knockainey Church, County Limerick, Ireland. (Photograph)

SACRED / TO THE MEMORY OF / STANDISH O'GRADY / 2ND VISCOUNT GUILLAMORE / COLONEL IN THE ARMY / A.D.C. TO THE QUEEN / SERVED IN THE PENINSULA / AND AT WATERLOO / WITH THE 7th HUSSARS / BORN 1792 / DIED JULY 22nd 1848

Cornet 21 Mar 1811. Lt 6 Aug 1812. Capt 20 Jul 1815. Bt Major 29 Oct 1825. Bt Lt Colonel 14 Apr 1829.

Served in the Peninsula Aug 1813 – Apr 1814. Present at Orthes and Toulouse. Present at Quatre Bras and Waterloo. At Quatre Bras covered the retreat of the infantry. When the infantry were through Genappe, O'Grady was left with his troop outside the town while the rest of the 7th Dragoons rode through Genappe. On O'Grady advancing to meet the French cavalry they turned and fled leaving the way clear for the troop to ride through Genappe. Later fierce cavalry action took place at Genappe and the 7th Dragoons lost many men including the Commanding Officer Major Hodge. O'Grady's account of the action is written in great detail in a letter and is printed in Siborne's *Waterloo Letters* (pp. 131–6). O'Grady was promoted Captain for his services at Waterloo. MGS medal for Orthes and Toulouse. MP for County Limerick 1820–1826 and 1830–1835. On the death of his father became Second Viscount Guillamore 21 Apr 1840. Half pay 14 Apr 1829. Married Gertrude Jane Paget, niece of Henry Paget, Marquis of Anglesey. Educated at Westminster.

REFERENCE: *Dictionary of National Biography.*

O'HARA, Patterson

Lieutenant. 59th (2nd Nottinghamshire) Regiment of Foot.

Memorial: Mount Jerome Cemetery, Dublin, Ireland. (Grave number C132–420). (Photograph)

SACRED / TO THE MEMORY OF / PATTERSON O'HARA ESQ / WHO DIED IN DUBLIN / AUGUST 10TH 1850 AGED 60

Ensign Louth Militia 8 Nov 1807. Ensign 59th Foot 8 Nov 1810. Lt 2 Sep 1812.

Served in the Peninsula Sep 1812 – Apr 1814. Present at Cadiz, Vittoria (wounded), San Sebastian (wounded), Nivelle, Nive (severely wounded 9 Dec 1813) and Bayonne. Present at Waterloo in reserve at Hal, the siege of Cambrai and the Capture of Paris. Half pay 25 Mar 1816. Retired to Cavan in Ireland where he became Paymaster of Cavan Militia. MGS medal for Vittoria, San Sebastian, Nivelle and Nive.

O'HARA, Robert
Captain. 88th (Connaught Rangers) Regiment of Foot.
Brass Memorial tablet: St Nicholas's Church, Galway, Ireland. (Photograph)

IN AFFECTIONATE MEMORY OF / ROBERT O'HARA / LIEUTENANT COLONEL / 88TH CONNAUGHT RANGERS / SON OF ROBERT O'HARA ESQ / OF RAHEEN CO. GALWAY. / DIED 1848. / HE SERVED DURING THE PENINSULAR WAR / IN THE 52ND LT INFANTRY AND / 88TH CONNAUGHT RANGERS / AND TOOK PART / IN THE FOLLOWING BATTLES AND SIEGES / "VIMIERA" "CORUNNA" / "TALAVERA" "COA" / "SABUGAL" "BUSACO" / "FUENTES D'ONOR" "REDINHA" / "MIRANDA DE CORVO" "BADAJOS" / ERECTED BY HIS SISTER / FLORINDA HENRIETTA LIVERSAY

Memorial: Mount Jerome Cemetery, Dublin, Ireland. (Grave number C153–998)

Ensign 15th Foot 29 Aug 1805. Ensign 52nd Foot 11 Sep 1805. Lt 3 Dec 1807. Capt 88th Foot 4 Apr 1811. Major 14 May 1829. Lt Colonel 10 Nov 1837. Lt Colonel 56th Foot 5 Jul 1839. Lt Colonel 88th Foot 16 Aug 1839.

Served in the Peninsula with 2/52nd Aug 1808 – Jan 1809 and 1/52nd Jul 1809 – Jun 1811. Present at Vimeiro, Vigo, Coa, Busaco, Pombal, Redinha, Casal Nova, Foz d'Arouce, Miranda de Corvo, Sabugal, Fuentes d'Onoro and second siege of Badajoz. MGS medal for Vimeiro, Busaco and Fuentes d'Onoro. Commanded 88th Foot 1839–1841.

O'HARE, Peter
Major. 95th Regiment of Foot.
Named on the Rifle Brigade Memorial: Winchester Cathedral, Winchester, Hampshire. (Photograph)

Lt 69th Foot 20 Jan 1797. Lt 95th Foot 28 Aug 1800. Capt 6 Aug 1803. Major 11 Apr 1811.

Served in the Peninsula with 1/95th Aug 1808 – Jan 1809 and Jul 1809 – Apr 1812. Present at Cacabellos, Corunna, Coa, Pombal, Redinha, Casal Nova, Foz d'Arouce, Sabugal, Fuentes d'Onoro (Mentioned in Despatches), Ciudad Rodrigo and Badajoz where he was killed at the siege 6 Apr 1812. Gold Medal for Fuentes d'Onoro, Ciudad Rodrigo and Badajoz. Also served in South America 1807 (present at Buenos Ayres).
REFERENCE: *Urban, Mark, Rifles, 2003.*

OLDHAM, Eli
Private. Royal Artillery Drivers.
Buried in St John the Baptist's Churchyard, Kirkheaton, Yorkshire. (Burial record)

Pte 1 Jul 1804.

Served in the Peninsula. Present at Salamanca, Vittoria, Pyrenees and Nivelle. Discharged 31 Aug 1818 due to an arm injury and awarded a pension of six pence per day. MGS medal for Salamanca, Vittoria, Pyrenees and Nivelle. Died 13 Nov 1859 aged 72 years.

O'LEARY, Arthur
Lieutenant. 24th (Warwickshire) Regiment of Foot.
Gravestone: St Mary's Cemetery, Cheltenham, Gloucestershire. (No longer extant). (M.I.)

"IN MEMORY OF MAJOR ARTHUR O'LEARY, LATE 55TH REGT, WHO DIED MARCH 5TH 1861, AGED 68 YEARS. HE RECEIVED THE SILVER WAR MEDAL WITH TWO CLASPS FOR CIUDAD RODRIGO AND SALAMANCA, THE MEDAL FOR INDIA, WHERE HE WAS SEVERELY WOUNDED, AND ALSO FOR CHINA."

Ensign 18 Apr 1811. Lt 25 Jan 1814. Lt 55th Foot 31 Jan 1825. Capt 27 Nov 1835. Bt Major 23 Dec 1842. Major 11 Nov 1845.

Served in the Peninsula Oct 1811 – Feb 1813. Present at Ciudad Rodrigo, Salamanca and retreat from Burgos. Also served in India (present in Nepal 1816 at Harrispore where he was severely wounded and the Mahratta Wars 1817–1818), China 1842 (present at Amoy, Chusan and Chinhai where he was Brigade Major to Colonel Craigie and then Brigade Major to the Chusan Field Force under Sir James Schoedde until the return of the 55th Foot in 1844). MGS medal for Ciudad Rodrigo and Salamanca. Medals for service in India and China.

O'LEARY, Edmund

Physician. Medical Department.
Headstone: St Mary the Virgin Churchyard, Carisbrooke, Isle of Wight. (Photograph)

EDMUND O'LEARY, M.D. PHYSICIAN TO THE FORCES AND PRINCIPAL OFFICER OF THE MEDICAL SERVICES AT THE ARMY DEPOT, DIED 27 JUNE 1823, AGED 40 YEARS.

Hospital Mate 23 Jul 1805. Asst Surgeon 52nd Foot 15 Aug 1805. Surgeon 47th Foot 1812. Physician 26 May 1814.

Served in the Peninsula Aug 1808 – Feb 1809, Mar – Oct 1811 and Mar 1813 – Apr 1814. Present at Vimeiro, Vittoria, San Sebastian, Nive and Bayonne. Also served at Copenhagen 1807. MD Edinburgh 1805. Retired on full pay 14 Feb 1822. Died in Albany Barracks Hospital Isle of Wight.

O'LEARY, John

Lieutenant. 91st Regiment of Foot.
Grave: St Mary's Churchyard, Athlone, County Westmeath, Ireland. (No longer extant). (M.I.) Graveyard has been redeveloped and graves removed to another church in Athlone, where most headstones are stacked.

"SACRED TO THE MEMORY OF LIEUT JOHN 0'LEARY OF THE 91ST REGIMENT WHO DIED AT ATHLONE ON THE 7TH JULY 1837, AGED 46 YEARS."

Ensign 27 Jun 1811. Lt 6 Oct 1813.

Served in the Peninsula Oct 1812 – Apr 1814. Present at Pyrenees, Nivelle, Nive, Orthes, Aire and Toulouse. Half pay 25 Mar 1817.

OLFERMANN, Johann Elias Hermann

Colonel Commandant. Brunswick Oel's Regiment.
Obelisk on a Pyramidal base: Nussberg Park, Brunswick, Lower Saxony, Germany. (Photograph)

DEM / ELIAS / FÜHRER / OLFERMANN / IN / GEBOREN / DER SCHLACHT / AM 2 TEN SEPTEMBER / VON / 1776 / WATERLOO / GESTORBEN / SEINE / AM 18 TEN OCTOBER / GEMEINDE / 1822

ELIAS OLFERMANN / LEADER / OF THE BATTLE OF WATERLOO / WAS BORN ON 2ND SEPTEMBER 1776 / AND DIED 18TH OF OCTOBER 1822

Tombstone: Blankenburg Cemetery, Harz, Lower Saxony, Germany. (Photograph)

HIER RUHT / DER HERZGL. BRAUNSCHW. GENERAL-MAJOR / JOHANN ELIAS HERMANN / OLFERMANN / GEB. 2. SEPT. 1776 / GEST. 18. OKT. 1822

HERE RESTS / THE DUKE OF BRUNSW. MAJOR-GENERAL / JOHANN ELIAS HERMANN / OLFERMANN / BORN 2. SEPT. 1776 / DIED 18. OCT. 1822

Sgt Major 90th Foot 1798. Ensign and Adjt 97th Foot 30 Dec 1799. Lt 2 Aug 1804. Capt 13 Dec 1810.

Served in the Peninsula Aug 1808 – Dec 1811 (DAAG Feb – Apr 1809. Brigade Major Lt Division Mar – Dec 1810. Brigade Major 4th Division Jan – Feb 1811. Brigade Major 7th Division Mar 1811). Present at Vimeiro, Albuera and second siege of Badajoz. Also served in Egypt 1801 (present at Alexandria where he was severely wounded). Olfermann was born in Brunswick and after meeting the Duke of Brunswick in Spain decided to join his Brunswick Infantry Regiment in 1815. After the Duke of Brunswick was killed at Quatre Bras Colonel Olfermann took command of the Brunswick contingent. They had lost many men at Quatre Bras and were held in reserve at the beginning of the battle on 18 July but gradually moved to the front line. Retired from the army in 1818. KCH. Died at Blankenburg 18 Oct 1822.

OLIVER, James Ward

Captain. 4th (King's Own) Regiment of Foot.

Ledger stone: British Cemetery, Elvas, Portugal. (Photograph)

SACRED TO THE / MEMORY OF / LIEUTENANT COLONEL / JAMES. W. OLIVER / WHO WAS MORTALLY / WOUNDED AT BADAJOS / AND DIED IN THIS CITY / THE 17TH JUNE / 1811. / DEDICADO A MEMORIA / DO / TENENTE-CORONEL / JAMES W. / OLIVER QUE FOI / MORTALMENTE FERIDO / NO CERCO DE BADAJOSE / MORREO NESTA CIDADE A17 DE / JUNHO DE 1811.

Family Memorial tablet: St Mary's Church, Paddington, London. (North wall left of the Altar). (Photograph)

THIS STONE RECORDS THE DUTY, AFFECTION, AND REGARD / OF THE SURVIVING SONS AND DAUGHTERS OF / THOMAS OLIVER, ESQUIRE / .... / JAMES WARD OLIVER, / THEIR SECOND SON, MAJOR ON THE STAFF OF THE BRITISH ARMY, / AND LIEUT. COL. IN THE PORTUGUESE SERVICE, / WHO AFTER ARDUOUS SERVICE IN NORTH AMERICA AND IN EUROPE, / IN THE 4TH OR KING'S OWN REGT OF INFANTRY, / HEROICALLY FELL / IN THE TRENCHES AT THE SIEGE OF BADAJOZ, / UNIVERSALLY BELOVED AND LAMENTED, / JUNE 17TH 1811, AGED 32 YEARS. / THOUGH FOR A SEASON; HEMISPHERES DIVIDE, / WHOM NATURE BY THE DEAREST BANDS HAS TIED. / THOUGH PROBITY AND HONOR SLUMBER HERE, / AND A FOND MOTHER'S LOVE RECALLS A TEAR. / THOUGH HERE REPOSES ONE WITHOUT THE NAME, / AND YET, IN ALL, A MOTHER'S CARE THE SAME / THOUGH A DEAR SISTER, ADORN'D THROUGH LIFE, / THE CHARACTERS OF DAUGHTER, MOTHER, WIFE. / THOUGH A BRAVE SOLDIER, BROTHER, MILD AS BRAVE, / PROVE HERE THEIR KINDRED, BY A KINDRED GRAVE. / WHILST DISTANT LANDS CONTAIN THE HONOR'D DUST, / OF HEARTS AS PURE, AS ARDENT, AND AS JUST / TIS FOR A SEASON SHORTLY SHALL THE SEA / COMMANDED TO GIVE UP ITS DEAD OBEY: / NOR, WHEN THE OCEAN SETS ITS PRISONERS LOOSE, / GANGES OR OCADIANA SHALL REFUSE: / THEN THE BLESSED SPIRITS SHALL UNITE, / TO LIVE REJOICING IN THE REALMS OF LIGHT. / ERECTED 1836

Named on Memorial tablet: Albuera Wall, British Cemetery, Elvas, Portugal. (Photograph)

Ensign 1 Oct 1794. Lt 1 Sep 1795. Capt 19 Aug 1799. Bt Major 9 Mar 1809. Portuguese Army: Lt Colonel 10th Line 24 Apr 1809. Lt Colonel 16th Line 11 Apr 1810. Lt Colonel 14th Line 2 May 1811.

Served in the Peninsula with 4th Foot Aug 1808 – Jan 1809. With Portuguese Army Apr 1809 – Jun 1811. Present at Corunna, Oporto, Busaco, Albuera, second siege of Badajoz where he was severely wounded in the trenches 31 May and died of his wounds 6 Jun 1811. Also served in America 1795 (on his voyage home captured by the French, spent a year in a French prison before escaping in Orleans. Travelled to Brittany helped by Royalists and returned to England in 1798), the Helder 1799, Hanover 1805, Copenhagen 1807 and Sweden 1808. In April 1809 became one of the British officers chosen to help reorganize the Portuguese Army. Oliver was successful with his Portuguese line regiment using methods he had acquired under Sir John Moore.
REFERENCE: *Hallidie, Nick, Lieutenant Colonel James Ward Oliver, Waterloo Journal, Vol. 33, No. 2, Summer 2011, pp. 2–24.*

OLIVER, Joseph
Private. 95th Regiment of Foot.
Headstone: St James's Churchyard, Stonesfield, Oxfordshire. (Photograph)

JOSEPH OLIVER / DIED AUGUST 13 1873 / AGED 80. / HE WAS IN THE 95TH REGIMENT / AT THE BATTLE OF WATERLOO

Served with the 3/95th at Waterloo in Captain J. Fullerton's company.

OLIVER, Nathaniel Wilmot
Captain. Royal Artillery.
Pennant tomb with marble cross at each end: St Andrew's Churchyard, Clifton, Bristol. (Grave number 0141). (Photograph)

IN MEMORY OF / MAJOR GENERAL NATHANIEL WILMOT OLIVER / COLONEL COMMANDANT ROYAL ARTILLERY / WHO DEPARTED THIS LIFE JANUARY 11TH 1854 / AGED 75 YEARS.

2nd Lt 2 Jun 1796. 1st Lt 13 Feb 1798. Capt 2 Mar 1804. Bt Major 4 Jun 1814. Major 14 Nov 1826. Bt Lt Colonel 4 Jun 1814. Lt Colonel 6 Nov 1827. Colonel 10 Jan 1837. Major General 9 Nov 1846.

Served at Walcheren 1809 (present at the siege of Flushing). Also served in Gibraltar 1796–1799, Minorca 1799–1800, Egypt 1800–1801, and Bermuda 1832–1835. Colonel Commandant Royal Artillery 18 Feb 1851.

O'LOGHLIN, Terence
Lieutenant Colonel and Colonel. 1st Life Guards.
Memorial tablet: All Saints' Church, Chalfont St Peter, Buckinghamshire. (Photograph)

IN THE VAULT UNDERNEATH / ARE DEPOSITED THE REMAINS OF / LIEUT. GENERAL O'LOGHLIN, / OF THE GRANGE, / DIED AUGUST 11TH 1843. / AGED 79. / ....

Ensign 45th Foot 1782. Ensign 27th Foot 1783. Lt 31 Oct 1789. Ensign 1st Life Guards 14 Dec 1792. Lt 7th Lt Dragoons 13 Mar 1793. Capt 1 Apr 1795. Major 14th Dragoons 19 Feb 1799. Bt Lt Colonel 14 Aug 1801. Lt Colonel and Colonel 1st Life Guards 1 Sep 1808. Major General 1 Jan 1812. Lt General 27 May 1825.

Served in the Peninsula Jan 1813 – Apr 1814. (O/c 1 Cavalry Brigade Jan – Jun 1813. On the Staff Jun – Oct 1813, then resumed command of 1 Cavalry Brigade until Apr 1814). Present at Toulouse. Also served in the Flanders campaign 1793–1794 with 7th Lt Dragoons (wounded at Tournai). Uncle of Lt Alexander A. Brice 23rd Foot.

O'MALLEY, George
Major. 44th (East Essex) Regiment of Foot.
Statue: Castlebar Parish Church, Castlebar, County Mayo. (Photograph)

TO THE MEMORY OF / MAJOR GENERAL GEORGE O'MALLEY, CB., / WHO EXPIRED IN LONDON / ON 16TH MAY 1843 / IN THE 63RD YEAR OF HIS AGE, / AND WHOSE MORTAL REMAINS ARE DEPOSITED / IN THE FAMILY BURIAL PLACE AT MURRISK ABBEY. / THIS STATUE IS ERECTED BY A NUMEROUS CIRCLE OF HIS / NAVAL, MILITARY AND CIVIL FRIENDS, / AMONGST WHOM ARE THE MEMBERS OF / THE ANCIENT AND MOST BENEVOLENT ORDER / OF THE FRIENDLY BROTHERS OF SAINT PATRICK / AS A SMALL TRIBUTE OF THEIR ESTEEM AND AFFECTION. / HE SERVED HIS COUNTRY IN EGYPT NORTH AMERICA / THE WEST INDIES THE MEDITERRANEAN ETC. / HE COMMANDED THE 2ND BATTALION OF THE 44TH REGT AT / WATERLOO, / WHERE HE WAS TWICE WOUNDED / AND SUBSEQUENTLY FOR MANY YEARS COMMANDED / THE 88TH REGT, OR CONNAUGHT RANGERS. / HE WAS A GOOD AND PIOUS CHRISTIAN / A ZEALOUS AND EXCELLENT SOLDIER / AND A SINCERE AND FIRM FRIEND.

Left pillar: (Photograph)

EGYPT / 13TH REGT / 13 APRIL / 1801 / N AMERICA / WT INDIES / 101 REGT

Right pillar: (Photograph)

WATERLOO / 44 REGT / 15 . 16. 17. 18. / JUNE / 1815 / MEDITERRANEAN / 88 REGT

Memorial tablet: Murrisk Abbey, Castlebar, County Mayo, Ireland. (In Chapel). (M.I.) (Photograph of Family Memorials in Murisk Abbey)

"SACRED / TO THE MEMORY OF / MAJOR GENERAL GEORGE O'MALLEY CB. / WHO EXPIRED IN LONDON / THE 16TH OF MAY 1843 / IN THE 63RD YEAR OF HIS AGE. / HE SERVED HIS COUNTRY IN EGYPT, NORTH AMERICA, / THE WEST INDIES, IONIAN ISLES ETC. ETC. ETC. / AND / HE COMMANDED THE 2ND BATTALION 44TH REGT AT WATERLOO / WHERE HE WAS TWICE WOUNDED / AND SUBSEQUENTLY COMMANDED THE 88TH REGT OF CONNAUGHT RANGERS / FOR SEVERAL YEARS. / THIS MONUMENT IS ERECTED / BY HIS SURVIVING BROTHER / MAJOR O'MALLEY."

Volunteer Castlebar Yeomanry 1798. Ensign 13th Foot 23 Feb 1800. Lt 2 Jun 1801. Capt 89th Foot 25 Apr 1805. Major 101st Foot 21 Aug 1806. Bt Lt Colonel 4 Jun 1813. Major 44th Foot 27 Apr 1815. Major 88th Foot 2 Jun 1825. Bt Colonel 22 Jul 1830. Major General 23 Nov 1841.

Present at Quatre Bras and Waterloo with 2/44th. Twice wounded in the battle and had two horses shot under him, but remained in command of the regiment after Lt Colonel Hamerton had been severely wounded. CB. Commanded 2nd Battalion in the Army of Occupation until it was disbanded in 1816 when he went on to half pay. Also serve in Ireland 1798 as a Volunteer when he joined the day before the French invasion (present in the Irish Rebellion and the French invasion of Ireland), Ferrol 1800, Egypt 1801 (severely wounded), North America 1808 and Jamaica 1810–1814. Lt Colonel commanding 88th Foot 2 Jun 1825 – Nov 1841 when he was promoted Major General. His younger brother Surgeon James O'Malley 11th Lt Dragoons also served at Waterloo.
Reference: Dictionary of National Biography. Gentleman's Magazine, Sep 1843, pp. 320–2. Annual Register, 1843, Appx, pp. 261–2.

O'MALLEY, James
Surgeon. 11th Regiment of Light Dragoons.
Pedestal tomb: Kacheri Cemetery, Cawnpore, India. (Grave number 610). (Photograph)

SACRED TO THE MEMORY / OF / JAMES O'MALLEY ESQR / SURGEON OF H. M. XI DRAGOONS / WHO / DEPARTED THIS LIFE / ON 27TH JULY 1820 AGED 42 YEARS. / ....

Asst Surgeon 16th Lt Dragoons 31 Dec 1803. Surgeon 50th Foot 11 Jul 1811. Surgeon 11th Lt Dragoons 11 Mar 1813.

Served in the Peninsula Apr 1809 – Jul 1810, Oct 1810 – Aug 1811 and Nov 1811 – Apr 1813. Present at Douro, Talavera, Redinha, Casal Nova, Foz d'Arouce, Sabugal, Fuentes d' Onoro, Almarez and Alba de Tormes. After Talavera the wounded in the hospitals and the surgeons were captured by the French and O'Malley was held prisoner until Jul 1810. Served with 11th Lt Dragoons at Quatre Bras, Waterloo and the Capture of Paris. Also served in India 1819 where he died in the following year. Younger brother of Major George O'Malley 44th Foot.

OMMANEY, Cornthwaite
Lieutenant. 1st (Royal) Regiment of Dragoons.
Memorial tablet: Chichester Cathedral, Sussex. (M.I.)

CAPTAIN CORNTHWAITE OMMANEY – AGED 48 YEARS, / DIED 11TH SEPTEMBER 1833. LATE OF 24TH LT DRAGOONS. / WOUNDED AT WATERLOO.

Cornet 11th Lt Dragoons 26 Sep 1811. Lt 1st Dragoons 29 Aug 1812. Capt 24th Lt Dragoons 24 Dec 1818.

Present at Waterloo where he was severely wounded. Half pay Dec 1818.

OMPTEDA, Christian von
Colonel. 5th Line Battalion, King's German Legion.
Named on the Regimental Memorial: La Haye Sainte, Waterloo. (Photograph)
Named on the Waterloo Column, Hanover, Germany. (Photograph)

Lt Colonel 1st Line 12 Jan 1805. Lt Col 1st Lt Infantry 29 Oct 1812. Bt Colonel 4 Jun 1813. Colonel 5th Line 17 Aug 1813.

Served in the Peninsula Dec 1808 – Jan 1809 and Feb 1813 – Apr 1814. Present at Vittoria, Tolosa, Bidassoa, Nivelle, Nive, St Etienne and Bayonne. Gold Medal for Vittoria, Nivelle and Nive. Also served at Hanover 1805, Mediterranean 1806–1807, the Baltic 1807–1808 and the Netherlands 1814. Present at Waterloo in command of 5th Line Battalion KGL where he was killed in an attempt to recapture La Haye Sainte. The Prince of Orange insisted that the 5th Light Battalion should attack even though Ompteda knew that the French cavalry was near. He had his infantry safe in a square because of this. Ompteda rode ahead of his two battalions knowing that he would be surrounded at any moment, but having been given the order obeyed. The French cavalry swept around the south west of the farm and the KGL were caught in line. Ompteda was killed and the 5th Battalion nearly all destroyed. A very brave and professional soldier, Ompteda died needlessly due to the Prince of Orange's inexperience.
Reference: Ompteda, Ludwig Friedrich Christian Carl von, A Hanoverian-English officer a hundred years ago: Memoirs of Baron Ompteda, 1892. Republished under the title In the King's German Legion: the memoirs of Baron Ompteda, Colonel, in the King's German Legion during the Napoleonic Wars, 1987.

OMPTEDA, Ferdinand von
Captain. 1st Line Battalion, King's German Legion.
Ledger stone: St John the Baptist's Churchyard, Egham, Surrey. (Photograph)

SACRED / TO THE MEMORY OF / BARON FERDINAND OMPTEDA, / CAPTAIN & BRIGADE MAJOR / IN / THE KING'S GERMAN LEGION / WHO DIED OCTOBER 31ST 1809.

Lt and Adjt 23 Apr 1805. Capt and Brigade Major 24 Apr 1808.

Served in the Peninsula Sep 1808 – Jun 1809. Brigade Major to Colonel Langwerth Sep – Oct 1808 and Brigade Major to Colonel Dreiberg Nov 1808 – Jun 1809. Also served at Hanover 1805, Copenhagen 1807 and Sweden 1808. Died at Egham 31 Oct 1809 aged 28.

O'NEILL, Charles

Lieutenant. 83rd Regiment of Foot.

Memorial tablet: Kilbarron Church, Ballyshannon Town, County Donegal, Ireland. (Photograph)

IN MEMORY OF CHARLES O'NEILL, OF ROCKVILLE, / FORMERLY CAPTAIN IN THE 83RD REGIMENT, / SECOND SON OF THE LATE JOHN O'NEILL OF PARKHILL, ESQR / HAVING SERVED THROUGHOUT THE PENINSULAR WAR / IN THE CONQUERING ARMS OF HIS COUNTRY / ON TWENTY-FOUR VICTORIOUS BATTLE FIELDS / HE DIED IN THE PEACEFUL RETIREMENT OF PRIVATE LIFE / BELOVED, HONOURED AND LAMENTED. / OB XXI MAR. MDCCCLII. AETAT LXVI. / THIS MONUMENT IS THE TRIBUTE OF THE AFFECTION / OF HIS WIDOW, HIS BROTHER AND HIS SISTER. / TALAVERA. BUSACO. OPORTO. POMBAL. LEIRA. CONDEIXA. / FLEUR DE LIS. GUARDA. SABUGAL. FUENTES D'ONOR. BADAJOZ. / CUIDAD RODRIGO (2ND SIEGE). SALAMANCA. VITTORIA. / PAMPELUNA. PYRENEES. NIVELLE. NIVE. SAUVETERRE. / VIC BIGORRE. TARBES. ORTHES. TOULOUSE. BADAJOZ.

Ensign 16 Jun 1808. Lt 4 Jan 1810. Lt 2nd Royal Veteran Battalion Oct 1823. Lt 33rd Foot Oct 1825. Capt 4 Jun 1827.

Served in the Peninsula Apr 1809 – Apr 1814. Present at Douro, Busaco, Redinha, Casal Nova, Foz d'Arouce, Sabugal, Fuentes d'Onoro, second siege of Badajoz, El Bodon, Ciudad Rodrigo, Badajoz (severely wounded), Salamanca, Vittoria, Pyrenees, Nivelle, Nive, Orthes, Vic Bigorre and Toulouse. Also served in Ceylon 1817–1818. Half pay 30 Jan 1835. MGS medal for Busaco, Fuentes d'Onoro, Ciudad Rodrigo, Badajoz, Salamanca, Vittoria, Pyrenees, Nivelle, Nive, Orthes and Toulouse.

Reference: O'Neill, Charles, The military adventures of Charles O'Neill, 1851, reprint 1997.

O'NEILL, John E.

Lieutenant. 1st (Royal Scots) Regiment of Foot.

Named on the Regimental Memorial: St Joseph's Church, Waterloo. (Photograph)

Lt 62nd Foot 21 Apr 1808. Lt 1st Foot 8 Jun 1809.

Served in the Peninsula with 3/1st 1810 – Apr 1814. Present at Busaco, Fuentes d'Onoro, Badajoz (wounded whilst serving as Acting engineer), Castrejon, Salamanca (wounded), Vittoria, San Sebastian (wounded), Bidassoa, Nivelle, Nive and Bayonne. Present at Waterloo where he was killed. Also served at Walcheren 1809.

O'NEILL, William

Ensign. 83rd Regiment of Foot.

Memorial: Mount Jerome Cemetery, Dublin, Ireland. (Grave number C3–3844)

Volunteer 83rd Foot 1 Feb 1812. Ensign 12 Aug 1812. Lt 22 May 1818. Capt 28 Dec 1841. Bt Major 20 Jun 1854. Bt Lt Colonel 10 May 1859. Bt Colonel Dec 1861.

Served in the Peninsula Feb 1812 – Apr 1814. Present at Badajoz, Salamanca (awarded Ensigncy), Vittoria, Pyrenees, Nivelle, Nive, Orthes, Vic Bigorre, Tarbes and Toulouse. Also served in Ceylon (present in the Kandian War 1817–1818 where he captured with his men two Kandian chiefs and their followers and brought the rebellion to an end. Received thanks from the Commander-in-Chief Sir Robert Brownrigg. During the rebellion the regiment only lost 12 men killed and wounded, but in the 2 years they lost 209 to death from disease). Half pay 28 Dec 1841. MGS medal for Badajoz, Salamanca, Vittoria, Pyrenees, Nivelle, Nive, Orthes and Toulouse. Staff Officer of Pensions for Armagh 15 Apr 1852. Died in Dublin 29 Sep 1869.

ONSLOW, Phipps Vansittart

1st Lieutenant. Royal Artillery.
Ledger stone: Kensal Green Cemetery, London. (20376/65 and 66/2). Inscription illegible. (Photograph)

2nd Lt 17 Dec 1807. 1st Lt 16 Dec 1808.

Present at Waterloo in Lt Colonel Sir Hew D. Ross's Troop. Half pay 9 Dec 1824. Died 10 May 1867.

ORANGE, HRH Prince William of

Commander. 1st Corps of Infantry at Waterloo.
Monument: Lion Mound, Waterloo. (Photograph)
Obelisk: Baarn, Holland. (End of a forest avenue, leading from the front of the Royal Soestdijk palace). (The four sides have the text engraved in Dutch, French, English and Latin). (Photograph)

IN GRATEFUL REMEMBRANCE / OF THE HEROIC EXERTIONS / OF WILLIAM FREDERICK GEORGE LEWIS / PRINCE OF ORANGE, / UNDER WHOSE AUSPICIOUS COMMAND / THE TROOPS OF THE NETHERLANDS / IN THE GLORIOUS FIELD / OF QUATRE BRAS, / REPULSED WITH UNBOUNDED FORTITUDE / THE FIERCE AND PERSEVERING EFFORTS / OF THE PUBLIC ENEMY, / AND PREPARED THE WAY / FOR THE TRIUMPHANT AND DECISIVE / VICTORY OF WATERLOO / BY WHICH OUR NATIONAL INDEPENDENCE / WAS FINALLY ESTABLISHED. / THE KING AND THE PEOPLE / OF THE NETHERLANDS / HAVE ERECTED THIS MONUMENT.

Lt Colonel 11 June 1811. Bt Colonel 17 Oct 1811. Major General 13 Dec 1813. Lt General 8 Jul 1814. General 25 Jul 1814.

Served in the Peninsula Jul 1811 – Jan 1814 (extra ADC to Lord Wellington). Present at Ciudad Rodrigo, Badajoz, Salamanca, Vittoria (Mentioned in Despatches), Pyrenees (Mentioned in Despatches) and Nivelle (Mentioned in Despatches). Present at Quatre Bras and Waterloo (wounded) where he was Commander of 1st Corps of Infantry, for diplomatic reasons. He was Commander-in-Chief of all forces in the Netherlands before Wellington arrived in Brussels in April 1815 to take overall command. At Quatre Bras he was responsible for placing the 69th Foot in line rather than square which led to the death of Colonel Morice and many men. Gave the order at Waterloo for the 5th Line King's German Legion to attack La Haye Sainte even though French cavalry was near. This led to the death of Colonel Ompteda and most of the 5th Line. Awarded Gold Cross for Ciudad Rodrigo, Badajoz, Salamanca, Vittoria, Pyrenees and Nivelle. GCB. Field Marshal in the British Army 28 Jul 1845. Succeeded his father to become King William II of the Netherlands in 1840. Died at Tilburg 1849 aged 56.
Reference: Royal Military Calendar, Vol. 2, pp. 80–5.

ORD, William Redman

Captain. Royal Engineers.
Low monument: Ford Park Cemetery, Plymouth, Devon. (Photograph)

TO THE BELOVED MEMORY OF GENERAL WILLIAM REDMAN ORD, COL. COMMANDANT OF THE CORPS OF ROYAL ENGRS BORN JULY 21ST 1791. DIED APRIL 1ST 1872.

2nd Lt 25 Apr 1809. 1st Lt 29 May 1810. Capt 20 Dec 1814. Bt Major 10 Jan 1837. Lt Colonel 18 Mar 1845. Colonel 17 Feb 1854. Major General 1 Nov 1858. Colonel Commandant Royal Engineers 20 Apr 1861.

Served in the Peninsula May – Nov 1810 and Apr 1811 – Apr 1814. Present at the sieges of Cadiz and Tarragona. Died at Stoke Damerell 11 Apr 1872.

O'REILLEY, John

Captain. 44th (East Essex) Regiment of Foot.
Memorial tablet: South Park Street Burial Ground, Calcutta, India. (Section 5 Grave number 158). (Photograph)

TO THE MEMORY OF / CAPT^{N} P. O'REILLEY, / H. M. 44TH REG^{T} / WHO DIED 25TH MAY 1823 / AGED 38 YEARS.

Volunteer with 44th Foot. Ensign 12 Dec 1811. Lt 22 Apr 1813. Capt 13 Jul 1820.
Served in the Peninsula Oct 1811 – Jun 1813. Present at Badajoz (wounded), Salamanca, Burgos and retreat from Burgos (present at Villa Muriel). Also served in North America 1814–1815 (present at Bladensburg, Washington and New Orleans) and India 1822 where he died in the following year. Changed his Christian name from John to Philip in 1816.

O'REILLEY, Philip see O'REILLEY, John

ORMISTON, John Andrew

Lieutenant. 91st Regiment of Foot.
Obelisk: Jedburgh Abbey Churchyard, Jedburgh, Roxburghshire, Scotland. (Photograph)

IN / MEMORY OF / LIEUTENANT / JOHN ANDREW ORMISTON / OF GLENBURNHALL. / LATE OF / THE 91ST REGIMENT OF FOOT / WHO DIED 19TH MARCH 1838 / AGED 40 YEARS.

Ensign 3 Oct 1811. Lt 29 Jul 1813.
Served in the Peninsula Oct 1812 – Apr 1814. Present at Pyrenees (wounded), Nivelle, Nive and Orthes. Half pay 25 Mar 1817.

ORMSBY, James

Captain. 52nd (Oxfordshire Light Infantry) Regiment of Foot.
Headstone: Kensal Green Cemetery, London. (3802/169/4). Inscription illegible.

Lt 17 Dec 1806. Capt 22 Jun 1813.
Served in the Peninsula Aug 1808 – Jan 1809 and Jul 1812 – Sep 1813. Present at Corunna (severely wounded), San Millan, Vittoria, Pyrenees and Vera. Died 1842.

ORR, John

Captain. 7th (Royal Fusiliers) Regiment of Foot.
Headstone: Cumbernauld Churchyard, Lanarkshire, Scotland. (Broken in two). (Photograph)

.... / MAJOR JOHN ORR AT KILMAN / LATE OF 7TH FUSILIERS / DIED AT GLASGOW 25TH NOV 1868 / AGED 89.

Ensign Royal Edinburgh Volunteers 1803. Lt 7th Foot 28 Aug 1804. Capt 27 Apr 1809. Bt Major 16 Mar 1815.
Served in the Peninsula with 2/7th Apr – Jul 1811 and 1/7th Aug 1812 – Apr 1814. Present at the first siege of Badajoz, Albuera (severely wounded and awarded pension of £200 per annum), Osma, Vittoria, Pyrenees (wounded), San Sebastian, Bidassoa, Nivelle, Nive and Orthes. Also served at Copenhagen 1807, Martinique 1809 and North America 1814. Half pay 25 Feb 1816. MGS medal for Martinique, Albuera, Vittoria, Pyrenees, San Sebastian, Nivelle, Nive and Orthes. Retired Apr 1826.

ORR, John
Lieutenant. 42nd (Royal Highland) Regiment of Foot.
Obelisk: Warriston Cemetery, Edinburgh, Scotland. (Photograph)

.... / AND OF / CAPTAIN JOHN ORR / LATE OF THE 42ND HIGHLANDERS / IN WHICH HE SERVED / DURING THE PENINSULAR AND AT / WATERLOO / BORN 3RD APRIL 1790 DIED 7TH DECEMBER 1879. / (VERSE)

Edinburgh Regiment of Militia 1809. Ensign 42nd Foot 3 Oct 1811. Lt 29 Apr 1813. Lt 94th Foot 3 Aug 1817. Lt 8th Veteran Battalion 6 Jul 1820. Capt Edinburgh Militia 20 Jun 1831.

Served in the Peninsula Apr 1812 – Oct 1813. Present at the siege of Salamanca Forts, Salamanca, Burgos (wounded), retreat from Burgos and Pyrenees. Present at Waterloo where he was wounded. MGS medal for Salamanca and Pyrenees. Superintendent of the Scottish Naval and Military Academy for 30 years. Was the last surviving officer of the Black Watch who fought at Waterloo, when he died 7 Dec 1879 aged 90.
REFERENCE: Obit. Scotsman, 8 Dec 1879.

OSBORN, Kean
Captain. 5th (Princess Charlotte of Wales's) Dragoon Guards.
Memorial tablet: St Peter's Church, Alley, Parish of Clarendon (formerly Vere Parish Church), Jamaica, West Indies. (Photograph)

.... / AND OF / KEAN OSBORN, A CAPTAIN IN THE VTH DRAGOON GUARDS, AND / A. Q. M. G. TO LT. GENL. SIR THOMAS PICTON'S DIVISION WHO / FELL AT THE BATTLE OF / SALAMANCA IN SPAIN ON THE XXIID DAY OF / JULY MDCCCXII, AFTER HAVING DISTINGUISHED HIMSELF AT THE BATTLE OF / VIMIERO AND THE SIEGES OF CIUDAD RODRIGO AND BADAJOS.

Cornet 4th Lt Dragoons. Lt 30 Jul 1805. Capt 5th Dragoon Guards 5 Jan 1809.

Served in the Peninsula Sep 1811 – Jul 1812. (DAAG Oct 1811. DAQMG Nov 1811 – Jul 1812). Present at Llerena and Salamanca where he was killed.

OSTEN, Baron William von
Lieutenant. 16th (Queen's) Regiment of Light Dragoons.
Interred in Catacomb B (Pub v Ave 10–12 1/171), Kensal Green Cemetery, London.

Lt 16th Lt Dragoons 17 Nov 1808. Capt 10 Oct 1816.

Served in the Peninsula Apr 1809 – Apr 1814 (ADC to Lt Gen Stapleton Cotton Sep – Oct 1810. Brigade Major 1st Cavalry Division Nov 1810 – Jul 1811 and Brigade Major 3 Brigade 1st Cavalry Division Aug 1811 – May 1813). Present at Douro, Talavera, Coa, Busaco, Albuera, Usagre, El Bodon, Salamanca, Vittoria, Nivelle, Nive and Bayonne. Present at Waterloo. Also served in India 1822 (present at the siege of Bhurtpore 1825–1826). Awarded Army of India medal. Retired from British army in 1834. KH. Became General in Hanoverian Army. MGS medal for Talavera, Busaco, Albuera, Salamanca, Vittoria, Nivelle and Nive. Died 24 Jan 1852.

OSWALD, Sir John
Colonel. 1st (Duke of York's) Greek Light Infantry Regiment.
Mural tablet: Old St Bryce's Kirkyard, Kirkcaldy, Fife, Scotland. (Interred in a vault under Pathhead Church, Kirkcaldy). (Photograph)

IN MEMORY OF / GENERAL SIR JOHN OSWALD OF DUNNIKIER / KNIGHT GRAND CROSS OF THE ORDER OF THE BATH / KNIGHT GRAND CROSS OF THE ORDER OF ST MICHAEL / AND

ST GEORGE AND COLONEL OF THE 35TH REG. / THIS DISTINGUISHED OFFICER, OLDEST SURVIVING / SON OF J. T. OSWALD ESQ., SERVED HIS COUNTRY / DURING THE WARS OF THE FRENCH REVOLUTION. / HE COMMANDED THE EXPEDITION WHICH TOOK / SIX OF THE IONIAN ISLANDS FROM THE FRENCH / AND WAS IN MANY OF THE ENGAGEMENTS / DURING THE PENINSULAR WAR. / AFTER AN ACTIVE LIFE HE SPENT THE EVENING OF / HIS DAYS AT DUNNIKIER, BELOVED BY HIS FAMILY, / RESPECTED AND ADMIRED BY ALL WHO KNEW HIM. / OBIIT MDCCXL AETAT. LXIX / .... / THIS STONE IS ERECTED BY THEIR SON J. T. OSWALD / IN MEMORY OF HIS PARENTS, WHOSE REMAINS ARE / INTERRED ALONG WITH AN INFANT DAUGHTER / IN A VAULT UNDER PATHHEAD CHURCH.

2nd Lt 23rd Foot Feb 1788. Lt 7th Foot 29 Jan 1789. Capt Independent Company 14 Jan 1791. Capt 35th Foot 23 Mar 1791. Major 1 Sep 1795. Lt Colonel 30 Mar 1797. Bt Colonel 30 Oct 1805. Colonel 1st Greek Lt Infantry 25 Feb 1811. Major General 4 Jun 1811. Lt General 12 Aug 1819. General 10 Jan 1837.

Served in the Peninsula Oct – Dec 1812 and Mar 1813 – Feb 1814 (GOC 5th Division). Present in the retreat from Burgos (present at Villa Muriel), Osma, Vittoria (Mentioned in Despatches), first and second assaults on San Sebastian (wounded and Mentioned in Despatches on 31 Aug 1813) and Nivelle. KCB. Gold Medal for Maida, Vittoria and San Sebastian. GCB. GCMG. Also served in the West Indies 1793–1796 (present at Martinique, St Lucia, Guadeloupe), the Helder 1799 (wounded at Krabbenhan), Malta 1800, Sicily 1806 (present at Maida where he commanded 3 Brigade), Egypt 1807 (present at Alexandria and Rosetta), Sicily 1809–1810, Ionian Islands 1809 (present at the Capture of St Maura). Colonel 35th Foot 9 Oct 1819.

REFERENCE: *Dictionary of National Biography. Royal Military Calendar, Vol. 3, pp. 46–56. Gentleman's Magazine, Oct 1840, pp. 427–9.*

O'TOOLE, Bryan

Captain. 39th (Dorsetshire) Regiment of Foot.

Ledger stone: St Martin's (Catholic) Churchyard, Piercestown, County Wexford, Ireland. (Photograph)
(Note: According to the recorded memorial inscription, this was originally an altar tomb, but now only part of the memorial remains, limited to the top nine lines of the inscription.)

BENEATH / ARE DEPOSITED THE MORTAL REMAINS / OF / LT COLONEL BRYAN O'TOOLE / WHO DIED THE 27TH OF FEBRUARY 1825. / HAVING CHOSEN IN EARLY YOUTH THE MILITARY PROFESSION, / HIS CAREER WAS SOON MARKED / BY THAT INTREPIDITY AND SKILL WHICH DISTINGUISHED IT / TO ITS CLOSE. / HIS SPLENDID SERVICES IN SPAIN AND IN PORTUGAL / WERE NOT INDEED UNREWARDED / FOR HE WAS / A ROMAN CATHOLIC. / (THE URN IS PLACED HERE) / THAT THE MEMORY OF SO MUCH WORTH / AND SUCH HEROIC VALOUR / MIGHT NOT PERISH ALTOGETHER. / THIS MONUMENT, / WHICH OUGHT TO HAVE BEEN THE TRIBUTE / OF PUBLIC GRATITUDE, / IS ERECTED / BY PRIVATE FRIENDSHIP. R.I.P. / ....

Brass Memorial tablet: Church of the Immaculate Conception, Wexford, County Wexford, Ireland. (Photograph)

A + M + D + G / OF YOUR CHARITY PRAY FOR THE SOULS OF COLONEL BRIAN O'TOOLE, (C.B. / KNIGHT G. CROSS OF THE TOWER & SWORD OF PORTUGAL, KNIGHT OF ST LOUIS OF / FRANCE, & SEVERAL OTHER ORDERS.) MOREOVER, OF HIS NEPHEW, CAPTN. MATHEW O'TOOLE / LATE 82ND REGT. THE FORMER DIED 27TH FEB 1825. THE LATTER DIED 23RD JUNE 1860. / BOTH BURIED IN THEIR TOMB AT PIERCESTOWN. UNIVERSALLY BELOVED, / THEIR CHARACTERS THROUGH LIFE WERE CONSPICUOUS FOR RELIGION AND BRAVERY. / READER. / THIS TRIBUTE TO THEIR MEMORY IS ERECTED FROM SINCERE FRIENDSHIP TO ASK PRAYERS / FOR THEIR SOULS. + R.I.P. + BY JOSH. H. TALBOT

Cornet Hompesch's Hussars 1793. Capt-Lt 31 Dec 1795. Capt 25 Mar 1796. Capt 39th Foot 9 Jul 1803. Bt Major 25 Apr 1808. Bt Lt Colonel 21 Jun 1813. Portuguese Army: Lt Colonel 2 Caçadores 9 Nov 1811. Lt Colonel 7 Caçadores 16 Oct 1812.

Served in the Peninsula with 1/39th Nov 1811 and with Portuguese Army Nov 1811 – Sep 1813. Present at Ciudad Rodrigo (Mentioned in Despatches), Salamanca, Burgos and retreat from Burgos, Osma, Vittoria and Pyrenees (severely wounded at Pamplona, Mentioned in Despatches and awarded pension of £300 per annum). Gold Cross for Ciudad Rodrigo, Salamanca, Vittoria and Pyrenees. CB. Also served in the Austrian Army 1792–1793 (present at Longwy, Thionville and Valmy), Flanders 1794–1795 (present at Maastricht, Charleroi, Boxtel and Nimwegen), West Indies 1796 (capture of part of St Domingo), Irish Rebellion 1798 (present at Vinegar Hill and Ballynahinch), Sicily 1806 (present at Maida) and Sicily 1809 (present at Ischia). Half pay 25 Dec 1816.

Reference: Gentleman's Magazine, Jun 1825, pp. 567–8.

OTTLEY, Benjamin Wynne

Lieutenant Colonel. 91st Regiment of Foot.

Grave: Holy Trinity Churchyard, Brompton, London. (M.I.)

"BENJAMIN WYNNE OTTLEY ESQ. COLONEL OF THE BRITISH ARMY. ALSO LATE LIEUT-COLONEL OF THE 70TH REGT. D. 22 JUNE 1840, AGED 75."

Ensign 87th Foot 19 Jan 1780. Lt 5 Feb 1783. Capt 2nd West India Regt 1 Jul 1795. Major 25 Jul 1801. Major 91st Foot 6 Dec 1806. Bt Lt Colonel 25 Apr 1808. Lt Colonel 91st Foot 2 Jan 1812. Bt Colonel 4 Jun 1814. Lt Colonel 70th Foot 12 Aug 1819.

Served in the Peninsula Aug 1808 – Jan 1809. Present at Rolica, Vimeiro, Cacabellos and Corunna. Also served in the West Indies 1795, St Vincent 1796, Walcheren 1809 and the Netherlands 1814 (present at Bergen-op-Zoom). Commanded 2nd battalion 91st Foot at Stralsund 1813 and went from there to Holland for the attack on Bergen-op-Zoom where he commanded 21st Foot, 37th Foot and 91st Foot. They succeeded in taking the outwork that covered the Strenbergen gate of Bergen-op-Zoom but Ottley was severely wounded and taken prisoner. Half pay 21 Oct 1816.

Reference: Gentleman's Magazine, Aug 1840, p. 209.

OTTLEY, Matthew

Paymaster. 82nd (Prince of Wales's Volunteers) Regiment of Foot.

Headstone: St John's Anglican Churchyard, Niagara, Ontario, Canada. Seriously eroded and part of inscription illegible. (Photograph)

SACRED / TO THE MEMORY OF / MATTHEW OTTLEY / WHO DIED JAN. 13, 1845 / IN THE 72ND YEAR OF HIS AGE / HIS EARLY LIFE WAS SPENT IN HIS MAJESTY'S SERVICE / AND AFTER A PERIOD OF 13 YEARS, HE HELD THE / RESPONSIBLE OFFICE OF PAYMASTER IN THE 82ND REGIMENT. / SINCE HIS REMOVAL TO CANADA IN 1827, HIS SUPERIOR / ....

Paymaster 15 Aug 1798.

Served in the Peninsula Aug 1808 – Jan 1809 and Jun 1812 – Apr 1814. (acting ACG Sep – Oct 1808). Present at Rolica, Vimeiro, Corunna, Burgos, Vittoria, Pyrenees, Nivelle and Orthes. Also served at Walcheren 1809 and North America 1814–1815.

OTWAY, Hon. Henry, Lord Dacre

Lieutenant Colonel. Coldstream Regiment of Foot Guards.

Memorial: Royal Military Chapel, Wellington Barracks, London. (M.I.) (Destroyed by a Flying Bomb 1944)

"IN MEMORY OF LIEUT.-GENERAL HENRY OTWAY, TWENTY-FIRST LORD DACRE, C.B. COLONEL OF THE 31ST (THE HUNTINGDONSHIRE) REGIMENT. BORN, 1777; DIED, 1853. COLDSTREAM GUARDS, 1793–1821. HE SERVED DURING THE CAMPAIGNS IN FLANDERS, OF 1793–4–5, IN THE EXPEDITION TO COPENHAGEN IN 1807, AND IN THE PENINSULA, 1809–10–11–12, BEING PRESENT AT THE BATTLES OF TALAVERA AND BUSACO, AND IN COMMAND OF THE 1ST BATTALION AT SALAMANCA. HE BECAME LIEUT.-COLONEL OF THE REGIMENT IN 1814. PLACED BY HIS SONS, THOMAS CROSBIE WILLIAM, TWENTY-SECOND LORD DACRE, AND THE RIGHT HON. HENRY BOUVERIE WILLIAM BRAND, M.P., SPEAKER TO THE HOUSE OF COMMONS, FORMERLY IN THE COLDSTREAM GUARDS."

Ensign 27 Apr 1793. Lt and Capt 23 Jun 1795. Capt and Lt Colonel 25 Oct 1806. Bt Colonel 4 Jun 1814. Lt Colonel 25 Jul 1814. Major General 19 Jul 1821. Lt General 10 Jan 1837. General 11 Nov 1851.

Served in the Peninsula Mar 1809 – Mar 1811 and Jul 1811 – Oct 1812. Present at Douro, Talavera, Busaco, Salamanca and Burgos. Gold Medal for Salamanca. Also served in Flanders 1793–1795 and Copenhagen 1807. MGS medal for Talavera and Busaco. CB. Colonel 31st Foot 12 Jul 1847. Served in the Coldstream Guards under the name of Hon. Henry Brand.

OTWAY, Sir Loftus William

Major. 18th Regiment of Light Dragoons.

Mausoleum: Highgate Cemetery, London. (West XIV). (Photograph)

TO THE MEMORY OF / GENERAL SIR LOFTUS WILLIAM OTWAY, CB, / COLONEL OF THE 84TH REGIMENT, / AND KNIGHT COMMANDER OF THE ORDER OF KING / CHARLES III. OF SPAIN. / BORN 28TH OF APRIL 1775, DIED 7TH OF JUNE 1854. / HIS DISTINGUISHED SERVICES TO HIS COUNTRY / THROUGHOUT THE IRISH REBELLION AND THE PENINSULAR WAR, / ARE RECORDED IN THE HISTORY OF HIS TIME. / BRAVE AND GENTLE, HONOURABLE, GENEROUS AND TRUE, / POSSESSED OF RARE AND HIGHLY CULTIVATED / MENTAL POWERS, HE HAS NOT LEFT ON EARTH A / KINDER HEART, OR A MORE GALLANT SPIRIT. / GONE TO THY REST, BRAVE SOLDIER, ESTEEMED BY ALL, / AND TRULY LOVED AND DEEPLY LAMENTED / BY THOSE WHO KNEW THEE BEST.

Cornet 5th Dragoon Guards 17 May 1796. Lt 2 Sep 1796. Capt 27 Oct 1798. Major 24 Feb 1803. Bt Lt Colonel 28 Mar 1805. Major 18th Lt Dragoons 12 Feb 1807. Bt Colonel 4 Jun 1813. Major General 12 Aug 1819. Lt General 10 Jun 1837. General 11 Nov 1851. Portuguese Army: Colonel of Cavalry 1810. Brigadier 4 and 10 Cavalry Sep 1810.

Served in the Peninsula with 18th Lt Dragoons Dec 1808 – Jul 1810. With Portuguese Army Aug 1810 – Jul 1813. Present at Rueda (captured the whole of a French cavalry picket 18 Dec 1808), Sahagun, Benevente, Campo Mayor (with his men he gained the rear of the enemy and captured 600 men and their battery train (sixteen 24 pounders), but had to abandon them as the enemy held the return road. Mentioned in Despatches), Busaco, Albuera (commanded three regiments of Portuguese cavalry. Mentioned in Despatches) and Usagre (Mentioned in Despatches). Also served in Ireland 1798 (AAG present in the Irish Rebellion at Vinegar Hill) and Canada 1805–1807 (DAG). MGS medal for Sahagun and Benevente, Busaco and Albuera. CB. Knight Commander of Charles III of Spain. Retired 10 Jul 1813. Knighted 15 Jan 1815. Colonel 84th Foot 30 Dec 1840.

REFERENCE: *Dictionary of National Biography. Gentleman's Magazine, Oct 1854, pp. 389–90. Annual Register, 1854, Appx, p. 308.*

OVENS, John

Lieutenant. 27th (Inniskilling) Regiment of Foot.

Memorial: Derrygonnelly Graveyard, County Fermanagh, Ireland. (M.I.)

"TO THE MEMORY OF BARBARA OVENS WIFE OF THE LATE JOHN OVENS OF RAHALTON .... / ALSO TO HER SON JOHN OVENS LATE CAPTAIN 27TH REGT OF FOOT ALSO DEPARTED THIS LIFE 3RD MARCH 1849 AGED 53 YEARS. ...."

Fermanagh Militia. Ensign 27th Foot 2 Jul 1812. Lt 5 Jul 1814. Lt 20th Foot 25 Mar 1824. Lt 57th Foot 16 Dec 1824. Capt 9 Sep 1837.

Served in the Peninsula with 3/27th Jan 1813 – Apr 1814. Present at Vittoria, Pyrenees (wounded at Sorauren 28 Jul 1813), Nivelle, Nive, Orthes and Toulouse. Served with the Army of Occupation 1815–1816. Also served in North America 1814–1815 (present at Plattsburgh), Australia 1824–1831 (with 57th Foot guarding convicts on voyage to Australia) and India 1831–1846. MGS medal for Vittoria, Pyrenees, Nivelle, Nive, Orthes and Toulouse.

OVENS, John
Captain. 74th (Highland) Regiment of Foot.
Monument in railed enclosure: St Thomas's Cemetery, Sydney, Australia. (Photograph)

West side:

UNDERNEATH LIE THE / MORTAL REMAINS OF / BT MAJOR JOHN / OVENS 57 REGT / AND OF SAINT CATHERINE / COUNTY OF FERMANAGH / IRELAND. / 37 YEARS / A BRAVE SOLDIER & PUBLIC / OFFICER OF TRIED AND UNBLE / MISHED INTEGRITY. / HE DIED THE 7 DAY OF DECR 1825 / AND ON A DEATHBED FAR REMOVED / FROM HOME, EXPRESSED A DESIRE TO / BE INTERRED IN THE TOMB OF HIS / EARLY FRIEND JUDGE BENT.

East side:

MAJOR OVENS / WHO IS REMEMBERED FOR HIS / RELIABILITY AND UNFAILING ENERGY / WAS IN THE 73RD REGT IN 1808 / ARRIVED IN THIS COLONY 1810 / WHERE HE WAS APPOINTED / ENGINEER BY GOVERNOR / MACQUARRIE. IN 1811. HE / RETURNED TO ENGLAND AND / EXCHANGED INTO THE 74TH REGT / WHERE IN SPAIN HE WAS DANGEROUSLY / WOUNDED AT THE BATTLE OF VITTORIA, / AND ON HIS RECOVERY WAS TAKEN / AN EXTRA-AID-DE-CAMP TO MAJOR / GENERAL SIR THOS BRISBANE ON / WHOSE STAFF HE CONTINUED THE / WHOLE OF THE PENINSULAR WAR. / HE ACCOMPANIED HIS GENERAL / TO THIS COLONY 1821 WHERE / HE WAS BRIGADE MAJOR, ENGINEER / AND PRIVATE SECRETARY TILL THE / CLOSE OF HIS (SIR THOMAS'S) GOVT / ON THE 1ST OF DECR 1825.

North side:

VITTORIA PAMPLUNA TOULOUSE PENINSULA

South side:

HONESTAS OPTIMA ROLITIA

Ensign 73rd Foot 9 Jun 1807. Lt 12 Jul 1808. Capt 23 Jul 1811. Capt 74th 13 Oct 1812. Capt 57th Foot 16 Sep 1824. Bt Major 1 Oct 1824.

Served in the Peninsula Feb 1813 – Apr 1814. Present at Vittoria (severely wounded), Pyrenees, Nivelle, Nive, Orthes, Vic Bigorre, Tarbes and Toulouse. Also served in Australia 1810 as an Engineer. Returned to England and went to the Peninsula in 1813. Served again in Australia in 1821 as ADC and Private Secretary to Major General Sir Thomas Brisbane, Governor of New South Wales. Chief Engineer in New South Wales 1824. Supervised the convict gangs, clearing the land for settlers to culti-

vate. Did excellent work but his health failed and he died 7 Dec 1825.
Reference: Australian Dictionary of Biography.

OWEN, Humphrey
Major. Royal Artillery.
Low monument: Kensal Green Cemetery, London. (15032/79/7). Inscription illegible. (Photograph)

2nd Lt 18 Sep 1793. 1st Lt 1 Jan 1794. Capt-Lt 16 Jul 1799. Capt 12 Sep 1803. Major 20 Dec 1814. Lt Colonel 23 Dec 1815.

Served in the Peninsula Jan 1810 – Aug 1812. Present at Cadiz as officer in charge of 8th Company 5th Battalion. Retired by sale of commission 27 Jun 1823. Died 2 Jul 1862.

OWEN, John
Corporal. 74th (Highland) Regiment of Foot.
Headstone with Cross on top: All Saints's Church, Berrington, Shropshire. (Relocated inside the church adjacent to main door). (Photograph)

IN MEMORY OF / JOHN OWEN, / LATE COLOR SERGEANT IN / THE 74TH HIGHLANDERS. WITH / WHICH REGIMENT HE SERVED IN / THE PENINSULAR WAR UNDER / ARTHUR DUKE OF WELLINGTON, / AND WAS ENGAGED IN THE BATTLES / OF SALAMANCA, VITTORIA, PYRENEES, / NIVELLE, ORTHES, TOULOUSE AND / AT THE SIEGES OF CUIDAD RODRIGO, / AND BADAJOZ FOR WHICH HE RECEIVED / THE MEDAL AND EIGHT CLASPS. / HE DIED AT SHREWSBURY / 16TH APRIL 1880 / AGED 88.

The gravestone was found buried in the churchyard in 2002, excavated, repaired and set in the Church. A brass plaque fixed to the wall has the following inscription:

THE GRAVESTONE OF / COLOR SERGEANT JOHN OWEN / A HEROIC SOLDIER OF THE NAPOLEONIC WARS / BURIED IN THIS CHURCHYARD IN 1880 / RESEARCHED AND REDISCOVERED BY PAUL RIDGLEY / A MEMBER OF THE ASSOCIATION OF FRIENDS / OF THE WATERLOO COMMITTEE, ASSISTED BY / PETER FISHER, DAVID McCORMICK AND ERIC BRAYNE. / ADDITIONALLY FINANCED BY THE ASSOCIATION OF / FRIENDS OF THE WATERLOO COMMITTEE / AND THE ROYAL HIGHLAND FUSILIERS. / PLACED IN THE CHURCH JULY 2002.

Volunteer Shropshire Militia. Private 74th Foot 2 May 1811. Cpl 25 Dec 1814. Sgt 25 Jun 1817. Asst Sgt Major Nov 1829.

Served in the Peninsula 1811 – Apr 1814. Present at Ciudad Rodrigo (member of the storming party). Badajoz (member of the storming party where he was wounded), Salamanca, Vittoria, Pyrenees, Nivelle, Orthes, Tarbes and Toulouse. Awarded 1st Class Regimental Medal for Peninsula. Also awarded Regimental Gold Cross for his brave and gallant conduct in the Forlorn Hope at Ciudad Rodrigo, Badajoz, Salamanca and Vittoria. MGS medal for Ciudad Rodrigo, Badajoz, Salamanca, Vittoria, Pyrenees, Nivelle, Orthes and Toulouse. Army Long Service and Good Conduct Medal 1832. Discharged 9 Jul 1832. Also served in Canada and Newfoundland 1818 and the West Indies 1825 and 1828–1830 (present in Bermuda). Died at Shrewsbury 16 Apr 1880 aged 88.
Reference: Ridgley, Paul, John Owen's Gravestone, Waterloo Journal, Summer 2003, pp. 13–20. Obit. Shrewsbury Journal, 21 Apr 1880.

OWEN, Richard
Private. Royal Staff Corps.
Gravestone: Galle Face Burial Ground, Colombo, Ceylon. (Burial ground is no longer extant). (M.I.)

"HERE LIES THE BODY OF RICHARD OWEN OF THE ROYAL STAFF CORPS, WHO WAS BORN AT LLANBERIS IN CARNARVONSHIRE, NORTH WALES, AND DIED AT COLOMBO ON THE 10TH OF JUNE 1812. HE WAS FOR SEVERAL YEARS AND IN MANY LABORIOUS CAMPAIGNS THE SERVANT OF LT. COL. WILLERMAN, WHO SINCERELY LAMENTED HIS DEATH, AND NOW LIES BY HIS SIDE."

Served in the Peninsula Aug 1808 – Jan 1809 and Jul – Aug 1811. Present at Rolica, Vimeiro and Corunna. Also served in the Baltic 1807, Sicily 1809 and Ceylon where he was the servant of Lt Colonel Willerman.

PACK, Sir Denis

Lieutenant Colonel. 71st (Highland Light Infantry) Regiment of Foot.
Memorial tablet: St Canice's Cathedral, Kilkenny, County Kilkenny, Ireland. (Photograph)

NEAR THIS PLACE ARE INTERRED THE MORTAL REMAIN OF / MAJOR GENERAL SIR DENIS PACK, / KNIGHT COMMANDER OF THE MOST HON. MILITARY ORDER OF THE BATH, / AND OF THE PORTUGUESE MILITARY ORDER OF THE TOWER AND SWORD, / KNIGHT OF THE IMPERIAL RUSSIAN ORDER OF WLADIMER AND OF THE / IMPERIAL AUSTRIAN ORDER OF MARIA THERESA: / COLONEL OF THE 84TH REGT OF FOOT AND LIEUTENANT GOVERNOR OF PLYMOUTH / WHO TERMINATED A LIFE DEVOTED TO THE SERVICE OF HIS KING AND COUNTRY / ON THE 24TH DAY OF JULY 1823 AGED FORTY EIGHT YEARS. / THE NAME OF THIS DISTINGUISHED OFFICER IS ASSOCIATED WITH ALMOST / EVERY BRILLIANT ACHIEVEMENT OF THE BRITISH ARMY DURING THE / EVENTFUL PERIOD OF CONTINUAL WARFARE BETWEEN THE YEAR 1791 / IN WHICH HE ENTERED HIS MAJESTY'S SERVICE AND THE YEAR 1823 IN / WHICH HE ENDED HIS HONOURABLE CAREER. THROUGHOUT THE CAMPAIGNS / IN FLANDERS IN 1794 AND 1795, HE SERVED IN THE 14TH REGIMENT OF LIGHT / DRAGOONS AT THE CAPTURE OF THE CAPE OF GOOD HOPE. IN 1806 AND IN / THE ARDUOUS AND ACTIVE CAMPAIGN WHICH IMMEDIATELY FOLLOWED. / IN SOUTH AMERICA HE COMMANDED THE 71ST REGIMENT OF HIGHLANDERS / IN A MANNER WHICH REFLECTED THE HIGHEST CREDIT ON HIS MILITARY / SKILL AND VALOUR AT THE HEAD OF THE SAME CORPS IN 1808. HE ACQUIRED / FRESH REPUTATION IN THE BATTLE OF ROLEIA AND VIMIERA, AND / IN THE FOLLOWING YEAR IN THE BATTLE OF CORUNNA. IN 1809 HE ACCOMPANIED / THE EXPEDITION TO WALCHEREN AND SIGNALIZED HIMSELF BY HIS ZEAL / AND INTREPIDITY AT THE SIEGE OF FLUSHING. HE WAS SUBSEQUENTLY / ENGAGED AT THE HEAD EITHER OF A BRIGADE, OR A DIVISION OF THE / ARMY IN EVERY GENERAL ACTION AND REMARKABLE SIEGE WHICH TOOK / PLACE DURING THE SUCCESSFUL WAR IN THE PENINSULA UNDER THE / CONDUCT OF THE GREAT DUKE OF WELLINGTON. HE FINALLY COMMANDED / A BRIGADE IN THE ACTION OF QUATRE BRAS AND AGAIN IN THE EVER / MEMORABLE AND DECISIVE BATTLE OF WATERLOO. / FOR THESE IMPORTANT SERVICES IN WHICH HE WAS NINE TIMES SEVERELY WOUNDED, / HE OBTAINED AT THE RECOMMENDATION OF HIS ILLUSTRIOUS CHIEF FROM THE / FOREIGN POTENTATES IN ALLIANCE WITH GREAT / BRITAIN THE HONOURABLE / TITLES OF DISTINCTION ABOVE MENTIONED, AND FROM HIS OWN SOVEREIGN, / BESIDES THE ORDER OF THE BATH AND A MEDAL IN COMMEMORATION OF / THE BATTLE OF WATERLOO, A GOLD CROSS WITH SEVEN CLASPS ON WHICH / ARE INSCRIBED THE FOLLOWING NAMES OF THE BATTLES AND SIEGES / WHEREIN HE BORE A CONSPICUOUS PART VIZ, ROLEIA, CORUNNA, / BUSACO, CUIDAD RODRIGO, SALAMANCA, VITTORIA, PYRENEES, NIVELLE, / NIVE, ORTHES, TOULOUSE. UPON FIVE DIFFERENT OCCASIONS / HE HAD ALSO THE HONOUR TO RECEIVE THE THANKS OF BOTH HOUSES OF / PARLIAMENT. ON THE 3RD FEBRUARY 1813 FOR HIS CONDUCT AT SALAMANCA, / ON THE 10TH FEBRUARY 1812 FOR HIS CONDUCT AT CUIDAD RODRIGO; / ON THE 8TH NOVEMBER 1813 FOR HIS CONDUCT AT VITTORIA, / ON THE 24TH

MARCH 1814 FOR HIS CONDUCT AT ORTHES; ON THE 23RD JUNE 1815 / FOR HIS CONDUCT AT WATERLOO. WHILST THESE MERITS AS AN OFFICER / ENSURE FOR HIM A PLACE IN THE RECORDS OF HIS GRATEFUL COUNTRY / AMONGST THOSE HEROES WHO HAVE BRAVELY FOUGHT HER BATTLES AND / ADVANCED HER MILITARY GLORY, HIS VIRTUES AS A MAN, / WHICH WERE / SECURELY FOUNDED UPON CHRISTIAN PIETY, ARE ATTESTED BY THE ESTEEM / OF HIS COMPANIONS IN ARMS AND BY THE LOVE OF ALL WHO WERE / INTIMATELY CONNECTED WITH HIM. / THIS MONUMENT IS ERECTED BY HIS WIDOW / THE LADY ELIZABETH PACK / DAUGHTER OF GEORGE DE LA POER MARQUIS OF WATERFORD / AS A TRIBUTE OF RESPECT TO ONE OF HIS MAJESTY'S / MOST DESERVED SOLDIERS AND SUBJECTS / AND IN TESTIMONY OF HER OWN AFFECTION.

Cornet 14th Dragoons 30 Nov 1791. Lt 12 Mar 1795. Capt 5th Dragoon Guards 27 Feb 1796. Major 4th Dragoon Guards 25 Aug 1798. Lt Colonel 71st Foot 6 Dec 1800. Bt Colonel 25 Jul 1810. Major General 4 Jun 1813.

Served in the Peninsula with 71st Foot Aug 1808 – Jan 1809 and on Staff Sep 1813 – Apr 1814. With the Portuguese Army Jun 1810 – Aug 1813 (Brigadier 1 Portuguese Brigade). Present at Rolica, Vimeiro (Mentioned in Despatches), Lugo, Corunna, Busaco, Almeida, Ciudad Rodrigo (Mentioned in Despatches), Salamanca (Mentioned in Despatches), Burgos and retreat from Burgos (covering the rear-guard), Vittoria (Mentioned in Despatches), Pyrenees (severely wounded), Bidassoa, Nivelle, Nive, Garris, Orthes, Nive and Toulouse (wounded). Gold Cross for Rolica, Vimeiro, Corunna, Busaco, Ciudad Rodrigo, Salamanca, Vittoria, Pyrenees, Nivelle, Nive, Orthes and Toulouse. The 71st Foot had suffered from Walcheren fever and were not fit to go back to the Peninsula in 1809, so Pack requested to go to Portugal and help Beresford with the Portuguese Army. Present at Quatre Bras and Waterloo (wounded), where he commanded the 9th British Brigade. KCB. KTS. KMT. Knight of St Vladimir of Russia and Knight of Maria Theresa of Austria. Also served at Quiberon Bay 1795, Flanders 1795–1796 (present at Boxtel), Ireland 1798, Cape of Good Hope 1805 (present at Blueberg), South America 1807 (present at Montevideo and Buenos Ayres where he was wounded) and Walcheren 1809 (present at the siege of Flushing. Commandant at Veere). Lieutenant Governor of Plymouth 12 Aug 1819 until his death in 1823. Colonel York Chasseurs 2 Jan 1816. Colonel 84th Foot 9 Sep 1822. The memorial is in the Cathedral church where his father had been Deacon.

Reference: Dictionary of National Biography. Royal Military Calendar, Vol. 3, pp. 268–86. Gentleman's Magazine, Sep 1823, pp. 372–4.

PACKE, George Hussey

Lieutenant. 13th Regiment of Light Dragoons.

Memorial tablet: St Andrew's Church, Prestwold, Leicestershire. (Photograph)

SACRED TO THE MEMORY OF / LIEUTENANT COLONEL GEORGE HUSSEY PACKE, OF PRESTWOLD, AND OF CAYTHORPE IN THE COUNTY OF LINCOLN. / BORN MAY 1ST 1796; DIED JULY 2ND 1874. / HE WAS THE SECOND SON OF CHARLES JAMES PACKE AND PENELOPE HIS WIFE. MARRIED IN 1824, MARY ANNE LYDIA, ELDEST DAUGHTER OF / JAMES HEATHCOTE ESQRE, OF CONINGTON CASTLE, IN THE COUNTY OF HUNTINGDON, AND HAD ISSUE TWO SONS AND ONE DAUGHTER; / THE ELDEST SON CHARLES HUSSEY PACKE, WAS CALLED TO REST AT THE AGE OF 15 / ....

Cornet 8 Jul 1812. Lt 6 Jan 1814. Capt 21st Dragoons 27 Jun 1816.

Present at Waterloo (wounded). Half pay 25 Mar 1817. MP for South Lincolnshire 1859–1868. Educated at Eton. Younger brother of Major Robert Christopher Packe Royal Horse Guards who was killed at Waterloo.

PACKE, Robert Christopher
Major. Royal Regiment of Horse Guards.
Memorial tablet: St Andrew's Church, Prestwold, Leicestershire. (Photograph)

TO THE MEMORY OF ROBERT CHRISTOPHER PACKE, / MAJOR OF THE ROYAL REGIMENT OF HORSE GUARDS BLUE, / WHO WAS KILLED AT THE BATTLE OF WATERLOO JUNE 18TH 1815, / AGED 32 YEARS: / HIS REMAINS LIE BURIED ON THE FIELD, AND HIS PARENTS / HAVE RAISED THIS COMMEMORATIVE MARBLE. / THE MANLY VIRTUE, WITHER'D IN THE BLOOM / HAS SUNK FOR EVER IN AN EARTHLY TOMB / WE WILL NOT MOURN FOR HIM, THAT RAISED HIS HAND / TO GUARD THE BLESSING OF HIS NATIVE LAND / AND SEAL'D OBSERVANT OF HIS COUNTRY'S CLAIM, / A LIFE OF HONOR WITH A DEATH OF FAME / PRIDE OF THY PARENTS GALLANT SPIRIT, REST / IN LIFE BELOW, AND IN THINE END HERE BLEST, / WHEN WILD AMBITION WAVED HIS BANNER HIGH, / FEARLESS AND FOREMOST, THOU HAST DARED TO DIE. / AND NOBLY WON, IN ENGLAND'S BRIGHTEST DAY, / A VICTOR-WREATH THAT SHALL NOT FADE AWAY.

Memorial tablet: St George's Chapel, Windsor, Berkshire. (On Ambulatory wall). (Photograph)

TO THE MEMORY / OF ROBERT CHRISTOPHER PACKE ESQUIRE, / SECOND SON OF CHARLES JAMES PACKE ESQUIRE, / OF PRESTWOLD LEICESTERSHIRE, / AND MAJOR IN THE ROYAL REGIMENT OF HORSE GUARDS BLUE, / WHO WAS KILLED AT THE HEAD OF HIS SQUADRON / WHEN CHARGING THE FRENCH CUIRASSIERS, AT THE EVER / MEMORABLE BATTLE OF WATERLOO, ON THE 18TH OF JUNE 1815. / IN THE XXXIIID YEAR OF HIS AGE. / THIS MONUMENT IS ERECTED BY THE OFFICERS OF THE REGIMENT / IN WHICH HE HAD SERVED MORE THAN FIFTEEN YEARS. / IN TESTIMONY OF THEIR HIGH VENERATION FOR / HIS DISTINGUISHED MILITARY MERIT. / AND OF THEIR SINCERE REGRET FO THE LOSS OF A COMPANION, / SO LONG ENDEARED TO THEIR AFFECTIONS, BY HIS / AMIABLE MANNERS AND PRIVATE VIRTUES.

Cornet 2 Nov 1799. Lt 20 Mar 1802. Capt 15 Dec 1804. Major 13 May 1813.

Served in the Peninsula Nov 1812 – Apr 1814. Present at Vittoria and Toulouse. Gold Medal for Vittoria. Present at Waterloo where he was killed. Educated at Eton. Elder brother of Lt George Hussey Packe 13th Lt Dragoons.

PAGAN, Samuel Alexander
Lieutenant. 33rd (1st Yorkshire West Riding) Regiment of Foot.
Mural memorial tablet: Dean Cemetery, Edinburgh, Scotland. (Photograph)

IN MEMORY OF / S. A. PAGAN, MD. FRCSE, / WHO WAS A LIEUTENANT IN THE 33RD REGIMENT / WAS SEVERELY WOUNDED AT THE / BATTLE OF WATERLOO, / AND AFTERWARDS STUDIED MEDICINE, / DIED 23RD SEPTEMBER 1867, AGED 74. / ………………..

Ensign 31 Oct 1811. Lt 7 Apr 1814.

Present at Waterloo where he was severely wounded and awarded pension of £70 per annum. Half pay 14 Feb 1822. Retired from the army and became a medical student and doctor in Edinburgh.

PAGET, Charles
Captain. Royal York Rangers.
Ledger stone: Kensal Green Cemetery, London. (8379/41/PS). Inscription illegible. (Photograph)

Ensign 52nd Foot 18 Feb 1808. Lt 16 Mar 1809. Capt Royal York Rangers 28 Oct 1813.

Served in the Peninsula with 2/52nd Aug – Sep 1808 and 1/52nd Oct 1808 – Jan 1809 and Oct – Nov 1813. Present at Vimeiro, Corunna, Nivelle and Nive. Also served at Walcheren 1809. MGS medal for Vimeiro, Corunna, Nivelle and Nive. Died Aug 1849.

PAGET, Hon. Sir Edward

Colonel. 80th (Staffordshire Volunteers) Regiment of Foot.
Low monument: Royal Hospital Graveyard, Chelsea, London. Inscription illegible. (Photograph)
Memorial tablet: Royal Military Chapel, Sandhurst, Berkshire. (Photograph)

IN MEMORY OF / GENERAL THE HONBLE SIR EDWARD PAGET G.C.B. / COLONEL 28TH FOOT / DIED 13TH MAY 1849 AGED 73 / HIS WAR SERVICES WERE AS FOLLOWS / HOLLAND NIMEGUEN GUELDERMALSEN 1794–95 / CAPE ST VINCENT 1797 MINORCA 1798 / EGYPT THREE ACTIONS WOUNDED 1801 BREMEN 1805 / SICILY 1806–7 SWEDEN AND PORTUGAL 1808 / CORUNNA AND PASSAGE OF THE DOURO LOST RIGHT ARM 1809 / SECOND IN COMMAND TO WELLINGTON / RETREAT FROM BURGOS TAKEN PRISONER 1812 / COMMANDER IN CHIEF IN INDIA 1822–5. / GOVERNOR OF THIS COLLEGE 1826–37 / AFTERWARDS GOVERNOR OF / CHELSEA HOSPITAL

Named on the Memorial tablet: Main Hall, Royal Hospital, Chelsea, London. (Photograph)

Cornet 1st Life Guards 23 Mar 1792. Captain 54th Foot 1 Dec 1792. Major 14 Nov 1793. Lt Colonel 28th Foot 30 Apr 1794. Bt Colonel 1 Jan 1798. Major General 1 Jan 1805. Lt General 4 Jun 1811. General 27 May 1825.

Served in the Peninsula Sep 1808 – Jan 1809, May – Jun 1809 and Oct 1812 – Apr 1814. Present at Corunna (O/c Reserve division), Oporto (severely wounded, his arm amputated and awarded pension of £400 per annum). Returned from England 1812 as Wellington's second in command, retreat from Burgos (present at San Munos, O/c 1 Division Oct – Nov 1812. Taken prisoner 17 Nov 1812 until Apr 1814). Gold Medal for Corunna. Also served in Flanders 1794–1795 (present at Nimwegan and Gueldermalsen), Naval action off Cape St Vincent 14 Feb 1797, Minorca 1798, Egypt 1801 (present at Cairo and Alexandria), Ireland 1803–1804, Hanover 1805, Sicily 1806–1807, Sweden 1808, Ceylon (Governor) 1821–1823 and India (present in the Burmese Campaign 1824–1825 and during the Barrackpore Barracks mutiny). KTS. GCB. Had been made Captain of Cowes Castle in 1818 and on his return from India in 1825 chose to live on the Isle of Wight where he died at Cowes 13 May 1849. Colonel 80th Foot 23 Feb 1808. Colonel 28th Foot 26 Dec 1815. Governor of Royal Military College 1826–1837. Governor of Chelsea Hospital 1837–1849. Younger brother of Lord Henry Paget Marquis of Anglesey Colonel 7th Lt Dragoons.

REFERENCE: *Dictionary of National Biography. Paget, H. M. and E. Paget, eds, Letters and memorials of General the Honourable Sir Edward Paget, 1898. Hylton, Lord (H. G. Jollife), The Paget Brothers, 1790–1840, 1918, reprint 2010. Gentleman's Magazine, Jul 1849, pp. 90–1. Annual Register, 1849, Appx, p. 238. Cole, John William, Memoirs of British Generals, Vol. 1, 1856, pp. 145–62.*

PAGET, Elijah

Private. 44th (East Essex) Regiment of Foot.
Headstone: All Saints' Churchyard, West Bromwich, Staffordshire. (Memorial destroyed when churchyard was landscaped). (M.I.)

"PAGET, ELIJAH / OF GUNS LANE / LATE OF THE 44TH REGIMENT OF FOOT / WOUNDED AT WATERLOO / AND BURIED HERE SEPT 2ND 1878 / ON WHOSE SOUL JESUS HAVE MERCY. AMEN."

Served in the Peninsula 1810 – Feb 1813. Present at Badajoz and Salamanca. Present at Waterloo

(wounded in Capt G. Crozier's Company). Died aged 86 with the bullet that he received at Waterloo still in his thigh. Granted a pension of 18 pence a day. MGS medal for Badajoz and Salamanca.
REFERENCE: *West Bromwich Weekly News, 7 Sep 1878.*

PAGET, Lord Henry William see UXBRIDGE, Henry William Earl of

PAKENHAM, Hon. Sir Edward Michael

Colonel. 6th West India Regiment.
Memorial monument: St Paul's Cathedral, London. (South Transept). (Joint memorial with Samuel Gibbs). (Photograph)

ERECTED AT THE PUBLIC EXPENSE / TO THE MEMORY OF / MAJOR GENERAL THE HONBLE. SIR EDWARD PAKENHAM, K.B. / AND OF / MAJOR GENERAL SAMUEL GIBBS / WHO FELL GLORIOUSLY ON THE 18TH JANUARY 1815 / WHILE LEADING THE TROOPS TO AN ATTACK / OF THE ENEMIES WORKS IN THE FRONT OF NEW ORLEANS.

Buried in the family vault: Killucan, Westmeath, Ireland.

Ensign Major General Grosbie's Regt 28 Feb 1794. Lt 28 May 1794. Capt in Lt Colonel Hewitt's Regt 1 Jun 1794. Major 33rd Lt Dragoons (Ulster) 6 Dec 1794. Major 23rd Lt Dragoons 1 Jan 1798. Lt Colonel 64th Foot 17 Oct 1799. Lt Colonel 7th Foot 5 May 1804. Bt Colonel 25 Oct 1809. Major General 1 Jan 1812. Colonel 6th West India Regt 21 May 1813.

Served in the Peninsula on Staff 1810 – Apr 1814. (Commanded 4 Brigade 1st Division Aug – Sep 1810, O/c 2 Brigade 4th Division Oct 1810 – Jun 1812, O/c 2 Brigade 3rd Division Jun – Jul 1812, GOC 3rd Division 22 Jul 1812 – Jan 1813, GOC 6th Division Jan – Apr 1813 and Adjutant General Apr 1813 – Apr 1814). Present at Busaco, Fuentes d'Onoro, Salamanca, Pyrenees, Bidassoa, Nivelle, Nive, Orthes and Toulouse. Also served in the West Indies 1803 (present at St Lucia where he was wounded), Copenhagen 1807, Martinique 1809 (wounded) and North America 1814–1815. Chosen to command the expedition when General Ross was killed at Baltimore. When he arrived in New Orleans he found the Army in a most unfavourable position between the Mississippi river and a swamp. Pakenham was killed in the ensuing battle, his body brought back and buried in Ireland. Gold Cross for Martinique, Fuentes d'Onoro, Salamanca, Pyrenees, Nivelle, Nive, Orthes and Toulouse. GCB. Edward Pakenham was the brother of Capt and Lt Colonel Hercules Pakenham Coldstream Guards and also Wellington's brother-in-law. Wellington said of him 'He may not be the brightest genius, but my partiality for him does not lead me astray when I tell you that he is one of the best we have.'
REFERENCE: *Dictionary of National Biography. Pakenham, Thomas, ed., The Pakenham letters, 1800–1815, (Consisting mainly of letters written by Sir Edward Michael Pakenham), 1914, reprint 2009. Cole, John William, Memoirs of British Generals, Vol. 2, 1856, pp. 325–67. Gentleman's Magazine, May 1815, p. 471.*

PAKENHAM, Hercules Robert

Captain and Lieutenant Colonel. Coldstream Regiment of Foot Guards.
Memorial tablet: Gartree Church, Gartree, Aldergrove, Northern Ireland. (Photograph)

TO THE MEMORY OF / LT. GENL. THE HONBLE SIR HERCULES ROBT. PAKENHAM, K.C.B. / COLONEL OF THE 43D. LT. INFANTRY DEPY. LIEUT. OF THE CO. OF ANTRIM, / AND FOR 8 YEARS LT. GOVR. OF PORTSMOUTH, COMMANDING THE S.W. DIST OF ENGLD. / HE WAS 3D. SON OF THE 2ND LORD LONGFORD, / AND GRANDSON OF THE COUNTESS OF LONG-FORD, WHO SURVIVED HER SON. / BORN IN 1781, HE ENTERED THE ARMY IN 1803, IN WHICH HE SERVED WITH THE HIGHEST DISTINCTION, HAVING / BEEN ENGAGED AT THE SIEGE AND CAPTURE OF COPENHAGEN IN 1807, ALSO IN THE PENINSULAR CAMPAIGNS

OF / 1809, 10, 11 AND 12, INCLUDING THE BATTLES OF OBIDOS, ROLEIA, VIMIERA, POMBAL, FOZ D'AROUCE, SABUGAL / BUSACO, AND FUENTES D'ONOR, SIEGE AND STORM OF CIUDAD RODRIGO, TWO SIEGES AND STORM OF BADAJOZ / AT THE ASSAULT OF WHICH HE WAS SEVERELY WOUNDED. HE RECEIVED THE GOLD MEDAL FOR BUSACO, FUENTES D'ONOR / CUIDAD RODRIGO, AND BADAJOZ, AND THE SILVER WAR MEDAL FOR ROLEIA AND VIMIERA, AND TWO CLASPS. / HE MARRIED THE HON[BLE] EMILY STAPLETON DAUGHTER OF LORD LE DESPENCER, / BY WHOM HE LEFT SIX SONS AND THREE DAUGHTERS. / HE DIED VERY SUDDENLY, AT LANGFORD LODGE, THE 8TH OF MARCH 1850, DEEPLY DEPLORED BY HIS WIFE AND CHILDREN, / AND MOST SINCERELY REGRETTED BY HIS FAMILY AND ALL WHO KNEW HIM. / HIS HOPE WAS TRULY IN THE LORD JESUS. / HE LIES IN THE VAULT BELOW THIS CHURCH, / WHICH WAS CHIEFLY BUILT AND ENDOWED BY HIM. / (VERSE)

Brass Memorial tablet: Royal Garrison Church, Portsmouth, Hampshire. (Back of a choir stall). (Photograph)

LIEUTENANT GENERAL / SIR HERCULES ROBERT / PAKENHAM K.C.B. EIGHT / YEARS LIEUT. GOVERNOR / OF PORTSMOUTH DIED / MAR 8 1850 AGE 68 / DD: HIS DAUGHTER / ELIZABETH THISTLETHWAYTE.

Ensign 40th Foot 23 Jul 1803. Lt 6th West India Regt 3 Mar 1804. Lt 95th Foot 28 Apr 1804. Capt 2 Aug 1805. Major 7th West India Regt 30 Aug 1810. Bt Lt Colonel 27 Apr 1812. Lt Colonel 26th Foot 3 Sep 1812. Capt and Lt Colonel Coldstream Guards 25 Jul 1814. Lt Colonel (unattached) 15 May 1817. Bt Colonel 27 May 1825. Major General 10 Jun 1837. Lt General 9 Nov 1846.

Served in the Peninsula with 2/95th Aug 1808 – Jan 1809, 1/95th Jul 1809 – Jan 1810 (DAAG Oct 1809 – Jan 1810) and AAG 3rd Division Apr 1810 – Jun 1812. Present at Obidos (wounded), Rolica, Vimeiro (wounded), Vigo, Busaco, Fuentes d'Onoro, El Bodon, Ciudad Rodrigo and Badajoz (severely wounded, Mentioned in Despatches and awarded a pension of £200 per annum). Gold Cross for Busaco, Fuentes d'Onoro, Ciudad Rodrigo and Badajoz. MGS medal for Rolica and Vimeiro. KCB 1838. Also served at Copenhagen 1807. Lt Governor of Portsmouth 1843. Brother of Colonel Sir Edward Pakenham who was killed at New Orleans and brother-in-law of the Duke of Wellington. Had six sons, one was killed at Inkerman and another in the relief of Lucknow. Colonel 43rd Foot 9 Sep 1844.
Reference: Dictionary of National Biography. Gentleman's Magazine, May 1850, pp. 532–3. Annual Register, 1850, Appx, p. 212.

PALLANDT, Baron William A. van
Captain. 4th Dragoons, Dutch Cavalry.
Memorial tablet: St Joseph's Church, Waterloo. (Photograph)

TER / NAGEDACHTENIS / WILLEM ANNE / BARON VAN PALLANDT / GEN[N] OP DEN HUIZE EERDE / DEN 4[DLM] JAN: MDCCLXXXV / ALS RITMEESTER / NY HET REGIMENT / LIGHT DRAGONDERS N° 4 / ROEMRYK / VOOR KONING EN VADERLAND / GESNEUVELD / DEN 18 JUN: MDCCCXV

Named on the Memorial to Dutch officers killed at Waterloo: St Joseph's Church, Waterloo. (Photograph)

PALMER, Charles
Lieutenant Colonel. 23rd Regiment of Light Dragoons.
Memorial tablet: Bath Abbey, Bath, Somerset. (North pier of Great West Door). (Photograph)

SACRED TO THE MEMORY OF / JOHN PALMER ESQ[R] / .... / AND OF HIS SONS /

………………. / MAJOR GEN[L] CHARLES PALMER, / FORMERLY OF THE 10TH HUSSARS, M.P. FOR THIS CITY, / OBITT APRIL 17TH 1851, AGED 74.

Interred in Kensal Green Cemetery, London. (9522/80/RS). (No longer extant)

Cornet 10th Lt Dragoons 17 May 1796. Lt 29 Mar 1797. Capt 17 May 1799. Major 22 Aug 1805. Lt Colonel 3 May 1810. Lt Colonel 23rd Lt Dragoons 12 Nov 1814. Bt Colonel 4 Jun 1814. Major General 27 May 1825.

Served in the Peninsula Nov 1808 – Jan 1809, Feb – Apr 1813 and Jul 1813 – Apr 1814. Present at Sahagun, Benevente, Orthes and Toulouse. ADC to the Prince Regent 1811. In command of the 10th Lt Dragoons in Spain from Feb 1813 until Colonel Quentin returned in July. Palmer had a reputation of being a most forward cavalry officer in all of the 10th Lt Dragoon's encounters with the French in the Pyrenees and South of France. As a consequence of differences over matters of discipline and other matters he was instrumental in trying to remove Colonel Quentin, the Commanding Officer of the regiment. At the subsequent court martial Quentin was found not guilty of some of the charges and allowed to remain in the regiment. His attackers were removed to other regiments and Palmer was transferred to the 23rd Lt Dragoons. This led to a duel between the two men which took place in France in Feb 1815. Quentin fired first and missed and in reply Palmer fired in the air. Quentin declared himself satisfied and they all returned back to Paris. Sold his commission in 1825 and retired from the army, becoming MP for Bath 1808–1826 and 1831–1837. In later life became a theatre manager in Bath and owner of a vineyard in Bordeaux. Educated at Eton.

REFERENCE: *Gentleman's Magazine, Jul 1851, p. 92. Buchanan, Brenda J., Charles Palmer (1777–1851): soldier, politician, vineyard owner and theatre proprietor, Journal of the Society for Army Historical Research, Vol. 90, No. 361, Spring 2012, pp. 11–24.*

PALMER, Thomas

Private. 32nd (Cornwall) Regiment of Foot.

Cross on stepped base: Milton Road Cemetery, Weston-Super-Mare, Somerset. (Photograph)

IN MEMORY OF / THOMAS PALMER / BORN 30TH NOVEMBER 1789 / DIED 10TH APRIL 1889 / HE SERVED 8 YEARS IN 32ND REGIMENT / AND WAS PRESENT WITH HIS CORPS / AT COPENHAGEN 1807, CORUNNA AND FLUSHING 1809 / BADAJOZ, SALAMANCA AND MADRID 1812, / HE WAS THE LAST SURVIVOR OF THE ARMY WHICH FOUGHT AT CORUNNA / UNDER SIR JOHN MOORE. / "THEN WAS THE PROOF OF BRITISH COURAGE SEEN "

Memorial Tablet: St Andrew's Church, Stogursey, near Bridgewater, Somerset. (Photograph)

IN / MEMORY / OF / THOMAS / PALMER: / BORN IN THIS PARISH / 30, NOVEMBER, 1789: / DIED AT WESTON-SUPER-MARE / 10 APRIL 1889. / HE SERVED IN THE 32ND REG[T], 1807–1814: / FOUGHT AT COPENHAGEN, 1807: / AT CORUNNA AND FLUSHING, 1809: / AT BADAJOZ, SALAMANCA, AND MADRID, 1812: / AND WAS THE LAST SURVIVOR OF / SIR JOHN MOORE'S ARMY.

Pte 15 Feb 1807.

Served in the Peninsula 1808 – Jan 1809 and 1811–1814. Present at Corunna, Badajoz (with 32nd Foot as a covering force only) and Salamanca. Also served at Copenhagen 1807 and Walcheren 1809 (severely wounded at the siege of Flushing). Discharged from the army 2 Jun 1814 on a pension of 9 pence a day. MGS medal for Corunna and Salamanca. Took up the trade of shoemaking and farming amd retired at the age of 75. Died 10 Apr 1889, the last survivor of Sir John Moore's army, and was given a military funeral.

PARBART, Hugh
Sergeant. 39th (Dorsetshire) Regiment of Foot.
Headstone: St Oswald's Churchyard, Malpas, Cheshire. (Photograph)

IN MEMORY OF / HUGH PARBART, OF MALPAS. / SERGEANT OF THE 39TH REGIMENT / OF FOOT; WHO DEPARTED THIS LIFE / JAN 13TH 1871. AGED 77 YEARS. / ....

Cpl 19 May 1806. Sgt 17 Sep 1806.
Served in the Peninsula 1809–1813. Present at Busaco, first and second sieges of Badajoz, Albuera (wounded), Arroyo dos Molinos and Campo Mayor. Served in France with the Army of Occupation until 1818. Discharged 6 Dec 1831 and became a shoe maker. MGS medal for Albuera.

PARDOE, Edward
Ensign. 1st Regiment of Foot Guards.
Memorial: Royal Military Chapel, Wellington Barracks, London. (M.I.) (Destroyed by a Flying Bomb 1944)

"IN MEMORY OF / EDWARD PARDOE, YOUNGEST SON OF JOHN PARDOE, ESQ, MP, OF LEYTON, ESSEX. / BORN 4TH APRIL, 1796. / ENSIGN, 1ST GUARDS, 1813. SEVERELY WOUNDED AT THE SIEGE OF BERGEN-OP-ZOOM, 1814. / KILLED AT WATERLOO. / PLACED BY HIS RELATIVES, H. PARDOE AND C. W. PARDOE, 1881."

Also named on Memorial Panel VIII for Waterloo: Royal Military Chapel, Wellington Barracks, London. (M.I.) (Destroyed by a Flying Bomb 1944)

Named on the Regimental Memorial: St Joseph's Church, Waterloo. (Photograph)

Ensign 29 Apr 1813.
Present at Waterloo where he was killed. Also served in the Netherlands 1814–1815 (present at Bergen-op-Zoom where he was wounded and Mentioned in Despatches).

PARKE, Charles
Captain. 3rd (East Kent) Regiment of Foot.
Pedestal tomb: Mount Jerome Cemetery, Dublin, Ireland. (Grave number 2320). (Photograph)
Memorial is seriously damaged, only the base of the memorial remaining. Inscription recorded from memorial inscription.

"SACRED TO THE MEMORY OF MAJOR CHARLES PARKE, FOURTH SON OF LIEUT-COL ROGER PARKE OF DUNALLY CO. OF SLIGO, WHO DEPARTED THIS LIFE ON THE 3RD DAY OF NOVEMBER 1858 IN HIS 71ST YEAR. THIS MONUMENT WAS ERECTED BY HIS NEPHEW JEMMETT DUKE AS A TRIBUTE OF AFFECTION AND GRATEFUL REMEMBRANCE."

Ensign 11 Dec 1802. Lt 16 Jun 1803. Capt 30 Jan 1806. Bt Major 12 Aug 1819.
Served in the Peninsula Jun 1809 – Jun 1810, Aug – Nov 1811 and Jan – Apr 1814. Present at Talavera. Also served in North America 1814–1815. MGS medal for Talavera.

PARKER, Edward
Captain. Royal Engineers.
Named on the Regimental Memorial: Rochester Cathedral, Rochester, Kent. (Photograph)
Named on the Memorial: St Andrew's Church (now Musée Historique), Biarritz, France. (Photograph)

2nd Lt 1 Jan 1804. Lt 1 Mar 1805. 2nd Capt 24 Jun 1809. Capt 21 Jul 1813.

Served in the Peninsula Jul 1812 – Feb 1814. Present at Orthes (acting as General Picton's ADC), where he was killed by a cannon shot 27 Feb 1814. Also served in Egypt 1807 and Sicily 1807–1811.

PARKER, Harry

Ensign. Coldstream Regiment of Foot Guards.
Memorial tablet: Holy Trinity Church, Long Melford, Suffolk. (Photograph)

………………. / LIEUTENANT HARRY PARKER. / COLDSTREAM GUARDS, / KILLED AT THE BATTLE OF TALAVERA, / 27TH JULY 1809. / ……………….

Named on Memorial Panel VI for Talavera: Royal Military Chapel, Wellington Barracks, London. (M.I.) (Destroyed by a Flying Bomb 1944)

Ensign 18 Apr 1805.

Served in the Peninsula Mar – Jul 1809. Present at Douro and Talavera where he was killed 28 Jul 1809. Brother of 2nd Capt John Boteler Parker Royal Artillery.

PARKER, Henry Thomas

Lieutenant. 9th Regiment of Light Dragoons.
Memorial tablet: St Mary's Church, Henley-on-Thames, Oxfordshire. (North wall of Font chapel at north-east corner of the church). (Photograph)

NEAR THIS PILLAR / LIES BURIED THE MORTAL REMAINS OF / HENRY THOMAS PARKER ESQR / WHO DIED 11TH FEBRUARY 1834. / THIS TABLET / ERECTED TO HIS MEMORY / BY HIS WIDOW / WHOSE CONSOLING BELIEF IS THAT / "HE IS NOT HERE, HE IS RISEN!"

Lt 29 Sep 1806.

Served in the Peninsula May 1812 – Apr 1813. Present at Alba de Tormes. Also served at Walcheren 1809. Half pay 30 Oct 1817.

PARKER, John Boteler

2nd Captain. Royal Artillery.
Family Memorial tablet: Holy Trinity Church, Long Melford, Suffolk. (Photograph)

………………. / MAJOR GENERAL JOHN BOTELER PARKER. C. B. / OF THE ROYAL ARTILLERY, / WHO LOST HIS LEFT LEG AT THE BATTLE OF WATERLOO, / AND DIED LIEUTENANT GOVERNOR / OF THE ROYAL MILITARY COLLEGE, WOOLWICH, / 25TH MARCH 1851: / ……………….

Memorial tablet: St Luke's Church, Charlton, Kent. (Photograph)

IN MEMORY OF / MAJOR GENERAL JOHN BOTELER PARKER, C.B. / LIEUT COLONEL OF THE ROYAL HORSE ARTILLERY. / LIEUT GOVERNOR OF THE ROYAL MILITARY ACADEMY / WHO DIED AT WOOLWICH / 25TH OF MARCH 1851; AGED 66 YEARS. / HIS REMAINS ARE DEPOSITED IN A VAULT ON THE NORTH SIDE OF THIS CHURCH. / HE WAS SECOND SON OF ADMIRAL SIR HYDE PARKER. / AND SERVED ON THE EXPEDITION TO WALCHEREN IN JULY 1809; / WAS PRESENT AT THE SIEGE OF FLUSHING, / COMMANDED A BRIGADE OF ARTILLERY AT THE BATTLE OF VITTORIA, / SERVED IN BOTH SIEGES OF ST SEBASTIAN, / THE BATTLE OF ORTHES, ACTION OF TARBES, / AND AT THE BATTLE OF TOULOUSE; / AND IN 1815 HE LOST HIS LEG AT THE / BATTLE OF WATERLOO.

Grave: St Luke's Churchyard, Charlton, Kent. (Grave number 281). (M.I.)

"MAJOR GENERAL JOHN BOTELER PARKER CB WHO DIED THE 25TH MARCH 1851 AGED 66."

2nd Lt 1 Apr 1802. 1st Lt 1 Sep 1803. 2nd Capt 5 Jun 1808. Bt Major 21 Sep 1813. Bt Lt Colonel 18 Jun 1815. Capt 29 Jul 1825. Lt Colonel 10 Jun 1837. Bt Colonel 10 May 1837. Major General 9 Nov 1846.

Served in the Peninsula Mar 1812 – Apr 1814. Present at Vittoria, first and second sieges of San Sebastian (Mentioned in General Graham's Despatches), Orthes, Tarbes and Toulouse. Gold Medal for Vittoria. MGS medal for San Sebastian, Orthes and Toulouse. CB. Present at Waterloo, where he lost his left leg. Also served at Walcheren 1809. Lt Governor of the Royal Military Academy at Woolwich 1 Apr 1846–1851. Brother of Ensign Harry Parker Coldstream Guards, killed at Talavera.
REFERENCE: *Gentleman's Magazine, Jun 1851, p. 665. Annual Register, 1851, Appx, p. 273. United Service Magazine, May 1851, p. 156.*

PARKER, Robert
Lieutenant. 76th Regiment of Foot.
Memorial tablet: St Bartholomew's Church, Colne, Lancashire. (Photograph)

.... / SACRED / TO THE MEMORY OF / LIEUT ROBERT PARKER, / OF THE 76TH REGT OF FOOT; / FIFTH SON OF THE ABOVE / THOMAS AND BETTY PARKER, / WHO DIED AT MIDDLEBURG; / THE 2ND OF SEPTR 1809, AGED 19 YEARS, / AND WAS INTERRED THERE.

Ensign 10 Nov 1808. Lt 8 Jul 1809.
Present at Walcheren 1809 where he died at Middleburg Sep 1809.

PARKER, Thomas
Captain. Royal Regiment of Horse Guards.
Chest tomb: Malvern Abbey Churchyard, Malvern, Worcestershire. (Photograph)

HERE REST THE REMAINS OF / THOMAS PARKER ESQUIRE / LATE COLONEL OF THE ROYAL CHESHIRE MILITIA / WHO DEPARTED THIS LIFE / ON THE FIRST DAY OF AUGUST 1840 / AGED 74 YEARS.

Cornet 22 Jun 1805. Lt 27 Feb 1806. Capt 11 May 1809.
Served in the Peninsula Nov 1812 – Nov 1813. Present at Vittoria. Resigned 18 Nov 1813. Later Colonel Royal Cheshire Militia.

PARKINSON, Henry
Corporal. 7th (Royal Fusiliers) Regiment of Foot.
Headstone: All Saints with St John the Baptist's Churchyard, Habergham, Padiham, Lancashire. Seriously eroded. (Photograph)

IN AFFECTIONATE MEMORY OF / HENRY PARKINSON, / OF HABERGHAM. / COLOR SERGEANT 7TH ROYAL FUSILIERS. / WHO DEPARTED THIS LIFE JULY 19TH 1868, / AGED 78 YEARS. / HE SERVED ** YEARS IN THE ARMY / AND TWENTY YEARS A YEOMAN OF HER / MAJESTY'S QUEEN'S BODYGUARD. HE WAS / THIRTEEN YEARS A COLOR SERGEANT / MAJOR OF THE 7TH FOOT HE BORE A CHAR- / ACTER CREDIBLE TO HIMSELF AND TO THE / REGIMENT AND ********** INTENDED TO / UPHOLD THE DISTINGUISHED RESPECTABILITY / OF THE CORPS. HE SERVED UNDER HIS GRACE / THE DUKE OF WELLINGTON IN THE PENINSULAR / CAMPAIGN AND HE WAS PRESENT AT THE / FOLLOWING ENGAGEMENTS. / ALBUHERA SABUGAL BADAJOS / SALAMANCA VITTORIA

RONCE – / VALLAS PYRENEES ST SEBASTIAN / NIVE NIVELLE TOULOUSE / ORTHES. / ALSO NEW ORLEANS NORTH AMERICA.

Served in the Peninsula 1811 – Apr 1814. Present at Albuera, Salamanca, Vittoria, Pyrenees, San Sebastian, Nivelle, Nive, Orthes and Toulouse. Also served in North America 1814–1815 (present at New Orleans). MGS medal for Albuera, Salamanca, Vittoria, Pyrenees, San Sebastian, Nivelle, Nive, Orthes and Toulouse. Awarded the Regimental medal for nine actions.
Reference: Orders and Medals Research Society Journal, Vol. 2, Spring 1990, No. 1.

PARKINSON, John
Ensign. 74th (Highland) Regiment of Foot.
Named on the Memorial: St Andrew's Church (now Musée Historique), Biarritz, France. (Photograph)
Named on the Regimental Memorial: St Giles's Cathedral, Edinburgh, Scotland. (Photograph)

Volunteer 6th Foot. Ensign 74th Foot 21 Oct 1813.
Served in the Peninsula Dec 1813 – Apr 1814. Present at Orthes, Vic Bigorre, Tarbes and Toulouse where he was severely wounded and died of wounds 11 Apr 1814.

PARRY, William Parry Jones
Captain. 48th (Northamptonshire) Regiment of Foot.
Obelisk: Locksbrook Cemetery, Bath, Somerset. (Grave number A BB 305). (Photograph)

WILLIAM PARRY JONES / BORN 12 MARCH 1790, DIED 6 JUNE 1867 / OF PLAS-YN-YALE DENBIGH, N. WALES / LT COLONEL 48TH FOOT / HE ENTERED THE ARMY / 1805, / AND SERVED WITH DISTINCTION / THROUGH THE PENINSULAR CAMPAIGN. / HE WAS IN NINE GENERAL ACTIONS, / "TALAVERA" "BUSACO" "ALBUHERA" / "VITTORIA" "PYRENEES" "NIVELLE" / "NIVE" "ORTHES" "TOULOUSE". / WAS SEVERELY WOUNDED AT PAMPELUNA, / AND HIS HORSE SHOT UNDER HIM. / HE RECEIVED THE GOLD MEDAL FOR ALBUHERA / AND THE WAR MEDAL WITH EIGHT CLASPS.

Note: Two panels of the memorial are missing. The top part of the inscription is recorded from a memorial inscription record.

Ensign 24 Sep 1805. Lt 16 Dec 1806. Capt 17 May 1808. Major 27 May 1825. Lt Colonel 28 Jun 1838.
Served in the Peninsula Apr 1809 – Aug 1811 and Sep 1812 – Apr 1814. Present at Douro, Talavera, Busaco, Albuera, Vittoria, Pyrenees (wounded at Pamplona), Nivelle, Nive, Orthes and Toulouse. Gold Medal for Albuera (as Captain of the Light Company of the 48th Foot, he took command of the battalion as all the senior officers were killed or wounded). MGS medal for Talavera, Busaco, Vittoria, Pyrenees, Nivelle, Nive, Orthes and Toulouse. Magistrate and Deputy Lieutenant of Denbighshire and High Sherriff 1833. Later assumed the name of Yale.
Reference: United Service Magazine, Sep 1867, pp. 129–30.

PARSONS, Charles
Captain. 27th (Inniskilling) Regiment of Foot.
Memorial tablet: St Lawrence's Church, Stretton Grandison, Herefordshire. (Photograph)

SACRED / TO THE MEMORY / OF / CHARLES PARSONS ESQ. / CAPTAIN OF HIS MAJESTYS 27 REGT OF INFANTRY / SECOND SON OF THE REV WILLIAM PARSONS / BY MARY HIS WIFE / DAUGHTER OF MORGAN GRAVES / OF MICKLETON IN THE COUNTRY OF GLOUCESTER ESQ. / AFTER A FEVER WHICH SUCCEEDED THE EXTRACTION OF / A MUSKET BALL RECEIVED IN HIS THIGH / DURING A SKIRMISH WITH THE FRENCH TROOPS / NEAR ALCO

IN VALENTIA / TERMINATED HIS VALUABLE LIFE / ON THE 28 DAY OF SEPTEMBER 1813 / IN THE 26 YEAR OF HIS AGE.

Lt 7 Jan 1806. Capt 13 Jul 1809.

Served in the Peninsula with 2/27th Dec 1812 – May 1813. Present at Alcoy where he was severely wounded and died of his wound 28 Sep 1813.

PARSONS, Edward

Captain. 48th (Northamptonshire) Regiment of Foot.

Family Memorial tablet: St Andrew's Church, Presteigne, Radnorshire, Wales. (Photograph)

SACRED TO THE MEMORY OF / EDWARD PARSONS / CAPTN. IN HIS MAJESTY'S 48TH REGT OF FOOT, / WHO AFTER HAVING SERVED IN SEVERAL CAMPAIGNS / IN SPAIN AND PORTUGAL / FELL AT THE BATTLE OF ALBUERA MAY 16TH 1812. / AGED 29 YEARS. / ....

West Essex Militia. Ensign 29 Foot 10 Sep 1799. Ensign 48 Foot 25 Feb 1800. Lt 16 Aug 1805. Capt 21 Nov 1805.

Served in the Peninsula Apr 1809 – May 1811. Present at Douro, Talavera, Busaco and Albuera where he was severely wounded and died of his wounds 4 Jun 1811. Brother of Capt Henry Parsons 47th Foot and Ensign Lucius Parsons 48th Foot.

Note that the date of his death at Albuera is incorrectly given as 1812 on the memorial tablet.

PARSONS, Henry

Captain. 47th (Lancashire) Regiment of Foot.

Family Memorial tablet: St Andrew's Church, Presteigne, Radnorshire, Wales. (Photograph)

.... / AND OF HENRY PARSONS, CAPTN IN THE 47TH REGT. OF FT. / WHO WAS WOUNDED AT THE BATTLE OF VITTORIA IN SPAIN / JUNE 21 1813 / AND DIED SERVING HIS COUNTRY IN THE WAR BETWEEN / THE ENGLISH AND BURMESE IN THE KINGDOM OF AVA / JULY 16TH 1824, AGED 39 YEARS / ....

Lt 28 Aug 1804. Capt 13 Jun 1811.

Served in the Peninsula Jan – Jul 1812 and Dec 1812 – Dec 1813. Present at Cadiz and Vittoria (wounded). Also served in India 1824 (present in the Burmese Campaign where he died 16 Jul 1824). Brother of Capt Edward Parsons 48th Foot and Ensign Lucius Parsons 48th Foot.

PARSONS, Lucius

Ensign. 48th (Northamptonshire) Regiment of Foot.

Family Memorial tablet: St Andrew's Church, Presteigne, Radnorshire, Wales. (Photograph)

.... / AND OF LUCIUS PARSONS AN ENSIGN IN THE SAME REGT / WHO WAS KILLED / AT THE BATTLE OF THE PYRENEES / JULY 28TH 1813, AGED 18 YEARS. / ....

Ensign 15 Aug 1811.

Served in the Peninsula Dec 1812 – Jul 1813. Present in the Pyrenees where he was killed at Sorauren. Brother of Capt Edward Parsons 48th Foot and Capt Henry Parsons 47th Foot.

PARTRIDGE, John

Corporal. 1st (Royal) Regiment of Dragoons.

Headstone laid flat: St Peter's Churchyard, Brighton, Sussex. (Photograph)

SACRED / TO THE MEMORY OF / CAPTAIN JOHN PARTRIDGE / LATE OF THE FIRST (OR) ROYAL DRAGOONS / WHO DEPARTED THIS LIFE / AUGUST 23RD 1863, / IN THE 70TH YEAR OF HIS AGE. / "HE IS NOT DEAD BUT SLEEPETH" / PRESENT AT THE GREAT BATTLE / OF WATERLOO JUNE 18TH 1815.

Present at Waterloo. Quartermaster in 1st Dragoons 18 Jul 1834. Half pay 1849. Became Honorary Captain 1 Jul 1859.

PASCHAL, George Frederick
Lieutenant. 2nd Line Battalion, King's German Legion.
Headstone: Brompton Cemetery, London. (Grave number BR 81798). (Photograph)

IN AFFECTIONATE REMEMBRANCE OF / LIEUT. COLONEL GEORGE FREDERICK PASCHAL / LATE 70TH REGT. / WHO DIED OCTOBER 23RD 1875, AGED 78 YEARS.

Ensign 17 Mar 1812. Lt 19 Oct 1812. Capt 70th Foot 23 Mar 1826.

Served in the Peninsula Oct 1813 – Apr 1814. Present at Nivelle, Nive, St Etienne and Bayonne. Present at Quatre Bras and Waterloo. MGS medal for Nivelle and Nive. Also served in the Netherlands 1814. Half pay 19 Dec 1834. Retired 11 Nov 1851.

PASLEY, Charles William
Lieutenant Colonel. Royal Engineers.
Monument: Kensal Green Cemetery, London. (5205/88/IC). (Photograph)

SACRED TO THE MEMORY OF / GENERAL / SIR CHARLES WILLIAM PASLEY KCB. / COLONEL COMMANDANT, ROYAL ENGINEERS, / DCL. FRS. ETC ETC / WHO DIED 19TH APRIL 1861, / IN HIS 81ST YEAR

2nd Lt Royal Artillery 1 Dec 1797. 2nd Lt Royal Engineers 1 Apr 1798. Lt 28 Aug 1799. 2nd Capt 1 Mar 1805. Capt 18 Nov 1807. Bt Major 8 Feb 1812. Bt Lt Colonel 27 May 1813. Lt Colonel 20 Dec 1814. Bt Colonel 22 Jul 1830. Colonel 12 Nov 1831. Major General 23 Nov 1841. Lt General 11 Nov 1851. Colonel Commandant 28 Nov 1853. General 20 Sep 1860.

Served in the Peninsula 1808–1809. Present at Corunna. Also served in Sicily 1806 (present at Maida), Copenhagen 1807, Walcheren 1809 (wounded twice, the second wound in his spine was so severe that he was never on active service again). From 1812 worked hard to improve the military engineering techniques with the support of Wellington. His ideas were introduced into the Engineering schools at Chatham. Director of Royal Sappers and Miners 1813. Director of the School of Military Engineering at Chatham. His publications included *A Course of Elementary Fortifications,* 2nd edn, 2 vols, 1822, and *Rules for Conducting the Practical Operations of a Siege*, 1829–1832. Also improved systems of telegraph communication, sapping, mining, pontooning and exploding gunpowder. His system of exploding gunpowder was credited by Sir Henry Hardinge with blowing the gates open at the siege of Ghuznee in 1840. Developed new kinds of cement which led to the manufacture of artificial cement such as Portland. MGS medal for Maida and Corunna. KCB.

Reference: Dictionary of National Biography. Kealy, Percival Hope, General Sir William Pasley, KCB, FRS, DCL, Colonel Commandant RE, 1780–1861, 1930. Harvey, A. D., Captain Pasley at Walcheren, Aug 1809, Journal of the Society for Army Historical Research, Vol. 69, No. 277, Spring 1991, pp. 16–21. Hancock, Major J. T., Roots – who was father of the Corps? Royal Engineers Journal, Vol. 91, No. 3, Sep 1977, pp. 177–83 (Sir Charles Pasley and the origin of the Corps). Gentleman's Magazine, Jul 1861, pp. 698–9. Annual Register, 1861, Appx, pp. 480–1.

Michael McCreagh Portuguese Army

Digby Mackworth 7th Foot

John McDonald 88th Foot

Peregrine Maitland 1st Foot Guards

Alexander McPherson 92nd Foot

Roderick McNeill 23rd Foot

Edward Macarthur 39th Foot

Donald McPherson 39th Foot

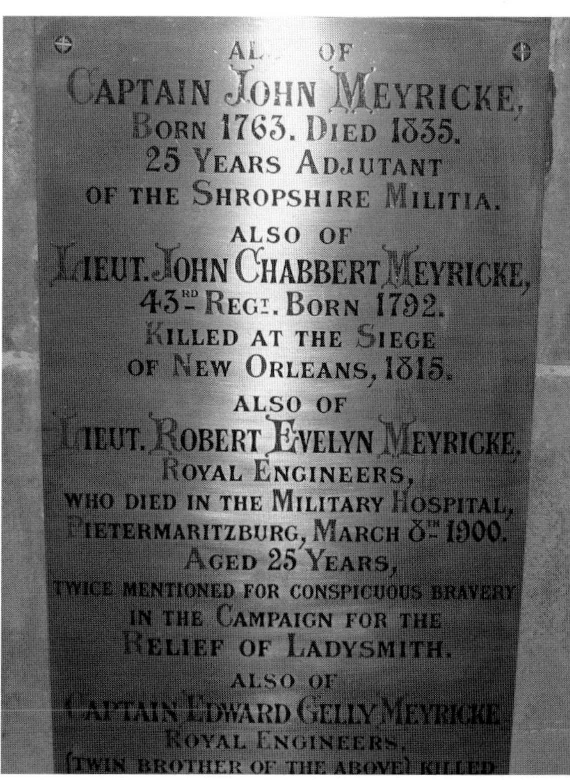

John C. Meyricke 43rd Foot

Robert Milligan 11th Dragoons

John Millar 43rd Foot

John Molloy 95th Foot

John Morgan 11th Dragoons

Roderick Murchison 36th Foot

Sir William Myers 7th Foot

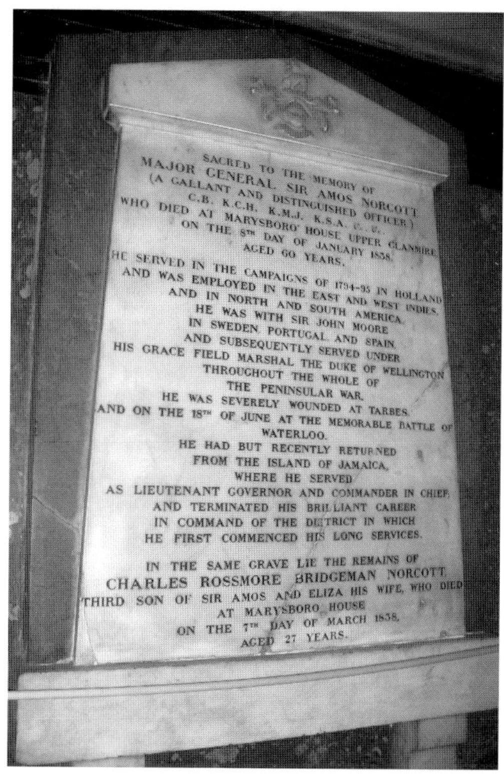

Sir Amos Norcott 95th Foot

William Offeney King's German Legion

James O'Malley 11th Dragoons

John Ormiston 91st Foot

John Orr 42nd Foot

Robert C Packe Royal Horse Guards

Sir Edward Paget 80th Foot

Hugh Parbart 39th Foot

Henry Parkinson 7th Foot

Hugh Patrickson 4th Dragoons

Alexander H. Pattison 74th Foot

Paul Peattie 42nd Foot

John and Robert Piper 4th Foot and R. Engineers

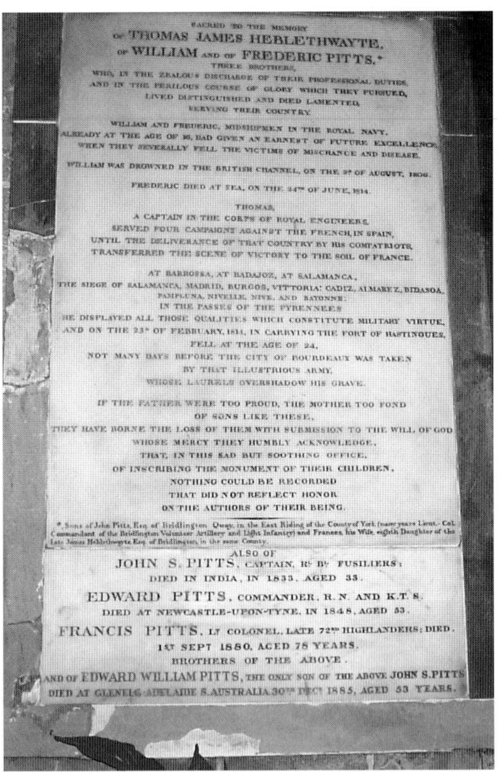

Thomas H. Pitts Royal Engineers

Edward Porteus Medical Department

Charles Pratt Commissariat Department

John Pring 27th Foot

Lucas Pulsford 18th Dragoons

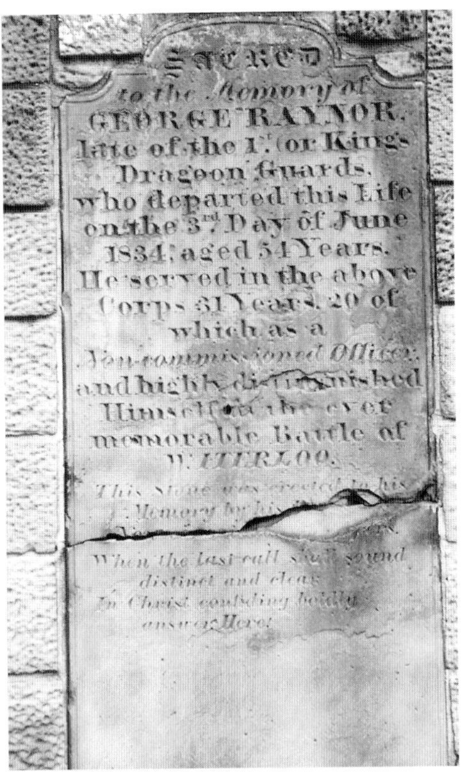

George Raynor 1st Dragoon Guards

Sir Thomas Reade 27th Foot

John Reed 62nd Foot

John Reeve 1st Foot Guards

John and William Riach 73rd & 79th Foot

Thomas Reynell 71st Foot

John S. Ribton 95th Foot

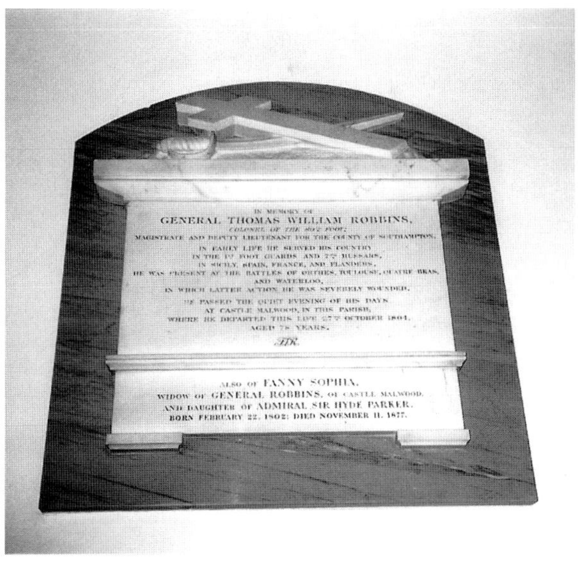

Thomas W. Robbins 7th Dragoons

John B. Riddlesden Royal Horse Guards

Alexander Rollo Royal Artillery

William Rowan 52nd Foot

Mathew Forster 85th Foot

James P. Gairdner 95th Foot

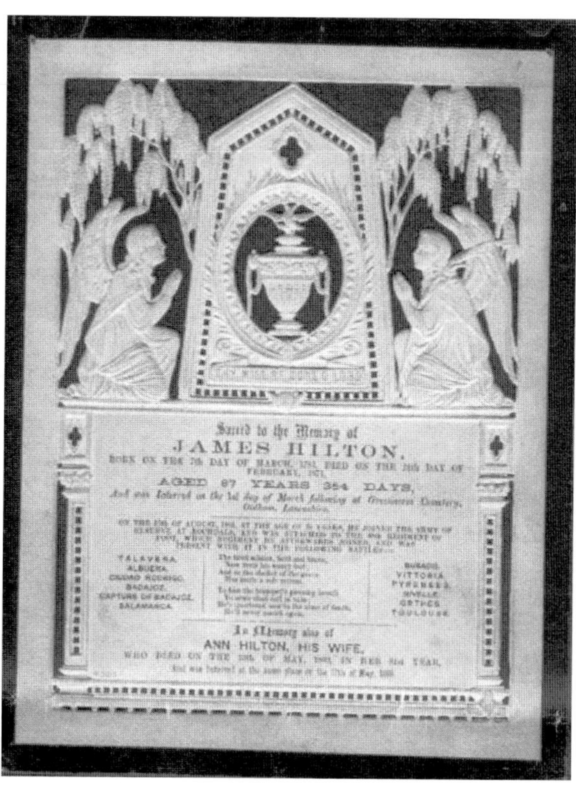

James Hilton 48th Foot

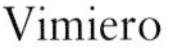
Vimiero

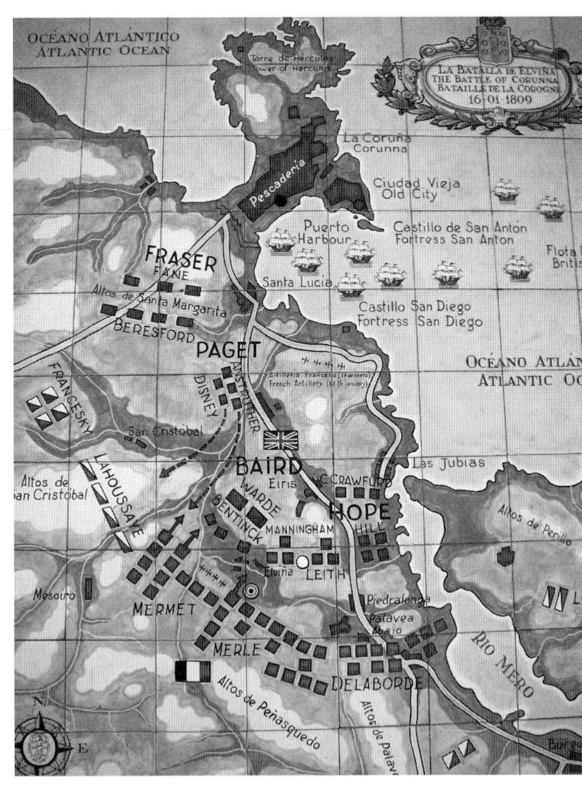

Corunna Tile Map

Busaco

Elvas [Albuera wall]

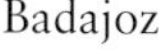

Badajoz

Salamanca

Toulouse

2nd (Queen's) Royal Regiment

Quatre Bras

Hougoumont (Coldstream Guards)

Waterloo 27th Foot

Sir Alexander Gordon 3rd Foot Guards

PATERSON, George

Captain and Lieutenant Colonel. 3rd Regiment of Foot Guards.
Memorial tablet: Longforgan Church, Longforgan, Perthshire, Scotland. (Photograph)

GEORGE PATERSON DIED 14 MARCH 1814 AGED 83. / .... / GEORGE LT COLONEL 3RD FOOT GUARDS / SON OF THE ABOVE DIED 14 JULY 1846 AGED 68. / ....

Lt and Capt 17 Sep 1799. Capt and Lt Col 1 Jun 1809.

Served in the Peninsula Mar – Jul 1809. Present at Douro. Retired 24 Oct 1811. Died 14 Jul 1846.

PATERSON, James

Assistant Surgeon. 45th (Nottinghamshire) Regiment of Foot.
Obelisk: Dean Cemetery, Edinburgh, Scotland. (Section F No. 583). (Photograph)

JAMES PATERSON MD. SURGEON 42ND (ROYAL HIGHLAND) REGT. DIED 26TH AUGUST 1866.

Hospital Mate 7 Jun 1810. Asst Surgeon 45th Foot 22 Aug 1811. Surgeon 13th Foot 25 May 1826. Surgeon 46th Foot 2 Jun 1833. Surgeon 42nd Foot 19 Jun 1835.

Served in the Peninsula Sep 1810 – Dec 1811. Also served in the Burmese Campaign 1824–1826 with 13th Foot. MD Glasgow 1816. Half pay 26 Feb 1841. Died in Edinburgh 26 Aug 1866.

PATERSON, James

Deputy Assistant Commissary General. Commissariat Department.
Family monument. St Michael's Church, Inveresk, Midlothian, Scotland. (Left of main path). (Photograph)

.... / ALSO OF / JAMES PATERSON / DEPUTY ASSISTANT COMMISSARY GENERAL / DURING THE SERVICE IN EGYPT, THE PENINSULA, AND AT WATERLOO / WHO DIED ON THE 25TH OF DECEMBER 1850 / AGED 73 YEARS. / HIS ENERGY, INDUSTRY AND INTEGRITY, WITH A HIGH / SENSE OF HONOUR AND MUCH KINDNESS OF DISPOSITION / GAINED FOR HIM GENERAL RESPECT AND ESTEEM AS / WELL WHEN ENGAGED WITH THE ARMY AS WHEN / EMPLOYED IN THE FISHING NET MANUFACTORY IN / MUSELBURGH, THE INGENIOUS MACHINERY FOR WHICH / WAS ALMOST EXCLUSIVELY HIS OWN INVENTION.

Dep Asst Comm Gen 11 Jan 1812.

Served in the Peninsula Oct – Jan 1809 and 1810 – Apr 1814. Present at Corunna, Busaco, Salamanca, Nivelle, Nive, Orthes and Toulouse. Present at Waterloo. Also served in Egypt. Employed in the fishing net industry in Musselburgh. MGS medal for Corunna, Busaco, Salamanca, Nivelle, Nive, Orthes and Toulouse.

PATERSON, Leeson

Lieutenant. 57th (West Middlesex) Regiment of Foot.
Ledger stone: St Nicholas's Churchyard, Galway, Ireland. (Photograph)

SACRED TO THE MEMORY OF LIEUT LEESON PATERSON / OF THE 57TH REGIMENT OF FOOT AND LATE OF THE RVB / WHO DEPARTED THIS LIFE 23 JANUARY 1826. / THIS TOMB WAS ERECTED BY HIS WIFE DOROTHEA.

Ensign 31 Dec 1805. Lt 4 Feb 1808.

Served in the Peninsula Jul 1809 – Aug 1811. Present at Busaco, first siege of Badajoz, and Albuera where he was severely wounded and awarded pension of £70 per annum.

PATOT, Tissot van
Captain. 4th Dragoons, Dutch Cavalry.
Named on the Memorial to Dutch officers killed at Waterloo: St Joseph's Church, Waterloo. (Photograph)

PATRICK, William
Private. 2nd (Royal North British) Regiment of Dragoons.
Family low monument: St Columba's Parish Churchyard, Stewarton, Ayrshire, Scotland. (Photograph)

"PATRICK FAMILY .... ALSO BROTHER WILLIAM LANCE SERGEANT SCOTS GREYS. 16TH APRIL 1855, AGED 66."

Pte 5 Jul 1808. Cpl 19 Oct 1815. Sgt 21 May 1821.
Present at Waterloo in Captain Barnard's Troop. Also served in Ireland. Discharged 11 Oct 1831 after 23 years service.

PATRICKSON, Christopher Clarges
Lieutenant Colonel. 43rd (Monmouthshire) Light Infantry Regiment of Foot.
Memorial tablet: St Peter's Church, Dublin, Ireland. (M.I.) (No longer extant). (Church demolished in 1980s. Bodies and gravestones removed to St Luke's Church in the Coombe, but this church is also now redundant and unlikely that any memorials will have survived)

"ERECTED TO THE MEMORY OF CHRISTOPHER PATRICKSON, C.B., LATE COLONEL OF H. M. 43RD REGIMENT. DIED 25TH SEPTEMBER 1856, AGED 78 YEARS."

Ensign 31st Foot 31 Aug 1793. Lt 25 Mar 1794. Lt 9th Dragoons 14 Jun 1794. Capt 23rd Lt Dragoons 25 Mar 1800. Capt 40th Foot 28 Aug 1801. Capt 43rd Foot 25 May 1803. Major 28 Sep 1809. Bt Lt Colonel 30 May 1811. Lt Colonel 17 Jun 1813. Colonel 19 Jul 1821.
Served in the Peninsula with 1/43rd Oct 1808 – Jan 1809, Jul 1809 – Aug 1811, Feb – Aug 1813 and Mar – Apr 1814. Present at Vigo, Coa, Busaco, Redinha, Casal Nova (Mentioned in Despatches), Foz d'Arouce, Sabugal (wounded and Mentioned in Despatches), Fuentes d'Onoro, Vittoria and Toulouse. Gold Medal for Toulouse where he commanded the regiment. Present at the Capture of Paris and with the Army of Occupation. CB. Also served in the Irish Rebellion with 9th Dragoons 1798, Copenhagen 1807 and North America 1814–1815 (present at New Orleans). Retired 1826. MGS medal for Busaco, Fuentes d'Onoro and Vittoria.

PATRICKSON, Hugh
Paymaster. 4th (Queen's Own) Regiment of Dragoons.
Memorial tablet: St Michael's Church, Stanwix, Carlisle, Cumbria. (Removed from church wall, and stored in boiler room in broken parts). (Photograph)

IN MEMORY OF / HUGH PATRICKSON ESQ. / LATE CAPTAIN OF THE 4TH LIGHT DRAGOONS / IN WHICH REGIMENT HE SERVED 32 YEARS. / HE DIED AT DUMFRIES 21ST JUNE 1821 / IN THE 63RD YEAR OF HIS AGE. / ....

Quartermaster. Promoted from the ranks. Cornet 18 Oct 1794. Lt 6 May 1795. Adjutant 3 Mar 1798. Capt-Lt 10 May 1800. Paymaster 30 Dec 1806.
Served in the Peninsula Apr 1809 – Apr 1814. Present at Talavera, Busaco, Albuera, Usagre, Aldea de Ponte, Llerena, Salamanca and Toulouse. Half pay 7 May 1819.

PATTENSON, Cooke Tylden
Captain. 43rd (Monmouthshire) Light Infantry Regiment of Foot.
Altar tomb: All Saints' Churchyard, Biddenden, Kent. (South side of church). (M.I.)

"UNDERNEATH ARE DEPOSITED THE REMAINS OF COOKE TYLDEN-PATTENSON OF IBORNDEN ESQUIRE, COLONEL IN THE ARMY, J.P. AND DEPUTY LIEUTENANT FOR THIS COUNTY WHO DIED JANUARY 23RD 1858 AGED 67. …………………

Ensign 43rd Foot 19 Feb 1807. Lt 9 Mar 1809. Capt 18 Aug 1814. Capt Rifle Brigade 19 Jun 1817. Bt Major 10 Jan 1837. Bt Lt Colonel 10 Nov 1851.

Served in the Peninsula with 1/43rd Oct 1808 – Jan 1809, Jul 1811 – Sep 1813 and Apr 1814. Present at Vigo, Ciudad Rodrigo (severely wounded), Badajoz, Salamanca, San Munos, Vittoria, Pyrenees and Toulouse. Half pay 25 Dec 1818. MGS medal for Ciudad Rodrigo, Badajoz, Salamanca, Vittoria, Pyrenees and Toulouse. Retired 4 Aug 1854. Magistrate and Deputy Lieutenant of Kent. Died at Brighton 23 Jan 1858.

PATTERSON, George see PATERSON, George

PATTESON, Robert Dossie
Captain. 6th (1st Warwickshire) Regiment of Foot.
Headstone: Drummond Hill Presbyterian Churchyard, Lundy's Lane, Niagara, Canada. (Photograph).

SACRED / TO THE MEMORY / OF / ROBERT DOSSIE / PATTESON, / CAPTAIN OF THE SIXTH / REGIMENT OF INFANTRY, / ROYAL 1ST WARWICKSHIRE, / WHO AFTER SERVING UNDER / SIR JOHN MOORE / AND / THE DUKE OF WELLINGTON, / THROUGHOUT / THE PENINSULAR WAR, / FELL BEFORE FORT ERIE / AT THE AGE OF XXVI. / XVI SEPTEMBER MDCCCXIV. / HE WAS THE FOURTH SON OF / JOHN PATTESON ESQ / OF THE CITY OF NORWICH, ENGLAND, / WHERE HIS NAME IS HELD IN HONOUR / BY ALL WHO KNEW HIM / ERECTED / BY ORDER OF / HIS SURVIVING BROTHERS / AND SISTERS / A.D. 1880 / T.C.P.

Named on the Monument at Fort Erie, Canada. (M.I.)

"OFFICERS KILLED DURING THE SIEGE OF FORT ERIE COL. HERCULES SCOTT, 103D REGT.; LIEUT. COL. WILLIAM DRUMMOND, 104TH REGT.; LIEUT. COL. JOHN GORDON, ROYAL SCOTS; CAPT. R. D. PATTESON, 6TH REGT.; CAPT. TORRENS, 8TH REGT.: CAPT J.M. WRIGHT, 824 REGT., CAPT. ED. WALKER, INCOR. MILITIA; LIEUT. COPLES RADCLIFFE, R. N.; LIEUT. NOEL, ROYAL SCOTS; LIEUT. J. RUTLEDGE, ROYAL SCOTS; LIEUT. BARSTOW, 8TH REGT.; LIEUT. PILLICHODY, DE WATTEVILLE REGT.; ENSIGN E. LANGFORD. 82D REGT."

2nd Lt 23rd Foot 7 Jan 1804. 1st Lt 1 Dec 1804. Capt in Major General Ramsay's Regt 27 Mar 1806. Capt 6th Foot 20 Nov 1806.

Served in the Peninsula Aug 1808 – Jan 1809 and Nov 1812 – Apr 1814. Present at Rolica, Vimeiro, Corunna, Vittoria, Pyrenees, Bidassoa, Nivelle, Orthes and Bordeaux. Also served at Walcheren 1809 and North America where he was killed at Fort Erie 17 Sep 1814. Educated at Eton.
Named as Pattison in Army Lists.

PATTISON, Alexander Hope
Lieutenant. 74th (Highland) Regiment of Foot.
Memorial tablet: St Mathew's Church, Nassau, New Providence, West Indies. (M.I.)

"ALEXANDER HOPE PATTISON, LIEUT.-COLONEL OF THE 2ND WEST INDIA REGIMENT, COMMANDING THE TROOPS IN THIS COLONY, SECOND SON OF JOHN PATTISON OF

KELVIN, DIED 11 JAN., 1835, AGED 48, BURIED WITH IMPRESSIVE CEREMONIAL IN ST MATHEW'S CHURCHYARD, NEW PROVIDENCE. HE WAS ONE OF THE 3RD DIVISION AND SERVED ON THE STAFF OF PICTON AND AT SALAMANCA ETC. HIS FELLOW CITIZENS FIRST ERECTED A MONUMENT IN THE NECROPOLIS OF GLASGOW, AND HIS WIDOW ANNA, SECOND DAUGHTER OF HIS HONOUR JUDGE ROBERT JOHNSON ERECTED THE STONE OVER HIS ASHES IN WHICH ALSO RESTS HIS NEPHEW."

Monument: Glasgow Necropolis, Glasgow, Scotland. (Photograph)

West side:

LIEUTENANT-COLONEL ALEXANDER HOPE PATTISON, K.H., / COMMANDER OF THE TROOPS IN THE BAHAMAS, &C, &C, / AFTER SERVING HIS COUNTRY TWENTY-SIX YEARS, / WITH HONOR AND FIDELITY, / DIED AT NASSAU, NEW PROVIDENCE, ON THE 11TH JANY. 1843, / AGED 48.

North side:

A.D. MDCCCXXXVIII / BY A GRANT FROM / THE MERCHANTS' HOUSE OF GLASGOW, / OF THE REQUISITE GROUND, / THE CONTRIBUTORS / WERE ENABLED TO PLACE COLONEL PATTISON'S MONUMENT / NEAR HIS FATHER'S TOMB. / SALAMANCA, MADRID, RETREAT OF ARANJUEZ, PYRENEES.

East side:

MASSENA'S RETREAT, CAMPO MAYOR, FUENTES D'ONORO, BADAJOZ.

South side:

BUSACO, REDINHA, CASAL NOVA, FOZ D'ARONCE.

Ensign 25 Sep 1807. Lt 26 Apr 1810. Capt 20 Mar 1823. Major 97th Foot 17 Sep 1826. Lt Colonel 2nd West India Regt 27 Sep 1831.

Served in the Peninsula Feb 1810 – Jul 1811 (extra ADC to General Picton) and Mar 1812 – Nov 1813. Present at Busaco, Redinha, Casal Nova, Foz d'Arouce, Fuentes d'Onoro, Campo Mayor, Badajoz (wounded), Salamanca and Pyrenees (severely wounded and awarded pension of £70 per annum). KH. Also served in the West Indies 1832–1835 (Commander of His Majesty's Forces in the Bahamas).

Reference: Gentleman's Magazine, Apr 1835, p. 446.

PATTON, Peter

Captain. Royal Engineers.

Named on the Regimental Memorial: Rochester Cathedral, Rochester, Kent. (Photograph)

2nd Lt 1 Apr 1799. Lt 18 Apr 1801. 2nd Capt 1 Mar 1805. Capt 24 Jun 1809.

Served in the Peninsula Aug 1808 – Jun 1811. Present at the first siege of Badajoz and second siege where he was severely wounded 8 Jun 1811 whilst inspecting the castle breach prior to conducting the storming party in the assault). Sent from Elvas to Lisbon for medical treatment but died of his wounds 17 Jun 1811.

PATULLO, William
Lieutenant. 6th (1st Warwickshire) Regiment of Foot.
Named on the Memorial: St Andrew's Church (now Musée Historique), Biarritz, France. (Photograph)

Ensign 83rd Foot 1 Jul 1805. Lt 6th Foot 4 Mar 1807.

Served in the Peninsula Nov 1812 – Feb 1814. Present at Vittoria, Pyrenees, Bidassoa, Nivelle and Orthes where he was killed 27 Feb 1814. Also served at Walcheren 1809.

PATY, George William
Major. Staff Appointment in Spain and Portugal not holding a Regimental Commission.
Low monument: Kensal Green Cemetery, London. (20915/87/IC). (Photograph)

SACRED / TO THE MEMORY OF / GENERAL SIR GEORGE W. PATY / K.C.B. K.H. / COLL OF THE 70TH REGIMENT / WHO DIED 8TH MAY 1868 / IN THE 80TH YEAR OF HIS AGE

Ensign 32nd Foot 28 Apr 1804. Lt 7 May 1805. Capt 28 Apr 1808. Major Spanish and Portuguese Staff 2 Jun 1814. Bt Lt Colonel 4 Sep 1817. Lt Colonel 96th Foot 29 Jan 1824. Lt Colonel 94th Foot 11 Jun 1826. Bt Colonel 10 Jun 1837. Major General 9 Nov 1846. Lt General 20 Jun 1854. General 14 Mar 1862. Portuguese Army: Major 9th Line 1811. Lt Colonel 5th Line 25 Jan 1814.

Served in the Peninsula with 32nd Foot Jun – Oct 1811 and Portuguese Army Oct 1811 – Apr 1814. Present at Badajoz, Salamanca, retreat from Burgos, Vittoria (Mentioned in Beresford's Despatches), Pyrenees, Nivelle and Nive. Also served at Copenhagen 1807. Commanded 94th Foot for 15 years from 1826–1841. MGS medal for Badajoz, Salamanca, Vittoria, Pyrenees, Nivelle and Nive. KCB, KTS and KH. Commander of St Benito d'Avis. Colonel 70th Foot 8 May 1854.

PAXTON, Archibald Frederic
Lieutenant. 11th Regiment of Light Dragoons.
Chest tomb: St Nicholas's Churchyard, Cholderton, Wiltshire. (Photograph)

IN MEMORY OF / ARCHIBALD FREDERIC PAXTON ESQRE / OF 5 DEVONSHIRE PLACE, LONDON, / AND CHOLDERTON HOUSE, WILTS, J.P. FOR THE COUNTY, / AND LATE OF THE 11TH LIGHT DRAGOONS. / ELDEST SON OF THE LATE SIR WILLIAM PAXTON, / OF MIDDLETON HALL, CARMARTHENSHIRE, / WHO DIED ON THE 11TH OF APRIL 1875, / IN THE 82ND YEAR OF HIS AGE. / ....

Cornet 26 Jun 1811. Lt 19 Dec 1811.

Served in the Peninsula May 1812 – Jun 1813. Present at Morales, Castrejon and Salamanca. MGS medal for Salamanca. Half pay 1814. Full pay 30 Mar 1815 and reverted to half pay 23 Jul 1817. Magistrate for Wiltshire. Died in 1875 still on half pay.

PAYNE, John
Quartermaster Sergeant. 1st Regiment of Foot Guards.
Memorial: Royal Military Chapel, Wellington Barracks, London. (M.I.) (Destroyed by a Flying Bomb 1944)

"CAPTAIN JOHN PAYNE / ENLISTED INTO THE 1ST GUARDS, 1801, BECAME QUARTER-MASTER-SERGEANT, 1810; QUARTERMASTER, / 1815; AND RETIRED, 1855. SERVED IN SICILY, AT CORUNNA, AT WALCHEREN, AND WITH THE 1ST BATTALION / IN SPAIN AND THE SOUTH OF FRANCE, FROM 1812–14, AND WITH THE 2ND BATTALION AS ACTING / QUARTERMASTER DURING THE WATERLOO CAMPAIGN".

Pte 28 May 1801. Cpl Jun 1803. Sgt Sep 1805. Quartermaster Sgt Aug 1810. Quartermaster 31 Aug 1815.

Served in the Peninsula 1808–1809 and Sep 1812 – Apr 1814. Present at Lugo, Corunna, Burgos, Pyrenees, San Sebastian, Bidassoa, Nivelle, Nive, Adour and Bayonne. Present at Quatre Bras, Waterloo, siege of Peronne, Capture of Paris and with the Army of Occupation. Also served in Sicily 1806–1807, Walcheren 1809 and Canada Apr 1838–1842. MGS medal for Corunna, Nivelle and Nive. Half pay 5 Dec 1855.

PEACHEY, James

Ensign. 1st Regiment of Foot Guards.

Memorial tablet: St Mary Magdalene's Church, Barkway, Hertfordshire. (M.I.)

"………… ALSO HIS ELDEST SON, THE HONOURABLE JAMES PEACHEY, LATE AN ENSIGN IN THE 1ST REGT. OF FOOT GUARDS, DIED AT NEWSELLS PARK, 8 NOV 1811 IN THE 27TH YEAR OF HIS AGE."

Ensign 18 Dec 1806.

Served in the Peninsula with 3rd Battalion Oct 1808 – Jan 1809. Present at Corunna. Retired 6 Apr 1809.

PEACOCKE, Nathaniel Levett

Lieutenant Colonel. 71st (Highland Light Infantry) Regiment of Foot.

Interred in Catacomb B (v103 c16), Kensal Green Cemetery, London.

Ensign 88th Foot 28 Jan 1783. Lt 50th Foot 4 Jan 1798. Capt Independent Company 27 Jan 1791. Capt 50th Foot 12 Mar 1794. Major 48th Foot 20 Dec 1796. Bt Lt Colonel 29 Apr 1802. Major 71st 25 Jun 1807. Lt Colonel 4 Jun 1811.

Served in the Peninsula Sep – Nov 1810 and Oct 1813 – Mar 1814. Present at Nivelle and Nive where he was wounded. Died 1 Nov 1847.

PEACOCKE, Stephen

Captain and Lieutenant Colonel. 3rd Regiment of Foot Guards.

Memorial tablet: St Mary's Church, Acton, London. (M.I.)

"TO THE MEMORY OF COLONEL STEPHEN PEACOCKE / LATE OF / THE THIRD REGIMENT OF FOOT GUARDS / WHO DISTINGUISHED HIMSELF / IN MANY OF THE SEVERAL ACTIONS / THAT TOOK PLACE IN THE PENINSULA / IN THE LATE WAR / UNDER THE COMMAND OF / HIS GRACE THE DUKE OF WELLINGTON. / HE DEPARTED THIS LIFE / THE 30TH NOV 1830 / AGED 56 YEARS."

Ensign 15 Feb 1794. Lt and Capt 9 Dec 1795. Capt and Lt Colonel 5 Jan 1804.

Served in the Peninsula Mar 1809 – Feb 1812. Present at Douro, Talavera, Busaco, Fuentes d'Onoro and Ciudad Rodrigo. Retired 8 Oct 1812.

PEACOCKE, Thomas

Captain. Sicilian Regiment of Foot.

Low monument: Tours Cemetery, Tours, France. (Photograph)

ICI REPOSE / UN VIEUX SOLDAT DE LA GUERRE DE / LA PENINSULE QUI A FAIT TOUTES LES / CAMPAGNES D ESPAGNE ET DE PORTUGAL / SOUS LES ORDRES DU MARECHAL / BERESFORD ET DU DUC DE WELLINGTON / THOMAS PEACOCKE, / ECUYER MAJOR GENERAL / AU SERVICE DE SA MAJESTE BRITANNIQUE / CHEVALIER DE LA TOUR ET DE LEPEE / ET DE PLUSIEURS AUTRES ORDRES / DECIDE A ST CYR LE 21 JUIN 1856 / AGE DE 80 ANS.

Ensign 9 Apr 1806. Lt 25 Feb 1808. Lt 44th Foot 14 Apr 1808. Capt Sicilian Regt 26 Aug 1813. Bt Lt Colonel 10 Jan 1837. Bt Colonel 11 Nov 1851. Major General 31 Aug 1855. Portuguese Army: Capt 23rd Line 11 Apr 1810. Major 5 May 1812.

Served in the Peninsula with Portuguese Army Apr 1810 – Apr 1814. Present at Busaco, Torres Vedras, Pombal, Redinha, Campo Mayor, Olivencia, Albuera, Ciudad Rodrigo, Badajoz (severely wounded and Mentioned in Beresford's Despatches), Aldea de Ponte, Vittoria, Pyrenees, Bidassoa, Nivelle and Nive. Also served at Ischa and Procida in the Bay of Naples 1809. O/c Convalescent Depot 26 Feb 1814. Half pay 25 Dec 1816. MGS medal for Busaco, Albuera, Ciudad Rodrigo, Badajoz, Vittoria, Pyrenees and Nivelle. KTS. Portuguese Gold Cross for Peninsular campaigns. Died 21 Jun 1856 aged 80.

PEACOCKE, Thomas Goodricke

Captain. 55th (Westmoreland) Regiment of Foot.
Family vault: St Brigid's Churchyard, Stillorgan, Dublin, Ireland. (Photograph)

THIS VAULT CONTAINS THE MORTAL REMAINS / OF THE UNDER MENTIONED MEMBERS OF THE / FAMILY OF P. A. LESLIE / .... / MAJOR THOMAS GOODRICKE PEACOCKE / HIS SON IN LAW DIED 19TH APRIL 1844

Ensign Jun 1807. Lt 3 Mar 1808. Capt 25 Oct 1814. Bt Major 4 Sep 1817. Portuguese Army: Capt 9th Line 19 Dec 1811.

Served in the Peninsula Oct 1811 – Aug 1812 (ADC to Major General Peacocke). With Portuguese Army Dec 1811 – Aug 1814. Present at Badajoz (severely wounded) and Orthes (Mentioned in Beresford's Despatches). Served with the Army of Occupation. Also served in North America 1814–1815 (ADC to Major General Sir Manley Power). Half pay 1823.

PEACOCKE, Warren Marmaduke

Captain and Lieutenant Colonel. Coldstream Regiment of Foot Guards.
Obelisk: Kensal Green Cemetery, London. (8534/113/PS). (Photograph)

SACRED TO THE MEMORY OF / GENL SIR WARREN MARMADUKE PEACOCKE / KCH – KTS. – KC. / COLONEL OF THE 19TH REGT OF FOOT, / AND LATE GOVERNOR OF KINSALE. / BORN ON THE 21ST SEPTEMBER A.D. 1766, / AND DIED ON THE 22ND AUGUST A.D. 1849. / HE SERVED IN THE COLDSTREAM GUARDS / AT THE LANDING IN EGYPT, / AND THE SUBSEQUENT ATTACKS IN THAT COUNTRY, / AND IN THE EXPEDITIONS TO HANOVER AND DENMARK. / HE WAS ALSO PRESENT AT THE PASSAGE OF THE DOURO, / AND OCCUPIED THE RESPONSIBLE POSITION OF / MILITARY GOVERNOR OF LISBON / DURING THE PENINSULA WAR.

Ensign 88th Foot 12 Dec 1780. Lt 22 May 1782. Capt-Lt 14 Apr 1783. Bt Major 1 Mar 1794. Lt and Capt Coldstream Guards 6 Nov 1795. Capt and Lt Colonel 9 May 1800. Bt Colonel 25 Apr 1808. Major General 4 Jun 1811. Lt General 19 Jul 1821. General 28 Jun 1838.

Served in the Peninsula Mar 1809 – Apr 1814. Present at Douro. Commandant at Lisbon from Jul 1809. Also served in Ireland 1796–1799 (present in the Irish Rebellion 1798 at Ballynahinch where he was ADC to General Sir G. Nugent), Egypt 1801 (present at Alexandria), Hanover 1805 and Copenhagen 1807. Knighted 27 Jul 1815. KCH, KTS and KC. Colonel 19th Foot 13 May 1843.
Reference: Gentleman's Magazine, Oct 1849, p. 420. Annual Register, 1849, Appx, p. 263.

PEACOCKE, William

Lieutenant. 71st (Highland Light Infantry) Regiment of Foot.
Ledger stone: St Mary's Churchyard, Dublin, Ireland. (Photograph)

SACRED / TO THE MEMORY OF THE LATE / W[M]. PEACOCKE ESQ[R] / 71ST REG[T], / DIED THE 3RD NOV[R] 1836 / AGED 52 YEARS. / HE WAS UNIVERSALLY BELOVED / AND RESPECTED BY ALL WHO KNEW HIM. / ....

Ensign 8 Nov 1809. Lt 14 May 1812.

Served in the Peninsula Apr 1812 – Apr 1814. Present at Almarez, Vittoria, Pyrenees (severely wounded), Nivelle, Nive, Garris, Orthes, Aire, Tarbes and Toulouse. Half pay 26 Dec 1816.

PEARCE, William

Captain. 60th (Royal American) Regiment of Foot.
Box tomb in railed enclosure: St Cattwg's Churchyard, Llanspyddid, Brecon, Wales. (Photograph)

SACRED TO THE MEMORY OF / MARY CHURCH PEARCE / OF FFRWDGRECH. / BORN 21ST MARCH 1800. / DIED 13TH DECEMBER 1868. / ALSO OF LIEU[T] COL WILLIAM PEARCE KH. JP / DIED 5TH FEB[RY] 1871. / AGED 81 YEARS.

Ensign 44th Foot 31 Dec 1807. Lt 21 Sep 1810. Capt 60th Foot 15 Aug 1813. Major 30 Aug 1825. Lt Colonel (unattached) 29 Aug 1826.

Served in the Peninsula Jan 1811 – Feb 1813. Present at Sabugal, Fuentes d'Onoro (wounded), Badajoz, Salamanca, Burgos and retreat from Burgos (present at Villa Muriel). While serving with the 44th Foot at Salamanca, he saw a French officer trying to hide the Eagle of the 62nd French Regiment of Line under his great coat. Pearce was nearly shot by another French soldier as he tried to take the Eagle. One of Pearce's men saw this and shot the Frenchman enabling Pearce to capture the Eagle. MGS medal for Fuentes d'Onoro, Badajoz and Salamanca. KH. Justice of the Peace. Half pay with rank of Lt Colonel 29 Aug 1826.

PEARSON, Isaac

Armourer Sergeant. 69th (South Lincolnshire) Regiment of Foot.
Headstone: Porch of St Nicholas' Churchyard, Harwich, Essex. (Photograph)

SACRED TO THE MEMORY OF / ISAAC PEARSON / MANY YEARS REGIMENTAL ARMOURER OF / THE 69TH REG[T] OF FOOT / AND WAS IN MANY ENGAGEMENTS / AND WAS WOUNDED IN HIS LEFT LEG AT / THE BATTLE OF WATERLOO. / HE DIED / MARCH 7TH 1848 / AGED 82 YEARS

Nottingham Fencibles 29 Feb 1795. Pte 69th Foot 22 Oct 1803. Armourer Sgt 1805.

Present at Waterloo where he was wounded in Capt Henry Cox's Company. Discharged 24 Oct 1816 on reduction of the battalion.
Note: Name also spelt as Pierson.

PEARSON, Thomas

Major. 23rd (Royal Welch Fusiliers) Regiment of Foot.
Memorial tablet: St Swithin's Church, Bath, Somerset. Interred in the Crypt. (Photograph)

SACRED TO THE MEMORY OF / LIEU[T] GEN[L] SIR THO[S] PEARSON, C.B. & K.C.H. / WHO DIED MAY 21ST 1847, / AGED 66 YEARS. / AND OF ANN ELIZA, HIS WIFE / WHO DEPARTED THIS LIFE NOV[R] 26TH 1859, AGED 70 YEARS. / THEIR MORTAL REMAINS REPOSE IN THE CRYPT OF THIS / CHURCH AWAITING THE DAY OF RESURRECTION. / (VERSE)

2nd Lt 23rd Foot 2 Oct 1796. Lt 25 Apr 1799. Capt 7 Aug 1800. Major 8 Dec 1804. Bt Lt Colonel 4 Jun 1811. Lt Colonel 43rd Foot 16 Nov 1815. Lt Colonel 23rd Foot 24 Jul 1817. Bt Colonel 19 Jul 1821. Major General 22 Jul 1830. Lt General 23 Nov 1841.

Served in the Peninsula with 1/23rd Dec 1810 – Nov 1811. Present at Redinha, Olivencia (severely wounded), first siege of Badajoz, Albuera (took command of the regiment when all senior officers were wounded – awarded Bt Lt Colonelcy), Fuente Guinaldo (severely wounded – his thigh bone was so severely shattered that he was sent home to recover). Also served in Canada 23 Feb 1812 as Inspecting Officer of Militia (present at Chrystler's Farm 11 Nov 1813). Second in command of troops under Lt Colonel Morrison, present at attack and Capture of Oswego 1813. Commanded the Light Brigade on the Niagara frontier 1814, present at Chippewa, Lundy's Lane (wounded) and Fort Erie where he was severely wounded by a rifle ball in the right side of his head which made him deaf on that side for the rest of his life and awarded pension of £300 per annum. Gold Medal for Albuera and Chrystler's Farm. CB and KCH. Colonel 85th Foot 21 Nov 1843. Also served at the Helder 1799, Ferrol 1800, Egypt 1801 (present at Aboukir where he was wounded). Copenhagen 1807, Martinique 1809 (present at Fort Bourbon where he was wounded). KCB. Served in the Army for 51 years.
Reference: Royal Military Calendar, Vol. 4, pp. 339–42. Gentleman's Magazine, Jul 1847, pp. 92–3. United Service Magazine, Jul 1847, p. 479. Annual Register, 1847, Appx, p. 232.

PEATTIE, Paul

Private. 42nd (Royal Highland) Regiment of Foot.
Headstone: Grange Cemetery, Edinburgh, Scotland. (Section J Row 7. Number 124). (Photograph)

ERECTED BY PAUL PEATTIE / LATE OF THE 42ND ROYAL HIGHLAND REGIMENT / IN MEMORY OF HIS WIFE / JANE DAVIDSON / WHO DIED 11TH SEPTEMBER 1867 AGED 78 YEARS / PAUL PEATTIE DIED 15TH MARCH 1875 AGED 90 / ....

Pte 1789.

Served in the Peninsula Jul 1809 – Apr 1814. Present at Busaco, Fuentes d'Onoro, Ciudad Rodrigo, Salamanca, Burgos, Pyrenees, Nivelle, Nive, Orthes and Toulouse. MGS medal for Busaco, Fuentes d'Onoro, Ciudad Rodrigo, Salamanca, Pyrenees, Nivelle, Nive, Orthes and Toulouse.

PEEBLES, Adam

Captain. 9th (East Norfolk) Regiment of Foot.
Family ledger stone: Greyfriars Burying Ground, Perth, Perthshire, Scotland. (Photograph)

.... / AND IN MEMORY OF / THEIR SON ADAM, THE ELDEST SON OF THE FAMILY. / HE WAS A LIEUT. COLONEL OF THE 9TH REGT / AND DIED IN LONDON ON 19TH APRIL 1835 / IN THE 54TH YEAR OF HIS AGE. / .... / THEY WERE BRAVE, HONOURABLE AND DEVOTED / TO THE SERVICE OF THEIR COUNTRY.

Emsign 90th Foot 1796. Lt 14 Feb 1797. Lt 9th Foot 26 Jan 1799. Capt 4 Aug 1804. Bt Major 7 Oct 1813. Bt Lt Colonel 26 Jan 1817.

Served in the Peninsula with 1/9th Aug 1808 – Jan 1809 and Mar 1810 – Apr 1814. Present at Rolica, Vimeiro, Corunna, Busaco, Fuentes d'Onoro, Castrejon, Salamanca, Bidassoa, Nivelle, Nive and Bayonne. Also served at Walcheren 1809 and North America 1814–1815. Half pay 10 Jun 1826.

PELLY, Raymond

Lieutenant Colonel. 16th (Queen's) Regiment of Light Dragoons.
Memorial: Mount Jerome Cemetery, Dublin, Ireland. (Grave number C28–624)

Ensign 27th Foot May 1800. Lt 3 Jul 1801. Capt York Hussars 6 Aug 1802. Capt 16th Lt Dragoons 25 Dec 1802. Major 1 Nov 1810. Lt Colonel 23 Apr 1812.

Served in the Peninsula Apr – Sep 1809, Jun 1810 – Sep 1811 (ADC to Major General G. Anson Apr – Sep 1809 and Jun 1810 – Feb 1811) and Oct 1812 – Apr 1814. Present at Douro, Talavera, Busaco,

Redinha, Casal Nova, Foz d'Arouce, Fuentes d'Onoro and retreat from Burgos (commanded rear guard of cavalry during the retreat). During a charge of cavalry at Venta del Pozo his horse was killed and he was wounded twice, Mentioned in Despatches, taken prisoner and not released until Apr 1814. Also served at Ferrol 1800, Egypt 1801 (present at Alexandria) and Ireland 1803–1805. CB. Half pay 1821. Died in Dublin 20 Dec 1845 aged 60.

Reference: *Royal Military Calendar, Vol. 4, p. 410. Gentleman's Magazine, Mar 1846, pp. 319–20. Annual Register, 1845, Appx, pp. 321–2.*

PEMBERTON, George Keating
1st Lieutenant. Royal Artillery.
Buried in Eccleshall Road Cemetery, Stafford, Staffordshire. (Burial record)

2nd Lt 5 Mar 1810. 1st Lt 17 Dec 1813. 2nd Capt 3 Oct 1831.
Served in the Peninsula Feb – Apr 1814. Present at Bayonne. Also served in Mauritius 1815–1822. Died 24 Aug 1860 at Stafford.

PENNINGTON, James Masterson
Lieutenant. 5th (Northumberland) Regiment of Foot.
Gravestone: Old Churchyard, Spital, Windsor. (Grave nmber: R22)

Ensign 5 Feb 1807. Lt 31 Mar 1808. Paymaster 25 Jan 1816.
Served in the Peninsula with 2/5th Jul 1809 – Jul 1812 and 1/5th Aug 1812 – Apr 1814 (Acting Paymaster). Present at Busaco, Torres Vedras, Redinha, Pombal, Condeixa, Casal Nova, Foz D'Arouce, Sabugal, Fuentes D'Onoro, first and second sieges of Badajoz, Campo Mayor, Ciudad Rodrigo (wounded), Badajoz, El Bodon, Salamanca, retreat from Burgos, Vittoria, Pyrenees, Nivelle, Nive, Adour, Orthes, Vic Bigorre and Toulouse. Served in France with the Army of Occupation 1815–1818. Also served in North America 1814–1815, West Indies 1819–1826, Gibraltar 1832–1834, Malta 1834–1837 and Ionian Islands 1837–1840. MGS medal for Busaco, Fuentes D'Onoro, Ciudad Rodrigo, Badajoz, Salamanca, Vittoria, Pyrenees, Nivelle, Nive, Orthes and Toulouse. Military Knight of Windsor and Honorary Major 7 Sep 1859. Died at Windsor 11 May 1862. Brother of Lt John Pennington 15th Light Dragoons.

PENNINGTON, John
Lieutenant. 15th (King's) Regiment of Light Dragoons.
Memorial tablet: Holy Trinity Church, Kendal, Cumbria. (Photograph)

SACRED / TO THE MEMORY OF / JOHN PENNINGTON ESQRE / LATE OF THE 15TH HUSSARS AND 44TH REGT., / WHO DEPARTED THIS LIFE AT CAWNPORE / IN THE EAST INDIES, / JUNE 6TH 1833 AGED 40 YEARS. / THIS TABLET / IS ERECTED BY HIS THREE SURVIVING BROTHERS / AS A TRIBUTE OF THEIR SINCERE AFFECTION.

Ensign 5th Foot 8 Jun 1808. Lt 8 Feb 1810. Lt 15th Lt Dragoons 13 Jan 1814.
Served in the Peninsula with 2/5th Jul 1809 – Aug 1812 and 1/5th Aug – Oct 1813. Present at Busaco, Redinha, Casal Nova, Foz d'Arouce, Sabugal, Fuentes d' Onoro, second siege of Badajoz, Ciudad Rodrigo, Badajoz (wounded) and Pyrenees. Present at Waterloo, siege of Cambrai and Capture of Paris. Also served in India. Brother of Lt James Masterson Pennington 5th Foot.

PENRICE, Thomas
Captain. 16th (Queen's) Regiment of Light Dragoons.
Memorial tablet: St Mary's Church, Pennard, Glamorgan, Wales. (Photograph)

IN MEMORY OF / THOMAS PENRICE / LATE OF KILVROUGH HOUSE IN THIS PARISH, ESQUIRE

/ HE WAS THE SECOND SON OF THOMAS PENRICE / OF GREAT YARMOUTH IN THE COUNTY / OF NORFOLK ESQUIRE / AND WAS THE PURCHASER OF / KILVROUGH / AND OTHER ESTATES IN THE COUNTY OF GLAMORGAN / EARLY IN LIFE / HE ENTERED THE 16TH OR QUEEN'S LANCERS / IN WHICH REGIMENT HE BECAME A CAPTAIN / AND DISTINGUISHED HIMSELF / IN THE PENINSULAR CAMPAIGNS / UNDER THE / DUKE OF WELLINGTON / HE DIED THE XIIITH DAY OF NOVEMBER MDCCCXLVI / IN THE LVIIITH YEAR OF HIS AGE

Cornet Mar 1808. Lt 16th Lt Dragoons 19 Oct 1808. Capt 60th Foot 18 Feb 1813. Capt 16th Lt Dragoons 29 Aug 1813.

Served in the Peninsula Apr 1809 – Jul 1812 and Sep 1813 – Apr 1814. Present at Douro, Talavera, Coa, Busaco, Redinha, Casal Nova, Foz d'Arouce, Sabugal, Fuentes d'Onoro, El Bodon, Llerena, Nivelle, Nive and Bayonne. Half pay 1814.

PERCEVAL, Philip Joshua

Lieutenant and Captain. 1st Regiment of Foot Guards.
Coat of Arms and Cross on Wall: St John's Wood Chapel, Marylebone, London. (M.I.)

"SACRED TO THE MEMORY OF / JOHN ROBERT PARKER, / LATE OF HARLEY STREET / .... / ALSO OF LT COL / PHILIP JOSHUA PERCEVAL / LATE OF GRENADIER GUARDS / THEIR SON-IN-LAW, WHO LEFT THIS WORLD / ON 10TH SEPT 1847. / (BURIED IN VAULT BENEATH)"

2nd Lt Royal Marines 2 Jul 1803. 1st Lt 15 Aug 1805. Ensign 1st Foot Guards 8 Aug 1811. Lt and Capt 10 Mar 1814. Capt and Lt Colonel 10 Jan 1837.

Served in the Peninsula with 3rd Battalion Dec 1812 – Apr 1814. Present at Bidassoa, Nivelle, Nive, Adour and Bayonne (severely wounded at the Sortie from Bayonne 14 Apr 1814 and awarded pension of £100 per annum). Retired 30 Dec 1845.

PERCEVAL, William

Lieutenant Colonel. 67th (South Hampshire) Regiment of Foot.
Ledger stone: Evere Cemetery, Brussels, Belgium. (Photograph)

SACRED / TO THE MEMORY OF / LIEUTENANT COLONEL / WILLIAM PERCEVAL CB. / HIS REMAINS **********. / RIFLE BRIGADE / WHO DIED 2ND JAN 1837

Ensign 67th Foot 1 Oct 1795. Lt 16 May 1796. Capt 1 Nov 1804. Capt 95th Foot 4 May 1809. Bt Major 21 Jun 1813. Major 14th Foot 12 Jan 1814. Lt Colonel 67th Foot 2 Mar 1815.

Served in the Peninsula with 95th Foot Feb – Dec 1810 and Sep 1811 – Sep 1813. Present at Cadiz, Sobral (severely wounded and had to return to England), Ciudad Rodrigo, Badajoz, Salamanca, San Millan, Vittoria, and Pyrenees (severely wounded 1 Aug 1813 when he lost the use of both arms and had to return to England again). Awarded two pensions of £300 and £100 per annum. At Sobral he was wounded in his leg and arm and was on the point of being captured by the French when he was rescued by Capt Brotherton who put him on his own horse, while Brotherton took the horse of a private who was the orderly of Sir Dennis Pack. Pack reprimanded Brotherton severely, but when he heard the explanation Pack apologised to Brotherton. Perceval never forgot this and as he lay dying in Brussels he said 'General Brotherton once saved my life.' Gold Medal for Ciudad Rodrigo, Badajoz and Salamanca. CB. On his return to England he joined the 14th Foot and on 2 Mar 1815 became Lt Colonel of 67th Foot and retired on half pay. Also served in the West Indies 1795–1800 (present at San Domingo 1796) and Walcheren 1809 (Brigade Major to Sir W. Stewart).
Reference: Royal Military Calendar, Vol. 5, p. 86.

PERCIVALL, William

Veterinary Surgeon. Royal Artillery Drivers.
Ledger stone: Brompton Cemetery, London. (Grave number BR 9963. Compartment AJ:25x105). (Photograph)

SACRED / TO THE MEMORY OF / WILLIAM PERCIVALL ESQ[RE] / VETERINARY SURGEON TO THE / 1ST REGIMENT OF LIFE GUARDS / WHO DIED AT RICHMOND, DEC[R] 11TH 1854, / AGED 67.

Veterinary Surgeon 30 Nov 1812. Veterinary Surgeon 1st Life Guards 30 May 1827.

Served in the Peninsula Sep 1813 – Apr 1814. Present at Orthes and Toulouse. Served in the 1815 campaign (present at the Capture of Paris). MGS medal for Orthes and Toulouse.

PERCY, Francis

Private. 12th (Prince of Wales's) Regiment of Light Dragoons.
Named on the Regimental Memorial: St Joseph's Church, Waterloo. (Photograph)

Present at Waterloo where he was killed.

PERCY, Hon. Henry

Captain. 14th (Duchess of York's Own) Light Dragoons.
Family vault: St Marylebone Parish Church, London. (In Crypt, second passage). (M.I.)

"THE FAMILY VAULT OF THE EARL OF BEVERLEY CONTAINING THE REMAINS OF ALGERNON PERCY, 1ST EARL OF BEVERLEY .... AND HIS SON HENRY, BORN 14 SEPT 1785, DIED 15 APRIL 1825."

Lt 7th Foot 16 Aug 1804. Capt 6th West India Regt 9 Oct 1806. Capt 7 Foot 6 Nov 1806. Capt 14th Lt Dragoons 21 Jun 1810. Bt Major 16 Aug 1810. Bt Lt Colonel 18 Jun 1815. Major 12 Oct 1820.

Served in the Peninsula Sep 1808 – Jan 1809 (ADC to Sir John Moore), with 2/7th Apr 1809 – Jul 1810 and with 14th Lt Dragoons Aug 1810 – Apr 1814. Present at Corunna, Douro and Talavera. Taken prisoner while reconnoitring near the heights of Busaco in 1810 and held in France until Mar 1814. Present at Waterloo (ADC to Wellington. Sent home after the battle with the despatches and captured eagles). Awarded Bt Lt Colonelcy and CB. Retired 13 Sep 1821. Educated at Eton. MP for Beeralston in Devon 1820–1825.

Reference: Gentleman's Magazine, Jun 1825, p. 567.

PERCY, Hugh

Sergeant. 51st (2nd Yorkshire West Riding) Light Infantry.
Named on the Regimental Memorial: KOYLI Chapel, York Minster, Yorkshire. (Photograph)

Served in the Peninsula. Present on the retreat from Burgos and taken prisoner 27 Nov 1812. He was not heard of again and it was assumed that he had died in captivity.

PERCY, John Samuel

Lieutenant. 51st (2nd Yorkshire West Riding) Light Infantry.
Named on the Regimental Memorial: KOYLI Chapel, York Minster, Yorkshire. (Photograph)

Ensign 20 Aug 1807. Lt 7 May 1809.

Served in the Peninsula Oct 1808 – Jan 1809 and Feb 1811 – Jun 1813. Present at Corunna, Fuentes d'Onoro, second siege of Badajoz, Moriscos, Salamanca, Burgos, San Millan and Vittoria where he was killed 21 Jun 1813.

PERRIN, Isaac Barrington

Lieutenant. 2nd (Queen's Royal) Regiment of Foot.
Headstone: St Mary the Virgin's Churchyard, Carisbrooke, Isle of Wight. Seriously eroded and inscription recorded from memorial inscription. (Photograph)

"LIEUT ISAAC BARRINGTON PERRIN OF QUEEN'S ROYAL REGT DROWNED OFF THE ISLE OF WIGHT 17 APRIL 1817 AGED 20 YEARS."

Ensign 27 Jul 1811. Lt 15 Sep 1813.

Served in the Peninsula Jan 1812 – Apr 1814. Present at the siege of Salamanca Forts, Salamanca, Burgos and retreat from Burgos. Taken prisoner at Tordesillas 31 Oct 1812 during the retreat and held prisoner until 1814. Drowned off the coast of the Isle of Wight 17 Apr 1817.

PERRY, John Philip

Captain. 38th (1st Staffordshire) Regiment of Foot.
Pedestal tomb: South Park Street Burial Ground, Calcutta, India. (Photograph)

SACRED / TO THE MEMORY OF / CAPTAIN J. P. PERRY / LATE OF H. M. 38TH REGIMENT / WHO DIED ON THE 12 APRIL 1824. / MOST DESERVEDLY REGRETTED.

Ensign 1801. Lt 1803. Capt 19 Apr 1808.

Served in the Peninsula with 2/38th Regiment Apr 1810 – Apr 1811 and Jan 1812 – Jan 1813. Present at Busaco, Badajoz, Castrejon, Salamanca, Burgos and retreat from Burgos (present at Villa Muriel). Served in Ireland and arrived too late for the Battle of Waterloo, but served at the Capture of Paris and with the Army of Occupation until Dec 1815. Also served in the Cape of Good Hope 1818 and India 1822 where he died in Bengal in 1824.

PETERS, Friedrich

Captain. 1st Regiment of Dragoons, King's German Legion.
Named on the Regimental Memorial: La Haye Sainte, Waterloo. (Photograph)
Named on the Waterloo Column, Hanover, Germany. (Photograph)
Named on the Memorial tablet: St Marien's Church, Celle, Lower Saxony, Germany. (Photograph)

Capt 21 Mar 1804.

Present at Waterloo where he was killed. Also served in Ireland 1806 (present at Tullamore where he was wounded) and the Netherlands 1814–1815.

PETERS, John

Private. 95th Regiment of Foot.
Memorial: St John's Church, Coolhurst, near Horsham. Sussex. (Photograph)

IN / LOVING REMEMBRANCE OF / JOHN PETERS, / WHO DIED JULY 3RD 1855, / AGED 64 YEARS.

Volunteer Sussex Militia. Pte 95th Foot 1814.

Present at Waterloo in Capt Charles Beckwith's Company. Discharged Apr 1821.

PETHICK, Edward

Sergeant. 59th (2nd Nottinghamshire) Regiment of Foot.
Ledger stone: St John's Churchyard, Bowmanville, Ontario, Canada. (Photograph)

IN MEMORY OF / EDWARD PETHICK / SERGEANT / IN THE 59TH REGT. FOOT / DIED NOV. 11 1853 / AET. 71 YRS. / HE RECEIVED A MEDAL FOR BATTLES / AT ST SEBASTIAN & VITTORIA, / COMMANDED BY / GEN. ROSS.

Memorial tablet: St John's Church, Bowmanville, Ontario, Canada. (South wall). (M.I.)

"IN MEMORY OF / EDWARD PETHICK / 1782–1853 / AND HIS WIFE / ELIZABETH BROWN / 1793–1848. / HE WAS A SERGEANT IN THE / 59TH REGIMENT OF FOOT. / HE RECEIVED A MEDAL FOR BATTLES / AT VITTORIA AND SAN SEBASTIAN / UNDER THE DUKE OF WELLINGTON. / FOR KING AND COUNTRY."

Pte 6th Garrison Battalion 1804. Cpl 59th Foot 1810. Sgt 1812.

Served in the Peninsula 1813. Present at Vittoria and San Sebastian (wounded). Discharged 16 Sep 1814 due to deafness and awarded pension of nine pence per day. Lived in Cornwall for 26 years before emigrating to Canada in 1842 aged 60. Every year on the anniversary of Vittoria Sgt Pethick would put on his red uniform jacket. MGS medal for Vittoria and San Sebastian.

PETIT, Peter Hayes

Lieutenant Colonel. 35th (Sussex) Regiment of Foot.
Headstone: St Leonard's Churchyard, Deal, Kent. (Near church). (Photograph)

HERE LIE THE REMAINS / OF / LIEUTT COLL PETER HAYES PETIT / LATE OF HIS MAJESTY'S / 35TH REGIMENT OF FOOT. / HE DIED AT DEAL / SEPT 2ND 1809 / IN THE 37TH YEAR OF HIS AGE / OF A WOUND / WHICH HE RECEIVED BEFORE FLUSHING

Ensign 12th Foot 6 Nov 1790. Lt 23 Jan 1793. Capt Independent Company 18 May 1793. Major 35th Foot 30 Mar 1797. Bt Lt Colonel 11 May 1802. Lt Colonel 35th Foot 1 May 1805.

Served at Walcheren 1809 (present at the siege of Flushing where he was severely wounded which later led to his death). Also served in Malta 1801 and the Mediterranean 1806.
Reference: Gentleman's Magazine, Sep 1809, p. 891.

PETRIE, Alexander

Major. 79th (Cameron Highlanders) Regiment of Foot.
Buried in St Mary the Virgin's Churchyard, Swainswick, near Bath, Somerset. (Burial record). (Photograph of church)

Lt 1st Foot 5 Sep 1795. Capt 79th Foot 26 Oct 1796. Major 28 May 1807. Bt Lt Colonel 30 May 1811.

Served in the Peninsula Aug 1808 – Jan 1809 and Jan 1810 – Oct 1811. Present at Corunna, Cadiz, Busaco, Foz d'Arouce and Fuentes d'Onoro. Awarded Bt Lt Colonelcy and Gold Medal for Fuentes d'Onoro when he succeeded to the command of the regiment after Colonel Phillips Cameron was mortally wounded. Also served at the Helder 1799 (present at Egmont-op-Zee), Egypt 1801 (present at Alexandria where he was awarded Gold Medal from the Sultan) and Walcheren 1809. Retired 20 Feb 1812. Died 29 Apr 1846. By his will he left £19,000 to the government.

PHELPS, James Henry

Captain. 51st (2nd Yorkshire West Riding) Light Infantry.
Headstone: Liverpool Pioneer Cemetery, New South Wales, Australia. (Photograph)

SACRED / TO THE MEMORY / OF / LT. COL. JAMES HENRY PHELPS / LATE OF THE 4TH REGT. / KT. OF HANOVER AND JP. / WHO DIED ON THE 19TH / NOV 1841. / AFTER THIRTY NINE YEARS / IN THE SERVICE OF HIS COUNTRY / IN THE COURSE OF WHICH / HE SHARED IN HER VICTORIES / DURING THE EUROPEAN WARS. / HE CLOSED / HIS JUST HONOURABLE UPRIGHT LIFE / AT LIVERPOOL IN THE 63RD / YEAR OF HIS AGE, / DESERVEDLY LAMENTED / BY ALL WHO KNEW HIM

Ensign 11 Oct 1798. Lt 1 Mar 1803. Capt 21 Sep 1809. Bt Major 22 Jul 1830. Major 4th Foot 26 Sep 1834. Lt Colonel 10 Nov 1837.

Served in the Peninsula Oct 1808 – Jan 1809, Feb 1811 – Dec 1812 and Sep 1813 – Apr 1814. Present at Lugo, Corunna, Fuentes d'Onoro, second siege of Badajoz, Moriscos, Salamanca and Nivelle. Taken prisoner at Nivelle 'through his own bravery which would not let him run till too late'. Was well treated by a French officer and subsequently escaped. He met his benefactor after Waterloo in the advance on Paris. Present at Waterloo, the siege of Cambrai, Capture of Paris and with the Army of Occupation. Also served in India 1800–1803, Walcheren 1809 (present at the siege of Flushing) and Ionian Islands 1823–1832. KH. Sailed for Australia 1831 with 4th Foot. Retired from the army 1838 and became a Police Magistrate in Liverpool, New South Wales, Australia.

PHELPS, Samuel

1st Lieutenant. Royal Artillery.
Memorial tablet: St Michael's Church, Rudbaxton, Wales. (Photograph)

SACRED TO THE MEMORY / OF SAMUEL PHELPS / THIRD SON OF JOHN MARTIN ESQR OF WITHY BUSH, / AND A LIEUTENANT IN THE ROYAL ARTILLERY / WHO AFTER AN ACTIVE SERVICE / IN DIFFERENT CAMPAIGNS, / WOUNDED EARLY IN THE MEMORABLE BATTLE OF WATERLOO / FELL A VICTIM TO THE PROTRACTED EFFECTS / OF THE WALCHEREN FEVER / ON THE 13TH DAY OF DECEMBER 1827 / IN THE 37TH YEAR OF HIS AGE.

2nd Lt 4 Apr 1808. 1st Lt 18 Sep 1809.

Present at Quatre Bras and Waterloo in Major Lloyd's Brigade (wounded) and with the Army of Occupation. Also served at Walcheren 1809. Half pay 4 Aug 1822. Died in 1827 from the effects of Walcheren fever.

PHILIPS, Frederick Charles

Captain. 15th (King's) Regiment of Light Dragoons.
Headstone: Anglican Churchyard, Bagni di Lucca, Tuscany, Italy. (Photograph)

SACRED TO THE MEMORY / OF / FREDERICK CHARLES PHILIPS ESQ / OF RHUAL / IN THE COUNTY OF FLINT N. WALES / LATE OF THE 15TH KING'S HUSSARS / IN WHICH REGT HE SERVED / IN THE PENINSULAR WAR AND AT / THE BATTLE OF WATERLOO / DIED JULY 13TH 1852 / (VERSE)

Cornet 13 Oct 1808. Lt 25 May 1809. Capt 16 Apr 1812. Major 11 Jul 1822. Lt Colonel 14 Jan 1826.

Served in the Peninsula Nov 1808 – Jan 1809 and Mar – Apr 1814. Present in the Corunna campaign and Toulouse. MGS medal for Toulouse. Present at Waterloo, the siege of Cambrai and with the Army of Occupation. Nearly killed at Cambrai when the ground gave way under his horse. He jumped off, but his horse fell down a 100 foot well. Went on a European tour and died in Italy 13 Jul 1852 aged 59. Nephew of Major Edwin Griffith 15th Lt Dragoons who was killed at Waterloo.

Reference: Glover, Gareth, From Corunna to Waterloo: the letters and journals of two Napoleonic Hussars, 2007.

PHILLIMORE, Robert William
Lieutenant and Captain. 1st Regiment of Foot Guards.
Interred in Catacomb B (v97 c8), Kensal Green Cemetery, London.

Ensign 13 Dec 1810. Lt and Capt 13 Dec 1813.

Served in the Peninsula with 3rd Battalion Jan – Dec 1812 and Aug – Sep 1813. Present at Cadiz and Seville. Present at Waterloo. Half pay 22 Jul 1824. Died 30 Nov 1846.

PHILLIPS, Grismond
1st Lieutenant. 23rd (Royal Welch Fusiliers) Regiment of Foot.
Memorial window: St David's Church, Abergwili, Carmarthenshire, Wales. (Photograph)

IN MEMORY OF GRISMOND PHILLIPS OF CURMGIRLE ESQ. / WHO DIED APRIL 28TH 1850 AGED 58. / HE SERVED ALL THROUGH THE PENINSULAR AND AT WATERLOO / AS AN OFFICER OF THE 23RD R W F / ………………..

2nd Lt 3 Aug 1809. 1st Lt 5 Sep 1811.

Served in the Peninsula with 1/23rd Apr – Oct 1811, Mar – Apr 1813 and Nov 1813 – Apr 1814. Present at the first siege of Badajoz, Albuera, Nivelle, Nive, Orthes and Toulouse. Present at Waterloo. Half pay 26 Aug 1819. Married niece of Sir Thomas Picton. MGS medal for Albuera, Nivelle, Nive, Orthes and Toulouse.

REFERENCE: Goodridge, Richard, Letters home (from Lt Phillips, 23rd Foot), Waterloo Journal, Aug 1999, pp. 20–6.

PHILLIPS, Roger Fryer
1st Lieutenant. Royal Artillery.
Ledger stone: Walcot Cemetery, Bath, Somerset. (Area 1 Row C). (Photograph)

SACRED / TO THE MEMORY OF / ROGER FRYER PHILLIPS, R. A. / WHO DEPARTED THIS LIFE / ON THE 8TH JANUARY 1856 / AGED 64 YEARS.

2nd Lt 4 Oct 1806. 1st Lt 1 Feb 1808. 2nd Capt 14 Nov 1826. Bt Major 28 Nov 1854.

Served in the Peninsula Mar 1812 – Dec 1813. Present at the siege of Salamanca Forts, Salamanca, Vittoria, Pyrenees, second siege of San Sebastian and Nivelle. Also served at Walcheren 1809, Malta and the Ionian Islands Jun 1814 – Jan 1823 and Gibraltar Apr 1828 – Feb 1833. MGS medal for Salamanca, Vittoria, Pyrenees, San Sebastian and Nivelle. Half pay 24 Oct 1834.

PHIPPS, Paul
Captain. 1st (Royal) Regiment of Dragoons.
Family Memorial tablet: All Saints' Church, Westbury, Wiltshire. (Photograph)

……………….. / PAUL PHIPPS, K. H. / THEIR THIRD SON. / LIEUTENANT-COLONEL IN / THE ARMY. SERVED WITH / HIS REGIMENT THE 1ST ROYAL / DRAGOONS THROUGHOUT / THE PENINSULAR WAR, / AND AT / THE BATTLE OF WATERLOO. HE WAS BORN / 18 JAN. 1788, / AND DIED 22 / NOV. 1858. / ………………..

Lt 24 Sep 1805. Capt 25 Jul 1811. Major 19 Dec 1826. Lt Colonel (unattached) 27 Oct 1829. Lt Colonel 3rd Dragoon Guards 14 Sep 1838.

Served in the Peninsula Aug 1810 – Apr 1814. Present at Fuentes d'Onoro, Aldea de Ponte, Maguilla, Vittoria and Toulouse. KH. Present at Waterloo. MGS medal for Fuentes d'Onoro, Vittoria and Toulouse.

PHIPPS, Robert
Private. 44th (East Essex) Regiment of Foot.
Buried in St Peter's Churchyard, Harborne, Staffordshire.

Present at Waterloo in Capt W. A. Grey's Company. Died 25 Feb 1882. Known as 'Waterloo Bob'.
REFERENCE: Milner, David, 'Waterloo Bob' – from an old Gentleman in the Midlands, Waterloo Journal, Aug 1999, pp. 29–30.

PICTON, Sir Thomas
Colonel. 77th (East Middlesex) Regiment of Foot.
Monument: St Paul's Cathedral, London. (North transept, West side). (Photograph)

ERECTED AT THE PUBLIC EXPENSE / TO LIEUTENANT-GENERAL SIR THOMAS PICTON, K.G. C.B. / WHO AFTER DISTINGUISHING HIMSELF IN THE VICTORIES OF / BUZACO, FUENTES DE ONOR, CUIDAD RODRIGO, BADAJOZ, VITORIA, / THE PYRENEES, ORTHES AND TOULOUSE; / TERMINATED HIS LONG AND GLORIOUS MILITARY SERVICE / IN THE EVER MEMORABLE BATTLE OF WATERLOO, / TO THE SPLENDID SUCCESS OF WHICH / HIS GENIUS AND VALOUR EMINENTLY CONTRIBUTED, / ON THE XVIII. OF JUNE MDCCCXV.

Memorial tablet: St Paul's Cathedral, London. (In floor). (Photograph)

LIEUTENANT GENERAL / SIR THOMAS PICTON. / FELL AT WATERLOO. / AGED 57.

Memorial stone: Mont St Jean, Waterloo. (Near crossroads). (Photograph)

TO THE GALLANT MEMORY OF / LIEUTENANT-GENERAL SIR THOMAS PICTON / COMMANDER OF THE 5TH DIVISION AND THE LEFT / WING / OF THE ARMY AT THE BATTLE OF WATERLOO / BORN 1758 / DIED NEAR THIS SPOT IN THE EARLY AFTERNOON / OF THE 18TH JUNE 1815 LEADING HIS MEN AGAINST / COUNT DROUET D'ERLON'S ADVANCE

Obelisk: Carmarthen, Wales. (Photograph)

Side 1: Inscription recorded from memorial inscription.

"SIR THOMAS PICTON, KNIGHT GRAND CROSS OF THE MILITARY ORDER OF THE BATH, OF THE PORTUGUESE ORDER OF THE TOWER AND SWORD, AND OF OTHER FOREIGN ORDERS, LIEUTENANT-GENERAL IN THE BRITISH ARMY, AND MEMBER OF PARLIAMENT FOR THE BOROUGH OF PEMBROKE: BORN AT POYSTON, IN PEMBROKESHIRE, IN AUGUST, 1758; DIED AT WATERLOO, ON THE 18TH OF JUNE, 1815, GLORIOUSLY FIGHTING FOR HIS COUNTRY AND THE LIBERTIES OF EUROPE. HAVING HONOURABLY FULFILLED, ON BEHALF OF THE PUBLIC, VARIOUS DUTIES IN VARIOUS CLIMATES, AND HAVING ACHIEVED THE HIGHEST MILITARY RENOWN IN THE SPANISH PENINSULA, HE THRICE RECEIVED THE UNANIMOUS THANKS OF PARLIAMENT, AND A MONUMENT, ERECTED BY THE BRITISH NATION IN ST PAUL'S CATHEDRAL, COMMEMORATES HIS DEATH AND SERVICES. HIS GRATEFUL COUNTRYMEN, TO PERPETUATE PAST AND INCITE TO FUTURE EXERTIONS, HAVE RAISED THIS COLUMN, UNDER THE AUSPICES OF HIS MAJESTY KING GEORGE THE FOURTH, TO THE MEMORY OF A HERO AND WELSHMAN. / THE PLANS AND DESIGN OF THIS MONUMENT WAS GIVEN BY OUR COUNTRYMAN, JOHN NASH, ESQ. R.A. AND THE WHOLE WAS ERECTED BY M. DANIEL MAINWARING, OF THE TOWN OF CARMARTHEN, IN THE YEARS 1826 AND 1827"

Side 2: PICTON / BORN AUGUST 24 1758 / FELL AT WATERLOO / JUNE 18 1815

Side 3: PICTON / ORTHES / TOULOUSE / WATERLOO

Side 4: PICTON / BUSACO / BADAJOS / VITTORIA

Foundation stone to Obelisk: Carmarthen, Wales. (M.I.)

"THIS, / THE FIRST STONE OF THE COLUMN / ERECTED TO THE MEMORY OF OUR GALLANT COUNTRYMAN / LIEUTENANT-GENERAL SIR THOMAS PICTON, / (KNIGHT GRAND CROSS OF THE BATH, AND OF SEVERAL FOREIGN ORDERS,) / WHO, AFTER SERVING HIS KING AND COUNTRY / IN SEVERAL CAMPAIGNS, / DIED GLORIOUSLY AT THE BATTLE OF WATERLOO, / WAS LAID / BY THE RIGHT HONOURABLE FRANCES BARONESS DYNEVOR, / ASSISTED BY / SIR CHRISTOPHER COLE, (KNIGHT COMMANDER / OF THE BATH, CAPTAIN IN THE ROYAL NAVY OF BRITAIN, MEMBER / OF PARLIAMENT FOR THE COUNTY OF GLAMORGAN, / AND PROVINCIAL GRAND MASTER OF / MASONS FOR SOUTH WALES,) / ON THE 16TH DAY OF AUGUST 1825."

The monument was originally erected in 1828 but fell into a dilapidated state and was taken down in 1846. Sculptures removed from this monument were neglected and forgotten until the 1940s when they were rescued and taken to the Museum. The present monument was erected in 1947. In 1984 the top section was declared unsafe, taken down and rebuilt on stronger foundations in 1988.

Statue: City Hall, Cardiff, Wales. (Photograph)

SIR / THOMAS PICTON / 1758–1815

Memorial tablet: St Michael's Church, Rudbaxton, Wales. (Photograph)

TO THE FAMOUS MEMORY OF / LIEUTENANT GENERAL SIR THOMAS PICTON K.G. C.B. / BORN AT POYSTON, IN THIS PARISH, 1758 AUG 24TH, / AND BAPTIZED IN THIS CHURCH, / FELL AT WATERLOO 1815 JUNE 18TH, / HE LIES BURIED IN THE CATHEDRAL / CHURCH OF ST PAUL'S, LONDON.

Ensign 12th Foot 1773. Lt 75th Foot 1776. Capt 1777. Lt Colonel 56th Foot 1 May 1796. Bt Colonel 1 Jan 1801. Colonel 77th Foot 13 Oct 1811. Major General 25 Apr 1808. Lt General 4 Jun 1813.

Served in the Peninsula Feb 1810 – Jul 1812 and Apr 1813 – Apr 1814 (GOC 3 Division). Present at Busaco (Mentioned in Despatches), Redinha, Casal Nova, Foz d'Arouce, Sabugal (Mentioned in Despatches), Fuentes d'Onoro (Mentioned in Despatches), second siege of Badajoz (Mentioned in Despatches), El Bodon, Ciudad Rodrigo (Mentioned in Despatches), Badajoz (wounded and Mentioned in Despatches), Vittoria (Mentioned in Despatches), Pyrenees (Mentioned in Despatches), Orthes (Mentioned in Despatches), Vic Bigorre and Toulouse. Did not take part at Salamanca as he was too ill with fever from the Walcheren expedition and was sent home. Gold Cross for Busaco, Fuentes d'Onoro, Ciudad Rodrigo, Badajoz, Vittoria, Pyrenees, Orthes and Toulouse. GCB. Present at Quatre Bras (wounded) and Waterloo where he was killed in command of the 5th Division. Also served in Gibraltar 1773–1776, West Indies 1794–1803 (present at St Vincent where he was wounded and St Lucia) and Walcheren 1809. Wellington said of him 'He was a rough foul mouthed devil as ever lived, but no man could do better in different services I assigned to him.'

Reference: Dictionary of National Biography. Robinson, Heaton Banstead, Memoirs of Lieutenant General Sir Thomas Picton, 2nd edn, 2 vols, 1836. Havard, Robert G., Wellington's Welsh General, a life of Sir Thomas Picton, 1966. Myatt, Frederick, Peninsular General: Sir Thomas Picton, 1758–1815, 1996.

Cole, John William, Memoirs of British Generals, Vol 2, 1856, pp. 1–86. Account of the ceremony of laying the foundation stone of the monument of Sir Thomas Picton at Carmarthen 8th August 1825, Waterloo Journal, Apr 1985, pp. 19–24.

PIERREPOINT, Charles Alphonso
Major. Permanent Assistant, Quartermaster General.
Chest tomb: St John the Evangelist Churchyard, Perlethorpe, Nottinghamshire. (Part of Thoresby Park Estate). (Photograph)

SACRED BE THIS SPOT / TO THE MEMORY OF / CHARLES ALPHONSO PIERREPOINT / A MAJOR IN THE BRITISH SERVICE. / WHO LOST HIS LIFE MOST GALLANTLY / WHILST STORMING AN OUTWORK NEAR BURGOS. / OF AN ANCIENT AND RESPECTABLE FAMILY / ON WHOM BY HIS EXCELLENT CONDUCT / HE CONFERRED HONOUR. / HE WAS INTERRED ON THE FIELD WHERE / HE FOUGHT AND FELL / SEPTEMBER 19TH 1812. / BY FOREIGN HAND DIE, THY HUMBLE GRAVE ORDERED, / STRANGERS HONOURED AND BY STRANGERS MOURNED.

Lt 20th Foot 31 Aug 1799. Capt 11 Sep 1806. Bt Major 26 Sep 1811.

Served in the Peninsula with 20th Foot Aug 1808 – Jan 1809 and May 1811 – Sep 1812 (AQMG). Present at Vimeiro and Corunna. Served as sketching officer for Quartermaster General Murray who was attempting to produce accurate maps for Wellington's campaigns. Killed at Burgos 19 Sep 1812.
REFERENCE: Glover, Gareth, ed., The Corunna diary of Captain C. A. Pierrepoint, 2005.

PILE, William
Private. 10th (Prince of Wales's Own Royal) Regiment of Light Dragoons.
Headstone: Ballyhennan Church Cemetery, Tarbet, Argyllshire, Scotland. (Photograph)

1854 / TO THE MEMORY OF / WILLIAM PILE / WHO DIED 12TH JANUARY 1854 / AGED 64 YEARS / THIS STONE IS ERECTED / BY HIS ORPHANED FAMILY

Present at Waterloo in Capt Grey's Troop No. 4.

PILLICHODY, Alexis
Lieutenant. 3rd (Prince of Wales's) Regiment of Dragoon Guards.
Named on the Monument at Fort Erie, Canada. (M.I.)

OFFICERS KILLED DURING THE SIEGE OF FORT ERIE COL. HERCULES SCOTT, 103D REGT.; LIEUT. COL. WILLIAM DRUMMOND, 104TH REGT.; LIEUT. COL. JOHN GORDON, ROYAL SCOTS; CAPT. R. D. PATTESON, 6TH REGT.; CAPT. TORRENS, 8TH REGT.: CAPT J.M. WRIGHT, 824 REGT., CAPT. ED. WALKER, INCOR. MILITIA; LIEUT. COPLES RADCLIFFE, R. N.; LIEUT. NOEL, ROYAL SCOTS; LIEUT. J. RUTLEDGE, ROYAL SCOTS; LIEUT. BARSTOW, 8TH REGT.; LIEUT. PILLICHODY, DE WATTEVILLE REGT.; ENSIGN E. LANGFORD. 82D REGT."

Lt De Watteville's Regt 21 Jan 1808. Lt 3rd Dragoon Guards 28 May 1812.

Served in the Peninsula Sep 1812 – Aug 1813. Present at Vittoria. Also served in North America (present at the siege of Fort Erie Aug – Sep 1814 where he was killed).

PIPER, John
Major. 4th (King's Own) Regiment of Foot.
Named on the Family Memorial tablet: St Andrew's Church, Colyton, Devon. (Photograph)

IN MEMORY OF / LIEUTENANT COLONEL / JOHN PIPER, C.B. / LATE COMMANDING / 4TH OR KING'S OWN REGIMENT / OF INFANTRY. / ………………..

Named on the Regimental Memorial to 4th Foot: St Michael's Cathedral, Bridgetown, Barbados, West Indies. (Photograph)

Ensign 6 Feb 1795. Lt 6 Sep 1795. Capt 21 Aug 1799. Major 16 Aug 1810. Bt Lt Colonel 17 Aug 1812.

Served in the Peninsula Aug 1808 – Jan 1809 and Nov 1810 – Jan 1814. Present at Corunna, Fuentes d'Onoro, Barba del Puerco, Badajoz (wounded), Salamanca, retreat from Burgos (wounded at Villa Muriel), Vittoria, San Sebastian (severely wounded), Bidassoa, Nivelle and Nive (severely wounded). Commanded the battalion at Badajoz and Salamanca as senior officers were wounded. At Nive on 10 Dec he took command of the 2nd Brigade in the 5th Division for the same reason. On 11th December he himself received a severe wound in the neck which left him paralysed. He was sent back to England with other wounded soldiers and their ship was captured by French pirates. When they discovered that there were only wounded men on board the pirates let them go on to England. Awarded pension of £300 per annum. Gold Cross for Badajoz, Salamanca, San Sebastian and Nive. CB. Also served at the Helder 1799 (present at Bergen and Alkmaar), Hanover 1805, Copenhagen 1807, Sweden 1808, Walcheren 1809 (severely ill from fever on his return) and the West Indies 1819 (present in Barbados where he died 1822). Brother of Capt Robert Sloper Piper Royal Engineers and Assistant Surgeon Samuel Ayrault Piper 30th Foot who served in India and was probably the original of Dr Slammer in *Pickwick Papers.*
REFERENCE: *Usher, H. Y., Lieut-Colonel John Piper, CB., 4th Foot, 1783–1821, Journal of the Society for Army Historical Research, Vol. 37, No. 152, Dec 1959, pp. 172–83. Royal Military Calendar, Vol. 4, pp. 406–9.*

PIPER, Robert Sloper
2nd Captain. Royal Engineers.
Named on the family Memorial tablet: St Andrew's Church, Colyton, Devon. (Photograph)

IN MEMORY OF / ……………….. / GENERAL ROBERT SLOPER PIPER / ROYAL ENGINEERS. / ………………..

2nd Lt 10 Jan 1809. Lt 1 Dec 1809. 2nd Capt 16 May 1814. Capt 15 Jan 1826. Bt Major 10 Jan 1837. Lt Colonel 28 Nov 1841. Bt Colonel 20 Jun 1854. Major General 30 May 1856. Lt General 20 Apr 1861. General 1 Jan 1868.

Served in the Peninsula Mar 1810 – Apr 1814. Present at Torres Vedras, Badajoz, Pamplona, Bidassoa, Nive, Bayonne and Toulouse. In command of a division of the Pontoon Train Jan 1812–1814. Responsible for the bridges across such rivers as the Guadiana, Tagus, Bidassoa, Gave D'Oleron and Garronne. Served with the Army of Occupation 1815–1816. In Jun 1815 was at Antwerp and then went to Paris after the Prussians and repaired bridges over the Seine. Also served in the Netherlands 1814–1815 and Ceylon 1816–1818 (commanding engineer in the third Kandian War 1817–1818). Retired on full pay 2 Feb 1848. MGS medal for Badajoz, Nive and Toulouse. Died in Brighton 26 Dec 1873 aged 84. Brother of Major John Piper 4th Foot and Asst Surgeon Samuel Ayrault Piper 30th Foot who served in India and was probably the original of Dr Slammer in *Pickwick Papers.*
REFERENCE: *Annual Register, 1873, Appx, p. 162.*

PITT, George Dean see DEAN, George

PITT, William Henry
Ensign. Coldstream Regiment of Foot Guards.
Ledger stone: Coldstream Guards Cemetery, St Etienne, Bayonne, France. (Photograph)

W. H. P.

Named on the Memorial: St Andrew's Church (now Musée Historique), Biarritz, France. (Photograph)
Named on Memorial Panel VII for the Sortie from Bayonne: Royal Military Chapel, Wellington Barracks, London. (M.I.) (Destroyed by a Flying Bomb 1944)

Ensign 5 Mar 1812.

Served in the Peninsula Mar – Apr 1814. Present at Bayonne where he was severely wounded at the Sortie from Bayonne on 14 Apr 1814 and died of his wound 24 Apr 1814.

PITTS, Thomas James Heblethwayte
2nd Captain. Royal Engineers.
Family Memorial tablet: Bridlington Priory, Bridlington, Yorkshire. (Photograph)

SACRED TO THE MEMORY / OF THOMAS JAMES HEBLETHWAYTE, / OF WILLIAM AND OF FREDERICK PITTS, * / THREE BROTHERS, / WHO, IN THE ZEALOUS DISCHARGE OF THEIR PROFESSIONAL DUTIES, / AND IN THE PERILOUS COURSE OF GLORY, WHICH THEY PURSUED, / LIVED DISTINGUISHED AND DIED LAMENTED, / SERVING THEIR COUNTRY. / WILLIAM AND FREDERICK, MIDSHIPMEN IN THE ROYAL NAVY, / ALREADY AT THE AGE OF 16, HAD GIVEN AN EARNEST OF FUTURE EXCELLENCE, / WHEN THEY SEVERALLY FELL THE VICTIMS OF MISCHANCE AND DISEASE. / WILLIAM WAS DROWNED IN THE BRITISH CHANNEL, ON THE 2D OF AUGUST, 1809. / FREDERICK DIED AT SEA, ON THE 24TH OF JUNE, 1814. / THOMAS, / A CAPTAIN IN THE CORPS OF ROYAL ENGINEERS, / SERVED FOUR CAMPAIGNS AGAINST THE FRENCH, IN SPAIN, / UNTIL THE DELIVERANCE OF THAT COUNTRY BY HIS COMPATRIOTS, / TRANSFERRED THE SCENE OF VICTORY TO THE SOIL OF FRANCE. / AT BARROSA, AT BADAJOZ, AT SALAMANCA, / THE SIEGE OF SALAMANCA, MADRID, BURGOS, VITTORIA, CADIZ, ALMAREZ, BIDASOA, / PAMPLUNA, NIVELLE, NIVE, AND BAYONNE: / IN THE PASSES OF THE PYRENNEES / HE DISPLAYED ALL THOSE QUALITIES WHICH CONSTITUTE MILITARY VIRTUE, / AND ON THE 23RD OF FEBRUARY, 1814, IN CARRYING THE FORT OF HASTINGUES, / FELL AT THE AGE OF 24, / NOT MANY DAYS BEFORE THE CITY OF BOURDEAUX WAS TAKEN / BY THE ILLUSTRIOUS ARMY, / WHERE LAURELS OVERSHADOW HIS GRAVE. / IF THE FATHER WERE TOO PROUD, THE MOTHER TOO FOND / OF SONS LIKE THESE, / THEY HAVE BORNE THE LOSS OF THEM WITH SUBMISSION TO THE WILL OF GOD / WHOSE MERCY THEY HUMBLY ACKNOWLEDGE, / THAT, IN THIS SAD BUT SOOTHING OFFICE, / ON INSCRIBING THE MONUMENT OF THEIR CHILDREN, / NOTHING COULD BE RECORDED / THAT DID NOT REFLECT HONOR / ON THE AUTHORS OF THEIR BEING. / * SONS OF JOHN PITTS, ESQ. OF BRIDLINGTON QUAY, IN THE EAST RIDING OF THE COUNTY OF YORK (MANY YEARS LIEUT-COL. COMMANDANT OF THE BRIDLINGTON VOLUNTEER ARTILLERY AND LT INFANTRY) AND FRANCES, HIS WIFE, EIGHTH DAUGHTER OF THE LATE JAMES HEBLETHWAYTE, ESQ. OF BRIDLINGTON, IN THE SAME COUNTY.

Named on the Regimental Memorial: Rochester Cathedral, Rochester, Kent. (Photograph)
Named on the Memorial: St Andrew's Church (now Musée Historique), Biarritz, France. (Photograph)

1st Lt 1 Jan 1808. 2nd Capt 21 Jul 1813.

Served in the Peninsula May 1810 – Feb 1814. Present at Cadiz, Barrosa, Badajoz, Salamanca Forts, Salamanca, Burgos where his arm was broken, retreat from Burgos (responsible for blowing up the bridges on the retreat), Pamplona, Pyrenees, Maya, Vera and Nivelle. Killed while on a reconnaissance looking for a crossing of the Gave d'Oleron 23 Feb 1814.

PLATT, George Edmund
Lieutenant. 26th (Cameronian) Regiment of Foot.
Memorial: St Andrew's Church, West Tarring, Sussex. (M.I.)

"GEORGE EDMUND PLATT, LATE LIEUTENANT IN THE 26TH REGIMENT OF FOOT (CAMERONIANS). HE SERVED UNDER SIR JOHN MOORE IN SPAIN, WITH CREDIT TO HIMSELF AND HONOR TO HIS REGIMENT. DIED AT SWISS COTTAGE, WORTHING, FEBRUARY 4TH 1850, AGED 70 YEARS."

Ensign 34th Foot 4 May 1805. Lt 26th Foot 3 Apr 1806.

Served in the Peninsula Oct 1808 – Jan 1809. Present at Corunna. Also served at Hanover 1805 and Walcheren 1809 (present at the siege of Flushing). Out of the battalion of 800 men who went to Walcheren only 7 officers and 95 rank and file returned. MGS medal for Corunna. Retired in 1813.
Reference: Gentleman's Magazine, Jun 1850, p. 682. Annual Register, 1850, Appx, p. 207.

PLAYFORD, Thomas
Private. 2nd Life Guards.
Headstone: Mitcham Cemetery, Adelaide, South Australia, Australia. (Photograph)

SACRED / TO THE MEMORY OF / THOMAS PLAYFORD / LATE PASTOR OF / BENTHAM CHAPEL ADELAIDE / BORN AUGUST 11TH 1795 / DIED SEPTEMBER 18TH 1873 / ………………..

Pte 25 Jun 1810. Cpl of Horse 9 Aug 1816.

Served in the Peninsula Nov 1812 – Jul 1814. Present at Vittoria. Present at Waterloo. Discharged 5 May 1834 due to ill health. Later settled in Australia and entered the church.
Reference: Glover, Gareth, The memoirs of Sergeant Thomas Playford, 2006.

PLENDERLEATH, John
Physician. Medical Department.
Memorial tablet: Westminster Abbey, London. (Photograph)

IN MEMORY OF / DR JOHN PLENDERLEATH, / (THIRD SON OF JOHN PLENDERLEATH, ESQR OF GLEN IN TWEDALE, SCOTLAND) / PHYSICIAN TO THE FORCES, SERVING UNDER THE MARQUIS OF WELLINGTON, IN PORTUGAL, / WHO DIED IN COIMBRA, OF A TYPHUS FEVER, ON THE 18TH JUNE, 1811 / AGED 28 YEARS. / HE WAS EMINENTLY DISTINGUISHED BY THE STRENGTH OF HIS MENTAL FACULTIES, / HIS GREAT CLASSICAL AND PROFESSIONAL KNOWLEDGE; / AND NO LESS SO BY THE HUMANITY OF HIS HEART, / WHICH MANIFESTED ITSELF ON ALL OCCASIONS: / AND ESPECIALLY TOWARDS THE NUMEROUS SICK AND WOUNDED / BOTH OF HIS COUNTRYMEN AND OF THE ENEMY, / WHICH WERE COMMITTED TO HIS CARE. / IN COMMEMORATION OF HIS PUBLIC VIRTUES, / AND OF HIS MANY AMIABLE QUALITIES IN PRIVATE LIFE / THIS MONUMENT IS ERECTED / AS A SMALL TRIBUTE OF PARENTAL AFFECTION.

Asst Surgeon 3rd Foot Guards 26 Jun 1801. Asst Surgeon 1st Foot 7 Nov 1805. Asst Surgeon 15th Lt Dragoons 15 May 1806. Surgeon 1st Foot 21 Jul 1808. Staff Surgeon 11 Aug 1808. Resigned 23 Feb 1809 and reappointed as Physician 24 Sep 1809.

Served in the Peninsula Nov 1808 – Jan 1809 and Jul 1810 – Jul 1811. Present in the Corunna campaign. Died at Coimbra of typhus fever Jun 1811. MD St Andrews 1808.
Reference: Gentleman's Magazine, Jul 1811, p. 92.

PODE, John Spurrell
Ensign. 57th (West Middlesex) Regiment of Foot.
Named on the Memorial: St Andrew's Church (now Musée Historique), Biarritz, France. (Photograph)

Ensign 11 Feb 1813.
Served in the Peninsula Nov – Dec 1813. Present at Nive where he was killed 13 Dec 1813.

POGSON, Peter see POXSON Peter

POLE, Edward Sacheverell Chandos
Lieutenant and Captain. 1st Regiment of Foot Guards.
Memorial: Royal Military Chapel, Wellington Barracks, London. (M.I.) (Destroyed by a Flying Bomb 1944)

"PLACED BY HIS GRANDSON, REGINALD WALKELYNE CHANDOS POLE, GRENADIER GUARDS, 1871–78, IN / MEMORY OF CAPTAIN EDWARD SACHEVERELL CHANDOS POLE, 1ST GUARDS, 1808–13. / "WALCHEREN," "PENINSULA."

Ensign 5 May 1808. Lt and Capt 28 Jan 1813.
Present in the Peninsula Sep 1812 – May 1813. Also served at Walcheren 1809. Resigned 8 Jul 1813. Became Captain of Derbyshire Yeomanry 7 Aug 1813.

POLLARD, Thomas
Private. Coldstream Regiment of Foot Guards.
Headstone laid flat: St James's Churchyard, Accrington. Lancashire. (Photograph)

SACRED / TO THE MEMORY OF / THE LATE THOMAS POLLARD / PENSIONER OF THE COLDSTREAM REGIMENT OF FOOT – / GUARDS, ENLISTED IN 1803, AND RETIRED IN 1814, / AND WAS THROUGH THE WHOLE OF THE PENINSULAR WAR / UNDER THE COMMAND OF HIS EXCELLENCY THE DUKE / OF WELLINGTON, BORN MARCH 24TH 1786 AND / DIED ON THE 21ST OF DECEMBER 1859. / ....

Pte 8 Oct 1803.
Served in the Peninsula Mar 1809 – Apr 1814. Present at Talavera, Busaco, Barrosa, Fuentes d' Onoro, Ciudad Rodrigo, Salamanca, Vittoria, Nivelle and Nive. Discharged 8 Sep 1814 after being wounded in his hand and awarded a pension of six pence per day. MGS medal for Talavera, Busaco, Barrosa, Fuentes d' Onoro, Ciudad Rodrigo, Salamanca, Vittoria, Nivelle and Nive.

PONSONBY, Hon. Frederick Cavendish
Lieutenant Colonel. 12th (Prince of Wales's) Regiment of Light Dragoons.
Buried in the Crypt: St Nicholas's Church, Hatherop, Gloucestershire. (Burial record)
Named on the Civil Commissioners and Governors of Malta, Grand Masters Palace, Valletta, Malta.

Cornet 10th Lt Dragoons Jan 1800. Lt 20 Jun 1800. Capt 20 Aug 1803. Capt 60th Foot 3 Apr 1806. Bt Major 25 Jun 1807. Major 23rd Lt Dragoons 5 Aug 1807. Lt Colonel 12th Lt Dragoons 11 Jun 1811. Bt Colonel 4 Jun 1814. Major General 27 May 1825.
Served in the Peninsula Jun 1809 – Jul 1811 and Sep 1811 – Apr 1814. Present at Talavera, Barrosa (AAG. Mentioned in General Graham's Despatches), Cadiz (AAG), Llerena, Salamanca, retreat from Burgos (severely wounded at Monasterio 13 Oct 1812 and Mentioned in Despatches), Venta del Poza, Vittoria, Tolosa, Nivelle, Nive, Adour and Bayonne. When the 23rd Lt Dragoons were withdrawn from the Peninsula after the disastrous charge at Talavera in 1809, Ponsonby transferred to the Staff and became

AAG at Barrosa and Cadiz. Present at Waterloo where he was severely wounded and lay on the battlefield during the night where he had many escapes from death. Half pay 26 Aug 1820. Also served in the Ionian Islands (Inspecting Field Officer 29 Jan 1824) and Malta (Governor 1825–1835). Gold Cross for Barrosa, Salamanca, Vittoria and Nive. KCB 1831. GCMG. KCH. KTS and Knight of Maria Theresa of Austria. Educated at Harrow. Was well liked by all ranks. Knowledgeable on all cavalry matters. In 1813 abridged *Instructions for Cavalry on Outpost Duty*, by Lt Colonel Von Arentschildt. His letters written from the Peninsula were printed in *Lady Bessborough and her family circle* edited by the Earl of Bessborough and A. Aspinall, 1940. Died 11 Jul 1837. Cousin of Lt Colonel the Hon. Sir Robert O'Callaghan 39th Foot and second cousin of Lt Colonel the Hon. Sir William Ponsonby 5th Dragoon Guards.
REFERENCE: *Dictionary of National Biography. Gentleman's Magazine, May 1837, pp. 543–5. Annual Register, 1837, Appx, pp 166–7. United Service Journal, Apr 1837, pp. 524–9. Collins, R. M., Colonel the Hon Frederick Cavendish Ponsonby, 12th Light Dragoons, Journal of the Society for Army Historical Research, Vol. 46, No. 185, Spring 1968, pp. 1–5.*

PONSONBY, Hon. Sir William
Lieutenant Colonel. 5th (Princess Charlotte of Wales's) Dragoon Guards.
Monument: St Paul's Cathedral, London. (Crypt south). (Photograph)

ERECTED AT THE PUBLIC EXPENSE TO THE MEMORY OF / MAJOR GENERAL THE HONBLE SIR WILLIAM PONSONBY, / WHO FELL GLORIOUSLY IN THE BATTLE OF WATERLOO / ON THE 18TH OF JUNE 1815.

Buried in the vault of the Molesworth family: St Mary Abbots Churchyard, Kensington, London (No longer extant). Church demolished in the 1860s, a new church built and all graves were covered.

Ensign Sir Vere Hunt's Regt 6 Mar 1794. Lt in Capt Davis's Independent Company 13 Dec 1794. Lt 12th Foot 16 May 1795. Capt 83rd Foot Sep 1795. Major Loyal Irish Fencible Infantry 15 Dec 1795. Major 5th Dragoon Guards 1 Mar 1798. Bt Lt Colonel 1 Jan 1800. Lt Colonel 5th Dragoon Guards 24 Feb 1803. Bt Colonel 25 Jul 1810. Major General 4 Jun 1813.

Served in the Peninsula Sep 1811 – Jan 1814 and Apr 1814. O/c 1 Cavalry Brigade 1st Division Jul 1812 – Jan 1813, 2 Cavalry Brigade 1st Division Feb – Mar 1813, 2 Cavalry Brigade Apr 1813 – Jan 1814 and Apr 1814. Present at Llerena, Salamanca (Mentioned in Despatches. After Le Marchant was killed Ponsonby took command of the Heavy Cavalry Brigade), Majalahonda (Mentioned in Despatches) and Vittoria. Gold Medal for Salamanca and Vittoria. KCB. Present at Waterloo in command of the Union Brigade of Cavalry where he was killed in the cavalry charge. MP of the Irish Parliament for Bandonbridge 1796–1798 and Fethard, County Tipperary until 1801 and MP for Londonderry in the House of Commons 1812 until his death. Cousin of Lt Colonel the Hon. Sir Robert O'Callaghan 39th Foot and second cousin of Lt Colonel the Hon. Frederick Cavendish Ponsonby 12th Light Dragoons.
REFERENCE: *Dictionary of National Biography. Gentleman's Magazine, 1815, Supplement Part 1, p. 644. Morewood, John, An ornament to his profession. Waterloo Journal, Apr 1996, pp. 1–7.*

POOLE, William Halstead
Lieutenant. Royal Artillery.
Memorial tablet: St Michael's Church, Marbury, Cheshire. (Photograph)

SACRED TO THE BELOVED MEMORY OF / WILLIAM HALSTEAD POOLE ESQUIRE, / OF TERRICK HALL, WHITCHURCH, SALOP / CAPTAIN HALF PAY, ROYAL ARTILLERY / BORN DECEMBER 12TH 1793, DIED JANUARY 28TH 1859, / AGED 65 YEARS. / HE SERVED THE CAMPAIGNS OF 1814 AND 1815, INCLUDING THE / BOMBARDMENT OF THE FRENCH FLEET AT ANTWERP AND / THE BATTLE OF WATERLOO, WHERE HE WAS SEVERELY WOUNDED. / FOR MANY YEARS HE FAITHFULLY FULFILLED THE DUTIES OF A / MAGISTRATE FOR THE

COUNTIES OF CHESHIRE AND SALOP, / OF THE LATTER COUNTY HE WAS A DEPUTY LIEUTENANT. / THIS TABLET IS ERECTED BY HIS SURVIVING CHILDREN.

2nd Lt 11 Sep 1812. 1st Lt 10 May 1815. Half pay 1819. Rejoined 24 Feb 1820. 2nd Capt 25 Nov 1833.

Present at Waterloo in Capt J. Sinclair's Brigade (wounded) and with the Army of Occupation. Also served in the Netherlands 1814–1815 (present at the bombardment of the Scheldt fleet at Antwerp). Half pay 22 Jan 1834. Magistrate for Cheshire and Deputy Lieutenant of Shropshire.

POPHAM, Samuel Taylor

Major. 24th (Warwickshire) Regiment of Foot.
Memorial tablet: St Michael's Cathedral, Bridgetown, Barbados, West Indies. (South wall). Photograph)

SACRED TO THE MEMORY OF / A FATHER AND DAUGHTER, / COLONEL S. T. POPHAM, / LATE QUARTERMASTER GENERAL TO THE ARMY, / OF THIS COMMAND, / HE DIED ON THE 25TH DECEMBER 1823, / AGED 50. / ....

Lt 58th Foot 5 Aug 1795. Capt 28th Foot 25 Apr 1799. Major 24th Foot 14 Sep 1804. Bt Lt Colonel 4 Jun 1811. Lt Colonel 10 Sep 1818.

Served in the Peninsula Apr 1809 – Apr 1814. Present at Talavera (wounded, taken prisoner and held prisoner until the end of the war). Also served at Capture of Guadeloupe 1815 under Sir James Leith and the Windward and Leeward Isles where he was DQMG 1818 until his death in 1825.

POPPLETON, Thomas William

Captain. 53rd Shropshire) Regiment of Foot.
Chest tomb: Killanin Churchyard, Rosscahill, County Galway, Ireland. (Photograph)

SACRED TO THE MEMORY OF MAJOR / THOMAS WILLIAM POPPLETON OF THE / 53RD REGT. AN OFFICER EMINENTLY / DISTINGUISHED AS A BRAVE ACCOMPLISHED / AND CHRISTIAN SOLDIER. HE SERVED IN / INDIA IN EGYPT AND ON THE PENINSULA / AND WAS HONOURED BY THE ESTEEM OF / NAPOLEON WHO WAS UNDER HIS PERSONAL / CHARGE FOR TWO YEARS IN ST HELENA. / OBIT OCTOBER THE 9TH 1827 / AGED 52 YEARS.

Ensign 10th Foot 16 Dec 1795. Lt 15 Aug 1798. Lt 66th Foot 9 Jul 1803. Capt 53rd Foot 23 Nov 1806. Bt Major 25 Dec 1817.

Served in the Peninsula Jun 1810 – Mar 1813. Present at Busaco, Fuentes d'Onoro, siege of Salamanca Forts, Salamanca (wounded), and Burgos. Also served in India 1798 with 10th Foot and from there joined Sir Ralph Abercrombie's expedition to Egypt 1801. Orderly Officer at Longwood, St Helena Dec 1815 – Jul 1817.

Reference: Gentleman's Magazine, Oct 1827, p. 382. Annual Register, 1827, Appx, p. 258.

PORTARLINGTON, John Dawson Earl of

Lieutenant Colonel. 23rd Regiment of Light Dragoons.
Interred in Catacomb B (v77 c11), Kensal Green Cemetery, London.

Ensign 20th Foot Mar 1798. Lt 20 Dec 1798. Capt 46th Foot 24 Mar 1800. Capt 23rd Lt Dragoons 24 Mar 1800. Major 4th Garrison Battalion 25 Nov 1806. Lt Colonel 10th Foot 1 Sep 1808. Lt Colonel 23rd Lt Dragoons 6 Apr 1809. Bt Colonel 4 Jun 1814.

Served in the Peninsula Jun – Dec 1809. Present at Talavera. Present at Waterloo where he commanded the regiment at Quatre Bras on 16th and 17th June but was ill, returned to Brussels and did not return until later on the 18th and missed his regiment's cavalry charge. He joined in with the 18th Hussars and fought with them at the end of the battle. Filled with remorse for missing most of the action on the 18th he retired

from the 23rd Lt Dragoons and purchased a half pay Ensigncy in the 86th Foot 21 Oct 1821. Lieutenant on half pay 10 Sep 1825 and Captain on half pay 9 Aug 1831. Also served at the Helder 1799 and Hanover 1805 (ADC to Lord Cathcart). He lost his fortune and died in reduced circumstances 28 Dec 1845.
REFERENCE: *Gentleman's Magazine, Feb 1846, pp. 201–2.*

PORTEOUS, Walter
Deputy Assistant Commissary General. Commissariat Department.
Grave: Sandpits Cemetery, Gibraltar. (M.I.)

"WALTER PORTEOUS, DEP. ASSISTANT COMMISSARY / GENL., D. 29 APRIL 1817, A. 35."

Deputy Asst Comm General 27 Jul 1811.
Served in the Peninsula Jan 1812 – Apr 1814. With the Royal Waggon Train Feb – Apr 1812 and with the Light Division May 1812 – Aug 1813.

PORTER, William
Captain. 3rd Royal Veteran Battalion.
Memorial tablet: St Stephen's Church, Saltash, Cornwall. (High on north wall of church). (Buried under the north aisle immediately below the tablet). (Photograph)

IN MEMORY OF / WILLIAM PORTER ESQR / OF THIS PARISH, & CAPTAIN IN THE 40TH REGIMENT, / IN WHICH HE SERVED / AT THE CAPTURE OF MONTE VIDEO, THE ATTACK ON / BUENOS AYRES, / AND IN THE PENINSULA UNDER THE DUKE OF WELLINGTON; / HE DIED ON THE 5TH OF APRIL, 1839, AGED 65 YEARS. / ………………..

Ensign Lord Landaff's Regt of Foot 1 Nov 1794. Lt 114th Foot 27 Jan 1795. Capt 40th Foot 9 Jul 1803. Capt 3rd Royal Veteran Battalion 23 Jul 1812.
Served in the Peninsula Aug 1808 – Dec 1809 and Aug – Oct 1811. Present at Rolica and Vimeiro. Also served at the Helder 1799 and South America 1807 (present at Montevideo and Buenos Ayres). Retired on full pay 1814.

PORTEUS, Edward
Deputy Inspector General of Army Hospitals. Medical Department.
Memorial: English Cemetery, Florence, Italy. (South-west section). (Grave number B16E). (Photograph)

SACRED TO THE MEMORY OF / EDWARD PORTEUS ESQRE DEPUTY INSPECTOR GENERAL OF ARMY HOSPITALS IN H. B. MAJESTY'S SERVICE / NEPHEW TO THE LATE RIGHT REVD RECTOR BEILBY PORTEUS / LATE BISHOP OF LONDON. DEPARTED THIS LIFE AT FLORENCE / ON THE 12 SEPT 1845 AGED 68 YEARS. / THIS MONUMENT TO THE MEMORY OF AN AFFECTIONATE HUSBAND A GOOD FATHER AND AN ABLE FRIEND / IS ERECTED BY HIS DISCONSOLATE WIDOW DOMENICA AND SURVIVING ONLY SON GEORGE

Hospital Mate 21 Dec 1797. Asst Surgeon 5th Foot 23 Aug 1799. Surgeon 17th Foot 18 Sep 1799. Staff Surgeon 17 Dec 1803. Deputy Inspector General of Hospitals 17 May 1813.
Served in the Peninsula Nov 1812 – Apr 1814. Present on the East coast of Spain (present at Tarifa and Genoa 1814). Also served in Egypt 1807 and the Ionian Islands 1829.

POWELL, Henry Weyland
Lieutenant and Captain. 1st Regiment of Foot Guards.
Memorial tablet: St Michael and All Angels' Church, Lyndhurst, Hampshire. (North transept). (Photograph)

SACRED TO THE MEMORY OF / HENRY WEYLAND POWELL ESQUIRE, / OF FOXLEASE IN THIS PARISH, / WHO DEPARTED THIS LIFE IN LONDON / ON THE 17TH OF JULY 1840, AGED 53 YEARS. / HIS REMAINS ARE INTERRED AT FULHAM MIDDLESEX; / HE WAS FORMERLY IN THE GRENADIER REGIMENT OF / FOOT GUARDS, / AND SERVED WITH THEM AT WALCHEREN, / IN THE PENINSULA / AND IN THE ACTIONS OF QUATRE BRAS, AND WATERLOO. / THIS TABLET IS ERECTED BY HIS AFFLICTED WIDOW / AS A LAST SAD TRIBUTE AND TOKEN OF AFFECTION, / TO HIM WHO AS A HUSBAND AND A FATHER, IS / DESERVING OF THE SINCEREST LOVE / AND GRATITUDE. / ALSO TO THE MEMORY OF / CLARISSA POWELL, / MOTHER OF HENRY WEYLAND POWELL, / WHO DIED THE 30TH OF JANUARY 1847, / AGED 81 YEARS. / THE BODIES OF THE ABOVE WERE REMOVED FROM FULHAM / TO A VAULT IN THIS CHURCH-YARD OCT 26TH 1865. / ALSO TO THE MEMORY OF ELIZA POWELL.

Ensign 7 Apr 1808. Lt and Capt 22 Jan 1813.

Served in the Peninsula Jul 1811 – May 1813. Present at Cadiz and Seville. Present at Quatre Bras and Waterloo. Also served at Walcheren 1809. Retired 11 Oct 1821.

POWELL, John

Quartermaster. 77th (East Middlesex) Regiment of Foot.
Buried in St George's Chapel, Windsor, Berkshire. (Burial register)

Quartermaster 21 Jun 1810.

Served in the Peninsula Jul 1811 – Apr 1814. Present at Badajoz and Bayonne. Also served in India 1788–1807 in the campaigns against Tippoo Sultan and Doondia Wao (present at Cochin 1795, Colombo 1796, Sedaseer 1799, Seringapatam, Panjalamcoorchy, Arrakeera and Wynaad 1801 where he was severely wounded). Half pay 7 Apr 1837. MGS medal for Badajoz. Military Knight of Windsor 24 Apr 1837. Died 27 Dec 1852 aged 83.

POWELL, Thomas

Captain. Glengarry Light Infantry.
Named on the Memorial tablet to 40th Foot: Afghan Memorial Church, St John the Evangelist, Cobala, Bombay, India. (M.I.)

Ensign 24th Foot 25 Aug 1807. Lt 14 Apr 1808. Capt Glengarry Lt Infantry 11 Mar 1813. Bt Major 11 May 1815. Capt Rifle Brigade 16 May 1816. Capt 57th Foot 27 Oct 1829. Major (unattached) 13 Aug 1830. Major 2nd Foot 29 Mar 1833. Lt Colonel 40th Foot 19 Feb 1836. Lt Colonel 6th Foot 23 Nov 1838.

Served in the Peninsula with 24th Foot Jul – Aug 1809 and Apr 1810 – Feb 1811 and with Staff Mar – Sep 1811 (ADC to Colonel Drummond). Present at Talavera, Busaco and Ciudad Rodrigo (severely wounded). Also served in North America with Glengarry Lt Infantry 1812–1815 (present at Fort Erie where he was wounded) and India 1837 (present at the Capture of Karachi). KH. Exchanged to 6th Foot 23 Nov 1838 but died of cholera in Karachi 23 Mar 1839 before he left the 40th Foot.

POWER, Sir Manley

Lieutenant Colonel. 32nd (Cornwall) Regiment of Foot.
Memorial tablet: Bath Abbey, Bath, Somerset. (Photograph)

SACRED / TO THE MEMORY OF / LIEUT. GENERAL SIR MANLEY POWER K.C.B. K.T.S. / HE WAS HIGHLY DISTINGUISHED AS AN OFFICER / THROUGH THE PENINSULAR WAR. / THE MILITARY COMMANDS ENTRUSTED TO HIM / BEAR TESTIMONY TO THE CONFIDENCE / REPOSED IN HIS VALOUR AND JUDGEMENT / AND HIS INTREPID DISCHARGE OF THEM / PROVED HOW SINCERE WAS HIS ZEAL AND DEVOTION TO HIS COUNTRY. / HE DIED AT

BERNE IN SWITZERLAND JULY 7TH 1826 / (AFTER A FEW HOURS ILLNESS) / RETURNING TO ENGLAND FROM MALTA, / WHERE HE HAD BEEN LIEUT. GOVERNOR SIX YEARS. / AN URBANITY OF MANNERS AND SACRED ATTACHMENT / TO ALL THAT WAS HONOURABLE ENDEAR HIS MEMORY / TO HIS CONNECTIONS AND FRIENDS / AND RENDER HIS LOSS IRREPARABLE / TO HIS AFFLICTED WIDOW / AND FAMILY.

Ensign 20th Foot 27 Aug 1785. Lt 4 May 1789. Capt Independent Company 28 Jun 1793. Capt 20th Foot 16 Jan 1794. Major 7 Oct 1799. Bt Lt Colonel 20 Jun 1801. Lt Colonel 32nd Foot 6 Jun 1805. Bt Colonel 25 Jul 1810. Major General 4 Jun 1813. Lt General 27 May 1825. Portuguese Army: Brigadier 12 Aug 1811. Field Marshal 10 Jul 1813.

Served in the Peninsula with the Portuguese Army Aug 1811 – Apr 1814 in command of the 3rd Brigade of the 8th Portuguese Division. Present at Badajoz (Mentioned in Despatches), Salamanca (Mentioned in Despatches), Vittoria (Mentioned in Despatches), Pyrenees, Nivelle (Mentioned in Despatches), Orthes (Mentioned in Despatches), Vic Bigorre and Toulouse. Gold Cross for Salamanca, Vittoria, Nivelle, Orthes and Toulouse. KCB and KTS. Also served at the Helder 1799 (present at Alkmaar), Minorca 1800, Egypt 1801 (present at Alexandria) and North America 1814–1815 (present at Plattsburgh). Lieutenant Governor of Malta 1820–1826.

REFERENCE: *Dictionary of National Biography. Royal Military Calendar, Vol. 3, pp. 312–13. Gentleman's Magazine, Aug 1826, pp. 182–3.*

POWER, Robert George

Lieutenant. Royal Engineers.

Named on the Regimental Memorial: Rochester Cathedral, Rochester, Kent. (Photograph)

Named on the Memorial: St Andrew's Church, (now Musée Historique), Biarritz, France. (Photograph)

2nd Lt 10 Jan 1809. Lt 2 Dec 1809.

Served in the Peninsula Feb – Nov 1813. Present at the Lines of Torres Vedras. In October 1813 was under orders to join the Army attached to the 5th Division. Present at Nivelle where he was killed near St Jean de Luz on 10 Nov 1813 in the last half hour of the battle. Also served at Walcheren 1809.

POWER, William Greenshields

Major. Royal Artillery.

Low monument with pedestal: Kensal Green Cemetery, London (14513/31/2). Inscription illegible. (Photograph)

Memorial tablet: Old Shanklin Church, Isle of Wight. (North transept). (Photograph)

IN MEMORY OF GENERAL / SIR WILLIAM GREENSHIELDS POWER / K.C.B. & K.H. COMMANDANT OF / 10TH BATTALION, ROYAL ARTILLERY; / BORN 1781, DIED AT SHANKLIN 23RD / JANUARY 1863. HIS REMAINS / ARE INTERRED IN THE FAMILY VAULT IN / KENSAL GREEN CEMETERY.

2nd Lt 31 May 1800. 1st Lt 11 Feb 1802. Capt 13 Jun 1807. Bt Major 21 Sep 1813. Bt Lt Colonel 21 Jun 1817. Lt Colonel 12 Jun 1835. Bt Colonel 10 Jan 1837. Colonel 4 May 1846. Major General 9 Nov 1846. Lt General 20 Jun 1854. General 4 Feb 1857.

Served in the Peninsula Oct 1808 – Apr 1814 and Jul 1810 – Dec 1813. Present at Talavera, Torres Vedras, Ciudad Rodrigo (wounded and Mentioned in Despatches), Badajoz, siege of Salamanca Forts, Salamanca, Burgos (wounded), Pyrenees, first and second sieges of San Sebastian (Mentioned in Despatches), Bidassoa, Nivelle, Nive, Adour and Toulouse. Led the reserve at Badajoz and received the surrender of the Fort of La Picurina from commandant. KCB and KH. MGS medal for Talavera, Ciudad Rodrigo, Badajoz, Salamanca, Pyrenees, San Sebastian, Nivelle, Nive and Toulouse. Also served in Ceylon 1829–1834. Colonel Commandant 10th Battalion 1826.

POWLING, John

Lieutenant. 79th (Cameron Highlanders) Regiment of Foot.
Named on the Regimental Memorial: St Joseph's Church, Waterloo. (Photograph)

Ensign 29 May 1811. Lt 15 Oct 1812.

Served in the Peninsula Jul 1811 – Apr 1813. Present at Salamanca and Burgos. Present at Quatre Bras and Waterloo where he was wounded. Died in England from the wounds he received at Waterloo 23 Oct 1815.

Named on the Regimental Memorial as John Rowling.

POXSON, Peter

Sergeant. 1st Regiment of Foot Guards.
Memorial: St Mary's Churchyard, Horncastle, Lincolnshire. (M.I.)

"IN MEMORY OF / PETER POXSON / A NATIVE OF THIS TOWN / LATE PAYMASTER SERGEANT IN THE FIRST / OR GRENADIER REGIMENT OF GRENADIER GUARDS, / IN WHICH HE SERVED TWENTY-ONE YEARS / WITH DISTINGUISHED CREDIT. / DURING HIS SERVICE HE WAS IN MORE THAN / TWENTY ENGAGEMENTS. / AT BAROSSA HE WAS MADE PAYMASTER SERGEANT. / AT BERGEN OP ZOOM HE WAS REWARDED WITH / THE BADGE OF HONOR, ENTITLING HIM TO / ADDITIONAL PAY, / AND AT WATERLOO HE RECEIVED THE MEDAL, / AND WAS ADMITTED AN OUT PENSIONER OF / CHELSEA HOSPITAL. / IN PRIVATE HIS CONDUCT WAS AS UPRIGHT AS IN / THE SERVICE OF HIS COUNTRY IT HAD BEEN BRAVE. / HE DIED APRIL 17TH 1822, / AGED 41 YEARS."

Pte 24 Oct 1799. Cpl 19 Oct 1803. Sgt 1808.

Served in the Peninsula Mar 1810 – May 1811. Present at Barrosa (made Paymaster Sergeant after Barrosa in Mar 1811). Present at Waterloo in Lt Colonel Colquitt's Company. Also served in the Netherlands 1814–1815 (present at Bergen-op-Zoom). Discharged 10 Aug 1819 as unfit for further service. Served in more than 20 engagements, and according to his wife, who accompanied him on his campaigns, never received a wound. He was killed at last, in his own house, by a blow in the pit of the stomach from a drunken man.

REFERENCE: Notes and Queries. Sixth Series, Vol. 6, 23 Sep 1882, p. 245.

POYNTZ, James

Ensign. 30th (Cambridgeshire) Regiment of Foot.
Ledger stone: Bridgetown, Nova Scotia, Canada. (M.I.)

"SACRED TO THE MEMORY OF COLONEL JAMES POYNTZ, / LATE OF H. M. 30TH REGIMENT, / WHO DIED AT WINDSOR, N. S., OCT. 5, 1889, / BELOVED AND RESPECTED BY ALL WHO KNEW HIM."

Volunteer 30th Foot. Ensign 14 Apr 1814. Lt 19 Jul 1815. Capt 28 Dec 1828. Bt Major 23 Nov 1841. Bt Lt Colonel 28 Nov 1854.

Served in the Peninsula Jan – Jun 1811 as a volunteer aged 12. Present at Torres Vedras, Sabugal, Almeida, Fuentes d'Onoro and Barba del Puerco. After 1811 he entered the Royal Military College at Sandhurst and rejoined his regiment as Ensign in 1814 but was allowed to continue his studies so he was not at Waterloo. Also served in India 1818–1829, West Indies 1834–1840, Halifax, Nova Scotia 1841–1843 and Ireland 1843. MGS medal for Fuentes d'Onoro. Retired on full pay 20 Sep 1844 and went to live in Bridgetown, Nova Scotia. James Poyntz was one of the last 10 surviving Peninsular officers. Brother of Lt Samuel Poyntz 30th Foot who also served in the Peninsula and Lt Arthur Poyntz 17th Foot. All sons of Quartermaster James Poyntz who served in America 1781 and who died in Madras 1812.

REFERENCE: Biographical sketch of Lieut-Colonel James Poyntz, 1799–1889, Royal Nova Scotia Historical Society Journal, Vol. 19, pp. 31–51.

PRATT, Charles
Lieutenant Colonel. 5th (Northumberland) Regiment of Foot.
Memorial: St Nicholas's Churchyard, Brighton, Sussex. (M.I.)

"SACRED TO THE MEMORY OF LIEUT-GENERAL SIR CHARLES PRATT KCB" (REMAINDER OF INSCRIPTION ILLEGIBLE)

Ensign 14 Apr 1794. Lt 3 Sep 1796. Capt 28 Feb 1798. Major 24 Aug 1804. Lt Col 25 Mar 1808. Bt Colonel 4 Jun 1814. Major General 27 May 1825. Lt General 28 Jun 1838.

Served in the Peninsula with 1/5th Jun 1812 – Apr 1814. Present at Salamanca, retreat from Burgos, Vittoria, Nivelle, Nive, Adour, Orthes, Vic Bigorre and Toulouse. Gold Cross for Salamanca, Vittoria, Nivelle, Orthes and Toulouse. KCB 1830. Also served in North America 1794 (present at Niagara), the Helder 1799 (wounded) Walcheren 1809, North America 1814 and West Indies (present at St Vincent). Colonel 95th Foot 24 Dec 1834. Died at Brighton 25 Oct 1838.
REFERENCE: Gentleman's Magazine, Feb 1839, p. 210.

PRATT, Charles
Deputy Commissary General. Commissariat Department.
Monument: Abbey Cemetery, Bath. (Photograph)

SACRED TO THE MEMORY OF / CHARLES PRATT ESQ: OF ELING, HANTS. / HE SERVED WITH GREAT DISTINCTION IN FLANDERS UNDER / H. R. H. THE DUKE OF YORK AND UNDER SIR DAVID BAIRD / AT THE CAPTURE OF THE CAPE OF GOOD HOPE AND WAS / SUBSEQUENTLY FOR MANY YEARS A COMMISSARY GENERAL / TO THE FORCES IN THE PENINSULA, UNDER HIS GRACE / THE DUKE OF WELLINGTON. HE WAS CREATED A KNIGHT / COMMANDER OF THE IMPERIAL ORDER OF CHRIST, AND OF THE / DISTINGUISHED MILITARY ORDER OF THE TOWER AND SWORD / OF PORTUGAL / HE DIED NEAR THIS CITY, ON THE 1 OF MAY 1844 / AGED 68 YEARS.

Asst Com General 26 Jul 1805. Dep Com General 3 Feb 1813.

Served in the Peninsula Sep 1808 – Nov 1811 and Feb 1812 – Apr 1814. Present at the Pyrenees and San Sebastian. Also served in Flanders 1793–1795 and the Cape of Good Hope 1805. MGS medal for Pyrenees and San Sebastian. KTS.

PRATT, Percy
Lieutenant. 94th Regiment of Foot.
Pedestal tomb: Lansdown Cemetery, Bath, Somerset. (Photograph)

SACRED / TO THE MEMORY OF / LIEUT COLONEL PERCY PRATT / OF SION PLACE IN THIS CITY / LATE OF HER MAJESTY'S 12TH / REGT OF INFANTRY AND / YOUNGEST SON OF THE LATE / LT GENERAL PRATT / OF STONEVILLE IN THE COUNTY / OF DUBLIN. / HE DEPARTED THIS LIFE ON / THE 21ST APRIL 1859 / IN THE 64TH YEAR / OF HIS AGE

Ensign 47th Foot 24 Sep 1812. Lt 8 Sep 1814. Lt 94th Foot 23 Feb 1815. Capt 26 Nov1818. Capt 81st Foot 8 Apr 1825. Major 29 Aug 1826. Bt Lt Colonel 23 Nov 1841. Lt Colonel 12th Foot 25 Oct 1842.

Served in the Peninsula Jan – Apr 1814. Present at Bayonne. Retired Oct 1842.

PRATT, Thomas Simson
Ensign. 26th (Cameronian) Regiment of Foot.
Low monument: Bath Abbey Churchyard, Bath, Somerset. (Photograph)

GENERAL SIR THOMAS SIMSON PRATT, K.C.B. COLONEL 37TH REGT / WHO AFTER A LONG AND DISTINGUISHED CAREER IN H. M. 26TH CAMERONIANS AND ON THE STAFF, / DIED AT BATH 2ND FEBRUARY 1879, AGED 82. / …………………

Volunteer 56th Foot. Ensign 26th Foot 2 Feb 1814. Lt 20 Apr 1820. Capt 17 Sep 1825. Bt Major 25 Dec 1835. Bt Lt Colonel 6 May 1841. Bt Colonel 11 Nov 1851. Major General 26 Oct 1858. Lt General 31 May 1865. General 26 May 1873.

Served in the Netherlands 1814–1815 (present at Merxem and the siege of Antwerp). Also served in China 1841–1842 (commanded the land forces at the capture of Fort Chuenpee and Boque Forts 26 Feb 1841). Commanded 26th Foot in attacks on Canton May – Jun 1841 and attacks on Ningpo (Mentioned in Despatches), Segonin, Chapoo (Mentioned in Despatches), Woosung, Shanghai and Chin Kiang Foo. Awarded CB for China. Also served in India Sep 1843–1855 (DAAG in Madras), Australia 1856–1861 (commander of British troops) and in New Zealand 1860 where he was awarded KCB for services in connection with the Waltara purchase. Colonel 37th Foot 30 May 1862.

REFERENCE: *Australian Dictionary of Biography. Dictionary of New Zealand Biography.*

PRENDERGAST, Charles O'Neil
Lieutenant and Captain. 3rd Regiment of Foot Guards.
Headstone: Mount Jerome Cemetery, Dublin, Ireland. (Grave number C80–1842). (Photograph)

HERE LIES / THE BODY OF / MAJOR GENERAL / CHARLES O'NEIL PRENDERGAST / LATE OF / THE SCOTS FUSILIER GUARDS / WHO DIED IN DUBLIN / THE 4TH DAY OF DECEMBER 1854 / AGED 61 YEARS

Ensign 26 Aug 1809. Lt and Capt 12 Jun 1814. Capt and Lt Colonel 26 Oct 1826. Bt Colonel 23 Nov 1841. Major General 11 Nov 1851.

Served in the Peninsula Feb 1812 – Apr 1814. Present at Badajoz, Salamanca, Madrid, Burgos, Osma, Vittoria, San Sebastian, Nivelle, Nive, Adour, siege and repulse of Sortie from Bayonne. Half pay 5 Jul 1849. MGS medal for Salamanca, Vittoria, Nivelle and Nive.

REFERENCE: *Gentleman's Magazine, May 1855, p. 526. Annual Register, 1854, Appx, p. 372.*

PRENDERGAST, Edward
Lieutenant. 30th (Cambridgeshire) Regiment of Foot.
Named on the Regimental Memorial: St Joseph's Church, Waterloo. (Photograph)

Ensign 25 Jun 1812. Lt 23 Nov 1814.

Present at Waterloo where he was killed.

PRESTON, George
Captain. 40th (2nd Somersetshire) Regiment of Foot.
Family chest tomb: All Saints Churchyard, Weston, Bath, Somerset. (Photograph)

SACRED / TO THE MEMORY OF / GEORGE PRESTON ESQ / LATE CAPTAIN IN THE 40TH / REGT OF FOOT. / ELDEST SON OF / ROBERT PRESTON ESQ / AND GRANDSON OF THE LATE / LIEUTENANT GENERAL / GEORGE PRESTON, / WHO DEPARTED THIS LIFE / MARCH 2ND 1812 / AGED 27 YEARS.

Cornet 2nd Dragoons 10 May 1800. Lt 8 Sep 1801. Capt 40th Foot 12 Jan 1805.

Served in the Peninsula Aug – Nov 1808 and Oct 1809 – Sep 1811. (ADC to Lt Gen Sir Brent Spencer Aug – Nov 1808 and Jun 1810 – May 1811). Present at Roḷica, Vimeiro, Busaco (wounded) and Fuentes d'Onoro. Died 2 Mar 1812.

PRICE, Hugh

Lieutenant. 11th Regiment of Light Dragoons.

Cross on stepped base: St Michael and All Angels' Churchyard, Lower Chapel, Brecon, Wales. (Photograph)

IN MEMORY OF HUGH PRICE OF CASTLE MADOC ESQ. / WHO DIED AUGUST 29 1856 AGED 70. / HE WAS A MAGISTRATE AND DEPUTY LIEUTENANT OF THIS / COUNTY AND SERVED WITH HONOUR IN THE 11TH DRAGOONS / AT THE BATTLE OF SALAMANCA AND OTHER ENGAGEMENTS / IN THE PENINSULAR WAR. / ....

Ensign 67th Foot 22 Sep 1808. Lt 3 Aug 1809. Lt 11th Lt Dragoons 17 May 1810.

Served in the Peninsula Oct 1811 – Oct 1812. Present at Moriscos, Castrejon, Salamanca and Venta del Poza. MGS medal for Salamanca. Retired 15 Dec 1812. Magistrate, Deputy Lieutenant and High Sheriff 1815 for Brecknockshire.

PRICE, Thomas Parry

Lieutenant. 4th Royal Veteran Battalion.

Headstone: St Michael and All Angels' Churchyard, Felton, Northumberland. (M.I.)

"LIEUTENANT THOMAS PRICE OF THE 4TH REGIMENT OF ROYAL VETERANS DIED 4TH MARCH 1819, AGED 46."

Quartermaster 1 Foot 1 Jan 1807. Lt 4th Veteran Battalion 8 Apr 1813.

Served in the Peninsula Apr 1810 – Feb 1812. Also served at Walcheren 1809.

PRINCE, John

Lieutenant and Captain. Coldstream Regiment of Foot Guards.

Altar tomb: St Paul's Churchyard, Clapham, London. (In Hibbert family enclosure). (M.I.)

"JOHN PRINCE, CAPTAIN IN THE COLDSTREAM GUARDS, SON OF GENERAL AND ANNE PRINCE. BORN 16 JUNE 1790, DIED 1 JAN 1818."

Memorial: Royal Military Chapel, Wellington Barracks, London. (M.I.) (Destroyed by a Flying Bomb 1944)

"THE ALTAR RAIL IS GIVEN BY MARY ANNE CAROLINE PRINCE IN MEMORY OF HER FATHER, / CAPTAIN JOHN PRINCE, COLDSTREAM GUARDS. / HE ENTERED, THE REGIMENT AT THE AGE OF 15, AND DURING THE CAMPAIGN IN SPAIN TOOK PART IN THE PASSAGE OF THE DOURO, THE BATTLES OF TALAVERA AND VITTORIA, AND THE SIEGE OF SAN SEBASTIAN. HE WAS ADJUTANT TO THE 2ND BATTALION WHEN QUARTERED IN FRANCE WITH THE ARMY OF OCCUPATION, AND DIED IN 1818, AGED 27."

Ensign 31 Oct 1805. Lt and Capt 29 Oct 1810.

Served in the Peninsula Mar 1809 – Mar 1810 and Jan 1813 – Jan 1814. Present at Douro, Talavera, Vittoria, San Sebastian, Bidassoa, Nivelle and Nive. Returned to England Jan 1814. Also served in France with the Army of Occupation (Adjutant to 2nd Battalion).

PRING, John
Captain. 27th (Inniskilling) Regiment of Foot.
Memorial tablet: St Michael and All Angels' Church, Awliscombe, Devonshire. (Photograph)

IN A VAULT NEAR THIS SPOT ARE DEPOSITED THE REMAINS OF / JOHN PRING ESQUIRE OF IVEDON. / LATE CAPTAIN IN THE 27TH OR ENNISKILLEN REGIMENT OF INFANTRY. / HE WAS ENGAGED AT THE BATTLE OF MAIDA UNDER SIR JOHN STEWART, / AND SUBSEQUENTLY SERVED IN THE PENINSULA UNDER THE DUKE OF / WELLINGTON, UNTIL THE 10TH MAY 1811, WHEN IN GALLANTLY / REPELLING A SORTIE MADE BY THE FRENCH TROOPS FROM THE WORKS / OF BADAJOZ HE RECEIVED THE WOUND WHICH OCCASIONED HIS / DEATH. HIS SUFFERINGS DURING THE NINE YEARS WERE OF ALMOST / UNPARALLELED SEVERITY, AND HE BORE THEM WITH UNCOMPLAINING / RESIGNATION AND FORTITUDE – DEVOTING THE INTERVALS OF / EASE TO ACTS OF CHARITY AND USEFUL BENEVOLENCE – HE WAS / EXEMPLARY IN ALL THE RELATIONS OF LIFE AND IN HIM WERE UNITED / THE CHARACTER OF THE CHRISTIAN, THE SOLDIER, AND THE GENTLEMAN. / HE DIED IN HIS NATIVE PARISH ON THE 2ND OF MAY 1820 / IN THE 38TH YEAR OF HIS AGE. / AND THIS TABLET IS DEDICATED TO HIS MEMORY AS A LAST OFFERING / OF FRATERNAL LOVE BY HIS ONLY SURVIVING BROTHER / CAPTAIN DANIEL PRING OF THE ROYAL NAVY. / BADAJOZ

Ensign 22 Foot 29 Nov 1803. Lt 27th Foot 31 Mar 1804. Capt 27 Apr 1809.

Served in the Peninsula with 3/27th Apr 1810 – Jun 1811. Present at Busaco, Redinha, Olivencia, and first siege of Badajoz (severely wounded and awarded pension of £100 per annum). Also served in Sicily 1806 (present at Maida).

PRINGLE, John Watson
1st Lieutenant. Royal Engineers.
Headstone with ringed cross: Smallcombe Cemetery, Bathwick, Bath, Somerset. (Photograph)

IN / MEMORY OF / MAJOR J .W. PRINGLE R .E. / WHO DIED OCTOBER 12TH 1861. / AGED 70 YEARS

2nd Lt 23 Aug 1809. Lt 1 May 1811. 2nd Capt 21 Jul 1815. Capt 16 Mar 1830. Major 28 Nov 1854.

Served in the Peninsula Feb 1811 – Apr 1814. Present at Nivelle, Nive (wounded), Orthes and Bayonne. Present at Waterloo where he was one of the few Engineers present and was severely wounded. Served with the Army of Occupation 1815–1817. Retired on full pay 14 Mar 1832. MGS medal for Nivelle, Nive and Orthes.
Reference: Gentleman's Magazine, Nov 1861, p. 577. Annual Register, 1861, Appx, p. 485.

PRINGLE, Sir William Henry
Captain and Lieutenant Colonel. Coldstream Regiment of Foot Guards.
Interred in Catacomb B (v95 c7), Kensal Green Cemetery, London.

Cornet 16th Lt Dragoons 6 Jul 1792. Lt 24 Feb 1793. Capt of Independent Company 15 Oct 1793. Major 111th Foot 19 Sep 1794. Bt Lt Colonel 5 Dec 1799. Capt and Lt Colonel Coldstream Guards 17 Sep 1802. Bt Colonel 25 Oct 1809. Major General 1 Jan 1812. Lt General 27 May 1825.

Served in the Peninsula Jun 1812 – Apr 1814 (GOC 2 Brigade 5th Division Jun 1812 – Jul 1813, Temporary GOC 5th Division Sep – Oct 1812 and GOC 3 Brigade 2nd Division Jul 1813 – Apr 1814). Present at Salamanca, Burgos, Pyrenees, Nivelle, Nive and Garris (wounded). Gold Cross for Salamanca, Pyrenees, Nivelle and Nive. KCB. Also served in Flanders 1793–1795, the Helder 1799, Hanover 1805 and the Baltic 1807. Colonel Royal Newfoundland Fencibles 12 May 1814. Colonel 64th Foot 1 Apr 1816.

Colonel 45th Foot 29 Nov 1837. MP for Cornwall at St Germans 1812–1818 and Liskeard 1818–1832. Died 22 Dec 1840.
REFERENCE: *Gentleman's Magazine, Mar 1841, p. 317. Annual Register, 1841, Appx, p. 177. Correspondence and papers, John Rylands Library, University of Manchester.*

PRIOR, Thomas Murray
Lieutenant. 18th Regiment of Light Dragoons.
Low monument: Highland Road Cemetery, Southsea, Hampshire. (Photograph)

North Side:

SACRED TO THE MEMORY OF / COLONEL THOMAS MURRAY PRIOR / OF RATHDOWNEY QUEENS CO IRELAND / WHO DEPARTED THIS LIFE JULY 16TH 1864 / AGED 73 YEARS

East and West Sides:

WATERLOO PENINSULA

Also commemorated on his daughter's low monument: Highland Road Cemetery, Southsea, Hampshire. (Photograph)

WATERLOO / 18TH HUSSARS. / PENINSULA. / 11TH DRAGOONS / SACRED / TO THE MEMORY OF / COLONEL THOMAS MURRAY PRIOR / OBIT 16TH JULY 1864 AGED 74. / ....

Cornet 11th Lt Dragoons 6 Aug 1803. Lt 22 Aug 1805. Lt 1st Foot 30 Sep 1813. Lt 18th Lt Dragoons 6 Jun 1814. Capt 28 Nov 1834. Bt Major 9 Nov 1846. Bt Lt Colonel 20 Jun 1854. Bt Colonel 20 Feb 1859.

Served in the Peninsula with 11th Lt Dragoons Jun 1811 – Sep 1812. Present at El Bodon, Morales, Castrejon and Salamanca. MGS medal for Salamanca. Transferred to the 1st Foot and then in Jan 1814 to the 18th Dragoons, with whom he fought at Waterloo. On 17th June, he commanded the skirmishers of the 18th Dragoons and received the first fire of the French army on that day. Also present at the Capture of Paris. Half pay 25 Oct 1850.
Note discrepancy in age of death on two monuments.

PROCTOR, Henry Adolphus
Major. 82nd (Prince of Wales's Volunteers) Regiment of Foot.
Memorial tablet: St Gwynog's Church, Aberhafesp, Montgomeryshire, Wales. (Photograph)

.... / ALSO OF LIEUTENANT GENERAL / HENRY ADOLPHUS PROCTOR C.B. / COLONEL H. M. 97TH (EARL OF ULSTER'S) REGT / DIED MAY 13 1859. AGED 74.

Cornet 2nd Life Guards 14 Jan 1801. Lt 25 Mar 1802. Capt 82nd Foot 16 May 1805. Major 30 Apr 1812. Bt Lt Colonel 17 Sep 1814. Bt Colonel 10 Jan 1837. Major General 9 Nov 1846. Lt General 20 Jun 1854.

Served in the Peninsula Feb – Mar 1811 and Jun – Oct 1812. Present at Barrosa (wounded) and Tarifa. Also served at Walcheren 1809 (present at the siege of Flushing), Gibraltar, North America (commanded the 82nd Foot at Fort Erie and for the rest of the American campaign. Awarded Bt Lt Coloncey for repelling attacks on the positions before Fort Erie). CB. MGS medal for Barrosa. Colonel 97th Foot 29 Nov 1852. Half pay 26 Nov 1818. Educated at Charterhouse.

PROCTOR, John
Captain. 43rd (Monmouthshire) Light Infantry Regiment of Foot.
Obelisk in railed enclosure: St James's Churchyard, Temple Sowerby, Cumbria. (Photograph)

IN MEMORY OF / LIEUT.-COL. JOHN PROCTOR / OF THE 30TH REGIMENT / BORN ON 18 MARCH 1788 / AND DIED ON 14 MARCH 1848 / HE SERVED HIS COUNTRY LONG AND FAITHFULLY, / AND WITH THE 43RD REGT / WAS IN VARIOUS ENGAGEMENTS / DURING THE WAR WITH FRANCE. / SWEETLY HE RESTS, THE SOLDIER NOW / FROM BATTLE, WOUND AND STRIFE / THE WREATH OF CONQUEST ON HIS BROW / WITH RAYS OF ENDLESS LIFE.

Ensign 3 Dec 1803. Lt 8 Jun 1804. Capt 4 May 1809. Capt 30th Foot 8 Jun 1826. Bt Major 22 Jul 1830. Major 30th Foot 5 Aug 1842. Bt Lt Colonel 9 Nov 1846.

Served in the Peninsula with 1/43rd Oct 1808 – Jan 1809 and Aug 1812 – Sep 1813. Present in the Corunna campaign, Vigo, San Millan and Vittoria. Also served at Copenhagen 1807 and North America 1814–1815. MGS medal for Vittoria. Retired 30 Jul 1847.

PULSFORD, Lewis

Assistant Surgeon. 18th Regiment of Light Dragoons.
Memorial tablet: St Cuthbert with St Mary's Church, Carlisle, Cumbria. (On gallery wall). (Photograph)

IN EXPRESSION OF THEIR ESTEEM FOR THEIR FRIEND AND COMPANION / AND IN SORROW FOR HIS LOSS THE OFFICERS OF THE 18TH HUSSARS / ERECT THIS TO THE MEMORY OF / LUCAS PULSFORD / LATE ASSISTANT SURGEON IN THAT REGIMENT. / HIS SUDDEN AND PREMATURE DEATH ON THE 20TH OF APRIL / 1819 AT THE AGE OF THIRTY ONE YEARS / AFFORDS BUT ANOTHER WARNING / 'THAT IN THE MIDST OF LIFE / WE ARE IN DEATH.'

Hospital Mate 12 Apr 1810. Asst Surgeon 8th Foot 17 Aug 1810. Asst Surgeon 18th Light Dragoons 14 Mar 1811.

Served in the Peninsula Feb 1813 – Apr 1814. Present at Morales, Vittoria, Nivelle, Nive, Orthes, Croix d'Orade and Toulouse. Present at Waterloo.

PURCHASE, John

Captain. 76th Regiment of Foot.
Headstone: Town Cemetery, Plattsburgh, United States of America. (Photograph)

CAPT. PURCHASE / 76TH REG. B. ARMY / 11 SEPT 1814

Ensign 20th Foot 2 Jun 1804. Lt 1806. Capt Royal York Rangers 18 Jun 1808. Capt 76th Foot 11 Aug 1808.

Served in the Peninsula Nov 1808 – Jan 1809 and Aug 1813 – Apr 1814. Present at Corunna, Bidassoa, Nivelle, Nive and Bayonne. Also served at Walcheren 1809 and North America 1814 where he was killed at the Battle of Plattsburgh 11 Sep 1814.

PURVIS, John

Captain. 1st (Royal Scots) Regiment of Foot.
Memorial tablet: Canterbury Cathedral, Kent. (Photograph)

SACRED TO THE MEMORY / OF CAPTAIN JOHN PURVIS, OF THE FIRST, OR ROYAL SCOTS REGIMENT, / WHO WAS MORTALLY WOUNDED ON THE NIGHT OF THE 8TH OF MARCH 1814, / WHILST GALLANTLY LEADING A DIVISION OF THAT BRAVE REGIMENT / TO THE CHARGE, AT THE SIEGE OF BERGEN OP ZOOM. / HE DESERVEDLY POSSESSED THE REGARD AND ESTEEM OF / HIS BROTHER OFFICERS, AND DIED, MUCH LAMENTED, / ON THE 16TH DAY OF THE SAME MONTH AT ROSENDAAL: / WHERE HIS REMAINS WERE INTERRED. / THUS IN THE 44TH YEAR OF HIS AGE, / AFTER A SERVICE OF 29 YEARS, IN DEFENCE OF HIS COUNTRY, / FELL A BRAVE MAN, A SINCERE FRIEND, AND MOST AFFECTIONATE HUSBAND: / WHOSE

GREATEST PRIDE WAS TO EMULATE OTHERS, BY THE HONOURABLE / AND ZEALOUS DISCHARGE OF HIS DUTY. / THIS HUMBLE TRIBUTE OF RESPECT TO HIS BELOVED MEMORY, / IS ERECTED BY MR. ALDERMAN BROWNE, BROTHER OF THE AFFLICTED WIDOW, / WHOSE LOSS IS MORE SEVERE, / FROM THE RECOLLECTIONS OF / HIS PRIVATE WORTH.

Pte 2nd Dragoons 1785. Troop Quartermaster 1796. Cornet and Adjt Royal Waggon Train 4 Sep 1802. Lt and Adjt 9 Jan 1804. Capt 27 Apr 1809. Capt 1st Foot 20 Aug 1811.

Promoted from the ranks. Served in North Germany 1813 (present at Stralsund), the Netherlands 1814 (present at Bergen-op-Zoom where he was severely wounded 8 Mar 1814 and died of his wounds on 16 Mar 1814).

PURVIS, Patrick

Captain. 79th (Cameron Highlanders) Regiment of Foot.
Named on the Memorial: St Andrew's Church (now Musée Historique), Biarritz, France. (Photograph)

Ensign 61st Foot. Lt 79th Foot 23 Jul 1807. Capt 11 Oct 1810.

Served in the Peninsula Jan 1810 – Dec 1812 and May 1813 – Apr 1814. Present at the siege of Cadiz, Busaco, Foz d' Arouce, Fuentes d' Onoro, Salamanca, Burgos, Pyrenees, Nivelle, Nive and Toulouse where he was killed Apr 1814, and is buried in the same grave in the Citadel at Toulouse as Captain John Cameron. Lt Duncan Cameron and Lt Ewen Cameron, all of the 79th Foot. Also served at Walcheren 1809.

PYM, John

Lieutenant. 13th Regiment of Light Dragoons.
Family Memorial tablet: St Swithun's Church, Sandy, Bedfordshire. (Photograph)

NEAR THIS PLACE ARE DEPOSITED THE REMAINS OF / FRANCIS PYM, ESQUIRE, / WHO DIED AT THE HASSELLS, IN THIS PARISH, ON THE 4TH DECEMBER, 1833, / IN THE 78TH YEAR OF HIS AGE / ALSO ANNE HIS WIFE / 3RD DAUGHTER OF ROBERT PALMER, ESQUIRE, OF HURST, IN THE COUNTY OF BERKS, / WHO DIED IN CLARGES STREET, LONDON, / ON THE 8TH OF SEPTEMBER, 1839, IN THE 79TH YEAR OF HER AGE. / THEY LEFT FOUR SONS / FRANCIS, WILLIAM WOLLASTON, ROBERT AND CHARLES, / AND TWO DAUGHTERS, ANNE AND CATHERINE, WHO SURVIVE THEM. / THEY HAD ONE SON WHO DIED IN INFANCY / AND JOHN, LIEUT. IN THE 13TH LT DRAGOONS, / WHO LOST HIS LIFE AT THE BATTLE OF WATERLOO, ON THE 18TH OF JUNE, 1815. / VERSE

Cornet 27 Jun 1811. Lt 23 Jul 1812.

Served in the Peninsula Jun 1812 – Apr 1814. Present at Alba de Tormes, Vittoria and Nivelle. Went on half pay in 1814, but returned to the regiment in 1815 and was present at Waterloo where he was killed.

PYNE, Robert

Captain. 66th (Berkshire) Regiment of Foot.
Named on the Memorial: St Andrew's Church (now Musée Historique), Biarritz, France. (Photograph)

Lt 83rd Foot 6 May 1805. Capt 66th Foot 6 Dec 1810.

Served in the Peninsula Apr 1809 – Mar 1810 and Apr – Nov 1813. Present at Douro, Talavera (wounded), Vittoria, Pyrenees (wounded) and Nivelle where he was severely wounded and died of his wounds 17 Nov 1813.

PYPER, Robert
Surgeon. 4th (Royal Irish) Dragoon Guards.
Low monument: Kensal Green Cemetery, London. Inscription illegible. (11790/79/10). (Photograph)

Hospital Asst 2 Dec 1795. Asst Surgeon 25 Jun 1797. Surgeon 11th Foot 30 Jan 1800. Surgeon 13th Lt Dragoons 16 Apr 1812. Surgeon 4th Dragoon Guards 3 Sep 1812.

Served in the Peninsula with 11th Foot and 13th Lt Dragoons Aug 1809 – Oct 1812 and 4th Dragoon Guards Nov 1812 – Apr 1814. Present at Busaco, Ciudad Rodrigo, Badajoz and Salamanca. Half pay 6 Apr 1826. MGS medal for Busaco, Ciudad Rodrigo, Badajoz and Salamanca. Died 3 Sep 1854.

QUICK, Francis
Sergeant Major. 3rd Battalion, 1st (Royal Scots) Regiment of Foot.
Named on the Regimental Memorial: St Joseph's Church, Waterloo. (Photograph)

Present at Quatre Bras 16 Jun 1815 where he was shot through the heart while holding the King's Colours after three Ensigns and one Lieutenant had all been killed whilst holding the colours.

QUILL, Henry
Lieutenant. 32nd (Cornwall) Regiment of Foot.
Obelisk: Glasnevin Cemetery, Dublin, Ireland. (Burial place J5). Seriously eroded and inscription recorded from memorial inscription. (Photograph)

"SERVED WITH HIS CORPS TO THE CLOSE OF THE PENINSULAR WAR. AT THE SIEGE OF BURGOS HIS LEG WAS SHATTERED AND HIS LEFT EYE CARRIED AWAY BY A BALL. HE RECEIVED TWO GUNSHOT WOUNDS IN THE CHEST AT WATERLOO. ONE OF THE BALLS FRACTURED THE COLLAR-BONE AND PENETRATED HIS LUNG, IN WHICH IT BECAME EMBEDDED. THE LONG TRAIN OF SUFFERING ENSUING, AND THE HAEMORRHAGE IT INDUCED, ULTIMATELY PROVED FATAL ON THE 26TH DAY OF MARCH, 1849, WHEN HE WAS SIXTY YEARS OF AGE."

Ensign 16 Mar 1809. Lt 17 Dec 1812.

Served in the Peninsula Jul 1811 – Apr 1814. Present at Salamanca (wounded), Burgos (severely wounded, lost an eye and awarded pension of £70 per annum). Present at Waterloo (severely wounded and awarded pension of £70 per annum). Half pay Dec 1817. His brother Maurice Quill served in the Peninsula as Surgeon of 31st Foot and died in Cork 15 Aug 1823.

RADCLIFF, Stephen
Lieutenant. 6th (1st Warwickshire) Regiment of Foot.
Ledger stone: Kilcommon Church of Ireland Churchyard, Kilcommon, Tinahely, County Wicklow, Ireland. (Photograph)

HERE LIES THE BODY OF / STEPHEN RADCLIFF / LATE LIEUTENANT OF THE / 6TH REGIMENT OF FOOT / WHO DEPARTED / THIS LIFE ON THE 19TH DAY OF JULY 1856 / AGED 63 YEARS. / ………………

Ensign 20 Jul 1810. Lt 16 Sep 1813.

Served in the Peninsula Nov 1812 – Apr 1814. Present at Vittoria, Pyrenees (wounded at Roncesvalles 25 Jul 1813), Bidassoa, Nivelle and Orthes. Half pay 1818. MGS medal for Vittoria, Pyrenees, Nivelle and Orthes.

RADCLIFFE, Robert

Private. 52nd (Oxfordshire) Light Infantry Regiment of Foot.
Ledger stone: St John the Baptist (Formerly Hey Chapel), Lees, Oldham, Lancashire. (Relocated from pathway and re-erected behind church). (Photograph)

………………. / ALSO ROBERT HIS SON, WHO WAS BURIED / SEPTEMBER 28TH 1817, AGED 40 YEARS. / HE FOUGHT IN 16 DIFFERENT ENGAGEMENTS / IN THE PENINSULA WAR AND ENDED / HIS MARTIAL CAREER AT WATERLOO. / ……………….

Pte 14 Nov 1799.

Served in the Peninsula 1808 – Jan 1809 and Jul 1809 – Apr 1814. Present at Vimeiro, Corunna, Busaco, Foz d'Arouce, Sabugal, Fuentes d'Onoro, Cuidad Rodrigo, Badajoz, Salamanca, Vittoria, Pyrenees, Bidassoa, Nivelle, Nive, Orthes and Toulouse. Present at Waterloo in Capt Charles Diggle's Company where he was wounded. Discharged 30 Aug 1816 aged 38 after 18 years and ten months' service with a pension of one shilling a day. He took his own life Sep 1817.

RADFORD, Henry Wyatt

Assistant Surgeon. 45th (Nottinghamshire) Regiment of Foot.
Buried in Christ Church Cathedral Churchyard, Newcastle, New South Wales, Australia. (Burial record)

Hospital Mate 24 Dec 1808. Asst Surgeon 45th Foot 19 Apr 1810. Asst Surgeon 56th Foot 10 Aug 1815. Asst Surgeon 65th Foot 25 Nov 1816. Surgeon 62nd Foot 21 Sep 1830. Surgeon 17th Foot 4 Mar 1836.

Served in the Peninsula Jun 1810 – Apr 1814. Present at Busaco, Fuentes d'Onoro, second siege of Badajoz, El Bodon, Badajoz, Salamanca, Vittoria, Pyrenees, Nivelle, Nive, Orthes, Vic Bigorre and Toulouse. Also served in India 1817–1818 (present in the Pindari War). Went to Australia in 1824 until his death at Patrick Plains, New South Wales, 15 Jan 1836 aged 44.

RAE, Thomas

Private. 92nd Regiment of Foot.
Memorial tablet and Cross: St Michael's Kirk, Queen's Aisle, Linlithgow, Scotland. (Photograph)

WELLINGTON / WATERLOO / JUNE 18 / 1815 / TO THE GLORY OF GOD / AND IN MEMORY OF / THOMAS RAE / BORN 1776 – DIED 1833 / A VETERAN OF WATERLOO / THOMAS RAE ENLISTED AT THE AGE / OF 18 HE WAS DISCHARGED AT EDINBURGH / CASTLE ON OCT 11TH 1816 FOUGHT WITH / THE HIGHLANDERS IN EGYPT SPAIN / AND AT WATERLOO WAS WOUNDED IN / VARIOUS ENGAGEMENTS AND WORN / OUT IN THE SERVICE OF HIS COUNTRY / DIED AND WAS BURIED IN THE KIRKYARD / OF ST MICHAEL'S / IN PROUD AND AFFECTIONATE MEMORY / THE ADJACENT CELTIC CROSS WAS / GIFTED BY COLIN C RAE HIS AMERICAN / GREAT GRANDSON

Pte 82nd Foot 2 Feb 1794. Pte 42nd Foot 27 Jun 1795. Pte 92nd Foot 29 Dec 1798.

Served in the Peninsula 1810 – Apr 1814. Present at Waterloo in Capt S. Maxwell's Company where he was wounded. Also served in Egypt 1801 (wounded). Discharged 11 Oct 1816.

RAGLAN, 1st Baron see SOMERSET, Lord Fitzroy James Henry

RAGLAND, Thomas Gajetan

Assistant Commissary General. Commissariat Department.
Memorial tablet: King's Chapel, Gibraltar. (Photograph)

SACRED / TO THE MEMORY OF / THOMAS GAJETAN RAGLAND / ACTING DEPUTY COMMIS-

SARY GENERAL / WHO FELL A VICTIM OF THE EPIDEMIC FEVER / ON THE 17TH OCTOBER 1814 / AGED 29 YEARS / (VERSE)

Grave: Trafalgar Cemetery, Gibraltar. (Grave number 21). (M.I.)

"THOS. GAJETAN RAGLAND, ACTING – DEP COMMISSARY GENERAL, OB. VICTIM TO THE EPIDEMIC FEVER, 17 OCT 1814, A.29."

Served in the Peninsula Apr 1810 – Apr 1811 at Lisbon. Also served in Gibraltar where he died of fever.

RAIKES, William Henley
Captain and Lieutenant Colonel. Coldstream Regiment of Foot Guards.
Gravestone: St Mary's Cemetery, Cheltenham, Gloucestershire. (No longer extant). (M.I.)

"SACRED TO THE MEMORY OF COL WILLIAM HENLEY RAIKES, LATE OF THE COLDSTREAM GUARDS, WHO DIED AT CHELTENHAM AUG 6TH 1854, AGED 69 YEARS."

Lt 3rd Foot 10 May 1800. Capt 26 Apr 1802. Capt 66th Foot 3 Feb 1803. Lt and Capt Coldstream Guards 13 Jun 1805. Capt and Lt Colonel 3 Jun 1813. Bt Colonel 27 May 1825.

Served in the Peninsula Mar 1809 – Jan 1812 and Jul 1812 – Jul 1813. Present at Douro, Talavera, Busaco and Fuentes d'Onoro. Retired 21 Jun 1826. MGS medal for Talavera, Busaco and Fuentes d'Onoro.

RAINES, Joseph Robert
Lieutenant. 8th West India Regiment of Foot.
Headstone: Old Churchyard, Spital, Windsor, Berkshire. (Photograph)

TO / COLONEL / JOSEPH ROBERT RAINES / M. K. W. / LATE 95TH REG. / WHO FOUGHT AT THE BATTLES / OF ROLEIA, VIMIERA AND CORUNNA. / HE DIED AT WINDSOR CASTLE / 14 JUNE 1874. / AGED 84. / ....

Brass Memorial tablet: Rutland Chapel, St George's Chapel, Windsor, Berkshire. (Photograph)

IN AFFECTIONATE REMEMBRANCE OF / COLONEL J. R. RAINES M. K. W. / LATE 95TH REGIMENT / WHO FOUGHT AT THE BATTLES OF / ROLICA, VIMIERO & CORUNNA. / HE DIED AT WINDSOR CASTLE, 14TH JUNE 1874, AGED 84. / THIS TABLET IS ERECTED BY HIS ONLY SON / MAJOR GENERAL JULIUS RAINES, C.B.

Ensign 82nd Foot 19 Sep 1805. Lt 28 May 1807. Lt 8th West India Regt 5 Oct 1809. Capt 95th Foot 2 Jun 1825. Bt Major 10 Jan 1837. Major 48th Foot 20 Apr 1848. Bt Lt Colonel 11 Nov 1851.

Served in the Peninsula Aug 1808 – Jan 1809. Present at Rolica, Vimeiro and Corunna. Also served at Walcheren 1809. MGS medal for Vimeiro and Corunna. Military Knight of Windsor 4 Feb 1864.

RAINEY, Henry
Captain. 55th (Westmoreland) Regiment of Foot.
Chest tomb: Kensal Green Cemetery, London. (13943/42/2). (Photograph)

IN MEMORY OF / LIEUT GENERAL HENRY RAINEY CB. KH. / COLONEL OF THE 23RD RT WELCH FUSILIERS / BORN 1779 DIED 1860 / ALSO MAJOR JOHN RAINEY / FORMERLY OF THE 82ND REGT / BURIED NEAR THIS GRAVE NO 12935

Ensign 82nd Foot 24 Aug 1804. Lt 23 Nov 1804. Capt 13 Apr 1809. Capt 55th Foot 10 Jun 1813. Bt Major 24 Jul 1813. Major 21 Jun 1817. Bt Lt Colonel 15 Aug 1822. Bt Colonel 10 Jan 1837. Major General 9 Nov 1846. Lt General 20 Jun 1854. Portuguese Army: On Staff as ADC to General Beresford.

Served in the Peninsula with 82nd Foot Aug 1808 – Jan 1809 and May 1812 – Jul 1813 and Portuguese Army Jul 1813 – Apr 1814 (ADC to General Beresford). Present at Rolica, Vimeiro, Corunna, siege of Salamanca Forts, Salamanca, Burgos and retreat from Burgos, Vittoria, Tolosa, first and second sieges of San Sebastian (wounded), Bidassoa, Nivelle and Nive (severely wounded and awarded pension of £200 per annum). MGS medal for Rolica, Vimeiro, Corunna, Salamanca, Vittoria, San Sebastian, Nivelle and Nive. CB. KH. Served in France with the Army of Occupation until 1818. Also served at Copenhagen 1807 and Walcheren 1809 (present at Middleburgh and siege of Flushing). Colonel 23rd Foot 22 May 1855. Half pay 4 May 1826. Died 26 Dec 1860. Brother of Major John Rainey 82nd Foot.

RAINEY, John
Major. 82nd (Prince of Wales's Volunteers) Regiment of Foot.
Headstone: Kensal Green Cemetery, London. (12935/49/5). Seriously eroded.

SACRED / TO / THE MEMORY OF / MAJOR JOHN RAINEY / FORMERLY OF THE 82ND REGIMENT / WHO DIED ON THE 11TH OF JANUARY 1856 / AGED 79 YEARS

Chest tomb: Kensal Green Cemetery, London. (13943/42/2). (Photograph – see Henry Rainey)

IN MEMORY OF / LIEUT GENERAL HENRY RAINEY CB. KH. / COLONEL OF THE 23RD RT WELCH FUSILIERS / BORN 1779 DIED 1860 / ALSO MAJOR JOHN RAINEY / FORMERLY OF THE 82ND REGT / BURIED NEAR THIS GRAVE NO 12935

Ensign 20 Mar 1798. Lt 28 Apr 1798. Capt 26 Apr 1800. Major 14 Mar 1805.

Served in the Peninsula Aug – Nov 1808 (AQMG). Present at Rolica and Vimeiro. Gold Medal for Rolica and Vimeiro. Also served at Walcheren 1809. Retired 1810. Brother of Capt Henry Rainey 55th Foot.

RAINFORTH, William
Lieutenant. 35th (Sussex) Regiment of Foot.
Grave: Old Churchyard, Spital, Windsor, Berkshire. (Grave Reference: C11)

Ensign 2 Dec 1812. Lt 23 Dec 1813. Capt 6 Feb 1835.

Present at Waterloo in reserve at Hal and at the Capture of Paris. Also served in the West Indies 1820–1832. Half pay 9 Jun 1838. Military Knight of Windsor 1866. Died 19 Mar 1870.

RAINSFORD, Michael
Private. 12th (Prince of Wales's) Regiment of Light Dragoons.
Named on the Regimental Memorial: St Joseph's Church, Waterloo. (Photograph)

Present at Waterloo where he was killed.

RAITT, George Edward
Major. 2nd (Queen's Royal) Regiment of Foot.
Interred in Kensal Green Cemetery, London. (No longer extant). (12948/79/13)

Ensign 10 Sep 1796. Lt 31 Jan 1797. Capt-Lt 28 Feb 1800. Capt 20 Aug 1801. Bt Major 1 Jan 1812. Major 19 Aug 1813. Bt Lt Colonel 25 Sep 1814. Lt Colonel (unattached) 15 Jun 1830.

Served in the Peninsula Aug 1808 – Jan 1809 and 1811–1812 (ADC to General Houston). Present at

Vimeiro, Corunna and Fuentes d'Onoro. Also served in the Irish Rebellion 1798 (present at Castlebar), the Helder 1799, Egypt 1801 (present at Aboukir, Alexandria, Fort St Julien and Rahmanie. Awarded Gold Medal from the Sultan and KC), Walcheren 1809 (Brigade Major to General Ackland) and Malta (DQMG 1814–1816 and DAG 3 Oct 1816). MGS medal for Egypt, Vimeiro, Corunna and Fuentes d'Onoro. Served in the army for 52 years. Died in 1859.
Reference: Gentleman's Magazine, Nov 1859, p. 541. Annual Register, 1859, Appx pp. 474–5.

RAM, Stopford
Ensign. 3rd Regiment of Foot Guards.
Named on Memorial Panel VI for Talavera: Royal Military Chapel, Wellington Barracks, London. (M.I.) (Destroyed by a Flying Bomb 1944)

Ensign 3 Apr 1806.
Served in the Peninsula Mar – Jul 1809. Present at Douro and Talavera where he was killed 28 Jul 1809.

RAMADGE, Benjamin
Lieutenant. 74th (Highland) Regiment of Foot.
Named on the Regimental Memorial: St Giles's Cathedral, Edinburgh, Scotland. (Photograph)

Ensign 29 Nov 1809. Lt 30 Oct 1811.
Served in the Peninsula Feb 1810 – Mar 1812. Present at Busaco, Casal Nova, Foz d'Arouce, Fuentes d'Onoro, second siege of Badajoz, El Bodon, Ciudad Rodrigo (wounded) and Badajoz where he was killed at the siege Mar 1812.

RAMSAY, George see DALHOUSIE, George Lord (in Supplement)

RAMSAY, George
Colonel. Royal Artillery.
Memorial tablet: Canterbury Cathedral. (South wall of Chapter House and family vault in Cloister Garth in south-east corner of Cathedral Church). (Photograph)

TO THE MEMORY OF / GEORGE RAMSAY / OF THE WHITE FRIARS CANTERBURY, / MAJOR GENERAL IN THE ARMY, / AND COLONEL / COMMANDANT OF THE 4TH BATTALION / OF THE ROYAL ARTILLERY; / WHO DEPARTED THIS LIFE / ON THE 6TH OF SEPTEMBER 1834, / AGED 71.

2nd Lt 30 Jun 1780. 1st Lt 22 Mar 1785. Capt-Lt 14 Aug 1794. Capt 1 Jun 1798. Major 28 Jan 1805. Lt Colonel 1 Jun 1806. Colonel 20 Dec 1814. Major General 19 Jul 1821.
Served in the Peninsula 1808–1811. Present at Cadiz. Also served in Canada and the West Indies 1781–1784, Gibraltar and West India 1785–1791, the Helder 1799 and Gibraltar 1805–1811. Colonel Commandant 10 Feb 1832.

RAMSAY, Thomas
Captain. 14th (Buckinghamshire) Regiment of Foot.
Family wall mural memorial tablet: East Church Graveyard, Banchory, Aberdeenshire, Scotland. (Wall on north side of family plot at north-east corner). (Photograph)

IN MEMORY OF / THOMAS RAMSAY, / SECOND SON OF SIR ALEXR RAMSAY OF BALMAIN, BART / AND OF HIS WIFE DAME ELIZABETH / DAUGHTER OF SIR ALEX BANNERMAN, BART. / HE WAS A CAPTAIN IN H. B. M.S ARMY, / SERVED IN THE PENINSULA AND AT WATERLOO: / BORN 24 FEB 1786. DIED 18TH DEC. 1857 AGED 71. / ………………

Ensign 52nd Foot 21 Jun 1806. Lt 16 Feb 1808. Capt 47th 26 May 1810. Capt 14th Foot 18 Oct 1810.
Served in the Peninsula with 52nd Foot Aug 1808 – Jan 1809 and with 47th Foot Oct 1810 – Mar 1811. Present at Vimeiro, Vigo, Corunna campaign and Cadiz. Present at Waterloo with 14th Foot. Also served at Copenhagen 1807 (present at Kiöge) and Walcheren 1809. Half pay 25 Mar 1816. MGS medal for Vimeiro.

RAMSAY, William Norman
Captain. Royal Artillery.
Sarcophagus memorial: St Michael's Churchyard, Inveresk, Midlothian, Scotland. (Photograph)

SACRED TO THE MEMORY OF / MAJOR WILLIAM NORMAN RAMSAY, / OF THE ROYAL HORSE ARTILLERY, / ELDEST SON OF CAPTAIN DAVID RAMSAY ROYAL NAVY / WHO HAVING SERVED THROUGHOUT THE VARIOUS CAMPAIGNS IN HOLLAND, EGYPT, PORTUGAL, SPAIN AND FRANCE, FROM THE YEAR 1799, / AND DISTINGUISHED HIMSELF IN ALL, FELL, IN THE BATTLE OF WATERLOO ON THE 18TH OF JUNE 1815, AGED 33. / HIS REMAINS PRESERVED THROUGH THE AFFECTION OF HIS BROTHER OFFICERS, AND THE RESPECT OF HIS TROOP WERE, TO FULFIL HIS OWN WISH / REMOVED TO THIS PLACE AND LAID BESIDE THOSE OF HIS BELOVED WIFE. / ALEXANDER RAMSAY, LIEUTENANT IN THE ROYAL ARTILLERY, / THIRD SON OF CAPTAIN RAMSAY, R. N. / GALLANTLY FELL, IN THE BATTERIES BEFORE NEW ORLEANS ON THE 1ST OF JANUARY 1815 IN HIS 24TH YEAR.

Named on the Regimental Memorial: St Joseph's Church, Waterloo. (Photograph)

2nd Lt 27 Oct 1798. 1st Lt 1 Aug 1800. 2nd Capt 24 Apr 1806. Capt 17 Dec 1813. Bt Major 22 Nov 1813.
Served in the Peninsula with 'I' Troop Royal Horse Artillery under Major Bull Aug 1809 – Feb 1814. Present at Busaco, Pombal, Redinha, Casal Nova, Foz d'Arouce, Sabugal, Fuentes d'Onoro (during the action his guns were encircled by the advancing French troops. By driving the guns at speed through the French he managed to save both his guns and his gunners), Salamanca, Burgos and retreat from Burgos, Venta del Pozo (Mentioned in Despatches. Major Bull was wounded and Ramsay took over command of the troop), Vittoria, Tolosa, Bidassoa, Nivelle and Nive (wounded 10 and 12 Dec). Present at Waterloo in command of 'H' Troop Royal Horse Artillery (wounded in the retreat from Quatre Bras and killed at Waterloo). Buried on the battlefield by his friend Sir Augustus Frazer. Later his body was returned to Scotland and buried at Inveresk. Also served at Ferrol 1800 and Egypt 1801. Brother of 1st Lt Alexander Ramsay Royal Artillery who was killed at New Orleans 1 Jan 1815 and Lt David Ramsay R.N. died at Jamaica 31 Jul 1815.
Reference: Dictionary of National Biography.

RAMUS, Charles Louis
Captain. 5th (Northumberland) Regiment of Foot.
Ledger stone in floor: St Mary's Churchyard, Tenby, Wales. (Photograph)

SACRED / TO THE MEMORY OF / CHARLES LOUIS RAMUS ESQR / OF CHELTENHAM / CAPTAIN (H. P) 5TH REGT OF FOOT / WHO / AFTER A LONG PERIOD OF SUFFERING / UNDER THE EFFECTS OF THE / WOUNDS WHICH HE RECEIVED IN / THE SERVICE OF HIS COUNTRY / DIED AT TENBY / ON THE 20 JULY 1831: / AGED 49 YEARS.

Ensign 40th Foot 5 Jul 1803. Lt 27 Aug 1804. Lt 50th Foot 1805. Capt 5th Foot 28 Sep 1809.
Served in the Peninsula with 40th Foot Aug 1808 – Oct 1809 and 2/5th Dec 1809 – Nov 1812. Present at Rolica, Vimeiro, Talavera, Busaco, Redinha, Casal Nova, Foz d'Arouce, Sabugal, Fuentes d'Onoro, second siege of Badajoz, El Bodon (wounded), Ciudad Rodrigo, Badajoz, Salamanca and retreat from Burgos. Also served in South America 1807 (present at Montevideo where he was wounded).

RAND, Samuel
Sergeant. 43rd (Monmouthshire) Light Infantry Regiment of Foot.
Buried in St George's Chapel, Windsor, Berkshire. (Burial record)

Quartermaster 8 Oct 1830.

Served in the Peninsula 1808 – Jan 1809 and 1811 – Apr 1814. Present at Vimeiro, Corunna, Badajoz (severely wounded in the storming party), Salamanca, Vittoria, Pyrenees, Nivelle, Nive and Toulouse. Also served at Walcheren 1809 and North America 1814–1815 (present at New Orleans). Retired 15 Aug 1848. Military Knight of Windsor 31 May 1849. MGS medal for Vimeiro, Corunna, Badajoz, Salamanca, Vittoria, Pyrenees, Nivelle, Nive and Toulouse. Died 31 Dec 1851 aged 70.

RANNIE, William
Lieutenant. 10th (North Lincolnshire) Regiment of Foot.
Headstone: Nunhead Cemetery, London. Inscription not recorded. (Grave number 2622 Sq80)

Ensign 21 May 1807. Lt 29 Jan 1808. Capt 5 Oct 1832.

Served in the Peninsula Aug 1812 – Apr 1814 on the East coast of Spain. Present at Alicante, Castalla, Ordal and Barcelona. Half pay 22 Feb 1839. Died 12 Dec 1853 aged 67.

RATCLIFFE, James
Private. 2nd (Royal North British) Regiment of Dragoons.
Buried in Holy Trinity Churchyard, Wetheral, Cumbria. Inscription not recorded.

Present at Waterloo in Capt Poole's Troop. One of the soldiers who carried the Marquis of Anglesey from the field when he was wounded. Enlisted in Edinburgh and marched to York via Carlisle. As he marched through Carlisle he saw a girl at a window and vowed to marry her, which he did after Waterloo. Died at Scotby near Carlisle 14 Mar 1869. One of the last surviving men of the Scots Greys at Waterloo.
Reference: Carlisle Journal, 19 Mar 1869.

RAVENSCROFT, Valentine
Captain. Royal Waggon Train.
Low monument: Green Street Cemetery, St Helier, Jersey, Channel Islands. (Plot F5 North stone). Seriously eroded and inscription recorded from memorial inscription. (Photograph)

"TO THE MEMORY OF CAPT VALENTINE RAVENSCROFT ROYAL WAGGON TRAIN, WHO DEPARTED THIS LIFE ON THE 15TH APRIL 18** AGED 42 YEARS."

Cornet 1806. Lt 26 Oct 1808. Capt 25 Feb 1815.

Served in the Peninsula Jun 1811 – Apr 1814. Attached to the Royal Artillery Dec 1811 – Apr 1812, 4th Division Sep 1812 – Feb 1813 and 7th Division Jun – Aug 1813.

RAWSON, William
Captain. 35th (Sussex) Regiment of Foot.
Memorial: St George's Churchyard, Doncaster, Yorkshire. (M.I.)

"IN MEMORY OF .... / ALSO HUSBAND WILLIAM RAWSON ESQUIRE / FORMERLY A CAPTAIN IN THE 35TH REGIMENT OF FOOT, AFTERWARDS / OF HALF PAY IN THE 27TH REGT OF FOOT AND CAPTAIN AND ADJUTANT / OF THE 3RD WEST YORK MILITIA. / HE DIED JULY 18, 1850 / AGED 73."

Ensign 16 Aug 1799. Lt 29 Mar 1804. Capt 4 May 1809.

Present with 2/35th at Waterloo in reserve at Hal and with the Army of Occupation. Also served in the Mediterranean 1806. Half pay 2 Jul 1818. Adjutant 3rd West Yorkshire Militia 1827.

RAYNER, Thomas
Deputy Assistant Commissary General. Commissariat Department.
Ledger stone: Kensal Green Cemetery, London. (661/169/RS). Inscription illegible. (Photograph)

Deputy Asst Comm General Apr 1813.
Served in the Peninsula Feb 1813 – Apr 1814. Present at Vittoria and Toulouse. MGS medal for Vittoria and Toulouse. Half pay 1814. Died 1854.

RAYNES, William Augustus
1st Lieutenant. Royal Artillery.
Slab on plinth from which railings have been removed: Malew Churchyard, Malew, Isle of Man. Seriously eroded and inscription recorded from memorial inscription. (Photograph)

"SACRED / TO THE MEMORY OF / MAJOR WILLIAM AUGUSTUS RAYNES / BARRACK MASTER, CASTLETOWN / ROYAL ARTILLERY / DIED 2ND OCTOBER 1850 AGED 61 / THIS TABLET IN HIS MEMORY / BY HIS AFFECTIONATE WIFE / ...."

2nd Lt 25 Apr 1806. 1st Lt 22 Oct 1806. 2nd Capt 26 Jun 1823. Capt 29 Dec 1834. Bt Major 28 Jun 1838.
Served in the Peninsula 1808–1809 and 1810–1814. Present in the Corunna campaign, Cadiz 1810, Barrosa, Tarifa, Seville, Vittoria, Pyrenees, Nivelle, Nive, Adour and siege of Bayonne. Also served at Copenhagen 1807, Sweden 1808, Halifax, Nova Scotia 1819–1820, and Corfu 1825–1828. Later became Barrack Master at Castletown, Isle of Man. Retired on full pay 4 Apr 1843. MGS medal for Corunna, Barrosa, Vittoria, Pyrenees, Nivelle and Nive.

RAYNOR, George
Private. 1st (King's) Dragoon Guards.
Memorial tablet: Old Hillsborough Barracks, Langset Road, Sheffield, Yorkshire. (On wall outside Barracks). (Photograph)

SACRED / TO THE MEMORY OF / GEORGE RAYNOR, / LATE OF THE 1ST (OR KING'S) / DRAGOON GUARDS, / WHO DEPARTED THIS LIFE / ON THE 3RD DAY OF JUNE / 1834, AGED 54 YEARS. / HE SERVED IN THE ABOVE / CORPS 31 YEARS, 20 OF / WHICH AS A / NON-COMMISSIONED OFFICER, / AND HIGHLY DISTINGUISHED / HIMSELF AT THE EVER / MEMORABLE BATTLE OF / WATERLOO. / THIS STONE WAS ERECTED TO HIS / MEMORY BY HIS FELLOW / NON-COMMISSIONED OFFICERS. / WHEN THE LAST CALL SHALL SOUND / DISTINCT AND CLEAR / IN CHRIST CONFIDING BOLDLY / ANSWER HERE!

Pte 16 Oct 1803. Cpl 30 Jan 1807. Pte 21 Feb 1809. Cpl 25 Dec 1815.
Present at Waterloo. Discharged 13 Aug 1833.

READ, William
Major. Permanent Assistant Quartermaster General.
Memorial: St George's Cathedral Cemetery, Madras, India. (M.I.)

"LIEUTENANT GENERAL WILLIAM READ, DEPUTY QUARTERMASTER-GENERAL OF THE KING'S TROOP, MADRAS, AGED 45 YEARS. HERE ALSO ARE DEPOSITED THE MORTAL REMAINS OF HIS DAUGHTER ELIZABETH MARGARET, THE DEARLY BELOVED WIFE OF BRIGADIER-GENERAL S. W. STEEL, CB., COMMANDING THE CEDED DISTRICTS DIVISION OF

THE MADRAS ARMY, WHO DIED OF SPASMODIC CHOLERA AT PALSAMOODRUM ON THE ROUTE TO BELLARY ON 15TH FEBRUARY 1849, AGED 41. HER REMAINS HAVING BEEN BROUGHT TO MADRAS WERE BURIED IN THIS HER FATHER'S GRAVE ON 10TH APRIL 1849."

Ensign Royal Staff Corps 4 Mar 1800. Lt 6 Jan 1801. Capt 19 Dec 1803. Bt Major and Permanent AQMG 9 Dec 1813. Bt Lt Colonel 2 Dec 1824.

Served in the Peninsula Dec 1812 – Dec 1813 and Jan – Apr 1814. Also served in India 1826–1827 as DQMG in Madras where he died 1 Aug 1827.

READE, Sir Thomas

Captain. 27th (Inniskilling) Regiment of Foot.
Memorial tablet: St Peter's Church, Congleton, Cheshire. (Photograph)

IN MEMORY OF / COLONEL SIR THOMAS READE, KNIGHT, C.B. / AND A KNIGHT OF THE SICILIAN ORDER / OF SAINT FERDINAND AND OF MERIT, / A NATIVE OF THIS TOWN, / WHO FOR 51 YEARS SERVED HIS COUNTRY / IN MANY DIFFERENT PARTS OF THE WORLD: / AND ESPECIALLY ON THE COAST OF SICILY, / WHERE IN COMMAND OF A FLOTILLA OF GUNBOATS, / HE REPELLED THE AGGRESSIONS OF THE FRENCH AND NEAPOLITANS. / SUBSEQUENTLY HE WAS DEPUTY ADJUTANT / OF THE TROOPS AT ST HELENA, / DURING THE CAPTIVITY THERE OF NAPOLEON BUONAPARTE. / IN LATER LIFE / SIR THOMAS READE SUSTAINED THE CHARACTER OF / AGENT AND CONSUL GENERAL / OF THE BRITISH GOVERNMENT AT TUNIS / AND ACQUIRING THE ENTIRE CONFIDENCE OF THE BEY, / INDUCED HIM TO ABOLISH SLAVERY, / THROUGHOUT HIS DOMINIONS. / HE DIED ON THE 20TH DAY OF JULY 1840, / IN CHRISTIAN FAITH AND IN CHARITY WITH ALL MEN, / AND WAS BURIED IN THE CEMETERY AT TUNIS. / AMIDST THE DEEP REGRETS OF A MULTITUDE / LAMENTING HIM / AS AN HONOURABLE, KIND AND FAITHFUL FRIEND.

Ensign Aug 1799. Lt 18 May 1800. Capt 8th Sep 1805. Bt Major 3 Jan 1811. Lt Colonel 19 Oct 1815. Bt Colonel 10 Jan 1837.

Served in the Peninsula with 1/27th Sep – Nov 1813 and 2/37th Dec 1813 – Apr 1814. Present at Barcelona. Also served at the Helder 1799, Ferrol 1800, Egypt 1801, Sicily 1810 (ADQMG). While in Sicily commanded a flotilla of gun boats near the straits of Messina and foiled attempts by the French to invade Sicily and was awarded 3rd Class of Order of St Ferdinand and Merit 1813. Present at St Helena (DAG during Napoleon's captivity). CB. Consul General in Tunis 1821 where he was successful in abolishing slavery. Died in Tunis 20 Jul 1840 and is buried in Tunis Cemetery.
Reference: Gentleman's Magazine, Sep 1849, pp. 316–17.

REBOW, Francis Slater

Supernumerary Lieutenant Colonel. 1st Regiment of Life Guards.
Family Memorial tablet: St Mary's Church, Colchester, Essex. (Photograph)

……………… / ALSO OF THE SAID FRANCIS SLATER REBOW / OF WIVENHOE PARK. A GENERAL IN THE ARMY / WHO DIED THE 7TH OCTOBER 1845 / IN THE 76TH YEAR OF HIS AGE / HE WAS SON OF R. SLATER OF CHESTERFIELD / AND ASSUMED THE NAME OF REBOW ON HIS / MARRIAGE TO THE BEFORE MENTIONED / MARY H. REBOW OF WIVENHOE PARK.

Ensign 60th Foot 12 Apr 1788. Lt 24 Oct 1789. Capt 22 Sep 1792. Major 60th Foot 20 Feb 1796. Major 2nd Life Guards 16 Feb 1797. Major and Lt Colonel 25 Sep 1799. Supernumerary Lt Colonel 1st Life Guards 20 Aug 1807. Bt Colonel 25 Oct 1809. Major General 1 Jan 1812. Lt General 27 May 1825. General 23 Nov 1841.

Served in the Peninsula Dec 1812 – Jan 1813 (O/c Household Cavalry Brigade). Also served in the West

Indies 1788–1796 (present at Martinique, St Lucia, and Guadeloupe where he was severely wounded). Retired in 1814 to his estates in Essex.
REFERENCE: Gentleman's Magazine, Dec 1845, p. 639. Annual Register, 1845, Appx, p. 300.

REED, John
Captain. 62nd (Wiltshire) Regiment of Foot.
Pedestal Monument: Dean Cemetery, Edinburgh, Scotland. (Section F). (Photograph)

ROLICIA / VIMIERO / ALMAREZ / BUSACO / SALAMANCA / NIVE / PENINSULA / TO THE MEMORY / OF / LIEUT COLONEL JOHN REED K.H. / LATE COMMANDING THE 62ND FOOT / AND FORMERLY OF THE 9TH FOOT / AND HIS SONS / DRUMMOND AND JOHN / WHO LIVED AND DIED IN THE SERVICE / OF THEIR COUNTRY. / ………………..

Grave: Rothesay Churchyard, Rothesay, Buteshire, Scotland. (M.I.)

"JOHN REED, LIEUT COL HM 62ND REGT DIED HERE 26 SEPT 1835 AGED 45."

Ensign 9th Foot 18 Nov 1806. Lt 29 Aug 1807. Capt 62nd Foot 25 Mar 1813. Major 27 Jul 1826. Lt Colonel 25 Jun 1829.

Served in the Peninsula with 1/9th Aug – Dec 1808, 2/9th Jan – Jun 1809, 1/9th Mar 1810 – Mar 1813 and 62nd Foot Oct 1813 – Apr 1814. Present at Rolica, Vimeiro, Douro, Busaco, Fuentes d'Onoro, Castrejon, Salamanca, retreat from Burgos (present at Villa Muriel), Nivelle, Nive and Bayonne. Also served at Walcheren 1809. KH. Died at Rothesay 26 Sep 1835.

REED, John
Captain. 68th (Durham) Regiment of Foot.
Buried in St Michael and All Angels' Churchyard, Bishopwearmouth, County Durham. (Burial record)

Ensign 26 Mar 1799. Lt 21 Mar 1800. Capt 12 May 1808. Bt Major 27 May 1825. Major 2 Jun 1825. Bt Lt Colonel 22 Jul 1830. Lt Colonel 54th Foot 1 Feb 1831. Bt Colonel 9 Nov 1846. Major General 20 Jun 1854.

Served in the Peninsula Jun 1811 – Dec 1813. Present at the siege of Salamanca Forts, Moriscos, Salamanca, Burgos and Vittoria (severely wounded). Also served in the West Indies 1800–1806 (present at Martinique, Barbados and St Lucia), Walcheren 1809 (present at the siege of Flushing), Canada 1818–1830 and India 1831–1840. MGS medal for Salamanca and Vittoria. Died 24 Mar 1859 aged 75.

REED, Samuel
Captain. 71st (Highland Light Infantry) Regiment of Foot.
Memorial: St Catherine's Churchyard, Ballure, Ramsey, Isle of Man. (M.I.)

"SAMUEL REED, BT LIEUT. COL. H.P. 71ST HIGHLAND LIGHT INFANTRY, DIED 13 JULY 1842, AGED 57."

Ensign 56th Foot 5 Feb 1801. Lt 36th Foot 24 Jul 1803. Capt 6th Garrison Battalion 29 Nov 1806. Capt 71st Foot 29 Sep 1808. Bt Major 18 Jun 1815. Bt Lt Colonel 10 Jan 1837.

Served in the Peninsula Dec 1812 – Sep 1813. Present at Vittoria (severely wounded). Present at Waterloo where he was awarded Bt Majority. Also served in South America 1807 (present at Buenos Ayres where he was wounded). Half pay 25 Oct 1821.

REED, William
Ensign. 14th (Buckinghamshire) Regiment of Foot.
Headstone: Sandpits Cemetery, Gibraltar. (M.I.)

"WILLIAM REED, ESQ., MAJOR, DIED 3RD NOV 1838 AET 40."

Ensign 13 Jan 1814. Lt 26 Jun 1815. Lt 48th Foot 18 Jul 1816. Capt 8 Jun 1825. Major 1 Dec 1837.
Present at Waterloo. Also served in Australia 1817–1824, India 1825–1835 (present at the Coorg Wars 1834), Malta and Gibraltar where he died in 1838.

REEVE, John
Captain and Lieutenant Colonel. 1st Regiment of Foot Guards.
Memorial tablet: St Swithin's Church, Leadenham, Lincolnshire. (Photograph)

SACRED / TO THE MEMORY / OF / GENERAL JOHN REEVE, / ELDEST SON OF THE LATE WILLIAM REEVE, ESQ. / OF LEADENHAM, IN THE COUNTY OF LINCOLN, / ALSO MILLICENT MARY HIS WIFE. / BORN JULY 28TH 1783. DIED OCTOBER 2ND 1864. / HE ENTERED THE ARMY AS ENSIGN IN THE / GRENADIER REGT OF FOOT GUARDS, 23RD OCTOBER 1800, / SERVED THROUGHOUT THE PENINSULAR CAMPAIGN, / WAS IN THE EXPEDITION TO WALCHEREN, / AND AT THE BATTLE OF WATERLOO. / ....

Memorial: Royal Military Chapel, Wellington Barracks, London. (M.I.) (Destroyed by a Flying Bomb 1944)

"IN MEMORY OF GENERAL JOHN REEVE, COLONEL 61ST (SOUTH GLOUCESTERSHIRE) REGIMENT. BORN 30TH JULY, 1783. DIED 2ND OCTOBER, 1864. 1ST GUARDS 1800 TO 1825. HE SERVED WITH THE 3RD BATTALION IN SICILY, 1806–7; THROUGHOUT THE CORUNNA CAMPAIGN, 1808–9; THE WALCHEREN EXPEDITION, 1809; THE DEFENCE OF CADIZ, 1811; REMAINING IN THE PENINSULA TILL 1814. HE WAS AT THE PASSAGE OF THE BIDASSOA, AND AT THE BATTLES OF THE NIVE AND THE NIVELLE; IN 1815 HE WAS PRESENT AT THE BATTLES OF QUATRE BRAS AND WATERLOO, AND COMMANDED THE 3RD BATTALION DURING THE MARCH TO PARIS, AND AT THE STORMING OF PERONNE. PLACED BY HIS SON, LIEUT. COLONEL JOHN REEVE, GRENADIER GUARDS, 1840 TO 1885, WHO SERVED WITH THE 3RD BATTALION, IN THE CRIMEA, AT THE BATTLES OF THE ALMA, BALAKLAVA, AND INKERMAN, AND AT THE SIEGE OF SEVASTOPOL".

Ensign 23 Oct 1800. Lt and Capt 11 Oct 1805. Capt and Lt Colonel 25 Dec 1813. Bt Colonel 22 Jul 1830. Major General 23 Nov 1841. Lt General 11 Nov 1851. General 7 Dec 1859.
Served in the Peninsula with 3rd Battalion Oct 1808 – Jan 1809 and Apr 1811 – Feb 1814. Present at Corunna, Cadiz, Seville, Bidassoa, Nivelle and Nive. Present at Quatre Bras, Waterloo, storming of Peronne, the Capture of Paris and with the Army of Occupation until 1818. MGS medal for Corunna, Nivelle and Nive. Also served in Sicily 1806–1807 and Walcheren 1809. Colonel 61st Foot 11 Oct 1852. Magistrate and Deputy Lieutenant for Lincolnshire and High Sherrif 1837. Educated at Eton.
Reference: Gentleman's Magazine, Nov 1864, p. 666. Household Brigade Journal, 1864, p. 334.

REEVES, George James
Lieutenant Colonel. 27th (Inniskilling) Regiment of Foot.
Interred in Catacomb B (v131 c8), Kensal Green Cemetery, London.

Ensign 8th Foot 9 Feb 1791. Lt 29 Jun 1793. Capt 18th Foot 20 Aug 1801. Major 27th Foot 10 Oct 1805. Bt Lt Colonel 1 Jan 1812. Lt Colonel 4 Jun 1813. Colonel 22 Jul 1830. Major General 28 Jun 1838.

Served in the Peninsula with 2/27th Dec 1812 – Apr 1814 on the East coast of Spain. Present at Alcoy, Biar, Castalla, Tarragona and Ordal (severely wounded and awarded a pension of £300 per annum). Also served in the West Indies 1793–1796 (present at St Lucia, Martinique and Guadeloupe where he was wounded), Ireland 1798 (present at Vinegar Hill), Egypt 1801 (present at Aboukir Bay, Alexandria, Rahmanie and Grand Cairo where he was awarded Medal from the Sultan) and the Capture of Ischia and Procida 1809. Became Inspecting Field Officer in 1815 and later Governor of Placentia in Newfoundland 14 Jun 1819. CB. KH. Died 14 Mar 1845.
Reference: Gentleman's Magazine, Jul 1845, p. 81. Annual Register, 1845, Appx, p. 260.

REID, Thomas
Captain. 33rd (1st Yorkshire West Riding) Regiment of Foot.
Buried in Cawdor Churchyard, Invernesshire.

Ensign 2 Jul 1805. Lt 20 Jun 1806. Capt 16 Jun 1815. Bt Major 10 Jan 1837. Major 10 Nov 1838.
Present at Quatre Bras and Waterloo where he was severely wounded. Also served in Germany 1813 (present at Stralsund) and the Netherlands 1814–1815 (present at Merxem and Bergen-op-Zoom). Retired 10 Jan 1837. Died at Nairn in 1881.

REID, William
2nd Captain. Royal Engineers.
Named on the Regimental Memorial: Rochester Cathedral, Rochester, Kent. (Photograph)

2nd Lt 10 Feb 1809. Lt 23 Apr 1810. 2nd Capt 20 Dec 1814. Bt Major 20 Mar 1817. Capt 28 Jan 1829. Bt Lt Colonel 10 Jan 1837. Lt Colonel 23 Nov 1841. Bt Colonel 11 Nov 1851. Colonel 17 Feb 1854. Major General 30 May 1856.
Served in the Peninsula Mar 1810 – Apr 1814. Present at Torres Vedras, first siege of Badajoz (wounded) and second siege of Badajoz (Mentioned in Despatches), Ciudad Rodrigo (wounded), Badajoz, siege of Salamanca Forts (Mentioned in Despatches), Salamanca, Burgos, Vittoria, San Sebastian (severely wounded), Nivelle, Nive, Adour and Toulouse. Present in France at the Capture of Paris and with the Army of Occupation until 1816. Also served in North America 1814–1815 (present at New Orleans and Fort Bowyer), Algiers 1816 (present at the attack on Algiers under Lord Exmouth – awarded NGS medal) and Spain 1835–1836. MGS medal for Ciudad Rodrigo, Badajoz, Salamanca, Vittoria, San Sebastian, Nivelle, Nive and Toulouse. KCB. Governor of Bermuda 1839–1846. Governor of Barbados and the Windward Islands 1846–1848. Chairman of the Executive Committee for the Great Exhibition 1851. Governor of Malta 1851–1858. Died in London 30 Oct 1858.

REIGNOLDS, Thomas
Captain. 2nd (Royal North British) Regiment of Dragoons.
Family Memorial tablet: St Mary's Church, Cowes, Isle of Wight. (Photograph)

SACRED TO THE MEMORY OF MARY REIGNOLDS, / .... / OF MAJOR REIGNOLDS, HER HUSBAND, / WHO FELL AT THE BATTLE OF WATERLOO / ....

Cornet 28 Nov 1797. Lt 5 Feb 1799. Capt 25 Dec 1804. Bt Major 4 Jun 1814.
Present at Waterloo (Brigade Major to Major General Sir William Ponsonby). Reignolds was riding back with Ponsonby after the cavalry charge. Sir William's horse was getting bogged down in the mud and when he saw the Polish Lancers bearing down on them he gave his watch and locket to Major Reignolds to take them home but both men were killed by the Lancers. They were found by Corporal Dickson of the Scots Greys (who is buried in Nunhead Cemetery) as he rode back after the charge. Major Reignolds's wife had died four months before and a pension was granted to the orphaned children.

REITH, Alexander

Sergeant. 6th (1st Warwickshire) Regiment of Foot.

Headstone with Celtic Cross: St Patrick's Church of Ireland Churchyard, Newry, Northern Ireland. (Photograph)

IN MEMORY OF / CR SERGEANT A. REITH, LATE VI REGT. / BORN AT ANNAPOLIS, ROYAL N. S. / 6 APR 1785, / DIED AT NEWRY 4TH DECEMBER 1882. / HE SERVED WITH THE VI FOOT IN THE / PENINSULAR WAR, AND WAS PRESENT AT / ROLEIA, VIMIERA, CORUNNA, VITTORIA, PYRENEES, / NIVELLE AND ORTHES. / ALSO THE AMERICAN WAR AT NIAGARA. / ERECTED AS A MARK OF SINCERE ESTEEM AND RESPECT / BY THE OFFICERS AND MEN / OF THE 1ST BATTALION ROYAL WARWICKSHIRE (VI) REGT.

Pte 11 Oct 1800. Sgt 1812.

Served in the Peninsula Aug 1808 – Jan 1809 and Nov 1812 – Feb 1814. Present at Rolica, Vimeira, Corunna, Vittoria, Pyrenees, Nivelle and Orthes. His regiment arrived too late for Waterloo but served with the Army of Occupation until 1818. MGS medal for Vittoria, Pyrenees, Nivelle and Orthes. Also served in Canada 1800 (he joined the 6th Foot when they were stationed in Canada between 1799–1806), Walcheren 1809, North America 1814–1815 (present at Niagara) and Cape of Good Hope 1821. The regiment was sent to St Helena in 1821 but on hearing of the death of Napoleon they were diverted to the Cape. He was injured on board ship before reaching the Cape and this was one of the reasons for his discharge 31 May 1825.

RESTON, James

Sergeant. 94th Regiment of Foot.

Headstone: Southern Necropolis, Glasgow, Scotland. (North-east corner). (Photograph)

IN MEMORY / OF / JAMES RESTON, / LATE SERGEANT 94TH REGIMENT. / WHO DIED / ON THE 24TH DAY OF OCTOBER 1834. / AGED 63 YEARS. / AND OF / AGNES HARKNESS. / HIS WIFE. / THE HEROINE OF MATAGORDA. / WHO DIED 24TH DECEMBER 1853. / AGED 85 YEARS. / FOR A DETAIL OF HER HEROISM / READ 'THE EVENTFUL LIFE OF A SOLDIER'

Pte 2nd Dragoons 17 Aug 1791. Pte 1st Foot 25 Dec 1793. Pte 94th Foot 26 Dec 1794. Cpl 1799. Sgt 1802.

Served in the Peninsula 1810 – Apr 1814. Present at the siege of Cadiz 1810 (present at Fort Matagorda), Ciudad Rodrigo, Badajoz, Salamanca, Vittoria, Orthes and Toulouse. After serving 20 years he was discharged 19 Dec 1814 as worn out and unfit for service on a pension of one shilling and ten pence per day.

His wife Agnes Harkness is also commemorated on the headstone. She was present at Fort Matagorda with her 4 year old son. She helped the surgeon with the wounded and carried water and ammunition to the soldiers defending the fort. The defence was not going to succeed as they only had 8 guns against 40. Of the 147 men in the fort 64 were wounded and General Graham ordered the evacuation. Agnes returned to Glasgow with her son and her husband joined her in 1814. She was persuaded to ask for a pension from the Secretary of State for War but it was turned down due to insufficient funds. When her husband died in 1834 Agnes went into the Glasgow Poor House. In 1845 a public appeal for funds for her raised a pension of £30 a year. She died 24 Dec 1856 aged 85 years.

Reference: Donaldson, J., Recollections of the eventful life of a soldier, 1857, reprint 2000.

REYNELL, Thomas

Lieutenant-Colonel. 71st (Highland Light Infantry) Regiment of Foot.

Low monument: St Multose's Church, Kinsale, County Cork, Ireland. (Photograph)

SACRED TO THE MEMORY OF / LIEUTENANT GENERAL SIR THOMAS REYNELL, BARONET,

/ KNIGHT COMMANDER OF THE HONORABLE ORDER OF THE BATH, / KNIGHT OF THE AUSTRIAN ORDER OF MARIA THERESA, / AND OF THE RUSSIAN ORDER OF ST GEORGE. COL. OF THE 71ST HIGHLAND LIGHT INFANTRY: / WHO DEPARTED THIS LIFE AT AVISFORD, NEAR ARUNDEL, SUSSEX, THE 10TH OF FEB. 1848 / AFTER A MILITARY SERVICE OF 54 YEARS / THIS DISTINGUISHED OFFICER ENTERED THE ARMY SEPT. 1793 AND DURING HIS MILITARY CAREER / WAS ACTIVELY EMPLOYED IN HOLLAND, THE WEST INDIES, / THE LANDING AND SUBSEQUENT ACTIONS IN EGYPT AND THE PENINSULA; / AT WATERLOO, WHERE HE WAS WOUNDED, HE COMMANDED THE 71ST REGT / AND ENTERED PARIS AT THE HEAD OF THE LIGHT BRIGADE. / AS A GENERAL OFFICER, SIR THOMAS COMMANDED A DIVISION OF THE ARMY IN THE EAST INDIES / AND HAVING ORGANISED THE FORCE WHICH BESIEGED BHURTPORE, HE WAS SECOND IN COMMAND / OF THE ARMY WHICH REDUCED THAT PLACE, AND LED THE PRINCIPAL COLUMN OF ASSAULT, / 18TH JAN 1828. FOR THIS SERVICE HE RECEIVED THE THANKS OF BOTH HOUSES OF PARLIAMENT. / SIR THOMAS WAS BORN THE 9TH OF APRIL, 1777, DURING THE PERIOD OF HOSTILITY IN AMERICA, / AND SUCCEEDED HIS BROTHER, SIR RICHARD, AS 6TH BARONET, SEPT. 1829, / HE MARRIED THE 12TH OF FEB. 1831, THE LADY ELIZABETH LOUISA / RELICT OF MAJOR GENERAL SIR DENIS PACK, KCB AND DAUGHTER OF GEORGE, / 1ST MARQUIS OF WATERFORD, BY WHOM HE LEAVES NO ISSUE, AND THE BARONETCY BECOMES EXTINCT. / HIS REMAINS ARE INTERRED IN CHICHESTER CATHEDRAL. / HE WAS AN AFFECTIONATE HUSBAND, A WARM FRIEND, A SINCERE CHRISTIAN / AND DIED TRUSTING IN THE MERITS AND ATONEMENT OF HIS SAVIOUR. / THIS MONUMENT IS ERECTED BY HIS WIDOW.

Ensign 38th Foot 30 Sep 1793. Lt 3 Dec 1794. Capt 2nd West India Regt Jul 1797. Capt 40th Foot Jul 1799. Bt Major 10 Mar 1805. Major 71st Foot 22 Sep 1808. Bt Colonel 4 Jun 1813. Lt Colonel 71st Foot 5 Aug 1813. Major General 12 Aug 1819. Lt General 10 Jan 1837.

Served in the Peninsula on the Staff Jun 1809 – Apr 1811. (Military Secretary to Lord Wellington Jan – May 1809), with the 4th Division Oct 1810 – Feb 1811 (AAG) and with Portuguese Army Mar – Apr 1811 (AAG). Present at Cadiz, Seville, Sobral (Mentioned in Despatches), Redinha and Olivencia. Present at Waterloo where he was wounded in command of 71st Foot. KCB. Knight of Maria Theresa of Austria and St George of Russia. Also served in Flanders 1795–1796, Trinidad 1796, San Domingo 1798 (AAG), the Helder 1799, Minorca 1800, Malta 1800, Egypt 1801 (commanded Lt Company of the 40th Foot), India 1804–1808, Cape of Good Hope 1811 (Military Secretary to Sir John Craddock), India 1821–1828 (Military Secretary at Madras and DQMG). Commanded the Meerut Division of the Bengal Army (present at the siege of Bhurtpore 1824–1826). Colonel 99th Foot 30 Jan 1832. Colonel 87th Irish Fusiliers 15 Aug 1834. Colonel 71st Foot 15 Mar 1841. Married widow of Major General Dennis Pack 1831.
REFERENCE: *Gentleman's Magazine, May 1848, p. 543. Annual Register, 1848, Appx, pp. 213–14. Royal Military Calendar, Vol. 4, pp. 37–9.*

REYNETT, James Henry
Captain. 45th (Nottinghamshire) Regiment of Foot.
Low monument: St John the Baptist's Churchyard, Paignton, Devon. (Photograph)

SACRED / TO THE MEMORY OF JAMES HENRY REYNETT / CAPTAIN 45TH REGT (LIGHT INF) / WHO DEPARTED THIS LIFE / ON THE 1ST DAY OF JANUARY 1855 / AGED 67 YEARS / …………………

Ensign 19 Jun 1804. Lt 4 Jun 1806. Capt 23 Jul 1812.

Served in the Peninsula Jan 1810 – Jun 1812. Present at Busaco, Redinha, Casal Nova, Foz d'Arouce, Sabugal, Fuentes d'Onoro, second siege of Badajoz, El Bodon, Ciudad Rodrigo and Badajoz (severely wounded). Half pay 25 Dec 1814 on reduction of the regiment. MGS medal for Busaco, Fuentes d'Onoro, Ciudad Rodrigo and Badajoz.

REYNOLDS, Barnard
Lieutenant. 88th (Connaught Rangers) Regiment of Foot.
Named on the Memorial: St Andrew's Church (now Musée Historique), Biarritz, France. (Photograph)

Leitrim Militia. Ensign 88th Foot 9 Jan 1812. Lt 1814.

Served in the Peninsula Jan 1813 – Mar 1814. Present at Vittoria, Pyrenees, Nivelle, Nive and Orthes, where he was severely wounded on 27th February and died of his wounds 1 Mar 1814.

REYNOLDS, James
Captain. 83rd Regiment of Foot.
Buried at Verdun Prison, France. (Burial record)

Ensign Prince of Wales's Fencible Infantry 4 Aug 1795. Ensign 83rd Foot 15 Sep 1804. Lt 8 Jun 1805. Capt 33rd Foot 16 Jul 1807.

Served in the Peninsula Apr 1809 – Dec 1812. Present at Douro and Talavera where he was severely wounded and his leg amputated. Along with most of the other wounded from the battle of Talavera he was captured by the French, and remained a prisoner until 27 Dec 1812 when he died in prison at Verdun.

RHODES, Charles Steech
Captain. Royal Engineers.
Memorial tablet: St Michael and All Angels' Church, Heavitree, Exeter, Devon. (Photograph)

SACRED TO THE MEMORY OF CHARLES STEECH RHODES, / CAPTAIN IN THE ROYAL ENGINEERS, / WHO WAS KILLED AT THE STORMING OF SAN SEBASTIAN, / AUGST THE XXXIST MDCCCXIII IN THE XXVIIITH YEAR OF HIS LIFE / WHILST LEADING THE STORMING PARTY TO THE ATTACK, / HIS LEFT ARM WAS SHATTERED TO PIECES BY A MUSKET BALL, / NOTWITHSTANDING WHICH HE MOUNTED THE BREACH, / AND FELL COVERED WITH WOUNDS. / HIS MORTAL REMAINS ARE DEPOSITED NEAR THE PLACE WHERE HE DIED. / THE DECEASED WAS THE FOURTH SON OF THE REVD GEORGE RHODES / LATE VICAR OF COLYTON. / VERSE

Monument to Fletcher, Rhodes, Collyer and Machell: San Sebastian, Spain. (Photograph)

TO FLETCHER, RHODES, COLLYER AND MACHELL

Named on the Regimental Memorial: Rochester Cathedral, Rochester, Kent. (Photograph)

Lt 1 Jul 1801. 2nd Capt 1 Jul 1806. Capt 1 May 1811.

Served in the Peninsula 1812–1813. Present at Torres Vedras (Senior Officer) and San Sebastian where he was killed leading the storming party 31 Aug 1813. Also served at Copenhagen 1807.

RIACH, John
Asst Surgeon. 73rd (Highland) Regiment of Foot.
Headstone: Greyfriars Burying Ground, Perth, Perthshire, Scotland. (Block D). (Photograph)

TO / THE MEMORY OF / JOHN RIACH, M.D., / LATE 67TH REGT / WHO DIED 14 MAY 1864, / AGED 73 YEARS. / ....

Hospital Mate 18 May 1812. Asst Surgeon 73rd Foot 2 Jul 1812. Asst Surgeon 19th Lancers 25 Sep 1817. Asst Surgeon 10th Hussars 24 Aug 1826. Surgeon 67th Foot 19 Nov 1830.

Present at Quatre Bras and Waterloo. Also served in Germany 1813 (present at Ghorde in Hanover)

and the Netherlands 1814 (present at Antwerp and Merxem). MD 1811. Half pay 19 Nov 1841. Brother of Lt William Alexander Riach 79th Foot.

RIACH, William Alexander

Lieutenant. 79th (Cameron Highlanders) Regiment of Foot.
Low monument: Greyfriars Burying Ground, Perth, Perthshire, Scotland. (Block D). (Photograph)

IN LOVING MEMORY OF / WILLIAM ALEXANDER RIACH / MAJOR 79TH REGIMENT CAMERON HIGHLANDERS / WHO DIED ON THE 14TH SEPTEMBER 1843 AGED 50 YEARS

Volunteer 79th Foot. Ensign 17 Oct 1811. Lt 17 Jul 1813. Capt 7 Apr 1825. Bt Major 28 Jun 1838. Major 8 Jun 1841.

Served in the Peninsula Oct 1811 – Apr 1814. Present at Salamanca, the siege of Burgos and retreat from Burgos, Nivelle, Nive and Toulouse. Present at Waterloo where he was severely wounded at Quatre Bras and afterwards served with the Army of Occupation. Also served in Canada 1825–1832. Retired 15 Jun 1842. Brother of Asst Surgeon John Riach 73rd Foot.

RIBTON, John Sheppey

Lieutenant. 95th Regiment of Foot.
Memorial tablet: St James's Church, Crinken, County Dublin, Ireland. (Photograph)

IN MEMORY OF / JOHN SHEPPEY RIBTON, BART. / OF WOODBROOK BRAY. / HE WAS BORN 7TH FEBY 1794, / AND DIED 1ST MAY 1877. / HE ENTERED THE ARMY IN 1811 / OBTAINING A COMMISSION IN THE RIFLE BRIGADE. / HE SERVED THROUGHOUT THE PENINSULAR CAMPAIGN, / AND TOOK AN ACTIVE PART / IN THE PRINCIPAL ENGAGEMENTS FROM 1811 TO 1814, / INCLUDING THE SIEGE OF BADAJOS, / AND THE BATTLE OF THE PYRENEES, / FOR WHICH SERVICES / HE RECEIVED THE WAR MEDAL WITH FOUR CLASPS. / AFTER THE PEACE HE WENT TO AMERICA, / WAS PRESENT AT THE SIEGE OF NEW ORLEANS, / WHERE HE WAS SEVERELY WOUNDED, / AND RETIRED ON HALF-PAY 1818. / (VERSE)

2nd Lt 6 Feb 1811. Lt 25 Jun 1812.

Served in the Peninsula with 2/95th Sep 1812 – Nov 1813 and 3/95th Dec 1813 – Apr 1814. Present at Badajoz, Pyrenees, Nivelle, Orthes, Tarbes (wounded) and Toulouse. Also served in North America 1814 (present at New Orleans where he was wounded and awarded pension of £70 per annum). MGS medal for Pyrenees, Nivelle, Orthes and Toulouse. Half pay 5 Feb 1818.

RICHARDS, Benjamin

Private. 39th (Dorsetshire) Regiment of Foot.
Buried in Shrewsbury Cemetery, Shrewsbury, Shropshire. (Grave number Plot 11A, Section 75).

Pte 6 Jan 1806.

Served in the Peninsula with 1/39th Oct 1811 – Apr 1814. Present at Vittoria, Pyrenees, Nivelle, Nive, Orthes and Toulouse. Also served in the Mediteranean and North America 1814–1815. Discharged 16 May 1834 with a pension of one shilling and three half pence a day. MGS medal for Vittoria, Pyrenees, Nivelle, Nive, Orthes and Toulouse. Later became Fife Major. Served in the army for 24 years. Buried 29 May 1864.

RICHARDS, John

Private. 1st Regiment of Foot Guards.
Memorial: St John the Baptist's Churchyard, Cardiff, Wales. (No longer extant). (M.I.)

"JOAN JONES DIED 1811 AGED 96 / ALSO JOHN RICHARDS HER GRANDSON, OF THE FIRST REGIMENT, / THIRD BATTALION OF GRENADIER GUARDS IN WHICH COMPANY HE SERVED 22 YEARS. / DIED 1836 AGED 47. / BILLETED HERE BY DEATH / WITH ORDERS TO REMAIN / TILL THE LAST TRUMPET SOUND / THEN RISE AND MARCH AGAIN. / ALSO JANE HIS WIFE DIED 1851"

Volunteer Glamorgan Militia. Pte 9 Dec 1813.

Served in the Peninsula 1814. Present at Bayonne. Present at Waterloo in the Light company of 3rd Battalion under Lt Colonel Lord Saltoun. Fought in the orchard at Hougoumont 18 June. Present at the Capture of Paris and with the Army of Occupation 1815–1818. Served in the regiment for 22 years. Discharged 8 May 1833.

RICHARDS, Thomas

Quartermaster. 4th (King's Own) Regiment of Foot.
Named on the Regimental Memorial to 4th Foot: St Michael's Cathedral, Bridgetown, Barbados, West Indies. (Photograph)

Quartermaster 22 Aug 1805.

Served in the Peninsula 1810 (present at the siege of Cadiz). Shipwrecked and taken prisoner off the coast of Cadiz 1810. Remained in prison until 1814. Also served at Walcheren 1809 and the West Indies 1819 where he died in Grenada 1820.

RICHARDSON, George Sant

Lieutenant. 4th (King's Own) Regiment of Foot.
Memorial tablet: St Werburgh's Church, Spondon, Derbyshire. (Photograph)

SACRED / TO THE MEMORY OF / LIEUTENANT / GEORGE SANT RICHARDSON, / OF THE 4TH KING'S OWN REGIMENT, / WHO DIED DECEMBER 27TH 1818, / CONSEQUENCE OF THE DANGEROUS WOUND / HE RECEIVED ON THE 18TH OF JUNE, 1815, / AND ALTHOUGH SUFFERING FROM / A SEVERE WOUND RECEIVED / AT NEW ORLEANS, HE PARTICIPATED IN THE / GLORIES OF THE CROWNING EVENT AT WATERLOO. / ....

Ensign 1 Jun 1807. Lt 26 May 1809.

Served in the Peninsula Aug 1808 – Jan 1809. Present at Corunna. Present at Waterloo where he was severely wounded, and subsequently died of his wounds. Also served in North America where he was present at New Orleans and was severely wounded.

RICHARDSON, John

Asst Surgeon. 18th (Royal Irish) Regiment of Foot.
Memorial: Mount Jerome Cemetery, Dublin, Ireland. (Grave number C4–2587)

Hospital Mate 9 Jul 1805. Asst Surgeon 20th Dragoons 18 Feb 1808. Hospital Mate General Service 2 Jul 1812. Asst Surgeon 18th Foot 6 Aug 1812. Surgeon 2nd West India Regt 5 Jan 1826. Staff Surgeon 20 Nov 1846. Deputy Inspector General of Hospitals 16 Feb 1855

Served in the Peninsula Aug 1808 – Jun 1809. Present at Rolica and Vimeiro. Also served in the Cape of Good Hope 1805, South America 1807 (present at Montevideo), West Indies 1809–1817, Mediterranean and again later in the West Indies. Served in the West Indies for 30 years. MGS medal for Rolica and Vimeiro. Retired on half pay with Honorary rank of Inspector General 1 Jan 1857.

RICHMOND, Charles Lennox 5th Duke of see MARCH, Charles Lennox

RICKETTS, Joseph
Private. 43rd (Monmouthshire) Light Infantry Regiment of Foot.
Buried in St Clement's Churchyard, Worcester, Worcestershire.

Pte Worcester Militia. Pte 43rd Foot 3 Sep 1807.

Served in the Peninsula Jul 1809 – Apr 1814. Present at Busaco, Pombal, Redinha, Casal Nova, Foz d'Arouce, Sabugal, Fuentes d'Onoro, Ciudad Rodrigo, Badajoz, Salamanca, Vittoria, Nivelle, Nive and Toulouse. Discharged 28 Oct 1814. MGS medal for Busaco, Fuentes d'Onoro, Ciudad Rodrigo, Badajoz, Salamanca, Vittoria, Nivelle, Nive and Toulouse. Died 8 Jan 1859 aged 79.

RIDDELL, Henry James
Major. Permanent Assistant Quartermaster General.
Mural memorial tablet: Greyfriars Churchyard, (8th Division), Edinburgh, Scotland. (Photograph)

SACRED / TO THE MEMORY / OF THOMAS RIDDELL, ESQ / OF BESSBOROUGH, / IN THE COUNTY OF BERWICK / .... / GENERAL HENRY JAMES RIDDELL, / KH. & & &, / DIED 8 MARCH 1861

Ensign 58th Foot 10 Mar 1798. Lt 66th Foot 19 Apr 1798. Captain 50th Foot 25 May 1803. Major 10 Dec 1807. Major 79th Foot 21 Apr 1808. Bt Major QMG's Staff 4 Jan 1810. Bt Lt Colonel 4 Jun 1813. Lt Colonel Royal West Indian Rangers 25 Dec 1814. Lt Colonel QMG's Staff 3 Jul 1823. Bt Colonel 22 Jul 1830. Major General 23 Nov 1841. Lt General 11 Nov 1851. General 26 Sep 1857.

Served in the Peninsula Nov 1813 – Apr 1814 (on Staff AQMG). Present on the East coast of Spain and Genoa 1813–1814. Also served at Copenhagen 1807 (DAQMG) and Ireland (AQMG). KH. Governor of Edinburgh Castle 1 Jan 1847. Colonel 6th Foot 25th Jun 1851.

RIDDICK, John
Private. 91st Regiment of Foot.
Headstone: St Michael's Churchyard, Dumfries, Dumfriesshire, Scotland. (South-east corner of churchyard). (Photograph)

SACRED / TO THE MEMORY OF / JOHN RIDDICK, / WHO DIED 11TH JULY 1875, AGED 83 YEARS. / ....

Served in the Peninsula 1808–1809 and 1812–1814. Present at Corunna. Present at Waterloo in reserve at Hal in Capt James Welsh's company, the Capture of Paris and with the Army of Occupation. Also served in the Netherlands 1814 (present at Bergen-op-Zoom). After his discharge returned to Dumfries and to his trade as a tailor. Received a pension of one shilling and six pence per day.

RIDDLESDEN, John Buck
Lieutenant. Royal Regiment of Horse Guards.
Celtic cross on base: St Oswald's Churchyard, Ashbourne, Derbyshire. (Photograph)

IN MEMORY OF / COL. JOHN BEECH RIDDLESDEN, / LATE OF THE ROYAL HORSE / GUARDS BLUE: / BORN SEP 3RD 1787, / DIED MAY 27TH 1879. / REQUIESCAT IN PACE. / WATERLOO. VITTORIA, TOULOUSE

Cornet 19 Jan 1809. Lt 4 Apr 1811. Capt 20 Jul 1815. Bt Lt Colonel 1 Aug 1826. Bt Colonel 23 Nov 1841.

Served in the Peninsula Mar 1813 – Apr 1814. Present at Vittoria and Toulouse. Present at Waterloo

in Capt Clayton's Troop. MGS medal for Vittoria and Toulouse. Half pay 1 Aug 1826.
Note: Named as John Beech Riddlesden on Memorial.

RIDER, John
Private. 1st (King's) Dragoon Guards.
Headstone: St Andrew's Churchyard, Twyford, Melton Mowbray, Leicestershire. (Right of church door). (Photograph)

IN MEMORY OF / JOHN RIDER / WHO DIED MARCH 21ST 1863 / AGED 76 YEARS. / SERVED TEN YEARS IN THE 1ST DRAGOON GUARDS. / RECEIVED FOUR WOUNDS AT WATERLOO. / ....

Pte 20 Jan 1807.

Present at Waterloo where he was wounded. Discharged 19 Jan 1817 owing to his wounds.

RIDER, Richard
Private. 15th (King's) Regiment of Light Dragoons.
Headstone: Auchtergaven and Moneydie Parish Churchyard, Perthshire, Scotland. (No longer extant). (M.I.)

"ERECTED / BY / RICHARD RIDER / IN MEMORY OF / ANN LOGIE HIS SPOUSE / WHO DIED AT MURTHLY COTTAGE / 11 NOVEMBER 1857 / AGED 62 YEARS. / THE ABOVE RICHARD RIDER / DIED AT TROCHRY STRATHBRAN / 17 MARCH 1866 AGED 84 YEARS."

Pte Royal Marines 1797. Volunteer Royal Navy 1800. Pte 15th Lt Dragoons 1804.

Served in the Peninsula Nov 1808 – Jan 1809 and Feb 1813 – Apr 1814. Present at Sahagun, Cacabellos, Morales, Vittoria and Toulouse. Present at Waterloo. Also present at the naval battle of Copenhagen 1801. MGS medal for Sahagun, Vittoria and Toulouse and NGS medal for Copenhagen. Assisted his Lieutenant, William Drummond Stewart at Waterloo, and when he was discharged at the end of the war was employed by Drummond Stewart as a coachman on his estate at Murthly Castle in Perthshire.

RIDESDALE, George
Surgeon. 79th (Cameron Highlanders) Regiment of Foot.
Tombstone: English Cemetery, Sonapur, Bombay, India. (M.I.)

"SACRED TO THE MEMORY OF GEORGE RIDESDALE, ESQUIRE, SURGEON OF HIS MAJESTY'S 47TH REGIMENT, WHO DEPARTED THIS LIFE ON THE 9TH OF OCTOBER 1820, AGED 40 YEARS."

Hospital Mate 12 Nov 1806. Asst Surgeon 68th Foot 10 Dec 1807. Surgeon 79th Foot 9 Sep 1813. Surgeon 47th Foot 5 Nov 1818.

Served in the Peninsula Jun 1811 – Apr 1814. Present at the siege of Salamanca Forts, Moriscos, Salamanca, Burgos, Vittoria, Pyrenees, San Marcial, Nivelle, Nive and Toulouse. Present at Quatre Bras and Waterloo. Also served at Walcheren 1809 and India.

RIDEWOOD, Henry
Lieutenant Colonel. 45th (Nottinghamshire) Regiment of Foot.
Memorial tablet: Chichester Cathedral, Sussex. (No longer extant). (M.I.)

"HENRY RIDEWOOD – AGED 31. DIED 11 JULY 1813 LATE LT. COL 45TH REGIMENT – DIED OF WOUNDS FROM BATTLE OF VITTORIA – AND BURIED THERE"

Family tombstone: Chichester Cathedral, Sussex. (M.I.)

"................... / OF HENRY RIDEWOOD (HIS STEPSON) / LATE LIEUT – COLONEL COMMANDER OF THE 45TH REGT., WHO / DIED OF THE WOUNDS HE RECEIVED WHILST LEADING ON / HIS BATTN. AT THE BATTLE OF VITTORIA IN SPAIN / ON THE 11TH OF JULY 1813, AND WAS BURIED IN THE TOWN. / AGED 31. / ...."

Ensign 52nd Foot 18 Dec 1792. Lt 8 Sep 1795. Capt-Lt 8 Apr 1800. Major 3 Jun 1806. Lt Colonel 45th Foot 2 Jul 1811.

Served in the Peninsula with 2/52nd Aug – Oct 1808, 1/52nd Nov 1808 – Jan 1809 and Jul 1809 – Apr 1811, 2/52nd Apr – Jul 1811 and 45th Foot Jul 1812 – Jul 1813. Present at Vimeiro, Corunna, Coa (wounded), Busaco, Pombal, Redinha, Casal Nova, Foz d'Arouce, Sabugal, Fuentes d'Onoro, Salamanca, Vittoria where he was severely wounded 21 Jun and died of his wounds 11 Jul 1813. Gold Medal for Salamanca and Vittoria. Step brother of Lt Edward Marcell Madden 95th Foot, Capt William Sterling Madden 52nd Foot and Lt Wyndham Carlyon Madden 43rd Foot.

RIDGWAY, Thomas Hughes

Surgeon. 95th Regiment of Foot.

Pedestal tomb: Kensal Green Cemetery, London. (4383/71/RS). Inscription largely illegible. (Photograph)

.... / DEPOSITED THE REMAINS OF / THOMAS HUGHES RIDGWAY M .D. / LATE NINETY FIFTH REGIMENT, / ********* / DIED / 10 SEPTEMBER 1843 AGED 60 YEARS

Northants Militia May 1803. Hospital Mate 9 Mar 1807. Asst Surgeon 95th Foot 30 Jul 1807. Surgeon 5 Nov 1812.

Served in the Peninsula with 2/95th Aug 1808 – Jan 1809, Jul 1810 – Jul 1811 and Apr – Nov 1812 and 3/95th Dec 1812 – Apr 1814. Present at Obidos, Rolica, Vimeiro, Vigo, Cadiz, Barrosa, Salamanca, San Millan, Vittoria, Pyrenees, Vera, Bidassoa, Nivelle, Nive, Orthes, Tarbes and Toulouse. Also served at Copenhagen 1807 and Walcheren 1809. MD Edinburgh 1820. Retired on half pay 14 Feb 1814.

RIDLEY, Matthew

Sergeant. Royal Artillery.

Grave: St Nicholas's Churchyard, Newcastle upon Tyne, Northumberland. (No longer extant). (M.I.)

"SACRED / TO THE MEMORY / OF MATTHEW RIDLEY / OF HALTWHISTLE / LATE COLOUR SERGEANT / IN THE ROYAL REGIMENT / OF ARTILLERY / WHO DEPARTED THIS LIFE MAY 17TH 1831 / AGED 50 YEARS."

Pte 25 Feb 1798. Cpl 1803. Sgt 1810.

Present at Waterloo where he served in Capt Ilbert's Company. Later promoted Colour Sergeant. Discharged 31 Mar 1819 being unfit for further service with a pension of two shillings and six pence per day.

RIDOUT, Cranstoun George

Captain. 11th Regiment of Light Dragoons.

Memorial tablet: St Stephen's Church, Baughurst, Hampshire. (Photograph)

OUTSIDE THE CHANCEL WALL AWAIT / THE REMAINS OF CRANSTOUN GEORGE RIDOUT, / LATE CAPTN 11TH LIGHT DRAGOONS AND 2ND / LIFE GUARDS, / SECOND SON OF JOHN CHRISTOPHER AND / CAROLINE RIDOUT OF BAUGHURST HOUSE. / ENTERED INTO REST AT BRIGHTON JUNE 3RD 1881, / AGED 95 YEARS. / HE JOINED THE ARMY IN 1801, SERVED

THROUGHOUT / THE PENINSULAR WAR, WAS ENGAGED AT / EL BODON, BADAJOZ AND CIUDAD RODRIGO / AND WAS WITH THE ARMY OF OCCUPATION / IN PARIS IN 1815. / THIS RECORD IS PLACED HERE IN LOVING / REMEMBRANCE BY HIS ONLY SURVIVING / CHILD AND HIS GRANDCHILDREN.

Cornet 29 Jan 1801. Lt 20 Jan 1803. Capt 2 Mar 1809. Capt 2nd Life Guards 1 Feb 1819.

Served in the Peninsula Jun 1811 – Jan 1812 and Dec 1812 – Jun 1813. Present at El Bodon where his horse was killed under him. Retired 17 Feb 1825.

RILEY, John

Driver. Royal Artillery.

Headstone: Staveley Cemetery, Chesterfield, Derbyshire. (Buried in the Open Ground Consecrated Section Grave number B 39). (Photograph)

TO THE MEMORY / OF JOHN RILEY. / BORN APRIL 26TH 1793 / DIED JULY 28TH 1888. / THIS STONE IS ERECTED BY THE / STAVELEY RIFLE CORPS AND THEIR FRIENDS / IN RECOGNITION OF THE SERVICE OF ONE / WHO FOUGHT AT WATERLOO AS A DRIVER / IN THE ROYAL ARTILLERY.

Pte 10 Feb 1808.

Present at Waterloo with Captain Mercer's 'G' Troop. Discharged 30 Nov 1818 owing to reduction of the regiment.

ROBARTS, George James

Major. 10th (Prince of Wales's Own Royal) Regiment of Light Dragoons.

Memorial tablet: St George's Chapel, Hyde Park Place, Cumberland Gate, London. (M.I.)

"LIEUT-COL GEORGE JAMES ROBARTS, DIED 16TH OCTOBER 1829 IN THE 48TH YEAR OF HIS AGE."

Cornet 23rd Lt Dragoons 8 Dec 1803. Lt in Hompesch's Mounted Rifles 19 Oct 1804. Lt 10th Lt Dragoons 23 Nov 1804. Capt 25 Apr 1806. Major 1 Aug 1811. Bt Lt Colonel 2 Jun 1813. Major 7th Lt Dragoons 12 Aug 1819.

Served in the Peninsula Nov 1808 – Jan 1809 (DAAG) and Feb – Sep 1813. Present at Sahagun, Benevente, Corunna, Morales (wounded and Mentioned in Despatches), Vittoria and Pyrenees. Commanded the 10th Lt Dragoons at Vittoria. Gold Medal for Vittoria. CB. Retired on half pay 1814. MP for Wallingford 1820–1826.

ROBBINS, Thomas William

Captain. 7th (Queen's Own) Regiment of Light Dragoons.

Memorial tablet: All Saints' Church, Minstead, Hampshire. (Photograph)

IN MEMORY OF / GENERAL THOMAS WILLIAM ROBBINS, / COLONEL OF THE 80TH FOOT: / MAGISTRATE AND DEPUTY LIEUTENANT IN THE COUNTY OF SOUTHAMPTON, / IN EARLY LIFE HE SERVED HIS COUNTRY / IN THE 1ST FOOT GUARDS AND 7TH HUSSARS, / IN SICILY, SPAIN, FRANCE AND FLANDERS, / HE WAS PRESENT AT THE BATTLES OF ORTHES, TOULOUSE, QUATRE BRAS, / AND WATERLOO, / IN WHICH LATTER ACTION HE WAS SEVERELY WOUNDED. / HE PASSED THE QUIET EVENING OF HIS DAYS / AT CASTLE MALWOOD, IN THIS PARISH, / WHERE HE DEPARTED THIS LIFE, 27TH OCTOBER 1864 / AGED 78 YEARS.

Ensign 1st Foot Guards 26 Sep 1805. Lt 7th Dragoons 5 May 1808. Capt 25 May 1809. Major 28 Jan 1818. Lieutenant Colonel 24 Oct 1821. Major General 9 Nov 1846. Lt General 10 Jun 1854. General 9 Feb 1862.

Served in the Peninsula Oct 1813 – Apr 1814. Present at Pampluna, Orthes and Toulouse. Present at Quatre Bras and Waterloo where he was severely wounded. Also served in Sicily 1806–1807. Half pay 24 Oct 1821. MGS medal for Orthes and Toulouse. Magistrate and Deputy Lieutenant for the County of Southampton. Colonel 80th Foot 12 Mar 1855.

Reference: Gentleman's Magazine, Dec 1854, p. 804.

ROBE, Alexander Watt

1st Lieutenant. Royal Engineers.

Memorial tablet: St Thomas's Church, St John's, Newfoundland, Canada.

Buried in St Thomas's Old Churchyard, St John's, Newfoundland, Canada.

2nd Lt 14 Dec 1811. 1st Lt Jul 1812. 2nd Capt 29 Jul 1825. Capt 10 Jun 1837. Lt Colonel 9 Nov 1846.

Served in the Peninsula Dec 1813 – Apr 1814. Present at Adour (employed on the Bridge of Boats used for Passage of the Adour) and Bayonne (present at the siege and sortie from Bayonne). Served with the Army of Occupation 1815–1818. Also served in North America 1814–1815 (present at New Orleans and Fort Bowyer). He returned to England and went to the Netherlands and the Battle of Waterloo but arrived too late to see his elder brother Lt William Livingstone Robe who was killed in action 18 Jun. Alexander remained in France until 1818. Appointed to the Ordnance Trigonometrical Survey after the war, based in the Ordnance Map Office in the Tower of London. Became a member of the Geographical and Geological Societies and the Society of Civil Engineers. Went to Halifax, Nova Scotia Apr 1841 as second in command of the Royal Engineers. Commander of the Royal Engineers at St John's May 1843. Had been in poor health for some years due to over exertion in a survey in the North of Scotland. The great fire of St John's broke out in 1848 and Alexander Robe worked without rest for days to protect lives and property of the inhabitants. This proved too much for him and he died 2 Apr 1849. Every house and shop was closed for his funeral and all the ships in the harbour had their flags at half mast as he was highly esteemed by the whole community. Son of Sir William Robe Royal Artillery, brother of Lt William Livingstone Robe Royal Artillery and Lt George M. S. Robe 27th Bengal Native Infantry who died in Burma Dec 1825.

ROBE, Sir William

Colonel. Royal Artillery.

Buried in the family vault: St Nicholas's Churchyard, Plumstead, Kent. (No longer extant. Destroyed by a flying bomb in the Second World War). (M.I.)

Named on the Regimental Memorial: St Nicholas's Church, Plumstead, Kent. (No longer extant. Destroyed by a flying bomb in the Second World War)

2nd Lt 24 May 1781. 1st Lt 22 Nov 1787. Capt-Lt 9 Sep 1794. Capt 2 Oct 1799. Major 1 Jan 1806. Lt Colonel 13 Jan 1807. Bt Colonel 4 Jun 1814. Colonel 16 May 1815.

Served in the Peninsula Aug 1808 – Sep 1811 and Mar – Oct 1812 (in command of the Artillery). Present at Rolica (Mentioned in Despatches), Vimeiro (Mentioned in Despatches), Douro, Talavera, Busaco, pursuit of Massena, Badajoz (Mentioned in Despatches), siege of Salamanca Forts, Salamanca, Madrid, Burgos (Mentioned in Despatches), and retreat from Burgos (severely wounded and had to return to England on 27 Oct 1812). Gold Cross for Vimeiro, Talavera, Busaco, Badajoz and Salamanca. KCB, KCH and KTS. Also served in Flanders 1793–1795 (present at Famars, Valenciennes, Cambria and Dunkirk), the Helder 1799 (present at Bergen and Alkmaar), Canada 1803–1806 (built the Protestant Cathedral in Quebec) and Copenhagen 1807. Died 5 Nov 1820. Father of Lt William Livingstone Robe who served with him in the Peninsula and was killed at Waterloo, Lt Alexander Watt Robe Royal Engineers and Lt George M. S. Robe 27th Bengal Lt Infantry.

Reference: Dictionary of National Biography. Dictionary of Canadian Biography.

ROBE, William Livingstone
1st Lieutenant. Royal Artillery.
Memorial tablet: St Joseph's Church, Waterloo. (Photograph)

ERECTED BY HIS BROTHER OFFICERS, / THIS STONE IS IN MEMORY OF / LIEUT WILLIAM LIVINGSTONE ROBE / OF THE BRITISH ROYAL HORSE ARTILLERY, / SON OF COL L SIR WM ROBE, K.C.B. & K.T.S. / HE FELL NOBLY AT WATERLOO 18TH JUNE 1815. / AGED 24 YEARS. / THIS WAS THE 33RD TIME HE HAD MET HIS COUNTRY'S FOE, / AMONG WHICH WERE / FUENTES DE ONORO SALAMANCA THE NIVELLE AND THE NIVE / 1812 & 1813. / HE WAS KNOWN TO AND / DISTINGUISHED BY / FIELD MARSHAL THE DUKE OF WELLINGTON. / PIOUS TO HIS GOD, / BELOVED BY HIS FRIENDS AND BY HIS SOLDIERS, / AND DEVOTED TO HIS COUNTRY. / HIS PARENTS AND FAMILY, / WHILE THEY GLORY IN THEIR COUNTRY'S TRIUMPHS, / MUST EVER DEPLORE HIS LOSS.

Named on the Regimental Memorial: St Joseph's Church, Waterloo. (Photograph)

2nd Lt 3 Oct 1807. 1st Lt 18 Jun 1808.

Served in the Peninsula Aug 1808 – Jan 1809, Jun 1811 – Mar 1813 and Aug 1813 – Apr 1814. Present at Vimeiro, Lugo, Corunna campaign, Pombal, Sabugal, Fuentes d'Onoro, El Bodon, first siege of Badajoz, Tarifa, siege of Salamanca Forts, Salamanca, Majalahonda, Burgos, Nivelle (wounded and Mentioned in Despatches 10 Nov 1813), Nive, Adour and Bayonne. Distinguished himself at the battle of Nivelle where he commanded a mountain battery of guns carried on mules. His gunners were all Portuguese and his drivers British. Gold Medal for Nivelle and Nive. Present at Waterloo in Major Ramsay's troop where he was killed. Also served in Sweden 1807 and Gibraltar 1807 from where he volunteered to go to Portugal and join his father who commanded the Artillery at Vimeiro. In 8 years service he was in action 33 times, sometimes at the same time as his father, Colonel Sir William Robe Royal Artillery. Brother of Lt George M. S. Robe 27th Bengal Native Infantry who died in Burma Dec 1825 and Lt Alexander Watt Robe Royal Engineers. William Livingstone Robe was one of the few Lieutenants to be Mentioned in Despatches.
Reference: Dictionary of National Biography.

ROBERTI
2nd Lieutenant. 35th Jager Battalion, Dutch Infantry.
Named on the Memorial to Dutch officers killed at Waterloo: St Joseph's Church, Waterloo. (Photograph)

ROBERTS, Charles see CURETON, Charles Robert

ROBERTS, Robert
Private. 1st Regiment of Foot Guards.
Headstone with cross laid flat: Garden of Rememberance, Whittington, Shropshire. (Photograph)

ROBERT / ROBERTS OF FRANKTON / DIED MARCH 2 1856 / AGED 75 / ....

Private 25 Dec 1800.

Served in the Peninsula Oct 1808 – Jan 1809. Present at Waterloo in 3rd Battalion Lt Edward Stables's Company. Discharged 17 Aug 1817 as a consequence of an injury to his leg in Spain in 1809.

ROBERTS, William
Captain. Royal Artillery.
Box tomb: Old Common Cemetery, Southampton, Hampshire. (K 07 059). (Photograph)

SACRED / TO THE MEMORY OF / LT COLONEL WILLIAM ROBERTS / LATE OF THE ROYAL

ARTILLERY / WHO DEPARTED THIS LIFE THE 9TH OF JULY 1851 / AGED 76. / THIS TOMB WAS ERECTED BY HIS SONS / AS A TRIBUTE OF AFFECTION TO THE MEMORY OF / THEIR BELOVED PARENT

2nd Lt 1 Dec 1795. 1st Lt 22 Apr 1797. Capt-Lieut 24 Oct 1803. Capt 1 Feb 1808. Bt Major 4 Jun 1814. Major 5 Nov 1825. Lt Colonel 6 Nov 1827.

Served in the Peninsula Apr 1810 – Oct 1812 and May 1813 – Jun 1814. Present at the defence of Cadiz, Barrosa (wounded) and Capture of Seville (Mentioned in Despatches). Gold Medal for Barrosa. Also served in Canada 1826–1831. Retired on full pay 4 Feb 1836.

ROBERTSON, Alexander

Ensign. 1st (Royal Scots) Regiment of Foot.
Named on the Regimental Memorial: St Joseph's Church, Waterloo. (Photograph)

Ensign 20 Oct 1814.

Present at Quatre Bras where he was killed while carrying the colours. His brother Lt John Robertson 9th Foot was Assistant Engineer at the siege of San Sebastian where he was severely wounded and died of wounds 6 Jul 1813.

ROBERTSON, Andrew

Lieutenant. 94th Regiment of Foot.
Family Memorial in Enclosure: Roxburgh Churchyard, Roxburghshire, Scotland. (Photograph)

WITHIN THIS ENCLOSURE / RESTS THE BODY / OF / .... / ANDREW ROBERTSON, FORMERLY A LIEUTENANT IN / THE SCOTS BRIGADE, IN WHICH CORPS HE / SERVED DURING NEARLY THE WHOLE OF THE / PENINSULAR WAR WHO DIED 17 MARCH 1832, / AGED 42 YEARS.

Ensign 4 May 1809. Lt 10 Feb 1814.

Served in the Peninsula Feb 1810 – Apr 1814. Present at Redinha, Foz d'Arouce, Sabugal, Fuentes d'Onoro, second siege of Badajoz, El Bodon, Ciudad Rodrigo, Badajoz, Salamanca, Vittoria, Pyrenees, Nivelle, Nive, Orthes, Vic Bigorre, Tarbes and Toulouse. Half pay 25 Dec 1818. Died at Ladyrig 17 Mar 1832.

ROBERTSON, Friedrich von

Ensign. 2nd Battalion Light Infantry, King's German Legion.
Named on the Regimental Memorial: La Haye Sainte, Waterloo. (Photograph)
Named on the Waterloo Column, Hanover, Germany. (Photograph)

Ensign 7 Dec 1813.

Present at Waterloo where he was killed. Also served in the Netherlands 1814.

ROBERTSON, William Sinclair

1st Lieutenant. 95th Regiment of Foot.
Named on the Family Memorial : St Mary's Churchyard, Burnham Market, Norfolk. (Photograph)

.... WILLIAM SINCLAIR ROBINSON / OF THE 95TH REGIMENT (RIFLE BRIGADE)

Ensign 59th Foot 22 Oct 1807. Lt 92nd Foot 11 Feb 1808. 1st Lt and Adjutant 95th Foot 8 Jun 1808.

Served in the Peninsula Sep 1812 – Jan 1813 where he died from typhus at Nave d'Aver on the retreat from Burgos 28 Jan 1813. Also served at Walcheren 1809. This probably contributed to his death as those who had served at Walcheren succumbed to typhus quicker than others.

ROBINSON, Sir Frederick Philipse
Colonel. 2nd Garrison Battalion.
Memorial tablet: Hove Churchyard, Hove, Sussex. (No longer extant). (M.I.)

"SACRED TO THE MEMORY OF / GENERAL / SIR FREDERICK PHILIPSE / ROBINSON / KNIGHT GRAND CROSS / OF THE MOST HONOURABLE ORDER / OF THE BATH / AND COLONEL OF THE 39TH REGIMENT / OF FOOT. / HE WAS THE OLDEST SOLDIER / IN THE BRITISH ARMY. / AFTER A SERIES OF BRILLIANT SERVICES / PERFORMED DURING HIS LONG MILITARY / CAREER OF SEVENTY FIVE YEARS / AND HAVING ESPECIALLY / DISTINGUISHED HIMSELF AT / STONY POINT / MARTINIQUE / ST LUCIA / GUADELOUPE / OSMA / VITTORIA / ST SEBASTIAN / BIDASSOA / NIVE / BAYONNE / HE DIED AT BRIGHTON FULL OF YEARS / AND HONOURS / ON THE 1ST JANUARY 1852. AGED 88 / BELOVED AND RESPECTED"

Ensign Loyal American Regt Feb 1777. Ensign 17th Foot 1 Sep 1778. Lt 60th Foot 1 Sep 1779. Lt 38th Foot 4 Nov 1780. Capt Mar 1794. Major 127th Foot 11 Sep 1794. Major 32nd Foot 1795. Bt Lt Colonel 1 Jan 1800. Bt Colonel 25 Jul 1810. Major General 4 Jun 1813. Colonel 2nd Garrison Battalion 12 Jan 1814. Lt General 27 May 1825. General 23 Nov 1841.

Served in the Peninsula Feb 1813 – Apr 1814 (O/c 2 Brigade 5th Division). Present at Osma, Vittoria (commanded a brigade which captured village of Gamarra Mayor and Mentioned in Despatches), first and second sieges of San Sebastian (wounded 31 Aug 1813 and Mentioned in Despatches), Bidassoa, Nive (severely wounded 10 Dec 1813), siege of Bayonne and repulse of the Sortie from Bayonne. Gold Medal for Vittoria, San Sebastian and Nive. KCB. Also served in First North American War in a regiment raised by his father (present at Stony Point where he was wounded and taken prisoner), West Indies 1794 (present at Martinique, St Lucia and Guadeloupe) and North America 1814–1815. Inspecting Field Officer for Recruiting Service in Bedford and London 1796–1800 (tried to improve the service and secure plentiful supply of recruits). Commander in Chief of Forces and Governor of Upper Province of Canada 1814–1816. Later Governor and Commander in Chief of Forces in Tobago 1816–1829. Colonel 59th Foot 1 Dec 1827. Colonel 39th Foot 15 Jun 1840. Served for 75 years becoming the oldest soldier in the British army, his first commission being of an earlier date than anyone else.

Reference: Dictionary of National Biography. Gentleman's Magazine, 1852, pp. 188–90. Annual Register 1854, pp. 249–51. Royal Military Calendar, Vol. 3, pp. 211–23. Atkinson, C. T. ed., A Peninsular Brigadier: Letters of Major General Sir F. P. Robinson, KCB, dealing with the campaign of 1813, Journal of the Society for Army Historical Research, Vol. 34, No. 140, Dec 1956, pp. 153–70.

ROBINSON, Frederick Philipse
Ensign. 59th (2nd Nottinghamshire) Regiment of Foot.
Named on the Regimental Memorial to 4th Foot: St Michael's Cathedral, Bridgetown, Barbados, West Indies. (Photograph)
Ledger stone: Government House, Scarborough, Tobago, West Indies. (M.I.)

"TO THE MEMORY OF / LIEUT F. P. ROBINSON OF / 4TH REGIMENT OF FOOT / AIDE DE CAMP AND PRIVATE SECRETARY TO HIS FATHER / SIR F. P. ROBINSON KCB, GOVERNOR OF TOBAGO / HE DIED OF A MALIGNANT / FEVER / MARCH 15TH 1820 IN THE 21ST YEAR OF HIS AGE."

Ensign 24 Sep 1813. Lt 12 Dec 1816. Lt 4th Foot Sep 1819.

Served in the Peninsula Feb – Apr 1814 (ADC to Major General Robinson). Present at Bayonne. Also served in the West Indies 1819 (present at Tobago where he was ADC and Secretary to his father Sir F. P. Robinson, Governor of Tobago). Died of fever 15 Mar 1820.

ROBINSON, Gilmour
Lieutenant. 59th (2nd Nottinghamshire) Regiment of Foot.
Tablestone: St Stephen's Churchyard, Tockholes, Lancashire. (Photograph)

IN MEMORY OF / THE REVEREND GILMOUR / ROBINSON, WHO DEPARTED THIS / LIFE ON THE 30TH DAY OF DECEMBER / A.D. 1856, AGED 61 YEARS HAVING / BEEN FOR TWENTY SIX YEARS INCUM / BENT OF THE CHURCH OF ST STEPHEN / TOCKHOLES. HE WAS FORMERLY AN / OFFICER IN THE 59TH FOOT AND SER / VED WITH HIS REGIMENT THROUGH / THE CAMPAIGN OF WATERLOO: AND / AT THE TIME OF HIS DEATH HELD / THE RANK OF D. G. M. OF THE FREE / MASONS FOR THE PROVINCE OF / WEST LANCASHIRE. / (VERSE)

Ensign 1 Jul 1813. Lt 1 Sep 1814.

Present at Waterloo in reserve at Hal, the siege of Cambrai and with the Army of Occupation. Later entered the church and for 26 years was the vicar of St Stephen's Church, Tockholes. Read the sermon at the memorial service in Preston on the Duke of Wellington's death. The service was attended by veterans of the Peninsular War from the north of England.

ROBINSON, James
Private. Coldstream Regiment of Foot Guards.
Headstone laid flat: Christchurch Churchyard, Burntwood, Staffordshire. (Photograph)

IN / LOVING MEMORY OF / JAMES ROBINSON, / A WATERLOO VETERAN, / WHO DIED DEC 24TH 1878 / AGED 88 YEARS / (VERSE)

Pte 6 May 1812.

Present at Waterloo where he was wounded in the Light Company of the 2nd Battalion, Coldstream Guards. Discharged 24 Aug 1821 due to his wounds and reduction of the regiment.

ROBINSON, Peter
Captain. 20th (East Devonshire) Regiment of Foot.
Gravestone: St James's Churchyard, Colchester, Essex. (M.I.)

"THIS MONUMENT / IS RAISED BY THE OFFICERS / OF THE XXTH REGT OF FOOT / TO THE MEMORY OF CAPT PETER ROBINSON / LATE OF THAT REGT / WHO DIED ON THE 1ST DAY OF / OCT 1809 / AGED 34"

Ensign 1799. Lt 1 Jul 1800. Capt 7 May 1807.

Served in the Peninsula Aug 1808 – Jan 1809. Present at Vimeiro and Corunna. Also served at the Helder 1799 and Walcheren 1809 and on his return to England died of Walcheren fever.

ROBINSON, Thomas
Private, 95th Regiment of Foot.
Headstone: All Saints' Churchyard, Marlow, Buckinghamshire. (Right of path from main gate). Seriously eroded. (Photograph)

IN LOVING MEMORY OF / THOMAS ROBINSON / OF THE RIFLE BRIGADE / IN WHICH HE SERVED FOR 17 YEARS. / BORN FEBY 20 1788. DIED **** 18*8 / AGED ** / SERVED DURING THE WHOLE OF THE PENINSULA WAR / AND WAS PRESENT AT THE BATTLE OF SALAMANCA? / ******GST WHICH HE WAS PLACED IN THE LINES OF / TORRES VEDRAS / THE BATTLE OF BUSACO ROLEICA AT THE SIEGE OF BURGOS BADAJOS / PRESENT AT THE PASSAGE OF THE DOURO / AT FUENTES D'ONORO ****** / SIEGE OF CIUDAD RODRIGO,

ALMAREZ, TOULOUSE, SALAMANCA, / VITTORIA, CASTALLA, TALAVERA, VIMIERO / OPORTO, PAMPELUNA, PYRENEES ******* / BAYONNE PASSAGE OF THE BIDASSOA, SAN SEBASTIAN / ****** ****** ****** / ALSO IN THE CAMPAIGN ******* THE ****** / AT QUATRE BRAS AND THE BATTLE OF WATERLOO. / ******* THE LATE ****** / LIEUT. GENERAL SIR WILLIAM ROBERT CLAYTON BART. / FOR ****** / WHO HAS ERECTED THIS TABLET TO COMMEMORATE / THE ACTIVE SERVICE OF THE ABOVE BRAVE SOLDIER / AND GOOD SERVANT.

Pte 1 Apr 1809.

Served in the Peninsula 1808 – Apr 1814. Present at Busaco, Fuentes d'Onoro, Ciudad Rodrigo, Badajoz, Salamanca, Vittoria, San Sebastian and Toulouse. Present at Quatre Bras and Waterloo in Captain E. Chawner's Company. Discharged 23 Jun 1823 due to ill health. MGS medal for Busaco, Fuentes d'Onoro, Ciudad Rodrigo, Badajoz, Salamanca, Vittoria, San Sebastian and Toulouse. Headstone erected by Sir William R. Clayton in recognition of his bravery.

ROBINSON, William

Private. 73rd (Highland) Regiment of Foot.

Headstone: Fleetwood Cemetery, Fleetwood, Lancashire. (Non-conformist section Grave number 203/204/205). (Photograph)

IN AFFECTIONATE REMEMBRANCE / OF / WILLIAM ROBINSON / OF CARLISLE, WATERLOO VETERAN / WHO DIED OCTR 10TH 1880 / AGED 85 YEARS. / ....

Royal Cumberland Militia. Pte 73rd Foot 2 Apr 1813.

Enlisted in the Regiment in 1813 joining it from the Royal Cumberland Militia when he lived in Carlisle. Present at Waterloo in Captain D. Dewer's company where he was wounded, aged 20, losing his left eye and awarded a pension of nine pence per day. Went to live with his son in Fleetwood and died there in 1880.

Reference: Lagden and Sly, The 2/73rd at Waterloo, 2nd edn, 1988, pp. 194–6. Obit. Fleetwood Chronicle, 15 Oct 1880. William Robinson (1795–1880), Waterloo veteran: Biography. Manuscript record in Lancashire Record Office. (DDX 1095)

ROCHE, Robert

Sergeant. 51st (2nd Yorkshire West Riding) Light Infantry.

Named on the Regimental Memorial: KOYLI Chapel, York Minster, Yorkshire. (Photograph)

Served in the Peninsula. Present in the Pyrenees where he was killed at Echellar Nov 1813.

RODWELL, Thomas

Private. 33rd (1st Yorkshire West Riding) Regiment of Foot.

Headstone: St Anne's Churchyard, East Gresford, New South Wales, Australia. (Photograph)

SACRED / TO / THE MEMORY OF / THOMAS RODWELL / WHO DEPARTED THIS LIFE / AUGUST 31ST 1861 AGED 71 YEARS / WHO WAS IN THE BATTLE OF / WATERLOO / IN 1815 / (VERSE) / ERECTED BY HIS SON JOHN

Pte Dec 1812.

Present at Waterloo where he was wounded and was discharged 6 Jun 1816 because of the wound he received. Awarded a pension of six pence a day. Joined the Royal New South Wales Veterans Corps and arrived in Australia for garrison duty 1826. Discharged 1830, he received a land grant of 100 acres. Later joined the Police Force.

ROE, John
Lieutenant. 30th (Cambridgeshire) Regiment of Foot.
Memorial: St Mary's Cemetery, Madras, India. (M.I.)

"JOHN ROE 2ND, HM'S 30TH REGIMENT, AGED 32 YEARS, DIED 30 DEC 1821."

Ensign 61st Foot 29 Aug 1809. Lt 30th Foot 18 Jul 1811.
Present at Quatre Bras and Waterloo (wounded). Later served in India where he died at Madras 30 Dec 1821.
Note: There were two men called John Roe, both Lieutenants and they joined the regiment within a few weeks of each other.

ROE, Samuel Crozier
Surgeon. 23rd (Royal Welch Fusiliers) Regiment of Foot.
Gravestone: St Mary's Cemetery, Madras, India. (M. I.)

SAMUEL CROZIER ROE. M. D. / DEPUTY INSPECTOR-GENERAL OF HOSPITALS, / WHO AFTER FAITHFULLY SERVING HIS COUNTRY / 43 YEARS AND 3 MONTHS IN THE PENINSULA, / WALCHEREN, IONIAN ISLANDS AND INDIA / AND HAVING OBTAINED THE WAR MEDAL / WITH 10 CLASPS DIED AGED 63 YEARS. / 4TH SEPT 1851.

Hospital Mate 4 Jun 1808. Asst Surgeon 4 Dec 1808. Surgeon 26 May 1814. Surgeon 28th Foot 29 Apr 1819. Surgeon 7th Dragoon Guards 15 Feb 1831. Surgeon 38th Foot 23 Nov 1832. Staff Surgeon 17 Sep 1839. Deputy Inspector General 30 Dec 1845.
Served in the Peninsula with 2/23rd Oct 1808 – Jan 1809 and 1/23rd Jul 1811 – Apr 1814. Present at Corunna, Ciudad Rodrigo, Badajoz, Salamanca, Vittoria, Pyrenees, Nivelle, Nive, Orthes and Toulouse. Also served at Walcheren 1809. MD Edinburgh 1832. MGS medal for Corunna, Ciudad Rodrigo, Badajoz, Salamanca, Vittoria, Pyrenees, Nivelle, Nive, Orthes and Toulouse.

ROGERS, Benjamin
Private. 66th (Berkshire) Regiment of Foot.
Headstone: St Margaret's Churchyard, Northam, Devon. (Photograph)

SACRED / TO / THE MEMORY OF / BENJAMIN ROGERS / OF THIS PARISH, / A PENSIONER AND GUARD / OF HONOUR TO NAPOLEON / AT ST HELENA, WHO FOUGHT / IN THE BATTLES OF / TOULOUSE, ORTHES, NIVE, / NIVELLE. PYRENEES, / ALBUERA AND BUSACO. / HE DIED APRIL 26TH 1877, / AGED 90 YEARS. / ……………….. /

Pte 4 Aug 1806.
Served in the Peninsula 1810 – Apr 1814. Present at Busaco, Albuera, Pyrenees, Nivelle, Nive, Orthes and Toulouse. Also served at St Helena Jul 1815 – Aug 1821 (member of the Guard of Honour at Napoleon's funeral). MGS medal for Busaco, Albuera, Pyrenees, Nivelle, Nive, Orthes and Toulouse. Discharged 1 Jun 1826.

ROGERS, Thomas
Paymaster. 88th (Connaught Rangers) Regiment of Foot.
Ledger stone: St George's Cemetery, Lisbon, Portugal. (Grave number E 13). (Photograph)

SACRED TO THE MEMORY OF / THOMAS ROGERS, ESQ, / PAYMASTER OF THE 1ST BATT. OF THE 88TH FOOT, / WHO DIED AT BELEM ON THE / 4TH DECEMBER 1812 AFTER A LONG / AND TEDIOUS ILLNESS, LEAVING A WIDOW AND / THREE CHILDREN TO LAMENT HIS LOSS

Paymaster 21 Mar 1805.

Served in the Peninsula with 1/88th Mar – Dec 1809 and May 1810 – Dec 1812. Present at Talavera, Busaco, Redinha, Casal Nova, Foz d'Arouce, Sabugal, Fuentes d'Onoro and El Bodon. Died of fever in Lisbon 4 Dec 1812.

ROKEBY, Henry 6th Lord see MONTAGU, Hon. Henry Robinson

ROLES, Richard

Driver. Royal Artillery Drivers.
Headstone laid flat: St Michael's Cemetery, Upper Bristol Road, Bath, Somerset. (Photograph)

IN / LOVING MEMORY OF / RICHARD ROLES / LATE OF THE R. A. D., WATERLOO / WHO DIED SEPT. 3RD 1863 / AGED 70 YEARS.

Pte Oct 1812.

Present at Waterloo. Discharged Mar 1816.

ROLLINGS, John

Private: 57th (West Middlesex) Regiment of Foot.
Headstone with ringed cross: St Mary's Churchyard, Syston, Lincolnshire. (Photograph)

IN MEMORY OF / JOHN ROLLINGS / BORN MARCH 25TH 1781 / DIED NOVEMBER 10TH 1871 / HE SERVED HIS COUNTRY LONG AND / FAITHFULLY IN THE 57TH REGIMENT / AND WAS PRESENT AT THE FOLLOWING / ENGAGEMENTS / BUSACO SEPTEMBER 1810 / ALBUERA MAY 1811 / BADAJOZ APRIL 1812 / BURGOS OCTOBER 1812 / VITTORIA JUNE 1813 / THE BATTLE OF THE PYRENEES 1813

Pte 1 Sep 1803.

Served in the Peninsula Jul 1809 – Apr 1814. Present at Busaco, Albuera, Badaojz, Burgos, Vittoria and Pyrenees where he was wounded. Discharged 10 Nov 1815 owing to his wounds. MGS medal for Busaco, Albuera, Vittoria and Pyrenees.

ROLLO, Alexander

Corporal, Royal Artillery.
Headstone: Tynemouth Priory Churchyard, Tynemouth, Northumberland. (Photograph)

IN MEMORY OF / ALEXANDER ROLLO / LATE CORPORAL OF ROYAL ARTILLERY / DIED MAY 26TH 1856 AGED 76 YEARS / .... / CORPORAL ROLLO HELD THE / LANTERN AT THE BURIAL OF / SIR JOHN MOORE / AT CORUNNA ON / 17TH JANUARY 1809

Pte 12 Mar 1794. Cpl 1805.

Present at Rolica, Vimeiro and Corunna. He held the lantern at the burial of Sir John Moore at Corunna 17 Jan 1809. Discharged 20 Jul 1820 with a pension of one shilling and seven pence per day. MGS medal for Rolica, Vimeiro and Corunna.

ROLT, John

Captain. 58th (Rutlandshire) Regiment of Foot.
Family Pedestal Monument: Kensal Green Cemetery, London. (3016/89/IC). (Photograph)

LIEUT-GENL SIR JOHN ROLT / KCB. KC. / COLONEL OF THE QUEEN'S ROYALS / DIED 8TH NOV 1856 / AGED 72 YEARS / THE FAMILY TOMB / OF / COLONEL ROLT / ERECTED A.D. 1841.

Ensign 58th Foot 1 Mar 1800. Lt 1 Jun 1801. Capt 5 Sep 1805. Bt Major 25 Nov 1813. Lt Colonel 2 Nov 1816. Bt Colonel 10 Jan 1837. Major General 9 Nov 1846. Lt General 20 Jun 1854. Portuguese Army: Major 13th Line 1810. Lt Colonel 17th Line 14 Apr 1812.

Served in the Peninsula with 2/58th Nov 1809 – Feb 1810 and with Portuguese Army Feb 1810 – Apr 1814. Present at Busaco, Vittoria, Pyrenees, Bidassoa, Nivelle, Nive (Mentioned in Despatches), Orthes and Toulouse. Gold Cross for Vittoria, Nivelle, Nive, Orthes and Toulouse. MGS medal for Egypt, Busaco and Pyrenees. Also served in Egypt 1801 where he was wounded. CB and KTS. Half pay 25 Dec 1816. Colonel 2nd Foot 29 Aug 1853.

REFERENCE: *Annual Register, 1862, Appx, p. 396.*

ROMER, William

2nd Captain. Royal Artillery.
Memorial tablet: Holy Trinity Church, Berwick-on-Tweed, Northumberland. (Photograph)

.... / THIS MARBLE IS ALSO DEDICATED IN REMEMBRANCE OF THEIR / SECOND SON WILLIAM ROMER, ESQUIRE, / LATE CAPTAIN OF THE ROYAL ARTILLERY; / WHO BORNE DOWN BY THE UNPARALLELED SUFFERINGS / OF THE PRECEDING CAMPAIGN, EXPIRED / AS THE BRITISH TROOPS WERE EMBARKING AT CORUNNA, / JANUARY 1809, / AETAT, XXVII.

2nd Lt 20 Dec 1798. 1st Lt 12 Nov 1800. 2nd Capt 1 Jun 1806.

Served in the Peninsula Oct 1808 – Jan 1809. Present at Corunna. Died on passage home from Corunna 16 Jan 1809.

RONALD, William

Lieutenant. 67th (South Hampshire) Regiment of Foot.
Upright stone and Cross: St Mungo's Burial Ground, Glasgow, Lanarkshire, Scotland. (M.I.)

"SACRED TO THE MEMORY OF WILLIAM RONALD, LATE CAPTAIN IN H. M. 67TH REGT OF FOOT WHO DEPARTED THIS LIFE ON THE 4TH DAY OF FEBY 1860 AGED 67."

Ensign 11 Jun 1807. Lt 13 Jan 1809. Capt 25 Mar 1817.

Served in the Peninsula Dec 1810 – Apr 1814 (Brigade Quartermaster Apr – Sep 1813). Present at Cadiz, Barrosa and Tarragona. Half pay 25 Mar 1817. MGS medal for Barrosa.

ROOKE, James

Lieutenant. Staff Corps of Cavalry.
Bust on plinth: Main square of Paipa, Boyaca Province, Columbia. (Photograph)

CORONEL / JAIME ROOK

Ensign 49th Foot 16 Jun 1792. Lt 15 Feb 1794. Capt 80th Foot 5 Apr 1794. Major 49th Foot 25 Oct 1797. Major 16th Lt Dragoons 10 Mar 1798. Lt Staff Corps of Cavalry 7 Aug 1813.

Served in the Peninsula Aug 1813 – Apr 1814 (attached to HQ Oct 1813 – Apr 1814). Present at Nive, Orthes and Toulouse. Present at Waterloo (ADC to Prince of Orange). Went absent without leave 23 Nov 1816 and his commission was superseded. Also served in Flanders 1793–1795. Ran into debt and fled to Paris where he was arrested in 1803 and sent to Verdun after the end of the Peace of Amiens. Escaped after ten years in custody and joined Wellington's forces in the Pyrenees. After Waterloo went to the West Indies and from there to Venezuela to aid Bolivar in his fight against Spain. Rooke was one of Bolivar's better recruits owing to his knowledge of warfare and his ability to speak Spanish. Soon promoted to Colonel but was severely wounded in Battle of Vargas and died of his wounds 1819.

REFERENCE: *Hughes, Ben, Conquer or Die: Wellington's Veterans and the liberation of the new world, 2010.*

ROOKE, John Charles

Captain and Lieutenant Colonel. 3rd Regiment of Foot Guards.
Named on the Memorial: St Andrew's Church (now Musée Historique), Biarritz, France. (Photograph)
Named on Memorial Panel VII for Nivelle: Royal Military Chapel, Wellington Barracks, London. (M.I.) (Destroyed by a Flying Bomb 1944)

Cornet Berkshire Fencible Cavalry. Ensign 3rd Foot Guards 18 Aug 1795. Lt and Capt 26 Dec 1798. Adjutant 2nd Battalion 1803 – Jan 1809. Capt and Lt Colonel 26 Jan 1809.

Served in the Peninsula Jan – Mar 1810 (Brigade Major to Major-General Stoppard) and Apr 1810 – Dec 1813 (AAG 2nd Division) Present at Busaco, Albuera (Mentioned in Despatches), Arroyo dos Molinos (Mentioned in Despatches), Almarez (Mentioned in Despatches), Alba de Tormes, Vittoria (Mentioned in Despatches), Pyrenees and Nivelle where he was severely wounded and died of his wounds 18 Dec 1813. Gold Cross for Albuera, Vittoria, Pyrenees and Nivelle.

ROOTH, Benjamin

Lieutenant and Adjutant. 76th Regiment of Foot.
Headstone: St Paul's Churchyard, Fort Erie, Canada. (Photograph)

HINDOOSTAN / BENJAMIN ROOTH / DIED MARCH 1849 / ....

Sgt Major 43rd Foot. Ensign and Adjutant 76th Foot 30 Jun 1808. Lt and Adjutant 10 May 1809. Capt 26 Feb 1828.

Served in the Peninsula Nov 1808 – Jan 1809 and Aug 1813 – Apr 1814. Present at Corunna, Bidassoa, Nivelle, Nive and Bayonne. Also served at Copenhagen 1807, Walcheren 1809 and North America 1814–1815 (present at Plattsburgh). Remained in Canada on garrison duty. Half pay Feb 1828. Became Town Major of Montreal 25 Jun 1828. After he retired he settled in Canada. MGS medal for Corunna, Nivelle and Nive which arrived five days after his death in 1849.

ROSE, Hugh Hay

Lieutenant. 92nd Regiment of Foot.
Grave: St George's Cemetery, Lisbon, Portugal. (Grave number D 216). (M.I.)

"SACRED TO THE MEMORY OF / LT COL. HUGH HAY ROSE / LATE CAPTAIN H. M. 92ND REGT / WHO DIED IN LISBON 17 APRIL 1851 / AGED 64 YEARS."

Ensign 14 Jul 1804. Lt 3 Oct 1805. Capt 25 Oct 1814. Bt Major 30 Dec 1826. Bt Lt Colonel 17 Sep 1839. Portuguese Army: Capt 10th Line 26 Aug 1809. Major 27 Aug 1813. Major 15th Line 15 Dec 1814.

Served in the Peninsula with 92nd Foot Aug 1808 – Jan 1809 and with Portuguese Army Aug 1809 – Apr 1814. Present at Corunna, Busaco, Albuera, first and second sieges of Badajoz, Arroyo dos Molinos, Vittoria, Pyrenees, Nivelle, Nive, Garris, Orthes and Toulouse. Half pay 1816. MGS medal for Corunna, Busaco, Albuera, Vittoria, Pyrenees, Nivelle, Nive, Orthes and Toulouse.

ROSS, Andrew Clark

Ensign. 59th (2nd Nottinghamshire) Regiment of Foot.
Named on the Regimental Memorial monument: Christ Church Churchyard, Tramore, County Waterford, Ireland. (Photograph)

Ensign 22 Sep 1813.

Served in the Peninsula Mar – Apr 1814. Present at Bayonne. Present at Waterloo with 2nd Battalion in reserve at Hal, siege of Cambrai and with the Army of Occupation. Drowned when the *Sea Horse* transport was wrecked in a storm in Tramore Bay 30 Jan 1816.

ROSS, Ewen Cameron
Lieutenant. 92nd Regiment of Foot.
Family Memorial headstone in railed enclosure: Kilmonivaig Churchyard, Spean Bridge, Invernesshire, Scotland. (Photograph)

……………… / LIEUTENANT EWEN CAMERON ROSS / 92ND HIGHLANDERS WHO SERVED WITH HIS / REGIMENT THROUGH THE PENINSULA CAMP / AIGN, AND AT THE BATTLE OF WATERLOO. DIED / AT FORT AUGUSTUS 29TH SEPTEMBER 1869, / AGED 79. / ………………

Ensign 13 Apr 1809. Lt 26 Nov 1812.

Served in the Peninsula Oct 1810 – Apr 1813. Present at Fuentes d'Onoro, Arroyo dos Molinos (severely wounded), Almarez and Alba de Tormes. MGS medal for Fuentes d'Onoro. Present at Quatre Bras (wounded) and Waterloo (wounded). Half pay 25 Mar 1817.

ROSS, George Charles
Captain. Royal Engineers.
Named on the Regimental Memorial: Rochester Cathedral, Rochester, Kent. (Photograph)

2nd Lt 1 Jul 1799. Lt 18 Apr 1801. 2nd Capt 1 Mar 1805. Capt 24 Jun 1809.

Served in the Peninsula Aug 1809 – Jan 1812. Present at Torres Vedras, first and second sieges of Badajoz and Ciudad Rodrigo. He set up a Telegraph signal system in the Lines. Then undertook training of the infantry as sappers. Responsible for work on the navigation of the River Douro Nov 1811. At the siege of Ciudad Rodrigo he was killed by a shell splinter 9 Jan 1812. His death was regarded as a great loss as he was one of the best engineers. Buried in the same grave in a valley near Ciudad Rodrigo as his friend Lt Thomas Skelton Royal Engineers who was also killed in the siege.

ROSS, Sir Hew Dalrymple
Captain. Royal Artillery.
Brass Memorial tablet: Royal Garrison Church of St George, Woolwich, Kent. (Photograph)

F. M .SIR HEW DALRYMPLE ROSS, GCB / COLONEL COMMANDANT OF THE ROYAL HORSE ARTILLERY, / AND LIEUTENANT GENERAL IN THE ARMY / HE WAS BORN 5TH JULY 1779 AND DIED 10TH DECEMBER 1868 …….. / THE COURSE OF WHICH HE ****** / WATERLOO ****** / LIEUT. GENERAL OF ARTILLERY / HE DIED DECEMBER 10TH 1868 MUCH RESPECTED & LAMENTED.

Cross on stepped base: Brompton Cemetery, London. (BR 54460 Compartment K:89.3x5). (Photograph)

FIELD MARSHAL / SIR HEW DALRYMPLE ROSS GCB / ROYAL HORSE ARTILLERY / BORN JULY 5TH 1779 / DIED DECEMBER 10TH 1868

Named on the Memorial tablet to Master Gunners: Royal Artillery Barracks, Woolwich, Kent. (Photograph)

Memorial window: Sir John Moore Library, Shorncliffe, Kent. (Photograph)

CHESTNUT TROOP / CAPTAIN H. D. ROSS / UBIQUE / A TROOP RHA

2nd Lt 6 Mar 1795. 1st Lt 10 May 1795. Capt-Lt 1 Sep 1803. Capt 24 Jul 1806. Bt Major 31 Dec 1811. Bt Lt Colonel 21 Jun 1813. Major 29 Jul 1825. Lt Colonel 29 Jul 1825. Bt Colonel 22 Jul 1830. Colonel 10 Jan 1837. Major General 23 Nov 1841. Lt General 11 Nov 1851. General 28 Nov 1854. Field Marshal 1 Jan 1868.

Served in the Peninsula Jul 1809 – Apr 1814 (O/c 'A' Troop (Chestnut Troop) attached to the Lt Division). Present at Coa (Mentioned in Despatches), Busaco, Pombal, Redinha (wounded), Casal Nova, Foz d'Arouce (wounded), Sabugal, Fuentes d'Onoro, Aldea de Ponte, Ciudad Rodrigo, Badajoz (severely wounded), siege of Salamanca Forts, Castrejon, Salamanca, Madrid, San Munos, San Milan, Osma, Vittoria (awarded Bt Lt Colonelcy), Pyrenees, Bidassoa, Nivelle, Nive and St Pierre. Present at Waterloo. KCB, KTS and Knight of St Anne of Russia. Also served in the Irish Rebellion 1798. Gold Cross for Busaco, Badajoz, Salamanca, Vittoria, Nivelle, and Nive. MGS medal for Fuentes d'Onoro, Ciudad Rodrigo and Pyrenees. Commanded Royal Artillery in Northern District 1825–1840. Deputy Adjutant General Royal Artillery 1840–1854. Acting Master General of Ordnance 1854–1856. Adjutant General of Royal Artillery 22 May 1855. GCB 1855. Master Gunner 1864–1868. Field Marshal of the Army 1 Jan 1868, the first such appointment from the Royal Artillery. Lt Governor Chelsea Hospital Jul 1868. Died 10 Dec 1868 aged 90. Uncle of Colonel Robert Ross 20th Foot.
REFERENCE: *Dictionary of National Biography. Ross, Sir Hew Dalrymple, Memoir of Field-Marshal Sir Hew Dalrymple Ross, reprint 2008.*

ROSS, James Kerr
Lieutenant. 92nd Regiment of Foot.
Memorial Cross: Grange Cemetery, Edinburgh, Scotland. (Section M Grave number 7). (Photograph)

SACRED / TO THE MEMORY OF / LT GEN JAMES KERR ROSS KH / BORN 18TH MARCH 1792 / DIED 26TH APRIL 1872 / ....

Ensign 19 Mar 1807. Lt 4 May 1808. Capt 22 Oct 1818. Bt Major 7 Jun 1831. Bt Lt Colonel 9 Nov 1846. Bt Colonel 20 Jun 1854. Major General 1 May 1861. Lt General 19 Nov 1870. Portuguese Army: Capt 16th Line 10 Jan 1814.
Served in the Peninsula with 92nd Foot Oct 1811 – Oct 1813 and with Portuguese Army Nov 1813 – Apr 1814. Present at Arroyo dos Molinos, Almarez, Alba de Tormes, Vittoria, Pyrenees (wounded at Maya), Nivelle (ADC to Sir John Buchan), Nive, Orthes, Aire and Toulouse. Present at Quatre Bras (wounded), Waterloo (wounded) and the Capture of Paris. Half pay 7 Jun 1831. MGS medal for Vittoria, Pyrenees, Nivelle, Nive, Orthes and Toulouse. KH.
REFERENCE: *Annual Register, 1872, p.148.*

ROSS, John
Major. 95th Regiment of Foot.
Mural wall tablet: Greyfriar's Burying Ground, Perth, Perthshire, Scotland. (Photograph)
Note: The centre tablet of the memorial is totally eroded. (Inscription recorded from memorial inscription.)

" SACRED TO THE MEMORY OF MAJOR-GENERAL SIR JOHN ROSS, K.C.B., DIED 21 APRIL 1835, AGED 52 YEARS. ...."

Named on the Rifle Brigade Memorial: Winchester Cathedral, Winchester, Hampshire. (Photograph)

Ensign 72nd Foot 24 Oct 1797. Lt 5 Jul 1800. Lt 95th Foot 2 Sep 1800. Capt 16 Jun 1803. Major 11 May 1808. Bt Lt Colonel 19 Jul 1811. Lt Colonel Cape Corps 8 Jan 1824. Major General 22 Jul 1830.
Served in the Peninsula with 1/95th Aug 1808 – Jan 1809 and 3/95th Mar 1810 – May 1811 and Oct 1812 – Apr 1814. Present at Cacabellos, Corunna, Cadiz, Barrosa (Mentioned in Despatches), San Millan, Vittoria, Pyrenees, Vera, Orthes, Tarbes and Toulouse. CB. Present at Waterloo where he was wounded. Gold Cross for Barrosa, Vittoria, Orthes and Toulouse. Also served at Hanover 1805, the Baltic 1807–1808 and the Cape of Good Hope 1824. KCB.
REFERENCE: *Gentleman's Magazine, Aug 1835, pp. 203–4.*

ROSS, John

Captain and Lieutenant Colonel. Coldstream Regiment of Foot Guards.
Named on Memorial Panel VI for Talavera: Royal Military Chapel, Wellington Barracks, London. (M.I.)
(Destroyed by a Flying Bomb 1944)

Capt Independent Company. Lt and Capt Coldstream Guards 12 Feb 1794. Bt Major 29 Apr 1802. Capt and Lt Col 25 Dec 1802.

Served in the Peninsula Mar – Jul 1809. Present at Douro and Talavera where he was killed 28 Jul 1809.

ROSS, John

Sergeant. 71st (Highland Light Infantry) Regiment of Foot.
Memorial tablet: St Michael's Churchyard, Inveresk, Midlothian, Scotland. (Photograph)

SACRED / TO THE MEMORY OF / QR. MASTER JOHN ROSS, / LATE OF THE 71ST REGT IN / WHICH HE SERVED 41 YEARS. / ON RETIRING FROM THE / REGT A SILVER VASE / WAS PRESENTED BY HIS BROTHER / OFFICERS, OUT OF RESPECT / TO HIM, AS A BRAVE SOLDIER / AND AGREEABLE COMPANION. / HIS KINDNESS TO HIS RELATIONS, / AND BENEVOLENCE TO THE POOR, / WILL BE LONG / REMEMBERED. / HE DIED / AT ESKSIDE MUSELBURGH, / ON THE 15TH MARCH 1857 / IN THE 81ST YEAR OF / HIS AGE.

Private Fife and Cromarty Fencible 8 Aug 1798. Pte 71st Foot 12 Aug 1800. Corporal 1809. Sgt 1814.

Served in the Peninsula 1809 – Apr 1814. Present at Talavera, Fuentes d'Onoro (wounded), Arroyo dos Molinos, Almarez, Vittoria, Pyrenees, Nivelle, Orthes and Toulouse. Present at Waterloo in Capt Campbell's Company. Regimental Medal for Good Conduct. Discharged 2 Feb 1819. MGS medal for Talavera, Fuentes d'Onoro, Vittoria, Pyrenees, Nivelle, Orthes and Toulouse.

ROSS, John

Private. 92nd Regiment of Foot.
Headstone: Penpont Churchyard, Penpont, Dumfries, Scotland. (Broken in two. The top half of the headstone lies to the foot of the rest of the headstone with the inscription to John Ross upright. The inscription on the reverse relates to other members of his family). (Photograph)

.... / SACRED TO THE MEMORY OF JOHN ROSS / DIED ON THE 24TH DECEMBER 1866 AGED 76 YEARS. IN THE 92ND HIGHLANDERS HE WAS PRESENT AND / SHARED IN THE BRILLIANT VICTORIES OF / ORTHES, NIVE, PYRENEES AND VITTORIA, AND / AWARDED PENINSULAR MEDAL WITH FOUR / CLASPS. HE ALSO FOUGHT IN THE BATTLE OF / WATERLOO, FOR WHICH HE HELD THAT MEDAL / AND THE SPECIAL PENINSULAR CLASP, AND / WAS ONE OF THE HEROIC FEW WHO SURVIVED / THE DEFENCE OF QUATRE BRAS FARM HOUSE / AND WAS SEVERELY WOUNDED WHILST CHEER / ING THE APPROACH OF THE PRUSSIAN ARMY / HE WAS AFTERWARDS FOR MORE THAN THIRTY / YEARS FORESTER WHICH SITUATION HE / MOST FAITHFULLY FILLED TO LAUDERDALE / MAITLAND ESQ. OF ECCLES BY WHOM HE WAS DEEPLY RESPECTED

Pte 5 Apr 1809.

Served in the Peninsula Oct 1810 – Apr 1814. Present at Vittoria, Pyrenees, Nive and Orthes. Present at Quatre Bras and Waterloo (severely wounded). MGS medal for Vittoria, Pyrenees, Nive and Orthes. Discharged 18 Feb 1816 owing to his wound. After leaving the army, worked for 30 years as a forester on a Highland estate at Eccles near Penpont, Dumfriesshire.

ROSS, Robert

Major. 4th (Royal Irish) Dragoon Guards.

Wall mural memorial tablet: St John the Evangelist, Lothian Road, Edinburgh, Scotland. (Right-hand side of first bay below church near Lothian Road). (Photograph)

SACRED TO THE MEMORY OF / COLONEL ROBERT ROSS, K.H., / OF THE 4TH ROYAL IRISH DRAGOON GUARDS, / FIFTH SON OF / ADMIRAL SIR JOHN LOCKHART ROSS, BART., / OF BALMAGOWAN, / WHO AFTER TWENTY FIVE YEARS PASSED IN THE / ARMY, DURING WHICH TIME HE SERVED IN EGYPT / AND THE PENINSULA, DEPARTED THIS LIFE AT / CASTLE BANK, LANARKSHIRE, / ON 18TH DEC. 1835, AGED 52 YEARS.

Lt 22nd Lt Dragoons 4 Mar 1801. Capt 24 Jul 1802. Capt 4th Dragoon Guards 27 Dec 1802. Major 16 Jul 1807. Bt Lt Colonel 4 Jun 1813.

Served in the Peninsula Aug 1811 – Feb 1812. Present at Llerena. Also served in Egypt 1801 with 22nd Lt Dragoons. KH.

ROSS, Robert

Colonel. 20th (East Devonshire) Regiment of Foot.

Chest tomb: Old Burial Ground, Halifax, Nova Scotia, Canada. (Grave number 1122). (Photograph)

HERE / ON THE 29TH OF SEPTEMBER 1814 / WAS COMMITTED TO THE EARTH / THE BODY / OF / MAJOR GENERAL ROBERT ROSS / WHO / AFTER HAVING DISTINGUISHED HIMSELF IN ALL RANKS AS AN OFFICER / IN / EGYPT, ITALY, PORTUGAL, SPAIN, FRANCE & AMERICA / WAS KILLED / AT THE COMMENCEMENT OF AN ACTION / WHICH TERMINATED THE DEFEAT AND ROUTE / OF / THE TROOPS OF THE UNITED STATES / NEAR BALTIMORE / ON THE 12TH OF SEPTEMBER / 1814 / AT / ROSSTREVOR / THE SEAT OF HIS FAMILY IN IRELAND / A MONUMENT / MORE WORTHY OF HIS MEMORY HAS BEEN ERECTED / BY / THE NOBLEMEN AND GENTLEMEN OF HIS COUNTRY / AND / THE OFFICERS OF A GRATEFUL ARMY / WHICH / UNDER HIS COMMAND / ATTACKED AND DISPERSED THE ENEMY / AT BLADENSBURG / ON THE 26TH OF AUGUST 1814 / AND / ON THE SAME DAY VICTORIOUSLY ENTERED / WASHINGTON / THE CAPITAL OF THE UNITED STATES / IN ST PAUL'S CATHEDRAL / A MONUMENT / HAS ALSO BEEN ERECTED TO HIS MEMORY / BY / HIS COUNTRY

Memorial: St Paul's Cathedral, London. (South transept). (Photograph)

ERECTED AT THE PUBLIC EXPENSE TO THE MEMORY / OF MAJOR GENERAL ROBERT ROSS, / WHO HAVING UNDERTOOK AND EXECUTED AN ENTERPRISE / AGAINST THE CITY OF / WASHINGTON, THE CAPITAL OF / THE UNITED STATES OF AMERICA WHICH WAS CROWNED / WITH COMPLETE SUCCESS WAS KILLED SHORTLY / AFTERWARDS WHILE DIRECTING A / SUCCESSFUL ATTACK / UPON A SUPERIOR FORCE NEAR THE CITY OF / BALTIMORE ON THE 12TH DAY OF SEPTEMBER 1814.

Memorial tablet: Parish Church, Rostrevor, County Down, Northern Ireland. (Photograph)

SACRED TO THE MEMORY / OF MAJOR GENERAL ROBERT ROSS / LATE LIEUT. COLONEL AND COMMANDING OFFICER / OF THE XX REGIMENT OF FOOT / WHO FELL ON THE 12TH OF SEPTEMBER 1814 / IN THE ATTACK ON BALTIMORE / THIS MONUMENT IS ERECTED / BY THE OFFICERS NON COMMISSIONED OFFICERS / AND PRIVATES OF THAT CORPS / TO PERPETUATE HIS WORTH / AND REMAIN IN TESTIMONY OF THEIR / ESTEEM AND SORROW

Obelisk: Rostrevor, County Down, Northern Ireland. (Photograph)

Front of Obelisk:

MAJOR-GENERAL / ROBERT ROSS / SERVED WITH DISTINCTION IN / HOLLAND, EGYPT, / ITALY, SPAIN, AND FRANCE. / CONQUERED IN AMERICA, AND / FELL VICTORIOUS AT / BALTIMORE. / BORN 1766, HELDER 1799, ALEXANDRIA 1801, MAIDA 1806, / CORUNNA 1809, VITTORIA 1813, / ORTHES 1813, PYRENEES 1813, / BLADENSBURG 1814, BALTIMORE 1814.

Rear of Obelisk:

THE OFFICERS OF A GRATEFUL ARMY / WHICH, UNDER THE COMMAND OF THE LAMENTED / MAJOR GENERAL ROBERT ROSS, / ATTACKED AND DISPERSED THE AMERICAN FORCES / AT BLADENSBURG ON THE 24TH AUGUST 1814, / AND ON THE SAME DAY VICTORIOUSLY ENTERED WASHINGTON, / THE CAPITAL OF THE UNITED STATES, / INSCRIBE UPON THIS TABLET / THEIR ADMIRATION FOR HIS PROFESSIONAL SKILL, / AND THEIR ESTEEM FOR HIS AMIABLE PRIVATE CHARACTER. / HIS WELL-EARNED FAME IS ALSO RECORDED / BY THE MONUMENT ERECTED AT HIS GRAVE / AT HALIFAX, NOVA SCOTIA, BY THE ARMY IN THAT COMMAND, / BY WHICH HIS MOURNING BROTHER OFFICERS OF THE 20TH FOOT / RAISED IN HIS PARISH CHURCH AT / ROSTREVOR; / AND / THAT PLACED IN ST PAUL'S CATHEDRAL, / AS THE LAST TRIBUTE OF A NATION'S PRAISE, / BY HIS COUNTRY.

Right side of Obelisk:

BORN 1766; ENSIGN 25TH FOOT 1788; LIEUTENANT 7TH FOOT 1791; CAPTAIN 1795; MAJOR 20TH / FOOT 1799; LIEUT. COLONEL (BREVET) 1808; AIDE-DE-CAMP TO THE KING 1810; MAJOR / GENERAL 1813; HELDER 1799; ALEXANDRIA 1804; MAIDA 1806; CORUNNA 1809; VITTORIA 1813; / ORTHES 1813; PYRENEES 1813; BLADENSBURG 1814 AND BALTIMORE 1814.

Left side of Obelisk:

ERECTED BY THE INHABITANTS OF THE COUNTY OF DOWN AND BY THE ARMY SERVING IN / AMERICA IN REMEMBRANCE OF MAJOR GENERAL ROSS, AS A TRIBUTE TO HIS WORK AND A / RECORD OF HIS MILITARY RECORD.

Ensign 25th Foot 1 Aug 1789 (aged 15). Lt 7th Foot 15 Jul 1791. Capt 19 Apr 1795. Major 90th Foot 23 Dec 1795. Major 20th Foot 6 Aug 1799. Bt Lt Colonel 1 Jan 1801. Lt Colonel 21 Jan 1808. Bt Colonel 25 Jul 1810. Major General 4 Jul 1813.

Served in the Peninsula Aug 1808 – Jan 1809, Nov 1812 – Jun 1813 and Jul 1813 – Apr 1814 (O/c 2 Brigade 4th Division). Present at Corunna, Vittoria, Pyrenees (present at Sorauren and Mentioned in Despatches), San Sebastian, Nivelle, Nive and Orthes (severely wounded at capture of village of St Boes). Gold Cross for Maida, Egypt, Corunna, Vittoria, Pyrenees and Orthes. After Corunna the regiment was decimated, but Ross brought it back to strength and retrained them, only for the same to happen after Walcheren and he again had to reform the regiment. Also served at the Helder 1799 (severely wounded at Krabbendam), Egypt 1801 (present at Alexandria), Sicily 1806 (present at Maida) and Walcheren 1809. Appointed to command British troops sent from Bordeaux to North America, May 1814. Defeated the Americans at Bladensburg, which resulted in the capture of Washington Aug 1814. He made sure that the private homes were not destroyed, only public buildings. Killed in the attack on Baltimore Sep 1814. He was an excellent linguist speaking both French and Spanish. On his death Rear Admiral George Cockburn said 'Our country has lost in him one of its best and bravest soldiers'. He was compared to General Wolfe. Both commanded the 20th Foot, both died young in America and their only fault was an excess of courage. Nephew of Lt General Hew Dalrymple Ross Royal Artillery.

Note: Andrew Robb, one of the soldiers who had served in the 20th Foot from the Helder to Toulouse was

put in charge of the monument erected at Ross Trevor to Major General Ross. He remained there until he died in 1856.
Reference: Dictionary of National Biography. Cole, John William, Memoirs of British Generals, Vol. 2, 1856, pp. 295–324. Gentleman's Magazine, Nov 1814, p. 483.

ROSS-LEWIN, Henry
Captain. 32nd (Cornwall) Regiment of Foot.
Family Memorial: Clondegad Churchyard, Clondegad, County Clare, Ireland. Seriously eroded. Inscription not recorded. (Photograph)

Limerick Militia 1793. Ensign 32nd Foot 4 Nov 1795. Lt 22 Aug 1797. Capt 6 Aug 1804. Bt Major 4 Jun 1814.

Served in the Peninsula Aug – Oct 1808, Jul 1811 – Jan 1813 and Jan – Apr 1814. Present at Rolica, Vimeiro, siege of Salamanca Forts, Salamanca (severely wounded), Burgos, retreat from Burgos and Orthes. Present at Quatre Bras and Waterloo. Also served in the West Indies 1796–1797 (promoted to Lieutenant when the regiment lost 32 officers to disease, present at St Domingo), Copenhagen 1807, Walcheren 1809 (present at the siege of Flushing) and the Ionian Islands 1818–1822. Retired 1828 on the death of his father and returned to the family estates in Ireland where he died in 1843. Brother of Lt Thomas Ross-Lewin 95th Foot who also served in the Peninsula and Waterloo and died in 1857. Wrote his autobiography published in 3 volumes in 1834.
Reference: Ross-Lewin, Henry, Life of a soldier: a narrative of twenty-seven years' service, by a field officer, 3 vols, 1834. Reprint with title 'With the Thirty Second in the Peninsula and other campaigns', 2000.

ROTTENBURG, Francis, Baron
Colonel. Roll's Regiment.
Memorial: Royal Garrison Church Graveyard, Portsmouth, Hampshire. (M.I.)

"HERE REST THE REMAINS OF LIEUTENANT GENERAL / FRANCIS, BARON DE ROTTENBURG / KCH / WHO DEPARTED THIS LIFE THE / 25TH APRIL 1832."

Major Hompesch's Hussars 25 Dec 1795. Lt Colonel 25 Jun 1796. Lt Colonel 60th Foot 30 Dec 1797. Bt Colonel 1 Jan 1805. Major General 25 Jul 1810. Colonel Roll's Regiment 2 Sep 1813. Lt General 12 Aug 1819.

Served at Walcheren 1809 in command of light troops (present at the siege of Flushing). Also served in Ireland 1798 (present in the Rebellion) and Surinam 1799. While in Ireland he formed a rifle corps out of the 5th Battalion of the 60th Foot. His rules and regulations for exercise of riflemen and light infantry were approved by the Commander in Chief and adopted in the army. On his return to England he continued to supervise the training of riflemen and formed three battalions of light infantry (68th Foot, 71st Foot and 85th Foot) and these he took to Walcheren. Also served in Canada May 1810 (in command of the garrison in Quebec) and in the American War of 1812 where he was in command of the garrison at Montreal. President of Upper Canada 1813. Returned to England in 1815. KCH.
Reference: Royal Military Calendar, Vol. 3, pp. 15–16.

ROTTON, Guy
Lieutenant. 20th (East Devonshire) Regiment of Foot.
Ledger stone: All Saints Churchyard, Weston, Bath, Somerset. (Photograph)

IN MEMORY OF / GUY ROTTON ESQ., / LATE CAPTAIN 17TH REGT. / WHO DEPARTED THIS LIFE AUGUST 16TH 1824 / IN THE THIRTY FIRST YEAR OF HIS AGE.

Ensign 7 Jul 1808. Lt 30 Mar 1809. Capt 17 Dec 1818. Capt 17th Foot 29 Apr 1824.

Served in the Peninsula Nov 1812 – Oct 1813. Present at Vittoria, and Pyrenees (wounded at Echalar 2 Aug 1813). Also served at Walcheren 1809.

ROUS, Hon. John Edward Cornwallis

Lieutenant and Captain. Coldstream Regiment of Foot Guards.
Memorial window: St Peter and St Paul's Church, Wangford, Suffolk. (Photograph)

TO THE GLORY OF ALMIGHTY GOD AND / IN AFFECTIONATE MEMORY OF JOHN EDWARD / CORNWALLIS ROUS EARL OF STRADBROOK / WHO DEPARTED THIS LIFE THE 27TH DAY OF JANR / 1886 AGED 91 YEARS. THIS WINDOW / DEDICATED BY HIS SORROWING WIDOW HIS / SON AND DAUGHTERS.

Ensign 28 Jun 1810. Lt and Capt 4 May 1814.

Served in the Peninsula. Present at Salamanca, Burgos, Vittoria, Bidassoa, Nivelle, Nive, Adour and Bayonne. Present at Quatre Bras where he was injured in an accident and unable to take part at Waterloo. Half pay 1818. Colonel East Suffolk Light Infantry Militia 1830–1844. MGS medal for Salamanca, Vittoria, Nivelle and Nive. Became 2nd Earl of Stradbrooke 1827. Lord Lieutenant of Suffolk 1844–1886. Developed his estate in Suffolk and devoted his time to his racing stables and packs of grey hounds from which several notable winners came in the nineteenth century. Died 27 Jan 1886.
Reference: Rous, John, A Guards Officer in the Peninsula: the Peninsular War letters of John Rous, edited by Ian Fletcher, 1992.

ROUS, Thomas Bates

Ensign. 1st Regiment of Foot Guards.
Box tomb: St Mary the Virgin's Churchyard, Llanwern, Monmouthshire, Wales. (Photograph)

SACRED TO THE MEMORY OF THOMAS BATES ROUS ESQ / OF COURT-YR-ALA, CO. / GLAMORGAN, / WHO DEPARTED THIS LIFE DEC 31ST 1850 AGED 66. / ………………..

Memorial tablet: St Michael and All Angels Church, Michaelston Le Pit, Glamorgan, Wales. (Photograph)

SACRED TO THE MEMORY OF / THOMAS BATES ROUS, ESQR / OF COURT YR-ALA CO:. GLAMORGAN, / WHO DEPARTED THIS LIFE, THE 31ST OF DECEMBER 1850, / AT LLANWERN, MONMOUTHSHIRE, AGED 66, / WHERE HE WAS INTERRED. / HE SERVED IN SPAIN UNDER SIR JOHN MOORE / IN THE GRENADIER GUARDS, / WAS WOUNDED AT CORUNNA IN 1809, / AND AFTERWARDS SERVED IN THE EXPEDITION TO WALCHEREN, / IN THE SAME YEAR. / THIS MONUMENT IS ERECTED / BY HIS AFFLICTED AND BEREAVED WIDOW.

Ensign 13 Nov 1804.

Served in the Peninsula with 3rd Battalion Oct 1808 – Jan 1809. Present at Corunna where he was wounded. Also served at Walcheren 1809. MGS medal for Corunna. Retired 24 Jan 1811.

ROUSE, John

Private. 95th Regiment of Foot.
Buried in Brompton Cemetery, London. (Chelsea In Pensioner)

Pte Oxford Militia. Pte 95th Foot 1 Apr 1810.

Served in the Peninsula 1810 – Apr 1814. Present at Busaco, Fuentes d'Onoro, Ciudad Rodrigo, Badajoz, Salamanca, Vittoria, Pyrenees, Nivelle, Nive and Toulouse. Present at Waterloo in Capt C. Beckwith's Company. Discharged 26 May 1818. MGS medal for Busaco, Fuentes d'Onoro, Ciudad

Rodrigo, Badajoz, Salamanca, Vittoria, Pyrenees, Nivelle, Nive and Toulouse. Died 16 Mar 1873 aged 92.

ROUTH, Randolph Isham

Deputy Commissary General. Commissariat Department.
Low monument: Kensal Green Cemetery, London. (14894/74 – 75/3 Square 77). (Photograph)

COMMISSARY-GENERAL SIR RANDOLPH ISHAM ROUTH KCB. / BORN POOLE, DORSET, 21 DECEMBER 1782. / DIED IN LONDON AT 19 DORSET SQUARE, 29 NOVEMBER 1858, AGED 75.

Asst Comm General 13 Nov 1805. Deputy Comm General 9 Mar 1812. Commissary General 15 Aug 1826.

Served in the Peninsula Jun 1810 – Dec 1813 (with 2nd Division Jun 1811 – Nov 1812 and 1st Division Jul – Dec 1813). Present at Busaco, Albuera and Nivelle. Present at Waterloo where he was senior Commissariat officer. Also served in the West Indies 1805, Walcheren 1809, West Indies 1822, Canada 1836–1841 and Ireland 1845–1848 (superintended famine relief during the potato famine). KCB Mar 1841. MGS medal for Busaco, Albuera and Nivelle. Author of *Observations on Commissariat Field Service and Home Defences, 2nd edn, 1852,* which became the standard work on the subject. Educated at Eton.
REFERENCE: *Dictionary of National Biography.*

ROWAN, Charles

Major. 52nd (Oxfordshire) Light Infantry Regiment of Foot.
Interred in Catacomb B (v168 c8), Kensal Green Cemetery, London.

Ensign 15 May 1797. Lt 15 May 1799. Capt 25 Jun 1803. Major 9 May 1811. Bt Lt Colonel 27 Apr 1812.

Served in the Peninsula with 1/52nd Aug 1808 – Jan 1809, Jul 1809 – May 1813 and Apr 1814. (Brigade Major 1 Brigade 3rd Division Jul 1809 – Feb 1810. Brigade Major Light Division Feb – Aug 1810. Brigade Major 2 Brigade Light Division Aug 1810 – Mar 1811. Assistant Adjutant General Light Division Mar 1811 – May 1813 and Apr 1814). Present at Corunna, Coa, Busaco, Pombal, Redinha, Casal Nova, Foz d'Arouce, Sabugal, Fuentes d'Onoro, Ciudad Rodrigo, Badajoz and Salamanca. Gold Medal for Ciudad Rodrigo, Badajoz and Salamanca. MGS medal for Corunna, Busaco and Fuentes d'Onoro. Present at Waterloo (wounded) and with the Army of Occupation. CB. Also served at Ferrol 1800, Sicily 1806 and the Baltic 1808. After the return of the regiment in 1818 they were mainly used for peace keeping in the Midlands owing to economic unrest. Rowan was appointed to the Committee to organise a Police Force set up by Sir Robert Peel, the Home Secretary in 1829. This was to ensure that the army did not have to deal with civil unrest. Rowan was able to organise this police force on military lines and became Chief Commissioner of the Metropolitan Police 1829–1850. KCB. Died 8 May 1852. Brother of Major William Rowan also in the 52nd Regiment.
REFERENCE: *Dictionary of National Biography. Gentleman's Magazine, Jul 1852, pp. 91–2. Annual Register, 1852, p. 279. Oxfordshire Light Infantry Chronicle, 1899, pp. 168–9.*

ROWAN, James

Captain. 1st (Royal Scots) Regiment of Foot.
Interred in Catacomb B 15391 (V168 C2), Kensal Green Cemetery, London.

Antrim Militia. Ensign 64th Foot 7 Feb 1800. Lt 11 Jan 1801. Capt 1st Foot 12 Apr 1807. Bt Major 1 Jun 1826. Portuguese Army: Capt 22nd Line 27 Jul 1810.

Served in the Peninsula with 1st Foot Oct 1808 – Jan 1809 and Apr – Jul 1810 and Portuguese Army Jul 1810 – Jul 1811. Retired from the Portuguese Army 17 Jul 1811. On Staff Jan 1812. Present at Corunna. Also served in the West Indies 1801–1807 (present at the Saints, St Lucia and Surinam), Walcheren 1809 (present at the siege of Flushing), North America 1812–1814 (DAAG. Present at Fort Erie) and Ireland 1817–1820. MGS medal for Corunna. Died Jul 1859.

ROWAN, William

Captain. 52nd (Oxfordshire) Light Infantry Regiment of Foot.
Low monument: Lansdown Cemetery, Bath, Somerset. (Photograph)

SACRED TO THE MEMORY OF / FIELD MARSHAL SIR WILLIAM ROWAN, / KNIGHT GRAND CROSS OF THE ORDER OF THE BATH / COLONEL OF THE 52ND REGIMENT OF LIGHT INFANTRY. / DIED THE 26TH SEPTEMBER 1879. / AGED 90.

Ensign 4 Nov 1803. Lt 15 Jun 1804. Capt 19 Oct 1808. Bt Major 3 Mar 1814. Bt Lt Colonel 21 Jan 1819. Major 58th Foot 27 Jul 1826. Bt Colonel 10 Jan 1837. Major General 9 Nov 1846. Lt General 20 Jun 1854. General 13 Aug 1862. Field Marshal 2 Jun 1877.

Served in the Peninsula Oct 1808 – Jan 1809, Mar – Jun 1811 (DAAG) and Apr 1813 – Apr 1814. Present at Vigo, Sabugal, Vittoria, Pyrenees, Vera, Bidassoa, Nivelle, Nive, Orthes, Tarbes and Toulouse. Present at Waterloo (wounded) and the Capture of Paris (appointed one of the commandants to govern Paris). CB. Also served in Sicily 1806–1807, Sweden 1808, Walcheren 1809 (present at the siege of Flushing) and Canada 1823–1829 (Civil and Military Secretary), 1832–1839 Military Secretary to Sir John Colborne who was Lt Governor of Upper Canada (present during the Canadian rebellion) and commanded Forces in Canada 1849–1855. MGS medal for Vittoria, Pyrenees, Nivelle, Nive, Orthes and Toulouse. KCB 1838. Colonel 19th Foot 15 Jun 1854. Colonel 52nd Foot 10 Mar 1861. Brother of Major Charles Rowan 52nd Foot. Grave restored by the Oxfordshire and Buckinghamshire Regimental Association.

REFERENCE: *Dictionary of National Biography. Milner, David, The lost warrior : Field Marshal Sir William Rowan, GCB, 52nd Regiment of Light Infantry, Waterloo Journal, Aug 1998, pp. 12–13. Annual Register, 1879, Part 2, p. 221. Oxfordshire Light Infantry Chronicle, 1899, pp. 168–9.*

ROWE, Benjamin

Captain. 50th (West Kent) Regiment of Foot.
Gravestone: Disused Graveyard at Up Park Camp, Kingston, Jamaica. West Indies. (M.I.)

"BT. MAJOR ROWE. DIED 3RD AUG 1819. AGED 34."

Lt 30 Oct 1802. Capt 26 Aug 1808. Bt Major 3 Mar 1814.

Served in the Peninsula Aug 1808 – Jan 1809 and Jul 1811 – Apr 1814. Present at Vimeiro, Corunna, Arroyo dos Molinos, Almarez, Alba de Tormes, Vittoria, Pyrenees, Nivelle, Nive, Garris, Orthes, Aire, Tarbes and Toulouse. Also served in Egypt 1801 and the West Indies 1819 where he died in a yellow fever epidemic in August 1819. Son-in-law of Paymaster John Montgomery 50th Foot.

ROWLAND, John

Captain. 32nd (Cornwall) Regiment of Foot.
Memorial: Clifton Hall, Bristol (Strangers) Burial Ground (Ancillary Cemetery to St Andrew's Parish Church), Bristol, Somerset. (M.I.)

"JOHN ROWLAND / LATE CAPTAIN 32ND FOOT / DIED OCT 1809 / FROM ILLNESS BROUGHT ON BY THE / MARCH WITH THE ARMY THROUGH / PORTUGAL AND SPAIN WITH / SIR JOHN MOORE"

Lt 1798. Capt 25 Jun 1803.

Served in the Peninsula Aug 1808 – Jan 1809. Present at Rolica, Vimeiro and Corunna. Died from the effects of retreat to Corunna.

ROWLING, John see POWLING, John

ROYCROFT, Robert

Private. 42nd (Royal Highland) Regiment of Foot.
Memorial Plaque: Shortland Cemetery, Thames, New Zealand. (Grave number 68). (Photograph)

R. ROYCROFT / NAPOLEONIC WARS PTE / 42ND REGT OF FOOT / DIED 18.10.1875 AGED 79 YRS

Pte 6 Sep 1814. Drummer 25 Dec 1821. Pte 25 Jun 1822.

Present at Waterloo in Capt John Campbell's Company and with the Army of Occupation. Also served in Gibraltar, Malta and Corfu. Remained in the Regiment for 25 years until 19 Apr 1839 when he was discharged with a pension of one shilling and two pence per day. In the 1830s there were schemes to settle ex-soldiers in Australia and New Zealand. Roycroft chose New Zealand and joined the New Zealand Fencibles in 1848. These men were given land in return for guard duties in various parts of the country. He settled first at Howick and then moved to Thames when the goldfield was opened in 1867. Died at Thames 18 Oct 1875 and was given a military funeral. In 1995 the Roycroft family rededicated the plaque as the original tombstone had disintegrated.
REFERENCE: *Northumberland and Durham Family History Society Journal, Summer 2008, Vol. 22, No. 2, p. 80.*

ROYLE, John Watson

Lieutenant. 52nd (Oxfordshire) Light Infantry Regiment of Foot.
Memorial tablet: St John the Baptist's Church, Aldford, Cheshire. (Photograph)

.... / ALSO IN MEMORY OF / LIEUT JOHN WATSON ROYLE .... / WHO / IN THE PRIME OF YOUTH / BELOVED BY HIS BROTHER OFFICERS AND / AS AFFECTIONATELY LAMENTED / BY HIS FAMILY / GLORIOUSLY FELL / AT THE ASSAULT AND CAPTURE / OF BADAJOS / VI APRIL MDCCCXII. / THE ABOVE WERE SONS OF THOS ROYLE ESQ / OF CHESTER AND MARGARET HIS WIFE.

Ensign 2 May 1810. Lt 5 Mar 1812.

Served in the Peninsula with 2/52nd Mar – May 1811 and 1/52nd Jun 1811 – Apr 1812. Present at Sabugal, Fuentes d'Onoro, Ciudad Rodrigo and Badajoz where he was killed at the assault 6 Apr 1812. Also known as Job Watson.

RUDD, John

Major. 77th (East Middlesex) Regiment.
Headstone: Auld Kirk, Ayr, Ayrshire, Scotland. Severely eroded. (Photograph)

SACRED TO THE MEMORY / OF / LIEUT-COL. JOHN RUDD CB. / DIED AT AYR / ON THE 17TH JANUARY 1827, / AGED 60 YEAR.S / FOR MANY YEARS / IN HIS MAJESTY'S 77TH REGIMENT / BOTH IN INDIA, AND IN / PORTUGAL AND SPAIN. / HE WAS AFTERWARD / INSPECTING FIELD OFFICER / OF THE / GLASGOW DISTRICT.

Volunteer 75th Foot 1788. Ensign 77th Foot 11 Apr 1792. Lt 25 Oct 1794. Capt 25 Jun 1803. Major 25 Jan 1810. Bt Lt Colonel 27 Apr 1812.

Served in the Peninsula Jul 1811 – Dec 1812 and Nov 1813 – Apr 1814. Present at El Bodon, Ciudad Rodrigo, Badajoz (severely wounded 26 Mar 1812 and Mentioned in Despatches) and Bayonne. CB. Also served as a volunteer in the 75th Foot in India. Present at Travengarry 1790, Seringapatam 1791–1792 (for these services he was recommended for an Ensigncy by Sir Robert Abercromby in 1792), the siege and

Capture of Fort Cochin 1795 and in Ceylon 1796 (present at the Capture of Colombo).
REFERENCE: *Royal Military Calendar, Vol. 4, pp. 413–14. Gentleman's Magazine, Feb 1827, p. 176. Rudd, Mary Amelia, Records of the Rudd family, 1920, pp. 256–7.*

RUDGE, Edward
2nd Assistant Surgeon. Ordnance Medical Department.
Headstone: St Peter and St Paul's Churchyard, Fakenham, Norfolk. (Photograph)

EDWARD RUDGE / DIED 29 NOVR 1854 / AGED 62 YEARS.

2nd Asst Surgeon 3 Dec 1812.

Served in the Peninsula 1812–1814. Present at Vittoria, San Sebastian, Nivelle and Nive. Present at Waterloo. MGS medal for Vittoria, San Sebastian, Nivelle and Nive. Half pay 1 Jun 1816.

RUDYERD, Charles William
Lieutenant Colonel. Royal Engineers.
Headstone: Trafalgar Cemetery, Gibraltar. (Photograph)

HERE / LIE THE REMAINS OF / LIEUT COLONEL RUDYERD / OF THE CORPS OF / ROYAL ENGINEERS / WHOSE VIRTUOUS LIFE / WAS TERMINATED / ON THE / 19TH OCTOBER 1845 / BY THE MALIGNANT FEVER / PREVALENT IN THIS / GARRISON

2nd Lt Royal Artillery 23 Jun 1793. 2nd Lt Royal Engineers 14 Jun 1793. Lt 1 Jun 1794. Capt-Lt 2 May 1800. 2nd Capt 19 Jul 1801. Capt 20 Jul 1804. Bt Major 1 Jan 1812. Lt Colonel 3 Mar 1812.

Served at Walcheren 1809. Also served in Flanders 1793–1795, the Helder 1799 and Gibraltar 1812 where he died 19 Oct 1813.

RUDYERD, Samuel
Captain. Royal Regiment of Artillery.
Ledger stone: St Hilda's Churchyard, Sneaton, near Whitby, Yorkshire. (East of church). (Photograph)

.... / ALSO OF THEIR SON / SAMUEL RUDYERD ESQ. / COLONEL OF THE / ROYAL ARTILLERY / WHO DEPARTED THIS LIFE / AT WHITBY JULY 19TH 1847

2nd Lt 15 Mar 1803. 1st Lt 12 Sep 1803. 2nd Capt 24 Mar 1809. Capt 29 Jul 1825. Bt Major 29 Jul 1830 Lt Colonel 10 Jan 1837. Colonel 9 Nov 1846.

Served in the Peninsula 1808. Present at Quatre Bras and Waterloo in Major Lloyd's Brigade. Also served on bomb vessels off the coast of France 1804, and the coast of Ceylon 1805–1812, North America 1814–1815 (present at New Orleans), St Helena 1821, Cape of Good Hope 1822 and the West Indies Dec 1831 – May 1834 and Dec 1839 – Jan 1843 (present in Jamaica).

RUMLEY, John
Lieutenant. 30th (Cambridgeshire) Regiment of Foot.
Memorial: Goomrapoondy, India.

Ensign 7 Jun 1809. Lt 25 Jun 1811.

Served in the Peninsula Apr 1810 – Jun 1813. Present at Tarifa, Cadiz, Sabugal, Fuentes d'Onoro, Barba del Puerco, Ciudad Rodrigo, Badajoz, Salamanca, Burgos and retreat from Burgos (present at Villa Muriel where he was severely wounded 25 Oct 1813). Also served in the Netherlands 1814 and at Waterloo where he commanded the Light Company (severely wounded). After the war he went with the regiment to India where he died 16 May 1819. Served in every action fought by the 30th Foot in the Peninsula. 'He was so mild, so good, so gallant a fellow that the whole regiment loved him' (Macready).

RUSSELL, Alexander
Sergeant. 83rd Regiment of Foot.
Gravestone: Galle Face Burial Ground, Colombo, Ceylon. (Burial ground is no longer extant). (M.I.)

"HERE LIES THE BODY OF ALEXANDER RUSSELL, SERGEANT IN THE 83RD REGT., WHO WAS BORN IN NEW MONKLAND IN THE COUNTY OF LANARK, RESIDED SOME YEARS IN HUNTLEY, ABERDEENSHIRE, AND DIED ON THE 1ST OF JUNE, 1818. HE HAD SERVED IN SPAIN AND PORTUGAL. HE WAS WOUNDED AT BADAJOS, AND WAS PRESENT IN ALMOST EVERY BATTLE WON BY THE DUKE OF WELLINGTON. FIGHTING FOR HIS COUNTRY LIKE A BRAVE SOLDIER, HE RECEIVED A MORTAL WOUND AT PANELLA, AND HE DIED AT COLOMBO LIKE A GOOD CHRISTIAN."

Served in the Peninsular Apr 1809 – Apr 1814. Present at Talavera, Busaco, Fuentes d'Onoro, Ciodad Rodrigo, Badajoz (wounded), Salamanca, Vittoria, Pyrenees, Nivelle, Nive, Orthes and Toulouse. Also served in Ceylon 1817 (present in the Kandian War 1817–1818 where he was severely wounded at Panella and died from his wounds 1 Jan 1818).

RUSSELL, William
Captain. 20th (East Devonshire) Regiment of Foot.
Buried in Christ Church Cathedral Churchyard, Newcastle, New South Wales, Australia. (Burial record)

Lt Derby Milita 1798. Ensign 20th Foot 10 Aug 1799. Lt 29 Oct 1799. Capt 21 Jan 1808. Bt Major 3 Mar 1814.

Served in the Peninsula Aug 1808 – Jan 1809 and Nov 1812 – Apr 1814. Present at Vimeiro, Corunna, Vittoria, Pyrenees, Nivelle, Nive, Orthes (commanded the battalion where he was wounded and awarded Bt Majority) and Toulouse. Gold Medal for Orthes and Toulouse. Also served in Egypt 1801, Sicily 1806 (present at Maida where he took command of the Light Company on the death of Capt McLeod) and Walcheren 1809. MGS medal for Egypt, Maida, Vimeiro, Corunna, Vittoria, Pyrenees, Nivelle and Nive. Half pay 11 Dec 1817. Emigrated to Australia with his family in 1837 where he acquired 1,000 acres of land which he called Orthes after the battle. 'Was as gallant an officer as ever drew a sword.'

RUTHERFORD, James
Lieutenant. 94th Regiment of Foot.
Headstone: St Michael's Churchyard, Dumfries, Scotland. (Photograph)

SACRED / TO THE MEMORY OF / NANCY ROBERTSON, WIFE OF / CAPTN JAMES RUTHERFORD, / OF THE OLD 94TH REGT SCOTCH BRIGADE / WHO DIED IN DUMFRIES, 29TH NOVR 1807, / AGED ** YEARS. / AND OF THE ABOVE / CAPTN JAMES RUTHERFORD / WHO DIED IN LIVERPOOL / ON THE 25TH FEBY 1875 AGED 86 YEARS. / ....

Ensign 15 Feb 1810. Lt 27 Oct 1814.

Served in the Peninsula Jun 1810 – Sep 1811 and Apr 1813 – Apr 1814. Present at Cadiz, Redinha, Casal Nova, Foz d'Arouce, Sabugal, Fuentes d'Onoro, second siege of Badajoz, Vittoria, Pyrenees, Nivelle, Nive, Orthes, Vic Bigorre and Toulouse. Half pay 15 Jun 1815. Later became Barrack Master at Newcastle upon Tyne. MGS medal for Fuentes d'Onoro, Vittoria, Pyrenees, Nivelle, Nive, Orthes and Toulouse.

RUTHERFORD, William Henry
Lieutenant. 88th (Connaught Rangers) Regiment of Foot.
Buried in (Catacomb B 4307 Public Vault 23), Kensal Green Cemetery, London.

Ensign 1 Sep 1808. Lt 22 Nov 1810. Capt 14 May 1829. Major 10 Aug 1839.

Served in the Peninsula with 2/88th Jan 1810 – Jun 1811 and with 1/88th Oct 1813 – Apr 1814. Present at Cadiz, Sabugal, Fuentes d'Onoro, Nivelle, Nive, Orthes, Vic Bigorre and Toulouse. Served with the Army of Occupation until 1817. Also served in North America 1814–1815 and the Ionian Islands 1825–1836. Half pay 1 Nov 1839. Died Jan 1844 aged 58.

RUTLEDGE, John
Sergeant. 95th Regiment of Foot.
Headstone: Holy Trinity Cathedral Churchyard, Elgin, Morayshire, Scotland. (Photograph)

SACRED / TO / THE MEMORY / OF COLOUR SERGEANT / JOHN RUTLEDGE, / GOVERNOR, / OF THE ELGIN COUNTY PRISON / FOR / A PERIOD OF THIRTY YEARS / WHO DIED AT ELGIN ON THE / 30TH DAY OF DECEMBER 1861 / IN THE 70TH YEAR OF HIS AGE. / ………………..

Pte 17 Jun 1807. Cpl 25 Mar 1813. Sgt 10 Jun 1814. Cpl 19 Apr 1819. Pte 28 Feb 1820. Cpl 10 Nov 1822. Sgt 25 Apr 1825. Colour Sgt 25 Dec 1825. Sgt 25 Sep 1827. Colour Sgt 25 Mar 1830.

Served in the Peninsula 1808 – Jan 1809 and Feb 1810 – Apr 1814. Present at Corunna, Barrosa (wounded), Tarifa, Vittoria, Pyrenees (wounded at Vera), Nivelle, Nive, Orthes, Tarbes and Toulouse. Present at Waterloo in Capt G. Miller's Company where he was wounded. Also served at Copenhagen 1807 and Walcheren 1809 (present at the siege of Flushing). MGS medal for Corunna, Barrosa, Vittoria, Pyrenees, Nivelle, Nive, Orthes and Toulouse. Governor of Elgin Prison 1831 and held the post for 30 years.
Reference: Obit. Forres Gazette. 1 Jan 1862.

RYAN, Thomas
Lieutenant. 50th (West Kent) Regiment of Foot.
Gravestone: No. 4 Cemetery, Kasauli, Ambala District, India. (M.I.)

"SACRED TO THE MEMORY OF LIEUTENANT COLONEL THOMAS RYAN, CB AND KH / OF HER MAJESTY'S 50TH REGIMENT WHO DIED AT KASSAULIE / ON THE 9TH APRIL 1846, OF A WOUND RECEIVED AT THE BATTLE / OF SOBRAON. THIS TABLET IS PLACED OVER THE REMAINS OF / THIS LAMENTED COMRADE BY HIS / BROTHER OFFICERS AS A / TOKEN OF THEIR RESPECT AND ESTEEM."

Ensign 104th Foot 10 Oct 1805. Lt 50th Foot 28 Apr 1808. Capt 30 Sep 1819. Major 13 Aug 1830. Bt Lt Colonel 30 Apr 1844.

Served in the Peninsula Sep 1810 – Apr 1814. Present at the Lines of Torres Vedras, Sobral and Fuentes d'Onoro (severely wounded and taken prisoner until Apr 1814). Also served at Walcheren 1809, Jamaica 1819–1827, Australia 1834–1840 (commanded troops in northern Van Diemen's Land 1835–1839 and Commandant of Norfolk Island 1839–1840) and India 1841–1846 (in command of 50th Foot in the first Sikh War, present at Maharajpore where he was awarded Bronze Star). Took part in the whole of the Sutlej campaign (present at Mudki, Ferozeshah where he commanded 2 Brigade, Aliwal and Sobraon where he was severely wounded and died of his wounds at Kussowlie 9 Apr 1846). KH 1834. Awarded CB 3 Apr 1846 but notification did not reach India until after his death.
Reference: Gentleman's Magazine, Aug 1846, p. 205. Australian Dictionary of Biography.

RYLANCE, Thomas
Captain. 43rd (Monmouthshire) Light Infantry Regiment of Foot.
Ledger stone: St Mary's Churchyard, Disley, Cheshire. (Photograph)

HERE LIETH THE BODY OF / ………………… / ALSO OF ELIZABETH, THE BELOVED WIFE OF / EDWARD GIBSON, AND ONLY CHILD OF THE LATE / CAPTAIN RYLANCE, OF H. M. 43RD REGT LIGHT INFANTRY / …………………

Ensign 6 Feb 1805. Lt 10 Dec 1805. Capt 14 May 1812.

Served in the Peninsula with 1/43rd Oct 1808 – Jan 1809 and Jul 1809 – Jun 1811. Present at Vigo, Coa, Busaco, Redinha, Casal Nova, Foz d'Arouce, and Sabugal where he was severely wounded. Also served in the Baltic 1807. Lost at sea Dec 1823 on passage home from Gibraltar.

SADLEIR, William
Lieutenant. 58th (Rutlandshire) Regiment of Foot.
Brass Memorial tablet: St Mary the Virgin Church, Carisbrooke, Isle of Wight. (Photograph)

SACRED / TO THE MEMORY OF / COLONEL WILLIAM SADLEIR / LATE OF THE 4TH KINGS OWN REGIMENT / WHO DIED AT CARISBROOKE / FEBRUARY 26TH 1863 / AGED 71 YEARS. / ………………

Ensign 2 Apr 1807. Lt 4 May 1809. Capt 25 Aug 1825. Major 4th Foot 4 Feb 1838. Bt Lt Colonel 11 Nov 1851. Colonel 1 Feb 1856.

Served in the Peninsula Aug 1812 – Apr 1814. Served on the East coast of Spain (present at Castalla and siege of Tarragona). Served with the Army of Occupation 1815–1818. Also served in Sicily 1808–1812 (present at the Capture of Ischia and Procida), North America 1814–1815 (present at Plattsburgh), Crimea 1854–1855 (present at Inkermann and the siege of Sebastopol). One of the oldest officers in the Crimea and awarded medal with two clasps. Died 1863 from an illness contracted in the trenches after 56 years service.

SAFFE, August von
Captain. 1st Line Battalion, King's German Legion.
Named on the Regimental Memorial: La Haye Sainte, Waterloo. (Photograph)
Named on the Waterloo Column, Hanover, Germany. (Photograph)

Lt 19 Aug 1805. Capt 11 Mar 1812.

Served in the Peninsula Dec 1808 – May 1812. Present at Douro, Talavera (wounded), Busaco, Fuentes d'Onoro, Ciudad Rodrigo, Moriscos and Salamanca. Present at Waterloo where he was killed. Promoted to Major during the battle, but the promotion did not reach him until after his death. Also served at Hanover 1805, Sicily 1806–1807, the Baltic 1807–1808, North Germany 1813–1814 and the Netherlands 1814.

ST AURIN, J. D. E.
Captain. 20th (East Devonshire) Regiment of Foot.
Named on the Memorial: St Andrew's Church (now Musée Historique), Biarritz, France. (Photograph)

Lt 29 Apr 1808. Capt 21 Oct 1813.

Served in the Peninsula Aug 1808 – Jan 1809 and Apr 1813 – Feb 1814. Present at Vimeiro, Corunna, Vittoria, Pyrenees, Nivelle, Nive and Orthes where he was killed 27 Feb 1814. Also served at Walcheren 1809.

ST CLAIR, Thomas Staunton
Captain. 1st (Royal Scots) Regiment of Foot.
Interred in Catacomb B (v75 c16), Kensal Green Cemetery, London.

Ensign 12 Aug 1803. Lt 6 Aug 1804. Capt 30 Sep 1807. Bt Major 2 Jun 1814. Bt Lt Col 4 Sep 1817. Major 94th Foot 29 Jun 1826. Lt Colonel (unattached) 9 Dec 1828. Bt Colonel 10 Jan 1837. Major General 9 Nov 1846. Portuguese Army: Major 21st Line 22 Jun 1810. Lt Colonel 5 Caçadores 27 Aug 1813.

Served in the Peninsula with 1st Foot Apr – Jun 1810 and Portuguese Army Jun 1810 – Apr 1814. Present at Busaco, Pombal, Sabugal, Fuentes d'Onoro, second siege of Badajoz, Nivelle, Nive (Mentioned in Beresford's Despatches) and Bayonne. Gold Medal for Nive. MGS medal for Busaco, Fuentes d'Onoro and Nivelle. CB. After the war he returned to Portugal until 1818, where he was appointed Colonel 7th Portuguese Regiment. KH 1834. Also served in the West Indies 1805–1808, Walcheren 1809 (present at the siege of Flushing) and Gibraltar 1827. Author of *A residence in the West Indies and America, with a narrative of the expedition to the Island of Walcheren*, 2 vols, 1834. Talented artist, published *A series of views of the principal occurrences of the campaign in Spain and Portugal – 12 coloured plates from the drawings of Lt Col St Clair*, 1812–1813. Died 5 Nov 1847.

Reference: Feibel, Robert M., Major General Thomas Staunton St Clair, Journal of the Society for Army Historical Research, Vol. 48, No. 193, Spring 1970, pp. 29–34. Gentleman's Magazine, Dec 1847, pp. 639–40. Annual Register, 1847, Appx, p. 259.

ST JOHN, Charles
Assistant Surgeon. 58th (Rutlandshire) Regiment of Foot.
Tombstone: Ambala Cemetery, India. (M.I.)

"SACRED TO THE MEMORY OF CHARLES ST JOHN MD. LATE INSPECTOR GENERAL H. M. HOSPITALS IN INDIA WHO DIED AT UMBALLA ON 12TH SEPTEMBER 1853 IN THE 63RD YEAR OF HIS AGE. THIS TOMB IS ERECTED BY THE MEMBERS OF THE MEDICAL DEPARTMENT WHO HAD SERVED WITH HIM IN INDIA &C AS A TOKEN OF THE ESTEEM IN WHICH HE WAS HELD BY THEM."

Hospital Mate 8 Aug 1811. Asst Surgeon 58th Foot 3 Sep 1812. Surgeon 61st Foot 14 Feb 1822. Staff Surgeon 9 Dec 1836. Asst Inspector General of Hospitals 4 Jan 1839. Deputy Inspector General 20 Oct 1843. Inspector General of Hospitals in India 19 Jul 1850.

Served in the Peninsula Sep 1811 – Apr 1814. Present at Castalla, Tarragona, Nivelle and Orthes. Present at the Capture of Paris and with the Army of Occupation in 1815. Also served in Canada 1814, Jamaica 1816–1822, Ireland 1822, Ceylon 1822 and India 1846 where he died at Ambala 12 Sep 1853. MD Edinburgh 1823.

ST JOHN, Henry Joseph
Ensign. 1st Regiment of Foot Guards.
Memorial tablet: St Mary the Virgin's Church, Hampton-on-Thames, London. (Photograph)

TO THE BELOVED MEMORY OF THE KINDEST HUSBAND AND FATHER / HENRY JOSEPH ST JOHN, / FORMERLY OF THE GRENADIER GUARDS. / HE WAS BORN JANUARY 15TH 1799, / AND DIED AT HAMPTON COURT PALACE JANUARY 2ND 1857. / (VERSE)

Ensign 25 Nov 1814.

Present at Waterloo. Half pay 3 Jan 1822.

SALL, William
Captain. 47th (Lancashire) Regiment of Foot.
Headstone: Old Churchyard, Spital, Windsor, Berkshire. (Photograph)

SACRED / TO THE MEMORY OF / COLONEL SALL / DIED 5 MAY 1862 / ********** / AGED 90 YEARS.

Ensign 30 Oct 1794. Lt 26 Nov 1794. Capt 2 Jul 1812. Bt Major 4 Jun 1814. Bt Lt Colonel 22 Jul 1830. Bt Colonel 28 Nov 1854.

Served in the Peninsula 1813 – Apr 1814. Present at Bayonne and the Sortie from Bayonne. Also served in South America 1807 (present at Montevideo) and Newfoundland. Commanded the Royal Newfoundland Veteran Companies and was made Lt Governor of Newfoundland. KH 1837. Military Knight of Windsor 1849.

SALMON, Thomas
Captain. 7th (Royal Fusiliers) Regiment of Foot.
Memorial tablet: All Saints' Church, Hollingbourne, near Maidstone, Kent. (Photograph)

TO THE MEMORY OF / ROBERT SALMON / A MIDSHIPMAN IN THE ROYAL NAVY / WHO DIED NEAR THE ISLAND OF CEYLON / FEBRUARY 1782. / AGED 18 YEARS. / ALSO OF / THOMAS, HIS YOUNGEST BROTHER / CAPTAIN IN THE 7TH REGT OF ROYAL FUSILIERS, / WHO DIED AT BELEM NEAR LISBON. / 1ST FEBRUARY 1811. / AGED 41 YEARS.

Ensign 9th Foot 26 Aug 1799. Lt 85th Foot 21 May 1801. Capt 7th Foot 21 Mar 1805.

Served in the Peninsula with 1/7th Oct 1810 – Jan 1811. Also served at Martinique 1809. Died in Lisbon 31 Jan 1811.

SALTOUN, Alexander George Fraser, Lord
Captain and Lieutenant Colonel. 1st Regiment of Foot Guards.
Mausoleum: Cluny Old Churchyard, Aberdeenshire, Scotland. (Photograph)
Memorial: Royal Military Chapel, Wellington Barracks, London. (M.I.) (Destroyed by a Flying Bomb 1944)

"IN MEMORY OF LIEUTENANT-GENERAL ALEXANDER GEORGE FRASER, LORD SALTOUN, K.T. K.C.B., G.C.H., KNIGHT OF MARIA THERESA OF AUSTRIA AND ST GEORGE OF RUSSIA. BORN, APRIL 22ND, 1785; DIED, AUGUST 18TH, 1853. FIRST OR GRENADIER GUARDS FROM 1804 TO 1837. HE TOOK PART IN THE EXPEDITION TO SICILY, THE BATTLE OF CORUNNA, THE WALCHEREN EXPEDITION, THE DEFENCE OF CADIZ, THE CAPTURE OF SEVILLE, AND IN THE ACTIONS OF THE GUARDS IN THE SOUTH OF FRANCE, 1813–14. HE COMMANDED THE LIGHT COMPANIES OF THE 1ST BRIGADE OF GUARDS AT QUATRE BRAS AND AT THE DEFENCE OF HOUGOUMONT; AND THE 3RD BATTALION, 1ST GUARDS, IN THE DEFEAT OF THE GRENADIERS OF THE OLD IMPERIAL GUARD AT THE BATTLE OF WATERLOO; AND HE LED THE ATTACK AT THE STORMING OF THE MAIDEN FORTRESS OF PERONNE. HE SERVED AS MAJOR-GENERAL IN THE WAR WITH CHINA, 1841–1842. PLACED BY HIS NEPHEW, ALEXANDER LORD SALTOUN."

Coat of Arms: St Peter's Church, Fraserborough, Aberdeenshire, Scotland.

Ensign 91st Foot 28 Apr 1802. Lt 35th Foot 2 Sep 1802. Lt 42nd Foot 25 Jun 1803. Capt 15 Sep 1804. Lt and Capt 1st Foot Guards 23 Nov 1804. Capt and Lt Colonel 25 Dec 1813. Bt Colonel 27 May 1825. Major 17 Nov 1825. Major General 10 Jan 1837. Lt General 9 Nov 1846.

Served in the Peninsula with 3rd Battalion Oct 1808 – Jan 1809, May 1811 – Feb 1813 and May 1813 – Apr 1814. Present at Corunna, Cadiz, Seville, Bidassoa, Nivelle, Nive, Adour, Bayonne and the Sortie from Bayonne. Present at Waterloo in command of the regiments outside Hougoumont in the wood and orchard. Later took part in the final charge of the Guards to defeat the Imperial Guard where he was wounded. Had four horses killed under him at Waterloo. Present at the storming of Peronne (wounded). Also served in Sicily 1806–1807, Walcheren 1809, China 1841–1842 (present in the first Opium War where he commanded a brigade at the attack and Capture of Chin Kiang Foo – awarded medal). Colonel 55th Foot 27 Feb 1846. Colonel 2nd Foot 7 Aug 1846. KT. KCB. GCH. KMT. KSTG. MGS medal for Corunna, Nivelle and Nive. Described by Wellington as a 'pattern to the army both as a man and soldier'. Died 18 Aug 1853.

REFERENCE: *Saltoun, Alexander, Waterloo campaign letters written by Lieutenant Colonel Alexander, Lord Saltoun, 1st Foot Guards 1815, edited by Gareth Glover, 2010. Dictionary of National Biography (Under Fraser). Gentleman's Magazine, Oct 1853, pp. 405–6. (Under Saltion). Annual Register, 1853, Appx, pp. 242–3. (Under Saltoun).*

SALVIN, Jeffrey

Lieutenant. 4th (King's Own) Regiment of Foot.

Memorial tablet: St Augustine of Canterbury Church, Alston, Cumbria. (Photograph)

TO THE MEMORY OF / JEFFERY SALVIN ESQUIRE / FORMERLY CAPTAIN / IN THE 4TH REGIMENT OF INFANTRY / WHO DEPARTED THIS LIFE SUDDENLY / NOVEMBER 29TH 1850 AGED 77 YEARS. / THIS MONUMENT / ERECTED BY HIS AFFECTIONATE TWIN BROTHER / HUGH SALVIN / VICAR OF THIS CHURCH / WITH WHOM AFTER MANY YEARS OF SEPARATION / THE LAST FEW YEARS OF HIS LIFE WERE PASSED.

Ensign 7th Battalion of Reserve 27 Mar 1804. Lieutenant 4th Foot 5 Feb 1805.

Served in the Peninsula with 1/4th Aug 1808 – Jan 1809 and Nov 1810 – Apr 1814. Present at Corunna, Fuentes d'Onoro, Barba del Puerco, Badajoz, Salamanca (wounded), retreat from Burgos (present at Villa Muriel), Vittoria, San Sebastian (wounded), Bidassoa, Nivelle (wounded) and Bayonne. Also served at Walcheren 1809 and North America 1814.

SALWEY, Henry

Ensign. Coldstream Regiment of Foot Guards.

Memorial tablet: St Bartholomew's Church, Richards Castle, Shropshire. (Photograph)

IN MEMORY OF HENRY SALWEY / COLONEL COLDSTREAM GUARDS. THIRD SON / OF THE LATE THEOPHILUS RICHARD SALWEY ESQ. / OF THE LODGE IN THIS PARISH. / HE SERVED WITH THE DUKE OF WELLINGTON / IN SPAIN, FRANCE AND HOLLAND 1813. 14. 15 AND / WAS PRESENT AT NEARLY ALL THE ACTIONS IN / THE PYRENEES, THE CROSSING OF THE BIDASSOA, / THE CAPTURE OF ST JEAN DE LUZ, THE BATTLE / OF THE NIVELLE, THE HEIGHTS OF BIDART, / THE CROSSING OF THE ADOUR, THE INVESTMENT / OF BAYONNE, AND THE REPULSE OF THE SORTIE. / HE REPRESENTED LUDLOW IN PARLIAMENT 1837–41 / AND 1847–52. BORN 20 JANY. 1794. DIED AT HIS / RESIDENCE RUNNYMEDE PARK EGHAM 10TH MARCH 1874.

Ensign 13 Jun 1811. Lt and Capt 20 Jul 1815. Capt and Lt Colonel 15 Feb 1827.

Served in the Peninsula Oct 1813 – Apr 1814. Present at Bidassoa, Nivelle, Nive, Adour and Bayonne. MGS medal for Nivelle and Nive. Half pay 1829. Member of Parliament for Ludlow 1837–1841 and 1847–1852. Educated at Eton.

SAMUEL, John
Sergeant. 1st (Royal Scots) Regiment of Foot.
Headstone: St David's Churchyard, Carmarthen, Wales. (Photograph)

IN / MEMORY OF / SERGEANT JOHN SAMUEL, / OF THE 1ST BATT. 1ST ROYAL REGIMENT OF / FOOT, WHO WAS BORN AT LLANGUNNOR IN / 1788, AND DIED AT CARMARTHEN, ON / OCTOBER 16TH 1874. / HE SERVED IN THE ARMY 25 YEARS, WAS / WOUNDED AT SAN SEBASTIAN, ON JULY 25TH / 1813, AND AT WATERLOO JUNE 18TH 1815. / ON THE CENTENARY OF WATERLOO, A WREATH / WAS LAID ON HIS GRAVE, BY / GENERAL SIR JAMES HILLS-JOHNES, V.C., / AND THIS STONE WAS ERECTED BY THE / VICAR, REV. GRIFFITH THOMAS, AND / D. DAVIES, SCULPTOR.

Pte Carmarthen Fusiliers 1807. Pte 1st Foot 1811.

Served in the Peninsula. Present at Salamanca, Vittoria and San Sebastian (wounded). Present at Waterloo where he was wounded. MGS medal for Salamanca and Vittoria. Discharged 8 Oct 1833.
Reference: Elmer, Bob, Rest in peace: Sgt John Samuel, Waterloo Journal, Dec 1993, p. 35.

SANDELL, Peter
Private. 73rd (Highland) Regiment of Foot.
Obelisk: Nunhead Cemetery, London. Inscription illegible. (Grave number 16888).

Present at Waterloo where he was wounded in Capt H. B. Lynch's Company. Afterwards resident in St Saviour's Workhouse, Southwark. Became friends there with James Lambourne, another Waterloo veteran. Buried in Nunhead Cemetery 22 Jul 1882, aged 97 years. The obelisk was found toppled over in a survey by the Friends of Nunhead Cemetery in 1996. Inscription illegible, but words 'Peter Sendells [sic], Waterloo Veteran' and a reference to the interest of Queen Victoria who was one of the contributors to the public appeal for the erection of a memorial. Sandell is buried below his old friend James Lambourne who resided at St Saviour's Workhouse with him. The grave was re-opened 12 Dec 1885 to inter James Lambourne.
Reference: Lagden, Alan and John Sly. 2/73rd at Waterloo. 2nd edn 1998, pp. 201–3.

SANDHAM, Charles Freeman
Captain. Royal Artillery.
Low monument: St Mary's Churchyard, Washington, near Worthing, Sussex. (Near north wall). (Photograph)

MAJOR CHARLES FREEMAN SANDHAM / OF ROWDELL / BORN 12 OCT 1782 DIED 14TH FEB 1869

Memorial window with brass plate below: St Mary's Church, Washington, near Worthing, Sussex. (Photograph)

IN MEMORY OF CHARLES FREEMAN SANDHAM / AND MARIA HIS WIFE / DEDICATED BY THEIR CHILDREN / FEAST OF PURIFICATION 1871

2nd Lt 27 Oct 1798. 1st Lt 7 Nov 1800. 2nd Capt 1 Jun 1806. Capt 14 Feb 1814. Bt Major 12 Aug 1819.

Served in the Peninsula Aug 1808 – Jan 1809. Present in the Corunna campaign. Present at Waterloo. The first shot fired by the Allied artillery was fired by Sandham's brigade. Also served at the Helder 1799, Copenhagen 1807, Walcheren 1809 and the Netherlands 1814–1815. Half pay 7 Jun 1822.

SANDILANDS, Patrick

Lieutenant and Captain. Coldstream Regiment of Foot Guards.
Headstone laid flat: St Luke's Churchyard, Charlton, Kent. (Grave S 7). (Photograph)

IN MEMORY OF / L^{T} COL^{L} PATRICK SANDILANDS / WHO DIED AT WOOLWICH / JANUARY 5 1847 / IN HIS 59TH YEAR.

Ensign 2 May 1803. Lt and Capt 19 Jul 1810.

Served in the Peninsula Mar – Nov 1809 and Mar 1812 – Apr 1814. Present at Douro, Talavera (severely wounded and taken prisoner until Nov 1809), Salamanca, Burgos, Vittoria, Bidassoa, Nivelle, Nive, Adour and Bayonne.

SANDILANDS, Philip

1st Lieutenant. Royal Artillery.
Low monument: St Peter and St Paul's Churchyard, Saltwood, Hythe, Kent. (Photograph)

TO THE MEMORY OF / L^{T} GENERAL PHILIP SANDILANDS, ROYAL ARTILLERY, / JUSTICE OF THE PEACE AND DEPUTY LIEUTENANT FOR THE COUNTY OF KENT, / ALSO JUSTICE OF THE PEACE FOR THE BOROUGH OF HYTHE, / BORN AT NUTHILL, PARISH OF FALKLAND, FIFESHIRE, 9TH SEP^{T} 1790, / DIED AT HYTHE, 30TH OCTOBER 1869

2nd Lt 4 Oct 1806. 1st Lt 1 Feb 1808. 2nd Capt 29 Jul 1825. Capt 4 Jun 1836. Bt Major 28 Jun 1838. Lt Colonel 1 Apr 1846. Bt Colonel 20 Jun 1854. Major General 26 Oct 1858. Lt General 24 Aug 1866.

Present at Quatre Bras where he covered the retreat and at Waterloo in Capt Norman Ramsay's Troop. After Ramsay had been killed and Alexander Macdonald and William Brereton wounded, Sandilands was left in command of the troop. Served with the Army of Occupation until Oct 1818. Also served at Walcheren 1809 and Malta 1827–1828. Retired on full pay 23 Jun 1846. Deputy Lieutenant for Kent and Justice of the Peace for Hythe.

SANDROCK, John Henry

Sergeant. 1st Regiment of Foot Guards.
Memorial: Hammersmith Churchyard, London. (M.I.)

TO THE MEMORY OF / JOHN HENRY SANDROCK / FORMERLY PAY SERGEANT / IN THE GRENADIER GUARDS / AND LATE SUPERINTENDENT / OF THE METROPOLITAN POLICE / WHO DEPARTED THIS LIFE / MAY 22ND 1849 / AGED 65. / HE WAS BY BIRTH A NATIVE OF HOPE CAPEL / AND BEING SHIPWRECKED IN EARLY LIFE / ON THE COAST OF SCOTLAND / HE ENTERED THE BRITISH ARMY IN 1807 / AND FOUGHT IN THE BATTLES OF CORUNNA / WALCHEREN, STORMING OF SEVILLE / NIVE, NIVELLE, BAYONNE, QUATRE BRAS / WATERLOO, STORMING OF PERONNE / TO THE SURRENDER OF PARIS. / A FEW PRIVATE FRIENDS HAVE UNITED / TO PAY THIS TRIBUTE TO HIS MEMORY. / J. A. S. 1849. G. A. MILLWOOD / HAMMERSMITH

Pte 11 May 1807. Cpl 1811. Sgt 1814.

Served in the Peninsula Oct 1808 – Jan 1809 and May 1811 – Apr 1814. Present at Corunna, Seville, Nive, Nivelle and Bayonne. Present at Waterloo in Lt Colonel E. Stables's Company, the siege of Peronne, Capture of Paris and with the Army of Occupation. Also served at Walcheren 1809 (present at the siege of Flushing). Discharged 11 Oct 1826.

Born near Hanover in 1785. Joined the navy but was shipwrecked off the coast of Scotland, and so decided to join the army by enlisting in the 1st Foot Guards 1807. Joined the Metropolitan Police Force 1829 and rose to be Superintendent of 'F' Division at Bow Street. Retired from the force in 1844 on a pension of £125 per annum. MGS medal for Corunna, Nivelle and Nive.

SANDS, Thomas
Sergeant. 1st (King's) Dragoon Guards.
Headstone: General Cemetery, Sharrowvale, Sheffield, Yorkshire. (On wall inside the Montague Street entrance. Buried in Grave number RR 79). (Photograph)

TO THE MEMORY OF / PERMANENT SERGEANT, / THOMAS SANDS, / OF THE SHEFFIELD SQUADRON OF THE FIRST / WEST YORKSHIRE YEOMAN CAVALRY, / WHO DIED 29TH MARCH 1850, / AGED 67 YEARS, / HAVING SERVED IN THE ABOVE REGIMENT, / UPWARDS OF 22 YEARS: / HE ALSO SERVED 24 YEARS / IN KING'S DRAGOON GUARDS, / AND HIGHLY DISTINGUISHED HIMSELF / AT THE EVER / MEMORABLE BATTLE OF WATERLOO. / THIS STONE IS ERECTED / BY THE NON-COMMISSIONED OFFICERS / AND PRIVATES OF THE SHEFFIELD SQUADRON / OF FIRST WEST YORKSHIRE YEOMAN CAVALRY.

Pte 20 May 1805.

Served with the regiment until 1827. Present at Waterloo and at the Capture of Paris. After retiring from the regiment he joined the Sheffield Squadron of the 1st West Yorkshire Yeomen Cavalry, becoming their Permanent Sergeant from 1827–1849.

SANDYS, Lord Arthur Moyse William Hill 2nd Baron see Hill, Lord Arthur Moyse William

SANDYS, Edwin W. T.
Captain. 12th (Prince of Wales's) Regiment of Light Dragoons.
Named on the Regimental Memorial: St Joseph's Church, Waterloo. (Photograph)

Cornet 1st Lt Dragoons 1805. Lt 4 Aug 1807. Lt 4th Garrison Battalion 20 Aug 1808. Capt 11th Foot 17 Sep 1808. Capt 12th Lt Dragoons 30 Mar 1809.

Served in the Peninsula Jun 1811 – Nov 1812 and Apr 1813 – Apr 1814. Present at Aldea de Ponte, Llerena, Castrejon, Salamanca, Venta del Poza, Nivelle, Nive, Adour and Bordeaux. Present at Waterloo where he was severely wounded and died later of his wounds. Educated at Eton.

SANDYS, Myles
Lieutenant. 29th (Worcestershire) Regiment of Foot.
Buried in the family vault: St Michael and All Angels' Churchyard, Hawkshead, Cumbria. (Photograph)

Ensign 29th Foot 1 Dec 1808. Lt 5 Apr 1810. Lt 11th Lt Dragoons 24 Jul 1817.

Served in the Peninsula with 29th Foot May 1809 – Nov 1811 and Apr 1813 – Feb 1814. Present at Talavera, Busaco, first siege of Badajoz, Albuera and Cadiz. Half pay 21 Apr 1818. Magistrate and Deputy Lieutenant for Lancashire. MGS medal for Talavera, Busaco and Albuera. Died 17 Aug 1853 aged 62.

SANDYS, Thomas Edwin
Lieutenant. 6th (1st Warwickshire) Regiment of Foot.
Headstone: Old Churchyard, Powerscourt, County Wicklow, Ireland. (Photograph)

SACRED / TO THE MEMORY OF / CAPTN THOS EDWIN SANDYS / OF H. M. 6TH REGT OF FOOT: / BORN JUNE 9TH 1786. / DIED JUNE 2ND 1832.

Ensign 6 Nov 1806. Lt 18 May 1809. Capt 1 Aug 1816.

Served in the Peninsula Aug 1808 – Jan 1809 and Nov 1812 – Oct 1813. Present at Rolica, Vimeiro, Corunna, Vittoria and Pyrenees where he was wounded 29 Jul 1813.

SANKEY, Andrew

Lieutenant. 57th (West Middlesex) Regiment of Foot.

Named on the Memorial: St Andrew's Church (now Musée Historique), Biarritz, France. (Photograph)

Ensign 6 Oct 1804. Lt 26 Dec 1805.

Served in the Peninsula Dec 1809 – Dec 1813. Present at Busaco, first siege of Badajoz, Albuera, Vittoria, Pyrenees, Nivelle (wounded) and Nive where he was killed 13 Dec 1813.

SANKEY, Samuel

Major. 9th (East Norfolk) Regiment of Foot.

Memorial tablet: Parish Church, Virginia, County Cavan, Ireland. (Photograph)

TO THE GLORY OF GOD AND IN MEMORY OF / SAMUEL SANKEY OF FORT FREDERICK. / MAJOR IX FOOT. SERVED IN PENINSULAR WAR. / 1808–1814. DIED 1861. / ....

Ensign in Lt Colonel O'Donnell's Regiment 15 Nov 1794. Lt 10 Jan 1795. Lt 72nd Foot 31 Oct 1800. Capt 2nd Battalion of Reserve 9 Jul 1803. Capt 9th Foot 2 Aug 1804. Major 2nd Sep 1813.

Served in the Peninsula with 1/9th Aug – Nov 1808. Present at Rolica (wounded 17 Aug 1808 and awarded pension of £100 per annum). Also served at Walcheren 1809. MGS medal for Rolica.

SANNERMAN, Henry Christian

Veterinary Surgeon. 10th (Prince of Wales's Own Royal) Regiment of Light Dragoons.

Memorial: St Paul's Churchyard, Dublin, Ireland. (M.I.) (Church deconsecrated in about 1990 and converted into an Enterprise Centre. Intact memorials were removed to St Michan's Church but many memorials are illegible or inaccessible around the perimeter wall).

"ERECTED BY THE STAFF OFFICERS OF TENTH ROYAL HUSSARS / AS A MARK OF RESPECT / TO THE MEMORY OF H. C. SANNERMAN ESQ / 22 YEARS VETERINARY SURGEON OF THIS REGIMENT. / HE DEPARTED THIS LIFE MARCH 20TH 1832 AT THE AGE OF 46 YEARS / LEAVING A WIDOW AND FIVE CHILDREN, THREE SONS AND TWO DAUGHTERS."

Grave: Holy Trinity Churchyard, Brompton, London. (M.I.)

"HENRY CHRISTIAN SANNERMAN OF THE ROYAL HUSSARS DIED MARCH 20TH 1832."

Veterinary Surgeon Brunswick Cavalry 7 Dec 1809. Veterinary Surgeon 10th Lt Dragoons 29 Mar 1810.

Served in the Peninsula Feb 1813 – Apr 1814. Present at Morales, Vittoria, Orthes and Toulouse. Present at Waterloo.

SAUNDERS, John Stratford

Lieutenant Colonel. 61st (South Gloucestershire) Regiment of Foot.

Memorial tablet: St John the Baptist's Church, Stratford, County Wicklow, Ireland. (M.I.)

" .... / IN MEMORY OF / GENERAL JOHN STRATFORD SAUNDERS / 61ST FT / AND J. S. SAUNDERS 56TH FT HER BELOVED FATHER AND BROTHER WHO / DIED AT GOLDEN FORT 1846 AND 1852"

Ensign 64th Foot 26 May 1779. Lt 90th Foot 2 Dec 1779. Capt 12 Sep 1782. Major 61st Foot 1 Mar 1794. Bt Lt Colonel 1 Jan 1798. Lt Colonel 61st Foot 7 Mar 1805. Bt Colonel 25 Apr 1808. Major General 4 Jun 1811. Lt General 10 Jul 1821. General 28 Jun 1838.

Served in the Peninsula Jun 1809 – Mar 1811. Present at Talavera in command of 61st Foot. Gold Medal

for Talavera. Also served in the West Indies 1779–1783, Gibraltar 1793, West Indies 1794 (present at Martinique and St Lucia), Cape of Good Hope 1798, Egypt 1801 (present at Alexandria) and Sicily 1806. Died 25 Mar 1846 aged 84.
Reference: Royal Military Calendar, Vol. 3, pp. 124–32.

SAUNDERS, William

1st Lieutenant. Royal Artillery.
Headstone and low monument: St Luke's Churchyard, Charlton, Kent. (Photograph)

TO THE MEMORY OF / MAJOR WILLIAM SAUNDERS / ROYAL HORSE ARTILLERY. / BORN 13TH MAY 1789 / DIED 12TH AUGUST 1839.

2nd Lt 13 Sep 1805. 1st Lt 1 Jun 1806. 2nd Capt 7 Nov 1820. Capt 17 Oct 1833. Bt Major 10 Jan 1837.

Served in the Peninsula Jan – Sep 1811 and Feb 1813 – Apr 1814 in 'F' Troop Royal Horse Artillery. Present at Pombal, Redinha, Sabugal, Fuentes d'Onoro, first siege of Badajoz (wounded), Vittoria, San Sebastian, Bidassoa, Nivelle and Bayonne.

SAUNDERSON, Hardress Robert

Captain. 39th (Dorsetshire) Regiment of Foot.
Chest tomb: Kensal Green Cemetery, London. Inscription illegible. (16854/102/IC). (Photograph)

Memorial tablet: St Nicholas's Church, Wickham, Hampshire. (Photograph)

TO THE / DEAR MEMORY OF / COL. HARDRESS SAUNDERSON / LATE GREN. GUARDS / SON OF COLONEL SAUNDERSON / OF CASTLE SAUNDERSON, IRELAND / DIED FEB 24TH 1865 / AND OF HIS WIFE / LADY MARIA SAUNDERSON / DAUGHTER OF / JOHN LAST EARL OF CARHAMPTON / DIED NOV 14TH 1861. / THIS TABLET IS ERECTED BY THEIR CHILDREN.

Ensign 15 Jun 1804. Lt 18 Feb 1806. Capt 5 May 1808. Lt and Capt 1st Foot Guards 22 Jul 1824. Bt Major 27 May 1825. Bt Lt Colonel 28 Jun 1838.

Served in the Peninsula with 2/39th Jul 1809 – Jan 1812. Present at Busaco, Campo Mayor, Badajoz, Albuera (wounded) and Arroyo dos Molinos (severely wounded, his skull fractured and sent back to England to recover). Returned to the Peninsula in 1813–1814 and acted as Deputy Judge Advocate. MGS medal for Busaco and Albuera. Also served in Malta, Sicily and Naples 1806 and Canada 1814 (QMG department, present at Plattsburgh). Half pay 30 Sep 1826. Died 24 Feb 1865.
Reference: Gentleman's Magazine, Apr 1865, p. 529.

SAYER, Stephen

Private. 1st (King's) Dragoon Guards.
Memorial tablet: Saint Eata's Church, Atcham, Shropshire. (Photograph)

SACRED TO THE MEMORY / OF STEPHEN SAYER / LATE OF THE 1ST REGIMENT OF KINGS DRAGOON GUARDS / HE FELL ON THE EVENING OF THE 18TH JUNE 1815 / AT WATERLOO. / AGED 44 YEARS. / (VERSE)

Present at Waterloo where he was killed.

SCANLON, Thomas

Sergeant Major. 12th (Prince of Wales's) Regiment of Light Dragoons.
Named on the Regimental Memorial: St Joseph's Church, Waterloo. (Waterloo)

Present at Waterloo where he was killed.

SCHARTROTH, J. Carl
Lieutenant. Duke of Brunswick's Oels' Corps.
Named on the Memorial: St Andrew's Church (now Musée Historique), Biarritz, France. (Photograph)

Ensign 27 Aug 1812. Lt 10 Jun 1813.

Served in the Peninsula Nov 1811 – Nov 1813. Present at Vittoria, Pyrenees, Bidassoa and Nivelle where he was killed Nov 1813.

SCHAUMANN, Friedrich Melchior Wilhelm
Captain. 2nd Battalion Light Infantry, King's German Legion.
Named on the Regimental Memorial: La Haye Sainte, Waterloo. (Photograph)
Named on the Waterloo Column, Hanover, Germany. (Photograph)

Lt 11 Sep 1807. Capt 25 May 1812.

Served in the Peninsula Aug 1808 – Jan 1809. Present at Vigo. Present at Waterloo where he was killed. Also served at Hanover 1805, the Baltic 1807–1808, Walcheren 1809, North Germany 1813–1814 and the Netherlands 1814.

SCHENLEY, Edward William Henry see SHENLEY, Edward William Henry

SCHOËDDE, James Holmes
Captain. 60th (Royal American) Regiment of Foot.
Headstone with Cross: St Michael and All Angels' Churchyard, Lyndhurst, Hampshire. (Photograph)

LIEUT-GENERAL / SIR JAMES HOLMES / SCHOEDDE K. C. B. / DIED NOV 15 1861 / AGED 75 / A GOOD SOLDIER / OF JESUS CHRIST

Brass Memorial tablet: St Michael and All Angels Church, Lyndhurst, Hampshire. (Photograph)

IN MEMORY OF LIEUT[T] GEN[L] SIR JAMES HOLMES SCHOEDDE K.C.B. / COLONEL OF THE 55TH REG[T] OF FOOT AND SOMETIME AIDE DE CAMP TO QUEEN VICTORIA. / DISTINGUISHED AS A SOLDIER AND BELOVED FOR HIS CHRISTIAN VIRTUES AND BENEVOLENCE / HE DIED MUCH LAMENTED AT ELCOMBS IN THIS PARISH NOV[R] 15TH 1861. AGED 75 YEARS. / HE BEQUEATHED £100 TO THE POOR OF LYNDHURST AND IS BURIED IN THE ADJOINING CHURCH-YARD.

Family Memorial monument: Warriston Cemetery, Edinburgh, Scotland. (Section E Grave number 248). (Photograph)

IN MEMORY OF / LIEUT GENERAL / SIR JAMES H. SCHOEDDE, KCB. / COLONEL 55TH REGIMENT / WHO DIED 15 NOVEMBER 1861. / HE SERVED IN EGYPT, THE PENINSULA / AMERICA, INDIA AND CHINA AND WAS / INTERRED AT LYNDHURST HAMPSHIRE. / ....

Ensign Lowenstein's Regiment May 1800. Lt 8 Oct 1801. Lt 60th Foot 25 Apr 1802. Capt 19 Sep 1805. Bt Major 21 Jun 1813. Major 20 Jan 1825. Lt Colonel 48th Foot 1 Jun 1830. Lt Colonel 55th Foot Mar 1833. Bt Colonel 23 Nov 1841. Major General 11 Nov 1851.

Served in the Peninsula Aug 1808 – Apr 1814 (attached to 3rd Division). Present at Rolica, Vimeiro, Douro, Talavera, Busaco, Redinha, Casal Nova, Foz d'Arouce, Sabugal, Fuentes d'Onoro, El Bodon, Ciudad Rodrigo, Badajoz, Salamanca, Vittoria, Pyrenees, Nivelle, Nive, Orthes, Vic Bigorre and Toulouse. Gold Medal for Nivelle. One of only ten officers who served throughout the Peninsular War. Also served in Egypt 1801, Gibraltar 1811–1818, Canada 1818–1824, India 1841 and China 1841–1844 (commanded

a Brigade at Chapoo, Wusung, Shanghai and Chin Kiang Foo and awarded medal). KCB 1842. MGS medal for Egypt, Rolica, Vimeiro, Talavera, Busaco, Fuentes d'Onoro, Ciudad Rodrigo, Badajoz, Salamanca, Vittoria, Pyrenees, Nive, Orthes and Toulouse. Colonel 55th Foot 30 May 1857.
REFERENCE: Rigaud, Major General Gibbs, Celer et Audax : a sketch of the services of the Fifth Battalion, Sixtieth Regiment (Rifles), 1879, reprint 2002. pp. 273–7.

SCHREIBER, George
Cornet. 11th Regiment of Light Dragoons.
Memorial: St Mary's Church, Cheltenham, Gloucestershire. (M.I.)

"LT COL GEORGE SCHREIBER MARCH 5TH 1878, AGED 83"

Cornet 23 Dec 1813. Lt 11 Jul 1816. Capt 18th Lt Dragoons 9 Nov 1821. Bt Lt Colonel 11 Nov 1851.
Present at Quatre Bras and Waterloo where his horse was shot under him. Afterwards ADC to Lt General Sir John Cameron. Half pay 9 Nov 1821. Brother of Capt James Alfred Schreiber and Capt William Frederick Schreiber both of 11th Lt Dragoons and cousin of Cornet Lemuel Shuldham 2nd Dragoons.

SCHREIBER, James Alfred
Captain. 11th Regiment of Light Dragoons.
Low monument: St Andrew's Old Churchyard, Melton, Suffolk. (Rear of Church). (Photograph)

SACRED / TO THE MEMORY OF / JAMES ALFRED SCHREIBER / WHO DIED 5TH JUNE 1840 / AGED 51 YEARS. / LT COL: AS CAPTAIN SCHREIBER / WAS PRESENT / AT THE BATTLE OF / WATERLOO / WITH HIS REGIMENT / THE XITH LIGHT DRAGOONS

Cornet 15 Mar 1806. Lt 29 May 1806. Capt 19 Nov 1812. Capt 6th Dragoon Guards 30 Dec 1819. Major (unattached) 23 Jun 1825. Bt Lt Colonel 28 Jun 1838.
Served in the Peninsula Jun 1811 – Jun 1813. Present at El Bodon, Moriscos, Castrejon, Salamanca and Venta del Pozo. Present at Quatre Bras and Waterloo (severely wounded). Brother of Capt William Frederick Schreiber and Cornet George Schreiber both of the 11th Lt Dragoons and cousin of Cornet Lemuel Shuldham 2nd Dragoons.

SCHREIBER, William Frederick
Captain. 11th Regiment of Light Dragoons.
Low monument: St Andrew's Churchyard, Rushmere, Suffolk. (Photograph)

WILLIAM FREDERICK / SCHREIBER / DIED / 14 JULY 1860 / AGED 76 YEARS

Cornet 22 Apr 1802. Lt 4 Aug 1804. Captain 11 May 1806.
Served in the Peninsula Jun 1811 – Apr 1813. Present at El Bodon, Moriscos, Castrejon, Salamanca and Venta del Pozo (wounded). Retired Oct 1813. MGS medal for Salamanca. Brother of Capt James Schreiber and Cornet George Schreiber both of 11th Lt Dragoons and cousin of Cornet Lemuel Shuldham 2nd Dragoons.

SCHRÖDER, Johann Christian von
Lieutenant Colonel. 2nd Line Battalion, King's German Legion.
Named on the Regimental Memorial: La Haye Sainte, Waterloo. (Photograph)
Named on the Waterloo Column, Hanover, Germany. (Photograph)

Lt Colonel 4 Jun 1813.

Present at Waterloo where he was severely wounded and died of his wounds 22 Jun 1815. Also served in the Baltic 1807, Mediterranean 1808–1814 and the Netherlands 1814.

SCHUCK, Johann Ludwig
Lieutenant and Adjutant. 5th Line Battalion, King's German Legion.
Named on the Regimental Memorial: La Haye Sainte, Waterloo. (Photograph)
Named on the Waterloo Column, Hanover, Germany. (Photograph)

Ensign and Adjutant 15 Oct 1812. Lt 25 Apr 1814.
Served in the Peninsula Dec 1812 – Apr 1814. Present at Vittoria, Tolosa, San Sebastian, Bidassoa, Nivelle, Nive, St Etienne and Bayonne. Present at Waterloo where he was killed. Also served in the Netherlands 1814.

SCHULZEN, Carl Detlef von
Lieutenant. Artillery, King's German Legion.
Named on the Regimental Memorial: La Haye Sainte, Waterloo. (Photograph)
Named on the Waterloo Column, Hanover, Germany. (Photograph)
Named on the Regimental Memorial to Royal Artillery and KGL Artillery, St Joseph's Church, Waterloo. (Photograph)

2nd Lt 22 Apr 1807. 1st Lt 11 Dec 1812.
Served in the Peninsula 1810 – Apr 1814. Present at Fuentes d'Onoro, Albuera, second siege of Badajoz, Ciudad Rodrigo, Badajoz, Salamanca, San Millan, Vittoria, San Sebastian, Pyrenees, Bidassoa, Nivelle, Nive, Orthes and Toulouse. Present at Waterloo where he was killed. Also served in the Baltic 1807–1808 and the Netherlands 1814.

SCOTT, Henry
Lieutenant. 6th (1st Warwickshire) Regiment of Foot.
Named on the Memorial: St Andrew's Church (now Musée Historique), Biarritz, France. (Photograph)

Ensign 1805. Lt 5 Mar 1807.
Served in the Peninsula Oct 1813 – Feb 1814. Present at Bidassoa, Nivelle and Orthes where he was killed 27 Feb 1814. Also served at Walcheren 1809.

SCOTT, Henry Alexander
2nd Captain. Royal Artillery.
Low monument: St Kenelm's Church, Alderley, Wotton-under-Edge, Gloucestershire. Inscription not recorded. (Photograph)

2nd Lt 28 Apr 1801. 1st Lt 30 Apr 1803. 2nd Capt 1 Feb 1808. Capt 26 Nov 1824. Bt Major 29 May 1825. Lt Colonel 20 May 1836. Colonel 9 Nov 1846. Major General 20 Jun 1854. Lt General 24 Jan 1863. General 12 May 1866.
Served at Ostend and Brussels 1815–1816. Also served in Jamaica 1805–1808, Walcheren 1809 (present at the siege of Flushing) and Gibraltar 1836–1839. Colonel Commandant Royal Artillery 26 Jun 1860. Died 1 Aug 1868 at Alderley, Wotton-under-Edge.

SCOTT, Henry Randolph
Assistant Surgeon. 82nd (Prince of Wales's Volunteers) Regiment of Foot.
Named on the Regimental Memorial: St Multose's Church, Kinsale, Ireland. (Photograph)

SACRED / TO THE MEMORY OF LIEUTS / EDMUND DAVENPORT, EDWIN HARDING / ASST

SURGEON HENRY RANDOLPH SCOTT / AND HIS WIFE / EIGHT SERJEANTS, NINE CORPORALS, / ONE HUNDRED AND FORTY PRIVATES, / THIRTEEN WOMEN AND SIXTEEN CHILDREN / OF THE 82^{D} REG^{T}, WHO PERISHED / ON BOARD THE BOADICEA TRANSPORT, / WRECKED ON GARRETSTOWN STRAND / ON THE NIGHT OF THE 30TH JAN^{Y} 1816 / THIS TRIBUTE IS ERECTED / BY THE OFFICERS OF THE REG^{T}

Buried in Old Court Burial Ground, Kinsale, Ireland.

Asst Surgeon 29 Jun 1809.

Served in the Peninsula Apr 1813 – Apr 1814. Present at Vittoria, Pyrenees, San Marcial, Nivelle and Orthes and with the Army of Occupation until Dec 1815. Also served in North America 1814 (present at Lundy's Lane). On 8 Dec 1815 the regiment marched from Paris en route to Calais to embark for England. Landed in Dover on 3 Jan 1816 and were immediately re-shipped for Ireland on 30 Jan on the transport ship *Boadicea*. The ship was wrecked at Kinsale off the coast of Ireland and of 289 people on board only 102 were saved.

SCOTT, James

Quartermaster. 9th (East Norfolk) Regiment of Foot.
Headstone: Old Churchyard, Spital, Windsor, Berkshire. (Grave number Q 5). (Photograph)

CAPTAIN / JAMES SCOTT MKW / LATE 9TH REGT IN WHICH HE SERVED 34 YEARS. / HE FELL ASLEEP IN JESUS ON THE / 18TH NOV 1863 IN HIS 84TH YEAR.

Quartermaster 17 Dec 1807.

Served in the Peninsula with 2/9th Aug 1808 – Jan 1809 and 1/9th Jan 1813 – Apr 1814. Present at Vimeiro, Douro, Osma, Vittoria, San Sebastian, Bidassoa, Nivelle, Nive and Bayonne. Also served at the Helder 1799 and North America 1814. Military Knight of Windsor 1851 and made Honorary Captain. MGS medal for Vimeiro, Vittoria, San Sebastian, Nivelle and Nive. Awarded pension for distinguished service.

SCOTT, James

Private. 91st Regiment of Foot.
Headstone: Langholm Churchyard, Langholm, Dumfries, Scotland. (Photograph)

IN MEMORY OF JAMES SCOTT, / WEAVER, WHO DIED / 22ND DECEMBER 1868, AGED 79 YEARS. / ALSO TWO CHILDREN WHO DIED IN / INFANCY. JEANNE HIS DAUGHTER AGED / 18 MONTHS. HELEN AGED 2 YEARS. / A SECOND HELEN AGED 9 YEARS. ALSO / JANET WHO DIED 3RD APRIL 1849 AGED / 19 YEARS. ALSO ANNE MURRAY, / WIFE OF THE ABOVE JAMES SCOTT, / WHO DIED 20TH MAY 1875, AGED 74 / YEARS. / THE ABOVE NAMED JAMES SCOTT PASSED / THROUGH MOST OF THE GREAT BATTLES OF THE / PENINSULAR WAR AND WAS PRESENT AT CORUNNA / WHEN SIR JOHN MOORE / MET HIS DEATH ON THE 16TH DAY OF JAN 1809.

Served in the Peninsula Aug 1808 – Jan 1809 and Oct 1812 – Apr 1814. Present at Rolica, Vimeiro, Corunna, Pyrenees (severely wounded in the head), Nivelle, Nive, Orthes, Aire and Toulouse. Discharged 23 Oct 1819. MGS medal for Rolica, Vimeiro, Corunna, Pyrenees, Nivelle, Nive, Orthes and Toulouse.

SCOTT, John F.

2nd Lieutenant. Royal Artillery.
Memorial: St Nicholas's Churchyard, Plumstead, Kent. (No longer extant. Destroyed by a flying bomb in the Second World War). (M.I.)

" JOHN F. SCOTT, LIEUT R. A. DIED ALICANTE 22 SEP 1813."

2nd Lt 13 Dec 1810.

Served in the Peninsula Jun 1812 – Sep 1813. Present on the East coast of Spain.

SCOTT, Richard Evans

1st Lieutenant. Royal Engineers.

Named on the Regimental Memorial: Rochester Cathedral, Rochester, Kent. (Photograph)

2nd Lt 22 Feb 1811. Lt 1 May 1811.

Served in the Peninsula Aug 1812 – Apr 1814. Present at Tarragona. Also served in Sicily 1811–1812 and Genoa 1814. Died at Corfu 16 Sep 1815.

SCOTT, Robert

Lieutenant. 59th (2nd Nottinghamshire) Regiment of Foot.

Named on the Regimental Memorial monument: Christ Church Churchyard, Tramore, County Waterford, Ireland. (Photograph)

Ensign 9 Sep 1813. Lt 20 Apr 1815.

Served in the Peninsula Mar – Apr 1814. Present at Bayonne. Present at Waterloo in reserve at Hal, siege of Cambrai and with the Army of Occupation. Drowned when the *Sea Horse* was wrecked in a storm in Tramore Bay 30 Jan 1816.

SCOTT, Samuel

Surgeon. 5th (Northumberland) Regiment of Foot.

Headstone: St Margaret's Churchyard, Restalrig, Edinburgh, Scotland. (Headstone fallen and broken in two). (Photograph)

SACRED / TO THE MEMORY OF / SAMUEL SCOTT ESQ., / SURGEON / OF THE 6TH DRAGOON GUARDS / WHO DIED AT PIERSHILL BARRACKS / ON THE 14TH OF AUGUST 1825, / IN THE 45TH YEAR OF HIS AGE. / THIS STONE WAS ERECTED BY / HIS BROTHER OFFICERS / IN THE REGIMENT, / IN TESTIMONY OF / THEIR REGARD AND ESTEEM.

Hospital Mate 30 Aug 1803. Asst Surgeon 23rd Lt Dragoons 17 Sep 1803. Surgeon 7th Garrison Battalion 27 Apr 1809. Surgeon 5th Foot 25 May 1809. Surgeon 6th Dragoons Guards 11 Jun 1816.

Served in the Peninsula with 2/5th Jul 1809 – Oct 1811 and 1812. Present at Busaco, Redinha, Casal Nova, Foz d'Arouce, Sabugal, Fuentes d'Onoro and the second siege of Badajoz.

SCOTT, Thomas

2nd Captain. Royal Artillery.

Memorial tablet: St Mary the Virgin's Church, Fordwich, Canterbury, Kent. (West end of north aisle). (Photograph)

THIS TABLET / IS PLACED HERE, / A TRIBUTE FROM HIS BROTHER OFFICERS, / TO RECORD THEIR ESTEEM / OF THE WORTH, TALENT, AND VIRTUES, / WHICH SO EMINENTLY CHARACTERIZED / THE LATE / MAJOR THOMAS SCOTT, / OF THE ROYAL REGIMENT OF ARTILLERY, / WHO DIED AT FORDWICH HOUSE / ON THE 28TH DECEMBER 1834, / AGED 46.

Ledger stone in floor below tablet: (Photograph)

BENEATH / LIE THE REMAINS OF / MAJOR / THOMAS SCOTT / OF THE ROYAL ARTILLERY / DIED DECEMBER 28TH 1834 / AGED 46 YEARS.

2nd Lt 3 Dec 1803. 1st Lt 10 Dec 1803. 2nd Capt 20 Jun 1812. Capt 12 Dec 1826. Bt Major 22 Jul 1830.
Served in the Peninsula Jun 1812 – Apr 1814. Served on the East coast of Spain (present at Castalla). Present at Quatre Bras where his horse was shot under him, Waterloo in Major Roger's Brigade and with the Army of Occupation until Nov 1815. Also served in Sicily and the Ionian Islands Jul 1806 – Jun 1812 where he was present at the siege of Ischia 1809 and siege of St Maura 1810.

SCOTT, Thomas
Lieutenant. 94th Regiment of Foot.
Headstone: Ashkirk and Lindean Churchyard, Selkirkshire, Scotland. (M.I.)

"IN MEMORY OF THOMAS SCOTT, FARMER SHIELDSWOOD, LATE CAPT 94TH REGT OF FOOT WHO DIED 19 DEC 1858 IN THE 70TH YEAR OF HIS AGE."

Ensign 25 Aug 1808. Lt 28 Feb 1812.
Served in the Peninsula Feb 1810 – Apr 1814. Present at Cadiz (wounded three times at Fort Matagorda and Mentioned in Despatches), Pombal, Redinha, Casal Nova, Foz d'Arouce, Sabugal, Fuentes d'Onoro, second siege of Badajoz, Campo Mayor, El Bodon, Ciudad Rodrigo (wounded), Badajoz, Salamanca Forts, Salamanca, Vittoria, Pyrenees, Nivelle, Nive, Vic Bigorre, Tarbes and Toulouse. Half pay 25 Dec 1818. MGS medal for Fuentes d'Onoro, Ciudad Rodrigo, Badajoz, Salamanca, Vittoria, Pyrenees, Nivelle, Nive and Toulouse.

SCOTT, William
Private. 3rd Regiment of Foot Guards.
Headstone: St Cuthbert with St Mary's Churchyard, Carlisle, Cumbria. (On wall on south side of church wall on flagged way). (Photograph)

IN MEMORY OF / .... / ALSO / THEIR SON WILLIAM WHO SERVED IN HIS MAJ / ESTY'S FOOTGUARDS, SIXYERS [*SIC*] DURING WHICH / TIME HAD BEEN AT HANOVER COPENHAG / EN SWEDEN, AND AFTERWARDS WENT TO / SPAIN IN GENERAL SHEAR-BROOKES DIV / ISION AND FELL IN THE BATTLE AT / TALAVERA / ON THE 28TH JULY 1809 AGED 23 YEARS. / ....

Private 1803 aged 17.
Served in the Peninsula in 1809. Present at Talavera where he was killed. Also served at Hanover 1805, Copenhagen 1807 and Sweden 1808.

SCOTT, William Henry
Lieutenant and Captain. 3rd Regiment of Foot Guards.
Memorial: Royal Military Chapel, Wellington Barracks, London. (M.I.) (Destroyed by a Flying Bomb 1944)

"GENERAL WILLIAM HENRY SCOTT, / COLONEL 36TH (THE HEREFORDSHIRE) REGIMENT. / BORN 3RD JANUARY, 1788; DIED 8TH NOVEMBER, 1868. / 3RD GUARDS, 1805–46. PRESENT AT THE PASSAGE OF THE DOURO AND BATTLE OF TALAVERA, WHERE HE WAS SHOT THROUGH THE BODY AND TAKEN PRISONER. HE COMMANDED THE REGIMENT FOR UPWARDS OF / THREE YEARS. / PLACED TO HIS MEMORY BY HIS WIDOW AND CHILDREN."

Ensign 27 Oct 1805. Lt and Capt 28 Mar 1811. Capt and Lt Colonel 5 Jul 1815. Bt Colonel 10 Jan 1837. Major General 9 Nov 1846. Lt General 20 Jun 1854. General 23 Mar 1861.
Served in the Peninsula Mar 1809 – Apr 1814. Present at Douro and Talavera where he was wounded and taken prisoner until Apr 1814. Commanding Officer 3rd Foot Guards 1841–1844. Served in the

regiment for 41 years. Colonel 36th Foot 31 Oct 1854. MGS medal for Talavera. Died in Brighton 8 Nov 1868.
Reference: Household Brigade Journal, 1868, p. 326.

SCOVELL, Sir George
Major. Staff Cavalry Corps.
Memorial tablet: Royal Military College, Sandhurst, Berkshire. (Photograph)

IN MEMORY / OF / GENERAL SIR GEORGE SCOVELL / G.C.B. / COLONEL OF THE 4TH LIGHT DRAGOONS / BORN 21ST MARCH 1774 / DIED 17TH JANUARY 1861 / HE WAS ON THE STAFF OF THE DUKE OF WELLINGTON / THROUGHOUT THE PENINSULAR WAR AND AT WATERLOO / AND WAS GOVERNOR OF THIS COLLEGE / FROM 1837 TO 1856

Obelisk: Royal Military College Churchyard, Sandhurst, Berkshire. (Photograph)

TO THE MEMORY / OF / GENERAL SIR GEORGE SCOVELL G.C.B. / COLONEL OF THE / 4TH QUEENS OWN LIGHT DRAGOONS / LATE GOVERNOR OF THE / ROYAL MILITARY COLLEGE / WHO DIED THE 17TH JANY 1861 / IN THE 87TH YEAR OF HIS AGE.

Warwickshire Fencible Cavalry. Cornet and Adjt 4th Dragoons 5 Apr 1798. Lt 4 May 1800. Capt 10 Mar 1804. Capt 57th Foot 12 Mar 1807. Bt Major 30 Mar 1811. Bt Lt Colonel 1 Aug 1812. Major Staff Corps of Cavalry 15 Jun 1813. Lt Colonel Commandant 22 Feb 1816. Bt Colonel 27 May 1825. Major General 10 Jan 1837. Lt General 9 Nov 1846. General 20 Jun 1854.

Served in the Peninsula Aug 1808 – Jan 1809 (DAQMG) and Apr 1809 – Apr 1814 (AQMG attached to Headquarters). Present at Sahagun, Benevente, Corunna, Douro, Talavera, Busaco, Fuentes d'Onoro, Ciudad Rodrigo, Badajoz, Salamanca (Mentioned in Despatches), Burgos, Vittoria, Pyrenees, Nivelle, Nive, Adour and Toulouse. Commanded the Corps of Guides and had charge of the postal service and communications until 1813. Then appointed to command the Staff Corps of Cavalry. CB. Was Wellington's chief code breaker. Gold Cross for Vittoria, Pyrenees, Nivelle, Nive and Toulouse. MGS medal for Sahagun and Benevente, Corunna, Talavera, Busaco, Fuentes D'Onoro, Ciudad Rodrigo, Badajoz and Salamanca. Present at Quatre Bras and Waterloo (AQMG) and with the Army of Occupation. Awarded 4th Class of St Wladimir. In command of the Royal Waggon Train 1820. Lt Governor of Royal Military College Sandhurst 1829–1837 and Governor 1837–1856. Colonel 4th Dragoons 18 Dec 1847. GCB 1860.
Reference: Dictionary of National Biography. Royal Military Calendar, Vol. 4, p. 430. Urban, Mark, The man who broke Napoleon's codes, 2001.

SCOVELL, Henry
Assistant Deputy Paymaster General. Paymaster General's Department.
Memorial in iron railed enclosure in the form of two oval marble tablets overlapping with part of the inscription across both. The second relates to his wife Ann Marie: St Brigid's Churchyard, Stillorgan, Dublin, Ireland. (M.I.)

"SACRED / TO THE MEMORY / OF / HENRY SCOVELL / WHO DIED / JANUARY 22ND / 1861 / AGED 70"

Asst Deputy Paymaster General 1811.

Served in the Peninsula Dec 1811 – Apr 1814 (attached to 2nd Division from Jul 1812). Present at Vittoria, Pyrenees, Nivelle, Orthes and Toulouse. MGS medal for Vittoria, Pyrenees, Nivelle, Orthes and Toulouse. Also served in Upper Canada 1814.

SEARLE, John
Private. 1st Regiment of Foot Guards.
Buried in St Mary's Churchyard, Rickinghall Inferior, Suffolk. (Burial Register)

Pte. 14 Jul 1795.
Present at Waterloo in Lt Colonel Henry Doyly's Company. Served for 21 years. Discharged 5 May 1816 aged 49 years.

SEATON, James see SETON, James

SEATON, Lord John see COLBORNE, John

SEDGWICK, Henry Bingley
Lieutenant. 5th (Northumberland) Regiment of Foot.
Memorial tablet: St John's Church, Hackney, London. (Photograph)

THIS TRIBUTE OF PARENTAL AFFECTION / IS ERECTED IN REMEMBRANCE OF / LIEUTENANT HARRY BINGLEY SEDGWICK, / OF THE 5TH REGIMENT OF FOOT, / ONLY SON OF HARRY SEDGWICK ESQRE OF HOMERTON; / WHOSE ARDENT MILITARY CAREER WAS SUDDENLY TERMINATED / ON THE 2ND OF JUNE, 1811, BY A CANNON-SHOT FROM / THE CASTLE OF BADAJOS, IN SPAIN, / WHILE BESIEGED BY THE BRITISH TROOPS / UNDER THE COMMAND OF THE ILLUSTRIOUS WELLINGTON, / IN THE PLENTITUDE OF YOUTH, HEALTH AND SPIRITS, / HE WAS TOTALLY UNCONSCIOUS OF HIS NEW APPROACH TO ETERNITY / (BEING IN THE ACT OF GIVING ORDERS TO HIS MEN / IN ONE OF THE TRENCHES) / WHEN HIS COUNTRY LOST A / GALLANT DEFENDER, / AT THE EARLY AGE OF 23 YEARS.

Ensign 29 Oct 1807. Lt 26 Sep 1809.
Served in the Peninsula with 1/5th Jul 1808 – Jan 1809 and 2/5th Nov 1810 – Jun 1811. Present at Rolica, Vimeiro, Redinha, Casal Nova, Foz d'Arouce, Sabugal, Fuentes d'Onoro and the second siege of Badajoz where he was killed 2 Jun 1811. Also served at Walcheren 1809.

SEDLEY, John Somner
Ensign. Royal Staff Corps.
Low monument: Kensal Green Cemetery, London. (20478/116/PS). (Photograph)

TO THE BELOVED MEMORY OF / MAJOR JOHN SOMNER SEDLEY / FORMERLY LIEUT. OF THE STAFF CORPS / LATE FIRST CLASS BARRACK MASTER OF / MAURITIUS / DEPARTED THIS LIFE 29TH JULY 1867.....................

Ensign 6 May 1813. Lt 23 Oct 1817.
Present at Waterloo. Half pay 25 Dec 1818. Later became Barrack Master in Mauritius 1833 with the rank of Major. Retired from this post in August 1860.

SELBY, William
Lieutenant. 3rd (King's Own) Regiment of Dragoons.
Memorial window: St Aidan's Church, Bamborough, Northumberland. (Photograph)

IN MEMORY OF WILLIAM SELBY THIRD & YOUNGEST SON OF GEORGE SELBY ESQR OF TWIZELL HOUSE WHO WAS KILLED AT THE BATTLE OF SALAMANCA ON THE 22ND JULY 1812 AGED 20 YEARS

Cornet 18 Jul 1807. Lt 7 Apr 1808.

Served in the Peninsula Aug 1811 – Jul 1812. Present at Castrejon and Salamanca where he was killed aged 20 years.

SENIOR, William

Private. 3rd (King's Own) Regiment of Dragoons.
Buried in St John the Baptist's Churchyard, Kirkheaton, Yorkshire. (Burial record)

Pte 1 Nov 1795.

Served in the Peninsula. Present at Salamanca, Vittoria and Toulouse. Discharged 24 Feb 1819 owing to reduction of the regiment and his long service. MGS medal for Salamanca, Vittoria and Toulouse. Died at Low Moor Lipton, Jun 1850 aged 79.

SERJEANTSON, William

Ensign. 28th (North Gloucestershire) Regiment of Foot.
Grave: Hobart, Tasmania, Australia. (Photograph of his property). (M.I.)

"SERJEANTSON CAPT 40TH REG FATHER IN LAW OF RICHARD WILLIS. D. 1.12.1835. CAMPBELL TOWN, WANSTEAD"

Ensign 26 Aug 1813. Lt 40 Foot 19 Jul 1815. Capt 17 Dec 1829.

Present at Waterloo and with the Army of Occupation. He went to Australia with his regiment in 1823 and remained there when the regiment went to India in 1829. He was murdered on his property at Hobart, Tasmania, Australia in 1835.

SETON, George

Lieutenant. 7th (Royal Fusiliers) Regiment of Foot.
Chest tomb: St Patrick's Churchyard, Newry, Northern Ireland. (Photograph)

HERE LIETH / THE REMAINS OF / GEORGE SETON / THE LINEAL DESCENDANT OF / THE EARLS OF WINTOUN AND TRANENT, / CAPTN IN THE 7TH REGT / ROYAL FUSILIERS – / AND S. INSPECTOR OF / CONSTABULARY / AT NEWRY / HE DIED ON THE 30TH DAY OF NOVR 1845./ AGED 58 YEARS. / THIS TOMB IS RAISED / TO HIS MEMORY / BY / HIS AFFECTIONATE WIDOW / ANN SETON.

Lt 31 May 1810. Capt 15 May 1827. Capt 35th Foot 21 Feb 1834.

Served in the Peninsula with 1/7th Sep – Nov 1809, 2/7th Dec 1809 – Jun 1811 and 1/7th Jul 1811 – Apr 1814. Present at Busaco, Albuera (wounded), Aldea de Ponte (severely wounded), Ciudad Rodrigo, Nivelle, Nive, Orthes and Toulouse. Retired 5 Aug 1836. Jointed the Police Force in Ireland and became an Inspector of Constabulary.

SETON, James

Captain 92nd Regiment of Foot.
Named on the Memorial: St Andrew's Church (now Musée Historique), Biarritz, France. (Photograph)

Ensign 12th Foot 30 Oct 1795. Lt 28 Jun 1796. Capt 92nd Foot 31 Dec 1803. Bt Major 14 Dec 1813.

Served in the Peninsula Aug 1808 – Jan 1809 and Dec 1811 – Mar 1814. Present at Corunna, Almarez, Alba de Tormes, Vittoria, Pyrenees (wounded), Nivelle, Nive, Garris where he was severely wounded and died of his wounds 22 Mar 1814. Gold Medal for Pyrenees where he took command 31 Jul 1813. Also served in India 1799 (present at Seringapatam with 12th Foot at the age of 15), Copenhagen 1807 and Walcheren 1809.

SETON, William Carden

Major. 88th (Connaught Rangers) Regiment of Foot.

Memorial: St Mary's Churchyard, Dublin, Ireland. (M.I.) (Church deconsecrated and is now a restaurant. Churchyard opened as a public space. Gravestones were removed and placed in three rows along a wall to the rear of the open space. Some slabs form part of the pavement, but this memorial not visible).

"TO THE MEMORY OF / WILLIAM CARDEN SETON ESQUIRE / COLONEL IN THE ARMY AND / COMPANION OF THE MOST HONOURABLE / MILITARY ORDER OF THE BATH / DIED MARCH 24TH 1841."

Ensign 90th Foot 11 Oct 1796. Lt 25 Oct 1797. Capt 9 Jul 1803. Capt 88th Foot 2 Aug 1804. Bt Major 30 Apr 1812. Major 30 Oct 1812. Bt Lt Colonel 27 May 1825. Bt Colonel 28 Jun 1838.

Served in the Peninsula Mar 1809 – Sep 1812. Present at Talavera, Busaco, Redinha, Casal Nova, Foz d'Arouce, Sabugal, Fuentes d'Onoro, second siege of Badajoz, El Bodon, Ciudad Rodrigo, Badajoz, Salamanca and retreat from Burgos. Also served in Egypt 1801 with 90th Foot and South America 1807 with 88th Foot (present at Buenos Ayres where he was wounded). Gold Medal for Badajoz and Salamanca. CB. Half pay 25 Feb 1816.

Reference: Gentleman's Magazine, May 1842, p. 561. Annual Register, 1842, Appx, p. 260. United Service Magazine, May 1842, p. 143.

SEWARD, Charles

Ensign. 69th (South Lincolnshire) Regiment of Foot.

Chest tomb: St Andrew's Churchyard, Enfield, London. (Photograph)

SACRED / TO THE MEMORY OF / CHARLES SEWARD ESQUIRE / OF / CHASE LAME. / 69TH REGT OF FOOT. / DIED 26TH AUG 1856 / AGED 67.

Ensign 24 Feb 1814. Lt 11 Aug 1815.

Present at Waterloo. Half pay 25 Nov 1816.

SEWARD, William

Lieutenant. 9th (East Norfolk) Regiment.

Memorial tablet: St Ouen's Church, St Ouen, Jersey, Channel Islands. (M.I.)

"MAJOR WILLIAM SEWARD SERVED WITH 9TH REGIMENT IN THE PENINSULA AUG 1808 – JAN 1809 AND WAS PRESENT AT THE BATTLE OF VIMIERA, ON THE EXPEDITION TO WALCHEREN IN 1808 – JAN 1809 AND SUBSEQUENTLY IN THE PENINSULA INCLUDING THE DEFENCE OF TARIFA, BATTLES OF BARROSA (WOUNDED), VITTORIA AND THE NIVE AND BLOCKADE OF BAYONNE. HE RECEIVED THE WAR MEDAL WITH FOUR CLASPS AND DIED AT DON PLACE, ST HELIER THE 16TH DAY OF OCTOBER 1857."

Headstone: Green Street, Cemetery, St Helier, Jersey, Channel Islands. (Plot 133 South stone). (Badly eroded and inscription recorded from memorial inscription. (Photograph)

"MAJOR WILLIAM SEWARD OF HIS MAJESTY'S 9TH REG. OF FOOT AFTER SERVING FOR MANY YEARS WITH DISTINCTION IN THE ABOVE CORPS THROUGH THE PENINSULAR WAR AND IN NORTH AMERICA. HE RETIRED ON HALF PAY AND DIED ON 16TH OCTOBER 1857 IN THE 66TH YEAR OF HIS AGE. BELOVED AND LAMENTED BY ALL."

Ensign 26 Mar 1808. Lt 26 Apr 1809. Capt 15 Jul 1819. Major 18 Oct 1832.

Served in the Peninsula with 2/9th Aug 1808 – Mar 1809 and Jun 1810 – Dec 1812 and 1/9th Jan 1813

– Apr 1814. Present at Vimeiro, Tarifa, Barrosa (wounded), Osma, Vittoria, Nive and Bayonne. Served with the Army of Occupation 1815–1818. Also served at Walcheren 1809, Gibraltar 1810 – Dec 1812, North America 1814–1815 and West Indies 1819–1821 and 1825–1826. MGS medal for Vimeiro, Barrosa, Vittoria and Nive. Half pay 12 Nov 1835.

SEWELL, William

Quartermaster. Staff Corps of Cavalry.
Chest tomb: St Mary and St Alkelda's Churchyard, Middleham, Yorkshire. (Photograph)

HERE / LIES THE REMAINS OF / ANN BUCKLE / ………………. / ALSO ON THE SOUTH SIDE OF THIS STONE LIES / THE REMAINS OF THE ABOVE NAMED / WILLIAM SEWELL, REGIMENTAL QUARTER MASTER / OF THE STAFF CORPS OF CAVALRY WHO DIED / ON THE 24TH DAY NOVEMBER 1853 / AGED 83 YEARS.

Quartermaster 4th Lt Dragoons. Quartermaster Staff Corps Cavalry 20 Jan 1814.
Served in the Peninsula with 4th Lt Dragoons Apr 1809 – Jan 1814 and Staff Corps of Cavalry Feb – Apr 1814. Present with 4th Lt Dragoons at Talavera, Albuera, Salamanca and Vittoria. Half pay 25 Feb 1819. MGS medal for Talavera, Albuera, Salamanca and Vittoria.

SEWELL, William Henry

Captain. 60th (Royal American) Regiment of Foot.
Low monument: English Cemetery, Florence, Italy. (Grave number E120). (Photograph)

UNDER THIS SACRED SYMBOL OF SALVATION REPOSE THE MORTAL REMAINS OF / GEN. SIR WILLIAM HENRY SEWELL, KCB, COLONEL OF THE / 79 HIGHLANDERS WHO DEPARTED THIS LIFE AT FLORENCE ON / 13 MARCH 1862.

Ensign 96th Foot 27 Mar 1806. Cornet 16th Lt Dragoons 17 Apr 1806. Lt 26 Feb 1807. Capt 12 Mar 1812. Capt 60th Foot 29 Apr 1813. Bt Major 3 Mar 1814. Bt Lt Colonel 21 Jun 1817. Capt 49th Foot 29 May 1828. Major 31st Foot 11 Aug 1829. Bt Colonel 10 Jan 1837. Lt Colonel 6th Foot 17 Sep 1839. Lt Colonel 94th Foot 30 Mar 1841. Major General 9 Nov 1846. Lt General 20 Jun 1854.
Served in the Peninsula Aug 1808 – Jan 1809 and Mar 1809 – May 1812. On the Staff of the Portuguese Army May 1812 – Apr 1814 (served throughout the campaign as ADC to Lord Beresford). Present in the Corunna campaign, Talavera, Coa, Agueda, Busaco, Ciudad Rodrigo, Badajoz, San Sebastian, Nivelle, Nive, Orthes, Bayonne and Toulouse. CB. Also served in South America 1807 (on the staff of Lord Beresford), Portugal 1814–1816 (remained in Portugal after the end of the war in command of a Portuguese Cavalry regiment) and India 1828–1854 (DQMG in command at Bangalore, then divisional commander at Madras and finally Commander-in-Chief of the Madras Army). MGS medal for Corunna, Talavera, Busaco, Ciudad Rodrigo, Badajoz, San Sebastian, Nivelle, Nive, Orthes and Toulouse. Returned to England in 1854 and became Colonel 79th Foot 24 Mar 1854. Retired 1856. KCB 1861. Educated at Westminster and Eton under the name of W. H. Robertson. On entering the army took the surname of Sewell.
Reference: Gentleman's Magazine, May 1862, p. 652. Annual Register, 1862, Appx, p. 396.

SHADFORTH, Thomas

Major. 57th (West Middlesex) Regiment of Foot.
Pedestal tomb in railed enclosure: near the University Farms, Greendale, New South Wales, Australia. (Relocated from St Mark's Cemetery). (Photograph)

IN MEMORY OF / THOMAS SHADFORTH / FORMERLY LIEUTENANT COLONEL / OF H. M.'S 57TH REGT / WHO DEPARTED THIS LIFE / 4TH AUGUST 1862 / AGED 90 YEARS / ……………….

Ensign 87th Foot 5 Jun 1798. Lt 47th Foot 6 Sep 1798. Capt 57th Foot 13 May 1802. Major 20 Jun 1811. Bt Lt Colonel 12 Aug 1819.

Served in the Peninsula Jul 1809 – Mar 1812. Present at Busaco, first siege of Badajoz and Albuera (wounded and awarded pension of £200 per annum). Served with the Army of Occupation until Nov 1817. Also served in the West Indies 1800, Gibraltar 1804, North America 1814–1815 and Australia 1826. In 1828 Shadforth was appointed by the Governor to investigate the problems with the commissariat notes which were circulating and being used as currency. He listed all those in circulation and then called them in and destroyed the plates from which they had been made. When the 57th went to India in 1831, Shadforth resigned his commission and stayed in Australia with his family. Became involved in local affairs including Honorary Secretary of the Australian Subscription Library, Director of the Bank of Australia and President of the Australian Wheat and Flour Company. MGS medal for Busaco and Albuera. His son Thomas Shadforth followed him into the 57th Foot and was killed as Lt Colonel of the regiment at Sebastopol.

Reference: Dictionary of Australian Biography. Johnson, Janice, Thomas Shadforth – one of the Die-Hards, Waterloo Journal, Winter 2012, pp. 32–3.

SHADWELL, John

Sergeant Major. 10th (Prince of Wales's Own Royal) Regiment of Light Dragoons.
Headstone: St Mary the Virgin's Churchyard, Mortlake, Surrey. (Seriously eroded and inscription recorded from memorial inscription). (Photograph)

"JOHN SHADWELL / R. S. M. ....REGT / SERVED PENINSULA AND AT WATERLOO / J. S. 1839"

Pte Surrey Fencible Cavalry 25 Apr 1797. Pte 10th Lt Dragoons 25 Mar 1800. Cpl 1803. Sgt 1805. Sgt Major 1814. Regt Sgt Major 1816.

Served in the Peninsula 1808–1809 and 1813–1814. Present at Sahagun, Benevente, Morales, Vittoria, Orthes and Toulouse. Present at Waterloo. Discharged owing to ill health 26 May 1822. Died 13 Dec 1839 aged 58 years.

SHANNON, Alexander

Assistant Surgeon. 14th (Buckinghamshire) Regiment of Foot.
Gravestone: Kacheri Cemetery, Cawnpore, India. (M.I.)

"A. SHANNON, ESQ. ASST SURGEON / 14TH H. M. FOOT DIED 19TH JUNE 1817 / AGED 21 YEARS. / SERVED AT WATERLOO."

Hospital Asst 4 Oct 1813. Asst Surgeon 27 Jan 1814.

Present at Waterloo. MD Edinburgh 1813. Also served in India where he died in 1817.

SHAW, Alexander Mackenzie

Lieutenant. Royal York Rangers.
Pedestal tomb: Borgue Churchyard, Dumfriesshire, Scotland. (Photograph)

GUADELOUPE CORUNNA MARTINIQUE / IN MEMORY OF / CAPTAIN ALEXANDER MACKENZIE SHAW / LATE OF MUIRTON ROSS-SHIRE / AND OF THE / 92ND HIGHLANDERS / WHO DIED AT / GATEHOUSE / THE 21ST JUNE 1852 / AGED 74 YEARS.

Ensign 92nd Foot 10 Feb 1808. Lt 3 Aug 1809. Lt Royal York Rangers 5 Aug 1813.

Served in the Peninsula Aug 1808 – Jan 1809. Present at Corunna. MGS medal for Corunna. Also served at Walcheren 1809.

SHAW, James

Captain. 43rd (Monmouthshire) Light Infantry Regiment of Foot.
Memorial tablet: Kirkmichael Churchyard, Kirkmichael, Ayrshire, Scotland. (Originally in the Kennedy mausoleum, the tablet was severely damaged, restored with financial help from the Waterloo Association and the Queen's Lancashire Regiment and is now located on a window sill inside the church). (Photograph)

SACRED / TO THE MEMORY OF / GENRL SIR JAMES SHAW-KENNEDY, K.C.B, / COLONEL OF THE 47RD REGIMENT, / BORN 13 OCTOBER 1788, / DIED 30 MAY 1865. / THIS TABLET IS ERECTED / BY HIS WIDOW / LADY SHAW KENNEDY, / OF KIRKMICHAEL.

Ensign 18 Apr 1805. Lt 23 Jan 1806. Capt 16 Jul 1812. Bt Major 18 Jun 1815. Bt Lt Colonel 21 Jan 1819. Major 16 Jul 1830. Bt Colonel 10 Jan 1837. Major General 9 Nov 1846. Lt General 20 Jun 1854.

Served in the Peninsula with 1/43rd Oct 1808 – Jan 1809, Jul – Nov 1809, Feb – Nov 1812 and Dec 1812 – Nov 1813 (Dec 1809 – Aug 1811 and Nov 1811 – Jan 1812 ADC to Major General Robert Craufurd. Dec 1812 – Nov 1813 ADC to Major General C. Alten). Present at Vigo, Coa (severely wounded), Ciudad Rodrigo, Badajoz, siege of Salamanca Forts, Salamanca and San Munos. Present at Waterloo (DAQMG where he was wounded). In command at Calais during the Army of Occupation. CB. Also served in the Baltic 1807 (present at Kiöge). MGS medal for Cuidad Rodrigo, Badajoz and Salamanca. Took the name of Shaw-Kennedy on marriage in 1820. Assistant Adjutant General in Manchester during the periods of unrest. Organised the Constabulary Force of Ireland. Colonel 47th Foot 27 Aug 1854.
Reference: Dictionary of National Biography (Under Kennedy). Gentleman's Magazine, Aug 1865, pp. 243–4. Annual Register, 1865, Appx, pp. 196–7 (Under Kennedy). Shaw-Kennedy, Sir James, Notes on the battle of Waterloo, 1865, reprint 2003.

SHAW, James Peter

Lieutenant. 44th (East Essex) Regiment of Foot.
Ledger stone: St Andrew's Presbyterian Cemetery, Niagara, Ontario, Canada. (Photograph)

IN MEMORY OF / LIEUT JAMES P. SHAW, / 44 REG'T FOOT. / LATE OF DRUMFORK, FORFARSHIRE, / SCOTLAND. / WHO DIED AT STAMFORD, / SEPT. 3, 1855, / AGED 71 YEARS.

Ensign 29 Feb 1804. Lt 8 Jan 1807.

Served in the Peninsula Aug 1813 – Apr 1814. Present at Tarragona. Half pay 29 Jun 1815.

SHAW, John

Corporal. 2nd Life Guards.
Pedestal tomb with obelisk: St Catherine's Churchyard, Cossall, Nottinghamshire. (Photograph)

WATERLOO / THIS MONUMENT IS ERECTED / TO THE MEMORY OF / JOHN SHAW & / RICHARD WAPLINGTON, / OF THE / LIFE GUARDS, / AND THOMAS WHEATLEY, / OF THE LIGHT DRAGOON GUARDS, / WHO LEFT THIS THEIR NATIVE HOME / IN DEFENCE OF THEIR COUNTRY, / THE TWO FORMER GLORIOUSLY / FELL AT WATERLOO, THE LATTER / RETURNED, AND LIES BURIED IN / THIS CHURCH / YARD

Pte 15 Oct 1807. Cpl 4 Dec 1812.

Served in the Peninsula Oct 1812 – Apr 1814. Present at Vittoria and Toulouse. Present at Waterloo where he was severely wounded. He was reported to have dragged himself to La Haye Sainte where he bled to death on the evening of 18 June and is buried there. Shaw was a powerfully built man over six feet tall, one of the 'Cossall Giants' like Richard Waplington. He was a boxer before he joined the army and once in the army was able to train and develop these skills and further his boxing career. His Colonel, Charles Barton introduced him to prize fighting and Shaw was soon winning fights with or without gloves.

He was about to meet the Champion of England, Tom Cribb when the regiment was ordered to Belgium and to the battle of Waterloo where Shaw fought his last fight against the French. The memorial to the three Waterloo men, John Shaw, Richard Waplington and Thomas Wheatley, was unveiled in 1877.
Reference: Dictionary of National Biography. Raynor, K. K., Waterloo men at Cossall, Waterloo Journal, Jan 1988, pp. 27–37 and Robinson, Apr 1988, pp. 4–5. Knollys, William W., Shaw: Life Guardsman Shaw, 1885, reprint 2003.

SHAWE, Charles Augustus
Lieutenant and Captain. Coldstream Regiment of Foot Guards.
Low monument: St Mary Magdalene's Churchyard, Torquay, Devon. (Photograph)

SACRED TO THE MEMORY OF GENERAL CHARLES AUGUSTUS SHAWE LATE OF THE COLDSTREAM GUARDS WHO / DEPARTED THIS LIFE AT HATLEY, TORQUAY ON THE 4TH APRIL 1876 IN HIS 85TH YEAR.

Memorial: Royal Military Chapel, Wellington Barracks, London. (M.I.) (Destroyed by a Flying Bomb 1944)

"GENERAL CHARLES AUGUSTUS SHAWE. / COLDSTREAM GUARDS, FROM 1808 TO 1846. COLONEL 74TH REGIMENT, 1856. / BORN, 1791; DIED 1876. "BUSACO," "FUENTES D'ONOR," "CIUDAD RODRIGO." / D. D. HIS WIDOW."

Ensign 26 May 1808. Lt and Capt 23 Apr 1812. Capt and Lt Colonel 28 Apr 1825. Colonel 8 Aug 1837. Major General 9 Nov 1846. Lt General 20 Jun 1854.

Served in the Peninsula with 1st battalion Feb 1810 – Jun 1812 (on his promotion left for England to join the 2nd battalion). Present at Busaco, Fuentes d'Onoro and Ciudad Rodrigo. Also served in the Netherlands 1813–1814 (present at Bergen-op-Zoom where he was wounded 9 Mar 1814). MGS medal for Busaco, Fuentes d'Onoro and Ciudad Rodrigo. Colonel 74th Foot 24 Nov 1856. Educated at Eton.
Reference: Household Brigade Journal, 1876, p. 309.

SHAWE, Charles Fielding
Captain. 6th (1st Warwickshire) Regiment of Foot.
Named on the Memorial: St Andrew's Church, (now Musée Historique), Biarritz, France. (Photograph)

Ensign 74th Foot 4 Jun 1803. Lt 10 Jul 1804. Capt 4th Garrison Battalion 15 Sep 1808. Capt 6th Foot 3 Nov 1808.

Served in the Peninsula with 6th Foot Nov 1812 – Mar 1813 and Oct 1813. Present at the crossing of the Bidassoa where he was killed 7 Oct 1813.

SHAWE, William Cunliffe
Lieutenant. Royal Regiment of Horse Guards.
Family Memorial tablet: Bath Abbey, Bath, Somerset. (South aisle of nave). (Photograph)

.... / ALSO OF WILLIAM CUNLIFFE SHAWE, / CAPTAIN ROYAL HORSE GUARDS BLUE / BORN JUNE 30TH 1793, / DEPARTED THIS LIFE DECR 25TH 1881.

Cornet 23 Nov 1809. Lt 26 Dec 1811. Capt 1 Feb 1816.

Served in the Peninsula Nov 1812 – Apr 1814. Present at Vittoria and Toulouse. Present at Waterloo where he was wounded. MGS medal for Vittoria and Toulouse.

SHEARD, Timothy
Private. 82nd (Prince of Wales's Volunteers) Regiment of Foot.
Buried in St John the Baptist's Churchyard, Kirkheaton, Yorkshire. (Burial record)

Pte 20 Nov 1809.

Served in the Peninsula. Present at Nivelle and Orthes (wounded). MGS medal for Nivelle. Also served in Mauritius 1823 – Jun 1824. Discharged 21 Sep 1824. Died 9 Dec 1852 aged 65 years.

SHEARMAN, Edward
Major. 26th (Cameronian) Regiment of Foot.
Chest tomb: Sandpits Cemetery, Gibraltar. (Photograph)

SACRED / TO THE MEMORY OF / BREVET LIEUT.COLONEL / EDWARD SHEARMAN, / OF THE / 26TH (OR CAMERONIAN) REGIMENT OF FOOT / WHO DIED ON THE 8TH MARCH / 1820 / AGED 46 YEARS. / HIS BROTHER OFFICERS / ERECTED THIS STONE TO MARK THEIR ***** / ***** AND THEIR REGRET FOR HIS DEATH.

Ensign 4 Nov 1795. Lt 23 Feb 1796. Capt 22 Oct 1803. Major 11 Jan 1810. Bt Lt Colonel 12 Aug 1819.

Served in the Peninsula Oct 1808 – Jan 1809 and Jul 1811 – Jun 1812. Present at Corunna. From 1811 the 26th Foot in the Peninsula were unable to fight as the result of Walcheren fever. Shearman took the rest of the troops back to Gibraltar. Also served in Canada 1796–1800 (on the voyage home Lt Shearman and Ensign Campbell were taken hostage by the French. The rest of the troops were permitted to continue their voyage home and Shearman and Campbell were taken to France where they were exchanged for French prisoners), Ireland 1803, Walcheren 1809 and Gibraltar 1811–1820.

SHEARMAN, John
Lieutenant. 62nd (Wiltshire) Regiment of Foot.
Headstone: Warriston Cemetery, Edinburgh, Scotland (Section A3 Grave number 126). (Photograph) Headstone fallen.

IN MEMORY OF / LIEUTENANT COLONEL / JOHN SHEARMAN / LATE OF THE 13TH FOOT / BORN AT KILKENNY IN 1774 / DIED AT EDINBURGH 5TH JUNE 1871 / SERVED IN THE PENINSULA WITH THE 13TH FOOT AND / WAS APPOINTED TO THE COMMAND OF THE CALABRIAN REGIMENT / WHICH WITH SOME BRITISH TROOPS WAS SENT TO GUARD / AN IMPORTANT PASS. THE LATTER BY SOME OVERSIGHT / WERE WITHDRAWN JUST AS THE FRENCH CAME FORWARD. / IN THE ENCOUNTER WHICH ENSUED CAPT SHEARMAN RECEIVED / TWO SABRE CUTS ON THE LEFT ARM, AND SOON AFTER STRUCK / DOWN BY A BULLET. HE FELL INSENSIBLE TO THE GROUND. / WHEN HE REVIVED HE FOUND HIMSELF A PRISONER OF WAR. / HIS CAPTORS WHO DID NOT RECOGNISE HIS NATIONALITY / PARADED HIM ABOUT AS "LE BRIGAND DE LA GUERRE". / EXHAUSTED BY HIS WOUND AND UNABLE TO MARCH WITH / THEM HIS GUARD PLACED HIM AGAINST A BANK TO SHOOT / HIM WHEN AN OFFICER CAME UP JUST IN TIME TO AVERT HIS / APPENDING FATE AND HAD HIM CARRIED TO PRISON WHERE / HE LANGUISHED FOR SOME MONTHS. AN IRISHMAN / IN THE FRENCH SERVICE BEING ON DUTY AT THE PRISON / DISCOVERED IN HIM A FELLOW COUNTRYMAN. HE WAS THEN / REMOVED TO BETTER QUARTERS, AND SOON AFTER SET FREE / HIS FIRST ACT ON REGAINING HIS LIBERTY WAS TO OBTAIN / THE RELEASE OF THE BROTHER OF THE OFFICER TO WHOM / HE OWED THE PRESERVATION OF HIS LIFE, AS HE WAS / THEN A PRISONER IN ENGLAND. HIS SERVICES WITH THE / ITALIAN REGIMENT WERE REWARDED IN HIS BEING MADE / A KNIGHT OF ST MAURICE AND ST LAZARRE AND HIS OTHER / ACTS OF BRAVERY INDUCED HIS OWN GOVERNMENT TO / OFFER HIM A BARONETCY WHICH HE DECLINED

Ensign 26th Foot 19 Feb 1806. Lt 4th Garrison Battalion 25 Nov 1806. Lt 62nd Foot 1 Nov 1807. Capt 60th Foot 15 Feb 1816. Capt 13th Foot 28 Mar 1816.

Served in the Peninsula Apr – Jun 1813 attached to the Calabrian Free Corps (wounded at St Vincente, taken prisoner and awarded pension of £100 per annum). Brigade Major to General La Tours Brigade Jul 1813 – Apr 1814. Present at Castalla and Tarragona. Awarded Knight of St Maurice and St Lazarre (from Sardinia). Half pay 20 Dec 1821.

SHEDDEN, John

Captain. 52nd (Oxfordshire) Light Infantry Regiment of Foot.
Memorial tablet: Holy Trinity Church, Hull, Yorkshire. (Photograph)

SACRED / TO THE MEMORY OF / MAJOR JOHN SHEDDEN, / OF THE 52ND LIGHT INFANTRY, / WHO DIED AT HULL JULY 12TH 1821, / AGED 42. / THIS STONE IS PLACED / BY HIS BROTHER OFFICERS, / IN TESTIMONY OF THEIR ADMIRATION / OF HIS ZEAL AND GALLANTRY / AS A SOLDIER; / PROVED IN ALMOST EVERY AFFAIR / OF THE PENINSULAR WAR; / AND OF / THEIR ESTEEM FOR HIS PRIVATE WORTH, / QUALITIES WHICH DURING / AN EVENTFUL SERVICE OF 17 YEARS, / WERE UNREMITTINGLY DEDICATED TO THE / INTERESTS OF THE / REGIMENT / AND HIS COUNTRY.

Ensign 6 Oct 1804. Lt 30 Apr 1805. Capt 9 May 1811. Bt Major 23 Jan 1819.

Served in the Peninsula with 1/52nd Aug 1808 – Jan 1809, Jul 1809 – May 1811, with 2/52nd Jun 1811 – Mar 1812, and 1/52nd Sep 1813 – Apr 1814. Present at Corunna, Coa, Busaco, Pombal, Redinha, Casal Nova, Foz d'Arouce, Sabugal, Fuentes d'Onoro, Ciudad Rodrigo, Bidassoa (wounded), Nivelle, Nive, Orthes, Vic Bigorre, Tarbes and Toulouse. Present at Waterloo where he commanded a company of the 1st Battalion.

SHEKLETON, Robert

Surgeon. 3rd (East Kent) Regiment of Foot.
Pedestal tomb: Mount Jerome Cemetery, Dublin, Ireland. (Grave number C62–2463). (Photograph)

TO THE MEMORY / OF / ROBERT SHEKLETON MD / FORMERLY / SURGEON 57TH REGT / FOR MANY YEARS / A PHYSICIAN IN THIS CITY / 22ND FEB 1789 / JULY 26TH 1867 / ....

Asst Surgeon 66th Foot 5 Nov 1807. Surgeon 3rd Foot 9 Sep 1813. Surgeon 51st Foot 13 Nov 1828.

Served in the Peninsula with 66th Foot Apr 1809 – Sep 1813 and 3rd Foot Oct 1813 – Apr 1814. Present at Douro, Albuera, Vittoria, Pyrenees, Nivelle, Nive (wounded), Garris, Orthes, Aire and Toulouse. Also served in North America 1814–1815. MD. Retired 25 Apr 1829. MGS medal for Albuera, Vittoria, Pyrenees, Nivelle, Nive, Orthes and Toulouse.

SHELTON, John

Captain. 9th (East Norfolk) Regiment of Foot.
Memorial tablet: St Peter's Church, Dublin, Ireland. (No longer extant. Church demolished in 1980s Bodies and gravestones removed to St Luke's Church in the Coombe, but this Church is also now redundant and unlikely that any memorials will have survived). (M.I.)

"SACRED TO THE MEMORY OF COLONEL JOHN SHELTON, WHO DIED IN COMMAND OF HER MAJESTY'S 44TH REGIMENT, ON THE 16TH OF MAY, 1845, AGED 54 YEARS, WHOSE REMAINS ARE DEPOSITED IN THE VAULT AT THE SOUTH SIDE OF THE CHURCH. THIS DISTINGUISHED SOLDER SERVED IN THE BATTLES OF ROLICIA, VIMIERA, THE RETREAT TO AND BATTLE OF CORUNNA, THE EXPEDITION TO WALCHEREN IN 1809, INCLUDING THE SIEGE OF FLUSHING: HE AFTERWARDS RETURNED TO THE PENINSULA AND WAS PRESENT

AT THE SIEGE AND CAPTURE OF BADAJOS, THE BATTLE OF SALAMANCA, THE CAPTURE OF MADRID, THE RETREAT FROM BURGOS, THE BATTLE OF VITTORIA, AND THE SIEGE AND CAPTURE OF ST SEBASTIAN, WHERE HE WAS SEVERELY WOUNDED AND LOST HIS RIGHT ARM. SUBSEQUENTLY HE SERVED IN THE CAMPAIGN OF 1814 IN CANADA, IN 1822 HE EMBARKED FOR THE EAST INDIES, WHERE HE SERVED 21 YEARS, AND WAS EMPLOYED IN THE CAMPAIGN IN AVA, AND THE TAKING OF ARRACAN. HE SERVED IN THE DISASTROUS RETREAT FROM CABOOL IN THE WINTER OF 1841–2. THIS TABLET IS ERECTED BY HIS NEPHEW WILLIAM SHELTON, FORMERLY OF THE ABOVE REG^T AND CAPT OF THE 9TH FOOT."

Ensign 21 Nov 1805. Lt 26 Aug 1807. Capt 17 Jul 1813. Major 44th Foot 6 Feb 1825. Lt Colonel 6 Sep 1827. Bt Colonel 23 Nov 1841.

Served in the Peninsula with 1/9th Aug 1808 – Jan 1809, Mar 1810 – Oct 1813 and Mar – Apr 1814. Present at Rolica, Vimeiro, Corunna, Castrejon, Salamanca, retreat from Burgos (present at Villa Muriel), Osma, Vittoria, San Sebastian (severely wounded where he lost his arm at the final assault on 31 Aug 1813 and awarded pension of £100 per annum) and Bayonne. Also served at Walcheren 1809 (present at the siege of Flushing), North America 1814, India 1822 (served in Ava and present at the Capture of Aracan), Afghanistan 1841–1842 (Second in Command in the disastrous campaign under Major General Elphinstone. Present in the retreat from Kabul and taken hostage so he survived the massacre). In command of 44th Foot 1827–1845. Accidentally killed in a riding accident in Dublin 16 May 1845.

REFERENCE: United Service Magazine, Jun 1845, p. 320. Annual Register, 1845, Appx, pp. 277–8.

SHELTON, John Willington

Lieutenant. 28th (North Gloucestershire) Regiment of Foot.

Family vault: Ballingarry Churchyard, Ballingarry, County Limerick. Ireland. (Photograph)

HERE LIE BURIED THE BODIES OF / ROBERT SHELTON ESQ^R OF ROSSMORE, / .... / AND OF / JOHN WILLINGTON, LATE A CAPT^N / IN HER MAJESTY'S SERVICE, ELDEST SON / OF JOHN, DIED JULY 19TH 1848 AGED 57 YR^S. / THIS MONUMENT IS ERECTED / BY THE FOND WIFE & CHILDREN / OF JOHN WILLINGTON SHELTON ESQ^R, / MARY FADDY, WIFE OF GENERAL FADDY, / ROYAL ARTILLERY & RELICT OF CAPT^N J. W. / SHELTON, DIED AT ROSSMORE 16TH MARCH 1871 / ÆTATIS 74.

Ensign 8th West India Regt 21 Jul 1808. Ensign 28th Foot 8 Oct 1808. Lt 22 Mar 1810.

Served in the Peninsula with 2/28th Jul 1809 – Aug 1811 and 1/28th Sep 1813 – Apr 1814. Present at Busaco, Lines of Torres Vedras, Campo Mayor, first siege of Badajoz, Albuera (severely wounded), Nivelle, Nive and Bayonne. Present at Waterloo where he was wounded four times, and severely wounded by a shell which broke his right arm and ribs. MGS medal for Busaco, Albuera, Nivelle and Nive. Half pay 27 Nov 1817. Later Capt and Adjt in 1st Regiment Royal Surrey Militia 17 Aug 1819. Died 19 Jul 1847 and his widow married General Peter Faddy, Royal Artillery. Elder brother of Ensign Jonathon Shelton 81st Foot.

SHELTON, Jonathan

Ensign. 81st Regiment of Foot.

Memorial tablet: Ballingarry Church, Ballingarry, County Limerick, Ireland. (Photograph)

SACRED / TO THE MEMORY OF / JONATHAN SHELTON ESQ^R. / LATE ENSIGN IN THE 81ST REGIMENT / WHO WAS WRECKED / AND LOST / IN THE SOVEREIGN TRANSPORT / ON HIS PASSAGE TO / AMERICA / ON THE 18TH OF OCTOBER 1814 / IN THE 20TH YEAR OF HIS AGE / THIS MONUMENT IS ERECTED / TO A BELOVED AND A CARING CHILD / BY HIS MUCH AFFLICTED / AND DISCONSOLATE / PARENTS

Ensign 28 Apr 1814.

Drowned in the shipwreck of *The Sovereign* in St Lawrence River 1814 on his way to the North American campaign. Younger brother of Lt John Shelton 28th Foot.

SHENLEY, Edward William Henry

2nd Lieutenant. 95th Regiment of Foot.
Chest tomb: Kensal Green Cemetery, London. (16950/42/RS). (Photograph)

EDWARD W. H. / SHENLEY ESQ / BORN MARCH 12 1799 / DIED JANY 31 1878 / AGED 78

2nd Lt 21 Apr 1814. Lt 4 Foot 13 Jul 1821.

Present at Waterloo (severely wounded at Quatre Bras). Half pay 25 Aug 1821. Retired 8 Oct 1825.

SHEPHERD, John

Lieutenant. 3rd (East Kent) Regiment of Foot.
Gravestone: Holy Trinity Churchyard, Cheltenham, Gloucestershire. (Burial record)

"18** JAN 23. SHEPHERD, JOHN CAPT., 3RD FT".

Ensign 4 May 1805. Lt 27 Nov 1806. Capt 1 Jan 1815.

Served in the Peninsula Sep 1808 – Jan 1809 and Jun 1809 – Apr 1814. Present at Corunna, Busaco, Albuera (wounded), Vittoria, Pyrenees, Nivelle, Nive, Garris, Orthes, Aire and Toulouse. Also served in North America 1814–1815.

SHEPHERD, Lynn

Private. 69th (South Lincolnshire) Regiment of Foot.
Memorial tablet: All Saints Anglican Churchyard, Sutton Forest, New South Wales, Australia. (Photograph)

IN MEMORY OF / PIONEERS / LYNN SHEPHERD BORN 1795 / ELISABETH (MARINER) BORN 1792 / LYNN WAS WOUNDED AT WATERLOO IN 1815 WHILE SERVING WITH THE 69TH REGIMENT. HE AND / ELISABETH WERE MARRIED AT ARNOLD, NOTTINGHAM IN 1817. IN 1826 THEY CAME TO N.S.W. IN / THE "ORPHEUS". LYNN WAS GRANTED 80 ACRES OF LAND AT BONG BONG IN 1830 (HARBY FARM). / THEIR CHILDREN WERE MARY, CHARLES, JOHN, LYNN, JAMES, SARAH AND WILLIAM. / IN 1838 LYNN WAS WRONGLY ACCUSED OF HIGHWAY ROBBERY AND IMPRISONED ON / NORFOLK ISLAND. HE WAS RELEASED IN 1841. / HE DIED AT MURRAY FLATTS IN 1845 AND WAS BURIED IN THIS CEMETERY. / ELISABETH WAS BURIED AT MANGARLOWE IN 1872. / LYNN AND ELISABETH'S DESCENDANTS HONOURED THEM ON / 17TH SEPTEMBER 1995 WITH THIS MEMORIAL STONE.

Pte 15 Feb 1812.

Present at Waterloo in Captain Charles Cuyler's company where he was wounded and discharged as unfit for service 27 May 1816 aged 20. Emigrated to Australia in 1826 and started a new life as a farmer.

SHEPPARD, Edmund

1st Lieutenant. Royal Artillery.
Memorial tablet: All Saints' Church, Market Place, Kingston upon Thames, Surrey. (Photograph)

SACRED TO THE MEMORY OF / MAJOR EDMUND SHEPPARD / ROYAL ARTILLERY / WHO DIED AT RUTLAND HOUSE IN THIS PARISH ON THE / 6TH NOVR A.D. 1858, / AGED 69 YEARS. / DURING A SERVICE OF UPWARD OF THIRTY YEARS / HE WAS ENGAGED IN THE / WALCHEREN EXPEDITION 1809, AND TOOK PART / IN THE ACTIONS OF CHIPPEWA LUNDY'S

/ LANE; FORT ERIE AND SNAKE HILL IN CANADA. / HIS REMAINS ARE INTERRED IN THE CEMETERY / BELONGING TO THIS TOWN / THIS TABLET WAS ERECTED TO HIS MEMORY BY HIS BEREAVED WIDOW

2nd Lt 1 Jul 1806. 1st Lt 1 Feb 1808. 2nd Capt 2 Mar 1825. Capt 4 Feb 1836. Bt Major 28 Jun 1838.

Served with the the Army of Occupation Jun 1817 – Dec 1818. Also served at Walcheren 1809, Canada 1812–1816 (present at Chippewa, Lundy's Lane, Fort Erie and Snake Hill), West Indies 1825 – Mar 1827 and Oct 1834 – Jul 1836. Half pay 19 Jun 1840.

SHEPPARD, Frederic

Lieutenant. 4th (King's Own) Regiment of Foot.
Memorial tablet: St John the Baptist's Church, Campsea Ash, Suffolk. (Photograph)

SACRED TO THE MEMORY OF / FREDERIC SHEPPARD / LIEUTENANT IN THE 4TH OR KINGS OWN REGIMENT OF FOOT / AND SON OF JOHN SHEPPARD OF CAMPSEY ASH / IN THE COUNTY OF SUFFOLK, ESQUIRE. / HIS CAREER WAS SHORT BUT GLORIOUS. IN 1806 HE ENTERED / INTO THE ARMY AND WAS PRESENT THE FOLLOWING YEAR / AT THE SIEGE AND CAPTURE OF COPENHAGEN. / HE AFTERWARDS SAILED WITH SIR JOHN MOORE TO GOTTENSBURGH / AND FROM THENCE TO PORTUGAL; / HE TRAVERSED THAT KINGDOM AND SPAIN AS FAR AS SALAMANCA / ENDURED THE HARDSHIPS OF THE RETREAT WITH THE GREATEST OF FORTITUDE / AND CARRIED THE KINGS COLOUR AT THE MEMORABLE BATTLE OF CORUNNA. / HE WENT UPON THE EXPEDITION TO ZEALAND WHERE HE BEHELD THE FALL OF / FLUSHING; WAS IN GARRISON AT GIBRALTAR AND THENCE REMOVED TO CEURTA / WHERE ANXIOUS TO DISTINGUISH HIMSELF IN THE FIELD OF HONOUR, HE / HASTENED TO JOIN THE ARMY SERVING UNDER LORD WELLINGTON / BEFORE BADAJOS, IN STORMING WHICH FORTRESS APRIL THE 6TH 1812, / HE RECEIVED A MUSQUET BALL THRO' HIS THIGH / OF WHICH WOUND TO THE UNIVERSAL REGRET OF THE REGIMENT / HE DIED SIX DAYS AFTER IN THE 22ND YEAR OF HIS AGE / AND HIS REMAINS WERE HONOURABLY INTERRED ON THE RAMPARTS / WHERE HE SO GLORIOUSLY FELL. / WHAT THO' THY BONES LAMENTED FREDERIC LIE / BENEATH THE ASPECT OF A FOREIGN SKY/ NEATH BADAJOS RAMPARTS WITH NO STONE TO TELL / OR MARK THE SPOT WHERE YOUTHFUL VALOUR FELL, / YET TO HIGH HEAVEN OUR THANKS WE STILL RETURN / FOR SHELTER NOBLER THAN SCULPTURED URN.

Ensign 4 Dec 1806. Lt 14 Dec 1808.

Served in the Peninsula Aug 1808 – Jan 1809 and Apr 1812 (with 1/4th). Present at Corunna (carrying the colours), Badajoz (severely wounded 6 Apr 1812 and died of his wounds 12 Apr 1812). Also served at Copenhagen 1807, Sweden 1808, Walcheren 1809 (present at the siege of Flushing) and Gibraltar 1810–1811.

SHERBROOKE, Sir John Coape

Colonel. 33rd (1st Yorkshire West Riding) Regiment of Foot.
Memorial tablet: St Wilfred's Church, Calverton, Nottinghamshire. (Photograph)

SACRED / TO THE MEMORY OF / SIR JOHN COAPE SHERBROOKE, / GENERAL IN THE ARMY, / COLONEL OF THE 33RD REGT OF FOOT, / AND KNIGHT GRAND CROSS OF THE / MOST HONORABLE MILITARY ORDER / OF THE BATH. / HE DIED ON THE 14TH OF FEBRUARY 1830, / AGED 63 YEARS. / HIS REMAINS ARE DEPOSITED / IN THE FAMILY VAULT AT OXTON, / IN THIS COUNTY.

Buried in the family vault: St Peter and St Paul's Church, Oxton, Nottinghamshire. (Photograph).

THE VAULT / OF THE / SHERBROOKE / FAMILY.

Ensign 4th Foot 7 Dec 1780. Lt 22 Dec 1781. Capt 85th Foot 6 Mar 1783. Capt 33rd Foot 23 Jun 1784. Major 30 Dec 1793. Lt Colonel 24 Mar 1794. Bt Colonel 1 Jan 1798. Major General 1 Jan 1805. Lt General 4 Jun 1811. General 27 May 1825.

Served in the Peninsula Jun 1809 – Apr 1810 (O/c 1 Division). Present at Oporto and Talavera where he was second in command to Wellington. Gold Medal for Talavera. GCB. Also served in Flanders 1794–1795, India 1799 (present at Malavelly and Capture of Seringapatam), Sicily 1805, Canada where he was Lt Governor of Nova Scotia 1810–1816, Commanded the expedition up the Penobscot River 1814 and Governor General of Canada 1816 – Aug 1818. He governed with great sense showing tact, diplomatic skills and avoided confrontation. Resigned owing to ill health and returned to England. Colonel Sicilian Regiment 5 Feb 1807. Colonel 33rd Regiment 1 Jan 1813.
Reference: Dictionary of National Biography. Dictionary of Canadian Biography. Gentleman's Magazine, Jun 1830, pp. 558–9. Royal Military Calendar, Vol. 2, pp. 193–6.

SHERER, Moyle
Captain. 34th Regiment of Foot.
Low monument: St Luke's Churchyard, Brislington, Bristol, Somerset. (Photograph)

"SACRED / TO THE / LOVED AND HONORED / MEMORY / OF / MAJOR MOYLE. SHERER FORMERLY OF H. M. 34TH REGIMENT / BORN FEBRUARY 18TH 1789. DIED NOVEMBER 14TH 1869."

Ensign 13 Jan 1807. Lt 4 Jun 1807. Capt 26 Mar 1812. Bt Major 22 Jul 1830. Capt 96th Foot 1831.

Served in the Peninsula Jul 1809 – Dec 1811 and Aug 1812 – Apr 1814. Present at Busaco, Olivencia, first siege of Badajoz, Albuera, Arroyo dos Molinos, Vittoria and Pyrenees (taken prisoner at Maya on 25th Jul 1813 and remained a prisoner of war until Apr 1814). MGS medal for Busaco, Albuera and Vittoria. Also served in India 1818 with 34th Foot. Wrote *Sketches of India*, 1821 (four edns), his very popular *Recollections of the Peninsula* 1823 (five edns), *Scenes and impressions in Egypt and Italy* 1824, *Notes and reflections during a Ramble in Germany*, 1826 and *Life of Wellington*, 1830–1832. His attempts at fiction were not successful. Half pay 6 Jul 1832.
Reference: Dictionary of National Biography. Sherer, Moyle, Recollections of the Peninsula, 1824, reprint, 1996.

SHERLOCK, Francis
Lieutenant Colonel. 4th (Royal Irish) Dragoon Guards.
Low monument: Southwell Minster, Southwell, Nottinghamshire. Inscription Illegible. (Photograph)

Memorial window: Southwell Minster, Southwell, Nottinghamshire. (Photograph)

TO THE GLORY OF GOD AND IN MEMORY OF A / BELOVED GRANDMOTHER ANNA SHERLOCK, WIDOW / OF COLONEL FRANCIS SHERLOCK KH. OF HER / GRANDCHILDREN JOHN, HENRY, GORDON, AND / ELIZABETH KATHARINE HODGKINSON, THE WIFE / OF GROSVENOR HODGKINS, HIS SISTER. THIS / ***************** / WILL AND TESTAMENT OF CHARLES FRANCIS GORDON

Cornet 8th Lt Dragoons Aug 1793. Lt/Capt 22 Dec 1793. Major 4 Jun 1801. Major 4th Dragoon Guards 28 Aug 1804. Lt Colonel 16 Feb 1809. Bt Colonel 4 Jun 1814.

Served in the Peninsula Aug 1811 – Apr 1813. Present at Llerena. Also served in Flanders 1794–1795 and Cape of Good Hope 1796–1803. KH. Died 15 Jan 1848.

SHERRIS, Alexander
Private. 2nd Garrison Battalion.
Buried at Old Meldrum, Aberdeenshire, Scotland.

Pte Aberdeen Militia 1803. Pte 92nd Foot 4 May 1805. Pte 2nd Garrison Battalion 2 May 1815.

Served in the Peninsula 1808 – Apr 1814. Present at Corunna, Fuentes d'Onoro, Vittoria, Pyrenees (wounded at Donna Maria Pass 31 Jul 1813). Discharged 24 Oct 1816. Chelsea Out-Pensioner (received a pension of six pence a day). MGS medal for Corunna, Fuentes d'Onoro, Vittoria and Pyrenees. Died at Old Meldrum 14 Jan 1851 aged 70.

SHERWOOD, Isaac
Lieutenant. 15th (King's) Regiment of Light Dragoons.
Named on the Regimental Memorial: St Joseph's Church, Waterloo. (Photograph)

Cornet 4 Oct 1809. Lt 13 Sep 1810.

Served in the Peninsula Feb 1813 – Apr 1814. Present at Morales, Vittoria, Orthes and Toulouse. Present at Waterloo where he was killed.

SHIFFNER, John Bridger
Lieutenant and Captain. 3rd Regiment of Foot Guards.
Memorial stone: 3rd Foot Guards Cemetery, Bayonne, France. (Photograph)

TO THE MEMORY / OF / CAPTAINS WHITE & SHIFFNER / THIRD GUARDS / WHO DIED OF WOUNDS RECEIVED IN / ACTION BEFORE BAYONNE / ON THE 14 APRIL / 1814

Memorial tablet: St Nicholas's Church, Tuxford, Nottinghamshire. (Photograph)

THE DESIGN ABOVE REPRESENTS THE BURIAL PLACE OF CAPTN WHITE AND THREE OF / HIS BROTHER OFFICERS. I. B. SHIFFNER FRANCIS R. HOLBURNE AND LUKE MAHON. / CAPTS WHITE AND SHIFFNER WERE BURIED TOGETHER IN THE GRAVE MARKED WITH THEIR / INITIALS, THE CROSS WAS FORMED OF A LARGE TREE AS IT GREW THE TOP BEING CUT OFF / AND PLACED ACROSS, ABOVE WHICH IT HAD BEEN PENETRATED BY A 24LB SHOT WHICH / REMAINED IN THE TREE AS REPRESENTED. – WITH THE DRUMS AND COLOURS AS PLACED / AT THE FUNERALS IN A VALLEY ABOUT A MILE FROM BAYONNE. / THERE WERE AFTER-WARDS STONES PLACED AT THE HEAD OF EACH GRAVE BY THE / SURVIVING OFFICERS OF THE REGIMENT / ....

(Remainder of this memorial refers exclusively to Lt and Capt Charles Lawrence White)

Named on Memorial Panel VII for the Sortie from Bayonne: Royal Military Chapel, Wellington Barracks, London. (M.I.) (Destroyed by a Flying Bomb 1944)

Named on the Memorial: St Andrew's Church (now Musée Historique), Biarritz, France. (Photograph)

Ensign 26 Oct 1805. Lt and Capt 27 Mar 1811.

Served in the Peninsula Mar 1809–1811 and Jul 1812 – Apr 1814. Present at Douro, Talavera, Busaco, Fuentes d'Onoro, Salamanca, Burgos, Bidassoa, Nivelle, Nive, Adour and Bayonne where he was severely wounded at the Sortie from Bayonne 14 Apr 1814 and died of his wounds 15 Apr 1814.

SHIP, John

Veterinary Surgeon. 23rd Regiment of Light Dragoons.
Memorial: St John's Church, Hackney, London. (In Crypt). Inscription not recorded.

Veterinary Surgeon 11th Lt Dragoons 25 Jun 1796. Veterinary Surgeon 23rd Lt Dragoons 3 Apr 1806.

Served in the Peninsula Jun 1809 – Jun 1810. Present at Talavera. Present at Waterloo. Wrote *Cases in farriery, in which the diseases of horse are treated on the principles of the Veterinary School of Medicine*, 1808. Half pay 1818. Died at Hackney 29 Nov 1834.
Note: Also known as John Shipp.
Reference: Gray, Ernest A., The trumpet of glory: the military career of John Shipp, first veterinary surgeon to join the British Army, 1985.

SHIPTON, Henry Noble

Ensign. 4th (King's Own) Regiment of Foot.
Memorial tablet: St Peter's Church, South Portishead, near Bristol, Somerset, (Photograph)

HENRY NOBLE SHIPTON SENIOR ENSIGN OF THE 4TH OR KINGS OWN REGIMENT / OF FOOT. HE WAS PERSONALLY ENGAGED AT THE SIEGE OF MAJORCA, MENORCA / AND NEW ORLEANS AND IN THE GLORIOUS BATTLE OF WATERLOO / ON THE EVE OF PROMOTION MERITED NOT LESS BY HIS AMIABLE QUALITIES AS A / MAN THAN BY HIS BRAVERY AS AN OFFICER HE FELL VICTIM TO THE YELLOW FEVER / IN BARBADOES DECEMBER 5TH 1821 AGED 26 YEARS.

Named on the Regimental Memorial to 4th Foot: St Michael's Cathedral, Bridgetown, Barbados, West Indies. (Photograph)

Memorial tablet: St Michael's Cathedral, Bridgetown, Barbados, West Indies. (Photograph)

SACRED TO THE MEMORY OF HENRY NOBLE SHIPTON, / SENIOR ENSIGN OF THE FOURTH OR KING'S OWN REGIMENT OF FOOT, / AND YOUNGEST SON OF THE REVEREND JOHN SHIPTON, / DOCTOR IN DIVINITY, RECTOR OF PORTISHEAD NEAR BRISTOL, VICAR OF / STANTON BURY, IN THE COUNTY OF BUCKINGHAM, AND ONE OF HIS MAJESTY'S / JUSTICES OF THE PEACE FOR THE COUNTY OF SOMERSET, IN ENGLAND. / HE WAS AN ACTIVE AND VALUED OFFICER, / AS WELL AS A SINGULARLY AMIABLE AND EXCELLENT YOUNG MAN: / WHO, ESCAPING THE DANGERS ESPECIALLY INCIDENT TO HIS PROFESSION, / PARTICULARLY THOSE OF THE SIEGE OF NEW ORLEANS, / AND THE EVER MEMORABLE BATTLE OF WATERLOO, / WAS CUT OFF, WHEN ON THE EVE OF PROMOTION, BY THE YELLOW FEVER, / AFTER ONLY FIVE DAYS OF ILLNESS, WHILST STATIONED WITH HIS REGIMENT / IN THIS ISLAND, ON THE FIFTH DAY OF DECEMBER 1821, / IN THE 26TH YEAR OF HIS AGE, / TO THE VERY DEEP REGRET OF HIS AFFLICTED PARENTS, / WHO HAVE CAUSED THIS TABLET TO BE ERECTED AS A TOKEN OF / THEIR AFFECTION FOR THEIR BELOVED SON.

2nd Lt Royal Marines 12 May 1812. Ensign 4th Foot 3 Aug 1815.

Present at Waterloo and with the Army of Occupation until 1818. Also served in America where he was drafted into 4th Foot from the Marines (present at New Orleans and Fort Bowyer), Majorca, Minorca and the West Indies 1819–1821 where he died of yellow fever on the eve of his promotion to Lieutenant.
Reference: Gentleman's Magazine, Feb 1822, p. 188.

SHIRLEY, John

Corporal. Royal Regiment of Horse Guards.
Low monument: St Chad's Churchyard, Prees, Shropshire. (Photograph)

IN MEMORY OF / JOHN SHIRLEY, CAP^T. N .S. Y. BORN AT ASTONFIELD, STAFFS. 15 APRIL 1784. / ENLISTED IN THE ROYAL REGT. HORSE GUARDS (BLUE) 16 DEC^R 1805, / SERVED IN PORTUGAL, SPAIN, FRANCE 1812–13, RETIRED FROM / THE BLUES 31 DEC^R 1830. ENTERED THE N. S. Y. JAN^Y 1831. GAZETTED / CAPTAIN AND ADJUTANT 6 JULY 1832. DIED AT PREES 22 FEB^Y 1861.

Inside the church in the vestry is a charity board inscribed:

A.D. 1861. THE SUM OF ONE HUNDRED POUNDS WAS LEFT / BY CAPT. JOHN SHIRLEY, THE INTEREST / TO BE GIVEN TO POOR WIDOWS OF PREES ON / ST THOMAS' DAY AT THE DISCRETION OF / THE MINISTER AND CHURCHWARDENS — £100-0-0.

Pte 16 Dec 1805.

Served in the Peninsula 1812–1813. MGS medal for Vittoria. After leaving the regiment in 1830 joined the North Shropshire Yeomanry becoming Capt and Adjutant 6 Jul 1832.

SHORT, Charles William

Ensign. Coldstream Regiment of Foot Guards.

Memorial cross: All Saints' Churchyard, Odiham, Hampshire. (Photograph)

LT COLONEL CHARLES WILLIAM SHORT / DIED 19 JAN 1857

Memorial window and brass tablet: All Saints Parish Church, Odiham, Hampshire. (Photograph)

THE PAINTED GLASS IN THE THREE EAST WINDOWS OF / THE CHANCEL WAS SET UP TO THE GLORY OF GOD / AND IN MEMORY OF HIS SERVANT CHARLES WILLIAM SHORT / L^T COL IN THE YEAR OF OUR LORD GOD 1838

Ensign 13 Oct 1814. Lt and Capt 17 Apr 1823. Capt and Lt Colonel 21 Sep 1830.

Present at Waterloo and with the Army of Occupation. Retired 1837. Wrote several pamphlets on military subjects such as outposts and patrolling translated from the German. Director of Royal West India Mail Steam Packet Company. Devoted himself to charitable work after 1837 such as helping to restore church buildings that had fallen into decay, especially at Christ Church Broadway in Westminster and the House of Charity in Soho for sons of gentlemen who had fallen on hard times. Retired to Odiham 1852 and repaired the village church and almshouses.

Reference: Gentleman's Magazine, Mar 1857, p. 364.

SHORTT, Thomas

Surgeon. 20th Regiment of Light Dragoons.

Buried in St Thomas's Churchyard, Newport, Isle of Wight. (Burial register)

Hospital Mate Jun 1806. Asst Surgeon Chasseurs Britanniques 4 May 1809. Asst Surgeon 20th Lt Dragoons 7 Dec 1809. Regimental Surgeon for a 'Particular Service' in Mediterranean 26 Jul 1813. Surgeon 20th Dragoons 7 Oct 1813. Physician 30 Nov 1815.

Served in the Mediterranean 1813. Also served in Egypt 1807 and St Helena 1815–1821. Half pay 25 Jun 1817. Principal Medical Officer at St Helena and was one of the five Army Medical Officers present at the autopsy on Napoleon 6 May 1821. Retired 1821. Died 5 Mar 1843 aged 54.

Reference: Chaplin, Arnold, Thomas Shortt, Principal Medical Officer in Helena, with biographies of some other medical men associated with the case of Napoleon from 1815–1821, 1914.

SHRAPNEL, Henry Scrope
Colonel. Royal Artillery.
Memorial tablet: Holy Trinity Church, Bradford-on-Avon, Wiltshire. (Floor of the chancel). (Photograph)

TO / THE MEMORY / OF / LIEUT GENERAL HENRY SHRAPNEL / COLONEL COMMANDANT / 6TH BATTALION OF ARTILLERY. / OBIT / 13TH MARCH 1842 / AETAT / 80 YEARS.

Family Memorial tablet: Holy Trinity Church, Bradford-on-Avon, Wiltshire. (Photograph)

.... / ALSO TO THE MEMORY OF / GENERAL HENRY SCROPE SHRAPNEL, / COLONEL COMMANDANT 6TH BATTALION OF ARTILLERY. / OBIT 13TH MARCH 1849, AETAT 80 YEARS.

2nd Lt 9 Jul 1779. 1st Lt 3 Dec 1781. Capt-Lt 14 Aug 1793. Capt 5 Oct 1795. Bt Major 29 Apr 1802. Major 1 Nov 1803. Lt Col 20 Jul 1804. Bt Colonel 4 Jun 1813. Colonel 20 Dec 1814. Major General 12 Aug 1819. Lt General 10 Jan 1837.

Served in Newfoundland 1784, Gibraltar 1787–1791, Flanders 1793 (wounded in the action near Dunkirk). He was chiefly engaged for many years in developing the destructive missile which bears his name and was to be used in every army in Europe. Proposed in 1799, by 1803 it was ready for use. First employed to good effect in the attack on Surinam in 1804, and from then on was used continually. 1st Asst Inspector of Artillery 1804. For his services to the country he was awarded a pension of £1,200 a year in 1814. He left the army 29 Jul 1825. Colonel Commandant Royal Artillery 6 Mar 1827. Died at Southampton 13 Mar 1842. (The date on the wall tablet at Bradford-on-Avon is in error).
Reference: Dictionary of National Biography. Gentleman's Magazine, Jul 1842, p. 95. Annual Register, 1842, Appx, p. 257.

SHULDHAM, Lemuel
Cornet: 2nd (Royal North British) Regiment of Dragoons.
Memorial tablet: St Andrew's Church, Marlesford, Suffolk. (Photograph)

LEMUEL SHULDHAM / CORNET IN THE SCOTS GREYS THE YOUNGER SON OF / WILLIAM SHULDHAM, OF MARLESFORD, ESQUIRE AND MARY HIS WIFE. / WAS BORN 27TH OF FEBRUARY 1794, AND FELL IN BATTLE ON / THE 18TH JUNE 1815, AT WATERLOO. / FAR IN ADVANCE WITHIN THE LINES RIGHT OF THE FRENCH / HIS BODY WAS FOUND THE NEXT MORNING AND BURIED ON THE SPOT. / TO PRESERVE IN HIS NATIVE VILLAGE A RECORD OF ONE SO EARLY AND SO NOBLY LOST / THIS MARBLE IS CONSECRATED / IN THE BLESSED HOPE AGAIN TO BEHOLD HIM IN THE BEAUTY OF IMMORTAL LIFE.

Cornet 19 Jan 1815.

Present at Waterloo, where he was killed when he became separated from his troop when the Scots Greys charged. Buried on the field of battle by the burial party under Lt Graham. Cousin of Cornet George Schreiber,Captain James Alfred Schreiber and Capt William Frederick Schreiber all of 11th Lt Dragoons.

SHUM, William
Captain. 3rd (Prince of Wales's) Dragoon Guards.
Table tomb: St Mary the Virgin's Churchyard, Bedfont, Middlesex, London. (M.I.)

SACRED / TO THE MEMORY OF / WILLIAM SHUM ESQUIRE / LATE CAPTAIN 3RD DRAGOON GUARDS / WHO DEPARTED THIS LIFE THE 18TH OF APRIL 1854 / AGED 64 YEARS

Cornet 10 Dec 1807. Lt 21 Feb 1810. Capt 27 May 1813.

Served in the Peninsula Apr 1809 – Apr 1814. Present at Talavera, Aldea de Ponte, Maguilla, Vittoria and Toulouse. Half pay 25 Mar 1816. MGS medal for Talavera, Vittoria and Toulouse.

SIBORNE, William
Ensign 9th (Norfolk) Regiment of Foot.
Headstone: Brompton Cemetery, London. (Photograph)

SACRED / TO THE MEMORY OF / CHARLOTTE SIBORNE / .... / ALSO TO THAT OF CAPT WILLIAM SIBORNE / SON OF THE ABOVE / WHO DIED ON THE 13TH DAY OF JANUARY 1849 / IN THE 51ST YEAR OF HIS AGE / THE DECEASED WAS SECRETARY OF / THE ROYAL MILITARY ASYLUM IN CHELSEA, / AUTHOR OF THE HISTORY OF THE WAR IN / FRANCE AND BELGIUM IN 1815 / AND CONSTRUCTOR OF THE WATERLOO MODELS.

Enign 9 Sep 1813. Lt 8 Nov 1815. Lt 47th Foot 11 Nov 1824.

Served with the Army of Occupation in France. Also served in Ireland 1826–1834 (Asst Military Secretary to the Commander in Chief). Interested in topography and model making. In 1830 Lord Hill suggested he made a model of the Waterloo battlefield while he was stationed in Ireland. By 1835 the model was finished and sent from Ireland to London for public display. The model was based on information that Siborne had from participants in the battle who had written to him in answer to questions he had raised. These letters are contained in the volume of *Waterloo Letters* edited by his son Major General H. T. Siborne in 1891. Further unpublished letters were found and edited by Gareth Glover in 2004. The letters are still controversial today. William Siborne also wrote *History of the Waterloo Campaign,* 3rd edn 1848. This edition contains corrections to his original work.
Reference: Dictionary of National Biography. Siborne, William, Waterloo letters, reprint 1983.

SICKER, George
Lieutenant and Adjutant. 11th Regiment of Light Dragoons.
Buried in St George's Chapel, Windsor, Berkshire. (Burial record)

Quartermaster Sgt. Cornet and Adjutant 4 Sep 1802. Lt 20 Feb 1805.

Served in the Peninsula Jun 1811 – Jan 1813. Present at El Bodon, Moriscos, Salamanca, Majalahonda and Venta del Pozo. Present at Waterloo. Also served in China 1792 as part of a detachment with Lord Macartney. Half pay 30 Jul 1818. Military Knight of Windsor. Died 13 Jan 1848 aged 80.

SIDDALL, John
Veterinary Surgeon. Royal Regiment of Horse Guards.
Headstone: Old Windsor Churchyard, Windsor, Berkshire. (Photograph)

SACRED / TO THE MEMORY OF / JOHN SIDDALL / VETERINARY SURGEON IN HER MAJESTY'S / ROYAL REGIMENT OF HORSE GUARDS / WHO DIED 2ND OCTOBER 1856 AGED 69 YEARS. / SCIENCE HAS LOST IN HIM A TALENTED MASTER / AND THE ARMY IN WHICH HE SERVED 53 YEARS / A FAITHFUL OFFICER.

Memorial tablet: Holy Trinity Parish and Garrison Church, Windsor, Berkshire. (Photograph)

AS A JUST TRIBUTE TO PRIVATE WORTH / AND GREAT PROFESSIONAL MERIT / THIS TABLET / IN MEMORY OF / JOHN SIDDALL, / IS INSCRIBED BY THE / OFFICERS OF THE ROYAL HORSE GUARDS (BLUE) / IN WHICH REGIMENT DURING A PERIOD OF / 53 YEARS. / HE DISCHARGED WITH ZEAL AND DILIGENCE THE DUTIES OF / VETERINARY SURGEON, / AND WAS THE LAST SURVIVING MEMBER OF ALL RANKS / IN THE HOUSEHOLD BRIGADE OF CAVALRY, PRESENT AT / WATERLOO. / HE DIED ON THE 2ND DAY OF OCTOBER 1856 /

IN THE 69TH YEAR OF HIS AGE / AND WAS INTERRED AT THE CHURCH OF OLD WINDSOR / IN THIS COUNTY.

Veterinary Surgeon 10 Oct 1812.

Present at Waterloo and with the Army of Occupation until 1816. Served for 53 years in Royal Horse Guards and was the last surviving officer of the regiment who served at Waterloo.

SIDLEY, George

Quartermaster. 23rd (Royal Welch Fusiliers) Regiment of Foot.
Ledger stone: St Columb's Cathedral, Londonderry, Northern Ireland. (Photograph)

UNDERNEATH ARE DEPOSITED / THE REMAINS / OF GEORGE SIDLEY / LATE LIEUTT AND QUARTERMASTER / OF THE / 23RD REGIMENT ROYAL WELCH FUSILIERS. / HE DEPARTED THIS LIFE ON THE 19TH OCTOBER 1839 / IN THE 71ST YEAR OF HIS AGE. / ....

Cork Militia. Quartermaster 23rd Foot 14 Apr 1808.

Served in the Peninsula with 2/23rd Oct 1808 – Jan 1809. Present at Corunna. Present at Waterloo. Retired on full pay 8 Nov 1827.

SIDNEY, Philip

Ensign. 43rd (Monmouthshire) Light Infantry Regiment of Foot.
Family Altar tomb: St Botolph's Churchyard, Aldgate, London. (M.I.)

"ENSIGN PHILIP SIDNEY OF THE 43RD REGIMENT, / SON OF JAMES AND MARGARET SIDNEY, DIED / 11 DECEMBER 1811, AGED 24 AT COIMBRA IN / PORTUGAL AND BURIED THERE."

Ensign 28 Jun 1810.

Served in the Peninsula with 1/43rd Jul 1810 – Dec 1811. Present at Coa, Busaco, Redinha, Casal Nova, Foz d'Arouce, Sabugal and Fuentes d'Onoro. Died from fever in the military hospital at Coimbra.

SIMCOE, Francis Gwillim

Lieutenant. 27th (Inniskilling) Regiment of Foot.
Monument: Exeter Cathedral, Exeter, Devon, (South aisle at the foot of a memorial to Lt General John Graves Simcoe). (Photograph)

.... / DURING THE ERECTION OF THIS MONUMENT HIS ELDEST SON FRANCIS GWILLIM SIMCOE, LIEUT IN THE 27TH REGIMENT OF FOOT, BORN AT WOLFORD LODGE / IN THIS COUNTY JUNE 6TH 1791, FELL IN THE BREACH AT THE SIEGE OF BADAJOZ, APRIL 6TH 1812, IN THE 21ST YEAR OF HIS AGE.

Ensign 6 Oct 1807. Lt 22 Dec 1808.

Served in the Peninsula with 3/27th Nov 1808 – Apr 1812. Present at Busaco, Redinha, Olivencia, first siege of Badajoz and Badajoz where he was killed on 6 Apr 1812. The regiment formed part of the 4th Division under Colville who stormed the breach in the Trinidad bastion. They met with disaster when leading columns jumped into the ditch filled with water, scores being drowned and then many being blown away by musketry and grape on the unfinished ravelin. Following the taking of the Castle, the 4th Division was ordered into the breaches once more meeting only limited resistance this time. The Inniskillings lost 303 casualties that night, one of whom was Simcoe. Educated at Eton.

SIMMONS, George
Lieutenant. 95th Regiment of Foot.
Memorial tablet: St Saviour's Church, St Helier, Jersey, Channel Islands. (Photograph)

IN MEMORY OF / MAJOR GEORGE SIMMONS, / LATE OF THE RIFLE BRIGADE, / WHO DIED AT ST HELIER / ON THE 4TH MARCH 1858 AGED 72. / HE SERVED IN THE PENINSULA / WITH THE OLD 95TH REGT FROM 1809 / TO THE END OF THE WAR IN 1814, / ALSO IN THE CAMPAIGN OF 1815, INCLUDING / THE ACTIONS OF THE 16TH 17TH 18TH JUNE, / AT QUATRE BRAS AND WATERLOO. / FOR HIS SERVICES HE RECEIVED / THE PENINSULA MEDAL WITH EIGHT CLASPS, / ORTHES, NIVELLE, PYRENEES, / VITTORIA, SALAMANCA, BADAJOZ / CIUDAD RODRIGO, FUENTES D'ONOR; / AND THE WATERLOO MEDAL. / THIS TABLET IS ERECTED BY HIS WIDOW, / ANNE CORBET, ELDEST DAUGHTER OF / SIR THOMAS LE BRETON OF BAGATELLE, / AND HIS AFFECTIONATE CHILDREN, / GEORGE, ANNE CORBET AND FRANCES ELIZA. / ....

Named on the Rifle Brigade Memorial: Winchester Cathedral, Winchester, Hampshire. (Photograph)

Asst Surgeon South Lincolnshire Militia 1805. 2nd Lt 95th Foot 25 Mar 1809. 1st Lt 25 Jul 1811. Capt 17 Apr 1828. Major 16 Feb 1838.

Served in the Peninsula with 1/95th Jun 1809 – Apr 1814. Present at Coa (wounded), Pombal, Redinha, Casal Nova, Foz d'Arouce, Sabugal, Fuentes d'Onoro, Ciudad Rodrigo, Badajoz, Salamanca, San Munos, San Millan, Vittoria, Pyrenees, Vera, Bidassoa, Nivelle, Orthes, Tarbes (wounded). Present at Waterloo (wounded) and with the Army of Occupation until 1818. Also served in Nova Scotia 1825. MGS medal for Fuentes d'Onoro, Ciudad Rodrigo, Badajoz, Salamanca, Vittoria, Pyrenees, Nivelle and Orthes. Retired 1845 after 36 years service. Brother of Lt Joseph Simmons 95th Foot and Lt Maud Simmons 34th Foot who both served in the Peninsula.

Reference: Simmons, G., A British rifleman : the journals and correspondence of Major George Simmons during the Peninsular War, edited by Colonel Willoughby Verner, London, 1899, reprint 2002. Annual Register, 1858, Appx, p. 394. Gentleman's Magazine, Apr 1858, p. 452.

SIMMONS, James
Private. 7th (Queen's Own) Regiment of Light Dragoons.
Pedestal tomb: All Saints' Churchyard, High Street, Carshalton, Surrey. (Photograph)

JAMES SIMMONS / LATE 7TH HUSSARS / DIED APRIL 6TH 1882 / AGED 90. / WATERLOO VETERAN

Present at Waterloo.

SIMPSON, Charles
Ensign. 3rd Regiment of Foot Guards.
Named on the Regimental Memorial, St Joseph's Church, Waterloo. (Photograph)

Ensign 3 Feb 1814.

Served with the 2nd Battalion at Waterloo where he was killed.

SIMPSON, Edward
Surgeon. Ordnance Medical Department.
Memorial in low walled enclosure: New Calton Burial Ground, Edinburgh, Scotland. (Photograph)

SACRED TO THE MEMORY OF / MRS MARY BOUTHRON / .... / ALSO OF / EDWARD SIMPSON, / LATE SENIOR SURGEON ROYAL ARTILLERY, / DIED 23 SEP 1854 / AGED 70 YEARS,

/ FIFTY OF WHICH WERE SPENT / IN THE SERVICE OF HIS COUNTRY. / ....

Supernumerary Asst Surgeon 25 Apr 1805. Asst Surgeon Ordnance Medical Department 1 Aug 1806. Surgeon 5 Aug 1813. Senior Surgeon 16 Jan 1841.

Present at Waterloo. Also served at Martinique 1809 and Guadeloupe 1810. MGS medal for Martinique and Guadeloupe. Retired 24 Jan 1844.

SIMPSON, James

Lieutenant and Captain. 1st Regiment of Foot Guards.
Headstone with ringed cross: St Leonard's Churchyard, Horringer, Suffolk. (Photograph)

SACRED / TO THE MEMORY / OF / GEN. SIR JAMES SIMPSON, / GCB / COLONEL 29TH REGIMENT / WHO DEPARTED THIS LIFE 18TH APRIL 1868, / AFTER A SERVICE OF NEARLY 60 YEARS / AGED 76.

Memorial: Royal Military Chapel, Wellington Barracks, London. (M.I.) (Destroyed by a Flying Bomb 1944)

"PLACED BY THE HON. W. O. STANLEY, LATE CAPTAIN AND ADJUTANT 2ND BATTALION / GRENADIER GUARDS, IN MEMORY OF THE FOLLOWING OFFICERS, WITH WHOM HE SERVED:- / GENERAL SIR JAMES SIMPSON, G.C.B. / COLONEL 87TH REGIMENT (ROYAL IRISH FUSILIERS); 1ST GUARDS, 1811–25; SERVED WITH THE 3RD BATTALION AT CADIZ AND IN THE SOUTH OF FRANCE, AND THE 2ND BATTALION AT THE BATTLE OF QUATRE BRAS, WHERE HE WAS WOUNDED. WAS ADJUTANT 1ST BATTALION, 1821–25; AND, AFTER CONSTANT SERVICE ON THE STAFF IN INDIA AND ELSEWHERE, WAS APPOINTED COMMANDER-IN-CHIEF OF THE ARMY IN THE CRIMEA, 1855".

Ensign 3 Apr 1811. Lt and Capt 11 Jan 1814. Lt Colonel (unattached) 28 Apr 1825. Lt Colonel 29th Foot 10 Jun 1826. Bt Colonel 28 Jun 1838. Major General 11 Nov 1851. Lt General 29 Jun 1855. General 8 Sep 1855.

Served in the Peninsula Jul 1812 – May 1813. Present at Cadiz and Seville. Present at Waterloo where he was severely wounded at Quatre Bras. Also served in Mauritius 1826–1837 and India 1842–1845. Commanded at Chatham 1846. Chief of Staff during the Crimean War in February 1855, but when Lord Raglan died in June 1855, took command of the British troops with some hesitation. After two unsuccessful assaults in the Redan he was criticised but the government promoted him to General and awarded him the GCB. Resigned in favour of Sir W. Codrington 10 Nov 1855. Awarded the Turkish Order of Medjidie, the Grand Cross of Military Order of Savoy and the Grand Cross of the Legion of Honour. Colonel 87th Foot 29 Jun 1855. Colonel 29th Foot 27 Jul 1863. Lived in retirement at Horringer until his death in 1868.
REFERENCE: Dictionary of National Biography. Household Brigade Journal, 1868, p. 323. Gentleman's Magazine, May 1868, p. 779.

SINCLAIR, James

Captain. 81st Regiment of Foot.
Headstone: Eyemouth Parish Churchyard, Eyemouth, Northumberland. (Photograph)

SACRED / TO THE MEMORY OF / CAPTAIN JAMES SINCLAIR LATE / OF THE 81ST REGT OF FOOT WHO DIED 18 / SEPTR 1851 AGED 59 YEARS / WHEN A SERGEANT IN THE 42D HE / HAD THE DISTINGUISHED HONOUR OF / CAPTURING THE FRENCH INVINCIBLE / STANDARD AT THE BATTLE OF ABOUKIR. / ....

Sgt 42nd Foot. Ensign 21 Jan 1804 . Lt 81st Foot 27 Aug 1807. Capt 10 Jun 1813.

Served in the Peninsula Aug 1812 – Jul 1813. Present in Eastern Spain. On duty in Brussels 16 Jun so not at Quatre Bras or Waterloo. Present in Paris with the Army of Occupation until the end of 1815 when the 2nd Battalion was brought home and disbanded in 1816. Retired on half pay. Also served in Egypt 1801 with 42nd Foot (present at Alexandria 21 Mar 1801 where the 42nd helped to defeat the French Grenadiers – the Invincibles and capture their standard). The standard was given to Sgt Sinclair who was told to stay near the French guns which had also been captured. The French cavalry appeared and attacked him re-capturing the standard. The standard was recovered eventually by Pte Lutz of the Minorca Regiment and is now in the Royal Chapel in Whitehall.

SINCLAIR, James

2nd Captain. Royal Artillery.
Obelisk: St Saviour's Churchyard, St Helier, Jersey, Channel Islands. (Photograph)

IN / MEMORY OF / LT COL JAMES SINCLAIR RA / WHO DIED AT ST HELIER / THE 15TH DAY OF MAY 1851 / AGED **/ ....

2nd Lt 9 Jun 1804. 1st Lt 15 Nov 1805. 2nd Capt 14 Feb 1814. Capt 22 Nov 1828. Bt Major 10 Jan 1837. Lt Colonel 26 Sep 1841.

Served in the Peninsula Aug 1808 – Jan 1809 (8th Company 3rd Battalion) and Feb 1811 – Apr 1814 (5th Company 5th Battalion). O/c Rocket Troop 1811. ADC to General Hay Sep 1813 – Apr 1814. Present at the retreat and battle of Corunna, Badajoz, Salamanca, retreat from Burgos (present at Villa Muriel), Vittoria (Adjutant of Artillery), Maya, Pyrenees, Bidassoa (ADC to Major General Hay), Nivelle, Nive and the Sortie from Bayonne. Present at Waterloo where he commanded Capt Frederick Gordon's Company who was in America and served with the Army of Occupation until 1818. Also served in the Baltic 1807, Walcheren 1809 and Mauritius Mar 1829 – Dec 1830. MGS medal for Corunna, Badajoz, Salamanca, Vittoria, Pyrenees, Nivelle and Nive. Retired on full pay 23 Dec 1841.
Reference: Annual Register, 1851, Appx, p. 289. United Service Magazine, Jul 1851, pp. 318–19. Haythornthwaite, Philip J. and Hall, John, A Waterloo Gunner: Second Captain James Sinclair, Royal Foot Artillery, Military History Society Bulletin, Vol. 44, No. 174, Nov 1993, pp. 88–92.

SINCLAIR, John

Captain. 79th (Cameron Highlanders) Regiment of Foot.
Named on the Regimental Memorial: St Joseph's Church, Waterloo. (Photograph)

Ensign 19 Nov 1803. Lt 14 Mar 1805. Capt 4 Jul 1811.

Served in the Peninsula Aug 1808 – Jan 1809 and Jan 1810 – Oct 1811. Present at Corunna, Cadiz, Busaco, Foz d'Arouce, Fuentes d' Onoro (wounded). Present at Quatre Bras where he died of his wounds 17 Jun 1815. Also served at Copenhagen 1807, Sweden 1808 and Walcheren 1809.

SINGER, Richard Oriel

Lieutenant. 32nd (Cornwall) Regiment of Foot.
Memorial tablet: St James's Church, North Wraxall, Wiltshire. (North Aisle). (Photograph)

IN MEMORY OF / RICHARD ORIEL SINGER ESQR / LATE OF HIS MAJESTY'S 32ND REGIMENT / WHO DIED OCTOBER 13TH 1818 / AGED 37 YEARS / WHOSE REMAINS ARE DEPOSITED / IN A VAULT IN THIS CHURCH YARD

Family Memorial tablet: St Andrew's Church, Chippenham, Wiltshire. (M.I.)

"................... ALSO IN MEMORY OF RICHARD ORIEL SINGER ESQUIRE, LATE OF HIS

MAJESTY'S 32ND REGT ONLY SON OF RICHARD SINGER BY MARIA PARRY HIS WIFE, WHO DIED OCTOBER 15TH 1818 AGED 37 YEARS. HIS REMAINS ARE DEPOSITED AT NORTH WRAXALL IN THIS COUNTY……………."

Ensign Coldstream Guards 3 Sep 1803. Lt 32nd Foot 8 May 1805.
Served in the Peninsula Aug 1808 – Jan 1809. Present at Rolica and Vimeiro. Half pay 1810.

SINGLETON, John
Lieutenant. 61st (South Gloucestershire) Regiment of Foot.
Buried in the Parish of Preston, Brighton, Sussex. (Burial record).

Ensign 60th Foot 11 Jan 1810. Ensign 61st Foot 5 Apr 1810. Lt 25 Jul 1812. Lt 62nd Foot 26 Apr 1820. Capt 15 Apr 1824. Major 10 Jan 1828. Lt Colonel 17 Jul 1840. Lt Colonel 30th Foot 26 Sep 1845. Bt Colonel 28 Nov 1854.
Served in the Peninsula Oct 1811 – Jan 1813. Present at the siege of Salamanca Forts (wounded) and Salamanca (twice wounded). MGS medal for Salamanca. KH. Commanded 30th Foot from 1845–1847. Buried on 12 Jul 1856 aged 62 years.

SISSONS, Marcus Jacob
Volunteer. 74th (Highland) Regiment of Foot.
Headstone: St Mary's Churchyard, Charlton Kings, near Cheltenham, Gloucestershire. (Photograph)

IN / MEMORY OF / MARCUS JACOB SISSONS, / DEPUTY ASSISTANT COMMISSARY GENERAL, / WHO DIED AT CHARLTON KINGS, / FEBRUARY 9TH 1862 / AGED 75 YEARS.

Volunteer 74th Foot Aug 1812–1813. Dep Asst Com Gen 22 Oct 1816.
Served in the Peninsula Aug – Dec 1812 with 74th Foot. Present at Salamanca, Vittoria and Pyrenees. MGS medal for Salamanca, Vittoria and Pyrenees.

SIVELL, James
Private. 12th (Prince of Wales's) Regiment of Light Dragoons.
Named on the Regimental Memorial: St Joseph's Church, Waterloo. (Photograph)

Present at Waterloo where he was killed.

SKEILL, David
Lieutenant. 3rd (East Kent) Regiment of Foot.
Family Memorial: St Michael's Churchyard, Inveresk, Midlothian, Scotland. (M.I.)

"CAPTAIN DAVID SKEILL, OF THE RIFLE BRIGADE, WHO DIED HERE 11TH JUNE 1824, AGED 40 YEARS".

Ensign 3rd Foot 23 Apr 1807. Lt 26 Dec 1809. Capt Rifle Brigade 10 Jan 1822. Portuguese Army: Capt 22nd Line 1810. Capt 7th Line 1813. Capt Portuguese and Spanish Staff 25 Oct 1814.
Served in the Peninsula with 3rd Foot Sep 1808 – Jan 1810. On the staff of the Portuguese Army Feb 1812 – Apr 1814. Present at Douro and Bayonne. Half pay 1816. Died at Musselburgh 11 Jul 1824.

SKELTON, Daniel Jones
2nd Captain. Royal Artillery.
Chest tomb: St Bridget's Churchyard, Bridekirk, Cumbria. (Photograph)

SACRED TO THE MEMORY OF ARNOLDUS JONES SKELTON, LATE 3RD GUARDS / OF BRANTHWAITE HALL .... ALSO OF DANIEL JONES SKELTON ESQ., THEIR / YOUNGEST SON, FORMERLY CAPTAIN OF THE ROYAL ARTILLERY, WHO DIED / AT DOVER 15TH MARCH 1859, AGED 73 YEARS, DEEPLY AND UNIVERSALLY LAMENTED.

2nd Lt 1 Apr 1802. 1st Lt 12 Sep 1803. 2nd Capt 29 Jun 1808.

Served in the Peninsula Mar 1813 – Apr 1814 on the East coast of Spain. Present at Tarragona. Retired 20 Nov 1823.

SKELTON, Thomas
1st Lieutenant. Royal Engineers.
Named on the Regimental Memorial: Rochester Cathedral, Rochester, Kent. (Photograph)

2nd Lt 1 Oct 1808. Lt 1 Aug 1809.

Served in the Peninsula Jan 1811 – Jan 1812. Present at the Lines of Torres Vedras. Then employed training the infantry in engineering work and at Ciudad Rodrigo. At the siege of Ciudad Rodrigo he was killed by a cannon ball whilst standing on the parapet encouraging the men to work. He was buried in the same grave as his friend Capt George Charles Ross, Royal Engineers near where they fell, in a valley near Ciudad Rodrigo.

SKELTON, Thomas Lowrey
Deputy Assistant Commissary General. Commissariat Department.
Memorial tablet: Dean Cemetery, Edinburgh, Scotland. (Photograph)

SACRED / TO THE MEMORY OF / THOMAS LOWREY SKELTON ESQ / WHO DIED AT EDINBURGH / SEP. 28. 1851. / AGED 70 YEARS.

Dep Asst Comm Gen 3 Feb 1813. Asst Com General 22 Nov 1816.

Served in the Peninsula 1811–1812. Present at Badajoz and Salamanca. Also served in Germany 1813–1814 and Flanders 1816. MGS medal for Badajoz and Salamanca.

SKENE, Alexander
Captain. 10th Royal Veteran Battalion.
Obelisk: Grange Cemetery, Edinburgh, Scotland. (Section S Row 15. Number 194). (Photograph)

IN MEMORY OF / MARGARET, / WIFE OF / ALEXANDER SKENE, / LATE OF THE 24TH FOOT, / .... / AND MAJOR ALEXANDER SKENE, / DIED 21ST MAY 1865, AGED 81. / ....

Ensign 24th Foot 25 Jan 1808. Lt 25 Jul 1809. Capt 10th Royal Veteran Battalion 11 Nov 1813. Bt Major 28 Nov 1854.

Served in the Peninsula Apr 1809 – Jul 1813. Present at Talavera (severely wounded 29 Jul 1809 where he was taken prisoner until Jul 1813 when he was exchanged). Awarded pension of £100 per annum for the loss of his leg. MGS medal for Talavera.

SKERRETT, John Byne
Lieutenant Colonel. 47th (Lancashire) Regiment of Foot.
Monument: St Paul's Cathedral (North transept). Joint memorial to Major General Arthur Gore and John Byne Skerrett. (Photograph)

ERECTED AT THE PUBLIC EXPENSE TO THE MEMORY OF / MAJOR GENERALS / ARTHUR

GORE, AND JOHN BYNE SKERRETT, / WHO FELL GLORIOUSLY / WHILE LEADING THE TROOPS TO THE ASSAULT / ON THE FORTRESS OF BERGEN-OP-ZOOM, / IN THE NIGHT OF THE 8TH AND 9TH OF MARCH 1814.

Memorial tablet: St Nicholas's Cathedral, Newcastle-upon-Tyne. (Photograph)

SACRED TO THE MEMORY / OF MAJOR GENERAL JOHN BYNE SKERRETT, / SON OF LIEUT GENL JOHN SKERRETT / OF NANTWICH IN CHESHIRE, / AND OF ANNE HIS WIFE / DAUGHTER OF HENRY BYNE ESQR OF CARSHALTON SURRY: / HE DIED ON THE 10TH DAY OF MARCH 1814 / IN THE 36TH YEAR OF HIS AGE / OF WOUNDS RECEIVED AT THE HEAD OF HIS BRIGADE / IN THE ASSAULT ON BERGEN OP ZOOM. / FROM THE AGE OF 15 YEARS / TO THE DAY OF HIS LAMENTED DEATH, / HIS LIFE WAS SPENT / IN THE SERVICE OF HIS KING AND COUNTRY, / IN EVERY QUARTER OF THE GLOBE. / DURING THE LONG AND SUCCESSFUL STRUGGLE OF / GENEROUS FREEDOM, / AGAINST TYRANNICAL OPPRESSION. / HIS SERVICES IN SPAIN WERE MOST CONSPICUOUS, / ESPECIALLY IN THE DEFENCE OF TARIFA AND IN THE CAPTURE OF SEVILLE. / HIS MILITARY CAREER WAS USEFUL, ACTIVE, BRILLIANT: / HIS PRIVATE LIFE EXEMPLARY. / READER! / IT IS A MOTHER WHO SURVIVES TO RAISE THIS MONUMENT / TO SUCH A SON HER ONLY CHILD. / BEREFT OF ALL EARTHLY FELICITY SHE LOOKS FORWARD / (IN HUMBLE HOPE) / TO A REUNION WITH THE OBJECT OF HER AFFECTIONS / IN THAT BLESSED WORLD, WHERE SEPARATE FRIENDS / AGAIN SHALL MEET; / AND WHERE GRIEF AND MOURNING CANNOT ENTER.

Memorial tablet: St Mary the Virgin's Church, Ponteland, Northumberland. (Photograph)

.... / MAJOR GENERAL JOHN BYRNE SKERRETT, / DISTINGUISHED BY HIS GALLANTRY / IN THE PENINSULAR WAR / UNDER LORD WELLINGTON, / WAS KILLED IN THE ATTACK ON / BERGEN OP ZOOM IN 1814 / ....

Lt 19th Foot 13 Sep 1791. Lt 48th Foot 3 Jan 1792. Capt 123rd Foot 14 Feb 1795. Capt 69th Foot 21 Apr 1795. Major 83rd Foot 20 Mar 1798. Lt Colonel 23 Oct 1800. Lt Colonel 47th Foot 16 Jan 1804. Bt Colonel 25 Jul 1810. Major General 4 Jun 1813.

Served in the Peninsula Jan 1811 – Oct 1813 (O/c Brigade May 1811 – Jul 1812, O/c 2 Brigade 4th Divison Nov 1812 – Jun 1813 and O/c 2 Brigade Lt Division Jul – Oct 1813). Present at Cadiz (Mentioned in Despatches), Tarifa (Mentioned in Despatches), Seville (Mentioned in Despatches), Vittoria, Pyrenees (Mentioned in Despatches) and Vera. At Vera he refused to send reinforcements down to the bridge at Vera resulting in the deaths of Captain Cadoux and his riflemen. Skerrett shortly afterwards returned to England. Gold Medal for Vittoria. Also served in the West Indies 1794, Cape of Good Hope, India and the Netherlands 1814 (in command of a Brigade in General Graham's force at Merxem and Bergen-op-Zoom where he was killed trying to take the Antwerp Gate).

Reference: Gentleman's Magazine, Apr 1814, p. 415.

SLADE, John

Lieutenant Colonel 1st (Royal) Regiment of Dragoons.
Memorial tablet: All Saints' Church, Norton Fitzwarren, Somerset. (Photograph)

TO THE GLORY OF GOD AND IN MEMORY OF / SIR JOHN SLADE, / OF MAUNSEL IN THE COUNTRY OF SOMERSET / BARONET. A GENERAL IN THE ARMY, / AND COLONEL OF THE 5TH DRAGOON GUARDS, / KNIGHT GRAND CROSS OF THE ROYAL / HANOVERIAN GUELPHIC ORDER, / EQUERRY TO H.R.H. THE DUKE OF CUMBERLAND / AFTERWARDS KING OF HANOVER, / ONLY SON OF THE LATE JOHN SLADE, / OF MAUNSEL, ESQRE AND CHARLOTTE / HIS WIFE, DAUGHTERS OF HENRY PORTAL, / OF FREEFOLK PRIORS, HANTS, ESQRE. / SIR

JOHN SLADE ENTERED THE ARMY 1780, / AND SERVED HIS COUNTRY WITH DISTINCTION IN / THE PENINSULA UNDER SIR JOHN MOORE, AND / LORD WELLINGTON. HE WAS TWICE MARRIED AND / LEFT TWELVE SURVIVING CHILDREN. HE WAS / A JUST AND CONSCIENTIOUS MAN IN ALL THE / RELATIONS OF LIFE, AND DESCENDED TO THE TOMB, / FULL OF YEARS AND UNIVERSALLY RESPECTED. / BORN 31ST DECEMBER 1762. / DIED 13TH AUGUST 1859. / AT MONTY'S COURT, IN THIS PARISH. / (VERSE)

Cornet 10th Lt Dragoons 11 May 1780. Lt 28 Apr 1783. Capt 24 Oct 1787. Major 1 Mar 1794. Lt Colonel 29 Apr 1795. Lt Colonel 1st Dragoons 18 Oct 1798. Bt Colonel 29 May 1802. Major General 25 Oct 1809. Lt General 4 Jun 1814. General 10 Jan 1837.

Served in the Peninsula Oct 1808 – Jan 1809 (O/c Cavalry Brigade), Sep 1809 – Jan 1812 and Jun 1812 – Apr 1813 (O/c 'B' Cavalry Brigade). Present at Sahagun (commanded 10th Dragoons) and Benevente, Corunna (Mentioned in Despatches), Busaco, Sabugal (Mentioned in Despatches), Fuentes d'Onoro, second siege of Badajoz (Mentioned in Despatches), Aldea de Ponte (Mentioned in Despatches), Maguilla, Nave d'Aver and El Bodon. Served as a volunteer at Corunna as the Cavalry were embarked before the battle. After his mistakes made at Maguilla in June 1812, Wellington wrote of 'the trick that officers of cavalry have acquired of galloping at everything'. Despite Slade's mistakes he remained in command of his brigade for another year. Ordered to return to England June 1813, he was sent to the Staff in Ireland and commanded the central district until June 1814. Gold Medal for Corunna and Fuentes d'Onoro. MGS medal for Sahagun and Benevente and Busaco. GCH. Colonel 5th Dragoon Guards 20 Jul 1831. Father of Lt John Henry Slade 12th Lt Dragoons.

REFERENCE: Dictionary of National Biography. Royal Military Calendar, Vol. 2, pp. 343–6. Gentleman's Magazine, Sep 1859, p. 307. Annual Register, 1859, Appx, pp. 480–1.

SLADE, John Henry

Lieutenant. 12th (Prince of Wales's) Regiment of Light Dragoons.

Memorial tablet: St Michael's Church, Michaelchurch, Sedgemoor, Somerset. (Photograph)

JOHN HENRY / ELDEST SON OF SIR JOHN SLADE / WHO DIED AT BARNES THE 30TH AUGUST 1843, AGED 47 / HE WAS A LIEUT COLONEL IN THE ARMY AND LATE MAJOR IN / THE 1ST DRAGOON GUARDS WHO SERVED IN THE PENINSULA / UNDER WELLINGTON, IN THE 12TH LANCERS AT THE BATTLE / OF WATERLOO, ONE OF THE REGIMENTS WHO SO / DISTINGUISHED ITSELF ON THAT MEMORABLE DAY / HE LEFT AN ONLY DAUGHTER.

Memorial Monument: St Mary's Church, Barnes, Berkshire. (M.I.)

"SACRED / TO THE MEMORY OF / JOHN HENRY SLADE ESQ / LIEUTENANT COLONEL IN HER MAJESTY'S ARMY, / AND LATE MAJOR IN THE FIRST DRAGOON GUARDS, / ELDEST SON OF / SIR JOHN SLADE, BART. GCH / WHO DIED AT BARNES ON THE 30TH AUGUST 1843 / AGED 47 AND WAS BURIED IN THE VAULTS / UNDER THIS CHURCH."

Cornet 1st Lt Dragoons 7 May 1812. Lt 25 Feb 1813. Lt 12th Lt Dragoons 6 Apr 1815. Capt 1st Dragoon Guards 24 Oct 1821. Major 5 Jun 1827. Bt Lt Colonel 30 Aug 1843.

Served in the Peninsula May 1813 – Apr 1814. Present at Toulouse. Present at Waterloo with 12th Lt Dragoons. Eldest son of General Sir John Slade.

SLADE, Richard

Private. 12th (Prince of Wales's) Regiment of Light Dragoons.

Named on the Regimental Memorial: St Joseph's Church, Waterloo. (Photograph)

Present at Waterloo where he was killed.

SLATER, Thomas
Sergeant. 6th (Inniskilling) Regiment of Dragoons.
Headstone (on reverse): Holy Trinity Parish Churchyard, Berwick-on-Tweed. (Photograph)

IN MEMORY OF / THOMAS SLATER, / LATE SERGEANT MAJOR / 6TH OR ENNISKILLEN DRAGOONS, / WHO DIED OCT 16TH 1840 / AGED 57 YEARS. / HE WAS MUCH BELOVED BY HIS / FELLOW SOLDIERS.

Pte 25 Mar 1803. Cpl 1810. Sgt 1813. Sgt Major 1822.

Present at Waterloo in Capt Henry Madox's Troop. Discharged 5 Oct 1827 owing to length of service.

SLESSOR, John
Major. 35th (Sussex) Regiment.
Memorial tablet: St Giles and St Nicholas's Church, Sidmouth, Devon. (Photograph)

SACRED TO THE MEMORY OF / H. E. SLESSOR, / RELICT OF GENERAL SLESSOR / .... / ALSO MAJOR GENERAL JOHN SLESSOR, / SON OF THE ABOVE, OBIT 11TH OCTOBER 1850, / ÆTAT 73.

1st Lt Royal Irish Artillery 14 Jun 1794. Capt-Lt 25 Jul 1795. Capt 35th Foot 16 May 1805. Bt Major 25 Apr 1808. Major 35th Foot 7 Oct 1813. Bt Lt Colonel 4 Jun 1814. Bt Colonel 10 Jan 1837. Major General 9 Nov 1846.

Present at Waterloo in reserve at Hal with 35th Foot after serving many years in the Royal Irish Artillery. Half pay 25 Jun 1817. Also served in Ireland 1798 (present in the Irish Rebellion where he was wounded), Sicily 1806–1807 (present at Scylla), Egypt 1807 (wounded), Ionian Islands 1809 (Civil Governor of Zante) and Italy 1813.
REFERENCE: *Gentleman's Magazine, Jan 1851, p. 96. Hayter Althea, editor, 'The Backbone' diaries of a military family in the Napoleonic wars, 1993.*

SLOW, David
Surgeon, Royal Regiment of Horse Guards.
Family chest tomb: St Mary's Churchyard, Huntingdon. (Near door of Church tower). (Photograph)

TO THE MEMORY OF / .... / DAVID SLOW ESQ. / (LATE SURGEON OF HIS / MAJESTY'S ROYAL REGIMENT OF HORSE GUARDS BLUE) WHO DEPARTED / THIS LIFE 6TH NOVEMBER 1829 AGED 60 YEARS

Hospital Mate 30 Jul 1795. Asst Surgeon Royal Regt of Horse Guards 4 Jul 1798. Surgeon 52nd Foot 23 Aug 1799. Surgeon Royal Regt of Horse Guards 18 Jul 1805.

Served in the Peninsula 1812 – Apr 1814. Present at Vittoria and Toulouse. Present at Waterloo. Half pay 12 Jan 1826.

SMAIL, George
Ensign. 34th (Cumberland) Regiment of Foot.
Family Memorial in railed enclosure: Kirkmichael Churchyard, Kirkmichael, Dumfriesshire, Scotland. (Photograph)

IN MEMORY OF / THE REVD JAMES SMAIL, MINISTER OF / KIRKMICHAEL, ... / ALSO GEORGE, THEIR FOURTH SON, ENSIGN / IN THE 34 REGT OF FOOT, KILLED IN PORTUGAL / 22ND DECEMBER, 1809 AGED 21 YEARS. / ....

Ensign 20 Jul 1809.

Served in the Peninsula Nov – Dec 1809. Murdered by persons unknown 22 Dec 1809. Official report – 'Assassinated by night in the streets of Lisbon on his return to his Quarters.'

SMITH, Andrew

Ensign. 91st Regiment of Foot.

Floor slab: St Catherine's Cathedral Church, Spanish Town, Jamaica, West Indies. (Photograph)

LIEUT ANDW SMITH / OF HIS MAJESTY'S / ARGYLLSHIRE REGIMENT. / DIED 13TH FEBRY 1825: / AGED 25 YEARS. /

Ensign 14 Apr 1814. Lt 5 Dec 1822.

Present at Waterloo, the siege of Cambrai and with the Army of Occupation. Also served in the West Indies 1823 where he died in Jamaica 13 Feb 1825 aged 25.

SMITH, Benjamin

Private. Royal Artillery.

Headstone: St John the Baptist's Churchyard, Kirkburton, Huddersfield, Yorkshire. (Photograph)

SACRED / TO THE MEMORY OF / BENJAMIN SMITH, ROYAL ARTILLERY / HE FOUGHT FOR HIS COUNTRY / UNDER THE COMMAND OF FIELD – / MARSHAL THE DUKE OF WELLINGTON / AT THE EVER MEMORABLE / BATTLE OF WATERLOO, / AND DIED NOVEMBER 27, 1845, / AGED 52 YEARS.

Pte 20 Oct 1812.

Present at Waterloo. Discharged 10 Feb 1819 owing to reduction of the corps.

Reference: Huddersfield Examiner, 18 Jun 1936.

SMITH, Charles

Volunteer. 95th Regiment of Foot.

Buried in the family vault: St Mary's Church, Whittlesey, Cambridgeshire.

CHARLES SMITH IS NOT NAMED ON THE VAULT INSCRIPTION / BORN 6TH JANUARY 1795. DIED 24TH DECEMBER 1854.

Volunteer Jun 1815. 2nd Lt 19 Jul 1815.

Present at Waterloo with 1st Battalion as a volunteer where he was wounded. Awarded a commission after Waterloo. Half pay 25 Dec 1817. Captain Commander of Whittlesey Troop Cambridgeshire Yeomanry Cavalry 1831. Lt Colonel Cambridgeshire Militia 1852. Resigned Aug 1854. Brother of Capt Harry Smith and 1st Lt Thomas Smith, both of whom were in the same regiment.

SMITH, Charles Felix

Captain. Royal Engineers.

Memorial: St Mary's Church, Broadwater, Sussex. (M.I.)

"LIEUT GENL SIR CHARLES FELIX SMITH, KCB. ROYAL ENGINEERS. DIED AUGUST 11TH 1858, AGED 72 YEARS."

2nd Lt 2 Jul 1801. 1st Lt 1 Oct 1802. 2nd Capt 18 Nov 1807. Capt 15 Apr 1812. Bt Major 31 Dec 1811. Bt Lt Colonel 21 Sep 1813. Lt Colonel 29 Jul 1825. Bt Colonel 22 Jul 1830. Colonel 10 Jan 1837. Major General 23 Nov 1841. Lt General 11 Nov 1851.

Served in the Peninsula Nov 1810 – Apr 1814. Present at Cadiz, Tarifa (Mentioned in Despatches), Osma, Vittoria, Tolosa and San Sebastian. Senior officer in charge of Cadiz at the time of Barrosa. Commanding Officer in the defence of Tarifa. Chief Engineer at the siege of Cadiz. Present at the Capture of Paris and with the Army of Occupation. Gold Medal for Vittoria and San Sebastian. MGS medal for Martinique. KCB. Also served in the West Indies 1807 (present at Santa Cruz, St Thomas and St John), Martinique 1809–1810 (wounded) and Syria 1840 where he was severely wounded at the Capture of St Jean d'Acre. Colonel Commandant 6 Mar 1856.
REFERENCE: *Gentleman's Magazine, Sep 1858, p. 310. Annual Register, 1858, Appx, p. 424.*

SMITH, Charles Hervey
Captain. 36th (Herefordshire) Regiment of Foot.
Memorial tablet: St Nicholas's Church, Hulcote, Bedfordshire. (Photograph)

IN MEMORY OF / CHARLES HERVEY SMITH, / (OF APSLEY HOUSE,) / LATE LIEUTENANT COLONEL, IN HER MAJESTY'S SERVICE: / MAGISTRATE AND DEPUTY LIEUTENANT, / FOR THE COUNTY OF BEDFORD: / BORN SEPTEMBER 9TH 1783: DIED NOVEMBER 23RD 1857; / AGED 74 YEARS. / HE LIVED AND DIED A CHRISTIAN GENTLEMAN. / .... / HAUD PROCUL HINC NATUS CONJUX PATER OPTIMUS, UXOR / HAUD PROCUL HINC TALI / CONJUGE DIGNA JACET

Ensign 7 May 1805. Lt 26 Dec 1805. Capt 40th Foot 26 May 1808. Capt 36th Foot 21 Oct 1812. Bt Major 27 May 1825. Bt Lt Colonel 28 Jun 1838.

Served in the Peninsula with 40th Foot Aug 1808 – Aug 1809. Present at Rolica and Vimeiro. MGS medal for Rolica and Vimeiro. Half pay 25 Feb 1826. Magistrate and Deputy Lieutenant of Bedfordshire.

SMITH, Charles Maitland
Private. 95th Regiment of Foot.
Headstone: Canonbie Old Churchyard, Canonbie, Dumfriesshire. Scotland. (Grave number 377). (Photograph)

ERECTED / IN MEMORY OF / CHARLES MAITLAND SMITH. BORN JULY 8TH 1791. DIED / 25TH FEBRUARY 1858. / ....

Dumfries Militia. Private 95th Foot 3 May 1808.

Served in the Peninsula 1809–1811. Present at Barrosa (severely wounded 5 Mar 1811 and returned to England). MGS medal for Barrosa. Chelsea Pensioner 5 Dec 1811.

SMITH, Francis
Captain. Royal Artillery.
Memorial tablet: St Luke's Church, Charlton, Kent. (M.I.)

IN MEMORY OF / COLONEL FRANCIS SMITH, RA. / DIED THE 22 JUNE 1837, / AGED 66 YEARS.

Altar tomb: St Luke's Churchyard, Charlton, Kent. (Grave number 295). (No longer extant). (M.I. with the same inscription).

2nd Lt Royal Irish Artillery. 1st Lt 8 Dec 1794. Capt-Lt 25 Dec 1801. Capt 7 Jul 1805. Bt Major 4 Jun 1813. Major 17 Jul 1823. Lt Colonel 29 Jul 1825. Colonel 10 Jan 1837.

Served in the Peninsula 1808. Present at Cadiz (joined the Peninsular Army from Gibraltar). Commanded a battery of nine pounders on the march from Ostend 1815, but did not arrive in time for Waterloo. Also served in Gibraltar 1806–1821 and Ceylon 1828–1834.

SMITH, Sir George
Lieutenant Colonel. 82nd (Prince of Wales's Volunteers) Regiment of Foot.
Memorial tablet: Town Church, St Peter Port, Guernsey, Channel Islands. (Photograph)

TOULON HOLLAND / ALEXANDRIA COPENHAGEN / COLONEL SIR GEORGE SMITH, KNIGHT. / LIEUT – COLONEL IN THE 82ND REGT OF FOOT, AND AID DE CAMP TO THE KING / BEING AT CADIZ, ON A DIPLOMATIC MISSION, DIED THERE, / THE 15TH FEBRUARY 1809, IN THE 49TH YEAR OF HIS AGE. / THIS MONUMENT IS ERECTED BY HIS WIDOW, AS A SMALL TESTIMONY OF HER / UNFEIGNED LOVE FOR THE BEST OF HUSBANDS AND HER RESPECT FOR HIS MEMORY.

Lt Colonel 14 Nov 1804. Bt Colonel 25 Aug 1808.

Served in the Peninsula Jan – Feb 1809. Died at Cadiz 15 Feb 1809 whilst on a diplomatic mission. Also served in Toulon 1793, Flanders 1794–1795, the Helder 1799, Egypt 1801 (present at Alexandria) and Copenhagen 1807.

SMITH, George
Asst Surgeon. Coldstream Regiment of Foot Guards.
Obelisk: Kensal Green Cemetery, London. (10160/89/IC). (Photograph)

SACRED / TO THE MEMORY OF / GEORGE CHENEVIX / ESQUIRE / OF BALLYCOMMON, KING'S COUNTY, IRELAND / AND SUSSEX GARDENS LONDON / LATE SURGEON MAJOR / OF THE COLDSTREAM GUARDS. / BORN 7TH OF JANUARY 1793. / DIED 31ST OF MARCH 1852. / HE ENTERED THE SERVICE DECEMBER 1812, / ACCOMPANIED THE COLDSTREAM GUARDS / ON THE EXPEDITION TO HOLLAND / AND SERVED IN THE NETHERLANDS AND FRANCE / FROM NOVEMBER 1813, UNTIL THE RETURN / OF THE ARMY OF OCCUPATION IN 1818, / HAVING BEEN PRESENT AT / THE BOMBARDMENT OF ANTWERP, / BATTLES OF QUATRE BRAS / AND WATERLOO. / AND CAPTURE OF PARIS. / ERECTED BY HIS AFFECTIONATE WIDOW.

Memorial tablet: Ballycommon Parish, County Offaly, Ireland. (Photograph)

SACRED / TO THE MEMORY OF / GEORGE CHENEVIX, ESQRE / OF THIS PARISH, AND SUSSEX GARDENS, LONDON, / LATE SURGEON MAJOR / OF THE COLDSTREAM GUARDS. / BORN 7 JAN 1793. DIED 31 MARCH 1852, / MUCH BELOVED AND REGRETTED. / HE ENTERED THE COLDSTREAM GUARDS DECEMBER 1812, / SERVED IN THE NETHERLANDS AND FRANCE, / AND WAS PRESENT AT / THE BOMBARDMENT OF ANTWERP, / THE STORMING OF BERGEN OP ZOOM, / BATTLE OF QUATRE BRAS AND WATERLOO, / AND CAPTURE OF PARIS. / ERECTED BY HIS AFFLICTED WIDOW MARIA SOPHIA / ………………..

Asst Surgeon 17 Dec 1812. Surgeon 24 Feb 1825. Surgeon Major Sep 1836.

Present at Quatre Bras, Waterloo (with the Coldstream Guards in Hougoumont throughout the battle on 18 June) and the Capture of Paris. Also served in the Netherlands 1813–1814 (present at Antwerp and the storming of Bergen-op-Zoom). Half pay 16 Mar 1838. Took the name of Chenevix instead of Smith 1836.

Reference: Gentleman's Magazine, May 1852, p. 534. Annual Register, 1852, Appx, pp. 269. (Both under name of Chenevix)

SMITH, Harry George Wakelyn
Captain. 95th Regiment of Foot.
Chest tomb in railed enclosure: Whittlesey Cemetery, Whittlesey, Cambridgeshire. (Photograph)

SACRED TO THE MEMORY OF L^T GENERAL / SIR HARRY G. W. SMITH B^T OF ALIWAL G.C.B. / B 28 JUNE 1788 D 12 OCT 1860

Engraved around the base of the tomb on four sides:

CORUNNA. BUSACO. FUENTES DE ONORO. NIVE. ORTHES. TOULOUSE. CIUDAD RODRIGO. BADAJOZ. SALAMANCA. VITTORIA. PYRENEES. NIVELLE. WATERLOO. MAHARAJPORE. FEROZESHUHAR. ALIWAL. SOBRAON. S. AFRICA.

On the reverse of the tomb is the text of a speech in the House of Lords giving thanks to the victors of Aliwal and Sobraon:

IN THE HOUSE OF LORDS 3^D APRIL 1846 THE DUKE OF WELLINGTON SAID "I WILL SAY, MY LORDS, WITH REGARDS TO THE MOVEMENTS OF SIR HARRY SMITH THAT I HAVE READ ACCOUNTS OF MANY BATTLES, BUT NEVER READ AN ACCOUNT OF ANY AFFAIR IN WHICH ANY OFFICER HAS EVER SHEWN HIMSELF MORE CAPABLE THAN THIS OFFICER DID ON COMMANDING TROOPS IN THE FIELD, OR IN WHICH EVERY DESCRIPTION OF TROOPS HAS BEEN BROUGHT TO BEAR WITH ITS ARM IN THE POSITION IN WHICH IT WAS MOST CAPABLE OF RENDERING SERVICE OR IN WHICH EVERYTHING WAS CARRIED ON MORE PERFECTLY, THE NICEST MANOEUVRES BEING PERFORMED UNDER THE ENEMY'S FIRE WITH THE UTMOST PRECISION. I MUST SAY OF THIS OFFICER THAT NEVER WAS ANY CASE OF ABILITY MANIFESTED MORE CLEARLY THAN IN THIS CASE. IT HAS BEEN SHEWN THAT SIR HARRY SMITH IS AN OFFICER CAPABLE OF RENDERING THE MOST IMPORTANT SERVICES, AND ULTIMATELY OF BEING AN HONOUR TO HIS COUNTRY."

Memorial tablet: St Mary's Church, Whittlesey, Cambridgeshire. (Photograph)

THIS MONUMENT WAS ERECTED / AND THIS CHAPEL RESTORED, IN 1863, BY PUBLIC SUBSCRIPTION / TO THE MEMORY OF LIEUTENANT GENERAL / SIR HARRY G. W. SMITH, BARONET, OF ALIWAL. / COLONEL OF THE 1ST BATTALION, RIFLE BRIGADE. / HE ENTERED THE 85TH REGIMENT IN 1805 / SERVED IN SOUTH AMERICA, SPAIN, PORTUGAL, FRANCE, / NORTH AMERICA, THE NETHERLANDS, INDIA / AND AT THE CAPE OF GOOD HOPE, / OF WHICH HE WAS GOVERNOR AND COMMANDER IN CHIEF FROM 1847 TO 1852, / AND ON THE HOME STAFF TO 1859, WHEN HE COMPLETED A MOST GALLANT / AND EVENTFUL CAREER OF 54 YEARS CONSTANT EMPLOYMENT. / HE WAS BORN AT WHITTLESEY 28TH JUNE 1788, / AND DIED IN LONDON, 12 OCTOBER 1860. / WITHIN THESE WALLS HE RECEIVED HIS EARLIEST EDUCATION / AND IN THE CEMETERY OF HIS NATIVE PLACE, HIS TOMB BEARS AMPLE RECORD / OF THE HIGH ESTIMATION OF WHICH HIS MILITARY TALENTS WERE HELD / BY HIS FRIEND AND CHIEF, THE GREAT DUKE OF WELLINGTON. / CORUNA, BUSACO, FUENTES DE ONORO, CIUDAD RODRIGO, BADAJOZ, SALAMANCA, / VITTORIA, PYRENEES, NIVELLE, NIVE, ORTHES, TOULOUSE, WATERLOO, / MAHARAJPORE, FEROZESHUHAR, ALIWAL, SOBRAON, SOUTH AFRICA. / "O LORD, IN THEE HAVE I TRUSTED LET ME NEVER BE CONFOUNDED."

Named on the Rifle Brigade Memorial: Winchester Cathedral, Winchester, Hampshire. (Photograph)

2nd Lt 8 May 1805. Lt 15 Aug 1805. Capt 28 Feb 1812. Bt Major 29 Sep 1814. Bt Lt Colonel 18 Jun1815. Major (unattached) 19 Dec 1826. Lt Colonel (unattached) 16 Jul 1830. Bt Colonel 10 Jun 1837. Major General 9 Nov 1846. Lt Gen 20 Jan 1854.

Served in the Peninsula Aug 1808 – Jan 1809 and Jul 1809 – Apr 1814 (Brigade Major 2 Brigade Lt Division Mar 1811 – Apr 1814). Present at Cacabellos, Corunna, Coa (severely wounded), Busaco,

Redinha, Casal Nova, Foz d'Arouce, Sabugal, Ciudad Rodrigo, Badajoz, Salamanca, Vittoria, Pyrenees, Vera, Bidassoa, Nivelle, Nive, Orthes, Tarbes and Toulouse. Present at Waterloo and with the Army of Occupation (Major of Brigade in General Lambert's Brigade). Also served in South America 1807 (present at Montevideo and Buenos Ayres), North America 1814–1815 (present at Bladensburg, Washington, New Orleans and Fort Bowyer), Halifax, Nova Scotia 1826, West Indies 1826–1827 (DAG), Cape of Good Hope 1827 (DQMG). Present in the Kaffir Wars 1834–1835, India 1839 (Adjutant General. Present at Gwalior and Maharajpore 1843). KCB. Sikh Wars 1845 where he was present at Moodki, Ferozepore, Aliwal (where he led the main charge and captured the Sikh guns) and Sobraon. Governor of the Cape of Good Hope 1847 (defeated the Boers at Boem Plaatz and remained in the Cape until 1852). Wellington said of him in 1846 after Smith's victory at Aliwal 'I never read an account of any affair in which an officer showed himself more capable than this officer did of commanding troops in the field.' MGS medal for Corunna, Busaco, Fuentes d'Onoro, Ciudad Rodrigo, Badajoz, Salamanca, Vittoria, Pyrenees, Nivelle, Nive, Orthes and Toulouse. Colonel 3rd Foot 13 May 1842. Colonel 47th Foot 18 Jun 1847. Colonel 2nd Battalion Rifle Brigade 16 Apr 1847. Colonel 1st Battalion Rifle Brigade 18 Jan 1855. Commanded Western District and Lt Governor of Plymouth 20 Jun 1853. Commanded Northern District 29 Sep 1854 – 30 Sep 1859. For most of his campaigns he was accompanied by his Spanish wife Donna Juana Maria de Leon whom he had rescued from the siege of Badajoz and married shortly afterwards. Ladysmith in Natal is named after her. Brother of Charles a Volunteer with 95th Foot and 1st Lt Thomas Lawrence Smith 95th Foot.

REFERENCE: *Dictionary of National Biography. Smith, G. C. Moore, ed, Autobiography of Lieutenant General Sir Harry Smith, 1787–1789 with an introduction by Philip Haythornthwaite, reprint 1999. Originally published 1910. Lehmann, Joseph R., Remember you are an Englishman: a biography of Sir Harry Smith, 1787–1789, 1977. Gentleman's Magazine, Nov 1860, p. 563. Annual Register, 1860, Part 2, pp. 488–9.*

SMITH, Henry Nelson

Lieutenant. Royal Engineers.

Pedestal tomb: Kensal Green Cemetery, London. (301/93/RS). Inscription not recorded. (Photograph)

2nd Lt 1 May 1810. 1st Lt 1 May 1811. Capt 26 Aug 1819.

Served in the Peninsula Apr 1813 – Apr 1814. Served in Eastern Spain (present at Tarragona). Half pay 1 Feb 1820. Died 21 Feb 1853.

SMITH, Hugh

Private. 12th (Prince of Wales's) Regiment of Light Dragoons.

Named on the Regimental Memorial: St Joseph's Church, Waterloo. (Photograph)

Present at Waterloo where he was killed.

SMITH, James

Lieutenant. 83rd Regiment of Foot.

Headstone: Galle Face Burial Ground, Colombo, Ceylon. (Burial ground is no longer extant). (M.I.)

"SACRED TO THE MEMORY OF LIEUT. JAMES SMITH, LATE HM'S 83RD REGT. IN WHICH HE HAD SERVED FROM THE FOUNDATION UNTIL THE DAY OF HIS DEATH, AND IN THE WEST INDIES AND THE CAPE OF GOOD HOPE AND THROUGH ALL THE CAMPAIGNS IN PORTUGAL AND SPAIN. HE DIED AT COLOMBO ON THE 3RD AUGUST 1818 AGED 42 YEARS, DEEPLY REGRETTED BY HIS BROTHER OFFICERS".

Pte 1793. Promoted from the ranks. Ensign 6 Aug 1807. Lt 23 Mar 1809.

Served in the Peninsula 1809 – Apr 1814. Present at Busaco, Fuentes d'Onoro, Ciudad Rodrigo, Badajoz, Salamanca, Vittoria, Nivelle, Orthes and Toulouse. Also served in the West Indies 1795–1802 (present in Jamaica in the Maroon War), Cape of Good Hope 1806 and Ceylon 1817 where he died in 1818. The 83rd Foot was raised in 1793 and Smith was one of the first men to enlist and was promoted from the ranks Aug 1807.

SMITH, James
Assistant Surgeon. 4th (King's Own) Regiment of Foot.
Grave: Ambala Cemetery, Ambala, India. (M.I.)

"SACRED TO THE MEMORY OF MAJOR JAMES SMITH ESQRE M.D. SURGEON H. Ms 61ST REGT WHO DEPARTED THIS LIFE ON THE 27TH NOVEMBER 1846 AGED 60 YEARS. THIS MONUMENT IS ERECTED BY HIS BROTHER OFFRICERS"

Hospital Mate General Service 10 Jun 1812. Asst Surgeon 4th Foot 25 Sep 1812. Asst Surgeon 29th Foot 25 Dec 1815. Asst Surgeon 17th Foot 10 May 1831. Surgeon 61st Foot 15 Feb 1839.

Served in France with 29th Foot in the Army of Occupation until 1818. Also served in Australia 1831, India 1836, Ceylon 1839, India 1845–1846 where he died in Ambala 27 Nov 1846 aged 60. MD Aberdeen 1822.

SMITH, James Webber
Captain. Royal Artillery.
Chest tomb: St Andrew's Churchyard, Hove, Sussex. Inscription illegible. (Photograph)

2nd Lt 6 Mar 1795. 1st Lt 1 Oct 1795. Capt-Lt 25 Nov 1802. Capt 1 Jun 1806. Bt Major 4 Jun 1813. Bt Lt Colonel 21 Sep 1813. Major 26 Dec 1824. Lt Colonel 29 Jul 1825. Bt Colonel 22 Jul 1830. Colonel 10 Jan 1837. Major General 25 Nov 1841. Lt General 11 Nov 1851.

Served in the Peninsula Feb 1813 – Apr 1814 (Officer in charge of 'F' Troop Royal Horse Artillery). Present at Vittoria, first and second sieges of San Sebastian (Mentioned in Despatches at the first siege), Bidassoa, Nivelle, Nive, Adour and Bayonne. Gold Medal for Vittoria and San Sebastian. MGS medal for Nivelle and Nive. CB. Present at Waterloo where he commanded a troop of the Royal Horse Artillery. Also served at Minorca 1798, Malta 1800, Walcheren 1809 (present at the siege of Flushing). Director-General of Artillery 1844–1848. Died in Brighton 21 Mar 1853.
REFERENCE: Gentleman's Magazine, Jun 1853, pp. 654–5. Annual Register, 1853, Appx, p. 221.

SMITH, John
Sergeant. 1st (Royal) Regiment of Dragoons.
Headstone: Holy Trinity Churchyard, Eccleshall, Staffordshire. Seriously eroded. (Photograph)

JOHN SMITH / WHO DEPARTED THIS LIFE / 31ST AUGUST 1843.

Served in the Peninsula Sep 1809 – Apr 1814. Present at Fuentes d'Onoro, Aldea de Ponte, Maguilla, Vittoria and Toulouse. Present at Waterloo in Capt A. Kennedy Clark's Troop where he had his horse shot under him.

SMITH, John
Private. 4th (Kings Own) Regiment of Foot.
Headstone with ringed cross: St Nicholas's Churchyard, Thelnetham, Suffolk. (Photograph)

JOHN SMITH / A BRAVE SOLDIER AND GOOD / CHRISTIAN. HE SERVED HIS KING AND / COUNTRY IN ALL THE BATTLES AND SIEGES / IN THE PENINSULAR WAR IN AMERICA AND WATERLOO. / HE DEPARTED THIS LIFE IN THE FAITH AND / FEAR OF CHRIST / JAN 12TH 1883 / AGE 92 YEARS. / (VERSE)

Pte 5 Apr 1810.

Served in the Peninsula 1812–1813. Present at the retreat from Burgos (wounded). Present at Waterloo where he was wounded by a lance. Also served in North America 1814–1815. Discharged 8 Jun 1818.

SMITH, John Weatherall

1st Lieutenant. Royal Artillery.
Memorial tablet: St Luke's Church, Charlton, Kent. (Photograph)

SACRED / TO THE MEMORY OF / JOHN WEATHERALL SMITH ESQRE / CAPTAIN OF THE ROYAL ARTILLERY / WHOSE BELOVED REMAINS ARE DEPOSITED / IN A VAULT NEAR THIS TABLET. / HE DEPARTED THIS LIFE / ON THE 22ND APRIL 1839, AGED 48 YEARS, / WAS THE ONLY SURVIVING SON OF / GENL SIR JOHN SMITH GCH / COLL COMMANDANT AND SENIOR OFFICER / OF THE SAME CORPS / SINCERELY REGRETTED & TRULY RESPECTED / BY ALL CLASSES AND DEEPLY DEPLORED / BY HIS AFFECTIONATE WIFE AND SON / ....

2nd Lt 17 Dec 1807. 1st Lt 1 Feb 1809. 2nd Capt 6 Nov 1827.

Served in the Peninsula Mar – Sep 1811 (ADC to Major General Howarth). Present at Fuentes d'Onoro May 1811. Served in Gibraltar 1808 – Mar 1811 and was sent to Portugal Mar 1811 to follow Massena's retreat into Spain from Torres Vedras. Afterwards returned to Gibraltar until Apr 1814.

SMITH, Joshua

Private. 40th (2nd Somersetshire) Regiment of Foot.
Headstone with ringed cross: St Nicholas's Churchyard, Kemerton, Gloucestershire. (Photograph)

THY WILL BE DONE / IN / MEMORY OF JOSHUA SMITH / WHO DIED JUNE 29TH 1837 AGED 54 YEARS / HE WAS SEVERELY WOUNDED / AT THE BATTLE OF ALBUERA / THY WILL BE DONE

Served in the Peninsula. Present at Waterloo in Captain J. Lowry's company.

SMITH, Michael

Sergeant. 51st (2nd Yorkshire West Riding) Light Infantry.
Named on the Regimental Memorial: KOYLI Chapel, York Minster, Yorkshire. (Photograph)

Served in the Peninsula where he was killed.

SMITH, Robert George Suckling

2nd Lieutenant. Royal Artillery.
Monument: English Cemetery, Florence, Italy. (Grave number D21N). Inscription recorded from memorial inscription. (Photograph)

"SACRED TO THE MEMORY OF CAPTAIN ROBERT GEORGE SUCKLING SMITH OF THE ROYAL ARTILLERY YOUNGEST AND LAST REMAINING SON OF THE LATE COLONEL WILLIAM PETER SMITH COMMANDANT OF THE ROYAL ARTILLERY IN NORTH BRITAIN AND ELIZABETH HIS WIFE WHO DEPARTED THIS LIFE AT THE BATHS OF LUCCA ON THE 16 SEPT 1840 AGED 47 THIS MONUMENT TO THE MEMORY OF A BELOVED BROTHER IS ERECTED BY HIS ONLY SURVIVING SISTER LOUISA SMITH"

2nd Lt 17 Dec 1812. 1st Lt 28 Jun 1815. 2nd Capt 25 Sep 1834.

Served with the Army of Occupation Jul 1815 – May 1816. Also served in Ceylon Feb 1823 – Apr 1829. Half pay 28 Nov 1837.

SMITH, Thomas Charlton

Ensign. 27th (Inniskilling) Regiment of Foot.
Memorial: Brompton Cemetery, London. (BR 115782 Compartment K:148x37.6)

Midshipman Royal Navy. Ensign 27th Foot 24 Jun 1813. Lt 5 Aug 1819. Capt 27 Mar 1835. Major 30 Sep 1842. Lt Colonel 15 Sep 1848. Bt Colonel 28 Nov 1854. Major General 21 Dec 1862. Lt General 25 Oct 1871.

Served in the Peninsula Sep 1813 – Apr 1814. Served on the East coast of Spain (present at Ordal and Barcelona). Present at Waterloo where he was severely wounded. Also served in the Royal Navy before 1813 (wounded three times) and Cape of Good Hope 1835–1846. Sent to Natal 1842 to maintain peace between the Boers and the Kaffirs. He set up camp at Port Natal (Durban) with only 263 offficers and men in a small enclosure and was under attack for weeks by hundreds of Boers who came from all over Natal to fight the British. A relief force from the rest of the Inniskilling regiment came to his rescue and the siege was raised a month later. Smith was awarded a Majority. Appointed a Frontier Commissioner but the Kaffirs broke out in rebellion again in the war of the Axe. Half pay 25 May 1846. Minor poet who published *Rude Rymes,* 1817 and *Bay Leaves,* 1824. Died in London11 Mar 1883 aged 89.

SMITH, Thomas Lawrence

1st Lieutenant and Adjutant. 95th Regiment of Foot.
Cross on stepped base: Military Cemetery, Aldershot. Hampshire. (Photograph)

.... / ALSO OF THEIR FATHER COLONEL THOMAS SMITH CB / WHO DIED APRIL 7TH 1877 AGED 85 YEARS. "HIS END WAS PEACE." / ....

2nd Lt 3 Mar 1808. 1st Lt 7 Jun 1809. Adjutant 15 Apr 1813.

Served in the Peninsula with 1/95th Nov 1808 – Jan 1809, Jul 1809 – Sep 1810 and Jan 1812 – Mar 1813. and 2/95th Apr 1813 – Apr 1814. Present at Cacabellos, Corunna, Coa (severely wounded), Ciudad Rodrigo, Badajoz, Salamanca, San Millan, Vittoria, Pyrenees, Vera, Bidassoa, Nivelle, Nive, Orthes, Tarbes and Toulouse. Present at Waterloo. When the Army marched into Paris on 7 Jul 1815 the 2/95th were the first corps to enter the city and Smith had the distinction to be the first British officer to ride into Paris. MGS medal for Corunna, Ciudad Rodrigo, Badajoz, Salamanca, Vittoria, Pyrenees, Nivelle, Nive, Orthes and Toulouse. Barrack Master in several Irish depots. Barrack Master First Class with rank of Major 2 Nov 1838 and then Principal Barrack Master at Aldershot with rank of Colonel 1865. CB. Retired 1868. Brother of Capt Harry Smith 95th Foot and Charles who was a volunteer at Waterloo with 95th Foot.
REFERENCE: The Times, 10 Apr 1877, p. 10.

SMITH, William

Major. 45th (Nottinghamshire) Regiment of Foot.
Memorial: Chirnside Churchyard, Chirnside, Berwickshire, Scotland. (Reverse of headstone at south-east corner of church near path). (Photograph)

.... / AND SACRED / TO THE MEMORY OF / WILLIAM SMITH LATE MAJOR / OF 45TH REGT OF FOOT, WHO GALL / ANTLY FELL IN PORTUGAL AT BATTLE OF / BUZACO SEPTR 27TH 1810, AGED / 37 YEARS DEEPLY REGRETTED BY / HIS RELATIONS, FRIENDS AND / BROTHER OFFICERS.

Ensign 2 Mar 1793. Lt 15 Oct 1794. Adjt 17 Aug 1802. Capt 25 Jun 1803. Major 13 Jul 1809.

Served in the Peninsula Aug 1808 – Sep 1810. Present at Rolica, Vimeiro, Talavera and Busaco where he was killed and Mentioned in Despatches.

SMITH, William

Private. 73rd Highland Regiment of Foot.

Family Headstone: Glencairn Churchyard, Dumfriesshire, Scotland. (Photograph)

WILLIAM SMITH, PENSIONER, WHO DIED AT MONIAIVE, / 31ST JANUARY 1874, IN HIS 80TH YEAR

Pte 1 Apr 1813.

Present at Waterloo in Capt R. Crawford's Company where he was wounded and with the Army of Occupation. Also served in the Netherlands 1814–1815 (present at Bergen-op-Zoom and siege of Antwerp). Discharged 24 Jun 1817 due to a wound received at Waterloo. Received a pension of six pence per day. Became an agricultural labourer and was well known in the area. He was always spoken of as 'Waterloo Smith'. Out Pensioner of Chelsea Hospital.

Reference: Glencairn Gazette, Jun/Jul 2009, p. 18.

SMITH, William Slayter

Lieutenant. 10th (Prince of Wales's Own Royal) Regiment of Light Dragoons.

Ledger stone in kerbed enclosure: Ripon Minster Churchyard, Ripon, Yorkshire. (Photograph)

TO THE MEMORY OF / SARAH BRADNEY SMITH / THE WIFE OF / WILLIAM SLAYTER SMITH / OF GREEN ROYD NEAR RIPON / .... / .... / ALSO OF THE ABOVE NAMED / WILLIAM SLAYTER SMITH / WHO DIED AT GREEN ROYD 18TH JULY 1865 / AGED 72 YEARS. / SERVED IN THE HUSSAR YEOMANRY IN THE YORKSHIRE REGIMENT / AND WAS ADJUTANT FROM 1822–1864. / SERVED UNDER WELLINGTON IN 13TH LIGHT / DRAGOONS IN THE PENINSULAR WAR IN THE / CAMPAIGNS OF 1810, 1811 AND 1812 AND WAS / ONCE SEVERELY AND TWICE SLIGHTLY WOUNDED. / AFTERWARDS SERVED WITH THE 10TH HUSSARS / AT THE BATTLE OF WATERLOO.

Ensign 2nd Garrison Battalion 25 Oct 1806. Lt 17 Nov 1808. Lt 13th Lt Dragoons 1 Feb 1810. Lt 10th Lt Dragoons 12 Nov 1814. Cornet and Lt 1st Life Guards 7 Jan 1819. Adjutant and Bt Capt Yorkshire Hussar Yeomanry 1822.

Served in the Peninsula Feb 1810 – May 1811 and Jun 1812 – Jan 1813. Present at Busaco, retreat to the Lines of Torres Vedras, Campo Mayor (severely wounded with sabre cuts and shot through the body. Awarded pension of £70 per annum). Returned to England on account of his wounds but returned to Spain in 1812. Wounded again in a cavalry action and went back to England and joined the senior department of the Royal Military Academy. Present at Waterloo with 10th Hussars (took part in cavalry actions during the retreat of infantry from Quatre Bras, was taken prisoner but managed to escape and was present at Waterloo 18 Jun). Also served with the Army of Occupation. After the battle he commanded a small observation party to gain information on the movements of the French army. Discovered General Lauriston, Napoleon's ADC and took him to Wellington and afterwards to Louis XVIII as a prisoner, not as a volunteer as the General wished. Half pay 7 Nov 1819. Joined the Yorkshire Hussar Yeomanry and was their Adjutant for many years.

SMITHIES, James

Private. 1st (Royal) Regiment of Dragoons.

Headstone: St Michael's Churchyard, Tonge, Lancashire. (Photograph)

IN / MEMORY / OF / JAMES SMITHIES FORMERLY OF / HER MAJESTY'S 1ST ROYAL DRAGOONS, / AN OLD VETERAN OF PORTUGAL, SPAIN, / FRANCE AND WATERLOO, WHO DIED JANR. / 3RD 1868, IN THE 81ST YEAR OF HIS AGE.

Pte 1804.

Served in the Peninsula 1809 – Apr 1814. Present at Busaco, Sabugal, Fuentes D'Onoro, Salamanca and Vittoria. Present at Waterloo in Capt Phipp's troop (taking part in the charge of the 'Union' Brigade. Smithies was wounded and taken prisoner and escaped the next morning). Returned to England Aug 1815 and was discharged from the Regiment. Received a pension for his wounds at Waterloo. MGS medal for Fuentes de Onoro, Vittoria and Toulouse. He was killed in 1868, knocked down by a colliery tramway coal wagon.

REFERENCE: Smithies, J., Adventurous pursuits of a Peninsular War and Waterloo Veteran: the story of Private James Smithies, 1st (Royal) Dragoons, 1808–1815, edited by Gareth Glover, 2011. Robson, Eric, James Smithies (1787–1868) 1st Royal Dragoons, Journal of the Society for Army Historical Research, Vol. 34, No. 137, Mar 1956, pp. 17–21.

SMYTH, George Barttelot

Lieutenant. Royal Artillery.

Memorial tablet: Church of St Mary the Virgin, Stopham, Sussex. (South wall of Nave). (Photograph)

SACRED / TO THE MEMORY OF / GEORGE BARTTELOT, / OF STOPHAM, ESQRE / WHO DIED NOVEMBER 28TH 1872 AGED 84 YEARS. / HE WAS THE THIRD BUT ONLY SURVIVING SON OF / WALTER BARTTELOT ESQRE / WHO ASSUMED THE NAME OF SMYTH IN COMPLIANCE / WITH THE WILL OF HIS GREAT-AUNT / MISS HAMILTON OF BINDERTON / HE SERVED IN THE ROYAL HORSE ARTILLERY THROUGH / THE PENINSULAR WAR FOR WHICH HE RECEIVED / THE WAR MEDAL AND FIVE CLASPS, / WAS ALSO FOR MORE THAN 55 YEARS A MAGISTRATE AND / A DEPUTY LIEUTENANT OF THE COUNTY OF SUSSEX. / HE MARRIED IN NOVEMBER 1819 EMMA / YOUNGEST DAUGHTER OF JAMES WOODBRIDGE ESQRE / OF RICHMOND SURREY / AND HAD ISSUE

2nd Lt 20 Dec 1805. 1st Lt 1 Jun 1806.

Served in the Peninsula Jul 1809 – Nov 1813 in 'A' Troop, Royal Horse Artillery. Present at Coa, Busaco, Pombal, Redinha, Casal Nova, Foz D'Arouce, Sabugal, Fuentes d'Onoro, Ciudad Rodrigo, Badajoz, Salamanca, San Munos, San Millan and Osma. Resigned 1 Dec 1813. Served in the Peninsula as George B. Smyth (see memorial), but later assumed his family name of Barttelot. MGS medal for Busaco, Fuentes d'Onoro, Ciudad Rodrigo, Badajoz and Salamanca. Educated at Eton.

SMYTH, Henry

Lieutenant and Adjutant. 39th (Dorsetshire) Regiment of Foot.

Chest tomb: St Mary the Virgin's Churchyard, Brading, Isle of Wight. (Photograph)

.... / ALSO TO THE MEMORY OF / MAJOR HENRY SMYTH / WHO SERVED IN H.M. 39TH REGT FROM 1804 / TO 1837 IN ALL ITS CAMPAIGNS / WHO DIED JULY 4TH 1867 AND WAS ENTOMBED / BY THE REMAINS OF HIS BELOVED WIFE / AGED 91 YEARS.

Lt 14 Jun 1807. Adjt 14 May 1812. Capt 17 Apr 1823. Major 16 Jan 1837.

Served in the Peninsula with 1/39th Oct 1811 – Apr 1814. Present at Vittoria, Pyrenees, Nivelle, Nive, Garris, Orthes, Aire and Toulouse. Served with the Army of Occupation in France. Also served in North America 1814 (present at Plattsburgh), Australia 1825–1831 and India 1831 (present in the Coorg Wars 1834). Half pay 1837. MGS medal for Vittoria, Pyrenees, Nivelle, Nive, Orthes and Toulouse.

SMYTH, James Carmichael

Lieutenant Colonel. Royal Engineers.

Memorial tablet: Georgetown Cathedral, British Guiana, West Indies. (M.I.)

"SACRED TO THE MEMORY OF / MAJOR-GENERAL / SIR JAMES CARMICHAEL SMYTH, / BARONET, / C.B., K.M.T., K.ST.W. / APPOINTED GOVERNOR OF BRITISH GUIANA, / 1833, / DIED 4 MARCH, 1838, / AGED 58 YEARS. / ERECTED BY PUBLIC SUBSCRIPTION"

2nd Lt Royal Artillery 20 Nov 1794. 2nd Lt Royal Engineers 13 Mar 1795. 1st Lt 3 Mar 1797. Capt-Lt 1 Jul 1802. 2nd Capt 19 Jul 1804. Capt 1 Jul 1806. Bt Major 4 Jun 1813. Lt Colonel 20 Oct 1813. Bt Colonel 29 Jun 1815. Major General 27 May 1825. Colonel Royal Engineeers 29 Jul 1825.

Served in the Peninsula Oct 1808 – Jan 1809. Present at Corunna. Present at Waterloo where he had already surveyed the ground for Wellington in 1814 and had drawn up the plans of the battlefield. CB. KCH 25 Aug 1825. Knight Commander of Maria Theresa and Fourth Class St Vladimir. Also served in the Cape of Good Hope 1805, the Netherlands 1814 (present at Merxem and Bergen-op-Zoom), West Indies 1823 (reported on the military defences), Canada 1825 (reported on the military defences) and Ireland 1828 (reported on military defences). Governor of the Bahamas 1829. Governor of British Guiana and died there 4 Mar 1838. Educated at Charterhouse.

REFERENCE: Dictionary of National Biography. Dictionary of Canadian Biography.

SNODGRASS, John James

Lieutenant. 52nd (Oxfordshire) Light Infantry Regiment of Foot.
Altar tomb: St Paul's Churchyard, Halifax, Nova Scotia, Canada. (Photograph)

BENEATH / THIS STONE / ARE DEPOSITED / THE MORTAL REMAINS OF / LIEUT. COLONEL / J. J. SNODGRASS / FOR SEVERAL YEARS / DY QR MR GENERAL / IN NOVA SCOTIA./ HE DIED ON THE 14TH JANUARY / A. D.1841. / AE 43.

Memorial tablet: St Paul's Church, Halifax, Nova Scotia, Canada. (M.I.)

"CONSECRATED TO THE MEMORY OF / LIEUTENANT-COLONEL JOHN JAMES SNODGRASS. / THIS OFFICER EQUALLY DISTINGUISHED FOR GALLANTRY IN THE FIELD, / TALENTS IN LITERATURE, AND THE VIRTUES WHICH ADORN PRIVATE LIFE, / COMMENCED HIS MILITARY CAREER IN THE YEAR 1812. / SERVED IN THE PENINSULA, FRANCE, AND FLANDERS WITH THE 52ND REGIMENT, / WAS ACTIVELY EMPLOYED DURING THE WHOLE OF THE BURMESE WAR / ON THE STAFF OF HIS FATHER-IN-LAW, / LIEUTENANT-GENERAL SIR ARCHIBALD CAMPBELL, BART., G. C. B. / HAD SUBSEQUENTLY HELD FOR SIX YEARS / THE OFFICE OF DEPUTY-QUARTERMASTER-GENERAL IN NOVA SCOTIA. / WHILE ASSIDUOUSLY DISCHARGING WITH HONOUR TO HIMSELF / AND BENEFIT TO HIS COUNTRY THE DUTIES OF HIS PUBLIC STATION, / IT PLEASED THE SOVEREIGN DISPOSER OF ALL EVENTS / TO BRING DOWN HIS STRENGTH IN HIS JOURNEY AND TO SHORTEN HIS DAYS / ON THE 14TH JANUARY, A.D. 1841. / AE. 43. / HE HAS LEFT A WIDOW AND AN ONLY SON TO LAMENT THEIR / IRREPARABLE LOSS."

Ensign 9 May 1812. Lt 7 Apr 1813. Lt 38th Foot 18 Oct 1821. Capt 91st Foot 22 Dec 1825. Major (unattached) 14 Nov 1826. Bt Lt Colonel 25 Dec 1826. Major 94th Foot 3 Aug 1830. Lt Colonel (unattached) 28 Jun 1833.

Served in the Peninsula with 1/52nd Foot Jun 1812 – Apr 1814. Present at San Munos, Vittoria, Pyrenees, Vera, Bidassoa, Nivelle, Nive, Orthes, Tarbes and Toulouse. Present at Waterloo with the 1/52nd Foot. Also served in India (present in the Burmese Campaign 1824–1826 on the staff of his father-in-law Lt General Sir Alexander Campbell) and Canada (DQMG at Halifax 12 Sep 1834) where he died 14 Jan 1841. In 1827 wrote *Narrative of the Burmese War, detailing the operation of Major Sir Archibald Campbell's army from May 1824 – February 1826.* Brother of Capt Kenneth Snodgrass 52nd Foot.

REFERENCE: Gentleman's Magazine, Aug 1841, p. 207. Annual Register, 1841, Appx, p. 205.

SNODGRASS, Kenneth

Captain. 52nd (Oxfordshire) Light Infantry Regiment of Foot.
Grave: Raymond Terrace Cemetery, Raymond Terrace, New South Wales, Australia. (Burial record)

Ensign 90th Foot 22 Oct 1803. Lt 43rd Foot 14 Aug 1804. Lt 52nd Foot 9 Aug 1804. Capt 20 Oct 1808. Bt Major 21 Sep 1813. Bt Lt Colonel 21 Jun 1817. Bt Colonel 10 Jan 1837. Portuguese Army: Major 13th Line 24 Nov 1812. Bt Lt Colonel 31 Aug 1813. Lt Colonel 1 Caçadores 9 Nov 1813.

Served in the Peninsula with 1/52nd Aug 1808 – Jan 1809, 2/52nd Mar 1811 – Mar 1812, 1/52nd Apr – Nov 1812 and Portuguese Army Nov 1812 – Apr 1814. Present at Corunna, Sabugal, Fuentes d'Onoro, Ciudad Rodrigo, San Munos, Vittoria, Tolosa, San Sebastian (wounded 31 Aug 1813 and Mentioned in Beresford's Despatches), Bidassoa, Nivelle, Nive (wounded 11 Dec 1813 and Mentioned in Beresford's Despatches), Orthes (severely wounded and Mentioned in Beresford's Despatches). Gold Cross for San Sebastian, Nivelle, Nive, Orthes. MGS medal for Corunna, Fuentes d'Onoro, Ciudad Rodrigo and Vittoria. CB. Also served in Sicily 1806, Sweden 1808 and Australia 1828 (Commandant of Mounted Police until 1830). Government Administrator of Tasmania 1836. Acting Governor of New South Wales 1837. He failed in his attempt to be made Governor, Sir George Gipps being appointed instead. So he resigned from the army and became a landowner, his wife and family having accompanied him to Australia. Remained there until his death 14 Oct 1853 aged 68. Brother of Lt John James Snodgrass 52nd Foot.
REFERENCE: *Australian Dictionary of Biography. Saunderson, Moira, The Corunna connection: Lieutenant Colonel Kenneth Snodgrass, Raymond Terrace Historical Society, 1988.*

SOMERSET, Lord Fitzroy James Henry

Captain and Lieutenant Colonel. 1st Regiment of Foot Guards.
Memorial tablet: Beaufort Estate Church, Badminton, Gloucestershire. (Not open to the public) (Photograph)

IN MEMORY OF / FIELD MARSHAL FITZROY JAMES HENRY SOMERSET, 1ST BARON RAGLAN, GCB, / AND OF SEVERAL FOREIGN ORDERS / WHO, HAVING ENTERED THE ARMY IN 1804, AND SERVED FROM 1807 TO 1815, / THROUGHOUT THE CAMPAIGNS OF THE PENINSULAR AND BELGIUM AS MILITARY SECRETARY, / WAS PRIVY TO ALL THE COUNCIL AND ASSOCIATED WITH ALL THE EXPLOITS OF / ARTHUR, DUKE OF WELLINGTON. / BY WHOSE SIDE, IN THE MOMENT OF VICTORY, HE LOST HIS RIGHT ARM AT WATERLOO. / DURING THE LONG PEACE WHICH THAT BATTLE PROCURED FOR EUROPE, / EMPLOYED SUCCESSFULLY IN HIGH DEPARTMENTS OF MILITARY ADMINISTRATION, / AND ALSO ON IMPORTANT DIPLOMATIC MISSIONS, / HE CONTINUED TO ENJOY THE WARM FRIENDSHIP AND UNBOUNDED CONFIDENCE / OF THAT ILLUSTRIOUS LEADER. / AFTER THIRTY SIX YEARS OF SUCH SERVICE, WHEN AN ENGLISH ARMY WAS SENT TO THE EAST, / AT THE BIDDING OF HIS SOVEREIGN AND THE CALL OF HIS COUNTRY, HE ACCEPTED COMMAND / AT THE HEAD OF THAT FORCE, HASTILY COLLECTED, AND ILL PROVIDED FOR DISTANT WAR / IN CONJUNCTION WITH OUR ALLIES, / HE UNDERTOOK AND CONDUCTED TO THE VERGE OF FINAL SUCCESS, / AN OPERATION IMMENSE IN MAGNITUDE, UNSURPASSED IN DIFFICULTY, THE CRIMEAN CAMPAIGN. / HAVING ESCAPED THE DANGERS OF ALMA AND INKERMAN, / AND FOR FIFTEEN MONTHS OF ARDUOUS STRUGGLE BEFORE SEBASTOPOL, WITH A GALLANT ARMY, / MAINTAINED THE HONOUR OF ENGLAND, / HE WAS STRUCK DOWN BY PAINLESS BUT RAPID DISEASE. / NONE BUT THOSE WHO HAD EXPERIENCE OF HIS QUALITIES IN PRIVATE LIFE, / CAN ESTIMATE THE AFFLICTION OF THIS EVENT TO RELATIVES AND FRIENDS. / IN ACTION CHIVALROUSLY BRAVE, SERENE IN ADVERSITY AND SUCCESS; / NOBLE IN HIS ADDRESS, AND LOYAL IN HIS DEALINGS, / HE ACQUIRED AND ENJOYED TO THE LAST / THE RESPECT AND CONFIDENCE OF HIS ALLIED CONFEDERATES, / THE ENTHUSIASTIC DEVOTION OF HIS TROOPS – THE LOVE OF ALL WHO KNEW HIM. / HE WAS THE YOUNGEST SON OF HENRY, 5TH DUKE OF BEAUFORT, / BORN 30TH SEPTEMBER 1788, / AND

DIED AT HIS HEADQUARTERS BEFORE SEBASTOPOL, 28TH JUNE, 1855. / THIS TABLET IS ERECTED BY HIS WIDOW, / EMILY HARRIETT 2ND DAUGHTER OF WILLIAM, 3RD EARL OF MORNINGTON, / TO HIS BELOVED AND REVERED MEMORY. / ALSO / EMILY HARRIET HIS WIDOW, DAUGHTER OF THE 5TH EARL OF MORNINGTON AND NIECE OF THE / DUKE OF WELLINGTON. BORN MAR 15TH 1792. DIED MARCH 6TH 1881.

Memorial window: St Nicholas's Church, Great Bookham, Surrey. (Photograph)

Memorial brass tablet: St Nicholas's Church, Great Bookham, Surrey. (Photograph)

"FITZROY JAMES HENRY SOMERSET, YOUNGEST SON OF THE 5TH DUKE OF BEAUFORT BORN 30TH SEPTEMBER 1778. ENTERED THE ARMY 1804 SERVED FROM 1801 TO 1815 THROUGHOUT THE CAMPAIGNS OF THE PENINSULAR AND BELGIUM AS MILITARY SECRETARY. HE WAS ASSOCIATED WITH THE EXPLOITS AND COUNCILS OF THE DUKE OF WELLINGTON BY WHOSE SIDE IN THE MOMENT OF VICTORY HE LOST HIS RIGHT ARM AT WATERLOO AND WHOSE FRIENDSHIP AND CONFIDENCE HE CONTINUED TO ENJOY UNTIL THE DUKE'S DEATH. HE WAS CREATED BARON RAGLAN ON THE 29TH OCTOBER 1852 AND LEFT ENGLAND IN 1854 AS COMMANDER IN CHIEF OF THE BRITISH ARMY IN THE EAST. HE FIRST PLACED THE FLAG IN THE CRIMEA AND BY HIS CONSTANT COURAGE AND SKILL BOTH AS GENERAL AND DIPLOMAT SUSTAINED THE HONOUR OF HIS COUNTRY. THE DEVOTION FELT BY THOSE WHO SERVED UNDER HIM WAS WARMLY SHARED BY THE SOLDIERS OF THE FRENCH ARMY. FROM THAT HUMBLE ABODE HIS HEADQUARTERS BEFORE SEBASTOPOL THERE RADIATED A MORAL FORCE A SERENE AND UNQUENCHABLE SPIRIT OF FAITH AND TRUST AND DUTY WHICH ALONE COULD HAVE RESISTED THE INNUMERABLE DIFFICULTIES BY WHICH THE BRITISH COMMANDER IN CHIEF AND HIS ARMY WERE ENCOMPASSED. NOTWITHSTANDING THE VICTORIES OF THE ALMA AND INKERMAN LORD RAGLAN EXPERIENCED IN THE CRIMEA DIFFICULTIES AND TRIALS OF NO ORDINARY CHARACTER WHICH WERE IN FACT ALMOST NATURAL CONSEQUENCES OF A DIVIDED COMMAND AND FOR WHICH IT WOULD BE HARD TO FIND A PARALLEL IN THE ANNALS OF WAR. THESE HE MET WITH CHRISTIAN FORTITUDE GALLANTRY AND FORBEARANCE HE SIMPLY CAST AWAY EVERY THOUGHT OF SELF AND REMEMBERED HIS OWN WORDS "HIS DUTY TO THE QUEEN". TOILING ALWAYS FROM EARLY MORNING AND CONTINUED HIS LABOURS DEEP INTO THE NIGHT AND BEARING HIS OWN NOBLE WAY THOSE CARES AND SORROWS FELL TO HIS LOT HE SANK AND DIED AT THIS HEADQUARTERS BEFORE SEBASTOPOL 28TH JUNE 1855". (VERSE)

Named on the Crimean Monument, Broad Sanctuary, outside Westminster Abbey, London. (Photograph)

FIELD – MARSHAL / LORD RAGLAN, G.C.B. / COMMANDER-IN-CHIEF – 1854–1855 / ………………..

Brass Memorial tablet: Royal Garrison Church, Portsmouth, Hampshire. (Back of a choir stall). (Photograph)

FIELD MARSHAL LORD / RAGLAN G.C.B. DIED / BEFORE SEBASTOPOL / JUNE 28 1855 AGED 66

Cornet 4th Lt Dragoons 9 Jun 1804. Lt 30 May 1805. Capt 43rd Foot 5 May 1808. Bt Major 9 Jun 1811. Bt Lt Col 27 Apr 1812. Capt and Lt Col 1st Foot Guards 25 Jul 1814. Bt Colonel 28 Aug 1815. Major General 27 May 1825. Lt General 28 Jun 1838. General 20 Jun 1854. Field Marshal 5 Nov 1854.

Served in the Peninsula 1808 – Jan 1809 and Apr 1809 – Apr 1814 (ADC to Wellington). Present at

Rolica, Vimeiro, Talavera, Busaco (wounded), Torres Vedras and following the retreat of Massena, Fuentes d'Onoro, first siege of Badajoz, El Bodon, Ciudad Rodrigo, Badajoz, Salamanca, Capture of Madrid, Burgos and retreat from Burgos, Vittoria, Pyrenees, Bidassoa, Nivelle, Nive, Orthes and Toulouse. Military Secretary to Wellington 1811. Gold Cross for Fuentes d'Onoro, Badajoz, Salamanca, Vittoria, Pyrenees, Nivelle, Nive, Orthes, and Toulouse. MGS medal for Rolica, Vimeiro, Talavera, Busaco and Ciudad Rodrigo. KCB. Present at Waterloo where he lost his right arm and awarded pension of £300 per annum. Married Lady Emily Harriet Wellesley-Pole, Wellington's niece 1814. Military Secretary at Horse Guards 1827–1852 under Lord Hill and then the Duke of Wellington. On Wellington's death in 1852 Fitzroy Somerset became Master General of Ordnance as Sir Henry Hardinge was preferred as Commander-in-Chief. Became Baron Raglan 1852. Commander-in-Chief of the Eastern Army Feb 1854. He went out with the troops to the Crimea 1854 and died at the siege of Sebastopol 28 Jun 1855. Colonel 53rd Foot 19 Nov 1836. Colonel Royal Horse Guards 8 May 1854. Educated at Westminster. His eldest son Major Arthur Somerset died from wounds at the Battle of Ferozeshahr 1845. Brother of Lt Colonel Lord Robert Edward Somerset 4th Lt Dragoons and Capt Lord John Somerset 60th Foot. Uncle of Lt Henry Somerset 18th Lt Dragoons, umcle of Lt Henry William Somerset Marquis of Worcester 10th Lt Dragoons.
Reference: Dictionary of National Biography. Royal Military Calendar, Vol. 4, pp. 245–6. Sweetman, J., Raglan: from the Peninsula to the Crimea, 1993. Gentleman's Magazine, Aug 1855, pp. 194–7. Annual Register, 1855, Appx, pp. 287–8. (Under Raglan)

SOMERSET, Henry

Lieutenant. 18th Regiment of Light Dragoons.
Memorial tablet: Beaufort Estate Church, Badminton, Gloucestershire. (Not open to the public). (Photograph)

LIEUT GENERAL SIR HENRY SOMERSET / KNIGHT COMMANDER OF THE BATH. KNIGHT OF HANOVER / AND COLONEL, OF THE 25TH (K .O .B.) REGIMENT OF FOOT. / BORN DECEMBER 30TH 1794 DIED AT GIBRALTAR FEBRUARY 15TH 1862 / SIR HENRY WAS ELDEST SON OF LORD CHARLES SOMERSET / AND GRANDSON OF HENRY 5TH DUKE OF BEAUFORT. / MARRIED FRANCES SARAH ELDEST DAUGHTER OF REAR ADMIRAL SIR HENRY HEATHCOTE / GRAND DAUGHTER OF SIR WILLIAM HEATHCOTE BART. OF HURSTEY PARK HANTS / ENTERED THE ARMY AS CORNET 10TH HUSSARS 1810. / SERVED THROUGH THE PENINSULAR WARS OF 18I3/1814 / WAS PRESENT AT THE BATTLES OF VITTORIA, ORTHES TOULOUSE AND WATERLOO. / APPOINTED AIDE DE CAMP IN 1818 TO HIS FATHER / LORD CHARLES SOMERSET GOVERNOR AND COMMANDER IN CHIEF AT THE CAPE OF GOOD HOPE / HE REMAINED ON THE STAFF UNTIL HE ASSUMED COMMAND OF A TROOP OF NATIVE CAVALRY / AND IN THIS SAME YEAR I8I9 ACTED AS MAGISTRATE FOR THE DISTRICT OF ALBANY, CAPE OF GOOD HOPE / AND LOCATED IN THAT SETTLEMENT THOSE BRITISH IMMIGRANTS WHO EVER AFTER / HELD HIM IN GRATEFUL ESTIMATION. / IN 1823 HE BECAME MAJOR OF THE CAPE CORPS CAVALRY WHICH HE HAD RAISED AND ORGANISED / AND AFTERWARDS COMMANDANT OF KAFFRARIA, PERFORMING THE DUTIES OF THAT IMPORTANT POST / THROUGHOUT THE WARS OF 1819, 1835, 1847–8 AND 1852. / PROMOTED TO THE RANK OF MAJOR GENERAL IN 1853 HE PROCEEDED TO INDIA WHERE HE ASSUMED / THE COMMAND OF A DIVISION AT GUZERAT AND SUBSEQUENTLY IN SCINDE. / IN 1855 HE BECAME COMMANDER IN CHIEF OF THE ARMY OF THE BOMBAY PRESIDENCY / AND HELD THAT COMMAND DURING THE MUTINY OF THE NATIVE ARMY OF BENGAL. / HE RECEIVED THE WAR MEDAL AND CLASPS FOR THE PENINSULAR, THE / WATERLOO MEDAL AND THE KAFFER WAR MEDAL. / FAITHFULLY AND ZEALOUS AS A SOLDIER, A DUTIFUL SON, / TENDERLY AFFECTIONATE AND INDULGENT AS A HUSBAND AND FATHER / A MOST EARNEST FRIEND, SIR HENRY SOMERSET WILL LIVE IN THE HEARTS OF ALL WHO KNEW HIM. / BRAVE LOYAL AND TRUE TO HIS DUTIES IN EVERY RELATION OF LIFE HE POSSESSED ABOVE ALL / THE MOST EXCELLENT GIFT OF CHARITY AND DIED AMID SORROWING

RELATIVES / IN SINCERE AND HUMBLE RELIANCE OF THE REDEEMING MERCY OF GOD HIS SAVIOUR. / THIS TABLET IS ERECTED BY HIS AFFLICTED AND AFFECTIONATE WIDOW.

Cornet 10th Lt Dragoons 3 Dec 1811. Lt 30 Dec 1812. Lt 18th Lt Dragoons 12 Nov 1814. Capt 6 Oct 1815. Major Cape Corps Cavalry 25 Mar 1823. Lt Col 17 Jul 1824. Bt Colonel 28 Jun 1838. Major General 11 Nov 1851. Lt General 29 Jan 1857.

Served in the Peninsula Feb 1813 – Apr 1814. (ADC to his uncle General Lord Edward Somerset Jul 1813 – Apr 1814). Present at Morales, Vittoria, Orthes and Toulouse. Present at Waterloo (again serving as ADC to Lord Edward Somerset). MGS medal for Vittoria, Orthes and Toulouse. Also served in the Cape of Good Hope 1818 (ADC to his father Lord Charles Somerset who was Governor of the Cape). He raised the Cape Corps Cavalry and took part in the Kaffir Wars. KCB and KH. Later went to India as Commander in Chief of the Army in Bombay during the Indian Mutiny 1857. Colonel 25th Foot 3 Sep 1856. Nephew of Lt Colonel Lord Robert Edward Somerset 4th Lt Dragoons, Capt and Lt Colonel Lord Fitzroy Somerset 1st Foot Guards and Capt Lord John Somerset 60th Foot. Cousin of Lt Henry William Somerset Marquis of Worcester 10th Lt Dragoons.
REFERENCE: *Journal of the Society for Army Historical Research, Vol. 22, No. 85, Spring 1943, pp. 27–34. (Refers mainly to his service in South Africa). Gentleman's Magazine, Apr 1862, p. 499. Annual Register, Appx, 1862, p. 399.*

SOMERSET, Lord John Thomas Henry
Captain. 60th (Royal American) Regiment of Foot.
Memorial tablet: Bristol Cathedral, Somerset. (East Cloister). (Photograph)

UNDER THIS STONE / ARE DEPOSITED THE REMAINS OF / COLONEL LORD JOHN THOMAS HENRY SOMERSET, SEVENTH SON OF HENRY FIFTH DUKE OF BEAUFORT. / BORN XXX AUGUST MDCCLXXXVII. HE DIED OCTOBER III MDCCCXLVI. / AT TALAVERA IN THE PENINSULA AND ON THE FIELD OF WATERLOO / HE DISPLAYED THE HEREDITARY VALOUR OF HIS RACE. / HE RESIDED FOR SOME YEARS AT BRISTOL INSPECTING OFFICER OF THE DISTRICT / WHERE THE KINDNESS OF HIS DISPOSITION; THE COURTEOUSNESS OF HIS MANNERS / AND THE WARMTH OF HIS HEART MADE HIM UNIVERSALLY BELOVED. / HIS FRIENDS IN THIS NEIGHBOURHOOD, BOTH MILITARY AND CIVIL, / DEDICATE THIS TABLET IN TESTIMONY OF THEIR REGARD FOR HIS MEMORY / AND THEIR GRIEF AT HIS LOSS.

Memorial tablet: Bristol Cathedral, Somerset. (Slab in floor of the South Aisle).

COLONEL / THE RIGHT HONBLE / LORD JOHN / THOMAS HENRY SOMERSET, / DIED AT WESTON. S. M. / OCTOBER 3RD 1846, / IN THE 60TH YEAR / OF HIS AGE.

Cornet 7th Dragoons 4 Aug 1804. Lt 14 Aug 1805. Capt 23rd Lt Dragoons 15 Apr 1808. Capt 60th Foot 15 May 1815. Bt Major 18 Jun 1815. Bt Lt Colonel 19 Jul 1821. Lt Colonel 16 Jul 1830. Bt Colonel 10 Jan 1837.

Served in the Peninsula Jun 1809 – Jun 1810 (ADC to Lt General Lord Charles Somerset). Present at Talavera. Present at Waterloo (ADC to the Prince of Orange). Inspecting Field Officer of Bristol Recruiting District 1843. Brother of Lt Colonel Lord Robert Edward Somerset 4th Lt Dragoons and Capt and Lt Colonel Lord Fitzroy Somerset 1st Foot Guards. Uncle of Lt Henry Somerset 18th Lt Dragoons and uncle of Lt Henry William Somerset Marquis of Worcester 10th Lt Dragoons.
REFERENCE: *Gentleman's Magazine, Dec 1846, pp. 645–6.*

SOMERSET, Lord Robert Edward Henry

Lieutenant Colonel. 4th (Queen's Own) Regiment of Dragoons.

Memorial tablet: Beaufort Estate Church, Badminton, Gloucestershire. (Not open to the public). (Photograph)

SACRED TO THE MEMORY OF / GENERAL LORD ROBERT EDWARD HENRY SOMERSET. / COLONEL 4TH LIGHT DRAGOONS, KNIGHT GRAND CROSS OF THE BATH / KNIGHT OF THE TOWER AND SWORD OF THE ORDER OF MARIA THERESA, / AND OF ST WLADIMIR OF RUSSIA. / HE WAS BORN ON THE 19TH DECEMBER 1776, / AND DIED ON THE 1ST SEPTEMBER 1842 / HE MARRIED IN 1805 LOUISA 7TH DAUGHTER OF VISC^{T} COURTENAY, / BY WHOM HE HAD EIGHT CHILDREN SEVEN OF WHOM SURVIVE HIM. / HE ENTERED THE 10TH LIGHT DRAGOONS AS CORNET IN THE YEAR 1793. / HE ACCOMPANIED HIS ROYAL HIGHNESS THE DUKE 0F YORK / TO HOLLAND IN 1799 AS ADC AND HE DISTINGUISHED HIMSELF / PARTICULARLY IN THE ACTION AT BERGEN OP ZOOM ON THE 19TH SEPTEMBER / AND EGMONT OP ZEE ON THE 2ND OCTOBER OF THAT YEAR. / ON HIS RETURN TO ENGLAND HE WAS APPOINTED TO A MAJORITY / OF THE 12TH LIGHT DRAGOONS. / HE OBTAINED HIS LIEUTENANT COLONELCY IN THE 5TH FOOT IN DECEMBER 1800, / ON THE 25TH SEPTEMBER 1801, HE WAS TRANSFERRED / TO THE 4TH QUEENS OWN DRAGOONS. / HE SUCCEEDED TO THE COMMAND OF THAT REGIMENT IN 1803, / AND CONTINUED IN COMMAND UNTIL JULY, 1813, WHEN HE ATTAINED THE RANK OF / MAJOR GENERAL AND WAS APPOINTED TO THE COMMAND CF THE HUSSAR BRIGADE. / DURING THE PERIOD OF HIS COMMAND OF THE 4TH HE SERVED IN THE / ACTIONS OF TALAVERA, BUSACO, USAGRE, SALAMANCA, / (WHERE HE CAPTURED SEVERAL PIECES OF CANNON) AND VITTORIA, / AT THE HEAD OF THE HUSSAR BRIGADE. / HE WAS PRESENT IN NUMEROUS ACTIONS AND SKIRMISHES, BOTH IN THE / PYRENEES AND IN THE SOUTH OF FRANCE AND HIS BRIGADE / DISTINGUISHED ITSELF ESPECIALLY AT THE BATTLE OF ORTHES. / IN 1815 LORD EDWARD WAS PLACED IN COMMAND OF THE / HOUSEHOLD BRIGADE OF CAVALRY AND ACQUIRED GREAT DISTINCTION IN THE / ACTION AT WATERLOO, BY A MOST BRILLIANT AND SUCCESSFUL CHARGE. / AT THE CLOSE OF THE WAR LORD EDWARD COMMANDED THE 1ST BRIGADE OF CAVALRY / OF THE ARMY OF OCCUPATION IN FRANCE, / AND ON HIS RETURN TO ENGLAND WAS APPOINTED INSPECTOR GENERAL OF CAVALRY. / DURING THE YEARS 1829, AND PART OF 1830, HE HELD THE APPOINTMENT OF / LIEUTENANT GENERAL OF THE ORDNANCE, / AND IN 1835, HE WAS SURVEYOR GENERAL OF THAT DEPARTMENT / HE SAT FOR THE BOROUGH OF MONMOUTH, AND REPRESENTED THE COUNTY OF GLOUCESTER / FROM 1803, UNTIL THE PASSING OF THE REFORM BILL IN 1831: / HE SUBSEQUENTLY SAT FOR CIRENCESTER IN TWO PARLIAMENTS. / THIS TABLET WAS ERECTED T0 HIS MEMORY BY HIS NEPHEW, / HENRY, 7TH DUKE OF BEAUFORT K.G. / IN COMPLIANCE WITH A WISH / EXPRESSED IN / LORD EDWARD'S / WILL.

Memorial tower: Hawkesbury Upton, Gloucestershire. (Photograph)

Inscription at Foot of Tower:

GENERAL LORD ROBERT EDWARD HENRY SOMERSET / G.C.B. K.M.T. K.T.S. K.S.W / THIS TOWER IS ERECTED ANNO DOMINI MDCCCXLVI

Inscription at Foot of the Internal Staircase:

THIS TOWER / WAS ERECTED BY THE UNITED CONTRIBUTIONS / OF / PRIVATE FRIENDSHIP, PROFESSIONAL ATTACHMENT, AND PUBLIC RESPECT, / TO COMMEMORATE / THE DISTINGUISHED MILITARY SERVICE / OF / GENERAL LORD ROBERT EDWARD HENRY SOMERSET,

/ FOURTH SON OF HENRY, FIFTH DUKE OF BEAUFORT, / KNIGHT GRAND CROSS OF THE ORDER OF THE BATH, / KNIGHT OF MARIA THERESA OF AUSTRIA, / OF THE TOWER AND SWORD OF PORTUGAL, / AND OF ST WLADIMIR OF RUSSIA, / AND / DURING TWENTY-SEVEN YEARS ONE OF THE REPRESENTATIVES OF THIS COUNTY IN PARLIAMENT. / HAVING, IN 1793, / CHOSEN THE PROFESSION OF ARMS, / HE COMMENCED HIS BRILLIANT CAREER OF FOREIGN SERVICE / IN 1799, / WITH THE BRITISH ARMY IN THE UNITED PROVINCES, / AND WAS PRESENT IN / THE ACTIONS OF BERGEN-OP-ZOOM AND EGMONT-OP-ZEE / IN 1809, IN COMMAND OF THE FOURTH DRAGOONS, / HE JOINED THE ARMY IN PORTUGAL / UNDER / THE DUKE OF WELLINGTON, / AND / EMINENTLY DISTINGUISHED HIMSELF / AT USAGRE AND SALAMANCA. / IN 1813, / HE WAS RAISED TO THE RANK OF MAJOR GENERAL, / AND, AT THE HEAD OF THE HUSSAR BRIGADE, / TOOK A PROMINENT PART IN / THE VARIOUS ACTIONS AND SKIRMISHES IN THE PYRENEES, / AND IN / THE MEMORABLE BATTLE OF ORTHES. / ON THE RENEWAL OF THE WAR WITH / NAPOLEON BONAPARTE, / IN 1815, / LORD EDWARD SOMERSET WAS APPOINTED TO / THE BRIGADE OF / LIFE GUARDS ROYAL HORSE GUARDS, AND FIRST DRAGOON GUARDS, / WHICH / HE COMMANDED IN THE DECISIVE BATTLE OF / WATERLOO. / HE HAD THE HONOR OF RECEIVING / IN HIS PLACE IN PARLIAMENT, / THE THANKS OF THE HOUSE OF COMMONS, ON THE 26TH JULY, 1814, / FOR HIS ABLE AND DISTINGUISHED CONDUCT / THROUGH THE OPERATIONS WHICH CONCLUDED WITH / THE ENTIRE DEFEAT OF THE FRENCH / AT ORTHEZ, / AND THE OCCUPATION / OF BORDEAUX, / AND / ON THE 29TH APRIL, 1816, / FOR HIS INDEFATIGABLE ZEAL AND EXERTIONS / AT WATERLOO / HE DIED IN LONDON, ON THE FIRST OF SEPTEMBER, 1842, / IN THE SIXTY-SIXTH YEAR OF HIS AGE; / AND HIS REMAINS WERE INTERRED IN THE / CHURCH OF ST PETER, / IN THE PARISH OF ST GEORGE, HANOVER SQUARE.

Cornet 10th Lt Dragoons 4 Feb 1793. Lt 10 Dec 1793. Capt 28 Aug 1794. Major 12th Lt Dragoons 23 Nov 1799. Lt Colonel 5th Foot 25 Dec 1800. Lt Colonel 4th Dragoons 3 Sep 1801. Bt Colonel 25 Jul 1810. Major General 4 Jun 1813. Lt General 27 May 1825. General 23 Nov 1841.

Served in the Peninsula Apr 1809 – Jan 1811 and May 1811 – Apr 1814. Present at Talavera, Busaco, Usagre (Mentioned in Despatches of Major General Lumley), Aldea de Ponte, Llerena, Salamanca (Mentioned in Despatches), Vittoria, Pyrenees, Orthes (Mentioned in Despatches) and Toulouse (from 1813 he commanded the Hussar Brigade (7th, 10th and 15th) at Orthes and Toulouse). Present at Waterloo in command of the Household Brigade of Cavalry (1st and 2nd Life Guards. Horse Guards and King's Dragon Guards) where he led the charge of the Brigade. Commanded 1st Brigade of Cavalry in the Army of Occupation until Nov 1818. Gold Cross for Talavera, Salamanca, Vittoria, Orthes and Toulouse. KCB. KTS. Order of Maria Theresa of Austria and Order of St Vladimir of Russia. Also served at the Helder 1799 (present at Bergen and Egmont-op-Zee). MP for Monmouth 1799–1802 and Gloucestershire 1803–1829. Lt General of Ordnance 1829–1830 and Surveyor General of Ordnance 1835. Colonel 21st Dragoons 15 Jan 1818. Colonel 17th Lancers 9 Sep 1822. Colonel 1st Dragoons 23 Nov 1829. Colonel 4th Lt Dragoons 31 May 1836. Brother of Capt and Lt Colonel Lord Fitzroy Somerset 1st Foot Guards and Capt Lord John Somerset 60th Foot. Uncle of Lt Henry Somerset 18th Lt Dragoons and uncle of Lt Henry William Somerset Marquis of Worcester 10th Lt Dragoons.

Reference: Dictionary of National Biography. Gentleman's Magazine, Feb 1843, p. 199. Annual Register, 1842, Appx, pp. 284–5.

SORRELL, William

Sergeant. 51st (2nd Yorkshire West Riding) Light Infantry.

Named on the Regimental Memorial: KOYLI Chapel, York Minster, Yorkshire. (Photograph)

Served in the Peninsula. Present in the Pyrenees where he was killed 30 Jul 1813.

SOTHEBY, Ambrose William

Captain and Lieutenant Colonel. 1st Regiment of Foot Guards.
Memorial: Royal Military Chapel, Wellington Barracks, London. (M.I.) (Destroyed by a Flying Bomb 1944)

"CHANCEL STALLS ARE GIVEN BY CHARLES WILLIAM HAMILTON SOTHEBY, IN MEMORY OF / .... / AND OF / LIEUT.-COLONEL AMBROSE WILLIAM SOTHEBY, HIS UNCLE, 1ST GUARDS, 1798–1812. / "SICILY," "CORUNNA," "WALCHEREN."

Ensign 19 Apr 1798. Lt and Capt 25 Nov 1799. Capt and Lt Colonel 3 Apr 1811.

Served in the Peninsula Oct 1808 – Jan 1809 and Sep – Dec 1812. Present at Corunna. Also served in Sicily 1806 and Walcheren 1809. Retired 25 Dec 1812.

SOUTER, David

Lieutenant. 71st (Highland Light Infantry) Regiment of Foot.
Memorial: Dalry Cemetery, Edinburgh, Scotland. (Grave number 642). (M.I.)

"DAVID SOUTER, CAPTAIN AND PAYMASTER 71ST HIGHLAND LIGHT INFANTRY, DIED AT MUSSELBURGH 16 DEC 1849, AGED 63. HE SERVED FOR 39 YEARS IN THE ARMY AND WAS AT THE BATTLE OF WATERLOO."

Ensign 16 May 1811. Lt 24 Sep 1812. Lt 88th Foot 7 Jan 1819. Capt 2 Feb 1830. Paymaster 71st Foot 12 Sep 1843.

Served in the Peninsula 1813 – Apr 1814. Present at Waterloo. Also served in the Ionian Islands 1825–1836. Half pay 26 Jan 1838. Returned to the 71st Foot as Paymaster in 1843 until his death in 1849.

SOUTH, Samuel

Major. 20th (East Devonshire) Regiment of Foot.
Ledger stone: St Michael and All Angels Churchyard, Heavitree, Exeter, Devon. (Photograph)

LIEUTT COLL / SAMUEL SOUTH / LATE OF H. M. XX REGT / DIED / 20TH JANUARY 1848 / AGED 87 YEARS. / ....

Sgt Major. Promoted from the ranks. Quartermaster 29 Mar 1794. Ensign and Adjutant 22 May 1797. Lt 10 Oct 1799. Capt 13 Feb 1805. Major 21 Oct 1813. Lt Colonel 17 Dec 1818.

Served in the Peninsula Aug 1808 – Jan 1809 (on staff as DAAG to Sir John Moore) and Nov 1812 – Apr 1814. Present at Vimeiro, Corunna, Vittoria, Pyrenees, Nivelle, Nive, Orthes and Toulouse. Also served in the West Indies 1794 (present at St Domingo), the Helder 1799 (present at Krabbendam where he was wounded), Egypt 1801, Sicily 1806 (present at Maida), Walcheren 1809 and St Helena. Commanded the Corps of 22nd Foot guarding Napoleon. Promoted from the ranks and rose to be Commanding Officer. MGS medal for Maida and Corunna. Half pay 21 Dec 1820.

SPALDING, John

Ensign. 71st (Highland Light Infantry) Regiment of Foot.
Headstone: Kettins Churchyard, Kettins, Perthshire, Scotland. (M.I.)

"CAPT JOHN SPALDING. DIED MARCH 1849 AGED 78."

Sgt Major 71st Foot. Promoted from the ranks. Ensign 20 Jan 1814. Lt 25th Foot 30 Mar 1826. Capt 6 Feb 1835.

Served in the Peninsula 1808 – Apr 1814. Present at Rolica, Vimeiro, Corunna, Almarez (wounded), Vittoria, Pyrenees, Garris, Orthes, Aire, Tarbes and Toulouse. Present at Waterloo. Also served in the Cape of Good Hope 1806 where he was wounded and South America 1807.

SPARKS, Frederick
Major. 51st (2nd Yorkshire West Riding) Light Infantry.
Named on the Regimental Memorial: KOYLI Chapel, York Minster, Yorkshire. (Photograph)

Ensign 44th Foot 6 Jun 1795. Lt 4 Sep 1795. Capt 6 Dec 1797. Capt 1st West India Regt 24 Mar 1803. Major 51st Foot 23 Nov 1809.
Served in the Peninsula Oct 1808 – Jan 1809 and Feb 1811 – Nov 1811. Present at Corunna, Fuentes d' Onoro and second siege of Badajoz. Died at Castello Branco 13 Nov 1811.

SPEAR, James
Private. 4th (King's Own) Regiment.
Buried in St Mary's Churchyard, Rickinghall Inferior, Diss, Suffolk. (Grave number 259 966). (Burial register)

"1877 JUNE 26TH – JAMES SPEAR, HERO OF WATERLOO, AGED 84."

Pte 1 Jun 1810.
Served in the Peninsula Nov 1810 – Apr 1814. Present at San Sebastian. Present at Waterloo in Captain Craig's Company No. 5 where he was severely wounded and his right arm amputated. MGS medal for San Sebastian. Discharged 17 Dec 1815 aged 20. Chelsea pensioner.

SPEARMAN, Charles
Lieutenant. Royal Artillery.
Named on the Regimental Memorial: St Joseph's Church, Waterloo. (Photograph)
Memorial tablet: Inside Mausoleum, Evere Cemetery, Brussels, Belgium. (Photograph)

LIEUTENANT / CHARLES / SPEARMAN / ROYAL ARTILLERY / AGED 20

2nd Lt 5 Jun 1809. 1st Lt 30 Aug 1812.
Present at Waterloo in Captain S. Bolton's Brigade, where he was severely wounded and died of his wounds in Brussels 27 Jun 1815. One of the select band of soldiers buried in the Mausoleum at Evere.

SPEARMAN, John
Captain. 5th (Northumberland) Regiment of Foot.
Interred in Kensal Green Cemetery, London. (8582/42/PS). (No longer extant). (Grave has been reused)

Ensign 22 Mar 1798. Lt 9 Aug 1799. Capt 28 Apr 1808.
Served in the Peninsula with 2/5th Jul 1809 – Aug 1812 and 1/5th Sep 1812 – Apr 1814. Present at Busaco, Redinha, Casal Nova, Foz d'Arouce, Sabugal, Fuentes d'Onoro, second siege of Badajoz, Ciudad Rodrigo, El Bodon, Badajoz, Salamanca, Vittoria, Nivelle, Adour, Orthes, Vic Bigorre and Toulouse. Also served at Hanover 1805 and North America 1814–1815. MGS medal for Busaco, Fuentes d'Onoro, Ciudad Rodrigo, Badajoz, Salamanca, Vittoria, Nivelle, Orthes and Toulouse. Died in 1849.

SPENCE, James
Lieutenant. 31st (Huntingdonshire) Regiment of Foot.
Obelisk: Lansdown Cemetery, Bath, Somerset. (Photograph.)

Side 1:

IN MEMORY OF LIEUT COLONEL JAMES SPENCE CB / LATE OF H.M. 31ST REGT / BORN JAN[Y] 30 1795 / DIED OCT[R] 8TH 1860 / THIS MONUMENT / ERECTED BY HIS SORROWING WIDOW / AS WELL TO RECORD THE GALLANTRY / OF A BRAVE MAN AND DISTINGUISHED SOLDIER / AS TO COMMEMORATE THE VIRTUES OF A GOOD SON / A KIND AND GENEROUS BROTHER, AN AFFECTIONATE HUSBAND / A TRUSTY FRIEND, AN UPRIGHT MAN, / AND A SINCERE CHRISTIAN.

Side 2:

COLONEL JAMES SPENCE / SERVED WITH DISTINCTION / IN THE MEMORABLE CAMPAIGN OF THE SUTLEJ / AND WAS IN COMMAND OF HIS REGIMENT / AT THE BATTLES OF MOODKEE, FEROZSHAH, AND ALIWAL / AND IN COMMAND OF A BRIGADE / AT THE GLORIOUS AND DECISIVE BATTLE / OF SOBRAON

Ensign 26 Nov 1808. Lt 29 Dec 1810. Capt 10 Feb 1825. Bt Major 28 Jun 1838. Lt Colonel 5 Jan 1846.

Served in the Peninsula on the East coast of Spain (present at the Capture of Genoa and Corsica 1814). Also served in India 1825–1848 (present in the first Sikh War where he commanded the 31st Foot at Moodkie, Ferozeshah, Buddiwal, Aliwal and Sobraon. His horses were killed at Ferozeshah and Sobraon but he was one of only five officers who escaped being wounded in all actions). CB. On his way to India in 1825 with part of the 31st Foot he was on board HMS *Kent* in the Bay of Biscay when fire broke out. Spence was one of the few survivors who escaped from the burning ship. Commanding Officer 31st Foot 1846–1849.

SPENCER, James

Lieutenant and Adjutant. 2nd (Queen's Royal) Regiment of Foot.
Named on the Regimental Memorial: St Michael's Cathedral, Bridgetown, Barbados, West Indies. (Photograph)

Sgt Major 2nd Foot. Promoted from the ranks. Ensign 25 Mar 1811. Adjt 20 Aug 1811. Lt 10 Jun 1813.

Served in the Peninsula Sep 1811 – Dec 1812. Present at the siege of Salamanca Forts, Salamanca, Burgos and retreat from Burgos. Also served at Walcheren 1809, West Indies 1816 where he died in Barbados 10 Dec 1816 during a yellow fever epidemic.

SPOTTISWOODE, George

Major. 71st (Highland Light Infantry) Regiment of Foot.
Memorial tablet: Westruther Old Parish Church, Berwickshire, Scotland. (Inside ruins of old church). (Photograph)

HERE LIE THE MORTAL REMAINS / OF / GEORGE SPOTTISWOODE / OF GLADSWOOD. / LIEUTENANT COLONEL IN HER MAJESTY'S SERVICE. / THIRD SON OF THE LATE / JOHN AND MARGARET PENELOPE / SPOTTISWOODE, OF SPOTTISWOODE, / WHO DIED AT GLADSWOOD / ON THE 10TH DAY OF JULY 1857 / IN THE 74TH YEAR OF HIS AGE. / ....

Ensign 52nd Foot 4 Jan 1804. Lt 15 Aug 1804. Capt 71st Foot 19 Jun 1806. Major 31 Mar 1814. Lt Colonel 22 Jul 1830.

Served in the Peninsula Aug 1808 – Jan 1809, Oct 1810 – Jun 1812 and Nov 1812 – Aug 1813 (ADC to Major General Colville). Present at Rolica, Vimeiro, Corunna, Fuentes d'Onoro, Badajoz (severely wounded and awarded pension of £200 per annum), Vittoria and Pyrenees. Also served at Walcheren 1809 (present at the siege of Flushing where he was wounded). At Badajoz he was severely wounded and was carried from the breach by Sgt John Hardy who was given a pension for life by the Spottiswoode family.

SPRY, William Frederick
Major. 77th (East Middlesex) Regiment.
Family Memorial tablet: St Peter's Church, Titchfield, Hampshire. (North aisle). (Photograph)

.... / INTERRED ON THE 21ST OF JANY 1814 / WILLIAM FREDERICK SPRY / MAJOR GENL IN THE ARMY / & SON OF GENL WM SPRY / ROYL ENGINEERS

Lt 64th Foot 6 Jun 1786. Capt-Lt 26 Jan 1788. Capt 77th Foot 8 Sep 1789. Major 12 Nov 1795. Bt Lt Colonel 1 Jan 1800. Bt Colonel 25 Jul 1810. Major General 4 Jun 1813. Portuguese Army: Brigadier 3 Portuguese Brigade 16 Aug 1810. Field Marshal 10 Jul 1813.

Served in the Peninsula in Portuguese Army 1810 – Dec 1813 (O/c 3 Brigade). Present at Badajoz (Mentioned in Beresford's Despatches), Salamanca (Mentioned in Despatches), retreat from Burgos (present at Villa Muriel), Vittoria (Mentioned in Beresford's Despatches), San Sebastian (Mentioned in Beresford's Despatches). Gold Medal for Salamanca, Vittoria and San Sebastian.

SQUIRE, John
Captain. Royal Engineers.
Named on the Regimental Memorial: Rochester Cathedral, Rochester, Kent. (Photograph)
Buried at Truxillo, Spain. (Church altar).

2nd Lt Royal Artillery 27 Apr 1796. 2nd Lt Royal Engineers 1 Jan 1797. 1st Lt 29 Aug 1798. Capt-Lt 2 Dec 1802. 2nd Capt 19 Jul 1804. Capt 1 Jul 1806. Bt Major 5 Dec 1811. Bt Lt Colonel 27 Apr 1812.

Served in the Peninsula Oct 1808 – Jan 1809 and Mar 1810 – May 1812. Present in the Corunna campaign, Torres Vedras, first siege of Badajoz (Mentioned in Despatches), Olivencia (Mentioned in Despatches), second siege of Badajoz, Arroyo dos Molinos (Mentioned in Despatches and awarded Bt Majority), Badajoz (Mentioned in Despatches for the attack on the ravelin of St Roque) and Almarez. Gold Medal for Badajoz. Died 19 May 1812 aged 32 from a fever brought on by excessive fatigue during the siege of Badajoz and was buried at Truxillo. Also served at the Helder 1799 (present at Bergen-op-Zee and Alkmaar), Egypt 1801 (present at Alexandria), South America 1807 (where he conducted the siege operations at Montevideo), the Baltic 1808 and Walcheren 1809 (present at the siege of Flushing). Author of *A short narrative of the late campaigns of the British Army under the orders of the Earl of Chatham, with preliminary remarks on the topography and channels of Zealand*, 1810.
Reference: Dictionary of National Biography. Gentleman's Magazine, Jul 1812, pp. 89–90.

SQUIRE, William
Captain. 94th Regiment of Foot.
Headstone: Church of Ireland Churchyard, Ballycarney, County Wexford, Ireland. (Photograph)

SACRED TO THE MEMORY OF / WILLIAM SQUIRE OF AUGHNAGALLY LODGE, / LATE CAPTAIN 94TH REGT. IN WHICH CORPS HE SERVED / MANY YEARS IN INDIA AND THROUGHOUT THE PENINSULAR WAR. / HE DEPARTED THIS LIFE ON THE / 5TH DAY OF OCTOBER 1839. / .... / THIS STONE IS ERECTED BY HIS SORROWING WIFE / MARIA SQUIRE / AS A SINCERE TRIBUTE OF RESPECT AND IN GRATEFUL REMEMBRANCE / OF THE BEST OF HUSBANDS. / (VERSE)

Ensign 20 Oct 1796. Lt 25 Oct 1799. Capt 29 Sep 1808.

Served in the Peninsula Feb 1810 – Jul 1812 and Nov 1813 – Apr 1814. Present at Cadiz, Redinha, Casal Nova, Foz d'Arouce, Sabugal, Fuentes d'Onoro, second siege of Badajoz, Orthes, Vic Bigorre and Toulouse. Retired 20 Oct 1814. Also served in India 1799 in 2nd Mysore War (present at Seringapatam).

SQUIRES, John
Private. 13th Regiment of Light Dragoons.
Buried in St Mary's Churchyard, Tenbury, Worcestershire. (Burial record)

Pte 14 Jan 1803.

Served in the Peninsula Apr 1810 – Apr 1814. Present at Campo Mayor, Albuera, Usagre, Arroyo dos Molinos, Alba de Tormes, Vittoria, Garris, Aire, St Gaudens and Toulouse. Present at Waterloo. Discharged 24 Sep 1817 on reduction of the regiment. MGS medal for Albuera, Vittoria and Toulouse.

STABLES, Edward
Captain and Lieutenant Colonel. 1st Regiment of Foot Guards.
Memorial tablet: Inside Mausoleum, Evere Cemetery, Brussels, Belgium. (M.I.)

COLONEL / EDWARD / STABLES / GRENADIER GUARDS

Named on the Regimental Memorial: St Joseph's Church, Waterloo. (Photograph)

Named on Memorial Panel VIII for Waterloo: Royal Military Chapel, Wellington Barracks, London. (M.I.) (Destroyed by a Flying Bomb 1944)

Chest tomb: Joli Bois. Behind a house on La Chaussée, Waterloo. (Photograph)

BENEATH THIS STONE LIES THE BODY OF / LIEUTENANT COLONEL EDWARD STABLES, / OF GREAT HORMEAD IN THE COUNTY OF HERTS. / HE SERVED IN THE CONTINENTAL WARS, / UNDER SIR JOHN MOORE AND THE DUKE OF WELLINGTON, / AND WAS KILLED ON THE 18TH OF JUNE, WHILST COMMANDING A BATTALION / OF GRENADIER GUARDS IN THE BATTLE OF WATERLOO, / AT THE CLOSE OF THAT MEMORABLE DAY. / HE FELL DISTINGUISHED / BY HIS SOLDIERS' BLESSING AND HIS COMRADES' TEARS / ÆTATIS SUÆ XXXIII / MDCCCXV / HIC JACET / EDUARDUS STABLES / OLIM DE HORMEADBURY IN COMITATU HERTFORDIENSI, / IN HISPANIA MILITIAM INIIT, SUB INSIGNI DUCE JOAN. MOORE, EQUIT BALN: / MOX, PER EAMDEM, PER VARIOS TRIUMPHOS GLORISSISSIMÈ LIBERATUM, / SUB INSIGNISSIMO PRINCIPE ARTHURO DUCE DE WELLINGTON, / GALLIAM FELICITER INTRAVIT: / TANDEM IN PRÆLIO WATERLOVIENSI, / AGMINI QUADRATO IMPERANS, / DÙM MONITU ET EXEMPLO MILITUM ANOMOS IN HOSTEM ACCENDEBAT, / EGREGIÀ MORTE PEREMPTUS EST / ABRUPTUM LUGENT AMICI, COMMILITIONES, PATRIA. / OBIIT ANNO ÆTATIS SUÆ XXXIII

Buried at Evere in 1894 when his body was removed from the tomb, and a new modified inscription placed on the tomb at Joli Bois.

BENEATH THIS STONE FOR NEARLY EIGHTY YEARS / LAY THE REMAINS OF / LT COLNL EDWARD STABLES OF GREAT HORMEADBURY HERTS / WHO SERVED IN THE CONTINENTAL WARS UNDER SIR JOHN MOORE / AND THE DUKE OF WELLINGTON, AND FELL GLORIOUSLY / ON THE 18TH JUNE 1815 / WHILE COMMANDING A BATTALION OF THE GRENADIER GUARDS / AT THE COST OF WHICH REGIMENT HIS REMAINS / WERE REMOVED TO THE WATERLOO MAUSOLEUM AT EVERE / DEC. 13TH 1894 AND THIS TOMB WAS REPAIRED / SIR FRANCIS PLUNKETT G.G.M.G. / H.B.M'S MINISTER AT BRUSSELS / A.M.B.

Memorial tablet: Marble plaque from his tomb at Joli Bois on the wall of the Wellington Museum, Waterloo. (Photograph)

HIC JACET / EDVARDUS STABLES / OLIM DE HORMEADBURY IN COMITATU / HERTFORDIENSI, / IN HISPANIA MILITIAM INIIT, SUB INSIGNI DUCE JOAN. MOORE, EQUIT BALN: / MOX, PER EAMDEM, PER VARIOS TRIUMPHOS GLORISSISSIMÈ LIBERATUM, / SUB INSIGNISSIMO PRINCIPE ARTHURO DUCE DE WELLINGTON, / GALLIAM FELICITER INTRAVIT: / TANDEM IN PRÆLIO WATERLOVIENSI, / AGMINI QUADRATO IMPERANS, / DÙM MONITU ET EXEMPLO MILITUM ANOMOS IN HOSTEM ACCENDEBAT, / EGREGIÀ MORTE PEREMPTUS EST / ABRUPTUM LUGENT AMICI, / OMMILITIONES, PATRIA./ OBIIT ANNO ÆTATIS SUÆ XXXIII

Memorial tablet: St Nicholas's Church, Great Hormead, Hertfordshire. (Photograph)

THIS SACRED TABLET IS THE TRIBUTE OF SORROW AND AFFECTION / TO THE MEMORY OF LIEUTENANT COLONEL STABLES, / OF GREAT HORMEADBURY IN THE COUNTY OF HERTS, / HE SERVED IN THE CONTINENTAL WARS / UNDER SIR JOHN MOORE AND THE DUKE OF WELLINGTON, / AND FELL GLORIOUSLY AT THE CLOSE OF THE ACTION / WHILE COMMANDING A BATTALION OF THE GRENADIER GUARDS / ON THE 18TH JUNE 1815 IN THE 33RD YEAR OF HIS AGE. / HIS BODY FOUND A SOLDIER'S GRAVE NEAR THE FIELD OF WATERLOO: / BUT HIS VIRTUES AND ENDEARING QUALITIES, / WILL LIVE EVER, IN MINDS OF HIS FAMILY AND OF HIS FRIENDS.

Ensign 31 May 1798. Lt and Capt 25 Nov 1799. Bt Major 4 Jun 1811. Capt and Lt Colonel 4 Jun 1812.

Served in the Peninsula with 1st Battalion Oct 1808 – Jan 1809, 3rd Battalion Feb – Dec 1813 and 1st Battalion Jan – Apr 1814. Present at Corunna, Bidassoa, Nivelle, Nive, Adour and Bayonne. Present at Waterloo where he was killed. One of the select band of soldiers buried in the Mausoleum at Evere. Educated at Eton.

Reference: Saunders, Derek, Restoring the Edward Stables tomb, Waterloo Journal, Dec 1992, pp. 24–5.

STAINFORTH, John

Captain. 57th (West Middlesex) Regiment of Foot.
Family Headstone: York Cemetery, York, Yorkshire. (Grave number M/19/03). (Photograph)

IN MEMORY OF / .... / ALSO OF / JOHN STAINFORTH ESQ. / LIEUTT COLONEL. LATE OF HER MAJESTY'S / 57 REGIMENT OF FOOT, / WHO DIED JANUARY 12TH 1865, / AGED 82 YEARS.

Ensign Mar 24 1803. Lt 23 Jul 1803. Capt 19 Feb 1807. Bt Major 10 Jan 1837. Bt Lt Colonel 10 Jan 1837 (backdated from 12 Nov 1844).

Served in the Peninsula Mar 1810 – Apr 1814. Present at the first siege of Badajoz, Albuera (severely wounded), Vittoria, Pyrenees (wounded), Nivelle, Nive, Orthes, Aire and Toulouse. Half pay 11 Jul 1816. MGS medal for Albuera, Vittoria, Pyrenees, Nivelle, Nive, Orthes and Toulouse.

STAINTON, Joseph

Lieutenant. York Chasseurs.
Gravestone: British Cemetery, Corfu, Greece. (Inscription not recorded)

Ensign 94th Foot 24 Jan 1811. Lt York Chasseurs 8 Nov 1813. Capt 2 Dec 1819. Capt 37th Foot 29 Mar 1821. Capt 95th Foot 8 Jun 1826.

Served in the Peninsula May 1811 – Feb 1813. Present at Fuentes d'Onoro, first and second sieges of Badajoz, El Bodon, Salamanca and Vittoria (severely wounded and Mentioned in Despatches). Also served in the West Indies 1814–1819 (present at Capture of Guadeloupe 1815), Canada 1821–1825 and Ionian Islands where he died in Corfu 28 Oct 1832.

STAMMEL, F. K.
1st Lieutenant. 2nd Nassau Regiment, Dutch Infantry.
Named on the Memorial to Dutch officers killed at Quatre Bras: St Joseph's Church, Waterloo. (Photograph)

STANDEN, George Douglas
Ensign. 3rd Regiment of Foot Guards.
Memorial: Royal Military Chapel, Wellington Barracks, London. (M.I.) (Destroyed by a Flying Bomb 1944)

"IN MEMORY OF / JOHN HAMILTON ELRINGTON, GEORGE DOUGLAS STANDEN, AND SIR / HUGH SEYMOUR BLANE, BART., / OF THE LIGHT COMPANY 3RD GUARDS, DURING THE DEFENCE OF HOUGOUMONT AT / THE BATTLE OF WATERLOO. / PLACED BY THE REVEREND WILLIAM FREDERICK ELRINGTON, B.A., / LATE LIEUT.-COLONEL SCOTS FUSILIER GUARDS."

Interred in Kensal Green Cemetery, London. (3870/144/2). (No longer extant).

Ensign 19 Mar 1812. Lt and Capt 6 Jul 1815. Capt and Lt Colonel 12 Jul 1827.
Present at Quatre Bras and Waterloo. Also served in the Netherlands 1814–1815 (present at Bergen-op-Zoom and Antwerp). Died in 1842.

STANDISH, Henry
Major. 39th (Dorsetshire) Regiment of Foot.
Family Pedestal tomb: Mount Jerome Cemetery, Dublin, Ireland. (Buried in vault C725–109). (Photograph)

THE FAMILY VAULT / OF / EDWARD WILLIAM CONNOR ESQRE / .... / ALSO HENRY STANDISH / WHO DIED APRIL 23RD 1853 / ....

Ensign 27th Foot 21 Oct 1795. Lt 20 Jan 1796. Bt Capt 24 Jul 1800. Capt 14 Aug 1800. Capt 39th Foot 25 May 1803. Bt Major 1 Jan 1812. Major 1 Apr 1813. Bt Lt Colonel 19 Jul 1821. Bt Colonel 10 Jan 1837. Half pay 25 Feb 1816.
Served in the Peninsula Oct 1811 – Jul 1813. Also served in Egypt 1801. MGS medal for Egypt.

STANHOPE, Hon. Charles Banks
Major. 50th (West Kent) Regiment of Foot.
Memorial tablet: Westminster Abbey, London. (Photograph)

TO THE MEMORY OF / THE HONBLE / CHARLES BANKS STANHOPE / SECOND SON OF / CHARLES, EARL STANHOPE, / AND NEPHEW OF / THE RIGHT HONBLE. WILLIAM PITT; / MAJOR OF THE 50TH REGIMENT OF FOOT, / WHO, / IN THE ACT OF GALLANTLY ENCOURAGING HIS MEN, / FELL BY A MUSQUET SHOT / IN THE BATTLE OF / CORUNNA; / THIS TABLET IS AFFECTIONATELY INSCRIBED / BY HIS AFFLICTED SISTER, / WHO CAN NEITHER DO JUSTICE TO / HIS VIRTUES, / NOR SUFFICIENTLY DEPLORE / HIS LOSS. / BORN 3RD JUNE 1785, / DIED 16TH JAN. 1809.

Memorial tablet: St Botolph's Church, Chevening, Kent. (Photograph)

TO THE MEMORY OF / THE HONOURABLE CHARLES BANKS STANHOPE, / SECOND SON OF CHARLES EARL STANHOPE, / WHOSE LIFE WAS SPENT WITH HONOR / IN THE SERVICE OF

HIS COUNTRY / WAS TERMINATED AS HE HAD WISHED / ON THE FIELD OF VICTORY. / HE WAS BORN JUNE 30TH 1785, / AND DIED IN THE BATTLE OF CORUNNA / JANUARY 16TH 1809.

Ensign 25th Foot 9 Feb 1802. Lt 57th Foot 24 Sep 1803. Lt 52nd Foot 9 Nov 1803. Capt 6 Feb 1804. Major 50th Foot 21 Apr 1808.

Served in the Peninsula Aug 1808 – Jan 1809. Present at Vimeiro and Corunna where he was killed. Also present at Sicily 1806–1807 and the Baltic 1808 (ADC to Sir John Moore). Brother of Capt and Lt Colonel James Hamilton Stanhope 1st Foot Guards and nephew of William Pitt.

STANHOPE, Hon. James Hamilton

Captain and Lieutenant Colonel. 1st Regiment of Foot Guards.
Memorial tablet: St Botolph's Church, Chevening, Kent. (In Stanhope Chantry – normally closed to the public). (Photograph)

IN THE SAME TOMB IS INTERRED / LIEUT COL. THE HONORABLE JAMES HAMILTON STANHOPE / THIRD SON OF CHARLES EARL STANHOPE / WHO DIED 6TH MARCH 1825 IN THE 37TH YEAR OF HIS AGE. / HIS AFFLICTED RELATIVES WOULD HAVE FELT A MELANCHOLY SATISFACTION / IN COMMEMORATING THE MANY TALENTS AND VIRTUES WHICH ADORNED HIM / BUT IN LAYING HIM BY THE SIDE OF HIS BELOVED WIFE / WITH NO OTHER RECORD THAT / THEY OBEY HIS LAST INJUNCTIONS

Memorial tablet: Guards Chapel, Wellington Barracks, London. (M.I.) (Destroyed by a Flying Bomb 1944).

"PLACED BY JAMES BANKS STANHOPE, IN MEMORY OF HIS FATHER, / LIEUT.-COLONEL THE HON. JAMES HAMILTON STANHOPE, THIRD SON OF CHARLES, THIRD EARL STANHOPE. / BORN, 1788; DIED, 1825. / 1ST GUARDS 1803–22. HE SERVED WITH THE 3RD BATTALION IN SICILY, 1806–7, AND WAS ON THE STAFF AT CORUNNA. HE WAS AIDE-DE-CAMP TO GENERAL THOMAS LORD LYNEDOCH, KB., APR 1810 – OCT, 1812; AND WAS AT BARROSA, THE ASSAULT OF CIUDAD RODRIGO, WHERE HE WAS WOUNDED, AND AT VITTORIA. HE WAS DEPUTY-ASST QUARTERMASTER-GENERAL, AND SEVERELY WOUNDED AT THE FIRST ASSAULT ON SAN SEBASTIAN. HE WAS ON THE STAFF AT BERGEN-OP-ZOOM, AND WITH THE 3RD BATTALION AT QUATRE BRAS AND WATERLOO."

Ensign 26 Oct 1803. Lt and Capt 14 Jan 1808. Bt Major 21 Jun 1813. Bt Lt Colonel 17 Mar 1814. Capt and Lt Colonel 25 Jul 1814. Lt Colonel 29th Foot 14 Feb 1822.

Served in the Peninsula Aug 1808 – Jan 1809 (ADC to Sir John Moore), Mar 1810 – Aug 1813 (Jun 1810 – Sep 1811 ADC to Lt General Graham), Sep 1811 – Jul 1812 (DAQMG) and Jul 1812 – Aug 1813 (AQMG). Present at Corunna, Cadiz, Barrosa, Ciudad Rodrigo (wounded), Vittoria and San Sebastian (severely wounded). Present at Quatre Bras and Waterloo. Also served in Sicily 1806–1807 and the Netherlands 1814–1815 (on staff at Bergen-op-Zoom). Half pay 28 Feb 1822. Brother of Major Charles Banks Stanhope 50th Foot who was killed at Corunna. Nephew of William Pitt.
Reference: Glover, Gareth, Eyewitness to the Peninsular War and the Battle of Waterloo: the letters and journals of Lieutenant Colonel James Stanhope 1803 to 1825 recording his service with Sir John Moore, Sir Thomas Graham and the Duke of Wellington, 2010. Gentleman's Magazine, Mar 1809, pp. 283–4.

STANSFIELD, James

Private. 2nd Life Guards.
Headstone: St Stephen's Churchyard, Acomb, Yorkshire. (Photograph)

SACRED / TO THE / MEMORY OF / JAMES STANSFIELD / PENSIONER, LATE OF / HER

MAJESTY'S 2ND REGT / OF LIFE GUARDS. / BORN AT CAWOOD IN 1788, / DIED AT ACOMB IN 1864, / AGED 76 YEARS. / HE SERVED 19 YEARS / IN THE ABOVE / DISTINGUISHED CORPS / AND SHARED IN THE / MEMORABLE AND DECISIVE / CHARGE OF THE / LIFE GUARDS, IN THE / BATTLE OF WATERLOO. / IN 1815. / SERVANT IN SPIRIT / ROM. C. XII. B XI

Pte 25 Sep 1809.

Served in the Peninsula Nov 1812 – Apr 1814. Present at Vittoria and Toulouse. Present at Waterloo. MGS medal for Vittoria and Toulouse. Discharged 28 Oct 1828 being unfit for further service.

STANWAY, Frank

2nd Captain. Royal Engineers.
Named on the Regimental Memorial: Rochester Cathedral, Rochester, Kent. (Photograph)

2nd Lt 1 Jun 1807. Lt 18 Nov 1807. 2nd Capt 21 Jul 1813. Capt 23 Mar 1825.

Served in the Peninsula Aug 1808 – Apr 1814. Present at Talavera (wounded), Torres Vedras, first and second sieges of Badajoz, Ciudad Rodrigo, Badajoz (Mentioned in Despatches) and San Sebastian. Present at Waterloo and with the Army of Occupation. Died at Limerick 9 Dec 1832.

STAPYLTON, Henry

Lieutenant. 68th (Durham) Regiment of Foot.
Named on the Memorial: St Andrew's Church (now Musée Historique), Biarritz, France. (Photograph)

Ensign Durham Militia. Ensign 68th Foot 28 Jul 1808. Lt 9 Nov 1809.

Served in the Peninsula Sep 1812 – Jan 1813 and Jan – Feb 1814. Present at Adour (severely wounded at Gave d'Oleron where he died of his wounds 26 Feb 1814). Also served at Walcheren 1809.

STARKEY, Walter W.

Lieutenant. 82nd (Prince of Wales's Volunteers) Regiment of Foot.
Memorial tablet: Church of Ireland Cathedral, Ross Carberry, County Cork, Ireland. (Photograph)

SACRED TO THE MEMORY OF / CAPT. WALTER W. STARKEY, / LATE OF THE 82ND REGT OF FOOT, THIRD AND YOUNGEST SON OF THE LATE / ROBERT STARKEY ESQ, OF BERGETIA / HE SERVED IN THE PENINSULA, AT THE SIEGE OF TARIFA AND AT THE BATTLES OF / ROLIEA, VIMIERO, VITTORIA, PYRENEES NIVELLE AND ORTHES. / HE RECEIVED THE WAR MEDAL WITH A CLASP FOR EACH OF THE ABOVE MENTIONED / ENGAGEMENTS. HE COMBINED THE CHARACTER. OF THE GALLANT SOLDIER AND ACCOMPLISHED / GENTLEMAN, WITH THE SINCERE FAITH OF THE TRUE CHRISTIAN. / HE DIED ON THE 23RD SEPT 1853 AGED 65 YEARS / RESPECTED AND DEEPLY REGRETTED BY ALL WHO KNEW HIM. / ....

Ensign Jun 1807. Lt 2 Jun 1808. Portuguese Army: Capt 19th Line 14 Sep 1813.

Served in the Peninsula with 82nd Foot Aug – Nov 1808, Apr 1810–1813 and with the Portuguese Army Sep 1813 – Apr 1814. Present at Rolica, Vimeiro, Cadiz, Tarifa, Vittoria, Pyrenees, Nivelle and Orthes. MGS medal for Rolica, Vimeiro, Vittoria, Pyrenees, Nivelle and Orthes.

STAVELEY, Thomas Kitchingman see HUTCHINSON, Thomas Kitchingman

STAVELEY, William

Captain. Royal Staff Corps.
Low monument in the form of a cross: St Stephen's Churchyard, Ootacamund, India. (Photograph)

BENEATH / LIE THE / REMAINS OF / LIEUTENANT-GENERAL / WILLIAM STAVELEY, CB. /

COLONEL OF / H. M. 94TH REGT / AND / COMMANDER / IN CHIEF / OF / THE MADRAS / ARMY / WHO DIED / AT / TIPPACAUDOO / THE 4TH DAY / OF APRIL / 1854 / AGED / 71 YEARS.

Memorial tablet: St George's Cathedral, Madras, India. Inscription not recorded.

Memorial tablet: Port Louis Protestant Church, Mauritius. (Photograph)

THIS MARBLE OWES ITS ERECTION / TO THE RESPECT AND ESTEEM OF MAURITIUS, / FOR HIS EXCELLENCY LT GENERAL WILLIAM STAVELEY, / COMPANION OF HER MAJESTY'S MOST / HONORABLE ORDER OF THE BATH, / COMMANDER IN CHIEF OF THE MADRAS ARMY, / COLONEL OF HER MAJESTY'S 84TH REGIMENT, / AND FOR TWENTY SIX YEARS A RESIDENT IN THAT ISLAND. / DISTINGUISHED ALIKE IN COUNCIL AS IN WAR, / AND ADORNED IN PRIVATE LIFE, / BY EVERY SOCIAL VIRTUE. / HE WAS BORN AT YORK, AND DIED AT TIPPICADOO IN THE MADRAS PRESIDENCY / ON THE 4TH OF APRIL 1854.

Ensign Royal Staff Corps 14 Jul 1804. Lt 21 Apr 1808. Capt Royal African Corps 6 May 1813. Bt Major 15 Dec 1814. Capt Royal Staff Corps 12 Jan 1815. Bt Lt Colonel 18 Jun 1815. Bt Colonel 10 Jan 1837. Major General 9 Nov 1846.

Served in the Peninsula Apr 1809 – Apr 1814. Present at Douro, Talavera, Pombal, Redinha, Foz d'Arouce, Fuentes d'Onoro, Ciudad Rodrigo (wounded whilst leading the storming party of the Light Division), Badajoz, Osma, Vittoria, Bidassoa, Nivelle, Nive, Adour, St Etienne, Bayonne, Vic Bigorre, Tarbes and Toulouse. Present at Waterloo and with the Army of Occupation. Appointed Commissioner with Colonel Torrens to enter Paris to see that the terms of the Convention were fulfilled, but wounded in a skirmish with French soldiers. CB and Bt Lt Colonelcy for Waterloo. MGS medal for Talavera, Fuentes d'Onoro, Ciudad Rodrigo, Badajoz, Vittoria, Nivelle, Nive and Toulouse. Also served in Mauritius 1821–1847 (DQMG), Hong Kong 1842–1850 (commanded the garrison), India 1851–1854 (commanded a division of the Bombay Army in 1851 and Commander in Chief of the Madras Army in 1853). Colonel 94th Regiment 1 Aug 1853. Served continuously in the East for 33 years.

REFERENCE: Dictionary of National Biography. Journal of the Society for Army Historical Research, Vol. 14, No. 55, Aug 1936, pp. 155–66. Gentleman's Magazine, Oct 1854, p. 390. Annual Register, 1854, Appx, p. 274.

STEELE, Henry

Assistant Surgeon. 11th Regiment of Light Dragoons.
Buried in the Meerut Cantonment Cemetery, Bombay, India. (Burial register)

Hospital Mate General Service 3 May 1810. Asst Surgeon 5th Foot 25 Jun 1812. Asst Surgeon 11th Dragoons 28 Apr 1814.

Served in the Peninsula with 5th Foot. Present at Waterloo with 11th Lt Dragoons. Also served in India 1819 where he died 17 Jan 1825.

STEELE, Samuel

Surgeon. 23rd Regiment of Light Dragoons.
Ledger Stone: St Faith's Churchyard, Llanfoist, Abergavenny, Monmouthshire. (Photograph)

HERE LIE THE REMAINS OF / SAMUEL STEELE ESQR. / LATE SURGEON OF THE 23RD DRAGOONS, / WHO DIED ON THE 11TH DAY OF JULY 1816 / IN THE 38TH YEAR OF HIS AGE. / FATIGUE AND PRIVATION IN THE DISCHARGE / OF HIS DUTY TO THE SICK AND WOUNDED, / DURING AND AFTER THE BATTLE OF / WATERLOO, BROUGHT ON DISEASE, WHICH, / ULTIMATELY DEPRIVED HIM OF HIS LIFE. / ....

Hospital Mate 11 Sep 1799. Asst Surgeon 89th Foot 7 Jun 1801. Surgeon 1st Division Lt Infantry Ireland 12 Nov 1801. Surgeon 6th Garrison Battalion 18 Dec 1806. Surgeon 23rd Lt Dragoons 20 Apr 1809.

Served in the Peninsula Jun 1809 – Jun 1810. Present at Talavera. Present at Waterloo. Died of disease brought on by excessive fatigue looking after the wounded at Waterloo.

STEEVENS, Charles
Lieutenant Colonel. 20th (East Devonshire) Regiment of Foot.
Memorial tablet: St Mary's Church, Cheltenham, Gloucestershire. (South transept). (Photograph)

IN MEMORY OF / LIEUT COLONEL CHARLES STEEVENS, / FORMERLY COMMANDING XXTH REGT OF FOOT / ………………. / WHO DIED IN THIS TOWN, MARCH 9TH 1861, AET 84. / ……………

Ensign 30 Dec 1795. Lt Sep 1798. Capt 23 Jan 1800. Major 9 Feb 1809. Bt Lt Colonel 26 Aug 1813. Lt Colonel 21 Oct 1813.

Served in the Peninsula Aug 1808 – Jan 1809 and Nov 1812 – Feb 1814. Present at Vimeiro, Corunna, Vittoria, Pyrenees, Nivelle and Nive. Also served at the Helder 1799 (present at Krabbendam and Egmont-op-Zee where he was severely wounded and taken prisoner), Egypt 1801 (present at Alexandria), Sicily 1806 (present at Maida) and Walcheren 1809. Retired in 1818. Gold Medal for the Pyrenees. MGS medal for Egypt, Maida, Vimeiro, Corunna, Vittoria, Nivelle and Nive. Two of his sons served in the same regiment, Lt Colonel George Steevens and Capt Nathaniel Steevens.
REFERENCE: Steevens, Charles, Reminiscences of my military life from 1795–1818, edited by his son Nathaniel Steevens, 1878.

STEPHENS, Maurice
Lieutenant. 51st (2nd Yorkshire West Riding) Light Infantry.
Named on the Regimental Memorial: KOYLI Chapel, York Minster, Yorkshire. (Photograph)
Named on the Memorial: St Andrew's Church (now Musée Historique), Biarritz, France. (Photograph)

Ensign 9 Jun 1808. Lt 7 Dec 1809.

Served in the Peninsula Oct 1808 – Jan 1809 and Feb 1811 – Nov 1813. Present at Corunna, Fuentes d'Onoro, second siege of Badajoz, Moriscos, Salamanca, Burgos, Vittoria, Pyrenees, San Marcial and Nivelle where he was killed Nov 1813. Also served at Walcheren 1809.

STEPNEY, John Cowell see COWELL, John Stepney

STEVENART, E. J.
Captain. Dutch Artillery.
Named on the Memorial to Dutch officers killed at Quatre Bras: St Joseph's Church, Waterloo. (Photograph)

STEVENSON, George
Lieutenant. 3rd (King's Own) Regiment of Dragoons.
Buried in St Andrew's Church, Hove, Sussex. (Vault T 3). (M.I.)

"SACRED TO THE MEMORY OF GEORGE STEVENSON ESQ / FORMERLY OF THE GRENADIER GUARDS / WHO DEPARTED THIS LIFE AT BRIGHTON / ON THE 25 JULY 1863 AGED 82"

Ensign 1st Foot Guards 14 May 1807. Lt 3rd Dragoons 1 Jun 1809.

Served in the Peninsula Oct 1808 – Jan 1809. Present at Corunna. Retired 1810. MGS medal for Corunna.

STEVENSON, William
Assistant Surgeon. 60th (Royal American) Regiment of Foot.
Memorial tablet: The Oratory, St James's Cemetery, Liverpool, Lancashire. (Section F Right / Grave number 118). (Photograph)

SACRED / TO THE MEMORY OF / WILLIAM STEVENSON / OF BIRKENHEAD, SURGEON, WHO DIED 6TH JUNE 1853 AGED 64 YEARS. / THIS MONUMENT IS ERECTED BY PUBLIC SUBSCRIPTION / AS A RECORD OF THE ESTEEM IN WHICH HE WAS REGARDED / BY HIS FELLOW TOWNSMEN.

Hospital Asst 25 Jun 1812. Asst Surgeon 60th Foot 25 Nov 1813. Asst Surgeon 21st Foot 9 Jul 1818.

Served in the Peninsula Jun 1813 – Apr 1814. Attached to 3rd Division from 18 Dec 1813. Present at Orthes, Vic Bigorre and Toulouse. Half pay 25 Dec 1818. MGS medal for Orthes and Toulouse. After the war was the first medical man to settle in Birkenhead. The memorial tablet was originally in St Mary's Church, Birkenhead, but removed to St James's Cemetery in 1977.

STEVENTON, Thomas
Private. 1st (Royal) Regiment of Dragoons.
Memorial: Claverley Churchyard, Shropshire. (M.I.)

"SACRED / TO THE MEMORY OF / THOMAS STEVENTON / LATE OF THE KINGS ROYAL DRAGOONS / WHO DEPARTED THIS LIFE 27 OCT / 1857 / AGED 75 YEARS / WHO SERVED HIS COUNTRY FAITHFULLY / FOR 21 YEARS AND WAS / ENGAGED IN THE FOLLOWING / BATTLES OF / TOULOUSE, VITTORIA / FUENTES D'ONOR / AND WATERLOO."

Private 1804.

Served in the Peninsula Sep 1809 – Apr 1814. Present at Fuentes d'Onoro, Aldea de Ponte, Maguilla, Vittoria and Toulouse. Present at Waterloo in Capt Clark's No. 8 Company. Discharged at Dublin 1826 aged 43. MGS medal for Fuentes d'Onoro, Vittoria and Toulouse.

STEWART, Alexander
Lieutenant. 42nd (Royal Highland) Regiment of Foot.
Gravestone: Kilmallie Churchyard, Kilmallie, Corpach, Invernesshire, Scotland. (M.I.)

"LIEUT ALEXANDER STEWART / 42ND REGT / DIED AT FORT WILLIAM 17TH MAY 1836 / AGED 46 YEARS."

Ensign 26 May 1808. Lt 27 Dec 1810.

Served in the Peninsula Jul 1809 – Apr 1814. Present at Busaco, Fuentes d'Onoro, Ciudad Rodrigo, Salamanca, Burgos, Pyrenees, Nivelle, Nive, Orthes, and Toulouse where he was severely wounded and awarded pension of £70 per annum.

STEWART, Alexander
Assistant Surgeon. 11th (North Devonshire) Regiment of Foot.
Monument: Kensal Green Cemetery, London. (17734/105/RS). (Photograph)

IN MEMORY / OF JAMES WILLIAM BROWN ESQ / .... / ALSO / ALEXR STEWART, ESQRE M. D. / INSPECTOR GENERAL OF ARMY HOSPITALS / WHO DIED 23RD AUGUST 1863 / AGED 73 YEARS / ....

Hospital Mate General Service 20 Jun 1809. Asst Surgeon 11th Foot 27 Dec 1810. Surgeon Royal African

Colonial Corps 13 May 1824. Staff Surgeon 24 Nov 1825. Deputy Inspector General of Hospitals 16 Dec 1845. Inspector General 12 Mar 1852.

Served in the Peninsula Jun 1811 – Apr 1814. Present at the siege of Salamanca Forts, Salamanca, Burgos, Pyrenees, Bidassoa, Nivelle, Nive, Bayonne, Orthes and Toulouse. MD Glasgow 1820. MGS medal for Salamanca, Pyrenees, Nivelle, Nive, Orthes and Toulouse. Half pay 12 Mar 1852.

STEWART, Archibald

Lieutenant. 95th Regiment of Foot.
Headstone: St Saviour's Churchyard, St Helier, Jersey, Channel Islands. (Photograph)

SACRED / TO THE MEMORY OF / ARCHIBALD STEWART ESQR / LATE MAJOR RIFLE BRIGADE AND K. H. / IN WHICH DISTINGUISHED REGIMENT / HE SERVED UPWARDS OF 26 YEARS, / THROUGHOUT THE WHOLE OF THE / PENINSULAR WAR, AT QUATRE BRAS, / AND WATERLOO. / HE DEPARTED THIS LIFE / ON THE 13TH OF JUNE 1836, / AGED 53 YEARS AND 11 MONTHS. / THIS STONE IS ERECTED BY HIS / AFFECTIONATE WIFE. / ....

Volunteer 95th Foot. 2nd Lt 13 Oct 1808. 1st Lt 2 Oct 1809. Capt 3 Dec 1818. Major 17 Dec 1829.

Served in the Peninsula with 2/95th Oct 1808 – Jan 1809 and 1/95th May 1811 – Apr 1814. Present at Vigo, Ciudad Rodrigo, Badajoz (wounded), Salamanca, San Millan, Vittoria, Pyrenees, Vera, Bidassoa, Nivelle, Nive, Tarbes and Toulouse. Present at Waterloo. Also served at Walcheren 1809. KH. Retired 22 May 1835.

STEWART, Charles

Lieutenant Colonel. 50th (West Kent) Regiment of Foot.
Memorial tablet: Coria Cathedral, Coria, Spain. (On Cathedral terrace). (Photograph)

MEMORIUM SACRUM / MILITIS / SUÆ PATRIA OPTIME MEMORIS / CAROLI STEWART / LIEUT COLONEL 50TH REGT / REGIS BRITANNICI / SERVICIO / DECESSIT 11TH DECEMBRIS ANNO DOM 1812 / ÆATIS XLVI

Lt 81st Foot. Lt 71st Foot 25 Jan 1791. Capt 109th Foot 3 Apr 1794. Capt 53rd Foot 2 Sep 1795. Major 4 Apr 1800. Lt Colonel 50th Foot 17 Feb 1805.

Served in the Peninsula Sep 1810 – Dec 1812 (O/c 1 Brigade 2nd Division Oct 1811 and Nov – Dec 1812). Present at Fuentes d'Onoro, Arroyo dos Molinos (Mentioned in Despatches), Almarez (Mentioned in Despatches), Alba de Tormes (Mentioned in Despatches). Died of a fever 11 Dec 1812. Also served in India 1791 (present at Seringapatam where he was severely wounded, Nundydroog, Savandroog and Pondicherry), West Indies 1795–1800 (present at Porto Rico and St Lucia where he was wounded) and Walcheren 1809 (Mentioned in Despatches). Uncle of Ensign William Stewart 50th Foot who died of wounds at Corunna while carrying the colours.
Reference: Dictionary of National Biography.

STEWART, Hon. Charles William

Colonel. 25th Regiment of Light Dragoons.
Statue: Durham. (Photograph)

Side 1:

CHARLES WILLIAM VANE STEWART / 3RD MARQUIS OF LONDONDERRY / 1ST EARL VANE AND BARON STEWART / OF STEWARTS COURT K.G. G.C.B. / LORD LIEUTENANT COUNTY OF DURHAM / AND FOUNDER OF SEAHAM HARBOUR / GENERAL IN THE ARMY / BORN MAY 8TH 1778 DIED / MARCH 6TH 1854

Side 2:

THIS PLAQUE WAS UNVEILED ON / THE 9TH DAY OF APRIL 1857 BY THE / EIGHTH MARQUESS OF LONDONDERRY / TO COMMEMORATE THE RESTORATION / OF THE STATUE FROM FUNDS RAISED /BY PUBLIC SUBSCRIPTION AND BY / THE CITY COUNCIL

Memorial tower: Mount Street, Strangford Lough, Belfast, Ireland. (Photograph)

CHARLES WILLIAM VANE STEWART / 3RD MARQUIS OF LONDONDERRY / EARL VANE AND BARON STEWART / OF STEWART'S COURT KCH GCB / LORD LIEUTENANT COUNTY OF DURHAM / AND FOUNDER OF SEAHAM HARBOUR / GENERAL IN THE ARMY / BORN MAY 8TH 1778 DIED MARCH 6TH 1854

Memorial tablet: St Mark's Church, Newtonards, County Down, Ireland. (In Chancel). (Photograph)

SACRED TO THE MEMORY OF / CHARLES WILLIAM VANE, / THIRD MARQUIS OF LONDONDERRY KG. GCB. GCH. / KNIGHT OF ST GEORGE OF RUSSIA, / KNIGHT OF THE BLACK AND RED EAGLE OF PRUSSIA, / KNIGHT OF THE TOWER AND SWORD OF PORTUGAL, / AND KNIGHT OF THE SWORD OF SWEDEN. / HE WAS BORN 18TH MAY 1776; / AND DIED 6TH MARCH 1854 / HIS REMAINS ARE INTERRED / IN THE FAMILY VAULT OF THE TEMPEST FAMILY, / AT LONG NEWTON, IN THE COUNTY OF DURHAM. / THIS TABLET IS PLACED HERE BY HIS SON FREDERICK, / FOURTH MARQUIS OF LONDONDERRY / A.D. 1855.

Memorial tablet: Mausoleum, Wynyard Hall, Long Newton. County Durham. (Photograph)

THIS ROOM IS / DEDICATED TO THE MEMORY OF / CHARLES WILLIAM VANE, / THIRD / MARQUIS OF LONDONDERRY / K.G. G.C.B. G.C.H. / GRAND CROSS OF THE BLACK EAGLE OF / PRUSSIA, / GRAND CROSS OF THE SWORD / SWEDEN, / KNIGHT OF ST GEORGE / RUSSIA, / KNIGHT OF THE TOWER AND SWORD / PORTUGAL, / BY HIS AFFECTIONATE AND MOURNING / WIDOW. / THE REWARDS OF HIS EARLY ACHIEVEMENTS / HAVE BEEN PLACED HERE, / AND WILL TELL THEIR TALE TO POSTERITY / THUS DOING JUSTICE TO THE HEROISM OF THE / GALLANT SOLDIER OF PENINSULAR FAME, / WHO NOBLY FOUGHT WITH / THE DUKE OF WELLINGTON AT / FUENTES DE ONOR, BENEVENTE, TALAVERA, / BADAJOS, BUSACO AND CORUNNA. / AND WHO AT / LEIPSIC, CULM, AND FERA CHAMPENOISE, / RECEIVED THE CROWNING HONOUR / OF HIS MILITARY CAREER. / SHEATHING HIS SWORD, / HE BECAME NO LEST DISTINGUISHED AS THE / FOUNDER / OF SEAHAM HARBOUR AND TOWN, / WHICH OWE THEIR EXISTENCE TO HIM / AND HIS TALENT, AND ENERGY, AND / INDOMITABLE PERSEVERANCE; / WERE AS REMARKABLE CHARACTERISTICS / OF HIS PRIVATE LIFE, / AS THE DARING AND BRAVERY / WERE CONSPICUOUS IN THE / FIELD OF BATTLE.

Surrounding the walls of the Mausoleum are tablets recording his military appointments and battles attended. (Photograph)

COLONEL 10TH HUSSARS / COLONEL 2ND LIFE GUARDS / LIEUT COLONEL 5TH LT DRAGOONS / COLONEL 25TH LT DRAGOONS / LT COLONEL 18TH HUSSARS / DOURO 1809 / CORUNNA 1809 / TALAVERA 1809. / BUSACO 1810 / FUENTES DE ONOR 1811.

In the floor is a tablet recording his presence at Badajoz 1812. (Photograph)

BADAJOS 1812

Ensign 108th Foot 11 Oct 1794. Lt 120th 30 Oct 1794. Capt 108th Foot 12 Nov 1796. Major 106th Foot 31 Jul 1795. Major 5th Dragoons 4 Aug 1796. Lt Colonel 1 Jan 1797. Lt Colonel 18th Lt Dragoons 12 Apr 1799. Bt Colonel 25 Sep 1803. Major General 25 Jul 1810. Lt General 4 Jun 1814. General 10 Jan 1837.

Served in the Peninsula Aug 1808 – Jan 1809 (O/c Cavalry Brigade) May – Nov 1809, May 1810 – Jan 1811 and Apr 1811 – Apr 1812 (Adjutant General). Present at Sahagun, Benevente (Mentioned in Despatches), retreat to Corunna, Douro (Mentioned in Despatches), Talavera (Mentioned in Despatches), Busaco (Mentioned in Despatches), Fuentes d'Onoro (Mentioned in Despatches), El Bodon, Ciudad Rodrigo (Mentioned in Despatches) and Badajoz. Ill health forced him to return to England, suffering from opthalmia. Wanted to return to the Peninsula in charge of the cavalry but Wellington refused. Military Commissioner to Eastern Allies 1813–1814. Served with the Prussian Army 1813–1814 (present at Lützen Bautzen, Haynau, Kulm (severely wounded) and Leipzig). Ambassador to Vienna 1814–1822 (as he was Castlereagh's half brother was successful in implementing his policies). Gold Cross for Sahagun and Benevente, Talavera, Busaco, Fuentes d'Onoro and Badajoz. GCB. GCH. KTS. Swedish Order of the Sword, Red Eagle of Prussia and Russian Order of St George. Also served in Flanders 1794–1796, Irish Rebellion 1798 and the Helder 1799 where he was wounded. One of the pall bearers at Wellington's funeral. Married Frances Vane 1819, an heiress with a considerable fortune owning most of County Durham. The coal mines alone brought in a vast income. Stewart used the money to improve the area including building a harbour at Seaham. Colonel 25th Lt Dragoons 20 Nov 1813. Colonel 10th Hussars 3 Feb 1820. Colonel 2nd Life Guards 23 Jun 1843. Author of several books including *Narrative of the Peninsular War from 1808–1813*, 2 vols, 1828.

REFERENCE: *Dictionary of National Biography. (Under Vane). Alison, Sir Archibald, Lives of Lord Castlereagh and Sir Charles Stewart, 3 vols, 1868. Gentleman's Magazine, Apr 1854, pp. 415–18. (Under Londonderry). Annual Register, 1854, Appx, pp. 270–3. (Under Vane)*

STEWART, George

Captain 42nd (Royal Highland) Regiment of Foot.

Memorial tablet: Wellpark Mid Kirk, Greenock, Renfrewshire, Scotland. (Photograph)

UPON THE 9TH OF DECR 1813, / AND IN THE 27TH YEAR OF HIS AGE, / GEORGE STEWART / OF / STEWARTFIELD, / CAPTAIN IN THE 42ND REGT OF FOOT / FELL IN FRONT OF BAYONNE, / IN THE KINGDOM OF FRANCE, / GLORIOUSLY FIGHTING / FOR THE INDEPENDENCE OF EUROPE. / ENDEARED TO ALL THOSE WITH WHOM / HE HAD EVER ASSOCIATED, AND / DISTINGUISHED IN A CORPS, IN WHICH / THE ORDINARY VIRTUES OF A SOLDIER / COMMAND NO PRE-EMINENCE, / HIS REMAINS WERE CONSIGNED / TO AN HONOURABLE GRAVE / IN A FOREIGN LAND, / AND / THE COMPANIONS OF HIS EARLY LIFE, / HAVE RAISED THIS MEMORIAL / TO HIS NAME, IN HIS / NATIVE TOWN.

Memorial tablet in walled enclosure: Ronachan Hill, Ronachan, Isle of Kintyre, Scotland. (North-facing slope of hill overlooking farm land of Stewartfield). (Photograph)

TO THE MEMORY / OF / ROBERT STEWART / OF RONACHAN AND STEWARTFIELD / BORN 1747 / DIED 1818 / WHO LIES BURIED HERE BY HIS OWN DESIRE / AND / OF HIS ONLY SON GEORGE STEWART / CAPTAIN IN THE 42ND REGIMENT OF FOOT / WHO FELL AT THE BATTLE OF THE NIVE / IN FRONT OF BAYONNE / DECEMBER 9TH 1813 / IN THE 27TH YEAR OF HIS AGE / AND WAS / THERE COMMITTED TO A SOLDIER'S GRAVE

Named on the Memorial: St Andrew's Church (now Musée Historique), Biarritz, France. (Photograph)

Ensign 8 Jun 1805. Lt 22 Apr 1806. Capt 3 Mar 1808.

Served in the Peninsula Jul 1809 – Feb 1812 and Nov 1812 – Dec 1813. Present at Busaco, Fuentes d'Onoro, Pyrenees, Nivelle and Nive where he was killed 9 Dec 1813. Gold Medal for Nive.

STEWART, James
Lieutenant. 42nd (Royal Highland) Regiment of Foot.
Named on the Memorial: St Andrew's Church (now Musée Historique), Biarritz, France. (Photograph)

Ensign 28 Jun 1808. Lt 21 Jun 1810.

Served in the Peninsula Jul 1809 – Dec 1813. Present at Busaco, Fuentes d'Onoro, Ciudad Rodrigo, Salamanca, Burgos (wounded), Pyrenees, Nivelle and Nive where he was killed 9 Dec 1813 at the same time as Capt George Stewart also 42nd Foot.

STEWART, James
Ensign. 53rd (Shropshire) Regiment of Foot.
Headstone: St Margaret's Churchyard, Bethersden, Kent. (Photograph)

SACRED TO THE MEMORY OF / LIEUTENANT JAMES STEWART / LATE OF 53RD REGIMENT OF / FOOT. / BORN AT DALKEITH IN SCOTLAND / DIED AT ASHFORD 29 MARCH 1848 / AGED 66 YEARS. / HE WAS A BRAVE SOLDIER AND WAS / AWARDED A MEDAL ON WHICH WAS ENGRAVED / TOULOUSE, ORTHES, NIVE, NIVELLE, PYRENEES, / VITTORIA, SALAMANCA, / BADAJOS, ALBUERA, TALAVERA, / THE NAMES OF THE BATTLES AND SIEGES / AT WHICH HE WAS PRESENT. / HE WAS A LOVING HUSBAND AND A / FAITHFUL FRIEND AND HIS PRIVATE VIRTUES / SECURED THE ESTEEM OF ALL / WITH WHOM HE WAS ASSOCIATED.

Pte 48th Foot. Cpl. Sgt. Ensign 53rd Foot 9 Jun 1814. Lt 16 Oct 1818.

Served in the Peninsula with 48th Foot 1809 – Apr 1814. Present at Talavera, Albuera, Badajoz, Salamanca, Vittoria, Pyrenees, Nivelle, Orthes and Toulouse. Commissioned from the ranks in 1814 and became Ensign in the 53rd Foot. Half pay 9 Sep 1824. MGS medal for Talavera, Albuera, Badajoz, Salamanca, Vittoria, Pyrenees, Nivelle, Orthes and Toulouse.

STEWART, James
Sergeant. 94th Regiment of Foot.
Headstone: Kirkton of Collace Churchyard, Perthshire, Scotland. (M.I.)

"IN MEMORY OF SGT JAMES STEWART, 94TH FOOT, DIED 3 MARCH 1859, AGED 77."

Pte 16 Aug 1800. Cpl 1808. Sgt 1812.

Served in the Peninsula 1810 – Apr 1814. Present at Cadiz, Redinha, Foz d'Arouce, Sabugal, Fuentes d'Onoro, Ciudad Rodrigo (wounded), Badajoz, Salamanca, Vittoria, Pyrenees, Nivelle (wounded), Nive, Orthes, Vic Bigorre, Tarbes and Toulouse. Also served in India 1802–1804 (present in the Mahratta Wars at Asseerghur, Argaum and Gawilghur where he was wounded). MGS medal for Fuentes d'Onoro, Ciudad Rodrigo, Badajoz, Salamanca, Vittoria, Pyrenees, Nivelle, Nive, Orthes and Toulouse. Army of India medal for Asseerghur, Argaum and Gawilghar. Discharged 20 Feb 1818 as unfil for service due to his wounds but an excellent soldier.

STEWART, Robert
Lieutenant. 91st Regiment of Foot.
Gravestone: Kinlochlaigh Old Churchyard, Kinlochlaigh, Argyllshire, Scotland. (M.I.)

"ROBERT STEWART, MAJOR 91ST REGIMENT. DIED 28TH MARCH 1851 AGED 63 YEARS."

Ensign 31 Aug 1805. Lt 13 May 1808. Capt 27 Apr 1820. Capt 94th Foot 21 Jul 1825. Bt Major 10 Jan 1837.

Served in the Peninsula Aug 1808 – Jan 1809 and Oct 1812 – Apr 1814. Present at Rolica, Vimeiro,

Cacabellos, Corunna, Pyrenees (wounded), Nivelle, Nive, Orthes, Aire and Toulouse. Present at Waterloo in reserve at Hal, the Siege of Cambrai and with the Army of Occupation. MGS medal for Rolica, Vimeiro, Corunna, Pyrenees, Nivelle, Nive, Orthes and Toulouse. Retired 30 Apr 1841.

STEWART, Hon. Sir William

Colonel. 95th Regiment of Foot.

Chest tomb: Churchyard of the Stewartry, Minnigaff, Newton Stewart, Dumfries and Galloway, Scotland. (Photograph)

IN MEMORY OF / LIEUT. GENERAL THE HON SIR WILLIAM STEWART, / 2ND SON OF JOHN, EARL OF GALLOWAY, K.G., C.B., AND K.T.S., / COL. OF THE 1ST BATN. RIFLE BRIGADE. HE WAS BORN ON THE 10TH JANUARY 1773, / AND DIED ON THE 6TH JANUARY 1827 AT CUMLODEN. / FROM 1792 TO THE CLOSE OF THE WAR IN 1814 HE WAS ACTIVELY ENGAGED IN THE / SERVICE OF HIS COUNTRY DURING SEVENTEEN FOREIGN CAMPAIGNS; IN THE WEST INDIES, / IN EGYPT, AND IN VARIOUS PARTS OF EUROPE; IN ITALY HE SERVED WITH THE / ALLIED ARMIES UNDER SUWARROW AND OTHERS; AT FERROL HE WAS SEVERELY WOUNDED; / AT COPENHAGEN HE COMMANDED THE TROOPS EMBARKED WITH LORD NELSON, AT / WALCHEREN THE LIGHT BRIGADE, AND IN SPAIN AND PORTUGAL THE 2ND DIVISION OF THE / ARMY UNDER THE DUKE OF WELLINGTON IN EIGHT GENERAL ACTIONS. HE REPRESENTED / THE COUNTY OF WIGTON IN THREE PARLIAMENTS, AND RECEIVED IN HIS PLACE THE THANKS / OF THE HOUSE OF COMMONS FOR THE ABLE AND GALLANT SERVICES HE HAD RENDERED / HIS COUNTRY. HIS HEALTH BEING GREATLY IMPAIRED BY ARDUOUS DUTY AND NUMEROUS / WOUNDS, HE SPENT THE LATTER YEARS OF HIS LIFE IN RETIREMENT WHEN HIS UNAFFECTED / BENEVOLENCE, PIETY, AND RESIGNATION PROVED HIM A SINCERE CHRISTIAN, AS HIS / PUBLIC LIFE HAD SHEWN HIM TO BE A TRUE PATRIOT AND A GALLANT SOLDIER. HE DIED / AT A PREMATURE AGE, A VICTIM TO HIS ZEAL FOR THE PUBLIC SERVICE, HONOURED AND / ADMIRED BY HIS COUNTRY, BELOVED AND LAMENTED BY HIS FRIENDS.

Memorial tablet: Parish Church of Stewartry, Minnigaff, Newton Stewart, Dumfries and Galloway, Scotland. (The inscription contains the same wording as the chest tomb, but the layout is slightly different). (Photograph)

Named on the Rifle Brigade Memorial: Winchester Cathedral, Winchester, Hampshire. (Photograph)

Ensign 42nd Foot 8 Mar 1786. Lt 67th Foot 14 Oct 1787. Capt Independent Company 24 Jan 1790. Capt 22nd Foot 31 Oct 1792. Major 31st Foot 14 Jan 1794. Bt Lt Colonel 14 Jan 1795. Lt Colonel 67th Foot 1 Sep 1796. Lt Colonel Rifle Corps 1 Jan 1800. Bt Colonel 2 Apr 1801. Major General 25 Apr 1808. Lt General 4 Jun 1813.

Served in the Peninsula Feb 1810 – Jul 1811 and Oct 1812 – Apr 1814 (GOC 2nd Division Sep 1810 – Jul 1811, 1st Division Nov 1812 – Apr 1813 and 2nd Division May 1813 – Apr 1814). Present at Cadiz, Campo Mayor, first siege of Badajoz (Mentioned in Despatches), Albuera (wounded and Mentioned in Despatches), Vittoria (wounded and Mentioned in Despatches), Pyrenees (wounded and Mentioned in Despatches), Nivelle (Mentioned in Dispatches), Nive (Mentioned in Despatches), Garris (Mentioned in Despatches), Orthes (Mentioned in Despatches), Aire (Mentioned in Despatches), Tarbes and Toulouse. Also served in the West Indies 1793–1794 (wounded, present at Martinique and Guadeloupe), Flanders 1795–1796, Ferrol 1800 (wounded), Copenhagen 1801 (commanded the troops employed in the Baltic Fleet), Sicily 1806, Egypt 1807 (wounded) and Walcheren 1809. KCB and KTS. Gold Cross for Albuera, Vittoria, Pyrenees, Nivelle, Nive and Orthes. Spanish Order of St Fernando. Served with the Russian and Austrian armies 1799 (present at Battle of Zurich). He was impressed with the riflemen he saw. Responsible with Colonel Coote Manningham for the training of the newly formed Corps of Rifleman 1800. The organ-

isation and training of this Corps was led by Stewart. It later became the 95th Rifles. Published *Outlines of a Plan for the General Reform of the British Land Forces,* 1805 which contained the methods he had adopted for the 95th Foot. MP for Saltash 1795–1796, Wigtonshire 1796–1802, 1803–1808 and 1812–1816. Colonel Commandant 3rd Battalion 95th Rifles 31 Aug 1809. Retired to his estate near Newton Stewart. Died 6 Jan 1827.
REFERENCE: *Dictionary of National Biography. Royal Military Calendar, Vol. 2, pp. 322–9. Gentleman's Magazine, Feb 1827, pp. 174–5. Stewart, Sir William. Cumloden papers: letters and papers of Sir William Stewart, Privately printed in Edinburgh, 1871.*

STEWART, William
Captain. 91st Regiment of Foot.
Gravestone: St Catherine's Cathedral Churchyard, Spanish Town, Jamaica, West Indies (Outside west door). (M.I).

WILLIAM STEWART. H. M. 91ST OR ARGYLLSHIRE REGT., / D. 1 JAN 1825 AGED 40.

Ensign 16 Jan 1804. Lt 6 Jun 1805. Capt 17 Apr 1806. Major 12 Aug 1819.
Served in the Peninsula Oct 1812 – Apr 1814. Present at the Pyrenees, Nivelle, Nive, Orthes, Aire and Toulouse. Present at Waterloo, the siege of Cambrai and with the Army of Occupation. Also served in the West Indies 1823 where he died 1 Jan 1825.

STEWART, William
Private. 12th (Prince of Wales's) Regiment of Light Dragoons.
Named on the Regimental Memorial: St Joseph's Church, Waterloo. (Photograph)

Present at Waterloo where he was killed.

STEWART, William Drummond
Lieutenant. 15th (King's) Regiment of Light Dragoons.
Buried in a vault of Chapel of St Anthony the Eremite, Murthley Castle, Perthshire, Scotland. (Burial register)

Cornet 6th Dragoon Guards 15 Apr 1813. Lt 15th Lt Dragoons 6 Jan 1814. Capt 15 Jun 1820.
Served in the Peninsula. Present at Orthes and Toulouse. Present at Waterloo. Half pay 25 Oct 1821. Travelled to America in 1832 and for the next four years sought adventure in the American West. Commissioned paintings of scenes in the Rocky Mountains and of Indian life and brought the paintings to Murthley Castle to hang in a gallery. Returned to England in 1838 on the death of his elder brother and became 7th Baronet. Visited America again in 1842–1843 but then returned to Scotland until his death in 28 Apr 1871. His son Capt W. D. Stewart 93rd Foot was awarded the V.C. for gallantry in the Indian Mutiny.

STEWART, William Henry
Lieutenant. 11th Regiment of Light Dragoons.
Memorial: Highgate Chapel Burial Ground, Hornsey, London. (M.I.)

"HERE LIE THE REMAINS OF / MAJOR WILLIAM HENRY STEWART / OF THE 19 LANCERS. / YOUNGEST SON OF / SIR JAMES STEWART BART. / OF FORT STEWART / IN THE COUNTY OF DONEGAL / IRELAND / WHO DEPARTED THIS LIFE / JUNE 6TH 1820 AGED 27 YEARS."

Cornet 8 Aug 1811. Lt 10 Dec 1812. Capt 100th Foot 21 Aug 1817. Bt Major 21 Jan 1819. Capt 19th Lancers 20 May 1819.

Served in the Peninsula Sep 1812 – Apr 1814 (attached to 16th Lt Dragoons from May 1813). Present at Vittoria, Nivelle, Nive and Bayonne. Present at Quatre Bras and Waterloo. Retired 1820.

STIBBERT, Thomas

Captain and Lieutenant Colonel. Coldstream Regiment of Foot Guards.
Memorial tablet: English Cemetery, Florence, Italy. (Grave location: A8GH). (Photograph)

QUI IACQUIRO LE SALME DI TOMMASO STIBBERT E LA SUA FIGLIA ERMINIA CHE DA FEDERIGO STIBBERT FIGLIO E FRATELLO FURANO TRASPORTATE NELLA CAPELLE DA LUI ERETTA NEL CIMITERO DEGLI ALLORI

Ensign 1st Foot 12 May 1790. Ensign Coldstream Guards 23 Jan 1793. Lt and Capt 5 Nov 1794. Capt and Lt Colonel 25 Jun 1803.

Served in the Peninsula Mar 1809 – Apr 1810. Present at Douro and Talavera where he was severely wounded. Also served at the Helder 1799, Egypt 1801 and Copenhagen 1807. Retired 27 Jun 1810.

STIRLING, George

Lieutenant. 9th (East Norfolk) Regiment of Foot.
Mural Family Memorial tablet: Greyfriars Churchyard, Edinburgh, Scotland. (Division 12 – North wall on exterior of church). (Photograph)

SIR ALEXANDER STIRLING / .... / CAPTAIN GEORGE STIRLING / LATE OF THE 9TH REGIMENT OF FOOT. / DIED AT PORTOBELLO ON THE 21ST FEBRUARY 1852 / AGED SIXTY SIX YEARS.

Ensign 85th 21 Sep 1808. Lt 9th Foot 19 Oct 1808.

Served in the Peninsula with 1/9th May 1811 – Jan 1813 and Oct 1813 – Apr 1814. Present at Bidassoa (wounded), Nive and Bayonne. Also served at Walcheren 1809 and North America 1814–1815. MGS medal for Nive.

STIRLING, Sir Gilbert

Captain and Lieutenant Colonel. Coldstream Regiment of Foot Guards.
Mural memorial tablet: Greyfriars Churchyard, Edinburgh, Scotland. (Photograph)

HERE LIES INTERRED / SIR GILBERT STIRLING / BARONET, / SECOND AND ONLY / SURVIVING SON OF THE SAID / SIR JAMES STIRLING / BARONET. / SIR GILBERT / ENTERED THE COLD-STREAM / REGIMENT OF GUARDS / AT AN EARLY AGE AND / SERVED WITH THAT CORPS / AT THE HELDER AND IN / EGYPT UNDER GENERAL / SIR RALPH ABERCROMBY, / AND AFTERWARDS IN THE / PENINSULA UNDER THE / DUKE OF WELLINGTON. / SIR GILBERT RETIRED / FROM THE SERVICE IN 1812, / IN WHICH HE ATTAINED / THE RANK OF LIEUT COLONEL / AND PURCHASED THE / ESTATE OF LARBERT IN / THE COUNTY OF STIRLING / WHERE HE DIED / ON 13TH FEBRUARY 1843, / AGED 64 YEARS.

Ensign 15 May 1795. Lt and Capt 16 Jan 1799. Adjt 18 Jun 1799 – 25 May 1803. Capt and Lt Colonel 12 May 1806.

Served in the Peninsula Apr 1809 – Dec 1811. Present at Talavera. Also served at the Helder 1799, Egypt 1801 and Copenhagen 1807. Retired by sale of his commission 1 Mar 1812 and returned to Scotland to buy his estate at Larbert near Stirling.

STIRLING, James

Lieutenant Colonel. 42nd (Royal Highland) Regiment of Foot.
Monument: St Michael's Churchyard, Inveresk, Midlothian, Scotland. (Photograph)

ALEXANDRIA / CORUNNA / PYRENEES / SACRED TO THE MEMORY OF MAJOR GENERAL JAMES STIRLING, LATE GOVERNOR OF CORK, / AND FOR 52 YEARS AN OFFICER IN THE XLIID, OR ROYAL HIGHLAND REGIMENT. / WITH A WING OF THAT NATIONAL CORPS HE ANNIHILATED THE FRENCH INVINCIBLES AT THE / BATTLE OF ALEXANDRIA, AND TOOK THEIR STANDARD WITH HIS OWN HAND. / HE COMMANDED IT THROUGHOUT THE WHOLE OF THE PENINSULAR WARS, AND, / AFTER 28 YEARS OF FOREIGN SERVICE, DURING WHICH HE WAS ONCE CAPTURED AT SEA, / TWICE WOUNDED, AND ONCE SHIPWRECKED, HE RETIRED IN 1813 INTO PRIVATE LIFE, WHERE, / CULTIVATING THE VIRTUES WHICH ADORN THE CHRISTIAN CHARACTER, / HE DIED, FULL OF YEARS AND HONOUR AT HIS VILLA OF ESKBANK 12 DEC 1834. / HIS REMAINS BORNE HITHER BY HIS VETERAN COMPANIONS IN ARMS ARE HERE INTERRED.

Volunteer 1774. Ensign 22 Apr 1777. Lt 3 Aug 1778. Capt 8 Aug 1792. Major 14 Dec 1796. Bt Lt Colonel 29 Apr 1802. Lt Colonel 7 Sep 1804. Bt Colonel 4 Jun 1811. Major General 4 Jun 1814.

Served in the Peninsula Aug 1808 – Jan 1809 and Apr 1812 – Nov 1813. (from Sep – Oct 1812 O/c 2 Brigade 1st Division and from Nov 1812 – Jun 1813 O/c 1 Brigade 6th Division). Present at Corunna, Salamanca, Burgos and Pyrenees. Gold Medal for Corunna, Salamanca and Pyrenees. Also served in North America 1776–1783 (present at Brooklyn, White Plains, Brandywine, Valley Forge and Rhode Island), Flanders 1793–1795 (present at Nieuport), Minorca 1798, Egypt 1801 (present at Grand Cairo and Alexandria where he was wounded) and Walcheren 1809. Lt Governor of Cork. Served for 42 years in 42nd Foot. Father of Captain James Stirling 42nd Foot and father-in-law of Paymaster John Home 42nd Foot.
Reference: Gentleman's Magazine, Dec 1835, pp. 668–9. Royal Military Calendar, Vol. 3, pp. 345–8.

STIRLING, James

Captain. 42nd (Royal Highland) Regiment of Foot.
Monument: St Michael's Churchyard, Inveresk, Midlothain, Scotland. (On reverse of monument to his father Sir James Stirling). (Photograph)

JAMES STIRLING, SON CAPTAIN 42ND R. H / DIED 20TH JAN 1818 AGED 25.

Ensign 8 Aug 1805. Lt 27 Aug 1807. Capt 11 May 1815. With Portuguese Army: Capt 11th Line 1813.

Served in the Peninsula Sep with 42nd Foot 1808 – Jan 1809 and May 1812 – Aug 1813 (from Oct 1812 ADC to his father Major General James Stirling). Present at Corunna, Salamanca, Burgos and Pyrenees. On his father's retirement in November 1813 joined the Portuguese Army as Captain 11th Line. Served with them Nov 1813 – Apr 1814. Also served at Walcheren 1809. Retired from the army in 1817. Died 20 Jan 1818 aged 25 years. One of the youngest officers to take part in the Peninsular War, he was only 15 years of age at Corunna.

STIRLING, William

Lieutenant. 1st (King's) Dragoon Guards.
Family vault: Parish Church, Carmunnock, Lanarkshire, Scotland. (Stirling Street vault). (M.I.)

"PANEL 8. CAPTAIN WILLIAM STIRLING, 1ST DRAGOON GUARDS (1789–1825). BORN AT KEIR 23RD AUG 1789."

Ensign 29th Foot 27 Oct 1808. Cornet 1st Dragoon Guards 1 Feb 1810. Lt 19 Mar 1812. Capt 20 Jul 1815.

Served in the Peninsula with 29th Foot Jun – Nov 1809. Present at Waterloo with 1st Dragoon Guards.

Sir Robert Macara 42nd Foot

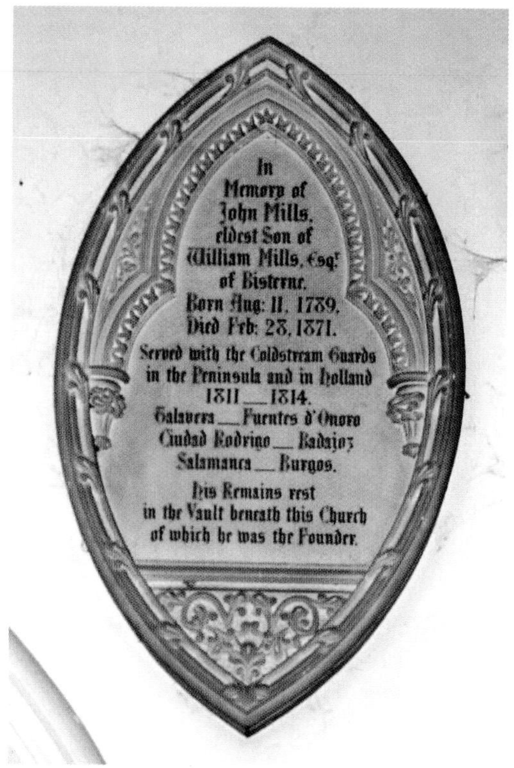

John Mills Coldstream Guards

Neil Macglashan 42nd Foot

George Maunsell 3rd Dragoon Guards

John Maclaine 73rd Foot

Sir John Moore 52nd Foot

Allan McNab 92nd Foot

Edward N. Macready 30th Foot

Sir Charles Napier 50th Foot

Sir Robert Nickle 88th Foot

John Ovens 74th Foot

John Proctor 43rd Foot

George T. Napier 3rd Foot Guards

Charles O'Neill 83rd Foot

William N. Ramsay Royal Artillery

Sir James McGrigor Army Medical Department

John P. Perry 38th Foot

Sir Thomas Picton 77th Foot

John Purvis 1st Foot

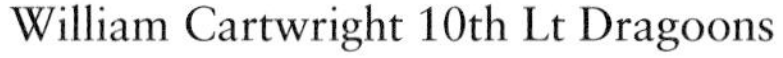

William Cartwright 10th Lt Dragoons

Copenhagen

Robert Ross 20th Foot

John E. C. Rous Coldstream Guards

Duke of Wellington

Moyle Sherer 34th Foot

John Ross 92nd Foot

James H. Schoedde 60th Foot

Alexander Lord Saltoun 1st Foot Guards

William Scott 3rd Foot Guards

William Selby 3rd Dragoons

John Shaw 2nd Life Guards

William Staveley Royal Staff Corps

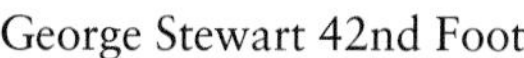

George Stewart 42nd Foot

Sempronius Stretton 40th Foot

John Stuart 9th Foot

Charles W. V. Stewart 25th Lt Dragoons

Henry Sunderland 52nd Foot

Joseph Thackwell 15th Lt Dragoons

William Tomkinson 16th Lt Dragoons

John Townsend 14th Lt Dragoons

William Wheatley 1st Foot Guards

William L. Walton Coldstream Guards

Earl of Uxbridge 7th Lt Dragoons

Gentle Vickers 95th Foot

James Weldon 3rd Foot

John G. Woodford 1st Foot Guards

Evere Mausoleum

3rd Foot Guards Cemetery

Biarritz memorial

Promoted to Captaincy in Jul 1815 as so many senior officers in his regiment were killed in the cavalry charge. Died in 1825 aged 36.

STISTED, Henry

Captain. 1st (Royal) Regiment of Dragoons.
Headstone in railed enclosure: Anglican Cemetery, Bagni di Lucca, Tuscany, Italy. (Photograph)

SACRED TO THE MEMORY OF COLONEL HENRY STISTED OF THE ROYAL DRAGOONS. TO THE QUALITIES OF A GALLANT SOLDIER /AND ACCOMPLISHED GENTLEMAN HE / UNITED THOSE OF A SINCERE CHRISTIAN / AND TO HIS EFFORTS IS THIS PLACE / MAINLY INDEBTED FOR POSSESSING / AN ENGLISH CHAPEL AND CEMETERY. / HE DEPARTED THIS LIFE IN ROME / ON THE 19TH OF MAY 1859 / IN HIS 73RD YEAR. / RESIGNING HIS SPIRIT IN THE BLESSED / HOPE OF GLORIOUS IMMORTALITY / THIS TRIBUTE IS ERECTED BY HIS AFFLICTED / WIDOW COMFORTED BY THE ASSURANCE / THAT THOSE WHO SLEEP IN JESUS / WILL GOD BRING WITH THEM

Cornet 8 Dec 1803. Lt 24 Jan 1805. Capt 5 Jan 1809. Major 25 Sep 1823. Lt Colonel 19 Dec 1826. Bt Colonel 28 Nov 1841.

Served in the Peninsula Sep 1811 – Apr 1814. Present at Maguilla, Vittoria and Toulouse. MGS medal for Vittoria and Toulouse. Half pay 19 Dec 1826. Later retired to Italy where with his wife Elizabeth he obtained permission from Carlo Lodovica, Prince of Lucca to build an Anglican church and cemetery for the British community living in Bagni di Lucca which opened in 1842. Died in Rome in 1859 and is buried in the Anglican churchyard that he built. Brother of Major Charles Stisted 3rd Lt Dragoons who also served in the Peninsula.

STOCKDALE, William

Lieutenant and Captain. 3rd Regiment of Foot Guards.
Memorial tablet: St Mary's Church, Wigton, Cumbria. (North aisle). (Photograph)

.... / WILLIAM STOCKDALE / LATE LIEUT COL IN 3RD REGT OF GUARDS / DIED OCT 17TH 1835, AGED 44. / ....

Ensign 31 May 1810. Lt and Capt 17 Mar 1814. Capt and Lt Colonel 12 Oct 1820.

Served in the Peninsula Apr 1812 – Apr 1814. Present at Salamanca, Burgos, Vittoria, Bidassoa, Nivelle, Nive, Adour and Bayonne. Retired 30 Aug 1831.

STODDART, Thomas

Sergeant. 2nd (Royal North British) Regiment of Dragoons.
Headstone: Grange Cemetery, Edinburgh, Scotland. (Section B. Number 61). (Photograph)

ERECTED BY / JANE RATCLIFFE / IN REMEMBRANCE OF / HER HUSBAND / THOMAS STODDART. / LATE SERGEANT SCOTS GRAYS / WHO DIED 3RD FEBRUARY 1852 / AGED 67 YEARS / ....

Pte 2 Jul 1803. Cpl 1813. Sgt 1815.

Present at Waterloo in Capt Poole's Troop where he was wounded. Discharged 21 Mar 1817 after 15 years and 317 days service due to his wounds at Waterloo, sabre cuts across his forehead had damaged his eyesight and fingers missing on his left hand.

STOKES, James Marshall

Lieutenant. 95th Regiment of Foot.
Named on the Rifle Brigade Memorial: Winchester Cathedral, Winchester, Hampshire. (Photograph)

Lt Shropshire Militia. 2nd Lt 95th Foot 20 Apr 1809. 1st Lt 2 May 1811.

Served in the Peninsula with 3/95th Feb 1810 – Sep 1811 and 1/95th Oct 1811 – Apr 1812. Present at Cadiz, Sobral, Fuentes d'Onoro, Ciudad Rodrigo and Badajoz where he was killed at the siege. Also served at Walcheren 1809.

STONE, Bayntun

Captain. 58th (Rutlandshire) Regiment of Foot.
Memorial tablet: St Saviour's Church, Larkhall, Bath, Somerset. (Photograph)

TO THE MEMORY OF / BAYNTUN STONE, / LATE OF THE 58TH REGIMENT, / HE FIRST SERVED IN THE CAMPAIGN IN EGYPT, / AND AFTERWARDS THROUGHOUT THE WHOLE OF THE PENINSULAR WAR. / HIS WORTH, AND BRAVERY AS A SOLDIER WAS ACKNOWLEDGED BY / MARKS OF FAVOUR CONFERRED UPON HIM; / IN EGYPT HE RECEIVED A GOLD MEDAL; FROM THE SULTAN SELIM THE III, / AND IN THE PENINSULAR FOR THE BATTLE OF THE NIVELLE / HE WAS PRESENTED WITH A GOLD MEDAL BY HIS / MAJESTY GEORGE THE III. / HE WAS RESPECTED BY ALL WHO KNEW HIM FOR HIS PRIVATE VIRTUES, / AND CLOSED AN HONOURABLE LIFE AT HIS HOUSE IN BATH, / ON THE 15TH DAY OF SEPTEMBER 1846, AGED 62 YEARS, / SINCERELY AND DEEPLY LAMENTED. / ………………..

Ensign 23 Nov 1799. Lt 54th Foot 21 Mar 1800. Lt 58th Foot 14 Dec 1802. Capt 1 Dec 1804. Bt Major 22 Nov 1813. Lt Col 22 Jul 1830.

Served in the Peninsula Jul 1809 – Apr 1814. Present at Salamanca, Burgos, Vittoria, Pyrenees, Nivelle, and Orthes. Gold Medal for Nivelle when in command of a Provisional Battalion. Also served in Egypt 1801 (awarded Sultan's Gold Medal). Half pay 25 Dec 1818.

STONE, Samuel

Private. Royal Regiment of Horse Guards.
Low monument: St Mary's Churchyard, Shrewsbury, Shropshire. (Photograph)

TO THE MEMORY OF SAMUEL STONE / DIED 10 MARCH 1842 AGED 56 YEARS. / HE WAS ONE OF THE SERJEANTS OF THE / SHROPSHIRE MILITIA AND FORMERLY OF THE ROYAL HORSE GUARDS (BLUES) / IN WHICH DISTINGUISHED REGIMENT HE SERVED AT WATERLOO.

Present at Waterloo in Lieutenant Colonel Clement Hill's Troop. Clement Hill was ADC to Lord Hill, so the troop was commanded by Captain William Tyrwhitt Drake. Later served as Sergeant in Shropshire Militia.

STOPFORD, Hon. Sir Edward

Captain and Lieutenant Colonel. 3rd Regiment of Foot Guards.
Memorial: Royal Military Chapel, Wellington Barracks, London. (M.I.) (Destroyed by a Flying Bomb 1944)

"IN MEMORY OF / LIEUT.-GENERAL SIR EDWARD STOPFORD, G.C.B., K.T.S., / COLONEL 41ST REGIMENT, 3RD GUARDS, 1784–1814. SERVED IN FLANDERS, SPAIN, AND PORTUGAL. COMMANDED 2ND BRIGADE OF GUARDS, 1812–14, IN SPAIN, AT THE SIEGE AND SORTIE OF BAYONNE. / BORN, 1766; DIED, 1837."

Ensign 20 Oct 1784. Lt and Capt 25 Apr 1792. Capt and Lt Colonel 28 May 1798. Bt Colonel 25 Apr 1808. Major General 4 Jun 1811. Lt General 19 Jul 1821.

Served in the Peninsula Mar 1809 – Apr 1812 and Nov 1812 – Apr 1814. (O/c 1 Brigade 1st Division Jul 1809 – Jun 1811. O/c 2 Brigade 4th Division Jul – Jul 1811. O/c 2 Brigade 1st Division Aug 1811 – Feb 1812 and Mar 1813 – Apr 1814). Present at Douro, Talavera, Busaco, Fuentes d'Onoro, Vittoria, Bidassoa (Mentioned in Dispatches), Nive, Adour and Bayonne (wounded). Gold Medal for Talavera, Vittoria and Nive. KTS. Also served in Flanders 1795. Colonel Royal African Corps 21 Sep 1818. Colonel 41st Foot 14 Jun 1819. MP for Marlborough 1810–1818. KCB 2 Jan 1815. GCB 28 Mar 1835. Equerry to the Queen 1795–1818. Died in Leamington Spa 14 Sep 1837. Educatd at Eton.
Reference: Gentleman's Magazine, Nov 1837, pp. 530–1.

STOPFORD, Hon. Edward

Ensign. 3rd Regiment of Foot Guards.
Memorial: Royal Military Chapel, Wellington Barracks, London. (M.I.) (Destroyed by a Flying Bomb 1944)

"................... / LIEUT.-COLONEL HON. EDWARD STOPFORD. / 2ND BATTALION 3RD GUARDS, 1811–32. SERVED AT THE PASSAGE OF THE ADOUR, AND SIEGE OF BAYONNE; AIDE-DE-CAMP TO MAJOR-GENERAL SIR E. STOPFORD, 1814. PRESENT AT THE BATTLES OF QUATRE BRAS AND WATERLOO; AIDE-DE-CAMP TO MAJOR-GENERAL SIR JOHN BYNG AT THE TAKING OF / PARIS, 1815; ADJUTANT OF THE BATTALION, 1822–26. / BORN 11TH JUNE, 1795; DIED 6TH JULY, 1840. / PLACED BY MEMBERS OF THE FAMILY, 1880."

Ensign 7 Nov 1811. Lt and Capt 3 Jul 1815. Capt and Lt Colonel 14 Dec 1826.

Served in the Peninsula Feb – Apr 1814 Present at Bayonne (ADC to Major General Stopford). Present at Waterloo and the Capture of Paris (ADC to Major General Byng).

STOPFORD, James

Major. 60th (Royal American) Regiment of Foot.
Gravestone: Old British Cemetery, Leghorn, Italy. (M.I.)

"IN MEMORY OF / LIEUT. COL JAMES STOPFORD / OF HIS BRITANNIC MAJESTY'S 60TH REGT., / WHO DIED AT PISA 14TH MAY 1823, / AGED 37. / THIS MONUMENT IS ERECTED OVER / HIS MORTAL REMAINS / BY HIS AFFECTIONATE AND MOURNING RELATIONS."

Ensign Sicilian Regt. Lt 29th Foot 27 Aug 1802. Capt 99th Foot 31 Mar 1808. Capt 60th Foot 9 Apr 1812. Major 10 Feb 1814. Lt Colonel 9 Nov 1815.

Served in the Peninsula Oct 1812 – Feb 1814. Present at Vittoria, Pyrenees and Nivelle where he was severely wounded.

STOPFORD, Roger

Lieutenant. 68th (Durham) Regiment of Foot.
Named on the Memorial: St Andrew's Church (now Musée Historique), Biarritz, France. (Photograph)

Ensign Durham Militia. Ensign 68th Foot 18 Apr 1809. Lt 21 Jun 1810.

Served in the Peninsula Jun 1811 – Nov 1813. Present at the siege of Salamanca Forts, Moriscos, Salamanca, Burgos, Vittoria, Pyrenees, San Marcial and Nivelle where he was killed Nov 1813. Also served at Walcheren 1809.

STOPFORD, William Henry
2nd Captain. Royal Artillery.
Low monument: Kensal Green Cemetery, London. (13358/117/RS). Inscription illegible. (Photograph)

2nd Lt 15 Sep 1804. 1st Lt 2 Jul 1805. 2nd Capt 1 Apr 1815. Capt 26 Jun 1829. Bt Major 10 Jan 1837. Lt Col 23 Nov 1841. Col 20 Jun 1854.

Present at Quatre Bras and Waterloo (wounded) in Capt Sandham's Brigade and at the Capture of Paris. Also served in South America 1807 and the Netherlands 1814–1815. Later changed his name to Stopford-Blair when he succeeded to estates in County Wigton. Married a daughter of Col Robert Bull, RA. Retired 20 Dec 1841. Died 12 Jul 1858.

STORER, Richard
Captain. 51st (2nd Yorkshire West Riding) Light Infantry.
Ledger stone: St John's Churchyard, Egham, Surrey. (Plot No. 38). (Photograph)

SACRED / TO THE MEMORY OF / CAPTN RICHARD STORER / LATE OF THE 51ST REGIMT / OF LIGHT INFANTRY / WHO DIED JANY 29TH 1844 / AGED 60 YEARS / ………………..

Ensign 19 Jul 1803. Lt 20 Jan 1804. Capt 13 Jul 1809.

Served in the Peninsula Oct 1808 – Jan 1809. Present at Corunna. Present at Waterloo, the siege of Cambrai and the Capture of Paris. Retired 1823.

STOREY, John
Lieutenant. 20th (East Devonshire) Regiment of Foot.
Tombstone: Colaba Cemetery, Bombay, India. (M.I.)

"SACRED TO THE MEMORY OF THE LATE CAPTAIN J. STOREY, HM'S 20TH REGIMENT, WHO DIED JUNE 16TH 1830 AGED 42 YEARS."

Sgt Major 20th Foot. Promoted from the ranks. Ensign and Adjutant 26 Aug 1813. Lt 1 Apr 1814. Capt 4 Oct 1827.

Served in the Peninsula Sep 1813 – Apr 1814. Present at Nivelle, Nive, Orthes and Toulouse. Also served in Ireland 1814, St Helena 1819 and India 1825 where he died in 1830.

STORY, Edmund Richard
Captain. 3rd (Prince of Wales's) Dragoon Guards.
Ledger stone: Kensal Green Cemetery, London. Inscription largely illegible. (9660/92/3). (Photograph)

COLONEL OF THE 3rd REGIMENT / 1784–1851 / **********.

Cornet 15 Oct 1803. Lt 12 Mar 1806. Capt 21 Dec 1809. Major 12 Jun 1823. Lt Colonel 8 Feb 1831.

Served in the Peninsula Nov 1809 – Apr 1814. Present at Redinha, Campo Mayor, Albuera, Usagre, Aldea de Ponte, Maguilla, Vittoria, Pamplona and Toulouse. MGS medal for Albuera, Vittoria and Toulouse. Commanding Officer 3rd Dragoon Guards 8 Feb 1831. Half pay 1838. Died July 1851.

STOTHERS, James
Sergeant. 51st (2nd Yorkshire West Riding) Light Infantry.
Named on the Regimental Memorial: KOYLI Chapel, York Minster, Yorkshire. (Photograph)

Served in the Peninsula. Present at Vittoria where he was killed.

STOTHERT, William
Lieutenant and Captain. 3rd Regiment of Foot Guards.
Named on the Regimental Memorial: St Joseph's Church, Waterloo. (Photograph)
Memorial tablet: Inside Mausoleum, Evere Cemetery, Brussels, Belgium. (Photograph)

CAPTAIN / WILLIAM STOTHERT / 3RD ROYAL FOOT GUARDS / AND BRIGADE MAJOR / TO THE 2ND BRIGADE OF GUARDS

Named on Memorial Panel VIII for Waterloo: Royal Military Chapel, Wellington Barracks, London. (M.I.) (Destroyed by a Flying Bomb 1944)

Ensign 3rd Foot Guards 1802. Capt 39th Foot 17 Dec 1803. Ensign 3rd Foot Guards 30 Oct 1805. Adjutant to 2nd Battalion 1809. Lt and Capt 11 Apr 1811.

Served in the Peninsula Mar 1809 – Jan 1812. Present at Douro, Talavera, Busaco, Fuentes d'Onoro. Present at Waterloo (Adjutant and Brigade Major to 2nd Brigade of Guards where he was severely wounded and died of his wounds 23 Jun 1815). Also served in the Netherlands 1814–1815 (present at Bergen-op-Zoom where he was severely wounded). One of the select band of soldiers buried in the Mausoleum at Evere. Author of *Narrative of the principal events of the campaigns of 1809, 1810 and 1811 in Spain and Portugal,* 1812, reprint 2009.

STOVIN, Sir Frederick
Captain. 28th (North Gloucestershire) Regiment of Foot.
Low monument: Kensal Green Cemetery, London. Inscription illegible. (19319/48/2). (Photograph)

Ensign 52nd Foot 22 Mar 1800. Lt 7 Jan 1801. Capt 62nd Foot 24 Jun 1802. Capt 28th Foot 9 Jul 1803. Bt Major 27 Apr 1812. Bt Lt Colonel 26 Aug 1813. Lt Colonel 92nd Foot 2 Sep 1819. Lt Colonel 90th Foot 9 Aug 1821. Bt Colonel 22 Jul 1830. Major General 23 Nov 1841. Lt General 11 Nov 1851. General 14 Aug 1859.

Served in the Peninsula with 1/28th Jul 1808 – Jan 1809, Apr – May 1810 and Sep 1811 – Apr 1814 (on staff as ADC to General Picton Oct 1811 – Jul 1812 and AAG to 3rd Division Aug 1812 – Apr 1814). Served with the 3rd Division without a day's leave of absence. Present at Corunna, Tarifa, Ciudad Rodrigo, Badajoz, Salamanca, Madrid, Vittoria, Pyrenees, Nivelle, Adour, Orthes, Vic Bigorre and Toulouse. He was detained in charge of a Court Martial in Dublin and so was not present at Waterloo. Also served at Ferrol 1800, Hanover 1805, Copenhagen 1807, Sweden 1808, Walcheren 1809 (ADC to Lt General Montague Fraser. Present at the siege of Flushing), North America 1814–1815 (DAG. Present at New Orleans where he was wounded), Jamaica with the 92nd Foot 1820–1821 and the Ionian Islands with 90th Foot 1821–1829. Gold Cross for Salamanca, Vittoria, Pyrenees, Nivelle, Orthes and Toulouse. MGS medal for Corunna, Ciudad Rodrigo and Badajoz. KCB 2 Jan 1815. KCMG. Colonel 83rd Foot 1 Sep 1848. GCB 1860. Died 16 Aug 1865.
REFERENCE: *Dictionary of National Biography. Gentleman's Magazine, Oct 1865, pp. 511–12.*

STOYTE, John
Lieutenant. 1st (Royal Scots) Regiment of Foot.
Obelisk: Walcot Cemetery, Lansdown, Bath, Somerset. (Area 1 Row G). (Photograph)

Side 1:

SACRED / TO THE MEMORY OF / LIEUT COLONEL / JOHN STOYTE / A DISTINGUISHED / OFFICER IN AN / EARTHLY WARFARE / & THROUGH DIVINE GRACE / A GOOD SOLDIER / OF JESUS CHRIST / HIS STEADFAST HOPE / WAS IN THE FINISHED / WORK OF HIS REDEEMER / AND HE ENTERED / IN FULL ASSURANCE / OF FAITH / UNTO HIS ETERNAL REST / DEC 13TH 1854

Side 2:

LIEU^T^. COLONEL STOYTE / COMMANDED THE 24TH AND 17TH REG^TS^ / AND WAS INSPECTING FIELD OFFICER / OF THE YORK DISTRICT. / HE WAS PRESENT AT THE STORMING OF BADAJOZ, / WOUNDED SEVERELY AT THE BATTLES / OF SALAMANCA & BERGEN OP ZOOM / PRESENT ON THE 16TH & 18TH JUNE 1815 AT WATERLOO.

Ensign 21 Mar 1811. Lt 4 Jul 1813. Capt 1st Foot 27 Jan 1825. Capt 24th Foot 19 May 1825. Bt Major 28 Jun 1838. Major 8 Jan 1841. Bt Lt Colonel 3 Apr 1846. Lt Colonel 17th Foot 7 Apr 1848.

Served in the Peninsula with 3/1st May 1811 – Nov 1812. Present at Badajoz, Castrejon and Salamanca (severely wounded while carrying the colours). Present at Quatre Bras and Waterloo (wounded). Also served in the Netherlands 1814–1815 (present at Bergen-op-Zoom where he was wounded, taken prisoner and awarded pension of £70 per annum) and India 1818–1821. MGS medal for Badajoz and Salamanca. Commanded 17th Foot 1848–1852.

STRAFFORD, John, EARL of STRAFFORD see BYNG, John

STRANGE, Alexander

Paymaster. 13th Regiment of Light Dragoons.
Buried in St George's Chapel, Windsor, Berkshire. (Burial record)

Promoted from the ranks. Paymaster 11 Apr 1811.

Served in the Peninsula Jul 1811 – Apr 1814. Present at Albuera, Usagre, Arroyo dos Molinos, Alba de Tormes, Vittoria and Nivelle where he was taken prisoner of war 10 Nov 1813 until Apr 1814. Present at Waterloo. Also served in Minorca 1782 (wounded at the siege of Fort Phillips), and the Irish Rebellion 1798. Retired 16 Aug 1831. Military Knight of Windsor 20 Nov 1835. Died 16 Dec 1840 aged 83.

STRANGWAYS, Thomas Fox

1st Lieutenant. Royal Artillery.
Gravestone: Cathcart's Hill Cemetery, Crimea, Ukraine. (M.I.)

"SACRED / TO THE MEMORY OF / BRIGADIER GENERAL / FOX STRANGWAYS / KILLED IN ACTION 5TH NOV. 1854."

Brass Memorial tablet: Royal Garrison Church, Portsmouth, Hampshire. (Back of a choir stall).

MAJOR GENL. THOMAS / FOX STRANGWAYS, / KILLED AT BATTLE IN / INKERMAN NOV 5 1855. / DD: FRIENDS.

2nd Lt 18 Dec 1806. 1st Lt 1 Feb 1808. 2nd Capt 12 Dec 1826. Capt 10 Jan 1837. Bt Major 23 Nov 1841. Lt Colonel 1 Aug 1846. Colonel 20 Jun 1854. Brigadier General 25 Aug 1854.

Served in Germany 1813–1814 with the Rocket Troop (present at Ghorde and Leipzig). Took command of the Rocket Troop after Major Borgue was killed. Swedish Order of the Sword. Present at Quatre Bras and Waterloo in Capt Whinyate's Rocket Troop (severely wounded). One of the few men to make the transition from Waterloo to the Crimea. At first in command of the Horse Artillery in the Crimea but on arrival succeeded to the command of the entire Artillery force. Present at Alma (greatly distinguished himself), Balaclava, the first bombardment of Sebastopol and Inkerman where he was severely wounded 5 Nov 1854 and died later the same day.
Reference: Annual Register, 1854, Appx, p. 353.

STRANGWAYS, William
Lieutenant. 3rd Garrison Battalion.
Memorial tablet: St Mary's Church, Kilkenny, Ireland. (Photograph)

SACRED TO THE MEMORY OF / WILLIAM STRANGWAYS, ESQ., / LATE OF 83RD REGIMENT, / AND OF SUTTONSRATH IN THE COUNTY, / WHO DIED ON THE 9TH OF NOVEMBER 1859. / …………………

Ensign 83rd Foot 15 Jun 1809. Lt 3 Jun 1812. Lt 3rd Garrison Battalion 29 Dec 1812.

Served in the Peninsula Oct 1809 – Jan 1812. Present at Redinha, Casal Nova, Foz d'Arouce, Sabugal, Fuentes d'Onoro, second siege of Badajoz and El Bodon. MGS medal for Fuentes d'Onoro.

STRATON, Sir Joseph see MUTER, Joseph

STRATENUS, A.
2nd Lieutenant. 4th Dragoons, Dutch Cavalry.
Named on the Memorial to Dutch officers killed at Waterloo: St Joseph's Church, Waterloo. (Photograph)

STREET, Alfred
Lieutenant. 40th (2nd Somersetshire) Regiment of Foot.
Chest tomb: St Andrew's Lower Churchyard (known as the Strangers Burial Ground), Clifton, Bristol, Somerset. (Grave number 3106). Seriously eroded. (Photograph)

TO THE MEMORY OF / LIEUTENANT ALFRED STREET 40TH FOOT / WHO DIED OF HIS WOUNDS / AT BADAJOZ / 9 APRIL 1812. / AGED **

Ensign 21 Jan 1806. Lt 10 Feb 1807.

Served in the Peninsula Aug 1808 – Apr 1812. Present at Rolica, Vimeiro, Talavera, Busaco, Redinha, first siege of Badajoz (wounded), Ciudad Rodrigo and Badajoz where he was severely wounded 6 Apr and died of his wounds 9 Apr 1812. Educated at Eton.

STRETTON, Edward
Private. 2nd Life Guards.
Headstone: Uxbridge Cemetery, Uxbridge, London. (Photograph)

EDWARD STRETTON / 2ND LIFE GUARDS / A VETERAN OF WATERLOO / DIED AUGUST ** 1871 / AGED 74 YEARS.

Pte 1 Aug 1814 – 27 Jul 1815, Pte 28 Jul 1815 – 31 Dec 1828, Pte 1 Jan 1829 – 27 Jul 1830, Pte 28 Jul 1830.

Present at Waterloo. Served a total of nearly 32 years in the regiment and received several distinguished marks for good conduct. Discharged 6 Feb 1845.

STRETTON, Sempronius
Captain. 40th (2nd Somersetshire) Regiment of Foot.
Gravestone: Parish Churchyard, Bromley, Kent. (No longer extant). (M.I.)

"COLONEL S. STRETTON CB., LATE OF LENTON PRIORY, NOTTS, WHO DIED AT CROYDON, 6TH FEBRUARY, 1842, AGED 59 YEARS. HIS DISTINGUISHED SERVICES IN THE PENINSULA AND MEMORABLE BATTLE OF WATERLOO OBTAINED FOR HIM SEVERAL DECORATIONS. INSCRIBED BY HIS AFFLICTED WIDOW."

Memorial tablet: Athlone Parish Church, Westmeath, Ireland. (Photograph)

SACRED TO THE MEMORY OF COLONEL S. STRETTON, C.B. / LATE 40TH REGT. OF LENTON PRIORY, NOTTS, WHO DIED AT / CROYDON SURREY, ON THE 6TH FEBY. 1842, AGED 59 YEARS. / HE SERVED HIS COUNTRY WITH ZEAL AND FIDELITY, IN DIFFERENT / PARTS OF THE WORLD FOR UPWARDS OF 40 YEARS, DURING WHICH / PERIOD HE WAS PRESENT AT THE FOLLOWING BATTLES, IN SEVERAL / OF WHICH HE HAD THE HONOR TO COMMAND THE ABOVE DISTINGUISHED / CORPS, VIZ. AT VITTORIA, PAMPELUNA, RONCESVALLES, THE SEVERAL / ACTIONS IN THE PYRENEES, HEIGHTS OF ST ANTONIO, THE PASSAGE / OF THE BIDASSOA AND HEIGHTS ABOVE VERA, IN SPAIN. THE BATTLE / OF SARA AND PASSAGE OF THE NIVELLE, BAYONNE, AND PASSAGE / OF THE NIVE, ORTHES, AND TOULOUSE IN FRANCE. THE EXPEDITION / TO NEW ORLEANS IN THE GULF OF MEXICO, AND LASTLY IN THE / MEMORABLE BATTLE OF WATERLOO, AFTER WHICH HE WAS APPOINTED / COMMANDANT OF THE 5TH ARRONDISSMENT OF PARIS. / HE MARRIED MARCH 3RD, 1821, / THE HON CATHERINE JANE MASSY, ELDEST DAUGHTER / OF GENERAL LORD CLARINA, OF ELM PARK, CO LIMERICK, / WHO DIED IN JULY FOLLOWING; AND SECONDLY / THE HON. ANNE HANDCOCK, YOUNGEST DAUGHTER / OF LORD CASTLEMAINE, OF THIS COUNTY / WHO SURVIVED HIM.

Named on Chest tomb: Old Lenton Churchyard, Nottingham, Nottinghamshire. (South-west corner of churchyard near the gateway). (Photograph)

IN MEMORY OF COLONEL SEMPRONIUS STRETTON, C.B., LATE OF THE 40TH REGIMENT, WHO DIED AT CROYDON, FEBRUARY 6, 1842, AGED 59 YEARS, AND WAS BURIED AT BROMLEY, IN KENT. HIS DISTINGUISHED SERVICES IN THE PENINSULA, AND AT THE MEMORABLE BATTLE OF WATERLOO, WERE REWARDED WITH SEVERAL HONORARY DECORATIONS, AND HE WAS ALSO MADE A COMPANION OF THE MOST HONOURABLE ORDER OF THE BATH

Ensign 6th Foot Nov 1800. Lt 49th Foot 18 Jul 1801. Capt 40th Foot 11 Sep 1806. Bt Major 22 Nov 1813. Major 18 Jun 1815. Bt Lt Colonel 21 Jun 1817. Bt Colonel 10 Jan 1837.

Served in the Peninsula Feb 1813 – Apr 1814. Present at Vittoria, Pyrenees, Vera, Bidassoa, Nivelle, Nive, Bayonne, Orthes and Toulouse. Gold Medal for Pyrenees where he commanded the 40th Foot. Present at Waterloo and with the Army of Occupation until 1818. (became one the Commandants of Paris). CB. Also served in North America 1814–1815 (present at New Orleans). Half pay 19 Feb 1824. Brother of Lt Severus William Lynam Stretton 68th Foot.

Reference: Gentleman's Magazine, Nov 1842, p. 546. Biography in Stretton, William, The Stretton manuscripts : being notes on the history of Nottinghamshire, privately printed, 1910.

STRETTON, Severus William Lynam

Lieutenant. 68th (Durham) Regiment of Foot.

Low monument: Old Common Cemetery, Southampton, Hampshire. (H51/1 and 16). (Photograph)

.... IN MEMORY OF LT. COL. SEVERUS WILLIAM LYNAM STRETTON LATE OF THE HAMPSHIRE MILITIA. DIED NOVEMBER 22ND 1881 AGED 91. HE WAS SEVERELY WOUNDED AT THE BATTLE OF VITTORIA WHILST SERVING IN THE 68TH L. I. IN THE PENINSULAR ON THE 13TH JUNE 1813 . AFTERWARDS COMDR. OF THE 64TH AND 40TH REGIMENTS.

Memorial tablet: All Saints' Church, Marlborough, Wiltshire. (Photograph)

TO THE / GLORY OF GOD / AND IN LOVING / MEMORY OF / LT COL. / S. W. L. STRETTON, /

LATE 40TH REGT / WHO DIED 22ND NOVR / 1884 / AGED 91 YEARS. / ERECTED / BY / HIS WIDOW AND CHILDREN.

Nottinghamshire Militia. Ensign 68th Foot 11 Jun 1812. Lt 6 Jan 1814. Capt 64th Foot 13 Aug 1825. Major 2 Dec 1831. Lt Colonel 64th Foot 6 May 1842. Lt Colonel 40th Foot 22 Dec 1848.

Served in the Peninsula Jan – Aug 1813 with 68th Foot. Present at Vittoria (severely wounded by two gun shots – one still lodged inside him at his death. Awarded pension of £50 per annum). MGS medal for Vittoria. Commanded 64th Foot 1842–1848 and 40th Foot from 1848–1852, but retired in Jan 1852 when the regiment went to Australia. Brother of Capt Sempronius Stretton 40th Foot.
Reference: Obit. The Times, 27 Nov 1884, p. 7.

STUART, John
Lieutenant Colonel. 9th (East Norfolk) Regiment of Foot.
Memorial tablet : Canterbury Cathedral, Kent. (Photograph)

SACRED TO THE MEMORY OF LIEUT. COLONEL JOHN STUART, / WHO FELL AT THE HEAD OF THE 9TH REGIMENT OF INFANTRY IN THE 32ND YEAR OF HIS AGE, / AT THE BATTLE OF ROLERA ON THE 17TH AUGUST 1808: / WHILE THE BRITISH ARMY WERE SUCCESSFULLY SUPPORTING / THE CAUSE OF PORTUGAL AGAINST THE USURPATION OF FRANCE. / HE WAS LOST TO HIS COUNTRY AT A PERIOD OF LIFE / WHEN HIS ATTAINMENTS AND NATURAL ENDOWMENTS MIGHT HAVE SECURED / TO HER BENEFIT THE MOST IMPORTANT ADVANTAGES / BUT IT IS THE PRIVATE LOSS THAT THE OFFICERS OF HIS REGIMENT / WOULD CHIEFLY DEPLORE, / IN PAYING THIS TRIBUTE OF VENERATION TO HIS BELOVED MEMORY / HE LIVES REVERED IN THE RECOLLECTION OF ALL WHO EVER KNEW HIM, / BUT THEY ARE ANXIOUS TO TRANSMIT IN LATER AGES, / SOME MEMORIAL OF A DISTINGUISHED EXAMPLE OF WORTH AND EXCELLENCE.

Capt 25th Foot 25 Feb 1793. Major 25th Foot 9 Sep 1798. Major 52nd Foot 1801. Bt Lt Colonel 13 Dec 1803. Lt Colonel 9th Foot 29 May 1806.

Served in the Peninsula with 1/9th Aug 1808. Present at Rolica where he was killed while leading the Regiment 17 Aug 1808. Gold Medal for Rolica. Also served at Ferrol 1800, Gibraltar, Sicily 1806–1807 and Copenhagen 1807. Senior Major of 52nd Foot on its formation as Light Infantry in Jan 1803. Took command of 9th Foot as Colonel de Bernierre and 260 men were still in prison in France after the shipwreck of the *Ariadne* on the French coast on their way to Hanover 1805.

STUART, Hon. William
3rd Major. 1st Regiment of Foot Guards.
Pedestal tomb: Erskine Churchyard, Erskine, Renfrewshire, Scotland. (Photograph)

HERE LIE THE REMAINS / OF / LIEUT GENERAL / THE HONBLE WILLIAM STUART, / LATE OF THE GRENADIER GUARDS. / THIRD SON OF / ALEXANDER TENTH LORD BLANTYRE / AND OF KATHARINE / DAUGHTER OF PATRICK LINDSAY / OF BALLESCARNNE / IN THE COUNTY OF HADDINGTON / BORN ERSKINE 20TH AUGUST 1775, / DIED ERSKINE 15 FEBRUARY 1837

Memorial: Royal Military Chapel, Wellington Barracks, London. (M.I.) (Destroyed by a Flying Bomb 1944)

"GENERAL THE HON. WILLIAM STUART, C.B., / GRENADIER GUARDS, 1794 TO 1821. / D.D. CHARLES STUART, TWELFTH LORD BLANTYRE, LATE GRENADIER GUARDS."

Ensign 30 Apr 1794. Lt and Capt 23 Jun 1797. Lt Colonel 14th Foot 25 Sep 1807. Capt and Lt Colonel

1st Foot Guards 1 Oct 1807. Bt Colonel 4 Jun 1814. 3rd Major 25 Jul 1814. Major General 19 Jul 1821. Lt General 10 Jan 1837.

Served in the Peninsula with 1st Battalion Sep 1812 – Nov 1812 and 3rd Battalion Nov 1812 – Apr 1814. Present at Pyrenees, Bidassoa, Nivelle, Nive, Adour and Bayonne. Gold Medal for Nive. Present at Quatre Bras (wounded and lost his arm and awarded pension of £300 per annum). CB. Also served in the Irish Rebellion 1798, the Helder 1799, Sicily 1806–1808 and Walcheren 1809. Educated at Winchester.
Reference: Gentleman's Magazine, May 1837, p. 545.

STUBBINS, John
Sergeant. 1st (King's) Dragoon Guards.
Brass Memorial tablet: St Peter and St Paul' Church, Warsop, Nottinghamshire. (Photograph)

IN MEMORY OF / SERGEANT JOHN STUBBINS / 1ST KING'S DRAGOON GUARDS / (1768–1849), / HE FOUGHT WITH WELLINGTON / AT WATERLOO – 18TH JUNE 1815.

Present at Waterloo.

STUBBS, Thomas William
Lieutenant. 50th (West Kent) Regiment of Foot.
Named on the Memorial tablet to Portuguese Commanders at Albuera: Albuera Wall, British Cemetery, Elvas, Portugal. (Photograph)

Ensign 27 Jul 1793. Lt 16 May 1795. Portuguese Army: Lt Colonel 23rd Line 28 May 1809. Colonel 20 Feb 1811. Brigadier 18 Jul 1813. Major General 10 Oct 1817.

Served in the Peninsula with Portuguese Army May 1809 – Apr 1814. Present at Busaco, Albuera, second siege of Badajoz, Ciudad Rodrigo, Badajoz, Castrejon, Salamanca (Mentioned in Despatches), Vittoria (Mentioned in Beresford's Despatches) and Pyrenees (Mentioned in Beresford's Despatches). Originally in 50th Foot and went with them to Portugal in 1797. He met his future wife there and resigned his commission when the Queen of Portugal offered him a company in her service. When in 1808 Beresford was looking for likely officers to command Portuguese soldiers he found Stubbs already a Lt Colonel in the Portuguese Army. He served with the Portuguese Army 1801–1841 rising to the rank of Lt General. During the reign of Don Miguel he returned to England but on the accession of Don Pedro went back to Portugal and became Governor of Oporto. Gold Cross for Albuera, Salamanca, Vittoria and Pyrenees. Knighted 10 Oct 1817. KCTS 24 Feb 1815. CB. Viscondé de Villa Nova de Gaio. Died in Lisbon 27 Apr 1844.
Reference: United Service Magizine, Jun 1844, p. 320. Gentleman's Magazine Jul 1844, p. 91. Annual Register, 1844, pp. 235–6.

STUPART, Francis
Lieutenant. 2nd (Royal North British) Regiment of Dragoons.
Headstone: Warriston Cemetery, Edinburgh, Scotland. (Section A2 Grave number 577). (Photograph)

IN MEMORY OF / ROBERT STUPART / .... / AND OF / MAJOR FRANCIS STUPART, / HIS FATHER / WHO DIED 21ST JULY 1860 / AGED 79 YEARS / THE LAST SURVIVING OFFICER IN SCOTLAND / OF THE SCOTS GREYS / PRESENT AT BATTLE OF WATERLOO / WHERE HE SERVED AS LIEUTENANT / AND WAS SEVERELY WOUNDED.

Cornet 3 May 1808. Lt 14 Dec 1809. Capt 20 Jul 1815. Bt Major 10 Jan 1837.

Present at Waterloo in Capt Cheney's Troop (wounded). The last surviving officer in Scotland of the Scots Greys who served at Waterloo. Half pay 25 Mar 1816.

STURGEON, Henry

Lieutenant Colonel. Royal Staff Corps.

Named on the Memorial: St Andrew's Church (now Musée Historique), Biarritz, France. (Photograph)

2nd Lt Royal Artillery 1 Jan 1796. Lt 21 Aug 1797. Capt Royal Staff Corps 25 Jun 1803. Major 1 Jun 1809. Bt Lt Colonel 6 Feb 1812.

Served in the Peninsula Apr 1809 – Mar 1814. (AQMG May 1813 – Mar 1814). Present at Busaco, Ciudad Rodrigo (Mentioned in Despatches), Badajoz, Salamanca (Mentioned in Despatches – especially for his bridge building over the Agueda, temporary bridge at Alcantara and the bridge of boats over the Adour) and Vic Bigorre where he was killed 19 Mar 1814. Gold medal for Ciudad Rodrigo and Badajoz. Also served at Ferrol 1800 and Egypt 1801 (present at Alexandria where he was wounded). Given command of a Corps of Guides and in charge of Post Office and Communications Apr 1813. Wellington called him a 'clever fellow'

Reference: Dictionary of National Biography. Stoneham, Martin, Lt Col Sturgeon and the Royal Staff Corps, Waterloo Journal, Summer 2010, pp. 3–5.

STURGEON, William

Private. Royal Artillery.

Memorial tablet: St Mary the Virgin's Church, Kirkby Lonsdale, Cumbria. (Photograph)

IN MEMORY OF / WILLIAM STURGEON / WHO WAS BORN AT WHITTINGHAM A.D. 1783 AND BURIED AT / PRESTWICH LANCASHIRE ON THE 8TH DAY OF DECEMBER 1850 / HE WAS THE SON OF PARENTS IN HUMBLE LIFE AND SERVED AS / A PRIVATE IN THE ROYAL ARTILLERY FOR NEARLY 20 YEARS. / AFTER COMPLETING HIS TERM OF SERVICE, HE SUCCESSFULLY / DEVOTED HIMSELF TO THE STUDY OF THE PHYSICAL SCIENCES, / WITH POWERS OF ORIGINALITY AND INDUSTRY RARELY EQUALLED. / BESIDES CONTRIBUTING NUMEROUS WORKS TO THE SCIENTIFIC / LITERATURE OF HIS COUNTRY, HE WAS THE DISCOVERER OF / THE SOFT IRON ELECTRO MAGNET, / THE AMALGAMATED ZINC BATTERY, / THE ELECTRO MAGNETIC COIL MACHINE AND / THE RECIPROCATING MAGNETIC ELECTRICAL MACHINE / INVENTIONS OF THE HIGHEST VALUE AND WHICH ALONG WITH / MANY OTHERS HE FREELY GAVE TO THE WORLD / HIS NAME WILL BE PERPETUATED AS LONG AS THE SCIENCE HE / CHERISHED CONTINUES TO EXIST

Westmoreland Militia 1803. Pte Royal Artillery 23 Apr 1805.

Served in the Peninsula 1812 – Apr 1814. Present at Salamanca, Vittoria, San Sebastian, Nivelle, Nive, Orthes and Toulouse. Discharged 30 Sep 1820. Before he joined the army he was apprenticed to a shoe maker. With very little education he decided to improve himself. While in the army he obtained a few books and started to study mathematics. Latin, Greek, French, German and Italian were also mastered to further his study of electicity and magnetism. Retired from the army 1820 and became Professor of Natural History in the Military Academy at Addiscombe. Later started to make scientific instruments at Woolwich and developed the first electro magnet amongst other inventions. Awarded Silver Medal from the Society of Arts. MGS medal for Salamanca, Vittoria, San Sebastian, Nivelle, Nive, Orthes and Toulouse. A collection of his essays *Scientific researches,* was published in 1850.

Reference: Dictionary of National Biography. Gentleman's Magazine, Jan 1851, pp. 101–3. Annual Register, 1850, Appx, p. 285.

STYLES, Sir Thomas

Ensign. 1st Regiment of Foot Guards.

Named on Memorial Panel VII: Royal Military Chapel, Wellington Barracks, London. (M.I.) (Destroyed by a Flying Bomb 1944)

Ensign 16 Apr 1812.

Served in the Peninsula with 1st Battalion Apr – Nov 1813. Died 8 Nov 1813 in Spain of disease. Educated at Eton.

SUCHOW, Arthur

Ensign. 1st Line Battalion, King's German Legion.

Named on the Regimental Memorial: La Haye Sainte, Waterloo. (Photograph)

Present at Waterloo where he was killed.

SULIVAN, George James

Captain. Royal Regiment of Horse Guards.

Memorial tablet: Church of St Lawrence, Abbots Langley, Hertfordshire. (Photograph)

SACRED / TO THE MEMORY OF / GEORGE JAMES SULIVAN ESQRE, / LATE CAPTAIN IN THE ROYAL HORSE GUARDS BLUE, / AND ELDEST SON OF THE LATE SIR BENJAMIN SULIVAN, / ONE OF THE JUDGES OF THE SUPREME COURT OF MADRAS. / BORN 14TH MARCH 1791. DIED 20TH DECEMBER 1858. / HIS MORTAL REMAINS LIE IN THE FAMILY VAULT / ON THE NORTH SIDE OF THE CHURCH. / VERSE

Lt 1st Life Guards 26 Sep 1811. Capt Royal Horse Guards 21 Apr 1815.

Served in the Peninsula Dec 1812 – Jan 1813 and Jul 1813 – Apr 1814. Present at Toulouse. MGS medal for Toulouse.

SULLIVAN, Sir Henry

Captain and Lieutenant Colonel. Coldstream Regiment of Foot Guards.

Ledger stone: Coldstream Guards Cemetery, St Etienne, Bayonne, France. (Photograph)

SIR H. S. BT M.P. / LIEUT. COL. 2D GUARDS

Memorial tablet: St Nicholas's Church, Thames Ditton, Surrey. (Photograph)

THIS TABLET IS ERECTED TO THE MEMORY OF / SIR HENRY SULLIVAN, BART, / LT COLONEL IN THE COLDSTREAM REGT OF GUARDS. M.P. FOR LINCOLN / AND SON OF THE LATE SIR RICHARD J. SULLIVAN, OF THAMES-DITTON, BART, / AGED 39. / HAVING SERVED THROUGHOUT THE WAR IN SPAIN AND PORTUGAL / UNDER THE DUKE OF WELLINGTON: / HE FELL AT ITS CLOSE BEFORE BAYONNE, ON THE 14TH OF APRIL, 1814, / AT THE MOMENT THE ENEMY WERE DRIVEN BACK TO THEIR ENTRENCHMENTS. / IN HIM THE ARDOR OF THE SOLDIER / WAS BLENDED WITH THE MOST CAPTIVATING AND REFINED MANNERS, / AND HE UNITED TO THE PRACTICE OF EVERY SOCIAL DUTY, / THE FIRM BELIEF AND HOPE OF A CHRISTIAN. / BORN 31ST OF MARCH 1785.

Named on Memorial Panel VII for the Sortie from Bayonne: Royal Military Chapel, Wellington Barracks, London. (M.I.) (Destroyed by a Flying Bomb 1944)

Named on the Memorial: St Andrew's Church (now Musée Historique), Biarritz, France. (Photograph)

Ensign 81st Foot 19 May 1798. Lt 25 Sep 1798. Capt 18 Jul 1801. Capt 66th Foot 7 Jun 1803. Ensign Coldstream Guards 8 Dec 1803. Lt and Capt 2 Dec 1805. Capt and Lt Colonel 24 Sep 1812.

Served in the Peninsula Mar 1809 – Nov 1811, Aug – Nov 1812 and Apr 1814. Present at Douro, Talavera, Busaco, Fuentes d'Onoro, Burgos and Bayonne where he was killed at the Sortie from Bayonne

14 Apr 1814. Also served at Copenhagen 1807 (ADC to Major General Hon E. Finch). Educated at Eton. Member of Parliament for Lincoln.

SUMNER, Edward

Lieutenant and Captain. Coldstream Regiment of Foot Guards.
Named on Memorial Panel VIII for Waterloo: Royal Military Chapel, Wellington Barracks, London. (M.I.) (Destroyed by a Flying Bomb 1944)

Ensign 20th Foot 3 Apr 1806. Lt 20 Aug 1807. Capt 7th Foot 24 Sep 1812. Lt and Capt Coldstream Guards 23 Sep 1813.

Served in the Peninsula Aug 1808 – Jan 1809. Present at Vimeiro and Corunna. Present at Waterloo, where he was severely wounded and died of his wounds in Brussels 26 June. Also served at Walcheren 1809.

SUNDERLAND, Henry

Sergeant Major. 52nd (Oxfordshire) Light Infantry Regiment of Foot.
Headstone: All Saints' Churchyard, Pontefract, Yorkshire. (Headstone laid flat and seriously damaged. Grave number 53). (Photograph)

IN MEMORY OF / HENRY SUNDERLAND / FORMERLY ADJUTANT IN H.M. 52ND REGT OF LT INFT / BORN HEPTONSTALL 31ST MAY 1787 / DIED AT PONTEFRACT 15TH OCT 1858 / AGED 77 YEARS. / HE SERVED WITH DISTINCTION AT THE FOLLOWING / BATTLES AND SIEGES AS A CPL AT FERROL, / AS A SERGT AT KIOGE, VIMIERA, SABUGAL / FUENTES DE ONORO, CIUDAD RODRIGO / AS SERGT MAJOR AT MERXEM. / HE WAS ADMIRED AS A GALLANT SOLDIER / AND DIED SINCERELY REGRETTED / THIS STONE IS ERECTED AS A TOKEN / OF AFFECTION BY HIS SON.

Cpl 1800. Sgt 1807. Sgt Major 1814. Promoted from the ranks. Ensign and Adjutant 26 Jul 1821.

Served in the Peninsula 1808 – Jan 1809 and Mar 1811 – Mar 1812. Present at Vimeiro, Vigo, Sabugal, Fuentes d'Onoro and Ciudad Rodrigo (wounded). Also served at Ferrol 1800, Copenhagen 1807 (present at Kiöge) and the Netherlands 1814–1815 (present at Merxem). Half pay 7 Mar 1822. MGS medal for Vimeiro, Fuentes d'Onoro and Ciudad Rodrigo.

Reference: Oxfordshire Light Infantry Chronicle, 1895, pp. 167–9.

SURMAN, John

Troop Sergeant Major. 10th (Prince of Wales's Own Royal) Regiment of Light Dragoons.
Chest tomb: St Mary the Virgin's Churchyard, Hawkesbury, Gloucestershire. (Photograph)

SACRED / TO THE MEMORY OF / JOHN SURMAN CAPTAIN / LATE OF PETTY FRANCE / DIED JUNE 1865 AGED 81 YEARS.

Hampshire Fencibles 1798. Pte 10th Lt Dragoons 25 Oct 1800. Sgt 1812. Troop Sgt Major 1814. Promoted from the ranks. Ensign Royal York Rangers 1819. Cornet 10th Hussars 25 Oct 1822. Lt 13 Apr 1825.

Served in the Peninsula with the 10th Lt Dragoons Nov 1808 – Jan 1809 and Feb 1813 – Apr 1814. Present at Sahagun, Benevente, Vittoria, Orthes and Toulouse. Present at Waterloo as Troop Sergeant Major with Captain Grey's Troop (No. 4) which brought the news of the Prussians retreat to Wavre after Ligny. Riding Master to the 10th Hussars from 1819. Served with the regiment for 31 years, retiring Jun 1831. MGS medal for Sahagun and Benevente, Vittoria, Orthes and Toulouse.

SURTEES, William

Quartermaster. 95th Regiment of Foot.
Memorial tablet: St Andrew's Church, Corbridge, Northumberland. (Photograph)

IN MEMORY OF / WILLIAM SURTEES, / QUARTERMASTER, RIFLE BRIGADE, / WHO DIED AT CORBRIDGE, HIS NATIVE VILLAGE, / MAY 28TH 1830; AGED 49 YEARS. / AUTHOR OF A WORK ENTITLED / "TWENTY FIVE YEARS IN THE RIFLE BRIGADE", / IN WHICH CORPS HE WAS ESTEEMED A BRAVE SOLDIER, / AND AN HONOURABLE MAN, / BUT HE LOOKED BEYOND THE GRAVE, / AND GAVE ASSURANCE THAT HE WAS A CHRISTIAN. / HIS REMAINS LIE INTERRED IN THE ADJACENT BURIAL GROUND.

Northumberland Militia 1795. Pte 56th Foot 1797. Cpl 95th Foot 1802. Sgt 1803. Quartermaster 8 Jun 1809. Ensign 4th Veteran Battalion 24 Feb 1820. Quartermaster 95th Foot Dec 1820.

Served in the Peninsula with 3/95th Aug 1810 – Aug 1811 and Feb 1812 – Apr 1814. Present at Cadiz, Barrosa, Badajoz, San Millan, Vittoria, Pyrenees, Vera, Bidassoa, Nivelle, Nive, Orthes, Tarbes (wounded) and Toulouse. Also served in North America 1814–1815 (present at New Orleans). Retired on full pay 25 Dec 1826. Author of *Twenty five years in the Rifle Brigade,* 1833, reprint 1996.

SUTHERLAND, William

Private. 42nd (Royal Highland) Regiment of Foot.
Family Headstone: Greyfriars Burying Ground, Perth, Perthshire, Scotland. (M.I.)

"ERECTED BY WILLIAM SUTHERLAND, LATE COLOUR SERGEANT 42ND ROYAL HIGHLAND REGIMENT IN MEMORY OF .... ALSO HIS BROTHER JOHN SUTHERLAND LATE OF THE 42ND REGIMENT WHO DIED IN SPAIN IN 1813 AND HECTOR, LATE SERGEANT MAJOR 7TH HUSSARS WHO DIED IN MONTREAL 24 MARCH 1850. ALSO THE ABOVE NAMED WILLIAM SUTHERLAND WHO DIED 1 FEBRUARY 1850 AGED 56 YEARS."

Pte 3 Oct 1811. Cpl 27 Sep 1817. Sgt 19 Nov 1821. Col Sgt 1 Jun 1829.

Served in the Peninsula Apr 1812 – Apr 1814. Present at Pyrenees, Nivelle, Nive, Orthes and Toulouse. Awarded Regimental medal. Present at Waterloo. Also served in Gibraltar 1825. Discharged 15 May 1832. MGS medal for Pyrenees, Nivelle, Nive, Orthes and Toulouse. Brother of Pte John Sutherland 42nd Foot killed in Spain 1813 and Sgt Major Hector Sutherland 7th Lt Dragoons who died in Montreal 1850.

SUTTON, Sir Charles

Lieutenant Colonel. 23rd (Royal Welch Fusiliers) Regiment of Foot.
Named on the Memorial tablet: Badajoz Wall, British Cemetery, Elvas, Portugal. (Photograph)

Ensign 3rd Foot Guards 10 Jul 1800. Lt and Capt 17 Dec 1802. Capt 23rd Foot 25 May 1803. Major 23 Apr 1807. Bt Lt Colonel 30 May 1811. Lt Colonel 23rd Foot 17 Jun 1813. Portuguese Army: Lt Colonel 9th Line 26 Aug 1809. Colonel 10 Jul 1813.

Present in the Peninsula with 2/23rd Oct 1808 – Jan 1809 and with Portuguese Army Jun 1809 – Apr 1814. Present at Corunna, Busaco (Mentioned in Despatches), Redinha, Foz d'Arouce, Sabugal, Fuentes d'Onoro, second siege of Badajoz, El Bodon, Badajoz (Mentioned in Beresford's Despatches), Salamaca, Vittoria, Pyrenees, Nivelle, Nive, Orthes (Mentioned in Beresford's Despatches), Vic Bigorre, Tarbes and Toulouse. Also served at the Helder 1799 and Hanover 1805. Gold Cross for Busaco, Fuentes d'Onoro, Badajoz, Salamanca, Vittoria, Nivelle and Toulouse. KCB. KTS. Inspecting Field Officer of Military in Ionian Islands. Was home on leave when he died suddenly 6 Apr 1828 at Bottesford.
Reference: Gentleman's Magazine, Apr 1828, pp. 368–9.

SWABEY, William

1st Lieutenant. Royal Artillery.

Brass Memorial tablet: St Mary the Virgin's Church, Langley, Slough, Buckinghamshire. (Photograph)

TO THE LOVED MEMORY OF WILLIAM SWABEY CAPTN / RHA. (3RD SON OF THE ABOVE MAURICE SWABEY D.C.L) WHO / SERVED HIS COUNTRY FROM 1805–1815 AT COPENHAGEN, / CIUDAD RODRIGO, SALAMANCA, VITTORIA, TOULOUSE / AND WATERLOO. HE WAS AFTERWARDS J.P. & DL BUCKS / CAPTAIN BUCKS YEOMANRY, SUBSEQUENTLY MEMBER / H. M. COUNCIL & ADJ-GENERAL OF THE MILITIA, / PRINCE EDWARD ISLAND, CANADA. / BORN 1789. DIED 1872. / ....

Brass Memorial tablet: St Mary's Church, Clifton Reynes, Buckinghamshire. (Photograph)

TO CAPTN. WM. SWABEY. LATE R. H. A. / A PENINSULAR AND WATERLOO OFFICER, / JP. AND D. L. FOR BUCKS, / AND MARIANNE, HIS WIFE, / WHO RESIDED AT CLIFTON HALL 1824 TO 1839 / AND TOOK THE GREATEST INTEREST IN THE / SPIRITUAL AND TEMPORAL WELFARE OF THIS PARISH. / THIS TABLET IS ERECTED BY / THEIR DAUGHTER EMILY FRANCES / WIFE OF SIR PAGET BOWMAN BART.

2nd Lt 1 Jun 1806. 1st Lt 13 Aug 1807. 2nd Capt 15 Nov 1824.

Served in the Peninsula Jul 1811 – Nov 1813 and Mar – Apr 1814. Present at Llerena, Ciudad Rodrigo, Salamanca, Vittoria (severely wounded) and Toulouse. Present at Quatre Bras and Waterloo in Lt Colonel Sir Robert Gardiner's Troop. Also served at Copenhagen 1807. Retired on half pay 28 Nov 1825. Became Captain in Buckinghamshire Yeomanry. Emigrated with his family to Prince Edward Island and became a successful farmer and politician. Served in the Legislative Council 1841–1861 until he returned to England.

Reference: Swabey, William, Diary of campaigns in the Peninsular for the years 1811, 12 and 13, 1895, reprint 1984. Annual Register, 1872, Part 2, p. 143. Dictionary of Canadian Biography.

SWANN, Frederick Dashwood

Ensign. 1st Regiment of Foot Guards.

Low monument: St John the Evangelist's Church, Ickham, Kent. (Photograph)

IN MEMORY OF FREDERICK DASHWOOD SWANN / OF REDHILL – SURREY – AND FORMERLY OF LEE PRIORY IN THIS PARISH / LATE CAPTAIN IN THE GRENADIER GUARDS. / HE SERVED WITH THAT REGT IN THE FINAL ACTIONS OF THE / PENINSULAR CAMPAIGN AND AT WATERLOO. / DIED MAY 22ND 1870 AGED 74.

Ensign 20 Oct 1813. Lt and Capt 16 Jul 1818.

Served in the Peninsula with 3rd Battalion Mar – Apr 1814. Present at Bayonne. Present at Waterloo. Half pay 25 Dec 1818. Retired 15 Sep 1839. Brother of Lt and Capt William Henry Swann 3rd Foot Guards.

SWANN, William Henry

Lieutenant and Captain. 3rd Regiment of Foot Guards.

Memorial tablet: St George's Church, Esher, Surrey. (M.I.)

"NEAR THIS SPOT ARE INTERRED THE MORTAL REMAINS OF / HENRY SCOTT SWANN ESQ / .... / ALSO TO THE MEMORY OF / WILLIAM HENRY ELDEST SON OF THE ABOVE AND / CATHERINE HIS WIFE. / CAPTAIN IN THE 3 REGIMENT OF FOOT / GUARDS. HE WAS KILLED AT THE BATTLE OF BARROSA / ON THE 5 OF MARCH 1811 IN THE 25 YEAR OF HIS LIFE. / (VERSE)"

Named on Memorial Panel VI for Barrosa: Royal Military Chapel, Wellington Barracks, London. (M.I.) (Destroyed by a Flying Bomb 1944)

Ensign 17 Jan 1804. Lt and Capt 22 Jun 1809.

Served in the Peninsula Mar 1809 – Aug 1809 and Apr 1810 – Mar 1811. Present at Cadiz and Barrosa where he was killed 5 Mar 1811. Educated at Eton. Brother of Ensign Frederick Dashwood Swann 1st Foot Guards.

SWANSON, John

Captain. 42nd (Royal Highland) Regiment of Foot.
Named on the Memorial: St Andrew's Church (now Musée Historique), Biarritz, France. (Photograph)

Ensign 71st Foot 1801. Lt 42nd Foot 9 Jul 1803. Capt 14 Dec 1809.

Served in the Peninsula Jul 1810 – May 1812 and Mar 1813 – Apr 1814. Present at Pyrenees, Nivelle, Nive, Orthes and Toulouse where he was killed Apr 1814. Also served at Walcheren 1809.

SWEENY, Charles Frederick

Lieutenant. 26th (Cameronian) Regiment of Foot.
Grave: Green Street Cemetery, St, Helier, Jersey, Channel Islands. (Plot 98 – Middle stone). (M.I.)

"SACRED TO THE MEMORY OF CHARLES FREDERICK SWEENEY ESQ. LATE CAPTAIN 83RD REGT WHO DEPARTED THIS LIFE ON THE 9TH DAY OF JUNE 1830. AGED 58 YEARS".

Ensign 12 Apr 1810. Lt 7 May 1812. Lt 3rd Royal Veteran Battalion 15 Jan 1824. Lt 48th Foot 9 Apr 1825. Lt 25th Foot 23 Nov 1825. Capt (unattached) 29 Dec 1837.

Served in the Peninsula Sep 1811 – Jun 1812. The regiment was unable to serve in any campaigns in the Peninsula as there were too many suffering from Walcheren fever and they were sent to Gibraltar 1812.

SWEENY, Francis Bernard

Ensign. 62nd (Wiltshire) Regiment of Foot.
Memorial Tablet: St Peter's Church, Bandon, County Cork, Ireland. (Photograph)

SACRED / TO THE MEMORY OF / FRANCIS BERNARD SWEENY, ESQ. / OF UNION HALL, BANDON. LATE OF THE 62ND FOOT / AND A MAGISTRATE OF THE COUNTY OF CORK FOR 26 YEARS / HE SERVED IN THE PENINSULA, AND RECEIVED / THE WAR MEDAL WITH TWO CLASPS, FOR NIVE AND NIVELLE. / HE WAS A TRULY GOOD MAN: A SINCERE AND / HUMBLE CHRISTIAN; OF THE STRICTEST PRINCIPLES OF / HONOUR; GENTLE, WARM HEARTED AND KIND. / HE DIED DEC.7TH 1863, AGED 69 YEARS / THIS MONUMENT IS ERECTED IN GRATEFUL REMEMBRANCE OF / A LOVING HUSBAND, BY HIS SORROWING AND AFFECTIONATE WIDOW / VERSE

Volunteer 62nd Foot. Ensign 20 Jan 1814.

Served in the Peninsula Oct 1813 – Apr 1814. Present at Nivelle, Nive and Bayonne. Half pay 25 Apr 1817. MGS medal for Nivelle and Nive. Magistrate for County Cork. Brother of Capt James Fielding Sweeny 62nd Foot.

SWEENY, James Fielding

Captain. 62nd (Wiltshire) Regiment of Foot.
Memorial Tablet: St Peter's Church, Bandon, County Cork, Ireland. (Photograph)

SACRED TO THE MEMORY OF / JAMES FIELDING SWEENY, / LATE MAJOR 70TH REGT. SERVED WITH THE 62ND REGT. / IN SICILY AND EGYPT: AT THE TAKING OF THE ISLANDS / ISCHIA

AND PROSETA: IN THE PENINSULA, AT THE PASSAGE / OF THE BIDASOA, BATTLES OF THE NIVELLE AND NIVE / AND INVESTMENT OF BAYONNE: MEDAL AND CLASPS: / WAS FOR MANY YEARS A MAGISTRATE / FOR COUNTIES OF CARLOW AND KILKENNY: / DIED MAY 14TH 1854 AGED 78. A CHRISTIAN SOLDIER. / (VERSE)

Ensign 31 Dec 1799. Lt 19 Oct 1804. Capt 22 Oct 1813. Bt Major 12 Aug 1819. Major 70th Foot 8 Feb 1831.

Served in the Peninsula Oct 1813 – Apr 1814. Present at Bidassoa, Nivelle, Nive and Bayonne. Also served in Sicily 1805, Egypt 1807 and Capture of Ischia and Procida 1809. MGS medal for Nivelle and Nive. Magistrate for Carlow and Kilkenny. Brother of Ensign Francis Bernard Sweeny 62nd Foot.

SWEETEN, Benjamin

Quartermaster. 52nd (Oxfordshire) Light Infantry Regiment of Foot.
Headstone: St Mary's Churchyard, Barnard Castle, Durham. (Photograph)

HERE LIE DEPOSITED THE REMAINS OF / BENJAMIN SWEETEN, / LATE QUARTER MASTER IN HIS MAJESTY'S / FIFTY SECOND LIGHT INFANTRY REGIMENT / AND HUSBAND OF SARAH SWEETEN HIS SURVIVING / AND DISCONSOLATE WIDOW, WHO IN RETURN FOR / THE GREAT SHARE OF HAPPINESS SHE ENJOYED / DURING THEIR UNION, CAUSED THIS STONE TO BE / ERECTED AS A TRIBUTE OF RESPECT AND AFFECTION / TO HIS DEPARTED WORTH. HE CEASED TO BE MORTAL / AT BARNARD CASTLE, DECEMBER 13TH 1832 / IN THE SIXTY FIRST YEAR OF HIS AGE. / ....

Reverse of headstone:

STUDIOUS TO FILL THE ROLE ASSIGNED / WITH PIOUS ZEAL HIS COURSE HE RAN / NOR OUGHT COULD WARP HIS EVEN HAND / NOR LOST THE CHRISTIAN IN THE MAN

Quartermaster Sgt. Quartermaster 22 Apr 1813.

Served in the Peninsula Jun 1813 – Apr 1814. Present at Vittoria, Pyrenees, Bidassoa, Nivelle, Nive, Orthes, Tarbes and Toulouse. Present at Waterloo.

SWEETMAN, J. Walter

Captain. 8th (The King's) Regiment of Foot.
Interred in Kensal Green Cemetery, London. (2592/108/RS). (No longer extant).

Ensign 9 Jul 1803. Lt 32nd Foot 8 Aug 1804. Capt 103rd Foot 5 Apr 1810. Capt 8th Foot 26 Jul 1810. Bt Major 22 Jul 1830.

Served in the Peninsula Aug 1808 – Aug 1809 (with 2nd Battalion detachment Feb – Aug 1809). Wounded and awarded pension of £70. Present at Rolica, Vimeiro, Douro and Talavera. Also served in the Irish Rebellion 1798 and Copenhagen 1807. Died Jul 1840.

SWETENHAM, Clement

Captain. 16th (Queen's) Regiment of Light Dragoons.
Memorial tablet: St Mary's Church, Astbury, Cheshire. (Photograph)

NEAR THIS PLACE / LIES INTERRED THE BODY OF / CLEMENT SWETENHAM, ESQ. / OF SOMERFORD BOOTH. / WHO DEPARTED THIS LIFE / NOVEMBER 17TH 1852 / AGED 65 YEARS. / THE ABOVE WAS A CAPTAIN / IN XVI REGIMENT OF LIGHT / DRAGOONS; HE SERVED IN THE / PENINSULAR WAR 1809–1813. WAS / PRESENT AT THE BATTLE OF / FUENTES D'ONOR, BUSACO, / TALAVERA AND WATERLOO.

Cornet 1803. Lt 20 Apr 1805. Capt 11 Jun 1807.

Served in the Peninsula Apr 1809 – Jan 1812 and Jul 1813 – Apr 1814. Present at Douro (wounded), Talavera, Coa, Busaco, Redinha, Casal Nova, Foz D'Arouce, Sabugal, Fuentes d'Onoro, El Bodon and Bayonne. MGS medal for Talavera, Busaco and Fuentes d'Onoro. Present at Waterloo. Retired in 1817. Magistrate for Cheshire. Major in Prince Regent's 2nd Regt of Cheshire Yeomanry Cavalry 3 Dec 1819.

SWINBURNE, Joseph

Lieutenant. 83rd Regiment of Foot.
Memorial Tablet: St Alphage's Church, Solihull, Warwickshire. (Photograph)

TALAVERA / SALAMANCA / BUSACO VITTORIA / FUENTES D'ONOR NIVELLE / CIUDAD RODRIGO ORTHES / BADAJOZ TOULOUSE / SACRED TO THE MEMORY OF / COLONEL JOSEPH SWINBURNE, / OF HER MAJESTY'S 83RD REGT. / BORN AT SOLIHULL, 19TH SEPTEMBER 1783. / AND AFTER DEVOTING 44 YEARS OF HIS LIFE TO THE SERVICE OF HIS COUNTRY, / DIED AT LICHFIELD, 7TH FEBRUARY 1860, AND IS BURIED HERE. / HIS DUTIES AS A SOLDIER ARE RECORDED IN THE ANNALS OF THE / GALLANT REGIMENT IN WHICH HE SERVED SO LONG AND WELL. / THE DUTIES OF A HUSBAND AND A FATHER WILL BE EVER / REMEMBERED BY HIS WIDOW AND HIS CHILDREN, / WHO HAVE ERECTED THIS TABLET AS A RECORD OF HIS PRIVATE WORTH / AND AS A HUMBLE TRIBUTE TO ONE WHOSE GOOD AND GENTLE NATURE / HAS MADE HIS MEMORY DEAR TO THEM AND THEIRS. / "I HAVE FOUGHT THE GOOD FIGHT, I HAVE FINISHED THE COURSE, / I HAVE KEPT THE FAITH."

Sergeant 25 Jun 1805. Sgt Major 1809. Ensign Aug 16 Aug 1809. Adjutant 30 Jul 1811. Lt 4 Jun 1812. Captain 6 Oct 1825. Bt Major 28 Jun 1838. Major 2 Aug 1842. Bt Lt Colonel 11 Nov 1851. Bt Colonel 28 Nov 1854.

Served in the Peninsula Apr 1809 – Apr 1814. Present at Douro, Talavera (wounded and promoted from the ranks for his bravery), Busaco, Redinha, Casal Nova, Foz d'Arouce, Sabugal, Fuentes d'Onoro, second siege of Badajoz, El Bodon, Ciudad Rodrigo, Badajoz, Salamanca, Vittoria, Nivelle, Orthes (wounded), Vic Bigorre and Toulouse. Also served in Ceylon 1817–1829. Served for 44 years in the regiment. MGS medal for Talavera, Busaco, Fuentes d'Onoro, Ciudad Rodrigo, Badajoz, Salamanca, Vittoria, Nivelle, Orthes and Toulouse.

SWINBURNE, Thomas Robert

Ensign. 1st Regiment of Foot Guards.
Mural memorial tablet: Dean Cemetery, Edinburgh, Scotland. (Interior boundary wall. Section I – BW No. 1933). (Photograph)

IN MEMORY OF / HELEN / THE BELOVED WIFE OF / THOMAS ROBERT SWINBURNE / OF PONTOP HALL DURHAM AND MARCUS FORFAR / MAJOR GENERAL IN HER MAJESTY'S ARMY / WHO DIED 10TH MARCH 1860 / AFTER A LONG AND PAINFUL ILLNESS BORNE WITH / TRUE CHRISTIAN PATIENCE AND RESIGNATION. ALSO OF THE ABOVE NAMED / THOMAS ROBERT SWINBURNE. / LIEUTENANT GENERAL IN HER MAJESTY'S ARMY / WHO SERVED UNDER THE DUKE OF WELLINGTON IN THE PENINSULAR / AND AT THE BATTLE OF WATERLOO. DEPUTY LIEUTENANT / OF THE COUNTY OF FORFAR WHO DIED 29TH FEBRUARY 1864 / IN THE 70TH YEAR OF HIS AGE.

Ensign 24 Jun 1813. Lt and Capt 26 Dec 1816. Capt 3rd Dragoon Guards 1823. Major 10 Sep 1825. Bt Lt Colonel 28 Jun 1838. Bt Colonel 11 Nov 1851. Major General 4 Jun 1857. Lt General 31 Jan 1864.

Served in the Peninsula and south of France. Present at Quatre Bras, Waterloo, the siege of Peronne (commanded a storming party), the Capture of Paris and with the Army of Occupation. Half pay 25 Dec

1818. Also served in Holland 1814–1815. Fellow of the Royal Society 1839. Magistrate and Deputy Lieutenant of Forfarshire.
Reference: Gentleman's Magazine, Apr 1864, p. 539.

SWINFEN, Francis
Lieutenant. 16th (Queen's) Regiment of Light Dragoons.
Cross on stepped base: All Saints' Churchyard, Lapley, Staffordshire. (Photograph)

FRANCIS SWINFEN ESQ / AND / MARRIANNE JOSEPHINE HIS WIFE / OF LAPLEY / 1886

Cornet 15 Dec 1808. Lt 1 Aug 1811.
Served in the Peninsula Apr – Oct 1809, Feb 1811 – Dec 1812 and Jul 1813 – Apr 1814. Present at Douro, Talavera, Redinha, Casal Nova, Foz d'Arouce, Fuentes d'Onoro, El Bodon, Llerena, Castrejon, Salamanca, Venta del Poza, Nivelle, Nive and Bayonne. Present at Waterloo. Half pay 25 May 1817. Died at Lapley Hall 20 Aug 1839.

SYMES, Joseph
Lieutenant. 1st (Royal Scots) Regiment of Foot.
Ledger stone: Kilcommon Church of Ireland Churchyard, Tinahely, County Wicklow, Ireland. (Photograph)

ERECTED TO THE MEMORY OF / JOSEPH SYMES OF HILLBROOK / WHO DEPARTED THIS LIFE / THE 28TH DAY OF NOVEMBER 1835 / IN THE ** YEAR OF HIS AGE / ....

Ensign 6 Apr 1812. Lt 23 Sep 1813.
Served in the Peninsula Nov 1812 – Apr 1814. Present at Osma, Vittoria, San Sebastian and Bayonne. Present at Quatre Bras where he was wounded. Half pay 25 Jun 1817 owing to the reduction of the regiment after Waterloo.

SYMON, Alexander
Sergeant. 92nd Regiment of Foot.
Headstone: Dunbennan Old Kirkyard, near Huntly, Aberdeenshire, Scotland. (Photograph)

IN MEMORY OF / .... / ALEXR SYMON LATE SERJT 92ND REGT DIED / 28TH MARCH 1870, AGED 93 YEARS. / ....

Pte 31 May 1793.
Served in the Peninsula 1808–1809 in one of the Corps of Detachments. Present at Douro and Talavera. Men who had been taken prisoner of the French and had escaped to Portugal on the retreat to Corunna formed the Battalion of Detachments; 3 officers, 8 sergeant and 71 other ranks from the 92nd formed part of the 1st Battalion of Detachments while the 92nd went to Walcheren. Napier states that they did good service at Oporto and Talavera. Also served in Egypt 1801. MGS medal for Egypt and Talavera.

SYMONS, Henry John
Chaplain to the Forces. Chaplain's Department.
Memorial tablet: St Martin's Church, Hereford, Herefordshire. (Photograph)

IN A VAULT BENEATH THE CHANCEL / ARE INTERRED THE REMAINS OF THE LATE / HENRY JOHN SYMONS, LL.D. D.C.L., CHAPLAIN TO THE FORCES, ALTERNATELY / TO THE GUARDS AND LIGHT DIVISION OF THE BRITISH / ARMY THROUGHOUT THE PENINSULAR CAMPAIGNS OF 1808–1814. / AFTERWARDS INCUMBENT FOR 35 YEARS OF THE / JOINT

PARISHES OF ALL SAINTS WITH ST MARTINS / AND RESTORER OF THIS CHURCH DESTROYED IN THE / CIVIL WARS OF 1646 / BORN JAN 25TH 1781 DIED MARCH 21ST 1857 / ....

Chaplain 1st Foot Guards 1808. Chaplain to the Forces 12 May 1808.

Served in the Peninsula Nov 1808 – Jan 1809 and Oct 1813 – Apr 1814 (attached to Light Division). Present at Corunna, Nivelle, Nive and Toulouse. Read the burial service at Corunna over Sir John Moore. MGS medal for Corunna, Nivelle, Nive and Toulouse. Retired from the Army 1816. Vicar of All Saints with St Martin's Church Hereford for 35 years. Restored the church of St Martin's which had been destroyed in the Civil War.

SYMPHER, Frederick

Major. Artillery, King's German Legion.

Named on the Memorial: St Andrew's Church (now Musée Historique), Biarritz, France. (Photograph)

Capt 14 Feb 1804. Major 17 Aug 1812.

Served in the Peninsula 1810–1814. Present at Salamanca, Vittoria, San Sebastian, Pyrenees, Nivelle, Orthes where he was killed 27 Feb 1814. Gold Cross for Salamanca, Vittoria, San Sebastian, Pyrenees, Nivelle and Orthes.

Reference: Beamish, N. L., History of the King's German Legion, Vol. 2, reprint 1997. No. 785.

TALBOT, William

Lieutenant. 27th (Inniskilling) Regiment of Foot.

Memorial: Glasnevin Cemetery, Dublin, Ireland. (M.I.)

"MAJOR WILLIAM TALBOT, OF CASTLE TALBOT, IN THE CO. WEXFORD, SERVED WITH THE 27TH OR INNISKILLING REGIMENT IN THE PENINSULAR WAR, AND WAS TWICE WOUNDED. HE DIED IN 1861, AT THE AGE OF 70 YEARS. . ..."

Ensign 48th Foot 3 Jun 1806. Lt 27th Foot 7 Feb 1808. Capt 7 Apr 1825.

Served in the Peninsula with 2/27th Dec 1812 – Apr 1814. Present at Alcoy, Castalla, Tarragona, Ordal (wounded 13 Sep 1813) and Barcelona. Present at Waterloo. Also served in North America 1814–1815, Gibraltar 1817 and West Indies 1823. Half pay 18 Jan 1827.

TAPP, Hammond Astley

2nd Captain. Royal Engineers.

Gravestone: Up Park Camp Military Cemetery, Kingston, Jamaica, West Indies. (M.I.)

"CAP. HAMMOND A. TAPP COMMANDING ROYAL ENGINEERS / D. 13 SEPT. 1831, AGED 40."

Named on the Regimental Memorial: Rochester Cathedral, Rochester, Kent. (Photograph)

2nd Lt 10 Feb 1809. Lt 1 Mar 1810. 2nd Capt 20 Dec 1814. Capt 29 Oct 1828.

Served in the Peninsula Mar 1810 – Apr 1814. Present at Torres Vedras and San Sebastian (severely wounded 13 Jul 1813). Also served in North America 1814–1815 (present at New Orleans and Fort Bowyer) and in the West Indies in command of the Royal Engineers where he died 13 Sep 1831.

TARLETON, Henry

Major. 60th (Royal American) Regiment of Foot.

Memorial tablet: St Oswald's Church, Malpas, Cheshire. (Photograph)

SACRED / TO THE MEMORY OF / LIEU^{T} COL. HENRY TARLETON, / YOUNGEST SON OF THOS TARLETON / OF BOLESWORTH CASTLE / IN THE COUNTY OF CHESTER ESQUIRE, / WHO DIED FEB 4TH 1829, / IN THE 41ST YEAR OF HIS AGE. / THIS MONUMENT / WAS ERECTED BY HIS WIDOW, ELEANOR AMELIA, / YOUNGEST DAUGHTER OF / PHILLIPS LLOYD FLETCHER / OF GWERNHAYLED / IN THE COUNTY OF FLINT ESQUIRE.

Cornet 1st Dragoon Guards 25 Feb 1804. Lt 21st Lt Dragoons 19 Sep 1805. Capt 4th Garrison Battalion 18 Aug 1808. Capt 7th Foot 7 Jun 1810. Major 60th Foot 21 Apr 1814. Lt Colonel 24 Feb 1817.

Served in the Peninsula with 2/7th Sep 1810 – Jul 1811 and 1/7th Oct 1812 – Apr 1814. Present at Busaco, Pombal, Condeixa, Olivencia, first siege of Badajoz, Albuera (wounded), Vittoria and Pyrenees (taken prisoner at Sorauren 27 Jul 1813 and remained a prisoner until Apr 1814). Half pay 25 Mar 1817.

TATHWELL, Tathwell Baker
Lieutenant. Royal Regiment of Horse Guards.
Buried in St Mary's Churchyard, Whitburn, County Durham. (Burial record)

Cornet 15 Oct 1812. Lt 9 Sep 1813.

Served in the Peninsula Sep 1813 – Apr 1814. Present at Toulouse. Present at Waterloo where he was taken prisoner but escaped two days later. Reputed to have captured a French Eagle but it was taken from him when he was captured. Died 23 Nov 1828 aged 32 years.

TATTON, Richard
Lieutenant. 77th (East Middlesex) Regiment of Foot.
Obelisk: Abbey Cemetery, Bath, Somerset. (Photograph)

SACRED / TO THE AFFECTIONATE MEMORY / OF LIEUT^{T} COLONEL / RICHARD TATTON / LATE OF THE 77TH REGIMENT / DIED 28TH MAY 1857 IN HIS 88TH YEAR. / (VERSE)

Ensign 62nd Foot 28 Dec 1809. Lt 77th Foot 7 Jun 1811. Capt 7 Apr 1825. Bt Major 28 Jun 1838. Bt Lt Colonel 28 Nov 1854.

Served in the Peninsula Sep 1811, Feb – Sep 1812 and Feb 1813 – Apr 1814. Present at the siege of Bayonne. Half pay 30 Oct 1840.

TAYLER, Samuel
Lieutenant. 13th Regiment of Light Dragoons.
Family Memorial tablet: St John's Church, Devizes, Wiltshire. (Photograph)

..................../ ALSO OF SAMUEL, ANOTHER SON, LIEUTENANT / IN THE 13TH REG^{T} L. D. WHO DIED IN PORTUGAL, / OCTOBER 11TH 1809. AGED 34 YEARS.

Adjt 62nd Foot 28 Jan 1795. Lt 1 Sep 1795. Lt 13th Lt Dragoons 7 Aug 1800.

Served in the Peninsula Apr – Oct 1809. Died from an accident in Lisbon 11 Oct 1809.

TAYLOR, Charles Douglas
Lieutenant Colonel. 20th Regiment of Light Dragoons.
Memorial tablet: Oxford Cathedral, Oxfordshire. (In Cloisters adjoining Christchurch College). (Photograph)

CHARLES TAYLOR ESQ^{RE} M.A. / FORMERLY STUDENT OF THIS HOUSE; / LIEUT. COLONEL OF HIS MAJESTY'S 20TH REGIMENT / OF LIGHT DRAGOONS. / HE HAD THE MERIT / OF HAVING FORMED AND DISCIPLINED THAT REGIMENT / HIMSELF: / AND AT THE HEAD OF A SMALL

PART OF IT / IN THE BATTLE OF VIMIERO / AUGUST 23RD 1808, / HE ATTACKED AND DEFEATED / A VERY SUPERIOR BODY OF THE ENEMY'S CAVALRY, / WHO WERE ADVANCING RAPIDLY / AGAINST THE FLANKS OF THE 50TH AND 52ND REGTS OF FOOT. / HE FELL IN THE MOMENT OF VICTORY. / HIS FIRST AND EARLIEST FRIENDS, / WHO KNEW THAT THEY WERE DEAR TO HIM, / AS HE WAS DEAR TO THEM, / HAVE PLACED THIS TABLET TO HIS MEMORY.

Named on Memorial tablet to his son Brigadier General Charles Cyril Taylor, Canterbury Cathedral, Kent. (Photograph).

TO THE MEMORY / OF BRIGADIER GENERAL CHARLES CYRIL TAYLOR, CB, / SON OF LIEUT COLN CHARLES TAYLOR. / BORN 29TH MARCH AD 1804. DIED 10TH FEBRUARY AD 1846. / THE FATHER FELL AT VIMIERO / THE FIRST TRIUMPH OF THE BRITISH ARMS IN THE WAR OF THE PENINSULA. / THE SON AT SOBRAON / ....

Memorial tablet: St Mary the Virgin, Reading, Berkshire. (South side of West Tower porch). (Photograph)

TO THE MEMORY OF / LIEUT. COL. CHARLES TAYLOR OF THE 20TH REGT OF LIGHT DRAGOONS / WHO FELL, IN THE MOMENT OF VICTORY, AT THE BATTLE OF VIMIERA, / AUGUST 21ST 1808, IN THE 36TH YEAR OF HIS AGE, / HAVING OBTAINED THE LOVE OF HIS FRIENDS BY HIS AMIABLE QUALITIES, / THE ESTEEM OF THE BRITISH ARMY, / AND EVEN THE ADMIRATION OF THE ENEMY, / BY HIS MILITARY SKILL AND INTREPIDITY. / THIS TABLET IS ERECTED / TO TESTIFY THE ATTACHMENT OF HIS NATIVE TOWN, / AND THE GRATITUDE OF HIS COUNTRY.

Cornet 7th Lt Dragoons 4 Nov 1794. Lt 29th Lt Dragoons Capt 7th Lt Dragoons. 16 Sep 1795. Major 16 May 1801. Lt Colonel 20th Lt Dragoons 24 Feb 1803.

Served in the Peninsula Aug 1808. Present at Rolica and Vimeiro where he was killed in a cavalry charge without infantry support against French cavalry. Gold Medal for Rolica and Vimeiro. Also served at the Helder 1799, Naples 1805 and Sicily 1806–1807. Educated at Westminster and Oxford University. His son Charles was killed at the Battle of Sobraon in the Sikh Wars 1846.

Reference: Bennett, Paul J., A Napoleonic soldier from Reading, Waterloo Journal, Winter 2008, pp. 30–3. Gentleman's Magazine, Nov 1808, pp. 963–4.

TAYLOR, James

Captain. 48th (Northamptonshire) Regiment of Foot.
Tombstone: Bellary, Madras, India. (M.I.)

"LT COL. JAMES TAYLOR / H.M.'S 48TH REGIMENT / DIED AUG 10TH 1829 / AGED 46 YEARS."

Ensign 9 Jun 1804. Lt 4 May 1805. Capt 4 Jun 1807. Bt Major 21 Sep 1813. Lt Colonel 6 Jun 1825.

Served in the Peninsula Apr 1809 – Nov 1813. (Brigade Major 2 Brigade, 2nd Division Aug 1809 – Jun 1811 and 1 Brigade, 5th Division Jul 1811 – Nov 1813). Present at Douro, Talavera, Busaco, Pombal, first siege of Badajoz, Albuera, Fuente Guinaldo, Badajoz, Salamanca, retreat from Burgos, Osma, Vittoria, first siege of San Sebastian (Mentioned in Despatches), second siege of San Sebastian (Mentioned in Despatches and awarded Bt Majority). Returned to England Dec 1813 sick with fever. Also served in India 1817 until his death in 1829.

TAYLOR, Jeremiah

Lieutenant. 9th (East Norfolk) Regiment of Foot.
Low monument: St Mary's Churchyard, Prestbury, Gloucestershire. (Photograph)

LIEUT GENERAL JEREMIAH TAYLOR: / DIED 1ST FEB. 1862 AGED 71 YEARS.

Ensign 28 Feb 1805. Lt 1 Oct 1807. Capt 2 Oct 1817. Major 1 Apr 1824. Lt Col 28 Mar 1827. Bt Colonel 23 Nov 1841. Major General 20 Jun 1854. Lt General 17 Jul 1859.

Served in the Peninsula with 2/9th Aug 1808 – Jun 1809, 1/9th Mar 1810 – Feb 1813 and Mar – Apr 1814. Present at Vimeiro (wounded), Busaco, Fuentes d'Onoro, Salamanca, retreat from Burgos (present at Villa Muriel where he was wounded) and the Sortie from Bayonne. MGS medal for Vimeiro, Busaco, Fuentes d'Onoro and Salamanca. Also served in North America 1814–1815. Colonel 59th Foot 8 Sep 1857.

TAYLOR, John

Lieutenant Colonel. 88th (Connaught Rangers) Regiment of Foot.
Memorial tablet: Adrahan Church, Adrahan, Galway, Ireland. (Photograph)

IN A VAULT / IN THIS CHURCHYARD / ARE DEPOSITED / THE REMAINS OF / LIEUT GENL / SIR JOHN TAYLOR K. C. B. / OF CASTLE TAYLOR / IN THIS PARISH / WHO DIED SUDDENLY / ON THE 6 DECR 1845. / (VERSE)

Ensign Colonel Pennington's Regt 25 Mar 1794. Lt 118th Foot 6 Dec 1794. Capt 102nd Foot 9 Sep 1795. Capt 25th Foot 8 Oct 1799. Bt Major 2 Sep 1801. Bt Lt Colonel 28 Feb 1805. Lt Colonel 88th Foot 18 May 1809. Bt Colonel 4 Jun 1813. Major General 12 Aug 1819. Lt General 10 Jan 1837.

Served in the Peninsula with 2/88th Jan – Dec 1810 and 1/88th Sep 1813 – Apr 1814. Present at Cadiz, Nivelle, Orthes (severely wounded) and Toulouse. Gold Medal for Nivelle, Orthes and Toulouse. KCB 17 Oct 1834. Also served in the Irish Rebellion 1798 (Brigade Major and ADC to Major General French), the Helder 1799 (ADC to Major General Hutchinson) and Egypt 1801 (awarded Brevet Majority). Gold Medal from Sultan. Colonel 80th Foot 15 Mar 1837.
Reference: Dictionary of National Biography. Royal Military Calendar, Vol. 4, p. 33.

TAYLOR, John

Lieutenant. 91st Regiment of Foot.
Memorial tablet: Stranraer Parish Church, Stranraer, Dumfries and Galloway, Scotland. (Photograph)

SACRED TO THE MEMORY / OF / CAPTAIN JOHN TAYLOR, / SON OF HUGH LEWIS TAYLOR, M. D. / BORN IN STRANRAER, 1ST JUNE, 1793, AND DIED THERE 30TH SEPR 1863, / AND IS INTERRED IN THE TOMB AT THE ENTRANCE TO THIS CHURCHYARD. / HE WAS ONE OF THE FEW REMAINING VETERANS OF THE PENINSULAR WAR, HAVING SERVED THROUGH THREE CAMPAIGNS / IN THE 91ST HIGHLANDERS, UNTIL DANGEROUSLY WOUNDED AT THE BATTLE OF ORTHES, THE BULLET BEING IN HIS HEAD FOUR YEARS. / VITTORIA, PAMPELUNA, PYRENEES, NIVE, NIVELLE, BAYONNE, TOULOUSE AND ORTHES / WERE SOME OF THE HARD FIELDS IN WHICH HE WAS ENGAGED, AND FOR WHICH HE RECEIVED A PENINSULAR MEDAL. / HE AFTERWARDS FILLED THE DUTIES OF STAFF OFFICER OF PENSIONERS IN THE CARLISLE DISTRICT / AND WAS FOR MANY YEARS A MAGISTRATE OF HIS NATIVE COUNTY, HE WAS A MAN OF GREAT BENEVOLENCE / AND THE STRICTEST INTEGRITY, ESTEEMED AND RESPECTED BY ALL WHO KNEW HIM, AND DEEPLY MOURNED / BY HIS WIDOW AND FAMILY. / ………………..

Family Memorial tablet: On vault in Churchyard, Stranraer Parish Church, Stranraer, Dumfries and Galloway, Scotland. (Photograph)

……………….. / ALSO CAPTAIN JOHN TAYLOR / WHO DIED 28 SEPR 1863. / ………………..

Ensign 30 Jul 1812. Lt 14 Jul 1814.

Served in the Peninsula Apr 1813 – Apr 1814. Present at Pyrenees, Nivelle, Nive and Orthes (severely wounded while carrying the colours, the bullet in his head was not extracted for four years). MGS medal for Pyrenees, Nivelle, Nive and Orthes. Half pay 25 Dec 1818. Staff Officer of Pensioners at Carlisle with the rank of Captain 1843. Held that post until 1860 when he returned to Stranraer, becoming a Magistrate for the last three years of his life. Brother of Lt Thomas Taylor 88th Foot.

TAYLOR, John

Sergeant. 4th (Queen's Own) Regiment of Dragoons.
Memorial tablet: St Mary's and All Saints' Church, Kidderminster, Worcestershire. (South wall of Nave). (Photograph)

SACRED TO THE MEMORY OF JOHN TAYLOR LATE A / SERGEANT IN THE 4TH (OR QUEENS OWN) REGT OF DRAGS, WHO / DEPARTED THIS LIFE, AT ELVAS, IN PORTUGAL, ON THE 14TH OF / NOVEMBER 1809 AT THE EARLY AGE OF 27. / HE FELL A SACRIFICE AMONG HUNDREDS, TO THE SICKNESS / WHICH VISITED THE ARMY, OF LT GENL LORD WELLINGTON, / AFTER THE RETREAT FROM TALAVERA, IN THE SPANISH DOMINIONS. / THIS HUMBLE MONUMENT IS ERECTED BY HIS OWN CAPTAIN, / AS A SMALL TRIBUTE OF RESPECT, FOR ONE, TO WHOM HE / WAS MUCH ATTACHED AND WHO WAS A MOST EXCELLENT / NON COMMISSIONED OFFICER AND AN HONEST, SOBER / UPRIGHT MAN. / (VERSE)

Served in the Peninsula Apr – Nov 1809. Present at Talavera. Died of disease at Elvas 14 Nov 1809.

TAYLOR, John Butt

Surgeon: 26th (Cameronian) Regiment of Foot.
Grave: Trafalgar Cemetery, Gibraltar. (Photograph).

JOHN BUTT TAYLOR; SURGEON 26TH REGT DIED OF THE EPIDEMIC FEVER, 4 OCT 1813 AGED 37

Hospital Mate 9 Feb 1800. Asst Surgeon 43rd 7 Nov 1805. Surgeon 25th Foot 23 Jun 1808. Surgeon 26th Foot 25 Aug 1809.

Served in the Peninsula Jul 1811 – Jun 1812. The Regiment was still suffering from Walcheren fever and was sent to Gibraltar in 1812 in order not to infect the other troops. However Surgeon Taylor caught the infection and died 4 Oct 1813.

TAYLOR, John D.

Lieutenant. 51st (2nd Yorkshire West Riding) Light Infantry.
Named on the Regimental Memorial tablet: KOYLI Chapel, York Minster, Yorkshire. (Photograph)
Named on the Memorial: St Andrew's Church (now Musée Historique), Biarritz, France. (Photograph)

Ensign 12 Dec 1811. Lt 16 Sep 1813.

Served in the Peninsula May 1812 – Nov 1813. Present at Moriscos, Salamanca, Burgos, San Munos, Vittoria, Pyrenees, San Marcial and Nivelle where he was killed Nov 1813.

TAYLOR, Philip C.

Captain. 81st Regiment of Foot.
Buried in Up Park Camp disused Graveyard, Kingston, Jamaica, West Indies. (M.I.)

"LT COL P. C. TAYLOR, 22ND REGT, DIED AT KINGSTON 7 DEC 1827 AGED 37."

Ensign 9th Foot 1 Apr 1806. Lt 69th Foot 30 Dec 1806. Lt 9th Foot 21 Mar 1807. Lt 13th Foot 13 Feb 1808.

Capt 81st Foot 26 Jan 1809. Major 16 May 1822. Lt Colonel 22nd Foot 27 Jul 1826.

Served in the Peninsula Oct 1812 – Apr 1814. Present on the East coast of Spain (present at Tarifa). Also served at Walcheren 1809, India 1816–1818 (present in the Pindari War) and the West Indies 1825 where he died in Jamaica in 1827.

TAYLOR, Thomas

Lieutenant. 88th (Connaught Rangers) Regiment of Foot.
Family Memorial tablet: On vault in Churchyard, Stranraer Parish Church, Stranraer, Dumfries and Galloway, Scotland. (Photograph)

……………… / TO THE MEMORY OF / LIEUTT THOMAS TAYLOR / WHO DIED 25TH MARCH 1846 / AGED 54 YEARS / ………………

Ensign 89th Foot 14 Jul 1808. Ensign 88th Foot 3 Oct 1811. Lt 6 Jan 1815.

Served in the Peninsula Apr 1814. Present at Toulouse. Half pay 25 Mar 1816. Brother of Lt John Taylor 91st Foot.

TAYLOR, Thomas John

Lieutenant. 36th (Herefordshire) Regiment of Foot.
Tombstone: Colaba Cemetery, Bombay, India. (M.I.)

"SACRED TO THE MEMORY OF MAJOR THOMAS JOHN TAYLOR 78TH HIGHLANDERS, WHO DIED AT COLABA ON THE 18TH OF JUNE A.D. 1850, AGED 60 YEARS. THIS MONUMENT IS ERECTED BY HIS BROTHER OFFICERS AS A MARK OF ESTEEM."

Ensign 12 Mar 1812. Lt 7 Sep 1814. Lt 96th Foot 25 May 1820. Capt 78th Foot 17 May 1830. Bt Major 9 Nov 1846. Major 2 Oct 1849.

Served in the Peninsula May 1813 – Apr 1814. Present at Pyrenees, Bidassoa, Orthes, Vic Bigorre, Tarbes, and Toulouse (severely wounded). Served in France with the Army of Occupation until 1817. Also served in the Ionian Islands and Malta 1817–1825, Ceylon 1826–1829 and India 1842–1850. MGS medal for Pyrenees, Orthes and Toulouse.

TAYLOR, Thomas William

Captain. 10th (Prince of Wales's Own Royal) Regiment of Light Dragoons.
Memorial tablet: St Mary the Virgin, West Ogwell, near Denbury, Devon. (In vestry). (Photograph)

IN MEMORY OF / THOMAS WILLIAM TAYLOR / OF WEST OGWELL MAJOR GENERAL IN THE ARMY / COMPANION OF THE BATH / COLONEL OF THE XVIITH LANCERS / AND FOR 17 YEARS LIEUT GOVERNOR / OF THE ROYAL MILITARY COLLEGE SANDHURST. / BORN JULY XIIITH MDCCLXXXV. / DIED JAN VIIITH MDCCCLIV. / (VERSE)

Cornet 6th Dragoon Guards 14 Jul 1804. Lt 12 Jun 1805. Capt 22 Jan 1807. Capt 24th Dragoons 25 Nov 1807. Bt Major 7 Jul 1814. Capt 10th Dragoons 12 Nov 1814. Bt Lt Colonel 18 Jun 1815. Major 10th Dragoons 21 Sep 1815. Bt Colonel 10 Jan 1837. Major General 9 Nov 1846.

Present at Waterloo (awarded Bt Lt Colonelcy). Also served in the Mediterranean 1805–1806 (AAG under Sir James Craig), India 1807–1814 (Military Secretary to the Governor General Lord Minto. Served in the expedition to capture Java in 1811 as ADC to General Gillespie). Commandant of Cavalry Riding Establishment 1826–1831. Lt Governor of Royal Military College Sandhurst 1837–1854. Colonel 17th Lancers 23 Sep 1853. MGS medal for Java. CB. Educated at Eton. Died 8 Jan 1854 at Haccombe, Devon aged 71.

TAYLOR, William Benjamin Sarsfield

Clerk. Commissariat Department.
Headstone: Kensal Green Cemetery, London. (9251/170/2). Inscription illegible. (Photograph)

Served in the Peninsula. Present at San Sebastian. Retired in 1814 and returned to Dublin to take up his life as an artist. Became a painter of landscapes and military subjects. Exhibited several sketches of the siege of San Sebastian. Later became an art critic. Wrote *Origin, Progress and Present conditions of the Fine Arts in Great Britain and Ireland,* 1841 and *History of the University of Dublin,* 1845. Died in London 23 Dec 1850.
Reference: Dictionary of National Biography.

TELFORD, Robert

Captain. 20th (East Devonshire) Regiment of Foot.
Grave: St Mary's Churchyard, Cheltenham, Gloucestershire. (No longer extant). (M.I.)

"CAPT. ROBERT TELFORD, 20TH REGT OF FOOT DIED 6TH JULY 1827 AGED 50."

Ensign 21 Jun 1800. Lt 25 Jul 1803. Capt 17 Oct 1811.

Served in the Peninsula Aug 1808 – Jan 1809 and Nov 1812 – Apr 1814. Present at Vimeiro, Corunna, Vittoria, Pyrenees, Nivelle, Nive and Orthes (wounded 27 Feb 1814 and awarded pension of £100 per annum).

TEW, William

Captain. 74th (Highland) Regiment of Foot.
Named on the Memorial: St Andrew's Church (now Musée Historique), Biarritz, France. (Photograph)
Named on the Regimental Memorial: St Giles's Cathedral, Edinburgh, Scotland. (Photograph)

Ensign 12th Foot 22 Mar 1806. Ensign 74th Foot 18 Nov 1806. Lt 5 Nov 1807. Capt 26 Aug 1813.

Served in the Peninsula Feb 1810 – Apr 1814. Present at Busaco, Casal Nova, Foz d'Arouce, Fuentes d'Onoro, second siege of Badajoz, El Bodon, Ciudad Rodrigo (severely wounded), Salamanca, Vittoria, Pyrenees (wounded), Nivelle, Nive, Orthes, Vic Bigorre, Tarbes and Toulouse where he was severely wounded 10 Apr and died of his wounds 16 Apr 1814.

THACKERAY, Frederick Rennell

Lieutenant Colonel. Royal Engineers.
Low monument: St Michael's Churchyard, Camberley, Surrey. (Photograph)

FREDERICK RENNELL THACKERAY, C.B. / GENERAL AND COMMANDANT R. E. BORN AT WINDSOR. 21ST JANY 1776. DIED AT WINDLESHAM. 19 SEPT 1860. / ....

2nd Lt Royal Artillery 18 Sep 1793. 2nd Lt Royal Engineers 1 Jan 1794. 1st Lt 18 Jun 1796. Capt-Lieut 18 Apr 1801. Capt 1 Mar 1805. Bt Major 9 May 1810. Lt Colonel 21 Jul 1813. Colonel 2 Jun 1825. Major General 10 Jan 1837. Lt General 9 Nov 1846. General 20 Jun 1854.

Served in the Peninsula Aug 1812 – Apr 1814. Present at Castalla and Tarragona (in command of Royal Engineers on East coast of Spain). Also served in Surinam 1799, Egypt 1807, Sicily 1807, Scylla Castle 1806 and Fortress of Santa Maura 1809. CB. Colonel Commandant 29 Apr 1846.
Reference: Annual Register, 1860, Part 2, p. 494.

THACKWELL, Joseph

Captain. 15th (King's) Regiment of Light Dragoons.
Memorial window: Gloucester Cathedral, Gloucestershire. (North Ambulatory). (Photograph)

IN THE REVERENCE OF GOD AND IN AFFECTIONATE MEMORY OF LIEUT GENERAL SIR JOSEPH THACKWELL KNIGHT GRAND CROSS OF THE / ORDER OF THE BATH AND KNIGHT OF HANOVER, COLONEL OF HER MAJESTY'S 16TH REGMT OF / LANCERS, WHO DIED APRIL 8TH 1859, AGED 77 YEARS

Cornet 23 Apr 1800. Lt 13 Jun 1801. Capt 9 Apr 1807. Major 19 Jun 1815. Bt Lt Colonel 21 Jun 1817. Lt Col 13 Jun 1820. Bt Colonel 10 Jan 1837. Major General 9 Nov 1838. Lt General 2 Jun 1854.

Served in the Peninsula Nov 1808 – Jan 1809 and Feb 1813 – Apr 1814. Present in the Corunna campaign, Morales, Vittoria (wounded), Orthes, Tarbes and Toulouse. Present at Waterloo where he was severely wounded charging a square of infantry, his left arm was amputated close to the shoulder. Awarded pension of £300 per annum. MGS medal for Vittoria, Orthes and Toulouse. Also served in India 1838 in command of cavalry during the Afghanistan campaign (present at Ghuznee and Kabul). KCB. Present at the Battle of Maharajapore 1843, the first Sikh War (present at Sobraon 1846), the second Sikh War (present at Ramnuggar 1848, Chillianwala 1849 and Gujerat 1849). Colonel-in-Chief of the 16th Lancers 10 Nov 1849. Inspector General of Cavalry 4 May 1854. GCB. KH. Died at Aghada Hall, County Cork, Ireland 8 Apr 1859.

REFERENCE: *Dictionary of National Biography. Wylly, H. C., Military memoirs of Lieut-General Sir Joseph Thackwell, 1908, reprint 2003. Gentleman's Magazine, May 1859, pp. 540–1 and Aug 1860, pp. 208–9. Annual Register, 1859, Appx pp. 490–1.*

THAIN, William

Ensign and Adjutant. 33rd (1st Yorkshire West Riding) Regiment of Foot.
Memorial tablet: Afghan Memorial Church, St John the Evangelist, Colaba, Bombay, India. (Photograph)

XXI / FOOT / MAJOR / W. THAIN

Memorial stone: St Mary's Churchyard, Wreay, Cumbria. (In Losh burial enclosure). (Photograph)

THIS KELAT PINE IS PLACED / IN MEMORY OF WM. THAIN, MAJOR / OF THE 33RD, AND WAS RAISED FROM / SEED TRANSMITTED BY HIM TO / ENGLAND. HE PERISHED IN THE / FATAL PASS OF KHOORD KABUL, / ESTEEMED AND LAMENTED BY ALL / WHO KNEW HIM.

Northumberland Militia. Ensign and Adjt 33rd Foot 13 May 1813. Lt 15 Aug 1815. Capt 17 Nov 1825. Bt Major 28 Jun 1838.

Present at Waterloo (wounded – shot through the arm) and with the Army of Occupation. Also served in North Germany 1813–1814 (present at Stralsund), the Netherlands 1814–1815 (present at Antwerp where he was Town Adjutant and Bergen-op-Zoom), Australia 1832 and India 1839. Joined one of the detachments of the 21st Foot sent out to Australia 1832 in charge of convicts. Proceeded from Australia to India 1839 where Major General Elphinstone has just been given command of an expedition to Afghanistan and chose Thain as his ADC. They had fought together at Waterloo. Thain was wounded at Kabul before setting out on the final retreat which ended in the massacre of the expedition. He was one of the last soldiers to be killed in the Jugdullock Pass on 12 Jan 1842. Described by the hostages taken from the retreat as 'an officer of rare merit, ever present at the post of danger and repeated charges were led by the gallant Major Thain'. He is commemorated in the church at Wreay in Cumbria built by his friend Sarah Losh.

REFERENCE: *Cumberland and Westmoreland Antiquarian and Archaeological Society Transactions, Vol. 78, 1978, p. 215. Matthews, Stephen, Sarah Losh and Wreay Church, 2007.*

THIELEN, A. van

Lieutenant Colonel. 6th National Militia Battalion, Dutch Infantry.
Named on the Memorial to Dutch officers killed at Waterloo: St Joseph's Church, Waterloo. (Photograph)

THILEE, Georg (or Tilee)
Captain. 2nd Line Battalion, King's German Legion.
Named on the Regimental Memorial: La Haye Sainte, Waterloo. (Photograph)
Named on the Waterloo Column, Hanover, Germany. (Photograph)

Lt 16 Jun 1804. Adjutant 19 Nov 1807. Capt 5 Mar 1812.

Served in the Peninsula Sep 1808 – Apr 1812. Present at Douro, Talavera, Busaco, Fuentes d'Onoro and Ciudad Rodrigo. Present at Waterloo where he was killed. Also served at Hanover 1805, the Baltic 1807–1808, North Germany 1813–1814 and the Netherlands 1814–1815.

THOMAS, Charles
Captain and Lieutenant Colonel. 1st Regiment of Foot Guards.
Named on the Regimental Memorial: St Joseph's Church, Waterloo. (Photograph)
Named on Memorial Panel VIII for Waterloo: Royal Military Chapel, Wellington Barracks, London. (M.I.) (Destroyed by a Flying Bomb 1944)

Ensign East Middlesex Militia 1799. Ensign 35th Foot 20 Dec 1799. Lt and Capt 1st Foot Guards 3 Dec 1803. Capt and Lt Colonel 25 Dec 1813.

Served in the Peninsula with 3rd Battalion Oct 1808 – Jan 1809 and Jul 1811 – Feb 1814. Present at Corunna, Cadiz, Seville, Bidassoa, Nivelle and Nive. Present at Quatre Bras and Waterloo where he was killed. Also served at the Helder 1799 where he served as a volunteer from the East Middlesex Militia. Given a commission for his gallant conduct at the Helder.

THOMAS, David
Private. 23rd (Royal Welch Fusiliers) Regiment of Foot.
Headstone: St Michael's Churchyard, Aberystwyth, Wales. (Photograph)

SACRED / TO THE MEMORY OF / DAVID THOMAS / GARDENER OF THIS TOWN. / WOUNDED AT WATERLOO / WHO DIED JUNE 23 / 1857 / AGED 74 YEARS / ....

Present at Waterloo where he was wounded in Capt Brown's Company, No. 4.

THOMAS, Evan
Private. 1st Regiment of Foot Guards.
Headstone: St Mellon's Churchyard, Cardiff, Glamorgan, Wales. (Photograph)

IN / MEMORY OF / EVAN THOMAS / OF THIS PARISH / LATE OF THE GRENADIER GUARDS / WHO DIED 3RD APRIL 1870 / AGED 80 YEARS / THIS MEMORIAL / TO ONE OF WELLINGTON'S VETERANS / WHO FOUGHT AT WATERLOO / IS ERECTED / BY THOSE WHO KNEW HIS WORTH. / ....

Pte Monmouth and Brecon Militia. Pte 1st Foot Guards 12 Dec 1813.

Present at Quatre Bras and Waterloo in Lt Colonel Sir Noel Hill's Company (wounded), siege of Peronne, Capture of Paris and with the Army of Occupation. Also served in the Netherlands 1814–1815. Discharged 9 Apr 1833 owing to ill health with a pension of one shilling a day.

THOMPSON, Alexander
Farrier. 2nd Life Guards.
Buried in Bethel Cemetery, Warwick, Lambton County, Ontario, Canada.

Present at Waterloo. Discharged 1822 and emigrated to Canada. Born at Kilmacolm, Renfrew, Scotland 10 Jan 1788. Died 1 Jun 1846.

THOMPSON, Charles William

Lieutenant and Captain. 1st Regiment of Foot Guards.
Named on the Memorial: St Andrew's Church (now Musée Historique), Biarritz, France. (Photograph)
Named on Memorial Panel VII for Nive: Royal Military Chapel, Wellington Barracks, London. (M.I.)
(Destroyed by a Flying Bomb 1944)

Memorial stone in railed enclosure: Garden of the former Mayor's House, Bidart, France. (Photograph)

CI GIT / LE LIEU COLONEL / S. C. MARTIN / LES CAPITAINES / THOMSON ET WATSON / DE LA GARDE ROYALE / DE S M BRITTANIQUE / TUE SUR LE CHAMP DE / BATAILLE LE 14 / DECEMBRE 1813.

Lt Sicilian Regt 12 Sep 1810. Capt 28 Feb 1812. Lt and Capt 1st Foot Guards 24 Sep 1812.

Served in the Peninsula with 1st Battalion Oct – Dec 1813. Present at Bidassoa, Nivelle and Nive where he was killed 12 Dec 1813. The three officers of the 1st Foot Guards were all buried in the same grave – Lt Colonel Samuel C. Martin, Capt Henry R. Watson and Capt Charles W. Thompson. The house where they are buried was the headquarters of General John Hope from Dec 1813 to Jan 1814.
Note: Thompson spelt without a 'p' on memorial stone.

THOMPSON, Claudius

Private. Coldstream Regiment of Foot Guards.
Obelisk: Presbyterian Cemetery, Campbell Town, Tasmania, Australia. (Photograph)

SACRED / TO / THE MEMORY OF / CLAUDIUS THOMPSON / FIRST WARDEN OF / CAMPBELL TOWN / ELECTED SEP 16 1866 / DIED OCT 16 1868 / AGED 78.

Present at Waterloo in Colonel Hon A. Abercromby's Company. Emigrated to Australia in 1824 where he received a grant of land and then moved to Van Diemen's Land in the same year and again received a grant of land. Appointed Pound keeper and special constable at Macquarie River in 1832 and for the last 15 years of his life resided at Campbell Town where he was a Magistrate and was elected First Warden in 1866.

THOMPSON, George

Corporal. Coldstream Regiment of Foot Guards.
Headstone: Holy Trinity Churchyard, Berwick-on-Tweed, Northumberland. (Photograph)

IN MEMORY OF / MARGARET WIFE OF / GEORGE THOMPSON / WHO DEPARTED THIS LIFE / MARCH 3RD 1817, AGED 69 YEARS / & SISTER TO MAJOR WOOD / LATE OF EMBLETON. / ALSO GEORGE THEIR SON / LATE SARGEANT ROYAL COLDSTREAM / GUARDS WHO DIED 17TH OCTOBER 1858 / AGED 79 YEARS.

Cpl 5th Foot 14 Aug 1799. Sgt 1801. Pte Coldstream Guards 6 Apr 1814. Cpl Jun 1814. Sgt 1819.

Present at Waterloo in Lt Colonel Hon. E. Acheson's Company. Discharged 16 Aug 1821 (worn out in the service and on the reduction of the regiment). Died 17 Oct 1858 aged 79.

THOMPSON, Ralph Keddy

Lieutenant. 95th Regiment of Foot.
Low monument: St Paul's Churchyard, Shurdington, Gloucestershire. (Photograph)

IN MEMORY OF / RALPH KEDDY THOMPSON. / WHO DIED 11TH DAY OF MARCH 1865. / AGED 68. / ....

Ensign 47th Foot 26 Mar 1812. Lt 21 Oct 1813. Lt 95th Foot 6 Apr 1815.

Served in the Peninsula Feb – Nov 1813. Present at Vittoria and San Sebastian. Half pay 1814. Exchanged to 95th Foot 6 Apr 1815 and served with them until 2 Apr 1818 when he again retired on half pay. MGS medal for Vittoria and San Sebastian.

THOMPSON, Robert

Captain. 83rd Regiment of Foot.
Gravestone: Galle Face Burial Ground, Ceylon. (Burial ground is no longer extant). (M.I.)

"SACRED TO THE MEMORY OF CAPT. ROBERT THOMPSON, LATE OF H M 83RD REGT, WHO DEPARTED THIS LIFE 4TH DAY OF OCT 1826 IN THE 65TH YEAR OF HIS AGE. HE WAS ON ACTIVE SERVICE FOR 48 YEARS. HIS KINDNESS AND AFFECTION AS A HUSBAND AND FATHER GAVE ADDITIONAL STRENGTH TO THE FIRMNESS AND INTREPIDITY OF THE SOLDIER".

Lt Royal Staff Corps 1799. Adjt 20 Dec 1803. Capt 83rd Foot 6 Jul 1809.

Served in the Peninsula Jul 1810 – Apr 1814. Present at Busaco, Redinha, Casal Nova, Foz d'Arouce, Sabugal, Fuentes d Onoro, second siege of Badajoz, El Bodon, Ciudad Rodrigo, Badajoz, Salamanca, Vittoria, Pyrenees, Nivelle, Nive, Orthes, Vic Bigorre and Toulouse. Also served in Ceylon 1817. Served in the army for 48 years.

THOMPSON, Thomas Perronet

Captain. 17th Regiment of Light Dragoons.
Low monument: Kensal Green Cemetery, London. (31/170–183/RS). Seriously eroded. (Photograph)

.... / THOMAS PERRONET THOMPSON / GENERAL IN HER MAJESTY'S ********* / BORN 15TH MARCH 1783 / DIED 6TH SEPTEMBER 1869 / ....

Midshipman Royal Navy 1803. 2nd Lt 95th Foot 1806. Lt 21 Jan 1808. Lt 14th Lt Dragoons 1 Oct 1812. Capt 17th Lt Dragoons 20 Oct 1814. Major 65th Foot 9 Jun 1825. Bt Lt Colonel 24 Feb 1829. Bt Colonel 9 Nov 1846. Major General 20 Jun 1854.

Served in the Peninsula with 14th Lt Dragoons Sep 1813 – Apr 1814. Present at Nivelle, Nive, Orthes, Vic Bigorre, Tarbes and Toulouse. Also served in the Royal Navy on HMS *Isis* 1803–1806, South America 1807 (present at Buenos Ayres where he was taken prisoner), Sierra Leone 1808–1810 (became Governor of Sierra Leone Colony set up by William Wilberforce for freed slaves. Thompson's father was a friend of Wilberforce. Recalled in 1810 as he threatened to reveal that slavery was still taking place), India 1815–1819 with 17th Lt Dragoons (present in the Pindari Wars). Then employed in the Persian Gulf as Political Agent. Returned home in 1822 and turned to radical reform. Wrote *Catechism on the Corn Laws* 1827 which ran to 18 editions by 1834. Fellow of of the Royal Society 1828. Editor of the *Westminster Review* 1829–1836. MGS medal for Nivelle, Nive, Orthes and Toulouse. After several unsuccessful attempts to enter Parliament became MP for Bradford 1847 and 1857–1859. He supported radical reform and free trade. Both his sons served in the army, Capt Charles Thompson 64th Foot in the Sikh Wars and Capt John Thompson 50th Foot in the Crimea.

REFERENCE: *Dictionary of National Biography. Thompson, L. G., General T. Perronet Thompson 1783–1869: his military, literary and political campaigns, 1957. Thompson, C. W., A sketch of the life of T. P. Thompson, Proceedings of the Royal Society, 1869, No. 116.*

THOMPSON, William

Assistant Surgeon. 38th (1st Staffordshire) Regiment of Foot.
Memorial: St Mary's Cemetery, Madras, India. (M.I.)

"WILLIAM THOMPSON MD., SURGEON OF / H.M.'S 94TH REGIMENT WHO AFTER SERVING / WITH THE HIGHEST PROFESSIONAL DISTINCTION / FOR 42 YEARS IN THE PENINSULA, CAPE AND INDIA / DIED AS ACTING DEPUTY INSPECTOR-GENERAL / OF H.M.'S HOSPITALS AT MADRAS, AGED 64 YEARS. / DIED ON 27TH MARCH 1852."

Hospital Mate 28 Sep 1809. Asst Surgeon 38th Foot 18 Oct 1810. Apothecary 12 Apr 1821. Asst Surgeon on Staff 10 May 1831. Surgeon 6th Foot 19 Jan 1838. Surgeon 94th Foot 11 Jul 1840.

Served in the Peninsula with 2/38th Dec 1810 – Jan 1813 and 1/38th Sep 1813 – Apr 1814. Present at Bidassoa, Nivelle and Bayonne. Also served at Walcheren 1809, Cape of Good Hope (present in the Kaffir Wars 1819 and 1835) and India 1839–1852 (Acting Deputy Inspector General of Madras Hospitals).

THOMSON, Alexander

Captain. 74th (Highland) Regiment of Foot.
Table tomb in railed enclosure: Protestant Graveyard, Salruck Church, Galway, Ireland. (Photograph)

TO THE MEMORY OF / HUGH THOMSON / OF BARCALDEN ARGYLLSHIRE / WHO DEPARTED THIS LIFE ON THE 25TH OF MAY 1838 / ALSO OF HIS SON / ALEXANDER THOMSON C.B. / LATE LIEUTENANT GENERAL IN THE ARMY / AND COLONEL OF HER MAJESTIES 74 / HIGHLANDERS WHO DEPARTED THIS LIFE / ON THE 23RD NOVEMBER 1856. / AND TO HIS GRANDSON / JAMES DOUGALD THOMSON / LATE LIEUTENANT AND ADJUTANT OF / HER MAJESTIES 32 LIGHT INFANTRY / WHO WAS KILLED AT CHENHUT NEAR LUCKNOW / EAST INDIES ON THE 30 JUNE 1857. / ....

Ensign 23 Sep 1803. Lt 29 Feb 1804. Capt 14 May 1807. Bt Major 9 Apr 1812. Bt Lt Colonel 21 Sep 1813. Bt Colonel 22 Jul 1830. Major General 23 Nov 1841. Lt General 11 Nov 1851.

Served in the Peninsula Feb 1810 – Apr 1814. Present at Busaco, Casal Nova, Foz d'Arouce (wounded), Fuentes d'Onoro, second siege of Badajoz, El Bodon, Ciudad Rodrigo (Mentioned in Despatches and awarded Bt Majority), Badajoz (led 300 men to storm and capture the Ravelin of St Roque where he was wounded), siege of Salamanca Forts (Mentioned in Despatches and wounded), Salamanca (severely wounded), Burgos and retreat from Burgos (present at Villa Muriel where he was entrusted with blowing the bridges), Vittoria, San Sebastian (awarded Bt Lt Colonelcy), Bidassoa, Nivelle, Nive and Orthes. Served as Assistant Engineer at the sieges in 1812–1813. Gold Medal for San Sebastian. MGS for Busaco, Fuentes d'Onoro, Ciudad Rodrigo, Badajoz, Salamanca, Vittoria, Nivelle, Nive and Orthes. CB. Half pay 1 Apr 1819. Colonel 74th Foot 15 Aug 1850.

THOMSON, Alexander

2nd Captain. Royal Engineers.
Named on the Regimental Memorial: Rochester Cathedral, Rochester, Kent. (Photograph)

2nd Lt 12 Apr 1808. Lt 24 Jun 1809. 2nd Capt 21 Jul 1813. Bt Major 21 Jan 1819. Capt 9 Apr 1825.

Served in the Peninsula Jan 1809 – Jun 1812. Present at Douro (taken prisoner but managed to escape), Torres Vedras, first and second sieges of Badajoz and Ciudad Rodrigo (severely wounded). Present at Waterloo and with the Army of Occupation (wounded at the siege of Cambrai Jun 1815). Died in Edinburgh 20 Jun 1839.

THOMSON, George

Captain. Royal Artillery.

Buried in the Town Church Graveyard, St Peter Port, Guernsey, Channel Islands. (No longer extant). (Burial register)

2nd Lt 19 Nov 1796. 1st Lt 8 Jan 1799. 2nd Capt 20 Jul 1804. Capt 1 Oct 1809. Bt Major 4 Jun 1814.

Served in the Peninsula Feb 1810 – Apr 1814. Present at Busaco, Fuentes d'Onoro (wounded), Ciudad Rodrigo, Castalla (Mentioned in General Murray's Despatch), Tarragona and Barcelona. Died in Guernsey 26 Nov 1814.

THOMSON, Robert

Captain. Royal Engineers.

Interred in Kensal Green Cemetery, London. (8082/33/-). (No longer extant).

2nd Lt 1 Nov 1804. 1st Lt 1 Mar 1805. 2nd Capt 10 Jul 1810. Capt 16 May 1814. Lt Col 26 Dec 1829. Colonel 1 Apr 1846.

Served in the Peninsula in 1812 on the North coast of Spain. Also served at Martinique 1809, the Netherlands 1813–1815 and Cape of Good Hope 1830–1836 (present in the Kaffir Wars). Died at Dover 13 Jul 1851.

THOMSON, Thomas

Deputy Inspector of Hospitals. Medical Department.

Low monument with cross: Holy Trinity Churchyard, Tunbridge Wells, Kent. (Photograph)

SACRED TO THE MEMORY OF LOUISA / WIFE OF THOMAS THOMSON ESQ. M. D. / OF TUNBRIDGE WELLS / WHO DIED AFTER A LONG AND PAINFUL ILLNESS / APRIL 26TH 1844. / ALSO OF THE ABOVE / THOMAS THOMSON ESQR. M. D. / INSPECTOR GENERAL OF HOSPITALS.

Hospital Mate Jun 1796. Asst Surgeon 3 Dragoons 19 Jul 1797. Asst Surgeon 17th Dragoons 21 Dec 1797. Asst Surgeon 21st Dragoons 20 Mar 1799. Staff Surgeon 23 Jun 1808. Deputy Inspector of Hospitals 21 Jan 1813. Bt Inspector of Hospitals 27 May 1825. Inspector General of Hospitals 22 Jul 1836.

Served in the Peninsula Sep 1808 – Jan 1809 and Oct 1813 – Apr 1814. Present at Nivelle, Nive and Orthes. Also served in Egypt 1801, Martinique 1809, Guadeloupe 1810 and North America 1814–1815 (present at New Orleans). MD Paris 1816. Half pay 22 Jul 1830. MGS medal for Egypt, Martinique, Guadeloupe, Nivelle, Nive, and Orthes. Died 4 Aug 1854.

THOREAU, John

Lieutenant. 40th (2nd Somersetshire) Regiment of Foot.

Memorial tablet: St James's Church, Jamestown, St Helena. (Photograph)

SACRED / TO THE MEMORY OF MAJOR THOREAU, / OF HER MAJESTY'S ST HELENA REGT / A NATIVE OF JERSEY, / WHO DIED ON THIS ISLAND, ON THE 29TH AUGT 1843, / IN THE 58TH YEAR OF HIS AGE. / HE SERVED HIS SOVEREIGN AND COUNTRY FOR 40 YEARS, / WITH ZEAL AND HONOR, AND RETAINED TO THE LAST, THE / SINCERE REGARD OF ALL WHO KNEW HIM / HE WAS IN THE 37TH REGT FOR UPWARDS OF 20 YEARS, BUT / DURING HIS ACTIVE SERVICE, HE BELONGED TO THE 40TH REGT / AND WAS WITH THAT CORPS THROUGHOUT THE / CAMPAIGNS OF THE PENINSULA, FROM 1809, TO THE / END OF THE WAR IN 1815. / HE WAS TWICE SEVERELY WOUNDED, AND WAS PRESENT / AT THE FOLLOWING GENERAL ACTIONS, / ROLICA, VIMIERA, BUSACO, BADAJOS, / CIUDAD RODRIGO, SALAMANCA, VITTORIA, / ORTHES, TOULOUSE. / AND / WATERLOO. / SIC TRANSIT GLORIA MUNDI. / THIS

TABLET IS ERECTED BY HIS BROTHER OFFICERS

Ensign 26 Oct 1804. Lt 28 May 1807. Capt 19 Jul 1815. Capt 37th Foot 3 May 1821. Bt Major 10 Jan 1837.

Served in the Peninsula Aug 1808 – Apr 1814. Present at Rolica, Vimeiro, Busaco, Redinha, first siege of Badajoz (severely wounded), Ciudad Rodrigo, Castrejon, Salamanca, Vittoria, Pyrenees (wounded), Nive, Orthes and Toulouse. Present at Waterloo. Also served at Hanover 1805 and North America 1814–1815 (present at New Orleans). Died at St Helena 29 Aug 1843.

THORN, Robert Brandon

Clerk of Stores. Field Train, Department of Ordnance.
Named on the Regimental monument: British Cemetery, Lisbon, Portugal. (Grave number D11). (M.I.)

"MR ROBERT BRANDON THORN, CLERK OF STORES, FIELD TRAIN, DEPT OF ORDNANCE WHO WAS KILLED IN ACTION AT THE SIEGE OF ALMEIDA 27 AUGUST 1810."

Served in the Peninsula where he was killed in an explosion at the fort of Almeida 27 Aug 1810.

THORNE, Peregrine Francis

Captain. 60th (Royal American) Regiment of Foot.
Memorial tablet: St Mary's Church, Bathwick, Bath, Somerset. (Photograph)

SACRED TO THE MEMORY OF / LIEUT COLL PEREGRINE FRANCIS THORNE, K.H. / WHO DIED AT CONSTANTINOPLE, / DEARLY LOVED AND DEEPLY LAMENTED, / JULY 11TH 1854, AGED 65.

Cornet 25 Dragoons 16 Jul 1807. Lt 1 Jan 1809. Capt 60th Foot 13 Aug 1813. Major 24 Feb 1817. Major 94th Foot 1 Dec 1828. Bt Lt Colonel 10 Jan 1837.

Served in the Peninsula in 1813 with 8/60th (on Staff of 2nd Division). Also served in America 1814–1815 (present at the attack on Castine, Bangor and Machias on River Penobscot). KH. Half pay 3 Aug 1830. Retired 16 Apr 1841.

THORNHILL, William

Major. 7th (Queens Own) Regiment of Light Dragoons.
Memorial tablet: Holy Trinity Church, Stanton-in-the-Peak, Derbyshire. Seriously eroded. (Photograph)

TO THE MEMORY OF LT. COLONEL / WILLIAM THORNHILL / SECOND SON OF / BACHE THORNHILL ESQ OF STANTON / IN THE PEAK HE WAS FIRST / A.D. C. TO THE MARQUIS OF ANGLESEY / AT THE BATTLE OF WATERLOO, THERE / HE WAS SEVERELY WOUNDED BY A / CANNON BALL IN THE NECK / HE WAS IN / NINETEEN GENERAL ENGAGEMENTS / WOUNDED THREE TIMES, / RECEIVED TWO / OF ********* GEORGE ALSO HONOURED IN / ******** BY ******** HIS SERVICE / WITH THE PRESENT SWORD.

Inscription on a natural gritstone outcrop between Stanton-in-the-Peak and Birchover, containing a memorial to Wellington and Thornhill. (Photograph)

FIELD MARSHAL / DUKE OF WELLINGTON / DIED 14 SEPT 1852. / AGED 82 YEARS. / LIEUT-COLONEL WILLIAM THORNHILL 7 HUSSARS / DIED 9 DEC, 1851 / AGED 71 / ASSAYE 1803. WATERLOO 1815. / T. MASTERS

The rock is called the Andle Stone (Anvil Stone) and is encircled by a deteriorating stone wall and obscured by natural rhododendron growth. The date on the inscription is incorrectly given as 1851. It should be 1850.

Needlework Sampler made by one of Colonel Thornhill's servants, M. Smith, Edensor, Bakewell, Derbyshire, 30 Dec 1851. (No longer extant)

"WIMBORNE, DECEMBER 27TH 1850 / THE LATE COLONEL THORNHILL C.B. / THIS DISTINGUISHED OFFICER SO WELL KNOWN AND HIGHLY ESTEEMED WAS INTERRED IN THE FAMILY VAULT AT YOULGREAVE CHURCH IN THE COUNTY OF DERBY ON THE 9TH DECEMBER. HE WAS BORN IN 1781 AND COMMENCED HIS MILITARY CAREER IN 1799 WHEN HE LEFT WESTMINSTER SCHOOL TO JOIN THE 23RD ROYAL WELSH FUSILIERS. HE WAS IN THE EXPEDITION TO WALCHEREN UNDER THE DUKE OF YORK AND UNDER SIR RALPH ABERCROMBIE IN EGYPT AND WITH SIR JOHN MOORE IN SPAIN UP TO THE RETREAT FROM CORUNNA. HE THEN WENT THROUGH THE PENINSULAR WAR UNDER THE DUKE OF WELLINGTON AND WAS BADLY WOUNDED AT ORTHES AND AT THE BATTLE OF WATERLOO. HE WAS FIRST AIDE-CAMP TO THE MARQUIS OF ANGLESEY. ON THAT OCCASION HE WAS RETURNED AS MORTALLY WOUNDED HAVING BEEN STRUCK ON THE SHOULDER TOWARDS THE CLOSE OF THE DAY BY A 12-POUNDER FROM WHICH HE SUFFERED SEVERELY AND WHICH EVENTUALLY SHORTENED HIS LIFE. FOR SEVERAL YEARS HE AFTERWARDS COMMANDED THE 7TH HUSSARS. HE DIED AT WIMBORNE IN DORSETSHIRE ON THE 9TH INST FROM WHENCE HIS REMAINS WERE BROUGHT TO BE INTERRED IN HIS NATIVE COUNTY."

2nd Lt 23rd Foot 20 Aug 1799. 1st Lt 28 Feb 1800. Capt 5 May 1804. Capt 7th Dragoons 12 Jun 1806. Major 8 Apr 1813. Bt Lt Colonel 18 Jun 1815. Lt Colonel 12 Aug 1819.

Served in the Peninsula Nov 1808 – Jan 1809 and Aug 1813 – Apr 1814. Present at Sahagun, Benevente, Orthes and Toulouse. Captured a French colour at Orthes but was severely wounded. Present at Waterloo where he was severely wounded (ADC to Lord Uxbridge). KH. Also served at the Helder 1799 and Egypt 1801. MGS medal for Sahagun and Benevente, Orthes and Toulouse. Died at Wimborne Minster 9 Dec 1850 aged 70.

Reference: Gentleman's Magazine, Mar 1851, p. 314. Annual Register, 1850, Appx, p. 285.

THORNTON, Henry

Lieutenant Colonel. 40th (2nd Somersetshire) Regiment of Foot.

Low monument: Kensal Green Cemetery, London. (12928/48/RS). (Photograph)

.... / ALSO OF / COLONEL HENRY THORNTON / FORMERLY OF 40th REGT LATE OF 82ND REGT / BELOVED SON OF THOMAS LEE THORNTON / DIED ON THE / 30TH DAY OF / FEBRUARY 1856 AGED 76 YEARS

Cornet 2nd Dragoons 8 Oct 1794. Lt 24 Jun 1795. Capt 40th Foot 23 Nov 1796. Major 1 Aug 1804. Bt Lt Colonel 4 Jun 1811. Lt Colonel 13 Jun 1811. Bt Colonel 27 May 1825.

Served in the Peninsula Aug 1808 – Jun 1811 and Jul 1813 – Apr 1814. Present at Rolica, Vimeiro, Talavera, Busaco, Redinha, first siege of Badajoz (wounded), Pyrenees, Bidassoa, Nivelle (severely wounded), Orthes and Toulouse. Gold Cross for Talavera, Nivelle, Orthes and Toulouse. CB. MGS medal for Rolica, Vimeiro, Busaco and Pyrenees. Also served in North America 1814–1815. The regiment returned in time for Waterloo, but Thornton was a witness in a court martial, was detained in London and so missed the battle. Joined the regiment afterwards, was present with the Army of Occupation and commanded it until 1827. Retired in 1828.

THORNTON, John
Lieutenant. 94th Regiment of Foot.
Mural Memorial tablet: Liberton Churchyard, Edinburgh, Scotland. (Photograph)

IN MEMORY / OF / LIEUT JOHN THORNTON / LATE OF HER MAJESTY'S 94TH REGT / BORN AT WOOLER, NORTHUMBERLAND, / 18TH AUGUST 1789 / DIED AT NIVELLE COTTAGE, LIBERTON, / 18TH NOVEMBER 1870. / LIEUT THORNTON JOINED THE ARMY / UNDER THE DUKE OF WELLINGTON IN 1807 / AND REMAINED IN IT TILL 1817. / HE WAS PRESENT AND ENGAGED IN / MANY OF THE GREAT BATTLES OF THE PERIOD / AND BEING DANGEROUSLY WOUNDED / AT THAT OF NIVELLE / HE WAS OBLIGED TO RETIRE FROM ACTIVE SERVICE / AND DURING THE REMAINDER OF HIS LIFE / HE CHIEFLY RESIDED IN THIS PARISH, / WHERE HE WAS MOST RESPECTED / AND DIED DEEPLY REGRETTED / BY ALL TO WHOM HE WAS KNOWN.

Ensign 27 Aug 1807. Lt 2 Aug 1810.

Served in the Peninsula Apr 1810 – Jan 1814. Present at Cadiz, Redinha, Casal Nova, Foz d'Arouce, Sabugal, Fuentes d'Onoro, second siege of Badajoz, El Bodon, Ciudad Rodrigo, Badajoz, Salamanca, Vittoria, Pyrenees and Nivelle (severely wounded and awarded pension of £70 per annum). Half pay 17 Jul 1817. MGS medal for Fuentes d'Onoro, Ciudad Rodrigo, Badajoz, Salamanca, Vittoria, Pyrenees and Nivelle.

THORPE, Samuel
Captain. 39th (Dorsetshire) Regiment of Foot.
Tomb: St Mary's Churchyard, Cheshunt, Hertfordshire. (Inscription not recorded)

Ensign 14th Foot 2 Apr 1807. Lt 10 Jan 1808. 1st Lt 23rd Foot 5 May 1808. Capt Royal York Rangers 16 Apr 1812. Capt 39th Foot 30 Jul 1812. Bt Major 22 Jul 1830.

Served in the Peninsula with 2/23rd Oct 1808 – Jan 1809, 1/23rd Apr 1811 – Oct 1811 and 1/39th Mar – Apr 1814. Present at Lugo, Corunna, first siege of Badajoz, Albuera (severely wounded), Aire and Toulouse (severely wounded). Also served at Walcheren 1809 and North America 1814–1815 (present at Plattsburgh). KH. MGS medal for Corunna, Albuera and Toulouse. Wrote about his military experiences in *Major Thorpe's Narrative*, 1854.
REFERENCE: *Cheshire Notes and Queries, Vol. 8, No. 2, pp. 57–9. Thorpe, Samuel, Narrative of incidents in the early life of the late Major S. Thorpe, 1854.*

THOYTS, John
Captain. Royal Regiment of Horse Guards.
Grave: Kensal Green Cemetery, London. (8163/83/2). (Inscription not recorded)

Cornet 14 Feb 1800. Lt 6 Apr 1803. Capt 22 Aug 1805. Major 18 Jun 1815. Bt Lt Colonel 18 Jun 1815.

Served in the Peninsula Nov 1812 – Apr 1814. Present at Vittoria and Toulouse. Present at Waterloo. During the cavalry charge his horse was shot from under him and he was taken prisoner. The French kept him at Charleroi for several days. Promoted Major 18 June 1815 and Bt Lt Colonel on the same day. Retired 1820. MGS medal for Vittoria and Toulouse. Died 15 May 1849 aged 77.
REFERENCE: *Gentleman's Magazine, Jul 1849, p. 104.*

TIDY, Francis Skelly
Major, 14th (Buckinghamshire) Regiment of Foot.
Ledger stone: Fort Henry, Kingston, Ontario, Canada. (Photograph)

TO / THE MEMORY / OF / COLONEL F. S. TIDY C.B. / WHO DIED WHILST IN COMMAND OF /

HIS MAJESTY'S 24TH REGIMENT OF FOOT / IN THE GARRISON / ON THE 9TH OCTOBER, 1835 / AT THE AGE OF / 60 YEARS / THIS TOMB WAS ERECTED BY / THE OFFICERS, NON COMMISSIONED OFFICERS & PRIVATES OF THE ABOVE CORPS / AS A TRIBUTE / OF / RESPECT AND ESTEEM / FOR / A GALLANT OFFICER / WHO SERVED HIS / KING AND COUNTRY / FAITHFULLY / FOR A PERIOD OF / 43 YEARS

Volunteer 43rd Foot. Ensign 41st Foot Sep 1792. Ensign 43rd Foot 31 Dec 1792. Lt 24 May 1794. Capt 1st West India Regt Dec 1798. Capt 1st Foot 8 Apr 1800. Major 8th West India Regt 9 Jun 1807. Major 14th Foot 10 Sep 1807. Bt Lt Colonel 4 Jun 1813. Lt Colonel 44th Foot 11 Nov 1825. Bt Colonel 22 Jul 1830.

Served in the Peninsula Nov 1808 – May 1809 (AAG to General Baird). Present at Corunna and Douro. Present at Waterloo where he commanded the 14th Foot. CB. Also served in the West Indies 1794 (present at Martinique, Guadeloupe where he was captured at Berville Oct 1794 when the entire garrison was taken prisoner by Victor Hugues and his men. Cruelly treated in prison on a hulk for 15 months then sent to France. Released on parole), West Indies May 1803 (present at St Lucia where he was Secretary to the Colony, Brigade Major to Sir William Myers and then ADC to Sir George Beckwith). Walcheren 1809, Malta 1813, Genoa 1814, Ionian Islands 1819, India 1822 (present in the 1st Burmese War) and Canada 1833 (in command of 24th Foot) where he died 9 Oct 1835. Served in the army for 43 years. Nephew of Major Francis Gordon Skelly 71st Foot who fought so well at Seringapatam with 94th Foot.

REFERENCE: *Ward, Harriet (his daughter), Recollections of an Old Soldier: a biographical sketch of Colonel Tidy 24th Regt, with anecdotes of his contempories, 1849. Gentleman's Magazine, May 1836, p. 548.*

TIDY, John

Private. 3rd (Prince of Wales's) Dragoon Guards.
Headstone: Holy Trinity Churchyard, Rolleston, Nottinghamshire. (Photograph)

TO / THE MEMORY OF / JOHN TIDY. / WHO DIED THE 10TH OF OCTR / 1823 / IN THE / 46 YEAR OF / HIS AGE. / CONQUEST I SHAR'D IN MANY DREADFUL SCENE. / WITH MATCHLESS WELLINGTON BY DURO STREAM. / LET ME ALONE AWHILE ASLEEP NOT SLAIN. / AND WHEN THE TRUMPET SOUNDS / I'LL MARCH AGAIN.

Pte 27 Jul 1803. Cpl 1816.

Served in the Peninsula 1809 – Apr 1814. Present at Talavera, Albuera, Usagre, Aldea de Ponte, Maguilla, Vittoria and Toulouse.

TIGHE, Daniel

Ensign, 1st Regiment of Foot Guards.
Memorial: Royal Military Chapel, Wellington Barracks, London. (M.I.) (Destroyed by a Flying Bomb 1944)

"DANIEL TIGHE. / BORN 11TH MAY, 1796. LIEUTENANT 1ST GUARDS, 1814–21. HE CARRIED THE KING'S COLOUR OF / THE 2ND BATTALION AT WATERLOO, AND WAS WOUNDED. HE DIED 16TH MARCH, 1874. / D. D. HIS WIDOW, 1881."

Ensign 26 Nov 1814.

Present at Waterloo where he was wounded carrying the King's colour. Half pay 15 Feb 1821. High Sheriff of County Wicklow 1829.

TILT, Andrew
Major. 37th (North Hampshire) Regiment of Foot.
Headstone: Paddington Street Burial Ground, London. (M.I.)

"IN MEMORY OF LIEUT COL ANDREW TILT, DIED 20TH OCTOBER 1853 AGED 73, OF HIS MAJESTY'S 37TH FOOT."

Ensign 1 Jan 1801. Lt 17 Sep 1802. Capt 4 Jun 1807. Major 37th Foot 20 Feb 1812. Lt Colonel 7 Dec 1815.
Served in the Peninsula Mar – Apr 1814. Present at Bayonne. Also served in the West Indies 1801–1809, Gibraltar 1811–1814 and Canada 1814–1826. Half pay 1826.

TINLING, George Vaughan
1st Lieutenant. Royal Engineers.
Low monument: St Paul's Churchyard, Shurdington, Gloucestershire. (Photograph)

………………. / SACRED TO THE MEMORY OF / MAJOR GEORGE VAUGHAN TINLING R. E. / BROTHER OF THE ABOVE / WHO DEPARTED THIS LIFE / JUNE 23RD 1864. / AGED 70 YEARS. / ……………….

2nd Lt 1 Jul 1812. 1st Lt 21 Jul 1813. 2nd Capt 19 Oct 1826. Capt 10 Jan 1837. Bt Major 28 Nov 1854.
Served in the Peninsula Dec 1813 – Apr 1814. Present at Adour and Bayonne. Served in France with the Army of Occupation until 1818. Also served in the Netherlands 1814–1815. Retired on full pay 28 Jul 1840.

TINLING, Isaac Pattison
Captain and Lieutenant Colonel. 1st Regiment of Foot Guards.
Memorial tablet: St Philip and St James's Church, Leckhampton, Gloucestershire. (Photograph)

SACRED / TO THE MEMORY OF / MAJOR GENERAL ISAAC PATTISON TINLING / FROM THE GRENADIER GUARDS / WHO DEPARTED THIS LIFE ON THE 22ND OF AUGUST 1822 / AGED 62

Ensign 20th Foot 1 Jun 1778. Lt 3 Dec 1785. Capt 14 Mar 1794. Lt and Capt 1st Foot Guards 24 Jan 1798. Bt Major 1 Oct 1803. Bt Lt Colonel 12 May 1804. Capt and Lt Colonel 14 Feb 1811. Bt Colonel 4 Jun 1813. Major General 12 Aug 1819.
Served in the Peninsula with 1st Battalion Sep 1812 – Dec 1813. Present at Bidassoa, Nivelle and Nive. Also served in North America (present at Saratoga and was a prisoner of war until 1780), the West Indies 1794 (present at St Domingo where he was severely wounded, sent home to England but taken prisoner on his way home and imprisoned in France for a year before he was exchanged), the Helder 1799 and Walcheren 1809.

TOD, George
Major. 29th (Worcestershire) Regiment of Foot.
Memorial tablet: All Saints' Church, Maidstone, Kent. (Tablet is partly obscured behind a wooden altar fixed to the floor. (Photograph)

TO THE MEMORY OF / COLONEL GEORGE TOD / 29TH FOOT: WHO DIED 3RD OF JUNE 1832 / ………………. / WIFE. WHO DIED 25TH DECEMBER 1840 / TOGETHER WITH THOSE OF THEIR INFANT SON / GEORGE GORDON / LIE UNDER THIS SPOT IN THE VAULT OF / JOSEPH HILLS. / COLONEL GEORGE TOD / SAW ACTION IN SPAIN AND PORTUGAL / UNDER WELLINGTON AND ALSO IN NORTH AMERICA. / HIS FATHER WILLIAM TOD ESQUIRE. FOCHABERS. N.B. / DEPUTY LIEUTENANT AND JUSTICE OF PEACE / BANFF MORAY AND INVERNESS.

Family ledger stone: Bellie Cemetery, Bellie, Morayshire, Scotland. (Photograph)

HERE ARE INTERRED THE REMAINS OF / WILLIAM TOD, FATHER OF .... / THE REMAINS OF THREE OF THEIR SONS / ARE INTERRED WILLIAM / CAPT^{N} 40TH FOOT AT DEPTFORD / WHERE HE DIED 25TH OCTOBER 1820 / GEORGE LIEUT. COLONEL 29TH FOOT / AT MAIDSTONE / WHERE HE DIED 3^{D} JUNE 1832 / AND ROBERT SURGEON 4TH LIGHT DRAGOONS / AT KAIRA BOMBAY / WHERE HE DIED 20TH FEBRUARY 1824.

Ensign 17 Apr 1795. Lt 2 Sep 1795. Capt 24 Jul 1803. Bt Major 31 Oct 1811. Major 2 Dec 1813. Bt Lt Colonel 12 Aug 1819.

Served in the Peninsula Jul 1808 – Nov 1811 and Apr 1813 – Feb 1814. Present at Rolica (taken prisoner), Douro, Talavera, Busaco, first siege of Badajoz, Albuera (severely wounded and awarded a pension of £100 per annum), Cadiz and Tarifa. On his return to England from North America in 1815 he was too late for Waterloo but served in France with the Army of Occupation. Also served in Ireland 1798 (present in the Irish Rebellion), the Helder 1799, North America 1801–1806 and 1814–1815 (present at the Capture of Castine and Fort Machias). Died at Maidstone 3 Jun 1832. Brother of Surgeon Robert Tod 52nd Foot and Capt William Tod 40th Foot.

REFERENCE: *Gentleman's Magazine, Jun 1832, pp. 562–3.*

TOD, Robert

Surgeon. 52nd (Oxfordshire) Light Infantry Regiment of Foot.
Family ledger stone: Bellie Cemetery, Bellie, Morayshire, Scotland. (Photograph)

HERE ARE INTERRED THE REMAINS OF / WILLIAM TOD .... / THE REMAINS OF THREE OF THEIR SONS / ARE INTERRED WILLIAM / CAPT^{N} 40TH FOOT AT DEPTFORD / WHERE HE DIED 25TH OCTOBER 1820 / GEORGE LIEUT. COLONEL 29TH FOOT / AT MAIDSTONE / WHERE HE DIED 3^{D} JUNE 1832 / AND ROBERT SURGEON 4TH LIGHT DRAGOONS / AT KAIRA BOMBAY / WHERE HE DIED 20TH FEBRUARY 1824.

Hospital Mate 10 Jun 1806. Asst Surgeon Royal Staff Corps 25 Jun 1806. Asst Surgeon 38th Foot 19 Feb 1807. Surgeon 52nd Foot 18 Feb 1813. Half pay 25 Jul 1816. Surgeon 83rd Foot 18 May 1820. Surgeon 4th Dragoons 20 Feb 1823.

Served in the Peninsula with 1/38th Aug 1808 – Jan 1809 and Jun 1812 – Feb 1813. Present at Rolica, Vimeiro, Castrejon, Salamanca and retreat from Burgos (present at Villa Muriel). Also served at Walcheren 1809 and in India with the 4th Dragoons Feb 1823. MD Edinburgh 1817. Died at Kaira, Bombay 20 Feb 1824. Brother of Major George Tod 29th Foot and Capt William Tod 40th Foot.

TOD, William

Captain. 92nd Regiment of Foot.
Family ledger stone: Bellie Cemetery, Bellie, Morayshire, Scotland. (Photograph)

HERE ARE INTERRED THE REMAINS OF / WILLIAM TOD .... / THE REMAINS OF THREE OF THEIR SONS / ARE INTERRED WILLIAM / CAPT^{N} 40TH FOOT AT DEPTFORD / WHERE HE DIED 25TH OCTOBER 1820 / GEORGE LIEUT. COLONEL 29TH FOOT / AT MAIDSTONE / WHERE HE DIED 3^{D} JUNE 1832 / AND ROBERT SURGEON 4TH LIGHT DRAGOONS / AT KAIRA BOMBAY / WHERE HE DIED 20TH FEBRUARY 1824.

Lt 100th Foot 21 Feb 1793. Capt 40th Foot 12 Aug 1799. Capt 92nd Foot 11 Oct 1804.

Served in the Peninsula Aug – Oct 1808. Retired 1808. Died at Deptford 25 Oct 1820. Brother of Major George Tod 29th Foot and Surgeon Robert Tod 52nd Foot.

TODD, Francis
Captain and Lieutenant Colonel. 1st Regiment of Foot Guards.
Grave: St James's Churchyard, Shirley, Southampton, Hampshire. (M.I.)

"LT COLONEL FRANCIS TODD. DIED 22 NOVEMBER 1871 AGED 93."

Ensign 11 Apr 1794. Lt and Capt 24 Nov 1796. Capt and Lt Colonel 18 Apr 1805.
Served in the Peninsula with 3rd Battalion Oct 1808 – Jan 1809. Present at Corunna. Retired 26 Oct 1809.

TOMKINSON, William
Captain. 16th (Queen's) Regiment of Light Dragoons.
Cross on stepped base: St Peter's Churchyard, Delamere, Cheshire. (Photograph)

LT COLONEL WILLIAM TOMKINSON / DIED 1872 AGED 82 YEARS. / THE MEMORY OF THE JUST IS BLESSED

Brass Memorial tablet: Abbey Church, Nuneaton, Warwickshire. (Photograph)

IN MEMORY OF LT COLONEL WILLIAM / TOMKINSON OF WILLINGTON HALL IN THE / COUNTY OF CHESTER, BORN 18 JANUARY 1790 / AN OFFICER IN HER MS 16TH LANCERS, / IN WHICH REGIMENT HE SERVED WITH / DISTINCTION IN THE PENINSULA WAR / DURING THE CAMPAIGN OF 1809–13 / AND AT THE BATTLE OF WATERLOO. / HE WAS SEVERELY WOUNDED AT THE CROSSING OF / THE DOURO 11 MAY 1809 AND RECEIVED THE / WATERLOO AND PENINSULA MEDALS WITH / CLASPS FOR THE BATTLES OF BUSACO, FUENTES, / SALAMANCA AND VITTORIA. IT WAS HIS / DESIRE, AS OWNER OF THE RUINS OF NUNEATON / ABBEY, TO SEE A CHURCH ERECTED ON THEM / AND FOR THAT PURPOSE HAD OFFERED THE SITE, / BUT DYING, UNIVERSALLY BELOVED / AND HONOURED AUG 26 1872: HE LEFT HIS / WISH TO BE CARRIED OUT BY HIS / SUCCESSOR.

Cornet 16 Dec 1807. Lt 4 Oct 1808. Capt 60th Foot 12 Mar 1812. Capt 16th Lt Dragoons 3 Jun 1812. Bt Major 21 Jan 1819. Bt Lt Colonel 10 Jan 1837.
Served in the Peninsula Apr – Sep 1809, Apr 1810 – Apr 1812 and Jul 1812 – Sep 1813. Present at Grijon (severely wounded 11 May 1809), Busaco, Redinha, Casal Nova, Rayengo (wounded 18 Jan 1811) Foz d'Arouce, Sabugal, Fuentes d'Onoro, El Bodon, Llerena, Castrejon, Salamanca and Vittoria. Present at Waterloo and with the Army of Occupation until Dec 1815. The 16th Lt Dragoons were the only cavalry regiment to serve throughout the Peninsular War and at Waterloo (although Tomkinson returned home from the Peninsula in Sep 1813). MGS medal for Busaco, Fuentes d'Onoro, Salamanca and Vittoria. Half pay 1821. Retired to his estates in Cheshire. Kept a diary which was edited by his son entitled *Diary of a Cavalry Officer, 1809–1815.*
Reference: Tomkinson, William, The Diary of a Cavalry Officer in the Peninsula and Waterloo Campaigns, 1809–1815, reprint 1999.

TOOLE, William
Captain. 40th (2nd Somersetshire) Regiment of Foot.
Table stone: Ardolm Church of Ireland Churchyard, Ardolm, County Wexford, Ireland. (Photograph)

BENEATH THIS STONE / REST / THE MORTAL REMAINS OF LIEUT COL WILLIAM TOOLE / CURRACLOE / LATE OF HER MAJESTY'S 40TH REGIMENT OF INFANTRY / OF WHICH HE LED THE GRENADIER COMPANY / AT THE STORMING OF BADAJOZ / WHERE HE RECEIVED HIS LAST AND FINALLY DISABLING WOUND / BUT LONG PERMITTED TO ENJOY THE BLESSING

OF THAT PEACE / HE CONTRIBUTED TO SECURE. / HE NOW SLEEPS THE SLEEP OF THOSE / WHOSE TRUST IS IN THE SON OF GOD. / HE DIED 3RD OF SEPTEMBER 1859 AGED 69. / ....

Ensign 5 Dec 1805. Lt 25 Aug 1807. Capt 9 Nov 1814. Bt Major 10 Jan 1837. Bt Lt Colonel 11 Nov 1851.

Served in the Peninsula Jan 1810 – Jul 1812 and Oct 1813 – Apr 1814. Present at Busaco, Redinha, first siege of Badajoz (wounded 10 May 1811), Ciudad Rodrigo, Badajoz (severely wounded 6 Apr 1812) and Nivelle. Served in France with the Army of Occupation until 19 Apr 1817 when he retired on half pay. MGS medal for Busaco, Ciudad Rodrigo, Badajoz and Nivelle.

TOOLE, William

Sergeant. 12th (Prince of Wales's) Regiment of Light Dragoons.
Named on the Regimental Memorial: St Joseph's Church, Waterloo. (Photograph)

Present at Waterloo where he was killed.

TOPP, Richard

Ensign. 94th Regiment of Foot.
Named on the Memorial: St Andrew's Church (now Musée Historique), Biarritz, France. (Photograph)

Ensign 11 Jun 1812.

Served in the Peninsula Nov 1812 – Feb 1814. Present at Vittoria, Pyrenees, Nivelle and Nive. Killed in the attack on the enemy's fortified posts on the left of the Gave d'Oloren 24 Feb 1814.

TORRENS, Sir Henry

Captain and Lieutenant Colonel. 3rd Regiment of Foot Guards.
Memorial tablet: St Paul's Church, Welwyn, Hertfordshire. (Photograph)

SACRED TO THE MEMORY / OF MAJOR GENERAL SIR HENRY TORRENS, / KNIGHT, COMMANDER OF THE BATH / AND OF THE TOWER AND SWORD, / AND COLONEL OF THE 2ND REGIMENT / OF QUEEN'S ROYAL; / HE WAS A SOLDIER FROM HIS EARLIEST YEARS, / AND SERVED HIS COUNTRY / IN ALL CLIMATES, AND IN ALL CAPACITIES: / HIS MERIT RAISED HIM, / WITHOUT THE AID OF PATRONAGE OR INFLUENCE, / TO THE HIGH AND RESPONSIBLE STATION / OF MILITARY SECRETARY TO / HIS ROYAL HIGHNESS THE DUKE OF YORK, / DURING THE EVENTFUL WAR / WHICH AROSE OUT OF THE / FRENCH REVOLUTION. / HE WAS BORN AT LONDONDERRY IN IRELAND, / IN THE MONTH OF OCTOBER 1776, / AND DIED 23RD AUGUST 1828, / ADJUTANT GENERAL TO THE FORCES; / BELOVED: LAMENTED: / A DISTINGUISHED SOLDIER; / A FAITHFUL FRIEND. / HIS REMAINS ARE INTERRED IN A VAULT UNDERNEATH THE / CHANCEL OF THIS CHURCH.

Ensign 52nd Foot 2 Nov 1793. Lt 92nd Foot 14 Jun 1794. Lt 63rd Foot 11 Dec 1795. Capt 6th West India Regiment 28 Mar 1797. Capt 20th Foot 8 Aug 1799. Major 86th Foot 4 Feb 1802. Bt Lt Colonel 1 Jan 1805. Major 89th Foot 19 Feb 1807. Capt and Lt Colonel 3rd Foot Guards 13 Jun 1811. Bt Colonel 20 Feb 1812. Major General 4 Jun 1814.

Served in the Peninsula Aug 1808 (Military Secretary to Wellington). Present at Rolica and Vimeiro (Mentioned in Despatches). Gold Medal for Rolica and Vimeiro. KTS. KCB. Also served in the West Indies 1795 (present at St Lucia and St Vincent where he was severely wounded), the Helder 1799 (present at Egmont-op-Zee where he was severely wounded), Egypt 1801 (crossed desert with Baird from India), India (present in the Mahratta Wars 1802–1803 and Scinde 1803–1805) and South America 1807 (Military Secretary to the Duke of York and present at Buenos Ayres 1807). On his return from the Peninsula became

Military Secretary to the Duke of York. Adjutant General of the Forces 25 Mar 1820. Revised the *Regulations for the exercise and field movement of the infantry of the army*. Colonel 2nd Garrison Battalion 5 Apr 1815. Colonel Royal African Colonial Corps 27 Nov 1815. Colonel 2nd West India Regiment 21 Sep 1818. Colonel 2nd Foot 26 Jul 1822.
Reference: Dictionary of National Biography. Royal Military Calendar. Vol 3, pp. 390–2. Gentleman's Magazine, Oct 1828, pp. 374–5. Annual Register, 1828, Appx, pp. 254–5.

TORRENS, S. B.
Captain. 1st (Royal Scots) Regiment of Foot.
Headstone: Drummond Hill Presbyterian Churchyard, Lundy's Lane, Niagara, Canada. (Photograph)

IN MEMORY OF / LT. COL. GORDON / AND / CAPT. TORRENS / OF / FIRST ROYAL SCOTS, / KILLED AT FORT ERIE / DURING THE CAMPAIGN / OF 1814. / ERECTED BY MAJOR BARRY FOX, / LATE OF SAID REGIMENT / THEIR FRIEND AND COMPANION / JUNE 20 1851.

Named on the Monument at Fort Erie, Canada. (M.I.)

"OFFICERS KILLED DURING THE SIEGE OF FORT ERIE COL. HERCULES SCOTT, 103D REGT.; LIEUT. COL. WILLIAM DRUMMOND, 104TH REGT.; LIEUT. COL. JOHN GORDON, ROYAL SCOTS; CAPT. R. D. PATTESON, 6TH REGT.; CAPT. TORRENS, 8TH REGT.: CAPT J.M. WRIGHT, 824 REGT., CAPT. ED. WALKER, INCOR. MILITIA; LIEUT. COPLES RADCLIFFE, R. N.; LIEUT. NOEL, ROYAL SCOTS; LIEUT. J. RUTLEDGE, ROYAL SCOTS; LIEUT. BARSTOW, 8TH REGT.; LIEUT.PILLICHODY, DE WATTEVILLE REGT.; ENSIGN E. LANGFORD. 82D REGT."

Lt Tyrone Militia. Ensign 1st Foot 5 May 1800. Lt 16 Mar 1802. Capt 13 Nov 1806.

Served in the Peninsula Oct 1808 – Jan 1809. Present at Corunna. Also served at Walcheren 1809 and North America 1812 (present at Niagara where he was killed at Fort Erie Sep 1814).

TORRIANO, William Edward
Lieutenant. 71st (Highland Light Infantry) Regiment of Foot.
Memorial tablet: All Saints' Church, East Budleigh, Devon. (M.I.)

"TO THE GLORY OF GOD / AND TO THE MEMORY OF WILLIAM EDWARD TORRIANO / LIEUTENANT 71ST REGIMENT HIGHLAND INFANTRY, / 3RD SON OF / CAPTAIN CHARLES TORRIANO / XXXTH REGIMENT OF FOOT, / AND HESTER DE LA FAUSILLE, HIS WIFE, / BORN AT MOUNT ROY, WELLS, SOMERSET / 14TH JULY 1793. / DIED AT BUDLEIGH SALTERTON 5TH FEBRUARY 1862. / HE SERVED FROM 1810–14 IN THE PENINSULAR WAR UNDER / THE GREAT DUKE OF WELLINGTON WAS THREE TIMES WOUNDED / AND WAS PRESENT AT THE ACTIONS OF ARROYO DES MOLINOS, / ALMAREZ, COVERING ARMY AT BADAJOS, VITTORIA, NIVE / BAYONNE, URT, ST PALAIS, ORTHES, AIRE, TARBES, TOULOUSE / AND MANY MINOR AFFAIRS, AND FINALLY FOUGHT AT THE BATTLE / OF WATERLOO WAS PRESENT AT THE SURRENDER OF PARIS / AND WAS WITH THE ARMY OF OCCUPATION IN FRANCE. / …………………"

Ensign 16 Oct 1809. Lt 12 Dec 1811. Adjutant 18 Oct 1821.

Served in the Peninsula Jul 1811 – Apr 1814. Present at Arroyo dos Molinos, Almarez, Vittoria (wounded), Nivelle, Nive (wounded), Bayonne (wounded), Orthes and Toulouse. MGS medal for Vittoria, Nivelle, Nive, Orthes and Toulouse. Present at Waterloo (where some men under his command captured a French gun, turned it round and fired on the fleeing Imperial Guard, reported to be the last French gun fired 18 Jun), the Capture of Paris and with the Army of Occupation. Retired in 1824.

TOWERS, Frederick

Lieutenant. 7th (Queen's Own) Regiment of Light Dragoons.
Memorial tablet: Parish Church, Laggan, Invernesshire, Scotland. (Photograph)

SACRED / TO THE MEMORY OF / MAJOR GENERAL FREDERICK TOWERS. / BORN AUGUST 15TH 1797. / DIED OCTOBER 13th 1859.

Cornet 18 Nov 1813. Lt 18 Apr 1815. Capt 8 Jul 1820. Bt Major 29 Aug 1826. Bt Lt Colonel 23 Nov 1841. Bt Colonel 20 Jun 1854. Major General 26 Oct 1858.

Present at Waterloo. Half pay 4 Sep 1821. Noted as the best deer-stalker of his day in the Highlands.

TOWNSEND, John

Captain. 14th (Duchess of York's Own) Regiment of Light Dragoons.
Memorial tablet: St Barrahane's Church, Castletownshend, near Skibbereen, West Cork, Ireland. (Photograph)

TO THE MEMORY OF / COLONEL / JOHN TOWNSEND, / LATE OF THE 14TH LIGHT DRAGOONS. / HE SERVED WITH DISTINCTION / IN PORTUGAL, SPAIN AND FRANCE. / HE DIED ON THE 25TH OF APRIL, / 1845. / THIS MONUMENT / IS ERECTED / BY HIS BROTHER OFFICERS.

Buried in St Peter's Churchyard, Dublin, Ireland. (Church was demolished in the 1980s)

Cornet 24 Jun 1805. Lt 27 Feb 1806. Capt 6 Jun 1811. Bt Major 21 Jan 1819. Major 13 Sep 1821. Lt Colonel 16 Apr 1829. Bt Colonel 23 Nov 1841.

Served in the Peninsula Dec 1808 – Jul 1813 and Oct 1813 – Apr 1814. Present at Douro, Talavera, Sexmiro, Coa, Busaco, Sobral, Pombal, Redinha, Casal Nova, Foz d'Arouce, Sabugal, Fuentes de Onoro (wounded), El Bodon, Badajoz, Llerena, Castrejon, Salamanca, Vittoria and Orthes. Taken prisoner near Pau in France 8 Mar 1814, where he remained until the end of the war. Also served in North America 1814–1815 (present at New Orleans), Ireland 1826 and India 1841. Commanded the regiment in India from 1841, and was appointed ADC to Queen Victoria Nov 1841. Returned from India in 1845 after 40 years service in the 14th Lt Dragoons.

Reference: Gentleman's Magazine, Aug 1845, pp. 196–7. Annual Register, 1845, Appx, p. 271.

TOWNSHEND, Hon. Horatio George Powys

Captain and Lieutenant Colonel. 1st Regiment of Foot Guards.
Family Memorial tablet: St Nicholas's Church, Chislehurst, Kent. (Photograph)

.... / THE HONBLE HORATIO GEORGE POWYS TOWNSHEND K.C.H. / BORN FEBRY 6TH 1780, DIED MAY 25th 1843. / A COLONEL IN THE ARMY. / LT GOVERNOR OF THE ROUND TOWER OF WINDSOR CASTLE.

Memorial: Royal Military Chapel, Wellington Barracks, London. (M.I.). (Destroyed by a Flying Bomb 1944)

"PLACED BY JOHN ROBERT EARL SYDNEY, G.C.B., IN MEMORY OF / COLONEL THE HON. SIR HORATIO GEORGE POWYS TOWNSHEND, K.C.H. / BORN, 1780; DIED, 1844. / LIEUT.-GOVERNOR OF WINDSOR CASTLE. HE SERVED IN THE 1ST GUARDS IN THE FOLLOWING CAMPAIGNS: – HOLLAND, 1799; SICILY, 1806; CORUNNA, 1809; WALCHEREN, 1809; PENINSULA, FROM 1811–1814; WATERLOO, 1815. HIS HORSE WAS KILLED UNDER HIM AT BARROSA, 1811. HE WAS TAKEN PRISONER AT THE SORTIE FROM BAYONNE, WHEN IN

COMMAND OF THE OUTLYING PICQUETS, 1814. / HE WAS WOUNDED AT QUATRE BRAS, 17TH JUNE, 1815. / HE COMMANDED THE GRENADIER GUARDS FROM 1821–29."

Ensign 23 Sep 1795. Lt and Capt 19 Sep 1799. Capt and Lt Colonel 26 Oct 1809. Bt Colonel 12 Aug 1819. Lt Colonel 25 Jul 1821.

Served in the Peninsula with 1st Battalion Oct 1808 – Jan 1809, 2nd Battalion Mar 1810 – May 1811 and 3rd Battalion Jun 1812 – Apr 1814. Present at Corunna, Cadiz, Barrosa, Seville, Bidassoa, Nivelle, Nive, Adour and Bayonne where he was severely wounded and taken prisoner at the Sortie from Bayonne 14 Apr 1814. Present at Waterloo (severely wounded at Quatre Bras) and with the Army of Occupation until 1818. Commanded Grenadier Guards from 1821–1829, but had to resign because of ill health due to wounds. Also served at the Helder 1799, Sicily 1806 and Walcheren 1809. Knighted 1834. KCH. Lt Governor of the Round Tower at Windsor Castle 1836. MP for Whitchurch 1816–1826 and 1831–1832. Educated at Eton. Died 25 May 1843.

Reference: United Service Magazine, Jul 1843, pp. 458–9. Gentleman's Magazine, Aug 1843, pp. 202–3.

TRAFFORD, Edmund

Lieutenant. 1st (Royal) Regiment of Dragoons.
Family Memorial tablet: Manchester Cathedral, Lancashire. (Photograph)

IN PIOUS REGARD / THIS MEMORIAL IS RAISED TO THE MEMORY OF / ELIZABETH TRAFFORD. / .... / NEAR THIS PLACE, ALSO, REST THE REMAINS, OF LIEUT EDMD TRAFFORD, / OF THE 1ST ROYAL DRAGOONS, WHO DIED 19TH DECR 1813, AGED 27 YEARS. / (VERSE)

Cornet 11 Aug 1808. Lt 25 Aug 1809.

Served in the Peninsula Feb – Oct 1811. Present at Fuentes d'Onoro and El Bodon. At Fuentes d'Onoro 'The Royal Dragoons did magnificently – Lieutenant Trafford headed a timely charge and extricated Capt. Belli's squadron of the 16th who were in difficulties near Pozo Bello.' (Atkinson, C. T., *History of the Royal Dragoons 1661–1934*). Died in Manchester 19 Dec 1813.

TRANT, Sir Nicholas

Captain. Royal Staff Corps.
Monument: St Mary's Church, Great Baddow, near Chelmsford, Essex. (M.I.)

"BENEATH THIS STONE LIE THE MORTAL REMAINS OF / MAJOR GENL SIR NICHOLAS TRANT / BORN AT CORK NOVR 12TH 1768 DIED AT GT BADDOW OCT 16TH 1839 / HAVING ENTERED THE ARMY AT A VERY EARLY AGE / HE SERVED HIS COUNTRY / IN FLANDERS, AT THE CAPTURE OF THE CAPE OF GOOD / HOPE, OF MINORCA 1798, IN EGYPT 1801–2, OF / VIMIERO 1808, WAS MADE BY THE DUKE OF WELLINGTON / GOVERNOR OF OPORTO 1809 AND SUBSEQUENTLY IN / 1810 AT THE HEAD OF AN UNDISCIPLINED FORCE OF / PORTUGUESE HE SURPRISED COIMBRA TOOK / 5000 FRENCH PRISONERS AND IN THE WORDS OF THE / MILITARY HISTORIAN OF THAT WAR BY HIS EXPLOIT AS / DARING AND HEARTY (?) AS ANY PERFORMED BY / PARTIZAN MILITIA BAD GENERALSHIP / AND TOOK HIS PLACE OF ********** AND ITS BASE / AT THE CONCLUSION OF THE WAR. / HE RETIRED FROM PUBLIC LIFE / BUT IT WAS MERCIFULLY GRANTED TO HIM TO END HIS / DAYS WITH THOSE WHOM HE LOVED BEST AND TO CLOSE / A SOLDIER'S ACTIVE LIFE / IN THE INDULGENCE OF A WARM AFFECTIONATE HEART / IN THE OFFICE OF AN UNBOUNDED GENEROSITY / AND IN THE DYING PEACE OF HUMANITY / AND CHRISTIAN HOPE."

Ensign Royal Staff Corps 25 Dec 1803. Lt 28 Nov 1805. Capt 1 Jun 1809. Bt Major 6 Jun 1815. Portuguese Army: Capt 25 Oct 1814. Brigadier General.

Served in the Peninsula Aug 1808 – Jan 1809 (on Staff as AQMG) and with the Portuguese Army Apr 1809–1813. Present at Rolica, Vimeiro (commanded the Portuguese at Rolica and Vimeiro), Corunna, Douro, Coimbra (captured the whole garrison with his corps of 2,000 militia, taking 5,000 French prisoners). Commandant at Oporto Mar 1810 – May 1812. Also served in Flanders 1792–1794 (Volunteer on Staff of the Duke of Brunswick 1792 and with Duke of York in Flanders 1794), Minorca 1796, Egypt 1801 and Cape of Good Hope 1805. Half pay 25 Dec 1816. Rose to the rank of Brigadier General in the Portuguese Army. KTS. Died 16 Oct 1839 aged 70.

REFERENCE: United Service Journal, Jan 1840, pp. 99–100. Gentleman's Magazine, Dec 1839, p. 653.

TRAVERS, Robert

Lieutenant Colonel. 10th (North Lincolnshire) Regiment of Foot.

Memorial tablet and window: St Finbarr's (Protestant) Cathedral, Cork, Ireland. (Photograph)

TO THE MEMORY OF / MAJOR GENERAL SIR ROBERT TRAVERS KCB KCMG & KCFM / AND HARRIETTE LETITIA HIS WIFE / THIS TABLET IS ERECTED BY THEIR CHILDREN IN TESTIMONY / OF THE GRATEFUL AND AFFECTIONATE REGARD IN WHICH THEIR / HONOURED NAMES ARE HELD. / SIR ROBERT TRAVERS ENTERED THE MILITARY SERVICE OF HIS / COUNTRY AD 1793, AND FROM THAT PERIOD UNTIL THE GENERAL PEACE IN 1815 / HE WAS CONSTANTLY EMPLOYED ON ACTIVE SERVICE IN ALL PARTS / OF THE GLOBE. ON FOUR DIFFERENT OCCASIONS HE WAS WOUNDED, / FIRST, WHILE SERVING (BEING THEN A CAPTAIN IN THE LINE) / AS A VOLUNTEER WITH THE SLIGO MILITIA IN THE IRISH REBELLION 1798; / AGAIN IN 1799 DURING THE CAMPAIGN IN HOLLAND / WHILE LEADING A COMPANY OF THE 79TH REGT. IN THE ATTACK ON FERROL. / IN 1800 HE RECEIVED A DANGEROUS WOUND IN THE HEAD / AND HE WAS WOUNDED AGAIN ON THE ATTACK ON BUENOS ARIES / IN 1807. HIS GALLANTRY AT THE / BATTLES OF ROLEIA AND VIMIERA / IN COMMAND OF THE 95TH RIFLE REGT, WAS ON THE RECOMMENDATION / OF THE DUKE OF WELLINGTON, REWARDED WITH THE LT COLONELCY / OF THE 10TH REGT OF FOOT AT THE HEAD OF WHICH CORPS HE WAS AGAIN / DISTINGUISHED FOR THE MASTERLY MANNER IN WHICH HE COVERED / THE RETREAT OF LORD WILLIAM BENTINCK'S ARMY IN THE FACE OF / A VASTLY SUPERIOR FORCE UNDER MARSHAL SUCHET. / HE WAS APPOINTED IN 1818 THE RESIDENT COMMANDANT OF CEPHALONIA AND ON / LEAVING THAT ISLAND, THE INHABITANTS PRESENTED HIM WITH A SWORD AND / MEDAL VALUE £300 IN TESTIMONY OF THEIR RESPECT AND ESTEEM. / THIS DISTINGUISHED SOLDIER WAS IN THE 64TH YEAR OF HIS HONOURABLE LIFE / ABRUPTLY TAKEN FROM HIS YOUNG AND NUMEROUS FAMILY, HAVING SURVIVED / BUT A FEW DAYS THE INJURIES RECEIVED IN A FALL FROM HIS HORSE / IN THE STREETS OF HIS NATIVE CITY. HE DIED DEC 25TH 1834. / THIS DEEP AND SUDDEN BEREAVEMENT (ITS FIRST STUNNING SHOCK RECOVERED) / DID BUT SERVE TO RENDER MORE EMINENTLY CONSPICUOUS, / THE VIRTUES AND MARKED ENERGY OF MIND OF HIS AFFLICTED LADY. / "HER CHILDREN RISE UP AND CALL HER BLESSED" PROV CHAP 31 V24 / SHE DEPARTED THIS LIFE 24TH MAY 1847, AND HER MORTAL REMAINS / TOGETHER WITH THOSE OF HER LAMENTED HUSBAND / REST IN THE FAMILY VAULT BENEATH THIS CATHEDRAL.

Ensign 85th Foot 19 May 1793. Lt 112th Foot 21 Jul 1794. Capt 1 Sep 1795. Capt 79th Foot 3 Jul 1799. Capt 95th Foot 25 Aug 1800. Major 4 May 1805. Lt Colonel 8th Garrison Battalion 22 Dec 1808. Lt Colonel 10th Foot 15 Feb 1810. Bt Colonel 4 Jun 1814. Major General 27 May 1825.

Served in the Peninsula with 95th Foot Aug 1808 and 10th Foot Aug 1812 – Dec 1813. Present at Obidos, Rolica, Vimeiro (Mentioned in Despatches), retreat from Sahagun, Alicante, Castalla, Ordal and Genoa (commanded Calabrian and Greek Corps). Gold Medal for Rolica and Vimeiro. CB. KCMG. Knight Commander of St Ferdinand and Merit. One of eight officers chosen by Sir John Moore to command one of the light companies of his newly formed 95th Regiment in 1800. Also served in Ireland 1798 (wounded

in the Irish Rebellion), the Helder 1799 with 79th Foot (present at Egmont-op-Zee where he was wounded), Ferrol 1800 (severely wounded, lost an eye and awarded pension of £300 per annum), Hanover 1805, Buenos Ayres 1807 (wounded), the Mediterranean 1810 and Ionian Islands 1819–1825 (Inspecting Officer). Retired in 1831. Died 24 Dec 1834 as a result of a fall from his horse.
Reference: Gentleman's Magazine, May 1835, p. 543. United Service Journal, Feb 1835, p. 253.

TRELAWNY, Harry Brereton
Lieutenant and Captain. 1st Regiment of Foot Guards.
Memorial: Royal Military Chapel, Wellington Barracks, London. (M.I.) (Destroyed by a Flying Bomb 1944)

"HARRY BRERETON TRELAWNY. / 1ST GUARDS, 1809–21. DIED, 1869. / "PENINSULA," 1811–12–13. "HOLLAND," 1814. WOUNDED AT BERGEN-OP-ZOOM, 1814."

Ensign 14 Sep 1809. Lt and Capt 7 Jul 1813.
Served in the Peninsula with 2nd Battalion Mar 1810 – May 1811 and 1st Battalion Sep 1812 – Jul 1813. Present at Cadiz and Barrosa. Also served in the Netherlands 1814–1815 (present at Bergen-op-Zoom where he was severely wounded). Retired 15 Mar 1821. MGS medal for Barrosa.

TRENCH, Hon. Sir Robert Le Poer
Lieutenant Colonel. 74th (Highland) Regiment of Foot.
Memorial tablet: St Mary's Church, Cheltenham, Gloucestershire. (North transept). (Photograph)

IN MEMORY OF / COL THE HONBLE SIR ROBT LE POER TRENCH KCB AND KTS / AND LIEUT COLONEL 74TH REGT. / THIS MONUMENT HAS BEEN ERECTED BY HIS BROTHER / RICHARD EARL OF CLANCARTY GCB / HE WAS BORN JULY 28TH 1782 AND DIED MARCH 14TH 1823. / OF THE 40 YEARS OF LIFE, / 23 WERE DEVOTED TO THE MILITARY PROFESSION. / HE COMMANDED THE 74TH REGT IN THE PENINSULAR WAR / DURING 5 YEARS AND IN EIGHT GENERAL ENGAGEMENTS. / IN 1818 HE ACCOMPANIED HIS REGT / TO NEW BRUNSWICK IN NORTH AMERICA, / WHERE THE SEVERITY OF THE CLIMATE, / ACTING ON A CONSTITUTION IMPAIRED BY / PREVIOUS HARDSHIP, / OBLIGED HIM TO RETURN TO ENGLAND IN 1821 / WHERE HE CLOSED HIS ACTIVE AND USEFUL LIFE. / HIS EXCELLENCE AS A FATHER, A HUSBAND, & A CHRISTIAN, / IS DEEPLY ENGRAVEN / ON THE MINDS OF HIS SURVIVING FAMILY & FRIENDS; / BUT IT IS THEIR WISH / THAT THE SOLDIER WHO GIVES THE TRIBUTE OF A TEAR / TO DEPARTED WORTH, / SHOULD KNOW THE PRINCIPLE THAT MADE HIM / VICTORIOUS IN DEATH. / "CHRIST CRUCIFIED" / WAS THE GREAT OBJECT OF HIS DEPENDENCE. / HE TRUSTED IN HIM ALONE FOR SALVATION / AN ENCREASED ATTACHMENT / TO THE DUTIES OF HIS PROFESSION, / AND AN ANXIETY FOR THE WELFARE, / BOTH SPIRITUAL AND TEMPORAL, / OF ALL UNDER HIS COMMAND, / MADE IT EVIDENT DURING THE LAST 5 YEARS THAT / "THE LOVE OF CHRIST CONSTRAINED HIM" / TO LIVE NOT UNTO HIMSELF BUT TO THE GLORY OF GOD; / AND WHEN DEATH APPROACHED HE WAS FOUND READY. / LET IT BE REMEMBERED THAT / OF ALL THE HONORS COMMEMORATED / ON THIS TABLET, / THAT OF A TRUE BELIEVER IN JESUS CHRIST / IS THE ONLY ONE / OF IMPORTANCE TO HIM NOW. / PYRENEES FUENTES D'ONOR SALAMANCA TOULOUSE / BADAJOZ VITTORIA NIVELLE BUSACO

Memorial tablet on vault: St Mary's Church, Cheltenham, Gloucestershire. (M.I.)

"WITHIN THIS VAULT LIE THE MORTAL REMAINS OF COLONEL THE HONORABLE SIR ROBERT LE POER TRENCH, KCB., YOUNGEST SON OF THE LATE EARL OF CLANCARTY, LT COL, OF THE 74TH REGT. ...."

Ensign 27th Foot 30 Oct 1799. Lt 67th Foot 9 Dec 1800. Capt 93rd Foot 25 May 1803. Major 96th Foot 25 Oct 1806. Lt Colonel 74th Foot 21 Sep 1809. Bt Colonel 4 Jun 1811.

Served in the Peninsula Feb 1810 – Apr 1814. Present at Busaco (Mentioned in Despatches), Casal Nova, Foz d'Arouce (Mentioned in Despatches), Fuentes d'Onoro, second siege of Badajoz, El Bodon (Mentioned in Despatches), Badajoz (severely wounded and Mentioned in Despatches), Salamanca, Vittoria, Pyrenees (wounded and Mentioned in Despatches), Nivelle, Nive, Vic Bigorre, Tarbes and Toulouse. Gold Cross for Busaco, Fuentes d'Onoro, Badajoz, Salamanca, Vittoria, Pyrenees, Nivelle and Toulouse. KCB and KTS. Also served in Canada 1818–1821. Commanded the 74th Foot from 1809–1823.

TRENCH, Samuel
Lieutenant. Royal Engineers.
Named on the Regimental Memorial: Rochester Cathedral, Rochester, Kent. (Photograph)

2nd Lt 10 May 1808. 1st Lt 24 Jun 1809.

Served in the Peninsula 1810–1811. Present at the Lines of Torres Vedras, Fuentes d'Onoro (where he was the only Engineer present) and Almeida May 1811. After the battle of Fuentes d'Onoro he was sent to Almeida to assess the damage caused by the French explosion. It was decided to destroy the remaining works as it would take longer to repair them. Trench was severely wounded when destroying the works due to lack of training of the infantry under him. Died 10 Jun 1811. Also served at Walcheren 1809.

TRESIDDER, Samuel
Lieutenant. 60th (Royal American) Regiment of Foot.
Gravestone: Old Lancer Lines Cemetery, Secunderabad, India. (M.I.)

"SACRED TO THE MEMORY OF SAML. TRESIDDER LIEUT H. M. 30TH REGT WHO DEPARTED THIS LIFE, 3RD DEC 1824, AGED 30 YEARS."

Lt Royal Cornwall Militia. Ensign 29th Foot 19 May 1812. Lt 60th Foot 6 Nov 1813. Adjutant 9 Jun 1814. Lt 30th Foot 25 Mar 1824

Served in the Peninsula with 29th Foot Feb – Dec 1813 and 8/60th Foot Jan – Apr 1814. Present at Cadiz. Half pay 25 Dec 1818. Joined the 30th Foot in India in 1824 where he died 3 Dec 1824.

TREVEVAN, Richard
Sergeant. 51st (2nd Yorkshire West Riding) Light Infantry.
Named on the Regimental Memorial: KOYLI Chapel, York Minster, Yorkshire. (Photograph)

Served in the Peninsula where he was killed.

TREVILIAN, Maurice Cely
Lieutenant. 1st (Royal) Regiment of Dragoons.
Memorial tablet: St Peter and St Paul's Church, Kilmersdon, Somerset. (Photograph)

I. M. / MAURICE CELY TREVILIAN, / OF MIDELNEY J.P. / LATE OF HM 14TH REGIMENT OF DRAGOONS, / AND SOMETIME RESIDING AT / NEWBERRY HOUSE IN THIS PARISH. / HE DIED AT PARKLANDS GLOUCESTERSHIRE, / ON THE 26TH DAY OF FEBRUARY AD 1861. / AET 64. / AND RESTS BY THE SIDE / OF HIS DEARLY BELOVED SON. / NEAR THE N.E. ANGLE OF THIS CHURCH.

At the bottom of the memorial is a bronze casting of a Military General Service Medal with a bar for Toulouse and the words: M. C. Trevilian, Lieut 1st Dragoons.

Memorial tablet: St Charetine's Church, Drayton, Somerset. (Photograph)

ANIMÆ / INNOCENTISSIMÆ DESIDERATISSIMÆ / CHARLOTTÆ / DIE XXVII^{MO} SEPT A.D. MDCCCLXXIV. / ÆATIS SUAÆ ANNO LXIX^{MO} / REVOCATÆ / CUJUS EXUVIAS JUXTA MARITUM / MAURICIUM CELY TREVILIAN / ET FILIUM PRIMOGENITUM / ANTE ECCLESIAM KILMERSDONENSEM / DEPOSUIMUS / FILII ET FILIA. / VERSE

Cornet 4 Mar 1813. Lt 30 Sep 1813. Capt 14th Lt Dragoons 13 Sep 1821.

Served in the Peninsula Mar – Apr 1814. Present at Toulouse. MGS medal for Toulouse. Half pay 1821. Justice of the Peace.

TRIBE, Richard

Captain. 82nd (Prince of Wales's Volunteers) Regiment of Foot.
Headstone: Trafalgar Cemetery, Gibraltar. (Grave number 139). (Photograph)

THIS STONE IS ERECTED / TO THE MEMORY OF / RICHARD TRIBE ESQ^{R} / CAPTAIN IN THE 82ND REG^{T} OF FOOT, / WHO DIED AT GIBRALTAR / ON THE 25TH MAY 1811 / AGED 30 YEARS.

Lt Devon and Cornwall Fencibles 30 May 1795. Ensign 82nd Foot 5 Dec 1795. Lt 27 Oct 1798. Capt 15 Aug 1804.

Served in the Peninsula Aug 1808 – Jan 1809. Present at Rolica, Vimeiro and Corunna. Also served at Walcheren 1809.

TRODT, F. van

2nd Lieutenant. 2nd Nassau Regiment, Dutch Infantry.
Named on the Memorial to Dutch officers killed at Waterloo: St Joseph's Church, Waterloo. (Photograph)

TROWARD, Thomas

Lieutenant. 51st (2nd Yorkshire West Riding) Light Infantry.
Grave: Kensal Green Cemetery, London. (Inscription not recorded) (4982/161/RS)

Ensign 29 Apr 1813. Lt 29 Sep 1814.

Served in the Peninsula Mar – Apr 1814. Present at Bordeaux. Present at Waterloo. Half pay 1818. Retired 1829. Died 17 Jun 1859.

TRYON, Charles

Lieutenant Colonel. 88th (Connaught Rangers) Regiment of Foot.
Memorial tablet: Christ Church, Alsager, Cheshire. (Photograph)

SACRED TO THE MEMORY OF / LIEU^{T} COLONEL CHARLES TRYON, 88 REG^{T}. / LATE ASSIS^{T} ADJUTANT GENERAL, TO THE FORCES / IN THE PENINSULA, AND AMERICA; / WHO DEPARTED THIS LIFE AT WHEELOCK, / ON THE 16TH DAY OF MARCH 1826, / SEVERELY LAMENTED. / AGED 41 YEARS. / ERECTED BY HIS AFFECTIONATE WIDOW / MARY ALSAGER TRYON.

Ensign 51st Foot 4 Apr 1800. Lt 81st Foot 12 Aug 1803. Capt 88th Foot 4 Apr 1805. Bt Major 17 Aug 1812. Bt Lt Colonel 26 Aug 1813.

Served in the Peninsula Jan 1810 – Oct 1812, Feb – Oct 1813 and Feb – Apr 1814. (Brigade Major 2 Brigade 4th Division Jun 1810 – Apr 1812, DAAG 4th Division Apr – Oct 1812 and DAAG 6th Division Feb – Oct 1813 and Feb – Apr 1814). Present at Cadiz, Busaco, Albuera, Ciudad Rodrigo, Badajoz, Salamanca (severely wounded) and Pyrenees (AAG). Gold Medal for Pyrenees. Also served in India 1800–1802 and Canada 1814–1815 (AAG to Sir John Kempt). Half pay 25 Oct 1821.

TUCKER, John Montmorency
Captain. 27th (Inniskilling) Regiment of Foot.
Buried in St Botolph's Churchyard, Northfleet, Kent. (No longer extant). (Burial register)

Lt Jul 1800. Capt 3 Mar 1808. Capt 8th Foot 23 May 1816.
Served in the Peninsula attached to the Spanish Army Aug 1810–1812. With 2/27th Foot Mar – Jul 1813. Present at Cadiz, Barrosa, Castalla and Tarragona. Present at Waterloo where he was wounded. Also served in Egypt 1801 and Sicily 1806 (present at Maida). MGS medal for Egypt, Maida and Barrosa. Author of *Life of the Duke of Wellington,* published in 1880 after his death, *Life and naval memoirs of Lord Nelson,* 1850 and *Tales of the camp and cabinet*, 1844. Died at Northfleet 22 Feb 1852 aged 71.

TURNER, Sir George
Captain. Royal Artillery.
Obelisk: Belhelvie Old Churchyard, Belhelvie, Aberdeenshire, Scotland. (Photograph)

SACRED / TO THE MEMORY OF / GENERAL SIR GEORGE TURNER KCB / OF MENIE, / COLONEL COMMANDANT 12TH BRIGADE / ROYAL ARTILLERY / BORN MARCH 22ND 1780. / DIED DECEMBER 9TH 1864 / ....

2nd Lt 14 Jan 1797. 1st Lt 16 Jul 1799. 2nd Capt 29 Jul 1804. Capt 8 May 1811. Bt Major 14 Jun 1814. Lt Colonel 25 Nov 1828. Colonel 28 Jun 1838. Major General 11 Nov 1851. Lt General 28 Nov 1854. General 24 Jan 1863.
Served in the Peninsula Dec 1813 – Apr 1814. Present at Orthes (thanked by Picton for his actions in the battle), Tarbes, Vic Bigorre and Toulouse. Gold Medal for Orthes and Toulouse. Awarded Brevet Majority. KCB. Also served in the Cape of Good Hope 1805–1810, Canada 1814–1817 and Gibraltar (Commander of Royal Artillery) 1834–1839. Colonel Commandant Royal Artillery 11 Aug 1852.
REFERENCE: *Gentleman's Magazine, Jan 1865, p. 124.*

TURNER, Michael
Captain. 1st (King's) Dragoon Guards.
Altar tomb: St Mathew's Churchyard, Ipswich, Suffolk. (No longer extant). (M.I.)

"IN MEMORY OF / MICHAEL TURNER ESQ. / LATE MAJOR OF THE 1ST / KING'S DRAGOON GUARDS / SON OF THE LATE NATHANIEL TURNER ESQ. / OF STOKE HALL / IN THE COUNTY. / HE DIED JULY 25TH 1865 / AGED 89 YEARS."

Cornet 26 Dec 1797. Lt 23 Jul 1799. Capt 4 Jul 1805. Major 7 Sep 1815.
Present at Waterloo. After the charge of the regiment, most of the officers had been killed and Capt Turner took command. Shortly afterwards, he too was wounded and awarded a pension of £200 per annum. Retired in 1818.

TURNER, William
Lieutenant. 13th Regiment of Light Dragoons.
Ringed Cross on pedestal: St Peter's Churchyard, Norbury, Staffordshire. (Photograph)

SACRED TO THE MEMORY OF MAJOR WILLIAM TURNER LATE 13TH LIGHT DRAGOONS WHO FOUGHT IN THE PENINSULA & WATERLOO. DIED 7TH DEC 1849 AGED 59 YEARS.

Cornet 23 May 1811. Lt 6 Feb 1812. Capt 3 Nov 1819. Bt Major 10 Jan 1837.
Served in the Peninsula Jun – Oct 1812 and Apr 1814. Present at Toulouse. MGS medal for Toulouse. Present at Waterloo. Half pay 27 Jun 1822.

TURNER, William

Lieutenant. 50th (West Kent) Regiment of Foot.
Grave: Military Burial Ground, Bhowanipore, India. (M.I.).

"TO THE MEMORY OF MAJOR WILLIAM TURNER, H. M. 50TH REGT. WHO DIED WHEN EMBARKED FOR ENGLAND OFF FORT WILLIAM, ON THE 17TH JUNE 1841, AGED 48 YEARS. THIS MONUMENT IS ERECTED BY HIS BROTHER OFFICERS, TO MARK THE ESTEEM FOR THEIR MUCH LAMENTED FRIEND, AND THEIR SENSE OF HIS GALLANT AND DISTINGUISHED SERVICES DURING A PERIOD OF 34 YEARS, IN HOLLAND, PORTUGAL AND SPAIN, AND PARTICULARLY AT THE BATTLES OF ROLEIA, VIMIERA, CORUNNA, THE SIEGE OF FLUSHING AND BATTLES OF FUENTES D'ONOR, ARROYO DE MOLINO, ALMAREZ, ALBA DE TORMES, AND VITTORIA, WHERE HE LOST HIS RIGHT ARM. HE ALSO SERVED FOR MANY LONG YEARS IN THE WEST INDIES AND NEW SOUTH WALES".

Ensign 9 Apr 1807. Lt 26 Aug 1808. Capt 4 Nov 1819. Bt Major 10 Jan 1837.

Served in the Peninsula Aug 1808 – Jan 1809 and Sep 1810 – Sep 1813. Present at Rolica, Vimeiro, Corunna, Fuentes d'Onoro, Arroyo dos Molinos, Almarez, Alba de Tormes, and Vittoria (severely wounded and his right arm amputated. Awarded a pension of £70 per annum). Also served at Walcheren 1809 (present at the the siege of Flushing), West Indies 1819–1827, Australia 1834 and India 1840 where he died in 1841.

TURNER, William Parks

Assistant Surgeon. 95th Regiment of Foot.
Family Memorial tablet: St Mary the Virgin, Wingham, Kent. (Photograph)

SACRED TO THE MEMORY OF / ………………. / WILLIAM PARKS TURNER, / SURGEON H.M. 95TH REGIMENT. DIED 1809 AGED 26. / ……………….

Asst Surgeon 95th Foot 28 Nov 1805.

Served in the Peninsula with 2/95th Nov 1808 – Jan 1809.
Present at Vigo and Corunna where he was severely wounded and died of his wounds 15 Feb 1809.

TURNOR, William

Captain. 14th (Buckinghamshire) Regiment of Foot.
Ledger stone: Kensal Green Cemetery, London. (Inscription illegible) (12101/123/4). (Photograph)

Ensign 15 Aug 1804. Lt 23 May 1805. Adjutant 1806. Capt 15 Aug 1811. Major 19 Dec 1826. Lt Colonel 22 Nov 1836. Major General 20 Jun 1854.

Served in the Peninsula Nov 1808 – Jan 1809. Present at Corunna. Present at Waterloo, siege of Cambrai and with the Army of Occupation. Also served at Hanover 1805–1806 and Walcheren 1809 (present at the siege of Flushing). MGS medal for Corunna. Died 12 Dec 1860.

TURTON, Richard

Captain. 40th (2nd Somersetshire) Regiment of Foot.
Family Memorial tablet: St Mary and St Nicholas's Church, Beaumaris, Anglesey, Wales. (Photograph)

SACRED TO THE MEMORY OF / RICHARD TURTON, / SON OF W H TURTON ESQRE OF BEAUMARIS, AND BARBARA HIS WIFE. / MAJOR IN HIS MAJESTY'S 40TH REGIMENT OF FOOT, WHO / AFTER AN ACTIVE SERVICE OF 27 YEARS IN EVERY / QUARTER OF THE GLOBE, FELL A VICTIM TO THE CLIMATE / OF INDIA, AND DIED ON HIS PASSAGE HOME FROM BOMBAY / ON THE 22ND OF MAY 1835, AGED 42 YEARS. / (VERSE) / ……………….

Ensign 26 Sep 1801. Lt 30 Jul 1803. Capt 10 Feb 1808. Bt Major 27 May 1825 Major 40th Foot 25 Jun 1827.

Served in the Peninsula Oct 1812 – Apr 1814. Present at Vittoria, Pyrenees, Bidassoa, Nivelle, Nive, Orthes and Toulouse (wounded). Also served in Australia 1823 and India 1829. Returned to England in May 1835 but died on his way home. Brother of Lt William Turton 40th Foot killed at San Sebastian.

TURTON, William

Lieutenant. 40th (2nd Somersetshire) Regiment of Foot.

Family Memorial tablet: St Mary and St Nicholas's Church, Beaumaris, Anglesey, Wales. (Photograph)

………………. / ALSO OF WILLIAM HIS ONLY BROTHER / A LIEUTENANT IN THE SAME REGIMENT WHO AFTER / BEING TWICE SEVERELY WOUNDED: VOLUNTEERING / HIS SERVICES IN THE FORLORN HOPE AT THE SIEGE OF / SAN SEBASTIAN FELL IN THE MOMENT OF VICTORY, / ON THE 2ND OF SEPTR 1813, AGED 21 YEARS. / THIS TABLET IS ERECTED BY CATHARINE THE AFFLICTED / WIDOW OF RICHARD TURTON, AND THE BEREAVED PARENTS / AS A TRIBUTE OF AFFECTION TO THEIR MEMORY.

Ensign Bewdly Volunteers 19 Oct 1806. Ensign 40th Foot 18 Apr 1807. Lt 8 Dec 1808.

Served in the Peninsula 1811–1813. Present at Badajoz (severely wounded), Salamanca (wounded), Vittoria and San Sebastian, where he volunteered for the Forlorn Hope and was killed 2 Sep 1813 aged 21 years. Brother of Capt Richard Turton 40th Foot.

Reference: Gentleman's Magazine, 1813, Supplement to Part 2, p. 699.

TWEEDIE, Michael

1st Lieutenant. Royal Artillery.

Tomb: St Mary the Virgin Churchyard, Rolvenden, Kent. (Beneath east window of South Chancel). (M.I.)

"MICHAEL TWEEDIE, CAPTAIN ROYAL ARTILLERY AND JP FOR KENT, DIED 3 FEB 1874, AGED 82."

Memorial window: St Mary the Virgin's Church, Rolvenden, Kent. (Photograph)

IN MEMORY OF CAPTAIN MICHAEL TWEEDIE, ROYAL ARTILL- / ERY, JP OF RAWLINSON, ROLVENDEN, FIFTH SON OF ALEXANDER / TWEEDIE OF QUARTER, PEEBLESSHIRE. BORN 11TH NOV 1791, / DIED 3RD FEB 1874. …………… HE SERVED UNDER WELLINGTON / IN SPAIN, FRANCE & ITALY.

Named on a Cross on stepped base to his son Alexander Tweedie: St Mary the Virgin Churchyard, Rolvenden, Kent. (Photograph)

………………. / ………………. THE LATE CAPTAIN MICHAEL TWEEDIE / OF RAWLINSON, J.P.

2nd Lt 1 May 1809. 1st Lt 17 Jul 1812. Capt 22 Jul 1830.

Served in the Peninsula Dec 1813 – Apr 1814. Present at Toulouse. Also served in Sicily Jul 1810 – May 1813, Marseilles May – Sep 1815, Genoa Oct 1815 – Feb 1816 and the Ionian Islands Aug 1816 – Dec 1822. MGS medal for Toulouse. Half pay 17 Dec 1833. Justice of the Peace for Kent.

TWINBERROW, Ralph John

Lieutenant. 44th (East Essex) Regiment of Foot.

Memorial tablet: North Park Street Burial Ground, Calcutta, India. (Burial Ground is no longer extant, having been redeveloped and built over). (M.I.)

"TO THE MEMORY OF / LIEUTENANT RALPH JOHN TWINBERROW, / H M 44TH REGT. WHO DIED 16TH NOV 1822"

Ensign 1 Oct 1807. Lt 30 Mar 1809.

Served in the Peninsula Apr 1810 – Jun 1813. Present at Cadiz (Fort Matagorda), Sabugal, Badajoz, Salamanca and retreat from Burgos (present at Villa Muriel). Present at Waterloo in Capt Mildmay Fane's Company. Also served in the Netherlands 1814–1815 (taken prisoner at Bergen-op-Zoom) and India 1822 where he died in the same year.

TWINING, William

Assistant Surgeon. Medical Department.
Tombstone: South Park Street Burial Ground, Calcutta, India. (M.I.)

"TO THE MEMORY OF WILLIAM TWINING, ESQ. / MEMBER OF THE ROYAL COLLEGE OF SURGEONS / IN LONDON, SURGEON IN THE SERVICE OF THE H. E. I. C. / COMPANY, BENGAL ESTABLISHMENT, FIRST PERMA- / NENT ASSISTANT SURGEON TO THE PRESIDENCY / GENERAL HOSPITAL AND SECRETARY TO THE MEDICAL / AND PHYSICAL SOCIETY OF CALCUTTA. / THIS MONUMENT IS ERECTED BY HIS PROFESSIONAL / BRETHREN IN INDIA TO MARK THE HIGH SENSE / WHICH THEY ENTERTAINED OF HIS CHARACTER AND OF HIS / EMINENT SERVICE, WHICH HE RENDERED IN THE CAUSE / OF MEDICAL IMPROVEMENT AND RESEARCH / IN THAT COUNTRY. / BORN A.D. 1790 DIED AT CALCUTTA 25TH AUGUST 1835, AGED 45 YEARS."

Memorial tablet: St John's Church, Calcutta, India. (Photograph)

IN GRATEFUL RECOGNITION / OF BENEFITS DERIVED FROM / THE SUCCESSFUL APPLICATION / OF PROFESSIONAL ABILITY: / AND / IN TESTIMONY OF RESPECT AND ESTEEM / FOR / MODEST WORTH AND MATURE PHILANTHROPY: / THIS TABLET, / ERECTED BY HIS FRIENDS AND PATIENTS, / IS CONSECRATED TO THE MEMORY OF / WILLIAM TWINING /. C. R. C. I. S. / OB. AUG 25. 1835 / AET: 45.

Hospital Mate 6 Feb 1812. Asst Surgeon Staff 10 Mar 1814. Asst Surgeon HEICS Bengal 1824.

Present at Waterloo. Became Surgeon to Lord Hill's family in 1815 and Surgeon to Sir Edward Paget in 1823. Accompanied him to India when Sir Edward was appointed to command the Indian Army. Joined the H.E.I.C.S. 1824 and still retained his rank in the British army but had to resign in 1830. Worked in the General Hospital in Calcutta but soon developed an extensive medical practice. Author of *Diseases in Bengal*, 1823, *Diseases of the Spleen*, 1828 and *Epidemic Cholera*, 1833.
Reference: Dictionary of National Biography. Gentleman's Magazine, Apr 1836, p. 445.

TYLDEN, Sir John Maxwell

Captain. 43rd (Monmouthshire) Light Infantry Regiment of Foot.
Memorial tablet: St Mary and the Holy Cross Church, Milstead, Kent. (Photograph)

IN THE / FAMILY VAULT / OUTSIDE THIS CHANCEL / ARE LAID THE MORTAL REMAINS OF / LIEUTENANT COLONEL / JOHN MAXWELL TYLDEN KNT FRS / ELDEST SON OF RICHARD TYLDEN ESQR / OF THE MANOR HOUSE IN THIS PARISH / BY JANE HIS SECOND WIFE. / BORN 25TH SEPTEMBER 1787. / DIED 18TH MAY 1866. / LEAVING ISSUE BY HIS FIRST WIFE / AN ONLY CHILD, ELIZABETH JANE, WIFE / OF CHARLES TYLDEN WRIGHT ESQR. / HE SERVED HIS COUNTRY WITH / DISTINCTION IN H.M. 43RD & 32ND REGT / IN THE PENINSULA, SOUTH OF FRANCE, / INDIA, NORTH & SOUTH AMERICA. / HE WAS MAJOR OF BRIGADE AT THE / CAPTURE OF MONTE VIDEO: / MILITARY SECRETARY TO HIS UNCLE / SIR SAML AUCHMUTY

G.C.B. AT THE / CAPTURE OF JAVA AND ASSIST ADJT GENL / AT THE ATTACK ON NEW ORLEANS. / IN 1826 HE RETIRED WHEN IN COMMAND / OF THE 32ND REGT / ....

Ensign 27 Aug 1804. Lt 23 Nov 1804. Capt 28 Sep 1809. Bt Major 19 Dec 1811. Major 52nd Foot 16 Jul 1818. Bt Lt Colonel 12 Aug 1819.

Served in the Peninsula with 1/43rd Oct 1808 – Jan 1809, Jul 1809 – Mar 1810 and Nov 1813 – Jul 1814 (attached to 52nd Foot Feb – Apr 1814). Present at Vigo, Nive, Orthes, Tarbes and Toulouse. Also served in South America 1807 (present at Montevideo and Buenos Ayres as Brigade Major to Sir Samuel Auchmuty), India 1810–1812 (served as Samuel Auchmuty's Secretary in the expedition to Java 1811. Present at the assault and Capture of Cornelius – awarded Bt Majority) and North America 1814–1815 (AAG – present at New Orleans). MGS medal for Java, Nive, Orthes and Toulouse. Knighted in 1812 when he stood proxy for Sir Samuel Auchmuty at the installation of Knights of Bath in 1812. Nephew of Sir Samuel Auchmuty. Magistrate. Deputy Lieutenant 1852. His younger brother Colonel Sir William Burton Tylden died in the Crimea in 1854.

REFERENCE: *Dictionary of National Biography. Royal Military Calendar, Vol. 5, pp. 180–1. Oxfordshire Light Infantry Chronicle, 1898, pp. 113–14.*

TYLER, John

Captain. 93rd Regiment of Foot.

Memorial tablet: St Paul's Church, Bridgetown, Barbados, West Indies. (Photograph)

SALAMANCA, ROLEIA, VIMIERA, / TORRES – VEDRAS, BUSACO, OPORTO, TALAVERA, / REDINHA, CASAL NOVA, CIUDAD-RODRIGO, / FOZ D'ARONCE, SABUGAL, BADAJOS, FUENTE-GUINALDO, / FUENTES D'ONOR, EL BODON, PYRENEES, / ALDEA DA PONTE, VITTORIA, LA BASTIDE, ORTHES, / VIC BIGORRE, / QUATRE BRAS, / TOULOUSE, WATERLOO. / SACRED / TO THE MEMORY OF / LIEUT COL: JOHN TYLER, K. H. / DEPUTY QUARTER MASTER GENERAL / IN THE WINDWARD AND LEEWARD COMMAND, / WHO DIED AT BARBADOS, JUNE 2ND 1842. / AGED 51 YEARS. / THIS TABLET IS ERECTED / BY LIEUT GEN: MAISTER AND HIS BROTHER OFFICERS AND FRIENDS / AS A MEMORIAL OF THEIR REGARD FOR THE DEPARTED WHILE LIVING / AND THEIR DEEP REGRET AT HIS LOSS.

Ensign 45th Foot 18 Feb 1808. Lt 28 Dec 1809. Capt 93rd Foot 11 Feb 1814. Bt Major 18 Jun 1815. Capt 97th Foot 27 Apr 1827. Major 18 Dec 1829. Bt Lt Colonel 12 Aug 1834.

Served in the Peninsula Aug 1808 – Apr 1814. (ADC to Lt General Picton Jun 1811 – Nov 1812 and Apr 1813 – Apr 1814). Present at Rolica, Vimeiro, Talavera, Busaco (severely wounded), Redinha, Casal Nova, Foz d'Arouce, Sabugal, Fuentes d'Onoro, second siege of Badajoz, El Bodon, Ciudad Rodrigo, Badajoz, Salamanca, Vittoria, Pyrenees, Nivelle, Nive, Orthes, Vic Bigorre and Toulouse. Present at Quatre Bras and Waterloo (wounded and awarded Bt Majority) where he was again Picton's ADC and was by his side when Picton was killed. Returned to England with Picton's body. KH. Also served in the West Indies (DQMG) and died there 2 Jun 1842.

UNIACKE, John

Captain. 95th Regiment of Foot.

Named on the Rifle Brigade Memorial: Winchester Cathedral, Winchester, Hampshire. (Photograph)

2nd Lt 19 Jul 1804. 1st Lt 9 May 1805. Capt 1 May 1811.

Served in the Peninsula with 1/95th Aug 1808 – Jan 1809, Jul 1809 – Oct 1810, 3/95th Nov 1810 – Jun 1811 and 1/95th Jul 1811 – Jan 1812. Present at Cacabellos, Corunna, Coa, Busaco, Fuentes d'Onoro (severely wounded), Ciudad Rodrigo where he was blown up by a mine which exploded on 12 Jan 1812 and died of his wounds at Gallegos 27 Jan 1812.

REFERENCE: *Urban, Mark, Rifles, 2003.*

UPTON, Hon. Arthur Percy

Captain and Lieutenant Colonel. 1st Regiment of Foot Guards.
Interred in Catacomb B (v57 c7), Kensal Green Cemetery, London.
Memorial: Royal Military Chapel, Wellington Barracks, London. (M.I.) (Destroyed by a Flying Bomb 1944)

"GENERAL THE HONOURABLE ARTHUR PERCY UPTON. / 1ST GUARDS, 1807–21. MAJOR 1ST BATTALION, 1814. / D.D. HIS NEPHEW, GENERAL THE HONOURABLE ARTHUR UPTON, COLD STREAM GUARDS / 1825–55."

Ensign Coldstream Guards 28 Apr 1793. Lt and Capt 2 Dec 1795. Lt Colonel 7th West India Regiment 14 May 1807. Capt and Lt Colonel 1st Foot Guards 21 May 1807. Bt Colonel 4th Jun 1814. First Major 1st Foot Guards 25 Jul 1814. Major General 19 Jul 1821. Lt General 10 Jan 1837. General 11 Nov 1851.

Served in the Peninsula Apr 1811 – Aug 1812 and Nov 1812 – Apr 1814 (AQMG 1st Division). Present at Cadiz, San Munos, Osma, Vittoria (Mentioned in Despatches), Tolosa, Bidassoa, Nivelle, Nive, Adour, St Etienne, Bayonne (Mentioned in Despatches) and Sortie from Bayonne. Gold Medal for Vittoria and Nive. MGS medal for Nivelle. CB. Also served in Flanders 1794–5, the Helder 1799 and Walcheren 1809 (AQMG). Died 22 Jan 1855.
Reference: Gentleman's Magazine, Mar 1855, p. 306.

URMSTON, Lambert Brabazon

Lieutenant. 45th (Nottinghamshire) Regiment of Foot.
Grave: Cemetery, Ambala, India. (M.I.)

"SACRED TO THE MEMORY OF / MAJOR URMSTON HR MS 31ST FOOT / WHO DEPARTED THIS LIFE / THE 26TH OF JUNE 1844 / AGED 50 YEARS. / THIS TOMB IS ERECTED BY HIS BROTHER OFFICERS / TO MARK THEIR ESTEEM."

Ensign 45th Foot 1 Apr 1813. Lt 11 May 1815. Lt 38th Foot 23 Jan 1823. Capt 31st Foot 12 Feb 1828. Bt Major 23 Nov 1841.

Served in the Peninsula Nov 1813 – Apr 1814. Present at Nive, Orthes, Vic Bigorre and Toulouse. Returned with the regiment to Ireland in 1814. Half pay 1817 owing to reductions in the regiment. Also served in India 1823 with 38th Foot (present in Burmese Campaign 1824–1826, Capture of Rangoon, attacks on Kemmerdyne and Kamaroot, battles of Kokein and Pagahm-Mew, Prome, Melloon, Sembike and Napadee) and India 1828 with 31st Foot (present in Afghanistan with General Pollock's Army of Retribution after massacre of Elphinstone's forces in Jan 1842, present at Mazeen, Jugdulluck, Tezin and Kabul). Served in India and Afghanistan until his death in 1844. Educated at Winchester.
Reference: Gentleman's Magazine, Nov 1846, pp. 547–8. United Service Magazine, Oct 1844, p. 318.

URQUHART, Donald

Captain. 84th (York and Lancaster) Regiment of Foot.
Tombstone: Agra Cemetery, India. (M.I.)

"SACRED TO THE MEMORY OF LIEUT COLONEL DONALD URQUHART H. M.'S 39TH REGIMENT WHO DIED AT AGRA ON THE 26TH AUGUST 1844. AGED 63 YEARS AND 11 MONTHS. ERECTED BY THE BROTHER OFFICERS."

Ensign 32nd Foot 25 Mar 1801. Lt York Rangers 17 Sep 1803. Lt 9th Foot 7 Mar 1805. Lt 9th Garrison Battalion 1 Dec 1806. Capt 84th Foot 31 May 1808. Capt 39th Foot 26 May 1825. Bt Major 27 May 1825. Bt Lt Colonel 28 Jun 1838. Major 39th Foot 24 Apr 1839.

Served in the Peninsula Jul 1813 – Apr 1814. Present at Bidassoa, Nivelle, Nive (severely wounded) and

Bayonne. Also served at Walcheren 1809 (present at the siege of Flushing), Australia 1825 and India 1831 (present in Coorg Wars 1834). Died of cholera 1844 after 34 years in the army.

UTTING, Samuel
Sergeant. 51st (2nd Yorkshire West Riding) Light Infantry.
Named on the Regimental Memorial: KOYLI Chapel, York Minster, Yorkshire. (Photograph)

Served in the Peninsula where he was killed.

UXBRIDGE, Lord Henry William Paget, Earl of
Colonel. 7th (Queen's Own) Regiment of Light Dragoons.
Brass Memorial tablet: Lichfield Cathedral, Lichfield, Staffordshire. (Photograph)

IN A VAULT BENEATH THIS PLACE, THE / MORTAL REMAINS OF FIELD MARSHAL / HENRY WILLIAM, FIRST MARQUIS / OF ANGLESEY, K.G., K.C.B. / WERE DEPOSITED MAY 1854.

Column: Plas Newydd, Anglesey, Wales. (Photograph)

THE INHABITANTS OF THE COUNTIES / OF ANGLESEY AND CAERNARVON / HAVE ERECTED THIS COLUMN / IN GRATEFUL COMMEMORATION / OF THE DISTINGUISHED MILITARY ACHIEVEMENTS / OF THEIR COUNTRYMAN / HENRY WILLIAM MARQUIS OF ANGLESEY / THE LEADER OF THE BRITISH CAVALRY IN SPAIN / THROUGHOUT THE ARDUOUS CAMPAIGN OF 1807 / AND THE SECOND IN COMMAND OF THE ARMIES / CONFEDERATED AGAINST FRANCE AT / THE MEMORABLE BATTLE OF WATERLOO / ON THE 18TH OF JUNE 1815.

Welsh Inscription on other side of the base of the column.

Y GOLOFN HON / A GYEODWYD GAN DRIGOLION MON ACARFON / O BARCH TW CYD WLADWR ENWOG / HENRY WILLIAM / ARDALYDD MON / AR ER COFFADWRIAETH / AM ER WROLDEB AI ORCHESTION / ***N F*** EN YMLADD YN HISPAEN / AC YN ENWEDIG / PAN DY WYSODD *** Y FARCH FYDDIN GYFENOL / AR FAES WATERLOO / 18 MEHEFIN 1815

Latin Inscription on other side of the base of the column.

INVICTO ET FORTISSIMO DUCE / HENRICO GULIELMO / MARCHION DE ANGLESEY / POPULARI SUO / OB PLURIMA / TAM IN BELLO HISPANICO / QUAM IN IPSO WATERLOOENSI PROELIO / EGREGIE GESTA / INCOLÆ HUJUSCE INSULE / ET VICINÆ ARVONIENSIS ORE / GRATI ET / TRIUMPHANTES / COLUMNAN HANC / EREXERUNT / AD 1816.

The column (without the statue on top) was finished two years after the battle of Waterloo. The statue was added in 1860 after the death of Uxbridge.

Memorial tablet: Garden of Waterloo Museum, Waterloo. (Photograph)

"HERE LIES THE LEG OF HIS MAJESTY'S ILLUSTRIOUS, BRAVE AND VALIANT / LIEUTENANT GENERAL THE EARL OF UXBRIDGE COMMANDER IN CHIEF OF / THE ENGLISH, BELGIAN AND DUTCH CAVALRY, WOUNDED ON THE 18TH OF / JUNE AT THE MEMORABLE BATTLE OF WATERLOO WHO BY HIS HEROISM / CONTRIBUTED TO THE TRIUMPH OF MANKIND'S CAUSE SO GLORIOUSLY / DECIDED BY THE BRILLIANT VICTORY OF THAT DAY".

"CI EST ENTERRÉE, LA JAMBE DE L'ILLUSTRE, BRAVE ET VALIANT COMTE / D'UXBRIDGE, LIEUTENANT GÉNÉRAL DE S. M. BRITANNIQUE, COMMANDANT / EN CHEF DE LA CAVALERIE ANGLAISE, BELGE ET HOLLANDAISE, BLESSÉ / 18 JUIN A LA MEMORABLE BATAILLE DE WATERLOO , QUI PAR SON / HÉROISME, A CONCOURU AU TRIOMPHE DE LA JUSTE CAUSE DU GENRE HUMAIN GLORIEUSEMENT DECIDÉE PAR L' ÉCLATANTE VICTOIRE DUDIT JOUR"

Lt 7th Foot 11 Mar 1793. Capt 23rd Foot 25 Mar 1793. Major 65th Foot 20 May 1793. Lt Colonel 16th Lt Dragoons 15 Jun 1794. Bt Colonel 30 May 1795. Lt Colonel 7th Lt Dragoons 6 Apr 1797. Colonel 16 May 1801. Major General 29 Apr 1802. Lt General 25 Apr 1808. General 12 Aug 1819. Field Marshal 9 Nov 1846.

Served in the Peninsula Sep 1808 – Jan 1809 (GOC Cavalry). Present at Sahugan and Benevente (Mentioned in Despatches), retreat to Corunna (until he retired with opthalmia). On his return from Corunna Paget left his wife and eloped with Lady Charlotte Wellesley who was married to Wellington's brother Henry. This scandal lasted many months with divorces and re-marriages. Paget went on the ill fated Walcheren expedition but took no further part in the Peninsular campaign as Wellington preferred Stapleton Cotton to lead the cavalry. Present at Waterloo (commanded the Allied cavalry and horse artillery). Not present at Quatre Bras but covered the retreat of the infantry on 17th June. Led the heavy cavalry charge against D'Erlon's infantry. Wounded in the evening of the battle and had his right leg amputated. Gold Medal for Sahagun and Benevente. GCB. GCH. KG. Order of Maria Theresa, Order of St George (2nd class) Russia. Also served in Flanders 1794–1795 (raised 80th Foot from his father's tenants), the Helder 1799 and Walcheren 1809. Became Earl of Uxbridge on the death of his father 1812. Created Marquis of Anglesey 1815. Master of Ordnance 1 Apr 1827 and again 1846–1852. Lord Lieutenant of Ireland 1828. Died 29 Apr 1854. Educated at Westminster. Brother of Colonel Sir Edward Paget 80th Foot.
Reference: Dictionary of National Biography (Under Paget). Royal Military Calendar, Vol. 2, pp. 105–15. (Under Anglesey). Anglesey, George C. H. V. P., One leg: the life and letters of Henry William Paget, 1961. Gentleman's Magazine, Jun 1854, pp. 638–44. (Under Anglesey). Cole, John William, Memoirs of British Generals, Vol. 1, 1856, pp. 107–44. United Service Magazine, May 1854, pp. 159–68. Illustrated London News, 15 Dec 1860. (Description and illustration of statue on top of memorial column).

VACHELL, Frederick
Ensign. Coldstream Regiment of Foot Guards.
Ledger stone: Coldstream Guards Cemetery, St Etienne, Bayonne, France. (Photograph)

F. V.

Named on Memorial Panel VII for the Sortie from Bayonne: Royal Military Chapel, Wellington Barracks, London. (M.I.) (Destroyed by a Flying Bomb 1944)

Named on the Memorial: St Andrew's Church (now Musée Historique), Biarritz, France. (Photograph)

Ensign 52nd Foot 27 Dec 1810. Ensign Coldstream Guards 19 Sep 1811.

Served in the Peninsula with the 1st Battalion Jul 1811 – Apr 1814. Present at Salamanca, Burgos, Nivelle, Nive, Adour and Bayonne where he was severely wounded at the Sortie from Bayonne 14 Apr and died of his wounds 13 May 1814.

VALE, Thomas
Private. 32nd (Cornwall) Regiment of Foot.
Headstone: Old Army Graveyard, Newcastle, Jamaica, West Indies. (M.I.)

"BARRACK SERGT THOS VALE, LATE SERGT 32ND REGT. DIED 26TH JANY 1844, AGED 47 YEARS."

Present at Waterloo in Capt Stopford Cane's Company and at the Capture of Paris. Also served in the West Indies.

VANCE, Richard Young
Staff Surgeon. Medical Department.
Interred in Kensal Green Cemetery, London. (2048/107/RS). (No longer extant)

Hospital Mate 21 Jan 1799. Asst Surgeon 1st West India Regt 12 Jun 1800. Surgeon 7th Foot 9 Jul 1803. Surgeon 10th Foot 1 Oct 1806. Staff Surgeon 1 Jun 1809.

Served in the Peninsula Feb 1812 – Apr 1813 and Oct 1813 – Apr 1814. Present at Cadiz. Also served at Walcheren 1809. Half pay 5 Nov 1814. Died 14 Jun 1839.

VANDELEUR, Sir John Ormsby
Lieutenant Colonel. 19th Regiment of Light Dragoons.
Granite monument: Mount Jerome Cemetery, Dublin, Ireland. (Grave number C65–1328)

Ensign 5th Foot Dec 1781. Lt 67th Foot 1783. Lt 9th Foot 1788. Capt 9 Mar 1792. Capt 8th Lt Dragoons Oct 1792. Major 1 Mar 1794. Lt Colonel 1 Jan 1798. Lt Colonel 19th Lt Dragoons 16 Apr 1807. Bt Colonel 25 Apr 1808. Major General 4 Jun 1811. Lt General 19 Jul 1821. General 10 Jan 1838.

Served in the Peninsula Sep 1811 – Jun 1813 (O/c 2 Brigade Lt Division) and Jul 1813 – Apr 1814 (O/c 'C' Cavalry Brigade). Present at Ciudad Rodrigo (wounded), Salamanca, Vittoria (Mentioned in Despatches) and Nive. Present at Waterloo in command of 4th Brigade of Cavalry (11th, 12th and 16th Lt Dragoons) and at the Capture of Paris. Commanded all British cavalry after Uxbridge was wounded. Gold Cross for Ciudad Rodrigo, Salamanca, Vittoria and Nive. GCB. Knight of 2nd Class of St Vladimir and Commander of Bavarian Order of Maximilian Joseph. Also served in the West Indies 1793, Flanders 1794, Cape of Good Hope 1796, India 1803–1805 (present at Laswareee and Futteghur) and the Netherlands 1814–1815. Colonel 14th Lt Dragoons 28 Oct 1823. Colonel 16th Lt Dragoons 18 Jun 1830. Served in the army for 68 years. Died in Dublin 1 Nov 1848.
Reference: Dictionary of National Biography. Royal Military Calendar, Vol. 3, pp. 149–51. Gentleman's Magazine, Jan 1850, pp. 88–9. Annual Register, 1849, Appx, p. 281.

VAN WYNBERGEN, William
Ritmeister. Light Cavallerie.
Named on the Memorial to Netherlands Light Cavalry Brigade at Waterloo: St Joseph's Church, Waterloo. (Photograph)

VANE, Charles William see STEWART, Charles William Vane

VANE, Walter
Lieutenant and Captain. 1st Regiment of Foot Guards.
Memorial tablet: St Bega's Church, Bassenthwaite, Cumbria. (Photograph)

WALTER VANE / THIS MONUMENT WAS ERECTED BY SIR E. E. VANE, BART. TO THE / MEMORY OF HIS SON WALTER VANE, ESQR LATE CAPTAIN / IN THE 1ST FOOT GUARDS, OR DUKE OF YORK'S REGIMENT. / WHO WAS MORTALLY WOUNDED AT THE BATTLE OF BAYONNE, / ON THE 14TH APRIL 1814, AND DIED ON THE 19TH OF THE / SAME MONTH, IN THE 19TH YEAR OF HIS AGE. / HIS REMAINS WERE INTERRED WITH MILITARY HONOURS, / BETWEEN THE CITY OF BAYONNE AND THE VILLAGE OF BOUCAT, / ALONG WITH MANY

OF HIS BROTHER OFFICERS, / WHO BRAVELY FELL IN THE SERVICE OF HIS COUNTRY / ON THE SAME MEMORABLE OCCASION.

Named on the Memorial: St Andrew's Church (now Musée Historique), Biarritz, France. (Photograph)

Named on Memorial Panel VII for Bayonne: Royal Military Chapel, Wellington Barracks, London. (M.I.) (Destroyed by a Flying Bomb 1944)

Ledger stone: Coldstream Guards Cemetery, St Etienne, Bayonne, France. (Photograph)

W. V.

Ensign 11 Sep 1811. Lt and Capt 15 Mar 1814.

Served in the Peninsula with the 3rd Battalion Mar 1813 – Apr 1814. Present at Bidassoa, Nivelle, Nive, Adour, Bayonne and Sortie from Bayonne (severely wounded 14 Apr and died of his wounds 19 Apr 1814 aged 19 years). Educated at Eton.

VARLEY, Thomas
Quartermaster. Royal Regiment of Horse Guards.
Buried in St George's Chapel, Windsor, Berkshire. (Burial record)

Quartermaster 20 Mar 1806.

Present at Waterloo where he was severely wounded and awarded pension of £50 per annum. Half pay 12 Dec 1822. Military Knight of Windsor 6 Aug 1831. Died at Windsor 25 Mar 1841 aged 69.

VAUGHAN-ARBUCKLE, Benjamin Hutchinson
1st Lieutenant. Royal Artillery.
Grave: St Luke's Churchyard, Charlton, Kent. (Grave number 31). (No longer extant). (M.I.)

"............... ALSO THE ABOVE NAMED BENJAMIN HUTCHINSON VAUGHAN-ARBUCKLE, LIEUTT – GENERAL RA, WHO DIED AT OLD CHARLTON 11 OCTOBER 1874 IN HIS 85TH YEAR."

2nd Lt 4 Oct 1806. 1st Lt 1 Feb 1808. 2nd Capt 29 Jul 1825. Capt 12 Jul 1836. Bt Major 28 Jun 1838. Lt Colonel 1 Apr 1846. Major General 26 Oct 1858. Lt General 24 Aug 1866.

Served in France May 1815 – Nov 1818 (present at the Capture of Paris and with the Army of Occupation). Also served in Malta 1807–1812, Antwerp 1815, Ceylon 1826–1828 and Jamaica 1845–1846. Retired on full pay 7 May 1847.

VEALL, William
Lieutenant. 59th (2nd Nottinghamshire) Regiment of Foot.
Named on the Regimental Memorial monument: Christ Church Churchyard, Tramore, County Waterford, Ireland. (Photograph)

Ensign 20 Feb 1812. Lt 23 Sep 1813.

Served in the Peninsula Sep 1812 – Apr 1814. Present at Cadiz, Vittoria, Nive and Bayonne. Present at Waterloo in reserve at Hal, siege of Cambrai and with the Army of Occupation. Lost in the *Sea Horse* shipwreck off the coast of Ireland 30 Jan 1816 aged 20.
Note: Name recorded on the memorial as William Neale.
Reference: Gentleman's Magazine, Mar 1816, pp. 278–9.

VERE, Charles Broke see BROKE, Charles

VERHELLOW, W. A.

1st Lieutenant. 6th Hussars, Dutch Cavalry.
Named on the Memorial to Dutch officers killed at Waterloo: St Joseph's Church, Waterloo. (Photograph)
Named on the Regimental Memorial to officers of the Dutch 6th Regiment of Hussars killed at Waterloo, St Joseph's Church, Waterloo. (Photograph)

VERLING, James

2nd Assistant Surgeon. Royal Artillery.
Box tomb in railed enclosure: Old Cemetery, Cobh, County Cork, Ireland. (Photograph)

JAMES VERLING M.D. F.R.C.S. / BORN 1787 / DIED AT "BELLAVISTA" COBH 1858 / OFFICIAL SURGEON TO NAPOLEON / ON ST HELENA 1818–1819 / R.I.P.

2nd Asst Surgeon 25 Jan 1810. 1st Asst Surgeon 24 Jun 1815. Surgeon 3 Jul 1827. Senior Surgeon 1 Jan 1843. Deputy Inspector General of Hospitals 1 Apr 1850. Inspector General of Hospitals 22 Feb 1854.

Served in the Peninsula Aug 1811 – Apr 1814. Present at Ciudad Rodrigo, Vittoria, San Sebastian, Bidassoa, Nivelle, Nive, and Bayonne. Also served at St Helena 1815. Succeeded Surgeon Barry O'Meara in medical charge of Napoleon at St Helena in 1818 after O'Meara had quarrelled with Hudson Lowe about his treatment of Napoleon. Verling remained there until 1820. Also served in Malta, Ionian Islands and Nova Scotia. MGS medal for Ciudad Rodrigo, Vittoria, San Sebastian, Nivelle and Nive. MD Edinburgh 1809. Retired on full pay 1 Apr 1854.

VERNER, Edward Donovan

2nd Assistant Surgeon. Ordnance Medical Department.
Interred in Catacomb B (v38 c10), Kensal Green Cemetery, London.

Temporary Asst Surgeon 9 Jun 1813. 2nd Asst Surgeon 29 Nov 1813.

Present at Waterloo. Half pay 30 Mar 1825. Died in London 9 Jul 1861.

VERNER, William

Captain. 7th (Queen's Own) Regiment of Light Dragoons.
Ledger stone: Loughgall Graveyard, Loughgall, County Armagh, Northern Ireland. (Photograph)

HERE LIETH THE BODY / OF / SIR WILLIAM VERNER, / 1ST BARONET OF CHURCHILL. / COLONEL 7TH HUSSARS. / SERVED IN PENINSULAR WAR / AND AT WATERLOO. / M.P. FOR THE COUNTY ARMAGH / 1832 – 1868. / BORN 25TH OCTOBER 1782. / DIED 20TH JANUARY 1871.

Cornet 1 May 1805. Lt 23 Jan 1806. Capt 27 Jul 1808. Bt Major 18 Jun 1815. Lt Colonel 12th Foot 24 Dec 1818.

Served in the Peninsula Nov 1808 – Jan 1809 and Aug 1813 – Apr 1814. Present at Benevente, retreat to Corunna, Nive, Orthes and Toulouse. Present at Waterloo where he was wounded and awarded Bt Majority. Retired from the army 13 May 1826. MGS medal for Benevente, Nive, Orthes and Toulouse. Entered Parliament in 1832. MP for County Armagh for 36 years. Deputy Lieutenant of Tyrone. High Sherriff of Monaghan 1820, Armagh 1821 and Tyrone 1823. KCH 1837.
Note: William Verner's charger *Constantia* is also commemorated with a memorial stone in the Orange Hall, Loughall, Co. Armagh, Northern Ireland.
Reference: Annual Register, 1871, Appx, p. 144. United Service Magazine, 1871, p. 443. Verner, Ruth, Reminiscences of William Verner (1782–1871) 7th Hussars, 1782–1871, Journal of the Society for Army Historical Research, 1965, (Special Publication No. 8).

VERNOR, Robert
Captain. 2nd (Royal North British) Regiment of Dragoons.
Family Memorial tablet: St Michael's Churchyard, Inveresk, Midlothian, Scotland. (Photograph)

SACRED / TO THE MEMORY OF / MAJOR ROBERT VERNOR, / LATE OF THE SCOTS GREYS, IN WHICH / DISTINGUISHED CORPS HE SERVED UPWARDS OF / THIRTY YEARS. DIED 10TH AUGUST 1827, / AGED 64 YEARS. / ....

Lt 28 Nov 1797. Capt 23 Nov 1804. Bt Major 4 Jun 1814.

Present at Waterloo where he was wounded in the cavalry charge and awarded pension of £200 per annum. Retired in 1817.

VETCH, James
2nd Captain. Royal Engineers.
Headstone: Highgate Cemetery London. (West XIV. Grave number 5276). (Seriously eroded and inscription not recorded). (Photograph)

2nd Lt 1 Jul 1807. 1st Lt 1 Mar 1808. 2nd Capt 21 Jul 1813.

Served in the Peninsula Oct 1810 – Apr 1814. Present at Cadiz, Barrosa, Badajoz. MGS medal for Barrosa and Badajoz. Designed British fortifications during the Peninsular War. Appointed to Ordnance Survey 1821. Consulting Engineer to the Admiralty 1846. Fellow of the Royal Geographical Society. Worked on an early Suez Canal scheme. Designed sewers and drainage systems for Leeds, Southwark and Windsor Castle. Appointed Conservator of Harbours 1853. Died 7 Dec 1869.

VEVERS, Charles Nicholas
Lieutenant. 59th (2nd Nottinghamshire) Regiment of Foot.
Memorial tablet: St Helen's Church, Lea, Lincolnshire. (M.I.)

"SACRED / TO THE MEMORY OF / CHARLES NICHOLAS VEVERS, LIEUTENANT / IN THE SECOND BATTN, OF HIS MAJESTY'S / FIFTY NINTH REGT OF FOOT, AND / SON OF THE REVD RICHARD VEVERS AND / THEODOSIA DOROTHY HIS WIFE, DAUGHTER / OF THE LATE REVD. SIR WILLIAM ANDERSON, BARONET / IN THE STORMING OF THE BREACH AT THE / MEMORABLE SIEGE OF ST SEBASTIAN, / ON THE THIRTIETH OF AUGUST 1813, / AMID NUMBERS OF HIS BRAVE AND / HEROIC COMRADES, HE FELL GLORIOUSLY / BUT DEEPLY LAMENTED BY ALL WHO / KNEW HIM, AT THE EARLY AGE OF TWENTY TWO YEARS. / AS A TRIBUTE OF AFFECTION TOWARDS THIS / AMIABLE AND PROMISING YOUTH AND TO / PERPETUATE A REMEMBRANCE OF THE GRIEF / EXPERIENCED BY HIS AFFLICTED PARENTS, AND / OTHER NUMEROUS RELATIVES UPON THE LOSS / THEY SUSTAINED. THIS TABLET IS ERECTED / BY HIS ONLY SURVIVING UNCLE / THE REVD SIR CHARLES ANDERSON, BARONET, / RECTOR OF THIS PARISH"

Ensign 29 Nov 1810. Lt 3 Sep 1812.

Served in the Peninsula Sep 1812 – Aug 1813. Present at Cadiz, Vittoria and San Sebastian where he was killed at the assault on the breach 31 Aug 1813 aged 22.

VICKERS, Gentle
Lieutenant. 95th Regiment of Foot.
Headstone: St Mary Bishophill Senior Churchyard, York, Yorkshire. (Photograph)

IN MEMORY OF / LIEUTENANT GENTLE VICKERS / WHO HAVING BRAVELY FOUGHT WITH THE / DUKE OF WELLINGTON IN SEVERAL / OF HIS ENGAGEMENTS IN SPAIN / AND ALSO AT

THE MEMORABLE BATTLEFIELD / OF WATERLOO, DIED IN THIS CITY, / ON 9TH MAY 1823, AGED 35 YEARS / ....

2nd Lt 4 Oct 1810. Lt 14 May 1813.

Served in the Peninsula with 3/95th Mar 1812 – Mar 1813 and Sep 1813 – Apr 1814. Present at Salamanca, Vittoria, Vera and Bidassoa (severely wounded). Present at Waterloo. Half pay 12 Jun 1817.

VICTOR, James Conway
1st Lieutenant. Royal Engineers.
Family obelisk: Dean Cemetery, Edinburgh, Scotland. (Photograph)

IN MEMORY OF / MAJOR GENERAL / JAMES CONWAY VICTOR. / ROYAL ENGINEERS, / BORN 17TH MARCH 1792. / DIED 4TH FEBRUARY 1864.

2nd Lt I Jun 1810. Lt 1 May 1811. 2nd Capt 19 Jun 1821. Capt 26 Oct 1834. Bt Major 10 Jan 1837. Lt Colonel 9 Apr 1846. Colonel 20 Jun 1854. Major General 13 Dec 1854.

Served in the Peninsula Feb 1813 – Apr 1814. Present at Nive, Orthes and Toulouse. Also served in Tasmania, Australia 1842 (commander of Royal Engineers). Director of Public Works, Roads and Bridges 1843. These responsibilities interfered with his military duties and he refused to do some of the works. Designed various buildings in Hobart including the gaol and Convict hospital. Returned to Edinburgh 1849. MGS medal for Nive, Orthes and Toulouse. Retired on full pay 13 Dec 1854.
Reference: Australian Dictionary of Biography.

VIGOUREUX, Charles Albert
Major. 30th (Cambridgeshire) Regiment of Foot.
Monument: Kensal Green Cemetery, London. (1919/89/RS). (Photograph)

IN MEMORY OF / COLONEL CHARLES / ALBERT VIGOUREUX / CB / LATE OF / THE 45TH REGT OF FOOT / MAJOR GENERAL / IN THE EAST INDIES / AND RECENTLY COMMANDING / THE MYSORE DIVISION / OF THE MADRAS ARMY / WHO AFTER 47 YEARS / SPENT IN THE SERVICE / OF HIS COUNTRY / DEPARTED THE LIFE / AT LONDON / ON THE 24TH FEBRUARY 1841 / AGED 64 YEARS

Ensign 3rd Foot 28 Dec 1793. Lt 19th Foot 17 Mar 1795. Capt 35th Foot 4 Apr 1795. Lt and Capt 1st Foot Guards 20 Dec 1799. Capt 42nd Foot 23 Nov 1804. Capt 6th Foot 16 May 1805. Capt 38th Foot 2 Jul 1807. Bt Major 25 Apr 1808. Major 30th Foot 4 Jun 1813. Bt Lt Colonel 21 Jun 1813. Lt Colonel 45th Foot 20 Dec 1826. Bt Colonel 22 Jul 1830.

Served in the Peninsula with 2/38th Apr 1810 – Jan 1813 and 1/38th Feb – Jun 1813. Present at Busaco, first siege of Badajoz, Fuentes d'Onoro, Badajoz, Castrejon, Salamanca and Vittoria. Gold Medal for Fuentes d'Onoro and Vittoria. CB. Present at Quatre Bras and Waterloo with the 30th Foot commanding the flank battalion of Halkett's Brigade where he was severely wounded, a bullet lodged in his spine which could not be extracted, and he suffered from this for the rest of his life. For his actions at Waterloo, he was gazetted for a second time as CB. Also served in Flanders 1793–1794, Corsica and Elba 1796, the Helder 1799, the Netherlands 1814–1815 (present at the siege of Antwerp), India 1829 (commanded the Mysore Division of the Madras Army) and in the 1st Burmese Campaign. Commanded 45th Foot from 1826–1839.
Reference: Gentleman's Magazine, Apr 1841, p. 441.

VIVIAN, Sir Richard Hussey
Lieutenant Colonel. 7th (Queen's Own) Regiment of Light Dragoons.
Memorial tablet: St Mary's Cathedral, Truro, Cornwall. (Photograph)

IN MEMORY OF L^T. GEN^L. THE RIGHT HON^BLE RICHARD HUSSEY BARON VIVIAN OF GLYNN AND TRURO, / GRAND CROSS OF THE BATH AND OF HANOVER AND KNIGHT OF THE AUSTRIAN ORDER OF MARIA THERESA / AND OF RUSSIAN ORDER OF S^T WLADIMER, BORN IN THIS TOWN JULY 28TH 1775, HE ENTERED THE ARMY IN / JULY 1793, AND IN 1794, AND IN 1795 SERVED AS CAPTAIN IN THE 28TH REGT IN FLANDERS AND HOLLAND / AND UNDER HRH THE DUKE OF YORK. IN 1799 AS A CAPTAIN IN THE 7TH HUSSARS, HE SERVED IN THE EXPEDITION TO THE HELDER. / IN 1808, HE, AS L^T. COL. OF THE 7TH HUSSARS, COMMANDED THAT REG^T IN THE EXPEDITION UNDER SIR JOHN / MOORE; IN 1813. HE AGAIN SERVED IN THE PENINSULA, WITH THE ARMY UNDER THE COMMAND OF LORD / WELLINGTON, AS A COLONEL ON THE STAFF, IN COMMAND OF A BRIGADE OF CAVALRY AND IN 1815, AS A / MAJOR GENERAL, HE COMMANDED A BRIGADE OF CAVALRY AT WATERLOO. HE HAD THE / HONOUR OF BEING APPOINTED ONE OF THE EQUERRIES TO HIS MAJESTY KING GEORGE IV, / AND A GROOM OF THE BED CHAMBER TO HIS MAJESTY KING WILLIAM IV. IN 1841 HE WAS / NAMED TO THE COMMAND OF THE ARMY IN IRELAND AND IN 1835 WAS BROUGHT FROM THERE / AND FILLED THE HIGH OFFICE OF MASTER GENERAL OF ORDNANCE. HE WAS A PRIVY COUNCILLOR / BOTH IN ENGLAND AND IRELAND AND DURING THE TIME HE COMMANDED IN THE LATTER COUNTRY / HE WAS SEVEN TIMES NAMED ONE OF THE LORD JUSTICES. HE SAT IN ALL THE PARLIAMENTS / WITH THE EXCEPTION OF ONE ONLY FROM 1820–1841 (WHEN HE WAS RAISED TO THE PEERAGE). / HAVING BEEN TWICE ELECTED FOR TRURO, TWICE FOR WINDSOR AND ONCE FOR THE EASTERN / DIVISION OF THE COUNTY OF CORNWALL. HIS NOBLENESS OF CHARACTER, HIS CHARITY, / BENEVOLENCE AND INTEGRITY ENDEARED HIM TO ALL WHO KNEW HIM. THE WIDOW / AND THE ORPHAN NEVER APPEALED TO HIM IN VAIN AND THE DESERVING SOLDIER / ALWAYS FOUND IN HIM A FRIEND. HE DIED AT BADEN BADEN ON 20TH AUGUST 1842 / REJOICING IN THE CERTAIN HOPE OF A BLESSED RESURRECTION TO EVERLASTING / LIFE, CONFIDENT IN THE MERITS OF HIS LORD AND SAVIOUR. / AT HIS OWN REQUEST HIS REMAINS WERE PLACED IN THE CHURCH BY THE SIDE OF / HIS BELOVED PARENTS, AND THIS MONUMENT IS ERECTED BY HIS WIDOW AND CHILDREN / WHO MOURN THE LOSS OF THE BEST AND MOST AFFECTIONATE HUSBAND AND FATHER.

Ledger stone: St Mary's Cathedral Churchyard, Truro, Cornwall. (Photograph)

JOHN VIVIAN / DIED 1826 AGED 77 / BETSY VIVIAN / HIS WIFE / DIED 1821 AGED 61 / THOMAS VIVIAN / THEIR SON / DIED 1821 AGED 21 / RICHARD HUSSEY VIVIAN / BARON VIVIAN / THEIR ELDEST SON / DIED 1842 AGED 67

Ensign 20th Foot 31 Jul 1793. Lt in Capt Grey's Independent Company of Foot 26 Oct 1793. Lt 54th Foot 2 Nov 1793. Capt 28th Foot 30 May 1794. Capt 7th Lt Dragoons 14 Aug 1798. Major 9 Mar 1803. Lt Colonel 25th Lt Dragoons 6 Oct 1804. Lt Colonel 7th Lt Dragoons 1 Dec 1804. Bt Colonel 20 Feb 1812. Major General 4 Jun 1814. Lt General 22 Jul 1830.

Served in the Peninsula Nov 1808 – Jan 1809 and Aug 1813 – Apr 1814 (O/c 'D' Cavalry Brigade Nov – Dec 1813 and O/c 'E' Cavalry Brigade Jan – Apr 1814). Present at Sahagun, Benevente, the Corunna campaign, Nive (Mentioned in Despatches), Orthes and Toulouse (severely wounded at the Bridge of Croix d'Orade. Mentioned in Despatches and awarded pension of £300 per annum). Present at Waterloo 17 Jun covering the retreat of infantry from Quatre Bras and 18 Jun in command of 6th Brigade of Cavalry (1st Dragoons, 10th Dragoons and 18th Dragoons). Also served in Flanders 1794–1795 (present at Nimwegen and Gueldermalsen), West Indies Dec 1795, Gibraltar 1796–1798 and the Helder 1799 (present at Bergen and Alkmaar). Gold Medal for Sahagun, Benevente and Orthes. GCB. GCH. Knight of Maria Theresa and Order of St Vladimar 3rd Class. Inspector General of Cavalry 1825–1830. Commander of Forces in Ireland 1831–1836. Master General of Ordnance 4 May 1835. MP for Truro 1820–1825 and Windsor 1826–1831 and later for the Eastern Division of Cornwall. Baronet 19 Jan 1828 and Baron 1841. Colonel 1st Dragoons 20 Jan 1837.

REFERENCE: *Dictionary of National Biography. Vivian, Claud H., Richard Hussey Vivian, first Baron Vivian: a memoir, 1897, reprint 2003. Vivian, R. H., Autobiographical memoir, in W. Scott, Letters addressed to R. Polwhele, edited by R. Polwhele, Dublin, 1832. Vivian, Richard Hussey, The experimental cavalry movements of Lt General Sir H. Vivian, arranged by Sgt Major Francis Haviland, 1831. Farmer, David, The warrior of the west: Richard Hussey Vivian, 2005. United Service Magazine, Sep 1847, pp. 145–6. Gentleman's Magazine, Nov 1842, pp. 543–4. Annual Register, 1842, Appx, pp. 298–9.*

VOIGT, August Wilhelm von
Captain. 8th Line Battalion, King's German Legion.
Named on the Regimental Memorial: La Haye Sainte, Waterloo. (Photograph)
Named on the Waterloo Column, Hanover, Germany. (Photograph)

Lt 13 May 1806. Capt 16 Apr 1809.
Present at Waterloo where he was killed. Also served in the Baltic 1807, Mediterranean 1808–1814 and the Netherlands 1814.

WADDELL, James George
Captain. 39th (Dorsetshire) Regiment of Foot.
Memorial tablet: Dromore Cathedral, County Down, Northern Ireland. (South wall). (Photograph)

SACRED TO THE MEMORY OF / JAMES GEORGE WADDELL ESQRE / OF ISLANDDERRY, / LATE MAJOR IN HER MAJESTY'S 39TH REGT. / DURING A LIFE SPENT / IN THE PATIENT AND UNOBTRUSIVE EXERCISE OF CHRISTIAN KINDNESS, / HE DREW CLOSELY AROUND HIM THE DEEP AND GRATEFUL AFFECTION / OF MANY HEARTS. / A DEVOTED BROTHER, A CHRISTIAN MASTER, A FAITHFUL FRIEND: / HE NEEDS NO MONUMENTAL RECORD OF HIS WORTH TO TESTIFY / HOW MUCH AND TENDERLY HE WAS BELOVED / AND HOW TRULY AND DESERVEDLY HE IS REGRETTED. / WASHED IN THE PRECIOUS BLOOD OF HIS DEAR LORD AND / "KNOWING HIM IN WHOM HE BELIEVED" / HIS CONSTANT DESIRE WAS THAT THOSE AROUND HIM SHOULD PARTICIPATE / IN HIS JOY: / AND HAVING SOUGHT THRO' YEARS OF SUFFERING / AND UNCOMPLAINING SUBMISSION TO HIS WILL / TO ADORN THE DOCTRINE OF GOD HIS SAVIOUR / IN ALL THINGS, / HE FELL ASLEEP IN JESUS / ON THE SIXTH DAY OF DECEMBER 1859, / AGED 77 YEARS. / (VERSE)

Ensign 105th Foot 26 Nov 1794. Lt in Lt Colonel Ward's Regt 20 Dec 1794. Lt 31st Foot 8 Sep 1795. Capt in Lt Colonel Ward's Regt 30 Apr 1796. Capt 46th Foot 9 Dec 1801. Capt 39th Foot 9 Jul 1803. Bt Major 25 Apr 1808.
Served in the Peninsula with 1/39th Oct 1811 – Dec 1812. Resigned 7 Jun 1813.

WADE, Hamlet
Lieutenant Colonel. 95th Regiment of Foot.
Named on the Rifle Brigade Memorial: Winchester Cathedral, Winchester, Hampshire. (Photograph)

Ensign 25th Foot 2 Feb 1791. Lt 25 Apr 1793. Capt 4 Apr 1795. Major 95th Foot 26 Aug 1800. Lt Colonel 6 May 1805. Bt Colonel 4 Jun 1813.
Served in the Peninsula with 2/95th Nov 1808 – Jan 1809, Sep 1812 – Aug 1813 and Feb – Apr 1814. Present at Vigo, San Millan, Vittoria, Orthes, Tarbes and Toulouse. Gold Medal for Vittoria, Orthes and Toulouse. CB. Also served as a Marine in 1792 on board HMS *Bogue* and HMS *Monarch* in the West Indies, Martinique 1795 and Grenada Apr 1795 – Sep 1796 (this long campaign resulted in losing every officer and man in his company apart from one drummer), the Helder 1799, Baltic 1807 and Walcheren 1809. Assisted in the formation of the Rifle Corps at Horsham after serving at the Helder. Retired 21 Sep 1815. Died 13 Feb 1821.

WAINMAN, William
Captain. 14th (Duchess of York's Own) Regiment of Light Dragoons.
Obelisk: Earl Crag, Cowling, Yorkshire. No inscription on obelisk. (Photograph)

Cornet 25 Sep 1806. Lt 1 Dec 1808. Capt 13 Feb 1812.

Served in the Peninsula Dec 1808 – Sep 1811 and Jun 1812 – Apr 1814. Present at Douro, Talavera (severely wounded), Sexmiro, Coa, Busaco, Sobral, Pombal, Redinha, Casal Nova, Foz d'Arouce, Sabugal, Fuentes d'Onoro, El Bodon, Castrejon, Salamanca, Vittoria, Pyrenees, Orthes, Vic Bigorre, Tarbes and Toulouse. Half pay Mar 1816. MGS medal for Talavera, Busaco, Fuentes d'Onoro, Salamanca, Vittoria, Pyrenees, Orthes and Toulouse. The Obelisk was erected by his father, Richard Wainman, as a memorial to the Battle of Waterloo and to mark his son's achievements in the Peninsular War. It seems fairly certain that the first Wainman's Pinnacle, or Cowling Pinnacle, was built in 1815–1816 by Mr Wainman of Carr Head Hall, Cowling to commemorate Wellington's victory at Waterloo. It was made of wood and became derelict after being struck by lightning. The present stone-built obelisk was erected in 1900.

WAINWRIGHT, Henry Maxwell
Lieutenant. 47th (Lancashire) Regiment of Foot.
Memorial tablet: St Mary Magdalene's Church, South Holmwood, Surrey. (Photograph)

SACRED TO THE MEMORY OF / MAJOR HENRY MAXWELL WAINWRIGHT, / FORMERLY OF THE 47TH REGT / IN WHICH REGT HE SERVED AT THE BATTLE OF BARROSA, / COMMANDING THE GRENADIER COMPANY, / COVERING THE GUNS, SIEGE OF CADIZ AND DEFENCE OF TARIFA, / ALSO IN SUBSEQUENT OPERATIONS IN INDIA, / WHERE HE FILLED THE IMPORTANT SITUATION / OF MILITARY SECRETARY TO THE MADRAS ARMY, / AND WAS ALSO A.D.C. TO LIEUT GENL SIR WILLOUGHBY COTTON, / DURING THE WAR IN AVA. / DIED 19TH NOVEMBER 1849, AGED 57 YEARS. / THIS TABLET IS ERECTED / BY SOME OF HIS BRETHREN IN ARMS, / AS A TOKEN OF THEIR REGARD FOR THE MEMORY / OF AN ESTEEMED FRIEND AND GALLANT SOLDIER.

Ensign 14 Jan 1808. Lt 3 Sep 1809. Capt 3 Jan 1826. Bt Major 23 Nov 1841.

Served in the Peninsula Oct 1810 – Feb 1812. Present at Cadiz, Barrosa and Tarifa. Also served in India (present in the Pindari War 1816–1818), the Expedition to the Persian Gulf under Sir Keir Grant 1819–1820 and in India 1821 (present in the Burmese Campaign 1825–1826 where he was ADC to Lt General Sir Willoughby Cotton). Returned to England in 1827. MGS medal for Barrosa. Half pay 26 Nov 1830. Died 19 Nov 1849.

WAKEFIELD, Joseph
Cornet. 13th Regiment of Light Dragoons.
Memorial tablet: Kamptee, India. (M.I.)

"SACRED TO THE MEMORY OF ANNE WAKEFIELD AND LIEUT-COL. JOSEPH WAKEFIELD OF HER MAJESTY'S XXXIX REGT WHO DIED AT KAMPTEE, THE FORMER OF THE XXV, THE LATTER OF THE XVIII MAY, MDCCCXL. THIS TABLET IS ERECTED BY A FRIEND R. MACKEN."

Cornet 26 May 1814. Lt 29 Aug 1815. Lt 19th Lt Dragoons 29 Aug 1816. Capt 39th Foot 29 Jul 1819. Major 27 May 1834. Lt Colonel 10 Mar 1837.

Present at Waterloo and the Capture of Paris. Also served in Australia 1825–1832 (Commandant of Norfolk Island Convict Settlement), India 1832 (present in Coorg Wars 1834 and Kurnaul 1839). Died in India of cholera 18 May 1840.

WAKELING, James
Private. 5th (Northumberland) Regiment of Foot.
Headstone: St Andrew's Churchyard, Hatfield Peverell, Essex. (Photograph)

SACRED / TO THE MEMORY OF / JAMES WAKELING / OF THE 5TH REGIMENT OF FOOT, / WHO DIED SEPTR 27TH 1865, / HE WAS IN THE FOLLOWING ENGAGEMENTS / IN 1799 UNDER H.R.H. THE DUKE OF YORK / IN HOLLAND, / IN 1806 UNDER GENERAL WHITLOCK, / IN SOUTH AMERICA / STORMING OF BUENOS AYRES, / IN 1809 UNDER THE EARL OF CHATHAM, / AT THE SIEGE OF FLUSHING, / THE FOLLOWING WERE UNDER / GENERAL MOORE AND LORD WELLINGTON, / IN FRANCE, SPAIN AND PORTUGAL, / BATTLE OF NIVE VIMIERA / NIVELLE ROLICA / PYRENEES CIUDAD RODRIGO / VITTORIA ORTHES / SALAMANCA TOULOUSE / CORUNNA / TOTAL NUMBER OF BATTLES 14.

Pte 23 Jul 1799.

Served in the Peninsula with 1/5th Aug 1808 – Jan 1809 and Jun 1812 – Apr 1814. Present at Rolica, Vimeiro, Corunna, Salamanca, retreat from Burgos, Vittoria, Pyrenees, Nivelle and Nive. Also served at the Helder 1799 (wounded), South America 1806 (present at Buenor Ayres) and Walcheren 1809 (present at the siege of Flushing). MGS medal for Rolica, Vimeiro, Corunna, Salamanca, Vittoria, Pyrenees, Nivelle and Nive. Discharged 15 Nov 1818 owing to the reduction of the regiment.
Note: Also known as James Wakeland.

WALBEOFFE, Thomas Wilkins
Lieutenant. 79th (Cameron Highlanders) Regiment of Foot.
Ledger stone in railed enclosure: St Helen's Churchyard, Llanellen, near Abergavenny, Monmouthshire, Wales. (Photograph)

.... / THOMAS WALBEOFFE, / FORMERLY LIEUT IN THE 79TH REG OF FOOT / OR CAMERON HIGHLANDERS. / DIED 20TH FEB 1871. / AGED 80.

Volunteer from 3rd Foot. Ensign 79th Foot 29 Nov 1810. Lt 13 Oct 1812.

Served in the Peninsula May 1811 – Sep 1813. Present at Salamanca, Burgos and Pyrenees.

WALCOTT, Edmund Yeamans
2nd Captain. Royal Artillery.
Memorial tablet: Christchurch Priory, Christchurch, Hampshire. (In Choir). (Photograph)

TO THE MEMORY OF / LIEUT .COLL EDMUND YEAMANS WALCOTT, ROYAL HORSE ARTILLERY / OF WINKTON: / ELDEST SON OF EDMUND WALCOTT SYMPSON, ESQRE. / HIS BEST MEMORIAL IS WRITTEN IN THE HEARTS / OF THOSE WHO KNEW AND LOVED HIM: / OTHER EPITAPHS HE WOULD HIMSELF DESIRE NOT. / A LOYAL SOLDIER, / AFTER A LONG AND HONOURABLE SERVICE, / HE DIED REGRETTED: / AND, AS WE HOPE, IS PASSED THITHER, WHERE HE, / WHO HAS FOUGHT BENEATH THE BANNERS OF CHRIST, / IS CROWNED IN IMMORTALITY / HE DEPARTED THIS LIFE ON THE 18TH FEBRY 1847, / AGED 60.

2nd Lt 20 Dec 1802. 1st Lt 12 Sep 1803. 2nd Capt 23 Mar 1809. Bt Major 15 Aug 1822. Capt 29 Jul 1825. Lt Colonel 10 Jan 1837.

Served in the Peninsula Nov 1808 – Jan 1809 and Apr 1811 – Jan 1812. Present in the Corunna campaign with Sir David Baird's division. After campaigning in the Peninsula he returned to home duties but did not find this exciting, so in March 1815 he became Secretary to Lt Colonel George Jenkinson of the Royal Artillery who was embarking on a mission to France to report on the state of Louis XVIII's Army. He returned to England in May but the same month was back in Ghent with Lt Colonel Webber-

Smith's Troop. Present at Waterloo. During the action he saw that his friend Norman Ramsay's Troop was in difficulty as all the officers including Ramsay were killed or wounded and only Lt Philip Sandilands was left. So he took command of Ramsay's Troop and was praised for this in a report by Lt Colonel Alexander MacDonald in command of the Horse Artillery of the Cavalry Division. Strongly recommended for promotion for Waterloo but did not receive it. After Waterloo given temporary command of the Rocket Troop and joined Blucher's forces outside Paris. In command of Mercer's Troop by 20 Sept while Mercer was on leave. Walcott returned to England Nov 1818 in command of F Troop. He wrote of his experiences at Waterloo in *A slight journal kept during the campaign of 1815*. Retired 10 Apr 1845.
Reference: Reid, William, The Walcott Jug, Journal of the Society for Army Historical Research, Vol. 57, Summer 1979, pp. 80–7. Walcott, Edmund Y., A slight journal kept during the campaign in 1815. (typescript copy in the National Army Museum).

WALDRON, John
Lieutenant. 4th (Queen's Own) Regiment of Dragoons.
Memorial tablet: Conigne Unitarian Chapel, Trowbridge, Wiltshire. (Church now demolished and tablet no longer extant). (M.I.)

"JOHN WALDRON DIED 26TH JANUARY 1827 IN HIS 81ST YEAR. HIS YOUNGEST SON JOHN WALDRON ESQ HAVING EMBRACED THE MILITARY LIFE AS A LIEUTENANT IN THE 4TH REGIMENT OF DRAGOON GUARDS THROUGHOUT THEIR BRILLIANT CAMPAIGN IN THE PENINSULA WHICH DISTINGUISHED THE LAST 4 YEARS OF THE WAR. DIED 13TH DAY OF APRIL 1830."

Cornet 12 Jul 1810. Lt 31 Oct 1811.
Served in the Peninsula Jul 1811 – Apr 1814. Present at Aldea de Ponte, Salamanca, Vittoria and Toulouse.
Note: Served in the 4th Lt Dragoons and not 4th Dragoon Guards as in inscription.

WALKER, Charles
Lieutenant. 5th (Princess Charlotte of Wales's) Dragoon Guards.
Chest tomb: St Andrew's Church, Aldringham, Suffolk. (Photograph)

SACRED TO THE MEMORY OF CHARLES WALKER ESQRE / LATE MAJOR OF THE 5TH DRAGOON GUARDS / WHO DIED SEPT 18TH 1859 AGED 72 YEARS / ....

Cornet 1 Jan 1807. Lt 20 Dec 1810. Capt 29 May 1817. Major 24 Jul 1825.
Served in the Peninsula Sep 1811 – Apr 1814. Present at Llerena (severely wounded), Vittoria and Toulouse. MGS medal for Vittoria and Toulouse.

WALKER, Sir George Townsend
Colonel. Meuron's Regiment.
Low monument: Kensal Green Cemetery, London. (15633/89/IC). (Photograph)
Re-interred from Marylebone Church, December 1859.

GENL SIR GEORGE TOWNSEND WALKER BART GCB. KCTS. / LT GOVR OF THE ROYAL HOSPITAL CHELSEA / BORN 25TH MAY 1764. DIED 14TH NOVR 1842.

Ensign 95th Foot 4 Mar 1782. Lt 13 Mar 1783. Lt 73rd Foot 22 Jun 1783. Lt 36th Foot 15 May 1785. Lt 35th Foot 25 Jul 1787. Capt 14th Foot 13 Mar 1789. Capt 60th Foot 4 May 1791. Major 28 Aug 1794. Lt Colonel 50th Foot 6 Sep 1798. Colonel 25 Apr 1808. Major General 4 Jun 1811. Colonel in Meuron's Regiment 24 Oct 1812. Lt General 19 Jul 1821. General 28 Jun 1838.

Served in the Peninsula Aug 1808 – Jan 1809, Sep 1810 – Aug 1812 (O/c 2 Brigade 5th Division) and Jul 1813 – Apr 1814 (O/c 1 Brigade 2nd Division, Aug – Oct 1813 and O/c 7 Division Nov 1813 – Mar 1814). Present at Rolica, Vimeiro (Mentioned in Despatches), Badajoz (Mentioned in Despatches, severely wounded and awarded pension of £300 per annum), Pyrenees (Mentioned in Despatches), Nivelle, Nive and Orthes (Mentioned in Despatches and severely wounded). Gold Medal for Vimeiro, Badajoz and Orthes. GCB. KCTS. Also served in India 1784–1787 (present in the Polygar War. DQMG), Flanders 1793 (present at Tournai), the Helder 1799, Baltic 1807, Walcheren 1809 and India (Commander in Chief in Madras 1825–1832). Colonel Commandant Rifle Brigade 21 May 1816. Colonel 84th Foot 13 May 1820. Colonel 52nd Lt Infantry 9 Sep 1822. Colonel 50th Foot 23 Dec 1839. Lieutenant Governor of Chelsea Hospital 24 May 1837. Died at Chelsea Hospital 14 Nov 1842.
REFERENCE: *Dictionary of National Biography. Royal Military Calendar, Vol. 3, pp. 177–80. United Service Magazine, Dec 1842, p. 583. Gentleman's Magazine, Jan 1843, pp. 88–90.*

WALKER, Harry
Captain. 67th (South Hampshire) Regiment of Foot.
Headstone: Green Street Cemetery, St Helier, Jersey, Channel Islands. (Plot F5 North stone). (Seriously eroded and inscription recorded from memorial inscription). (Photograph)

"HARRY WALKER, LATE CAPT OF THE 1ST ROYAL VETERAN BATTALION, WHO DIED 16TH DEC 1840 IN THE 63RD YEAR OF HIS AGE."

Cornet Royal Waggon Train 16 Jan 1804. Lt 28 Aug 1804. Lt Nova Scotia Fencibles 19 Feb 1807. Lt 23rd Foot 20 Sep 1808. Capt 67th Foot 22 Jul 1813. Capt 2nd Royal Veteran Battalion 29 Aug 1815. Capt 1st Royal Veteran Battalion Nov 1819.
Served in the Peninsula with 1/23rd Aug 1811 – Jun 1812. Present at Badajoz (severely wounded). Retired on full pay with 1st Royal Veteran Battalion.

WALKER, James
Captain. 42nd (Royal Highland) Regiment of Foot.
Ledger stone: Erskine Churchyard, Erskine, Renfrewshire, Scotland. (M.I.)

"MAJOR JAMES WALKER, LATE 42ND REGT ROYAL HIGHLANDERS, DIED 21 NOV 1818 AGED 44."

Lt 1798. Capt 20 Sep 1804. Bt Major 12 Apr 1814.
Served in the Peninsula 1808 – Jan 1809 and Mar 1813 – Apr 1814. Present at Rolica, Vimeiro, Corunna, Pyrenees, Nivelle, Nive, Orthes (wounded) and Toulouse (wounded). Also served in Egypt 1801 and Walcheren 1809.

WALKER, James Perriman
Lieutenant. 20th (East Devonshire) Regiment of Foot.
Family Headstone: Linton Churchyard, Linton, Roxburghshire, Scotland. (Photograph)

IN MEMORY OF / ROBERT WALKER OF WOODEN DIED 18 JULY 1825 / .... / JAMES PERRIMAN, THEIR 4TH SON, LT 20TH REGT KILLED AT VITTORIA / 19TH OCT 1813.

Ensign 9 Feb 1809. Lt 23 Nov 1809.
Served in the Peninsula Nov 1812 – Oct 1813. Present at Vittoria and Pyrenees (severely wounded at Roncesvalles 25 Jul 1813 and died of his wounds 18 Oct 1813). Also served at Walcheren 1809.
Note: The inscription reference to his death at Vittoria is in error.

WALKER, Samuel
Lieutenant and Captain. 3rd Regiment of Foot Guards.
Memorial monument: St Peter's Church, Leeds, Yorkshire. (Photograph)

TO THE MEMORY OF / CAPTAIN SAMUEL WALKER OF THE 3RD REGIMENT OF GUARDS / AND / RICHARD BECKETT OF THE COLDSTREAM REGT OF GUARDS / NATIVES OF LEEDS / WHO / HAVING BRAVELY SERVED THEIR COUNTRY TOGETHER / IN EGYPT, GERMANY, DENMARK AND PORTUGAL / FELL IN THE PRIME OF LIFE / AT THE GLORIOUS BATTLE OF TALAVERA, SPAIN / ON THE 28TH JULY 1809. / THEIR FELLOW TOWNSMEN DEDICATED THIS MONUMENT

Named on Memorial Panel VI for Talavera: Royal Military Chapel, Wellington Barracks, London. (M.I.) (Destroyed by a Flying Bomb 1944)

Ensign 20 Aug 1796. Lt and Capt 11 Oct 1799.

Served in the Peninsula Mar – Jul 1809. Present at Douro and Talavera where he was killed 28 Jul 1809. Also served in Egypt 1801, Hanover 1805 and Copenhagen 1807.

WALKER, William
Private. Royal Artillery.
Ledger stone: St Helen's Churchyard, Tarporley, Cheshire. (Photograph)

Pte 22 Nov 1803.

Served in the Peninsula 1810 – Apr 1814. Present at Busaco, Fuentes d'Onoro, Salamanca and Vittoria. Discharged 10 Aug 1814 as unfit for further service with a pension of nine pence a day which was increased to one shilling a day in 1852. MGS medal for Busaco, Fuentes d'Onoro, Salamanca and Vittoria.

WALL, Thomas
Sergeant. 95th Regiment of Foot.
Family Headstone: St John's Churchyard, Winster, Derbyshire. (Photograph)

IN MEMORY OF / THOMAS WALL / .... / THEIR SON THOMAS. FEB. 11 1853. AGED 67

Memorial tablet: St John's Church, Winster, Derbyshire. (Photograph)

IN MEMORY OF / THOMAS WALL, WHO DIED FEBRUARY 11TH 1853, / AGED 67 YEARS. / HIS REMAINS LIE IN THE ADJOINING GROUND. / THROUGH THE MERCY OF GOD HE WAS PERMITTED TO / RETURN TO HIS NATIVE TOWN, AFTER A LONG ABSENCE / SPENT, IN THE SERVICE OF HIS COUNTRY. / HE HAD THE HONOR OF BEING ENGAGED IN MOST OF THE / GREAT ACTIONS DURING THE PENINSULAR WAR, WAS / APPOINTED COLOUR SERGEANT IN H.M.'S 95TH RIFLE BRIGADE. / AND HIGHLY ESTEEMED BY HIS OFFICERS, AND / COMRADES, HE MAINTAINED THROUGHOUT THE CHARACTER / OF A BRAVE SOLDIER, SEVERELY WOUNDED / IN SEVERAL ACTIONS, HE WAS PRESENTED WITH THE / MEDAL AWARDED BY THE GOVERNMENT, HAVING THE FOLLOWING / VICTORIES INSCRIBED UPON ITS CLASP. / TOULOUSE. BADAJOZ. PYRENEES. / NIVE. ORTHES. SALAMANCA. / ST SEBASTIAN. NIVELLE. BARROSA. / VITTORIA. CIUDAD RODRIGO. / HE LIVED AND DIED A PATRIOT AND A CHRISTIAN.

Pte 4 Apr 1807. Cpl 1810. Sgt 1811.

Served in the Peninsula Feb 1810 – Apr 1814. Present at Barrosa, Ciudad Rodrigo, Badajoz, Salamanca,

Vittoria, Pyrenees (wounded), San Sebastian, Nivelle, Nive, Orthes and Toulouse (wounded). Also served in North America 1814–1815 (present at New Orleans where he was wounded). MGS medal for Barrosa, Ciudad Rodrigo, Badajoz, Salamanca, Vittoria, Pyrenees, San Sebastian, Nivelle, Nive, Orthes and Toulouse. Awarded pension of nine pence per day. Discharged 14 Jan 1819.

WALLACE, James Maxwell
Captain. 23rd Regiment of Light Dragoons.
Ringed Cross on a pedestal base: St Helen's Churchyard, Ainderby Steeple, Yorkshire. (Photograph)

SACRED / TO THE MEMORY OF / GENERAL SIR MAXWELL WALLACE K.H. / WHO DIED FEBRUARY 3RD 1867 / IN HIS 82ND YEAR.

Cornet 9th Dragoons 14 Aug 1805. Lt 11th Dragoons 5 Jun 1806. Capt 22 Oct 1807. Capt 21st Dragoons 25 Dec 1808. Capt 23rd Dragoons 20 Apr 1815. Bt Major 1 Jan 1817. Major 1st Dragoons 11 Jun 1818. Lt Colonel 25 Sep 1823. Bt Colonel 28 Jun 1838. Major General 11 Nov 1851. Lt General 6 Feb 1855. General 8 Jun 1863.

Present at the retreat from Quatre Bras and Waterloo (ADC to Major General Dornberg). KH. Knighted 1831. Also served in the Cape of Good Hope 1812 (present on the Kaffir frontier). Commanded 5th Dragoon Guards 1824–1840. Colonel 17th Lancers 28 Jun 1854.
Reference: Gentleman's Magazine, Mar 1867, pp. 400–1.

WALLACE, John
Private. 2nd (Royal North British) Regment of Dragoons.
Memorial: Whithorn Old Kirkyard, Whithorn, Dumfries and Galloway, Scotland. (Photograph)

ERECTED / BY / ANN WALLACE, / WHITHORN, IN MEMORY OF HER HUSBAND / JOHN WALLACE, / SERGEANT 2D R.N.B. DRAGOONS / WHO DIED 3D AUGUST 1846 / AGED 66 YEARS. / ....

Pte 24 Jun 1798. Cpl 1815. Sgt 1816.

Present at Waterloo in Capt Cheney's Troop where he was severely wounded. Showed great gallantry during the battle and was promoted Corporal. Discharged 21 Mar 1817 owing to the wounds received at Waterloo.

WALLACE, Peter Margetson
Captain. Royal Artillery.
Memorial tablet: St Mary's Church, Cheltenham, Gloucesteshire. (M.I.)

"SACRED TO THE MEMORY OF CAPTAIN GEORGE HARRIS WALLACE LATE OF H M 16TH REGT OF FOOT THIRD SON OF LT GEN P. M. WALLACE ROYAL ARTILLERY DIED MONTPELIER MANSIONS CHELTENHAM 10 OCT 1857 AGED 45. ALSO OF PETER MARGETSON WALLACE, GENERAL ROYAL ARTILLERY FATHER OF THE ABOVE, DIED 14 DEC 1864 AGED 84 YEARS."

2nd Lt 10 May 1797. 1st Lt 16 Jul 1799. 2nd Capt 15 Nov 1804. Capt 16 Mar 1812. Bt Major 4 Jun 1814. Lt Colonel 30 Dec 1828. Colonel 23 Nov 1841. Major General 20 Jun 1854. Lt General 28 Nov 1854. General 22 Feb 1863.

Served at Walcheren 1809 (present at the siege of Flushing). Also served in the West Indies 1800–1801, Sicily 1806–1808, Canada 1812–1815 (present at the attack on Sacketts Harbour) and 1823–1829 and Malta 1834–1840. Colonel Commandant Royal Artillery 21 Jun 1853.

WALLACE, Robert Clerke
Captain. 1st (King's) Dragoons Guards.
Grave: Christ Church Churchyard, Worthing, Sussex. (M.I.)

"COLONEL ROBERT CLERKE WALLACE, LATE OF THE KING'S DRAGOON GUARDS AND KNIGHT OF THE THIRD CLASS OF THE ROYAL HANOVERIAN GUELPHIC ORDER DIED MARCH 25TH 1865, AGED 73 YEARS."

Cornet 4 Dec 1806. Lt 25 Mar 1808. Capt 20 Oct 1814. Major 5 Nov 1825. Lt Colonel 31 Dec 1828.

Present at Waterloo (one of the three Captains of the regiment who were not killed or wounded in the various charges. Wallace is noted for not killing a wounded Frenchman as he rode by, even though the Frenchman had attacked him). KH. Half pay 31 Dec 1828. Lived in York after his retirement.

WALLETT, Charles
Captain. 32nd (Cornwall) Regiment of Foot.
Ledger stone: Abbey Cemetery, Bath, Somerset. (Photograph)

SACRED / TO THE MEMORY OF / MAJOR CHARLES WALLETT / FORMERLY / OF THE CEYLON RIFLES / WHO DEPARTED THIS LIFE / ON THE 31ST DAY / OF DECEMBER 1847 / AGED 68 YEARS. / BRAVE SOLDIER, A MOST AFFECTIONATE / HUSBAND AND FATHER AND A SINCERE / FRIEND.

Ensign 16 Aug 1804. Lt 9 Oct 1806. Capt 23 Mar 1815. Capt 61st Foot 24 Apr 1828. Capt Ceylon Rifle Regiment 18 Sep 1835. Bt Major 10 Jan 1837.

Served in the Peninsula Aug 1808 – Feb 1809 (with 2nd Battalion of Detachment Feb 1809) and Jul 1811 – Apr 1814. Present at Rolica, Vimeiro, Pyrenees, Pamplona, Bidassoa, Nivelle and Nive. Present at Waterloo (severely wounded at Quatre Bras). Also served at Walcheren 1809 (present at the siege of Flushing). MGS medal for Rolica, Vimeiro, Pyrenees, Nivelle and Nive.

WALLEY, William
1st Lieutenant. 23rd (Royal Welch Fusiliers) Regiment of Foot.
Memorial tablet: Chester Cathedral, Cheshire. (West wall of north transept). (Photograph)

HERE LIE THE REMAINS OF / WILLIAM WALLEY, ESQR / (LATE CAPTAIN IN THE 23RD REGIMENT OF FOOT / OR ROYAL WELSH FUSILIERS) / WHO DEPARTED THIS LIFE AT BIRKENHEAD / IN THIS COUNTY / ON THE 28TH DAY OF JULY, IN THE YEAR OF OUR LORD 1827 / AGED 44 YEARS. / THE MILITARY CAREER OF THIS GALLANT OFFICER / (WHICH COMMENCED AT THE CAPTURE OF COPENHAGEN, / AND AFTER BEING EXTENDED THROUGHOUT THE PENINSULAR WAR / TERMINATED GLORIOUSLY AT WATERLOO, / AND THE CONSEQUENT CAPITULATION OF PARIS) / WAS DISTINGUISHED BY THE UNION OF MANY OF THE BEST / QUALITIES WHICH AT ONCE CHARACTERIZE AND ENNOBLE THE GENUINE BRITISH SOLDIER. / TO PERPETUATE THE MEMORY OF HIS VALOUR AS AN OFFICER / AND THE STERLING MERIT AS A MAN / THIS MONUMENT HAS BEEN ERECTED / BY HIS AFFECTIONATE SISTERS.

2nd Lt 13 May 1807. 1st Lt 10 Dec 1807. Capt 19 Jul 1815.

Served in the Peninsula with 2/23rd Oct 1808 – Jan 1809 and 1/23rd Apr 1811 – Apr 1814. Present at Corunna, first siege of Badajoz, Albuera, Aldea de Ponte, Ciudad Rodrigo, Badajoz (severely wounded), Vittoria, Pyrenees, Nivelle, Nive, Orthes and Toulouse. Present at Waterloo and the Capture of Paris. Also served at Walcheren 1809. Half pay 6 Apr 1820.

WALLINGTON, John Clement
Lieutenant. 10th (Prince of Wales's Own Royal) Regiment of Light Dragoons.
Low monument: Tachbrook Road Cemetery, Leamington Spa, Warwickshire. (Photograph)

……………… / IN AFFECTIONATE REMEMBRANCE OF / LIEUT COLONEL / JOHN CLEMENT WALLINGTON / OF THE 10TH ROYAL HUSSARS / WHO DIED / 25TH AUGUST 1872 / AGED 82 YEARS. / VERSE / ………………

Cornet 21 Oct 1813. Lt 27 Dec 1814. Capt 16 Dec 1824. Major 3 Apr 1833. Lt Colonel 3 Apr 1846.

Present at Waterloo. Also served in Portugal 1826–1828 with Lt General William Clinton's expedition. Commanded 10th Hussars 1846 but retired shortly afterwards. Cousin of Capt Thomas Noel Harris 36th Foot.

WALLIS, John
Private. 34th (Cumberland) Regiment of Foot.
Low monument on pedestal: St Mary and All Saints' Churchyard, Boxley, Kent. (Photograph)

IN LOVING MEMORY OF / JOHN WALLIS, LATE OF H. M. 34TH REGT / WHO DIED OCTOBER 26TH 1861 AGED 80 YEARS. / ………………

Served in the Peninsula. Present at Vittoria and Pyrenees. MGS medal for Vittoria and Pyrenees.
Note: Also known as John Wallace.
REFERENCE: Kent Messenger, 21 Feb 1997.

WALPOLE, Hon. John
Captain and Lieutenant Colonel. Coldstream Regiment of Foot Guards.
Ledger stone: Kensal Green Cemetery, London. (15602/112/2). (Photograph)

SACRED / TO THE MEMORY OF / COL THE HONBLE / JOHN WALPOLE / DIED 10TH DEC 1859 / AGED 73 YEARS

Ensign 18 Feb 1804. Lt and Capt 23 Jun 1808. Capt and Lt Colonel 25 Jul 1814.

Served in the Peninsula Apr 1810 – Nov 1812. Present at Cadiz, Barrosa, Ciudad Rodrigo, Salamanca and Burgos (severely wounded and awarded pension of £100 per annum). Also served in the Netherlands 1814–1815. Retired 27 Apr 1825. MP for King's Lynn 1827–1831. Private Secretary to Lord Palmerston 1830–1833. Consul General in Chile 1833. Promoted to Chargé d'Affaires 1841. MGS medal for Barrosa, Ciudad Rodrigo and Salamanca.
REFERENCE: Annual Register, 1859, Appx, p. 43.

WALSH, Pearson Lyons
Captain. 4th Garrison Battalion.
Memorial tablet: King's Chapel, Gibraltar. (South side). (Photograph)

SACRED TO THE MEMORY OF / PEARSON LYONS WALSH, ESQUIRE, / LATE CAPTAIN IN THE IVTH GARRISON BATTALION, / TOWN MAJOR OF THIS GARRISON, DEPUTY JUDGE ADVOCATE, / AND ACTING JUDGE OF HIS MAJESTY'S COURTS / OF VICE-ADMIRALTY AND CIVIL JUDICATURE. / AS A PUBLIC TESTIMONY OF HIS ZEAL, ABILITY, AND PERSEVERANCE, / IN THE FAITHFUL DISCHARGE OF THE VARIOUS DUTIES / OF THESE ARDUOUS AND IMPORTANT OFFICES, / AND UNDER TWO AWFUL VISITATIONS OF A MALIGNANT FEVER. / AND AS A TRIBUTE OF ESTEEM AND GRATITUDE FOR HIS UNWEARIED / ATTENTION TO THEIR COMMERCIAL INTERESTS, / THIS MONUMENT IS ERECTED BY THE MERCHANT'S SOCIETY

/ TO RECORD THE VIRTUES OF THE DEAD, AND THE / GRATEFUL REMEMBRANCES OF THE LIVING. / OB. XVTH JANUARY MDCCCXIV. ÆT XXXVII.

Cornet 11th Lt Dragoons 30 Apr 1794. Lt 16 Apr 1795. Lt 2nd Foot 1798. Capt 25 Jun 1803. Capt 4th Garrison Battalion 7 Jun 1810.

Served in the Peninsula Oct 1808 – Jan 1809 (on Staff as DAAG to Sir John Moore). Present at Corunna. Also served in the West Indies 1795–1797 (present at the Capture of Trinidad 1797) and Gibraltar (Town Major and Deputy Judge Advocate). Died in Gibraltar 15 Jan 1814 aged 37.

WALSH, Robert

Clerk of Stores. Field Train, Department of the Ordnance.
Named on the Regimental Memorial: British Cemetery, Lisbon, Portugal. (Grave number D11). (M.I.)

".................MR ROBERT WALSH, CLERK OF STORES FIELD TRAIN ORDNANCE DEPARTMENT WHO DIED AT LISBON 9 JUNE 1809 .. .."

Served in the Peninsula 1809.

WALTER, John

Captain. 62nd (Wiltshire) Regiment of Foot.
Pedestal Tomb: Kensal Green Cemetery, London. (11592/100/IC). (Photograph)

SACRED TO THE MEMORY OF / LIEUTENANT COLONEL JOHN WALTER, / LATE OF THE 62ND REGIMENT / WHO DIED AT BOULOGNE SUR MER ON THE 9TH DAY OF OCTR 1853 / IN THE 60TH YEAR OF HIS AGE

Ensign 15 Jul 1806. Lt 3 Sep 1807. Capt 24 Mar 1813. Major 95th Foot 26 May 1831. Lt Colonel 9 Nov 1846.

Served in the Peninsula Oct 1813 – Apr 1814. Present at Bidassoa, Nivelle, Nive and Bayonne. MGS medal for Nivelle and Nive. Half pay 19 Apr 1831.

WALTER, Philip

Staff Surgeon. Medical Department.
Family Memorial tablet: St Helen's Church, Abbotsham, Devon. (Photograph)

SACRED TO THE MEMORY OF THE REVND JOHN WALTER, / .... / AND TO THE MEMORY OF THEIR YOUNGEST SON PHILIP, LATE / STAFF SURGEON IN THE BRITISH ARMY, HAVING SERVED HIS MAJESTY IN THE / LATE WARS OF SPAIN AND PORTUGAL AND IN THE EAST AND WEST INDIES / HE DIED SEPTR 14TH 1823, AGED 44, AND HIS REMAINS / LIE UNDERNEATH THIS TABLET, WHICH IS PLACED HERE BY HIS, / AND THEIR AFFECTIONATE RELATIVES.

Hospital Mate 19 Nov 1805. Asst Surgeon 1st Foot 5 Dec 1805. Staff Surgeon (Portuguese Army) 6 Aug 1812. Staff Surgeon 25 Sep 1814.

Served in the Peninsula with 3/1 Foot May 1811 – Aug 1812. With Portuguese Army Aug 1812 – Apr 1814. Present at Castrejon and Salamanca. Also served in the West Indies 1805 and India 1807.

WALTON, John

Private. 38th (1st Staffordshire) Regiment of Foot.
Buried in Carlisle Cemetery, Carlisle, Cumbria. (Grave: Ward 3 Section R No. 114). (Burial record)

Served in the Peninsula 1812 – Apr 1814. Present at Salamanca, Burgos and retreat from Burgos (present at Villa Muriel), Vittoria, San Sebastian, Bidassoa, Nivelle, Nive and Bayonne. Was wounded twice in the Peninsula. MGS medal for Salamanca, Vittoria, San Sebastian, Nivelle and Nive.
Lived in Caldewgate, Carlisle, where he worked as a weaver and died Feb 1860.
Reference: Carlisle Journal, 24 Feb 1860, p. 5.

WALTON, William Lovelace
Lieutenant and Captain. Coldstream Regiment of Foot Guards.
Ledger stone: Brompton Cemetery, London. (BR 39917). (Photograph)

TO THE MEMORY OF / WILLIAM LOVELACE WALTON / 5TH (NORTHUMBERLAND) FUSILIERS / FORMERLY – COLONEL / COMMANDING COLDSTREAM GUARDS, / IN WHICH REGIMENT HE SERVED / THROUGH THE PENINSULA AND AT WATERLOO. / BORN JUNE 16TH 1788. DIED JANUARY 11TH 1865, / AGED 75.

Memorial: Royal Military Chapel, Wellington Barracks, London. (M.I.) (Destroyed by a Flying Bomb 1944)

"PLACED BY MAJOR-GENERAL GEORGE BRYAN MILMAN, C.B., / ………………… IN MEMORY OF HIS FATHER-IN-LAW, / GENERAL WILLIAM LOVELACE WALTON, / BORN 1788; DIED, 1863. / FOR 40 YEARS IN THE COLDSTREAM GUARDS, SERVING WITH IT THROUGH THE PENINSULA, AT TALAVERA, / AND AT BUSACO; ADJUTANT TO THE 2ND BATTALION AT WATERLOO; / COLONEL OF THE 5TH FUSILIERS, 1856."

Ensign 8 May 1806. Lt and Capt 7 Mar 1811. Capt and Lt Colonel 20 Feb 1823. Colonel 10 Jan 1837. Major General 9 Nov 1846. Lt General 20 Jun 1854. General 13 Feb 1863.

Served in the Peninsula with 1st Battalion Mar 1809 – Jan 1810 and 2nd Battalion Mar 1810 – Apr 1811. Present at Douro, Oporto, Talavera, Busaco, Lines of Torres Vedras and the pursuit of Massena. Present at Quatre Bras and Waterloo where he was Acting Adjutant of the 2nd Battalion. Brigade Major to 2nd Brigade of Guards after Waterloo to the Capture of Paris on the death of Capt William Stothert at Waterloo. Also served at Copenhagen 1807, the Netherlands 1813–1814 (present at Antwerp and Bergen-op-Zoom). Served in the Coldstream Guards for 40 years and commanded the regiment from 1839–1846. MGS medal for Talavera and Busaco. Colonel 5th Foot 20 Feb 1856. Died 11 Jan 1865.
Reference: Household Brigade Journal, 1865, p. 319. Gentleman's Magazine, Feb 1865, p. 261. Military History Society Bulletin, No. 23, Vol. 6, No. 23, Feb 1956, pp. 49–51.

WAPLINGTON, Richard
Private. 2nd Life Guards.
Pedestal tomb with obelisk: St Catherine's Churchyard, Cossall, Nottinghamshire. (Photograph)

WATERLOO / THIS MONUMENT IS ERECTED / TO THE MEMORY OF / JOHN SHAW & / RICHARD WAPLINGTON, / OF THE / LIFE GUARDS, / AND THOMAS WHEATLEY, / OF THE LIGHT DRAGOON GUARDS, / WHO LEFT THIS THEIR NATIVE HOME / IN DEFENCE OF THEIR COUNTRY, / THE TWO FORMER GLORIOUSLY / FELL AT WATERLOO, THE LATTER / RETURNED, AND LIES BURIED IN / THIS CHURCH / YARD.

Pte 1809.

Served in the Peninsula Nov 1812 – Dec 1813. Present at Vittoria. Returned home Dec 1813. Present at Waterloo where he was killed. He joined the army to escape life as a coal miner, having worked in the pits since the age of 12. Working 15 hours a day in the mines, this hard physical work developed his muscles. He was over six feet tall and was known as the 'Cossall Giant' along with John Shaw who was in the same regiment. The last sighting of him at Waterloo, where he was killed, was of him holding onto a French Eagle surrounded by cuirassiers. The memorial to the three Waterlooo men, John Shaw, Richard Waplington and Thomas Wheatley was unveiled in 1877.

REFERENCE: Raynor, K. K., Waterloo men at Cossall, Waterloo Journal, Jan 1988, pp. 27–37. Robinson, G., Waterloo Journal, Apr 1988, pp. 4–5.

WARBERTON, James
Private. 95th Regiment of Foot.
Died at Brindle Workhouse, Chorley, Lancashire.

Pte 15 Apr 1805.

Served in the Peninsula 1808 – Apr 1814. Present at Corunna, Fuentes d'Onoro, Ciudad Rodrigo, Badajoz, Vittoria, Nivelle, Nive and Toulouse. Present at Waterloo in Capt H. Lee's Company. Discharged 26 Oct 1816. MGS medal for Corunna, Fuentes d'Onoro, Ciudad Rodrigo, Badazoz, Vittoria, Nivelle, Nive and Toulouse. Died 5 May 1869.

WARD, Adam
1st Lieutenant. Royal Artillery.
Memorial: Merrion Cemetery, Bellone, Dublin, Ireland.

2nd Lt 1 Jun 1808. 1st Lt 9 Sep 1810.

Served in the Peninsula Feb – Apr 1814. Present at Orthes, Vic Bigorre and Tarbes where he was severely wounded and lost a leg. Present at Waterloo in Capt Edward Whinyates Rocket Troop. Died in Dublin 28 Feb 1827.

WARD, William Cuthbert
2nd Captain. Royal Engineers.
Headstone: Candie Cemetery, St Peter Port, Guernsey, Channel Islands. (Inscription not recorded). (Photograph)

2nd Lt 10 May 1808. 1st Lt 24 Jun 1809. 2nd Capt 21 Jul 1813. Bt Major 10 Jan 1837. Lt Colonel 9 Dec 1837. Colonel 11 Nov 1851. Major General 18 Aug 1858.

Served in the Peninsula Aug 1812 – Sep 1813. Present at Castalla, Denia and siege of Tarragona. Also served in Sicily 1811–1812 and the Netherlands 1814–1815. Died in Guernsey 6 Sep 1867.

WARDE, Francis
1st Lieutenant. Royal Artillery.
Pedestal tomb: Holy Trinity Churchyard, Amersham, Berkshire. (Photograph)

PENINSULA / WATERLOO / TO THE MEMORY OF GENERAL SIR FRANCIS WARDE / KNIGHT COMMANDER OF THE / MOST HONOURABLE ORDER OF THE BATH, / WHO DIED AT READING MAY 1879, / AGED 89 YEARS.

2nd Lt 4 Mar 1809. 1st Lt 8 Mar 1812. 2nd Capt 3 Jul 1830. Capt 15 Jun 1840. Bt Major 9 Nov 1846. Lt Colonel 7 May 1847. Colonel 13 Sep 1854. Major General 8 Mar 1860. Lt General 24 Aug 1866. General 15 Apr 1877.

Served in the Peninsula Jun 1812 – Apr 1814. (Brigiade Major 6/9th Brigade Apr – Oct 1813. AAG Oct 1813 – Apr 1814). Present at Cadiz. Present at Waterloo in Lt Colonel Sir Hew Dalrymple Ross's Troop and with the Army of Occupation. Also served in Malta 1830–1832. KCB 24 May 1873. Colonel Commandant Royal Artillery 12 May 1866.

WARDE, Sir Henry

Colonel. 68th (Durham) Regiment of Foot.

Memorial tablet and Stained glass window: Royal Military Chapel, Wellington Barracks, London. (M.I.) (Destroyed by a Flying Bomb 1944) (Photograph of Stained glass window in the Apse. The only original part of the Chapel)

"GENERAL SIR EDWARD WARDE, G.C.B., TO THE MEMORY OF / HIS DISTINGUISHED FATHER, GENERAL SIR HENRY WARDE, K.C.B., / WHO ENTERED THE 1ST GUARDS 2ND APRIL, 1783, AND SERVED WITH THEM CONTINUOUSLY UNTIL HE COMMANDED THE BRIGADE AS MAJOR-GENERAL IN THE CORUNNA CAMPAIGN, 1808 AND 1809, DURING WHICH THEY MORE THAN MAINTAINED THEIR HIGH CHARACTER FOR GALLANTRY AND DISCIPLINE, UNDER CIRCUMSTANCES OF GREAT TRIAL AND PRIVATION. HE SERVED WITH MUCH DISTINCTION DURING THE WARS IN THE LOW COUNTRIES, UNDER FIELD-MARSHAL H.R.H. THE DUKE OF YORK, AND WAS DANGEROUSLY WOUNDED WHILST HEADING THE STORMING PARTY AT THE SIEGE OF VALENCIENNES. HE WENT TO INDIA, 1809, AND WAS SELECTED TO ACCOMPANY THE EXPEDITION THAT WAS SENT FROM THENCE TO CAPTURE THE ISLE OF FRANCE, AS SECOND IN COMMAND, AND WAS THE FIRST CIVIL GOVERNOR AND COMMANDER-IN-CHIEF OF THAT ISLAND. HE SUCCEEDED LORD COMBERMERE AS CIVIL GOVERNOR AND COMMANDER-IN-CHIEF OF THE WEST INDIES, 1831. HE THREE TIMES RECEIVED THE THANKS OF PARLIAMENT, AND DIED 1834."

Ensign 1st Foot Guards 2 Apr 1783. Lt and Capt 6 Jul 1790. Capt and Lt Colonel 15 Oct 1794. Bt Colonel 1 Jan 1801. Major General 25 Apr 1808. Third Major 14 Feb 1811. Colonel 68th Foot 1 Jun 1813. Lt General 4 Jun 1813. General 22 Jul 1830.

Served in the Peninsula Oct 1808 – Jan 1809 (GOC 1 Brigade, 1st Division). Present at Corunna (Mentioned in Despatches). Gold Medal for Corunna. Also served in Flanders 1793–1794 (present at Valenciennes where he was severely wounded), the Helder 1799, Baltic 1807, India 1809, Capture of Mauritius 1810 (remained as Acting Governor 1811–1813) and the West Indies 1821–1827 (Governor of Barbados). GCB. Colonel 31st Foot 13 Apr 1831. Died 1 Oct 1834.

Reference: Dictionary of National Biography. Royal Military Calendar, Vol. 2, pp. 294–5. Gentleman's Magazine, Feb 1835, p. 207.

WARDLAW, John

Lieutenant Colonel. 76th Regiment of Foot.

Memorial tablet: Bath Abbey, Bath, Somerset. (Photograph)

ERECTED BY HIS CHILDREN / IN MEMORY OF / LIEUTENANT GENERAL JOHN WARDLAW, / COLONEL OF HER MAJESTY'S 55TH REGIMENT OF FOOT; / WHO DIED AT TORQUAY, / ON THE 28TH OF NOVEMBER 1848, IN HIS 73RD YEAR. / (VERSE)

Lt 20th Foot 26 Oct 1796. Capt 11th Foot 24 May 1798. Major 64th Foot 16 Jan 1806. Lt Colonel 76th Foot 10 May 1810. Bt Colonel 12 Aug 1819. Major General 22 Jul 1830. Lt General 9 Nov 1846.

Served in the Peninsula Aug 1813 – Jan 1814. Present at Bidassoa, Nivelle, Nive and Bayonne. Commanded 76th Foot at Nive and awarded Gold Medal. Half pay 18 Aug 1814. Colonel 55th Foot 7 Aug 1846.

WARNE, George

Private. 69th (South Lincolnshire) Regiment of Foot.

Headstone: St Mary's Churchyard, Tasburgh, Norfolk. (Right of main entrance about three rows against the hedge). (Photograph)

IN LOVING MEMORY OF / GEORGE WARNE, / A WATERLOO VETERAN / WHO DEPARTED THIS LIFE / OCTOBER 4TH 1883 / AGED 87 YEARS / ....

Present at Quatre Bras and Waterloo in Capt William Hamilton West's Company.

WARRE, William

Captain. 23rd Regiment of Light Dragoons.
Grave: Old St Andrew's Churchyard, Bishopthorpe, York, Yorkshire. (No longer extant). (M.I.)

"SACRED TO THE MEMORY / OF / LIEUTENANT-GENERAL SIR WILLIAM WARRE / C.B., K.T.S., K.C., ST BENTO D'AVIS / COLONEL OF THE 94TH REGIMENT / DIED AT YORK, 26TH JULY 1853, AGED 69 YEARS."

Ensign 52nd Foot 5 Nov 1803. Lt 2 Jun 1804. Capt 98th Foot 25 Apr 1806. Capt 23rd Lt Dragoons 7 Aug 1806. Bt Major 30 May 1811. Bt Lt Colonel 13 May 1813. Major 3 Jul 1823. Bt Colonel 22 Jul 1830. Major General 23 Nov 1841. Lt General 11 Nov 1851. Portuguese Army: Major 21 Jan 1809. Lt Colonel 3 Jul 1811.

Served in the Peninsula Aug 1808 – Jan 1809 (ADC to General Ferguson). With Portuguese Army Mar 1809 – May 1813 (on staff as ADC to Marshal Beresford 21 Mar 1809). Present at Rolica, Vimeiro, retreat to Corunna and battle of Corunna (one of the last soldiers to embark after the battle). Warre's ability to speak Portuguese was invaluable to General Beresford when, in Madrid in 1809, Beresford was given command of the Portuguese troops. Present at Douro, second siege of Badajoz, Ciudad Rodrigo, Badajoz, siege of Salamanca Forts and Salamanca. Returned to England. Also served in the Cape of Good Hope 1813–1821 (DQMG), Ireland 1823 (AQMG), Portugal 1826–1828 (AQMG on Lt General William Clinton's staff), Ireland 1830–1836 (on Lt General William Clinton's staff) and Chatham 1836–1851. MGS medal for Rolica, Vimeiro, Corunna, Ciudad Rodrigo, Badajoz and Salamanca. KTS. CB. Colonel 94th Foot 29 Sep 1847. Knighted 1839.

REFERENCE: *Dictionary of National Biography. Royal Military Calendar, Vol. 4, pp. 442–4. Gentleman's Magazine, Nov 1853, pp. 531–2. Annual Register, 1853, Appx, pp. 238–9. Warre, Sir William, Letters from the Peninsula: 1808–1812, 2nd edn by William Acheson Warre, 1999.*

WARREN, Francis

Captain. 9th Regiment of Light Dragoons.
Ledger stone: St Mary's Churchyard, Bunclody, Wexford, Ireland. (Photograph)

SACRED / TO THE MEMORY OF / FRANCIS WARREN / LATE CAPTAIN IN HIS MAJESTY'S 9TH LANCERS / WHO DEPD THIS LIFE THE 7TH DAY OF MAY 1837 / AGED 55 YEARS

Cornet 31 May 1808. Lt 18 Aug 1808. Capt 5 Nov 1812.

Served in the Peninsula Jul 1811 – Jul 1812. Present at Arroyo dos Molinos. Also served at Walcheren 1809. Half pay 1817.

WARREN, Lemuel

Lieutenant Colonel. 27th (Inniskilling) Regiment of Foot.
Grave: Kensal Green Cemetery, London. (Section 164 Grave number 59). (Inscription not recorded).

Ensign 17th Foot 10 Mar 1787. Lt 14 Mar 1789. Capt 27th Foot 2 Jan 1794. Major 31 Dec 1799. Lt Colonel 16 Aug 1804. Bt Colonel 4 Jun 1813. Major General 12 Aug 1819.

Served in the Peninsula with 1/27th Nov 1812 – Jun 1813 and on Staff Jul 1813 – Apr 1814. Present at Castalla, Tarragona, Barcelona, Bayonne and Bordeaux. Present at the Capture of Paris. Also served in the Royal Navy as a Marine 1789–1792, Flanders 1793–1796 (present at Nimwegen and Geldermalsen

Jan 1796), West Indies 1796 (present at St Lucia), the Helder 1799, Ferrol 1800, Egypt 1801 (present at Alexandria), Hanover 1806 and Sicily 1809–1812. Died 29 Oct 1833.
REFERENCE: Royal Military Calendar Vol. 3, pp. 410–11. Gentleman's Magazine, Feb 1834, pp. 226–7.

WARRINGTON, Thornhill

Captain. 8th (King's Royal Irish) Light Dragoons.
Obelisk: Kensal Green Cemetery, London. (Inscription illegible). (14978/24/4). (Photograph)

Cornet 5th Dragoon Guards 13 Nov 1798. Lt 5 Nov 1800. Capt 8th Lt Dragoons 23 Jan 1812.

Served in the Peninsula with 5th Dragoons Sep 1811 – Jan 1812. Also served in India 1812 (present in the Nepaul War 1814, Pindari War 1816–1817 and siege of Hattras 1819) Half pay 2 Jul 1823. Died Jan 1859 aged 80.

WASDELL, John

Staff Surgeon. Medical Department.
Headstone: St Mary's Churchyard, Swansea, Glamorgan, Wales. (Churchyard was bombed during the Second World War and memorial no longer extant). (M.I.)

SACRED / TO THE MEMORY OF / JOHN WASDELL / OF BIRMINGHAM / SURGEON TO H.M. FORCES / WHO DIED AUGST 15TH 1819 / AGED 36 YEARS

Hospital Mate 8 Sep 1803. Asst Surgeon 57th Foot 3 Dec 1803. Surgeon 66th Foot 4 Jun 1810. Staff Surgeon 28 May 1812.

Served in the Peninsula Nov 1809 – Jun 1811 and Apr 1812 – Apr 1814. (attached to 2nd Division Cavalry Jul 1812 – Nov 1813). Half pay 1816.

WATERS, John

Major. Staff Appointment in Spain and Portugal not holding a Regimental Commission.
Chest Tomb: Kensal Green Cemetery, London. (Inscription largely illegible). (3848/87/IC). (Photograph)

IN THIS TOMB ARE INTERRED / LT GENL SIR JOHN WATERS KCB. / SON OF THOMAS WATERS ESQUIRE / ....

Ensign 1st Foot 2 Aug 1797. Lt 15 Feb 1797. Capt York Rangers 24 Sep 1803. Capt 1st Foot 28 Feb 1805. Major 16 Feb 1809. Bt Lt Colonel 30 May 1811. Capt and Lt Colonel Coldstream Guards 15 May 1817. Bt Colonel 19 Jul 1821. Major General 22 Jul 1830. Lt General 23 Nov 1841. Portuguese Army: Lt Colonel 1st Line 1809 (employed on intelligence work).

Served in the Peninsula with Staff Aug 1808 – Jan 1809 (ADC to Brigadier Charles Stewart). With Portuguese Army and Staff Feb 1809 – Apr 1814 (from Apr 1811 as AAG). Present at Corunna, Douro (Mentioned in Despatches), Talavera, Busaco, Sabugal (taken prisoner of war but escaped two days later, Mentioned in Despatches), Ciudad Rodrigo, Badajoz (AG), Salamanca (AG) (Mentioned in Despatches), Vittoria, Pyrenees (wounded), Nivelle, Nive, Orthes and Toulouse. Present at Waterloo as Assistant Adjutant General, where he was wounded. Became Adjutant General when Sir Edward Barnes was wounded and remained in this post until the Capture of Paris. CB. Order of St Anne. Also served at the Helder 1799, Ferrol 1800, Egypt 1801, Gibraltar 1802 and West Indies 1803. Awarded Gold Cross for Badajoz, Salamanca, Vittoria, Pyrenees, Nivelle, Nive, Orthes and Toulouse. Captain of Yarmouth Castle 1831. KCB 1832. Colonel 81st Foot 15 Jun 1840. Died in London 21 Nov 1842. One of Wellington's most successful intelligence officers. In 1808 obtained a dispatch which had been taken from the French by the Spanish. This dispatch gave Sir John Moore vital information of the true situation in Spain and deployment of French troops, thus enabling him to retreat to Corunna and save the British army. Obtained barges at the passage of the Douro so that Wellington's troops could cross the river after it was feared that the

French had burnt all the boats. His fluency in Spanish and Portuguese and his knowledge of the customs of these countries combined with his daring made him invaluable to Wellington. Died 24 Nov 1842 aged 68.

REFERENCE: *Dictionary of National Biography. United Service Magazine, Jan 1843, pp. 95–9. Gentleman's Magazine, Feb 1843, p. 201.*

WATERS, Marcus Antonius

Lieutenant. Royal Engineers.
Chest tomb: Kensal Green Cemetery, London. (20946/127/RS). (Photograph)

TO THE LOVED AND HONOURED MEMORY OF / MAJOR GENERAL / MARCUS ANTONIUS WATERS, / ROYAL ENGINEERS. / THIS GALLANT OFFICER WAS THE LAST SURVIVING OFFICER / OF HIS CORPS WHO WAS ENGAGED / IN THE BATTLES OF / QUATRE BRAS AND WATERLOO. / HE DEPARTED THIS LIFE ON / JANUARY 14TH 1868 AGED 73.

2nd Lt 30 Sep 1809. Lt 1 May 1811. 2nd Capt 11 Nov 1816. Capt 2 Jun 1830. Major 10 Jan 1837. Lt Colonel 15 Jul 1845. Colonel 20 Jun 1854. Major General 21 May 1855.

Served in the Peninsula Apr 1812 – Sep 1814. Present at the siege of Cadiz. Present at Quatre Bras, Waterloo, the siege of Peronne (led one of the columns of the assault 26 Jun 1815), the Capture of Paris and with the Army of Occupation. Also served in the Netherlands 1814–1815. Retired on full pay 21 May 1855. Last surving officer of the Royal Engineers at Waterloo.

WATSON, Amos

Corporal. 43rd (Monmouthshire) Light Infantry Regiment of Foot.
Buried in Braintree Cemetery, Braintree, Essex. (Grave 732 – no headstone). (Burial register)

Volunteer from Essex Militia.

Served in the Peninsula Jun 1810 – Dec 1813. Present at Ciudad Rodrigo, Badajoz, Salamanca, Vittoria, Pyrenees (wounded by a shell). Served in the 43rd Foot for seven and a half years. MGS medal for Ciudad Rodrigo, Badajoz, Salamanca, Vittoria and Pyrenees. Died 5 Jun 1863.

WATSON, George

Chaplain to the Forces. Chaplains Department.
Memorial tablet: St Mary's Church, Barnard Castle, Durham. (Photograph)

TO THE MEMORY OF / THE REVD GEORGE WATSON OF PEMBROKE COLL. CAMBRIDGE / SON OF JOHN AND ELIZABETH WATSON OF THIS TOWN, / WHO TERMINATED A SHORT, BUT USEFUL AND VIRTUOUS LIFE, / ON THE 28TH OF MARCH 1815 IN THE 27TH YEAR OF HIS AGE. / HE COMMENCED HIS PASTORAL CARES AT TIVERTON IN DEVON: AND IN THE SPRING OF 1814, JOINED / THE DUKE OF WELLINGTON'S ARMY IN THE SOUTH OF FRANCE AS / CHAPLAIN TO THE FORCES, / AND AFTERWARDS ACCOMPANIED THE EXPEDITION TO AMERICA / UNDER THE COMMAND OF GENERAL ROSS. / HIS UNAFFECTED PIETY AND ZEAL, / ENDEARED HIM TO ALL WHO KNEW HIM. / HE DIED ON HIS PASSAGE HOME / NEAR DAUPHIN ISLE IN THE GULF OF MEXICO / SINCERELY REGRETTED BY HIS FRIENDS, / WHO OFFER THiS FEEBLE TRIBUTE TO THE MEMORY / OF DEPARTED WORTH

Chaplain to the Forces 1 Apr 1814.

Served in the Peninsula Apr 1814 attached to 7 Division. Also served in North America 1814–1815. Died on his voyage home 28 Mar 1815.

WATSON, Henry

Captain. 48th (Northamptonshire) Regiment of Foot.
Interred in Catacomb B (v103 c2&3), Kensal Green Cemetery, London.
Named on the Memorial tablet: Albuera Wall, British Cemetery, Elvas, Portugal. (Photograph)

Cornet 3rd Lt Dragoons 6 May 1795. Lt 10 Feb 1796. Capt 25 Jun 1803. Capt 48th Foot 25 Dec 1807. Bt Major 18 Jan 1810. Bt Lt Colonel 28 Jul 1814. Bt Colonel 22 Jul 1830. Major General 28 Jun 1838. Portuguese Army: Major 4 Cavalry 16 Sep 1809. Lt Colonel 5 Cavalry 12 Mar 1810. Lt Colonel 7 Cavalry 1810. Lt Colonel 1 Cavalry 24 Mar 1812.

Served in the Peninsula with 48th Foot May – Sep 1809 and Portuguese Army Sep 1809 – Oct 1812 and Sep 1813 – Apr 1814. Present at Douro, Campo Mayor, Olivencia, Los Santos, Usagre, Albuera, Salamanca (severely wounded and awarded pension of £300 per annum) and Toulouse. Gold Medal for Salamanca. CB and KTS. MGS medal for Albuera and Toulouse. Also served in Ireland 1809 (Brigade Major). Died 31 Aug 1851.

Reference: Gentleman's Magazine, Oct 1851, p. 432. Annual Register, 1851, Appx, p. 326. United Service Magazine, Oct 1851, p. 319.

WATSON, Henry Robert

Captain. 3rd Regiment of Foot Guards.
Memorial stone in railed enclosure: Garden of the former Mayor's House, Bidart, France. (Photograph)

CI GIT / LE LIEUT COLONEL / S. C. MARTIN / LES CAPITAINES / THOMSON ET WATSON / DE LA GARDE ROYALE / DE HM BRITTANIQUE / TUE SUR LE CHAMP DE / BATAILLE LE 14 / DECEMBRE 1813.

Named on the Memorial: St Andrew's Church (now Musée Historique), Biarritz, France. (Photograph)
Named on Memorial Panel VII for the Nive: Royal Military Chapel, Wellington Barracks, London. (M.I.) (Destroyed by a Flying Bomb 1944)

Ensign 25 Dec 1807. Adjutant 1st Battalion 5 Mar 1812. Lt and Capt 9 Oct 1812.

Served in the Peninsula Apr 1810 – May 1811 and May 1812 – Dec 1813. Present at Cadiz, Barrosa (wounded), Salamanca, Vittoria, Nivelle and Nive where he was killed 12 Dec 1813 (date wrong on memorial stone). Educated at Charterhouse. The three officers of the 1st Foot Guards were all buried in the same grave – Lt Colonel Samuel C. Martin, Capt Henry R. Watson and Capt Charles W. Thompson. The house where they are buried was the headquarters of General John Hope from Dec 1813 to Jan 1814.

WATSON, J. Lewis

Captain. 69th (South Lincolnshire) Regiment of Foot.
Buried in a vault in St Andrew's Churchyard, Leasingham, Lincolnshire. (Photograph)

Cornet 7th Lt Dragoons 1798. Lt 25 Aug 1798. Capt 69th Foot 9 Jul 1803. Bt Major 4 Jun 1813. Bt Lt Colonel 18 Jun 1815. Major 69th Foot 10 Aug 1815. Major 54th Foot 19 Dec 1816. Major 71st Foot 18 Mar 1819.

Present at Quatre Bras, Waterloo and with the Army of Occupation (awarded Bt Lt Colonelcy). Also served in the Netherlands 1813–1814. Half pay 1829. Died 12 Apr 1842.

WATSON, James

Lieutenant. 42nd (Royal Highland) Regiment of Foot.
Named on the Memorial: St Andrew's Church (now Musée Historique), Biarritz, France. (Photograph)

Ensign 20 May 1812. Lt 1814.

Served in the Peninsula Sep 1813 – Apr 1814. Present at Nivelle, Nive, Orthes and Toulouse where he was severely wounded and died of his wounds 11 Apr 1814.

WATSON, Thomas Creswick
Captain. 3rd (King's Own) Regiment of Dragoons.
Memorial: St John's Wood Chapel Cemetery, London. (M.I.)

"THOMAS CRESWICK WATSON, OF THE 3RD LT DRAGOONS."

Lt 4 Apr 1805. Capt 25 Jul 1811.
Served in the Peninsula Oct 1811 – May 1812. Died 1831 aged 61.

WATSON, William
Private. Coldstream Regiment of Foot Guards.
Headstone: St Mary's Churchyard, Richmond, Yorkshire. (Photograph)

IN MEMORY OF / SERJEANT WILLIAM WATSON / WHO DIED SEPT 19 1844 / AGED 57 YEARS. / EARLY IN LIFE ENTERED THE COLDSTREAM / GUARDS AND FOUGHT IN THE PENINSULAR / WAR AND WATERLOO AND SUBSEQUENTLY / SERVED FOR SOME TIME IN THE WEST / INDIES, AND RETIRED WITH A PENSION. / HE WAS A KIND UPRIGHT AND PIOUS / MAN HIGHLY RESPECTED. / ………………..

Pte 25 Mar 1806. Cpl 1817. Sgt 1822. Sgt 96th Foot 12 Feb 1824.
Served with the Coldstream Guards in the Peninsula and at Waterloo. Also served with 96th Foot in Nova Scotia where he was injured in a fall and discharged 5 Mar 1827.

WATSON, William Henry
Lieutenant. 1st (Royal) Regiment of Dragoons.
Chest tomb: Christ Church Churchyard, Welshpool, Montgomeryshire, Wales. (Photograph)

BENEATH THIS STONE LIE THE MORTAL REMAINS OF / THE HON. SIR WILLIAM HENRY WATSON KNT: / BARON OF THE EXCHEQUER. / BORN JULY 1 1796 – DIED MARCH 13 1860. / SERVED IN EARLY LIFE AS LIEUTENANT OF DRAGOONS / IN SPAIN, FRANCE, AND BELGIUM: / ADMITTED STUDENT OF LINCOLN-INN AT THE AGE OF 21. / WAS MEMBER OF THE HOUSE OF COMMONS IN TWO PARLIAMENTS: / APPOINTED QUEEN'S COUNSEL 1843. / CREATED BARON OF THE / EXCHEQUER 1856. / HE DIED SUDDENLY IN THIS TOWN WHILST FULFILLING HIS DUTY AS / JUSTICE OF ASSIZE.

Cornet 11 Nov 1811. Lt 7 May 1812. Lt 6th Lt Dragoons 1816.
Served in the Peninsula Oct 1813 – Apr 1814. Present at Toulouse. Served with the Army of Occupation. MGS medal for Toulouse. Half pay 25 Mar 1816. Entered the legal profession and was called to the Bar 1832. QC 1843. MP for Kinsale 1841–1847 and Hull 1854–1856.
Reference: Dictionary of National Biography. Gentleman's Magazine, Apr 1860, p. 422. Annual Register, 1860, Appx, p. 499.

WATT, George
Private. Royal Artillery.
Memorial: Monymusk Churchyard (Lower part), Aberdeenshire. (M.I.)

"HERE LIES THE BODY OF GEORGE WATT, ROYAL HORSE ARTILLERY. HE DID HIS DUTY TO HIS KING AT WATERLOO 18 JUNE 1815."

Pte 14 Aug 1803

Present at Waterloo in Captain Mercer's 'D' Troop. Discharged 2 Sep 1817 on reduction of the regiment. Died Jul 1879 aged 84.

WATTS, John James

Lieutenant. 85th (Buckinghamshire Volunteers) Light Infantry Regiment of Foot.
Gravestone: Old Churchyard, Spital, Windsor, Berkshire. (Grave number: E 110)

Ensign 21st Foot 1 Feb 1810. Lt 12 Nov 1812. Lt 85th Foot 25 Jan 1813. Capt 6 Nov 1823.

Served in the Peninsula Aug 1813 – Apr 1814. Present at San Sebastian, Bidassoa, Nivelle, Nive and Bayonne. MGS medal for San Sebastian, Nivelle and Nive. Also served in North America 1814–1815 (present at Bladensburg, Capture of Washington, Baltimore and New Orleans). Military Knight of Windsor 1870. Died 2 Oct 1873.

WATTS, Michael

Ensign. Coldstream Regiment of Foot Guards.
Named on Memorial Panel VI for Barrosa: Royal Military Chapel, Wellington Barracks, London. (M.I.) (Destroyed by a Flying Bomb 1944)

Ensign 20 Oct 1808.

Served in the Peninsula Apr 1810 – Mar 1811. Present at Cadiz and Barrosa where he was killed 4 Mar 1811.

WAY, Sir Gregory Holman Bromley

Lieutenant Colonel. 29th (Worcestershire) Regiment of Foot.
Low monument: St Mary's Churchyard, Denham, Buckinghamshire. (Photograph)

TO THE MEMORY OF / .... / LIEUT GENERAL SIR GREGORY WAY / K.C.B. FEB 19TH 1844.

Ensign 26th Foot 24 Aug 1797. Lt 35th Foot 3 Nov 1799. Capt 13 Aug 1802. Capt 5th Foot 20 Jan 1803. Major 29th Foot 25 Feb 1808. Bt Lt Colonel 30 May 1811. Lt Colonel 4 Jul 1811. Colonel 19 Jul 1821. Major General 22 Jul 1830. Lt General 23 Nov 1841.

Served in the Peninsula Jul – Oct 1808, Apr 1809 – Aug 1811 and Apr 1813 – Feb 1814. Present at Rolica (wounded), Douro, Talavera, Busaco, first siege of Badajoz and Albuera (wounded and awarded pension of £200 per annum). Succeeded to the command of the 29th Foot during the battle of Albuera and was awarded Gold Medal. His career was marked by a number of imprisonments. At the start of his career in the 26th he sailed to Canada to join his regiment and was captured on the way and spent a year in a French prison. In 1805 he went with the 5th Foot on the Hanover expedition, was shipwrecked off the Dutch coast and taken prisoner. He was also taken prisoner at Rolica and released at the Convention of Cintra. Also served in Malta 1800 (present at the siege of Valetta), Hanover 1805, St Helena and Cape of Good Hope 1806 and South America (AQMG – present at Buenos Ayres). CB. KTS. Knighted 1814. Retired on half pay 1814 and became Deputy Adjutant General in Scotland. Colonel 1st West India Regt 21 Nov 1843.

Reference: Dictionary of National Biography. Royal Military Calendar, Vol. 4, pp. 343–4. Gentleman's Magazine, May 1844 pp. 537–8. Annual Register, 1844, Appx, pp. 212–13.

WEARE, Thomas

Captain. 35th (Sussex) Regiment of Foot.
Memorial tablet: St Andrew's Church, Hampton Bishop, Herefordshire. (Right-hand side of Chancel adjacent to altar). (Photograph)

IN THIS CHANCEL REST THE REMAINS OF / COLONEL THOMAS WEARE, K.H. / AIDE-DE-CAMP TO THE QUEEN / LATE COMMANDANT OF THE / PROVISIONAL BATTALION, CHATHAM / AND A MAGISTRATE OF THIS COUNTY. / BORN 16 APRIL 1785. / DIED 27 MARCH 1850. / IN EARLY LIFE HE SERVED IN THE GREAT CAUSE OF / THE COUNTRY IN EGYPT, THE IONIAN ISLANDS / IN SPAIN AND IN FRANCE, WITH HONOUR TO / HIMSELF. DURING HIS LATER YEARS HE DISCHARGED / WITH SINGULAR SUCCESS AND WARMEST / APPROBATION OF THE HIGHEST MILITARY AUT- / HORITIES / OF THE COUNTRY, THE DUTIES OF / AN ARDUOUS AND IMPORTANT COMMAND. / BELOVED & HONOURED BY ALL CONNECTED / WITH HIM / IN LIFE HE EVER STROVE TO DO HIS DUTY / TO GOD & MAN. IN HIS DEATH HE / WAS "HAPPY": FULL OF HOPE IN GOD'S / MERCY THROUGH JESUS CHRIST OUR LORD. / "THE LORD BE PRAISED" / ....

Ensign 14 Sep 1804. Lt 25 Jun 1805. Capt 19 Apr 1810. Bt Major 21 Jun 1813. Major 1 Jun 1826. Bt Lt Colonel 22 Jun 1830. Lt Colonel 13 Apr 1838. Bt Colonel 23 Nov 1841.

Served in the Peninsula Oct – Dec 1812 and Mar 1813 – Feb 1814 (ADC to Major General Oswald). Present at the retreat from Burgos (present at Villa Muriel), Osma, Vittoria (awarded Bt Majority), first and second sieges of San Sebastian, Nivelle and Bidart. Also served in Italy 1805, Egypt 1807 (present at Rosetta), Ischia and Procida 1809, Ionian Islands 1809–1810 and West Indies 1820–1832. MGS medal for Vittoria, San Sebastian and Nivelle. KH. Commanded the Provisional Battalion at Chatham 1836. Magistrate for the County of Herefordshire.

REFERENCE: Gentleman's Magazine, Jun 1850, pp. 662–4. Annual Register, 1850, Appx, p. 214.

WEAVER, Thomas

Corporal. 30th (Cambridgeshire) Regiment of Foot.
Headstone: Holy Trinity Churchyard, Bembridge, Isle of Wight. (Photograph)

THOMAS WEAVER / DIED 9TH MAR 1868 / AGED 75 YEARS / (VERSE) / ERECTED IN MEMORY OF HIS FAITHFUL SERVICES / AS SEXTON OF THIS CHURCH FOR 28 YEARS.

Pte 15 Jun 1807. Cpl 25 May 1824. Pte 4 Jun 1825. Cpl 14 Aug 1827.

Served in the Peninsula 1809 – Jun 1813. Present at Cadiz, Fuentes d'Onoro, Badajoz (wounded), Salamanca, Burgos (wounded) and retreat from Burgos (present at Villa Muriel). Present at Quatre Bras and Waterloo. Also served in the Netherlands 1814–1815 and India 1823–1829. Discharged 8 Jun 1831. MGS medal for Fuentes d'Onoro, Badajoz and Salamanca.

WEBB, Vere

1st Lieutenant. 95th Regiment of Foot.
Low monument: Locksbrook Road Cemetery, Bath, Somerset. (Grave number Fa 468). (Photograph)

VERE WEBB, DIED 4 OCT 1875 AGED 82. MAJOR RIFLE BRIGADE.

2nd Lieutenant 12 May 1812. 1st Lt 9 Dec 1813. Capt 19 Aug 1830. Bt Major 9 Nov 1846.

Present at Waterloo where he was wounded. Also served in the Netherlands 1814–1815 (present at Merxem and the siege of Antwerp). Adjutant Royal Cardigan Rifles Militia 1831–1851. Retired 17 Jan 1851.

WEBBER, William

2nd Captain. Royal Artillery.
Memorial tablet: St John the Baptist's Church, Stowford, Devon. (In alcove behind organ). (Photograph)

TO THE MEMORY / OF / WILLIAM WEBBER / (ELDEST SON OF / THE ABOVE WILLIAM WEBBER

AND JANE FRANCIS HIS WIFE) / LIEUT. COLONEL H. P. OF THE ROYAL HORSE ARTILLERY; / WHICH SERVICE HE ENTERED ON THE 8TH OF SEPTEMBER 1803. / HE SERVED / AT THE TAKING OF SURINAM, WHERE HE WAS WOUNDED; / IN THE CAMPAIGN OF SPAIN AND BATTLE OF CORUNNA, / UNDER SIR JOHN MOORE, WHERE HE WAS AGAIN WOUNDED; / THROUGHOUT THE PENINSULA CAMPAIGN AND / BATTLE OF WATERLOO, UNDER THE DUKE OF WELLINGTON, / WHERE HE WAS SEVERELY WOUNDED. / HE DIED MARCH 1ST 1847, / AT HEXWORTHY, IN THE COUNTY OF CORNWALL, / THE RESIDENCE OF HIS BROTHER, G. W. WEBBER ESQRE. / AGED 59. / AND LIES BURIED BY THE SIDE OF HIS PARENTS.

2nd Lt 8 Sep 1803. Lt 6 Dec 1803. 2nd Capt 17 Apr 1812. Bt Major 21 Jan 1819. Bt Lt Colonel 10 Jan 1837.

Served in the Peninsula Nov 1808 – Jan 1809 and May 1812 – Apr 1814. Present at Benevente and the Corunna campaign (embarked before the battle of Corunna), Vittoria, Pyrenees, St Palais, Orthes and Toulouse. Present at Waterloo in Major Bean's 'D' Troop Royal Horse Artillery, where he was severely wounded and his horse killed under him. Also served in the West Indies 1804 and Surinam (wounded and returned to Barbados only to catch yellow fever). Seriously ill and was sent back to England. Later served in Canada and North America 1811 and 1814. Wrote a war journal while in the Peninsula. Half pay 1826. *Reference: Webber, William, With the guns in the Peninsula: the Peninsular War journal of Captain William Webber, Royal Artillery, reprint 1991.*

WEBSTER, Henry Vassal
Lieutenant. 9th Regiment of Light Dragoons.
Low monument: Kensal Green Cemetery, London. (6797/100/2). (Photograph)

SACRED / TO THE MEMORY OF / LIEUT COL SIR HENRY VASSAL WEBSTER KTS KB KW / WHO DIED ON THE 19TH APRIL 1847, / AGED 54 YEARS.

Cornet 27 Mar 1810. Lt 13 Jun 1811. Capt 14 Dec 1815. Bt Major 22 Apr 1826. Bt Lt Colonel 9 Aug 1831.

Served in the Peninsula Jan 1812 – Aug 1813 (extra ADC to Major General Long Apr – Aug 1813). Present at Alba de Tormes and Vittoria (wounded). Present at Waterloo (extra ADC to the Prince of Orange). KTS. KW. Order ot St Bento d'Avis. Committed suicide in April 1847 in a fit of temporary insanity. *Reference: Gentleman's Magazine, Jul 1847, p. 93. Annual Register, 1847, Appx, p. 51 and pp. 223–4.*

WEBSTER, Thomas
Sergeant. 51st (2nd Yorkshire West Riding) Light Infantry.
Named on the Regimental Memorial: KOYLI Chapel, York Minster, Yorkshire. (Photograph)

Served in the Peninsula. Present at Nivelle where he was killed Nov 1813.

WEDDERBURN, Alexander
Lieutenant and Captain. Coldstream Regiment of Foot Guards.
Family Mural Memorial: St Michael's Churchyard, Inveresk, Midlothian, Scotland. (Photograph)

SACRED TO THE MEMORY OF / COLONEL ALEXANDER WEDDERBURN / LATE OF THE COLDSTREAM GUARDS / AND FIFTH SON OF THE LATE / SIR JOHN WEDDERBURN BARONET / OF BLACKNESS AND BALINDEAN / WHOSE REMAINS LIE HERE INTERRED / BORN 18 JUN 1791 DIED 3O JULY 1839 / ………………..

Ensign 17 Sep 1807. Lt and Capt 7 Nov 1811. Adjutant 8 Jan 1818. Bt. Major 21 Jan 1819. Capt and Lt Colonel 17 Apr 1823.

Served in the Peninsula Oct 1809 – Dec 1811 and Oct 1813 – Apr 1814 (ADC to Lt General Sir John Hope). Present at Busaco, Fuentes d'Onoro, Nive and Bayonne (Mentioned in Despatches).
Reference: Gentleman's Magazine, Sep 1839, p. 327. Annual Register, 1839, Appx, p. 355.

WEDGWOOD, Thomas
Ensign. 3rd Regiment of Foot Guards.
Memorial fountain: The Square, Tenby, Wales. (No longer extant)

The drinking fountain originally erected to his memory in the middle of Tudor Square at Tenby was erected by the Mayor in 1867 to commemorate Lt Colonel Thomas Wedgwood who fought at Waterloo.

Ensign 11 Jan 1814. Lt and Capt 28 Dec 1820. Capt and Lt Colonel 31 Dec 1830.
Present at Waterloo. Died at Tenby 7 Nov 1860. Younger son of Thomas Josiah Wedgwood.

WEIR, James
Ensign. 36th (Herefordshire) Regiment of Foot.
Headstone: St Aidans's Churchyard, Broughty Ferry, Dundee, Angus, Scotland. (Photograph)

IN MEMORY OF / CAPT JAMES WEIR. / LATE OF / HIS MAJESTY'S 50TH REGIMENT. / WHO DIED AT BROUGHTY FERRY / 18 NOV 1853.

Volunteer 42nd Foot Nov 1812. Ensign 36th Foot 13 May 1813. Lt 30 Dec 1819. Capt 50th Foot 27 Nov 1838.
Served in the Peninsula with 42nd Foot Nov 1812 – May 1813 and 36th Foot Jun 1813 – Apr 1814. Present at Nivelle and Orthes. Served with the Army of Occupation until 1817. Also served in the Ionian Islands and Malta 1817–1825 and West Indies and North America 1830–1839. Retired 27 Oct 1843. MGS medal for Nivelle and Orthes.

WEIR, John Laing
Major. 59th (2nd Nottinghamshire) Regiment of Foot.
Buried in the Garden of the Convent in Vittoria, Spain. (M.I.)

"OF WOUNDS RECEIVED AT THE BATTLE OF VITTORIA LT COL JOHN LAING WEIR, MAJOR OF THE 59TH FOOT, 4TH SON OF THE LATE R. LAING ESQ OF STRONGE IN ORKNEY"

Lt 17th Lt Dragoons. Capt 8th West India Regt 20 Oct 1801. Capt 86th Foot. Bt Major 3 Nov 1804. Capt 59th Foot 25 Apr 1805. Bt Lt Colonel 25 May 1806. Major 19 May 1808.
Served in the Peninsula Sep 1812 – Jul 1813. Present at Cadiz and Vittoria where he was severely wounded and died of his wounds 4 Jul 1813. His remains were interred in the garden of the Convent at Vittoria by the side of his Commanding Officer, Lt Colonel Charles Fane who also died of his wounds from the battle.

WELDEN, James
Private. 3rd (East Kent) Regiment of Foot.
Headstone: St Mary Magdalene's Churchyard, Elmstone Hardwick, Gloucestershire. (Beneath yew tree). (Photograph)

IN MEMORY OF / JAMES WELDEN / WHO SERVED IN THE 3RD / FOOT (THE BUFFS) FROM / 1793 TO 1814, AND WAS / ENGAGED IN THE BATTLES / OF ALBUHERA, BUSACO, & / TALAVERA. / DIED AUGT 12TH 1874. / AGED 97 YEARS. / ....

Pte 1 Apr 1805.

Served in the Peninsula Sep 1808 – Apr 1814. Present at Talavera, Busaco, Albuera (severely wounded with sabre cuts to the head). Served with the Army of Occupation. Also served in North America 1814–1815 and Australia 1821–1827. Discharged in Sydney 7 Jul 1827 being no longer fit after serving 22 years in the army. MGS medal for Talavera, Busaco and Albuera.

WELDON, William
Sergeant. 13th Regiment of Light Dragoons.
Buried in Great Yarmouth Cemetery, Yarmouth, Norfolk. (Row 96). (Burial record)

Pte Pembroke Fencible Cavalry 6 Sep 1795–18 Aug 1800. Pte Durham Fencible Infantry 19 Aug 1800 – 22 May 1802. Trumpeter 13th Lt Dragoons 4 Jun 1802. Sgt 1810.

Served in the Peninsula 1810 – Apr 1814. Present at Campo Mayor, Albuera, Usagre, Arroyo dos Molinos, Alba de Tormes, Vittoria, Nivelle, Nive, Garris, Orthes, Aire, St Gaudens and Toulouse. Present at Waterloo as Trumpet Major and with the Army of Occupation. Discharged 24 Jun 1818 with a pension of one shilling and eight pence, due partly to an injury he sustained in 1816 when he was kicked by a horse. After leaving the army became a Baptist Minister first at Thorpe St Chapel Birmingham and then moved to Great Yarmouth where he died 18 May 1845.

REFERENCE: Weldon, William, Jehovah Nissi, the Lord my Banner, Parts 1 – 3, 1818–1820. Norfolk Chronicle and Norwich Gazette, 24 May 1845, p. 2.

WELLINGTON, Arthur, Duke of
Field Marshal. Commander of the Forces.

London
Memorial: St Paul's Cathedral, London. (Nave North). (Photograph)

ARTHUR FIRST DUKE OF WELLINGTON

The following battle honours are recorded on a bronze strip around the base of the Memorial:

ASSAYE, GAWILGHUR, ARGAUM, ZUBIRI, VIMIERO, KIOGE, BUSACO, TALAVERA, / TORRES VEDRAS, PONT CIBERTE, CANIZAL, CASAL NUOVA, BURGOS, EL RETIRO, ARETESOUI, / RONCEVALLES, SAN SEBASTIAN, BADAJOS, BIDASSOA, PAMPELUNA, SALAMANCA, ADOUR, / NIVELLE, QUATRE BRAS, WATERLOO, ORTHES, PERONNE, NIVE, TOULOUSE, GARONNE, / BAYONNE, VITTORIA, CUIDAD RODRIGO, HOMANZA, TORMES, ALDEA DA PONTE, / ARREYO MOLINOS, FONS D'ARONCE, SABUGAL, MORALES, FUENTES D'ONOR, DOURO, ALMEIDA, / EL BODEN, ROLICA, BURGOS, CONAGUL, AHMEDNUGGAR.

Alfred Stevens undertook the original design of the memorial but he died midway through the construction in the 1860s. Lord Leighton the painter and sculptor selected the final position of the memorial and it was eventually completed in 1912 with the erection of Wellington mounted on his horse Copenhagen at the top. The bronze sarcophagus looks like a coffin but Wellington is buried in the Crypt. It is reputed to have been made from captured French cannon. The whole memorial is surrounded by a railing incorporating 12 lions.

Tomb: St Paul's Cathedral, London. (Photograph)

ARTHUR / DUKE OF / WELLINGTON / BORN MAY 1 MDCCLXIX / DIED SEPT XIV MDCCCLII

Two inscriptions in mosaic on the floor of the area around the tomb:

NUNC UMBRATA CERIS CIVILI TEMPORA QUERCU: / UT DEBIT FAMAE GLORIA NULLA TRUAE

CONSERVATA TUIS ASIA ATQUE EUROPA / TRIUMPHIS INVICTUM BELLO TE COLUERE DUCEM

English translation:

NOW YOU MAY WEAR YOUR TEMPLES SHADED WITH THE CIVIL OAK WREATH SO THAT THE GLORY OF YOUR FAME MAY NEVER DECLINE / HAVING BEEN SAVED BY YOUR VICTORIES EUROPE AND ASIA HAVE PROMOTED YOU AS A INVINCIBLE LEADER

Also on the mosaic are four shields each with the inscription:

VIRTUTIS FORTUNA COMES

Monument: Facing Apsley House, Duke of Wellington Place, London. (Photograph)

The plinth is inscribed on one side:

WELLINGTON

On the reverse:

1769–1852

At each corner is the figure of a soldier from:

23RD ROYAL WELSH FUSILIERS / 1ST GUARDS / 6TH INNISKILLING DRAGOONS / 42ND ROYAL HIGHLANDERS

Foreign Office

Statue: Ghurkha Staircase, Foreign Office, London. (Photograph)

WELLINGTON

Guildhall

Statue: Guildhall, City of London. (Photograph)

ARTHUR WELLESLEY / DUKE OF WELLINGTON. / BORN 1769. DIED 1852.

Hyde Park

Victory Arch: Hyde Park Corner, London. (Photograph)

The Wellington Arch was built in 1825–7 as part of a campaign to improve the Royal Parks. Intended as a victory arch proclaiming Wellington's defeat of Napoleon, it is crowned by the largest bronze sculpture in Europe, depicting the Angel of Peace descending on the 'Quadriga', the four-horsed chariot of War.

Statue of Achilles: Hyde Park, London. (Photograph)

TO ARTHUR, DUKE OF WELLINGTON, / AND HIS BRAVE COMPANIONS IN ARMS. / THIS

STATUE TO ACHILLES / CAST FROM CANNON TAKEN IN THE VICTORIES / OF SALAMANCA, VITTORIA, TOULOUSE AND WATERLOO, / IS INSCRIBED / BY THEIR COUNTRYWOMEN. / PLACED ON THIS SPOT / ON THE XVIII DAY OF JUNE MDCCCXXII / BY COMMAND OF / HIS MAJESTY GEORGE III.

Cast from twelve 24-pounder French guns taken at Vittoria, Salamanca, Toulouse and Waterloo, it was erected by the women of England at a cost of £10,000. The pedestal, of two tiers of granite, is massive and well proportioned. It was unveiled 18 Jun 1822.

Royal Exchange
Statue: Outside Royal Exchange, London. (Photograph)

WELLINGTON / ERECTED 18 JUNE / 1844

Sculpted from French cannon captured during Wellington's victories battles. The sculptor, Sir Francis Chantry, was commissioned to do the work, but died before it was finished and his assistant Henry Weekes completed the statue in 1846.

Tower of London
Memorial tablet: Chapel Royal of St Peter-Ad-Vincula, Tower of London, London. (Photograph)

FIELD MARSHAL / THE DUKE OF WELLINGTON / KG / VICTOR OF WATERLOO / CONSTABLE / OF THE / TOWER OF LONDON / 1826–1852

Statue: Tower of London. (Lithograph)

Foundation stone: Tower of London, London. (Photograph)

THIS FIRST STONE WAS LAID BY / FIELD MARSHAL / THE DUKE OF WELLINGTON / KG, GCB, GCH, / CONSTABLE OF THE TOWER / COMMANDER IN CHIEF OF HM FORCES / ON THE 14TH JUNE MDCCCXIV

Wellington Barracks
Statue, Wellington Barracks, London. (Photograph)

THIS STATUE OF THE DUKE OF WELLINGTON / WAS MOVED FROM IT'S POSITION IN THE PORCHWAY OF / THE CHURCH OF ST MICHAEL AND ALL SAINTS, CATERHAM / TO IT'S PRESENT POSITION IN WELLINGTON BARRACKS / ON 22ND JANUARY 1996. / DEDICATED TO THE GLORY OF GOD / AND PLACED IN THIS CHAPEL BY / LIEUT/ COL. LORD GLANUSK. D.S.O. / LATE GRENADIER GUARDS. / COMMANDANT GUARDS' DEPOT 1901–1903. / AND / LIEUT. E. G. CHRISTIE-MILLER. / COLDSTREAM GUARDS. / ADJUTANT GUARD'S DEPOT 1902–1904.

Woolwich
Wellington Memorial: Royal Arsenal, Woolwich, Kent. (Reported to be kept in store). (Photograph)

The marble statue of Wellington sculptured by Thomas Milnes was presented to the Board of Ordnance in 1848 and erected in the south-west corner of the Parade Ground at the Tower of London. In 1861 it was moved again to a site near the White Tower and moved again two years later to the Royal Arsenal. For 112 years it stood south of the Grand Store, originally the Headquarters of the Ordnance Department.

The Wellington Memorial plaque was unveiled Jun 1874. The cast-iron work incorporated in the wall originated from the buildings which sometime adjoined the central pavilions of the Royal Laboratory. The larger cannon are Smooth Bore Brass 6-pounder of the type uses at the Battle of Waterloo. One is dated 1850 and probably saw service in the Crimean War and the Indian Mutiny. The other, dated 1855, probably never was in action. The carriages are modern. (Wesley, Harry, *The Royal Arsenal Woolwich* 1987).

Aldershot

Statue: Aldershot, Hampshire. (Photograph)

WELLINGTON

The origins of the statue go back to the end of the Napoleonic Wars, when various memorials to the British triumph were begun, including Nelson's Column in Trafalgar Square and the victory arch at Hyde Park Corner. In 1837 a committee was formed under the Chairmanship of the Duke of Rutland to raise funds for a military memorial to the Duke of Wellington. The sculptor was Matthew Cotes Wyatt, a highly controversial choice at the time. The monument was made on a massive scale, the largest equestrian statue hitherto to be seen in Britain. The final statue was 30 feet high, 26 feet from nose to tail, and 21 feet in girth. It weighed 40 tons. In 1840 the statue was moved in a grand procession from Wyatt's workshop to Hyde Park Corner where it was erected on the unfinished victory arch, again amidst much controversy, for many believed it was completely out of scale. However, it could not be moved as this would be an insult to the ageing Duke of Wellington and by the time of his death the public had become used to the statue and the controversy died down. In 1882 traffic congestion at Hyde Park Corner resulted in the re-alignment of the victory arch. The controversy about the Wellington statue was re-ignited and the Government decided to replace it with a figure of Victory.

After removal from the arch, the statue was left in Green Park until a decision was made on its future, as no sites in London were considered suitable. In 1883 the Prince of Wales suggested that the statue should be taken to the great military camp at Aldershot 'where it will be highly regarded by the Army'. This was agreed and the statue was brought to Aldershot in pieces in August 1884. The re-assembled monument was handed over to the care of the Army in August 1885. Standing out against the skyline, the Wellington Statue rapidly became a well-known landmark and a symbol of military Aldershot.

The Statue fell into decline through the second half of the twentieth century. By the millennium the monument was in a poor state and largely hidden by overgrown bushes and trees. At the beginning of 2004 Aldershot Garrison, in partnership with local conservation groups and volunteers, began a major project to restore the Wellington Statue to its former glory. Overgrown bushes were cleared by volunteers, while restorers cleaned and re-bronzed the statue so it could be seen as intended, with the remarkable details revealed and the skill of Matthew Cotes Wyatt once again fully appreciated.

Baslow

Stone Cross: On bridleway on Blackstone Edge, above Baslow, Derbyshire. (The old Baslow to Chesterfield turnpike overlooking the present A619 Baslow to Sheffield road). (Photograph)

WELLINGTON / BORN 1769 DIED 1852

The cross was erected by E. M. Wrench of the 34th Foot in 1866 to commemorate the Duke of Wellington. On nearby Birchen Edge is a monument erected in 1810 to honour Lord Horatio Nelson.

Brighton

Monument: St Nicholas's Church, Brighton, Sussex. (Photograph)

ASSAYE – TORRES VEDRAS – VITTORIA – WATERLOO / IN MEMORIAM / HAEC DOMUS SACROSANCTA / MAXIMI DUCIS WELLINGTON / QUA IPSE ADOLESCENS / DEUM COLEBAT / REAEDIFICATUR

Memorial raised to commemorate the association between Sir Arthur as a boy when he was taught by the then Vicar. He was also a member of the Choir.

Durham

Obelisk: Wynyard Hall Park, Long Newton, County Durham. (Photograph)

WELLINGTON

THIS STONE / IS DEDICATED TO / ENGLAND'S GREATEST GENERAL / ARTHUR DUKE OF WELLINGTON / TO COMMEMORATE HIS VISIT TO / CHARLES MARQUIS OF LONDONDERRY / WHO SERVED / AS ADJUTANT GENERAL / DURING HIS CAMPAIGNS / IN THE PENINSULAR

Reference: Liddell, A., An illustrated history of Wynyard estate...., 1989.

Leeds

Statue: Woodhouse Moor at junction of Moorland Road and Clarendon Road, Leeds, Yorkshire. (Photograph)

WELLINGTON / 1859

Erected in 1855 in front of the Leeds Town Hall and relocated to its present postion in 1937.

Liverpool

Statue: Liverpool, Lancashire. (Near to St George's Hall). (Photograph)

Side 1:
WELLINGTON

Side 2:
ASSAYE. TALAVERA. / ARGAUM. BUSACO. / ROLICA. FUENTES D'ONOR. / VIMIERO./ CUIDAD RODRIGO. / OPORTO. BADAJOS.

Side 3:
SALAMANCA. BAYONNE. / VITTORIA. ORTHEZ. / SAN SEBASTIAN. QUATRE BRAS. / WATERLOO.

Side 4:
BRONZE RELIEF DEPICTING THE DUKE ORDERING THE FINAL CHARGE AT WATERLOO

Designed by Mr Lawson of Glasgow the monument was inaugurated in May 1863, and took two years to erect.The statue is 14 feet high, and cast from cannon taken at Waterloo. It stands on a column 81 feet high.

Manchester

Statue: Piccadilly Circus, Manchester, Lancashire. (Photograph).

WELLINGTON / BORN / MAY 1 MDCCLXIX / DIED / SEPTEMBER XIV MDCCCLII / ERECTED / BY PUBLIC SUBSCRIPTION / MDCCCLVI

Four bronze reliefs at foot of statue represent:
Battle of Assaye 1803

Wellington receiving thanks from House of Commons in Parliament 1814
Battle of Waterloo
Wellington as a diplomat at the Congress of Vienna.

Norwich
Statue: Norwich Cathedral Close, Norfolk. (Photograph)

WELLINGTON

Portsmouth
Brass Memorial tablet: Royal Garrison Church, Portsmouth, Hampshire. (Back of a choir stall). (Photograph)

FIELD MARSHAL ARTHUR / DUKE OF WELLINGTON / K.G. G.C.B. G.C.H. DIED / SEP. 14 1852. AGED 83. / D.D. FIELD MARSHAL / H.R.H. THE DUKE OF / CAMBRIDGE. K.G.

Southam
Statue: Church of the Ascension, Southam, near Cheltenham, Gloucestershire. (Photograph)

ARTHUR / DUKE OF WELLINGTON

Memorial brass tablet: below the statue on a wall to the left.

IN MEMORY OF THE DUKE OF WELLINGTON

Stanton-in-the-Peak
Inscription on a natural gritstone outcrop between Stanton-in-the-Peak and Birchover, Derbyshire, containing a memorial to Wellington and Lt Colonel Thornhill. (Photograph)

FIELD MARSHAL / DUKE OF WELLINGTON / DIED 14 SEPT 1852. / AGED 82 YEARS. / LIEUT-COLONEL WILLIAM THORNHILL 7 HUSSARS / DIED 9 DEC, 1851 / AGED 71 / ASSAYE 1803. WATERLOO 1815. / T. MASTERS

The rock is called the Andle Stone (Anvil Stone) and is encircled by a deteriorating stone wall and obscured by natural rhododendron growth. The date on the inscription is incorrectly given as 1851. It should be 1850.

Stratfield Saye
Column: Entrance to Stratfield Saye House, Berkshire. (No inscription recorded). (Photograph)

Pedestal monument: Grounds of Stratfield Saye House, near to a tree planted by the 1st Duke. (Photograph)

IN MEMORY / OF THE GALLANT BRITISH SOLDIERS / WHO GAVE THEIR LIVES / FOR THE GREATNESS OF THEIR OWN COUNTRY / AND FOR INDEPENDENCE / AND LIBERTY OF SPAIN.

Bust from the Officers' Mess, Knightsbridge Barracks, which were demolished 1966.

The bust was originally placed on the Old Jubilee Drive by Gerald, 7th Duke of Wellington after the completion of the new Jubilee Drive and Lodges. It was moved by Arthur Valerian 8th Duke of Wellington to this spot, where it commemorates the planting of this cedar of Lebanon (Cedris Libani) by Arthur, 1st Duke of Wellington on his first visit to the estate in September 1817. The Bust was purchased by the 8th Duke when the Barracks were being demolished, as a gift for his father.

Headstone: To Copenhagen, Wellington's horse in the grounds of Stratfield Saye. (Photograph)

HERE LIES / COPENHAGEN / THE CHARGER RIDDEN BY / THE DUKE OF WELLINGTON / THE ENTIRE DAY, AT THE / BATTLE OF WATERLOO. / BORN 1808. DIED 1836. / GOD'S HUMBLER INSTRUMENT THOUGH MEANER CLAY / SHOULD SHARE THE GLORY OF THAT GLORIOUS DAY.

Walmer

Hatchment: Blessed St Mary's Church, Walmer, Kent. (Photograph)

VIRTUTE FORTUNA HOMEN

Wellington

Obelisk: Wellington, Somerset. (Erected on the highest point of the Blackdown Hills). (Photograph)

Now in the care of the National Trust, the foundation stone was laid in 1817, but the plans were too elaborate for the money available and it was left uncompleted for many years until the death of the Duke in 1852, when there was renewed effort to complete the project. It was finally completed in 1892, standing at a height of 175 feet. In 2008 the National Trust reported that cracks had been discovered and the landmark was in a dangerous state and may have to be pulled down or even replaced with a fibreglass replica. It is now closed to the public and safety barriers have been erected.
Reference: Milner, David L., The Wellington monument in Somerset, Waterloo Journal, Apr 2000, p. 28. Adams, H. W. and C. P., Wellington's monument at Wellington, Waterloo Journal, Summer 2008, p. 30. Bush, Robin and Allen, Gillian, The book of Wellington, 1981, pp. 113–17.

Woodhall Spa

Obelisk: Woodhall Spa, Lincolnshire. Inscription not recorded. (Photograph)

IRELAND

Dublin

Obelisk: Phoenix Park, Dublin, Ireland. (Photograph)
East Face. (Photograph)

ASIA AND EUROPE SAVED BY THEE, PROCLAIM / INVINCIBLE IN THE WAR, THY BREATHLESS NAME, / NOW ROUND THY BROW THE CIVIC OAK WE TWINE / THAT EVERY EARTHLY GLORY BE THINE. / WELLINGTON / CONSERVATA TUIS ASIA ATOUE EUROPA TRIUMPHIS / INVICTUM BELLO TE COLUERE DUCEM, / NUNE UMBRATA CERIS CIVILI TEMPORA QUERCU UT DEBIT FAMAE GLORIA NULLA TRUAE. / THIS TESTIMONIAL TO THE SERVICE OF ARTHUR, DUKE OF WELLINGTON WAS ERECTED BY PRIVATE SUBSCRIPTION OF HIS COUNTRYMEN.

South Face. (Photograph)
Shows Wellington the statesman and simply has the inscription

MDCCCXXIX

West Face.
Shows action in India. (Photograph)

North Face.
Shows a depiction of Waterloo. (Photograph)

On each face of the obelisk itself are the names of the battles:

EAST: BIDASSOA, NIVELLE, NIVE, ADOUR, ORTHES, TARBES, TOULOUSE.

NORTH: TALAVERA, FUENTOS D'ONARO, CUIDAD RODRIGO, BADAJOS, SALAMANCEA, VITTORIA, PYRENEES.

WEST: CANANGUL, POONAH, AHMEDNAGAR, ASSAYE, ARGAUM, GAWILGHUR, MONKASEER.

SOUTH: ROLICA, VIMIERO, OPORTO, BUSACO, TORRES VEDRAS, REDHINA, SABUGAL.

The obelisk was begun in 1817 and finished in 1861. The inscription was written in honour of his brother by Richard, Marquis Wellesley. The sculptures were executed by Irish artists and cast from cannon taken in battle.

Grange

Tower: Kilcooley Abbey, Grange, County Tipperary, Ireland. (Near summit of Slieveardagh Hills). (Photograph)

THIS BUILDING / WAS ERECTED BY / SIR WILLIAM BARKER BART / 1817 / IN THE 80TH YEAR OF HIS AGE / TO HIS GRACE / THE DUKE OF WELLINGTON / IN COMMEMORATION OF HIS GLORIOUS VICTORY / OVER THE FRENCH AT WATERLOO / JUNE THE 18TH ANNO DOMINI / 1815

Erected in 1817, the Wellington Monument, as it is known locally, was constructed by Sir William Barker who also built the near-by mansion of Kilcooley Abbey.The tower commemorates the military successes of the Duke of Wellington.

Trim

Statue: Trim, Ireland. (Photograph)

THIS COLUMN / ERECTED IN THE YEAR / MDCCCXVII / IN HONOUR / OF THE ILLUSTRIOUS / DUKE OF WELLINGTON / BY THE GRATEFUL CONTRIBUTION / OF THE COUNTY MEATH.

SCOTLAND

Edinburgh

Statue: Princes Street, Edinburgh, Scotland. (Photograph)

WELLINGTON

Glasgow

Statue: Queen Street, Royal Exchange Flags, Glasgow, Lanarkshire, Scotland. (Photograph)

WELLINGTON

Erected 1844.

Peniel Heugh
Monument: Summit of Peniel Heugh Hill, Crailing, Roxburghshire, Scotland. (Photograph)

TO THE / DUKE OF WELLINGTON / AND THE BRITISH ARMY / WILLIAM KERR / VI MARQUESS OF LOTHIAN / AND HIS TENANTRY / DEDICATE THIS MONUMENT / XVIII JUNE MDCCCXV

Built between 1817 and 1824. No access to the Tower.

WALES

Brecon
Statue: Town Square, Brecon, Wales. (Photograph)

Front Face:

WELLINGTON / MDCCCLII / THIS STATUE WAS MODELLED FROM LIFE / BY THE LATE JOHN EVAN THOMAS FSA JP / DEPUTY LIEUTENANT AND HIGH SHERIFF / OF THE COUNTY OF BRECKNOCK / WAS PRESENTED BY HIM / TO HIS NATIVE TOWN IN THE YEAR 1856

WELLINGTON
MDCCCLII

Left Face Bas relief plaque:

PENINSULAR

Rear Face:

PICTON / MDCCCXV

Right Face Bas Relief Plaque:

WATERLOO

Tredegar
Clock Tower: Tredegar, Monmouthshire, Wales. (Photograph)

WELLINGTON / ENGLAND'S / HERO

GIBRALTAR

Statue: Alameda Gardens, Gibraltar. (Photograph)

IMAGINEM HANC ARTHURI WELLESLEY / WELLINGTONIÆ DUCIS / AD MDCCCXLX POSUERUNT BRITANNI / NAM CIVILIA QUAM MILITARI MUNERE / IN HAC ARCHEO HUNGENTES / P******* RES GESTAS ADMIRATI / IMPERATORUS SUMMI INVICTI / QUI ANNUEVENTE DEO OPTIMO MAXIMO / IMPERANTE GEORGIO TERTIO / BRITANNARIUM REGI PATRE PATRIA / ET SOCUS HISPANIS ATIQUE LUSITANIS / HAS REGIONES / A DIRIS GALLIÆ EXERCITIBUS / TUM FŒDE OPPRESSAS / IN REBUS VEL MAXIME ARDUIS ET PENE DESPÈRATIS / POST LONGAM ET DURAM MILITIAM / ET PRÆLIA INNUMERA TOTIDEMQUE FERE VICTORIAS / PULSIS GALLIS A GADIBUS USQUE / ULTRA PYRENÆOS MONTES ET GARUMNAM FLUVIUM / AB IMMANI TANDEM HOSTE FELIX LIBERAVIT / RENATUM

DENIQUE IN GALIA ET BELGIO / ATROCISSIMUDE BELLUM CONFECIT / UNO PRÆLIO WATERLOO / ET SURQPAM AB INSTANTE TYRANNIDE VINDICAVIT / ET IMMORTALENI / NON SIBI SOLI SETI ARMIS BRITANNICIS / GLORIANE PEPERIT / DE REGE FT PATRIA ET GENFRE HUMANE / OPTIME MERITUS

Inscription on base:

WELLINGTON

Sir George Don, the Governor of Gibraltar unveiled the statue in 1819. The bust was cast in bronze under the direction of Sir Richard Westmascott from guns captured by the Duke of Wellington. Funds for the monument had been obtained by deducting a day's pay from all the members of the Garrison.

INDIA

Bombay

Ornamental Fountain: Esplanade, Bombay, India. (M.I.)

An ornamental fountain of stone. The basin which is octagonal in shape is about 37 feet in diameter resting on a circular base approached by a flight of six steps all round. The sides of the central octagonal column are panelled and on each alternate panel are inscribed the names of battles in which the Duke of Wellington took part, the intermediate panels being filled in with representative figures in bas relief.

N.W. Side:

"VIMIERA. DOURO. BUSACO. ROLICA."

S.W. Side:

"GONAGHULL. ASSAYE. AHMEDNUGGAR. ARGAUM. GAWILGHUR. SERINGAPATAM. POWANGHUR".

S.E. Side:

"NIVELLE. NIVE. TOULOUSE. WATERLOO."

N.E. Side:

"TALAVERA. BADAJOZ. CIUDAD RODRIGO. SALAMANCA. VITTORIA. BIDASSOA. ST SEBASTIAN."

PORTUGAL

Busaco

Memorial plaque: near the Cruz Alta (High Cross) on the Busaco heights, Portugal. (Photograph)

PORTO DE COMANDO DO MARECHAL GENERAL / ARTHUR WELLESLEY DUQUE DE WELLINGTON, / COMMANDANTE EM CHEFEDAS FORCAS / ANGLO-LUSAS NA BATALHA DO BUCACO / TRAVADA EM 27 DE SEPTEMBRO DE 1810 / COLOCADA EM 27 X 1947

("COMMAND POST OF MARSHAL GENERAL ARTHUR WELLESLEY / DUKE OF WELLINGTON,

/ COMMANDER-IN-CHIEF OF THE / ANGLO-PORTUGUESE FORCES AT THE BATTLE OF BUSACO, / OCCUPIED ON 27 SEPTEMBER 1810")

SPAIN

Freneida

Statue: Freneida, Spain. (Photograph)

LORD WELLINGTON / TERROR, HOSTIUM LUSITANIÆ / ARTHUR WELLESLEY, 1^E DUQUE DE WELLINGTON / (1769–1852), MARQUES DO DOURO E DE / TORRES VEDRAS, / MARECHAL GENERAL DOS / EXERCITOS DE SUA ALTOZA REAL O PRINCIPE / REGENTE DE PORTUGAL, CONTRIBUIU CAM O SOU / GENIO PARA A DERROTA NAPOLEONICA

Fuentes d'Onoro

Memorial: Fuentes d'Onoro. (Photograph)

BICENTENARIA / DE LA GUERRA / DE LA / INDEPENCIA / 5 DE MAYO DE 2011

FUENTES DE OÑORO / VILLA HEROICA / 1811–2011 / MONUMENTO / HOMENAJE A LAS TROPAS / ANGLO LUSAS / FRANCESAS Y ESPANOLOS, / QUE LUCHARON CON / VALOR Y HONOR / EN LA HISTÓRICA BATALLA / DEL 3 AL 5 DE MAYO DE 1811 / LORD WELLINGTON / ALFONSO IX / J. S. EL CHARRO

Memorial unveiled 2011 to commemorate the bicentenary of the Battle of Fuentes d'Onoro. Lord Wellington, Alfonso IX and J. S. Charro are portrayed in relief on three sides.

Salamaca

Plaque to Wellington in Square at Salamanca, Spain. (Photograph)

Ensign 73rd Foot 7 Mar 1787. Lt 76th Foot 25 Dec 1787. Lt 41st Foot 23 Jan 1788. Lt 12th Lt Dragoons 25 Jun 1789. Capt 58th Foot 30 Jun 1791. Capt 18th Lt Dragoons 31 Oct 1792. Major 33rd Foot 30 Apr 1793. Lt Colonel 30 Sep 1793. Bt Colonel 3 May 1796. Major General 29 Apr 1802. Lt General 25 Apr 1808. General 31 Jul 1811. Field Marshal 21 Jan 1813.

Present in the Peninsula Jul – Aug 1808 and Apr 1809 – Apr 1814. Present at Quatre Bras, Waterloo and with the Army of Occupation. Also served in Ireland 1788–1794, Flanders 1794–1795, India 1797–1805, Hanover Dec 1805 – Feb 1806. (His service records are not fully recorded here as they have been so well documented elsewhere). KG, GCB, GCH. Gold Cross and nine clasps for Rolica, Vimeiro, Talavera, Busaco, Fuentes d'Onoro, Ciudad Rodrigo, Badajoz, Salamanca, Vittoria, Pyrenees, Nivelle, Nive, Orthes and Toulouse. Held the First and Highest Class of nearly every Order in Europe. MP for Trim 1790, Rye 1806, Mitchell (Cornwall) 1807, Newport (Isle of Wight) 1807–1809. Prime Minister 9 Jan 1828–16 Nov 1830. Colonel 33rd Foot 30 Jan 1806. Colonel Royal Horse Guards 1 Jan 1813. Colonel Rifle Brigade 19 Feb 1820. Colonel Grenadier Guards 22 Jan 1827. Constable of the Tower of London 29 Dec 1826. Commander-in-Chief Jan – May 1827, Aug 1827 – Feb 1828. Reappointed 15 Aug 1842. Lord Warden of Cinque Ports 27 Dec 1828. Died at Walmer Castle, Kent 22 Sep 1852.

REFERENCE: *Dictionary of National Biography. Gurwood, John, The dispatches of Field Marshall the Duke of Wellington, during the various campaigns in India, Denmark, Portugal, Spain, the Low Countries and France from 1799–1818, 13 vols, 1837–1839. Longford, Elizabeth, Wellington: the Years of the Sword, 1969. Wellington: pillar of state, 1975. Hibbert, Christopher, Wellington: a personal history, 1997. Gentleman's Magazine, Oct 1852, pp. 413–24. Annual Register, 1852, Appx, p. 30. Life of the Duke of Wellington, Annual Register, 1853, pp. 437–518 and Public funeral of Field Marshal Arthur Duke of Wellington, pp. 482–96. Favret, Leo, The life and campaigns of the Duke of Wellington: a brief guide to the literature, Part 1 – Sources of Information (1), Waterloo Journal, Summer 2008, pp. 3–16. Part 2- Secondary Sources (1), No. 1, Spring 2009, pp. 3–13.*

WELLS, John Neave
2nd Captain. Royal Engineers.
Interred in Catacomb B 11359 (v99 c8), Kensal Green Cemetery, London.

2nd Lt 6 Nov 1806. 1st Lt 1 May 1807. 2nd Capt 20 May 1812. Bt Major 21 Jan 1819. Lt Colonel 10 Jan 1837. Bt Colonel 11 Nov 1851.

Served in the Peninsula Aug 1808 – Jan 1809 and Mar 1810 – Apr 1814. Present at Rolica, Vimeiro, (taken prisoner but released after the Convention of Cintra), Corunna, Cadiz, Barrosa, Badajoz, Bidassoa and Bayonne. Present in France with the Army of Occupation 1815. Also served at Walcheren 1809 (present at the siege of Flushing). MGS medal for Rolica, Vimeiro, Corunna, Barrosa and Badajoz. CB. Died at Woodstock 25 Feb 1854. Cousin of Lt and Capt John Fremantle Coldstream Regiment of Foot Guards.

WELLS, Rees
Sergeant. 51st (2nd Yorkshire West Riding) Light Infantry.
Named on the Regimental Memorial tablet: KOYLI Chapel, York Minster, Yorkshire. (Photograph)

Served in the Peninsula where he was killed.

WELLS, Samuel
Sergeant Major. 10th (Prince of Wales's Own Royal) Regiment of Light Dragoons.
Pedestal tomb: Mount Jerome Cemetery, Dublin, Ireland. (Photograph)

SACRED / TO THE MEMORY OF / SAMUEL WELLS ESQRE / PAYMASTER 10TH ROYAL HUSSARS / IN WHICH REGT HE SERVED 42 YEARS. / HE WAS PROMOTED TO A CORNETCY / AND THE ADJUTANCY IN 1816 / AND TO PAYMASTERSHIP IN 1826. / HE WAS PRESENT WITH THE REGIMENT / AT THE SEVERAL ACTIONS INSCRIBED / ON EITHER SIDE OF THIS MONUMENT / HE DEPARTED THIS LIFE / AT PORTOBELLO BARRACKS, DUBLIN / ON THE 8TH FEBRUARY 1842 / AGED 61 YEARS. / THIS TABLET IS ERECTED / TO HIS MEMORY AS / A TRIBUTE OF RESPECT / BY / HIS BROTHER OFFICERS / VITTORIA / PYRENEES / ORTHES / TARBES / TOULOUSE / SAHAGUN / MAYORGA / BENEVENTE / CORUNNA / MORALLES

Pte 1798. Sgt 1800. Sgt Major 1808. Cornet and Adjutant 6 Feb 1816. Paymaster 25 Jun 1826.

Served in the Peninsula Nov 1808 – Jan 1809 and Feb 1813 – Apr 1814 (Acting Adjutant during the 1813 campaign). Present at Sahagun, Mayorga, Benevente, Corunna, Morales, Vittoria, Pyrenees, Orthes, Tarbes and Toulouse. Paymaster of the regiment in 1826 and held this appointment until his death 8 Feb 1842 after 43 years service.

WELSH, John
Private. 12th (Prince of Wales's Own) Regiment of Light Dragoons.
Named on the Regimental Memorial: St Joseph's Church, Waterloo. (Photograph)

Present at Waterloo where he was killed.

WEMYSS, James
Lieutenant. 2nd (Royal North British) Regiment of Dragoons.
Buried in St Mary le Bow's Churchyard, North Bailey, Durham. (Burial record)

Cornet 30 Aug 1810. Lt 15 Sep 1814. Capt 10 Oct 1816. Major 10 Jun 1826.

Present at Waterloo where he commanded his troop at the final charge of the Scots Greys as so many of the other officers were killed or wounded. Although severely wounded himself he led his men into the fight, but his horse was shot under him. Half pay 8 Mar 1827. Moved from Scotland to Durham in 1837. Durham was one of the earliest counties to take advantage of the 1839 Act of Parliament to set up police forces to quell civil unrest and Wemyss became the first Chief Constable of Durham Dec 1839. Under him the police force became one of the most efficient and well disciplined in the country. He remained there until his untimely death in 1848, when out walking in the countryside, he had a stroke and lay out all night in the rain. He was found next day but was not moved back into the city quickly enough. He died on 24 Sep 1848, shortly after being carried back to his home in Durham.

REFERENCE: Gentleman's Magazine, Nov 1848, pp. 546–7. Inquest report, Durham Advertiser, 29 Sep 1848, p. 5. Brown, M. F., One life at Waterloo, Durham County Local History Society Bulletin, 1989, pp. 18–23.

WEMYSS, Thomas James

Captain. 50th (West Kent) Regiment of Foot.
Low monument: Abbey Cemetery, Bath, Somerset. (Photograph)

LIEUT GENERAL WEMYSS / C.B. / COLONEL OF THE 17TH FOOT / DIED AT BATH JULY 19TH 1860 / AGED 74. / THIS BRAVE OFFICER WAS THE SON OF / THE LATE COLONEL CHARLES JAMES WEMYSS / ROYAL MARINES

Ensign 65th Foot 9 Jun 1803. Lt 19th Foot 1 Mar 1804. Capt 6th Garrison Battalion 30 Nov 1806. Capt 50th Foot 12 Nov 1807. Bt Major 21 Jun 1813. Bt Lt Colonel 21 Jan 1819. Major 50th Foot 4 Nov 1819. Bt Colonel 10 Jan 1837. Major General 9 Nov 1846. Lt General 20 Jun 1854.

Served in the Peninsula Sep 1810 – Apr 1814 (Brigade Major to 1 Brigade, 2nd Division Feb 1811 – Apr 1814). Present at Pombal, Redinha, Foz d'Arouce, Fuentes d'Onoro, Arroyo dos Molinos, Almarez (Mentioned in Despatches), Alba de Tormes, Vittoria (awarded Bt Majority). Pyrenees (severely wounded), Nivelle, Nive, St Pierre (wounded), Garris, Orthes, Aire (Mentioned in Despatches), Tarbes and Toulouse. CB. Also served at Walcheren 1809 and Ceylon (present in the third Kandian War 1817–1818). Half pay 10 Feb 1820. MGS medal for Fuentes d'Onoro, Vittoria, Pyrenees, Nivelle, Nive, Orthes and Toulouse. Colonel 17th Foot 31 May 1854.

REFERENCE: Gentleman's Magazine, Sep 1860, pp. 324–5. Annual Register, 1860, Appx, p. 499.

WEMYSS, William

Major. 93rd Regiment of Foot
Tomb in railed enclosure: St Mary's Churchyard, Wimbledon, London. (M.I.)

TO THE MEMORY / OF / .... / ALSO / LIEUTENANT GENERAL / WILLIAM WEMYSS / COLONEL OF THE 93RD HIGHLANDERS / DIED NOVEMBER 30TH 1852 AGED 62 YEARS / ....

Ensign 93rd Foot 3 Jul 1803. Lt 12 Sep 1805. Capt 6th Garrison Battalion 18 Aug 1808. Major 93rd Foot 27 May 1813. Bt Lt Colonel 16 Mar 1815. Bt Colonel 22 Jul 1830. Major General 23 Nov 1841. Lt General 11 Nov 1851.

Served in the Peninsula on Staff Sep 1810 – Jan 1813 (ADC to General Sir William Erskine). Present at Sobral, Pombal, Redinha, Miranda de Corvo, Foz d'Arouce, Sabugal, Fuentes d'Onoro, Arroyo dos Molinos and Almarez. Also served at Walcheren 1809 (ADC to Sir William Erskine). MGS medal for Fuentes d'Onoro. Half pay 25 Feb 1840. Appointed to the Royal Household to control Prince Albert's

equestrian and agricultural establishments. Colonel 93rd Foot 10 Apr 1850. Nephew of General Sir William Erskine. Died at Windsor 30 Nov 1852.
REFERENCE: Gentleman's Magazine, Jan 1853, p. 93. Annual Register, 1852, Appx, p. 333.

WEMYSS, William
Deputy Commissary General. Commissariat Department.
Family Mural Monument: Grange Cemetery, Edinburgh, Scotland. (Section J Grave number 311. Centre Panel). (Photograph)

TO THE MEMORY OF WILLIAM WEMYSS, / DEPUTY COMMISSARY GENERAL TO THE FORCES / WHO DIED 6, SALISBURY ROAD, / 8TH APRIL 1862 AGED 86.

Asst Comm General 7 Nov 1809. Dep Comm General 25 Dec 1814.
Served in the Peninsula Aug 1808 – Jan 1809 and Jul 1809 – Apr 1814 (from Aug 1810 attached to 1st Division). Present at Rolica, Vimeiro, Corunna, Talavera, Busaco, Fuentes D'Onoro, Salamanca, Vittoria, Nivelle and Nive. Half pay 25 Dec 1814. MGS medal for Rolica, Vimeiro, Corunna, Talavera, Busaco, Fuentes d'Onoro, Salamanca, Vittoria, Nivelle and Nive.

WERGE, John
Captain. 38th (1st Staffordshire) Regiment of Foot.
Memorial tablet: St Andrew's Church, Newcastle upon Tyne, Northumberland. (Photograph)

SACRED TO THE MEMORY OF / JOHN WERGE / MAJOR OF THE 38TH REGIMENT OF INFANTRY. / HE LOST HIS LIFE AT THE ASSAULT OF ST SEBASTIAN / .... / JOHN WERGE / BORN 26TH AUGUST 1772, DIED 31ST AUGUST 1813. / ....

Cornet 17th Lt Dragoons 20 Oct 1796. Lt 1799. Capt 10 Jul 1802. Capt 38th Foot 26 Dec 1805. Major 4 Jun 1813.
Served in the Peninsula with 1/38th Jun 1808 – Jan 1809 and Jun 1812 – Aug 1813. Present at Rolica, Vimeiro, Corunna, Castrejon, Salamanca, Osma, Vittoria and San Sebastian where he was killed 31 Aug 1813. Also served at Walcheren 1809.

WERNER, G. J.
1st Lieutenant. 8th National Militia Battalion, Dutch Infantry.
Named on the Memorial to Dutch officers killed at Waterloo: St Joseph's Church, Waterloo. (Photograph)

WEST, Charles Augustus
Lieutenant Colonel. 1st Royal Veteran Battalion.
Ledger stone: Kensal Green Cemetery, London. (Inscription illegible). (11606/92.7). (Photograph)

Ensign 3rd Foot Guards 20 Mar 1794. Acting Adjutant to 2nd Battalion Jul 1794. Lt and Capt Feb 1797. Capt and Lt Colonel 5 May 1804. Lt Colonel 1st Royal Veteran Battalion 13 Aug 1811.
Served in the Peninsula Mar – Aug 1809. Present at Douro, Salamonde and Talavera. Also served in Flanders 1794–1796, the Helder 1799 (present at Alkmaar where he was wounded), Ireland 1800, Egypt 1801, Hanover 1805 and the Baltic 1807. MGS medal for Egypt and Talavera. Lieutenant Governor of Landguard Fort 1811, which post he occupied until his death 20 Jun 1854, the longest period that it had ever been held. Born 22 Jun 1766. Died 20 Jun 1854. Father of Charles Edward West Capt and Lt Colonel 3rd Regiment of Foot Guards.
REFERENCE: Gentleman's Magazine, Aug 1854, p. 193. Royal Military Calendar, Vol. 4, p. 320.

WEST, Charles Edward
Captain and Lieutenant Colonel. 3rd Regiment of Foot Guards.
Obelisk: General Cemetery, Folkestone, Kent. (Photograph)

TO THE MEMORY OF / CHARLES EDWARD WEST / LIEUTENANT COLONEL / 3RD REGT OF GUARDS. / DIED OCTOBER 11TH 1872 / AGED 83 YEARS. / …………………

Ensign 8 Nov 1804. Lt and Capt 25 Aug 1809. Capt and Lt Colonel 25 Jul 1814.

Served in the Peninsula Mar – Aug 1809 and Apr 1812 – Apr 1814. Present at Douro, Talavera, Salamanca, Burgos, Vittoria, Bidassoa, Adour, Bayonne and the Sortie from Bayonne where he was severely wounded. Present at Waterloo (severely wounded while commanding No. 8 Company at Hougoumont). Also served at Hanover 1805 and the Baltic 1807. MGS medal for Talavera, Salamanca and Vittoria. Retired Aug 1829. Son of Lt Colonel Charles Augustus West 3rd Regiment of Foot Guards. Both father and son fought in the battle of Talavera.
REFERENCE: Household Brigade Journal, 1872, pp. 328–9.

WEST, James Dawson
Captain and Lieutenant Colonel. 1st Regiment of Foot Guards.
Memorial tablet: St John the Baptist's Church, Mathon, Herefordshire. (Photograph)

SACRED TO THE MEMORY / OF JAMES DAWSON WEST / COLONEL OF THE FIRST REGIMENT OF GRENADIER GUARDS / WHO DEPARTED THIS LIFE / AUGUST THE II MDCCCXXXI / AGED LII. / THIS INSCRIPTION IS DEDICATED / AS A SINCERE TRIBUTE OF AFFECTION / FROM HIS AFFLICTED RELATIVES / TO HIS MANY VIRTUES AND AMIABLE DISPOSITION / THAT ENHANCED HIM TO ALL THOSE / WHO KNEW HIS WORTH.

Ensign 60th Foot 25 May 1796. 2nd Lt 23rd Foot 4 Jun 1796. 1st Lt 25 Jan 1797. Lt and Capt 1st Foot Guards 22 Dec 1799. Capt and Lt Colonel 27 Aug 1812. Bt Major 4 Jun 1811. Major 25 Jul 1821.

Served in the Peninsula with 1st Battalion Oct 1808 – Jan 1809 and May 1813 – Apr 1814. Present at Corunna, Bidassoa, Nivelle, Nive, Adour and Bayonne. Gold Medal for Nive.

WESTBY, Edward
Cornet. 2nd (Royal North British) Regiment of Dragoons.
Memorial tablet: St Peter's Church, Dublin, Ireland. (M.I.) (No longer extant. Church demolished in 1980s and bodies and gravestones removed to St Luke's Church in the Coombe, but this Church is also now redundant and unlikely that any memorials will have survived)

"SACRED TO THE MEMORY OF GEORGE WESTBY …………… ALSO OF EDWARD WESTBY, CORNET IN HIS MAJESTY'S 2ND OR ROYAL NORTH BRITISH DRAGOONS WHO WAS KILLED AT THE BATTLE OF WATERLOO ON THE 18TH OF JUNE 1815 AGED 20. THIS MONUMENT WAS ERECTED BY THEIR FATHER WILLIAM WESTBY OF MERRION SQUARE, ESQRE AS A TRIBUTE OF RESPECT TO THE MEMORY OF TWO BELOVED SONS WHO THUS UNTIMELY FELL IN THE SERVICE OF THEIR COUNTRY."

Cornet 12 May 1814.

Present at Waterloo where he was killed. Brother of 1st Lt George William Westby 95th Foot.

WESTBY, George William
1st Lieutenant. 95th Regiment of Foot.
Memorial tablet: St Peter's Church, Dublin, Ireland. (M.I.) (No longer extant. Church demolished in 1980s and bodies and gravestones removed to St Luke's Church in the Coombe, but this Church is also now redundant and unlikely that any memorials will have survived)

"SACRED TO THE MEMORY OF GEORGE WESTBY, FIRST LIEUTENANT IN HIS MAJESTY'S 95TH OR RIFLE REGIMENT WHO WAS KILLED AT THE BATTLE OF FUENTES D'HONOR IN SPAIN ON 5TH OF MAY 1811, AGED 20. ALSO OF EDWARD WESTBY .... THIS MONUMENT WAS ERECTED BY THEIR FATHER WILLIAM WESTBY OF MERRION SQUARE, ESQRE AS A TRIBUTE OF RESPECT TO THE MEMORY OF TWO BELOVED SONS WHO THUS UNTIMELY FELL IN THE SERVICE OF THEIR COUNTRY."

2nd Lt 8 Dec 1808. 1st Lt 3 Nov 1809.

Served in the Peninsula with 3/95th Feb 1810 – May 1811. Present at Cadiz, Sobral and Fuentes d'Onoro where he was killed. Brother of Cornet Edward Westby 2nd Dragoons.

WESTERNHAGEN, Thilo von
Captain. 8th Line Battalion, King's German Legion.
Named on the Regimental Memorial: La Haye Sainte, Waterloo. (Photograph)
Named on the Waterloo Column, Hanover, Germany. (Photograph)

Lt 29 Jun 1806. Capt 10 Sep 1814.

Present at Waterloo where he was killed. Also served in the Baltic 1807, Mediterranean 1808–1814 and the Netherlands 1814.

WESTMORE, Richard
Lieutenant. 33rd (1st Yorkshire West Riding) Regiment of Foot.
Altar tomb: Hendon Cemetery, London. (M.I.)

"COLONEL RICHARD WESTMORE, 33RD FOOT DIED 1867 AGED 75"

Ensign 28 May 1812. Lt 1 Apr 1813. Capt 23 Jun 1825. Bt Major 28 Jun 1838. Major 30 Oct 1840. Lt Colonel 14 Jun 1842. Bt Colonel 28 Nov 1854.

Present at Waterloo where he was severely wounded. Also served in North Germany 1813 and the Netherlands 1814 (present at Merxem and Bergen-op-Zoom). Retired on full pay 1842.

WESTROPP, Ralph
Lieutenant. 51st (2nd Yorkshire West Riding) Light Infantry.
Named on the Regimental Memorial tablet: KOYLI Chapel, York Minster, Yorkshire. (Photograph)

Cornet 12th Lt Dragoons 23 Jul 1803. Lt 29 May 1805. Lt 51st Foot 7 Aug 1809.

Served in the Peninsula Feb – Jun 1811. Present at Fuentes d'Onoro and the second siege of Badajoz where he was killed 5 Jun 1811 while rescuing a wounded soldier from the siege lines.

WEYLAND, Richard
Captain. 16th (Queen's) Regiment of Light Dragoons.
Buried at Holy Rood, Woodeaton, Oxfordshire. (Burial register). (Named on his wife's memorial tablet only). (Photograph)

Ensign 9th Foot 31 Dec 1805. Lt 4th Garrison Batalion 17 Dec 1806. Lt 16th Lt Dragoons 26 Mar 1807.

Capt 99th Foot 18 Jul 1811. Capt 16th Lt Dragoons 5 Sep 1811. Bt Major 21 Jan 1819.

Served in the Peninsula Apr 1809 – Apr 1814 (ADC to Major General G. Anson Sep 1809 – May 1810, Jul 1811 – Jan 1812 and Jun 1812 – Jul 1813). Present at Douro, Talavera, Coa, Busaco, Leyria (wounded and Mentioned in Despatches 9 Mar 1811), Fuentes D'Onoro (severely wounded), Castrejon, Salamanca, Vittoria, Nivelle, Nive and Bayonne. Present at Waterloo where he was wounded). MGS medal for Talavera, Busaco, Fuentes D'Onoro, Salamanca, Vittoria, Nivelle and Nive. Retired in 1820. Died 25 Oct 1864.

WHATMOUGH, Joseph

Private. 95th Regiment of Foot.
Headstone: Melbourne General Cemetery, Australia. (Photograph)

SACRED / TO THE MEMORY OF / JOSEPH WHATMOUGH / OF THE / 95TH REGT RIFLE BRIGADE / DIED JULY 26TH 1861 AGED 75 YEARS. / THIS STONE IS ERECTED BY / STEPHEN WHATMOUGH / OF RICHMOND / AS A TOKEN OF AFFECTION FOR THE RESPECT / AND OF PRIDE FOR THE / SOLDIER / OF TOULOUSE / PYRENEES / VITTORIA / SALAMANCA / BADAJOZ / CIUDAD RODRIGO / FUENTES D'ONORO / BUSACO / ....

Served in the Peninsula Aug 1810 – Apr 1814. Present at Busaco, Fuentes d'Onoro, Ciudad Rodrigo, Badajoz, Salamanca, Vittoria, Pyrenees and Toulouse. Present at Waterloo in Capt W. Johnston's Company. Went to live in Australia and died in Melbourne 26th Jul 1861 aged 75. MGS medal for Busaco, Fuentes d'Onoro, Ciudad Rodrigo, Badajoz, Salamanca, Vittoria, Pyrenees and Tououse.
Note: Also known as Joseph Whatnuff and Joseph Wattripp.

WHEATLEY, Henry

Captain and Lieutenant Colonel. 1st Regiment of Foot Guards.
Memorial tablet: St John the Baptist's Church, Erith, Kent. (South wall). (Photograph)

SACRED / TO THE MEMORY OF / MAJOR GENERAL SIR HENRY WHEATLEY, BART., C.B. & G.C.H. / DIED MARCH 21ST 1852, AGED 74. / SINCERELY LOVED AND LAMENTED / LOUISA / RELICT OF THE ABOVE, / .... / THEIR REMAINS ARE INTERRED IN THE FAMILY VAULT IN THIS CHURCH.

Floor tablet of Family Vault: St John the Baptist's Church, Erith, Kent. (Wheatley Chapel). (Photograph)

FAMILY VAULT / OF / MAJOR GENERAL / SIR HENRY WHEATLEY / BARONET

Named on the Family Memorial window: St John the Baptist's Church, Erith, Kent. (Photograph)

The window contains two panels. One to the Wheatley family which also records the battles that the Wheatley family took part in. The second panel illustrates Wellington mourning over the grave of William Wheatley.

ST AMAND / LINCELLES / COPENHAGEN / VIMIERA / CORUNNA / BARROSA / SALAMANCA / CHILLIANWALLAH / GOJERAAT / DELHI / REMEMBER YE IN THE LORD ALL / THOSE OF THE FAMILY OF WHEATLEY / WHO REST IN THIS CHAPEL, AND / IN OTHER COUNTRIES: ESPECIALLY / WILLIAM WHEATLEY MAJOR GENERAL / AND SIR HENRY WHEATLEY BART / C.B. G.C.H. : HIS BROTHER. ALSO THOMAS RANDALL WHEATLEY / AND ELIZA HIS WIFE, AND FRANCES COLQUHOUN THEIR DAUGHTER: IN / LOVING RECOLLECTION OF WHOM THIS / WINDOW IS DEDICATED

Memorial: Royal Military Chapel, Wellington Barracks, London. (M.I.) (Destroyed by a Flying Bomb 1944)

"MAJOR-GENERAL SIR HENRY WHEATLEY, BART., C.B., G.C.H., BROTHER OF THE / ABOVE, / BORN 1777; DIED 1852. SERVED IN THE 1ST GUARDS FROM 1795 UNTIL 1812; WAS A.D.C. TO SIR HARRY BURRARD, AT COPENHAGEN, LISBON, AND CADIZ, AND WAS PRESENT AT THE BATTLE OF BARROSA. HE WAS FOR MANY YEARS KEEPER OF THE PRIVY PURSE TO KING WILLIAM IV, AND TO QUEEN VICTORIA. / GIVEN BY THEIR SURVIVING RELATIVES."

Ensign 22 May 1795. Lt and Capt 31 Aug 1798. Capt and Lt Colonel 4 May 1809. Bt Lt Colonel 14 Sep 1826.

Served in the Peninsula Aug – Nov 1808 (ADC to Lt General Burrard) and Mar 1810 – May 1811 with 2nd Battalion. Present at Vimeiro, Cadiz and Barrosa. Also served in Flanders 1795 and Copenhagen 1807 (ADC to Lt General Burrard). Retired 29 Oct 1812. Returned to England, possibly due to his brother William's death. MGS medal for Vimeiro and Barrosa. CB. GCH. Major General in Hanoverian Army 1830. Educated at Charterhouse. Keeper of the Privy Purse to William IV and Queen Victoria. Brother of Major General William Wheatley 1st Foot Guards who died in Madrid Sep 1812.
Reference: Gentleman's Magazine, May 1852, p. 519. Annual Register, 1852, Appx, p. 267.

WHEATLEY, Thomas

Private. 23rd Regiment of Light Dragoons.
Pedestal tomb with obelisk: St Catherine's Churchyard, Cossall, Nottinghamshire. (Photograph)

WATERLOO / THIS MONUMENT IS ERECTED / TO THE MEMORY OF / JOHN SHAW & / RICHARD WAPLINGTON, / OF THE / LIFE GUARDS, / AND THOMAS WHEATLEY, / OF THE LIGHT DRAGOON GUARDS, / WHO LEFT THIS THEIR NATIVE HOME / IN DEFENCE OF THEIR COUNTRY, / THE TWO FORMER GLORIOUSLY / FELL AT WATERLOO, THE LATTER / RETURNED, AND LIES BURIED IN / THIS CHURCH / YARD

Present at Waterloo in Capt John Martin's Troop. Thomas Wheatley was a stocking weaver by trade as was his father. He joined the army after trying to shoot his father who broke the strike of stocking workers in Nottingham. Thomas was in sympathy with the strikers. After Waterloo he returned to his village as a blacksmith and joined the Yeomanry Cavalry. This was a time of civil unrest in the country and Wheatley played a prominent part in preventing the mob from burning down Wollaton Hall in Nottingham after they had burnt down Nottingham Castle in 1832. He lived for the rest of his life in the area and was buried in the churchyard. The memorial to the three Waterlooo men, John Shaw, Richard Waplington and Thomas Wheatley was unveiled in 1877.
Reference: Raynor, K. K., Waterloo men at Cossall, Waterloo Journal, Jan 1988, pp. 27–37, and Robinson, Apr 1988, pp. 4–5.

WHEATLEY, William

Captain and Lieutenant Colonel. 1st Regiment of Foot Guards.
Memorial tablet: Garden of the Friars, El Escorial Monastery, near Madrid, Spain. (Photograph)

TO THE MEMORY OF / MAJOR GENERAL WILLIAM WHEATLEY, / FIRST GUARDS, / OF LESNESS, IN THE COUNTY OF KENT, / BORN 14TH AUGUST 1771, / DIED AT THE ESCORIAL, 1ST SEPTEMBER 1812, / AND WAS BURIED AT THIS SPOT. / HE WAS PRESENT AT THE BATTLES OF / CORUNNA, BARROSA, AND SALAMANCA, / BESIDES MANY OTHERS. / LORD WELLINGTON / DESIRED THAT A STONE TO HIS MEMORY / SHOULD BE PLACED IN THIS WALL. / IN CONSEQUENCE OF THE SHORT STAY OF / THE ENGLISH ARMY IN MADRID / THIS

WAS NOT DONE AT THE TIME / BUT WAS CARRIED OUT BY / COLONEL MORETON WHEATLEY, C.B., R.E., / HIS GRANDSON IN THE YEAR / 1905.

Memorial tablet: St John the Baptist's Church, Erith, Kent. (South wall). (Photograph)

SACRED TO THE MEMORY OF / MAJOR GENERAL WILLIAM WHEATLEY, / OF LESNEY, IN THIS COUNTY, / CAPTAIN IN THE FIRST REGT OF FOOT-GUARDS; / WHO, HAVING FOUGHT WITH HONOR AND DISTINCTION, / IN SEVERAL ENGAGEMENTS, / PARTICULARLY AT THE BATTLES / OF LINCELLES AND BARROSA, / DIED, OF A FEVER AT MADRID, / BELOVED AND LAMENTED BY THE WHOLE ARMY, / WHILE IN COMMAND UNDER THE MARQUIS OF WELLINGTON, / SEPTEMBER THE 1ST 1812, AGED 41 YEARS.

Memorial window: St John the Baptist's Church, Erith, Kent. (Photograph)
The window contains two panels. One to the Wheatley family which also records the battles that the Wheatley family took part in. The second panel illustrates Wellington mourning over the grave of William Wheatley.

HERE LORD WELLINGTON VISITS THE / GRAVE OF HIS COMRADE AND FRIEND / MAJOR GENERAL WILLIAM WHEATLEY / IN THE GARDEN OF THE ESCORIAL ON / THE 1ST OF SEPTEMBER MDCCCXII.

ST AMAND / LINCELLES / COPENHAGEN / VIMIERA / CORUNNA / BARROSA / SALAMANCA / CHILLIANWALLAH / GOJERAAT / DELHI / REMEMBER YE IN THE LORD ALL / THOSE OF THE FAMILY OF WHEATLEY / WHO REST IN THIS CHAPEL, AND / IN OTHER COUNTRIES: ESPECIALLY / WILLIAM WHEATLEY MAJOR GENERAL / AND SIR HENRY WHEATLEY BART / C.B. G.C.H. : HIS BROTHER. ALSO THOMAS RANDALL WHEATLEY / AND ELIZA HIS WIFE, AND FRANCES COLQUHOUN THEIR DAUGHTER: IN / LOVING RECOLLECTION OF WHOM THIS / WINDOW IS DEDICATED

Memorial: Royal Military Chapel, Wellington Barracks, London. (M.I.) (Destroyed by a Flying Bomb 1944)

"MAJOR-GENERAL WILLIAM WHEATLEY. / BORN 1771. / SERVED IN THE 1ST GUARDS FROM 1790 UNTIL HIS DEATH FROM FEVER, AT MADRID, IN 1812. HE TOOK PART IN THIRTY-FOUR ENGAGEMENTS; INCLUDING THE BATTLES OF LINCELLES, CORUNNA, WHERE HE COMMANDED THE 3RD BATTALION, AND BARROSA, WHERE HE WAS IN COMMAND OF A BRIGADE".

Named on Memorial Panel VI: Royal Military Chapel, Wellington Barracks, London. (M.I.) (Destroyed by a Flying Bomb 1944)

Ensign 23 Jun 1790. Lt and Capt 14 Aug 1793. Capt and Lt Colonel 25 Nov 1799. Bt Colonel 25 Oct 1809. Major General 1 Jan 1812.

Served in the Peninsula with 3rd Battalion Oct 1808 – Jan 1809 and Mar 1810 – Sept 1812 (O/c 3 Brigade Aug 1810 – Apr 1811 and O/c 2 Brigade 1st Division May – Sep 1812). Present at Corunna, Cadiz, Barrosa (Mentioned in Despatches) and Salamanca. Also served in Flanders 1793–1795 (present at Lincelles). Gold Medal for Barrosa and Salamanca. Died in Madrid 1 Sep 1812 of typhoid fever. Brother of Capt and Lt Colonel Sir Henry Wheatley 1st Foot Guards.

WHEELER, William
Sergeant. 51st (2nd Yorkshire West Riding) Light Infantry.
Headstone: St Mark's Churchyard, Bath, Somerset. (Photograph)

TO THE MEMORY OF / WILLIAM WHEELER / WHO DIED APRIL 13TH 1851 / AGED 70 / HIS END WAS PEACE

Pte 4 Apr 1809. Cpl 1813. Sgt 1815.

Served in the Peninsula Feb 1811 – Apr 1814. Present at Fuentes d'Onoro, second siege of Badajoz, Salamanca, retreat from Burgos (present at San Munos), Vittoria, Pyrenees and Nivelle. Present at Waterloo (wounded) and with the Army of Occupation until Dec 1815. Also served at Walchern 1809, Malta 1822, Ionian Islands (present in Corfu 1823). Discharged 31 May 1828 with a pension of one shilling and ten pence a day. Retired to Bath where he became a Porter to the Walcot Commissioners. Author *of Letters of Private Wheeler 1809–1828* relating his experiences in the Army.
Reference: Wheeler, William, Letters of Private Wheeler 1809–1828, edited by B. H. Liddell Hart, 1951, reprint 1997.

WHICHCOTE, George
Lieutenant. 52nd (Oxfordshire) Light Infantry Regiment of Foot.
Low monument: St Laurence's Churchyard, Meriden, Warwickshire. (Photograph)

SACRED TO THE MEMORY OF / GENERAL GEORGE WHICHCOTE, / BORN 21ST DECEMBER 1794 AT ASWARBY, LINCOLNSHIRE, / DIED AT MERIDEN 26TH AUGUST 1891 / SERVED WITH THE 52 REGT. IN THE PENINSULAR / AND FRANCE IN THE CAMPAIGN, AND AT THE BATTLE OF WATERLOO.

Volunteer 52nd Foot Dec 1810. Ensign 10 Jan 1811. Lt 8 Jul 1812. Capt 3rd Foot 22 Jan 1818. Capt 4th Dragoon Guards 25 Jul 1822. Major 29 Oct 1825. Bt Lt Colonel 28 Jun 1838. Bt Colonel 11 Nov 1851. Major General 4 Jun 1857. Lt General 31 Jan 1864. General 5 Dec 1871.

Served in the Peninsula with 2/52nd Mar – Jul 1811 and 1/52nd Jul 1811 – Apr 1814. Present at Sabugal, El Bodon, Ciudad Rodrigo, Badajoz (wounded), Salamanca, retreat from Burgos, San Millan, Vittoria, Pyrenees, Vera, Bidassoa, Nivelle, Nive, Orthes, Tarbes and Toulouse. Present at Waterloo where he was wounded. Half pay 29 Oct 1825. MGS medal for Ciudad Rodrigo, Badajoz, Salamanca, Vittoria, Pyrenees, Nivelle, Nive, Orthes and Toulouse. Received the Queen's Jubilee medal in 1887. One of the last four surviving officers who served at Waterloo. Educated at Rugby School where he was the 'fag' for William McCready, the future actor. Known as 'Father of the British Army' when he died on 26 Aug 1891.
Reference: Dictionary of National Biography. Annual Register, 1891, Appx, pp. 177–8. Oxfordshire Light Infantry Chronicle, 1895, pp. 118–21.

WHINYATES, Edward Charles
Captain. Royal Artillery.
Headstone: St Mary's Churchyard, Prestbury, Gloucestershire. (Photograph)

SACRED / TO THE MEMORY OF / GENERAL / SIR EDWARD CHARLES WHINYATES / K. C. B. & K.H. / COLONEL COMMANDANT OF B. BRIGADE / ROYAL HORSE ARTILLERY. / WHO WAS BORN NEAR CALCUTTA 6 MAY 1782 / AND DIED AT CHELTENHAM 25TH DECEMBER 1865 / IN HIS 84TH YEAR. / HE WAS THE THIRD SON OF MAJOR THOMAS WHINYATES / BY CATHARINE SIXTH DAUGHTER OF ADMIRAL SIR THOMAS / FRANKLAND BART, AND ENTERED THE ARMY AS SECOND / LIEUTENANT IN THE ROYAL ARTILLERY AT THE AGE OF / SIXTEEN & SAW MUCH ACTIVE SERVICE. HE SERVED IN THE / EXPEDITION TO THE HELDER, & CAMPAIGN IN NORTH / HOLLAND IN 1798, THE EXPEDITION TO MADEIRA IN

1801 / & AT THE SIEGE & CAPTURE OF COPENHAGEN IN 1807, / THE PENINSULAR CAMPAIGNS FROM FEBY 10TH 1810 TO JULY / 1813, INCLUDING THE BATTLES OF BUSACO & ALBUERA / AFFAIRS AT USAGRE, ALDEA DE PONTE, AND SAN MUNOZ, / ATTACK & DEFEAT OF GENERAL LALLEMAND'S CAVALRY / AT RIBERA & MANY OTHER AFFAIRS, BEING ALWAYS / ON THE ADVANCE OR REAR GUARDS. HE SERVED ALSO THE / CAMPAIGN OF 1815 IN THE NETHERLANDS AND FRANCE / AND WAS SEVERELY WOUNDED IN THE LEFT ARM AT WATERLOO / WHERE HE COMMANDED THE ROCKET TROOP ROYAL HORSE / ARTILLERY. HE WAS REWARDED WITH MILITARY HONOURS: / HAVING BEEN NOMINATED A KNIGHT OF THE ROYAL / GUELPHIC ORDER FOR DISTINGUISHED MILITARY SERVICES IN 1825. / A KNIGHT COMMANDER OF THE BATH ON 18 MAY 1860. / HE ALSO RECEIVED THE SILVER WAR MEDAL WITH TWO CLASPS / FOR BUSACO & ALBUERA & MEDAL FOR THE BATTLE OF WATERLOO. / THUS, AFTER A SERVICE OF NEARLY SIXTY EIGHT YEARS / IN THE ROYAL REGIMENT OF ARTILLERY, HE CLOSED, AT CHELTENHAM, / A LONG AND USEFUL & HONOURABLE CAREER / FULL OF YEARS & FULL OF HONOURS / MUCH LOVED & RESPECTED BY ALL WHO KNEW HIM.

2nd Lt 1 Mar 1798. 1st Lt 2 Oct 1799. 2nd Capt 8 Jul 1805. Capt 24 Jan 1813. Bt Major 18 Jun 1815. Lt Colonel 22 Jul 1830. Colonel 23 Nov 1841. Major General 20 Jun 1854. Lt General 7 Jun 1856. General 10 Dec 1864.

Served in the Peninsula Feb 1810 – Jul 1813. Present Busaco, Albuera, Usagre, Aldea de Ponte, San Munos and Ribera (Mentioned in Despatches 24 Jul 1812). Present at Waterloo (commanded the Rocket Troop and was severely wounded) and with the Army of Occupation until 1818. Also served at the Helder 1799, Maderia 1801, Copenhagen 1807 and the Netherlands 1814–1815. MGS medal for Busaco and Albuera. KCB. KH. Director General of Artillery and Commandant at Woolwich 15 Aug 1852 – 1 Jun 1856. Died in Cheltenham 25 Dec 1865.

REFERENCE: *Dictionary of National Biography. Gentleman's Magazine, Mar 1866, pp. 426–7.*

WHITE, Andrew

Private. 2nd (Royal North British) Regiment of Dragoons.

Obelisk: Private family graveyard at "Gowrie", Singleton, New South Wales, Australia. (Photograph)

IN MEMORY OF / ANDREW WHITE / WHO DIED 20TH NOV 1862 AGED 72 YEARS. / HE SERVED AT WATERLOO / IN THE SCOTS GREYS / OF WHICH REGT HE WAS THE MOST SEVERELY / WOUNDED SURVIVOR BUT ONE. / HE RECEIVED THIRTEEN SABRE, GUNSHOT & LANCE WOUNDS / SAVED THE LIFE OF AN OFFICER & OTHERWISE / GREATLY DISTINGUISHED HIMSELF. / ....

Pte 1 Mar 1808.

Present at Waterloo in Captain J. Poole's Troop where he was severely wounded with sabre cuts, shell shot and gun shot wounds. Discharged 1815 at the age of 23 owing to his wounds. Described by his Commanding Officer as 'a gallant soldier, desperately wounded in the head, and not likely to be able to earn his bread'. Despite his condition he was one of the first immigrants to go to New South Wales under the Military Commutation Scheme, arriving in Sydney in 1832. He later farmed at Singleton and died in 1862.

WHITE, Andrew Douglas

Lieutenant. Royal Engineers.

Chest tomb: Liverpool Pioneer Cemetery, New South Wales, Australia. (Photograph)

SACRED TO THE MEMORY OF / CAPTAIN A.D. WHITE / OF THE ROYAL ENGINEERS / WHO DIED 24TH NOV. 1837 / AGED 44 YEARS.

2nd Lt 1 Jul 1812. 1st Lt 21 Jul 1813. 2nd Capt 6 Dec 1826.

Present at Waterloo and with the Army of Occupation until 1818. The small corps of Royal Engineers were used in the various sieges on the way to Paris. Also served in the Netherlands 1813–1815. Son of Surgeon John White of the Royal Navy and Rachel Turner who was a convict. His father took him to England when he was very small. In February 1823 he returned to Australia to find his mother. Half pay 6 Oct 1831 and remained in Australia. Became known as Australia's first returned soldier. Died at Parramatta, New South Wales 25 Nov 1837. In his will he left his Waterloo medal to his mother.

WHITE, Charles Lawrence

Lieutenant and Captain. 3rd Regiment of Foot Guards.

Memorial tablet: St Nicholas's Church, Tuxford, Nottinghamshire. (Photograph)

THE DESIGN ABOVE REPRESENTS THE BURIAL PLACE OF CAPTN WHITE AND THREE OF / HIS BROTHER OFFICERS. I. B. SHIFFNER FRANCIS R. HOLBURNE AND LUKE MAHON. / CAPTS WHITE AND SHIFFNER WERE BURIED TOGETHER IN THE GRAVE MARKED WITH THEIR / INITIALS, THE CROSS WAS FORMED OF A LARGE TREE AS IT GREW THE TOP BEING CUT OFF / AND PLACED ACROSS, ABOVE WHICH IT HAD BEEN PENETRATED BY A 24LB SHOT WHICH / REMAINED IN THE TREE AS REPRESENTED. – WITH THE DRUMS AND COLOURS AS PLACED / AT THE FUNERALS IN A VALLEY ABOUT A MILE FROM BAYONNE. / THERE WERE AFTER-WARDS STONES PLACED AT THE HEAD OF EACH GRAVE BY THE / SURVIVING OFFICERS OF THE REGIMENT. / SACRED TO THE MEMORY / OF CHARLES LAWRENCE WHITE ESQR LIEUT AND CAPT IN HIS MAJESTY'S 3RD REGIMENT / OF FOOT GUARDS, WHO, AFTER HAVING BEEN ENGAGED IN THE TAKING OF COPENHAGEN, / IN THE DEFENCE OF CADIZ; AT THE BATTLE OF BARROSA UNDER SIR THO. GRAHAM / AND IN MOST OF THE BATTLES IN PORTUGAL AND SPAIN UNDER THE DUKE OF WELLINGTON / PARTICULARLY AT SALAMANCA WHERE HE WAS SEVERELY WOUNDED IN THE FACE, WAS MORTALLY / WOUNDED IN THE RIGHT BREAST IN A SORTIE MADE BY THE FRENCH FROM BAYONNE / ABOUT 4 O'CLOCK IN THE MORNING OF THE 14TH OF APRIL 1814 AND DIED THE NEXT DAY / IN THE 32ND YEAR OF HIS AGE, BEING BORN 19TH SEPR 1782 AND WAS BURIED AS ABOVE / DESCRIBED ON THE 16TH OF APRIL 1814. / HIS CHARACTER WILL BE BEST DESCRIBED BY THE FOLLOWING EXTRACT FROM THE LETTER OF / HIS COMMANDING OFFICER ACQUAINTING HIS FAMILY WITH THE MELANCHOLY EVENT. / "CAMP CLOSELY INVESTING BAYONNE. APRIL 16TH 1814. / "TO OFFER CONSOLATION ON SO DISTRESSING AN OCCASION IS FRUITLESS AND / "UNAVAILING, BUT PERMIT ME TO SAY HIS LOSS IS MOST DEEPLY FELT AND / "REGRETTED BY MYSELF AND THE REST OF HIS BROTHER OFFICERS, AS A MORE / "PROMISING OFFICER FOR BRAVERY, INTELLIGENCE AND ENTERPRISE NEVER ENTERED / "THE SERVICE, WHILST THE AMIABILITY OF HIS CHARACTER ENDEARED HIM TO / "EVERY ONE WHO KNEW HIM. HE WAS BURIED THIS EVENING WITH EVERY / "MILITARY HONOR THAT CIRCUMSTANCES WOULD PERMIT. / "I HAVE THE HONOR TO BE SIR, / "YOUR MOST OBEDIENT SERVANT / "J. GUISE / "COLL COMMANDING 1ST BATTN 3RD GUARDS & PRO TEMPORE 2ND BRIGADE OF GUARDS."

Low monument: 3rd Foot Guards Cemetery, St Etienne, Bayonne, France. (Photograph)

TO THE MEMORY / OF / CAPTAINS WHITE & SHIFFNER / THIRD GUARDS / WHO DIED OF WOUNDS RECEIVED IN / ACTION BEFORE BAYONNE / ON THE 14 APRIL / 1814

Named on Memorial Panel VII for the Sortie from Bayonne: Royal Military Chapel, Wellington Barracks, London. (M.I.) (Destroyed by a Flying Bomb 1944)

Named on the Memorial: St Andrew's Church (now Musée Historique), Biarritz, France. (Photograph)

Ensign 10 Jan 1804. Lt and Capt 8 Aug 1808.

Served in the Peninsula Apr 1810 – May 1811 and Feb 1812 – Apr 1814. Present at Cadiz, Barrosa, Salamanca (severely wounded), Burgos, Vittoria, Bidassoa, Nivelle, Nive, Adour and Bayonne where he was severely wounded at the Sortie from Bayonne 14 Apr 1814 and died of his wounds 15 Apr 1814. Also served at Copenhagen 1807. Miss Holburne, sister of Lt and Capt Holburne, restored his original tombstone.

WHITE, Daniel

Lieutenant Colonel. 29th (Worcestershire) Regiment of Foot.
Ledger stone: British Cemetery, Elvas, Portugal. (Photograph)

HERE LIES THE BODY / OF / LIEUTENANT COLONEL DANIEL WHITE / WHO DIED IN ELVAS ON 3RD JUNE 1811 / OF WOUNDS RECEIVED / WHILE LEADING THE 29TH FOOT / AT THE BATTLE OF / ALBUERA / AQUI JAZ / TENENTE CORONEL DANIEL WHITE / QUE MORREU EM ELVAS / NO DIA 3 DE JUNHO DE 1811 / DE FERIMENTOS SOFRIDOS, / COMANDANDO / 0 29º REGIMENTO DE / INFANTERIA / NA BATALHA DE / ALBUERA

Ensign 27 Sep 1787. Lt 25 Aug 1790. Capt-Lt and Capt 5 Feb 1793. Capt 1 Mar 1794. Major 5 Dec 1799. Bt Lt Colonel 1 Jan 1805. Lt Colonel 2 Sep 1808.

Served in the Peninsula Jul 1808 – Jun 1811. Present at Rolica, Vimeiro, Douro, Oporto, Talavera, first siege of Badajoz and Albuera where he was severely wounded 16 May 1811 and died of his wounds at Elvas 8 Jun 1811. Gold Cross for Rolica, Vimeiro, Talavera and Albuera. Also served on board HMS *Egmont* 1790. With the fleet again on HMS *Duke* in the expedition to Martinique 1793, Grenada 1795–1796 and the Helder 1799 (present at Bergen where he was wounded). Gravestone placed in his memory May 2003.

WHITE, George

Captain. 3rd (Prince of Wales's) Dragoon Guards.
Memorial tablet: St Mildred's Church, Whippingham, Isle of Wight. (Photograph)

NEAR THIS SPOT LIE THE REMAINS OF / GEORGE WHITE, ESQRE / WHO WAS BORN ON THE 20TH MARCH 1782 / AND DIED ON THE 10TH FEBRUARY 1845. / HE WAS COLONEL IN THE PORTUGUESE SERVICE / AND WAS 3D SON OF THE LATE JOHN WHITE ESQRE / OF FAIRLEE, IN THIS PARISH. / SACRED / TO HIS CHERISHED MEMORY / THIS TABLET IS AFFECTIONATELY RAISED BY / HIS SORROWING WIDOW AND ORPHAN CHILDREN, / THE LAST SAD TRIBUTE OF THEIR LOVE, RESPECT AND ESTEEM / FOR THE TENDEREST OF HUSBANDS, / AND THE MOST AFFECTIONATE OF FATHERS.

Lt 11 Mar 1806. Capt 16 Nov 1809. Portuguese Army: Major 10th Cavalry 7 Jul 1810. Lt Colonel 3rd Cavalry 23 May 1812. Lt Colonel 5th Cavalry 15 Dec 1814.

Served in the Peninsula with 3rd Dragoon Guards May 1809 – Jul 1810 and with Portuguese Army Jul 1810 – Apr 1814. Present at Talavera. Retired 1816.

WHITE, Henry

Lieutenant. 74th (Highland) Regiment of Foot.
Buried in the Grounds of the Royal Garrison Chapel, Portsmouth, Hampshire.
Memorial tablet: English Heritage Store, Fort Brockhurst, Gosport, Hampshire. (EH Reference No 87900143). (M.I.)

IN MEMORY OF TOWN MAJOR HENRY WHITE OF PORTSMOUTH / AND FORMALLY OF THE 74TH HIGHLANDERS / WHO DIED 23RD MARCH 1849 AGE 69 / AFTER MUCH ACTIVE SERVICE

IN THE WARS OF HOLLAND / AND THE PENINSULA WHERE HE WAS FOUR TIMES SEVERELY / WOUNDED. HE WAS 25 YEARS TOWN MAJOR OF THIS GARRISON. / GREATLY HONOURED AND ESTEEMED. / ALSO IN MEMORY OF JEAN HIS WIFE / WHO DIED AT DURHAM 14TH JANUARY 1870 AGED 90 YEARS. / THIS TABLET IS DEDICATED BY THEIR AFFECTIONATE SON / LT COLONEL GEORGE FRANCIS WHITE, / LATE OF THE 31ST REGT.

Pte 1st Foot Guards 11 Mar 1791. Commissioned from the ranks. Ensign and Adjt 74th Foot 5 Apr 1810. Lt 29th Apr 1812. Lt 7th Royal Veteran Battalion 28 Dec 1815.

Served in the Peninsula 1808 – Jan 1809 and Jul 1810 – Aug 1813. Present at Benevente, Lugo, Corunna, Busaco, Pombal, Redinha, Casal Nova, Foz d'Arouce, Sabugal, Fuentes d'Onoro (wounded), Aldea de Ponte, first siege of Badajoz, El Boden, Ciudad Rodrigo, Salamanca (wounded) and Vittoria (severely wounded and awarded pension of £70 per annum). Also served in Flanders 1793–1795 (present at St Amand, Famars, Valenciennes, Lincelles, Dunkirk, Cateau, Roubaix, Lannoi, Malines, Boxtel and Nimwegen), the Helder 1799 (present at Zyp Dyke, Bergen, Kallantzoog where he was severely wounded and Alkmaar). Town Major of Hull and later Town Major of Portsmouth 2 Oct 1823 where he served for 25 years. Served in the army for 56 years. MGS medal for Corunna, Busaco, Fuentes d'Onoro, Ciudad Rodrigo, Salamanca and Vittoria. Died 23 Mar 1849.

WHITE, William

Captain. 13th Regiment of Light Dragoons.
Memorial tablet: All Saints' Church, High Wycombe, Buckinghamshire. (Located immediately behind, but obscured by the altar). (Photograph)

CAPTAIN WILLIAM WHITE OF HIS / MAJESTY'S 13 REGT OF LIGHT DRAGOONS, / AND D.A.Q.M.G. OF CAVALRY / UNDER HIS GRACE THE DUKE OF WELLINGTON / WAS MORTALLY WOUNDED AT THE BATTLE OF SALAMANCA / THE 22ND JULY 1812 / IN THE 30TH YEAR OF HIS AGE / OF WHOM HIS BRAVE COMPANIONS IN ARMS HAVE BORNE THIS HONORABLE TESTIMONY / THAT "HE FELL NOBLY, ACTING WITH DISTINGUISHED BRAVERY, IN A GLORIOUS CAUSE, / WITH A CHARACTER UNBLEMISHED AS A MAN; AND, AS A SOLDIER, ADORNED WITH / UNSULLIED INTEGRITY AND UNDAUNTED COURAGE" / A TESTIMONY AMPLY CORROBORATED BY THE OFFICIAL GAZETTES OF / SEPT 18TH 1810 AND MAY 9TH 1812. HE SURVIVED TILL / THE NIGHT OF THE 23RD AND ERE HE BREATHED HIS LAST / HAD THE SATISFACTION OF KNOWING THAT HE DIED AS HE HAD LIVED, / THE COMPANION OF VICTORY. / LIEUTENANT GILLESPIE WHITE OF THE SAME REGIMENT / TWIN BROTHER OF THE ABOVE, AND HOLDING SIMILAR RANK / ON THE STAFF OF THE ARMY IN EGYPT, COMMANDED BY SIR RALPH ABERCROMBIE KB, / DIED AT DAMIETTA OCTOBER 15TH 1801, AT THE AGE OF 20 YEARS"

Cornet 23 May 1797. Lt 16 Jan 1800. Capt 18 Feb 1804.

Served in the Peninsula Apr 1810 – Jul 1812 (DAQMG of Cavalry Nov 1810 – Jul 1812). Present at Ladocra 22 Aug 1810 (Mentioned in Despatches). Llerena (Mentioned in Despatches) and Salamanca where he was killed 22 Jul 1812. His twin brother Lt Gillespie White 13th Lt Dragoons died in Egypt 1801.

WHITE, William Edward

Lieutenant. 51st (2nd Yorkshire West Riding) Light Infantry.
Memorial: Regimental Memorial: KOYLI Chapel, York Minster, Yorkshire. (Photograph)

Ensign 18 Apr 1800. Lt 3 Apr 1803.

Served in the Peninsula Oct 1808 – Jan 1809. Present in the Coruuna campaign where he was killed.

WHITEHEAD, Samuel

Corporal. 3rd Regiment of Foot Guards.
Headstone: St Mary's Churchyard, Ilkeston, Derbyshire. (South-west corner). (Photograph)

IN / LOVING MEMORY OF / SAMUEL WHITEHEAD, / LATE CORP^{L} OF H.M. 3RD FOOT GUARDS, / AND 21 YEARS CLERK OF THIS PARISH, / BORN DEC^{R} 2ND 1777. DIED OCT^{R} 27TH 1870. / HE SERVED HIS COUNTRY IN EGYPT, / AT TALAVERA, BUSACO, / FUENTES D'ONORO & WATERLOO

Pte 20 Aug 1798. Cpl 1813.

Served in the Peninsula 1809 – May 1811. Present at Oporto, Talavera, Busaco, Fuentes d'Onoro (severely wounded and took no further part in the Peninsular War). Present at Quatre Bras, Waterloo and the Capture of Paris. Also served at the Helder 1799, Egypt, 1801, and Copenhagen 1807. Discharged 12 May 1818 with a pension of one shilling and two pence per day. MGS medal for Egypt, Talavera, Busaco and Fuentes d'Onoro. Parish Clerk of Ilkeston for 21 years.
REFERENCE: *Ilkeston and District Local History Society Journal, No. 5, September/October 2010, pp. 4–5.*

WHITMORE, Henry

Private. 23rd (Royal Welch Fusiliers) Regiment of Foot.
Headstone: St Mary's Churchyard, Snettisham, Norfolk. (Photograph)

SACRED / TO THE MEMORY OF / ANN WHITMORE / WHO DEPARTED THIS LIFE / JUNE 9TH 1875 AGED 79 YEARS / ALSO / HENRY WHITMORE / HER HUSBAND / WHO DEPARTED THIS LIFE / DEC 9TH 1875 AGED 81 YEARS.

West Norfolk Volunteers. Private 23rd Foot 1 Jun 1813.

Present at Waterloo in Capt Brown's Company No. 4. Discharged 18 Nov 1816. At the age of 77 with the help of the local vicar he applied for, and was granted a pension of one shilling per day.

WHITNEY, John

Lieutenant. 71st (Highland Light Infantry) Regiment of Foot.
Box tomb: Adamstown Churchyard, County Wexford, Ireland. (M.I.)

"HERE LIETH THE REMAINS OF / JOHN WHITNEY / LATE LIEUTENANT IN HIS MAJESTY'S 71ST / REGIMENT OF HIGHLAND LIGHT INFANTRY / WHO DEPARTED THIS LIFE ON / THE 20TH DAY OF APRIL 1821 / AGED 35 YEARS"

Ensign 11th Foot 5 Oct 1806. Lt 71st Foot 19 Oct 1809.

Served in the Peninsula Sep 1813 – Apr 1814. Present at Nivelle, Nive and Toulouse. Present at Waterloo and with the Army of Occupation.
Note: Also known as Witney.

WHITTAM, Samuel

Private. 52nd (Oxfordshire) Light Infantry Regiment of Foot.
Buried in Christ Church Churchyard, Healey, Rochdale, Lancashire. (Burial record)

Pte 1807.

Served in the Peninsula Aug 1808 – Jan 1809 and Jul 1809 – Apr 1814. Present at Rolica, Vimeiro, Douro, Busaco, the Lines of Torres Vedras, Ciudad Rodrigo, Badajoz, Salamanca, Burgos, Vittoria and the Pyrenees. Present at Waterloo in Captain Charles Diggle's Company. One of the members of the

Rochdale Veterans Association. MGS medal for Ciudad Rodrigo, Badajoz, Salamanca and the Pyrenees. Died in Rochdale 19 Nov 1862 aged 80.

WHITTING, William

Captain. 74th (Highland) Regiment of Foot.
Named on the Regimental Memorial: St Giles's Cathedral, Edinburgh, Scotland. (Photograph)

Lt 53rd Foot 29 Aug 1805. Lt 74th Foot 26 Jul 1806. Capt 15 Apr 1813.

Served in the Peninsula Mar – Jul 1813. Present at Vittoria and Pyrenees where he was killed 30 Jul 1813.

WHITTINGHAM, Sir Samuel Ford

Major. Staff Appointment in Spain and Portugal not holding a Regimental Commission.
Memorial tablet: St Mary's Church, Fort St George, Madras, India. (Photograph)

SACRED / TO THE MEMORY OF / LIEUT. GENERAL SIR S. F. WHITTINGHAM, / K. C. B. AND K. C. H. / COLONEL H. M. 71ST HIGHLAND LIGHT INFANTRY / AND / COMMANDER-IN-CHIEF OF THE MADRAS ARMY, / WHO DEPARTED THIS LIFE / ON THE 19TH JANUARY 1841, / AGED 66.

Lt 1st Life Guards 10 Mar 1803. Capt 13th Lt Dragoons 13 Jun 1805. Bt Colonel 4 Jun 1814. Major General 27 May 1825. Lieutenant General 28 Jun 1838. Spanish Army: Major 12 Mar 1810. Lt Colonel 30 May 1811.

Served in the Peninsula Aug 1808 – Jan 1809 and Jul – Oct 1809 (on Staff as DAQMG). Attached to the Spanish Army in charge of the Cavalry Division Nov 1809 – Apr 1814. Present with the British Army at Corunna, Talavera (Mentioned in Despatches and severely wounded), Barrosa (Mentioned in Despatches), Castalla (wounded), Tarragona and Alicante. Present with the Spanish Army at Baylen (ADC to General Castanos), Tudela, Mora, Cousalga, and Medellin. His appointments in the Spanish army reflected his ability to speak Spanish fluently and understand the customs of the country owing to the fact that his wife was Spanish. His services to Spain were recognised by his appointment as Major General of the Spanish army and awarded the Grand Cross of the Order of St Ferdinand. KCH. KCB. Also served in South America 1807 (present at Buenos Ayres), West Indies 1819 (Governor of Dominica), India 1822 (QMG, present at the siege and Capture of Bhurtpoore),West Indies 1835 (Governor of Windward and Leeward Islands) and India 1839 (present at Madras). On his return to England in 1835 he challenged Napier to a duel over Napier's comments about the conduct of the Spanish troops in the Peninsula, but the affair was amicably settled. Colonel 71st Highland Lt Infantry 28 Mar 1838. Commander-in-Chief of the Madras Army 1839, but died a few months after arriving back in India.
Reference: Dictionary of National Biography. Gentleman's Magazine, Jun 1841, p. 654. Annual Register, 1841, Appx, p. 182. Whittingham, F., ed., Memoir of the services of Lieutenant-General Sir Samuel Ford Whittingham, 1868.

WHITTLE, Robert

Lieutenant. 59th (2nd Nottinghamshire) Regiment of Foot.
Ledger stone: St Mary and All Saints' Churchyard, Whalley, Lancashire. (Photograph)

SACRED / TO THE MEMORY OF / MARGARET BOOTH WHITTLE / .... / ALSO OF ROBERT WHITTLE ESQ / LATE CAPTAIN OF THE 59TH / REGT WHO DIED JUNE 17TH 1853 / AGED 61 YEARS.

Ensign 69th Foot 25 Aug 1808. Lt 59th Foot 22 Feb 1810. Capt 22 Dec 1824.

Served in the Peninsula Sep 1812 – Apr 1814. Present at Cadiz. Also served at Walcheren 1809 (present at the siege of Flushing), and India 1817–1818 (present in the Mahratta Wars). Half pay 6 Dec 1827.

WHITWORTH, John

Sergeant. 7th (Royal Fusiliers) Regiment of Foot.
Mural memorial tablet: St George's Churchyard, Mossley, Lancashire. (Photograph)

PENINSULAR ACHIEVEMENTS / MARTINIQUE. BADAJOZ. SALAMANCA. / BUSACO. VITTORIA. MONTABELLA. / BURLADA. CIUDAD-RODRIGO. FONTA-DE-LA-PENNA. / OLIV-ERIA. PYRENEES. RONCESVALLES. / ALBUERA. / ORTHES ST SEBASTIAN. / ALDI-DE-PONT TOULOUSE. / COPENHAGEN NEW ORLEANS. / SACRED TO THE MEMORY OF / JOHN WHIT-WORTH, / OF MOSSLEY, LATE OF MANCHESTER; / WHO DEPARTED THIS LIFE ON THE 2ND DAY OF AUGUST, A.D. 1848, IN THE / 64TH YEAR OF HIS AGE. / HE ENTERED THE SERVICE AS A DRUMMER IN THE YEAR MDCCCIV, / AND WAS DISCHARGED IN MDCCCXXV; HE WAS FIELD / BUGLER DURING THE PENINSULAR AND PYRENEES / WARS, AND LATE DRUM-MAJOR OF THE / VIITH ROYAL FUSILIERS. / BRITONS! AT PEACE WITHIN HIS HALLOW'D GRAVE, / LIE THE COLD ASHES OF A SOLDIER BRAVE; / HIS SOUL, 'TIS HOP'D HAS JOIN'D A HAPPIER CORPS, / WITH HEAVEN'S HIGH HOST, ON CANAAN'S PEACEFUL SHORE. / HIS DRUM, AND BUGLE'S VOICE, WITH WARLIKE CHEERS, / TO ACTION, ROUS'D THE ROYAL FUSILIERS; / AND BY HIS VALOUR GAINED HIS COUNTRY'S LOVE, / IN GLORIOUS BATTLES AS INSCRIBED ABOVE. / HIS BUGLE NOTES, WHEN FOES WERE ON THE GROUND, / RE-ECHO'D HIS COMMANDER'S MARTIAL WORD; / AND BRITISH TROOPS, FOR BATTLE FORMING ROUND, / SOON BRAV'D THE FOE WITH MUSKET, GUN, AND SWORD. / AND WHEN RESTLESS DEATH HE DAUNTLESS FAC'D, / NOR DANGER FEAR'D WHEN FOEMEN FIERCE WERE NIGH, / HE IN THE FIELD HIS COLOURS NE'ER DISGRAC'D, / BUT BRAVELY FOUGHT, NOR EVERY FEAR'D TO DIE! / HE LEFT HIS HOME, WITH ALL ITS VARIED PLEA-SURES, / TO SERVE HIS KING, HIS COUNTRY, AND FOR FAME; / BOLDLY HE MARCHED BY LONG AND TEDIOUS MEASURES / TO JUSTIFY, OLD ENGLAND'S GLORIOUS NAME! / HUNGER, AND THIRST, AND EVERY DREAD PRIVATION, / MIGHT OFT HAVE CAUS'D HIS LOYAL HEART TO SIGH, / BUT HE RESOLV'D FOR HIS VICTORIOUS NATION, / WHEN DUTY CALL'D "TO CONQUER OR TO DIE!" / REST, WARRIOR, REST!

Ledger stone: St George's Churchyard, Mossley, Lancashire. (Photograph)

.... / IN MEMORY OF / JOHN WHITWORTH, LATE / DRUM MAJOR SERGEANT OF / THE 7TH ROYAL FUSILIERS, OF / MOSSLEY LATE OF MANCHESTER, / WHO DEPARTED THIS LIFE, ON / THE 2ND DAY OF AUGUST A.D. 1848 / IN THE 64TH YEAR OF HIS AGE. / HIS SWORD IS SHEATHED, HIS DUTY'S DONE, / HIS VICTORIES ARE O'ER; / HIS BUGLE NOTES THE MARSHALLED BANKS, / TO ARMS SHALL ROUSE NO MORE. / HE SLEEPS AT PEACE, AND SILENCE REIGNS, / WITHIN HIS HALLOWED GRAVE; / THE DESTINED PLACE OF ALL ON EARTH, / THE MONARCH AND THE SLAVE.

Pte 4 Feb 1804. Cpl 1814. Sgt 1814.

Served in the Peninsula Apr 1809 – Apr 1814. Present at Talavera, Albuera, Badajoz, Salamanca, Vittoria, Pyrenees, Orthes and Toulouse. Served with the Army of Occupation until 1818. Also served at Copenhagen 1807, the West Indies 1808 – Apr 1809 (present at Martinique) and North America (present at New Orleans). Joined the regiment in 1804 as a drummer but served in most of the campaigns in the Peninsula as a Field Bugler. At the storming of Badojoz he was bugler to Edward Pakenham. MGS medal for Talavera, Albuera, Badajoz, Salamanca, Vittoria, Pyrenees, Orthes and Toulouse. Became Drum Major of the 7th Royal Fusiliers. Discharged 5 Apr 1825.

Reference: Yorke, Colin, John Whitworth: a Peninsular hero, Waterloo Journal, Summer 2007, pp. 25–30. Oxfordshire and Buckinghamshire Light Infantry Chronicle, 1901, p. 179.

WHYMPER, William

Surgeon. Coldstream Regiment of Foot Guards.
Interred in Catacomb B (v160 c2), Kensal Green Cemetery, London.

Asst Surgeon 14 Nov 1805. Surgeon 25 Dec 1813. Surgeon Major 24 Feb 1825.

Served in the Peninsula Mar 1809 – Oct 1810, Apr – May 1811 and May 1813 – Jan 1814. Present at Douro, Talavera (taken prisoner but escaped to rejoin his regiment on 20 Dec 1809), Busaco, Cadiz, Vittoria, Bidassoa, Nivelle and Nive. Present at Waterloo and with the Army of Occupation until 1818. MGS medal for Talavera, Busaco, Vittoria, Nivelle and Nive. Also served in the Netherlands 1814–1815. Knighted 1832. Retired 4 Sep 1836. MD Aberdeen 1817. Died at Dover 20 Nov 1850.

Reference: Gentleman's Magazine, Jan 1851, p. 96. Annual Register, 1850, Appx, p. 283.

WIDDOP, John

Private. 33rd (1st Yorkshire West Riding) Regiment of Foot.
Headstone: All Souls' Churchyard, Boothtown, Halifax, Yorkshire. (Photograph)

IN MEMORY OF / JOHN WIDDOP / OF HALIFAX WHO DIED 18TH JUNE 1868 / AGED 73 YEARS. / HE FOUGHT AT THE BATTLE OF WATERLOO. / ………………

Pte 10 Dec 1813.

Present at Quatre Bras and Waterloo where he was severely wounded. Also served in the West Indies 1822–1832 (present in Jamaica). Discharged 30 Oct 1835 owing to ill health aged 41 years.

WIEGMANN, Heinrich

Captain. 2nd Battalion Light Infantry, King's German Legion.
Named on the Regimental Memorial: La Haye Sainte, Waterloo. (Photograph)
Named on the Waterloo Column, Hanover, Germany. (Photograph)
Named on the memorial tablet in St Dionysius's Church, Adensen, Lower Saxony, Gemany. (Photograph)

Lt 7 Jan 1806. Capt and Brigade Major 24 Oct 1811.

Served in the Peninsula Aug 1808 – Jan 1809, Mar 1811 – Apr 1814. (Brigade Major, 1 Brigade 7th Division Dec 1811 – Nov 1812 and Brigade Major 3 Brigade 1st Division Dec 1812 – Apr 1814). Present at Vigo, Albuera, second siege of Badajoz, siege of Salamanca Forts, Moriscos, Salamanca, Burgos, Vittoria, Tolosa, St Sebastian, Bidassoa, Nivelle, Nive, St Etienne and Bayonne. Present at Waterloo where he was killed. Also served in the Baltic 1807–1808, Walcheren 1809 and the Netherlands 1814.

WIGGINS, James

Private. 12th (Prince of Wales's) Regiment of Light Dragoons.
Named on the Regimental Memorial: St Joseph's Church, Waterloo. (Photograph)

Present at Waterloo where he was killed.

WIGHTMAN, James

Sergeant Major. Royal Artillery.
Buried in St George's Chapel, Windsor, Berkshire. (Burial record)

Promoted from the ranks. Quartermaster 11 May 1825. Adjutant Invalid Battalion 11 May 1825. Lt and Adjutant Field Train Department 30 Aug 1834.

Served in the Peninsula 1811 – Apr 1814. Present at Ciudad Rodrigo, Badajoz, Salamanca, Vittoria, Burgos, San Sebastian, Nivelle, Nive and Bayonne (wounded). Present at Waterloo where he was wounded.

Retired 1 Jul 1847. MGS medal for Ciudad Rodrigo, Badajoz, Salamanca, Vittoria, San Sebastian, Nivelle, and Nive. Military Knight of Windsor 23 Mar 1848. Died 20 Apr 1848.

WIJNBERGEN, W. L. van

Captain. 6th Hussars, Dutch Cavalry.
Named on the Memorial to Dutch officers killed at Waterloo: St Joseph's Church, Waterloo. (Photograph)
Named on the Regimental Memorial to officers of the Dutch 6th Regiment of Hussars killed at Waterloo, St Joseph's Church, Waterloo. (Photograph)

WILD, John

Ensign and Adjutant. 48th (Northamptonshire) Regiment of Foot.
Pedestal tomb in railed enclosure: Heber Churchyard, Cobbity, Queensland, Australia. (Photograph)

TO / THE MEMORY OF / JOHN WILD. / LATE LIEUT AND ADJT 48TH REGT / WHO DIED AT VANDERVILLE / 4TH MARCH 1834. / AGED 53. / ....

Pte 1797 (aged 15). Promoted from the ranks. Quartermaster 22 Jun 1810. Ensign and Adjutant 7 Jul 1814. Lt 2 Mar 1820.

Served in the Peninsula 1809 – Jul 1811. Present at Douro, Talavera, Busaco and Albuera. The regiment returned to England after the Battle of Albuera in May 1811. Also served in Australia 1817. Retired 25 Sep 1822 and became Principal Overseer of Government Stock at Cawdor cattle station. Granted 2,000 acres of land on Wernberri Creek 1826 where he died 4 Mar 1834.

WILDMAN, Thomas

Captain. 7th (Queen's Own) Regiment of Light Dragoons.
Monument: Mansfield Cemetery, Mansfield, Nottinghamshire. (Photograph)

COLONEL THOMAS WILDMAN DIED SEP XX: MDXXXLIX: AGED LXXII:

Cornet 9th Lt Dragoons 5 Mar 1807. Lt 7th Lt Dragoons 29 Sep 1808. Capt 18 Feb 1813. Major 18 Jul 1816. Lt Colonel 23 Dec 1819. Bt Colonel 10 Jan 1837.

Served in the Peninsula Nov 1808 – Jan 1809 and Oct 1813 – Apr 1814. Present at Sahagun, Mayorga, Benevente, retreat to Corunna, Orthes and Toulouse. Present at Quatre Bras 17 June covering the retreat of the infantry and at Waterloo where he was wounded (ADC to Lord Uxbridge). MGS medal for Sahagun and Benevente, Orthes and Toulouse. Half pay 23 Dec 1819. Purchased the Newstead Abbey estates in Nottinghamshire, formerly the home of Lord Byron. Deputy Lieutenant of Nottinghamshire. High Sheriff 1821. Died 20 Sep 1859.
Reference: Birks, M., The young Hussar: the Peninsular War journal of Colonel Wildman, 2007. Gentleman's Magazine, Dec 1859, pp. 645–6. Annual Register, 1859, Appx, p. 496.

WILKIE, Peter

Captain. 92nd Regiment of Foot.
Low monument: Holy Trinity with St Edmund's Churchyard, Horfield, Bristol, Somerset. (Grave number 1073). (North side of church near perimeter bank). (Seriously eroded). (Photograph)

PETER WILKIE / LATE BARRACK MASTER / AND FORMERLY OF THE 92ND HIGHLANDERS / WHO DEPARTED THIS LIFE / ON THE 4TH NOVEMBER 1852 / IN THE 67TH YEAR OF HIS AGE / (VERSE)

Ensign 23 Nov 1799. Lt 26 May 1801. Capt 21 May 1806. Major 21 Jan 1819.

Served in the Peninsula Oct – Nov 1811 and May 1813 – Apr 1814. Present at Arroyo dos Molinos,

Vittoria, Pyrenees, Nivelle, Nive, Garris, Orthes, Aire, Tarbes and Toulouse. Present at Waterloo (severely wounded). Also served in Egypt 1801 (present at the Capture of Cairo and Alexandria where he was wounded and awarded Gold Medal from the Grand Seignjor). Later Barrack Master at Bristol. MGS medal for Egypt, Vittoria, Pyrenees, Nivelle, Nive, Orthes and Toulouse. Died 4 Nov 1852.
Reference: Gentleman's Magazine, Jan 1853, p. 105.

WILKIE, Thomas Fletcher
Captain. 38th (1st Staffordshire) Regiment of Foot.
Headstone: St John the Baptist's Churchyard, Batheaston, Bath, Somerset. (Seriously eroded and inscription recorded from memorial inscription). (Photograph)

"TO THE MEMORY OF / ELIZABETH WIFE OF / LT COLONEL THOMAS WILKIE / HE SERVED IN THE REVOLUTIONARY WAR / AND IN THE PENINSULAR WAR"

Lt 35th Foot 18 Nov 1795. Capt-Lt 20 Mar 1800. Capt 3rd Battalion of Reserve 5 Nov 1803. Capt 38th Foot 2 Aug 1804. Bt Major 1 Jan 1811. Lt Col 19 Jul 1821.

Served in the Peninsula with 1/38th Aug 1808 – Jan 1809. Present at Rolica, Vimeiro and Corunna. Present at the Capture of Paris 1815. Also served at the Helder 1799, Capture of Malta 1800, Cape of Good Hope 1806, South America 1807 (present at the siege of Montevideo and Buenos Ayres) and Walcheren 1809 (present at the Siege of Flushing). MGS medal for Rolica, Vimeiro and Corunna. Died in Bath 16 May 1862 aged 80.
Reference: Bath Chronicle, 15 May 1867

WILKINS, George
Major. 95th Regiment of Foot.
Grave: St James's Churchyard, Shirley, Southampton, Hampshire. (M.I.)

"GEORGE WILKINS, LIEUT COLONEL CB. KH. DIED 8 NOVEMBER 1862 AGED 83."

2nd Lt 82nd Foot 14 Sep 1794. Lt 7 Jan 1795. Lt 31st Foot 10 Sep 1795. Capt in McDonnell's Regt 1 Jun 1796. Capt 85th Foot 18 May 1800. Bt Major 25 Apr 1808. Major 95th Foot 10 May 1809. Bt Lt Colonel 4 Jun 1814.

Served in the Peninsula with 2nd Battalion Mar – Jul 1810 and May 1811 – Sep 1813. Present at Cadiz, Salamanca, San Millan, Vittoria, Pyrenees and Vera. Gold Medal for Salamanca. CB. KH. Present at Waterloo (wounded in command of 2nd Battalion and awarded pension of £300 per annum). Also served in the Irish Rebellion 1798 (wounded), Madeira 1801 and Walcheren 1809. Retired 23 Dec 1819. MGS medal for Vittoria and Pyrenees.

WILKINSON, John
Private. 2nd Life Guards.
Headstone: Maitland Cemetery, Campbell's Hill, New South Wales, Australia. (Photograph)

SACRED / TO THE MEMORY OF / JOHN WILKINSON / WHO DEPARTED THIS LIFE / ON THE 8TH APRIL A.D. 1855. / AGED 66 YEARS. / (VERSE) / ....

Pte 25 Jun 1810. Cpl of Horse 19 Mar 1817.

Served in the Peninsula Nov 1812 – Jul 1814. Present at Vittoria. Present at Waterloo. MGS medal for Vittoria. Joined the Royal Veterans Corps, posted to the new settlement of Bathurst in Australia and was promoted to Corporal. Discharged 1 Feb 1833. Awarded a grant of land in 1831, which he farmed until 1839. Then given the licence of a new hotel in High St Maitland, which he called the Waterloo Inn.

WILKINSON, Thomas
Captain. 85th (Buckinghamshire Volunteers) Light Infantry Regiment of Foot.
Memorial tablet: St Mary the Virgin's Church, Baldock, Hertfordshire. (Photograph)

SACRED / TO THE MEMORY OF / THOMAS WILKINSON, / CAPTAIN IN H. M. 85TH REGIMENT OF INFANTRY, / AND MAJOR OF BRIGADE TO / MAJOR GENERAL GIBBS, / IN THE EXPEDITION AGAINST NEW ORLEANS. / SLAIN WITH HIS GALLANT GENERAL / AT THE ATTACK ON THE AMERICAN LINES. / JANUARY 8TH 1815, / AGED 21 YEARS.

Ensign 4th Garrison Battalion 1 Sep 1808. Lt 43rd Foot 18 Jan 1810. Lt 85th Foot 25 Jan 1813. Capt 26 Apr 1814.

Served in the Peninsula Jul 1811 – Feb 1813 and Aug 1813 – Apr 1814. Present at Ciudad Rodrigo, Badajoz (wounded), Salamanca, San Munos, Nivelle, Nive and Bayonne. Also served in North America 1814–1815 (present at Bladensburg and New Orleans where he was killed 8 Jan 1815).

WILKINSON, William
Captain. 60th (Royal American) Regiment of Foot.
Grave: Holy Trinity Churchyard, Brompton, London. (M.I.)

"WILLIAM WILKINSON, CAPTAIN LATE OF HER / MAJESTY'S (MILITARY) DIED 14 MAR 1848 / IN HIS 75TH YEAR."

Lt 7th Foot 29 Aug 1807. Capt 2 Sep 1813. Capt 60th Foot 16 Dec 1813. Capt 8th Veteran Battalion 24 Feb 1820 (disbanded 1821). Capt 3rd Veteran Battalion 25 Dec 1821.

Served in the Peninsula with 1/7th Aug 1810 – Dec 1813 and 5/60th Apr 1814. Present at Aldea de Ponte, Ciudad Rodrigo, Badajoz, Vittoria, Pyrenees, Bidassoa, Nivelle and Nive. Retired on full pay 1826. MGS medal for Ciudad Rodrigo, Badajoz, Vittoria, Pyrenees, Nivelle and Nive.

WILL, Andrew
Lieutenant. 92nd Regiment of Foot.
Mural memorial tablet: Holy Trinity Cathedral Churchyard, Brechin, Angus, Scotland. (West side of church near north gate). (Photograph)

TO THE MEMORY OF / ANDREW WILL / LATE LIEUTENANT 92ND / (HIGHLAND REGIMENT), / WHO, AFTER SERVING FOUR YEARS / IN THE PENINSULAR WAR / WHERE HE WAS SEVERELY WOUNDED / IN THE HEAD / AND AT THE BATTLES OF / QUATRE BRAS & WATERLOO, / FELL IN JAMAICA ON THE 7TH OF OCTR, /1819 / A VICTIM TO THE / CLIMATE.

Forfarshire Militia. Ensign 91st Foot 29 Sep 1807. Lt 92nd Foot 18 Feb 1808.

Served in the Peninsula Oct 1810 – Apr 1814. Present at Fuentes d'Onoro, Arroyo dos Molinos, Almarez, and Alba de Tormes (severely wounded). Present at Quatre Bras and Waterloo. Also served in the West Indies where he died in Jamaica of yellow fever 7 Oct 1819.

WILLATS, Peter John
Captain. Bourbon Regiment.
Memorial tablet: St James's Church, Cheltenham, Gloucestershire. (Photograph)

IN AFFECTIONATE REMEMBRANCE OF / PETER JOHN WILLATS LT COLONEL, / (OF ST OSWALD'S CHELTENHAM) / H.M. 48TH REGT HE SERVED IN THE PENINSULA, / (UNDER THE DUKE OF WELLINGTON) / AT BADAJOS, CUIDAD RODRIGO, / IN INDIA & AT THE CAPE OF GOOD HOPE, / HE DIED FEBRY 20 1875. / (VERSE)

Ensign 8th Foot 31 Aug 1809. Lt 77th Foot 2 Jun 1811. Capt Bourbon Regt 22 Dec 1814. Capt 48th Foot 26 Mar 1824. Bt Major 10 Jan 1837. Major 4 Nov 1838. Bt Lt Colonel 28 Nov 1854.

Served in the Peninsula Dec 1811 – Apr 1814. Present at Ciudad Rodrigo, Badajoz and Bayonne. Also served in India 1824–1835 (present in the Coorg Wars 1834) and the Cape of Good Hope. MGS medal for Ciudad Rodrigo and Badajoz.

WILLERMAN, William

Captain. 2nd Ceylon Regiment.
Obelisk: Galle Face Burial Ground, Ceylon. (Burial ground is no longer extant). (M.I.)

"SACRED TO THE MEMORY OF LIEUT.-COL. WILLIAM WILLERMAN, D. Q. M. G., WHO DIED ON THE 13TH OF JUNE 1815, AGED 41. TO AN ARDENT ZEAL IN THE PERFORMANCE OF HIS MILITARY DUTIES LIEUT.-COL. WILLERMAN UNITED MANY ACQUIREMENTS, WHICH GRACE THE CHARACTER AND ELEVATE THE PROFESSION OF A SOLDIER. HE HAD AN EXTENSIVE KNOWLEDGE OF ANCIENT AND MODERN LANGUAGES, MATHEMATICAL AND TOPOGRAPHICAL DRAWING AND WAS EMINENTLY SKILFUL. HE HAD SERVED WITH DISTINCTION IN FLANDERS, PORTUGAL, AND SPAIN, AND DECISIVE SUCCESS OF THE LATE KANDIAN WAS ATTRIBUTED BY HIS GRATEFUL COMMANDER TO HIS ARRANGEMENTS AND COMBINATION. HIS MANNERS WERE MILD AND POLISHED, HIS MORAL CONDUCT HONOURABLE AND UPRIGHT. HIS RELIGIOUS OPINIONS WERE FOUNDED ON A FIRM BELIEF IN THE GOSPEL AND AN HUMBLE RELIANCE ON THE MEDIATION OF OUR BLESSED SAVIOUR. THE CHARACTER OF SUCH A MAN WAS REGARDED WITH AFFECTIONATE ESTEEM, HIS UNTIMELY DEATH WITH DEEP REGRET. HE WAS BURIED AT HIS OWN DESIRE CLOSE TO THE GRAVE OF HIS FAITHFUL SERVANT, AND THIS MONUMENT WAS ERECTED BY LIEUT.-GEN. SIR ROBERT BROWNRIGG, G.C.B., WHO LONG HAD KNOWN HIS WORTH, AND WILL EVER DEPLORE HIS LOSS."

Lt Royal Staff Corps 1803. Capt 3 Sep 1807. Bt Major 18 Feb 1813. Capt 2nd Ceylon Regt 22 Apr 1813.

Served in the Peninsula Aug 1808 – Jan 1809 (DAQMG) and Jul – Aug 1811. Present at Rolica, Vimeiro and Corunna. Also served in the Baltic 1807, Sicily 1809 and Ceylon 1815 (DQMG, present in the second Kandian War 1815). Formerly served in the Dutch Guards but obtained a commission in the British Army. Was an excellent draughtsman and linguist.
Reference: Lewis, J. Penry, List of inscriptions on tombstones and monuments in Ceylon, 1913, reprint 1994, pp. 28–9.

WILLETT, George

Private. 2nd (Royal North British) Regiment of Dragoons.
Memorial headstone: British Military Burying Ground, Ballincollig, County Cork, Ireland. (Photograph)

SACRED TO THE MEMORY OF / GEORGE WILLETT LATE SERGEANT AND / MASTER TAILOR OF THE ROYAL SCOTS GREYS / WHO DEPARTED THIS LIFE ON 28TH JANUARY 1840 / AGED 46 YEARS. HE SERVED IN THE REGIMENT / AND WAS PRESENT WITH IT AT THE / BATTLE OF WATERLOO. HE WAS A KIND AND / AFFECTIONATE HUSBAND AND HIS DEATH / WAS MUCH REGRETTED BY THE REGIMENT. / THIS STONE IS ERECTED BY HIS BELOVED / WIFE AS A MEMORIAL AS TO THE AFFECTION SHE / HAD FOR HIM AS A TRIBUTE OF RESPECT / TO HIS MEMORY. / WHY SHOULD WE MOURN DEAR FRIENDS / OR SHRINK AT DEATH'S ALARMS. / T'IS BUT THE VOICE THAT JESUS SENDS / TO CALL US TO HIS ARMS.

Headstone: Sydney Burial Ground, Sydney, New South Wales, Australia. (M.I.) (No longer extant. Now site of Sydney Town Hall).

"GEORGE WILLETT, SERGEANT AND MASTER TAILOR, ROYAL SCOTS GREYS. DIED JAN 28TH 1840 AGED 46. SERVED AT WATERLOO."

Pte 31 Jul 1811.

Present at Waterloo in Captain Payne's Troop. Also served in Australia. Discharged 4 Jun 1839.

WILLIAMS, David
Jobbing Smith. Royal Artillery Drivers.
Headstone: Holy Trinity Churchyard, Coalbrookdale, Shropshire. (Photograph)

IN / AFFECTIONATE / REMEMBRANCE / OF / SARAH / THE WIFE OF DAVID WILLIAMS / OF COALBROOKE / WHO DIED 13TH APRIL 1866 / AGED 65 YEARS / ALSO OF THE ABOVE / DAVID WILLIAMS / WHO SERVED AT WATERLOO / DIED APRIL 22ND 1878 / IN THE 87TH YEAR OF HIS AGE / ....

New headstone: Holy Trinity Churchyard, Coalbrookdale, Shropshire. (Photograph)

IN / AFFECTIONATE / REMEMBRANCE / OF / SARAH / THE WIFE OF / DAVID WILLIAMS / (OF COALBROOKE DALE) / WHO DIED 13TH APRIL 1866 / AGED 65 YEARS / ALSO / DAVID WILLIAMS / WHO SERVED AT WATERLOO / WITH THE / ROYAL HORSE ARTILLERY / WHO DIED 22ND APRIL 1878 / IN THE 87TH YEAR OF HIS LIFE

Pte 18 Jan 1810.

Served in the Peninsula. Present at Toulouse. Present at Waterloo in Capt W. H. Humphrey's 'H' Troop and with the Army of Occupation until 1818. Discharged 18 Nov 1818. He worked for the Coalbrookdale Company until he was 80 years old. Awarded pension by the Army of one shilling and six pence a day in 1874. A new headstone (Photograph) has been erected to take the place of the badly eroded headstone, the latter being laid flat on the grave. A ceremony to mark the restoration took place on Saturday 16 Jun 2007. The project was organised by the Shropshire War Memorial Association.

Reference: Shrewsbury Chronicle, 11 Mar 1915. Shropshire Star, 18 Jun 2007.

WILLIAMS, Sir Edmund Keynton
Captain. 81st Regiment of Foot.
Memorial tablet: St Tewdric's Church, Mathern, Monmouthshire, Wales. (Photograph)

IN MEMORY OF / MAJOR GENERAL / SIR EDMUND KEYNTON WILLIAMS K.C.B. & K.T.S. / COLONEL OF HER MAJESTY'S 80TH REGIMENT OF FOOT. / BORN IN THIS PARISH DURING THE CURACY OF HIS FATHER THE / REVD HENRY WILLIAMS LATE VICAR OF UNDY IN THIS COUNTY / DECEASED DEC 7TH 1830 AGED 71. / BEING INTENDED FOR HOLY ORDERS HE ENTERED AND RESIDED AT / ORIEL COLLEGE OXFORD IN THE YEAR 1798, BUT SUBSEQUENTLY JOINED / THE EXPEDITION INTO HOLLAND UNDER THE LATE DUKE OF YORK, IN THE / YEAR 1799: AFTER A LONG AND ARDUOUS SERVICE THROUGH THE WHOLE / OF THE PENINSULAR CAMPAIGN, DURING WHICH HE GAINED HIGH AND / HONOURABLE DISTINCTION FROM HIS OWN COUNTRY, AS WELL AS THAT OF / PORTUGAL, HE CONCLUDED HIS MILITARY CAREER AS GENERAL OF THE / CENTRAL DIVISION OF THE MADRAS ARMY EAST INDIES.

Ensign 4th Foot 30 Aug 1799. Lt 18 Apr 1800. Lt 81st Foot 9 Jul 1803. Capt 25 Sep 1807. Bt Major 8 Oct 1812. Bt Lt Colonel 21 Jun 1813. Major 4th Foot 21 Mar 1822. Lt Colonel 41st Foot 9 Aug 1827. Bt Colonel 22 Jul 1830. Major General 23 Nov 1841. Portuguese Army: Major 4th Caçadores 7 May 1810. Lt Colonel 14 Apr 1812.

Served in the Peninsula with Portuguese Army May 1810 – Nov 1811 and Feb 1812 – Jan 1814. Present at Busaco (wounded), Redinha, Almeida, Badajoz, Salamanca (wounded), Burgos (wounded and Mentioned in Despatches), retreat from Burgos, Vittoria, Tolosa (Mentioned in Despatches), San Sebastian (wounded), Bidassoa, Nivelle, Nive, Adour and Bayonne (wounded). Gold Cross for Busaco, Salamanca, Vittoria, San Sebastian and Nive. MGS medal for Maida, Badajoz and Nivelle. KCB. KTS. Also served at the Helder 1799 (present at Egmont-op-Zee and Alkmaar where he was wounded), Sicily 1806 (present at Maida), Ischia 1809, West Indies 1822, India 1828 and in 1842 on Staff of Madras Presidency. Colonel 80th Foot 24 Oct 1848.

Reference: Gentleman's Magazine, Mar 1850, p. 319. Annual Register, 1849, Appx, p. 296.

WILLIAMS, Henry

1st Lieutenant. Royal Artillery.

Memorial tablet: St Paul's Church, Bridgetown, Barbados, West Indies. (Photograph)

SACRED TO THE MEMORY OF / LIEUTENANT COLONEL HENRY WILLIAMS, / COMMANDING THE ROYAL ARTILLERY IN THE WEST INDIES, / WHO DIED OF YELLOW FEVER / ON THE 10TH NOVR 1852, AGED 60 YEARS / ....

Low monument: St Paul's Churchyard, Bridgetown, Barbados, West Indies. (Photograph)

SACRED / TO THE MEMORY OF / LIEUTENANT COLONEL / HENRY WILLIAMS, / COMMANDING THE / ROYAL ARTILLERY IN THE WEST INDIES, / WHO DIED OF YELLOW FEVER / ON THE 10TH NOVR 1852 / AGED 60.

2nd Lt 17 Dec 1812. 1st Lt 20 May 1815. 2nd Capt 17 Dec 1833. Capt 16 Sep 1841. Bt Major 9 Nov 1846. Lt Col 1 Nov 1848.

Present at Waterloo, the Capture of Paris and with the Army of Occupation. Also served in North America 1814 (present at New Orleans, Fort Bowyer and Mobile Bay) the Ionian Islands May 1834 – Nov 1841 and Mar 1843 – May 1849 (Resident of Ithaca Apr 1845 – Sep 1846 and Resident of Santa Maura Sep 1846 – Feb 1849) and the West Indies Mar – Nov 1852 where he died of yellow fever.

WILLIAMS, John

Ensign. 74th (Highland) Regiment of Foot.

Named on the Regimental Memorial: St Giles's Cathedral, Edinburgh, Scotland. (Photograph)

Ensign Oct 1809.

Served in the Peninsula Feb – Sep 1810. Present at Busaco where he was killed 27 Sep 1810.

WILLIAMS, John

Staff Surgeon. Medical Department.

Monument: English Cemetery, Florence, Italy. (Grave number D29R). (Photograph)

IOANNI WILLIAMS LONDINENSI / SANCTIS MORIBUS HUMANIS LITTERIS / NATURA ET PHILOSOPHIA PRAETARO / CUI AD MEDICAM ET CHIRUGIAM / MILIT BRITANNIC RELICTO MEDICA / DOCTOR XXXV ANNOS PERITUM ******** AL AD AMORE / MORBIS RAPITOS / HONESTA MISSIONI DONATVS FLORENTIAE / VBI LENIRE COARCTATIONIS MAGNORUM CORDIS VASORUM / INCREMENTVM PASSVS / DIEM OBIIT EXTREMVM / XV FEBRVARI ANNO MDCCCXXXX1 AET SVAE LVIII / RESVRRECTIONEM A.D.J. CHRISTO PROMISSAM EXPECTANS / CONIVGI DILECTISSIMO PAVLA VXOR CVM LACRYMIS

Hospital Mate May 1805. Asst Surgeon 52nd Foot 20 Jun 1805. Surgeon 9th Foot 3 Sep 1812. Surgeon 94th Foot 28 Oct 1813. Staff Surgeon 26 May 1814.

Served in the Peninsula with 1/52nd Aug – Dec 1808, 1st Battalion Detachments Jan – Dec 1809, 1/52nd Dec 1809 – Oct 1812, 1/9th Oct 1812 – Oct 1813 and 94th Foot Nov 1813 – Apr 1814. Present at Douro, Coa, Busaco, Fuentes d'Onoro, Ciudad Rodrigo, Badajoz, Salamanca, Osma, Vittoria, San Sebastian, Orthes, Vic Bigorre and Toulouse. Also served in North America 1814–1815. MD Glasgow 1825. Retired 1 Nov 1838. Died in Florence 15 Feb 1841.

WILLIAMS, John

Private. Coldstream Regiment of Foot Guards.

Memorial tablet: St Andrew's Church, St Andrews Major, Glamorgan, Wales. (In porch). (Photograph)

SACRED TO THE MEMORY OF JOHN WILLIAMS OF THIS PARISH WHO DIED / 4TH JUNE 1861 AGED 84 YEARS. ONE OF THE MANY UNCONSCIOUS HEROES WHO HAVE MADE / ENGLAND WHAT SHE IS: JOHN WILLIAMS SERVED AS A PRIVATE IN THE COLDSTREAM GUARDS / IN THE PENINSULAR WAR TAKING PART IN THE BATTLE OF BUSACO ON 17TH JUNE 1810, THE / BATTLE OF FUENTES DE ONORO 3RD TO 5TH MAY 1811, THE SIEGE & CAPTURE OF CIUDAD RODRIGO ON / 19TH JANUARY 1812, THE BATTLE OF SALAMANCA 22ND JULY 1812, THE BATTLE OF VITTORIA / 26TH JUNE 1813, THE SIEGE AND CAPTURE OF ST SEBASTIAN 17TH JULY TO 31ST AUGUST 1813 & FINALLY / LOST A LEG THROUGH A WOUND RECEIVED AT THE SIEGE OF BAYONNE DURING THE SORTIE / MADE BY THE FRENCH ARMY ON 14TH APRIL 1814. THIS TRIBUTE OF RESPECT FOR A SOLDIER IS / OFFERED BY ANOTHER SOLDIER A.D. 1893.

Pte 9 Sep 1793 – 11 Mar 1805. Pte 11 Dec 1808 – 7 Feb 1818.

Served in the Peninsula with 1st Battalion Mar 1809 – Apr 1814. Present at Busaco, Fuentes d'Onoro, Ciudad Rodrigo, Salamanca, Vittoria, San Sebastian and Sortie from Bayonne (severely wounded). MGS medal for Busaco, Fuentes d'Onoro, Ciudad Rodrigo, Salamanca and Vittoria. Discharged 7 Feb 1818 as unfit after his long period of service.

WILLIAMS, John

Private. 23rd (Royal Welch Fusiliers) Regiment of Foot.

Headstone: St Mar's Churchyard, Llanfor, Merioneth, Wales. (Photograph)

IN MEMORY / OF / JOHN WILLIAMS / PENSIONER, 23RD ROYAL WELSH / FUSILIERS REGIMENT OF FOOT / DIED 27TH DAY OF JANUARY 1864 / AGED 87 YEARS. / HE FOUGHT FOR HIS COUNTRY AT / 27 BATTLES AMONG WHICH WERE / MARTINIQUE. / ALBUHERA. / CIUDAD RODRIGO. / BADAJOZ. / SALAMANCA. / VITTORIA. / PYRENEES. / ST: SEBASTIAN. / NIVELLE. / ORTHES. / TOULOUSE. / WATERLOO.

Pte 28 Apr 1805.

Served in the Peninsula Dec 1810 – Apr 1814. Present at Albuera, Ciudad Rodrigo, Badajoz, Salamanca, Vittoria, Pyrenees, San Sebastian (wounded), Nivelle, Orthes and Toulouse. Present at Waterloo. Also served in the West Indies 1808–1809 (present at Martinique). MGS medal for Martinique, Albuera, Ciudad Rodrigo, Badajoz, Salamanca, Vittoria, Pyrenees, San Sebastian, Nivelle, Orthes and Toulouse. Discharged 25 Jun 1823 as unfit for further service and received a pension of one shilling per day.

WILLIAMS, John

Private. 95th Regiment of Foot.

Headstone: St Asaph's Churchyard, Flint, Wales. (Photograph)

.... / ALSO OF JOHN WILLIAMS, WHO / DIED APRIL 1ST 1861 AGED 76 / THE ABOVE NAMED J. W. / FOUGHT IN GENERAL ACTIONS / UNDER THE DUKE / OF WELLINGTON.

Pte 12 Mar 1805.

Served in the Peninsula 1810 – Apr 1814. Present at Busaco, Fuentes D'Onoro, Ciudad Rodrigo, Badajoz, Salamanca, Vittoria, Pyrenees (wounded) and Toulouse. Present at Waterloo in Captain E. Chawner's Company. Discharged 24 Sep 1816. MGS medal for Busaco, Fuentes D'Onoro, Ciudad Rodrigo, Badajoz, Salamanca, Vittoria, Pyrenees and Toulouse.

WILLIAMS, John Archer

2nd Captain. Royal Engineers.
Named on the Regimental Memorial: Rochester Cathedral, Rochester, Kent. (Photograph)

2nd Lt 1 Jan 1804. Lt 1 Mar 1805. 2nd Capt 24 Jun 1809.

Served in the Peninsula Aug 1808 – Sep 1812. Present at Torres Vedras, Ciudad Rodrigo, Badajoz (severely wounded at the third siege when he was guiding the Light Division in the assault on the Maria flank 6 Apr 1812 and Mentioned in Despatches) and Burgos where he was killed 24 Sep 1812 directing operations for the siege.

WILLIAMS, Peter

Private. 2nd (Queen's Royal) Regiment of Foot.
Low monument: Abbey Cemetery, Bath, Somerset. (Photograph)

IN MEMORY OF / PETER WILLIAMS / VETERAN OF THE PENINSULAR CAMPAIGN / BORN 1789 DIED 1861 / ....

Pte Apr 1809.

Served in the Peninsula Mar 1811 – Apr 1814. Present at Salamanca, Vittoria, Pyrenees and Nivelle (severely wounded 10 Nov 1813). MGS medal for Salamanca, Vittoria, Pyrenees and Nivelle. Discharged 8 May 1815 owing to his wounds from the Pyrenees.

WILLIAMS, Thomas Molyneux see MOLYNEUX, Thomas

WILLIAMS, Sir William

Lieutenant Colonel. 13th (1st Somersetshire) Regiment of Foot.
Memorial tablet: St Swithin's Church, Bath, Somerset. (Photograph)

SACRED / TO THE MEMORY OF / MAJOR GENL SIR W. WILLIAMS C.B. / WHO DIED IN THIS CITY / JUNE 17TH 1832 / AGED 56. / ....

Ensign 40th Foot 23 Jun 1794. Lt 7 Apr 1795. Capt 23 Sep 1799. Bt Major 24 Jun 1802. Major 81st Foot 26 Oct 1804. Lt Colonel 60th Foot 15 Nov 1809. Lt Colonel 13th Foot 25 Jun 1812. Bt Colonel 12 Aug 1819. Major General 22 Jul 1830.

Served in the Peninsula with 81st Foot Nov 1808 – Jan 1809 and 60th Foot Jun 1810 – Jul 1812. Present at Corunna (wounded), Busaco (wounded), Pombal, Redinha, Casal Nova (Mentioned in Despatches), Foz d'Arouce (Mentioned in Despatches), Sabugal (Mentioned in Despatches), Fuentes d'Onoro (severely wounded and Mentioned in Despatches), El Bodon (Mentioned in Despatches), Badajoz, and Salamanca (wounded and Mentioned in Despatches). By 3 May 1812 was O/c Light Troops 3rd Division. Gold Cross for Corunna, Fuentes d'Onoro Ciudad Rodrigo, Badajoz and Salamanca. KCB. KTS. Also served in Flanders 1793–1794, West Indies 1795–1796 (present at St Vincent), Irish Rebellion 1798, Ferrol 1800,

Egypt 1801, Walcheren 1809 and North America 1814–1815 (commended for his defence of posts on the River Richelieu when attacked by Americans under General Wilkinson).
Reference: Royal Military Calendar, Vol. 4, pp. 271–2.

WILLIAMS, William Freke
Captain. 85th (Buckinghamshire Volunteers) Light Infantry Regiment of Foot.
Headstone: St Thomas a Becket's Churchyard, Widcombe, Bath, Somerset. (Photograph)

SACRED / TO THE CHERISHED MEMORY OF / MAJOR GENERAL / W. FREKE WILLIAMS, K.H. / AND HIS YOUNGEST CHILD / FREKE ALISTER WILLIAMS / DIED DECEMBER 12TH / AND DECEMBER 22ND 1860.

Ensign Royal African Corps 30 Aug 1810. Lt 10 Jun 1811. Lt 85th Foot 25 Jan 1813. Capt 31 Oct 1814. Major 6 Apr 1825. Bt Lt Colonel 28 Jun 1838. Bt Colonel 11 Nov 1851. Major General 14 Apr 1857.

Served in the Peninsula Aug 1813 – Apr 1814. Present at San Sebastian, Bidassoa, Nivelle, Nive and Bayonne. Also served in Senegal, Goree and Sierra Leone 1811–1812 and North America 1814. At the end of the Peninsular War he went to America with the 85th Foot, under the command of General Robert Ross (present at Bladensburg where he was wounded). Served in Canada during the Rebellion 1838–1839 (sent on 'Particular Service'). On special service in Ireland 1843 (AAG). Half pay Jul 1843. MGS medal for San Sebastian, Nivelle and Nive. KH.
Reference: Gentleman's Magazine, Feb 1861, p. 228. Annual Register, 1860, Part 2, p. 500.

WILLIAMSON, Donald
Captain. 42nd (Royal Highland) Regiment of Foot.
Tablestone in enclosure: Halkirk Churchyard, Halkirk, Caithness, Scotland. (M.I.)

"LT. COL. WILLIAMSON, BARRISKIRK, DIED AT BAMBURGH 7 MARCH 1823. .... HIS SONS CAPT. DONALD 42ND ROYAL HIGHLANDERS AND CAPT JAMES 94TH REGT., BOTH DIED IN SPAIN 1812."

Ensign 42nd Foot 26 May 1801. Lt 10 Sep 1803. Capt 18 Feb 1804. Bt Major 8 Oct 1812.

Served in the Peninsula Aug 1808 – Jan 1809 and Apr – Oct 1812. Present at Corunna, Salamanca and Burgos where he was severely wounded 24 Sep and died of his wounds 2 Oct 1812. Awarded Brevet Majority but did not live long enough to be told of this honour. Brother of Capt James Williamson 94th Regiment.
Reference: Gentleman's Magazine, Nov 1812, p. 494.

WILLIAMSON, James
Captain. 94th Regiment of Foot.
Tablestone in enclosure: Halkirk Churchyard, Halkirk, Caithness, Scotland. (M.I.)

"LT. COL. WILLIAMSON, BARRISKIRK, DIED AT BAMBURGH 7 MARCH 1823. .... HIS SONS CAPT. DONALD 42ND ROYAL HIGHLANDERS AND CAPT JAMES 94TH REGT., BOTH DIED IN SPAIN 1812."

Ensign 42nd Foot 28 Dec 1804. Lt 79th Foot 25 Mar 1805. Capt 8 Jun 1809. Capt 94th Foot 18 Jan 1810.

Served in the Peninsula Aug 1808 – Jan 1809 and Apr 1810 – Jan 1812. Present at Corunna, Cadiz, Redinha, Casal Nova, Foz d'Arouce, Sabugal, Fuentes d'Onoro, second siege of Badajoz, El Bodon and Ciudad Rodrigo where he was killed 19 Jan 1812. Brother of Captain Donald Williamson 42nd Foot.

WILLIAMSON, John Sutherland

Major. Royal Artillery.

Grave: St Nicholas's Churchyard, Plumstead, Kent. (No longer extant. Destroyed by a flying bomb in the Second World War). (M.I.)

Named on the Regimental Memorial: St Nicholas's Church, Plumstead, Kent. (No longer extant. Destroyed by a flying bomb in the Second World War)

2nd Lt 1 Jan 1794. 1st Lt 11 Apr 1794. Capt-Lt 2 Oct 1799. Capt 12 Sep 1803. Bt Major 4 Jun 1811. Major 20 Dec 1814. Bt Lt Colonel 13 Oct 1814. Lt Colonel 24 Mar 1817. Colonel 20 Jul 1825.

Served in the Peninsula Aug 1812 – Apr 1814 (officer in charge of Royal Artillery in Catalonia). Present on the East coast of Spain, Saragossa, Ordal, Castalla (Mentioned in General Murray's Despatches) and Tarragona. Present at Waterloo in command of the Artillery with the 3rd Division. CB for Waterloo. Also served at Quiberon Bay 1795, Cape of Good Hope 1806, Ischia 1809 and the Ionian Islands 1809–1810. Half pay 1 May 1817. Rejoined 21 Apr 1820. Became Superintendent of the Royal Military Repository where he prepared new courses of instructions for the Artillery. Died at Woolwich 26 Apr 1836.

WILLIAMSON, Joseph

Private. 12th (Prince of Wales's) Regiment of Light Dragoons.

Named on the Regimental Memorial: St Joseph's Church, Waterloo. (Photograph)

Present at Waterloo where he was killed.

WILLINGTON, James

Captain. 3rd (East Kent) Regiment of Foot.

Obelisk: Culver Hill, Beekmantown, Plattsburgh, United States of America. (Photograph)

CULVER HILL / SEPTEMBER 6 / 1814 / NEAR THIS SPOT FELL / CORPORAL / STEPHEN PARTRIDGE / OF THE ESSEX COUNTRY / NEW YORK MILITIA / ALSO / BREVET LIEUT COLONEL / JAMES WILLINGTON / ALSO ENSIGN / JOHN CHAPMAN / OF THE / 3RD FOOT BRITISH ARMY / ……………….

Ledger stone: Town Cemetery, Plattsburgh, United States of America. (Photograph)

LT. COL. J. WILLINGTON / 3RD REGT, BUFFS / B. ARMY / 6TH SEPT. 1814 / B. CO. TIPPERARY, IRELAND

Lt in Lt Colonel Craddock's Regt 3 Nov 1794. Capt in Lt Colonel Charles McDonnell's Regt 12 Apr 1796. Capt 3rd Foot 9 Jul 1803. Bt Major 25 Apr 1808. Bt Lt Colonel Apr 1814.

Served in the Peninsula Sep 1808 – Apr 1814. Present at Douro, Talavera, Busaco, Albuera, Vittoria, Pyrenees, Nivelle, Nive, Garris, Orthes, Aire and Toulouse. Also served in North America where he was killed at the Battle of Plattsburgh 6 Sep 1814.

WILLIS, George Brander

1st Lieutenant. Royal Artillery.

Memorial tablet: St Michael's Church, Sopley, Hampshire. (Photograph)

IN MEMORY OF / GEORGE BRANDER WILLIS, ESQRE / ELDEST SON OF THE REVD JAMES WILLIS, / FORMERLY OF SOPLEY PARK AND / VICAR OF THIS PARISH. / AS AN OFFICER OF THE ROYAL ARTILLERY / HE SERVED HIS COUNTRY DURING WAR / IN HOLLAND, SPAIN AND AMERICA. / HE DIED THE 29TH DAY OF AUGUST 1868 / IN THE 79TH YEAR OF HIS AGE. / ……………….

2nd Lt 2 May 1808. 1st Lt 17 Nov 1809.

Served in the Peninsula Apr 1811 – Sep 1812 and Nov 1813 – Apr 1814. Present at the first siege of Badajoz, Badajoz, Burgos and the siege and repulse of the Sortie from Bayonne. Also served at Walcheren 1809 (present at the siege of Flushing) and North America 1814–1815. Half pay 3 Apr 1823. MGS medal for Badajoz.

WILMOT, James

Private. 12th (Prince of Wales's) Regiment of Light Dragoons.
Named on the Regimental Memorial: St Joseph's Church, Waterloo. (Photograph)

Present at Waterloo where he was killed.

WILSON, Sir James

Major. 48th (Northamptonshire) Regiment of Foot.
Memorial tablet: St Michael's Church, Burnett, Bath, Somerset. (Photograph)

TO THE MEMORY OF / MAJOR GENERAL SIR JAMES WILSON, K.C.B. / WHO, AFTER SERVING HIS COUNTRY, IN THE CAMPAIGNS OF / HOLLAND, EGYPT, AND THE PENINSULA, / FROM THE YEAR 1799 TO 1815, / RETIRED TO PRIVATE LIFE IN THE SECLUSION / OF THIS VILLAGE, BURNET: / HAVING HAD CONFERRED UPON HIM MANY HONORABLE / MILITARY DISTINCTIONS, BY HIS SOVEREIGN, / HE DEPARTED THIS LIFE ON 7: FEBRUARY 1847 IN HIS 67: YEAR. / THAT THOSE WHO READ THESE LINES MAY STRIVE TO SERVE / THEIR EARTHLY AND HEAVENLY PRINCE WITH THE ZEAL, AND / CHRISTIAN HUMILITY THAT CHARACTERIZED THIS GALLANT MAN, / IS THE HOPE OF HIS BEREAVED WIDOW, / BY WHOM THIS TABLET IS ERECTED.

Ensign 27th Foot 12 Dec 1798. Lt 31 Aug 1799. Capt 27 May 1801. Capt 48th Foot 9 Jul 1803. Major 20 Jun 1811. Bt Lt Colonel 27 Apr 1812. Bt Colonel 22 Jul 1830. Major General 28 Jun 1838.

Served in the Peninsula Jul 1809 – Apr 1814. Present at Talavera, Busaco, Albuera (severely wounded in command of the 48th Foot after the death of Lt Colonel Duckworth), Ciudad Rodrigo, Badajoz (wounded), Castrejon, Salamanca, Vittoria, Pyrenees (severely wounded 26 Jul 1813) and Toulouse (wounded). Also served at the Helder 1799, Ferrol 1800 and Egypt 1801. Gold Cross for Albuera, Badajoz, Salamanca, Vittoria and Toulouse. KCB. Half pay 25 Sep 1814. No longer able to serve owing to the severity of his wounds from the Peninsula. Awarded pension of £250 per annum for wounds at Albuera, Badajoz, Pamplona and Toulouse.
Reference: Dictionary of National Biography. Royal Military Calendar, Vol. 4, p. 418. United Service Magazine, Mar 1847, p. 480. Gentleman's Magazine, Apr 1847, pp. 424–5. Milner, David and Life, Page, Missing grave of Sir James Wilson, Waterloo Journal, Apr 1999, pp. 30–2.

WILSON, Sir John

Lieutenant Colonel. Royal York Rangers.
Interred in Catacomb B (v198, c 13, 14 and 15), Kensal Green Cemetery, London.

Ensign 28th Foot 26 Mar 1794. Lt 12 Aug 1795. Capt 97th Foot 18 Jan 1799. Major 27 May 1802. Lt Colonel Royal York Rangers 22 Dec 1808. Bt Colonel 4 Jun 1814. Major General 27 Mar 1825. Lt General 28 Jun 1838. General 20 Jun 1854.

Served in the Peninsula with 97th Foot Aug – Dec 1808 and with the Loyal Lusitanian Legion and Portuguese Army Jan 1809 – Apr 1814. Present at Vimeiro (severely wounded), Barba ded Puerco, Coimbra, Celorico, San Sebastian, Bidassoa, Nivelle and Bayonne (severely wounded). Commanded 1st Portuguese Brigade of Infantry at San Sebastian, Bidassoa and Nivelle. Also served in the West Indies 1796 (present at St Lucia and St Vincent), Minorca 1798, Cadiz 1800, Egypt 1801 and Ceylon 1830–1838.

Gold Medal for San Sebastian. MGS medal for Egypt, Vimeiro and Nivelle. Awarded Bt Colonelcy and knighted Jun 1814. CB 1815. Knight Commander of the Portuguese Order of the Tower and Sword. Order of St Bento d'Avis. Colonel 82nd Foot 5 Dec 1836. Colonel 11th Foot 10 May 1841. Educated at Winchester. Died 22 Jun 1856.
REFERENCE: Dictionary of National Biography. Royal Military Calendar, Vol. 4, pp. 234–5. Annual Register 1856, Appx, p. 260.

WILSON, John
Corporal. 71st Highland Regiment, Light Infantry
Buried in St Michael's Churchyard, Stanwix, Carlisle, Cumbria (Burial Register)

Served in the Peninsula Sep 1810 – Apr 1814. Present at Vittoria, Pyrenees, Nivelle, Nive, Orthes and Toulouse. Present at Waterloo in Captain James Henderson's Company. Wounded during the battle and in 1816 was discharged with a pension. MGS Medal for Vittoria, Pyrenees, Nivelle, Nive, Orthes and Toulouse. Died in Carlisle 29 Apr 1879.

WILSON, John Morillyon
Captain. 1st (Royal Scots) Regiment of Foot.
Low monument: Brompton Cemetery, London. (BR 52192). (Photograph)

IN MEMORY OF / COL. SIR JOHN MORILLYON / WILSON, GCB, KH, / WHO DIED / AT THE ROYAL HOSPITAL / CHELSEA / ON THE 8TH MAY 1868 / AGED 85 YEARS.

Brass Memorial tablet: Royal Hospital, Chelsea, London. (Photograph)

TO THE MEMORY OF / COLNL SIR JOHN MORILLYON WILSON, CB, KH, / OF THE ROYAL HOSPITAL, CHELSEA. / HE WAS BORN IN 1783, ENTERED THE ROYAL NAVY / AND SERVED AS MIDSHIPMAN IN THE EXPEDITION / TO THE HELDER 1799, AND IN THE MEDITERRANEAN / AND EGYPT 1801 (MEDAL) INVALIDED FROM ROYAL NAVY 1803. / HE ENTERED THE ARMY AS ENSIGN FIRST ROYALS, 1804. / SERVED WITH HIS REGIMENT AT WALCHEREN, / AND SEIGE OF FLUSHING, THRICE WOUNDED. / HE AFTERWARDS SERVED IN THE PENINSULAR WAR / BATTLES OF BUSACO, TORRES VEDRAS, FUENTES D'ONOR / AND OTHER MINOR ACTIONS. HE SERVED WITH / THE ROYALS IN AMERICAN WAR 1812–13–14. / WAS ENGAGED AT THE CAPTURE OF FORT NIAGARA. / ACTIONS AT BUFFALO AND CHIPPEWA (WOUNDED 7 TIMES. / LEFT FOR DEAD ON THE FIELD AND TAKEN PRISONER). / APPOINTED ADJUTANT ROYAL HOSPITAL CHELSEA 1822 / AND MAJOR 1855. DIED THERE IN 1868. / THIS TABLET IS PLACED HERE BY HIS YOUNGEST DAUGHTER LADY AUBREY-FLETCHER, WIFE OF RIGHT HON-SIR HENRY AUBREY-FLETCHER CB. MP. / AUGUST 1907.

Midshipman Royal Navy 1798–1803. Ensign 1st Foot 1 Sep 1804. Lt 28 Feb 1805. Capt 1 Jan 1807. Bt Major 5 Jul 1814. Lt Colonel 27 Nov 1815. Bt Colonel 10 Jan 1837.

Served in the Royal Navy 1798–1803. Present at the Helder, Mediterranean and Egypt (wounded three times and left the navy in consequence of his wounds). On recovery joined the army in 1804. Served in the Peninsula Apr 1810 – Jul 1811. Present at Busaco, Pombal, Redinha, Condeixa, Casal Nova, Foz d'Arouce, Sabugal, Almeida and Fuentes d'Onoro. Also served in Canada 1812–1814 (present at Sacketts Harbour, Black Rock Buffalo, and Chippewa Jul 1814, where he received seven wounds and was left for dead on the battlefield. Taken prisoner, not released until Dec 1814 at the end of the American War and awarded a Brevet Majority). MGS medal for Busaco and Fuentes d'Onoro. Adjutant of the Royal Hospital Chelsea 1822. CB. KH. Major and Commandant of the Royal Hospital Chelsea 14 Jul 1855. Also served at Walcheren (twice wounded at the siege of Flushing). Half pay 25 Jul 1822. Died 8 May 1868.
REFERENCE: Dictionary of National Biography. Gentleman's Magazine, May 1868, p. 782.

WILSON, Richard
Lieutenant. 51st (2nd Yorkshire West Riding) Light Infantry.
Named on the Regimental Memorial: KOYLI Infantry Chapel, York Minster, Yorkshire. (Photograph)

Ensign 16 May 1811. Lt 1812.
Served in the Peninsula. Died on the retreat from Burgos Nov 1812.

WILSON, Richard Goodwin Bowen
2nd Lieutenant. Royal Artillery.
Grave: St Saviour's Churchyard, St Helier, Jersey, Channel Islands. (Burial register)

2nd Lt 17 Dec 1812. Lt 20 Jun 1815. Capt 8 Jul 1834. Major 9 Nov 1846. Lt Colonel 1 Nov 1848. Colonel 28 Nov 1854. Major General 7 Feb 1855.

Present at Quatre Bras and Waterloo (in Major T. Roger's Brigade attached to Picton's 5th Division). Also served in the Netherlands 1813–1815, Jamaica Oct 1816 – Oct 1819 (placed on temporary half pay and rejoined 11 May 1820), Gibraltar Jun 1822 – May 1828, Canada Apr 1829 – Jul 1834, Malta Aug 1836 – Dec 1841, West Indies (present at Bermuda Apr 1844 – Jan 1847 and Jamaica 1851–1854 (commanded Royal Artillery). Superintendent of School of Gunnery at Shoeburyness 1854. Died in Jersey 24 Oct 1876.

Reference: Annual Register, 1876, Appx, p. 158.

WILSON, Robert Thomas
Lieutenant Colonel. 22nd Regiment of Light Dragoons.
Brass floor tablet: Westminster Abbey, London. (North aisle). (Photograph)

HERE RESTETH SIR ROBERT THOMAS WILSON, KNIGHT. BORN 17 AUGUST 1777. DIED 9 MAY 1849. / ALSO THE DAME JEMIMA HIS WIFE DAUGHTER AND / CO-HEIRESS OF COLONEL BELFORD OF HARBLEDOWN IN KENT BORN 21 JUNE 1777. DIED 12 AUGUST 1823. / IN CHRIST / A GENERAL IN THE BRITISH ARMY, COLONEL OF THE 15TH (THE KING'S) REGIMENT OF (LIGHT) / DRAGOONS, GOVERNOR AND COMMANDER IN CHIEF OF THE FORTRESS OF GIBRALTAR / 14 YEARS REPRESENTATIVE IN PARLIAMENT OF THE BOROUGH OF SOUTH-WARK, HE WON ON THE / FIELDS OF BATTLE THE TITLES OF KNIGHT GRAND CROSS OF THE ORDER OF THE RED EAGLE OF / PRUSSIA AND OF THE MILITARY ORDER OF ST ANNE OF RUSSIA, COMMANDER OF THE IMPERIAL / MILITARY ORDER OF MARIA THERESA OF AUSTRIA. BARON OF THE HOLY ROMAN EMPIRE / KNIGHT COMMANDER OF THE IMPE-RIAL RUSSIAN ORDER OF ST GEORGE, OF / THE ROYAL PORTUGUESE MILITARY ORDER OF THE TOWER AND SWORD, OF THE / TURKISH CRESCENT AND OF THE ORDER OF MERIT OF SAXONY.

Cornet 15th Dragoons Apr 1794. Lt 31 Oct 1794. Capt 21 Sep 1796. Major in Hompesch's Rifles 28 Jun 1800. Lt Colonel 19th Lt Dragoons Aug 1804. Lt Colonel 20th Lt Dragoons 7 Mar 1805. Bt Colonel 25 Jul 1810. Lt Colonel 22nd Lt Dragoons 10 Dec 1812. Major General 4 Jun 1813. Lt General 27 May 1825. General 23 Nov 1841. Portuguese Army: Brigadier 3, 4, 6, Caçadores 11 May 1809. Loyal Lusitanian Legion and 5 Caçadores 18 Jun 1809.

Served in the Peninsula with Portuguese Army Aug 1808 – Dec 1809. Present in the Corunna campaign, Banos and Talavera. Given command of the Loyal Lusitanian Legion raised from Portuguese refugees in England under British officers 1808. The Legion was absorbed into Beresford's new organisation of the Portuguese Army Dec 1809 and Wilson returned home. Went on various military missions to the allied armies in Europe 1810–1814. Also served in Flanders 1794–1795 (present at Villars-en-Couche, Cateau, Lannoy and Boxtel), Ireland 1798 (ADC to Major General St John in the Irish Rebellion), the Helder 1799 (present at Egmont-op-Zee), Egypt 1801 (present at Aboukir and Alexandria), Cape of Good Hope 1806,

Battle of Eylau 1807, Friedland 1807, Russia 1812 (present at Smolensk), Lutzen 1813, Bautzen 1813, Leipzig 1813, Italy 1814 and Spain 1823.

In 1816 Wilson took part with Lt Bruce and Lt and Capt Hely-Hutchinson in the escape from Paris of Count Lavalette who had been condemned to death. They escorted the Count to the frontier disguised as a British officer. All three were sentenced to three months' imprisonment for their conduct. MP for Southwark 1818. Received many foreign awards and honours including Knight Commander of the Tower and Sword, Cross of St George of Russia, Knight Grand Cross of the Red Eagle of Prussia, but he received no awards from his own country. Although the government realised that he had exceptional knowledge of the Russian and Prussian armies, they were wary of him. He was too much of an independent person, not carrying out orders as he should, but his bravery was never in doubt. Wellington called him 'a very slippery fellow'. In 1821 after the funeral of Queen Caroline the Household Cavalry and some members of the public clashed at Hyde Park and shots were fired. Wilson intervened and stopped the soldiers. Next month in September 1821 he was dismissed from the army. Reinstated on the accession of William IV. Colonel 15th Hussars 29 Dec 1835. Governor and Commander in Chief of Forces in Gibraltar 1841 until his death in 1849. Educated at Winchester. Wrote extensively on military events including *History of the British expedition to Egypt,* 1802. *Narrative of events during the invasion of Russia by Napoleon Bonaparte and the retreat of the French army,* 1812, edited by H. Randolph, 1860 and various private diaries and autobiographical memoirs. Son of Benjamin Wilson the eminent Victorian painter.

REFERENCE: *Dictionary of National Biography. Gentleman's Magazine, Jul 1849, pp. 91–4. Annual Register, 1849, Appx, pp. 236–7. Wilson, Sir Robert Thomas, General Wilson's journal: 1812–1814, edited by Anthony Brett-James, 1964. Glover, M., 'A very slippery fellow': the life of Sir Robert Wilson 1777–1849, 1978. Samuel, L., An astonishing fellow: the life of Sir Robert Wilson, 1985. Costigan, Giovanni, Sir Robert Wilson: a soldier of fortune in the Napoleonic Wars, 1932. Chartrand, Rene, Sir Robert Wilson and the Loyal Lusitanian Legion, 1808–1811, Journal of the Society for Army Historical Research, Vol. 79, No. 319, Autumn 2001, pp. 197–208.*

WILSON, Thomas

Captain. 28th (North Gloucestershire) Regiment of Foot.
Grave: St Peter's Churchyard, Titchfield, Hampshire. (Section E 25). (M.I.)

"………………. IN MEMORY OF THOMAS WILSON MAJOR ETC AND FORMERLY OF THE 28TH REGT WHO DIED DECEMBER 6TH 1871 AGED 89."

Ensign 28 Oct 1800. Lt 7 Jan 1801. Capt 14 Nov 1805. Major 12 Aug 1819.

Served in the Peninsula with 2/28th Jul 1809 – Jul 1811 and 1/28th Aug 1811 – Sep 1813. Present at Busaco, Lines of Torres Vedras, Campo Mayor, Olivencia, first siege of Badajoz, Albuera, Arroyo dos Molinos, Miravete, Almarez, retreat from Burgos and Vittoria (severely wounded and awarded pension of £100 per annum). Also served in Egypt 1801 and Hanover 1805. Half pay 10 May 1821. MGS medal for Egypt, Busaco, Albuera and Vittoria.

WIMBRIDGE, John

Purveyor. Commissariat Department.
Box tomb: All Saints' Churchyard, Curry Mallet, Somerset. (Photograph)

UNDER THIS STONE MOULDER THE REMAINS OF / JOHN WIMBRIDGE ESQ / PURVEYOR TO HIS MAJESTY'S FORCES IN PORTUGAL AND SPAIN. / HE DEPARTED THIS LIFE MAY 27TH 1809. / AGED 40 YEARS. / HIS DEATH WAS OCCASIONED BY THE FATIGUE HE SUFFERED / IN HIS MARCH THROUGH SPAIN / WITH THE ARMY UNDER THE COMMAND OF / SIR JOHN MOORE KB / HE WAS A MOST DUTIFUL SON, AN AFFECTIONATE HUSBAND / A TENDER FATHER, AN ESTIMABLE MAN. / SPECTEMUR AGENDO.

Purveyor 28 May 1807.

Served in the Peninsula Aug 1808 – Jan 1809. Present on the retreat to Corunna. Died on his return to England.

WINCHESTER, Robert

Lieutenant. 92nd Regiment of Foot.

Headstone: Warriston Cemetery, Edinburgh, Scotland. (Section A 3. Grave number 58). (Photograph)

IN MEMORY / OF / LT COLONEL / ROBERT WINCHESTER KH / 92ND HIGHLANDERS / WHO DIED AT EDINBURGH / ON THE 23RD OF JULY / 1846 / ....

Obelisk, Grounds of Tornaveen House, near Torphins, Aberdeenshire, Scotland. (Photograph)

COLONEL ROBERT WINCHESTER K.H. / BORN A.D. 1783 ~ DIED A.D. 1846 / DURING 37 YEARS OF ACTIVE SERVICE, WITH A / SPIRIT WHICH SHUNNED NO DANGER, HE ACCOM· / PANIED IN SIEGES, & IN MANY MARCHES & BATTLES, / THE 92ND REGT. GORDON HIGHLANDERS. LIEUT.-GEN· / ERAL THE HONORABLE SIR WILLIAM STEWART G.C.B. / THUS RECORDS HIS MERITS. "MANY MEMORABLE / "SERVICES WERE RENDERED TO THE DIVISION OF THE / "ARMY UNDER MY COMMAND. DURING THE ARDUOUS / "CAMPAIGNS OF THE YEARS 1813·14 IN THE PENINSULA / "& SOUTH OF FRANCE, BY HIM, & THE GALLANT LIGHT / "INFANTRY UNDER HIS ORDERS. I SHOULD BE TRULY / "UNGRATEFUL IF I WERE EVER TO FORGET THE VALU / "ABLE AID THAT I RECEIVED FROM HIM, ON THAT 25TH OF / "JULY, WHEN WE SO NEARLY LOST THE ROCK & PASS / "OF MAYA. BUT HIS, & HIS NOBLE CORPS CONDUCT, / "ON THAT, & ON EVERY OCCASION. WHERE VALOUR & / "SELF DEVOTION WERE EMINENTLY CALLED FOR, DUR· / "ING THOSE CAMPAIGNS & IN THE DECISIVE CONFLICT / "OF WATERLOO, ARE ON RECORD & EVER WILL BE SO, / "IN THE MILITARY ANNALS OF THOSE DAYS." / TO WHOM / THIS MEMORIAL IS ERECTED BY HIS NEPHEW / WILLIAM NATHANIEL FRASER ESQR. / 1865.

Ensign 18 Sep 1805. Lt 6 Feb 1808. Capt 19 Jul 1815. Major 16 Aug 1825. Bt Lt Colonel 28 Jun 1838.

Served in the Peninsula Oct 1810 – Apr 1814. Present at Arroyo dos Molinos, Almarez, Alba de Tormes, Vittoria, Puerto de Maya, Pyrenees (wounded), Nivelle, Nive (severely wounded), Garris, Orthes, Aire, Tarbes and Toulouse. Present at Quatre Bras (wounded) and Waterloo (severely wounded). Also served at Copenhagen 1807, Walcheren 1809, Jamaica 1819–1820 and 1825–1827, Malta 1839–1841 and the West Indies 1841–1842. KH. Retired 1 Nov 1842.

Reference: Gentleman's Magazine, Oct 1846, p. 431. Annual Register, 1846, Appx, p. 270.

WINDOW, Richard

Private. 43rd (Monmouthshire) Light Infantry Regiment of Foot.

Died at the Union Workhouse, Cheltenham, Gloucestershire.

Pte 29 Oct 1800.

Served in the Peninsula 1809 – Apr 1814. Present at Fuentes d'Onoro, Ciudad Rodrigo, Badajoz, Vittoria, Pyrenees and Toulouse. Discharged 8 Nov 1814. MGS medal for Fuentes d'Onoro, Ciudad Rodrigo, Badajoz, Vittoria, Pyrenees and Toulouse. Died 30 May 1855.

WINDSOR, Edward Charles

Captain. 1st (Royal) Regiment of Dragoons.

Memorial tablet: St Mary's Church, Shrewsbury, Shropshire. (In Chancel. Possibly destroyed in the late Victorian reconstruction of the church). (M.I.)

"..................... / OF HIS ELDEST SON EDWARD CHARLES WINDSOR, CAPTAIN / IN THE 1ST OR ROYAL DRAGOONS, WHO BRAVELY FELL ON THE 18TH JUNE 1815, / IN THE 24TH YEAR OF HIS AGE, WHILST CHARGING THE ENEMY WITH HIS REGIMENT / IN THE EVER MEMORABLE BATTLE OF WATERLOO. / HE DIED MOST DESERVEDLY AND MOST DEEPLY LAMENTED BY HIS MOTHER / AND EVERY OTHER MEMBER OF HIS FAMILY; AND MOST SINCERELY REGRETTED / BY MANY FRIENDS, WHO HIGHLY ESTEEM HIM / FOR HIS HONOURABLE, AMIABLE AND MANLY DISPOSITION."

Cornet 7 Feb 1807. Lt 22 Sep 1808. Capt 18 Jun 1812.

Served in the Peninsula Sep 1810 – Mar 1813. Present at Fuentes d'Onoro, Aldea de Ponte and Maguilla. Captured by the French at the disastrous cavalry action under General Slade at Maguilla Jun 1812, and remained a prisoner until Mar 1813. Present at Waterloo where he was killed. His mother received a pension of £50 a year as she had used all her money to buy her son's commission. Educated at Shrewsbury School.

WINGFIELD, Hon. John

Ensign. Coldstream Regiment of Foot Guards.
Named on Memorial Panel VI for Fuentes D'Onoro: Royal Military Chapel, Wellington Barracks, London. (M.I.) (Destroyed by a Flying Bomb 1944)

Ensign 16 Apr 1807.

Served in the Peninsula Oct 1809 – May 1811. Died at Coimbra 4 May 1811 aged 20.

WINTERBOTTOM, John

Lieutenant and Adjutant. 52nd (Oxfordshire) Light Infantry Regiment of Foot.
Memorial tablet: St Chad's Church, Saddleworth, near Rochdale, Yorkshire. (Photograph)

IN MEMORY OF / JOHN WINTERBOTTOM. / PAYMASTER OF THE 52ND LIGHT INFANTRY, / WHO DIED AT THE HEADQUARTERS OF THE REGIMENT, / IN THE ISLAND OF BARBADOS, ON THE 26th NOVEMBER 1838. / BORN AT SADDLEWORTH 17TH NOVEMBER 1781. / PRIVATE SOLDIER 52ND 17TH OCTOBER 1799. / CORPORAL APRIL 1803. / SERGEANT DEC. 1803. / SERGEANT MAJOR 11TH JUNE 1805./ ENSIGN AND ADJUTANT 24TH NOVEMBER 1808. / LIEUTENANT AND ADJUTANT 28TH FEBRUARY 1810. / PAYMASTER 31ST MAY 1821. / HE SERVED WITH DISTINCTION AT THE FOLLOWING BATTLES AND SIEGES, / AS A PRIVATE AT FERROL, AS SERGEANT MAJOR AT COPENHAGEN AND VIMIERO, / AS ADJUTANT AT CORUNNA, THE COA, BUSACO, POMBAL, REDINHA, / CUIDAD RODRIGO, BADAJOZ, SALAMANCA, SAN MUNOZ, VITTORIA, / THE HEIGHTS OF VERA, THE NIVELLE, THE NIVE, / ORTHEZ, TARBES, TOULOUSE AND / WATERLOO / AS WELL AS SIX OTHER ACTIONS OF LESS NOTE, / IN WHICH THE 52ND REGIMENT ENGAGED DURING THE WAR, / AND HE WAS NEVER ABSENT FROM HIS REGIMENT, / EXCEPT IN CONSEQUENCE OF WOUNDS RECEIVED AT REDINHA, / BADAJOZ AND WATERLOO. / ONE HUNDRED AND THIRTY OFFICERS WHO HAD SERVED WITH HIM IN THE 52ND / AND OTHER MILITARY FRIENDS AND ADMIRERS / OF HIS EXTRAORDINARY TALENTS AS AN OFFICER, / AND HIS ACKNOWLEDGED WORTH AS A MAN, / HAVE DIRECTED THIS MONUMENT TO BE RAISED TO HIS MEMORY.

Named on the Regimental memorial tablet: St Paul's Church, Bridgetown, Barbados, West Indies. (Photograph)

SACRED TO THE MEMORY OF / .... / PAYMSR J. WINTERBOTTOM & PENELOPE HIS WIFE / ALL OF WHOM FELL VICTIMS TO YELLOW FEVER / DURING THE TERM OF THE 52ND LIGHT INFANTRY'S / SERVICE IN THE WEST INDIES / BETWEEN NOVEMBER 1838, AND

MARCH 1843. / THIS TABLET IS ERECTED BY THE OFFICERS / OF THE REGIMENT AS A SMALL TOKEN OF SINCERE / REGARD AND ESTEEM FOR THEIR / DEPARTED FRIENDS.

Headstone: St Paul's Churchyard, Bridgetown, Barbados, West Indies. (Photograph)

SACRED TO THE MEMORY OF / JOHN WINTERBOTTOM / PAYMASTER 52ND REGT / DIED 26TH NOVEMBER 1838

Pte 17 Oct 1799. Cpl Apr 1803. Sgt Dec 1803. Sgt Major 11 Jun 1805. Promoted from the ranks. Ensign and Adjt 24 Nov 1808. Lt and Adjt 28 Feb 1810. Paymaster 31 May 1821.

Served in the Peninsula 1808 – Jan 1809 and Jul 1809 – Apr 1814. Present at Vimeiro, retreat and battle of Corunna, Coa, Busaco, Pombal, Redinha (wounded), Cuidad Rodrigo, siege of Badajoz, (wounded), Salamanca, San Munos, Vittoria, Vera, Nivelle, Nive, Orthes, Tarbes and Toulouse. Present at Waterloo where he was severely wounded. Resigned as Adjutant because of his Waterloo wound Jul 1816, but Sir John Colborne who was then in command of the 52nd Light Infantry requested him to become Adjutant again in Sep 1819 until 1821. He then became Paymaster. Also served at Ferrol 1800, Copenhagen 1807, Canada 1823–1829 and West Indies 1838 where he died of yellow fever. 'He was never absent from his regiment from his enrolment to his death from yellow fever in Barbados in 1838.'

WINTERSCALE, John

Assistant Surgeon. 71st (Highland Light Infantry) Regiment of Foot.
Headstone with Cross: Dean Cemetery, Edinburgh, Scotland. (Section D. No 327). (Photograph)

SACRED / TO THE MEMORY OF / JOHN WINTERSCALE ESQ. / LATE SURGEON OF THE 2D DRAGOONS. / IN EARLY LIFE HE SERVED IN THE / 71ST HIGHLANDERS UNDER THE / DUKE OF WELLINGTON / AND WAS PRESENT AT / THE NUMEROUS ENGAGEMENTS / IN WHICH THAT REGIMENT TOOK A PART / IN THE COURSE OF THE PENINSULAR WAR. / AT ALL THESE OBTAINING THE RESPECT / AND ESTEEM OF THE OFFICERS / AND MEN OF HIS CORPS. / HE DIED AT EDINBURGH / ON THE 14TH MARCH 1858 / AGED 68.

Hospital Assistant 17 Sep 1809. Asst Surgeon 71st Foot 8 Feb 1810. Surgeon 2nd Dragoons 12 Jun 1828.

Served in the Peninsula Sep 1810 – Dec 1812. Present at Sobral and Fuentes d'Onoro. Present at Waterloo. Also served at Walcheren 1809. MGS medal for Fuentes d'Onoro.

WINTERTON, John

Private. 95th Regiment of Foot.
Headstone: Welford Road Cemetery, Leicester, Leicestershire. (Grave number CE 131). (Photograph)

IN / REMEMBRANCE OF / JOHN WINTERTON. / WHO DEPARTED THIS LIFE / FEBY 16th 1870. / IN THE 74th YEAR OF HIS AGE. / HE WAS SEVERELY WOUNDED AT / THE BATTLE OF WATERLOO, / AND AFTER LYING THREE DAYS / AND TWO NIGHTS ON THE FIELD / HAD HIS LEFT LEG AMPUTATED / AT BRUSSELS / MAY HE REST IN PEACE.

Pte 5 Apr 1814.

Present at Waterloo in Captain C. Eaton's Company, where he was severely wounded. Discharged 11 Dec 1815 owing to severe wounds at Waterloo including loss of his leg.

WISELEY, William

Saddle Sergeant. 1st (Royal) Regiment of Dragoons.
Family memorial: St John's Churchyard, Manchester, Lancashire. (Grave number 756). (M.I.)

"………………. WILLIAM WISELEY SERGEANT / MAJOR 1ST ROYAL (DRAGOONS) / OBIT NOVEMBER 23RD 1826. AETAT 42 YEARS. / IN THE FIELDS OF PORTUGAL / SPAIN AND FRANCE HE / DID ……………. / PROUD."

Served in the Peninsula 1809 – Apr 1814. Present at Fuentes d'Onoro, Aldea de Ponte, Maguilla, Vittoria and Toulouse. Present at Waterloo in Capt C. E. Radclyffe's No. 1 Troop.

WISHART, Alexander
Lieutenant. 15th (Yorkshire East Riding) Regiment of Foot.
Wall tablet: Ramshorn New Burying Ground, Glasgow, Scotland. (Outer wall). (M.I.)

"SACRED TO THE MEMORY OF HELEN DICK ………………. AND CAPTAIN ALEXANDER WISHART OF THE 15TH REGT OF FOOT."

Ensign 14 Nov 1805. Lt 42nd Foot 26 May 1808. Lt 15th Foot 29 Jun 1809. Capt 6 Sep 1821.
Served in the Peninsula Aug 1808 – Jan 1809. Present at Corunna. Half pay 6 Sep 1821.

WITHERINGTON, Henry
Lieutenant. 63rd (West Suffolk) Regiment of Foot.
Pedestal monument: St George's Churchyard, Deal, Kent. (Photograph)

THIS IS THE TOMB OF HENRY WITHERINGTON ESQ. / LIEUTENANT 63RD REGIMENT OF INFANTRY. / HE DIED ON 15 SEPTEMBER 1809 AGED 31 YEARS. / HE SERVED IN THE DISASTROUS WALCHEREN EXPEDITION / COMMANDED BY THE EARL OF CHATHAM WHICH EMBARKED FROM / DEAL. HE WAS ONE OF HUNDREDS WHO / DIED OF WOUNDS AND SICKNESS. / MANY OF WHOM ARE BURIED HERE.

Lt Royal Lancashire Militia 30 Jan 1804. Lt 63rd Foot 6 Dec 1808.
Served at Walcheren 1809 and died on his return to England.

WITNEY, JOHN see WHITNEY, John

WOLF, Pierre Frederic
Lieutenant. Chasseurs Britanniques.
Headstone with Cross: Vorges, near Laon, Aisne, France. (Photograph)

………………. / PIERRE FREDERIC / WOLF / ……. A LAON / ………………. / 1871 / ……………….

Pte 24 Sep 1805. Sgt 14 Jul 1811. Ensign 13 Aug 1812. Lt 26 Apr 1814.
Served in the Peninsula Sep 1812 – Apr 1814. Present at Vittoria, Pyrenees, Nivelle and Orthes. Also served in Sicily and Cadiz. Half pay 1814. Mayor of Vorges. Died in 1871.

WOLF, W.
2nd Lieutenant. 6th Hussars, Dutch Cavalry.
Named on the Memorial tablet to the Dutch-Belgian officers killed at Quatre Bras: St Joseph's Church, Waterloo. (Photograph)
Named on the Regimental Memorial to officers of the Dutch 6th Regiment of Hussars killed at Waterloo, St Joseph's Church, Waterloo. (Photograph)

WOLFF, Willem

Luitenant. Light Cavallerie.

Named on the Regimental Memorial to officers of the Dutch 6th Regiment of Hussars killed at Waterloo, St Joseph's Church, Waterloo. (Photograph)

WOOD, Charles

Captain. 10th (Prince of Wales's Own Royal) Regiment of Light Dragoons.

Cross on stepped base: St Michael the Archangel's Churchyard, Carlton, Pontefract, Yorkshire. (Photograph)

IN LOVING MEMORY OF / CHARLES WOOD

Memorial tablet: St Michael the Archangel's Church, Carlton, Pontefract, Yorkshire. (Photograph)

AT THE EAST END OF THIS CHURCHYARD / AWAITING THE GENERAL RESURRECTION / LIE THE MORTAL REMAINS OF / LIEUTENANT COLONEL COLONEL CHARLES WOOD, / YOUNGEST SON OF THOMAS WOOD, ESQ / AND MARY HIS WIFE, / OF LITTLETON, / IN THE COUNTY OF MIDDLESEX. / HE SERVED IN THE LIGHT DIVISION OF / THE ARMY IN THE PENINSULA WAR FROM / 1809 TO THE END OF 1812 AND WAS / PRESENT AT THE BATTLES OF COA AND / BUSACO, IN WHICH LATTER CARRYING THE / KING'S COLOR OF THE 52ND LIGHT INFANTRY / HE WAS WOUNDED AT FUENTEZ D'ONORE / AT THE STORMING OF CIUDAD RODRIGO, / AND OF BADAJOS. / LEAVING THE PENINSULA, IN 1813, / HE WAS PRESENT IN GERMANY AS A.D.C. TO / LORD STEWART, WITH THE ALLIED ARMIES / AT THE BATTLES OF GROSS BEEREN, / DENNEWITZ AT THE SIEGE OF WITTENBERG, / AND AT THE BATTLE OF LEIPSIC, / AT THE CAPTURE OF HANOVER, / AT THE BATTLES OF BRIENNE MONTEREAU, / ARCIS-SUR-AUBE. FERE-CHAMPENOISE AND AT / THE CAPTURE OF PARIS, BESIDES DAILY AFFAIRS / AT THE OUTPOSTS. / HE WAS SEVERELY WOUNDED / WHILST IN COMMAND OF A TROOP OF THE / 10TH ROYAL HUSSARS, AT THE BATTLE OF / WATERLOO. / BORN DEC 4, 1790 / DIED DEC 13, 1877. / ....

Ensign 52nd Foot 16 Mar 1809. Lt 7 Mar 1810. Capt 68th Foot 17 Sep 1812. Capt 18th Lt Dragoons 29 Jul 1813. Capt 10th Lt Dragoons 12 Nov 1814. Bt Major 16 Mar 1815. Bt Lt Colonel 10 Jan 1837.

Served in the Peninsula Aug 1809 – Dec 1810, May 1811 – Jan 1812 (ADC to Major General Robert Craufurd) and Feb 1812 – Apr 1813 (DAAG). Present at Coa, Busaco (wounded), Fuentes D'Onoro, Ciudad Rodrigo, Badajoz, Salamanca and Burgos. Present at Waterloo. While on picket duty 17 Jun was one of the first to discover that the Prussians were retreating from Ligny and informed Wellington. Severely wounded at the head of his troop 18 Jun. Also served in Germany 1813 (ADC to Lord Stewart). Present at Gross Beeren, Dennewitz, Wittenberg and Leipzig where he saved a Prussian General and his staff from being captured for which he was awarded the Prussian Military Order of Merit. Entered Paris with the Allies Mar 1814. After Waterloo appointed Brigade Major on the staff of the Northern District at Pontefract. His house in Pontefract was named *Leipzig Lodge*. Half pay 5 Apr 1821. Educated at Charterhouse School where he was expelled 4 Feb 1809. He had been a member of the Sixth Form who on Founder's Day 1808 'broke out into acts of great outrage and riot'. Four weeks later he was an officer in the 52nd Foot and his military career had begun. He retained his interest in the regiment to the end of his life, leaving them a collection of books and pictures of the period. Died in Pontefract 13 Dec 1877 aged 87.

REFERENCE: Oxfordshire and Buckinghamshire Light Infantry Chronicle, 1910, pp. 213–14.

WOOD, John

Captain. 4th (King's Own) Regiment of Foot.

Memorial tablet: St Mary the Virgin's Church, Chislet, Kent. (Photograph)

SACRED / TO THE MEMORY OF / JOHN WOOD ESQUIRE / CAPT. OF THE 4TH OR KING'S OWN REG. / HE DIED AT MAFRA IN PORTUGAL / JANUARY 10TH 1811, AGED 32 / AND LIES BURIED AT / TORRES VEDRAS

Ensign 16 Oct 1798. Lt 1 Jan 1799. Capt 17 Feb 1803.

Served in the Peninsula Aug 1808 – Jan 1809 and Nov 1810 – Jan 1811. Present at Corunna. Died at Mafra of fever 10 Jan 1811 and was buried in Torres Vedras.

WOOD, John Manley

Ensign. 14th (Buckinghamshire) Regiment of Foot.
Interred in Catacomb B (v172 c16), Kensal Green Cemetery, London.

Ensign Nottingham Militia. Ensign 14th Foot 19 May 1814. Lt 6 Sep 1821. Lt 67th Foot 28 Feb 1825. Capt 10 Sep 1825. Bt Major 28 Jun 1838. Major 14th Foot 28 Aug 1840. Bt Lt Colonel 11 Nov 1851. Bt Colonel 28 Nov 1854.

Present at Waterloo with 14th Foot. Also served with 67th Foot in Gibraltar, West Indies and Canada (present in the Canadian Rebellion). Transferred to 14th Foot and continued to serve in Canada and Nova Scotia until 1848. Retired 28 Nov 1854. Died 9 Mar 1867.

WOOD, William

Lieutenant Colonel. 85th (Buckinghamshire Volunteers) Light Infantry Regiment of Foot.
Pedestal tomb: Kensal Green Cemetery, London. (Inscription illegible). (22296/124/PS). (Photograph)

Ensign 14th Foot 22 Jan 1797. Lt 27 Dec 1797. Capt 3 Dec 1802. Major 14 May 1807. Lt Colonel 85th Foot 8 Apr 1813. Bt Colonel 22 Jul 1830. Major General 23 Nov 1841. Lt General 11 Nov 1851. General 31 Aug 1855.

Served in the Peninsula with 14th Foot Nov 1808 – Jan 1809 and 85th Foot Apr 1814. Present at Corunna. Also served in the West Indies 1798–1804, Hanover 1805, Walcheren 1809 (where he volunteered to storm the entrenchments at the siege of Flushing with success and supervised the embarkation of troops from Walcheren), Mediterranean 1810–1813 and America 1814–1815 (present at Bladensburg where he was wounded four times and taken prisoner). CB. KH. MGS medal for Corunna. Colonel 3rd West India Regt 8 Feb 1849. KCB. Died 8 Aug 1870.

WOOD, William

Private. 95th Regiment of Foot.
Headstone: Bong Bong Church of England Cemetery, Moss Vale, New South Wales, Australia. (Photograph)

SACRED / TO / THE MEMORY OF / WILLIAM WOOD / DIED 25 MARCH 1854 / AGED 66 YEARS / THIS LANGUISHING HEART IS AT REST / ITS THINKING AND ACHING ARE OER / THIS QUIET IMMOVABLE BREAST / IS HEAVD BY AFFLICTION NO MORE / THIS HEART IS NO LONGER THE SEAT / OF TROUBLE AND TORTURING PAIN / IT CEASES TO FLUTTER AND BEAT / IT NEVER SHALL FLUTTER AGAIN. / ....

Pte 33rd Foot 1811. Pte 95th Foot 1815. Pte Royal Staff Corps 1819.

Present at Waterloo in Capt MacNamara's Company. Returned to England in 1818, but in 1825 sailed for Australia as part of the escort for Governor Darling. Part of an expedition to form a settlement in Western Australia 1826. Discharged from the army 1829, and was given an 80 acre veteran's grant. Apart from farming he was the local shoemaker and also carried the mail from Liverpool to Berrima.

WOOD, William Leighton

Captain. 4th (King's Own) Regiment of Foot.

Grave: St Luke's Churchyard, Charlton, Kent. (Grave number 75 in grave named for Johnson). (No longer extant). (M.I.)

"ALSO OF LIEUT[T] COL WILLIAM LEIGHTON WOOD KH. WHO DIED 19 SEPT 1843 AGED 58 YEARS."

Ensign 19 Nov 1803. Lt 24 Apr 1804. Capt 1 Jan 1807. Bt Major 21 Jan 1819. Bt Lt Colonel 10 Jan 1837. Served in the Peninsula with 1/4th May 1812 – Apr 1814. (ADC to General Frederick Robinson from Jun 1813). Present at Salamanca, retreat from Burgos (present at Villa Muriel), Vittoria, San Sebastian, Bidassoa, Nivelle, Nive and Bayonne. KH. Half pay 29 Apr 1819.

WOODFORD, Alexander George

Second Major. Coldstream Regiment of Guards.

Low monument: Kensal Green Cemetery, London. (22148/143/PS). (Photograph)

SACRED TO THE MEMORY OF / FIELD MARSHAL SIR ALEXANDER WOODFORD G.C.B. G.C.M.G / COLONEL OF THE SCOTS FUSILIER GUARDS, GOVERNOR OF CHELSEA HOSPITAL / ELDEST SON OF THE LATE COLONEL JOHN WOODFORD GRENADIER GUARDS / AND SUSAN DOWAGER COUNTESS OF WESTMORELAND. HE DIED / AT THE ROYAL HOSPITAL CHELSEA AUGUST 26TH 1870 IN THE 89TH / YEAR OF HIS AGE TO THE GREAT SORROW OF HIS CHILDREN AND FRIENDS, / HIGHLY HONOURED IN LIFE HE WAS WIDELY LAMENTED IN DEATH.

Brass Memorial tablet: Royal Hospital, Chelsea, London. (Photograph)

IN MEMORY OF FIELD MARSHAL SIR ALEXANDER WOODFORD / G.C.B., G.C.M.G., LIEUTENANT GOVERNOR OF CHELSEA HOSPITAL / 1854–1868. GOVERNOR 1869–1870. COLONEL SCOTS / FUSILIER GUARDS, BORN 1782 DIED 1870. ALSO OF HIS WIFE / CHARLOTTE, DAUGHTER OF CHARLES HENRY FRASER / OF H. M. DIPLOMATIC SERVICE, BORN 1795 DIED 1870. / THIS MEMORIAL IS ERECTED BY THEIR GRANDSON FRANCIS ALEXANDER NEWDIGATE NEWDEGATE.

Named on the Memorial tablet: Main Hall, Royal Hospital, Chelsea, London. (Photograph)

Memorial: Royal Military Chapel, Wellington Barracks, London. (M.I.) (Destroyed by a Flying Bomb 1944)

"IN MEMORY OF FIELD MARSHAL SIR ALEXANDER WOODFORD, G.C.B., G.C.M.G., KNIGHT OF MARIA THERESA, KNIGHT OF ST GEORGE OF RUSSIA. HE ENTERED THE ARMY, 1794, AND SERVED AS CAPTAIN LIEUTENANT OF 9TH FOOT IN NORTH HOLLAND, WHERE HE WAS SEVERELY WOUNDED, 19TH SEPTEMBER, 1799. HE SERVED IN THE COLDSTREAM GUARDS, 1799–1825, AT COPENHAGEN, AND ON THE STAFF IN SICILY, COMMANDING THE LIGHT BRIGADE OF GUARDS AT CIUDAD RODRIGO, BADAJOS, SALAMANCA, WHERE HIS DEFENCE OF THE VILLAGE OF ARAPILES WAS SPECIALLY MENTIONED BY THE DUKE OF WELLINGTON; AT THE CAPTURE OF MADRID, AND AT THE SIEGE OF BURGOS, THE REAR GUARD IN THE SUBSEQUENT RETREAT, THE 1ST BATTALION AT VITTORIA, SAN SEBASTIAN, IN THE PYRENEES, AT THE NIVELLE, THE NIVE, AND BAYONNE, AND THE 2ND BATTALION AT WATERLOO, WHERE HE TOOK THE COMMAND AT HOUGOUMONT EARLY IN THE DAY. COLONEL SCOTS FUSILIER GUARDS, 1861. HE DIED 1870. GOVERNOR OF CHELSEA

HOSPITAL. / PLACED BY HIS SURVIVING DAUGHTER AND SONS, THE VISCOUNTESS TEMPLETOWN, A. F. A. WOODFORD, J. W. G. WOODFORD, AND BY HIS SONS-IN-LAW, GENERAL THE VISCOUNT TEMPLETON, K.C.B., AND LIEUT. COLONEL FRANCIS NEWDIGATE, BOTH LATE COLDSTREAM GUARDS."

Brass Memorial tablet: Royal Garrison Church, Portsmouth, Hampshire. (Back of a choir stall)

FIELD MARSHAL SIR / ALEXANDER WOODFORD / G.C.B., G.C.M.G. DIED / AUG 26 1870 AGE 88. / DD: VISCOUNTESS TEMPLETOWN / (HIS DAUGHTER) & LIEUT GENL / VISCOUNT TEMPLETOWN K.C.B.

Ensign 9th Foot 6 Dec 1794. Lt 22nd Foot 8 Sep 1795 (placed on half pay in 1795 as he was only 12 years old). Lt 4 Sep 1799. Capt-Lt 14 Dec 1799. Lt and Capt Coldstream Guards 20 Dec 1799. Capt and Lt Colonel 8 Mar 1810. Bt Colonel 4 Jun 1814. Second Major 25 Jul 1814. First Major 18 Jan 1820. Lt Colonel 25 Jul 1821. Major General 27 May 1825. Lt General 28 Jun 1838. General 20 Jun 1854. Field Marshal 1 Jan 1868.

Served in the Peninsula Jan 1812 – Apr 1814. Present at Ciudad Rodrigo, Salamanca (Mentioned in Despatches), Burgos, Vittoria, Bidassoa, Nivelle, Nive, Adour and Bayonne (Mentioned in Despatches). From Vittoria commanded the 1st Battalion. Present at Quatre Bras and Waterloo (defence of Hougoumont), siege of Cambrai, the Capture of Paris and with the Army of Occupation. From Quatre Bras commanded the 2nd Battalion. Gold Medal for Salamanca, Vittoria and Nive. MGS medal for Ciudad Rodrigo and Nivelle. GCB. GCMG. Also served at the Helder 1799 (wounded at Bergen), Copenhagen 1807, Sicily 1809 (ADC to Sir James Forbes), Malta 1825, Corfu 1827, Ionian Islands 1832 and Gibraltar 1835–1848 (Governor). Lt Governor of Chelsea Hospital 1856. Governor of Chelsea Hospital 3 Aug 1868 on the death of Sir Edward Blakeney. Colonel 40th Foot 25 Apr 1842. Colonel Scots Guards 15 Dec 1861. Elder brother of Capt and Lt Colonel John George Woodford 1st Foot Guards.
REFERENCE: Dictionary of National Biography. Household Brigade Journal, 1870, pp. 317–19.

WOODFORD, John George

Captain and Lieutenant Colonel. 1st Regiment of Foot Guards.
Headstone: St Kentigern's Churchyard, Crosthwaite, Keswick, Cumbria. (Photograph)

SACRED / TO THE MEMORY OF / MAJOR GENERAL / SIR JOHN GEORGE WOODFORD KCB KCH. / LATE GRENADIER GUARDS / OF DERWENT BAY, KESWICK / SON OF COLONEL WOODFORD / GRENADIER GUARDS. / AND / SUSAN, COUNTESS OF WESTMORELAND, / BORN 28TH FEBRUARY 1785. / DIED 22ND MARCH 1879.

Memorial: Royal Military Chapel, Wellington Barracks, London. (M.I.) (Destroyed by a Flying Bomb 1944)

"IN MEMORY OF / MAJOR-GENERAL SIR JOHN GEORGE WOODFORD, K.C.B., K.C.H., / ENSIGN 1ST GUARDS, 1800. DEPUTY-ASSISTANT ADJUTANT-GENERAL, COPENHAGEN; DEPUTY-ASSISTANT QUARTERMASTER-GENERAL, CORUNNA; ASSISTANT QUARTERMASTER-GENERAL, NIVELLE, NIVE, ORTHES, TOULOUSE, WATERLOO. MAJOR, GRENADIER GUARDS, 1823. LIEUT.-COLONEL, 1830–1837. / PLACED BY HIS NEPHEWS A. F. A. WOODFORD, J. W. G. WOODFORD, 1880"

Ensign 23 May 1800. Lt and Capt 13 Nov 1804. Capt and Lt Colonel 1 Jul 1813. Major 20 Nov 1823. Bt Colonel 20 Nov 1823. Lt Colonel 12 Feb 1830. Major General 10 Jan 1837.

Served in the Peninsula Nov 1808 – Jan 1809 and Jul 1813–1814. Present at Corunna (DAQMG and ADC to Sir John Moore. Woodford was wounded and his horse shot under him at the same time that

Moore was killed. Awarded pension of £100 per annum). Served as AQMG at Nivelle, Nive, Orthes and Toulouse. Present at Waterloo (Extra ADC to Wellington) and with the Army of Occupation until 1818. Also served at Copenhagen 1807 (DAAG) and Ireland 1821. Gold Cross for Nivelle, Nive, Orthes and Toulouse. MGS medal for Corunna. When he became Colonel in 1823 he was able to set in motion reforms in the regiment. In 1830 under his own initiative he abolished the punishment of 'standing under arms'. Wellington strongly disapproved of this abolition, but it was never restored. In 1835 he presented evidence before H. M. Commissioners enquiring into the system of military punishment. He published a pamphlet *Remarks on military flogging, it's causes and effects with some considerations on the propriety of the entire abolition*, 1835. He was against flogging and in favour of solitary confinement and seclusion. Recommended recreation for soldiers in barracks, teaching of useful trades and establishment of regimental libraries. He was not able to make the changes to the uniforms and abolition of the purchasing of commissions, but this happened during his retirement. When he retired in 1841 he sold his commission at half price to show his dislike for the system. Retired to the Lake District and for the next 30 years spent his time on antiquarian research. KH. KCB 1838. Served in the army for 41 years. Younger brother of Second Major Alexander Woodford Coldstream Guards. Died 22 Mar 1879 aged 94.
Reference: Dictionary of National Biography. Crosthwaite, J. F., Brief memoir of Major General Sir John George Woodford, Keswick, 1881. Household Brigade Journal, 1879, pp. 306–7. Annual Register, 1879, Appx, p. 183.

WOODHOUSE, Uriah
Sergeant. Coldstream Regiment of Foot Guards.
Headstone: St Andrew's Churchyard, Clewer, Windsor, Berkshire. (Photograph)

………………../ ALSO OF OUR GRANDFATHER / URIAH WOODHOUSE / LATE COLOUR SERGEANT / 2ND BATTALION / COLDSTREAM GUARDS / DIED MARCH 19TH 1869 / AGED 80. / REST IN PEACE.

Pte 25 Jun 1806. Cpl 5 May 1809. Sgt 22 Aug 1812.

Served in the Peninsula with the 2nd Battalion 1809–1814. Present at the Douro, Talavera, Busaco, Fuentes d'Onoro, Ciudad Rodrigo, Salamanca, siege of Burgos, Vittoria, Bidassoa Nivelle, Nive and Bayonne. Also served at Copenhagen 1807. Discharged 12 Oct 1830. MGS medal for Talavera, Busaco, Fuentes d'Onoro, Ciudad Rodrigo, Salamanca, Vittoria, Nivelle and Nive. Later became Colour Sergeant.
Reference: Gentleman's Magazine, May 1868, p. 685.

WOODS, William
Lieutenant. 4th (Royal Irish) Dragoon Guards.
Memorial tablet: St Nicholas's Cathedral, Newcastle upon Tyne, Northumberland. (Photograph)

SACRED TO THE MEMORY / OF / WILLIAM WOODS ESQR / WHO HAVING IN EARLY YOUTH SERVED HIS COUNTRY / WITH DISTINCTION AS AN OFFICER IN THE PENINSULAR WAR / AT THE CLOSE, ESTABLISHED HIMSELF IN THIS TOWN, WHERE HE TOOK A / HIGH PLACE AS A MERCHANT AND BANKER, AND BY THE / INTEGRITY OF HIS PURPOSE, THE CLEARNESS OF HIS INTELLECT / AND THE KINDNESS OF HIS DISPOSITION / WON THE REGARD OF ALL. / AT THE SAME TIME / NOT FORGETTING THAT HE HAD BEEN A SOLDIER / AND AMID THE ENGROSSING PURSUITS OF BUSINESS, HE CONTINUED / TO HIS COUNTRY THE BENEFITS OF MILITARY ACQUIREMENTS BY THE / EFFICIENT DISCHARGE OF HIS DUTIES OF ADJUTANT TO THE N. N. Y. CAVALRY / FOR THE LONG SPACE OF FORTY THREE YEARS. / HE DIED ON THE TWELFTH DAY OF JUNE / ONE THOUSAND EIGHT HUNDRED AND SIXTY FOUR / AGED SEVENTY SEVEN YEARS, MOST DEEPLY REGRETTED. / THIS TRIBUTE TO HIS MEMORY / ATTESTS THE GRATEFUL AFFECTION OF HIS ELDEST SON / JOHN ANTHONY WOODS ESQUIRE.

Ensign 48th Foot 7 Apr 1808. Lt 28 Dec 1809. Lt 4th Dragoon Guards 23 Jan 1812.

Served in the Peninsula Nov 1810 – Jul 1811 and Dec 1812 – Apr 1813. Present at Olivencia, first siege of Badajoz and Albuera where he was taken prisoner but managed to escape. Later joined the 4th Dragoon Guards. After he retired from the army in 1814 he became a merchant and banker in Newcastle and was much respected. Adjutant of the Newcastle and Northumberland Yeomanry for 43 years. MGS medal for Albuera.

Reference: Cooke, Timothy, A second prisoner at Albuera: a letter from Lieutenant Woods of the 48th Foot May 29th 1811, Waterloo Journal, Winter 2004, pp. 3–10.

WOOLRICHE, Stephen

Deputy Inspector of Hospitals. Medical Department.

Ledger stone: St Mary Magdalene's Churchyard, Quatford, Shropshire. (Photograph)

STEPHEN WOOLRICHE C.B. / INSPECTOR GENERAL OF / ARMY HOSPITALS / DIED FEBRUARY 29TH / 1856

Regimental Mate 1794. Surgeon 111th Foot 30 May 1794. Surgeon 4th Foot 22 May 1806. Staff Surgeon 18 Jun 1807. Deputy Inspector of Hospitals 26 May 1814. Inspector of Hospitals 9 Dec 1823. Inspector General of Hospitals 22 Jul 1830.

Served in the Peninsula Sep 1812 – Nov 1813 and Feb – Apr 1814. Present at Vittoria and Pyrenees. Present at Waterloo. Also served in Flanders 1795, the Helder 1799, Copenhagen 1807 and Portugal 1827. MGS medal for Vittoria and Pyrenees. CB.

WORCESTER, Henry William Somerset, Marquis of

Lieutenant. 10th (Prince of Wales's Own Royal) Regiment of Light Dragoons.

Memorial tablet: Beaufort Estate Church, Beaufort, Gloucestershire. (Not open to the public). (Photograph)

THIS TABLET / IS ERECTED TO THE MEMORY OF / HENRY 7TH DUKE OF BEAUFORT K. G. / BY HIS SON / HENRY CHARLES FITZROY, 8TH DUKE / AS A SMALL TRIBUTE OF AFFECTION / TO THE KINDNESS OF FATHERS / HIS AMIABILITY AND COURTESY IN HEALTH / AND HIS PATIENCE AND GENTLENESS / DURING THE THREE YEARS OF CONSTANT SUFFERING / WHICH PRECEDED HIS DEATH / ENDEARED HIM TO ALL WHO HAD THE HAPPINESS / OF KNOWING HIM / HE WAS MANY YEARS IN THE ARMY / TO WHICH PROFESSION HE WAS DEVOTEDLY ATTACHED / HE SERVED IN THE 10TH AND 7TH REGIMENTS OF HUSSARS / AND ON THE STAFF OF THE DUKE OF WELLINGTON / AS AIDE DE CAMP / DURING A CONSIDERABLE PART OF THE PENINSULAR WAR. / HE RECEIVED A MEDAL AND FIVE CLASPS FOR THE BATTLES OF / BUSACO, SALAMANCA, / VITTORIA, THE PYRENEES AND THE NIVELLE / HE WAS ALSO PRESENT WITH HIS SQUADRON OF THE 10TH HUSSARS / FORMING THE ADVANCE GUARD OF THE HUSSAR BRIGADE / AT THE BRILLIANT CAVALRY ACTION / OF MORALES DEL TORO JUNE 1813 / AND WAS SEVERAL TIMES ENGAGED IN MINOR AFFAIRS / HE AFTERWARDS COMMANDED THE GLOUCESTERSHIRE YEOMANRY / FOR MORE THAN TWENTY YEARS. / HE WAS BORN FEBRUARY 5TH, 1792 / SUCCEEDED HIS FATHER HENRY CHARLES 6TH DUKE OF BEAUFORT KG. / IN 1835 / AND DIED 17TH NOVEMBER 1853 / BELOVED AND REGRETTED BY FAMILY, FRIENDS / BUSACO / SALAMANCA / VITTORIA / PYRENEES / NIVELLE.

Cornet Aug 1810. Lt 21 Aug 1811. Bt Major 30 Dec 1819.

Served in the Peninsula 1812–1813 (Extra ADC to the Duke of Wellington). Sent there by his family to remove him from his attachment to Harriette Wilson, the celebrated courtesan. Present at Salamanca, Vittoria, Morales, Pyrenees and Nivelle. Half pay 25 Oct 1821. Returned to England in 1813 to become

MP for Monmouth which he held until 1832 and MP for West Gloucestershire 1835. KG. MGS medal for Salamanca, Vittoria, Pyrenees and Nivelle. Educated at Westminster. Married Georgina Fitzroy, niece of the Duke of Wellington 1814. Nephew of Lt Colonel Lord Robert Edward Henry Somerset 4th Lt Dragoons, nephew of Capt Lord John Thomas Henry Somerset 60th Foot and nephew of Capt and Lt Colonel Lord Fitzroy James Henry Somerset 1st Foot Guards and cousin of Lt Henry Somerset 18th Lt Dragoons. Later became the 7th Duke of Beaufort in 1835.

WORSLEY, Henry

Major. 34th (Cumberland) Regiment of Foot.
Family Memorial tablet: St Olave's Church, Gatcombe, Isle of Wight. (Photograph)

TO THE MEMORY / OF / .... / HENRY, BREVET LIEU^{T}. COL^{L}. C B. H M. 34TH REG^{T} / AFTER A COURSE OF ARDUOUS SERVICE, / (PARTICULARLY AT WALCHEREN & IN THE PENINSULAR / WAR,) / FOR HIS GALLANT CONDUCT IN WHICH, HE WAS / REWARDED BY HIS SOVEREIGN WITH MANY MEDALS / DIED OF CONSUMPTION, MAY 13TH 1820 / ....

North Hampshire Militia (aged 15) 1797. Ensign 5th Foot 13 Aug 1799. Lt 96th Foot 24 Apr 1800. Capt 7 Sep 1804. Capt 89th Foot 8 Dec 1804. Capt 85th Foot 9 Aug 1806. Major 4th Garrison Battalion 13 Jun 1811. Major 34th Foot 23 Jan 1812. Bt Lt Colonel 21 Jun 1813.

Served in the Peninsula with 85th Foot Apr – Aug 1811 (on Staff as Brigade Major 1 Brigade 7th Division) and 34th Foot Jun 1812 – Apr 1814. Present at Fuentes d'Onoro (rescued Capt George Fitz-Clarence 10th Lt Dragoons from being captured by the French), second siege of Badajoz, retreat from Burgos, Vittoria, Pyrenees, Nivelle, Nive, Orthes and Toulouse. Gold Cross for Pyrenees, Nivelle, Nive and Orthes. CB. Also served at the Helder 1799 (present at Bergen where he carried the colours), West Indies 1804–1808, Walcheren 1809 (present at the siege of Flushing) and India 1816 (had to return immediately because of his health). All through his service in the Peninsula he was affected by the fever he caught at Walcheren and this contributed to his death from consumption in 1820. Captain of Yarmouth Castle 1818.
Reference: Royal Military Calendar, Vol. 4, pp. 471–4.

WRAY, Thomas Fawcett

Lieutenant. 7th (Royal Fusiliers) Regiment of Foot.
Memorial tablet: St Andrew's Church, Aysgarth, Yorkshire. (Photograph)

TO THO. FAWCETT WRAY / SON OF GEORGE WRAY ESQ / OF TOWN HEAD, THORALBY. / WHO IN THE 25 YEAR OF HIS AGE, / WHEN LIEUT. IN THE 7 FUSILIERS / GALLANTLY FELL / ON THE 2 DAY OF APRIL 1812, / IN A STORMING PARTY AT / BADAJOZ. / THIS MARBLE IS ERECTED / IN ESTEEM AND REGRET / BY HIS BROTHER OFFICERS / OF THE LOYAL DALES / VOLUNTEERS.

Brass Memorial tablet: St Andrew's Church, Aysgarth, Yorkshire. (In Lady Chapel under East Window). (Photograph)

..................THOMAS FAWCETT WRAY LIEUT H. M. 7TH FUSILIERS BORN 1786 KILLED AT THE STORMING OF BADAJOS 1812 UNMARRIED. ....

Lt North Yorkshire Militia. Lt 7th Foot 13 Apr 1809.

Served in the Peninsula with 2/7th Aug 1809 – Jun 1811 and 1/7th Jul 1811 – Jul 1812. Present at Busaco, Pombal, Condeixa, Olivencia, first siege of Badajoz, Albuera (severely wounded), Cuidad Rodrigo and Badajoz where he was killed in the storming party 6 Apr 1812.

WRENCH, William Handfield

Lieutenant. 38th (1st Staffordshire) Regiment of Foot.

Pedestal tomb: St Cynfarch's Churchyard, Hope, Flintshire, Wales. (Photograph)

IN / MEMORY OF / WILLIAM HANDFIELD WRENCH / OF TALYN GLAS IN THIS PARISH / CAPTAIN IN HER MAJESTY'S 38TH REGT / WHO DIED ON THE 9TH DAY OF JUNE / 1848. AGED 57 YEARS.

Ensign 1 Apr 1807. Lt 22 Oct 1807. Capt 7 May 1818.

Served in the Peninsula with 1/38th Sep 1813 – Apr 1814. Present at Bidassoa, Nivelle, Nive and Bayonne. Half pay 29 Nov 1821.

WRIGHT, Peter

Lieutenant. Royal Engineers.

Family Ledger stone. St John's Churchyard, Knutsford, Cheshire. (Centre of Churchyard behind the Church and Church Hall). (Photograph)

.... / PETER WRIGHT A LIEUTENANT IN THE ROYAL / ENGINEERS KILLED AT THE ATTACK AT NEW ORLEANS / BY HIS MAJESTY'S FORCES UNDER THE COMMAND / OF SIR EDWARD PAKENHAM K.C.B ON THE 30TH / DAY OF DECEMBER 1814 AGED 22 YEARS.

2nd Lt 24 Jun 1809. 1st Lt 25 Mar 1811.

Served in the Peninsula Nov 1810 – Apr 1814. Present at Torres Vedras, first and second sieges of Badajoz (wounded at second siege), Ciudad Rodrigo, Badajoz, Almarez (wounded and Mentioned in Despatches), Vittoria (wounded) and Pyrenees. Also served in North America 1814 (present in the New Orleans Campaign. On 30 Dec 1814 he was sent through a swamp to reconnoitre the enemy position but never returned. During the subsequent fighting his body was discovered, killed by a single shot with his weapons and telescope intact).

WRIGHT, Thomas

Captain. Royal Staff Corps.

Ledger stone: Holy Trinity Churchyard, Cheltenham, Gloucestershire. (In path outside door to the Church. Seriously eroded). (Photograph)

IN MEMORY OF / LT COLONEL / THOMAS WRIGHT / ROYAL STAFF CORPS / DIED AT CHELTENHAM / JULY 2ND 1850 / AGED 72 YEARS / ....

Ensign 5 May 1804. Lt 3 Sep 1807. Capt 23 Dec 1813. Major 25 Jun 1830.

Present at Waterloo where he was wounded (DAQMG). Half pay 5 Nov 1830.

WRIXON, Nicholas

Lieutenant. 10th (North Lincolnshire) Regiment of Foot.

Memorial tablet: Castlemanger Church, County Cork, Ireland. (No longer extant. Church now disused and memorials removed). (M.I.)

"MAJOR NICHOLAS WRIXON, LATE OF 21ST FUSILIERS, WHO DIED AT CORK, 6 JUNE 1864."

Ensign 4 Apr 1811. Lt 13 May 1813. 1st Lt 21st Foot 8 Apr 1825. Capt 1 May 1840. Bt Major 11 Nov 1851.

Served in the Peninsula Apr 1812 – Apr 1814. Present at Tarragona, Alicante, Castalla, Ordal and Barcelona. Also served at the siege of Genoa 1814. Retired 11 Nov 1851.

WURMB, Ernst Christian Carl von
Captain. 5th Line Battalion, King's German Legion.
Named on the Regimental Memorial: La Haye Sainte, Waterloo. (Photograph)
Named on the Waterloo Column, Hanover, Germany. (Photograph)

Lt 25 May 1805. Adjutant 21 Jan 1806. Capt 7 Dec 1809.

Served in the Peninsula Aug 1808 – Apr 1814. (ADC to Major General Murray Aug – Oct 1808, ADC to Col Dreiberg Nov 1808 – Jun 1809 and ADC to Major General Low Jul 1809 – Jun 1811). Present at Douro, Talavera, Busaco, Fuentes d'Onoro, Ciudad Rodrigo, Moriscos, Salamanca, Burgos, Vittoria, Tolosa, San Sebastian, Bidassoa, Nivelle, Nive, St Etienne and Bayonne. Present at Waterloo where he was killed. Also served at Hanover 1805, the Baltic 1807–1808 and the Netherlands 1814.

WYATT, James
Private: 50th (West Kent) Regiment of Foot.
Headstone: St Mary's Church, Appledore, Kent. (Re-erected in Nave north side). (Photograph)

IN MEMORY OF / JAMES WYATT / OF APPELEDORE / WHO DIED JANY 12TH 1848 / AGED 65 YEARS.

Memorial tablet: St Mary's Church, Appledore, Kent. (Photograph)

THIS TOMBSTONE OF JAMES WYATT WHO FOUGHT AT / WATERLOO WAS MOVED INTO THIS POSITION IN / THE CHURCH (THE SITE OF THE OLD NORTH DOOR) / IN 1971 TO PREVENT FURTHER DETERIORATION OF / THE INSCRIPTION. THIS ORIGINALLY READ: / IN MEMORY OF / JAMES WYATT / OF APPLEDORE / WHO DIED JANUARY 12 1848 / AGED 65 YEARS / HE SERVED IN THE ROYAL STAFF CORPS 23 YEARS / AND WAS PRESENT IN ALL THE PENINSULAR / CAMPAIGNS / AND AT THE FINAL VICTORY OF WATERLOO, / AND WAS DISCHARGED IN CONSEQUENCE OF / THE DISBANDING OF THE COMPANY. / THIS STONE IS ERECTED AS A TRIBUTE OF RESPECT TO HIS MEMORY / BY RICHD. ASHBEE AND WM. CHAMBERS. / WILLIAM CHAMBERS OF WOODCHURCH HAD EMPLOYED / JAMES WYATT AS A MASTER BRICKLAYER.

Pte 50th Foot 4 Apr 1809. Pte Royal Staff Corps 30 Nov 1817.

Served in the Peninsula 1809 – Apr 1814. Present at Almarez, Vittoria, Pyrenees, Orthes and Toulouse where he was wounded. Present at Waterloo. Also served at Walcheren 1809, Malta and Corfu 1817–1823 and North America (present at Halifax for four and a half years). MGS medal for Vittoria, Pyrenees, Orthes and Toulouse. Discharged 9 Dec 1833.

WYATT, William Edgell Richard
Lieutenant Colonel. 23rd (Royal Welch Fusiliers) Regiment of Foot.
Chest tomb: St John's Churchyard, Egham, Surrey. Inscription illegible. (Plot 109). (Photograph)

Ensign 29th Foot 22 Feb 1793. Lt 5 Feb 1794. Capt-Lt 25 Apr 1795. Major 24 Jul 1804. Lt Colonel 23rd Foot 18 Feb 1808. Bt Colonel 4 Jun 1814.

Served in the Peninsula with 2/23rd Oct 1808 – Jan 1809. Present at Corunna where he commanded the 23rd Foot as part of the expedition under Sir David Baird. Gold Medal for Corunna. CB. Also served in the West Indies 1794–1796 under Sir Ralph Abercromby, the Helder 1799 and Halifax, Nova Scotia 1801. Inspecting Field Officer Andover Recruiting District 1814. Died in 1821.

WYLDE, John Newman

Captain. 56th (West Essex) Regiment of Foot.
Interred in Kensal Green Cemetery, London. (1606/46/2). (No longer extant)

Ensign 5th Foot 22 Jan 1807. Lt 15 Sep 1808. Capt 56th Foot 9 Nov 1813.

Served in the Peninsula with 1/5th Jul 1808 – Jan 1809 and 2/5th Jul 1809 – Apr 1812. Present at Rolica, Vimeiro, Corunna, Busaco, Redinha, Casal Nova, Sabugal, Fuentes d'Onoro, second siege of Badajoz, El Bodon and Ciudad Rodrigo where he was severely wounded and awarded pension of £70 per annum. Died 21 Aug 1838 aged 55.

WYLDE, Ralph

Captain. 89th Regiment of Foot.
Grave: Paddington Street Cemetery, London. (M.I.)

"RALPH WYLDE, ESQ., LATE CAPTAIN IN THE 89TH REGT AND MAJOR IN THE PORTUGUESE INFANTRY, SEVERELY WOUNDED AT THE BATTLE OF SALAMANCA, DIED 1814."

Lt 13th Foot 29 Dec 1804. Capt Royal York Rangers 8 Dec 1808. Capt 89th Foot 28 Feb 1811. Portuguese Army: Major 8th Line 30 Aug 1811 and Major 14th Line 9 Nov 1813.

Served in the Portuguese Army in the Peninsula Aug 1811 – Nov 1813. Present at Salamanca (severely wounded) and Pyrenees. Retired 22 Dec 1813 and returned to England.

WYLDE, William

2nd Captain. Royal Artillery.
Low monument: Brompton Cemetery, London. (BR 88400). (Photograph)

IN MEMORY OF / GENERAL WILLIAM WYLDE. C.B. / COLONEL COMMANDANT ROYAL ARTILLERY. / KNIGHT GRAND CROSS OF THE ORDER OF ISABELLA AL CATOLICA, / AND KNIGHT OF THE ORDERS OF CHARLES III AND SAN FERNANDO OF SPAIN. / FOR SOME TIME ATTACHED TO THE HOUSEHOLD OF H.R.H. THE PRINCE CONSORT, / FIRST AS EQUERRY AND SUBSEQUENTLY AS GROOM OF THE BEDCHAMBER. / HE DEPARTED THIS LIFE ON THE 14TH DAY OF APRIL, 1877, AGED 89 YEARS.

Named on the Memorial tablet to Master Gunners: Royal Artillery Barracks, Woolwich, Kent. (Photograph)

2nd Lt 8 Sep 1803. 1st Lt 6 Dec 1803. 2nd Capt 16 Mar 1812. Capt 4 Aug 1826. Bt Major 16 Jul 1830. Lt Colonel 20 Nov 1839. Colonel 8 Jan 1849. Major General 20 Jun 1854. Lt General 22 Feb 1863. General 24 Aug 1866.

Served with the Army of Occupation in France. Also served in the Netherlands 1814 (present at Antwerp and Bergen-op-Zoom), Portugal 1826–1828, Spain 1834–1840 and Portugal 1846. CB 1840. First to suggest that the electric telegraph should be used in the field. Colonel Commandant Royal Artillery 1 Jun 1863. Master Gunner 1868–1877. Knight of Charles III, Second Class of St Fernando, and Grand Cross of Isabella the Catholic, all awarded for his services in Portugal and Spain after the Peninsular War.
Reference: Annual Register, 1877, Appx, p. 144.

WYNCH, James

Lieutenant Colonel. 4th (King's Own) Regiment of Foot.
Grave: St George's Cemetery, Lisbon, Portugal. (Grave number C32). (M.I.)

"COLONEL J. WYNCH / OF THE 4TH REGIMENT OF FOOT / WHO DIED 6 JAN 1811. AGED 46 YEARS."

Lt 2nd Troop Royal Horse Guards. Capt 7 Jan 1786. Capt 10th Foot 16 Jun 1787. Capt 36th Foot 24 Apr 1790. Bt Major 15 Nov 1797. Major 4th Foot 13 Dec 1797. Lt Colonel 4th Foot 15 Nov 1799.

Served in the Peninsula Aug 1808 – Jan 1809 and Nov 1810 – Jan 1811 in command of the 2nd Brigade Light Division. Present at Corunna (severely wounded). Also served at the Helder 1799 (severely wounded), Copenhagen 1807 (Lt Governor) and Walcheren 1809. He never recovered from his wounds from Corunna and died of typhoid fever in Lisbon 8 Jan 1811. Gold Medal for Corunna. Promoted to command a brigade and placed on the Staff a short time before his death.

WYNDHAM, Charles
Lieutenant. 14th (Duchess of York's Own) Regiment of Light Dragoons
Low monument. Cockermouth Cemetery, Cockermouth, Cumbria. (Photograph)

COL. CHARLES WYNDHAM, / BORN 8TH OCT 1792. DIED 17TH APRIL 1876. / ....

Cornet 10th Lt Dragoons 17 Oct 1811. Lt 5 Nov 1812. Lt 14th Lt Dragoons 12 Nov 1814. Capt 2nd Life Guards 24 Feb 1817. Major 67th Foot 20 Dec 1821. Lt Colonel (unattached) 26 Jun 1823. Bt Colonel 28 Jun 1838.

Served in the Peninsula 1813 – Apr 1814. Present at Morales, Vittoria, Orthes, Tarbes and Toulouse (wounded at Espinasse 4 Apr 1814). Half pay 28 Jun 1838. MGS medal for Vittoria, Orthes and Toulouse.

WYNDHAM, Hon. George
Lieutenant Colonel. 20th Light Dragoons.
Memorial tablet: St Mary the Virgin's Church, Petworth, Sussex. (Photograph)

TO THE MEMORY OF / COLONEL GEORGE WYNDHAM, / ELDEST SON OF GEORGE CHARLES, EARL OF EGREMONT, / CREATED BARON LECONFIELD OF LECONFIELD IN THE COUNTY OF YORK / AD 1830. / BORN JUNE 5TH 1787. / DIED MARCH 18TH 1869, AGED 81. / HIS LORDSHIP SERVED IN THE ROYAL NAVY AS A MIDSHIPMAN / IN THE AMELIA FRIGATE AND IN THE MALTA. / AT THE AGE OF 15, HE JOINED THE ARMY, / AND SERVED IN THE WEST INDIES, ON THE STAFF OF SIR EYRE COOTE, / ACCOMPANIED THE EXPEDITION TO STRALSUND, / ON SIR JAMES MCDONALD'S STAFF; / WAS PRESENT AT THE BOMBARDMENT OF COPENHAGEN, / THE SIEGE OF FLUSHING, / AND THE CAPTURE OF THE DANISH FLEET, 1807. / SERVED IN THE WALCHEREN EXPEDITION, 1809, / AT THE STORMING OF CIUDAD RODRIGO, 1812, / AND WITH THE ARMY UNDER THE COMMAND OF / LORD WILLIAM BENTINCK, / IN CATALONIA, GENOA, MALTA AND SICILY. / HIS LORDSHIP MARRIED APRIL 25TH 1815, MARY FANNY, / ONLY DAUGHTER OF THE REVD W. BLUNT, OF CRABBETT, SUSSEX. / THIS TABLET IS ERECTED TO THEIR FATHER, BY HIS AFFECTIONATE SONS / HENRY AND PERCY WYNDHAM.

Midshipman Royal Navy 1799. Cornet 5th Dragoon Guards 31 Mar 1803. Capt 72nd Foot 19 Sep 1805. Lt and Capt 1st Foot Guards 13 Nov 1807. Major 78th Foot 31 Jan 1811. Major 12th Lt Dragoons 25 Apr 1811. Lt Colonel in Meuron's Regt 13 Mar 1812. Lt Colonel 20th Lt Dragoons 10 Dec 1812. Bt Colonel 22 Jul 1830.

Served in the Peninsula with 12th Lt Dragoons Jun 1811 – Jan 1812, and 20th Lt Dragoons Nov 1813 – Apr 1814. Present at Aldea de Ponte, Ciudad Rodrigo and the East coast of Spain. Also served as a Midshipman in Royal Navy on HMS *Amelia* and HMS *Malta* 1799, West Indies 1803, Copenhagen 1807, Walcheren 1809 (present at the siege of Flushing), Genoa, Malta and Sicily. Half pay 25 Jun 1816. Became Baron Leconfield 1859. Brother of Capt and Lt Colonel Hon Henry Wyndham Coldstream Guards and Lieutenant Charles Wyndham 2nd Dragoons.
Reference: Royal Military Calendar, Vol. 4, pp. 405–6. Mollo, John and Boris, Three Peninsula brothers, Journal of the Society for Army Historical Research, Vol. 37, No. 152, Dec 1959, pp. 183–4. (Notes on portraits at Petworth).

WYNDHAM, Hon. Henry

Captain and Lieutenant Colonel. Coldstream Regiment of Foot Guards.
Memorial tablet: St Mary the Virgin's Church, Petworth, Sussex. (Photograph)

TO THE MEMORY OF / GENERAL SIR HENRY WYNDHAM K.C.B. / BORN MAY 12TH 1790. DIED THURSDAY AUGUST 2ND 1860. / ENTERED THE GRENADIER GUARDS / WAS IN THE DUKE OF YORK'S OFFICE, WHEN COMMANDER IN CHIEF / WAS MADE AID-DE-CAMP TO SIR ARTHUR WELLESLEY, AND WAS AT / THE BATTLE OF VIMIERA AND ROLEIA / WAS MADE AID-DE-CAMP TO SIR JOHN MOORE, AND BROUGHT HOME THE / DISPATCHES AFTER THE BATTLE OF CORUNNA: AND BROUGHT OVER / AS PRISONER, THE FRENCH GENERAL LEFEVRE. / WAS AT THE BATTLE OF ALBUERA, IN THE PORTUGUESE CAVALRY. / HAVING BEEN APPOINTED TO THE 10TH HUSSARS, HE WAS IN THAT REGIMENT / IN THE HUSSAR BRIGADE UNDER COLONEL GRANT AT THE BRILLIANT / CAVALRY AFFAIR AT MORALES-DE-TORO ON THE 2ND OF JUNE 1813; ALSO AT / VITTORIA, AND IN JULY WITH THE HUSSAR BRIGADE (THEN COMMANDED / BY MAJOR GENERAL LORD EDWARD SOMERSET) PRESENT AT THE BATTLES / OF THE PYRENEES. / ON THE 8TH SEPTEMBER, 1813, HE LEFT THE 10TH HUSSARS IN CONSEQUENCE / OF PROMOTION AS MAJOR IN AN INFANTRY REGIMENT. / IN JULY 1814 HE WAS TRANSFERRED INTO THE COLDSTREAM GUARDS AS / CAPTAIN AND LIEUT: COLONEL, AND WAS WITH THAT REGIMENT AT THE / BATTLE OF WATERLOO, BEING SEVERELY WOUNDED AT HOUGOUMONT / WAS MADE KING'S AID-DE-CAMP IN 1825 / HE COMMANDED THE 19TH LANCERS AFTER THEIR RETURN FROM INDIA UNTIL THEY / WERE DISBANDED. / HE COMMANDED THE CAVALRY IN PORTUGAL IN THE LAST EXPEDITION UNDER / LIEUT-GENERAL SIR W. CLINTON, WHEN GENERAL CLINTON COMMANDED THE ARMY. / HE COMMANDED THE 10TH HUSSARS AFTER SIR GEORGE QUENTIN'S RETIREMENT / IN MARCH 1824, TILL APRIL 1833. / BECAME A MAJOR GENERAL 10TH JANUARY 1837. LIEUT-GENERAL 9TH NOVEMBER 1840. / COLONEL OF THE 11TH HUSSARS 19TH NOVEMBER 1847. GENERAL 20TH JUNE 1854 / COMMANDED THE DUBLIN DISTRICT IN 1843. 1844. 1845 AND 1846 / DIED A FULL GENERAL K.C.B. AND COLONEL OF THE 11TH HUSSARS. / RECEIVED THE WATERLOO MEDAL – MEDAL WITH 4 CLASPS, / VITTORIA, ALBUERA, VIMIERA, ROLEIA, SPANISH MEDAL FOR ALBUERA. / THIS TABLET IS PLACED BY HIS AFFECTIONATE BROTHER, / LECONFIELD.

Memorial tablet: All Saints' Church, Cockermouth, Cumbria. (Photograph)

TO THE MEMORY OF GENERAL SIR HENRY WYNDHAM, KNIGHT OF THE / CROSS, AND COLONEL OF THE 11TH HUSSARS AND MEMBER OF PARLIAMENT / FOR THE WESTERN DIVISION OF THE COUNTY OF CUMBERLAND. BORN MAY 12 1790 / ENTERED THE GRENADIER GUARDS IN 1806, WAS SHORTLY AFTERWARDS EMPLOYED / IN THE OFFICE OF COMMANDER IN CHIEF THE H.R.H. DUKE OF YORK / APPOINTED AIDE-DE-CAMP TO SIR JOHN MOORE. BROUGHT HOME THE DESPATCHES / AFTER THE BATTLE OF CORUNNA, TOGETHER WITH THE FRENCH GENERAL LEFEVRE / AS PRISONER OF WAR / APPOINTED AIDE DE CAMP TO SIR ARTHUR WELLESLEY AND WAS WITH HIM IN SPAIN / SERVED WITH THE HUSSAR BRIGADE AS CAPTAIN IN THE 10TH HUSSARS AND ALSO / WITH THE PORTUGUESE CAVALRY. / SERVED THROUGHOUT THE PENINSULAR CAMPAIGN OF 1808, '9, '11 AND '13, / INCLUDING THE ACTIONS OF CORUNA ROLEIA VIMIERO BENEVENTE ALBUERA USAGRE MORALES DE TORO VITTORIA AND THE PYRENEES / SERVED ALSO THE CAMPAIGN OF 1815 AS LIEUT. COLONEL OF THE COLDSTREAM / GUARDS. WAS SEVERELY WOUNDED AT WATERLOO DURING THE MEMORABLE / DEFENCE OF THE FARM HOUSE AT HOUGOUMONT BY A WING OF THAT REGIMENT. / MADE KING'S AIDE-DE-CAMP IN 1825. COMMANDED THE 10TH HUSSARS AND THE 19TH LANCERS. COMMANDED THE CAVALRY IN PORTUGAL IN 1827, AND THE DUBLIN DISTRICT IN 1843 '44 '45 AND '46, / WAS RETURNED

FOR COCKERMOUTH IN 1852, SAT FOR THAT BOROUGH TILL / 1857, WHEN HE WAS ELECTED FOR WEST CUMBERLAND, / DIED AT COCKERMOUTH CASTLE ON THURSDAY AUG 2ND 1860, IN THE 71ST YEAR OF HIS AGE / REQUIESCAT IN PACE.

Ensign 31st Foot 27 Mar 1806. Ensign 1st Foot Guards 25 Apr 1806. Capt 71st Foot 8 Jun 1809. Capt 10th Lt Dragoons 6 Jul 1809. Major 60th Foot 9 Aug 1813. Lt Colonel in Dillon's Regt 20 Jun 1814. Capt and Lt Colonel Coldstream Guards 25 Jul 1814. Lt Colonel 19th Lt Dragoons 11 Jul 1816. Lt Colonel 10th Lt Dragoons 18 Mar 1824. Bt Colonel 27 May 1825. Major General 10 Jan 1837. Lt General 9 Nov 1846. General 20 Jun 1854.

Served in the Peninsula 1808–1809, 1811 – May 1812 (with Portuguese Army as Major 8th Cavalry) and 1813. Present at Rolica, Vimeiro (ADC to Sir Arthur Wellesley), Benevente, Corunna (ADC to Sir John Moore). Brought home the despatches from Corunna and also the captured French General Lefebure-Desnouettes, Albuera, Usagre, Morales, Vittoria and Pyrenees. Present at Waterloo with the Coldstream Guards in the defence of Hougoumont where he was severely wounded and awarded pension of £300 per annum. Surgeons wanted to amputate his arm but he said only Dr Jenks of the 10th Lt Dragoons could decide. Dr Jenks said it was not necessary and Wyndham in future always held Dr Jenks in gratitude for his good advice. Also served in Portugal 1827 (commanding cavalry in Sir William Clinton's expedition) and Ireland 1843–1846 (commanding the Dublin District). KCB. MGS medal for Rolica, Vimeiro, Albuera and Vittoria. Spanish medal for Albuera. Colonel 11th Hussars 19 Nov 1847. Henry Wyndham was the illegitimate son of the Earl of Egremont and succeeded to his Cumbrian estates. MP for Cockermouth 1852–1857 and West Cumberland 1857–1860. Brother of Lt Colonel George Wyndham 26th Lt Dragoons who served in the Peninsula and Lt Charles Wyndham 2nd Dragoons who served at Waterloo.

Reference: Gentleman's Magazine, 1860, p. 328. Annual Register Appx, pp. 512–13. Mollo, John and Boris, Three Peninsula brothers, Journal of the Society for Army Historical Research, Vol. 37, No. 152, Dec 1959, pp. 183–4. (Notes on portraits at Petworth).

WYNN, Henry

Captain. 23rd (Royal Welch Fusiliers) Regiment of Foot.
Memorial tablet: St Mary's Church, Flint, Wales. (M.I.)

"SACRED TO THE MEMORY OF HENRY / WYNN, ESQ., LATE CAPTAIN IN THE 23RD REGIMENT, OR 'ROYAL WELSH / FUSILIERS,' SON OF WILLIAM WYNN, ESQ., OF RHAGATT, IN THE COUNTY / OF MERIONETH, WHO DIED JUNE 18TH, 1832, AGED 44"

2nd Lt 22 Apr 1803. 1st Lt 24 Mar 1804. Adjt 24 May 1806. Capt 29 Sep 1808.

Served in the Peninsula with 1/23rd May 1813 – Apr 1814. Present at Subijana de Morrillos, Vittoria, Pyrenees, Nivelle, Nive and Orthes where he was severely wounded 27 Feb 1814. Half pay between 1818–1823. In the report of the inspection of the regiment on 16 May 1810, officers born in Wales are mentioned for the first time, amongst them is Capt Henry Wynn.

Reference: Cambrian Quarterly Magazine, Vol. 4, 1832, p. 554.

WYNN, William

Private. 38th (1st Staffordshire) Regiment of Foot.
Obelisk: General Cemetery, Sheffield. (On main path near to Anglican Chapel). (Photograph)

WILLIAM WYNN / BROTHER OF / EDWARD WYNN. / DIED 1ST MARCH 1869 / AGED 81 YEARS. / HE FOUGHT IN THE PENINSULAR WAR / CAMPAIGN, AND WAS AT THE / PASSAGE OF THE DOURA, / OPORTO, TALAVERA. AND / VITTORIA. / ....

Served in the Peninsula 1810–1814. Present at Busaco, Salamanca, siege of Burgos, retreat from Burgos (present at Villa Muriel), Vittoria and San Sebastian. MGS medal for Busaco, Salamanca, Vittoria and San Sebastian. Died 1 Mar 1869 aged 81.

WYNOLDY, A.

1st Lieutenant. 5th National Militia Battalion, Dutch Infantry.
Named on the Memorial to Dutch officers killed at Quatre Bras. St Joseph's Church, Waterloo. (Photograph)

YALE, William Parry see PARRY, William Parry Jones

YATES, Samuel

Sergeant. 20th (East Devonshire) Regiment of Foot.
Gravestone: St Leonard's Churchyard, Hythe, Colchester, Essex. (M.I.)

"SACRED TO THE MEMORY OF / SAMUEL YATES / LATE SERGEANT OF H. M. 20TH / OR EAST DEVON REGT. OF FOOT. / WHO DEPARTED THIS LIFE / MARCH 15 1810 / AGED 35 YEARS. / HERE LIES WITHIN THIS SILENT GRAVE, / ONCE A SOLDIER LOVED, JUST AND BRAVE, / IN HOLLAND, EGYPT AND ON MAIDA'S PLAIN. / HE FOUGHT ALSO IN PORTUGAL AND SPAIN. / BUT WALCHEREN'S DREADFUL AND DESTRUCTIVE RAGE / ...." / (REST OF INSCRIPTION ILLEGIBLE)

Served in the Peninsula 1808 – Jan 1809. Present at Vimeiro, retreat to Corunna and Corunna. Also served at the Helder 1799, Egypt 1801, Sicily 1806 (present at Maida) and Walcheren 1809. Died from Walcheren fever 15 Mar 1810.

YONGE, William Crawley

Lieutenant. 52nd (Oxfordshire) Light Infantry Regiment of Foot.
Low monument with cross: St Matthew's Churchyard, Otterbourne, Hampshire. (Photograph)

WILLIAM CRAWLEY YONGE OF H. M. 52 REGIMENT / BORN 2 JUNE 1795 DIED 26 FEBRUARY 1854.

Ensign 14 May 1812. Lt 29 Apr 1813.
Served in the Peninsula Sep 1813 – Apr 1814. Present at Bidassoa, Nivelle, Nive, Orthes, Tarbes and Toulouse. Present at Waterloo and with the Army of Occupation. MGS medal for Nivelle, Nive, Orthes and Toulouse. Half pay 13 Feb 1823. Designed the local church with John Keble, opened in 1839. Author of *Memoirs of Lord Seaton's services*, privately published in 1853. No known copies survive. Father of Charlotte Mary Yonge, the Victorian novelist.
REFERENCE: Oxfordshire Light Infantry Chronicle, 1903, pp. 139–43.

YORKE, Charles

Captain. 52nd (Oxfordshire) Light Infantry Regiment of Foot.
Low monument: Kensal Green Cemetery, London. (24993/54/RS). (Photograph)

CHARLES YORKE / .... / (1790–1880)

Memorial tablet: Chapel Royal of St Peter-Ad Vincula, Tower of London, London. (Photograph)

IN MEMORY OF / FIELD MARSHAL / SIR CHARLES YORKE / KNIGHT GRAND CROSS / OF THE / ORDER OF THE BATH / COLONEL COMMANDANT OF / THE RIFLR BRIGADE / CONSTABLE OF THE TOWER OF LONDON LEUTENANT / AND/ CUSTOS ROTULOREM / OF THE TOWER

HAMLETS / SERVED THROGHOUT THE PENINSULAR / AND WATERLOO CAMPAIGNS / AND CAPE WAR 1852–3 / BORN 7TH DECEMBER 1790 / DIED 20TH NOVEMBER 1880

Ensign 35th Foot 22 Jan 1807. Lt 18th Feb 1808. Lt 52nd Foot 25th Feb 1808. Capt 24 Dec 1813. Major 9 Jun 1825. Lt Colonel 30 Nov 1826. Bt Colonel 23 Nov 1841. Major General 11 Nov 1851. Lt General 13 Feb 1859. General 5 Sep 1865. Field Marshal 2 Jun 1877.

Served in the Peninsula with 2/52nd Aug 1808 – Jan 1809 and Apr 1811 and 1/52nd May 1811 – Mar 1814. Present at Vimeiro, Vigo, Fuentes d'Onoro, Ciudad Rodrigo, Badajoz (wounded), Salamanca, San Munos, Vittoria, Pyrenees, Vera, Bidassoa, Nivelle (wounded), Nive and Orthes (severely wounded). Present at Waterloo as extra ADC to Major General Adam who was in command of the brigade in which the 52nd took part. After a period on half pay became Inspecting Field Officer of Militia 1826. MGS medal for Vimeiro, Fuentes d'Onoro, Ciudad Rodrigo, Badajoz, Salamanca, Vittoria, Pyrenees, Nivelle, Nive and Orthes. Also served in Ireland, AQMG at Cork and also at Manchester 1842–1851 and Cape of Good Hope (second in command under General Cathcart in the Kaffir War 1852–1853), Military Secretary at Headquarters May 1854–1860. KCB 1856. GCB 1860. Colonel 33rd Foot 27 Feb 1855. Colonel Commanding 2nd Battalion Rifle Brigade 1 Apr 1863. Constable of the Tower of London 1875. Died 20 Nov 1880 and was buried in Kensal Green Cemetery 24 Nov 1880.
REFERENCE: Dictionary of National Biography. Oxfordshire Light Infantry Chronicle, 1901, p. 179. Annual Register, 1880, Part 2, p. 215.

YOUNG, JAMES

Lieutenant and Adjutant. 42nd (Royal Highland) Regiment of Foot.
Buried in Canongate Cemetery, Edinburgh, Scotland. (Burial Register)

Ensign 22 Oct 1805. Lt 25 May 1808. Adjutant 31 Mar 1814.

Served in the Peninsula May 1812 – Apr 1814 (Acting Quartermaster May – Nov 1813). Present at Salamanca, Burgos, Pyrenees, Nivelle, Nive, Orthes and Toulouse. Present at Waterloo where he was wounded. Half pay 1819. Died at Edinburgh 15 Jun 1846.

YOUNGS, John

Private. 23rd (Royal Welch Fusiliers) Regiment of Foot.
Headstone: St Andrew's Churchyard, Sutton, Cambridgeshire. (Photograph)

IN MEMORY OF / JOHN YOUNGS / OF THIS PARISH, / LATE 23RD REGIMENT / ROYAL WELSH FUSILIERS / WHO SERVED HIS COUNTRY / GALLANTLY AND FAITHFULLY / THROUGHOUT THE PENINSULAR WAR / AND TOOK PART IN THE BATTLE / OF WATERLOO. / HE DIED APRIL 13th 1878. / AGED 82 YEARS.

Pte Cambridge Volunteers. Pte 23rd Foot 2 Apr 1813.

Served in the Peninsula. Present at Waterloo in Capt Harrison's Company No. 3 aged 16 years.
REFERENCE: Saunders, Derek, Rest in peace, Waterloo Journal, Aug 1995, p. 8.

YUILL, William

Colour Sergeant. 1st Regiment of Foot Guards.
Named on the Memorial: St Andrew's Church (now Musée Historique), Biarritz, France. (Photograph)

Mural memorial tablet: Guards Cemetery, St Etienne, Bayonne, France. (Photograph)

1814 / WM YUILL / CR SERJ 3RD BATTN 1ST FOOT / GUARDS. KILLED BY A / GRAPE SHOT 7TH APRIL. / BELOVED BY THE REGT IN / WHICH HE SERVED 20 YEARS. / A FRIEND TO TRUTH / HE LOVED HIS KING, ZEALOUS / FOR HIS COUNTRY AND IN ITS / JUST CAUSE HE BREATHD HIS LAST /

ADUE MY FRIEND. / THIS STONE RECOVERED / FROM A WASHING FOUNTAIN IN / A WOOD WHERE THE 1ST FOOT / GUARDS WERE ENCAMPED / IN 1814 WAS REMOVED TO / THIS CEMETERY MAY 28TH 1881 / BY P. A. HURT.

Pte 1794.

Served in the Peninsula Oct 1808 – Jan 1809 and Apr 1811 – Apr 1814. Present at Corunna, Bidassoa, Nivelle, Adour and Bayonne where he was killed 9 Apr 1814. Served in the regiment for 20 years.

Place Index

ENGLAND

Hawkshead: Sandys, Myles
Kendal: Pennington, John
Keswick: Woodford, Sir John George
Kirkby Lonsdale: Sturgeon, William
Kirkbride: Metcalfe, Henry
Morland: Nicholson, Edward
Penrith: Macleod, George Francis
Temple Sowerby: Proctor, John
Wetheral: Ratcliffe, James
Wigton: Stockdale, William
Wreay: Thain, William

Derbyshire
Ashbourne: Riddlesden, John Buck
Baslow: Wellington
Chesterfield: Riley, John
Heanor: Meakin, Joseph
Ilkeston: Whitehead, Samuel
Spondon: Richardson, George Sant
Stanton-in-the-Peak: Thornhill, William
Winster: Wall, Thomas

Devon
Abbotsham: Walter, Philip
Awliscombe: Pring, John
Colyton: Piper, John
Colyton: Piper, Robert Sloper
Dartmouth: Mountsteven, William T. B.
East Budleigh: Torriano, William Edward
Exeter: Manley, John
Exeter: Mercer, Alexander Cavalié
Exeter: Rhodes, Charles Steech
Exeter: Simcoe, Francis Gwillam
Exeter: South, Samuel
Ilfracombe: McKenzie, George Davis
Ilfracombe: McKenzie, John Holland
Northam: Rogers, Benjamin
Paignton: Reynett, James Henry
Plymouth: Macgregor, Malcolm
Plymouth: Murray, Hon. Henry
Plymouth: Ord, William Redman
Sidmouth: Slessor, John
Stowford: Webber, William
Torquay: Macdonald, George
Torquay: Shawe, Charles Augustus
West Ogwell: Taylor, Thomas William

Dorset
Christchurch: Walcot, Edmund Yeamans
Kimmeridge: Mansel, John

Durham
Barnard Castle: Murchison, Roderick Impey
Barnard Castle: Sweeten, Benjamin
Barnard Castle: Watson, George
Bishop Auckland: Nixon, Edward
Bishopwearmouth: Reed, John
Durham: Stewart, Hon. Charles William
Durham: Wemyss, James
Long Newton: Stewart, Hon. Charles William
Long Newton: Wellington
Staindrop: Nesham, Matthew
Whitburn: Tathwell, Tathwell Baker

Essex
Braintree: Watson, Amos
Colchester: Rebow, Francis Slater
Colchester: Robinson, Peter
Colchester: Yates, Samuel
Grear Baddow: Trant, Sir Nicholas
Harwich: Pearson, Isaac
Hatfield Peverell: Wakeling, James

Gloucestershire
Almondsbury: Master, William Chester
Badminton: Somerset, Lord Fitzroy J.H.
Badminton: Somerset, Henry
Badminton: Somerset, Lord Robert E. H.
Beaufort: Worcester, Henry W. S. Marquess
Charlton Kings: Sissons, Marcus Jacob
Cheltenham: Manners, Charles
Cheltenham: Moore, Richard
Cheltenham: Myers, Sir William James
Cheltenham: Nichols, George
Cheltenham: O'Leary, Arthur
Cheltenham: Raikes, William Henley
Cheltenham: Schreiber, George
Cheltenham: Shepherd, John
Cheltenham: Steevens, Charles
Cheltenham: Telford, Robert
Cheltenham: Trench, Robert Le Poer
Cheltenham: Wallace, Peter Margetson
Cheltenham: Willatts, Peter John
Cheltenham: Window, Richard
Cheltenham: Wright, Thomas
Elmstone Hardwick: Welden, James
Frampton-Cottrell: Morgan, John
Gloucester: Nightingall, Miles
Gloucester: Thackwell, Joseph
Hatherop: Ponsonby, Frederick Cavendish
Hawkesbury: Somerset, Lord Robert E. H.
Hawkesbury: Surman, John

Kemerton: Smith, Joshua
Leckhampton: Macready, Edward Nevil
Leckhampton: Nicolay, William
Leckhampton: Tinling, Isaac Pattison
Prestbury: Morgan, Hugh
Prestbury: Obins, Hamlet
Prestbury: Taylor, Jeremiah
Prestbury: Whinyates, Sir Edward Charles
Shurdington: Thompson, Ralph Keddy
Shurdington: Tinling, George Vaughan
Southam: Napier, Charles James
Southam: Murray, Sir George
Southam: Wellington
Thornbury: Maclaine, Hector
Wotton-under-Edge: Scott, Henry Alexander

Guernsey
St Peter Port: Smith, Sir George
St Peter Port: Thomson, George
St Peter Port: Ward, William Cuthbert

Hampshire
Aldershot: Wellington
Aldershot: Smith, Thomas Lawrence
Alverstoke: Mackrell, Thomas
Andover: Moore, Sir John
Baughurst: Ridout, Cranstoun George
Bisterne: Mills, John
Christchurh: Walcott, Edmund Yeamans
Gosport: Madden, George Allan
Gosport: White, Henry
Lyndhurst: Powell, Henry Weyland
Lyndhurst: Schoëdde, James Holmes
Minstead: Robbins, Thomas William
Odiham: Short, Charles William
Otterbourne: Yonge, William Crawley
Portsmouth: Macgregor, George
Portsmouth: MacDonald, John
Portsmouth: McGrigor, Sir James
Portsmouth: Mill, James
Portsmouth: Miller, William
Portsmouth: Moore, Sir John
Portsmouth: Napier, Charles James
Porstmouth: Napier, George Thomas
Portsmouth: Napier, William Francis Patrick
Portsmouth: Pakenham, Hercules Robert
Portsmouth: Rottenburg, Francis
Portsmouth: Somerset, Lord Fitzroy J. F.
Portsmouth: Strangways, Thomas Fox
Portsmouth: Wellington
Portsmouth: White, Henry
Portsmouth: Woodford, Alexander George
Sopley: Willis, George Brander
Southampton: McNeil, Roderick
Southampton: Manners, Russell
Southampton: Mee, John
Southampton: Robarts, William
Southampton: Stretton, Severus W. L.
Southampton: Todd, Francis
Southampton: Wilkins, George
Southsea: Prior, Thomas Murray
Titchfield: Spry, William Frederick
Titchfield: Wilson, Thomas
Wickham: Saunderson, Hardress Robert
Winchester: Manningham, Coote
Winchester: Miller, George
Winchester: Mitchell, Samuel
Winchester: Moore, Sir John
Winchester: Norcott, Amos Godsil Robert
Winchester: O'Hare, Peter
Winchester: Ross, John
Winchester: Smith, Harry George Wakelyn
Winchester: Stewart, Hon. Sir William
Winchester: Stokes, James Marshall
Winchester: Uniacke, John
Winchester: Wade, Hamlet

Herefordshire
Hampton Bishop: Weare, Thomas
Hereford: Symons, Henry John
Mathon: West, James Dawson
Stretton Grandison: Parsons, Charles

Hertfordshire
Abbots Langley: Sulivan, George James
Ardeley: Murray, John
Baldock: Wilkinson, Thomas
Barkway: Peachey, James
Cheshunt: Thorpe, Samuel
Great Hormead: Stables, Edward
Welwyn: Torrens, Henry

Huntingdonshire
Huntingdon: Slow, David
Waresley: Offley, Francis Needham

Isle of Man
Ballure: Reed, Samuel
Malew: Raynes, William Augustus

Isle of Wight
Bembridge: Moreton, Augustus John Francis

Bembridge: Weaver, Thomas
Brading: Smyth, Henry
Carisbrooke: McIntosh, Hugh
Carisbrooke: Murray, Thomas
Carisbrooke: O'Leary, Edmund
Carisbrooke: Perrin, Isaac Barrington
Carisbrooke: Sadleir, William
Cowes: Mainwaring, John Montague
Cowes: Reignolds, Thomas
Gatcombe: Worsley, Henry
Newport: Shortt, Thomas
Ryde: Macandrew, John
Ryde: Milligan, Robert
Shanklin: Power, William Greenshields
Whippingham: White, George

Jersey
St Helier: Mitchell, Robert
St Helier: Ravenscroft, Valentine
St Helier: Seward, William
St Helier: Simmons, George
St Helier: Sinclair, James
St Helier: Stewart, Archibald
St Helier: Sweeny, Charles Frederick
St Helier: Walker, Harry
St Helier: Wilson, Richard Goodwin B.
St Ouen: Seward, William

Kent
Appledore: Wyatt, James
Bethersden: Stewart, James
Biddenden: Pattenson, Cooke Tylden
Boxley: Wallis, John
Bromley: Stretton, Sempronius
Canterbury: Mead, Charles
Canterbury: Purvis, John
Canterbury: Ramsay, George
Canterbury: Stuart, John
Canterbury: Taylor, Charles Douglas
Charlton: Maule, George Silvester
Charlton: Parker, John Boteler
Charlton: Sandilands, Patrick
Charlton: Saunders, William
Charlton: Smith, Francis
Charlton: Smith, John Wetherall
Charlton: Vaughan-Arbuckle, Benjamin H.
Charlton: Wood, William Leighton
Cheriton: Mansel, Robert Christopher
Chevening: Stanhope, Hon. Charles Banks
Chevening: Stanhope, Hon. James Hamilton
Chiselhurst: Townshend, Hon. Horatio G. P.
Chislet: Wood, John
Deal: Petit, Peter Hayes
Deal: Witherington, Henry
Erith: Wheatley, Henry
Erith: Wheatley, William
Folkestone: West, Charles Edward
Fordwich: Scott, Thomas
Hollingbourne: Salmon, Thomas
Hythe: Mackenzie, Kenneth
Hythe: Sandilands, Philip
Ickham: Swann, Frederick Dashwood
Maidstone: Tod, George
Milstead: Tylden, John Maxwell
Northfleet: Tucker, John Montmorency
Plumstead: Martin, Donald N.
Plumstead: May, Sir John
Plumstead: Napper, George
Plumstead: Robe, Sir William
Plumstead: Scott, John F.
Plumstead: Williamson, John Sutherland
Rochester: McDonald, Donald
Rochester: Machell, Lancelot
Rochester: Marshall, Anthony
Rochester: Melhuish, Samuel Camplin
Rochester: Melville, David
Rochester: Mudge, Richard Zachary
Rochester: Mulcaster, Edmund R.
Rochester: Nicholas, William
Rochester: Parker, Edward
Rochester: Patton, Peter
Rochester: Pitts, Thomas James Heblethwaite
Rochester: Power, Robert George
Rochester: Reid, William
Rochester: Rhodes, Charles Steech
Rochester: Ross, George Charles
Rochester: Scott, Richard Evans
Rochester: Skelton, Thomas
Rochester: Squire, John
Rochester: Stanway, Frank
Rochester: Tapp, Hammond Astley
Rochester: Thomson, Alexander
Rochester: Trench, Samuel
Rochester: Williams, John Archer
Rolvenden: Monypenny, Thomas Gybbon
Rolvenden: Tweedie, Michael
Sandgate: Macdonald, Stephen
Sandgate: Moore, Sir John
Shorncliffe: Mackenzie, Kenneth
Shorncliffe: Moore, Sir John
Shorncliffe: Ross, Sir Hew Dalrymple
Tunbridge Wells: Middlemore, George

Tunbridge Wells: Molyneux, Thomas
Tunbridge Wells: Thomson, Thomas
Walmer: Wellington
Wingham: Miller, William
Wingham: Turner, William Parkes
Woolwich: Ross, Sir Hew Dalrymple
Woolwich: Wellington
Woolwich: Wylde, William

Lancashire
Accrington: Pollard, Thomas
Bolton: Murray, Donald
Chorley: Warberton, James
Colne: Parker, Robert
Fleetwood: Robinson, William
Liverpool: Stevenson, William
Liverpool: Wellington
Manchester: Trafford, Edmund
Manchester: Wellington
Manchester: Wiseley, William
Mossley: Whitworth, John
Oldham: Radcliffe, Robert
Padiham: Parkinson, Henry
Rochdale: Whittam, Samuel
Southport: Munro, Charles
Tockholes: Robinson, Gilmour
Tonge: Smithies, James
Whalley: Whittle, Robert

Leicestershire
Leicester: Winterton, John
Melton Mowbray: Rider, John
Prestwold: Packe, George Hussey
Prestwold: Packe, Robert Christopher

Lincolnshire
Horncastle: Poxson, Peter
Lea: Vevers, Charles Nicholas
Leadenham: Reeve, John
Leasingham: Myddleton, Richard Wharton
Leasingham: Watson, J. Lewis
Syston: Rollings, John

London
Arranged under: Brompton, Kensal Green, Royal Military Chapel and Other London locations

Brompton Cemetery
Macarthur, Edward
Montague, John
Murchison, Robert Impey
Murray, Sir Archibald John
Paschal, George Frederick
Percivall, William
Ross, Sir Hew Dalrymple
Rouse, John
Sannerman, Henry Christian
Siborne, William
Smith, Thomas Charlton
Walton, William Lovelace
Wilkinson, William
Wilson, John Morillyon
Wylde, William

Kensal Green Cemetery
Macdonald, John
Macdonell, James
McGrigor, Sir James
McInnes, Alexander
Mackenzie, Alexander
Mackinnon, Daniel
Maclean, George
McLeod, Swinton
McMahon, Thomas
Magenis, Henry Arthur
Marshall, John
Matson, Edward
Maunsell, John Edward
Mence, Haffey
Methold, Edward
Mudie, Charles
Murray, Sir George
Muttlebury, George
Naylor, James Franklin
Norcliffe, Norcliffe
Northey, Lewis Augustus
Onslow, Phipps Vansittart
Ormsby, James
Osten, Baron William von
Owen, Humphrey
Paget, Charles
Palmer, Charles William
Pasley, Charles William
Paty, George William
Peacocke, Nathaniel Levett
Peacocke, Warren Marmaduke
Phillimore, Robert William
Portarlington, John Dawson Earl of
Power, William Greenshields
Pringle, William Henry
Pyper, Robert
Rainey, Henry

Rainey, John
Raitt, George Edward
Rayner, Thomas
Reeves, George James
Ridgway, Thomas Hughes
Rolt, John
Routh, Randolph Isham
Rowan, Charles
Rowan, James
Rutherford, William Henry
St Clair, Thomas Staunton
Saunderson, Hardress Robert
Sedley, John Somner
Shenley, Edward William Henry
Smith, George
Smith, Henry Nelson
Spearman, John
Standen, George Douglas
Stewart, Alexander
Stopford, William Henry
Storey, Edward Richardson
Stovin, Sir Frederick
Sweetman, J. Walter
Taylor, William Benjamin Sarfield
Thompson, Thomas Perronet
Thomson, Robert
Thornton, Henry
Thoyts, John
Troward, Thomas
Turnor, William
Upton, Arthur Percy
Vance, Richard Young
Verner, Edward Donovan
Vigoureux, Charles Albert
Walker, Sir George Townshend
Walpole, Hon. John
Walter, John
Warren, Lemuel
Warrington, Thornhill
Waters, John
Waters, Marcus Antonius
Watson, Henry
Webster, Henry Vassal
Wells, John Neave
West, Charles Augustus
Whymper, William
Wilson, Sir John
Wood, John Manley
Wood, William
Woodford, Sir Alexander
Wylde, John Newman
Yorke, Charles

Royal Military Chapel
McDonald, Hon. James
Macdonell, James
Mackinnon, Henry
Mahon, Luke
Maitland, Peregrine
Martin, Samuel Coote
Mercer, Douglas
Mercer, Robert
Miller, William
Milman, Francis Miles
Milnes, William Henry
Montgomery, Hugh Bernard
Morant, Edward
Murray, Sir George
Northey, Edward Richard
Otway, Hon. Henry
Pardoe, Edward
Parker, Harry
Payne, John
Pitt, William Henry
Pole, Edward Sacheverell Chandos
Prince, John
Ram, Stopford
Reeve, John
Rooke, John Charles
Ross, John
Saltoun, Alexander George Fraser Lord
Scott, William Henry
Shawe, Charles Augustus
Shiffner, John Bridger
Simpson, James
Sotheby, Ambrose William
Stables, Edward
Standen, George Douglas
Stanhope, Hon. James Hamilton
Stopford, Edward
Stopford, Hon. Sir Edward
Stothert, William
Stuart, Hon. William
Styles, Sir Thomas
Sullivan, Sir Henry
Sumner, Edward
Swann, William Henry
Thomas, Charles
Thompson, Charles William
Tighe, Daniel
Townshend, Horatio George Powys
Trelawny, Harry Brereton

Other London locations

Middlesex see London

Norfolk

Yarmouth: Weldon, William

Northumberland
Bamborough: Selby, William
Berwick-on-Tweed: Romer, William
Berwick-on-Tweed: Slater, Thomas
Berwick-on-Tweed: Thompson, George
Corbridge: Surtees, William
Eyemouth: Sinclair, James
Felton: Price, Thomas Parry
Newcastle: Maxwell, Archibald Montgomery
Newcastle: Ridley, Matthew
Newcastle: Skerrett, John Byne
Newcastle: Werge, John
Newcastle: Woods, William
Ponteland: Skerrett, John Byne
Tynemouth: Rollo, Alexander

Nottinghamshire
Calverton: Sherbrooke, Sir John Coape
Cossall: Shaw, John
Cossall: Waplington, Richard
Cossall: Wheatley, Thomas
Mansfield: Wildman, Thomas
Nottingham: Madin, George
Nottingham: Stretton, Sempronius
Perlethorpe: Pierrepont, Charles Alphonso
Rolleston: Tidy, John
Southwell Minster: Sherlock, Francis
Tuxford: Mahon, Luke
Tuxford: Shiffner, John Bridger
Tuxford: White, Charles Lawrence
Warsop: Stubbins, John

Oxfordshire
Henley-on-Thames: Parker, Henry Thomas
Oxford: Taylor, Charles Douglas
Stonesfield: Oliver, Joseph
Witney: Moulder, Patrick William
Witney: Moulder, Robert
Woodeaton: Weyland, Richard

Rutland
Belvoir: Manners, Lord Charles Somerset
Belvoir: Manners, Hon. Lord Robert William

Shropshire
Atcham: Sayer, Stephen
Berrington: Owen, John
Claverley: Steventon, Thomas
Coalbrookdale: Williams, David
Ludlow: Meyricke, John Chabbert
Prees: Shirley, John
Quatford: Woolriche, Stephen
Richards Castle: Salwey, Henry
Shifnal: Mealling, Thomas
Shrewsbury: Richards, Benjamin
Shrewsbury: Stone, Samuel
Shrewsbury: Windsor, Edward Charles
Whittingham: Roberts, Robert

Somerset
Bath: Mackay, Honeyman
Bath: Madox, Henry
Bath: Morewood, George Alexander
Bath: Nichols, William
Bath: Nooth, John Mervin
Bath: Palmer, Charles
Bath: Parry, William Parry Jones
Bath: Pearson, Thomas
Bath: Phillips, Roger Fryer
Bath: Power, Sir Manley
Bath: Pratt, Charles
Bath: Pratt, Percy
Bath: Pratt, Thomas Simson
Bath: Preston, George
Bath: Pringle, John Watson
Bath: Roles, Richard
Bath: Rotton, Guy
Bath: Rowan, William
Bath: Shawe, William Cunliffe
Bath: Spence, James
Bath: Stone, Bayntun
Bath: Stoyte, John
Bath: Tatton, Richard
Bath: Thorne, Peregrine Francis
Bath: Wallett, Charles
Bath: Wardlaw, John
Bath: Webb, Vere
Bath: Wemyss, Thomas James
Bath: Wheeler, William
Bath: Wilkie, Thomas Fletcher
Bath: Williams, Peter
Bath: Williams, Sir William
Bath: Williams, William Freke
Bath: Wilson, Sir James
Brislington: Sherer, Moyle
Bristol: Oliver, Nathaniel Wilmot
Bristol: Rowland, John
Bristol: Somerset, Lord John Thomas H.
Bristol: Street, Alfred
Curry Mallet: Wimbridge, John

Drayton: Trevilian, Maurice Cely
Horfield: Wilkie, Peter
Kilmersdon: Trevilian, Maurice Cely
Norton Fitzwarren: Slade, John
Portishead: Shipton, Henry Noble
Ruishton: Napier, Hon. Charles
Sedgemoor: Slade, John Henry
Stogursey: Palmer, Thomas
Swainswick: Petrie, Alexander
Taunton: Mills, John
Wellington: Wellington
Weston-Super-Mare: Palmer, Thomas

Staffordshire
Burntwood: Robinson, James
Eccleshall: Smith, John
Harborne: Phipps, Robert
Lapley: Swinfen, Francis
Leek: Malkin, William
Lichfield: Uxbridge, Henry William, Earl of
Norbury: Turner, William
Stafford: Pemberton, George Keating
West Bromwich: Paget, Elijah
Wolverhampton: Morrison, William

Suffolk
Aldringham: Walker, Charles
Bury St Edmunds: Middleditch, William M.
Campsea Ash: Sheppard, Frederic
Horringer: Simpson, James
Ipswich: Turner, Michael
Long Melford: Parker, Harry
Long Melford: Parker, John Boteler
Marlesford: Shuldham, Lemuel
Melton: Schreiber, James Alfred
Rickinghall Inferior: Searle, John
Rickinghall Inferior: Spear, James
Wangford: Rous, John Edward Cornwallis
Rushmere: Schreiber, William Frederick
Thelnetham: Smith, John

Surrey
Camberley: Thackeray, Frederick Rennell
Carshalton: Simmons, James
Egham: Ompteda, Ferdinand von
Egham: Storer, Richard
Egham: Wyatt, William Edgell Richard
Epsom: Northey, Edward Richard
Esher: Swann, William Henry
Great Bookham: Somerset, Fitzroy, J. H.
Kingston upon Thames: Sheppard, Edmund
Leatherhead: Manningham, Coote
Mortlake: Shadwell, John
Petersham: Moore, William George
South Holmwood: Wainwright, Henry M.
Thames Ditton: Sullivan, Sir Henry
Tongham: Maitland, Peregrine

Sussex
Brighton: Partridge, John
Brighton: Pratt, Charles
Brighton: Singleton, John
Brighton: Wellington
Broadwater: Smith, Charles Felix
Chichester: Madden, Edward Marcell
Chichester: Madden, William Sterling
Chichester: March, Charles Lennox (Earl)
Chichester: Nicolls, Jasper
Chichester: Ommaney, Cornthwaite
Chichester: Ridewood, Henry
Coolhurst: Peters, John
Hartfield: Maitland, Frederick
Hastings: Newland, Robert
Hove: Robinson, Sir Fredrick Philipse
Hove: Stevenson, George
Hove: Smith, James Webber
Petworth: Wyndham, Hon. George
Petworth: Wyndham, Hon. Henry
Stopham: Smyth, George Bartellot
West Tarring: Platt, George Edmund
Worthing: Sandham, Charles Freeman
Worthing: Wallace, Robert Clarke

Warwickshire
Edgehill: Miller, Fiennes Sanderson
Leamington Spa: Macdonald, Alexander
Leamington Spa: Wallington, John Clement
Meriden: Whichcote, George
Nuneaton: Tomkinson, William
Radway: Miller, Fiennes Sanderson
Solihull: Swinburne, Joseph

Wiltshire
Bradford-on-Avon: Shrapnel, Henry Scrope
Chippenham: Singer, Richard Oriel
Cholderton: Paxton, Archibald Frederic
Devizes: Tayler, Samuel
Lacock: Montagu, Frederick Augustus C.
Marlborough: Stretton, Severus W. L.
North Wraxall: Singer, Richard Oriel
Trowbridge: Waldron, John
Westbury: Phipps, Paul

Worcestershire
Kidderminster: Taylor, John
Malvern: Parker, Thomas
Tenbury: Squires, John
Worcester: Ricketts, Joseph

Yorkshire
Acomb: Stansfield, James
Ainderby Steeple: Wallace, James Maxwell
Aysgarth: Wray, Thomas Fawcett
Beverley: Machell, John Thomas
Beverley: Machell, Lancelot
Beverley: Marten, Thomas
Bridlington: Pitts, Thomas James H.
Carlton: Wood, Charles
Cowling: Wainman, William
Doncaster: Rawson, William
Halifax: Milton, Daniel
Halifax: Nutter, Robert
Halifax: Widdop, John
Huddersfield: Smith, Benjamin
Hull: Newmarch, William
Hull: Ogle, James Gordon
Hull: Shedden, John
Kirkheaton: Oldham, Eli
Kirkheaton: Senior, William
Kirkheaton: Sheard, Timothy
Kirkburton: Smith, Benjamin
Kirkleatham: Macbean, Forbes
Leeds: McCreagh, Michael
Leeds: Walker, Samuel
Leeds: Wellington
Kirkleatham: Macbean, Forbes
Masham: Morton, Harcourt
Middleham: Sewell, William
Pontefract: Sunderland, Henry
Richmond: Watson, William
Ripon: Maister, John
Ripon: Smith, William Slayter
Saddleworth: Winterbottom, John
Sheffield: Moreton, William
Sheffield: Raynor, George
Sheffield: Sands, Thomas
Sheffield: Wynn, Edward
Sneaton: Rudyerd, Samuel
Whalley: Whittle, Robert
York: McCabe, John
York: McCarthy, Owen
York: McPherson, Philip
York: Marsland, Henry
York: Mercer, Charles Wilkinson
York: Mills, John
York: Minskiull, John
York: Moore, Sir John
York: Nicholson, Thomas
York: Percy, Hugh
York: Percy, John Samuel
York: Roche, Robert
York: Smith, Michael
York: Sorrell, William
York: Sparks, Frederick
York: Stainforth, John
York: Stephens, Maurice
York: Stothers, James
York: Taylor, John D.
York: Trevevan, Richard
York: Utting, Samuel
York: Vickers, Gentle
York: Warre, William
York: Webster, Thomas
York: Wells, Rees
York: Westropp, Ralph
York: White, William Edward
York: Wilson, Richard

SCOTLAND

Aberdeenshire
Aberdeen: McGrigor, Sir James
Banchory: Ramsay, Thomas
Belhelvie: Turner, Sir George
Cluny: Saltoun, Alexander George F.
Dunbennan: Symon, Alexander
Hatton of Fintray: Milne, Alexander
Huntly: March, Charles Lennox, Earl of
Marnoch: Murray, William
Monymusk: Watt, George
Old Meldrum: Sherris, Alexander
Stonehaven: Moncur, William
Torphins: Winchester, Robert

Angus
Brechin: Will, Andrew
Dundee: Mancor, Andrew
Dundee: Weir, James
Forfar: Nash, James
Montrose: Macneill, Archibald

Argyllshire
Kinlochlaigh: Stewart, Robert
Tarbet: Pile, William

Ayrshire
Ayr: Rudd, John
Kirkmichael: Shaw, James
Largs: McLean, Donald
Stair: Miller, William
Stewarton: Patrick, William

Berwickshire
Chirnside: Smith, William
Eccles: Nisbet, Robert
Lauder: Murray, James
Westruther: Spottiswoode, George

Buteshire
Rothesay: Mackay, John
Rothesay: Reed, John

Caithness
Dingwall: Murchison, Roderick Impey
Dunn: Munro, John
Halkirk: Williamson, Donald
Halkirk: Williamson, James
Reay: Mackay, Joseph
Reay: Mackay, Robert Faro[r]

Dumbartonshire
Arrochar: Macfarlane, Andrew Angus
Dumbarton: McKenzie, Roderick

Dumfriesshire and Galloway
Borgue: Shaw, Alexander Mackenzie
Canonbie: Mein, Nicol Alexander
Canonbie: Mein, William
Canonbie: Smith, Charles Maitland
Dumfries: Maxwell, Hamilton
Dumfries: Nicholson, William
Dumfries: Riddick, John
Dumfries: Rutherford, James
Gatehouse of Fleet: McWhan, Samuel
Glencairn: Smith, William
Kirkmichael: Smail, George
Langholm: Scott, James
Minnigaff: Stewart, Hon. Sir William
Mochrum: McMillan, William
Penpont: Ross, John
Stranraer: Taylor, John
Stranraer: Taylor, Thomas
Whithorn: Wallace, John

Edinburgh see Midlothian

Fife
Kirkcaldy: Oswald, Sir John

Galloway see Dumfriesshire and Galloway

Invernesshire
Cawdor: Reid, Thomas
Cille Choirill: Macdonald, Ronald
Inverness: Macarthur, Charles
Inverness: Mackay, Joseph
Inverness: Mackay, William
Inverness: McKenzie, Donald
Kilmallie: Stewart, Alexander
Kilmonivaig: Mitchell, James
Kilmonivaig: Ross, Ewan Cameron
Kinrara: Macara, Robert
Laggan: Macpherson, Alexander Laggan
Laggan: Macpherson, Donald
Laggan: Towers, Frederick
Rothiemurchus: Macbean, Alexander

Kincardineshire
Caterline: Mercer, James
St Cyrus: Muter, Joseph

Lanarkshire
Bothwell: Moore, Sir John
Carmunnock: Stirling, William
Cumbernauld: Orr, John
Glasgow: Macintosh, Alexander Fisher
Glasgow: McNair, James
Glasgow: Malcolm, John
Glasgow: Middleton, William
Glasgow: Millar, John
Glasgow: Miller, William
Glasgow: Moffat, William
Glasgow: Moore, Francis
Glasgow: Moore, Sir John
Glasgow: Pattison, Alexander Hope
Glasgow: Reston, James
Glasgow: Ronald, William
Glasgow: Wellington
Glasgow: Wishart, Alexander
Lanark: Miller, James

Midlothian
Edinburgh: Macdermid, John
Edinburgh: Macdonald, A.
Edinburgh: Macdonald, Donald
Edinburgh: Macgregor, Malcolm

Edinburgh: Maclagan, David
Edinburgh: Maclaine, Archibald
Edinburgh: Maclaine, Hector
Edinburgh: Maclaine, John
Edinburgh: McNeill, Donald
Edinburgh: Macnish, William
Edinburgh: McPherson, Daniel
Edinburgh: Macpherson, Evan
Edinburgh: Maxwell, Robert
Edinburgh: Maxwell, William
Edinburgh: Middleton, John
Edinburgh: Mitchell, John
Edinburgh: Munro, David
Edinburgh: Orr, John
Edinburgh: Pagan, Samuel Alexander
Edinburgh: Parkinson, John
Edinburgh: Paterson, James
Edinburgh: Peattie, Paul
Edinburgh: Ramadge, Benjamin
Edinburgh: Reed, John
Edinburgh: Riddell, Henry James
Edinburgh: Ross, James Kerr
Edinburgh: Ross, Robert
Edinburgh: Schoedde, James Holmes
Edinburgh: Shearman, John
Edinburgh: Simpson, Edward
Edinburgh: Skelton, Thomas Lowrey
Edinburgh: Skene, Alexander
Edinburgh: Souter, David
Edinburgh: Stirling, George
Edinburgh: Stirling, Sir Gilbert
Edinburgh: Stoddart, Thomas
Edinburgh: Stupart, Francis
Edinburgh: Swinburne, Thomas Robert
Edinburgh: Tew, William
Edinburgh: Victor, James Conway
Edinburgh: Wemyss, William
Edinburgh: Whitting, William
Edinburgh: Williams, John
Edinburgh: Winchester, Robert
Edinburgh: Winterscale, John
Edinburgh: Young James
Inveresk: Macdonald, Donald
Inveresk: McNiven, Thomas W. Ogilvy
Inveresk: Patterson, James
Inveresk: Ramsay, William Norman
Inveresk: Ross, John
Inveresk: Skeill, David
Inveresk: Stirling, James (Lt Colonel)
Inveresk: Stirling, James (Captain)
Inveresk: Vernor, Robert
Inveresk: Wedderburn, Alexander
Liberton: Thornton, John
Linlithgow: Rae Thomas
Portobello: McGregor, Hugh
Restalrig: Scott, Samuel

Morayshire
Bellie: MacLeod, Alexander
Bellie: MacLeod, William
Bellie: Marshall, George
Bellie: Marshall, John
Bellie: Marshall, William
Bellie: Tod, George
Bellie: Tod, Robert
Bellie: Tod, William
Elgin: Rutledge, John

Perthshire
Auchtergaven: Rider, Richard
Blairgowrie: Menzies, William
Comrie: Macnab, John
Kettins: Spalding, John
Killin: McNab, Allan
Kilmadock: Murdoch, James Campbell
Kinloch Rannoch: McDonald, John
Kirkton of Collace: Stewart, James
Longforgan: Paterson, George
Methven: McGlashan, John
Murthly Castle: Stewart, William Drummond
Perth: Peebles, Adam
Perth: Riach, John
Perth: Riach, William Alexander
Perth: Ross, John
Perth: Sutherland, William
Trinity Gask: Macowen, James

Renfrewshire
Erskine: Stuart, Hon. William
Erskine: Walker, James
Greenock: Stewart, George
Ronachan: Stewart, George

Ross and Cromarty
Avoch: Munro, William (78 Ft)
Avoch: Munro, William (R.A.)

Roxburghshire
Crailing: Wellington
Jedburgh: Murray, John
Jedburgh: Ormiston, John A.
Linton: Walker, James Perriman

Roxburgh: Robertson, Andrew

Selkirkshire
Ashkirk and Lindean: Scott, Thomas

Skye
Cill Chriosd: McDonald, John

Stirlingshire
Stirling: Mackenzie, Hugh

Sutherland
Dornoch: Murray, James

WALES
Abergavenny: Steele, Samuel
Aberystwyth: Thomas, David
Abergwili: Phillips, Grismond
Aberhafesp: Proctor, Henry Adolphus
Beaumaris: Turton, Richard
Beaumaris: Turton William
Brecon: Price, Hugh
Brecon: Wellington
Cardiff: Picton, Sir Thomas
Cardiff: Richards, John
Cardiff: Thomas, Evan
Carmarthen: Picton, Sir Thomas
Carmarthen: Samuel, John
Flint: Wynn, Henry
Hope: Wrench, William Handfield
Llanblethian: Nicholl, Edward
Llanellen: Walbeoffe, Thomas
Llanfor: Williams, John
Llanhennock: Mackworth, Digby
Llansantffraid-ym-Mechain: Morris, Thomas
Llanspyddid: Pearce, William
Llanwern: Rous, Thomas Bates
Lower Machen: Milman, Francis Miles
Mathern: Williams, Sir Edmund Keynton
Michaelston Le Pit: Rous, Thomas Bates
Newport: Morgan, David
Penarth: Minchin, John Paul
Pennard: Penrice, Thomas
Plas Newydd: Uxbridge, Henry W., Earl of
Presteigne: Parsons, Edward
Presteigne: Parsons, Henry
Presteigne: Parsons, Lucius
Rudbaxton: Phelps, Samuel
Rudbaxton: Picton, Sir Thomas
St Andrew Major: Williams, John
St Asaph: Williams, John
Swansea: Wasdell, John
Tenby: Ramus, Charles Louis
Tenby: Wedgwood, Thomas
Tredegar: Wellington
Trefeglwys: Manuel, John
Trefeglwys: Morgan, Reese
Welshpool: Watson, William Henry
Wtexham: McNulty, John

NORTHERN IRELAND
Belfast: Stewart, Hon. Charles William V.
Carrickfergus: Millar, John
Derrygonnelly: Ovens, John
Donaghmore: McCurdy, Thomas
Dromore: Waddell, James George
Gartree: Pakenham, Hercules Robert
Londonderry: McClintock, James
Londonderry: Sidley, George
Loughgall: Verner, William
Newtownabbey: Nunn, Loftus
Newtownards: Hon. Stewart, Charles W. V.
Newry: Reith, Alexander
Newry: Seton, George
Rostrevor: Ross, Robert

IRELAND REPUBLIC OF
Adamstown: Whitney, John
Ardolm: Toole, William
Adrahan: Taylor, John
Athlone: McCulloch, William
Athlone: O'Leary, John
Athlone: Stretton, Sempronius
Ballincollig: Willett, George
Ballingarry: Shelton, John Willington
Ballingarry: Shelton, Jonathon
Ballycarney: Squire, William
Ballycommon: Smith, George
Ballyshannon Town: Montgomery, Knox
Ballyshannon Town: O'Neill, Charles
Bandon: Sweeny, Francis Bernard
Bandon: Sweeny, James Fielding
Buncara: O'Donnell, William
Bunclody: Warren, Francis
Castlebar: O'Malley, George
Castlemanger: Wrixon, Nicholas
Castletownshend: Townsend, John
Clondegad: Ross-Lewin, Henry
Clontarf: O'Dell, Henry Edward
Cobh: Verling, James
Cork: Norcott, Amos Godsil Robert
Cork: Travers, Robert

Crinken: Ribton, John Sheppey
Dublin: McGowan, William
Dublin: Meighan, Michael William
Dublin: Nicholson, Benjamin Walker
Dublin: Nicholson, Huntly
Dublin: O'Hara, Patterson
Dublin: O'Hara, Robert
Dublin: O'Neill, William
Dublin: Parke, Charles
Dublin: Patrickson, Christopher Clarges
Dublin: Peacocke, Thomas Goodricke
Dublin: Peacocke, William
Dublin: Pelly, Raymond
Dublin: Prendergast, Charles O'Neil
Dublin: Quill, Henry
Dublin: Richardson, John
Dublin: Sannerman, Henry Christian
Dublin: Scovell, Henry
Dublin: Seton, William Carden
Dublin: Shekleton, Robert
Dublin: Shelton, John
Dublin: Standish, Henry
Dublin: Talbot, William
Dublin: Townsend, John
Dublin: Vandeleur, Sir John Ormsby
Dublin: Ward, Adam
Dublin: Wellington
Dublin: Wells, Samuel
Dublin: Westby, Edward
Dublin: Westby, George William
Eglish: Mitchell, Andrew
Galway: O'Hara, Robert
Galway: Paterson, Leeson
Grange, Tipperary: Wellington
Kilkenny: Pack, Sir Denis
Kilkenny: Strangways, William
Killucan: Pakenham, Edward Michael
Kinsale: Reynell, Thomas
Kinsale: Scott, Henry Randolph
Knockainey: O'Grady, John Thomas
Knockainey: O'Grady, Standish
Limerick: Maunsell, Frederick
Limerick: Maunsell, George
Lismore: O'Callaghan, Sir Robert William
Newcastle: Morris, Samuel
New Ross: Napper, Alexander
Piercestown: O'Toole, Bryan
Powerscourt: Sandys, Thomas Edwin
Preban: Newton, Hibbert
Rosscahill: Poppleton, Thomas William
Ross Carberry: Starkey, Walter W.
Salruck: Thomson, Alexander
Stratford Co. Wicklow: Saunders, John S.
Taghmon: Miller, Arthur
Thomastown: Nicolls, William Dann
Tinahely: Radcliff, Stephen
Tinahely: Symes, Joseph
Tramore: McGregor, James
Tramore: Ross, Andrew Clark
Tramore: Scott, Robert
Tramore: Veall, William
Trim: Wellington
Virginia: Sankey, Samuel
Whitegate: O'Connor, Ogle Nesbit

OVERSEAS MEMORIALS

AUSTRALIA
Adelaide: Playford, Thomas
Busselton: Molloy, John
Campbell Town: Thompson, Claudius
Campbell's Hill: Wilkinson, John
Cobbity: Wild, John
East Gresford: Rodwell, Thomas
Greendale: Shadforth, Thomas
Hobart: Millar, Henry
Hobart: Serjeantson, William
Ipswich: North, William
Kelso: Morisset, James Thomas
Liverpool: Moore, Samuel
Liverpool: Phelps, James Henry
Liverpool: White, Andrew Douglas
Melbourne: Nickle, Robert
Melbourne: Whatmough, Joseph
Morisset: Morisset, James Thomas
Moss Vale: Wood, William
Newcastle: Radford, Henry Wyatt
Newcastle: Russell, William
Parramatta: McDonald, George
Parramatta: Macarthur, Edward
Raymond Terrace: Snodgrass, Kenneth
Ross: Maher, Philip
Rostella: Neilley, William
Singleton: White, Andrew
Sutton Forest: Shepherd, Lynn
Sydney: Mackay, George
Sydney: Mitchell, James
Sydney: Mitchell, Thomas Livingstone
Sydney: Ovens, John
Sydney: Willett, George
York: Meares, Richard Goldsmith

BELGIUM

Evere
Maclaine, John
Miller, William
Milnes, William Henry
Perceval, William
Spearman, Charles
Stables, Edward
Stothert, William

Waterloo
Gordon, Sir Alexander
Gunning, John
Mercer, Alexander Cavalié
Orange, Prince W.
Picton, Sir Thomas
Stables, Edward
Uxbridge, Henry William, Earl of

Waterloo
St Joseph's Church
McDonald, Edward
Macfarlane, John
McLasher, James
MacNab, Alexander
Macpherson, Duncan
Manners, Robert
Marsh, William
Mascheck, C.
Matthewson, Robert
Merlen, J. B. van
Miller, William
Milnes, William Henry
Murphy, Daniel
Murphy, Philip
Myers, Arthur
Nelson, Robert
Nichols, Samuel
Norbert, J. C.
Nugent, John
O'Neill, John E.
Pallandt, Baron W. A. van
Pardoe, Edward
Patot, Tissot van
Percy, Francis
Powling, John
Prendergast, Edward
Quick, Francis
Rainsford, Michael
Ramsay, William Norman
Robe, William L.
Robertson, Alexander
Roberti
Sandys, Edwin W. T.
Scanlon, Thomas
Sherwood, Isaac
Simpson, Ensign
Sinclair, John
Sivell, James
Slade, Richard
Smith, Hugh
Spearman, Charles
Stables, Edward
Stammel, F. K.
Stevenart, E. J.
Stewart, William
Stothert, William
Stratenus, A.
Thielen, A. van
Thomas, Charles
Toole, William
Trodt, F. van
Verhellow, Willem
Von Schulzen, Carl D.
Welsh, John
Werner, G. J.
Wiggins, James
Wijnbergen, W. L. van
Williamson, Joseph
Wilmot, James
Wolf, W.
Wolff, Willem
Wynbergen, Willem van
Wynoldy, A.

KGL memorial – La Haye Sainte
Marenholz, Wilhelm von
Marschalck, Heinrich von
Meyer, Friedrich Ludwig
Ompteda, Christian von
Peters, Friedrich
Robertson, Friederich von
Saffe, August von
Schaumann, Friedrich M. W
Schröder, Johann C. von
Schuck, Johann Ludwig
Schulzen, Cart Detlef von
Suchow, Arthur
Thilee, Georg (or Tilee)
Voigt, August Wilhelm von
Westernhagen, Thilo von

Jeffrey Salvin 4th Foot

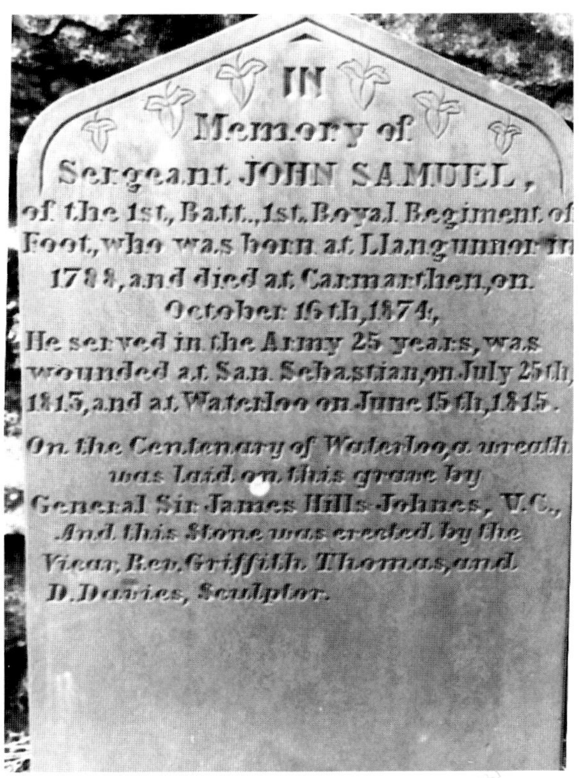

John Samuel 1st Foot

Thomas Slater 6th Dragoons

John B. Skerrett 47th Foot

William Stewart 95th Foot

Frederic Sheppard 4th Foot

George Simmons 95th Foot

David Slow Royal Horse Guards

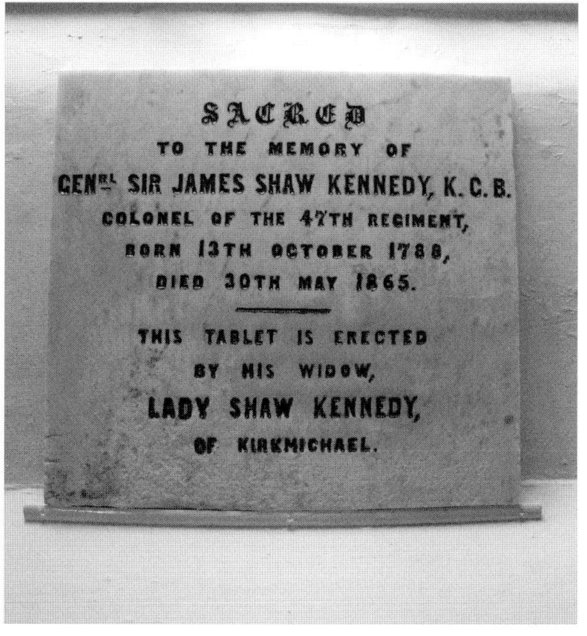

James Shaw 43rd Foot

Sir George Scovell Staff Corps of Cavalry

Thomas Shadforth 57th Foot

Alexander M. Shaw Royal York Rangers

Lemuel Shuldham 2nd Dragoons

John Siddal Royal Horse Guards

Lord Robert Somerset 4th Dragoons

John W. Smith Royal Artillery

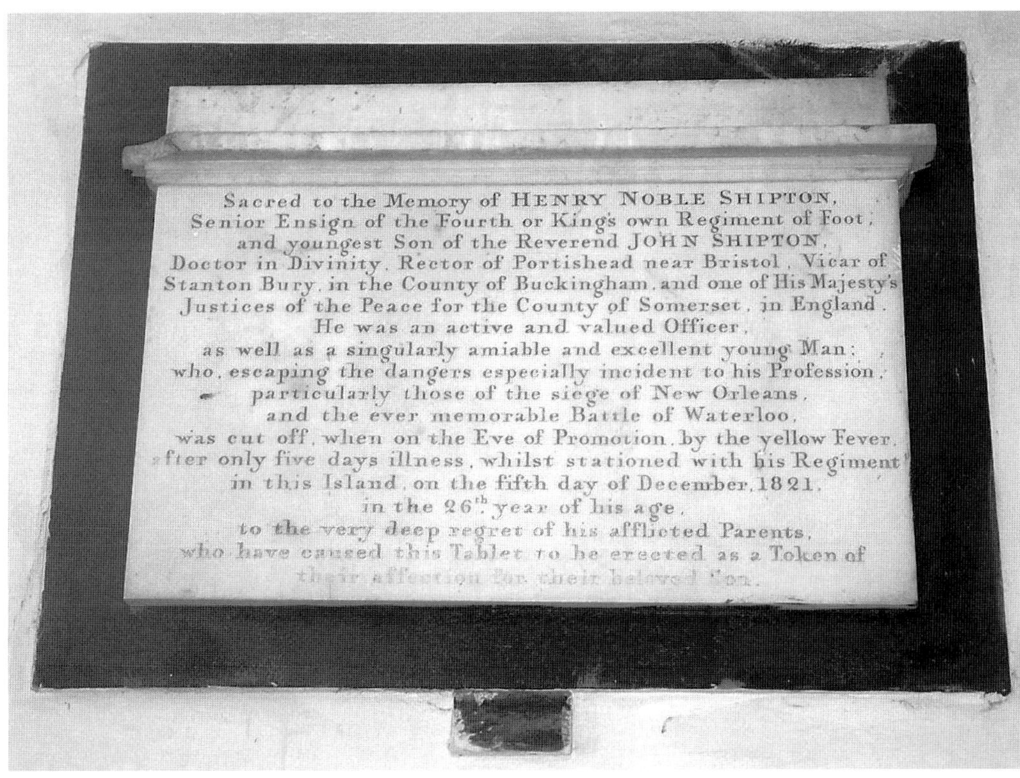

Henry N. Shipton 4th Foot

Sir Harry Smith 95th Foot

James Spence 31st Foot

George B. Smyth Royal Artillery

Joshua Smith 40th Foot

James Stansfield 2nd Life Guards

Sir Gilbert Stirling Coldstream Guards

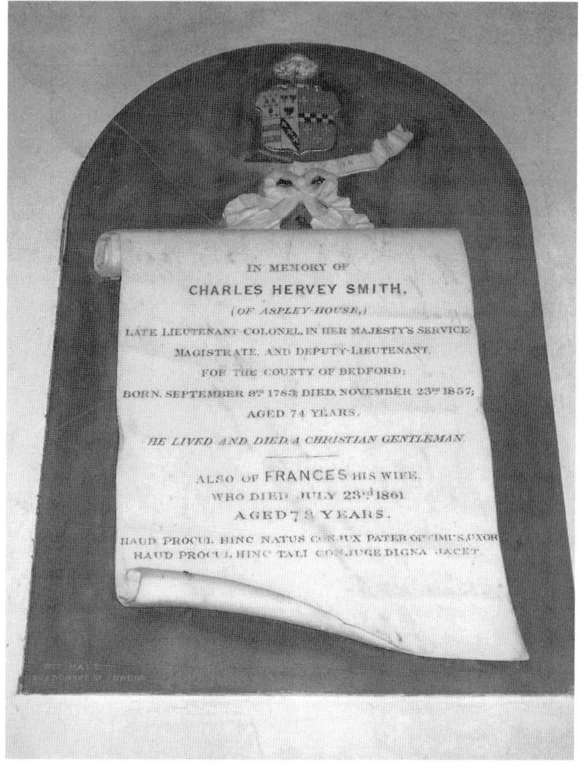

Charles H. Smith 36th Foot

James F. Sweeny 62nd Foot

Henry Stisted 1st Dragoons

James Stirling 42nd Foot

William Surtees 95th Foot

Joseph Swinburne 83rd Foot

Henry Tarleton 60th Foot

Alexander Thomson 74th Foot

John Thoreau 40th Foot

John Thornton 94th Foot

Charles Tryon 88th Foot

Robert Travers 10th Foot

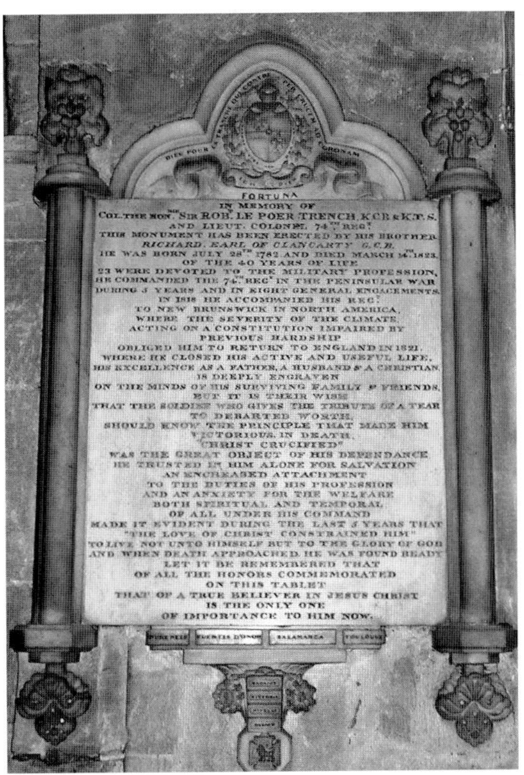

Sir Robert P. Trench 74th Foot

Maurice C. Trevilian 1st Dragoons

Walter Vane 1st Foot Guards

James C. Victor Royal Engineers

James G. Waddell 39th Foot

William Watson Coldstream Guards

Sir Henry Warde 68th Foot

William H. Watson 1st Dragoons

Samuel Walker 3rd Foot Guards

George White 3rd Dragoon Guards

John Wild 48th Foot

Peter J Willatts Bourbon Regiment

George B. Willis Royal Artillery

Edmund K. Williams 81st Foot

James Willington 3rd Foot

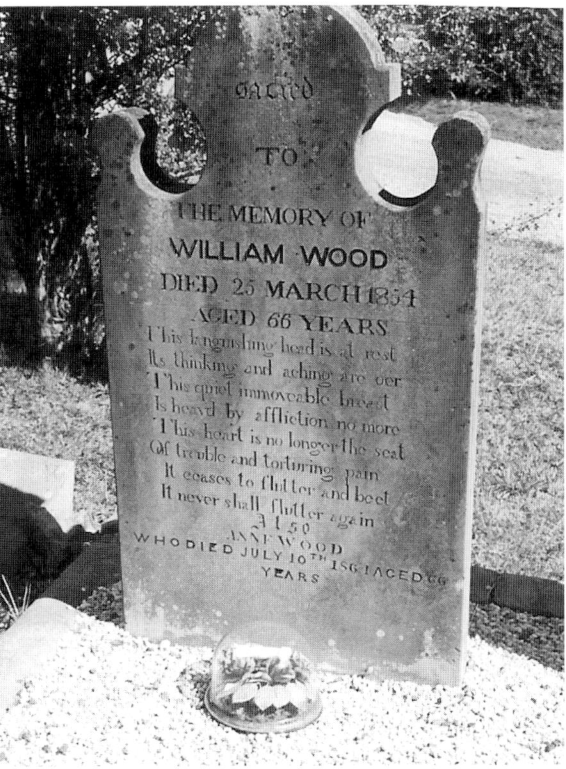

William Wood 95th Foot

Uriah Woodhouse Coldstream Guards

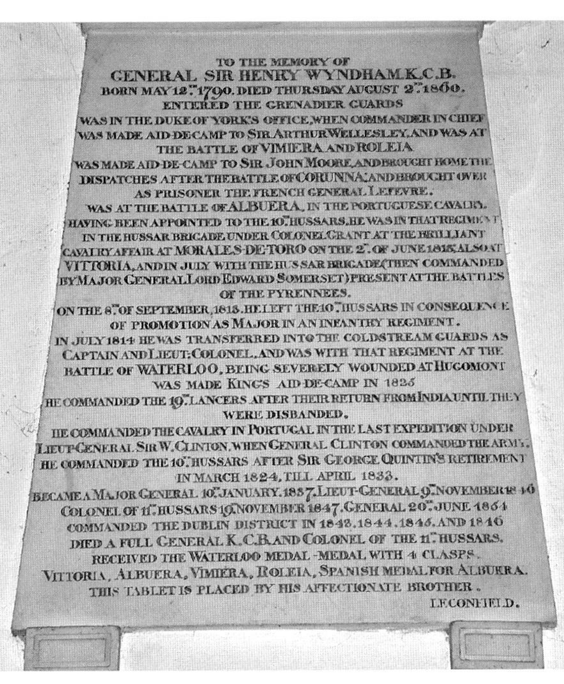

Henry Wyndham Coldstream Guards

John Youngs 23rd Foot

William Yuill 1st Foot Guards

Wiegmann, Heinrich
Wurmb, Ernst C. C. von

CANADA
Bowmanville: Pethick, Edward
Bridgetown: Poyntz, James
Fort Erie: Pillichody, Alexis
Fort Erie: Rooth, Benjamin
Halifax: Ross, Robert
Halifax: Snodgrass, John James
Hudson: Mathison, John Augustus
Kingston: Tidy, Francis Skelly
Niagara: Melville, Robert
Niagara: Ottley, Matthew
Niagara: Patteson, Robert Dossie
Niagara: Shaw, James Peter
Niagara: Torrens, S. B.
Quebec: Monckton, Carleton Thomas
St John's: Robe, Alexander Watt
Warwick (Ontario): Thompson, Alexander

CEYLON (SRI LANKA)
Galle Face, Colombo: Owen, Richard
Galle Face, Colombo: Russell, Alexander
Galle Face, Colombo: Smith, James
Galle Face, Colombo: Thompson, Robert
Galle Face, Colombo: Willerman, William
Kandy: McGlashan, James Edwin

CHINA
Chusan: Oglander, Henry

COLUMBIA
Paipa: Rooke, James

FRANCE
Biarritz
McBarnett, William
McCrimmon, Donald
McDermott, Henry
McDonald, Allan
McDonnell, Duncan
Macintyre, David
Mackenzie, Maxwell
McPherson, Duncan
McPherson, John
Mahon, Luke
Martin, Samuel Coote
Metcalfe, John
Meyer, Johann
Millius, Charles
Mitchell, Thomas
Moore, George A.
Moriarty, James
Müller, Henrich
Murchison, Robert P.
Murray, James
Myers, John
Myles, John
Parker, Edward
Parkinson, John
Patullo, William
Pitt, William Henry
Pitts, Thomas James Hebblethwayte
Pode, John Spurrell
Power, Robert George
Purvis, Patrick
Pyne, Robert
Reynolds, Barnard
Rooke, John Charles
St Aurin, J. D. E.
Sankey, Andrew
Schartroth, J. Carl
Scott, Henry
Seton, James
Shawe, Charles Fielding
Shiffner, John Bridger
Stapylton, Henry
Stephens, Maurice
Stewart, George
Stewart, James
Stopford, Roger
Sturgeon, Henry
Sullivan, Sir Henry
Swanson, John
Sympher, Frederick
Taylor, John D.
Tew, William
Thompson, Charles William
Topp, Richard
Vachell, Frederick
Vane, Walter
Von Drechsell, Frederick
Von Schulzen, Carl Detlef
Watson, Henry Robert
Watson, James
White, Charles Lawrence
Yuill, William

Other French Locations
Bidart: Martin, Samuel Coote
Bidart: Thompson, Charles William

Bidart: Watson, Henry Robert
Laon: Wolf, Pierre Frederic
St Etienne: Mahon, Luke
St Etienne: Pitt, William Henry
St Etienne: Shiffner, John Bridger
St Etienne: Sullivan, Sir Henry
St Etienne: Vachell, Frederick
St Etienne: Vane, Walter
St Etienne: White, Charles Lawrence
St Etienne: Yuill, William
Tours: Peacocke, Thomas
Verdun: Reynolds, James
Vorges: Wolf, Pierre Frederic

GIBRALTAR
Alameda Gardens: Wellington
King's Chapel: Ragland, Thomas Gajetan
King's Chapel: Walsh, Pearson Lyons
Sandpits Cemetery: McGilliwie, James
Sandpits Cemetery: Porteous, Walter
Sandpits Cemetery: Reed, William
Sandpits Cemetery: Shearman, Edward
Trafalgar Cemetery: Northern, Lewis
Trafalgar Cemetery: Ragland, Thomas Gajetan
Trafalgar Cemetery: Rudyerd, Charles William
Trafalgar Cemetery: Taylor, John Butt
Trafalgar Cemetery: Tribe, Richard

GREECE
Corfu: Stainton, Joseph

HOLLAND
Baarn: Orange, HRH Prince William

INDIA
Agra: Urquhart, Donald
Ambala: Ryan, Thomas
Ambala: St John, Charles
Ambala: Smith, James
Ambala: Urmston, Lambert Brabazon
Bangalore: Macgregor, Duncan
Bellary: Moss, John Irving
Bhowanipore: Mountgarrett, William
Bhowanipore: Turner, William
Bombay: Mackrell, Thomas
Bombay: Moorhouse, Joseph William
Bombay: Powell, Thomas
Bombay: Ridesdale, George
Bombay: Steele, Henry
Bombay: Storey, John
Bombay: Taylor, Thomas John
Bombay: Thain, William
Bombay: Wellington
Calcutta: Macleod, Donald
Calcutta: O'Reilley, John
Calcutta: Perry, John Philip
Calcutta: Twinberrow, Ralph John
Calcutta: Twining, William
Cawnpore: Murray, George Home
Cawnpore: O'Malley, James
Cawnpore: Shannon, Alexander
Dinapore: Murray, John
Goomrapoondy: Rumley, John
Madras: Marshall, John
Madras: Mill, Charles
Madras: Morphett, Mars
Madras: Read, William
Madras: Roe, John
Madras: Roe, Samuel Crozier
Madras: Staveley, William
Madras: Taylor, James
Madras: Thompson, William
Madras: Wakefield, Joseph
Madras: Whittingham, Samuel F.
Mirzapur: Macdonald, Archibald
Octacumund: Staveley, William
Peshawar: MacLeod, Alexander
Ranipet: McElroy, Peter
Secunderabad: Mallock, John McGrigor
Secunderabad: Tresidder, Samuel
Tangacherry: Moulson, Edward
Trichinopoly: Mandilhon, Philip

ITALY
Bagni di Lucca: Philips, Frederick Charles
Bagni di Lucca: Stisted, Henry
Florence: Porteus, Edward
Florence: Sewell, William Henry
Florence: Smith, Robert George S.
Florence: Stibbert, Thomas
Florence: Williams, John
Leghorn: Stopford, James
Naples: Mercer, Douglas

MALTA
Floriana: Mein, John Alexander
Valletta: Ponsonby, Frederick Cavendish

MAURITIUS
Port Louis: Staveley, William

NEW ZEALAND

Thames: Roycroft, Robert
Wellington: O'Connell, Richard

PERU
Lima: Miller, William

PORTUGAL
Busaco: Wellington
Elvas: Macbean, William
Elvas: McCreagh, Michael
Elvas: McDonald, Donald
Elvas: Oliver, James Ward
Elvas: Stubbs, Thomas William
Elvas: Sutton, Sir Charles
Elvas: Watson, Henry
Elvas: White, Daniel
Elvas: Wyndham, Hon. Henry
Lisbon: Macglashan, Neil
Lisbon: Moore, Edward
Lisbon: Offeney, William
Lisbon: Rogers, Thomas
Lisbon: Rose, Hugh Hay
Lisbon: Thorn, Robert Brandon
Lisbon: Walsh, Robert
Lisbon: Wynch, James

RUSSIA
Ekaterinburg: Murchison, Roderick Impey

SAINT HELENA
Jamestown: Thoreau, John

SPAIN
Coria: Stewart, Charles
Corunna: McKenzie, John
Corunna: Moore, Sir John
Freneida: Wellington
Madrid: Wheatley, William
Salamanca: Wellington
San Sebastian: Machell, Lancelot
San Sebastian: Rhodes, Charles Steech
Truxillo: Squire, John
Vittoria: Weir, John Laing

SWITZERLAND
Geneva: Napier, George Thomas

UKRAINE
Cathcart's Hill: Strangways, Thomas Fox

UNITED STATES OF AMERICA
Plattsburgh: Purchase, John
Plattsburgh: Willington, James

WEST INDIES
Barbados: Massie, Thomas
Barbados: Norman, John Ballentine
Barbados: Piper, John
Barbados: Popham, Samuel Taylor
Barbados: Richards, Thomas
Barbados: Shipton, Henry Noble
Barbados: Spencer, James
Barbados: Tyler, John
Barbados: Williams, Henry
Barbados: Winterbottom, John
Bermuda: Mercer, Cavalie Shorthose
British Guiana: Nooth, John Mervin
British Guiana: Smyth, James Carmichael
Grenada: Mair, John Hastings
Jamaica: Marshall, George
Jamaica: Montgomery, Henry
Jamaica: Montgomery, John
Jamaica: Osborn, Kean
Jamaica: Rowe, Benjamin
Jamaica: Smith, Andrew
Jamaica: Stewart, William
Jamaica: Tapp, Hammond Astley
Jamaica: Taylor, Philip C.
Jamaica: Vale, Thomas
Nassau: Pattison, Alexander Hope
Tobago: Robinson, Frederick Philipse

Regimental Index M – Z

WELLINGTON, ARTHUR, DUKE OF – COMMANDER OF THE FORCES

WILLIAM, PRINCE OF ORANGE COMMANDER 1ST CORPS

1st Life Guards

O'Loghlin, Terence	Lt Col and Col
Rebow, Francis Slater	Supernum Lt Col

2nd Life Guards

McInnes, Alexander	Cornet
Marten, Thomas	Cornet
Meares, Richard G.	Lt
Playford, Thomas	Pte
Shaw, John	Cpl
Stansfield, James	Pte
Stretton, Edward	Pte
Thompson, Alexander	Farrier
Waplington, Richard	Pte
Wilkinson, John	Pte

Royal Regiment of Horse Guards

Nutter, Robert	Pte
Packe, Robert C.	Major
Parker, Henry Thomas	Capt
Riddlesden, John B.	Lt
Shawe, William Cunliffe	Lt
Shirley, John	Cpl
Siddall, John	Vet Surgeon
Slow, David	Surgeon
Stone, Samuel	Pte
Sulivan, George James	Capt
Tathwell, Tathwell Baker	Lt
Thoyts, John	Capt
Varley, Thomas	Quartermaster

1st (King's) Dragoon Guards

Meakin, Joseph	Pte
Naylor, James Frank	Capt
Nicholson, Thomas	Pte
Raynor, George	Pte
Rider, John	Pte
Sands, Thomas	Pte
Sayer, Stephen	Pte
Stirling, William	Lt
Stubbins, John	Sgt
Turner, Michael	Capt
Wallace, Robert Clarke	Capt

3rd (Prince of Wales's) Dragoon Guards

Macintosh, Alexander F.	Lt
Maunsell, George	Capt
Pillichody, Alexis	Lt
Shum, William	Capt
Story, Edmund Richard	Capt
Tidy, John	Pte
White, George	Capt

4th (Royal Irish) Dragoon Guards

Pyper, Robert	Surgeon
Ross, Robert	Major
Sherlock, Francis	Lt Colonel
Woods, William	Lt

5th (Princess Charlotte of Wales's) Dragoon Guards

Osborn, Kean	Capt
Ponsonby, Sir William	Lt Colonel
Walker, Charles	Lt

1st (Royal) Regiment of Dragoons

Mealling, Thomas	Sgt
Ommaney, Cornthwaite	Lt
Partridge, John	Cpl
Phipps, Paul	Capt
Slade, John	Lt Colonel
Smith, John	Sgt
Smithies, James	Pte
Steventon, Thomas	Pte
Stisted, Henry	Capt
Trafford, Edmund	Lt
Trevilian, Maurice Cely	Lt
Watson, William Henry	Lt
Windsor, Edward C.	Capt
Wiseley, William	Saddle Sgt

2nd (Royal North British) Regt of Dragoons

McMillan, William	Troop Sgt Major
Mills, John	Lt
Patrick, William	Pte
Ratcliffe, James	Pte
Reignolds, Thomas	Capt
Shuldham, Lemuel	Cornet
Stoddart, Thomas	Sgt
Stupart, Francis	Lt
Vernor, Robert	Capt
Wallace, John	Pte
Wemyss, James	Lt
Westby, Edward	Cornet
White, Andrew	Pte
Willett, George	Pte

3rd (King's Own) Regiment of Dragoons

Manners, Lord Charles S.	Lt Colonel
Selby, William	Lt
Senior, William	Pte
Stevenson, George	Lt
Watson, Thomas C.	Capt

4th (Queen's Own) Regiment of Dragoons

Norcliffe, Norcliffe	Lt
Patrickson, Hugh	Paymaster
Somerset, Lord Robert E.	Lt Colonel
Taylor, John	Sgt
Waldron, John	Lt

6th (Inniskilling) Regiment of Dragoons

Madox, Henry	Capt
Miller, Fiennes S.	Major
Muter, Joseph	Lt Colonel
Slater, Thomas	Sgt

7th (Queen's Own) Regt of Lt Dragoons

Myers, Arthur	Lt and Adj
O'Grady, Standish	Lt
Robbins, Thomas W.	Capt
Simmons, James	Pte
Thornhill, William	Major
Towers, Frederick	Lt
Uxbridge, Paget H. W., Lord	Colonel
Verner, William	Capt
Vivian, Sir Richard H.	Lt Colonel
Wildman, Thomas	Capt

8th (King's Royal Irish) Regt of Lt Dragoons

Warrington, Thornhill	Capt

9th Regiment of Light Dragoons

Macandrew, John	Asst Surgeon
Parker, Henry Thomas	Lt
Warren, Francis	Capt
Webster, Henry Vassal	Lt

10th (Prince of Wales's Own Royal) Regt of Lt Dragoons

Manners, Hon. Robert W.	Lt Colonel
Pile, William	Pte
Robarts, George James	Major
Sannerman, Henry C.	Vet Surgeon
Shadwell, John	Sgt Major
Smith, William Slayter	Lt
Surman, John	Troop Sgt Major
Taylor, Thomas W.	Capt
Wallington, John C.	Lt
Wells, Samuel	Sgt Major
Wood, Charles	Capt
Worcester, H. Marquess	Lt

11th Regiment of Light Dragoons

Milligan, Robert	Lt
Money, Archibald	Major
Morgan, John	Pte
O'Grady, John Thomas	Lt
O'Malley, James	Surgeon
Paxton, Archibald F.	Lt
Price, Hugh	Lt
Ridout, Cranstoun George	Capt
Schreiber, George	Cornet
Schreiber, James Alfred	Capt
Schreiber, William F.	Capt
Sicker, George	Lt and Adjt
Steele, Henry	Asst Surgeon
Stewart, William Henry	Lt

12th (Prince of Wales's) Regt of Lt Dragoons

McDonald, Edward	Pte
Macfarlane, John	Pte
McLasher, James	Pte
Madden, George Allan	Major
Marsh, William	Cpl
Matthewson, Robert	Pte
Murphy, Daniel	Pte
Murphy, Philip	Pte
Nelson, Robert	Sgt Major
Nichols, Samuel	Sgt
Nugent, John	Pte
Percy, Francis	Pte
Ponsonby, Frederick C.	Lt Colonel

Rainsford, Michael	Pte
Sandys, Edwin W. T.	Capt
Scanlon, Thomas	Sgt Major
Sivell, James	Pte
Slade, John Henry	Lt
Slade, Richard	Pte
Smith, Hugh	Pte
Stewart, William	Pte
Toole, William	Sgt
Welsh, John	Pte
Wiggins, James	Pte
Williamson, Joseph	Pte
Wilmot, James	Pte

13th Regiment of Light Dragoons

McElroy, Peter	Cpl
Moss, John Irving	Lt
Nisbet, Robert	Lt
Packe, George Hussey	Lt
Pym, John	Lt
Squires, John	Pte
Strange, Alexander	Paymaster
Tayler, Samuel	Lt
Turner, William	Lt
Wakefield, Joseph	Cornet
Weldon, William	Sgt
White, William	Capt

14th (Duchess of York's Own) Regt of Lt Dragoons

Molyneux, Thomas	Lt
Percy, Hon. Henry	Capt
Townsend, John	Capt
Wainman, William	Capt
Wyndham, Charles	Lt

15th (King's) Regiment of Light Dragoons

Moulder, Patrick William	Sgt
Moulder, Robert	Pte
Pennington, John	Lt
Philips, Frederick Charles	Capt
Rider, Richard	Pte
Sherwood, Isaac	Lt
Stewart, William D.	Lt
Thackwell, Joseph	Capt

16th (Queen's) Regiment of Light Dragoons

Mallock, John M.	Asst Surgeon
Mathews, Thomas	Pte
Monckton, Carleton T.	Lt
Murray, George Home	Major
Osten, Baron William von	Lt
Pelly, Raymond	Lt Colonel
Penrice, Thomas	Capt
Swetenham, Clement	Capt
Swinfen, Francis	Lt
Tomkinson, William	Capt
Weyland, Richard	Capt

17th Regiment of Light Dragoons

Thompson, Thomas P.	Capt

18th Regiment of Light Dragoons

Machell, John Thomas	Lt
Moore, Edward	Lt
Moore, Hon. Henry	Lt Colonel
Murray, Hon, Henry	Lt Colonel
Otway, Sir Loftus W.	Major
Prior, Thomas Murray	Lt
Pulsford, Lucas	Asst Surgeon
Somerset, Henry	Lt

19th Regiment of Light Dragoons

Vandeleur, Sir John O.	Lt Colonel

20th Regiment of Light Dragoons

Shortt, Thomas	Surgeon
Taylor, Charles Douglas	Lt Colonel
Wyndham, Hon. George	Lt Colonel

22nd Regiment of Light Dragoons

Wilson, Robert Thomas	Lt Colonel

23rd Regiment of Light Dragoons

McNeil, Roderick	Capt
Martin, John	Capt
Palmer, Charles	Lt Colonel
Portarlington, John D.	Lt Colonel
Ship, John	Vet Surgeon
Steele, Samuel	Surgeon
Wallace, James Maxwell	Capt
Warre, Sir William	Capt
Wheatley, Thomas	Pte
Youngs, John	Pte

25th Regiment of Light Dragoons

Stewart, Hon. Charles W.	Colonel

Staff Corps of Cavalry

McDermott, Thomas	Lt
Rooke, James	Lt
Scovell, George	Major

Sewell, William	Quartermaster

Royal Waggon Train

Ravenscroft, Valentine	Capt

1st Regiment of Foot Guards

McDonald, Hon. James	Capt and Lt Colonel
Maitland, Peregrine	Capt and Lt Colonel
Martin, Samuel Coote	Lt Colonel
Middleditch, William M.	Sgt
Miller, William	Capt and Lt Colonel
Milnes, William Henry	Capt and Lt Colonel
Moore, Francis	Pte
Moore, William George	Lt and Capt
Morant, Edward	Ensign
Moreton, Augustus J. F.	Capt and Lt Colonel
Pardoe, Edward	Ensign
Payne, John	Quartermaster Sgt
Peachey, James	Ensign
Perceval, Philip Joshua	Lt and Capt
Phillimore, Robert W.	Lt and Capt
Pole, Edward S. C.	Lt and Capt
Powell, Henry Weyland	Lt and Capt
Poxson, Peter	Sgt
Reeve, John	Capt and Lt Colonel
Richards, John	Pte
Roberts, Robert	Pte
Rous, Thomas Bates	Ensign
St John, Henry Joseph	Ensign
Saltoun, Alexander G. F.	Capt and Lt Colonel
Sandrock, John Henry	Sgt
Searle, John	Pte
Simpson, James	Lt and Capt
Somerset, Lord Fitzroy J.	Capt and Lt Colonel
Sotheby, Ambrose W.	Capt and Lt Colonel
Stables, Edward	Capt and Lt Colonel
Stanhope, Hon. James H.	Capt and Lt Colonel
Stuart, Hon. William	3rd Major
Styles, Sir Thomas	Ensign
Swann, Frederick D.	Ensign
Swinburne, Thomas R.	Ensign
Thomas, Charles	Capt and Lt Colonel
Thomas, Evan	Pte
Thompson, Charles W.	Lt and Capt
Tighe, Daniel	Ensign
Tinling, Isaac Pattison	Capt and Lt Colonel
Todd, Francis	Capt and Lt Colonel
Townshend, Hon. G.	Capt and Lt Colonel
Trelawny, Harry B.	Lt and Capt
Upton, Hon. Arthur P.	Capt and Lt Colonel
Vane, Walter	Lt and Capt
West, James Dawson	Capt and Lt Colonel
Wheatley, Henry	Capt and Lt Colonel
Wheatley, William	Capt and Lt Colonel
Woodford, John George	Capt and Lt Colonel
Yuill, William	Colour Sgt

Coldstream Regiment of Foot Guards

Macdonell, James	Capt and Lt Colonel
Mackinnon, Daniel	Capt and Lt Colonel
Mackinnon, Henry	Colonel
Mills, John	Lt and Capt
Milman, Frances Miles	Capt and Lt Colonel
Nixon, Edward	Asst Surgeon
Otway, Hon. Henry	Lt Colonel
Pakenham, Hercules R.	Capt and Lt Colonel
Parker, Harry	Ensign
Peacocke, Warren M.	Capt and Lt Colonel
Pitt, William Henry	Ensign
Pollard, Thomas	Pte
Prince, John	Lt and Capt
Pringle, William Henry	Capt and Lt Colonel
Raikes, William Henley	Capt and Lt Colonel
Robinson, James	Pte
Ross, John	Capt and Lt

	Colonel
Rous, John Edward C.	Lt and Capt
Salwey, Henry	Ensign
Sandilands, Patrick	Lt and Capt
Shawe, Charles Augustus	Lt and Capt
Short, Charles W.	Ensign
Smith, George	Asst Surgeon
Stibbert, Thomas	Capt and Lt Colonel
Stirling, Sir Gilbert	Capt and Lt Colonel
Sullivan, Sir Henry	Capt and Lt Colonel
Sumner, Edward	Lt and Capt
Thompson, Claudius	Pte
Thompson, George	Cpl
Vachell, Frederick	Ensign
Walpole, Hon. John	Capt and Lt Colonel
Walton, William L.	Lt and Capt
Watson, William	Pte
Watts, Michael	Ensign
Wedderburn, Alexander	Lt and Capt
Whymper, William	Surgeon
Williams, John	Pte
Wingfield, Hon. John	Ensign
Woodford, Alexander G.	Second Major
Woodhouse, Uriah	Sgt
Wyndham, Hon. Henry	Capt and Lt Colonel

3rd Regiment of Foot Guards

Mahon, Luke	Lt and Capt
Master, William Chester	Capt and Lt Colonel
Mercer, Douglas	Capt and Lt Colonel
Mercer, Robert	Capt and Lt Colonel
Montagu, Hon. Henry R.	Ensign
Montgomery, Hugh B.	Lt and Capt
Moorhouse, Joseph W.	Lt and Capt
Murray, Sir Archibald J.	Lt and Capt
Napier, George Thomas	Capt and Lt Colonel
Paterson, George	Capt and Lt Colonel
Peacocke, Stephen	Capt and Lt Colonel
Prendergast, Charles O.	Lt and Capt
Ram, Stopford	Ensign
Rooke, John Charles	Capt and Lt Colonel
Scott, William	Pte
Scott, William Henry	Lt and Capt
Shiffner, John Bridger	Lt and Capt
Simpson, Charles	Ensign
Standen, George Douglas	Ensign
Stockdale, William	Lt and Capt
Stopford, Hon. Sir Edward	Capt and Lt Colonel
Stopford, Hon. Edward	Ensign
Stothert, William	Lt and Capt
Swann, William Henry	Lt and Capt
Torrens, Sir Henry	Capt and Lt Colonel
Walker, Samuel	Lt and Capt
Watson, Henry Robert	Capt
Wedgwood, Thomas	Ensign
West, Charles Edward	Capt and Lt Colonel
White, Charles Lawrence	Lt and Capt
Whitehead, Samuel	Cpl

1st (Royal Scots) Regiment of Foot

Mackay, Joseph	Ensign
Mathias, George	Lt
Mudie, Charles	Ensign
O'Neill, John E.	Lt
Purvis, John	Capt
Quick, Francis	Sgt Major
Robertson, Alexander	Ensign
Rowan, James	Captain
St Clair, Thomas S.	Capt
Samuel, John	Sgt
Stoyte, John	Lt
Symes, Joseph	Lt
Torrens, S. B.	Capt
Wilson, John Morillyon	Capt

2nd (Queen's Royal) Regiment of Foot

Norman, John Ballantine	Lt
Perrin, Isaac B.arrington	Lt
Raitt, George Edward	Major
Spencer, James	Lt and Adjt
Williams, Peter	Pte

3rd (East Kent) Regiment of Foot

Nicholls, William	Capt
Parke, Charles	Capt
Shekleton, Robert	Surgeon
Shepherd, John	Lt

Skeill, David	Lt
Welden, James	Pte
Willington, James	Capt

4th (King's Own) Regiment of Foot

Macgregor, Duncan	Asst Surgeon
Moore, Richard	Capt
Oliver, James Ward	Capt
Piper, John	Major
Richards, Thomas	Quartermaster
Richardson, George Sant	Lt
Salvin, Jeffrey	Lt
Sheppard, Frederick	Lt
Shipton, Henry Noble	Ensign
Smith, James	Asst Surgeon
Smith, John	Pte
Spear, James	Pte
Wood, John	Capt
Wood, William Leighton	Capt
Wynch, James	Lt Colonel

5th (Northumberland) Regiment of Foot

McKenzie, George Davis	Capt
McKenzie, John	Lt Colonel
McKenzie, John Holland	Lt
O'Dell, Henry Edward	Lt
Pennington, John M.	Lt
Pratt, Charles	Lt Colonel
Ramus, Charles Louis	Capt
Scott, Samuel	Surgeon
Sedgwick, Henry Bingley	Lt
Spearman, John	Capt
Wakeling, James	Pte

6th (1st Warwickshire) Regiment of Foot

Miller, Arthur	Major
Patteson, Robert Dossie	Capt
Patullo, William	Lt
Radcliff, Stephen	Lt
Reith, Alexander	Sgt
Sandys, Thomas Edwin	Lt
Scott, Henry	Lt
Shawe, Charles Fielding	Capt

7th (Royal Fusiliers) Regiment of Foot

Mackworth, Digby	Capt
Magenis, Henry Arthur	Lt
Mair, John Hastings	Capt
Myers, Sir William James	Lt Colonel
Nantes, Richard	Lt
Nooth, John Mervin	Lt Colonel
Orr, John	Capt
Parkinson, Henry	Cpl
Salmon, Thomas	Capt
Seton, George	Lt
Whitworth, John	Sgt
Wray, Thomas Fawcett	Lt

8th (King's) Regiment of Foot

Sweetman, J. Walter	Capt

9th (East Norfolk) Regiment of Foot

Peebles, Adam	Capt
Sankey, Samuel	Major
Scott, James	Quartermaster
Seward, William	Lt
Shelton, John	Capt
Siborne, William	Ensign
Stirling, George	Lt
Stuart, John	Lt Colonel
Taylor, Jeremiah	Lt

10th (North Lincolnshire) Regiment of Foot

Rannie, William	Lt
Travers, Robert	Lt Colonel
Wrixon, Nicholas	Lt

11th (North Devonshire) Regiment of Foot

Stewart, Alexander	Asst Surgeon

12th (East Suffolk) Regiment of Foot

Myddleton, Richard W.	Lt

13th (1st Somersetshire) Regiment of Foot

Williams, Sir William	Lt Colonel

14th (Buckinghamshire) Regiment of Foot

Manley, John	Sgt
Marlay, George	Capt
Meek, Jacob	Lt
Morton, Harcourt	Capt
Nicolls, Jasper	Lt Colonel
Ramsay, Thomas	Capt
Reed, William	Ensign
Shannon, Alexander	Asst Surgeon
Tidy, Francis Skelly	Major
Turnor, William	Capt
Wood, John Manley	Ensign

15th (Yorkshire East Riding) Regt of Foot

Wishart, Alexander	Lt

17th (Leicestershire) Regiment of Foot

McMahon, Thomas	Lt Colonel

18th (Royal Irish) Regiment of Foot

Richardson, John	Asst Surgeon

20th (East Devonshire) Regiment of Foot

Murray, James	Lt
Murray, John	Major
Oakley, Richard Cater	Lt
Obins, Hamlet	Capt
O'Donnell, William	Lt
Robinson, Peter	Capt
Ross, Robert	Colonel
Rotton, Guy	Lt
Russell, William	Capt
St Aurin, J. D. E.	Capt
South, Samuel	Major
Steevens, Charles	Lt Colonel
Storey, John	Lt
Telford, Robert	Capt
Walker James Perriman	Lt
Yates, Samuel	Sgt

23rd (Royal Welch Fusiliers) Regt of Foot

Methold, Edward	1st Lt
Montagu, Frederick A. C.	Capt
Morgan, Reese	Pte
Morris, Thomas	Pte
Offley, Francis Needham	Major
Pearson, Thomas	Major
Philipps, Grismond	1st Lt
Roe, Samuel Crozier	Surgeon
Sidley, George	Quartermaster
Sutton, Sir Charles	Lt Colonel
Thomas, David	Pte
Walley, William	1st Lt
Whitmore, Henry	Pte
Williams, John	Pte
Wyatt, William Edgell R.	Lt Colonel
Wynn, Henry	Capt
Youngs, John	Pte

24th (Warwickshire) Regiment of Foot

O'Leary, Arthur	Lt
Popham, Samuel Taylor	Major

25th (King's Own Borderer's) Regt of Foot

Mitchell, John	Capt

26th (Cameronian) Regiment of Foot

Marshall, John	Lt
Nash, James	Capt
Nicholson, William	Cpl
Platt, George Edmund	Lt
Pratt, Thomas Simson	Ensign
Shearman, Edward	Major
Sweeny, Charles F.	Lt
Taylor, John Butt	Surgeon

27th (Inniskilling) Regiment of Foot

Macdonald, George	Lt
McGowan, William	Drummer
Mill, Charles	Major
Ovens, John	Lt
Parsons, Charles	Capt
Pring, John	Capt
Reade, Sir Thomas	Capt
Reeves, George James	Lt Colonel
Simcoe, Francis Gwillam	Lt
Smith, Thomas Charlton	Ensign
Talbot, William	Lt
Tucker, John M.	Capt
Warren, Lemuel	Lt Colonel

28th (North Gloucestershire) Regt of Foot

Moore, Samuel	Lt
Morris, Samuel	Capt
Mountsteven, William T.	Ensign
Serjeantson, William	Ensign
Shelton, John Willington	Lt
Stovin, Sir Frederick	Capt
Wilson, Thomas	Capt

29th (Worcestershire) Regiment of Foot

Sandys, Myles	Lt
Tod, George	Major
Way, Sir Gregory H.	Lt Colonel
White, Daniel	Lt Colonel

30th (Cambridgeshire) Regiment of Foot

Macnab, Alexander	Capt
Macready, Edward Nevil	Ensign
Monypenny, Thomas G.	Lt
Neville, Park Percy	Lt
Nicholson, Benjamin W.	Lt
Poyntz, James	Ensign
Prendergast, Edward	Lt
Roe, John	Lt
Rumley, John	Lt

Vigoureux, Charles A.	Major
Weaver, Thomas	Cpl

31st (Huntingdonshire) Regiment of Foot

Murray, John	Pte
Nunn, Loftus	Lt
Spence, James	Lt

32nd (Cornwall) Regiment of Foot

Meighan, Michael W.	Lt
Metcalfe, Henry	Ensign
Newton, Hibbert	Lt
Palmer, Thomas	Pte
Power, Sir Manley	Lt Colonel
Quill, Henry	Lt
Ross-Lewin, Henry	Capt
Rowland, John	Capt
Singer, Richard Oriel	Lt
Vale, Thomas	Pte
Wallett, Charles	Capt

33rd (1st Yorkshire West Riding) Regiment of Foot

Madin, George	Cpl
Ogle, James Gordon	Lt
Pagan, Samuel A.	Lt
Reid, Thomas	Capt
Rodwell, Thomas	Pte
Sherbrooke, Sir John C.	Colonel
Thain, William	Ensign
Westmore, Richard	Lt
Widdop, John	Pte

34th (Cumberland) Regiment of Foot

Maister, John	Lt Colonel
Sherer, Moyle	Capt
Smail, George	Ensign
Wallis, John	Pte
Worsley, Henry	Major

35th (Sussex) Regiment of Foot

Macleod, Henry George	Capt
Petit, Peter Hayes	Lt Colonel
Rainforth, William	Lt
Rawson, William	Capt
Slessor, John	Major
Weare, Thomas	Capt

36th (Herefordshire) Regiment of Foot

Macpherson, Evan	Ensign
Murchison, Roderick I.	Capt
Smith, Charles Hervey	Capt
Taylor, Thomas John	Lt
Weir, James	Ensign

37th (North Hampshire) Regiment of Foot

Tilt, Andrew	Major

38th (1st Staffordshire) Regiment of Foot

Minchin, John Paul	Capt
Perry, John Philip	Capt
Thompson, William	Asst Surgeon
Walton, John	Pte
Werge, John	Capt
Wilkie, Thomas Fletcher	Capt
Wrench, William H.	Lt
Wynn, William	Pte

39th (Dorsetshire) Regiment of Foot

Macarthur, Edward	Lt
Macpherson, Donald	Capt
O'Callaghan, Robert W.	Lt Colonel
O'Toole, Bryan	Capt
Parbart, Hugh	Sgt
Richards, Benjamin	Pte
Saunderson, Hardness R.	Capt
Smyth, Henry	Lt and Adjt
Standish, Henry	Major
Thorpe, Samuel	Capt
Waddell, James George	Capt

40th (2nd Somersetshire) Regiment of Foot

Mill, James	Lt
Millar, Henry	Lt
Neilley, William	Lt
Oglander, Henry	Major
Preston, George	Capt
Smith, Joshua	Pte
Street, Alfred	Lt
Stretton, Sempronius	Capt
Thoreau, John	Lt
Thornton, Henry	Lt Colonel
Toole, William	Capt
Turton, Richard	Capt
Turton, William	Lt

42nd (Royal Highland) Regiment of Foot

Macara, Sir Robert	Lt Colonel
McCrimmon, Donald	Ensign
MacDonald, Donald	Capt
McGlashan, John	Pte
MacGlashan, Neil	Capt
Mackay, John	Pte

Mackay, Robert Faro[r]	Pte
Mackenzie, Alexander	Capt
McKenzie, Roderick	Pte
McLean, Donald	Pte
McLeod, Swinton	Surgeon
McNiven, Thomas W. O.	Lt
Macowen, James	Pte
Malcolm, John	Lt
Maxwell, Hamilton	Capt
Middleton, William	Capt
Munro, John	Pte
Nicholson, Huntly	Lt
Orr, John	Lt
Peattie, Paul	Pte
Roycroft, Robert	Pte
Stewart, Alexander	Lt
Stewart, George	Capt
Stewart, James	Lt
Stirling, James	Lt Colonel
Stirling, James	Capt
Sutherland, William	Pte
Swanson, John	Capt
Walker, James	Capt
Watson, James	Lt
Williamson, Donald	Capt
Young, James	Lt and Adjt

43rd (Monmouthshire) Light Infantry Regiment of Foot

Macdonald, John	Major
Maclean, John Leyburn	Lt
Macleod, Charles	Lt Colonel
McPherson, Philip	Lt
Madden, Wyndham C.	Lt
Mein, Nicol Alexander	Major
Meyricke, John Chabbett	Lt
Murchison, Robert P.	Capt
Napier, William F. P.	Major
Nesham, Mathew	Sgt
O'Connell, Richard	Lt
Patrickson, Christopher C.	Lt Colonel
Pattenson, Cooke Tylden	Capt
Proctor, John	Capt
Rand, Samuel	Sgt
Ricketts, Joseph	Pte
Rylance, Thomas	Capt
Shaw, James	Capt
Sidney, Philip	Ensign
Tylden, Sir John Maxwell	Capt
Watson, Amos	Cpl
Window, Richard	Pte

44th (East Essex) Regiment of Foot

Mackrell, Thomas	Capt
Mence, Haffey	Lt
O'Malley, George	Major
O'Reilley, John	Capt
Paget, Elijah	Pte
Phipps, Robert	Pte
Shaw, James Peter	Lt
Twinberrow, Ralph John	Lt

45th (Nottinghamshire) Regiment of Foot

Malkin, William	Cpl
Metcalfe, John	Lt
Munro, Charles	Lt
Paterson, James	Asst Surgeon
Radford, Henry Wyatt	Asst Surgeon
Reynett, James Henry	Capt
Ridewood, Henry	Lt Colonel
Smith, William	Major
Urmston, Lambert B.	Lt

47th (Lancashire) Regiment of Foot

McCurdy, Thomas	Asst Surgeon
Norris, George	Lt
Parsons, Henry	Capt
Sall, William	Capt
Skerrett, John Byne	Lt Colonel
Wainwright, Henry M.	Lt

48th (Northamptonshire) Regiment of Foot

McDonald, George	Sgt
Mackay, George	Capt
Middlemore, George	Major
Moffat, William	Asst Surgeon
Morisset, James Thomas	Capt
Parry, William Parry J.	Capt
Parsons, Edward	Capt
Parsons, Lucius	Ensign
Taylor, James	Capt
Watson, Henry	Capt
Wild, John	Ensign and Adjt
Wilson, Sir James	Major

50th (West Kent) Regiment of Foot

McDonald, John	Capt
McDonnell, Duncan	Lt
Mitchell, Andrew	Capt
Montgomery, Henry	Capt
Montgomery, John	Paymaster
Morgan, David	Asst Surgeon
Myles, John	Lt and Adj

Napier, Charles James — Lt Colonel
Rowe, Benjamin — Capt
Ryan, Thomas — Lt
Stanhope, Hon. Charles B. — Major
Stewart, Charles — Lt Colonel
Stubbs, Thomas William — Lt
Turner, William — Lt
Wemyss, Thomas J. — Capt
Wyatt, James — Pte

51st (2nd Yorkshire West Riding) Lt Infantry

McCabe, John	Capt
McCarthy, Owen	Sgt
Maher, Philip	Pte
Mainwaring, John M.	Lt Colonel
Marsland, Henry	Sgt
Mercer, Charles W.	Capt
Mills, John	Lt and Q. Master
Minchin, Francis	Lt
Minskiull, John	Sgt
Mitchell, Hugh Henry	Lt Colonel
Percy, Hugh	Sgt
Percy, John Samuel	Lt
Phelps, James Henry	Capt
Roche, Robert	Sgt
Smith, Michael	Sgt
Sorrell, William	Sgt
Sparks, Frederick	Major
Stephens, Maurice	Lt
Storer, Richard	Capt
Stothers, James	Sgt
Taylor, John D.	Lt
Trevevan, Richard	Sgt
Troward, Thomas	Lt
Utting, Samuel	Sgt
Webster, Thomas	Sgt
Wells, Rees	Sgt
Westropp, Ralph	Lt
Wheeler, William	Sgt
White, William Edward	Lt
Wilson, Richard	Lt

52nd (Oxfordshire) Lt Infantry Regt of Foot

Mackenzie, Kenneth	Lt Colonel
McNair, James	Capt
Madden, William S.	Capt
March, C. L., Earl of	Capt
Massie, Thomas	Ensign
Mein, William	Major
Montague, John	Ensign
Moore, Sir John	Colonel
Northey, Edward Richard	Lt
Ormsby, James	Capt
Radcliffe, Robert	Pte
Rowan, Charles	Major
Rowan, Sir William	Capt
Royle, John Watson	Lt
Shedden, John	Capt
Snodgrass, John James	Lt
Snodgrass, Kenneth	Capt
Sunderland, Henry	Sgt
Sweeten, Benjamin	Quartermaster
Tod, Robert	Surgeon
Whichcote, George	Lt
Whittam, Samuel	Pte
Winterbottom, John	Lt and Adjt
Yonge, William Crawley	Lt
Yorke, Charles	Capt

53rd (Shropshire) Regiment of Foot

Mansel, John	Major
Mansel, Robert C.	Capt
Morphett, Mars	Ensign
Poppleton, Thomas W.	Capt
Stewart, James	Ensign

54th (West Norfolk) Regiment of Foot

Mandilhon, Philip	Lt

55th (Westmoreland) Regiment of Foot

Peacocke, Thomas G.	Capt
Rainey, Henry	Capt

56th (West Essex) Regiment of Foot

Wylde, John Newman	Capt

57th (West Middlesex) Regiment of Foot

Maclaine, Hector	Capt
Myers, John	Lt
Paterson, Leeson	Lt
Pode, John Spurrell	Ensign
Rollings, John	Pte
Sankey, Andrew	Lt
Shadforth, Thomas	Major
Stainforth, John	Capt

58th (Rutlandshire) Regiment of Foot

Rolt, John	Capt
Sadleir, William	Lt
St John, Charles	Asst Surgeon
Stone, Bayntun	Capt

59th (2nd Nottinghamshire) Regiment of Foot

Macgregor, George	Lt Colonel
McGregor, James	Capt
Mancor, Andrew	Capt
Murray, Donald	Sgt
O'Hara, Patterson	Lt
Pethick, Edward	Sgt
Robinson, Frederick P.	Ensign
Robinson, Gilmour	Lt
Ross, Andrew Clark	Ensign
Scott, Robert	Lt
Veall, William	Lt
Vevers, Chares Nicholas	Lt
Weir, John Laing	Major
Whittle, Robert	Lt

60th (Royal American) Regiment of Foot

Mitchell, Robert	Capt
Murray, Sir George	Col Commandant
Pearce, William	Capt
Schoedde, James Holmes	Capt
Sewell, William Henry	Capt
Somerset, Lord John T. H.	Capt
Stevenson, William	Asst Surgeon
Stopford, James	Major
Tarleton, Henry	Major
Thorne, Peregrine F.	Capt
Tresidder, Samuel	Lt
Wilkinson, William	Capt

61st (South Gloucestershire) Regt of Foot

MacLeod, Alexander	Lt
Murray, James	Sgt
Saunders, John Stratford	Lt Colonel
Singleton, John	Lt

62nd (Wiltshire) Regiment of Foot

Reed, John	Capt
Shearman, John	Lt
Sweeny, Francis Bernard	Ensign
Sweeny, James Fielding	Capt
Walter, John	Capt

63rd (West Suffolk) Regiment of Foot

Macnish, William	Surgeon
Witherington, Henry	Lt

66th (Berkshire) Regiment of Foot

Nicholls, George	Capt
Pyne, Robert	Capt
Rogers, Benjamin	Pte

67th (South Hampshire) Regiment of Foot

Moore, Charles	Capt
Perceval, William	Lt Colonel
Ronald, William	Lt
Walker, Harry	Capt

68th (Durham) Regiment of Foot

Mackay, Honeyman	Lt
Mackay, William	Capt
Melville, Robert	Capt
Miller, James	Capt
North, William	Capt
Reed, John	Capt
Stapylton, Henry	Lt
Stopford, Roger	Lt
Stretton, Severus W. L.	Lt
Warde, Sir Henry	Colonel

69th (South Lincolnshire) Regiment of Foot

Morice, Charles	Lt Colonel
Muttlebury, George	Major
Nightingall, Sir Miles	Lt Colonel
Pearson, Isaac	Armourer Sgt
Seward, Charles	Ensign
Shepherd, Lynn	Pte
Warne, George	Pte
Watson, J. Lewis	Capt

71st (Highland Light Infantry) Regt of Foot

Mackenzie, Hugh	Capt and Paymaster
Mackenzie, Maxwell	Major
Moncur, William	Sgt
Napier, Hon. Charles	Lt
Pack, Sir Dennis	Lt Colonel
Peacocke, Nathaniel L.	Lt Colonel
Peacocke, William	Lt
Reed, Samuel	Capt
Reynell, Thomas	Lt Colonel
Ross, John	Sgt
Souter, David	Lt
Spalding, John	Ensign
Spottiswoode, George	Major
Torriano, William E.	Lt
Whitney, John	Lt
Wilson, John	Cpl
Winterscale, John	Asst Surgeon

73rd (Highland) Regiment of Foot

Maclaine, John	Major
Riach, John	Asst Surgeon

Robinson, William	Pte
Sandell, Peter	Pte
Smith, William	Pte

74th (Highland) Regiment of Foot

McQueen, John Donald	Capt
Manners, Russell	Major
Maxwell, Robert	Lt
Maxwell, William	Sgt
Mein, John Alexander	Major
Ovens, John	Capt
Owen, John	Cpl
Parkinson, John	Ensign
Pattison, Alexander H.	Lt
Ramadge, Benjamin	Lt
Sissons, Marcus Jacob	Volunteer
Tew, William	Capt
Thomson, Alexander	Capt
Trench, Hon. Sir Robert	Lt Colonel
White, Henry	Lt
Whiting, William	Capt
Williams, John	Ensign

76th Regiment of Foot

Parker, Robert	Lt
Purchase, John	Capt
Rooth, Benjamin	Lt and Adjt
Wardlaw, John	Lt Colonel

77th (East Middlesex) Regiment of Foot

Mathison, John Augustus	Lt
Picton, Sir Thomas	Colonel
Powell, John	Quartermaster
Rudd, John	Major
Spry, William Frederick	Major
Tatton, Richard	Lt

78th (Highland) Regiment of Foot

Macgregor, Malcolm	Capt
Mackenzie, John Randoll	Colonel
Munro, William	Surgeon

79th (Cameron Highlanders) Regt of Foot

Macarthur, Charles	Lt
McBarnett, William	Lt
McKenzie, Donald	Sgt
MacPherson, Duncan	Lt
Manuel, John	Pte
Marshall, William	Capt
O'Connor, Ogle Nesbit	Lt
Petrie, Alexander	Major
Powling, John	Lt
Purvis, Patrick	Capt
Riach, William A.	Lt
Ridesdale, George	Surgeon
Sinclair, John	Capt
Walbeoffe, Thomas W.	Lt

80th (Staffordshire Volunteers) Regt of Foot

Paget, Hon. Sir Edward	Colonel

81st Regiment of Foot

Montgomery, Knox	Lt
Napper, Alexander	Lt
Shelton, Jonathon	Ensign
Sinclair, James	Capt
Taylor, Philip C.	Lt
Williams, Sir Edmund K.	Capt

82nd (Prince of Wales's Volunteers) Regt of Foot

Marshall, George	Capt
Northern, Lewis	Capt
Ottley, Mathew	Paymaster
Proctor, Henry Adolphus	Major
Rainey, John	Major
Scott, Henry Randolph	Asst Surgeon
Sheard, Timothy	Pte
Smith, Sir George	Lt Colonel
Starkey, Walter W.	Lt
Tribe, Richard	Capt

83rd Regiment of Foot

O'Neill, Charles	Lt
O'Neill, William	Ensign
Reynolds, James	Capt
Russell, Alexander	Sgt
Smith, James	Lt
Swinburne, Joseph	Lt
Thompson, Robert	Capt

84th (York and Lancaster) Regiment of Foot

Nicholl, Edward	Capt
Urquhart, Donald	Capt

85th (Buckinghamshire Volunteers) Light Infantry Regiment of Foot

Macdougall, Sir Duncan	Capt
McGilliwie, James	Lt and Adjt
Maunsell, Frederick	Lt
Watts, John James	Lt
Wilkinson, Thomas	Capt

Williams, William Freke | Capt
Wood, William | Lt Colonel

87th (Prince of Wales's Own Irish) Regt of Foot

Mountgarrett, William	Lt

88th (Connaught Rangers) Regt of Foot

McClintock, James	Ensign
McDermott, Henry	Capt
McDonald, John	Capt
McNulty, John	Pte
Moriarty, James	Lt
Nickle, Robert	Capt
O'Hara, Robert	Capt
Reynolds, Barnard	Lt
Rogers, Thomas	Paymaster
Rutherford, William H.	Lt
Seton, William Carden	Major
Taylor, John	Lt Colonel
Taylor, Thomas	Lt
Tryon, Charles	Lt Colonel

89th Regiment of Foot

Moulson, Edward	Ensign
Wylde, Ralph	Capt

91st Regiment of Foot

McDonald, Donald	Capt
Macfarlane, Andrew A.	Capt
McGregor, Hugh	Capt
Macintyre, David	Capt
McNeil, Donald	Major
MacNeill, Archibald	Capt
Marshall, John	Lt
Murdoch, James C.	Capt
Murray, Thomas	Lt
O'Leary, John	Lt
Ormiston, John Andrew	Lt
Ottley, Benjamin Wynne	Lt Colonel
Riddick, John	Pte
Scott, James	Pte
Smith, Andrew	Ensign
Stewart, Robert	Lt
Stewart, William	Capt
Taylor, John	Lt

92nd Regiment of Foot

Macdonald, Allan	Lt
Macdonald, Donald	Major
Macdonald, Ronald	Capt
McNab, Allan	Lt
McPherson, Alexander	Lt
McPherson, Duncan	Lt
McPherson, John	Major
Marshall, George	Lt
Milne, Alexander	Pte
Mitchell, James	Lt Colonel
Mitchell, Thomas	Lt
Murray, William	Pte
Rae, Thomas	Pte
Rose, Hugh Hay	Lt
Ross, Ewen Cameron	Lt
Ross, James Kerr	Lt
Ross, John	Pte
Seton, James	Capt
Symon, Alexander	Sgt
Tod, William	Capt
Wilkie, Peter	Capt
Will, Andrew	Lt
Winchester, Robert	Lt

93rd Regiment of Foot

Tyler, John	Capt
Wemyss, William	Major

94th Regiment of Foot

Macnab, John	Lt
Munro, David	Capt
Pratt, Percy	Lt
Reston, James	Sgt
Robertson, Andrew	Lt
Rutherford, James	Lt
Scott, Thomas	Lt
Squire, William	Capt
Stewart, James	Sgt
Thornton, John	Lt
Topp, Richard	Ensign
Williamson, James	Capt

95th Regiment of Foot

Macdermid, John	Capt
McWhan, Samuel	Cpl
Madden, Edward Marcell	Lt
Manningham, Coote	Colonel
Mercer, James	1st Lt
Middleton, John	1st Lt
Miller, George	Capt
Milton, David	Pte
Mitchell, Samuel	Major
Mitchell, Thomas L.	1st Lt
Molloy, John	1st Lt
Neal, William	Pte

Norcott, Amos G. R.	Major
O'Hare, Peter	Major
Oliver, Joseph	Pte
Peters, John	Pte
Ribton, John Sheppey	Lt
Ridgeway, Thomas H.	Surgeon
Robertson, William S.	1st Lt
Robinson, Thomas	Pte
Ross, John	Major
Rouse, John	Pte
Rutledge, John	Sgt
Shenley, Edward W. H.	2nd Lt
Simmons, George	Lt
Smith, Charles	Volunteer
Smith, Charles Maitland	Pte
Smith, Harry George W.	Capt
Smith, Thomas Lawrence	1st Lt and Adjt
Stewart, Archibald	Lt
Stewart, Hon. Sir William	Colonel
Stokes, James Marshall	1st Lt
Surtees, William	Quartermaster
Thompson, Ralph Keddy	Lt
Turner, William Parks	Asst Surgeon
Uniacke, John	Capt
Vickers, Gentle	Lt
Wade, Hamlet	Lt Colonel
Wall, Thomas	Sgt
Warberton, James	Pte
Webb, Vere	1st Lt
Westby, George W.	Lt
Whatmough, Joseph	Pte
Wilkins, George	Major
Williams, John	Pte
Winterton, John	Pte
Wood, William	Pte

96th Regiment of Foot

Macmahon, William O.	Capt

101st (Duke of York's Irish) Regiment of Foot

McIntosh, Hugh	Capt

Permanent Assistant Quartermaster Generals

Northey, Lewis Augustus	Lt Colonel
Pierrepoint, Charles A.	Major
Read, William	Major
Riddell, Henry James	Major

Staff Appointments in Spain and Portugal not holding a Regimental Commission

Macbean, William	Major
McCreagh, Michael	Major
Paty, George William	Major
Whittingham, Sir Samuel	Major
Waters, John	Major

Royal Staff Corps

Nicolay, William	Lt Colonel
Owen, Richard	Pte
Sedley, John Somner	Ensign
Staveley, William	Capt
Sturgeon, Henry	Lt Colonel
Trant, Nicholas	Capt
Wright, Thomas	Capt

Paymaster General's Department

Scovell, Henry	Asst Dep P M G

3rd West India Regiment of Foot

Murray, Sir John	Colonel

6th West India Regiment of Foot

Pakenham, Hon. Sir E.	Colonel

7th West India Regiment of Foot

Maclaine, Archibald	Lt Colonel

8th West India Regiment of Foot

Raines, Joseph Robert	Lt

Royal York Rangers

Paget, Charles	Capt
Shaw, Alexander M.	Lt
Wilson, Sir John	Lt Colonel

York Chasseurs

Stainton, Joseph	Lt

1st Ceylon Regiment

Maitland, Frederick	Colonel

2nd Ceylon Regiment

Willerman, William	Capt

1st Garrison Battalion

Macdonald, Archibald	Major

2nd Garrison Battalion

Robinson, Sir Frederick	Colonel
Sherris, Alexander	Pte

3rd Garrison Battalion
Strangways, William — Lt

4th Garrison Battalion
Walsh, Pearson Lyons — Capt

5th Garrison Battalion
Mee, John — Lt

1st Royal Veteran Battalion
Newmarch, William — Pte
West, Charles Augustus — Lt Colonel

3rd Royal Veteran Battalion
Porter, William — Capt

4th Royal Veteran Battalion
Price, Thomas Parry — Lt

10th Royal Veteran Battalion
Skene, Alexander — Capt

13th Royal Veteran Battalion
Macleod, William — Capt

Glengarry Light Infantry Fencibles
McPherson, Daniel — Capt
Powell, Thomas — Capt

King's German Legion

1st Regiment of Dragoons
Peters, Friedrich — Capt

2nd Regiment of Dragoons
Mitchell, William — Paymaster

3rd Regiment of Hussars
Meyer, Friederich L. — Lt Colonel

1st Battalion Light Infantry
Macdonald, Stephen — Lt
Marschalck, H. von — Capt
Suchow, Arthur — Ensign

2nd Battalion Light Infantry
Macbean, Alexander — Lt
McGlashan, James Edwin — Lt
Robertson, Friedrich von — Ensign
Schaumann, Friedrich M. — Capt

1st Line Battalion
Ompteda, Ferdinand von — Capt
Saffe, August von — Capt

2nd Line Battalion
Müller, Heinrich — Capt
Paschal, George F. — Lt
Schröder, Johann C. Von — Lt Colonel
Thilee, Georg — Capt
Wiegmann, Heinrich — Capt

5th Line Battalion
Meyer, Johann — Lt
Ompteda, Christian von — Colonel
Schuck, Johann Ludwig — Lt and Adjt
Wurmb, Ernst C. C. von — Capt

7th Line Battalion
Offeney, William — Lt Colonel

8th Line Battalion
Marenholz, Wilhelm von — Lt
Voigt, August W. von — Capt
Westernhagen, Thilo von — Capt

KGL Artillery
Schulzen, Carl von — Lt
Sympher, Friedrich — Major

Duke of Brunswick Oels' Corps (Infantry)
Olfermann, Johann J. H. — Col Commandant
Schartroth, J. Carl — Lt

Roll's Regiment
Rottenburg, Francis — Colonel

Bourbon Regiment
Willats, Peter John — Capt

Meuron's Regiment
Walker, Sir George T. — Colonel

Chasseurs Britannique
Millius, Charles — Capt
Wolf, Pierre Frederic — Lt

Sicilian Regiment
Peacocke, Thomas — Capt

1st (Duke of York's) Greek Lt Infantry Regt
Oswald, Sir John — Colonel

Royal Artillery

Macbean, Forbes	2nd Capt
MacDonald, Alexander	Lt Colonel
Manners, Charles	1st Lt
Manners, Robert	1st Lt
Martin, Donald N.	1st Lt
Maule, George Silvester	1st Lt
Maunsell, John Edward	1st Lt
Maxwell, Archibald M.	2nd Capt
May, Sir John	Capt
Menzies, William	Cpl
Mercer, Alexander C.	2nd Capt
Miller, William	1st Lt
Montagu, Willoughby	1st Lt
Moore, George A.	1st Lt
Moreton, William	Pte
Morgan, Hugh	1st Lt
Morrison, William	Capt
Munro, William	Pte
Napper, George	Asst Surgeon
Newland, Robert	2nd Capt
Nicholson, Edward	Gunner
Nicolls, William Dann	Capt
Nixson, Philip	Pte
Oliver, Nathaniel Wilmot	Capt
Onslow, Phipps Vansittart	1st Lt
Owen, Humphrey	Major
Parker, John Boteler	Capt
Pemberton, George K.	1st Lt
Phelps, Samuel	1st Lt
Phillips. Roger Fryer	1st Lt
Poole, William Halstead	Lt
Power, William G.	Major
Ramsay, George	Colonel
Ramsay, William Norman	Capt
Raynes, William A.	1st Lt
Ridley, Matthew	Sgt
Riley, John	Driver
Robe, Sir William	Colonel
Robe, William L.	1st Lt
Roberts, William	Capt
Rollo, Alexander	Cpl
Romer, William	2nd Capt
Ross, Sir Hew Dalrymple	Capt
Rudyerd, Samuel	Capt
Sandham, Charles F.	Capt
Sandilands, Philip	1st Lt
Saunders, William	1st Lt
Scott, Henry Alexander	2nd Capt
Scott, John F.	2nd Lt
Scott, Thomas	2nd Capt
Sheppard, Edmund	1st Lt
Shrapnel, Henry Scrope	Colonel
Sinclair, James	2nd Capt
Skelton, Daniel Jones	Capt
Smith, Benjamin	Pte
Smith, Francis	Capt
Smith, James Webber	Capt
Smith, John Wetherall	lst Lt
Smith, Robert G. S.	2nd Lt
Smyth, George Barttelot	Lt
Spearman, Charles	Lt
Stopford, William Henry	2nd Capt
Strangways, Thomas Fox	1st Lt
Sturgeon, William	Pte
Swabey, William	1st Lt
Thomson, George	Capt
Turner, Sir George	Capt
Tweedie, Michael	1st Lt
Vaughan-Arbuckle, B. H.	1st Lt
Verling, James	2nd Asst Surgeon
Walcott, Edmund Y.	2nd Capt
Walker, William	Pte
Wallace, Peter Margetson	Capt
Ward, Adam	1st Lt
Warde, Francis	1st Lt
Watt, George	Pte
Webber, William	2nd Capt
Whinyates, Sir Edward C.	Capt
Wightman, James	Sgt Major
Williams, Henry	lst Lt
Williamson, John S.	Major
Willis, George Brander	1st Lt
Wilson, Richard G. B.	2nd Lt
Wylde, William	2nd Capt

Royal Artillery Drivers

Mead, Charles	2nd Lt Commissary
Oldham, Eli	Driver
Percivall, William	Veterinary Surgeon
Roles, Richard	Driver
Williams, David	Jobbing Smith

Field Train Department of Ordnance

Miller, William	Dep Asst Com Gen
Thorn, Robert Brandon	Clerk of Stores
Walsh, Robert	Clerk of Stores

Ordnance Medical Department

Rudge, Edward	2nd Asst Surgeon
Simpson, Edward	Surgeon
Verner, Edward Donovan	2nd Asst Surgeon

Royal Engineers

McCulloch, William	2nd Capt
Macdonald, Donald	2nd Capt
Machell, Lancelot	Lt
Macleod, George F.	Capt
Marshall, Anthony	2nd Capt
Matson, Edward	Lt
Melhuish, Samuel C.	2nd Capt
Melville, David	2nd Lt
Mercer, Alexander Cavalié	Capt
Mudge, Richard Z.	2nd Capt
Mulcaster, Edmund R.	2nd Capt
Nicholas, William	Capt
Ord, William Redman	Capt
Parker, Edward	Capt
Pasley, Charles William	Lt Colonel
Patton, Peter	Capt
Piper, Robert Sloper	2nd Capt
Pitts, Thomas James H.	2nd Capt
Power, Robert George	Lt
Pringle, John Watson	Lt
Reid, William	2nd Capt
Rhodes, Charles Steech	Capt
Robe, Alexander Watt	1st Lt
Ross, George Clarke	Capt
Rudyard, Charles W.	Lt Colonel
Scott, Richard Evans	Lt
Skelton, Thomas	Lt
Smith, Charles Felix	Capt
Smith, Henry Nelson	Lt
Smyth, James C.	Lt Colonel
Squire, John	Capt
Stanway, Frank	2nd Capt
Tapp, Hammond Astley	2nd Capt
Thackeray, Frederick R.	Lt Colonel
Thomson, Alexander	2nd Capt
Thomson, Robert	Capt
Tinling, George Vaughan	Lt
Trench, Samuel	Lt
Vetch, James	2nd Capt
Victor, James Conway	Lt
Ward, William Cuthbert	2nd Capt
Waters, Marcus Antonius	Lt
Wells, John Neave	2nd Capt
White, Andrew Douglas	Lt
Williams, John Archer	2nd Capt
Wright, Peter	Lt

Commissariat Department

Maclean, George	Treasury Clerk
Miller, William	DACG
Murray, John	Commissary Gen
Paterson, James	DACG
Porteous, Walter	DACG
Pratt, Charles	Dep Com Gen
Ragland, Thomas Gajetan	Asst Com Gen
Rayner, Thomas	DACG
Routh, Randolph Isham	Dep Com Gen
Skelton, Thomas Lowrey	DACG
Taylor, William B. S.	Clerk
Wemyss, William	Dep Comm Gen
Wimbridge, John	Purveyor

Medical Department

McGrigor, James	Director General
Maclagan, David	Staff Surgeon
Macleod, Donald	Staff Surgeon
Millar, John	Hospital Assistant
Mitchell, James	Hospital Asst
Morewood, George	Physician
O'Leary, Edmund	Physician
Plenderleath, John	Physician
Porteus, Edward	Dep Insp Gen
Thomson, Thomas	Dep Insp of Hosp
Twining, William	Asst Surgeon
Vance, Richard Young	Staff Surgeon
Walter, Philip	Staff Surgeon
Wasdell, John	Staff Surgeon
Williams, John	Staff Surgeon
Woolriche, Stephen	Dep Insp of Hosp

Chaplains Department

Symons, Henry John	Chaplain
Watson, George	Chaplain

Other Names

Orange, HRH Prince W.	Commander 1st Corps

Dutch Officers
Cavalry – Staff

Merlen, J. B. van	Major Gen

Light Cavellerie

Wolff, William	2nd Lt

1st Carabineers Regiment

Norbert, J. C.	1st Lt

4th Dragoons

Mascheck, C.	Capt
Pallandt, Baron W. A. van	Capt
Patot, Tissot van	Capt
Stratenus, A.	2nd Lt

6th Hussars

Verhellow, W. A.	1st Lt
Wijnbergen, W. L. van	Capt
Wolf, W.	2nd Lt

35th Jager Battalion

Roberti	2nd Lt

5th National Militia Battalion

Wynoldy, A.	1st Lt

6th National Militia Battalion

Thielen, A. Van	Lt Colonel

8th National Militia Battalion

Werner, G. J.	1st Lt

2nd Nassau Regiment

Stammel, F. K.	1st Lt
Trodt, F. Van	2nd Lt

Artillery

Stevenart, E. J.	Capt

Supplement A – L

New records found since the publication of Vol. I.

ALLAN, James
Major. 94th Regiment of Foot.
Memorial stone: St Mary's Churchyard, Cheltenham, Gloucestershire. (Part 3, Section 4). (M.I.)

"BENEATH THIS STONE ARE DEPOSITED THE REMAINS OF MAJOR-GENERAL JAMES ALLAN, C.B. COLONEL OF THE 50TH QUEENS OWN REGT, WHO DEPARTED THIS LIFE FEBRUARY THE 17TH 1853 IN THE 76TH YEAR OF HIS AGE. ...."

Ensign Independent Company 31 Dec 1794. Lt 94th Foot 13 Mar 1795. Capt 16 Sep 1799. Major 20 Jul 1809. Bt Lt Colonel 4 Jun 1814. Lt Colonel (unattached) 29 Jun 1826. Lt Colonel 57th Foot 20 Mar 1828. Bt Colonel 10 Jan 1837. Major General 9 Nov 1846.

Served in the Peninsula Feb – Aug 1810 and Mar – Apr 1814. Present at Cadiz, Vic Bigorre, Tarbes and Toulouse. Gold Medal for Toulouse. CB. Also served in the Cape of Good Hope 1795, India 1799 (present in the Mysore campaign, Mallavelly, siege of Seringapatan – awarded medal), Tranquebar, Cape of Good Hope 1806 (present at Blauberg) and India 1808 (present in the Polygar Wars). Commanded 57th Foot 1828–1846. Colonel 50th Foot 11 Oct 1852.
Reference: Gentleman's Magazine, 1853, pp. 437–8. Annual Register, 1853, Appx, p. 213.

ARDEN, William
Private. 1st Regiment of Foot Guards.
Headstone: St John the Baptist's Churchyard, Hillmorton, Warwickshire. (Against churchyard boundary). (Photograph)

THIS STONE WAS / ERECTED BY A FEW / FRIENDS TO THE MEMORY OF / WILLIAM ARDEN / A PENINSULAR WAR / AND WATERLOO VETERAN / BORN IN HILLMORTON 1789 / DIED NOVEMBER 18TH 1874 / AGED 85 YEARS / (VERSE)

Served in the Peninsula Oct 1812 – Apr 1814. Present at Nivelle and Nive. Served at Waterloo in Lt Colonel Hon. H. P. Townshend's Company. MGS medal for Nivelle and Nive.

ARMSTRONG, Abraham
Assistant Surgeon. 13th Regiment of Light Dragoons.
Buried in the Royal Garrison Church Graveyard, Portsmouth, Hampshire. (M.I.)

"SACRED / TO THE MEMORY OF / ABRAHAM ARMSTRONG / STAFF SURGEON OF THE GARRISON / WHO DIED 18TH OCTOBER 1849 / AGED 70."

Hospital Mate 15 Apr 1809. Asst Surgeon 13th Lt Dragoons 18 May 1809. Surgeon 76th Foot 7 Mar 1816. Surgeon 87th Foot 24 Apr 1826. Staff Surgeon 19 Nov 1830.

Served in the Peninsula Apr 1810 – Apr 1814. Present at Campo Mayor, Albuera, Usagre, Alba de Tormes, Vittoria, Garris, Orthes, Aire, St Gaudens and Toulouse. Present at Waterloo. Later Staff Surgeon at Portsmouth Garrison. MGS medal for Albuera, Vittoria, Orthes and Toulouse. Retired 14 Jul 1843. Died at Southsea 18 Oct 1849.

ARSCOTT, John
Paymaster. 3rd (Prince of Wales's) Regiment of Dragoon Guards.
Memorial tablet: St Andrew's Church, Sampford Courtney, Devon. (Photograph)

NEAR THIS SPOT / ARE DEPOSITED / THE MORTAL REMAINS / OF JOHN ARSCOTT ESQRE / PAYMASTER / OF THE 3RD OR P. W. REGIMENT / OF DRAGOON GUARDS, / WHO DIED NOV 16 1824, / AGED 54.

Paymaster 23 Jun 1808.

Served in the Peninsula May 1809 – Apr 1814. Present at Talavera, Albuera, Usagre, Aldea de Ponte, Maguilla (taken prisoner 11 Jun 1812 but released two days later in a second attack on French cavalry by the 1st Dragoons and 3rd Dragoon Guards), Vittoria and Toulouse. Half pay 1817.

BAILEY, Benjamin
Corporal. 15th (King's) Regiment of Light Dragoons.
Headstone: St Mary's Churchyard, Barnsley, Yorkshire. (Photograph)

SACRED TO THE MEMORY / OF / BENJAMIN BAILEY / LATE 15TH KINGS HUSSARS IN WHICH / REGIMENT HE SERVED HIS COUNTRY FOR 18 YEARS / DURING THE PENINSULA WAR / WAS WOUNDED AT THE BATTLE OF TOULOUSE / AND AFTERWARDS WAS PERMANENT SERGEANT / OF THE BARNSLEY TROOP / OF YEOMANRY CAVALRY FOR 33 YEARS / DIED SEPTEMBER 5TH 1855 / AGED 73 YEARS.

Pte Berkshire Fencible Cavalry 1798. Pte 15th Lt Dragoons 19 Mar 1800.

Served in the Peninsula Nov 1808 – Jan 1809 and Feb 1813 – Apr 1814. Present at Sahagun, Vittoria, Orthes and Toulouse (severely wounded). Discharged 1818. Became Sergeant of the Barnsley Troop of Yeomanry Cavalry for 33 years. MGS medal for Sahagun, Vittoria, Orthes and Toulouse.

BAKEWELL, Robert
Lieutenant. 27th (Inniskilling) Regiment of Foot.
Box tomb: St Edmund the Martyr's Churchyard, Castle Donington, Leicestershire. (Photograph)

LIEUT. ROBERT BAKEWELL / LATE 27TH REGT. FOOT. / DIED FEBY 24TH 1853 / AGED 77 YEARS

Ensign 12 Apr 1810. Lt 22 Oct 1812. Ensign 27th Foot 17 Jan 1815.

Served in the Peninsula with 3/27th Nov 1810 – Sep 1811. Present at Pombal, Redinha, Olivencia and first siege of Badajoz. Retired in 1813 but rejoined in Jan 1815 as an Ensign. Shortly after the Battle of Waterloo the first battalion received reinforcements from England as their losses in officers and men had been so great. Bakewell came over with them and served with the Army of Occupation in Paris.
Reference: Robertson, Ian, Exploits of Ensign Bakewell with the Inniskillings in the Peninsula, 1810–1811 and in Paris 1815, 2012.

BARKER, Frederick
Private. 18th Regiment of Light Dragoons
Headstone: St Catherine's Churchyard, Dublin, Ireland. (No longer extant). (M.I.)

"SACRED TO THE MEMORY OF MR FREDERICK BARKER DIED 1800 .... HIS ELDEST SON FREDERICK WAS KILLED BY THE FRENCH AT RUGHEDA IN SPAIN DEC 13TH 1808, AGED 27 YEARS."

Served in the Peninsula Sep – Dec 1808. Present at Rueda 13 Dec 1808 where he was killed in action when the 18th Lt Dragoons encountered part of Francescki's cavalry division and captured them all. This was the first action of Sir John Moore's advance into Spain.

BARNARD, Henry William
Ensign. 1st Regiment of Foot Guards.
Tomb with Cross: Rajpura Cemetery, Delhi, India. (M.I.)

"BENEATH THIS CROSS ARE BURIED THE MORTAL REMAINS OF MAJOR GENERAL SIR HENRY BARNARD, KCB ETC. ETC., WHO DIED ON THE VTH JULY MDCCCLVII WHEN IN CHIEF COMMAND OF THE TROOPS BESIEGING DELHI. THIS MONUMENT IS ERECTED TO HIS MEMORY BY BROTHER OFFICERS WHO SERVED WITH HIM BEFORE SEBASTOPOL"

Memorial tablet in Cemetery wall: Rajpura Cemetery, Delhi, India. (M.I.)

"SIR HENRY BARNARD 5TH OF JULY 1857"

Brass Memorial tablet: Royal Garrison Church, Portsmouth, Hampshire. (Back of a choir stall). (Photograph)

LIEUTENANT GENERAL / SIR HENRY WILLIAM / BARNARD K.C.B. DIED / IN COMMAND OF THE / FORCE BEFORE DELHI / JULY 5 1857 AGE 57 / DD: COL. W. A. MOORE BARNARD

Ensign 9 Jun 1814. Lt and Capt 29 Aug 1822. Capt and Lt Colonel 17 May 1831. Bt Colonel 9 Nov 1846. Major General 20 Jun 1854.

Served in France with the Army of Occupation until 1818 (on staff of his uncle Sir Andrew Barnard). Also served in the West Indies 1824–1825 (ADC to Sir John Keane), Canada 1838–1842 (during the Rebellion), served in various regions of the United Kingdom 1847–1854, Crimea 1855 (Commanded 1 Brigade 3rd Division. Chief of Staff to General Simpson, Raglan's successor Jul 1855. CB, medal and clasp for the Crimea. Commanded 2nd Division 1856. KCB May 1856) and India 1857 (in command of Sirhind Division where there was already disaffection in native troops). When General Anson died on his way from Simla, Barnard was put in charge of the army. He defeated mutineers at Badli-Ki-Serai and seized the ridge overlooking Delhi and maintained his position. Died of cholera 5 Jul 1857. Nephew of Lt Colonel Sir Andrew Barnard 95th Foot and Colonel Sir Moore Disney 15th Foot. Educated at Westminster.

BARNETT, John Henry
Captain. 40th (2nd Somersetshire) Regiment of Foot.
Buried in the Royal Garrison Church Graveyard, Portsmouth, Hampshire. (M.I.)

"SACRED / TO THE MEMORY OF / MAJOR JOHN BARNETT / LATE OF HER MAJESTY'S 40TH REGT / WHO DIED THE 15TH APRIL 1848 / AGED 73"

Lt 28 Sep 1804. Capt 13 Jun 1811. Bt Major 22 Jul 1829.

Served in the Peninsula Aug 1808 – Apr 1814. Present at Rolica, Vimeiro, Talavera, Busaco, Redinha, first Siege of Badajoz, Bidassoa, Nivelle (severely wounded), Orthes and Toulouse (wounded). Present at Waterloo where he was wounded.

BARR, John
Sergeant Major. 7th (Queen's Own) Regiment of Light Dragoons.
Headstone: St Michael's Churchyard, Lowther, Cumbria. (Section AA Row 6 No. 2). (M.I.)

"SACRED TO THE MEMORY OF / JOHN BARR / LATE SERGEANT MAJOR IN THE / SEVENTH OR QUEEN'S OWN HUSSARS / WHO DIED JUNE 9TH 1835 / AGED 58 YEARS."

Pte 12 Apr 1795. Cpl 1803. Sgt 1805. Sgt Major 1811.

Served in the Peninsula 1813 – Apr 1814. Present at Orthes and Toulouse. Also served at the Helder 1799 (Orderly to General Sir David Dundas). Discharged 4 Mar 1820 after 25 years service.

BASDEN, Samuel Taylor
Lieutenant. 84th (York and Lancaster) Regiment of Foot.
Headstone: St Paul's Churchyard, Paget, Bermuda, West Indies. (M.I.)

"SACRED / TO / THE MEMORY OF CAPTAIN / SAMUEL TAYLOR BASDEN / LATE OF THE 84TH REGT OF FOOT / WHO DEPARTED THIS / LIFE ON THE 26TH DAY / OF SEPTEMBER 1847 / AGED 62 YEARS. / IN PACE REQUIESCANT / REQUIESCANT IN PACE."

Ensign 21 May 1807. Lt 9 Oct 1808. Capt 3 Oct 1827.

Served in the Peninsula Jul 1813 – Apr 1814. Present at Bidassoa, Nivelle, Nive and Bayonne. Also served at Walcheren 1809 (present at the siege of Flushing) and the West Indies 1827–1837. Retired and settled in Bermuda where he died 26 Sep 1847.

BELL, John
Sergeant: 1st Regiment of Foot Guards.
Buried in Carlisle Cemetery, Carlisle, Cumbria.

Pte 8 Jan 1798. Cpl 1804. Sgt 1807.

Served in the Peninsula Oct 1808 – Jan 1809 and Oct 1812 – Apr 1814. Present at Corunna, Nivelle and Nive. Present at Waterloo in Lt Colonel Edward Stable's Company. Discharged 24 Aug 1824 aged 41. MGS medal for Corunna, Nivelle and Nive. Died in Carlisle Oct 1848 aged 69.

BELSON, Sir Charles Philip
Lieutenant Colonel. 28th (North Gloucestershire) Regiment of Foot.
Buried in St Martin-in-the-Fields's Church, London. (Burial record)

Ensign 13 Foot 17 Feb 1794. Lt 6th West India Regt Jul 1795. Capt 9 Foot 14 Jan 1797. Capt 7th Lt Dragoons 23 Apr 1799. Major 28th Foot 20 Mar 1804. Lt Colonel 24 Nov 1804. Bt Colonel 4 Jun 1813. Major General 12 Aug 1809.

Served in the Peninsula Aug 1808 – Jan 1809, Feb – Mar 1811, Jul – Sep 1811 and Dec 1812 – Apr 1814. Present at Corunna, Tarifa, Barrosa, Vittoria, Pyrenees, Nivelle and Nive. Present at Quatre Bras and Waterloo where he commanded the 28th Foot. After the death of Picton he commanded Major General Sir James Kempt's Brigade (28th, 32nd, 79th and 95th). Also served in the West Indies 1794–1795 (present at St Lucia, Martinique, St Vincent (wounded) and St Domingo), the Helder 1799 (wounded) and Walcheren 1809. Gold Cross for Corunna, Barrosa, Vittoria, Pyrenees, Nivelle and Nive. KCB 25 Jul 1821. Died in London 5 Nov 1830 aged 56.
Reference: Gentleman's Magazine, 1830 p. 564. Royal Military Calendar Vol. 4, pp. 14–15.

BETTESWORTH, John
2nd Captain. Royal Artillery.
Headstone: St Saviour's Church, Torquay, Devon. (M.I.)

"SACRED / TO THE MEMORY OF / CAPTAIN JOHN BETTESWORTH / ROYAL ARTILLERY / WHO DIED 16 JANUARY 1823 / AGED 40 YEARS"

2nd Lt 20 Dec 1800. 1st Lt 3 Jun 1802. 2nd Capt 1 Feb 1808. Capt 30 Sep 1816.
Present in the Waterloo campaign where he was stationed at Ostend.

BIRTWHISTLE, John
Ensign. 32nd (Cornwall) Regiment of Foot.
Headstone: Borough Cemetery, Cheltenham. (M.I.)

"SACRED TO THE MEMORY OF MAJOR GENERAL JOHN BIRTWHISTLE, LATE H.M. 32ND LIGHT INFANTRY WHO DIED OCTOBER 6TH 1867 AGED 75"

Ensign 14 Apr 1813. Lt 14 Jun 1819. Capt 13 May 1824. Bt Major 28 Jun 1838. Major 19 Jan 1839. Bt Lt Colonel 11 Nov 1851. Bt Colonel 20 Nov 1854. Major General 28 Aug 1865.
Served in the Peninsula Apr 1814. Present at Quatre Bras (wounded) and Waterloo where he was severely wounded while carrying the regimental colours. Served with the Army of Occupation until 1816. Also served in the Ionian Islands 1817–1825, Ireland 1827–1830 and Canada 1830–1841 (present during the Rebellion). Half pay 12 Mar 1841.

BLACK, Samuel James John
Lieutenant. 6th (Inniskilling) Regiment of Dragoons.
Headstone: St Mary's Churchyard, Buckden, Huntingdonshire. (M.I.)

"SACRED / TO THE MEMORY OF SAMUEL JAMES JOHN BLACK / LATE CAPTAIN IN THE 6TH DRAGOONS / WHO DIED NOV 2ND 1853"

Cornet 5 Apr 1810. Lt 8 Jul 1813. Capt 28 Jul 1825.
Present at Waterloo and in France with the Army of Occupation. Returned home 1 Jan 1816. Also served in Ireland 1819–1823. Retired on half pay 8 Apr 1826.

BLOIS, Charles
Lieutenant. 1st (Royal) Regiment of Dragoons.
Memorial tablet: St Peter's Church, Yoxhall, Suffolk. (Photograph)

IN MEMORY / OF / SIR CHARLES BLOIS / SEVENTH BART OF COCKFIELD HALL SUFFOLK, BORN IN 1794, DIED 12TH JUNE 1855, / HE ENTERED THE ARMY EARLY IN LIFE, SERVING THROUGH / THE PENINSULAR WAR, AND WAS SEVERELY WOUNDED / AT THE BATTLE OF WATERLOO. / HE WAS ALSO / COLONEL OF THE EAST SUFFOLK MILITIA, / A BRAVE SOLDIER, A KIND LANDLORD, / AND A FAITHFUL FRIEND. / (VERSE)

Cornet 10 Dec 1812. Lt 2 Sep 1813. Capt 25 Sep 1823. Major 27 Oct 1829.
Served in the Peninsula Oct 1813 – Apr 1814. Present at Toulouse. Present at Waterloo where he was wounded. Retired 1 Sep 1830. Lt Colonel East Suffolk Militia 6 Feb 1844. MGS medal for Toulouse. Became Sir Charles Blois 7th Baronet of Cockfield Hall Suffolk 1850. Deputy Lieutenant of Suffolk 21 Dec 1853.

BOLTON, George
Captain. 14th (Buckinghamshire) Regiment of Foot.
Low monument: Holy Trinity Churchyard, Ilfracombe, Devon. (Photograph)

SACRED TO / MAJOR GEORGE BOLTON / FORMERLY OF THE 14TH AND LATE OF THE 20TH REGT / WHO DEPARTED THIS LIFE FEBRUARY 24TH 1849 / AGED 67 YEARS / ....

Ensign 27 Mar 1806. Lt 11 Dec 1806. Capt 4 Apr 1815. Capt 20th Foot 4 Dec 1823. Bt Major 10 Jan 1837.

Served in the Peninsula Nov 1808 – Jan 1809. Present at Corunna. Also served at Walcheren 1809 (present at the siege of Flushing), Gibraltar (with two companies sent to Tarifa), Malta, Sicily, Capture of Genoa 1814 and India 1817–1818 (present in the Pindari War at the siege of Hattrass). Served in India until 1834.

BOND, Isaac

Sergeant. 52nd (Oxfordshire) Light Infantry Regiment of Foot.
Buried in St Mary's Churchyard, Tidenham, Gloucestershire. (Burial record)

Pte 16 Oct 1799. Cpl 1802. Sgt 1814.

Present at Waterloo in Capt George Young's Company and with the Army of Occupation. Discharged 24 Feb 1819 on the reduction of the regiment. Died 15 Aug 1841.

BOWCOCK, Samuel

Private. 92nd Regiment of Foot.
Buried in Old Cemetery, Leek, Staffordshire. (Grave Number 2194). (Burial register)

Pte 1792.

Served in the Peninsula 1808 – Jan 1809 and Oct 1810 – Apr 1814. Present at Corunna, Fuentes d'Onoro, Almarez, Alba de Tormes, Vittoria, Maya, Orthes and Aire. Present at Quatre Bras and Waterloo in Capt Claud Alexander's Company. Also served at the Helder 1799 and Egypt 1801 (wounded). MGS medal for Egypt, Corunna, Fuentes d'Onoro and Vittoria. Promoted to Corporal. Discharged 25 Nov 1818 aged 44. Died 23 Dec 1858 aged 84.
Note: Also known as Bancock or Beaucock.

BOWLBY, Peter

Lieutenant. 4th (King's Own) Regiment of Foot.
Memorial: New Cemetery, Cheltenham, Gloucestershire. Inscription not recorded.

Ensign 7 Jun 1808. Lt 31 May 1809. Capt 23 Oct 1824.

Served in the Peninsula with 1/4th Mar – June 1812, with 2/4th Jul 1812 – Jan 1813 and with 1/4th Sep 1813 – Apr 1814. Present at Badajoz, Salamanca, retreat from Burgos (present at Villa Muriel), San Sebastian, Bidassoa, Nivelle, Nive and Bayonne. Present at Waterloo and with the Army of Occupation. Also served at Walcheren 1809, North America 1814–1815 (present at Bladensburg where he was wounded, New Orleans where he was wounded and Fort Bowyer). Half pay 25 Mar 1823. MGS medal for Badajoz, Salamanca, San Sebastian, Nivelle and Nive. Died 8 Nov 1877.

BRICE, Alexander Adair

1st Lieutenant. 23rd (Royal Welch Fusiliers) Regiment of Foot.
Gravestone: English Cemetery, Nice, France. (M.I.)

"ALEXANDER ADAIR BRICE OF THE 23RD / ROYAL WELSH FUSILIERS / IN WHICH HE SERVED IN THE PENINSULA AND WAS PRESENT / ON THE STAFF OF HIS UNCLE GENERAL O'LOGHLIN. / AT THE BATTLE OF WATERLOO"

2nd Lt 8 Aug 1811. 1st Lt 21 May 1812.

Served in the Peninsula with 1/23rd May 1812 – Aug 1813. On Staff Sep 1813 – Apr 1814 as ADC to his uncle Major General Terence O'Loghlin. Present at Salamanca, Vittoria and Pyrenees where he was wounded at Sorauren 28 Jul 1813. Present at Waterloo. Half pay 5 Oct 1820. MGS medal for Salamanca, Vittoria and Pyrenees. Died 1864. Nephew of Lt Colonel and Colonel Terrence O'Loghlin 1st Life Guards.

BRIDGE, Cyprian
2nd Captain. Royal Artillery.
Memorial tablet: St Philip and St James's Church, Cheltenham, Gloucestershire. (M.I.)

"SACRED / TO THE MEMORY OF / LIEUT COL CYPRIAN BRIDGE / OF THE ROYAL REGT OF ARTILLERY / WHO HAVING SERVED HIS SOVEREIGN AND COUNTRY / WITH HONOR AND FIDELITY FOR 43 YEARS / DEPARTED THIS LIFE DEC 31ST 1843 / AGED 59 YEARS / DEEPLY AND SINCERELY REGRETTED"

2nd Lt 20 Dec 1800. 1st Lt 8 Aug 1802. 2nd Capt 1 Feb 1808. Capt 24 Mar 1817. Bt Major 27 May 1825. Lt Colonel 4 Jun 1836.

Served with the Army of Occupation 1815–1816. Also served in North America 1812–1814 (present on the Niagara frontier campaign where he was wounded and brought back the dispatches from Fort Erie 1814) and Portugal 1826–1828. Served in the army for 43 years.

BROWN, William
2nd Captain. Artillery, King's German Legion.
Named on the Memorial tablet to Portuguese Commanders at Albuera: Albuera Wall, British Cemetery, Elvas, Portugal. (Photograph)

2nd Lt 5 May 1804. 1st Lt 9 Jul 1808. 2nd Capt 11 Dec 1812.

Served in the Peninsula 1808–1812 (with Portuguese Artillery 1810–1812). Present at Fuentes d'Onoro, Albuera and Ciudad Rodrigo. Present at Waterloo (severely wounded). Also served at Hanover 1805, the Baltic 1807–1808 and North Germany 1813–1814. Gold Medal for Albuera. Portuguese Cross for distinguished services. KH. Spanish Cross for distinguished service. King William's Cross. Became Bt Lt Colonel Hanoverian Artillery. Died in 1845.

Reference: Beamish, N. L., History of the King's German Legion, Vol. 2, reprint 1997. No. 38.

BROWNE, Gore
Lieutenant Colonel. 40th (2nd Somersetshire) Regiment of Foot.
Memorial: St Mary's Churchyard, Weymouth, Dorset. (M.I.)

"SACRED / TO THE MEMORY OF / GENERAL GORE BROWNE / COLONEL OF H. M. 44TH REGT / DIED AT WEYMOUTH 12 JAN / 1843 AGED 79"

Ensign 35th Foot 5 Jul 1780. Lt 3 Mar 1789. Capt 83rd Foot 8 Jun 1793. Major 15 Jun 1794. Lt Colonel 7th West India Regt 30 Nov 1796. Lt Colonel 40th Foot 5 Aug 1799. Bt Colonel 1 Jan 1805. Major General 25 Jul 1810. Lt General 12 Aug 1819. General 10 Jan 1837.

Present at Walcheren 1809 (wounded). Also served in North America 1780, West Indies 1784–1789, 1794–1795 and 1798, the Helder 1799 and South America 1807 (commanded Brigade at Monte Video). Lt Governor of Plymouth 1813. Colonel 44th Foot 29 Jan 1820.

Reference: Gentleman's Magazine, May 1843, p. 543. Annual Register, Appx, pp. 226–7.

BROWNING, John
Private. 52nd (Oxfordshire Light Infantry) Regiment of Foot.
Headstone: St Andrew's Churchyard, West Stoke, Sussex. (Photograph)

"SACRED / TO THE MEMORY OF / JOHN BROWNING / DIED MARCH 3RD 1868 / AGED 83 YEARS / THE ABOVE JOHN BROWNING WAS A / FINE SOLDIER OF THE 52ND REGIMENT / AND SERVED HIS COUNTRY IN THE / PENINSULAR AND AT WATERLOO"

Pte 1 Apr 1809.

Served in the Peninsula 1811 – Apr 1814. Present at Ciudad Rodrigo, Badajoz, Salamanca, San Munos, Vittoria, San Sebastian, Pyrenees, Orthes (wounded) and Toulouse. Volunteered for a storming party on more than one occasion. Present at Waterloo in Capt Love's Company. Discharged 12 Jun 1816. MGS medal for Ciudad Rodrigo, Badajoz, Salamanca, Vittoria, San Sebastian, Pyrenees, Orthes and Toulouse. Note: Also known as John Brown.

BUCKLEY, Edward Pery
Lieutenant and Captain. 1st Regiment of Foot Guards.
Memorial tablet: St Andrew's Church, Nunton, Wiltshire. (M.I.)

"MAJOR GENERAL EDWARD PERY BUCKLEY / DIED 28 MAY 1873, BORN 7 OCT 1796 / COLONEL OF 83RD REGIMENT"

Memorial window: St Andrew's Church, Nunton, Wiltshire. (Photograph)

Memorial tablet: St Andrew's Church, Nunton, Wiltshire. (Photograph)

THE PRESENT EAST WINDOW / REPLACES ONE GIVEN BY / MAJ: GEN: EDWARD PERY BUCKLEY / WHEN HE RESTORED THE CHURCH / IN 1854–55

Ensign 24 Jun 1812. Lt and Capt 23 Mar 1814. Bt Major 19 Jul 1821. Lt Colonel 26 Sep 1826 (unattached). Bt Colonel 23 Nov 1841. Major General 11 Nov 1851. Lt General 26 Oct 1858. General 17 Aug 1865.

Served in the Peninsula May 1813 – Apr 1814. Present at Bidassoa, Nivelle, Nive, Adour and Bayonne. Present at Quatre Bras, Waterloo and siege of Peronne. Half pay 9 Nov 1830. MGS medal for Nivelle and Nive. Equerry to the Queen. MP for Salisbury 1853–1865. Colonel 83rd Foot 17 Aug 1865.

BURGH, Sir Ulysses
Captain and Lieutenant Colonel. 1st Regiment of Foot Guards.
Family vault: St Ann's Church, Dublin, Ireland. (Vault V).

Ensign 54th Foot 31 Mar 1804. Lt 12 Nov 1804. Capt 60th Foot 9 Jul 1806. Capt 54th Foot 6 Oct 1806. Capt 92nd Foot 25 Nov 1808. Bt Major 31 Mar 1811. Bt Lt Colonel 5 Sep 1812. Capt and Lt Colonel 1st Foot Guards 25 Jul 1814. Bt Colonel 27 May 1825. Major General 10 Jan 1837. Lt General 9 Nov 1846. General 20 Jun 1854.

Served in the Peninsula Jan – Apr 1809 (ADC to Lt General Cradock) and May 1809 – Apr 1814 (ADC and Assistant Military Secretary to Lord Wellington). Present at Talavera (wounded), Busaco (Mentioned in Despatches, took despatches home and awarded Brevet Majority), Fuentes d'Onoro, El Bodon, Ciudad Rodrigo, Badajoz, Salamanca, Majalahonda (Mentioned in Despatches and carried the despatches home), Burgos, Vittoria, Pyrenees, Bidassoa, Nivelle, Nive and Toulouse (wounded). Gold Cross for Vittoria, Pyrenees, Nivelle, Nive and Toulouse. KCB Jan 1815. MGS medal for Talavera, Busaco, Fuentes d'Onoro, Ciudad Rodrigo, Badajoz and Salamanca. Also served in Gibraltar 1805 and Jamaica 1807. Half pay 5 Jul 1827. MP for Carlow County 1818–1826 and Queensborough 1826–1830. Surveyor General of Ordnance Mar 1820. Became second Baron Downes in 1826. One of the pall bearers at Raglan's funeral in 1855. Member of the committee to administer Raglan's Memorial Fund that acquired Kifntella Estate for the Raglan family. Russian Order of St Anne 2nd class 1856. Colonel 54th Foot 4 Apr 1845. Colonel 29th Foot 15 Aug 1850. Died 26 Jul 1863.
Reference: Dictionary of National Biography.

CALDER, Stewart
Lieutenant. Royal Engineers.
Buried in St Mary's, Churchyard, Carlisle, Cumbria. (Burial Register)

Sub Lt Jul 1811. Appointed from the Royal Artillery.

Served in the Peninsula Nov 1811 – Apr 1814. Present at Cadiz, Pyrenees (present at Roncesvalles and Maya), Bidassoa, Nivelle, Nive, Orthes and Toulouse. Commended by Burgoyne at Nive for building bridges of casks over the Nive. Appointed Master Gunner at Carlisle Castle. Died at Carlisle 16 Oct 1822.

CAMPBELL, Allan William
Major. 74th (Highland) Regiment of Foot.
Named on the Memorial tablet to Portuguese Commanders at Albuera: Albuera Wall, British Cemetery, Elvas, Portugal. (Photograph)

Ensign 31 May 1800. Lt 20 Oct 1801. Capt 74th Foot 23 Sep 1803. Major 5 Apr 1810. Bt Lt Colonel 26 Aug 1813. Portuguese Army: Lt Colonel 4 Line 4 Jun 1810.

Served in the Peninsula on Staff May – Jun 1809 (ADC to General A. Campbell) and Jun 1809 – May 1810 (DAAG I Division). With Portuguese Army Jun 1810 – Oct 1813 (one of the British officers chosen to train and lead units of the Portuguese Army). Present at first siege of Badajoz, Albuera, Vittoria and Pyrenees (severely wounded 30 Jul 1813 and died of his wounds 9 Oct 1813). Awarded a Bt Lt Colonelcy for the Pyrenees but the promotion did not reach him until after his death. Gold Medal for Albuera, Vittoria and Pyrenees. His father was General Sir Alexander Campbell who served in the Peninsula as Divisional Commander. His elder brother Lt John Campbell was killed in India with the 74th Foot at the Battle of Assaye.
Reference: Gentleman's Magazine, Nov 1813, p. 506.

CAMPBELL, John
Hospital Assistant. Medical Department.
Obelisk: Grange Cemetery, Edinburgh, Scotland. (Section J Row 5. No. 392). (Photograph)

SACRED / TO THE MEMORY / OF / JOHN CAMPBELL MD. LATE SURGEON / 93RD HIGHLANDERS / DIED 20TH OCTOBER 1870 / AGED 78 / ....

Hospital Asst 25 Mar 1813. Asst Surgeon 7th West India Regt 27 Jul 1815. Asst Surgeon 30th Foot 20 Feb 1823. Asst Surgeon 45th Foot 15 Mar 1827. Surgeon 55th Foot 27 Dec 1833. Surgeon 93rd Foot 20 Mar 1835.

Served in the Peninsula Apr 1813 – Apr 1814. Present at Pyrenees and Orthes. Also served in North America 1814–1815 (present at New Orleans), India 1826, Canada with 93rd Foot 1836–1848 (present in the Canadian Rebellion 1838) and in the West Indies. While on half pay 1816–1823 took his MA and MD at Glasgow University. MGS medal for Pyrenees and Orthes. Retired on half pay 30 Mar 1849 and was employed as Medical Officer at Greenlaw Military Prison near Penicuick.

CARR, James
Private: 64th (2nd Staffordshire) Regiment of Foot.
Headstone: New Burying Ground, Belfast, Northern Ireland. (No longer extant). (M.I.)

"SACRED TO THE MEMORY OF JAMES CARR, LATE QUARTER MASTER 64TH REGT WHO DIED 22ND AUGUST 1845, AGED 65 YEARS."

Pte 1794. Quarter Master 2 Nov 1826.

Served in the Peninsula Jul 1808 – Jan 1809 and Oct 1812 – Apr 1814. Present at Vimeiro, Corunna, Vittoria, Pyrenees, Orthes and Toulouse. Also served at the Helder 1799 (wounded and taken prisoner at Egmont-op-Zee), Egypt 1801 and Maida 1806. Half pay 6 Sep 1839.

CHAMBERLAINE, Frederick
Lieutenant. 16th (Queen's) Regiment of Light Dragoons.
Family memorial tablet: St Leonard's Church, Keevil, Wiltshire. (Photograph)

.... / ALSO OF / FREDERICK CHAMBERLAINE / MA TRIN. COLL. CAMBRIDGE / LIEUTENANT 16TH LIGHT DRAGOONS / DIED 26 JANUARY 1815 AGED 29 / ....

Cornet 23 Jan 1812. Lt 3 Dec 1812.
Served in the Peninsula Dec 1812 – Apr 1814. Present at Nivelle, Nive and Bayonne. Retired on half pay Dec 1814. Died of consumption brought on by fatigue in the Peninsula. Educated at Charterhouse and Cambridge.

CHEEK, Jabez
Farrier. Royal Waggon Train.
Headstone: St Mary the Virgin's Churchyard, Carisbrooke, Isle of Wight. (Seriously eroded and inscription recorded from memorial inscription). (Section D. Grave Number 216). (Photograph)

"JABEZ CHEEK, LATE FARRIER THE ROYAL WAGGON TRAIN. DIED 1 SEPT 1823 AGED 41".

Present at Waterloo.
Note: Also known as Thabus Check.

CHENEY, William
Captain. 1st (Royal Scots) Regiment of Foot.
Memorial: St Mary Magdalene's Church, Somerby, near Grantham, Lincolnshire. (Photograph)

IN A VAULT OUTSIDE OF THE CHURCH, / LIE THE REMAINS OF WILLIAM, YOUNGER SON / OF THE LATE ROBERT CHENEY ESQR., AND LATE / CAPTAIN IN THE FIRST REGIMENT OF GUARDS. BORN DECEMBER 2 1780. DIED AT SOMERBY / DECEMBER 17 1822 / ....

Ensign 1st Foot Guards 26 Dec 1799. Lt and Capt 12 May 1803. Capt 1st Foot 13 Apr 1809.
Served in the Peninsula with 1st Battalion Oct 1806 – Jan 1809. Present at Corunna. Retired 3 Feb 1810. Son of Capt and Lt Colonel Robert Cheney 1st Foot Guards and brother of Capt Edward Cheney 2nd (Royal North British) Regiment of Dragoons.

CHISHOLM, Donald
Lieutenant. 42nd (Royal Highland) Regiment of Foot.
Low monument: Canongate Burial Ground, Edinburgh, Scotland. (Photograph)

.... / ALSO CAPTAIN DONALD CHISHOLM FORMERLY OF THE 42ND REGIMENT. / DIED 21 AUGUST 1853. AGED 87 YEARS.

Lt 10 Oct 1805. Capt 29 Jul 1815.
Served in the Peninsula Aug 1808 – Jan 1809 and May 1813 – Apr 1814. Present at Corunna. Present at Waterloo where he was wounded. Also served at Walcheren 1809. Retired on full pay 1821.

CLINTON, Lord Robert Cotton St John Trefusis
Major. 41st Regiment of Foot.
Memorial tablet: Mylor Parish Church, Mylor, Cornwall. (Photograph)

ROBERT COTTON ST JOHN TREFUSIS / BARON CLINTON AND SAYE / DIED IN ITALY 7TH OCTOBER 1832 AGED 45 / TRUSTING IN THE MERCY OF HIS REDEEMER / THIS TABLET IS ERECTED AND INSCRIBED / BY HIS WIDOW / IN GRATEFUL REMEMBRANCE OF / MANY YEARS OF / HAPPINESS / (VERSE)

Lt 16th Lt Dragoons 18 Dec 1805. Capt 18 Jun 1807. Major 41st Foot 13 Aug 1812. Bt Lt Colonel 20 Aug 1812.

Served in the Peninsula Mar 1810 – Mar 1811 and Oct 1811 – Jul 1812 (Extra ADC to Wellington). Present at Busaco, Ciudad Rodrigo, Badajoz and Salamanca (brought the Despatches to England from Salamanca and awarded Bt Lt Colonelcy). Half pay 1814. Died 9 Oct 1832 in Italy near Florence on the way to Naples. His remains were brought back for burial in the family estate in Cornwall.

CLUES, Josiah
Cornet and Adjutant. 2nd Life Guards.
Ledger Stone: Deconsecrated Churchyard behind All Saints Church, Kingston, Surrey. (Photograph)

TO THE MEMORY OF / LIEUT JOSIAH CLUES / WHO SERVED 1812–1814 UNDER / THE DUKE OF WELLINGTON / AT / VITTORIA PAMPLONA PYRENEES / IN SPAIN / WAS AT THE SURRENDER OF PARIS 1814 / AND / ADJUTANT 2ND LIFE GUARDS AT WATERLOO / DIED 25TH MARCH 1842 AGED 62

Promoted from the ranks. Adjutant 24 Jun 1813. Cornet 12 Apr 1815. Lt 15 Oct 1816.

Served in the Peninsula Dec 1812 – Apr 1814. Present at Vittoria, Pamplona, Pyrenees and Toulouse. Present at Waterloo. Half pay 25 Jan 1817.

CONNOLLY, James
Major. 26th (Cameronian) Regiment of Foot.
Named on the Memorial tablet: St Michael's Cathedral, Barbados, West Indies. (Photograph)

Lt 7 Dec 1796. Capt 9 Feb 1804. Major 2 Jan 1812.

Served in the Peninsula Oct 1808 – Jan 1809 and Jun 1811 – Jun 1812. Present at Corunna. Also served at Walcheren 1809 and Gibraltar 1811–1812. Exchanged to 2nd Foot in 1816 and went to the West Indies where he died in 1817 in a yellow fever epidemic.

COOPER, John Spencer
Sergeant. 7th (Royal Fusiliers) Regiment of Foot.
Memorial stone: Carlisle Cemetery, Carlisle, Cumbria. (Grave Number D 6 G 18). (Photograph)

IN AFFECTIONATE MEMORY OF / JOHN SPENCER COOPER / AGED 87 YEARS. DIED JANUARY 17TH 1875 / ....

Pte. North York Militia Jun 1806. Pte 7th Foot 21 Aug 1807.

Served in the Peninsula Apr 1809 – Apr 1814. Present at Oporto, Talavera, Busaco, Torres Vedras, Albuera, Ciudad Rodrigo, Badajoz, Vittoria, Pyrenees, Pamplona, Orthes and Toulouse. Also served in Ireland 1808 and North America 1814–1815 (present at New Orleans). Discharged Jul 1815. Did not receive a pension for 50 years. After a third application in Aug 1865 he was awarded a pension of one shilling per day as a Chelsea Out-Pensioner. MGS medal for Talavera, Busaco, Albuera, Ciudad Rodrigo,

Badajoz, Vittoria, Pyrenees, Orthes and Toulouse. Wrote *Rough notes of Seven Campaigns in Portugal ...* describing his military experience in the Peninsula and North America.

REFERENCE: Cooper, John Spencer, Rough notes of seven campaigns in Portugal, Spain, France and America during the years 1809–10–12–13–14–15, 1869, reprint 1912. Obit. Carlisle Journal, 2 Feb 1875, p. 2.

CRAWLEY, William

Lieutenant. 27th (Inniskilling) Regiment of Foot.
Named on the Memorial: St Andrew's Church (now Musée Historique), Biarritz, France. (Photograph)

Ensign 32nd Foot 7 Nov 1811. Lt 27th Foot 31 Dec 1812.

Served in the Peninsula Aug 1813 – Apr 1814. Present at Nivelle where he was taken prisoner of war 10 Nov 1813, reported missing believed killed and entered in the records as such. Released at the end of the war but the records were not amended. He was mistakenly entered on the Biarritz memorial as William Lewanley. MGS medal for Nivelle.

CREIGHTON, R.

Private. 74th (Highland) Regiment of Foot.
Headstone: St George's Military Cemetery, St George's, Bermuda, West Indies. (M.I.)

"PENINSULA / MEMORIA SACRUM / OF / R. CREIGHTON LATE PRIVATE / LT CY 74TH ASSAYE REGT WHO / DEPARTED THIS LIFE THE 10TH OF MAY / 1829. AGED 37 YEARS AND 6 MONTHS. / HE SERVED IN THE REGT 20 YEARS DURING / WHICH PERIOD HE SERVED 4 YEARS AND A HALF / IN THE PENINSULA AND WAS IN SEVEN / GENERAL ENGAGEMENTS IN ONE OF / WHICH HE RECEIVED A SEVERE WOUND. / (VERSE) / ERECTED BY HIS COMRADES OF THE COY."

Pte 1809.

Served in the Peninsula Feb 1810 – Apr 1814. Present at Fuentes d'Onoro, Ciudad Rodrigo, Badajoz, Salamanca, Vittoria, Nivelle and Toulouse. Also served in Canada 1818, Newfoundland and Bermuda. Died in 1829 just before 74th Foot left Bermuda in 1830.

CRINGAM, William

Surgeon. 25th (King's Own Borderers) Regiment of Foot.
Family headstone: St Bride's Churchyard, Sanquhar, Dumfriesshire, Scotland. (Headstone severely damaged, broken in two and centre part not visible. Inscription recorded from a Memorial Inscription). (Photograph)

"................... / AT RYEHILL, BY SANQUHAR THE 13TH JANUARY 1828 IN THE 40TH YEAR OF HIS AGE WILLIAM CRINGAM ESQ TENANT THERE AND LATE SURGEON OF THE 2ND BATTALION 25TH REGIMENT ...."

Hospital Mate 8 Jan 1807. Asst Surgeon 69th Foot 31 Mar 1808. Surgeon 25th Foot 17 Mar 1814.

Served in the Netherlands 1814–1815 where he was wounded and awarded a pension for loss of his right eye. Also served in Travancore 1809, Mauritius 1810 and Java 1811. Retired 25 Jun 1816. Died at Ryehill, near Sanquhar 13 Jan 1828 aged 40.

CROLL, Francis

Private. 42nd (Royal Highland) Regiment of Foot.
Family Memorial Monument: St Michael's Churchyard, Inveresk, Midlothian, Scotland. (Photograph)

SACRED / TO THE MEMORY OF / FRANCIS CROLL, / MERCHANT, OF FISHERROW, / WHO DIED 28TH MARCH 1873, AGED 89 YEARS. / ....

Pte 21 Jan 1804.

Served in the Peninsula 1808 – Jan 1809 and Apr 1812 – Apr 1814. Present at Corunna, Salamanca, Orthes and Toulouse (severely wounded). Also served at Walcheren 1809. Discharged 24 Aug 1814 owing to injuries received at Toulouse. MGS medal for Corunna, Salamanca, Orthes and Toulouse. Returned to Musselburgh and resumed his trade as a weaver, setting up his own business. He also established a successful property business, owning 11 properties by 1867. His son, also named Francis Croll was a well-known artist and engraver.

Reference: Millar, Suzi, Battling on (the Croll family). Your Family Tree, Mar 2012, pp. 44–6.

CROSS, JOHN

Captain. 52nd (Oxfordshire) Light Infantry Regiment of Foot.
Memorial tablet: St Mark's Church of Ireland, Killylea, County Armagh, Northern Ireland. (M.I.)

"SACRED TO THE MEMORY OF / LIEUT COLONEL JOHN CROSS K.H. / BORN 17TH JAN^{Y} 1787 DIED 27TH SEP^{R} 1850 / SON OF THE LATE WILLIAM CROSS OF DARTAN / (TWENTY YEARS A DEPUTY GOVERNOR OF THIS COUNTY) / COL CROSS WAS A MEMBER OF THE ROYAL HANOVERIAN GUELPHIC ORDER / SOME TIME L^{T} GOVERNOR OF JAMAICA AND A MAGISTRATE OF THIS COUNTY. / HE SERVED WITH DISTINCTION IN THE 52ND L^{T} INFANTRY WITH THE LIGHT DIVISION DURING / THE PENINSULAR WAR IN THE CAMPAIGNS OF 1808, 9, 10, 11, 12, 13, 14 & 15 (THREE TIMES WOUNDED) / INCLUDING THE CAPTURE OF PARIS, AND SUBSEQUENT OCCUPATION. / WAS PRESENT AT THE BATTLES OF CORUNNA, ALMEIDA, ON THE COA, BUSACO, / POMBAL, REDINHA, MIRANDA, DE CORVO, FOZ, D'AROUCE, SABUGAL, / FUENTES D'ONOR, 3RD AND 5TH MAY1811 SIEGE AND ASSAULT OF CUIDAD-RODRIGO, / BATTLES OF SAN MUNOZ, SAN MILAN, VITTORIA, LESACA-BRIDGE, / BIDASSOA, VERA, NIVELLE, NIVE, 9TH 10TH 11TH 12TH & 13TH DEC^{R} 1813, / ORTHES, TARBES, TOULOUSE, WATERLOO, / AS WELL AS OTHER ACTIONS OF LESS NOTE IN WHICH THE 52ND REG^{T} WAS ENGAGED DURING THE WAR; / FROM WHICH REG^{T} HE WAS PROMOTED TO THE COMMAND OF THE 68TH L^{T} INFANTRY FEB^{Y} 8TH 1831, / COLONEL CROSS ENTERED THE SERVICE AS A VOLUNTEER, FROM / THE ARMAGH MILITIA AS ENSIGN IN THE 52 L^{T} INFANTRY 9TH JULY 1805 / HE RECEIVED THE WAR MEDAL WITH TEN CLASPS, ALSO THE WATERLOO MEDAL. / THIS TABLET IS PLACED HERE BY HIS NEPHEW / WILLIAM CROSS LT COLONEL COMMANDANT / OF THE MILITIA OF THIS COUNTY AS A TRIBUTE OF RESPECT AND AFFECTION 1867"

Ensign Armagh Militia. Ensign 52nd Foot 9 Jul 1805. Lt 29 May 1806. Capt 31 Dec 1812. Major 25 Jun 1825. Lt Colonel 68th Foot 8 Feb 1831.

Served in the Peninsula with 1/52nd Aug 1808 – Jan 1809, Jul 1809 – Feb 1812, 2/52nd Feb – Mar 1812 and 1/52nd Aug 1812 – Apr 1814. Present at Corunna, Coa, Busaco, Pombal, Redinha (wounded), Miranda de Covo, Foz d'Arouce, Sabugal, Fuentes d'Onoro, Ciudad Rodrigo, San Munos, San Millan, Vittoria, Pyrenees, Bidassoa, Vera, Nivelle, Nive, Orthes, Vic Bigorre, Tarbes and Toulouse. Present at Waterloo (wounded) and with the Army of Occupation until Sep 1816. Also served in the Baltic 1808, North America 1823–1824 and 1827–1829. MGS medal for Corunna, Busaco, Fuentes d'Onoro, Ciudad Rodrigo, Vittoria, Pyrenees, Nivelle, Nive, Orthes and Toulouse. KH. Commanded 68th Foot from 1831 until he retired as Colonel in 1843. Appointed Lt Governor commanding forces in Jamaica. Magistrate for County Armagh. Died in Brighton 27 Sep 1850.

CROYDEN, William
Private. 23rd Regiment of Light Dragoons.
Buried in All Saints' Churchyard, Claverley, Shropshire. (Burial record)

Pte 1803.

Served in the Peninsula Jun – Nov 1809. Present at Talavera where he was injured by his horse. Present at Waterloo in Capt Hamilton's No. 4 Troop. Discharged 1817 owing to the disbandment of the regiment and being unfit for further service due to his injury at Talavera. Died 1833 aged 59 years.

CUNNINGHAM, John
Private. 27th (Inniskilling) Regiment of Foot.
Headstone: Mauchline Churchyard, Mauchline, Ayrshire, Scotland. (Photograph)

TO THE MEMORY OF / PRIVATE JOHN CUNNINGHAM / OF THE 27TH FOOT / WHO FOUGHT AT TOULOUSE ORTHES NIVELLE / PYRENEES VITTORIA SALAMANCA AND BADAJOZ / DIED AT MAUCHLINE 28 OCT 1868 AGED 81 / ....

Pte 1802. Pte 2nd Royal Veteran Battalion Dec 1821.

Served in the Peninsula 1809 – Apr 1814. Present at Badajoz, Salamanca, Vittoria, Pyrenees, Nivelle, Orthes and Toulouse. Present at Waterloo. Discharged 24 Apr 1826 on reduction of the battalion. MGS medal for Badajoz, Salamanca, Vittoria, Pyrenees, Nivelle, Orthes and Toulouse

CUYLER, George
Lieutenant Colonel. 11th (North Devonshire) Regiment of Foot.
Buried in the Royal Garrison Church Graveyard, Portsmouth, Hampshire. (M.I.)

"TO THE MEMORY OF / COLONEL GEORGE CUYLER CB / 11TH REGIMENT OF FOOT / WHO DIED NOVEMBER 12TH 1818 / AGED 46 YEARS"

Ensign 55th Foot 6 Oct 1787. Lt in Major General Cuyler's Regt 16 Nov 1793. Capt 86th Foot 26 Jul 1794. Bt Major 11 May 1802. Major 86th Foot 1 Jun 1805. Bt Lt Colonel 28 Jan 1808. Lt Colonel 11th Foot 16 Nov 1809. Bt Colonel 4 Jun 1814.

Served in the Peninsula Jan 1811 – Sep 1812 and Jan – Apr 1814. Present at Fuentes d'Onoro, siege of Salamanca Forts, Salamanca (severely wounded and awarded pension of £300 per annum), Orthes and Toulouse (severely wounded). Also served in the West Indies 1793, Quiberon Bay 1795, India 1799 (present at Seringapatam), Egypt 1801, India 1802–1807 (present in the Mahratta Wars) and Nova Scotia 1808 where he was Inspecting Field Officer of Militia. Gold Medal for Salamanca, Orthes and Toulouse. CB.

DALHOUSIE, George Lord
Colonel. 26th (Cameronian) Regiment of Foot.
Buried in the Family vault: Panbride Church, Carnoustie, Angus, Scotland.

Cornet 3rd Dragoon Guards 5 Jul 1788. Capt Independent Company 27 Jan 1791 (raised by himself). Capt 1st Foot 7 May 1791. Major 2nd Foot 27 Jun 1792. Lt Colonel 22 Aug 1794. Bt Colonel 1 Jan 1800. Major General 25 Apr 1808. Colonel 26th Foot 21 May 1813. Lt General 4 Jun 1813. General 22 Jul 1833.

Served in the Peninsula Oct 1812 – Oct 1813 and Feb – Apr 1814 (GOC 7th Division). Present at Vittoria, Pyrenees and Bidassoa. Gold Medal for Vittoria and Pyrenees. GCB. Also served in the West Indies 1794–1797 (present at Trinidad and Martinique where he was wounded 1795), Irish Rebellion 1798, Helder 1799, Ferrol 1800, Egypt 1801 (present at Aboukir), Walcheren 1809 and North America 1819 (Capt General and Governor in Chief of the Forces on the death of the Duke of Richmond). Colonel 60th

Foot 30 Aug 1809. Died 21 Mar 1838 at Brechin Castle.
Reference: Dictionary of National Biography (under George Ramsay). Dictionary of Canadian Biography (under George Ramsay). Royal Military Calendar, Vol. 2, pp. 248–9.

DAVIDSON, James
Hospital Assistant. Medical Department.
Obelisk: Dean Cemetery, Edinburgh, Midlothian, Scotland. (Photograph)

IN MEMORY OF / SURGEON MAJOR JAMES DAVIDSON / LATE OF THE 50TH FOOT / HE SERVED IN BELGIUM IN 1815 / GIBRALTAR WEST INDIES / WESTERN AUSTRALIA / BURMAH AND GWALIOR / SUTLEJ CAMPAIGNS / AND UPPER INDIA / UNDER LORD ELLENBOROUGH / AND LORD GOUGH / BORN 10TH MARCH 1796 / DIED 25TH MARCH 1868

Hospital Asst 24 Jun 1815. Asst Surgeon 21st Foot 30 Jun 1825. Surgeon 50th Foot 28 Jul 1840.
Served in France with the Army of Occupation, treating the wounded after Waterloo. Also served in Gibraltar, West Indies, Australia, India 1840 in the Gwalior Campaign (present at the Battle of Punniar 1843 where he was awarded a medal) and the Sutlej campaign Dec 1845 (present at Moodki and Ferozeshah where he was awarded a medal). Retired 30 Jun 1848. Died 25 Mar 1868.

DENNIS, William
1st Lieutenant. Royal Artillery.
Memorial tablet: St Mary's Church, Bramshott, Hampshire. (Photograph)

SACRED TO THE MEMORY OF / WILLIAM DENNIS, FIRST LIEUTENANT / ROYAL ARTILLERY, WHO DIED JUNE 3RD 1817, / AGED 25 YEARS. / ....

2nd Lt 1 Oct 1808. 2nd Lt 11 Jul 1811.
Served in the Peninsula Oct 1810 – Sep 1813. Present on the East coast of Spain and second siege of San Sebastian 31 Aug 1813.

DICKSON, Sir Jeremiah
Lieutenant Colonel. Permanent Assistant Quartermaster General.
Pedestal tomb: Mauchline Churchyard, Ayrshire, Scotland. (Photograph.)

PENINSULA WATERLOO / SACRED / TO THE MEMORY OF / LIEUTENANT GENERAL / SIR JEREMIAH DICKSON / KNIGHT COMMANDER OF THE BATH / AND COLONEL / OF THE SIXTY FIRST REGIMENT / DIED 17TH MARCH 1848 / AGED 73 / ....

Cornet 8th Lt Dragoons 25 Oct 1798. Lt 2nd Dragoon Guards 6 Aug 1799. Capt 2 Mar 1803. Major QMG Department 16 Sep 1806. Lt Colonel 1 Aug 1811. Bt Colonel 27 May 1825. Major General 10 Jan 1837. Lt General 9 Nov 1846.
Served in the Peninsula Nov 1812 – Apr 1814 (on Staff as AQMG). Present at Vittoria, Pyrenees, Nivelle, Orthes, Tarbes and Toulouse. Present at Waterloo and Capture of Paris. Gold Cross for Vittoria, Pyrenees, Nivelle, Orthes and Toulouse. KCB. Also served in Hanover 1805, Stralsund and Copenhagen 1807, Walcheren 1809, India 1827 (QMG) and Nova Scotia 1841 in command of forces. Colonel in Chief 61st Regt 20 Jan 1844. Served in the Army for 50 years.
Reference: Gentleman's Magazine, May 1848, pp. 544–5.

DIEPENBROICK, Augustus Friedrich von
Captain. 5th Line Battalion, King's German Legion.
Headstone: All Saints' Churchyard, Freshwater, Isle of Wight. (Photograph)

IN MEMORY OF / CAPT AUGUSTUS VON DIEPENBROICK / OF THE 5TH LINE BATTALION / KING'S GERMAN LEGION / WHO WAS BORN AT HANOVER IN / THE YEAR 1770 / AND DIED AT COLWELL BARRACKS / ON THE 21 SEPTEMBER / 1811.

Capt 5th Line 1 Jul 1806.

Served in the Peninsula Sep 1808 – Sep 1811. Present at Douro, Talavera and Busaco. Also served in the Baltic 1807–1808. Died from illness at Colwell Barracks, Isle of Wight, 21 Sep 1811.
Reference: Beamish, N. L., History of the King's German Legion, Vol. 2, reprint 1997. No. 1093.

DIX, Thomas

Lieutenant. 57th (West Middlesex) Regiment of Foot.
Memorial tablet: St George's Chapel of Ease, Hill Street, Dublin, Ireland. (M.I.)

" .... AND OF THEIR SON THOMAS DIX, A CAPTAIN IN HIS MAJESTY'S 57TH REGT, OBIT 15 SEPT 1820 AGED 35 YEARS"

Ensign 15 Dec 1804. Lt 5 Mar 1807. Capt 10 Feb 1820.

Served in the Peninsula Dec 1809 – Aug 1811 and Mar 1813 – Apr 1814. Present at Busaco, first siege of Badajoz, Albuera (wounded), Vittoria (wounded), Pyrenees, Nivelle and Nive (severely wounded 13 Dec 1813). In charge of telegraph system Jan – Apr 1814.

D'OLBREUSE, Christophe Henri Desmier

Lieutenant. Chasseurs Britanniques.
Headstone with Cross: Vorges, near Leon, Aisne, France. (Photograph)

ICI REPOSE / .... / LE CORPS DE / CHRISTOPHE HENRI / DESMIER D'OLBREUSE / ..... A VORGES LE 18 OCBRE / DANS SA 76TH ANNEE / ....

Ensign 17 Oct 1810. Lt 15 Oct 1812.

Served in the Peninsula Mar 1812 – Apr 1814. Present at Moriscos, Salamanca, Burgos, Vittoria, Pyrenees, Nivelle and Orthes. Half pay 1816 when the regiment was disbanded.

DONALDSON, Andrew

Lieutenant. 44th (East Essex) Regiment of Foot.
Buried in Up Park Camp disused Graveyard, Kingston, Jamaica, West Indies. (M.I.)

"SACRED TO THE MEMORY OF CAPTAIN ANDREW DONALDSON – THE 92ND REGIMENT. DIED IN CAMP ON THE 16TH JULY 1825 IN THE 34TH YEAR OF HIS AGE. BELOVED AND RESPECTED. ERECTED BY HIS WIDOW."

Ensign 44th Foot 1 Dec 1804. Lt 22 Jan 1807. Capt 92nd Foot 11 Dec 1818.

Served in the Peninsula Aug 1813 – Apr 1814. Present on the eastern coast of Spain (present at Tarragona). Also served in the West Indies 1819 (present at Jamaica until his death in 1825).

DOUGLAS, Neil

Lieutenant Colonel. 79th (Cameron Highlanders) Regiment of Foot.
Buried in Dalry Cemetery, Edinburgh, Scotland. (Section I. Headstone no longer visible). (Inscription not recorded)

2nd Lt 21st Foot 28 Jan 1801. Lt 9th Foot 16 Jul 1802. Lt 42nd Foot 9 Jul 1803. 1st Lt 95th Foot 2 Dec 1803. Capt 79th Foot 19 Apr 1804. Major 31 Jan 1811. Lt Colonel 3 Dec 1812. Bt Colonel 27 May 1825. Major

General 10 Jan 1837. Lt General 9 Nov 1846.

Present in the Peninsula Aug 1808 – Jan 1809, Jan – Dec 1810 and Jun 1813 – Apr 1814. Present at Corunna, Cadiz (Brigade Major to Major General Hoghton Jun – Jul 1810), Busaco (severely wounded and awarded pension of £300 per annum), Pyrenees, Nivelle, Nive and Toulouse. Commanded 79th Foot at Quatre Bras (severely wounded) and Waterloo. Also served at Copenhagen 1807, Sweden 1808 and Walcheren 1809 (present at the siege of Flushing). Gold Cross for Pyrenees, Nivelle, Nive and Toulouse. MGS medal for Corunna and Busaco. KCB. KCH. Cross of St Vladimir 4th Class and Cross of Knight Companion of Maria Theresa. Governor of Edinburgh Castle 17 Feb 1837. Colonel 78th Foot 20 Dec 1851. Died 1 Sep 1853 at Brussels but interred in Dalry Cemetery, Edinburgh, one of the first burials there.
Reference: United Service Journal, Oct 1853, p. 314. Gentleman's Magazine, Oct 1853, pp. 416–7. Annual Register, 1853, Appx, p. 252.

DOWBIGGIN, William Henry
Lieutenant. 12th (Prince of Wales's) Regiment of Light Dragoons.
Memorial: Warriston Cemetery, Edinburgh, Scotland. (Section C2. Grave Number 117). (M.I.)

"WILLIAM DOWBIGGIN ESQ. DIED AT EDINBURGH 4 MAR 1849 AGED 59. LATE OF H. M. 12TH LT DRAGOONS IN WHICH REGIMENT HE SERVED AT WATERLOO ...."

Ensign 52nd Foot 22 Mar 1810. Lt 8 Aug 1811. Lt 12th Lt Dragoons 31 Dec 1811.

Served in the Peninsula Mar 1811 – Mar 1812 and Sep 1812 – Apr 1814. Present at Sabugal, Fuentes d'Onoro, Vittoria, Nivelle, Nive, Adour and Bordeaux. Present at Waterloo in Capt Houston Wallace's Troop (wounded) and with the Army of Occupation. Half pay 1821. MGS medal for Fuentes d'Onoro, Vittoria, Nivelle and Nive.

DOWNHAM, John
Private. 1st (King's) Dragoon Guards.
Buried in Greywell Churchyard, near Odiham, Hampshire. (Burial record)

Pte 28 Jul 1812 – 26 Nov 1817. Pte 27 Jul 1820.

Present at Waterloo and with the Army of Occupation. Joined the regiment at the age of 16 but deserted 27 Nov 1817. Rejoined three year later on 22 Jul 1820 when he was pardoned and not tried for desertion. Served from 22 Jul 1820 – 10 Aug 1838 when he was finally discharged 26 Aug 1838. Died 12 Jan 1873.

DOWNES, Second Baron see BURGH, Sir Ulysses

DRUMMOND, John
Lieutenant and Captain. Coldstream Guards.
Memorial tablet: St Mary's Church, Dymock, Gloucestershire. (Photograph)

IN SACRED MEMORY / OF / JOHN DRUMMOND / OF THE / BOYCE COURT / GENERAL IN THE ARMY / CHIEF OF THE DRUMMONDS / OF CONCRAIG AND LENNOCH. / BORN 5TH OCT. 1793 / DIED 15TH APRIL 1875. / THIS TABLET WAS ERECTED / BY HIS AFFECTIONATE GRANDSON / HORACE DEANE-DRUMMOND / 1911.

Ensign 22 Nov 1810. Lt and Capt 26 May 1814. Capt and Lt Colonel 22 Jun 1826. Bt Colonel 23 Nov 1841. Major General 11 Nov 1851. Lt General 26 Oct 1858. General 10 Feb 1865.

Served in the Peninsula Feb 1813 – Apr 1814. Present at Vittoria, Bidassoa, Nivelle, Nive, Bayonne and the Sortie from Bayonne. Served with the Army of Occupation in France. Also served in the Netherlands 1814. Half pay 13 Apr 1832. MGS medal for Vittoria, Nivelle and Nive.

DRURY, George
Ensign. 33rd (1st Yorkshire West Riding) Regiment of Foot. (M.I.)
Ledger stone: General Cemetery, Bruges, Belgium.

"SACRED TO THE MEMORY OF LIEUT. GEORGE DRURY, LATE OF THE 33RD REGIMENT OF FOOT, WHO DIED HERE, AFTER A FEW HOURS ILLNESS, OF CHOLERA MORBUS, ON THE 5TH DAY OF OCTOBER 1832, IN THE 44TH YEAR OF HIS AGE, DEEPLY AND SINCERELY LAMENTED BY HIS FAMILY AND FRIENDS."

Ensign 9 Feb 1815. Lt 23 Nov 1815.
Present at Waterloo where he was severely wounded. Half pay 1817.

DU HEAUME, William
Hospital Mate. Medical Department.
Headstone: St Peter's Churchyard, Jersey, Channel Islands. (Photograph)

SACRED / TO THE MEMORY OF / WILLIAM DU HEAUME ESQ / SURGEON OF / HIS MAJESTY'S 84TH REGIMENT OF FOOT / THROUGHOUT THE PENINSULAR WAR / ALSO IN AMERICA. HE DIED / ON THE 20TH DAY OF JANUARY 1830 / IN THE 37 YEAR OF HIS AGE / AND LIES HERE IN PEACE TOGETHER / WITH FIVE OF HIS CHILDREN / THE ELDEST OF WHOM A SON / DIED IN HIS 7TH YEAR

Hospital Mate 3 Nov 1813. Hospital Assistant 9 Nov 1815.
Served in the Peninsula. Also served in America. Half pay 2 Dec 1816. Half pay 1823.

DUNKIN, John Henry
Lieutenant Colonel. 77th (East Middlesex) Regiment of Foot.
Grave: Dhaka Cemetery, Bengal, India. (M.I.)

"BR GEN J. H. DUNKIN, HM 44TH REGT. 11 NOV 1825"

Cornet 12th Lt Dragoons 19 Feb 1794. Lt 28th Lt Dragoons 20 Feb 1796. Capt 7 Aug 1799. Major 9th Foot 27 May 1802. Major 51st Foot 25 Jun 1803. Lt Colonel 77th Foot 16 Nov 1809. Lt Colonel 34th Foot 5 Mar 1818. Bt Colonel 12 Aug 1819. Lt Colonel 44th Foot 25 Mar 1824.
Served in the Peninsula Oct 1808 – Jan 1809, Jul 1811 – Jun 1812 and Dec 1812 – Apr 1814. Present at Corunna, El Bodon, Ciudad Rodrigo, Badajoz (wounded) and Bayonne. Gold Medal for Ciudad Rodrigo. CB. Also served in Ceylon 1803, Walcheren 1809, Ireland 1815 and India 1824.

ELTON, William
Captain. 1st (King's) Dragoon Guards.
Interred in Catacomb B (v203 c9), Kensal Green Cemetery, London.

Cornet 12 May 1804. Lt 17 Dec 1805. Capt 13 May 1809. Major 7 Sep 1820. Lt Colonel (unattached) 5 Nov 1825.
Present at Waterloo. Half pay 5 Nov 1825. Died 4 Jun 1847.

ERSKINE, John Francis Miller
Ensign. 1st Regiment of Foot Guards.
Memorial tablet: St John's Episcopal Church, Alloa, Clackmannanshire, Scotland. (M.I.)

"SACRED TO THE MEMORY OF JOHN FRANCIS MILLER ERSKINE, NINTH EARL OF MAR,

AND ELEVENTH EARL OF KELLIE, WHO DIED ON THE 19TH DAY / OF JUNE, 1866, IN THE 71ST YEAR OF HIS AGE. THIS TABLET WAS ERECTED BY THE FOUNDER OF THIS CHURCH, WALTER CONINGSBY ERSKINE, TWELFTH EARL OF KELLIE, &C., AS A MARK OF ESTEEM AND AFFECTION FOR HIS COUSIN, WHOSE REMAINS REST IN THE NEIGHBOURING FAMILY VAULT."

Ensign 1 Dec 1813. Lt and Capt 10 Feb 1820.

Present at Quatre Bras and Waterloo where he was wounded. Retired 12 Jul 1821. Became 9th Earl of Marr 1828.

EVANSON, Edward Alleyn

Lieutenant. 54th (West Norfolk) Regiment of Foot.

Memorial tablet: St John the Baptist's Church, Inglesham, Wiltshire. (Photograph)

………………. / ALSO OF AN AFFECTIONATE BROTHER / CAPTN EDWARD ALLEYN EVANSON 54TH REGT / WHO DIED DECR 26TH 1826 AGED 37 YEARS. / ……………….. / THIS TABLET IS ERECTED BY / THE REVD WILLIAM ALLEYN EVANSON M.A. / VICAR OF THIS PARISH 1840.

Lt 20 Apr 1809. Capt 24 May 1824.

Present at Waterloo in reserve at Hal, the storming of Cambria and the Capture of Paris. Also served in the Netherlands 1813–1815.

EYRE, Charles

Lieutenant. 1st (Royal Scots) Regiment of Foot.

Buried in the Royal Garrison Church Graveyard, Portsmouth, Hampshire. (M.I.)

"SACRED / TO THE MEMORY OF CHARLES EYRE ESQ / LATE CAPTAIN IN HIS MAJESTY'S / 1ST OR ROYAL REGIMENT OF FOOT / IN WHICH DISTINGUISHED CORPS / HE SERVED 27 YEARS / OBIT MARCH 13TH 1833 / AETAT 42 YEARS"

Memorial: St Andrew's Church, Landford, Wiltshire. (M.I.)

"CAPTAIN CHARLES EYRE. BORN 23 OCTOBER 1793 / DIED 15 MARCH 1833 OF ROYAL REGT OF FOOT / SON OF REV HENRY EYRE AND HIS SECOND WIFE."

Ensign 17 Jul 1809. Lt 18 Oct 1810. Capt 23 Nov 1823.

Served in the Peninsula Nov 1812 – Oct 1813. Present at Osma, Vittoria, first siege of San Sebastian (wounded and taken prisoner 25 Jul 1813 when he was recorded as missing). Also served in India in the Mahratta Wars 1816 where he was wounded (present at Nagpore and Maheidpore). Returned from India 1826 and retired 1827 owing to his Peninsular wounds.

FAIRWEATHER, Thomas

1st Lieutenant. 21st (Royal North British Fusiliers) Regiment of Foot.

Mural Memorial tablet: Dean Cemetery, Edinburgh, Scotland. (Inner Boundary wall. No. 1857). (Photograph)

SACRED / TO THE MEMORY OF / MAJOR THOMAS FAIRWEATHER / LATE OF THE 21ST FOOT / WHO DIED 20TH SEPTEMBER 1846 / AGED 59 YEARS

2nd Lt Jul 1805. 1st Lt 6 Aug 1807. Capt 26 Oct 1820. Major 6 Nov 1827.

Served in the Peninsula Dec 1812 – Apr 1813. Present on the East coast of Spain. Present at the

Occupation of Paris and remained in France until 1817. Also served in North America 1814–1815 (present at the Battle of Bladensburg, Capture of Washington 1814 and New Orleans 1815) and West Indies 1819–1827.

FALCONER, Hugh

Major 82nd (Prince of Wales's Volunteers) Regiment of Foot
Memorial tablet: St Mary's Church, Storrington, Sussex. (Photograph)

SACRED TO THE BELOVED MEMORY OF / MAJOR HUGH FALCONER. / WHO SERVED MANY YEARS IN THE 71ST HIGHLAND REGIMENT / AND ON THE STAFF IN EGYPT WITH ZEAL AND HONOR. / HE WAS BORN IN INVERNESS N.B. ON THE 12TH OF JUNE 1770 / AND DEPARTED THIS LIFE AT / BRIGHTON / ON THE 23RD OF JANUARY 1827. / A BRAVE SOLDIER AND FAITHFUL FRIEND, / AND IN EVERY RELATION OF LIFE / A JUST, HONOURABLE, AND GOOD MAN. / ....

Family Vault: St Mary's Churchyard, Storrington, Sussex. (Photograph)

IN MEMORY OF / MAJOR HUGH FALCONER, 71ST HIGHLANDERS / DIED 23RD JANUARY 1827, AGED / 57. / ....

Ensign 35th Foot. Lt 71st Foot 9 Feb 1791. Adjt 2 Jan 1798. Capt 9 Oct 1800. Bt Major 8 Mar 1809. Major 82nd Foot 5 May 1810.

Served in the Peninsula with 71st Foot Aug 1808 – Jan 1809. Present at Rolica, Vimiero and Corunna. Also served on the Staff in Egypt.

FARRINGTON, Charles Henry

Lieutenant. 4th (King's Own) Regiment of Foot.
Memorial: On Rajpur-Mussoorie-Landour Road, Landour, Uttarakhand, India. (Near 3rd mile stone – memorial reported to have been destroyed in a land slip). (M.I.)

"SACRED TO THE MEMORY OF CHARLES HENRY FARRINGTON, BART, LATE CAPTAIN HIS MAJESTY'S 31ST REGIMENT, WHO DEPARTED THIS LIFE 26TH DAY OF MARCH 1828 IN THE 35TH YEAR OF HIS AGE."

Ensign 30 Oct 1810. Lt 29 Jul 1813. Capt 31st Foot 21 Apr 1825.

Served in the Peninsula with 1/4th Jul 1812 – Apr 1814. Present at Salamanca, retreat from Burgos, (present at Villa Muriel), San Sebastian, Bidassoa, Nivelle, Nive (wounded) and Bayonne. Also served in North America 1814–1815 (present at New Orleans where he was wounded) and India 1826 (one of the first officers to take troops up to Landour). Half pay 29 Jul 1815. Later inherited the title to become Sir Charles Henry Farrington 3 Nov 1823.

FAUNCE, Edmund

Lieutenant Colonel. 4th (King's Own) Regiment of Foot.
Memorial: St Oswald's Churchyard, Oswestry, Shropshire. (No longer extant). (M.I.)

"SACRED TO THE MEMORY OF JANE, ELDEST DAUGHTER OF EDMUND FAUNCE ESQ. LATE LIEUTENANT-COLONEL OF THE 4TH OR KING'S OWN REGIMENT .... / ALSO SACRED TO THE MEMORY OF THE ABOVE NAME EDMUND FAUNCE ESQ OF ST MARY'S HALL, COUNTY OF KENT LATE LIEUTENANT-COLONEL IN THE 4TH OR KING'S OWN REGIMENT. HE DIED SEPTEMBER 29TH 1838 AGED 72."

Lt 10 Aug 1793. Capt 4 Dec 1798. Major 15 Aug 1804. Lt Colonel 1 Aug 1811.

Served in the Peninsula Aug 1808 – Jan 1809. Present at Corunna. Also served at Walcheren 1809 and Gibraltar. Retired in 1813. Cousin of Major Alured Dodsworth Faunce 4th Foot.

FEARON, Peter

Captain. 31st (Huntingdonshire) Regiment of Foot.

Named on Memorial tablet: Albuera Wall, British Cemetery, Elvas, Portugal. (Photograph) British Cemetery, Elvas, Portugal. (Photograph)

Ensign 69th Foot 27 Mar 1804. Ensign 31st Foot 21 Apr 1804. Lt 21 Dec 1804. Capt 17 Aug 1809. Bt Major 26 Dec 1813. Portuguese Army: Major 7th Caçadores 22 Jul 1810. Major 1st Line 8 Feb 1812. Bt Lt Colonel 3 Aug 1813. Lt Colonel 6th Caçadores 27 Aug 1813.

Served in the Peninsula with 31st Foot Jan – Jun 1810 and with Portuguese Army Jul 1810 – Feb 1814. Present at Albuera, Ciudad Rodrigo, Salamanca, Burgos, Vittoria, Pyrenees, Nivelle, Nive (wounded at St Pierre 13 Dec 1813 and Mentioned in Beresford's Despatches) and Garris where he was killed in action 15 Feb 1814. Gold Medal for Albuera, Nivelle and Nive.

FENDALL, William

Lieutenant. 4th (Queen's Own) Regiment of Dragoons.

Cross on stepped base: St Nicholas's Church, Child Okeford, Dorset. (Photograph)

……………….. AND IN MEMORY OF / LIEUT COL W. FENDALL / BORN 26 MARCH 1793 DIED 14 JAN 1888 / ………………..

Brass memorial tablet: St Nicholas's Church, Child Okeford, Dorset. (M.I.)

IN MEMORY OF / COLONEL WILLIAM FENDALL / BORN MARCH 26TH 1793 / DIED JANUARY 14TH 1888, AGED 94. / THE SUM OF £38 HAS ALSO BEEN ADDED / TO THE BELL FUND BY HIS / FRIENDS AND RELATIVES

Cornet 29 Sep 1808. Lt 3 Oct 1809. Capt 3 Feb 1820. Major 2 Jun 1825. Lt Colonel 24 Dec 1832.

Served in the Peninsula Apr 1809 – Nov 1811 and May 1812 – Apr 1814. Present at Talavera, Albuera, Usagre, Aldea de Ponte, Vittoria and Toulouse. Retired 24 Dec 1832. MGS medal for Talavera, Albuera, Vittoria and Toulouse. Died 14 Jan 1888 aged 94.

FIELDING, George

Lieutenant. 23rd (Royal Welch Fusiliers) Regiment of Foot.

Memorial tablet: Holy Trinity Church, Startforth, County Durham. (M.I.)

"……………….. / AND TO GEORGE FIELDING, MAJOR IN THE 23RD REGIMENT OF WELCH FUSILIERS WHO DIED IN 1830, ALSO OF STARTFORTH HALL."

2nd Lt 24 May 1810. Lt 7 Nov 1811. Capt 6 Jun 1822. Bt Major 22 Jul 1830.

Served in the Peninsula Aug 1811 – May 1812 and Aug 1813 – Apr 1814. Present at Aldea de Ponte, Ciudad Rodrigo, Badajoz (wounded), Pyrenees, Nivelle, Nive, Orthes and Toulouse. Present at Waterloo where he was wounded. Died at Bath 29 Nov 1830 in command of the Depot Companies in Brecon.

FITZGERALD, John Forster

Major. 60th (Royal American) Regiment of Foot.

Low monument: Tours Cemetery, Tours, France. (Photograph)

IN MEMORY OF / SIR JOHN FORSTER FITZGERALD CB. / COL 18TH REGT ROYAL IRISH / OF THE CARRIGORAN FAMILY COUNTY CLARE IRELAND / BORN IN 1785 / DIED AT TOURS MARCH 24 1877 / HE RECEIVED HIS FIRST COMMISSION IN THE BRITISH / ARMY AS ENSIGN IN 1793 DIED A FIELD MARSHAL / AFTER 84 YEARS SERVICE. HE SERVED WITH DISTINCTION / IN THE PENINSULA WAR IN INDIA AND OTHER PARTS OF / THE BRITISH EMPIRE HIS LAST YEARS WERE SPENT / IN FRANCE AND AT HIS DEATH THE FRENCH GOVERNMENT / AS A MARK OF PERSONAL RESPECT / BETWEEN THE FRENCH AND ENGLISH NATIONS / ORDERED HIS FUNERAL BE ATTENDED WITH THE CEREMONY / AND MILITARY HONOURS BEFITTING HIS RANK

Ensign Capt Shee's Independent Company 29 Oct 1793. Lt 31 Jan 1794. Capt 79th Foot 9 May 1794. Capt 46th Foot 31 Oct 1800. Capt New Brunswick Fencible Regt 9 Jul 1803. Bt Major 25 Sep 1803. Major 60th Foot 9 Nov 1809. Bt Lt Colonel 25 Jul 1810. Bt Colonel 12 Aug 1819. Lt Colonel 20th Foot 5 Feb 1824. Major General 22 Jul 1830. Lt General 23 Nov 1841. General 20 Jun 1854. Field Marshal 29 May 1875.

Served in the Peninsula Mar 1812 – Apr 1814. Present at Badajoz (wounded and Mentioned in Despatches), Salamanca, Vittoria, Pyrenees (O/C 1 Brigade 2nd Division Jul 1813, Mentioned in Despatches but was taken prisoner 31 Jul 1813 until Apr 1814). Gold Cross for Badajoz, Salamanca, Vittoria and Pyrenees. CB. Also served in Canada (Commandant of Quebec 1818 and then Commandant of Montreal), India 1824–1830 (commanded 20th Foot), India 1838 (present at Madras and Bombay. GOC of a Division of Bombay Army) and Windward and Leeward Islands 1852 (in command of troops). KCB 1831. MP for County Clare 1852–1857. Colonel 18th Foot 9 Mar 1850. GCB 1862. Retired to France where he died at the age of 92. Served in the army for 84 years. The Garrison at Tours buried him with the same honours due to a Marshal of France.

Reference: Dictionary of National Biography.

FORSTER, Mathew

Lieutenant. 85th (Buckinghamshire Volunteers) Light Infantry Regiment of Foot.
Obelisk: St John's Churchyard, New Town, Tasmania, Australia. (Photograph)

SACRED / TO THE MEMORY OF / MATTHEW FORSTER, / WHO DIED THE SIXTH OF JANUARY, MDCCCXLVI, / AGED 49. / HE ENTERED THE 85TH REGT AS AN ENSIGN IN HIS SIXTEENTH YEAR. / HE SERVED IN THE PENINSULA AND AT NEW ORLEANS AND / WAS AFTERWARDS MAJOR OF BRIGADE IN IRELAND. / IN THIS COLONY / HE SUCCESSIVELY FILLED THE RESPONSIBLE OFFICES OF / CHIEF POLITICAL / MAGISTRATE, COLONIAL SECRETARY & / CONTROLLER GENERAL ON CONVICTS. / THIS MONUMENT / HAS BEEN ERECTED BY HIS PRIVATE FRIENDS AS A / TESTIMONIAL OF THEIR REGARD.

Ensign 46th Foot 19 Dec 1811. Lt 12th Foot 24 Dec 1812. Lt 85th Foot 25 Jan 1813. Capt (unattached) 26 Dec 1822. Capt 85th Foot 24 Apr 1823.

Served in the Peninsula Aug 1813 – Apr 1814. Present at Nivelle, Nive and Bayonne. Also served in North America 1814–1815 (present at New Orleans) and Ireland 1815–1830. Half pay 8 Jun 1830. Left for Australia in 1831, having married the niece of Colonel Sir George Arthur, Lt Governor of Van Diemen's Land. Appointed Chief Police Magistrate on his arrival. Ran the Police Department efficiently at first. Appointed Director of the Probation Service 1841 to organise the convict labour gangs and Controller General of Convicts 1842. Between 1842–1844 convict numbers were increasing rapidly and soon Forster no longer had control. Died 11 Jan 1846.

Reference: Australian Dictionary of Biography.

FOULKES, Thomas
Private. 18th Regiment of Light Dragoons.
Headstone: St Paul's Churchyard, North King Street, Dublin, Ireland. (M.I.)

"TO THE / MEMORY OF / THOMAS FOULKES FARRIER / 18TH HUSSARS WHO DEPARTED THIS LIFE / ON THE 15TH DEC 182* / AGED 45 YEARS. / TO PEACEFUL QUARTERS BILLETED AM I / AND HERE FORGETFUL OF PAST LABOURS LIE / LET ME ALONE WHILE SLEEPING I REMAIN / AND WHEN THE TRUMPET SOUNDS I'LL MARCH AGAIN"

Served in the Peninsula 1808 – Jan 1809 and 1813 – Apr 1814. Present at Benevente, Morales, Vittoria, Nivelle, Nive, Orthes and Toulouse. Present at Waterloo in Capt Arthur Kennedy's Troop.

FRASER, Donald
Corporal. 79th (Cameron Highlanders) Regiment of Foot.
Pedestal Monument: Grange Cemetery, Edinburgh, Scotland. (Section M, Row 14. No 187) (Photograph)

IN MEMORY / OF / DONALD FRASER / LATE COLOUR SERGEANT / 79TH CAMERON HIGHLANDERS / WHO DIED AT EDINBURGH / ON THE 27TH APRIL 1862 / AGED 73 YEARS. / …………………

Pte 25 Dec 1807. Cpl 1813. Sgt 1817.
Served in the Peninsula Mar 1810 – Apr 1814. Present at Busaco, Fuentes d'Onoro (wounded), Salamanca, Burgos, Pyrenees, Nivelle, Nive and Toulouse. Present at Waterloo in Capt P. Innes's Company No 5. MGS medal for Busaco, Fuentes d'Onoro, Salamanca, Pyrenees, Nivelle, Nive and Toulouse. Discharged 22 Aug 1828 after 22 years and 262 days service.

FREDERICK, Prince of the Netherlands
Commander. Netherlands Corps.
Memorial tablet: St Joseph's Church, Waterloo. (Photograph)

AUSPICE ILLUSTRISSOMO PRINCIPE / FREDERICO NASSOVIO / IN PERPETUAM MEMORIAM / ENSIGNIS VICTORIÆ / ANNO DDCCCXV DIE JUNII XVIII / RELATÆ / WATERL. SODAL. AERE ET CURA / HON MONUMENTUM EST ERECTUM

Present at Waterloo in reserve at Hal. Younger brother of the Prince of Orange. He was only 18 years old and took no part in the battle.

GAIRDNER, James Penman
Lieutenant. 95th Regiment of Foot.
Obelisk: Summerville Cemetery, Augusta, Richmond County, Georgia, United States of America. (Photograph)

JAMES PENMAN / GAIRDNER / DIED APRIL 21 1862 / AGED 69 YEARS. / AN OFFICER IN THE ENGLISH ARMY / AND SERVED WITH DISTINCTION / UNDER LORD WELLINGTON IN THE / PENINSULAR WAR AND AT THE / BATTLE OF WATERLOO. / "HE WALKED THE PATHS IN / RIGHTEOUSNESS AND GENTLY / FELL ASLEEP"

2nd Lt 23 Aug 1810. Lt 12 May 1812.
Served in the Peninsula Jan 1812 – Apr 1814. Present at Ciudad Rodrigo, Badajoz (wounded), Salamanca, San Millan, Vittoria (severely wounded), Pyrenees, Vera, Bidassoa, Nivelle, Nive, Orthes, Tarbes and Toulouse. Present at Waterloo (wounded) and with the Army of Occupation. Half pay 1 Jul

1819. Retired 30 Dec 1826. MGS medal for Ciudad Rodrigo, Badajoz, Salamanca, Vittoria, Pyrenees, Nivelle, Nive, Orthes and Toulouse.

GEILS, Thomas

Captain and Lieutenant Colonel. 3rd Regiment of Foot Guards.
Family Memorial: Geilston Family enclosure, Cardross Churchyard, Dumbartonshire, Scotland. (North-east corner of church). Seriously eroded. (M.I.)

"THOMAS GEILS OF GEILSTON, COL HM 3RD FOOT GUARDS. BORN 16 JAN 1778, DIED 28 MAR 1828"

Ensign 73rd Foot 30 Apr 1799. Lt 60th Foot 29 Sep 1799. Capt 12 Aug 1800. Lt and Capt 3rd Foot Guards 16 Dec 1800. Capt and Lt Colonel 9 Aug 1813.

Served in the Peninsula Mar 1809 – Apr 1814. Present at Douro and Talavera where he was wounded and taken prisoner until Apr 1814.

GIBBONS, James

Private. 57th (West Middlesex) Regiment of Foot.
Headstone: Sandhills Burial Ground, Sydney, New South Wales, Australia. (Burial Ground no longer extant. Now site of Sydney Town Hall). (M.I.)

"JAMES GIBBONS DIED 12 NOVEMBER 1857...................."

Pte 3 Apr 1809. Cpl 25 Jan 1821. Pte 3 Jun 1821.

Served in the Peninsula 1812–1814. Present at Vittoria, Nivelle (severely wounded in thigh) and Nive. Served in France with the Army of Occupation Aug 1815 – Nov 1817. Also served in North America 1814–1815 and New South Wales 1823 where the regiment was stationed on Melville Island to man the garrison in the convict settlement. Discharged 31 Jul 1831 after having served 22 years. Remained in Australia after leaving the army and died in Sydney 12 Oct 1857.

GIBSON, Samuel

Private: 27th (Inniskilling) Regiment of Foot.
Low monument: St Mary's Churchyard, Caterham, Surrey. (Inscription engraved on all four sides of the grave) (Photograph)

TO THE GLORY OF GOD AND IN MEMORY OF SAMUEL GIBSON LATE PRIVATE. AT THE TIME OF HIS DEATH HE WAS ONE OF THE LAST SURVIVORS OF WATERLOO. ENLISTED IN THE 27TH INNISKILLINGS 1803 AND SERVED THROUGHOUT THE PENINSULAR AND WATERLOO CAMPAIGN IN THAT DISTINGUISHED REGIMENT. BORN AT TANDRAGEE CO. ARMAGH IN 1790. DIED AT CATERHAM ASYLUM IN 1891. SAMUEL GIBSON WHOSE FATHER WAS IN THE MONAGHAN MILITIA. THIS MONUMENT WAS ERECTED BY OFFICERS NON-COMMISSIONED OFFICERS AND MEN OF THE 27TH INNISKILLINGS 1892.

Pte 1803.

Served in the Peninsula and at Waterloo. Discharged 1815 with a pension of one shilling a day. Died at Caterham 24 Dec 1891 aged 101 years. He was the last Waterloo veteran from the ranks to die. Samuel Gibson is mentioned in the regimental history of the Royal Inniskilling Fusiliers as one of the last two men who fought at Waterloo. 'The other veteran, Gibson, had as a boy enlisted very early in the nineteenth century, and served throughout the Peninsular War. On his death the officers erected a memorial to his memory.' No other records have been found.

GILDER, Frederick
Assistant Surgeon. Coldstream Regiment of Foot Guards.
Memorial: Kirk Christ Church, Lezayre, Ramsey, Isle of Man. (M.I.)

"IN LOVING REMEMBRANCE OF / FREDERICK GILDER / LATE SURGEON OF THE COLDSTREAM GUARDS / (WATERLOO) / WHO DIED FEBRUARY 18TH 1876 / AGED 81 YEARS. / (VERSE) / ……………….."

Asst Surgeon 9 Jun 1814. Half pay 1818–1838. Surgeon Coldstream Guards 16 Mar 1838.
Present at Waterloo. Retired on half pay 14 Apr 1843.

GILLIES, John
Corporal. Royal Artillery.
Buried in Plumstead Churchyard, Plumstead, Kent. (Burial Register)

Pte 17 Apr 1808. Cpl 1 Oct 1811. Sgt 1 Aug 1825. Sgt Major 14 Apr 1842.
Served at Waterloo in Major Lloyd's Company. When he was finally discharged on 11 Jul 1854 he was the last soldier serving in the Royal Artillery who had been present at the Battle of Waterloo. Awarded annuity of £20 for long service and good conduct having served 48 years. Also served at Walcheren 1809 and Gibraltar. Died in Woolwich 1858 aged 71.

GORDON, John Robert
Lieutenant. 7th (Queen's Own) Regiment of Light Dragoons.
Memorial: St Mary's Church, Donhead, Wiltshire. (M.I.)

"CAPT J. R. GORDON OF 7TH HUSSARS / DIED 13 SEPT 1824 AGED 30 / ELDEST SON OF J. GORDON OF WINCOMBE PARK."

Cornet 15 Feb 1812. Lt 15 Sep 1813. Capt 12 Dec 1816.
Served in the Peninsula Aug 1813 – Apr 1814. Present at Orthes and Toulouse. Present at Waterloo where he was wounded.

GOULD, John
Lieutenant. 76th Regiment of Foot.
Ledger stone: Abbey Cemetery, Bath, Somerset. (Plot No. SM 37). (Photograph)

LIEUT COL^{L} GOULD / 88TH REG^{T} CONNAUGHT RANGERS / DIED MARCH 6TH 1855 / AGED 64.

Ensign 31 Aug 1807. Lt 22 Mar 1809. Capt 8th Foot 13 Feb 1827. Bt Major 23 Jan 1841. Capt 88th Foot 27 Jan 1843. Bt Lt Colonel 11 Nov 1851.
Served in the Peninsula Aug 1813 – Apr 1814. Present at Bidassoa, Nivelle, Nive and Bayonne. Also served at Walcheren 1809 (present at Flushing) and North America 1814–1815 (present at Plattsburg). Half pay 13 Apr 1849. MGS medal for Nivelle and Nive.

GROSVENOR, Thomas
Colonel. 65th (2nd Yorkshire North Riding) Regiment of Foot.
Tomb within railings: St Mary's Churchyard, Wimbledon, London. (M.I.)

"HERE LIES FIELD MARSHAL THOMAS GROSVENOR / WHO DIED AT RICHMOND ON THE 20TH DAY OF JANUARY 1851 / AGED 86 / AS A SOLDIER HE SERVED HIS KING AND / COUNTRY ABROAD WITH HONOUR AND DISTINCTION / HIS KIND AND BENEVOLENT DISPOSITION

ENDEARED / HIM TO ALL WHO KNEW HIM ESPECIALLY / TO HIS FAMILY AND NEAR CONNECTIONS BY WHOM / HE WAS FONDLY CHERISHED / HIS FAITH AND TRUST IN HIS REDEEMER WERE EVER / STEADFAST THROUGHOUT HIS LIFE / AND GREW STRONGER AS HIS BODILY STRENGTH DECAYED / HE DIED IN PEACE BELOVED AND LAMENTED / VALE A.G. / ………………."

Ensign 3rd Foot Guards 1 Oct 1779. Lt and Capt 20 Oct 1784. Capt and Lt Colonel 25 Apr 1793. Bt Colonel 3 May 1796. Major General 29 Apr 1802. Lt General 25 Apr 1808. General 12 Aug 1819. Field Marshal 9 Nov 1846.

Served at Walcheren 1809 (present at the siege of Flushing where he was second in command to Sir Eyre Coote). Also served in Flanders 1793–1796 (present at St Amand and Nimwegen), the Helder 1799 (present at Zuype where he was wounded and Alkmaar), Ireland 1799, Ferrol 1800 and Copenhagen 1807. MP for Chester 1795–1825 and Stockbridge 1826–1830. Colonel 97th Foot 25 Feb 1807. Colonel 66th Foot 8 Feb 1814. Educated at Westminster.

Reference: Dictionary of National Biography. Gentleman's Magazine, Mar 1851, pp. 312–13. Annual Register, 1851, Appx, p. 254. Royal Military Calendar, Vol. 2, pp. 94–5.

HAMILTON, Thomas

Lieutenant. 29th (Worcestershire) Regiment of Foot.

Memorial: Cimitero di Pinte, Pisa, Italy. (M.I.)

"IN LOVE AND RESPECT / TO THE MEMORY OF / THOMAS HAMILTON, ESQUIRE / WHO HERE LIES BURIED / DIED AT PISA ON THE / SEVENTH OF DECEMBER 1842 / IN HIS FIFTY THIRD YEAR"

Ensign 2 Aug 1810. Lt 31 Oct 1811.

Served in the Peninsula Oct 1810 – Nov 1811 and Apr 1813 – Feb 1814. Present at the first siege of Badajoz, Albuera (severely wounded) and Cadiz. Served with the Army of Occupation. Half pay Mar 1818. Author of *Cyril Thornton,* (a novel about his military experiences), 1827, *Annals of the Peninsular Campaign,* 3 vols, 1829, *Men and Manners in America*, 1833 (a very popular account of his travels in America which was translated into French and German).

Reference: Dictionary of National Biography.

HAMILTON, William Charles

Lieutenant. 10th (Prince of Wales's Own) Regiment of Light Dragoons.

Memorial tablet in walled enclosure: Kirkcowan Kirkyard (Old Section), Kirkcowan, Dumfries and Galloway, Scotland. (Photograph)

SACRED TO THE MEMORY OF / WILLIAM CHARLES HAMILTON / OF CRAIGHLAW, / WHO DEPARTED THIS LIFE ON THE / 1ST OCTOBER 1850. / HE SERVED IN THE 10TH ROYAL HUSSARS / DURING THE LATE WAR, / WAS PRESENT AT THE BATTLE OF WATERLOO / AND AFTERWARDS HONOURABLY FULFILLED / HIS DUTIES AS A COUNTRY GENTLEMAN AND MAGISTRATE. / THIS MONUMENT IS ERECTED / AS A LAST TRIBUTE OF RESPECT / BY HIS TRULY ATTACHED AND DEVOTED FAMILY /. …………….

Lt 29 Dec 1814. Capt 21 Nov 1822.

Present at Waterloo. Justice of the Peace and Deputy Lieutenant for County of Wigton.

HANCOX, Skinner

Captain. 15th (King's) Regiment of Light Dragoons.

Tombstone: St Oswald's Churchyard, Oswestry. (No longer extant). (M.I.)

"SACRED TO THE MEMORY OF SKINNER HANCOX ESQ. LATE COLONEL OF THE 7TH DRAGOON GUARDS, WHO DEPARTED THIS LIFE JANUARY 27TH 1843, AGED 55."

Lt 20 Jun 1805. Capt 11 May 1809. Bt Major 18 Jun 1815. Major 12 Aug 1819. Lt Colonel 7th Dragoon Guards 18 Dec 1823.

Served in the Peninsula Nov 1808 – Jan 1809 and Feb 1813 – Apr 1814. Present at Sahagun, Corunna campaign, Morales, Vittoria (wounded), Orthes and Toulouse. Present at Waterloo where he commanded the regiment at the end of the day as senior officers were either killed or wounded. Awarded Brevet Majority. Commanded 7th Dragoon Guards from 1823–1830.

HART, Francis Henry
Lieutenant. 39th (Dorsetshire) Regiment of Foot.
Headstone with low monument: Spital Cemetery, Chesterfield, Derbyshire. (Photograph)

O GOD THE LORD / THE STRENGTH OF MY SALVATION / THOUGH HAST COVERED MY HEAD / IN THE DAY OF BATTLE. / TOULOUSE PYRENEES / ORTHES VITTORIA / NIVE ALBUERA / NIVELLE BUSACO. / FRANCIS HENRY HART / MAJOR LATE OF HER MAJESTY'S 39TH REGIMENT / DIED JUNE 10TH 1867.

Ensign 9 Jan 1805. Lt 18 Jun 1807. Capt 8 Apr 1825. Bt Major 28 Jun 1838.

Served in the Peninsula with 2/39th Jul 1809 – Jul 1811 and 1/39th Apr 1813 – Apr 1814. Present at Busaco, first siege of Badajoz, Albuera (wounded), Vittoria, Pyrenees (wounded at Maya 25 Jul 1813), Nivelle, Nive, Garris, Orthes, Aire and Toulouse. Awarded pension of £70 for wound at Albuera and Pyrenees. Also served in North America 1814–1815. Half pay 26 May 1825. MGS medal for Busaco, Albuera, Vittoria, Pyrenees, Nivelle, Nive, Orthes and Toulouse.

HATCHER, John
Private. 95th Foot.
Buried in St George's Churchyard, Benenden, Kent. (Burial Register)

Served in the Peninsula. Present at Vittoria, Pyrenees, San Sebastian (wounded in the right ear) and Toulouse. Also served in North America 1814–1815 (present at New Orleans where he was wounded in the right arm). Died 8 Sep 1867 aged 82.

HAY, William
Captain. 47th (Lancashire) Regiment of Foot.
Memorial tablet: Greyfriars Churchyard, Edinburgh, Scotland. (On exterior west wall of church). (Photograph)

IN MEMORY OF / CAPTAIN WILLIAM HAY / ELDEST SON OF / GENERAL SIR JAMES HAY / DIED 11TH APRIL 1844 / ....

Cornet 7th Dragoon Guards 11 Aug 1804. Lt 11 Sep 1805. Capt 47th Foot 11 Nov 1813. Major 3 Feb 1825. Lt Colonel 10 Jun 1826.

Served in the Peninsula Feb 1813 – Apr 1814 (ADC to Major General Brisbane). Present at Vittoria (wounded), Pyrenees, Nivelle, Nive, Orthes, Vic Bigorre, and Toulouse. Half pay 10 Jun 1826. Son of General Sir James Hay Colonel 2nd Dragoon Guards.

HAYWOOD, Charles
Private. 82nd (Prince of Wales's Volunteers) Regiment of Foot.
Buried in St Mary the Virgin's Churchyard, Deane, Bolton. (Burial Register)

Pte 10 Apr 1809.

Served in the Peninsula Jun 1812 – Apr 1814. Present at Vittoria and the Pyrenees. MGS medal for Vittoria and Pyrenees. Discharged 12 Oct 1814. Died 2 Oct 1877.

HEIDEN, F. M. Van

Captain. 6th Hussars, Dutch Cavalry.
Named on the Memorial to Dutch officers killed at Waterloo: St Joseph's Church, Waterloo, Belgium. (Photograph)
Named on the Regimental Memorial to officers of the Dutch 6th Regiment of Hussars killed at Waterloo, St Joseph's Church, Waterloo. (Photograph)

HIGGINS, Summers

Deputy Inspector of Hospitals, Medical Department.
Buried in the Crypt of Trinity Church, Cheltenham, Gloucestershire. (Burial record)

Asst Surgeon 23rd Dragoons 1 Sep 1797. Asst Surgeon 22nd Dragoons 1 Dec 1797. Asst Surgeon 59th Foot 25 Dec 1802. Surgeon 3rd Foot 15 Oct 1803. Surgeon 6th Dragoon Guards 17 Jul 1806. Staff Surgeon 5 Jan 1809. Deputy Inspector of Hospitals 12 Nov 1812. Bt Inspector General of Hospitals 27 May 1825. Inspector General of Hospitals 22 Jul 1830.

Served in the Peninsula May 1809 – June 1810, Sep 1810 – Oct 1811 and Feb 1813 – Apr 1814. (7th Division Mar – Oct 1811 and Cavalry Division Feb – Oct 1813). Present at Talavera, Fuentes d'Onoro, Vittoria and San Sebastian. Present at Waterloo where he was in charge of the wounded at Brussels. After Talavera he was taken prisoner by the French while in charge of the wounded and was released by Napoleon in 1810 for his care of the French wounded at Talavera. He was presented with a silver cup by 23 of the wounded British officers and it became known as the Talavera Cup which his son presented to the RAMC. MD 1816. Also served in Egypt 1801 and North America 1814–1815. Retired on half pay 22 Jul 1830. Died at Cheltenham 5 Apr 1843.

HILL, Charles

Private. 58th (Rutlandshire) Regiment of Foot.
Headstone: St Margaret's Church, Roath, Wales. Inscription not recorded.

Served in the Peninsula. MGS Medal for Salamanca, Vittoria, Pyrenees, Nivelle and Orthes. Died 1862 aged 85 years.

HILL, John Humphrey Edward

Major. 23rd (Royal Welch Fusiliers) Regiment of Foot.
Memorial tablet: St Mary the Virgin's, Hennock, Devon. (North wall above Rood screen). (Photograph)

TO THE MEMORY OF / LIEUTT COLL JOHN HUMPHREY HILL, CB. / LATE OF THE 23RD REGT, ROYAL WELSH FUSILIERS. / ELDEST SON OF THE REVD JOHN HILL, / FORMERLY VICAR OF THIS PARISH. / THIS GALLANT OFFICER COMMENCED HIS PROFESSIONAL / CAREER IN 1796, IN H. M. 23RD REGT OF FOOT, AND SHARED / IN THE RENOWN, THAT DISTINGUISHED CORPS ACQUIRED / IN EGYPT, THE PENINSULA, AMERICA, AND LASTLY / AT WATERLOO, ON WHICH MEMORABLE DAY HE WAS / DANGEROUSLY WOUNDED BY A GRAPE SHOT IN THE / SHOULDER, WHILST LEADING THE BRAVE FUSILIERS / TO VICTORY. / THE 4TH PORTUGUESE REGT OF CACADORES, WHICH / HE FORMED, WAS COMMANDED BY HIM IN SEVERAL / OF THE PENINSULAR CAMPAIGNS, IN WHICH HIS ZEAL / AND ABILITY WERE SO EMINENTLY CONSPICUOUS, / AS TO OBTAIN FOR HIM MANY HONORABLE MARKS / OF DISTINCTION FROM HIS OWN AND FOREIGN / SOVEREIGNS. / HAVING FOR SOME

YEARS RETIRED FROM THE / ARMY, HE WAS IN THE ENJOYMENT OF THE SOCIETY / OF AN AFFECTIONATE FAMILY, AND A N EXTENSIVE / CIRCLE OF FRIENDS: AND HIS DISCHARGE OF ALL / THE RELATIONS OF LIFE WAS EXEMPLARY, AS HIS / CONDUCT IN THE FIELD HAD BEEN GLORIOUS. / HE DIED SUDDENLY, / ON THE 21ST OF JANUARY 1838, / AGED 59 YEARS.

Named on the Family box tomb: St Mary the Virgin's Churchyard, Hennock, Devon. Seriously eroded and inscription not recorded). (Photograph)

2nd Lt 29 Jul 1796. Lt 6 Apr 1797. Capt 3 Sep 1803. Major 12 Mar 1812. Bt Lt Colonel 21 Sep 1813. Major 49th Foot 2 Oct 1823. With Portuguese Army: Major 5 Caçadores 3 Aug 1811. Lt Colonel 4th Line 15 Nov 1813.

Served in the Peninsula with 1/23rd Dec 1810 – Aug 1811 and with Portuguese Army Sep 1811 – Apr 1814. Present at Redinha, Olivencia, first siege of Badajoz, Albuera, Ciudad Rodrigo, Badajoz, Salamanca, Burgos, Osma, Vittoria, Tolosa, San Sebastian Nivelle, Nive (Mentioned in Beresford's Despatches) and Orthes. Present at Waterloo where he was wounded and awarded pension of £200 per annum. Also served at the Helder 1799 (on return to England was shipwrecked on the Dutch frigate *Valk*. Hill was the only officer saved from the shipwreck. Three companies of the regiment were lost – only 25 people were saved out of 554), Ferrol 1800, Egypt 1801 (awarded Gold Medal from Sultan), Hanover 1805, Copenhagen 1807 (wounded by one of his regiment in the dark) and West Indies (present at Martinique 1809). Gold Cross for Salamanca, San Sebastian, Nivelle and Nive. CB.

Reference: Hill, J. H. E., Letters to a vicarage 1796–1815, reprint 1988.

HILTON, James

Private: 48th (Northamptonshire) Regiment of Foot.

Family Memorial headstone: Greenacres Cemetery, Oldham, Lancashire. (Grave Section G3, Grave Number 75). (Photograph)

………………. / ALSO THE AFORESAID JAMES HILTON / WHO DIED FEBRUARY 24TH 1871 / AGED 88 YEARS

……………….

Memoriam Card. (Photograph)

SACRED TO THE MEMORY OF / JAMES HILTON, / BORN ON THE 7TH DAY OF MARCH, 1783, DIED ON THE 24TH DAY OF / FEBRUARY, 1871, / AGED 87 YEARS 354 DAYS, / AND WAS INTERRED ON THE 1ST DAY OF MARCH FOLLOWING AT GREENACRES CEMETERY, / OLDHAM, LANCASHIRE. / ON THE 13TH OF AUGUST 1804, AT THE AGE OF 20 YEARS, HE JOINED THE ARMY OF / RESERVE, AT ROCHDALE, AND WAS ATTACHED TO THE 48TH REGIMENT OF / FOOT, WHICH REGIMENT HE AFTERWARDS JOINED, AND WAS / PRESENT WITH IT IN THE FOLLOWING BATTLES:- / TALAVERA, ALBUERA, CIUDAD RODRIGO, CAPTURE OF BADAJOZ, SALAMANCA, / BUSACO, VITTORIA, PYRENEES, NIVELLE, ORTHES, TOULOUSE. / THE TIRED SOLDIER, BOLD AND BRAVE, / NOW REST HIS WEARY FEET; / AND TO THE SHELTER OF THE GRAVE / HAS MADE A SAFE RETREAT / TO HIM THE TRUMPET'S PIERCING BREATH / TO ARMS SHALL CALL IN VAIN; / HE'S QUARTERED NOW IN THE ARMS OF DEATH, / HE'LL NEVER MARCH AGAIN. / ……………….

Pte 13 Aug 1804.

Present in the Peninsula Jul 1809 – Apr 1814. Present at Talavera, Albuera, Ciudad Rodrigo, Badajoz, Salamanca, Vittoria, Pyrenees, Nivelle, Orthes and Toulouse. Also served in Ireland 1814 and Australia 1817–1824. Discharged Nov 1824 with a pension of one shilling per day. MGS medal for Talavera, Albuera, Ciudad Rodrigo, Badajoz, Salamanca, Vittoria, Pyrenees, Nivelle, Orthes and Toulouse. Worked

as a handloom weaver for 10 years and then as a weaver on power looms until the age of 82. Was never injured throughout his military service. Died 24 Feb 1871.
Reference: Obit. Oldham Chronicle, 4 Mar 1871, p. 7.

HOLMES, George Washington
Captain. 92nd Regiment of Foot.
Box tomb: St Brendan's Cemetery, Birr, County Offaly, Ireland. (Photograph)

SACRED TO THE MEMORY OF / GEORGE WASHINGTON HOLMES / LATE MAJOR IN THE 92ND FOOT / DIED AT PARSONTOWN ON THE / 1ST JANUARY 1852 / AGED 82 YEARS / ………………

Ensign 2 Mar 1799. Lt 10 Oct 1799. Capt 28 Mar 1805. Major 18 Jun 1815.

Served in the Peninsula Oct 1810 – Apr 1814. Present at Arroyo dos Molinos, Almarez, Alba de Tormes, Vittoria, Pyrenees (wounded 25 Jul 1813 and severely wounded 30 Jul 1813) and Nive (severely wounded 13 Dec 1813). Present at Quatre Bras where he took command of 92nd after senior officers were killed or wounded and Waterloo where he was wounded. Also served in Egypt 1801 and Walcheren 1809. MGS medal for Egypt, Vittoria, Pyrenees and Nive. Half pay 1818.

HORSELL, Bartholomew
Captain. Royal Waggon Train.
Memorial tablet: St Bartholomew and All Saints' Church, Wootton Bassett, Wiltshire. (M.I.)

"SACRED TO THE MEMORY OF CAPTAIN BARTHOLOMEW HORSELL DIED 22 APRIL 1851 AGED 83."

Headstone: St Bartholomew and All Saints' Churchyard, Wootton Bassett, Wiltshire. (Photograph)

SACRED / TO THE MEMORY OF / CAPT BARTHOLOMEW HORSELL / ……………… / A MONUMENT TO WHOSE / REMEMBRANCE IS ERECTED / IN THE CHURCH

Lt 12 Jan 1804. Capt 26 Nov 1812.

Served in the Peninsula Apr 1810 – Mar 1813 and Apr 1814. Present at Busaco, Badajoz and Toulouse. Half pay 1814. MGS medal for Busaco, Badajoz and Toulouse. Justice of the Peace.

HOUGHTON, Edward
Captain. 5th (Princess Charlotte of Wales's) Dragoon Guards.
Tombstone: St Selskar's Abbey, Wexford, County Wicklow, Ireland. (M.I.)

"WITHIN THIS TOMB / LIE THE MORTAL / REMAINS OF CAPTN EDWARD HOUGHTON / FORMERLY OF THE 5TH DRAGOON GUARDS / WHO DEPARTED THIS LIFE / ON THE 17TH MARCH / 1840"

Dumfriesshire Fencible Cavalry. Adjt 5th Dragoon Guards 12 Aug 1800. Cornet and Adjt Nov 1801. Lt 18 Jul 1805. Capt 22 Apr 1813.

Served in the Peninsula Apr 1814. Present at Toulouse.

HOWARD, John
51st (2nd Yorkshire West Riding) Light Infantry.
Buried in Old Cemetery, Leek, Staffordshire. (Grave Number 1672). (Burial register)

Pte 1808.

Present at Waterloo (wounded three times) in Capt James Campbell's Company. Discharged 1816 due to his wounds. Died 29 Mar 1879 aged 86.

HUGHES, David

Private. 95th Regiment of Foot.
Headstone: St Michael's Church, Eglwys Fach, Cardiganshire, Wales. (Photograph)

SACRED / TO THE MEMORY OF / DAVID HUGHES / OF MELIN-Y-GARREG IN THIS / PARISH WHO DEPARTED / THIS LIFE MARCH 24TH 1847. / AGED 65 YEARS.

Pte 1805.

Served in the Peninsula 1808 – Jan 1809 and 1810 – Apr 1814. Present at Vimeiro, Corunna, Barrosa Vittoria, Pyrenees and Toulouse. Present at Waterloo in Capt Henry Lee's Company and with the Army of Occupation. Also served in South America 1807. Discharged 1824. MGS medal for Vimeiro, Corunna, Barrosa, Vittoria, Pyrenees and Toulouse.

HUNT, Robert

Lieutenant. Royal Engineers.
Family Memorial tablet: St Saviour's Church, Dartmouth, Devon. (Photograph)

.... / ROBERT, LIEUTENANT IN THE ROYAL ENGINEERS, / WHO DIED ON HIS PASSAGE TO CEYLON, / ON THE 6TH OF SEPTEMBER 1819, AGED 27 YEARS, / ....

2nd Lt 1 Jul 1812. Lt 1 Mar 1813.

Served in France 1815–1818 (present at the siege of Peronne and with the Army of Occupation). Died at sea on his way to Ceylon with his regiment in 1819.

JACKSON, Sir Richard Downes

First Major. Coldstream Regiment of Foot Guards.
Buried on his estate 'William Henry' at Sorel, Montreal, Canada.

Ensign 9 Jul 1794. Lt and Capt 31 May 1798. Capt and Lt Colonel 4 Aug 1808. First Major 25 Jul 1814. Bt Colonel 4 Jun 1814. Major General 27 May 1825. Lt General 28 Jul 1838.

Served in the Peninsula Apr 1810 – Mar 1811, Apr 1811 – May 1813 (AQMG) and Oct 1813 – Apr 1814 (AQMG 2nd Division). Present at Cadiz, Barrosa (Mentioned in Despatches), Fuentes d'Onoro, Salamanca, Nivelle, Nive (Mentioned in Despatches), Adour, Garris, Orthes, Aire and Toulouse. Also served in Ireland 1798 (present in the Rebellion), Hanover 1805 and Copenhagen 1807. Gold Medal for Barrosa, Fuentes d'Onoro, Salamanca, Nivelle, Nive and Orthes. KCB. Colonel Royal Staff Corps 18 Jan 1820. Colonel 81st Foot 8 Jan 1829. Colonel 35th Foot 15 Jun 1840. In command of Northern Military District in Britain during Chartist riots and unrest in 1830. Commander in Chief of Forces in Canada 1839 to replace Sir John Colbourne. He tried to strengthen the border between Canada and America, but by 1842 tensions had eased between the two countries. He asked for a recall to England in 1845 but died suddenly on 9 Jun 1845 and is buried on his Canadian estate.
REFERENCE: Dictionary of Canadian Biography. Gentleman's Magazine, Sep 1845, p. 309. Annual Register, 1845, Appx, p. 282.

JAMES, Joseph

Private. 40th (2nd Somersetshire) Regiment of Foot.
Headstone: St John's Church of England Cemetery, Parramatta, New South Wales, Australia. (Photograph)

.... / ALSO / JOSEPH JAMES / WHO DIED 19TH DECEMBER 1852 / AGED 55 YEARS / LEAVING A WIDOW AND EIGHT CHILDREN TO / LAMENT THEIR LOSS.

Pte 1811.

Served in the Peninsula 1811 – Apr 1814. Present at Pyrenees and Toulouse. Present at Waterloo in Captain S. Stretton's Company. Also served in North America 1814–1815. MGS medal for Pyrenees and Toulouse. Discharged in 1820, he went to Australia in 1826 and enlisted in the New South Wales Royal Veteran Company. After his discharge in 1831 he received a veterans grant of 60 acres of land.

JARMY, Robert

Private. 43rd (Monmouthshire) Light Infantry Regiment of Foot.
Headstone: St Bartholomew's Churchyard, Shipmeadow, Suffolk. (Photograph)

SACRED / TO THE MEMORY OF / WILLIAM JARMY / WHO DEPARTED THIS LIFE 8TH SEPR 1850 / AGED 84 YEARS / ALSO SARAH HIS 1ST WIFE WHO / DIED 8TH AUGUST 1794 AGED 42 YEARS / ALSO MARY HIS 2ND WIFE WHO / DIED 18TH SEPT 1831 AGED 81 YEARS / THIS STONE IS ERECTED BY THEIR / AFFECTIONATE SON ROBERT WHO WAS A / SOLDIER 42 YEARS. / (VERSE)

Pte 4 May 1801. Cpl 11 May 1811. Sgt 25 Mar 1812. Pte 20 Jun 1814. Cpl 25 Sep 1815. Pte 18 Feb 1816. Cpl 7 Mar 1821. Sgt 8 May 1821. Pte 13 Sep 1822. Pte 7 Feb 1823. Cpl 28 Dec 1826. Pte 9 Jun 1827. Cpl 7 Jan 1832. Sgt 10 May 1832. Pte 15 Nov 1832. Cpl 4 Nov 1837. Sgt 15 Dec 1837. Colour Sgt 1 Feb 1840.

Served in the Peninsula Feb 1813 – Jun 1814. Present at Vittoria, Pyrenees, San Sebastian, Nivelle, Nive, Bayonne (distinguished himself in a skirmish 23 Nov 1813) and Toulouse. Present with the Army of Occupation until Oct 1818. Also served in North America (present at New Orleans where he was wounded 8 Jan 1815), Gibraltar 1823–1827, Portugal 1827 – Mar 1828 and Gibraltar 1828–1831. MGS medal for Vittoria, Pyrenees, San Sebastian, Nivelle, Nive and Toulouse. Awarded Regimental medal. His fondness for drink was the main reason for so many reductions in rank. He was tried by a Regimental Court Martial in Dec 1822 for being drunk and missing a morning parade which led to him being imprisoned for six weeks. He was tried again for being drunk and neglectful of his duties in 1832. The army persevered with him as he had proved to be trustworthy and in the end he apparently overcame his drink problems and was discharged with a very good character reference 28 Jun 1841. Served in the army for 42 years.
Note: Named as Jermy in regimental records.

JERMY, Robert see JARMY, Robert

JOHNSON, Samuel

Lieutenant. 48th (Northamptonshire) Regiment of Foot.
Buried in St George's Chapel, Windsor, Berkshire.

Pte 1794. Promoted from the ranks. Ensign 13 Jun 1811. Lt 6 Jan 1814. Quartermaster 14 Dec 1815.

Served in the Peninsula 1809 – Apr 1814. Present at Talavera, Aldea de Ponte, Albuera, Ciudad Rodrigo and Badajoz (wounded and awarded a pension of £50 per annum). Also served in North America 1814–1815. Served as Quartermaster from 1815 – 9 Mar 1838 when he retired. Died 24 Jul 1847.

JOHNSTONE, George

Captain. 43rd (Monmouthshire) Light Infantry Regiment of Foot.
Pedestal tomb topped with urn: Warriston Cemetery, Edinburgh, Scotland. (Section A 2. No. 528). (Photograph)

IN MEMORY OF / MAJOR GEORGE JOHNSTONE / LATE OF THE 43RD LIGHT INFANTRY / WHO DIED 2 JAN 1863 / AGED 84. / ………………..

Ensign 23 Oct 1804. Lt 29 May 1805. Capt 16 Aug 1810. Major 29 Jun 1830.

Served in the Peninsula with 1/43rd Oct 1808 – Jan 1809, Jul 1809 – Sep 1812 and Apr 1814. Present at Vigo, Coa (wounded), Busaco, Pombal, Redinha, Casal Nova, Foz d'Arouce, Sabugal, Fuentes d'Onoro, Ciudad Rodrigo, Badajoz (wounded) and Salamanca. Present with the Army of Occupation until Nov 1818. Also served at Copenhagen 1807, North America 1814–1815 (present at New Orleans), Gibraltar 1822–1826 and 1828–1829. Retired 23 Dec 1831. MGS medal for Busaco, Fuentes d'Onoro, Ciudad Rodrigo, Badajoz and Salamanca.

JONES, Charles

Captain. 15th (King's) Regiment of Light Dragoons.
Buried in St Mary's Churchyard, Lancaster.

Troop Quartermaster. Promoted from the ranks. Cornet and Adjt 27 Aug 1807. Lt 10 Mar 1808. Capt 7 Oct 1813.

Served in the Peninsula Nov 1808 – Jan 1809 and Feb 1813 – Apr 1814 (Brigade Major Cavalry Brigade 8 May 1813 – Apr 1814). Present at Sahagun (wounded), Corunna campaign, Morales, Vittoria, Orthes and Toulouse. Present at Waterloo as Brigade Major to 5th Cavalry Brigade commanded by Major General Sir Colquhoun Grant with whom he had served in the Peninsula as Adjutant. They were known as the Black Giant and the Red Dwarf, Jones being very small with red hair. After the war Jones was a witness at the court martial of Colonel Quentin of the 10th Hussars. Compiled the Adjutant's Journal of the 15th (King's) Light Dragoons 1799–1815. Died 27 Jan 1840 aged 65 and buried in St Mary's Church, Lancaster 1 Feb 1840.

REFERENCE: *Jones, Charles, Cavalry in the Corunna campaign as told in the Diary of the Adjutant of the 15th Hussars, edited by Major Lord Carnock, Journal of the Society for Army Historical Research, 1936, (Special Publication No. 4).*

JONES, Charles

Major. 18th Regiment of Light Dragoons.
Memorial Vault: Kensal Green Cemetery, London. (3970/58/ -). (Photograph)

Cornet 5th Lt Dragoons 26 Apr 1796. Lt 18th Lt Dragoons 16 Apr 1799. Capt 29 Oct 1802. Major 19 Sep 1811.

Served in the Peninsula Sep 1808 – Jan 1809 and Jan – May 1811 (Extra ADC to Major General Nightingall). Present at Benevente, and Fuentes d'Onoro. Resigned 1812. Became Equerry to the Duke of Cumberland 22 Nov 1817. Died in 1843. His son Ernest Jones was the Chartist radical and poet.

JONES, Thomas

Captain. 32nd (Cornwall) Regiment of Foot.
Gravestone: Old Kilbride Cemetery, Arklow, County Wicklow, Ireland. (M.I.)

"UNDERNEATH ARE DEPOSITED THE REMAINS OF / THOMAS JONES ESQ. LATE CAPTAIN IN H. M. / 32ND REGIMENT OF INFANTRY WHO DIED 1ST OF / MAY 1832 AGED 60 YEARS"

Ensign 1801. Lt 24 Nov 1803. Capt 27 Jul 1809.

Served in the Peninsula Aug 1808 – Jan 1809 and Jul 1811 – Apr 1814. Present at Rolica, Vimeiro, Corunna, Bidassoa, Nivelle, Nive and Orthes.

JONES, William
Private. 1st (Royal) Regiment of Dragoons.
Headstone: St Mary Magdalene's Churchyard, Albrighton, Shropshire. (Photograph)

HERE LIETH THE BODY OF / WILLIAM JONES / PENSIONER – LATE A PRIVATE IN THE FIRST / REGIMENT OF ROYAL DRAGOONS, / WHO DIED JUNE 12TH 1851 AGED 70. / HE SERVED IN THE PENINSULAR WAR / UNDER THE DUKE OF WELLINGTON / AT DOURO. TALAVERA. TORRES VEDRAS. / BUSACO. FUENTES D'ONORE. ALBUERA. / SALAMANCA. BADAJOZ. VITTORIA. / PYRENEES. ORTHES. TOULOUSE. / FOR ENGLAND SCORNING WOUNDS AND DEATH / HE FOUGHT HER BATTLES WELL / AND NOW HE FIGHTS THE FIGHT OF FAITH / THE JUDGEMENT DAY WILL TELL. / .... / THIS HEADSTONE IS ERECTED BY / RICHARD YATES ESQ. TO THE / MEMORY OF / A GOOD AND FAITHFUL SERVANT IN HIS FAITH.

Served in the Peninsula Sep 1809 – Apr 1814. Present at Fuentes d'Onoro, Aldea de Ponte, Maguilla, Vittoria and Toulouse. MGS medal for Fuentes d'Onoro and Vittoria.

KEPPEL, George Thomas
Ensign. 14th (Buckinghamshire) Regiment of Foot.
Low monument in railed enclosure: St Andrew's Churchyard, Quidenham, Norfolk. (Photograph)

GENERAL GEORGE THOMAS 6TH EARL OF ALBERMARLE / BORN JUNE 13 1799. DIED FEBRUARY 21 1891 / SERVED IN THE 14TH REGIMENT AT WATERLOO

Ensign 4 Apr 1815. Ensign 22nd Foot 5 Feb 1818. Lt 22nd Foot 25 May 1820. Lt 24th Foot 26 Oct 1820. Lt 20th Foot 27 Nov 1821. Capt 62nd Foot 17 Feb 1825. Major (Unattached) 20 Mar 1827. Bt Lt Colonel 23 Nov 1841. Bt Colonel 20 Jun 1854. Major General 26 Oct 1858. Lt General 31 Mar 1866. General 7 Feb 1874.

Present at Waterloo at the age of 16 after leaving Westminster School, and with the Army of Occupation. Also served in the Ionian Islands 1817, Mauritius and Cape of Good Hope 1818, India 1821 (ADC to Governor General the Marquis of Hastings. When Hastings resigned in 1823, Keppel was granted leave to return home overland via Persia and Russia) and Ireland 1825 (ADC to Marquis of Wellesley). Half pay 20 Mar 1827. Travelled extensively in Turkey and the Balkans. MP for East Norfolk 1832–1835 and Lymington 1847–1850. Private Secretary to the Prime Minister Lord John Russell 1846. Became 6th Earl of Albemarle 15 Mar 1851. Trustee of Westminster School 1854. Deputy Lieutenant of Norfolk 1859. Wrote *Personal Narrative of a Journey from India to England,* 2 vols, 1825, *Narrative of a Journey across the Balkans,* 1830 and *Fifty Years of my Life,* 2 vols, 1876. Died 21 Feb 1891.

Reference: Dictionary of National Biography. Keppel, George, Fifty Years of my Life, 2 vols, 1876.

KIELMANNSEGGE, Friedrich Otto Gothard Graf von
Colonel Commander. 1st Hanoverian Brigade.
Chest tomb: Gartenfriedhof, Marienstrasse, Hanover, Germany. (Photograph)

CHARLOTTE WILHELMINE HEDWIG GRAF VON KIELMANSEGGE / GEB. VON SPORKEN / GEB. 28 APRIL 1744. GEST 27 DECEMB. 1830 / FRIEDRICH OTTO GOTHARD GRAF VON KIELMANSEGGE KONIGL. HANNOV: GENERAL DER INFANTERIE / GEB. 15 DECEMB 1768. GEST 18 JULI 1851.

Present at Waterloo in command of the 1st Hanoverian Brigade in Alten's 3rd Division. Present at Quatre Bras where they reinforced the 95th Foot and re-took the Farm of Piraumont but suffered heavy losses. In 1813 he had raised the Kielmannseggeschen Jaeger Corps. These were men who were known for their

sharp shooting and were included in his 1st Hanoverian Brigade.. On the 18th June Kielmannsegge deployed these men in the woods around Hougoumont. His Luneburg battalion was sent to help Major Baring and the King's German Legion at La Haye Sainte but they were heavily defeated by French cuirassiers. Later in the day when Alten and Halkett were wounded and Ompteda was killed, Kielmannsegge was in charge of the division but he too was wounded. Appointed Major General in the Hanoverian Army in 1815 and Lt General in 1816. Died in Hanover 18 Jul 1851.
Reference: Allgemeine Deutsche Biographie.

KING, John Duncan
Lieutenant. 7th (Royal Fusiliers) Regiment of Foot.
Buried in St George's Chapel, Windsor, Berkshire. (Burial Register)

Ensign 71st Foot 28 Aug 1806. Lt 18 Feb 1808. Lt 1st Foot 28 Jul 1808. Lt 7th Foot 13 Jun 1811. Lt 8th Foot 20 Apr 1826. Lt 75th Foot 14 May 1829. Capt 18 Mar 1830.

Served in the Peninsula with 1st Foot Aug 1810 – Mar 1811 and with 7th Foot Sep – Oct 1811 and Jan 1813 – Apr 1814. Present at Busaco, Fuente Guinaldo, Aldea de Ponte, Vittoria, Osma and the Pyrenees (severely wounded at Sorauren 27 Jul 1813). Served in France 1815 with the Army of Occupation. Also served at Walcheren 1809 (present at the siege of Flushing). MGS medal for Busaco, Vittoria and Pyrenees. King was an excellent water colour artist. His paintings were exhibited at the Royal Academy. Eight of his water colours were presented to George V by his grandson and are now in the Royal Library at Windsor Castle. Retired 28 Dec 1830. Military Knight of Windsor 28 Jan 1851. Died 21 Aug 1863. Buried in Windsor Castle 29 Aug 1863.

KING, Thomas Newton
1st Lieutenant. Royal Artillery.
Ledger stone in railed enclosure: St Selskar's Abbey, Wexford, County Wicklow, Ireland. (M.I.)

"........... / AND ALSO THE BODY OF THE ABOVE NAMED / CAPT THOMAS N. KING / WHO DEPARTED THIS / LIFE ON THE 8TH DAY OF MAY 1851 / IN THE 66TH YEAR OF HIS AGE"

2nd Lt 4 Oct 1806. 1st Lt 1 Feb 1808. 2nd Capt 5 Aug 1826.

Served in the Peninsula Oct 1808 – Jan 1809. Present at Corunna. Also served in the Netherlands 1815–1816 and the West Indies 1826 – Apr 1827. Half pay 30 Jun 1830.

KORFES, Georg Ludwig
Lieutenant Colonel. Duke of Brunswick Oel's Regiment of Infantry.
Memorial: Ottenstein on Weser, Lower Saxony, Germany. (Photograph)

GEORG LUDWIG KORFES / GEBOREN IN OTTENSTEIN AM 29. OKTOBER / 1769, LEISTETE IN DEUTSCHER TREUE GROS- / SES AUF DEM FELDZUGE DES HERZOGS / FRIEDRICH WILHELM IM JAHRE 1809 UND / STARB ALS BEFEHLSHABER DES BRAUN- / SCHWEIGISCHEN INFANTERIEREGIMENTS / AM 31. DEZEMBER 1810 IN LISSABON

GEORG LUDWIG KORFES / BORN AT OTTENSTEIN ON THE 29TH OCTOBER / 1769, SERVED WITH GERMAN LOYALTY GREAT / DEEDS ON THE CAMPAIGN OF THE DUKE / FRIEDRICH WILHELM IN THE YEAR 1809 AND / DIED AS COMMANDER OF THE BRUNS – / WICK INFANTRY REGIMENT / ON 31ST DECEMBER 1810 AT LISBON

Memorial tablet: On house in Korfes. (Photograph)
(This is not the original house but a later reconstructed building).

HIER WURDE / GEBOREN AM 29 OKTOBER 1769 / MAJOR KORFES / DER TREUE DIENER SEINES HERZOG / IM DEUTSCHEN FREIHEITSKRIEGE

MAJOR KORFES / WAS / BORN HERE / ON 29TH OCTOBER 1769 / / THE FAITHFUL SERVANT OF HIS DUKE / IN THE GERMAN WAR OF LIBERATION

Capt Brunswick Artillery 1806. Major 1809. Lt Colonel Brunswick Oel's Infantry Regt 1810.

Served in the Peninsula 1810 and died in Lisbon 31 Dec 1810. Also served in the Artillery in North Germany under Duke Wilhelm of Brunswick (present at the battle of Ölper 1808).

KORTRIGHT, William

Ensign. Coldstream Regiment of Foot Guards.
Buried in St Mary's Churchyard, Fryerning, Essex. (Burial Register)

Ensign 68th Foot 26 Mar 1812. Ensign Coldstream Guards 26 Nov 1812. Capt 93rd Foot 11 Sep 1817. Lt and Capt Coldstream Guards 25 Feb 1819.

Served in the Peninsula Dec 1812 – Apr 1814. Present at Vittoria, Bidassoa, Nivelle, Nive, Adour and Bayonne. Joined 93rd Foot on reduction of the Coldstream Guards in 1817 but rejoined the Coldstream Guards 1819. MGS medal for Vittoria, Nivelle and Nive. Died 21 Dec 1866.

LAMONT, John Henry

Lieutenant Colonel. 92nd Regiment of Foot.
Buried in the family vault: St Kilfinan's Church, Ardlamont, Argyllshire, Scotland.

Ensign 42nd Foot 1793. Lt 16th Foot 1793. Capt 97th Foot 11 Feb 1794. Major Clan Alpine Fencible Infantry 7 Sep 1799. Major 92nd Foot 2 Jun 1804. Bt Lt Colonel 1 Jan 1805. Lt Colonel 92nd Foot Jan 1809. Bt Colonel 4 Jun 1813. Major General 12 Aug 1819.

Served in the Peninsula Aug 1808 – Jan 1809. Present at Corunna where he was promoted to Lt Colonel 92nd Foot when Lt Colonel Alexander Napier was killed during the battle. Also served in Flanders 1794–1795, Helder 1799 (present at Bergen), Ferrol 1800, Copenhagen 1807 (present at Kioge) and Sweden 1808. After Corunna he took command of the 2nd Battalion and went to Ireland until 1811 when the battalion went to Scotland and remained there until 1814. Half pay 1814. Died in Robroyston, Glasgow 31 Mar 1829.

LAW, James Smith

1st Lieutenant. Royal Artillery.
Memorial: St Mary's Churchyard, Cheltenham, Gloucestershire. (Part III Section 4). (M.I.)

"SACRED TO THE MEMORY OF LT COLONEL JAMES SMITH LAW ROYAL ARTILLERY WHO DEPARTED THIS LIFE (AT BAYSHILL CHELTENHAM) ON THE 31ST OF JULY 1862 IN THE 73RD YEAR OF HIS AGE"

2nd Lt 3 Nov 1807. 1st Lt 16 Jul 1808. 2nd Capt 6 Nov 1827. Capt 10 Jan 1837. Bt Major 23 Nov 1841. Lt Colonel 28 Nov 1854.

Served at Walcheren 1809 (services highly commended on the evacuation). Also served in Malta 1815–1817, Newfoundland 1825–1827 and Malta 1835–1836. Retired on full pay 13 Apr 1842.
Reference: Gentleman's Magazine, Sep 1862, p. 373.

LAW, Robert

Lieutenant. 71st (Highland) Regiment of Foot.
Memorial: St Michan's Churchyard, Dublin, Ireland. (M.I.)

"GENERAL ROBERT LAW, KH, KCB. 71ST HIGHLANDERS"

Ensign 8 Jun 1809. Adjt 6 Dec 1810. Lt 27 May 1811. Capt 18 Oct 1821. Capt 33rd Foot 20 Mar 1823. Capt Ceylon Rifles 25 Sep 1824. Major 20 Aug 1834. Lt Colonel 2 Feb 1844. Bt Colonel 20 Jun 1854. Major General 17 Jul 1859. Lt General 30 Mar 1868.

Served in the Peninsula 1808 – Jan 1809 and Sep 1810 – Apr 1814. Present at Corunna, Sobral, Fuentes d'Onoro (wounded), Arroyo dos Molinos, Almarez, Alba de Tormes, Pyrenees, Nivelle, Nive, Garris, Orthes, Aire and Tarbes (severely wounded). Present at Waterloo (severely wounded) and with the Army of Occupation. Also served at Walcheren 1809 (present at the siege of Flushing) and Newfoundland 1834 where he was Commandant of the Garrison for 25 years until he returned to England in 1859. The Garrison was formed from former invalid soldiers from Chelsea, mainly to assist civil power in time of unrest. Law also took part in the political life of the colony. Lt Colonel Royal Newfoundland Veteran Companies. MGS medal for Corunna, Fuentes d'Onoro, Pyrenees, Nivelle, Nive and Orthes. KH. KCB. Colonel 2nd West India Regt 26 Jan 1865. Died 16 May 1874.
Reference: Dictionary of Canadian Biography.

LAWSON, Hugh

2nd Captain. Royal Engineers.
Memorial tablet: St Peter and St Paul's Church, Fareham, Hampshire. (Photograph)

SACRED TO THE MEMORY / OF / LIEUT DOUGLAS LAWSON / OF THE ROYAL ENGINEERS / WHO DIED IN THE ISLAND OF TOBAGO / IN THE WEST INDIES THE 15TH OF JULY 1794 / IN THE 34TH YEAR OF HIS AGE. / ALSO OF HIS SON CAPTN HUGH LAWSON / OF THE SAME CORPS WHO DIED JANY 4TH / 1812 AGED 21 YEARS.

2nd Lt 1 Aug 1806. Lt 1 Dec 1806. 2nd Capt 18 Jul 1811.

Served in Sicily 1807–1812 where he died at Messina 1 Jan 1812.

LE TOLLER, Henry

Lieutenant. 83rd Regiment of Foot.
Memorial: St Mary's Church, Bunclody, Wexford, County Wicklow, Ireland. (M.I.)

"DEPARTED THIS LIFE ON THE 24TH OF MARCH 1821 / LIEUTENANT HENRY LE TOLLER OF HIS MAJESTIES 83RD REGIMENT OF FOOT"

Ensign 16 Mar 1809. Lt 30 May 1811.

Served in the Peninsula Apr 1809 – Apr 1814. Present at Douro and Talavera where he was wounded and taken prisoner until Apr 1814. Half pay 30 May 1818.

LEWANLEY, William see CRAWLEY, William

LEWIS, Joseph

Sergeant. 3rd (Prince of Wales's) Regiment of Dragoon Guards.
Buried in St Mary's Churchyard, Kingswinford, Shropshire. (Burial record)

Pte 18 Jul 1797. Cpl Nov 1809. Sgt 1810.

Served in the Peninsula Apr 1809 – Apr 1814. Present at Talavera, Albuera, Usagre, Aldea de Ponte, Maguilla, Vittoria and Toulouse. Recruiting Sergeant in Liverpool district 1816. Discharged 27 Jul 1825 as unfit for further service. MGS medal for Talavera, Albuera, Vittoria and Toulouse. Died 1857 aged 80.

LIGHTBODY, John

Surgeon. 28th (North Gloucestershire) Regiment of Foot
Family Pedestal monument: Warriston Cemetery, Edinburgh, Scotland. (Section A3. No. 65). (Photograph)

IN MEMORY OF / JANE / THIRD DAUGHTER OF / JOHN LIGHTBODY ESQR / SURGEON TO THE FORCES / .... / THE AFORESAID / JOHN LIGHTBODY ESQ / (RETIRED) STAFF SURGEON MAJOR / DIED AT EDINBURGH 21ST APRIL 1865 / IN THE 78TH YEAR OF HIS AGE.

Hospital Mate 20 Aug 1804. Asst Surgeon 10th Foot 20 Jun 1805. Asst Surgeon 71st Foot 23 Aug 1810. Surgeon 28th Foot 13 Oct 1812. Surgeon 80th Foot 7 May 1818. Surgeon 2nd Dragoon Guards 4 Dec 1835. Staff Surgeon 3 Mar 1837.

Served in the Peninsula with 71st Foot Apr – Nov 1812 and with 28th Foot Dec 1812 – Jun 1813. Present at Almarez and retreat from Burgos. Also served in Sicily 1806–1807. Retired on half pay 2 Aug 1842.

LINTON, John

Lieutenant. 6th (Inniskilling) Regiment of Dragoons.
Memorial tablet: St Mary's Church, Buckden, Huntingdonshire. (North wall). (M.I.)

"IN HOPE OF A GLORIOUS RESURRECTION LOUISA THE BELOVED WIFE OF COLONEL LINTON OF STIRTLOE .... ALSO TO THE MEMORY OF THE ABOVE COLONEL LINTON A WATERLOO SOLDIER WHO DIED JUNE 1877 IN THE 86TH YEAR OF HIS AGE."

Cornet 3 Sep 1808. Lt 25 Jan 1809. Capt 15 May 1817. Major 21 Jul 1825. Lt Colonel 31 Aug 1830. Bt Colonel 9 Nov 1846.

Present at Waterloo, Capture of Paris and with the Army of Occupation until 1816. Also served in Ireland 1809–1814 and 1819–1823 (present in the 'White Boys' Insurrection 1822). Half pay 31 Aug 1830.

LISTON, Alexander

Private. 94th Regiment of Foot.
Family Headstone: Canongate Cemetery, Edinburgh, Scotland. (Photograph)

.... / ALEXANDER LISTON LATE SERGEANT IN THE 94TH REGIMENT / BORN 17 FEB 1780 DIED 5 MAY 1871 AGED 91 YEARS / HE SERVED IN THE ARMY UPWARDS OF 27 YEARS / PRESENT AT THE STORMING OF SERINGAPATAM GAWILGHUR ASSEERGHUR / UNDER SIR DAVID BAIRD IN 1799

Served in the Peninsula. Present at Fuentes d'Onoro. Also served in India 1799–1804. Present at the siege of Seringapatam, siege of Gawilghur, siege of Asseerghur and battle of Argaum. Awarded MGS medal for Fuentes d'Onoro and Army of India medal for Asseerghur, Arguam and Gawilghur. Died 5 Mar 1871.

LITTLE, John

Lieutenant. 27th (Inniskilling) Regiment of Foot.
Fractured Ledger stone: St Selskar's Abbey, Wexford, County Wicklow, Ireland. (M.I.)

"SACRED / TO THE MEMORY OF / JOHN LITTLE ESQUIRE / LIEUTENANT IN THE 27TH ENNISKILLEN REGT / OF FOOT WHO DIED AT WEXFORD ON 25TH SEPTEMBER 1857"

Ensign 27 Apr 1809. Lt 9 Sep 1812.

Served in the Peninsula with 1/27th Nov 1812 – Apr 1814. Present at Castalla, Tarragona and Barcelona. Also served in North America 1814–1815. Half pay 25 Jul 1817.

LOCKWOOD, Purefoy
Lieutenant. 30th (Cambridgeshire) Regiment of Foot.
Buried in the Officer's Graveyard, Royal Hospital, Kilmainham, Dublin, Ireland.

Ensign Tipperary Militia. Ensign 30th Foot 18 Apr 1811. Lt 22 Apr 1813.

Served in the Peninsula Oct 1811 – Jun 1813. Present at Badajoz, Salamanca, Burgos and the retreat from Burgos (present at Villa Muriel). Present at Waterloo where he was shot through the top of his head and severely wounded at Quatre Bras. After trepanning he was fitted with a silver plate in his skull which remained until his death. The plate was engraved with the words 'Bomb Proof' and he became known as 'Bomb Proof Lockwood'. Also served in the Netherlands 1814–1815. Half pay 25 Aug 1816. Became Captain of Invalids at the Royal Hospital at Kilmainham in Dublin. His son Augustus served as Surgeon with the 7th Foot in the Crimea. MGS medal for Badajoz and Salamanca. Died 14 Aug 1859.

LONGDEN, John
Captain. 33rd (1st Yorkshire West Riding) Regiment of Foot.
Marble slab: General Cemetery, Bruges, Belgium. (M.I.)

"SACRED TO THE MEMORY OF MAJOR JOHN LONGDEN LATE OF THE 33RD REGIMENT WHOSE SUDDEN DEATH BY CHOLERA MORBUS TOOK PLACE AT BRUGES ON THE 6TH DAY OF OCTOBER 1832 AGED 50 YEARS. DEEPLY LAMENTED BY HIS FAMILY AND UNIVERSALLY BY HIS FRIENDS"

Lt 16 Apr 1806. Capt 8 Sep 1814. Bt Major 1 Nov 1821.

Present at Waterloo. Also served in the Netherlands 1814–1815. Half pay 1 May 1827. Died in Bruges in a cholera epidemic 6 Oct 1832.

LONSDALE, James
Paymaster. 4th (King's Own) Regiment of Foot.
Buried in the Royal Garrison Church Graveyard, Portsmouth, Hampshire. (M.I.)

"TO THE MEMORY OF / JAMES LONSDALE ESQ / LATE PAYMASTER, KING'S OWN REGT / WHO DIED 23RD SEPTEMBER 1836 / AGED 62"

Paymaster 20 Dec 1798.

Served in the Peninsula Aug 1808 – Jan 1809, with 1/4th Nov 1810 – Dec 1812 and Sep 1813 – Apr 1814. Present at Corunna, Barba del Puerco, Fuentes d'Onoro, Badajoz, Salamanca, retreat from Burgos (present at Villa Muriel), Bidassoa, Nivelle, Nive and Bayonne. Present at Waterloo. Also served at Walcheren 1809 and North America 1814–1815.

LOWRIE, Robert
Captain. 91st Regiment of Foot.
Memorial tablet: St Martin's Church, Lincoln, Lincolnshire. (The church is no longer extant). (M.I.)

"PYRENEES / ERECTED BY THE OFFICERS OF THE 91ST REGIMENT AS A MARK OF THEIR ESTEEM TO THE MEMORY OF CAPTAIN ROBERT LOWRIE OF THAT CORPS, WHO DIED AT VITTORIA THE 3RD OF OCTOBER 1813 IN CONSEQUENCE OF A WOUND RECEIVED IN ACTION WITH THE ENEMY ON THE 28TH OF JULY PRECEDING, AGE 34 YEARS."

Ensign 3 Oct 1798. Lt 10 May 1799. Capt 26 Oct 1804.

Served in the Peninsula Aug 1808 – Jan 1809 and Oct 1812 – Oct 1813. Present at Rolica, Vimeiro, Cacabellos, Corunna and the Pyrenees (severely wounded 28 Jul 1813 at Sorauren). Died of his wounds 3 Oct 1813 at Vittoria. Also served at Walcheren 1809. One of four officers selected to raise a number of men for the regiment in 1804. Promoted to Captain for this service.

Supplement Place Index A – L

London – Other sources
St Martin-in-the Fields: Belson, Sir Charles
Wimbledon: Grosvenor, Thomas

Norfolk
Keppel, George Thomas

Shropshire
Albrighton: Jones, William
Claverley: Croyden, William
Kingswinford: Lewis, William
Oswestry: Faunce, Edmund
Oswestry: Hancox, Skinner

Somerset
Bath: Gould, John

Staffordshire
Leek: Bowcock, Samuel
Leek: Howard, John

Suffolk
Shipmeadow: Jarmy, Robert
Yoxhall: Blois, Charles

Surrey
Caterham: Gibson, Samuel
Kingston: Clues, Josiah

Sussex
Storrington: Falconer, Hugh
West Stoke: Browning, John

Warwickshire
Hillmorton: Arden, William

Wiltshire
Donhead: Gordon, John
Inglesham: Evanson, Edward Alleyn
Keevil: Chamberlaine, Frederick
Landford: Eyre, Charles
Nunton: Buckley, Edward Pery
Wootton Bassett: Horsell, Bartholomew

Yorkshire
Barnsley: Bailey, Benjamin

Northern Ireland
Belfast: Carr, James
Killylea: Cross John

Ireland
Arklow, Co. Wicklow: Jones, Thomas
Birr, Co. Offaly: Holmes, George Washington
Bunclody Wexford: Le Toller, Henry
Dublin: Barker, Frederick
Dublin: Burgh, Sir Ulysses
Dublin: Dix, Thomas
Dublin: Foulkes, Thomas
Dublin: Law, Robert
Dublin: Lockwood, Purefoy
Wexford, Co. Wicklow: Houghton, Edward
Wexford, Co. Wicklow: King, Thomas N.
Wexford, Co. Wicklow: Little, John

Scotland
Alloa: Erskine, John Francis Miller
Ardlomant: Lamont. John Henry
Edinburgh: Campbell, John (Medical Dept)
Edinburgh: Chisholm, Donald
Edinburgh: Davidson, James
Edinburgh: Douglas, Neil
Edinburgh: Dowbiggin, William
Edinburgh: Fairweather, Thomas
Edinburgh: Fraser, Donald
Edinburgh: Hay, William
Edinburgh: Johnstone, George
Edinburgh: Lightbody, John
Edinburgh: Liston, Alexander
Inveresk: Croll, Francis
Kirkcowan: Hamilton, William Charles
Mauchline: Cunningham, John
Mauchline: Dickson, Sir Jeremiah
Panbride: Dalhousie, George Lord
Sanquhar: Cringam, William

Wales
Eglwys Fach: Hughes, David

Australia
New Town, Tasmania: Forster, Matthew
Parramatta: James, Joseph
Sydney: Gibbons, James

Belgium
Bruges: Drury, George
Bruges: Longden, John
Waterloo: Frederick, Prince of Netherlands
Waterloo: Heiden, F. M. van

Canada
Montreal: Jackson, Sir Richard Downes

France
Biarritz: Crawley, William
Nice: Brice, Alexander Adair
Tours: Fitzgerald, John Forster
Vorges: D'Olbreuse, Christope Henry D.

Germany
Hanover: Kielmannsegge, F. O. Graf von
Ottestein on Weser: Korfes, Georg Ludwig

India
Delhi: Barnard, Henry William
Dhaka: Dunkin, John Henry
Rajpur: Farrington, Charles Henry

Italy
Pisa: Hamilton, Thomas

Portugal
Elvas: Brown, William
Elvas: Campbell, Allan William
Elvas: Fearon, Peter

United States of America
Augusta: Gairdner, James Penman

West Indies
Barbados: Connolly, James
Bermuda: Basden, Samuel Taylor
Bermuda: Creighton, R.
Jamaica: Donaldson, Andrew

Supplement Regimental Index A – L

2nd Life Guards

Clues, Josiah	Cornet

1st (King's) Dragoon Guards

Elton, William	Capt
Downham, John	Pte

3rd (Prince of Wales's) Dragoon Guards

Arscott, John	Paymaster
Lewis, Joseph	Sgt

5th (Princess Charlotte of Wales's) Dragoon Guards

Houghton, Edward	Capt

1st (Royal) Regiment of Dragoons

Blois, Charles	Lt
Jones, William	Pte

4th (Queen's Own) Regiment of Dragoons

Fendall, William	Lt

6th (Inniskilling) Regiment of Dragoons

Black, Samuel	Lt
Linton, John	Lt

7th (Queen's Own) Regiment of Light Dragoons

Barr, John	Sgt Major
Gordon, John Robert	Lt

10th (Prince of Wales's Own) Regiment of Light Dragoons

Hamilton, William C.	Lt

12th Light Dragoons

Dowbiggin, William	Lt

13th Regiment of Light Dragoons

Armstrong, Abraham	Asst Surgeon

15th (King's) Regiment of Light Dragoons

Bailey, Benjamin	Cpl
Hancox, Skinner	Capt
Jones, Charles	Capt

16th (Queen's) Regiment of Light Dragoons

Chamberlaine, Frederick	Lt

18th Regiment of Light Dragoons

Barker, Frederick	Pte
Foulkes, Thomas	Pte
Jones, Charles	Major

23rd Regiment of Light Dragoons.

Croyden, William	Pte

Royal Waggon Train

Cheek, Jabez	Farrier
Horsell, Bartholomew	Capt

1st Regiment of Foot Guards

Arden, William	Pte
Barnard, Henry William	Ensign
Bell, John	Sgt
Buckley, Edward Pery	Lt and Capt
Burgh, Sir Ulysses	Capt and Lt
Colonel	
Erskine, John F. M.	Ensign

Coldstream Regiment of Foot Guards

Drummond, John	Lt and Capt
Gilder, Frederick	Asst Surgeon
Jackson, Richard Downes	First Major
Kortright, William	Ensign

1st (Royal Scots) Regiment of Foot

Cheney, William	Capt
Eyre, Charles	Lt

4th (King's Own) Regiment of Foot

Bowlby, Peter	Lt
Farrington, Charles Henry	Lt
Faunce, Edmund	Lt Colonel
Lonsdale, James	Paymaster

7th (Royal Fusiliers) Regiment of Foot.

Cooper, John Spencer	Sgt
King, John Duncan	Lt

11th (North Devonshire) Regiment of Foot	
Cuyler, George	Lt Colonel

14th (Buckinghamshire) Regiment of Foot	
Bolton, George	Capt
Keppel, George Thomas	Ensign

18th Regiment of Light Dragoons	
Jones, Charles	Major

21st (Royal North British Fusiliers) Regt of Foot	
Fairweather, Thomas	1st Lt

23rd (Royal Welch Fusiliers) Regiment of Foot.	
Brice, Alexander Adair	1st Lt
Croyden, William	Pte
Fielding, George	Lt
Hill, John Humphrey E.	Major

25th (King's Own) Regiment of Foot	
Cringam, William	Surgeon

26th (Cameronian) Regiment of Foot	
Connolly, James	Major
Dalhousie, George Lord	Lt Colonel

27th (Inniskilling) Regiment of Foot	
Bakewell, Robert	Lt
Crawley, William	Lt
Cunningham, John	Pte
Gibson, Samuel	Pte
Little, John	Lt

28th (North Gloucestershire) Regiment of Foot	
Belson, Sir Charles P.	Lt Colonel
Lightbody, John	Surgeon

29th (Worcestershire) Regiment of Foot	
Hamilton, Thomas	Lt

30th (Cambridgeshire) Regiment of Foot	
Lockwood, Purefoy	Lt

31st (Huntingdonshire) Regiment of Foot.	
Fearon, Peter	Capt

32nd (Cornwall) Regiment of Foot	
Birtwhistle, John	Ensign
Jones, Thomas	Capt

33rd (1st Yorkshire West Riding) Regt of Foot	
Drury, George	Ensign
Longden, John	Capt

39th (Dorsetshire) Regiment of Foot	
Hart, Francis Henry	Lt

40th (2nd Somersetshire) Regiment of Foot	
Barnett, John Henry	Capt
Browne, Gore	Lt Colonel
James, Joseph	Pte

41st Regiment of Foot	
Clinton, Lord Robert	Major

42nd (Royal Highland) Regiment of Foot	
Chisholm, Donald	Lt
Croll, Francis	Pte

43rd (Monmouthshire) Lt Infantry Regt of Foot	
Jarmy, Robert	Pte
Johnstone, George	Capt

44th (East Essex) Regiment of Foot	
Donaldson, Andrew	Lt

47th (Lancashire) Regiment of Foot	
Hay, William	Capt

48th (Northamptonshire) Regiment of Foot	
Hilton, James	Pte
Johnson, Samuel	Lt

52nd (Oxfordshire) Lt Infantry Regt of Foot	
Bond, Isaac	Sgt
Browning, John	Pte
Cross, John	Capt

54th (West Norfolk) Regiment of Foot	
Evanson, Edward Alleyn	Lt

57th (West Middlesex) Regiment of Foot	
Dix, Thomas	Lt
Gibbons, James	Pte

60th (Royal American) Regiment of Foot	
Fitzgerald, John Forster	Major

64th (2nd Staffordshire) Regiment of Foot	
Carr, James	Pte

65th (2nd Yorkshire North Riding) Regt of Foot
Grosvenor, Thomas Colonel

71st (Highland Light Infantry) Regt of Foot
Law, Robert Lt

74th (Highland) Regiment of Foot
Campbell, Allan W. Major
Creighton, R Pte

76th Regiment of Foot
Gould, John Lt

77th (East Middlesex) Regiment of Foot
Dunkin, John Henry Lt Colonel

79th (Cameron Highlanders) Regiment of Foot
Douglas, Neil Lt Colonel
Fraser, Donald Cpl

82nd (Prince of Wales's Volunteers) Regt of Foot
Falconer, Hugh Major
Haywood, Charles Pte

83rd Regiment of Foot
Le Toller, Henry Lt

84th (York and Lancaster) Regiment of Foot
Basden, Samuel Taylor Lt

85th (Buckinghamshire) Regiment of Foot
Forster, Matthew Lt

91st Regiment of Foot
Lowrie, Robert Capt

92nd Regiment of Foot
Bowcock, Samuel Pte
Holmes, George W. Capt
Lamont, John Henry Lt Colonel

94th Regiment of Foot
Allan, James Major
Liston, Alexander Pte

95th Regiment of Foot
Gairdner, James Penman Lt
Hatcher, John Pte
Hughes, David Pte

Permanent Assistant Quarter Master General
Dickson, Sir Jeremiah Lt Colonel

King's German Legion Artillery
Brown, William 2nd Capt

Duke of Brunswick Oel's Corps (Infantry)
Korfes, Georg Lt Colonel

Chasseure Brittaniques
D'Olbreuse, Christophe Lt

Hanoverian Brigade
Kielmannsegge, F. O. G. Colonel Commandant

Royal Artillery
Bettesworth, John 2nd Capt
Bridge, Cyprian 2nd Capt
Dennis, William 1st Lt
Gillies, John Cpl
King, Thomas Newton 1st Lt
Law, James Smith 1st Lt

Royal Engineers
Hunt, Robert Lt
Lawson, Hugh 2nd Capt

Medical Department
Campbell, John Hospital Asst
Davidson, James Hospital Asst
Du Heaume, William Hospital Mate
Higgins, Summers Dep Insp of Hosp

Dutch Officers
Frederick, Prince Commander

6th Hussars
Heiden, F. M. van Capt

Addenda

New information found for entries already in Vol. I.

ANDERSON, Andrew
Surgeon. 61st Regiment of Foot.
Memorial tablet: Grange Cemetery, Edinburgh, Scotland. (Photograph added)

ANSON, Sir George
Colonel. 23rd Regiment of Light Dragoons.
Named on the memorial tablet: Main Hall, Royal Hospital, Chelsea, London. (Photograph)

GENERAL SIR GEORGE ANSON G.C.B. K.T.S.

ARABIN, Frederick
2nd Captain. Royal Artillery.
Memorial tablet: St Peter's Church, Bermuda, West Indies. (M.I.)

"IN THE ADJOINING CHURCHYARD LIE THE REMAINS OF / FREDERICK ARABIN LIEUTENANT COLONEL ROYAL ARTILLERY / SIXTH SON OF HENRY ARABIN ESQRE OF MOYGHARE CO. MEATH IRELAND / WHO WHILE IN COMMAND OF H. M.'S FORCES IN THESE ISLAND / DIED AUG 17TH 1843 IN HIS 57TH YEAR."

BARTON, Alexander
Captain. 12th (Prince of Wales's) Regiment of Light Dragoons.
Grave: Colmonell Kirkyard, Colmonell, Ayrshire, Scotland. (Grave number 272). (Photograph added)

BATTY, Robert
Ensign. 1st Regiment of Foot Guards.
Revised inscription on refurbished obelisk (Photograph)

TO THE / LOVING MEMORY OF / LT-COL ROBERT BATTY / 1ST FOOT GUARDS. PENINSULA & WATERLOO / BORN 5TH AUGUST 1789 / DIED 20TH NOVEMBR 1848, / IN THE 60TH YEAR OF HIS AGE / AFTER A LONG AND PAINFUL ILLNESS

Reference Error: Annual Register, 1848, Appx, p. 264 not pp. 201.

BLACKLIN, Richard
Volunteer. 1st (Royal Scots) Regiment of Foot
Memorial tablet: St George's Chapel, Windsor.
Additional Memorial tablet: St Michael's Church, Heighington, Durham. (Photograph)

Family stained glass window:

TO THE GLORY OF GOD AND IN MEMORY OF COLONEL / RICHARD BLACKLIN YOUNGEST SON OF THE REV ROBERT / BLACKLIN WHO DIED MAY 18 1867 AGED 77 YEARS ………………..

Brass memorial tablet below family stained glass window: St Michael's Church, Heighington, Durham. (Photograph)

ON DECEMBER 18TH 1839 THE BODY OF THE REV ROBERT BLACKLIN WAS INTERRED IN THIS CHURCHYARD. HE HAD CHARGE OF THIS PARISH FOR 32 YEARS AND WAS 40 YEARS MASTER OF THE ANCIENT ELIZABETHAN GRAMMAR SCHOOL. HIS SON COLONEL RICHARD BLACKLIN MILITARY / KNIGHT OF WINDSOR WAS INTERRED IN THE CATACOMBS OF ST GEORGE'S CHAPEL, WINDSOR ON MAY 22ND 1867, WITH MILITARY HONOURS. HE SERVED AS ENSIGN WITH THE 3RD BATTALION, ROYAL SCOTS AT THE BATTLE OF QUATRE BRAS JUNE 16TH 1815, AT THE RETREAT ON THE 17TH AND CARRIED THE KING'S COLOURS AT WATERLOO. ON THE 18TH, AFTER FOUR OFFICERS HAD BEEN KILLED, AND HIMSELF WOUNDED. AT THE CAPTURE OF PARIS HE WAS ONE OF ONLY FIVE OFFICERS REMAINING WITH HIS REGIMENT, THIRTY FOUR HAVING PREVIOUSLY / FALLEN. HE ALSO SERVED IN INDIA WITH 2ND BATTALION ROYAL SCOTS THROUGH THE MAHATTA WAR 1817–1824, AND LED THE STORMING PARTY AT THE CAPTURE OF NAGPORE. HE AFTERWARDS SERVED IN THE WEST INDIES AND AS A STAFF OFFICER IN TURKEY DURING / THE RUSSIAN CAMPAIGN 1854–1856. HE SERVED HIS COUNTRY UNDER FOUR SOVEREIGNS FOR UPWARDS OF 56 YEARS AND HELD MANY MEDALS, AMONGST WHICH WERE, THE WATERLOO MEDAL, THE INDIAN WAR MEDAL WITH CLASPS FOR NAGPORE AND ASSERGHUR

BLAKENEY, Sir Edward
Additional memorial.
Lieutenant Colonel. 7th (Royal Fusiliers) Regiment of Foot.
Named on the memorial tablet: Main Hall, Royal Hospital, Chelsea, London. (Photograph)

FIELD MARSHAL THE RT. HON / SIR EDWARD BLAKENEY G.C.B. G.C.H. K.T.S.

BLOOD, Thomas
Additional memorial tablet: Wall of his former house, 69, Cheadle Road, Upper Tean, Staffordshire. (M.I.)
Memorial erected September 2003.

ERECTED IN MEMORY OF / LIEUTENANT THOMAS BLOOD / BORN IN CHEADLE 18TH APRIL 1775 / ENLISTED INTO 16TH LIGHT DRAGOON LANCERS 1793 / SAW ACTION AT FLANDERS, TALAVERA, / BUSACO, FUENTES D'ONORO, SALAMANCA, TOULOUSE, / PYRENEES, WATERLOO, BHURTPORE. / EARNED TESTIMONIALS FROM SIR F. / PONSONBY, / LORD COMBERMERE, COLONEL R. ARNOLD, / AND THE DUKE OF YORK. / BUILT THIS ROW OF COTTAGES KNOWN AS BLOOD'S ROW AND LIVED HERE / DIED 20TH JUNE 1840, AGED 65, / BURIED AT ST GILES THE ABBOT, CHEADLE / 16TH L/DRAGOON LANCERS ARE NOW PART OF THE QUEEN'S ROYAL LANCERS.

Reference: 42 Years a soldier 1793–1835, Cheadle Soldier, Lieut Thomas Blood 16th Light Dragoons. 2001, Privately printed.

BROWN, Thomas
Lieutenant and Captain. 1st Regiment of Foot Guards.
Memorial tablet: Inside Mausoleum, Evere Cemetery, Brussels, Belgium. (Photograph added).

BRUNSWICK, Frederick William Duke of
Colonel in Chief. Duke of Brunswick's Oels' Corps.
Obelisk: Park on the Löwenwall, Braunschweig, Lower Saxony, Brunswick, Germany. (Photograph)

DES VATERLANDES / VOM FEINDE / NEU BEDROHTES GLÜCK / SCHÜTZEN / IN RETTENDER SCHLACHT / SANK / BRAUNSCHWEIGS /WELFE / FRIEDRICH / WILHELM / AN / SEINER KRIEGER SPITZE

TO PROTECT THE FATHERLAND FROM THE NEWLY THREATENED MENACE OF THE ENEMIES FREDERICK WILLIAM IN THE DECISIVE BATTLE FELL IN FRONT OF HIS BRUNSWICK WARRIORS

CADOUX, Daniel
Captain. 95th Regiment of Foot.
Additional photograph
Restored headstone on bridge and Box tomb in railed enclosure: Vera Churchyard, Spain. (Photograph)

CARTWRIGHT, William
Additional memorial
Lieutenant. 10th (Prince of Wales's Own) Regiment of Light Dragoons.
Memorial tablet: St Michael's Church, Aynho, Northamptonshire. (Photograph added)

Note: Lt William Cartwright did not acquire one of Napoleon's dinner services as quoted in Volume 1!

CHENEY, Edward Hawkins
Captain. 2nd (Royal North British) Regiment of Dragoons.
Memorial tablet and statue: St Luke's Church, Gaddesby, Leicestershire. (Photograph)
Brother of Capt William Cheney 1st Foot (see Supplement) and son of Capt and Lt Colonel Robert Cheney 1st Foot Guards (see Vol. 1)

CHENEY, Robert
Captain and Lieutenant Colonel. 1st Regiment of Foot Guards.
Memorial tablet: St Mary's Church, Beverley, Yorkshire. (South-west end of south transept). (Photograph)
Father of Capt William Cheney 1st Foot. (see Supplement) and Capt Edward Hawkins Cheney 2nd Lt Dragoons (see Vol. I).

CLYDE, John
1st Lieutenant. 23rd (Royal Welch Fusiliers) Regiment of Foot.
Memorial: Inside Mausoleum, Evere Cemetery, Brussels, Belgium. (Photograph added).

COLQUITT, John Scrope
New memorial: Seville (Photograph)
Inscription is the same as the headstone in Vol. I.

CUBITT, Thomas
2nd Captain. Royal Artillery.
Memorial tablet: All Saints' Church, Catford, Norfolk.
Photograph added.

ELDER, Sir George
Major. Staff Appointment in Spain and Portugal.
Additional memorial tablet: Badajoz Wall, British Cemetery, Elvas, Portugal. (Photograph)

ELLISON, Robert
Lieutenant and Captain. 1st Regiment of Foot Guards.
Kensal Green Cemetery, London and Royal Military Chapel, London.

Additional memorial tablet: St Edmund's Chapel, Gateshead, County Durham. (South wall). (M.I.)

"THIS TABLET IS INSCRIBED BY / CUTHBERT ELLISON OF HEBBURN HALL ESQRE / TO THE MEMORY OF HIS BELOVED BROTHER / COLONEL ROBERT ELLISON, / OF THE GRENADIER GUARDS, / IN WHICH REGIMENT / HE COMMENCED AND CLOSED HIS MILITARY CAREER / OF THIRTY SIX YEARS IN DURATION. / HE DISTINGUISHED HIMSELF ON MANY OCCASIONS, / PARTICULARLY AT THE DEFENCE OF HOUGOUMONT / IN THE BATTLE OF WATERLOO; / AND AT THE CAPTURE OF THE FORTRESS OF PERONNE / ON THE ADVANCE OF THE BRITISH ARMY TO PARIS. / MUCH AS HE WS ADMIRED FOR HIS GALLANTRY, / HE WAS EQUALLY BELOVED IN HIS REGIMENT / FOR HIS STRICT SENSE OF DUTY AND JUSTICE, / **** CHARACTER THE QUALITIES THAT **** / BLENDED WITH THE AFFABILITY / THAT GRACES HUMAN STATURE. / HIS REMAINS INTERRED WITH MILITARY HONORS AT / KENSAL GREEN IN THE COUNTY OF MIDDLESEX / A MONUMENT HAS BEEN ERECTED / BEARING THE FOLLOWING INSCRIPTION: / TO THE MEMORY OF COLONEL ROBERT ELLISON / WHO DIED ON 3RD JULY 1843 / IN THE ACTUAL EXECUTION OF HIS DUTY, AGED 54 / THIS MONUMENT IS ERECTED BY THOSE / WHO COULD BEST APPRECIATE HIS MERITS / FIELD MARSHAL, THE DUKE OF WELLINGTON / AND THE OFFICERS OF HIS REGIMENT / OF GRENADIER GUARDS"

EPPES, William Randolph
Treasury Clerk. Commissariat Department.
Low monument: Old Army Base Graveyard, Newcastle, Jamaica, West Indies. (Additional Photograph).

EVANS, Sir George De Lacy
Captain. 5th West India Regiment of Foot.
Kensal Green Cemetery, London.
Additional Brass Memorial tablet: Royal Garrison Church, Portsmouth, Hampshire. (Back of a choir stall).

D.D. TWO FRIENDS / TO THE GLORY OF GOD AND IN MEMORY OF GENERAL / SIR DE LACY EVANS G.C.B. WHOSE LONG/ AND GALLANT SERVICES WON THE / ADMIRATION OF / HIS COUNTRY

FAUNCE, Alured Dodsworth
Major 4th (King's Own) Regiment of Foot.
Cousin of Lt Colonel Edmund Faunce 4th Foot. See Supplement.

FLETCHER, Sir Richard
Royal Engineers.
Ledger stone used as a paving stone in floor of Cemetery adjacent to a Box tomb: San Sebastian, Spain. (Photograph)

LIEUT COLONEL RICHD FLETCHER / CAPTAIN C. RHODES / CAPTAIN G. COLLYERS / LIEUTENANT E. MACHEL

Note: Additional photograph to image in Vol. I indicates that the railings have been removed.

FRAMINGHAM, Sir Haylett
Additional data: *REFERENCE: One of Norfolk's Forgotten sons ... Major General Sir Haylett Framingham, Norfolk Fair Country Magazine, November 1968, pp. 49–51.*

FRANKLAND, Frederick William
Lieutenant. 2nd (Queen's Royal) Regiment of Foot.
Additional Family Memorial tablet: St Mary's Church, Thirsk, Yorkshire. (Photograph)

.... THE BELOVED SON OF / SIR FREDERICK WILLIAM FRANKLAND / VIII BARONET / LATE CAPTAIN 20TH REGIMENT / ....

REFERENCE: Frankland, Frederick William, A memoir of the early military life of Sir William Franklin, Private circulation, 1874.

FREMANTLE, John
Lieutenant and Captain. Coldstream Regiment of Foot Guards.
Additional data: Buried in St Marylebone's Parish Church, London on 6 April 1845.

GIBBS, Sir Samuel
Lieutenant Colonel. 59th (2nd Nottinghamshire) Regiment of Foot.
Memorial statue: St Paul's Cathedral, London. (Joint statue with Sir Edward Pakenham). (Photograph)
Additional data: Buried in the Royal Garrison Church, Portsmouth, Hampshire 18 Mar 1815.

GIBSON, John
Additional data: *REFERENCE: Webb-Carter, Sir Evelyn, Colour Sergeant John Gibson 33rd Regiment of Foot, Waterloo Journal, Winter 2012, pp. 34–5.*

GORDON, Hon. Sir Alexander
Captain and Lieutenant Colonel. 3rd Regiment of Foot Guards. Photographs of restored monument at La Haye Sainte added.

GOUGH, Hugh
Lieutenant Colonel. 87th (Prince of Wales's Own Irish) Regiment of Foot.
Additional *REFERENCE: Soldiers of the Victorian Age Volume 1, 1880, pp. 222–59.*

GRAHAM, Sir Thomas
Colonel. 90th Regiment of Foot.
Mausoleum, Methven, Perthshire, Scotland. (Additional photograph)

GRIFFITH, Edwin
Major. 15th (King's) Regiment of Light Dragoons.
Additional data: *REFERENCE: Glover, Gareth, From Corunna to Waterloo: the letters and journals of two Napoleonic Hussar: Major Edwin Griffith and Capt Frederick Phillips 15th (King's) Hussars 1801–1816, 2007.*

GRIFFITHS, Richard
Private. 1st Foot Guards.
Bettws Cedewain, Montgomeryshire, Wales. (Additional Photograph)

HACKET, William
Staff Surgeon. Medical Department.
Additional data: Box tomb in railed enclosure: Sandpits Cemetery, Gibraltar. (Photograph)

TO MARK THE SPOT WHERE THE / REMAINS / OF / WILLIAM HACKET M.D. / MAJOR GENERAL / OF / MILITARY HOSPITALS / HE SERVED AT WALCHEREN. / AND DURING THE AMERICAN WAR. / ALSO IN 1814 IN HOLLAND

HALKETT, Sir Colin
Colonel. 2nd Battalion Light Infantry, King's German Legion.
Named on the memorial tablet: Main Hall, Royal Hospital, Chelsea, London. (Photograph)

HILL, Dudley St Leger
Captain. Royal West India Rangers.
Additional memorial tablet: Badajoz Wall, British Cemetery, Elvas, Portugal. (Photograph)

KYNOCK, John
Lieutenant and Adjutant. 79th (Cameron Highlanders) Regiment of Foot.
Grave: Dean Cemetery, Edinburgh, Scotland. (Section E Grave Number 404). (Photograph added)

Battlefield Memorials

PORTUGAL

Busaco

Monument: Busaco, Portugal. (Photograph)

AO EXERCITO / LUSO-BRITANNICO / CAMPANHAS / DA / GUERRA PENINSULAR / 1808 A 1814 / 6 BLOQUEIOS / 12 DEFENSAS / 14 CERCOS / 18 ASSALTOS / 215 COMBATES / 15 B: TALH : S /

Inscription on laurel wreath: (Photograph)

CENTENARIO / 1810 / 1910 / PENINSULAR

Memorial tablet at foot of monument: (Photograph)

175 ANIVERSARIO DA / BATALHA DO BUÇACO / 27 DE SETEMBRO DO 1985 / REGIAO MILITAR DO CENTRA / MUSEU MILITAR

Memorial tablet: On outside of a windmill at Busaco, Portugal. (Photograph)

IT WAS HERE / THAT THE / BRITISH GENERAL / CRAUFORD / ESTABLISHED HIS / COMMAND POST / DURING THE / BUSACO BATTLE IN 1810

Cascais Fort

Memorial outside Cascais Fort. Inscription only partly recorded. Appears as a band below the figure on top of memorial. (Photograph)

GUERRA PENINSULAR / 1807–14

Coa

Memorial: Coa Bridge, near Almeida, Portugal. (Photograph)

2010 / 1810 – 2010 / BATALHA DO COA CERCO DE ALMEIDA / ....

New memorial erected 2010 in commemoration of the bicentenary of the Battle of the Coa.

Elvas

Memorial tablet: Entrance to British Cemetery, Elvas, Portugal. (Photograph)

IN SPRING 1811 NAPOLEON'S ARMY HAD / BEEN DRIVEN FROM PORTUGAL BEFORE / ADVANCING INTO SPAIN, WELLINGTON / WISHED TO SECURE THE MAIN CROSSING / POINTS – ALMEIDA/CIUDAD RODRIGO IN / THE NORTH, ELVAS/BADAJOZ IN THE SOUTH. / MARSHAL BERESFORD WAS RESPONSIBLE / FOR THE SOUTH BEFORE THIS GATEWAY / WAS CLOSED, BADAJOZ WAS BESIEGED / TWICE AND THE BLOODY BATTLE OF / ALBUERA HAD BEEN FOUGHT. / SOME 11,000 BRITISH, PORTUGUESE, SPANISH / AND GERMAN SOLDIERS FELL IN THESE BATTLES. / TWO OF THE OFFICERS BURIED HERE FELL / AT BADAJOZ AND ALBUERA.

The memorial also contains the same text in Portuguese.

Memorial tablet: Elvas British Cemetery, Elvas, Portugal. (Photograph)

TO LIVE IN HEARTS WE LEAVE BEHIND US IS NOT TO DIE. / THOMAS CAMPBELL / IN REMEMBRANCE OF THE 60,000 / OFFICERS AND MEN OF THE BRITISH / AND PORTUGUESE ARMIES WHO / DIED ALONGSIDE THEIR SPANISH / ALLIES IN THE CAUSE OF FREEDOM / AND INDEPENDENCE IN THE / PENINSULAR WAR OF 1808–1814. / ERECTED BY PENINSULAR 200 / 14 MAY 2011

Memorial tablet: Albuera Wall, British Cemetery, Elvas, Portugal. (Photograph)

TO THE IMMORTAL MEMORY OF / THE OFFICERS AND MEN / WHO FOUGHT SO VALIANTLY AT / ALBUHERA / 16 MAY 1811 / "1500 UNWOUNDED MEN THE / REMNANT OF 6000 UNCONQUERABLE / BRITISH SOLDIERS STOOD / TRIUMPHANT ON THE FATAL HILL" / SIR WILLIAM NAPIER / ERECTED BY THE PRINCESS OF / WALES'S ROYAL REGIMENT 14 MAY 2000

Memorial tablet: Albuera Wall, British Cemetery, Elvas, Portugal. (Photograph)

THE BATTLE OF ALBUHERA
16 MAY 1811
IN IMMORTAL MEMORY OF THE
OFFICERS AND MEN OF

ROYAL ARTILLERY
CAPT LEFEBURE'S TP RHA
CAPT HAWKER'S BDE RHA

CAVALRY
3RD DRAGOON GUARDS
4TH QUEEN'S OWN DRAGOONS
13TH LIGHT DRAGOONS

2ND DIVISION
FOUR COYS 60TH (ROYAL AMERICAN)
REGIMENT ONE TO EACH BDE

COLBURNE'S BRIGADE
1/3RD THE BUFFS
2/48TH NORTHAMPTONSHIRE
2/31ST HUNTINGDONSHIRE
2/66TH BERKSHIRE

HOGHTON'S BRIGADE
29TH WORCESTERSHIRE
1/57TH WEST MIDDLESEX
1/48TH NORTHAMPTONSHIRE

ABERCROMBIE'S BRIGADE
2/28TH NORTH GLOUCESTERSHIRE
2/39TH DORSETSHIRE
2/34TH CUMBERLAND

CAPT CLEEVE'S BDE KGA
CAPT SYMPHER'S BDE KGA

ALTEN'S INDEPENDENT BRIGADE
1ST 2ND LIGHT BATTS. KING'S
GERMAN LEGION

4TH DIVISION
MYERS FUSILIERS BRIGADE
1/7TH ROYAL FUSILIERS
2/7TH ROYAL FUSILIERS
1/23RD ROYAL WELCH FUSILIERS

JAMES KEMMIS'S BRIGADE
1 COY EACH OF
2/27TH INNISKILLING
1/40TH 2ND SOMERSETSHIRE

97TH QUEEN'S GERMAN

Memorial tablet: Albuera Wall, British Cemetery, Elvas, Portugal. (Photograph)

BATALHA DE ALBUERA
16 MAIO 1811

EM MEMÓRIA DOS MILITARES DA
DIVISÃO PORTUGUESA COMANDADA PELO
TENENTE GENERAL JOÃO HAMILTON

REGIMENTOS DE ARTILHARIA
CAP SEBASTIÃO ARRIAGA RA1
CAP GUILHERME BROWN RA2

REGIMENTOS DE CAVALARIA
TCOR MIGUEL AMARAL RC1
TCOR HENRIQUE WATSON RC7
MAJ HENRIGUE WYNDHAM EC8 EC5

REGIMENTOS DE INFANTARIA
TCOR FRANCISCO SILVA R15
TCOR MIGUEL MC GREAG BCAÇ5

REGIMENTOS DE INFANTARIA
TCOR ALAN CAMPBELL R14
COR CONDE DE RESENDE R110

REGIMENTOS DE INFANTARIA
TCOR DONATE MC DONALD R111
COR THOMAS STUBBS R123
MAJ AGREGADO FEARON BCAÇ7

REGIMENTOS DE INFANTARIA
COR ANTONIA COSTA R12
T COR JAMES OLIVIER R114

Memorial tablet: Spanish Forces present at Albuera, Albuera Wall, British Cemetery, Elvas, Portugal. (Photograph)

FUERZAS DEL EJERCITO ESPA OL
PRESENTES EN LA BATALLA DE LA
ALBUERA (18 DE MAYO DE 1811)

4° EJERCITO
(TTE GRAL BLAKE)
R.I. DE MURCIA
R.I. DE CANARIAS
R.I. DE LEÓN
R.I. DE CAMPO MAYOR
R.I. 2° DE BARBASTRO
R.I. PRAVIA
R.I. LENA
R.I. CASTROPOL
R.I. CANGAS DE TINEO
R.I. INFIESTO
R.I. IRLANDA
R.I. VOLUNTARIOS DE
LA PATRIA
R.I. IMPERIALES DE TOLEDO
R.I. CIUDAD RODRIGO
R. GUARDIAS VALONAS
2° Y 4° BON. GUARDIAS
ESPA OLAS

5° EJERCITO
(CAP. GRAL. CASTRA OS)
R.I. DEL RAY
R.I. DE ZAMORA
R.I. VOLUNTARIOS DE NAVARRA
R.I. 1° DE CATALU A
LEGIÓN EXTREME A
R.C. DE LA REINA
R.C. DE BORBON
R.C. 2° DEL ALGARVE
R.C. 2° HUSARES DE
EXTREMADURA
DRAGONES DE CÀCERES
R.C. CARABINEROS REALES
BIA DEL 4° REGIMENTO
DE ARTILLERIA
ZAPADORES Y GUIAS

BAJAS EN LA BATALLA
1,376 HOMBRES

CAMPA IA DE ZAPADORES	258 MUERTOS
BATERIA DE ARTILLERIA	1,118 HERIDOS
4° EJÉRCITO	
R.C. DEL REY	HONOR Y GLORIA
(PROVIS. DE SANTIAGO)	
R.C. GRANADEROS DE	LA BRIGADA
FERNANDO VII	"EXTREMADURA" XI
ESCUADRÒN DE INSTRUCCIÒN	
GRANADEROS A CABALLO	
4° EJÉRCITO	ELVAS, 14 DE MAYO DE 2004
LEGIÓN DE EXTRANJEROS	

Memorial tablet: Albuera Wall, British Cemetery, Elvas, Portugal. (Photograph)

IN MEMORY OF / THE OFFICERS AND MEN / OF / THE FUSILIERS BRIGADE / 1ST AND 2ND BNS, THE ROYAL FUSILIERS – 7TH FOOT / 1ST BN, THE ROYAL WELCH FUSILIERS – 23RD FOOT / WHO AT GRIEVOUS COST / TURNED THE TIDE OF BATTLE AT / ALBUHERA / 16 MAY 1811 / THEN WAS SEEN WITH WHAT A / STRENGTH AND MAJESTY /THE BRITISH SOLDIER FIGHTS / NOTHING COULD STOP THAT ASTONISHING INFANTRY / SIR WILLIAM NAPIER / ERECTED BY BOTH REGIMENTS ON 14TH MAY 2000

Memorial tablet: 3rd Siege of Badajoz, Badajoz Wall, British Cemetery, Elvas, Portugal. (Photograph)

3° CERCO A BADAJOZ
6 ABRIL 1812
EM MEMÓRIA DOS MILITARES PORTUGUESES

REGIMENTO ARTILHARIA N° 1
REGIMENTO ARTILHARIA N° 2
REGIMENTO ARTILHARIA N° 3
REGIMENTO ARTILHARIA N° 4

REGIMENTOS DE CAVALARIA
TCOR JOÃO LACERDA RC 3
TCOR VISCONDE BARBACENA RC 7

BATALHÖES DE CACADORES
MAJ JOÃO ALGEO BCAÇ1
TCOR JORGE ELDER BCAÇ3
TCOR JOÃO CASTRO BCAÇ7
MAJ DUDLEY HILL BCAÇ8
TCOR THOMAS DURSBACH BCAÇ11

REGIMENTOS DE INFANTARIA
COR JORGE AVILEZ R12
COR JOÃO TAVARES R13
TCOR HENRIQUE MULLER R15
TCOR CARLOS SUTTON R19
TCOR DONALD MC DONALD R11
TCOR JOAQUIM DO CÂMARA R113
TCOR JOÃO MC DONALD R114
COR LUÍS BARRETO R115
MAJ FRANCISCO SILVA R117
TCOR JOSÉ BACELAR R121
TCOR LUÍS BAIA R123
COR GUILHERME MCBEAN R124

Memorial tablet: Badajoz Wall, British Cemetery, Elvas, Portugal. (Photograph)

THE STORMING OF BADAJOZ
6 APRIL 1872
IN HELL BEFORE DAYLIGHT

ROYAL ARTILLERY
MAJ BULL'S TROOP RHA

CAPT GARDINER'S COY RA

MAJ ROSS'S TROOP RHA
CAPT HOLCOMBE'S COY RA
SKIRMISHERS
60TH ROYAL AMERICAN
BRUNSWICK OELS
3RD DIVISION
KEMPT'S BRIGADE
1/48TH 1ST NOTTINGHAMSHIRE
3/60TH ROYAL AMERICAN
74TH HIGHLANDERS
1/88TH CONNAUGHT RANGERS
CAMPBELL'S BRIGADE
2/5TH NORTHUMBERLAND
77TH EAST MIDDLESEX
2/83RD (ROYAL IRISH RIFLES)
94TH SCOTCH BRIGADE
4TH DIVISION
KEMMIS'S BRIGADE
3/27TH INNISKILLING
1/49TH 2ND SOMERSETSHIRE
BOWE'S BRIGADE
1/7TH ROYAL FUSILIERS
1/23RD ROYAL WELCH
FUSILIERS
1/48TH NORTHAMPTONSHIRE
CAPT GLUBB'S COY RA
(CAPT POWER)
CAPT RETTBERG'S COY KGA
ROYAL ENGINEERS
ROYAL MILITARY ARTIFICERS
5TH DIVISION
HAY'S BRIGADE
3/1ST THE ROYAL SCOTS
1/9TH EAST NORFOLK
2/38TH 1ST STAFFORDSHIRE
WALKER'S BRIGADE
1/4TH OR THE KING'S OWN
2/30TH CAMBRIDGESHIRE
2/44TH EAST SUSSEX
LIGHT DIVISION
1/38TH 1ST STAFFORDSHIRE
1/43RD MONMOUTHSHIRE
LIGHT INFANTRY
1/52ND OXFORD LIGHT
INFANTRY
95TH RIFLE BRIGADE TWO
BATTALIONS

5th (Northumberland) Regiment of Foot
Memorial tablet: Badajoz Wall, British Cemetery, Elvas, Portugal. (Photograph)

QUO FATA VOCANT / ERECTED BY THE FIFTH FUSILIERS / IN MEMORY OF THE / SECOND BATTALION, FIFTH / (NORTHUMBERLAND) / REGIMENT OF FOOT / WHOSE INDOMITABLE COURAGE / AT THE CAPTURE / OF THE CITADEL MADE CERTAIN THE FALL OF / BADAJOZ, 6TH APRIL 1812. / "THOUGH LADDER AFTER LADDER WAS FLUNG DOWN BY / THE DEFENDERS, AND THE RUNGS WERE SLIPPERY / WITH BLOOD, THOSE BELOW TOOK THE PLACES OF / THOSE WHO FELL, SO SWIFTLY THAT IN THE END / A LODGEMENT WAS MADE AND THE RAMPARTS CLEARED" / ARTHUR BRYANT / DEDICATED 14TH MAY 2000

Reference: Walker, H. M., History of the Northumberland Fusiliers, 1674–1902, 1919, reprint 2012.

48th (Northamptonshire) Regiment of Foot
Regimental memorial tablet: Badajoz Wall, British Cemetery, Elvas, Portugal. (Photograph)

THIS PLAQUE HAS BEEN ERECTED / IN PROUD AND HONOURED MEMORY / OF ALL THE OFFICERS / NON-COMMISSIONED OFFICERS / AND MEN OF THE / 48TH FOOT / THE NORTHAMPTONSHIRE REGIMENT / WHO MADE THE SUPREME SACRIFICE / AT / ALBUHERA AND BADAJOZ / IN / 1811 AND 1812

Reference: Gurney, Russell, History of the Northamptonshire Regiment, 1742–1934, 1935.

Foz d'Arouce
Obelisk: In village near bridge, Foz d'Arouce, Portugal. (Photograph)

3[d] / INVASÁO / FRANCESA / COMBATE / DE / FOZ DE AROUCE / 1811

Obelisk: On hill overlooking village, Foz d'Arouce, Portugal. (Photograph)

15 DE MARCO DE 1811 / *** HEROICOS DEFENSORES / DA PATRIA / DE O CONDE DE FOZ DE AROUCE / 15 DE MARCO DE 1898

Lavos
Mural tiled plaque: Town Hall, Lavos, Figueira de Foz, Portugal. (Photograph)

DISEMBARQUE DAS TROPAS INGLESAS NAS PRAIAS DEE LAVOS / AGOSTA 1808

Lisbon
Monument: Heroes of the Peninsular War, Praça de Entrecampos, Lisbon, Portugal. (Photograph)

GUERRA PENINSULAR / MDCCCVIII / A / MDCCCXIV / AO / DUQUE DA TERCEIRA / MDCC-CLXXVII LONDON

Monument: Duque da Terceira, Praça Duque da Terceira, Belem, Lisbon, Portugal. (Photograph)

AO / DUQUE DA TERCEIRA / MDCCCLXXVII / GUERRA PENINSULAR / MDCCCVIII / A / MDCC-CXIV

Oporto
Monument to the Peninsular War: Boavista, Portugal. (Photograph)

D.A.D. 2 / NO DIA 11 DE / MAIS XI 1809 / WELLESLEY / CONTEMPL A NDO / DO ALTO DA SERRA / DO PILLOR O FORMOSO / PANORAMA DO PORTO / PENSOU QUE DAQULO / *********** / ACHIJAVA AP / GEN DO RESTO DO / EXERCITO / 20 – 2 1931

Redinha
Memorial near bridge: Redinha, Portugal. (Photograph)

1811 – 2006 HOMENAGEM / A TODAS QUANTOS PERECERAM / NO COMBATE DA REDINHA

Mural tiled memorial: Redinha, Portugal. (Photograph)

REDINHA / 1811

Rolica
Mural tiled memorial: Rolica, Portugal. No Inscription. (Photograph)

Torres Vedras
Monument: Main Square, Torres Vedras, Portugal. (Photograph)

AO EXERCITO / LUSO-BRITANICO / CAMPANAS / DA / GUERRA PENINSULAR / 1809–1814 / LINHAS DE TORRES / 12 – X – 1810 a 5 – II – 1811

Memorial tablet: Fort at Torres Vedras. (Photograph)

ON 19TH OCTOBER 1992, ON THE OCCASION OF THE / COMMEMORATION OF THE DEFENSE OF THE LINES OF TORRES, THIS / FORTRESS AND THE CITY OF TORRES VEDRAS WERE VISITED BY SIR / ARTHUR VALERIAN, DUKE OF WELLINGTON, MARQUIS OF TORRES VEDRAS

Text also in Portuguese.

Vimeiro

Monument to the Battle of Vimeiro, Vimeiro Hill, Portugal. (Photograph)

BATALHA / DO / VIMEIRO / 1E / CENTENARIO / 21 AGOSTO 1808 / A EXPEDICAO BRITANNICO SOB O COMMANDO DO / GENERAL WELLESLEY, TENDO DESEMBARCADO EM / LAVOS E REUNIDO A SI TROPAS PORTUGUEZAS / MARCHOU SOBRE LISBOA BATEU AS / AVANÇADAS INIMICAS / NO ROLICA E SENDO ATACADA PELO EXERCITO / DO COMMANDA DE JUNOT N'ESTE SITIOS DO VIMERO, / ALÇANCOU SOBRE ELLE UNA GLORIOSA VICTORIA.

SPAIN

Albuera

Mural tiled memorial: Albuera, Spain. (Photograph)
The inscription is provided in Spanish, English, French and Portuguese. The English text reads:

OH ALBUERA, GLORIOUS FIELD OF GRIEF! / LORD BYRON – "CHILDE HAROLD'S PILGRIMAGE" / IN ROWS, JUST LIKE / THEY FOUGHT THEY LAY / LIKE THE HAY IN THE / OPEN COUNTRYSIDE WHEN / THE NIGHT FALLS AND THE / MOWER FALLS SILENT. THAT / IS HOW THEY WERE SLAIN / BATTLE OF ALBUERA, MAY 16TH 1811, MEMORIAL IN VILLAGE.

Regimental memorial: Albuera, Spain. (Photograph)

2ND / 31ST FOOT / HUNTINGDONSHIRE / (LATER BECAME) / THE EAST SURREY REGIMENT / "AFTER WHEN THE REST OF THE BRIGADE WAS SWEPT / OFF BY CAVALRY THE LITTLE BATTALION ALONE / HELD ITS GROUND

Regimental memorial: Albuera, Spain. (Photograph)

57TH FOOT / THE MIDDLESEX REGIMENT / "DIE HARD 57TH DIE HARD" / TO THE IMMORTAL MEMORY / AT ALBUERA ALSO REMEMBER AND PAY HOMAGE TO THOSE / BRAVE SOLDIERS OF THE ALLIANCE – SPAIN AND PORTUGAL

Also on another face:

THE PRINCESS OF WALES'S / ROYAL REGIMENT / "OH ALBUHERA / GLORIOUS FIELD OF GRIEF" / THIS MONUMENT IS ERECTED TO THE IMMORTAL MEMORY OF / OUR PREDECESSOR REGIMENTS WHO FOUGHT SO BRAVELY / AT THE BATTLE OF ALBUERA – 16 MAY 1811 / ERECTED BY THE PRINCESS OF WALES'S REGIMENT / 16 MAY 2001

Memorial to Spanish Officers killed at Albuera: Albuera, Spain. (Photograph)

EN MEMORIA DE LOS / PRIMEROS OFICIALES / DE E. M. MUERTOS / EN COMPA A D EMETERIA VELARDE / Y. D. MARTIN PARRAGA / BATALLA DE LA / ALBUERA 1811 LOS DIPLOMANDOS DE / E. M. DE LA BRIMZ XXI / BADAJOZ 1978 / IN AUGURADO EL DIA 28-11-1978 CON / ASISTENCIA DEL GENERAL PROFESORES / Y ALUMNOS DE LA /PROMOTION 76 / DE LA ESCUELA DE ESTADO MAYOR

Badajoz
Obelisk: Albuera, Santa Maria Bastion, Badajoz, Spain. (Photograph)

TO THOSE WHO TOOK PART IN THE DEFENCE, / ASSAULTS AND OCCUPATIONS DURING THE SIEGES OF BADAJOZ, 1811–1812 / 2012

Brass plaques on four faces show the inscription in English, Spanish, Portuguese and French.

New Obelisk was erected 21 Apr 2012. It consists of four sides; each dedicated to one of the four principal countries involved: Spain, United Kingdom, Portugal and France. Each face has a bronze plaque, 50 x 50cm, with the same text in the country's language below and the national insignia/coat of arms above. The obelisk is made of silver/yellow coloured granite, with a diameter of 30cm and was cut at Eleuterio Deogracias's quarry at Quintana de la Serena (Badajoz).

Memorial wall: Badajoz, Spain. (Photograph)

1812

Barrosa
Monument: Barroso Hill, Spain. (Photograph)

"EL PUERCO" HILL / ON THE 5TH MARCH 1811 / THE BAROSSA OR CHICLANA BATTLE / WAS FOUGHT AROUND THIS PLACE, / DURING THE PENINSULAR WAR / AGAINST NAPOLEON. / THOUSANDS OF BRITISH, FRENCH, / SPANISH, PORTUGUESE, / POLISH AND GERMAN SOLDIERS / SHED THEIR BLOOD ON THIS HILL. / NOWADAYS, IN A NEW MILLENNIUM, / THE DESCENDENTS OF THOSE / WHO FOUGHT HERE ARE LIVING / TOGETHER IN AN UNITED / AND PEACEFUL EUROPE. / ON OCCASION OF THE / VII CENTURY OF THE TOWN OF / CHICLANA DE LA FRONTERA / 1303 – 2003

Monument: Bermeja Beach, Spain. (Photograph)

1811 2011 / BATTALLA DE CHICLANA

Ciudad Rodrigo
Memorial tablet: Walls of Ciudad Rodrigo, Spain. (Above breach where Craufurd is buried). (Photograph)

MAJOR GENERAL ROBERT CRAUFURD / TO THE MEMORY OF MAJOR GENERAL ROBERT CRAUFORD AND THOSE OF THE 43RD AND 52ND LIGHT INFANTRY AND THE 95TH RIFLES OF THE LIGHT DIVISION, WHICH HE COMMANDED WITH SUCH DISTINCTION, AND THEIR COMRADES OF THE 60TH, ALL OF WHOM FELL IN THE STORMING OF THE BREACHES THROUGH WHICH CIUDAD RODRIGO WAS LIBERATED ON 19TH JANUARY 1812. / THIS PLAQUE IS ERECTED BY THEIR HEIRS THE ROYAL GREEN JACKETS MINDFUL OF THE HISTORIC EFFORTS OF THE SPANISH AND BRITISH TO FREE THE PENINSULA 1808–1813.

Memorial tablet in wall: Ciudad Rodrigo, Spain. (Photograph)

175 ANNIVERSARIO / CIUDAD RODRIGO / RINDE HOMENAJE / A QUIENES LIBERARON / ESTA PLAZA / 1–1–1812 1–1–1987

Memorial tablet in wall: Ciudad Rodrigo, Spain. (Photograph)

Commemoration of the Bicentenary of the Siege of Ciudad Rodrigo and Peninsular War.

"BRECHA PEQUÑENA" / 1812–2012 / CIUDAD RODRIGO, A TODAS LAS VÍCTIMAS / DE LA GUERRA DE LA INDEPENDENCIA / CON MOTIVO DEL BICENTENARIO / DE SU LIBERACION. / 19 DE ENERO DE 2012

Mural Monument to Spanish: In wall, Ciudad Rodrigo, Spain. (Photograph)

ESTA GUERRILLA Y ELEJER / CITO SABRAN DEFENDER / HASTA SU ULTIMO ALIEN / TO SU RELIGION SU LEGI / TIMO Y AMADO REY Y / LA LIBERTAD DE LA / PATRIA

CIUDA RODRIGO / A / JULIAN SÁNCHEZ / "EL CHARRO"

Memorial tablet in wall: Ciudad Rodrigo, Spain, (Photograph)

CENTENARIO / DEL SITO DE ESTA PLAZA / EN 1810 CIUDAD RODRIGO / ASUS HEROICOS / DEFENSORES

Corunna

Memorial tablet: Via Zapatiera, Corunna, Spain. (Photograph)

BATALLA DE ELVINA / 16 DE ENERO DE 1809 / A SIR JOHN MOORE / EN PERMANENTE RECUERAO / LA CORUNA 16 DE ENERO DE 1996.

Memorial tablet: Via Zapatiera, Corunna, Spain. (Photograph)

Tablet 1:

EL EXCM° SR. EMBAJADOR DE S. M. BRITANICA / MR. A. DAVID BRIGHTY C.M.G. GVO / DESCUBRIO AMBAS PLACAS / EN COLABORACION CON / LAS ASOCIACIONES CULTURALES / AMIGOS DE SIR JOHN MOORE / ARMADA INVENCIBLE / ORDEN DE CABALLEROS DE MARIA PITA / ROYAL GREEN JACKETS DE LA CORUNA

Tablet 2:

XVI JANUARI MDCCCIX / XIX JANUARI MCMXXXI JOANNES MOORE / EXERCYTUS BRYTANNYCY DUX

Tablet 3:

BATTALLA DE ELVINA / 16 DE ENERO DE 1809 / A SIR JOHN MOORE / EN PERMANENTE RECUERDO / LA CORUNA 16 DE ENERO DE 1996

Tablet 4: Inscription not recorded.

Memorial tablet: San Vicente, Elvina, Corunna, Spain. (Photograph)

190 ANIVERSARIO DE LA BATALLA DE ELVINA
En memoria de los caidos en la batalla de Elvina
el 16 de Enero de 1809
En memoire des morts tombes durant la bataille de la Corogne
le 16 janvier 1809
La Coruna, 15 de Enero de 1999

Ayuntamiento de La Coruña
Cuartel General de la Region Militar Noroeste
Universidad de La Coruña
Enbajado de Francia en Espano en España
Emabajado de Su Majestad Britanica en Espana

Associacion Historico Cultural
"The Royal Green Jackets"
Orden de Caballeros de Maria Pita
Napoleonic Association
Asociacion Historico Cultural
Batalla de Elviña

Memorial tablet: San Vicente, Elvina, Corunna, Spain. (Photograph)

ROLICA
VIMEIRO
SAHUGUN
CORUNA
BUSSACO
FUENTES DE OÑORO
ALMAREZ
CIUDAD RODRIGO
TALAVERA
BADAJOZ
SALAMANCA
VICTORIA
LA ALBUERA
PIRINEOS
ORTHEZ
TOULOUSE

PENINSULAR WAR 1808–1814
IN MEMORY
OF BRIGADIER GENERAL ROBERT ANSTRUTHER, WHO FORMED PART
OF THE RESERVE UNDER GENERAL SIR JOHN MOORE,
AND DIED IN CORUNNA ON 14 JANUARY 1809,
AND LIEUTENANT COLONEL JOHN MACKENZIE, 5TH FOOT
WHO DIED IN PALAVEA DE ABAIXO, CORUNNA, ON 15 JANUARY 1809.
200TH ANNIVERSARY OF THE BATTLE OF CORUNNA 1809 – 2009

Excmo. Ayuntamiento de A Coruña Embajada de S. M. Britanica en Espana.

Asociation Historico Cultural "The Royal Green Jackets" Asociacion Napoleonica Española.

Memorial tablet: San Vicente, Elvina, Corunna, Spain. (Photograph)

DE LA PROCLAMA QUE ET GENERAL INGLES LORD WELLINGTON / DIAICIÓ AL EVERCITO DESPOES DE LA GLORIOSA BATALLA DE SAN MARCIAL / EN 31 DE AGOSTO DE 1813. / GUERREROS DEL MUNDO CIVILIZADA / APRENDED A SERLO DE LOS INDIVIDUOS DEL 4° EJÊRATO QUE TENGO / LA DICHA DE MANDAR: CADO SOLADO DE EL MERECE CON MAS JUSTO MOTIVA / QE YO BASTON QUE EMPUÑO, TODAS SOMOS TESTIGOS DE UN VALOR / DESCONOCIDO HASTA AHORA .... / ESPAÑOLES DEDICAOS TODOS A IMITAR A LOS INIMITABLES GALLEGOS. / WELLINGTON. / CUARTEL GENERAL DE LESCA. 4 DE SEPTEMBRE DE 1913

Memorial tablet: Corunna, Spain. (Memorial tablet to commemorate the bicentenary of the Retreat to Corunna, 2009).

LA CUIDAD DE A CORUÑA, / ORGULLOSA DE SU HISTORIA, / EN CONMEMORACIÓN / DEL BICENTENARIO DE LA BATALLA / QUE ENFRENTÓ ANTE SUS PUERTAS / A BRITÁNICOS Y FRANCESES / EL 16 ENERO DEL AÑO 1809 / A CORUÑA, 16 DE ENERO DE 2009 / EXCMO.

AYUNTAMIENTO DE A CORUÑA / EMBAJADAS DE FRANCIA Y GRAN BRETAÑA EN ESPAÑA / ASSOCIACIÔN HISTORICO CULTURAL "THE ROYAL GREEN JACKETS"

El Bodon
Memorial on Battlefield, Spain. (Photograph)

"COMBATE DE EL BODON" / ENTRE TROPAS ALIADOS / Y NAPOLEONICAS. / 25 – SEPTEMBRE – 1811

Erected to commemorate the bicentenary of the Battle.

Fuentes d'Onoro
Memorial: In village square near to Church, Fuentes d'Onoro, Spain. (Photograph)

EN MEMORIA DE LAS TROPAS / "ANGLO LUSO GERMANO ESANOLAS" / QUE EN LA BATALLA DEL – 5 – MAYO 1811 / AL MANDO DE LORD WELLINGTON / DERROTARON A LAS FRANCESAS DE MASSENA / FUENTES DE ONÓRO A 28 – 6 – 1986

Memorial obelisk: On main road next to old border crossing and Customs House. Fuentes d'Onoro, Spain. (Photograph)

Side 1:

FUENTES DE OÑORO / VILLA HEROICA / 1811 – 2011 / MONUMENTO / HOMENAJE A LAS TROPAS / ANGLO LUSAS / FRANCESAS Y ESPAÑOLOS, / QUE LUCHARON CON / VALOR Y HONOR / EN LA HISTÓRICA BATALLA / DEL 3 AL 5 DE MAYO DE 1811 / LORD WELLINGTON / ALFONSO IX / J. S. EL CHARRO

Side 2:

BICENTENARIA / DE LA GUERRA / DE LA / INDEPENDENCIA / 5 DE MAYO DE 2011

Memorial unveiled 2011 to commemorate the bicentenary of the battle of Fuentes d'Onoro. Lord Wellington, Alfonso IX and J. S. Charro are portrayed in relief on three sides.

Salamanca
Obelisk on summit of Greater Arapile: Salamanca, Spain. (Photograph)

ARAPILES / 22 JULIO 1812

San Sebastian
Memorial tablet: San Sebastian, Spain. (Photograph)

REPRESENTACIONES MILITARES DE FRANCIA, INGLATERRA, / PORTUGAL Y ESAPAÑA, HERMANADAS EN LA CONCORDIA. / DESCUBREN ESTA LAPIDA EN RECUERDO DEL HEROISMO DE / LOS SOLDADOS QUE LUCHARON BRAVAMENTE AL PIE / DE ESTOS MUROS DEFENDIENDO EL HONOR Y LA INDEPENDENCIA / DE SUS PATRIAS: Y RINDEN HOMENAJE DE ADMIRACION / Y RESPETO A LA CIUDAD DE SAN SEBASTIAN QUE DESPUES DE / PATRIR PACIENTEMENTE EN LA GUERRA SUPO ALCANZAR LOS / LAURELES DE SU RESURGIMIENTO EN EL EFEUERZO DE LA PAZ. / 31 DE AGOSTO DE 1813 – 31 DE AGOSTO DE 1963.

Monument: San Sebastian, Spain. (Photograph)

IN MEMORY / OF THE GALLANT BRITISH SOLDIERS / WHO GAVE THEIR LIVES / FOR THE GREATNESS OF THEIR OWN COUNTRY / AND FOR INDEPENDENCE / AND LIBERTY OF SPAIN.

INGLATERRA NOS CONFIA SUS GLORIOSOS RESTOS / NUESTRA GRATITUD VELARA SU ETERNO ROPOSA

ENGLAND HAS CONFIDED TO US THEIR HONOURED REMAINS / OUR GRATITUDE WILL WATCH OVER THEIR ETERNAL REPOSE

Talavera

The 'Pyramid' at Talavera. (Photograph)

3RD (PRINCE OF WALES'S) DRAGOON GUARDS
4TH OR QUEEN'S OWN DRAGOONS
14TH OR DUCHESS OF YORK'S OWN LIGHT INFANTRY
18TH OR THE QUEEN'S LIGHT DRAGOONS
ROYAL REGIMENT OF ARTILLERY
COLDSTREAM REGIMENT OF FOOT GUARDS
3RD REGIMENT OF FOOT GUARDS
3RD (EAST KENT – THE BUFFS) REGIMENT OF FOOT
7TH (ROYAL FUSILIERS) REGIMENT OF FOOT
24th (2nd WARWICKSHIRE) REGIMENT OF FOOT
29TH (WORCESTERSHIRE) REGIMENT OF FOOT
31ST (HUNTINGDONSHIRE) REGIMENT OF FOOT
40TH (2ND SOMERSETSHIRE) REGIMENT OF FOOT
45TH (1ST NOTTINGHAMSHIRE) REGIMENT OF FOOT
48TH (NORTHAMPTONSHIRE) REGIMENT OF FOOT
53RD (SHROPSHIRE) REGIMENT OF FOOT
60TH REGIMENT OF FOOT
61ST (SOUTH GLOUCESTERSHIRE) REGIMENT OF FOOT
66TH (BERKSHIRE) REGIMENT OF FOOT
83RD REGIMENT OF FOOT
87TH (PRINCE OF WALES'S IRISH) REGIMENT OF FOOT
88TH (CONNAUGHT RANGERS) REGIMENT OF FOOT
KING'S GERMAN LEGION (CAVALRY, ARTILLERY & INFANTRY)

Spanish, Portuguese, and French Regiments are also named on the Memorial.

Old memorial on hillside above battlefield. No inscription. (Photograph)

Vittoria

Monument to the Battle: Town Square, Vittoria, Spain. (Photograph)

A LA / BATALLA / DE / VITORIA / A LA INDEPENENCIA DE ESPANA / 21 DE JUNIO DE 1813

FRANCE

Arcangues

Cross in kerbed enclosure in churchyard: British and French Troops in the Battle of Nive, Arcangues, France. (Photograph)

A / LA MEMOIRE / DES SOLDATS / ANGLAIS ET FRANÇAIS / QUI SONT TOMBES LE CHAMP D'HONNEUR DANS LES / BATAILLES DE LA NIVE LES 10.11 ET 12 DEC[BRE] 1813 / ENSEVELIS DANS CE CIMETIERE. / TO MARK THE RESTING PLACE OF BRAVE MEN. / THIS CROSS WAS PLACED HERE BY LT COLONEL W. HILL JAMES / (LATE 31ST REGIMENT) / APRIL 1897 / THE 60TH YEAR OF / THE REIGN OF / QUEEN VICTORIA

Bayonne

Memorial tablet: Coldstream Guards Cemetery, Bayonne, France. (Photograph)

"IN REMEMBRANCE" / PENINSULAR WAR 200 & BAYONNE 1814 / 14 Apr 2014

Erected by Peninsular War 200 in commemoration of the bicentenary of the Sortie from Bayonne, 14 April 2014.

Memorial tablet: Wall of St Etienne Church, Bayonne, France. (Photograph)

IN MEMORIUM / 14 AVRIL 1814–14 AVRIL 2014 / PENINSULAR WAR 200 / BAYONNE 1814

Biarritz

Memorial: Catholic Old Parish Churchyard. (On hill towards the Négresse Station, France). (Notes and Queries, 16 Mar 1912)

"HERE ARE INTERRED THE REMAINS OF SEVERAL SOLDIERS OF THE ALLIED ARMY, WHO DIED IN HOSPITAL IN BIARRITZ IN THE YEAR 1814. THEIR REMAINS WERE REMOVED HITHER IN 1864 ON THE LEVELLING OF THE ATALAYE, THEIR ORIGINAL PLACE OF SEPULTURE."

Memorial: Porch of St Andrew's Church (now Musée Historique), Biarritz, France. (Photograph)

PRISTINAE VIRTUTIS MEMOR / THIS PORCH / DEDICATED TO THE MEMORY OF THE / OFFICERS, NON-COMMISSIONED OFFICERS AND MEN, OF / THE BRITISH ARMY / WHO FELL IN THE SOUTH OF FRANCE / FROM THE 7TH OCTOBER 1813 TO THE 14TH APRIL 1814 / WAS ERECTED BY THEIR FELLOW SOLDIERS AND COMPATRIOTS AD 1882. / "GIVE PEACE IN OUR TIME, O LORD".

The memorial contains names of the officers killed or died of wounds in the various battles fought in the Pyrenees and South of France from November 1813 to April 1814. All are listed by name in Vol. I (A – L) and Vol. II (M – Z}

Orthes

Memorial tablet on battlefield: Orthes, France. (Photograph)

ICI REPOSENT DES SOLDAT / FRANCAIS ANGLAIS / PORTUGAIS ESPAGNOLS / BATAILLE D'ORTHEZ / 27 FEVRIER 1814

SOUVENIR FRANÇAIS / DELEGATION / DES PYRENEES ATLANTIQUES / COMITES / D'ORTHEZ PAU ANGLET / 16 MAI 1998

Memorial tablet on tree: Orthes, France. (Photograph)

SOUS CETTE MOTTE, AVEC / ARMEE ET MONTURE, REPOSENT / DEUX OFFICIERS ANGLAIS DE L'ARMEE DU WELLINGTON TUES / DURANT LA BATAILLE D'ORTHEZ / 27 FEVRIER 1814.

Toulouse

Obelisk, Toulouse, France. (Photograph)

BATAILLE / DU 10 AVRIL 1814

BELGIUM

Brussels

Mausoleum: Evere Cemetery, Brussels, Belgium. (Located at cross roads of 10th and 8th Avenue). (Photograph)

IN MEMORY / OF THE BRITISH OFFICERS, NON COMMISSIONED OFFICERS / & MEN WHO FELL DURING THE WATERLOO CAMPAIGN IN 1815 / & WHOSE REMAINS WERE TRANSFERRED TO THE CEMETERY IN 1889. / THIS MONUMENT IS ERECTED BY HER BRITANNIC MAJESTY / QUEEN VICTORIA, EMPRESS OF INDIA & BY THEIR COUNTRYMEN / ON A SITE GENEROUSLY PRESENTED BY THE CITY OF BRUSSELS

In the interior of the mausoleum are the names of 17 of the fallen buried there:

CAPT AND LT COLONEL WILLIAM HENRY MILNES – 1ST FOOT GUARDS. / LIEUTENANT COLONEL SIR ALEXANDER GORDON – 3RD ROYAL FOOT GUARDS. AGED 29. / COLONEL SIR WILLIAM HOWE DE LANCEY – QUARTERMASTER GENERAL OF THE BRITISH ARMY. / LIEUTENANT JOHN CLYDE – 23RD ROYAL WELSH FUSILIERS. AGED 22. / LIEUTENANT CHARLES SPEARMAN – ROYAL ARTILLERY. AGED 20. / MAJOR JOHN MCLAINE – 73RD REGIMENT. / CAPTAIN W. STOTHERT-- 3RD ROYAL FOOT GUARDS AND BRIGADE MAJOR TO THE 2ND BRIGADE OF GUARDS. / MAJOR WILLIAM JOHN LLOYD – ROYAL ARTILLERY. AGED 35. / CAPTAIN J. LUCIE BLACKMAN – COLDSTREAM GUARDS. AGED 21. / CAPTAIN E. GROSE – 3RD BATTALION 1ST FOOT GUARDS. / ENSIGN JAMES LORD HAY. A.D.C.- 3RD BATTALION 1ST FOOT GUARDS. / CAPTAIN T. BROWN – 1ST FOOT GUARDS / LIEUTENANT THE HONORABLE SAMUEL SHUTE BARRINGTON – 2ND BATTALION 1ST FOOT GUARDS. / SERGEANT MAJOR EDWARD COTTON – 7TH HUSSARS. / COLONEL EDWARD STABLES – GRENADIER GUARDS. / CAPTAIN THE HONOURABLE HASTINGS BRUDENEL FORBES – 3RD ROYAL FOOT GUARDS. AGED 22. / LIEUTENANT MICHAEL THOMAS CROMIE – ROYAL HORSE ARTILLERY. AGED 25.

The inscription in the interior reads:

PEACE TO THE SOUL, AND BLESSED GLORY CROWN / THY SHADE, O BRAVE AND VIRTUOUS HERO! / WHOSE COUNTRY MOURNS, THE WHILE GLAD VICTORY / IN SMILES TRIUMPHANT WOULD ADORN HER BROW, / FOR THOU ART FALLEN, AND HER BRIGHTEST HOPES / WHICH, NURSED IN JOY, HAD WATCHED THY YOUNG CAREER / AND MARKED THEE FOR ANOTHER WELLINGTON, / ARE SUNK BENEATH THY TOMB. / FRIENDS TO THE BRAVE, COMPANIONS IN THE FIELD, / COMRADES OF WATERLOO, REVERE THE TOMB / WHERE, EMBLEM OF BRITTANIA'S GRIEF AND PRIDE, / WREATH WE IN CYPRESSES THE LAUREL CROWN: / BELOVED BY MANY HERE, A FOE TO NONE, / HIS BROTHER'S VOICE NEED NOT

INVOKE YOUR TEARS / TO GRACE THE MEMORY OF A GALLANT YOUTH, / AND SHED THEIR HALLOWED TRIBUTE O'ER HIS GRAVE.

After the Battle of Waterloo some of the British soldiers who died in Brussels of their wounds were buried in local cemeteries such as St Josse-ten-Noode and St Gilles. Toward the end of the nineteenth century there were schemes to widen some of the roads in Brussels and this involved moving some of the graves. In 1887 it was decided to move the British soldiers to a plot in Evere Cemetery and on 26 Aug 1890 the mausoleum was inaugurated. In the crypt there are plaques to the 17 officers who are buried there.
Reference: The Times, 27 August 1890, p. 3.

Quatre Bras
Monument: Near Quatre Bras Farm, Waterloo. (Photograph)

THIS MEMORIAL WAS ERECTED / AT THE INSTIGATION OF / BRIGADIER HIS GRACE THE DUKE OF WELLINGTON KC LVO OBE MC DL / PRINCE OF WATERLOO / IT WAS DESIGNED AND FINANCED THROUGH / THE ASSOCIATION OF FRIENDS OF THE WATERLOO COMMITTEE / WITH THE SUPPORT OF THE REGIMENTS THAT PARTICIPATED IN THE BATTLE / THE PLANNING WAS CARRIED OUT BY THE WATERLOO COMMITTEE IN ENGLAND AND BELGIUM

IN MEMORY OF / THE OFFICERS AND MEN / OF THE / BRITISH AND HANOVERIAN FORCES / WHO, UNDER THE COMMAND OF / FIELD MARSHAL, THE DUKE OF WELLINGTON / FOUGHT AT QUATRE BRAS / 16TH JUNE 1815

1815 Title	**2000 Title**
1ST BRITISH DIVISION – MAJOR GENERAL GEORGE COOKE	
1ST GUARDS BRIGADE – MAJOR GENERAL PEREGRINE MAITLAND	
2/1st Guards	Grenadier Guards
3/1st Guards	Grenadier Guards
2ND GUARDS BRIGADE – MAJOR GENERAL SIR JOHN BYNG	
2/Coldstream Guards	Coldstream Guards
2/3rd Guards	Scots Guards
Sandham's Brigade of Guns. Royal Artillery	16 Battery (Sandham's Company) RA
Kuhlmann's Horse Troop. King's German Legion	
3RD BRITISH DIVISION – LIEUTENANT GENERAL BARON CHARLES VON ALTEN	
5TH BRITISH BRIGADE – MAJOR GENERAL SIR COLIN HALKETT	
2/30th Foot (Cambridgeshire Regiment)	The Queen's Lancashire Regiment
33rd Foot (1st Yorkshire (West Riding Regiment)	The Duke of Wellington's Regiment (West Riding)
2/69th Foot (South Lincolnshire Regiment)	The Royal Regiment of Wales
2/73rd Foot (Highland Regiment)	The Black Watch (Royal Highland Regiment)
1ST HANOVERIAN BRIGADE – MAJOR GENERAL COUNT KIELMANSEGGE	
Bremen, Grubenhagen, Lüneburg, Osnabrück and Verden Field Battalions.	
Jäger Corps	

1815 Title	2000 Title
Lloyd's Brigade of Guns. Royal Artillery	43 Battery (Lloyd's Company) RA
Cleeves's Brigade of Guns. King's German Legion	

5TH BRITISH DIVISION – LIEUTENANT GENERAL SIR THOMAS PICTON

8TH BRITISH BRIGADE – MAJOR GENERAL SIR JAMES KEMPT

1/28th Foot (North Gloucestershire Regiment)	The Royal Gloucestershire. Berkshire & Wiltshire Regiment
1/32nd Foot (Cornwall Regiment)	The Light Infantry
1/79th Foot (Cameron Highlanders)	The Highlanders
1/95th (Rifle Regiment)	The Royal Green Jackets

9TH BRITISH BRIGADE – MAJOR GENERAL SIR DENIS PACK

3/1st Foot (The Royal Scots	The Royal Scots (The Royal Regiment)
1/42nd Foot (The Royal Highland Regiment)	The Black Watch (Royal Highland Regiment)
2/44th Foot (East Essex Regiment)	The Royal Anglian Regiment
1/92nd Foot (Gordon Highlanders)	The Highlanders

4TH HANOVERIAN BRIGADE – COLONEL CARL BEST

Lüneberg, Münden, Osterode and Verden Landwehr Battalions	
Roger's Brigade of Guns, Royal Artillery	30 Battery (Roger's Company) RA
Braun's Brigade of Guns, Hanoverian	
von Rettberg's Brigade of Guns. Hanoverian	

THE TRANSPORTATION OF THE MONUMENT FROM THE UNITED KINGDOM / WAS EXECUTED BY / 151 (GREATER LONDON) LOGISTIC SUPPORT REGIMENT RLC (V)

Monument: Quatre Bras. (Photograph)

1815–16 JUNE. IN MEMORY OF THE BELGIAN SOLDIERS KILLED AT THE BATTLE OF QUATRE BRAS FOR THE DEFENSE OF THE FLAG AND THE HONOUR OF ARMS.

TER NAGEDACHTENIS DER BELGEN TE / QUATRE BRAS / VOOR DE VERDEDIGING VAN HET VAANDEL / EN DE EER DER WAPENS GESNEUVELD
ZIG STREDEN ALS LEEUWEN / TEGEN TROEPEN STERKER IN GETAL

Statue: Quatre Bras. (Photograph)

FRIEDRICH WILHELM / HERZOG ZU BRAUNSCHWEIG UND LÜNEBERG / KAMPFTE UND FIEL UNWEIT DIESER STÄATE / AN DER SPITZE SEINER TRUPPEN / AM XVI JUNI MDCCCXV

English translation of German text.

"FREDERICK-WILLIAM, DUKE OF BRUNSWICK AND LUNEBURG, FELL NEAR THIS PLACE WHILE FIGHTING AT THE HEAD OF HIS TROOPS, ON 16 JUNE 1815."

Reverse side of monument:

"IN MEMORY OF THE HERO AND HIS WARRIORS WHO FELL WITH HIM FOR GERMANY. THE GRATEFUL HOMELAND. MDCCCMXXXX."

Memorial tablet on wall: Quatre Bras, Waterloo. (Photograph)

AAN DE NEDERLANDERS EN / HUN MEDESTRYDERS VERDEDISERS / VAN QUATRE BRAS / 15–16 – VI – 1815 / A LA MEMOIRE DES / NEERLANDAIS ET LEURS / ALLIES DEFENSEURS DE / QUATRE BRAS

Memorial: Dutch Cavalry, Quatre Bras, Waterloo. (Photograph)

TER NAGEDACHTENIS EN HULDE / AAN DE GEVALLENEN VAN DE / NEDERLANDSE CAVALERIE / REGIMENTEN / HUZAREN NO 6 EN NO 8 / KARABINIERS NO 1, NO 2 EN NO 3 / LIGHTE DRAGONDERS NO 4 EN NO 5 / IN DE VELDSLAGEN BIJ / QUATRE BRAS 16–6–1815 EN / WATERLOO / 18–6–1815 / OPGERICHT / 21–9–1990 / REG HUZEREN VAN BOREEL / REG HUZAREN VAN SYTZAMA / REG HUZAREN PRIME ALEXANDER

THIS MEMORIAL WAS ERECTED ON THE INITIATIVE OF THE FONDATION DE LA CAVALERIE QUATRE-BRAS ET WATERLOO (QUATRE-BRAS AND WATERLOO CAVALRY FOUNDATION), DESIGNED BY WILLIAM VAN ROOIJEN IN MEMORY OF AND IN HOMAGE TO THE WAR CASUALTIES OF THE DUTCH CAVALRY REGIMENTS WHO DIED HERE IN THE BATTLES OF 16 AND 18 JUNE 1815.

IN MEMORY OF AND IN HOMAGE OF THE CASUALTIES OF THE DUTCH CAVALRY REGIMENTS. / 6TH AND 8TH HUSSARS / 1ST, 2ND AND 3RD CARABINEERS / 4TH AND 5TH LIGHT DRAGOONS / ON THE BATTLEFIELD OF QUATRE BRAS AND WATERLOO 16.6.1815 18.6.1815 / ERECTED ON / 21.9.1990 / HUZAREN VAN BORELL REGIMENT / HUZAREN PRINS ALEXANDER REGIMENT

Hougoumont

Memorial plaque: Hougoumont Chapel, Waterloo. (Photograph)

VISITORS ARE EARNESTLY REQUESTED TO TREAT THIS CHAPEL / WITH RESPECT, FOR WITHIN ITS WALLS ON THE MEMORABLE / 18TH JUNE 1815, MANY OF THE BRAVE DEFENDERS OF / HOUGOUMONT PASSED TO THEIR REST. / TO THE MEMORY OF THEIR BRAVE DEAD / THIS TABLET WAS ERECTED BY HIS / BRITANNIC MAJESTY'S BRIGADE OF / GUARDS, AND BY COMTE CHARLES VAN DER BURCH 1907

Text also in French and German.

Regimental memorial plaque: 1st Regiment of Foot Guards, Hougoumont, Waterloo. (Photograph)

FIRST REGIMENT OF FOOT GUARDS / IN MEMORY OF / THE OFFICERS AND MEN / OF THE LIGHT COMPANIES / OF THE 2ND AND 3RD BATTALIONS / WHO DIED DEFENDING HOUGOUMONT / 18TH JUNE 1815 / THIS TABLET WAS ERECTED IN 1977 / BY THEIR SUCCESSOR OF THE / FIRST OR GRENADIER GUARDS

Regimental memorial tablet: Coldstream Guards, Hougoumont, Waterloo. (Photograph)

IN MEMORY / OF THE OFFICERS AND MEN OF THE / 2ND BATTALION COLD STREAM GUARDS / WHO, WHILE DEFENDING HOUGOUMONT FARM / SUCCESSFULLY HELD THIS SOUTH GATE / FROM SUCCESSIVE ATTACKS THROUGHOUT: / 18TH JUNE 1815 / A LA MEMOIRE / DES OFFICIERS ET SOLDATS DU / 2EME BATAILLON DES COLDSTREAM GUARDS / QUI ONT PARTICIPE A LA DEFENSE DE HOUGOUMONT / ET ONT RESISTE A TOUTES LES ATTAQUES / DIRIGEES CONTRE LA PORT SUD / LE 18 JUIN 1815

Regimental memorial tablet: 3rd Regiment of Foot Guards, Hougoumont, Waterloo. (Photograph)

3RD REGIMENT OF FOOT GUARDS / IN MEMORY OF / THE OFFICERS AND MEN / OF THE 2ND BATTALION / WHO DIED / DEFENDING THIS FARM / JUNE 18TH 1815

Regimental memorial tablet: Royal Waggon Train, Hougoumont, Waterloo. (Photograph)

ROYAL WAGGON TRAIN / IN MEMORY OF / THE OFFICERS AND MEN / OF THE ROYAL WAGGON TRAIN / WHO TOOK PART IN THE / DEFENCE OF HOUGOUMONT / 18TH JUNE 1815. / THIS TABLET WAS ERECTED IN 1979 / BY THE ROYAL CORPS OF TRANSPORT / THE SUCCESSORS OF / THE ROYAL WAGGON TRAIN

Memorial tablet: Lt and Capt Thomas Gage Craufurd, 3rd Regiment of Foot Guards. (On wall of orchard at Hougoumont). (Photograph)

IN MEMORY OF / CAPTAIN THOMAS CRAUFURD / OF THE 3RD GUARDS / ELDEST SON OF THE BARONET OF KILBIRNIE, / KILLED IN THE EXTREME SOUTH WEST ANGLE OF THIS WALL. / THIS STONE WAS PLACE BY HIS KINSMAN / SIR WILLIAM FRASER / OF MORAR / 1889

La Haye Sainte

Monument: Sir Alexander Gordon. 3rd Regiment of Foot Guards. (Photograph)

Regimental Monument: King's German Legion Opposite La Haye Sainte Farm, Waterloo. (Photograph)

TO THE MEMORY / OF THEIR COMPANIONS IN ARMS / WHO GLORIOUSLY FELL ON THE MEMORABLE / 18TH DAY OF JUNE 1815 / THIS MONUMENT / IS ERECTED BY THE OFFICERS OF THE KING'S / GERMAN LEGION

Memorial tablet: 2nd Light Battalion, Kings' German Legion, La Haye Sainte outer wall, Waterloo. (Photograph)

DER / OFFICIERE / DES 2TEN / LEICHTEN BATAILLONS, / KONIGLICH DEUTSCHER LEGION, IHREN / IN DER VERTHEIDIGUNG DIESER MEYEREY / AN 18 TEN JUNI 1815 GEFADLENEN / WAFFENBRÜUDERN: MAJOR H. BÖSEWIEL / CAPTAIN W. SCHAUMANN / FAHNDRICH F. VON ROBERTSON / UND 46 UNTEROFFICIERE END JÄGER VOM 2TEN LEICHTEN BATAILLON. WIEDERHERGESTELLT / DURCH SEINE KÖNINLICHE HOHETT / DEN KRONPRINZEN GEORG VON HANNOVER AM 18TEN JUNI 1847 / UND ZUGLEICH GEWIDMET DEN EBENDASELBST BEI / DIESER GEDEGENHEIT GEFALLENEN: / CAPTAIN H. VON MARSCHALCK / VOM 1TEN LEICHTEN BATAILLON, / CAPTAIN C. VON WURMB / VOM 5TEN LINIEN BATAILLON / IN ANERKENNUNG DES VOM / IHNEN BEWIESENEN / HANNOVERSCHEN / HELDENMUTHS.

English translation:

THE / OFFICERS / OF THE 2ND / LIGHT BATTALION / TO THEIR COMRADES-IN-ARMS WHO FELL IN THE DEFENCE OF / THIS FARMHOUSE / ON THE 18TH JUNE : MAJOR H. BOSEWIEL / CAPTAIN W. SCHAUMANN / ENSIGN F. VON.ROBERTSON / AND 46 NCOS AND RIFLEMEN OF THE 2ND LIGHT BATTALION / RAISED AGAIN BY HIS ROYAL HIGHNESS / CROWN PRINCE GEORGE OF HANOVER ON 18TH JUNE 1847 / DEDICATED AT THE SAME TIME / TO THOSE WHO ALSO FELL: CAPTAIN H. VON MARSCHALK / FROM THE 1ST LIGHT BATTALION / CAPTAIN VON WURMB / FROM THE 5TH LINE BATTALION / IN RECOGNITION OF THE HANOVERIAN HEROISM THEY SHOWED.

Memorial stone: Sir Thomas Picton, Mont St Jean, Waterloo. (Near crossroads). (Photograph)

TO THE GALLANT MEMORY OF / LIEUTENANT-GENERAL SIR THOMAS PICTON / COMMANDER OF THE 5TH DIVISION AND THE LEFT / WING / OF THE ARMY AT THE BATTLE OF WATERLOO / BORN 1758 / DIED NEAR THIS SPOT IN THE EARLY AFTERNOON / OF THE 18TH JUNE 1815 LEADING HIS MEN AGAINST / COUNT DROUET D'ERLON'S ADVANCE

Regimental memorial stone: 27th (Inniskilling) Regiment of Foot. Mont St Jean, Waterloo. (Photograph)

IN MEMORY OF THE HEROIC STAND BY / THE 27TH (INNISKILLING) REGIMENT OF / FOOT AT THE BATTLE OF WATERLOO ON / 18TH JUNE 1815 WHEN, OF THE 747 / OFFICERS AND MEN OF THE REGIMENT / WHO JOINED BATTLE, 495 WERE KILLED OR / WOUNDED. A NOBLE RECORD OF / STUBBORN ENDURANCE. / OF THEM THE DUKE OF WELLINGTON SAID, / "AE, THEY SAVED THE CENTRE OF MY LINE." / ERECTED BY THEIR SUCCESSORS / THE ROYAL IRISH RANGERS / (27TH INNISKILLING) 83RD, 87TH / 18 JUNE 1990

REFERENCE; Royal Inniskilling Fusiliers, being the History of the Regiment from December 1688 to July 1914, revised edn, 1934.

Memorial tablet: Deputy Inspector General of Hospitals John Gunning, Mont St Jean Farm, Waterloo. (Photograph)

IN MEMORY OF / DEPUTY INSPECTOR GUNNING / PRINCIPAL MEDICAL OFFICER OF THE 1ST CORPS / THE SURGEONS AND OTHER MEMBERS / OF THE FIELD HOSPITAL / WHICH WAS ESTABLISHED IN THIS FARM / TO CARE FOR THE WOUNDED OF THE BATTLEFIELD / 18TH UNE 1815. / THIS TABLET WAS ERECTED IN 1981 / BY THE ROYAL ARMY MEDICAL CORPS.

Memorial stone marking position of Capt Alexander Cavalié Mercer's Troop at Waterloo. (Photograph)

THIS STONE MARKS THE LAST POSITION / OF G TROOP ROYAL HORSE ARTILLERY / COMMANDED BY CAPTAIN A. C. MERCER / DURING THE BATTLE OF WATERLOO / 18 JUNE 1815. FROM HERE THE TROOP / TOOK A CONSPICUOUS PART IN DEFEATING / THE ATTACKS OF THE FRENCH CAVALRY

Marker stone opposite the Visitor Centre, Waterloo.

DE JUAN 1815–1915 / WATERLOO / N.B.

Lion Mound, Waterloo, Belgium. (Photograph)

XVIII JUIN MDCCCXV

The Lion Monument is located on the Plain of Waterloo where the Prince of Orange was wounded. It simply bears the date of the battle, and is set on a man-made mound 50 metres high, bearing at the top the gigantic Lion of Waterloo. It measures 4.5 metres in height, and is made of cast iron from the captured French cannon. The plaster work was done by Mr J. F. van Geel.

Memorial tablet: Entrance lobby of Wellington Museum, Waterloo. (Photograph)

PENDANT LA BATAILLE / DE WATERLOO / CETTE AUBERGE / BATIE EN 1705 / ABRITA LE QUARTIER GENERAL / DU DUC DE WELLINGTON / QUI Y PASSA LES NUITS / DES 17 ET 18 JUIN 1815 / IL REDIGEA ICI / LA PREMIERE PARTIE / DE LA DEPECHE / ANNONCANT / LA VICTOIRE DES ALLIES. / LE COMITTE DE WATERLOO / THE WATERLOO COMMITTEE / A PLACE CETTE PLAQUE / EN 1996

Low monument: Garden of the Waterloo Museum, Waterloo. (Photograph)

TO THE MEMORY OF / COLONEL SIR H. W. ELLIS KCB. / 23RD REG^T^. R. WELSH FUSILIERS / KILLED IN ACTION AT WATERLOO / 18 JUNE 1815.

Pedestal tomb: Major Arthur Rowley Heyland, Garden of Waterloo Museum, Waterloo. (Originally buried in the garden of the old Auberge du Cheval Blanc, the grave was removed to make way for a road and relocated in 1889). (Photograph)

SACRED / TO THE MEMORY OF / MAJOR ARTHUR ROWLEY HEYLAND / OF HIS BRITANNIC MAJESTY'S / FORTIETH REGIMENT OF FOOT / WHO WAS BURIED ON THIS SPOT. / HE FELL GLORIOUSLY IN THE BATTLE OF / WATERLOO / ON THE 18TH JUNE 1815. / AT THE MOMENT OF VICTORY / AND IN COMMAND OF HIS REGIMENT / AGED 34 YEARS.

Memorial plaque to Capt and Lt Capt Edward Stables from his tomb at Joli Bois now on the wall of the Wellington Museum, Waterloo. (Photograph)

HIC JACET / EDVARDUS STABLES / OLIM DE HORMEADBURY IN COMITATU / HERTFORDIENSI, / IN HISPANIA MILITIAM INIIT, SUB INSIGNI DUCE JOAN. MOORE, EQUIT BALN: / MOX, PER EAMDEM, PER VARIOS TRIUMPHOS GLORISSISSIMÈ LIBERATUM, / SUB INSIGNISSIMO PRINCIPE ARTHURO DUCE DE WELLINGTON, / GALLIAM FELICITER INTRAVIT: / TANDEM IN PRÆLIO WATERLOVIENSI, / AGMINI QUADRATO IMPERANS, / DÙM MONITU ET EXEMPLO MILITUM ANOMOS IN HOSTEM ACCENDEBAT, / EGREGIÀ MORTE PEREMPTUS EST / ABRUPTUM LUGENT AMICI, / OMMILITIONES, PATRIA./ OBIIT ANNO ÆTATIS SUÆ XXXIII

Memorial tablet: Belle Alliance, Waterloo. (Photograph)

BELLE ALLIANCE / RENCONTRE / DES GENERAUX / WELLINGTON ET BLUCHER / LORS / DE LA MEMORABLE / BATAILLE DU XVIII JUIN / M.D.CCC.XV / LUANT MUTELLEMENT / VAINQUEURS

St Joseph's Church, Waterloo
Memorial tablet to All British Officers: St Joseph's Church, Waterloo. (Photograph)

IN HONORED MEMORY OF / ALL BRITISH OFFICERS / NON COMMISSIONED OFFICERS AND SOLDIERS / WHO FELL IN BATTLE, / UPON THE 16TH 17TH AND 18TH OF JUNE 1815. / THIS TABLET WAS ERECTED / BY A FEW BROTHERS IN ARMS AND COUNTRYMEN / A.D. MDCCCLVIII / GLORY ENCIRCLES WITH THE SAME DIADEM / THE HUMBLE AS WELL AS THE EXALTED

St Joseph's Church is in the village of Waterloo opposite the Wellington Museum. It contains memorials to British and allied soldiers who died in the Battle of Waterloo. They are all listed by name in Vol. I (A – L) and Vol. II (M – Z) and illustrated in the Battlefield Memorial file.

UNITED KINGDOM – Waterloo Memorials

BERKSHIRE

Windsor
Waterloo Gallery, Windsor Castle, Windsor, Berkshire. (Photograph)

The Waterloo Gallery was built in the 1830s during the reign of William IV to display all of the portraits by Sir Thomas Lawrence of the sovereigns, military commanders and statesmen who were associated with the downfall of Napoleon. The Prince Regent had commissioned this as early as 1814 and Lawrence had to travel around Europe in order to finish the project.

DEVON

Great Torrington
Obelisk: In valley near Great Torrington, Devon. (Photograph)

ERECTED JUNE 1818 / TO COMMEMORATE / THE BATTLE OF / WATERLOO / JUNE 1815 / PEACE TO THE / SOULS OF THE / HEROES!!!

ESSEX

Harwich
Memorial: Church Gate, All Saints' Churchyard, Dovercourt, Harwich, Essex. (Photograph)

ERECTED BY HER MAJESTY QUEEN VICTORIA EMPRESS OF INDIA TO / THE MEMORY OF BRITISH SOLDIERS BURIED IN THIS CHURCH YARD / PARTICULARLY THOSE WHO DIED FROM DISEASE / CONTRACTED DURING THE WALCHEREN 1809 – 1810 EXPEDITION.

Memorial: All Saints Churchyard, Dovercourt, Harwich, Essex. (Photograph)

AT OR NEAR THIS PLACE / THE BRITISH AND GERMAN SOLDIERS / WHO DIED IN THIS PARISH FROM DISEASE / CONTRACTED DURING THE WALCHEREN EXPEDITION 1809–1810

Stained Glass Window: All Saints' Church, Dovercourt, Harwich, Essex. (M.I.)

PRESENTED BY THE GERMAN EMPEROR IN MEMORY OF THE BRITISH AND GERMAN SOLDIERS WHO DIED OF DISEASE AS A RESULT OF THE WALCHEREN EXPEDITION

GLOUCESTERSHIRE

Wooton-under Edge

Copse of trees at Wooton-under-Edge, Gloucestershire. (Photograph)

WOOTON-UNDER-EDGE TOWN TRUST / TREES WERE PLANTED HERE IN 1815, TO COMMEMORATE THE / VICTORY AT WATERLOO. THEY HAD BECOME THIN BY THE / END OF THE CRIMEAN WAR AND WERE FELLED FOR A BONFIRE. / THIS WALLED ENCLOSURE WAS ERECTED AND THE SITE / RE-PLANTED WITH TREES TO COMMEMORATE THE JUBILEE / OF HER LATE MAJESTY QUEEN VICTORIA. (1887) FOLLOWING / THE BURNING IN THIS SPOT OF ONE OF A CHAIN OF / CELEBRATION BEACONS WHICH THEN SPANNED THE COUNTRY. / INTERPLANTED WITH NEW TREES 1952 BY SUBSCRIPTION OF:- / THE FAMILY OF THE LATE REVD. JAMES HARDYMAN. / THE FAMILY OF THE LATE W. J. WILLIAMS ESQ., / MRS A. G. BURY. / BRIG. AND MRS ALAN DURAND. / A. H. JOTCHAM ESQ., / WOOTON-UNDER-EDGE TRADERS ASSOCIATION. / WOOTON-UNDER-EDGE TOWN TRUSTEES.

HAMPSHIRE

Portsmouth

Memorial plaque: Memorial Gardens, Royal Hospital, Haslar, Portsmouth, Hampshire. (Photograph)

ROYAL HOSPITAL HASLAR BURIAL GROUND / IN MEMORIAM / FROM 1753 UNTIL 1826 THE AREA BEYOND THIS WALL, KNOWN AS THE / PADDOCK WAS USED AS A BURIAL GROUND TO LAY TO REST MANY THOUSANDS OF / SICK AND WOUNDED WHO ENDED THEIR DAYS IN HASLAR HOSPITAL. / AMONGST THOSE INTERRED HERE ARE SOLDIERS AND SAILORS / WHO GAVE THEIR LIVES FOR THEIR COUNTRY DURING THE TURBULENT DAYS / OF TRAFALGAR, CORUNNA AND WATERLOO. / THEY LIE SIDE BY SIDE, HAMMOCKS THEIR SHROUDS AND COFFINS, / BROTHERS IN ARMS IN DEATH AS IN LIFE. / THIS PLAQUE WAS UNVEILED BY / ADMIRAL SIR ALAN WEST GCB, DSC, ADC / FIRST SEA LORD / 10 JUNE 2005

Romsey Abbey

Column: Grounds of Romsey Abbey, Hampshire. (Photograph)

THIS COLUMN WAS ERECTED / BY A YOUNG ARCHITECT / OF THIS TOWN / IN COMMEMORATION / OF THE VICTORIOUS BATTLE OF / WATERLOO / IN WHICH BRITISH VALOUR / WAS TRIUMPHANT / AND SECURED / FOR THE CONTENDING POWERS / OF EUROPE / TRANQUILLITY AND PEACE / JUNE 18TH 1815

KENT

Isle of Thanet

Memorial Tower: Waterloo Tower, Quex Park, Isle of Thanet, Kent (Photograph)

Tower built in 1818–1819 by John Powell Powell, owner of Quex Park. He was very interested in bell ringing. The Waterloo Tower had a ring of 12 bells, more than any other place in Kent. Even Canterbury Cathedral only had 10. The bell tower is surmounted by a white metal spire, and contains the 12 bells.

Tunbridge Wells

Low monument: Trinity Cemetery, Tunbridge Wells, Kent. (Photograph)

SACRED TO THE MEMORY OF / LIEUT GENERAL MIDDLEMORE C.B. / COLONEL OF H. M. 48 REG^{T} OF FOOT. / DEPARTED THIS LIFE 18 NOVEMBER 1850 / IN THE 81 YEAR OF HIS AGE.

At the head of the low monument is a slate tablet erected in 1907 by the 1st Northamptonshire Regiment, (formerly 48th Foot), commemorating the battle of Talavera. Now badly flaked the inscription is not readable, but the inscription has been recorded from a memorial inscription:

"TALAVERA / IT WAS ON THE ADVANCE OF THE BATTALION TO THE RESCUE OF THE GUARDS THAT COL. DONELLAN WAS STRUCK AND PAINFUL AS MUST HAVE BEEN THE WOUND, HIS COUNTENANCE NOT ONLY DID NOT BETRAY HIS SUFFERING BUT PRESERVED HIS USUAL EXPRESSION. CALLING MAJOR MIDDLEMORE THE NEXT SENIOR OFFICER, COL DONELLAN SEATED ERECT IN HIS SADDLE, TOOK OFF HIS HAT, BOWED, AND SAID, MAJOR MIDDLEMORE, YOU WILL HAVE THE HONOUR OF LEADING THE 48TH TO THE CHARGE. THE BATTALION CHARGED AND RESCUED THE GUARDS, WHILST COL. DONELLAN WAS CONDUCTED TO THE REAR AND DIED AT TALAVERA. / GRAVE RESTORED AND THIS TABLET ERECTED BY THE OFFICERS OF THE 1ST NORTHAMPTONSHIRE REGIMENT IN 1907."

LANCASHIRE

Billinge

Bispham Hall Estate, Crank Road, Billinge, Merseyside. (M.I.)
Square Obelisk on pedestal and base in Gardens.

West face:

ENGLAND CONFESSES / TO THE MOST NOBLE ILLUSTRIOUS / ARTHUR / DUKE OF WELLINGTON / AND THE BRAVE HEROES OF BRITAIN AND THE CONTINENT / WHO UNDER HIS AUSPICIOUS GENIUS AND COMMAND / SO GLORIOUSLY ACCOMPLISHED THE DOWNFALL OF / TYRANNY AND THE RESTORATION OF LIBERTY TO EUROPE / ON THE PLAINS OF WATERLOO. / JUN 18, A.D. 1815 / PARCERE

South face:

ON THAT DAY / BRITISH / HILL, PICTON, UXBRIDGE, GORDON, / SOMERSET, PONSONBY, F. SOMERSET, / CAMERON, ELLIS, MAITLAND, PACK, / HALKETT, KEMPT, COOKE, BYNGE, GRANT,
CLINTON, ALTON, ADAM, BARNES, / DELANCY, VIVIAN AND / SUBJECTIS ET

East face:

EACH MAN DID / CONTINENTAL / BRUNSWICK, ORANGE, BLUCHER, / BULOW, TRIP, VANHOPE, DORNBERG, / OMPTEDA, POSSO DI BORGO, / DEBELLARE

North face:

HIS DUTY / TO THOSE WHO FELL, / THE IMMORTAL HEROES ON WHOSE LATEST BREATH / GLOWED THE PATRIOT FEELING STRONG IN DEATH. / BUT THAT MOMENT WAS IN ALL THE PAST / SAVE MY COUNTRY HEAVEN, / WAS YOUR LAST. / DULCE ET DECORUM EST PRO PATRIA MORI. / SUPERBOS

Memorial was erected in 1816 by John and Robert Holt who owned and lived at the Hall and estate at Bispham.

Todmorden

Monument on Stoodley Pike, Todmorden, Lancashire. (Photograph)

STOODLEY PIKE / A PEACE MONUMENT / ERECTED BY PUBLIC SUBSCRIPTION / COMMENCED IN 1814 TO COMMEMORATE THE SURRENDER OF PARIS TO THE ALLIES / AND FINISHED AFTER THE BATTLE OF WATERLOO WHEN PEACE WAS ESTABLISHED IN 1815. / BY A STRANGE COINCIDENCE THE PIKE FELL ON THE DAY THE RUSSIAN AMBASSADOR LEFT LONDON BEFORE / THE DECLARATION OF WAR WITH RUSSIA IN 1854, AND IT WAS REBUILT WHEN PEACE WAS PROCLAIMED IN 1856. / REPAIRED AND LIGHTENING CONDUCTOR FIXED 1889.

Reference: Savage, E. M., Stoodley Pike, Todmorden Antiquarian Society, 1993. (Pamphlet).

LINCOLNSHIRE

Leasingham

An obelisk by the front door of Leasingham Hall commemorates some box wood trees said to have been brought back from Hougoumont. Various box wood trees are located nearby, but cannot specially be identified as connected with the original trees. (Photograph)

THIS / BOXWOOD / GREW IN THE / GARDEN AT / HOUGOMONT / DURING THE / BATTLE / OF / WATERLOO / 18TH JUNE 1815

LONDON

Buckingham Palace

Frieze depicting Battle of Waterloo on Palace Cornice. (No inscription). (Photograph)

Waterloo Vase: Garden of Buckingham Palace, London. (Photograph)

The Waterloo Vase is a large urn 15 feet high, weighing 20 tons carved from one piece of Carrara marble and forms a garden ornament in the grounds of Buckingham Palace. Originally intended to show Napoleon's victories in the panels around the sides, it was presented to the Prince Regent in 1815 and he wanted to display it in the new Waterloo Chamber at Windsor Castle. However the floor could not withstand the weight and it was presented to the National Gallery in 1836. It was eventually returned to Buckingham Palace in 1906.

Reference: Gentleman's Magazine, 1836, pp. 186–7.

Chelsea

Memorial tablet: Royal Hospital, Chelsea, London. (Photograph)

PENINSULAR WAR / 1808–1811 / ROLICA VIMIERA / SAHAGUN / CORUNNA DOURO / BUSACO / BARROSA / FUENTES D'ONOR / ALBUHERA / ARROYO DOS MOLINOS / TARIFA

PENINSULAR WAR / 1812–1814 / CIUDAD RODRIGO / BADAJOZ / ALMAREZ SALAMANCA / VITTORIA / PYRENEES ST SEBASTIAN / NIVELLE / NIVE / ORTHES TOULOUSE / PENINSULA

Horse Guards Parade

Monument: Horse Guards Parade, London. (Photograph)

English text on Left-hand side:

TO COMMEMORATE / THE RAISING OF THE SIEGE OF CADIZ IN CONSEQUENCE OF THE

GLORIOUS VICTORY GAINED BY THE / DUKE OF WELLINGTON / OVER THE FRENCH NEAR SALAMANCA ON THE XXII OF JULY MDCCCXII. / THIS MORTAR, CAST FOR THE DESTRUCTION OF THAT GREAT PORT, WITH POWERS SURPASSING ALL OTHERS, / AND ABANDONED BY THE BESIEGERS ON THEIR RETREAT, / WAS PRESENTED AS A TOKEN OF RESPECT AND GRATITUDE. BY THE SPANISH NATION / TO HIS ROYAL HIGHNESS THE PRINCE REGENT. / CONSTRUCTED BY THE CARRIAGE DEPARTMENT, ROYAL ARSENAL. / EARL OF MULGRAVE MASTER GENERAL 1814.

Latin text on Right-hand side:

DEVICTIS, A. WELLINGTON DUCE PROPE SALAMANCAM, GALLIS, / SOLUTAQUE EXINDE GADIUM OBSIDIONE, HANC, QUAM APSICTIS / BASI SUPERIMPOSITAM BOMBARDUM. VI PRAEDITAM ADHUC INAUDITA / AD URBEM PORTUMQUE GADITANUM DESTRUENDUM, CONFLATUM, / ET A COPTIS TURBATIS RELICTAM / CORTES HISPANICI PRISTINORUM HAUDQUAQUAM / BENEFICTOIORUM OBLITI, SUMMAI VENERATIONIS TESTIMONIO DONAVERUNT, / GEORGIO: ILLUS: BRIT: PRINC: / QUI IN PERPETUAM REI MEMORIAM, HOC LOCO PONENDAM, ET HIS ORNAMENTIS DECORANDUAM IUSSIT.

Marble March

Commemorative Arch: Marble Arch, London. (Photograph)

Waterloo Bridge, London. (Photograph)

The Waterloo Bridge is the national memorial to Waterloo and was chosen after designs for monuments were turned down owing to the expense. The bridge was financed by the shareholders of the Strand Bridge Company who were already building a bridge that started in 1811. It was officially opened on 18 June 1817 in the presence of the Prince Regent and the Duke of Wellington who returned from France for the occasion. By the 1920s the bridge was found to have so many cracks that it was proposed by the London County Council to demolish it. This led to great controversy but in 1934 the Labour led LCC. had its way and it was dismantled and a new bridge put in its place. The official opening was 10 Dec 1945 although it had been used during the Second World War, but there was no mention of Waterloo on the commemorative plaque.

Reference: Foster, R. E., Waterloo bridge: national memorial or national disgrace? Waterloo Journal, Vol. 35, No. 3, Winter 2013, pp. 8–12.

NORTHAMPTONSHIRE

Burton Latimer

Plaque: On side of The Round House, Burton Latimer, Northamptonshire. (Photograph)

PANORAMA / WATERLOO / VICTORY / JUNE 18 / A.D. / 1815

SOMERSET

Sedgemoor

Memorial: Sedgemoor, Somerset. (Photograph)

WATERLOO / 1815

SURREY

Kew

Memorial: Kew Gardens, Kew Road, Kew, Surrey. King William's Temple, Southern Part of the Garden. (M.I.)

External Tablet

KING WILLIAM'S TEMPLE / THIS TEMPLE WAS DESIGNED BY SIR GEORGE WYATVILLE / FOR KING WILLIAM IV AND BUILT IN 1837. / THE INNER WALLS ARE DECORATED WITH A SERIES OF IRON / PLAQUES COMMEMORATION THE ACTIONS AND CAMPAIGNS / FOUGHT BY THE BRITISH ARMY 1760–1815.

Internal Tablets

Tablet 2: 808 / ROLIEA / VIMIERO / SAHAGUN / 1809 / CORUNNA / DOURO / OPORTO

Tablet 3: 1809 / TALAVERA / 1810 / BUSACO / 1811 / BAROSSA / LIBERATION OF PORTUGAL

Tablet 4: 1811 / FUENTES D'ONOR / ALMEIDA / ALBUERA / EL BODON / ARROYO DE MOLINO / TARIFA

Tablet 5 CIUDAD RODRIGO / BADAJOS / ALMAREZ / FORTS OF SALAMANCA / SALAMANCA / MADRID

Tablet 6: 1812 / RETIRO / ALBA DE TORMES / 1813 / CASTALLA / MORALES / VITTORIA

Tablet 7: 1813 / PYRENEES / ST. SEBASTIAN / BIDASSOA / THE NIVELLE / THE NIVE

Tablet 8: 1814 / GARRIS / ORTHES / AIRE / TARBES / TOULOUSE

Tablet 9: 1815 / QUATRE BRAS / WATERLOO

YORKSHIRE

Cowling

Obelisk: Earl Crag, Cowling, Yorkshire. (No inscription on obelisk). (Photograph)

The Obelisk was erected by Richard Wainman as a memorial to the Battle of Waterloo and to mark his son William's achievements in the Peninsular War. It seems fairly certain that the first Wainman Pinnacle, or Cowling Pinnacle, was built in 1815–1816 by Mr Wainman of Carr Head Hall, Cowling to commemorate Wellington's victory at Waterloo. It was made of wood and became derelict after being struck by lightning. The present stone built obelisk was erected in 1900.

York

Memorial: 2nd Division, Seven Arch Wall, York Minster, York, Yorkshire. (Photograph)

Seven Arch Wall originally formed part of the Archbishop's of York's Medieval Palace. It was restored and a dedicatory plaque placed to the left of the Wall. Plaques with battle honours are placed in each archway. Behind the fourth arch is a low obelisk with inscription. On a tablet attached near the top iron railings between each archway are the names of campaigns fought.

LEFT OF 1ST ARCH: THIS MEMORIAL TO THE SECOND DIVISION / WAS UNVEILED BY / HER MAJESTY, QUEEN ELIZABETH, THE QUEEN MOTHER / 24TH JUNE 1987

ARCH 1: MEMORIAL TO THE SECOND DIVISION / RAISED IN PORTUGAL AT ALBUERA / 18TH JUNE 1809

ARCH 2: TALAVERA 1809 VITTORIA 1813 / SALAMANCA 1812 PYRENEES 1814 / WATERLOO / 1815

SCOTLAND

DUMFRIESSHIRE

New Abbey

Monument on hillside south -west of New Abbey, Dumfriesshire, Scotland. (Photograph).

ERECTED A.D. 1816 / TO RECORD THE VALOUR / OF THOSE BRITISH, BELGIAN / AND PRUSSIAN SOLDIERS / WHO UNDER / WELLINGTON AND BLUCHER / ON THE 18TH JUNE 1815 / GAINED THE VICTORY / OF / WATERLOO / BY WHICH, FRENCH TYRANNY / WAS OVERTHROWN / AND PEACE RESTORED / TO THE WORLD

The monument at New Abbey was erected in part because of the local connections with Colonel Stewart of New Abbey, whose 43rd Regiment, which included many men from the parish took part in the battle and suffered heavy casualties. The foundation stone was laid 6 Oct 1815 by the Provincial Grand Master of the southern district of the Freemasons in Scotland. Following the ceremony, which was preceded by a church service, and village fete, a new road in New Abbey was named Waterloo Place. Work was completed in 1816. A glass bottle containing further details of the battle was laid in the foundation stone. *REFERENCE: Dumfries and Galloway Courier, 10 Oct 1815. Dumfries Weekly Journal, 4 Jan 1817.*

EDINBURGH

National Monument, Calton Hill. (Photograph)
Based on the Parthenon in Athens, it was intended to be a memorial church with catacombs for the dead of the Napoleonic Wars. The project was abandoned in 1826 when money ran out.

Communal Water Pump and Waterloo Pyramid. Junction of St Leonard's Street, and Parkside Street, Edinburgh. (Photograph)

WATERLOO 1815

ROXBURGHSHIRE

Peniel Heugh

Tower: Peniel Heugh, Roxburghshire, Scotland. (Photograph)

TO THE / DUKE OF WELLINGTON / AND THE BRITISH ARMY. / WILLIAM KERR / VI MARQUIS OF LOTHIAN / AND HIS TENANTRY / DEDICATE THIS MONUMENT / XXX JUNE MDCCCXV

The tower is 150 feet high built between 1817 and 1824 to commemorate the Battle of Waterloo. It was started in 1815 but by 1816 it had collapsed and building recommenced in 1817. It stands on the site of an Iron Age fortified settlement. Although it is one of the best man-made features in the central Borders, there is no public access.

WALES

CONWAY

Betws-Y-Coed

Waterloo Bridge, Betws-Y-Coed, Conway, Wales. (Photograph)

THIS ARCH WAS CONSTRUCTED IN THE SAME YEAR THE BATTLE OF WATERLOO WAS FOUGHT

Waterloo Bridge is an early cast-iron bridge, located half a mile south-east of Betws-Y-Coed, spanning the River Conwy, constructed by the civil engineer Thomas Telford. Although designed and constructed in 1815 its erection was not completed that year. It was raised during the building of the road from London to Holyhead (now the A5). It Is made from cast iron (apart from the stone bastions) and was only the seventh such bridge to be built.

POWYS

Llanrhaedr-Ym-Mochant

Memorial: Llanrhaedr-Ym-Mochant, Powys, Wales. (Photograph)

WATERLOO / 1815

Regimental Memorials

2nd (Royal North British) Regiment of Dragoons
Memorial: St Giles' Cathedral, Edinburgh, Midlothian, Scotland. (Photograph)

WATERLOO / THE REGIMENTAL GUIDON OR STANDARD / OF / THE ROYAL SCOTS GREYS / PLACED IN THIS CHURCH 1907

REFERENCE: *Almack, Edward, History of the Second Dragoons "Royal Scots Greys", 1908. Mellor, Stuart, Grey's Ghosts: men of the Scots Greys at Waterloo, 2012.*

3rd (Prince of Wales's) Dragoon Guards
Named on the Battlefield memorial: Talavera, Spain. (Photograph)

4th (Queen's Own) Dragoons
Named on the Battlefield memorial: Talavera, Spain. (Photograph)

6th (Inniskilling) Regiment of Dragons
Obelisk: Edgehill, Warwickshire. (Photograph)

THIS OBELISK WAS ERECTED BY / CHARLES CHAMBERS ESQ^{RE} R. N. / IN 1834 TO COMMEMORATE THE / BATTLE OF WATERLOO, / WHERE THE VITH INNISKILLING DRAGOONS / WERE COMMANDED BY / LIEUT. COL. F. S. MILLER / WHO, FOR HIS GALLANT CONDUCT / DURING THE ACTION IN WHICH HE WAS / VERY SEVERELY WOUNDED / WAS MADE A COMPANION OF THE MOST / HONORABLE ORDER OF THE BATH.

REFERENCE: *Jackson, E. S., Inniskilling Dragoons, the Records of an Old Heavy Cavalry Regiment, 1909, reprint, 2002.*

7th (Queen's Own) Regiment of Light Dragoons
Memorial stone with Celtic cross on top: St Keverne, Ireland. (Photograph)

IN MEMORY OF / THE OFFICERS AND MEN / OF HIS MAJESTY'S NAVAL AND / MILITARY FORCES WHO LOST THEIR / LIVES IN THE WRECK OF H.M. BRIG / OF WAR "PRIMROSE", ON THE / MANACLE ROCKS, 22ND OF JANUARY / 1809

The *Dispatch* and the *Primrose* were both wrecked on 22 Jan 1809. Troops were returning from Corunna and among them 3 officers and 70 men of the 7th Lt Dragoons in the *Dispatch*. They were all drowned and their bodies washed ashore and buried in St Keverne churchyard. The *Primrose* was carrying despatches to Spain and there was only one survivor out of a crew of 126 men.

12th (Prince of Wales's) Regiment of Light Dragoons
Regimental memorial: St Joseph's Church, Waterloo. (Photograph)

THIS MONUMENT WAS ERECTED / BY THE 12TH L^{T}. DRAGOONS TO THE MEMORY OF / THE OFFICERS AND SOLDIERS BELONGING TO THE / REGIMENT WHO WERE KILLED AT THE BATTLE OF WATERLOO / 18TH JUNE, 1815. / CAPTAIN EDWARD SANDYS / LIEUTENANT

LINDSAY BERTIE / CORNET JOHN E. LOCKHART / SERJEANT MAJORS / ROBERT NELSON THOMAS SCANLON / SERJEANTS / WILLIAM BAIRD THOMAS FINLAY / JAMES KIRBY / WILLIAM COX WILLIAM TOOLE / CORPORALS / WILLIAM HORSTON WILLIAM MARSH / SAMUEL NICHOLS / PRIVATES JOHN BAXTER ISAAC BISHOP WILLIAM BURLEY CHARLES CLARE THOMAS CLARKE CHARLES COCHRAN WILLIAM DAXTER GUY DEVITT HUGH DONNEGAN EDWARD EADIE JOHN EARLY JAMES FISHER FRANCIS FOSTER JOHN GLASS EDWARD GROWCOCK JEREMIAH HICKEY THOMAS HALFORD GEORGE HURST ROBERT KELLY JOHN KING FRANCIS LANG EDWARD M^C^DONALD JOHN MACFARLANE JAMES M^C^LASHER ROBERT MATTHEWSON DANIEL MURPHY PHILIP MURPHY JOHN NUGENT FRANCIS PERCY MICHAEL RAINSFORD JAMES SIVELL RICHARD SLADE HUGH SMITH WILLIAM STEWART JOSEPH WILLIAMSON JAMES WIGGINS JAMES WILMOT JOHN WELLS A TOTAL OF 3 OFFICERS AND 48 MEN.

REFERENCE: *Stewart, Patrick Findlater, History of the XII Royal Lancers (Prince of Wales's), 1950.*

14th (Duchess of York's Own) Regiment of Light Dragoons
Named on the Battlefield memorial: Talavera, Spain. (Photograph)

15th (King's) Regiment of Light Dragoons
Regimental memorial: St Joseph's Church, Waterloo. (Photograph)

TO / THE MEMORY / OF / MAJOR EDWIN GRIFFITH / LIEUTENANT ISAAC SHERWOOD & / LIEUTENANT HENRY BUCKLEY / OFFICERS IN THE XVTH KINGS REGT OF HUSSARS / (BRITISH) / WHO FELL IN THE BATTLE OF / WATERLOO / JUNE XVIIITH MDCCCXV. / THIS STONE WAS ERECTED BY THE OFFICERS / OF THAT REGIMENT / AS A TESTIMONY OF THEIR RESPECT / DULCE ET DECORUM EST PRO PATRIA MORI.

REFERENCE: *Wylly, H. C., XVth (The King's) Hussars, 1769–1913, 1914.*

16th (Queen's) Regiment of Light Dragoons
Regimental memorial tablet: Canterbury Cathedral, Canterbury, Kent. (Photograph)

TALAVERA / FUENTES D'ONOR / SALAMANCA / VITTORIA NIVE / PENINSULA WATERLOO / THE QUEEN'S LANCERS

REFERENCE: *Graham, Henry, History of the Sixteenth, the Queen's Light Dragoons, 1759 to 1912, Privately printed, 1912.*

18th Regiment of Light Dragoons
Named on the Battlefield memorial: Talavera, Spain. (Photograph)

Guard's Chapel, Wellington Barracks, Birdcage Walk, London.

The Guard's Chapel in Wellington Barracks was built for the Brigade of Guards in 1839–1840. Constructed on the model of a Grecian temple, it was given a thorough restoration in the late 1870s. This transformed the Chapel into a kind of military Valhalla, with marble tablets, brass panels and memorial windows commemorating virtually every Guard's officer of the previous half century. The chapel was destroyed by a flying bomb in 1944, and all of the memorials were used to form the foundations for the rebuilt Chapel.

The memorials relating to officers who served in the Peninsular and at Waterloo have been recorded from a volume of memorial inscriptions published by the Guards in 1887. None are still extant. Two stained glass windows in the east end of the Apse survived the bomb, and include six brass plates of which four commemorate General Sir Edward Bowater, Lt General Robert Cheney, Major General Francis Ker Hepburn and General Sir Henry Warde and are incorporated into the designs for the new Guard's Chapel, which was dedicated and opened for worship in 1963. (Photographs).

All of the memorial tablets and memorial windows commemorating officers of the Guards who served in the Peninsular and at Waterloo are recorded in the alphabetical section under the names and ranks that they held at Waterloo, or earlier if they did not serve at Waterloo. In addition, the following men, with the exception of ten who are also remembered on memorials individually are commemorated exclusively on Panels in the Chapel.

REFERENCE: *Royal Military Chapel. Wellington Barracks, 1882. Wilkinson, Sir Neville Rodwell, The Guards' Chapel, 1838–1938, 1938.*

PANEL VI.

CAPTAIN KEATING JAMES BRADFORD / BRIGADIER-GEN. ROBERT ANSTRUTHER / ENSIGN PAUL HARRY DURELL BURRARD / LIEUT.-COLONEL JOHN ROSS / CAPTAIN RICHARD BECKETT / CAPTAIN F. EDWARD JENKINSON / CAPT. AND ADJT. GEORGE BRYAN / ENSIGN HARRY PARKER / CAPTAIN SAMUEL WALKER / CAPTAIN JAMES BUCHANAN / CAPTAIN ROBERT DALRYMPLE / ENSIGN AND ADJT. THE HON. EDWARD METHUEN IRBY / ENSIGN STOPFORD RAM / ENSIGN EDWARD NOEL LONG / ENSIGN HON. JOHN ASHBURNHAM / LIEUT.-COL. GEORGE G. DONALDSON / ENSIGN E. MORANT / ENSIGN WILLIAM HENRY COMMERELL / ENSIGN GERVASE ANTHONY EYRE / ENSIGN MICHAEL WATTS / CAPTAIN WILLIAM HENRY SWANN / ENSIGN GEORGE PARKER COOKSON / ENSIGN THE HON. JOHN WINGFIELD / MAJOR EDWARD DALLING

PANEL VII.

MAJOR-GENERAL HENRY MACKINNON / CAPTAIN EDWARD HARVEY / ENSIGN WENTWORTH NOEL BURGESS / ENSIGN JOHN CHARLES BUCKERIDGE / MAJOR-GENERAL WILLIAM WHEATLEY / MAJOR-GENERAL RICHARD HULSE / LIEUT.-COL. JOHN SCROPE COLQUITT / ENSIGN WILLIAM BURRARD / LIEUT.-COL. JOHN CHARLES ROOKE / LIEUT.-COL. SAMUEL COOTE MARTIN / CAPTAIN CHARLES WILLIAM THOMPSON / CAPTAIN CAREY LE MARCHANT / ENSIGN JAMES OLIVER LAUTOUR / CAPTAIN AND ADJUTANT HENRY ROBERT WATSON / LIEUT.-COL. THE HON. JOHN DE COURCY / ENSIGN WYNDHAM KNATCHBULL / ENSIGN SIR THOMAS STYLES, BART / CAPTAIN WILLIAM HENRY CLITHEROW, / LIEUT-COL. THE HON. FRANCIS WHEELER HOOD / CAPTAIN WALTER VANE / LIEUT.-COL. GEORGE COLLIER / LIEUT.-COLONEL SIR HENRY SULLIVAN, BART / CAPTAIN HON. WILLIAM GEORGE CROFTON / CAPTAIN WILLIAM BURROUGHS / ENSIGN FREDERICK VACHELL / ENSIGN WILLIAM PITT / CAPTAIN CHARLES LAURENCE WHITE / CAPTAIN JOHN BRIDGER SHIFFNER / CAPTAIN LUKE MAHON / CAPTAIN AND ADJUTANT FRANCIS RALPH THOMAS HOLBURNE

PANEL VIII.

LIEUT.-COL. THE HON. JAMES MACDONALD / LIEUT.-COL. GEORGE CLIFTON / CAPTAIN JOHN BULTEEL / LIEUT.-COL. ROBERT MERCER / LIEUT.-COL. WILLIAM MILLER / CAPTAIN EDWARD GROSE / CAPTAIN ROBERT ADAIR / CAPTAIN THOMAS BROW / ENSIGN JAMES LORD HAY / ENSIGN THE HON. SAMUEL P. BARRINGTON / LIEUT.-COL. SIR FRANCIS D'OYLEY, K.C.B. / LIEUT.-COL. WILLIAM HENRY MILNES / LIEUT.-COL. EDWARD STABLES / LIEUT.-COL. CHARLES THOMAS / CAPTAIN NEWTON CHAMBERS / ENSIGN EDWARD PARDOE / CAPTAIN JOHN LUCIE BLACKMAN / CAPTAIN EVERARD SUMNER / LIEUT.-COL.

HON. SIR ALEXANDER GORDON, K.C.B. / LIEUT.-COL. CHARLES FOX CANNING / CAPTAIN HON. HASTINGS FORBES / CAPTAIN THOMAS CRAUFORD / CAPTAIN JOHN ASHTON / CAPTAIN WILLIAM STOTHERT / ENSIGN C. SIMPSON / LIEUT. GEORGE RICHARD BUCKLEY / LIEUT.-COL. SIR HENRY HOLLIS BRADFORD, K.C.B.

1st Regiment of Foot Guards

Regimental memorial plaque: Hougoumont, Waterloo. (Photograph)

FIRST REGIMENT OF FOOT GUARDS / IN MEMORY OF / THE OFFICERS AND MEN / OF THE LIGHT COMPANIES / OF THE 2ND AND 3RD BATTALIONS / WHO DIED DEFENDING HOUGOUMONT / 18TH JUNE 1815 / THIS TABLET WAS ERECTED IN 1977 / BY THEIR SUCCESSOR OF THE / FIRST OR GRENADIER GUARDS

Memorial tablet: St Joseph's Church, Waterloo. (Photograph)

SACRED / TO THE MEMORY / OF / LIEUT. COLONEL EDWARD STABLES. / LIEUT. COLONEL SIR FRANCIS D'OYLY KCB. / LIEUT. COLONEL CHARLES THOMAS. / LIEUT. COLONEL WILLIAM MILLER. / LIEUT. COLONEL WILLIAM HENRY MILNES. / CAPTAIN ROBERT ADAIR. / CAPTAIN EDWARD GROSE. / CAPTAIN NEWTON CHAMBERS. / CAPTAIN THOMAS BROWN. / ENSIGN EDWARD PARDOE. / ENSIGN JAMES LORD HAY. / ENSIGN THE HONBLE S. S. P. BARRINGTON. / OF / HIS BRITANNIC MAJESTY'S / 1ST REGIMENT OF FOOT GUARDS / WHO FELL GLORIOUSLY IN THE BATTLES / OF QUATRE BRAS AND WATERLOO ON / THE 16TH AND 18TH OF JUNE / 1815. / THE OFFICERS OF THE / REGIMENT HAVE ERECTED THIS / MONUMENT IN COMMEMORATION / OF THE FALL OF THEIR / GALLANT COMPANIONS.

Memorial: Guards Cemetery, St Etienne, Bayonne, France. (Photograph)

SACRED TO THE MEMORY OF THE UNDER-NAMED BRITISH / OFFICERS WHO GALLANTLY FELL AT / THE SORTIE MADE BY THE GARRISON / FROM THE CITADEL OF / BAYONNE ON THE 14TH OF APRIL 1814 / COLDSTREAM GUARDS / LIEUT-COLONELS / G. COLLIER / SIR H. SULLIVAN, BART AND M. P. / CAPTAINS / HONBLE W. G. CROFTON / W. BURROUGHS, ADJT / ENSIGNS / K. VACHELL W. PITT. / 1ST REGT OF GUARDS / ENSIGN / W. VANE / 3RD REGT OF GUARDS / CAPTAINS / C. L. WHITE. J. B. SHIFFNER. / LIEUT / F. HOLBURNE, ADJT / 60TH REGT / LIEUT / J. HAMILTON / THIS TABLET / WAS PLACED TO THE MEMORY OF THE / ABOVE-NAMED OFFICERS BY THEIR / FRIEND AND COMPANION AT THE SORTIE / J. V. HARVEY / FORMERLY CAPTAIN IN THE / COLDSTREAM GUARDS AND SINCE / H. M. CONSUL AT BAYONNE / 1830.

Reference: Hamilton, Sir Frederick William, Origin and History of the First or Grenadier Guards, 3 vols, 1874.

Coldstream Guards

Regimental memorial tablet: Hougoumont, Waterloo. (Photograph)

IN MEMORY / OF THE OFFICERS AND MEN OF THE / 2ND BATTALION COLD STREAM GUARDS / WHO, WHILE DEFENDING HOUGOUMONT FARM / SUCCESSFULLY HELD THIS SOUTH GATE / FROM SUCCESSIVE ATTACKS THROUGHOUT: / 18TH JUNE 1815 / A LA MEMOIRE / DES OFFICIERS ET SOLDATS DU / 2EME BATAILLON DES COLDSTREAM GUARDS / QUI ONT PARTICIPE A LA DEFENSE DE HOUGOUMONT / ET ONT RESISTE A TOUTES LES ATTAQUES / DIRIGEES CONTRE LA PORT SUD / LE 18 JUIN 1815

Memorial: Guards Cemetery, St Etienne, Bayonne, France. (Photograph)

SACRED TO THE MEMORY / OF THE UNDER-NAMED BRITISH / OFFICERS WHO GALLANTLY FELL AT / THE SORTIE MADE BY THE GARRISON / FROM THE CITADEL OF / BAYONNE ON THE 14TH OF APRIL 1814 / COLDSTREAM GUARDS / LIEUT-COLONELS / G. COLLIER / SIR H. SULLIVAN, BART AND M. P. / CAPTAINS / HON^{BLE} W. G. CROFTON / W. BURROUGHS, ADJ^{T} / ENSIGNS / K. VACHELL W. PITT. / 1ST REG^{T} OF GUARDS / ENSIGN / W. VANE / 3RD REG^{T} OF GUARDS / CAPTAINS / C. L. WHITE. J. B. SHIFFNER. / LIEUT / F. HOLBURNE, ADJ^{T} / 60TH REG^{T} / LIEUT / J. HAMILTON / THIS TABLET / WAS PLACED TO THE MEMORY OF THE / ABOVE-NAMED OFFICERS BY THEIR / FRIEND AND COMPANION AT THE SORTIE / J. V. HARVEY / FORMERLY CAPTAIN IN THE / COLDSTREAM GUARDS AND SINCE / H. M. CONSUL AT BAYONNE / 1830.

Named on the Battlefield memorial: Talavera, Spain. (Photograph)
Reference: Mackinnon, Daniel, Origin and services of the Coldstream Guards, 2 vols, 1833, reprint, 2010.

3rd Regiment of Foot Guards
Memorial: Guards Cemetery, St Etienne, Bayonne, France. (Photograph)

BURIAL PLACE / OF THE / OFFICERS OF THE THIRD GUARDS / WHO FELL IN THE SORTIE / FROM THE / CITADEL OF BAYONNE / ON THE 14TH OF APRIL 1814. / THIS GROUND FORMED PART OF THE SITE / OF THE CAMP OF THEIR REGIMENT / AND ENCLOSED BY THE LAST SURVIVING SISTER / OF CAPTAIN HOLBURNE / A.D. 1876

Memorial: Guards Cemetery, St Etienne, Bayonne, France. (Photograph)

SACRED TO THE MEMORY OF THE UNDER-NAMED BRITISH / OFFICERS WHO GALLANTLY FELL AT / THE SORTIE MADE BY THE GARRISON / FROM THE CITADEL OF / BAYONNE ON THE 14TH OF APRIL 1814 / COLDSTREAM GUARDS / LIEUT-COLONELS / G. COLLIER / SIR H. SULLIVAN, BART AND M. P. / CAPTAINS / HON^{BLE} W. G. CROFTON / W. BURROUGHS, ADJ^{T} / ENSIGNS / K. VACHELL W. PITT. / 1ST REG^{T} OF GUARDS / ENSIGN / W. VANE / 3RD REG^{T} OF GUARDS / CAPTAINS / C. L. WHITE. J. B. SHIFFNER. / LIEUT / F. HOLBURNE, ADJ^{T} / 60TH REG^{T} / LIEUT / J. HAMILTON / THIS TABLET / WAS PLACED TO THE MEMORY OF THE / ABOVE-NAMED OFFICERS BY THEIR / FRIEND AND COMPANION AT THE SORTIE / J. V. HARVEY / FORMERLY CAPTAIN IN THE / COLDSTREAM GUARDS AND SINCE / H. M. CONSUL AT BAYONNE / 1830.

Regimental memorial plaque: Hougoumont, Waterloo. (Photograph)

3RD REGIMENT OF FOOT GUARDS / IN MEMORY OF / THE OFFICERS AND MEN / OF THE 2ND BATTALION / WHO DIED / DEFENDING THIS FARM / JUNE 18TH 1815

Memorial tablet: St Joseph's Church, Waterloo. (Photograph)

TO THE MEMORY / OF THE UNDER MENTIONED GALLANT OFFICERS / OF THE SECOND BATTALION / OF HIS BRITANNIC MAJESTY'S / THIRD REGIMENT OF FOOT GUARDS, / WHO BRAVELY FELL / IN THE BATTLE OF WATERLOO, / ON THE 18TH JUNE 1815: / THIS TABLET IS INSCRIBED BY / THEIR COLONEL / HIS ROYAL HIGHNESS / PRINCE WILLIAM FREDERICK, / DUKE OF GLOUCESTER AND EDINBURGH / &c. &c. &c. &c. / FIELD MARSHAL OF HIS MAJESTY'S FORCES. / LIEUT. COLONEL THE HON^{BLE} SIR ALEX^{R} GORDON K.C.B. / CHARLES

FOX CANNING. / CAPTAINS WILLIAM STOTHERT. / THE HON^BLE HASTINGS FORBES. / THOMAS CRAUFURD. / JOHN ASHTON. / ENSIGN SIMPSON.

Named on the Battlefield memorial: Talavera, Spain. (Photograph)

REFERENCE: Maurice, Sir Frederick Barton, History of the Scots Guards from the Creation of the Regiment to the end of the Great War, 2 vols, 1934.

1st (Royal Scots) Regiment of Foot
Regimental memorial tablet: St Joseph's Church, Waterloo. (Photograph)

TO THE MEMORY OF / THE UNDERNAMED OFFICERS ON THE 3RD BATTALION OF HER / BRITANNIC MAJESTY'S REGIMENT OF ROYAL SCOTS, / WHO FELL IN THE BATTLE OF / QUATRE BRAS AND WATERLOO, / ON THE 16TH AND 18TH JUNE 1815 / AND OF THE GALLANT SERGEANT MAJOR, / (WHO WAS SHOT THROUGH THE HEART / WHILE HOLDING THE KING'S COLOUR, / IN THE ACT OF BEARING WHICH / ONE LIEUTENANT AND THREE ENSIGNS / HAD SUCCESSIVELY FALLEN) / THIS TABLET IS INSCRIBED. / AS A TESTIMONY OF PERSONAL REGARD FOR THE INDIVIDUALS / AND OF THE ADMIRATION OF THE GALLANT SERVICES OF THE CORPS / BY THEIR COLONEL / HIS ROYAL HIGHNESS, / PRINCE EDWARD, / DUKE OF KENT AND STRATHEARN / & & & & / FIELD MARSHAL OF HIS MAJESTY'S FORCES / AND GOVERNOR OF GIBRALTAR. / CAPTAIN BUCKLEY / LIEUTENANTS ARMSTRONG O'NEILL YOUNG / ENSIGNS ROBERTSON KENNEDY ANDERSON / SERGEANT MAJOR QUICK

REFERENCE: Leask, J. C. and M. McCance, Regimental records of the Royal Scots (The First Royal Regiment of Foot), 1915, reprint 2011.

2nd (Queen's) Royal Regiment of Foot
Regimental memorial tablet: St Michael's Cathedral, Barbados, West Indies. (South wall). (Photograph)

SACRED / TO THE MEMORY OF THE FOLLOWING OFFICERS / OF THE 2ND (OR QUEEN'S) ROYAL REGIMENT / BURIED NEAR THIS SPOT, / WHO AFTER A SERIES OF MERITORIOUS SERVICES / UNDER HIS GRACE THE DUKE OF WELLINGTON / AND IN ALMOST EVERY QUARTER OF THE GLOBE / FELL TOGETHER WITH MANY OLD & VALUABLE / NON-COMM^D OFFICERS & SOLDIERS EARLY / VICTIMS TO A DESTRUCTIVE FEVER RAGING IN / BARBADOS A. D. 1816. / CAPT^N J. GORDON SEN^R LIEU^T GRANT. / LIEU^T CLUTTERBUCK LIEU^T ADJ^T SPENCER / LIEU^T MCDOUGALL LIEUT MASSIE / LIEUT GRAY ENSIGN RICHMOND / LIEUT NORMAN ASST SURG^N PRENDERGAST. / BRAVE MEN / YE DESERVED A BRIGHTER FIELD, YET SHALL THE / PALE ROSE SHED ITS DEWS UPON YOUR UNTIMELY / GRAVE, & MEMORY CHERISH YOUR CONTEMPLATION / WITH NO LESS DIGNITY THAT YE FELL BEFORE / AN ALMIGHTY HAND. / THIS STONE / IS PLACED HERE / AS A TRIBUTE OF REGARD TO DEPARTED MERIT BY / LT COL. H. C. E. VERNON GRAHAM / COMMANDING THE REG^T. / C. ASHMEAD, SCULP. QUEENS.

Memorial tablet: St Michael's Cathedral, Barbados, West Indies. (Photograph)

MAJOR JAMES CONNOLLY. CAPT^N JOHN GORDON. LIEUT^T WILL^M CLUTTERBUCK. LIEUT^T DUNCAN M^CDOUGALL. LIEUT^T WILLIAM GRAY. LIEUT^T JOHN NORMAN. LIEUT^T JOHN ADAMS. LIEUT^T CHARLES GRANT. LIEUT^T THOMAS MASSIE. LIEUT^T ANDREW RICHMOND. ADJ^T JAMES SPENCER. ASST SURG^N JOHN PRENDERGAST.
SACRED TO THE MEMORY OF THE ABOVE NAMED OFFICERS / WHO HAVING FAITHFULLY SERVED THEIR KING AND COUNTRY / IN VARIOUS PARTS OF THE WORLD, FELL VICTIMS

TO THE FATAL CLIMATE, / IN THE YEAR OF OUR LORD 1816 AND 1817. / THIS MONUMENT IS ERECTED / AS A TESTIMONY OF AFFECTIONATE ESTEEM, BY THEIR BROTHER OFFICERS. / OF THE 2ND OR QUEEN'S ROYAL REGIMENT OF FOOT.

Regimental memorial tablet: Afghan Memorial Church, St John the Evangelist, Colaba, Bombay, India. (M.I.)

CAPTAIN H. D. KEITH. LIEUTENANTS T. GRAVATT. H. HALKETT. E. W. SPARKES. T. A. NIXON. ASSISTANT SURGEON W. HIBBERT MD.

Reference: Davis, John, The History of the Second Queen's Royal Regiment, now the Queen's Royal West Surrey) Regiment, 9 vols, 1887–1961.

3rd (East Kent) Regiment of Foot
Named on the Battlefield memorial: Talavera, Spain. (Photograph)

4th (King's Own) Regiment of Foot
Regimental memorial brass: St. Michael's Cathedral, Barbados, West Indies. (South wall). (Photograph)

IN MEMORY OF / LT COL J. PIPER, MAJOR J. W. FLETCHER, CAPT J. EDGELL. / LIEUTENANTS / W. BLAGROVE, J. DUTHY, F. ROBINSON, I. BEER, R .E. COTTON. / ENSIGNS / F. CLARKE, R. GAMBLE, H.M. SHIPTON, J. LORAINE. / QUARTER MASTERS / T. RICHARDS, B. DORAN, E. KELLY. / 21 SGTS 1 DR 245 RANK AND FILE / 4TH THE KING'S OWN / WHO DIED WHEN THE REGIMENT WAS QUARTERED IN THE / WEST INDIES, FROM 14TH APRIL 1819, TO 10TH FEN 1826. / (VERSE)

Reference: Cowper, L. I., The King's Own. The Story of a Royal Regiment, Vol. 1 1680–1814, Vol. 2 1814–1914, 1939.

5th (Northumberland) Regiment of Foot
Memorial tablet: Badajoz Wall, British Cemetery, Elvas, Portugal. (Photograph)

QUO FATA VOCANT / ERECTED BY THE FIFTH FUSILIERS / IN MEMORY OF THE / SECOND BATTALION FIFTH / (NORTHUMBERLAND) / REGIMENT OF FOOT / WHOSE INDOMITABLE COURAGE / AT THE CAPTURE / Of THE CITADEL MADE CERTAIN THE FALL OF / BADAJOZ, 6TH APRIL 1812. / "THOUGH LADDER AFTER LADDER WAS FLUNG DOWN BY / THE DEFENDERS, AND THE RUNGS WERE SLIPPERY / WITH BLOOD, THOSE BELOW TOOK THE PLACES OF / THOSE WHO FELL, SO SWIFTLY THAT IN THE END / A LODGEMENT WAS MADE AND THE RAMPARTS CLEARED" / ARTHUR BRYANT / DEDICATED 14TH MAY 2000

Reference: Walker, H. M., History of the Northumberland Fusiliers, 1674–1902, 1919, reprint 2012.

7th (Royal Fusiliers) Regiment of Foot
Memorial tablet: Albuera Wall, British Cemetery, Elvas, Portugal. (Photograph)

IN MEMORY OF / THE OFFICERS AND MEN / OF / THE FUSILIERS BRIGADE / 1ST AND 2ND BNS, THE ROYAL FUSILIERS – 7TH FOOT / 1ST BN, THE ROYAL WELCH FUSILIERS – 23RD FOOT / WHO AT GRIEVOUS COST / TURNED THE TIDE OF BATTLE AT / ALBUHERA / 16 MAY 1811 / THEN WAS SEEN WITH WHAT A / STRENGTH AND MAJESTY /THE BRITISH SOLDIER FIGHTS / NOTHING COULD STOP THAT ASTONISHING INFANTRY / SIR WILLIAM NAPIER / ERECTED BY BOTH REGIMENTS ON 14TH MAY 2000

Named on the Battlefield memorial: Talavera, Spain. (Photograph)

Cross on Pedestal monument in railed enclosure: On road near the Ermita de los Martires, Valverde. Portugal. No inscription on the memorial. (Photograph)

Reported that the memorial was erected when the bones of families in Valverde, together with bones of Peninsular War dead which had been buried in 1811 were removed to the new Cemetery outside of the town. Believed to contain the bones of William Myers.

23rd (Royal Welch Fusiliers) Regiment of Foot.
Memorial tablet: Albuera Wall, British Cemetery, Elvas, Portugal. (Photograph)

IN MEMORY OF / THE OFFICERS AND MEN / OF / THE FUSILIERS BRIGADE / 1ST AND 2ND BNS, THE ROYAL FUSILIERS – 7TH FOOT / 1ST BN, THE ROYAL WELCH FUSILIERS – 23RD FOOT / WHO AT GRIEVOUS COST / TURNED THE TIDE OF BATTLE AT ALBUHERA / 16 MAY 1811 / THEN WAS SEEN WITH WHAT A / STRENGTH AND MAJESTY /THE BRITISH SOLDIER FIGHTS / NOTHING COULD STOP THAT ASTONISHING INFANTRY / SIR WILLIAM NAPIER / ERECTED BY BOTH REGIMENTS ON 14TH MAY 2000

24th (2nd Warwickshire) Regiment of Foot
Named on the Battlefield memorial: Talavera, Spain. (Photograph)

27TH (Inniskilling) Regiment of Foot
Regimental memorial tablet: Mont St Jean, near cross roads, Waterloo. (Photograph)

IN MEMORY OF THE HEROIC STAND BY / THE 27TH (INNISKILLING) REGIMENT OF / FOOT AT THE BATTLE OF WATERLOO ON / 18TH JUNE 1815 WHEN, OF THE 747 / OFFICERS AND MEN OF THE REGIMENT / WHO JOINED BATTLE, 495 WERE KILLED OR / WOUNDED. A NOBLE RECORD OF / STUBBORN ENDURANCE. / OF THEM THE DUKE OF WELLINGTON SAID, / "AE, THEY SAVED THE CENTRE OF MY LINE." / ERECTED BY THEIR SUCCESSORS / THE ROYAL IRISH RANGERS / (27TH INNISKILLING) 83RD, 87TH / 18 JUNE 1990

REFERENCE: *Royal Inniskilling Fusiliers, being the History of the Regiment from December 1688 to July 1914, revised edn, 1934.*

28th (North Gloucestershire) Regiment of Foot
Regimental memorial tablet: St Joseph's Church, Waterloo. (Photograph)

28th / REGIMENT. / TO THE MEMORY / OF THE OFFICERS AND / PRIVATES OF THE 28TH / REGIMENT, WHO FELL IN / THE BATTLES OF QUATRE / BRAS, AND WATERLOO, ON THE / 16TH AND 18TH JUNE 1815. / THIS PYRAMID IS ERECTED BY / COLONEL SIR PHILIP BELSON, AND THE / OFFICERS OF THAT CORPS, WHO WERE / ENGAGED IN THAT MEMORABLE VICTORY. / HIC MANUS, OB PATRIAM PUGNANDO VULNERA PASSI.

REFERENCE: *Cadell, Charles, Narratives of the Campaigns of the Twenty-Eighth Regiment since their return from Egypt in 1802, 1835.*

29th (Worcestershire) Regiment of Foot
Named on the Battlefield memorial: Talavera, Spain. (Photograph)

30th (Cambridgeshire) Regiment of Foot
Regimental memorial tablet: St Joseph's Church, Waterloo. (Photograph)

SACRED / TO THE MEMORY OF THE OFFICERS / OF THE 2ND BATTALION 30TH REGIMENT OF FOOT / WHO FELL IN THE / BATTLE OF WATERLOO / 18 JUNE 1815. / MAJOR T. W. CHAMBERS. / CAPTAIN A. M^{C}NAB / LIEU^{TS} H. BEERE. / EDW^{D} PRENDERGAST. / ENS^{NS} J. JAMES / J. BULLEN / AND OF / 18 NON COMMISSIONED OFFICERS AND / 11 PRIVATES OF THE SAME CORPS / WHO ALSO FELL ON / THAT MEMORABLE DAY.

Memorial: St Mylor's Churchyard, Mylor, Falmouth, Cornwall. (Photograph)

TO THE / MEMORY OF THE WARRIORS, / WOMEN AND CHILDREN, / WHO ON THEIR RETURN TO ENGLAND / FROM THE COAST OF SPAIN; / UNHAPPILY PERISHED / IN THE WRECK OF THE / QUEEN TRANSPORT / ON TREFUGIS POINT, JAN^{Y} 14 1814. / THIS STONE IS ERECTED AS A TESTIMONY / OF REGRET FOR THEIR FATE BY THE / INHABITANTS OF THE PARISH.

The *Queen Transport* was wrecked in a storm on 14 Jan 1814 off Trefugis Point, Falmouth. The ship broke up in 45 minutes and of the 315 men, women and children aboard, only 124 reached the safety of the shore. She was bringing home mainly wounded Royal Artillery men from Lisbon. There were also 32 men from the 30th Foot. Among them was Robert Daniel, his wife and five children. They were all drowned except Lt Daniel who reached shore. He died in 1852 and is buried in Kensal Green Cemetery.

Catherine Daniel is buried in Mylor Churchyard, Cornwall. (M.I.)

"IN MEMORY OF CATHERINE, WIFE OF LIEUT. ROBERT DANIEL, 30TH REGT. ALSO THEIR CHILDREN VIZ. MARGARET, ELEANOR, WILLIAM, ROBERT AND EDWARD ALEXANDER, WHO UNHAPPILY PERISHED IN THE WRECK OF THE 'QUEEN' TRANSPORT ON THE AWFUL MORNING OF THE 14TH JAN 1814. LEAVING AN UNFORTUNATE HUSBAND AND FATHER TO LAMENT THEIR LOSS TO THE END OF HIS EXISTENCE."

Memorial stone near sea shore: Mylor, Falmouth, Cornwall. (Photograph)

T. B.

Memorial: Penryn, Cornwall. (M.I.)

"BENEATH THIS STONE, (PLACED BY THE INHABITANTS OF PENRYN AS A MEMORIAL OF THE AWFUL DISPENSATION) WERE INTERRED IN ONE GRAVE THE BODIES OF TWENTY SHIPWRECKED STRANGERS! THESE UNFORTUNATE PERSONS, INVALIDS AND FOLLOWERS OF THE BRITISH ARMY IN SPAIN, HAD RECENTLY ARRIVED AT FALMOUTH FROM LISBON, IN THE QUEEN TRANSPORT. EARLY IN MORNING OF JANUARY 14TH, 1814, DURING A VIOLENT SNOW STORM THE SHIP PARTED FROM HER ANCHOR, WAS DASHED IN PIECES ON TREFUSIS POINT".

Reference: Divall, Carole, Inside the Regiment: the officers and men of the 30th Regiment during the Revolutionary and Napoleonic Wars, 2011. Divall, Carole, Redcoats against Napoleon: the 30th Regiment during the Revolutionary and Napoleonic Wars, 2009.

31st (Huntingdonshire) Regiment of Foot
Obelisk: Albuera, Spain. (Photograph)

2ND / 31ST FOOT / HUNTINGDONSHIRE / (LATER BECAME) / THE EAST SURREY REGIMENT / "AFTER WHEN THE REST OF THE BRIGADE WAS SWEPT / OFF BY CAVALRY THE LITTLE BATTALION ALONE / HELD ITS GROUND"

Named on the Battlefield memorial: Talavera, Spain. (Photograph)

33rd (1st Yorkshire West Riding) Regiment of Foot
Regimental memorial tablet: St Joseph's Church, Waterloo. (Photograph)

TO THE MEMORY / OF / CAPTAINS / JOHN HAIGH / HENRY RISHTON BUCK / LIEUTENANTS JOHN BOYCE / JAMES HART / ARTHUR GORE / THOMAS HAIGH / JOHN CAMERON / OF THE 33RD REGIMENT OF FOOT / WHO WERE KILLED AT THE BATTLES OF / QUATRE BRAS AND WATERLOO. / THIS STONE IS ERECTED BY THEIR BROTHER / OFFICERS AS A MARK OF THEIR ESTEEM / AND REGARD.

REFERENCE: Lee, Albert, History of the Thirty-Third Foot, Duke of Wellington's (West Riding) Regiment, 1922.

38th (1st Staffordshire) Regiment of Foot
Memorial: Lichfield Cathedral. (Photograph)

XXXVIITH / STAFFORDSHIRE REGIMENT / NOW / 1ST BATT. SOUTH STAFFORDSHIRE REGIMENT / TO THE GLORY OF GOD / AND IN MEMORY OF / THE OFFICERS, NON-COMMISSIONED OFFICERS AND MEN / OF THE ABOVE REGIMENT / WHO FELL IN ACTION OR WHO DIED OF THEIR WOUNDS / IN THE FOLLOWING CAMPAIGNS / PENINSULA, / BURMA, / CRIMEA, / INDIAN MUTINY, / EGYPT 1882. / THIS WINDOW IS DEDICATED / BY THE OFFICERS PAST AND PRESENT / OF THE ABOVE REGIMENT. / 1884.

REFERENCE: Jones, James P., History of the South Staffordshire Regiment (1705–1923), 1923.

40th (2nd Somersetshire) Regiment of Foot
Obelisk: Chicksands Priory, Chicksands, Bedfordshire. (Photograph)

Side One:

TO THE MEMORY OF / THE OFFICERS NON-COMMISSIONED OFFICERS AND PRIVATE SOLDIERS / OF THE FORTIETH REGIMENT OF FOOT / WHO GLORIOUSLY FELL IN THE CONTEST / MAINTAINED BY GREAT BRITAIN AGAINST REVOLUTIONARY FRANCE, / COMMENCING IN THE YEAR 1793, / AND TERMINATING IN THE YEAR 1815 / BY THE BATTLE OF WATERLOO AND THE CAPTURE OF PARIS. / THIS PILLAR IS ERECTED / BY GENERAL SIR GEORGE OSBORN BART THEIR COLONEL / IN HUMBLE GRATITUDE TO DIVINE PROVIDENCE / FOR THE SUCCESS OF HIS MAJESTY'S ARMS / AND THE RESTORATION OF THE BLESSINGS / OF PEACE.

Side Two:

FOR PEACE RESTORED TO EUROPE / AND FREEDOM TO THE NATIONS, / OPPRESSED, INSULTED, / BY THE AMBITION OF ONE MAN; / WHO IN THE END MIGHT HAVE DEFIED

RESISTANCE, EXTINGUISHED HOPE, / BUT FOR THEIR HEROIC EFFORTS, / AIDED BY THE COUNSELS AND VALOUR OF THIS COUNTRY, / WHICH CLAIMS SO PROUD A SHARE IN THE GLORY OF THEIR DELIVERANCE / FOR THESE BLESSINGS, / LONG AND ARDUOUSLY CONTENDED FOR. / LET GRATITUDE BE FELT / TO THOSE WHETHER OF THIS OR FOREIGN LANDS, / WHO NOBLY CONTRIBUTED TO PROCURE THEM, / BUT ABOVE ALL / TO THE POWER INVISIBLE SUPREME

Side Three:

THIS PILLAR / WAS RESTORED AND REMOVED TO ITS PRESENT SITE / BY SIR GEORGE ROBERT OSBORNE BARONET / IN COMMEMORATION OF A / TREATY OF PEACE / SIGNED AT PARIS / ON THE THIRTEENTH DAY OF MARCH, 1856 / BETWEEN THE ALLIED POWERS OF / GREAT BRITAIN, FRANCE, SARDINIA AND TURKEY / ON THE ONE SIDE AND / RUSSIA / ON THE OTHER AT THE TERMINATION / OF THE ARDUOUS AND MEMORABLE CAMPAIGN OF THE / CRIMEA / ALMA BALACLAVA INKERMANN SEBASTOPOL.

Side Four:

THIS MONUMENT / WAS RESTORED AND REMOVED IN 1975/76 TO THIS / LOCATION BY MEMBERS OF / THE UNITED STATES AIR FORCE STATIONED AT / ROYAL AIR FORCE CHICKSANDS / IN RECOGNITION OF THE LASTING BONDS OF / FRIENDSHIP BETWEEN THE PEOPLES OF AMERICA / AND TO COMMEMORATE / 25 YEARS OF OPERATIONS HERE BY THE UNITED STATES / AIR FORCE SECURITY SERVICE, THE BICENTENNIAL OF / AMERICAN INDEPENDENCE AND EUROPEAN / ARCHITECTURAL HERITAGE YEAR.

Named on the Battlefield memorial: Talavera, Spain. (Photograph)

Memorial tablet: Afghan Memorial Church, St John the Evangelist, Colada, Bombay, India. (M.I.)

"LIEUTENANT COL T. POWELL KH, LIEUTENANT H. F. VALIANT, R. ARMSTRONG, A. J. MAGNAY, ENSIGN W. IRWIN, R.A. LINDSAY, Q/M C. PHILIP"

Reference: Smythies, R. H., Historical Record of the 40th (2nd Somersetshire) Regiment, now 1st Battalion the Prince of Wales's Volunteers (South Lancashire Regiment) from its Formation in 1717 to 1893, 1894.

42nd (Royal Highland) Regiment of Foot
Memorial tablet: Dunkeld Cathedral, Dunkeld, Scotland. (Photograph)

IN MEMORY OF / THE OFFICERS NON-COMMISSIONED OFFICERS / AND / PRIVATE SOLDIERS / OF THE / 42ND ROYAL HIGHLANDERS – THE BLACK WATCH / WHO FELL IN WAR / FROM THE CREATION OF THE REGIMENT / TO / THE CLOSE OF THE INDIAN MUTINY / 1859. / THE TEN INDEPENDENT COMPANIES OF THE PREACADAN / DUCH, OR BLACK WATCH, WERE FORMED INTO A / REGIMENT ON THE / 25TH OCTOBER 1739, AND THE / FIRST MUSTER TOOK PLACE MAY 1740, / IN A FIELD BETWEEN TAYBRIDGE / AND ABERFELDY. / HERE, IT IS 'MONG THE HILLS THAT NURSED EACH HARDY GAEL, / OUR VOTIVE MARBLE TELLS THE SOLDIERS TALE: / ART'S MAGIC POWER EACH PERISHED FRIEND RECALLS, AND HEROES HAUNT THESE OLD CATHEDRAL WALLS. / ERECTED BY THE OFFICERS OF THE CORPS / 1872 / FONTENOY FLANDERS TICONDEROGA MARTINIQUE GUADELOUPE HAVANNAH EGYPT / CORUNNA FUENTES D'ONOR PYRENEES NIVELLE NIVE ORTHES TOULOUSE PENINSULA / WATERLOO ALMA SEVASTOPOL LUCKNOW.

Reference: *Stewart, John, The Royal Highland Regiment, the Black Watch, formerly 42nd and 73rd Foot, Medal Roll, 1801–1911, 1913. Naval and Military Press reprint.*

43rd (Monmouthshire) Light Infantry Regiment of Foot
Memorial hatchment: St Mary's Church, New Plymouth, New Zealand. (Photocopy illustration)

43 / MONMOUTHSHIRE LIGHT INFANTRY / VIMIERA. CORUNNA. BUSACO. F. D'ONOR. C RODRIGO. BADAJOZ. / SALAMANCA. VITTORIA. NIVELLE. / NIVE. TOULOUSE. PENINSULA.

Reference: *Oxfordshire and Buckinghamshire Light Infantry Chronicle, 1901, p 101.*

Memorial plaque: Ciudad Rodrigo, Spain. (On walls above breach). (Photograph)

MAJOR GENERAL ROBERT CRAUFURD / TO THE MEMORY OF MAJOR GENERAL ROBERT CRAUFURD AND THOSE OF THE 43RD AND 52ND LIGHT INFANTRY AND THE 95TH RIFLES OF THE LIGHT DIVISION, WHICH HE COMMANDED WITH SUCH DISTINCTION, AND THEIR COMRADES OF THE 60TH, ALL OF WHOM FELL IN THE STORMING OF THE BREACHES, THROUGH WHICH CIUDAD RODRIGO WAS LIBERATED ON 19TH JANUARY 1812. / THIS PLAQUE IS ERECTED BY THEIR HEIRS, THE ROYAL GREEN JACKETS, MINDFUL OF THE HISTORIC EFFORTS OF THE SPANISH AND BRITISH TO FREE THE PENINSULA 1808–1813.

Reference: *Levine, Sir Richard, Historical records of the Forty-Third Regiment Monmouthshire Light Infantry with a roll of the Officers and their services from the period of Embodiment to the close of 1867, 1868, reprint 2012.*

45th (1st Nottinghamshire) Regiment of Foot
Named on the Battlefield memorial: Talavera, Spain. (Photograph)

48th (Northamptonshire) Regiment of Foot
Regimental memorial tablet: Badajoz Wall, British Cemetery, Elvas, Portugal. (Photograph)

THIS PLAQUE HAS BEEN ERECTED / IN PROUD AND HONOURED MEMORY / OF ALL THE OFFICERS / NON-COMMISSIONED OFFICERS / AND MEN OF THE / 48TH FOOT / THE NORTHAMPTONSHIRE REGIMENT / WHO MADE THE SUPREME SACRIFICE / AT / ALBUHERA AND BADAJOZ / IN / 1811 AND 1812

Slate tablet: Trinity Cemetery, Tunbridge Wells, Kent. (Photograph)
At the head of the grave to Lt General Middlemore is a slate tablet erected in 1907 by the 1st Northamptonshire Regiment, (formerly 48th Foot), commemorating the Battle of Talavera. Now badly flaked the inscription is not readable, but the inscription has been recorded from a memorial inscription:

"TALAVERA / IT WAS ON THE ADVANCE OF THE BATTALION TO THE RESCUE OF THE GUARDS THAT COL. DONELLAN WAS STRUCK AND PAINFUL AS MUST HAVE BEEN THE WOUND, HIS COUNTENANCE NOT ONLY DID NOT BETRAY HIS SUFFERING BUT PRESERVED HIS USUAL EXPRESSION. CALLING MAJOR MIDDLEMORE THE NEXT SENIOR OFFICER, COL DONELLAN SEATED ERECT IN HIS SADDLE, TOOK OFF HIS HAT, BOWED, AND SAID, MAJOR MIDDLEMORE, YOU WILL HAVE THE HONOUR OF LEADING THE 48TH TO THE CHARGE. THE BATTALION CHARGED AND RESCUED THE GUARDS, WHILST COL. DONELLAN WAS CONDUCTED TO THE REAR AND DIED AT TALAVERA. / GRAVE RESTORED AND THIS TABLET ERECTED BY THE OFFICERS OF THE 1ST NORTHAMPTONSHIRE REGIMENT IN 1907."

Named on the Battlefield memorial: Talavera, Spain. (Photograph)
REFERENCE: Gurney, Russell, History of the Northamptonshire Regiment, 1742–1934, 1935.

51st (2nd Yorkshire West Riding) Light Infantry
Named on the Regimental Memorial: KOYLI Chapel, York Minster, Yorkshire. (Photograph)

CORUNNA FUENTES DONOR SALAMANCA VITTORIA PYRENEES SAN SEBASTIAN NIVELLE ORTHES / THIS MEMORIAL WAS ERECTED IN 1913 BY / THE KING'S OWN YORKSHIRE LIGHT INFANTRY / TO THE FOLLOWING OFFICERS AND NON- / COMMISSIONED OFFICERS OF THE 51ST / LIGHT INFANTRY WHO LOST THEIR LIVES FOR / THEIR COUNTRY IN THE WARS OF 1808–1814 / LIEU GENERAL SIR JOHN MOORE K.B. / MAJOR FREDERICK SPARKS / CAPTAIN CHARLES WILKINSON MERCER / CAPTAIN JAMES HENRY BLOOMFIELD / CAPTAIN JOHN McCABE / CAPTAIN CHARLES AYTOYNE DOUGLAS / LIEUT AND ADJUTANT J. JENNINGS / LIEUT WILLIAM EDWARD WHITE / LIEUT THOMAS KEPPE CHALMLEY / LIEUT RALPH RESTROPP / LIEUT RICHARD WILSON / LIEUT JOHN SAMUEL PERCY / LIEUT ROBERT DODD / LIEUT MAURICE STEPHENS / LIEUT JOHN D. TAYLOR / LIEUT J. H. DREW / LIEUT HENRY HONEY / LIEUT AND QUARTERMASTER MILLS / ASSISTANT SURGEON ROBERT HAMILTON / SERGT REES WELLS SERGT JOSEPH BEECHAM / SERGT OWEN McCARTHY SERGT WILLIAM SORRELL / SERGT JOHN FITTON SERGT RICHARD FORRESTER / SERGT THOMAS BUTCHER SERGT ROBERT ROCHE / SERGT JAMES DOWNS SERGT ANDREW CURSON / SERGT DANIEL LANE SERGT HUGH PERCY / SERGT THOMAS DOYLE SERGT JAMES STOTHERS / SERGT JOHN MINSKUILL SERGT WILLIAM HANKS / SERGT JOHN BRAUND SERGT RICHARD TRELEVAN / SERGT JAMES BALL SERGT HENRY MARSLAND / SERGT SAMUEL UTTING SERGT THOMAS WEBSTER / SERGT JOHN HANGER SERGT MICHAEL SMITH / ALSO TO 610 RANK AND FILE OF THE / REGIMENT WHOSE NAME INSCRIBED ON A / REGIMENTAL ROLL ARE DEPOSITED WITH / THE MINSTER AUTHORITIES

REFERENCE: Wheater, W., A Record of the Services of the Fifty-First (Second West York), the King's Own Light Infantry Regiment, 1870.

52nd (Oxfordshire) Light Infantry Regiment of Foot
Memorial plaque: Ciudad Rodrigo, Spain. (On walls above breach). (Photograph)

MAJOR GENERAL ROBERT CRAUFURD / TO THE MEMORY OF MAJOR GENERAL ROBERT CRAUFURD AND THOSE OF THE 43RD AND 52ND LIGHT INFANTRY AND THE 95TH RIFLES OF THE LIGHT DIVISION, WHICH HE COMMANDED WITH SUCH DISTINCTION, AND THEIR COMRADES OF THE 60TH, ALL OF WHOM FELL IN THE STORMING OF THE BREACHES, THROUGH WHICH CIUDAD RODRIGO WAS LIBERATED ON 19TH JANUARY 1812. / THIS PLAQUE IS ERECTED BY THEIR HEIRS, THE ROYAL GREEN JACKETS, MINDFUL OF THE HISTORIC EFFORTS OF THE SPANISH AND BRITISH TO FREE THE PENINSULA 1808–1813.

Memorial tablet: Oxford Cathedral, Oxford. (Photograph)

DEDICATED TO THE / MEMORY OF ALL RANKS OF / THE OXFORDSHIRE / AND BUCKINGHAMSHIRE / LIGHT INFANTRY / WHO HAVE GIVEN THEIR / LIVES FOR THEIR COUNTRY / AND IN THE SERVICE OF / THE REGIMENT SINCE ITS / FORMATION IN 1741

REFERENCE: Moorsom, W. S., Historical record of the Fifty-Second Regiment (Oxfordshire) Light Infantry) from the Year 1755 to the Year 1858, 1860, reprint 1996.

53rd (Shropshire) Regiment of Foot
Named on the Battlefield memorial: Talavera, Spain. (Photograph)

57th (West Middlesex) Regiment of Foot
Regimental memorial: St Paul's Cathedral, London. (Photograph)

57TH / WEST MIDDLESEX REGT / ALBUHERA VITTORIA / PYRENEES NIVELLE / NIVE PENINSULA / INKERMAN SEVASTOPOL / NEW ZEALAND

Regimental memorial: Albuera, Spain. (Photograph)

57TH FOOT / THE MIDDLESEX REGIMENT / "DIE HARD 57TH DIE HARD" / TO THE IMMORTAL MEMORY / AT ALBUERA ALSO REMEMBER AND PAY HOMAGE TO THOSE / BRAVE SOLDIERS OF THE ALLIANCE-SPAIN AND PORTUGAL

Also on another face:

THE PRINCES OF WALES'S / ROYAL REGIMENT / "OH ALBUHERA / GLORIOUS FIELD OF GRIEF" / THIS MONUMENT IS ERECTED TO THE IMMORTAL MEMORY OF / OUR PREDECESSOR REGIMENTS WHO FOUGHT SO BRAVELY / AT THE BATTLE OF ALBUERA–16 MAY 1811 / ERECTED BY THE PRINCESS OF WALES'S REGIMENT / 16 MAY 2001

REFERENCE: *Woollwright, Henry Herriott, History of the Fifty-Seventh (West Middlesex) Regiment of Foot, 1955–1888, 1893.*

59th (2nd Nottinghamshire) Regiment of Foot
Regimental memorial stone: Drumcannon, Tramore, County Waterford, Ireland. (Photograph)

A memorial was originally erected on the shore in the cliff face by Lt Colonel Austin, Lt Colonel Hoysted and the other serving Officers of the Battalion. The text of the memorial is almost identical to the inscription on the Obelisk, with the addition of a note that it was removed from Crest of the beach 1912 and restored 1955.

BENEATH THIS STONE / ARE DEPOSITED THE REMAINS OF / MAJOR CHARLES DOUGLAS 29 / CAPT JAMES MCGREGOR 23 / LIEUT & ADJT ABRAHAM DENT 26 / LIEUT WILLIAM VEALL 21 / LIEUTENANT ROBERT SCOTT 21 / LIEUTENANT JAMES GEDDES 21 / LIEUTENANT WILLIAM GILLESPIE 19 / ENSIGN ANDREW ROSS 19 / ENSIGN ROWLAND HILL 19 / SURGEON JAMES HAGAN 30 / ASSISTANT SURGEON LAMBE 26 / QUARTERMASTER WILLIAM BAIRD 38 / OF HER MAJESTY'S 2ND BATTALION 59TH FOOT / WHO PERISHED IN THE BAY OF TRAMORE / ON THE 30TH DAY OF JANUARY 1816 / BY THE WRECK OF THE SEA HORSE TRANSPORT / THIS MONUMENT IS ERECTED BY / LIEUT COLONEL AUSTIN, LIEUT COLONEL HOYSTED / AND THE OTHER SURVIVING OFFICERS OF THE BATTALION / ALSO A MONUMENT AT THE CHURCH OF TRAMORE / RETURNING TO THEIR NATIVE LAND / WHERE THEY LOOKED FOR SOLACE AND REPOSE / AFTER ALL THE TOILS AND DANGERS THEY HAD ENDURED / FOR THE SECURITY OF THE BRITISH EMPIRE / AND THE DELIVERANCE OF EUROPE / THEIR LIVES WERE SUDDENLY CUT SHORT / BY THE AWFUL DISPENSATION / OF AN ALL-WISE BUT INSCRUTABLE PROVIDENCE / BUT THE MEMORY OF THOSE GALLANT ACHIEVEMENTS / IN WHICH THEY BORE SO DISTINGUISHED A PART / UNDER THE GUIDANCE OF THE / ILLUSTRIOUS WELLINGTON / WILL NEVER BE FORGOTTEN, BUT SHALL CONTINUE TO ILLUMINATE / THE HISTORIC PAGE, AND ANIMATE THE HEARTS OF BRITONS / THE MOST REMOTE PERIOD OF TIME / REMOVED FROM CREST OF BEACH / 1912 / RESTORED 1955

Regimental memorial: Obelisk, Christ Church, Drumcannon, Tramore, County Waterford, Ireland. (Photograph)

South side:

THIS MONUMENT WAS RESTORED IN OCTOBER 1881 / BY GENERAL HOPE GRAHAM C.B. / WHO AS LIEUT. COL. COMMANDED / THE 59TH REGIMENT FOR SEVEN YEARS / AND AGAIN BY THE REGIMENT IN 1955. / THIS MONUMENT WAS ERECTED BY / LIEUT COLONEL AUSTIN, LIEUT COLONEL HOYSTED / AND THE OTHER SURVIVING OFFICERS / OF THE 2ND BATTALION OF HER MAJESTY'S 59TH REGIMENT / AS A TESTIMONIAL OF THEIR PROFOUND SORROW / FOR THE LOSS OF THEIR GALLANT BROTHER OFFICERS / WHO PERISHED BY THE WRECK OF THE SEA HORSE TRANSPORT / IN THE BAY OF TRAMORE / ON THE 30TH DAY OF JANUARY 1816 / AND AS A TRIBUTE TO THE HEROIC AND SOCIAL VIRTUES WHICH ADORNED / THEIR SHORT BUT USEFUL LIVES. / RESTORED 1955 / LUGO 6TH AND 7TH OF JANUARY 1809 / CORUNNA 16TH OF JANUARY 1809 / WALCHEREN AUGUST 1809

West side:

THE 2ND BATTALION OF THE 59TH REGIMENT / COMMENCED THEIR MILITARY CAREER IN THE AUTUMN OF 1808 / WHEN THEY ACCOMPANIED SIR DAVID BAIRD TO CORUNNA / AND WERE CONSPICUOUSLY BRAVE IN THE ARDUOUS CAMPAIGN / UNDER LIEUT GENERAL SIR JOHN MOORE / THEY PARTOOK OF THE FATE OF THE EXPEDITION TO WALCHEREN / THEY ALSO BORE A DISTINGUISHED PART IN THE PRINCIPAL ACTIONS / THAT WERE FOUGHT ON THE PENINSULA IN 1813 & 1814 / UNDER THE COMMAND OF / THE ILLUSTRIOUS WELLINGTON / AND FINALLY PARTICIPATED IN THE RENOWN OF THE / EVER MEMORABLE DAY OF WATERLOO AND THE / SECOND SURRENDER OF THE FRENCH CAPITAL / WATERLOO 18TH JUNE 1815 / CAMBRAY 24TH JUNE 1815 / SURRENDER OF PARIS 6TH JULY 1815.

North side:

SACRED TO THE MEMORY OF / MAJOR CHARLES DOUGLAS, LIEUT WM GILLESPIE, / CAPTAIN JAMES MCGREGOR, ENSIGN ANDREW ROSS, / LIEUT & ADJT / ABRAHAM DENT, ENSIGN ROWLAND HILL, / LIEUT WM VEALL, SURGEON JAMES HAGAN, / LIEUT ROBERT SCOTT, ASS SURGEON LAMBE, / LIEUT JAMES GEDDES, / QTR MASTER WILLIAM BAIRD / OF THE 2ND BATTN. 59TH REGT, WHO WERE LOST BY THE WRECK OF THE SEAHORSE TRANSPORT. / YOUR HEROIC DEEDS, BRAVE WARRIORS! / WILL NEVER BE ERASED FROM THE PAGES OF HISTORY: AND THOUGH / CYPRESS INSTEAD OF LAURELS ENCIRCLE YOUR TEMPLES, YOUR CENOTAPH / IS ERECTED IN THE BOSOM OF YOUR COUNTRYMEN. / NIVELLE, 10TH OF NOVEMBER 1813 / NIVE, 9TH, 10TH, 11TH AND 12TH DECEMBER 1813 / BAYONNE, FEBRUARY AND MARCH 1814.

East side:

"ON THE 30TH DAY OF JANUARY 1816, THE SEAHORSE TRANSPORT, CAPTAIN GIBBS, / WAS WRECKED IN TRAMORE BAY; / (UPON WHICH MELANCHOLY OCCASION) / 12 OFFICERS, 264 NON COMMISSIONED OFFICERS AND PRIVATES / OF HIS MAJESTY'S 2ND BATTN, 59TH REGIMENT, TOGETHER WITH LIEUT ALLEN R.N. 15 SAILORS AND 71 / WOMEN & / CHILDREN, / PERISHED WITHIN A MILE OF THE SHORE. / OF THE HAPLESS INMATES OF THIS ILL-FATED VESSEL, / ONLY 4 OFFICERS AND 26 SOLDIERS AND SEAMEN / WERE PROVIDENTIALLY RESCUED / FROM THE RAGING OCEAN! / VITTORIA, 21ST JUNE 1813 / ST SEBASTIAN, 31ST AUGUST, 1813 / BIDASSOA, 7TH OCTOBER, 1813"

The brig *Sea Horse* left Deal bound for Ireland on 25 Jan 1816. The 59th Foot were returning from Waterloo with 16 officers and nearly 340 men, women and children aboard. She ran into a storm 30 Jan off the coast of Ireland and broke up in one and a half hours. People at Tramore tried to help but the sea was too rough. Only 24 men and 4 officers were saved; 12 officers and 267 men, 33 women and 31 children were drowned.

REFERENCE: Ingham, David, Sudden Death, Sudden Glory: the 59th Regiment, 1793–1830. 1996. Entract, J. P., The Tramore and Kinsale Tragedies 30th January 1816 (His Majesty's 59th, 62nd and 82nd Regiments). Journal of the Society for Army Historical Research. Winter 1968, pp. 225–34.

60th (Royal American) Regiment of Foot

Named on the Battlefield memorial: Talavera, Spain. (Photograph)
Memorial: Guards Cemetery, St Etienne, Bayonne, France. (Photograph)

SACRED TO THE MEMORY OF THE UNDER-NAMED BRITISH / OFFICERS WHO GALLANTLY FELL AT / THE SORTIE MADE BY THE GARRISON / FROM THE CITADEL OF / BAYONNE ON THE 14TH OF APRIL 1814 / COLDSTREAM GUARDS / LIEUT-COLONELS / G. COLLIER / SIR H. SULLIVAN, BART AND M. P. / CAPTAINS / HONBLE W. G. CROFTON / W. BURROUGHS, ADJT / ENSIGNS / K. VACHELL W. PITT. / 1ST REGT OF GUARDS / ENSIGN / W. VANE / 3RD REGT OF GUARDS / CAPTAINS / C. L. WHITE. J. B. SHIFFNER. / LIEUT / F. HOLBURNE, ADJT / 60TH REGT / LIEUT / J. HAMILTON / THIS TABLET / WAS PLACED TO THE MEMORY OF THE / ABOVE-NAMED OFFICERS BY THEIR / FRIEND AND COMPANION AT THE SORTIE / J. V. HARVEY / FORMERLY CAPTAIN IN THE / COLDSTREAM GUARDS AND SINCE / H. M. CONSUL AT BAYONNE / 1830.

Memorial plaque: Ciudad Rodrigo, Spain. (On walls above breach). (Photograph)

MAJOR GENERAL ROBERT CRAUFURD / TO THE MEMORY OF MAJOR GENERAL ROBERT CRAUFURD AND THOSE OF THE 43RD AND 52ND LIGHT INFANTRY AND THE 95TH RIFLES OF THE LIGHT DIVISION, WHICH HE COMMANDED WITH SUCH DISTINCTION, AND THEIR COMRADES OF THE 60TH, ALL OF WHOM FELL IN THE STORMING OF THE BREACHES, THROUGH WHICH CIUDAD RODRIGO WAS LIBERATED ON 19TH JANUARY 1812. / THIS PLAQUE IS ERECTED BY THEIR HEIRS, THE ROYAL GREEN JACKETS, MINDFUL OF THE HISTORIC EFFORTS OF THE SPANISH AND BRITISH TO FREE THE PENINSULA 1808–1813.

61st (South Gloucestershire) Regiment of Foot

Named on the Battlefield memorial: Talavera, Spain. (Photograph)

66th (Berkshire) Regiment of Foot

Named on the Battlefield memorial: Talavera, Spain. (Photograph)

68th (Durham) Regiment of Foot

Memorial tablet: Durham Cathedral, Durham. (M.I.)

1758 1968 / DLI / THE DURHAM LIGHT INFANTRY / IN 1968 MERGED INTO / THE LIGHT INFANTRY. / AFTER TWO HUNDRED AND TEN YEARS / OF PROUD AND HAPPY ASSOCIATION WITH / THE COUNTY OF DURHAM. / THE GALLANTRY AND DISTINGUISHED WAY IN WHICH / THE REGIMENT DISCHARGED ITS DUTY OVER / THE YEARS IS PLAIN FOR ALL TO SEE / WHO ENTER THIS CHAPEL. / GREATER LOVE HATH NO MAN / THAN THIS THAT HE / LAY DOWN HIS LIFE / FOR HIS FRIENDS. / DULCE ET DECORUM / EST PRO PATRIA MORI.

69th (South Lincolnshire) Regiment of Foot

Memorial tablet: St Paul's Cathedral, Barbados, West Indies. (Photograph)

BATTLES AND CAMPAIGNS / 69 SOUTH LINCOLN / WATERLOO INDIA / SACRED TO THE MEMORY OF / THE OFFICERS OF THE SERVICE COMPANIES / OF THE 69TH REGIMENT, / WHO HAVE DIED DURING THE FOUR YEARS / THE REGIMENT HAD SERVED IN THE WEST INDIES, / FROM 1851, TO 1855, VIZ: / LIEUTENANT J. W. L. PAXTON, / COMMANDING 69TH REGIMENT, / WHO DIED AT TRINIDAD, OF YELLOW FEVER, / ON THE 24TH AUGUST 1853; / CAPTAIN C. J. CARMICHAEL, / WHO JUST AFTER REACHING ENGLAND FROM BARBADOS, / DIED ON THE 2ND DECEMBER 1852, / LIEUTENANT H. C. STRICKLAND, / WHO DIED AT BARBADOS, OF YELLOW FEVER, / ON THE 14TH SEPTEMBER 1852: / AND SURGEON A. B. CLELAND, M. D. / WHO DIED AT TRINIDAD, OF YELLOW FEVER, / ON THE 25TH AUGUST 1853. / THIS TABLET IS ERECTED / BY THEIR BROTHER OFFICERS. / ALSO / LTS C. R. DORINGTON AND H. T. ALLEN, WHO DIED / OF YELLOW FEVER, AT BARBADOS, ON THE 12TH & / 15TH AUGUST, 1855.

74th (Highland) Regiment of Foot

Regimental Memorial tablet: St Giles' Cathedral, Edinburgh, Midlothian, Scotland. (Photograph)

IN MEMORY OF / THE OFFICERS N.C. OFFICERS AND MEN OF THE / 74TH HIGHLANDERS / (NOW 2ND BATTN HIGHLAND LIGHT INFANTRY) / WHO WERE KILLED OR MORTALLY WOUNDED IN THE VARIOUS ACTIONS IN / WHICH THE REGIMENT WAS ENGAGED. / ………………. / IN THE PENINSULA AND FRANCE 1810–1814 / CAPT BASSETT COLLINS / CAPT W. WHITTING / CAPT T. ANDREWS / CAPT WILLIAM TEW LIEUT ROBT MAXWELL / LIEUT DANIEL EWING / LIEUT HUGH JOHNSON / LIEUT B. RAMADGE / LIEUT H. S. HAMILTON / ENSIGN ALEX GRANT / ENSIGN JOHN WILLIAMS / ENSIGN J. PARKINSON / ALSO 146 N.C.O. AND MEN / ……………….

Reference: *Oatts, L. B., Proud Heritage, The Story of the Highland Light Infantry, Vol. 2, The 74th Highlanders, 1787–1882, 1959.*

79th (Cameron Highlanders) Regiment of Foot

Regimental memorial tablet: St Joseph's Church, Waterloo. (Photograph)

SACRED TO THE MEMORY / OF CAPTAINS / NEIL CAMPBELL, JOHN SINCLAIR, JOHN CAMERON / LIEUTENANTS / DONALD CAMERON, DUNCAN MACPHERSON, / JOHN KYNOCK, JOHN BOWLING, EWEN KENNEDY, / AND OF NINE NON-COMMISSIONED OFFICERS / AND SEVENTY FIVE PRIVATES OF THE 79TH REGT OF HIGHLANDERS / WHO FELL IN THE MEMORABLE BATTLES OF / QUATRE BRAS & WATERLOO / 16TH AND 18TH JUNE 1815. / IN WHICH ACTIONS THERE WERE ALSO WOUNDED OF THE / SAME CORPS 24 OFFICERS, 375 NON-COMMISSIONED / OFFICERS AND PRIVATES. / IN TESTIMONY OF THE VALOUR OF THEIR DECEASED / BRETHREN IN ARMS, THIS TABLET IS INSCRIBED / BY THE SURVIVING OFFICERS OF THE REGIMENT. / "HOW SLEEP THE BRAVE, WHO SINK TO REST / BY ALL THEIR COUNTRY'S WISHES BLEST!!!"

Reference: *Groves, Percy, History of the 79th Queen's Own Cameron Highlanders, now the First Battalion Queen's Own Cameron Highlanders, 1794–1893, 1893. Mackenzie, T. A., J. S. Ewart and C. Findlay, Historical Records of the 79th Queen's Own Cameron Highlanders, 1887, reprint 2011. Historical Records of the Queen's Own Cameron Highlanders, 6 vols 1909–1952, Vol. 7 1949–1961. Contains Biographical Notes on all Officers from the Formations, 1961.*

82nd (Prince of Wales's Volunteers) Regiment of Foot
Memorial tablet: St. Multose's Church, Kinsale, County Cork, Ireland. (Photograph)

SACRED / TO THE MEMORY OF LIEU^{TS} / EDMUND DAVENPORT, EDWIN HARDING / ASS^{T} SURGEON HENRY RANDOLPH SCOTT / AND HIS WIFE / EIGHT SERJEANTS, NINE CORPORALS, / ONE HUNDRED AND FORTY PRIVATES, / THIRTEEN WOMEN AND SIXTEEN CHILDREN / OF THE 82^{D} REG^{T}, WHO PERISHED / ON BOARD THE BOADICEA TRANSPORT, / WRECKED ON GARRETSTOWN STRAND / ON THE NIGHT OF THE 30TH JAN^{Y} 1816 / THIS TRIBUTE IS ERECTED / BY THE OFFICERS OF THE REG^{T}

The *Boadicea* left Deal bound for Cork on 25 Jan 1816 with men of the 82nd Foot. They ran into a storm off Old Head Kinsale on 30 January. The ship was seen in difficulties and the militia was called out but they had to march six miles to reach the coast. By that time it was dark and nothing could be seen. At dawn the ship had disappeared from view but 50 survivors were seen clinging to a rock and were eventually brought ashore; 198 men lost their lives.
Reference: Jarvis, Samuel Peters, Historical Record of the Eighty-Second Regiment or Prince of Wales's Volunteers, 1866, pp. 114–15.

83rd Regiment of Foot
Named on the Battlefield memorial: Talavera, Spain. (Photograph)

86th (Royal County Down) Regiment of Foot
Named on the Battlefield memorial: Talavera, Spain. (Photograph)

87th (Princes of Wales's Irish) Regiment of Foot
Regimental Memorial tablet: St James's Cathedral, Port Louis, Mauritius.

THIS MONUMENT IS ERECTED / BY THE OFFICERS OF THE 87TH ROYAL IRISH FUSILIERS, / TO THE MEMORY OF / THOSE OFFICERS OF THE REGIMENT / WHO DIED DURING THE PERIOD OF ITS SERVICE / IN THIS COLONY, VIZ: / MAJOR JAMES KENNELLY DIED MAR 5TH 1843 / CAPT LORD ARTHUR CHICHESTER DIED JULY 21ST 1840 / CAPT JOHN H. HASSARD DIED DEC^{R} 7TH 1842 / CAPT ROGER S. KEATING DIED MAY 4TH 1842 / LIEUT WILLIAM L. STAFFORD DIED AUG 12TH 1837 / LIEUT HENRY P. FAUNT DIED SEP^{R} 11TH 1843 / PAYMASTER THOMAS DRURY DIED FEB^{Y} 20T^{H} 1841

Named on the Battlefield memorial: Talavera, Spain. (Photograph)
Reference: Cunliffe, Marcus, The Royal Irish Fusiliers, 1793–1950, 1952.

88th (Connaught Rangers) Regiment of Foot
Named on the Battlefield memorial: Talavera, Spain. (Photograph)

Reference: Jourdain, H. F. N., and Edward Fraser, History of the Connaught Rangers, 3 vols, 1924–1928.

90th (Perthshire Volunteers) Regiment of Foot
Obelisk: North Inches, Perthshire, Scotland. (Photograph)

IN HONOUR OF / THE 90TH LIGHT INFANTRY / (PERTHSHIRE VOLUNTEERS) / RAISED MAY 1794 BY / THOMAS GRAHAM / OF BALGOWAN / WHO WAS PROMOTED FOR HIS / SERVICES IN ITALY SPAIN / AND HOLLAND / TO THE RANK OF GENERAL 1809 / MADE A KNIGHT OF THE BATH 1812 / AND CREATED BARON LYNEDOCH / 1814.

95th Regiment of Foot
Regimental Memorial tablet: Battles and Campaigns, Winchester Cathedral, Winchester, Hampshire. (Photograph)

95 / BATTLES AND CAMPAIGNS / 1800 FERROL. 1801 COPENHAGEN. / 1807 MONTE VIDEO. BUENOS AYRES / DENMARK. 1808 OBIDOS. / ROLICA VIMEIRO. 1809 CACABELOS. / CORUNA. DOURO. TALAVERA. / WALCHEREN. THE COA. BUSACO. / TARIFA. 1811 BARROSA. REDINHA. / SABUGAL. FUENTES DE ONORO. / 1812 CIUDAD RODRIGO. BADAJOZ. / SALAMANCA. 1813 VITORIA. / SAN SEBASTIAN. PYRENEES. PASS OF VERA. / NIVELLE. NIVE. 1814 ANTWERP / ORTHEZ. TARBES. TOULOUSE. / NEW ORLEANS QUATRE BRAS / PENINSULA. WATERLOO / 1846–7 51–53 SOUTH AFRICA. / 1848 BOOM PLAATZ. 1854 ALMA. INKERMANN / 1855 REDAN. 1854–55 SEBASTOPOL. / 1857 CAWNPORE. 1858 LUCKNOW. / 1858–9 CENTRAL INDIA. / 1864. 77. 81. 97 N. W. FRONTIER / 1873–4 ASHANTEE. 1878 ALI MUSJID. / 1898 KHARTOUM. 1899–1900 LADYSMITH. TUGELA. BERGENDAL / 1899–1900 SOUTH AFRICA.

Regimental Memorial tablet: Roll of Fame, Winchester Cathedral, Winchester, Hampshire. (Photograph)

ROLE OF FAME / MAJ. GEN. COOTE MANNINGHAM 1809 / CAPT. J. UNIAKE 1812 / MAJ. P. O'HARE 1812 / LT. J. M. STOKES 1812 / SJT. MAJ. ADAMS 1813 / COL. H. WADE 1821 / RFN. TOM PLUNKET 1825 / LT. GEN SIR W. STEWART 1827 / LT. GEN SIR T. S. BECKWITH 1834 LT. COL. S. MITCHELL 1833 / MAJ. GEN. SIR J. ROSS 1835 / MAJ. GEN. SIR A. G. R. NORCOTT 1838 / LT. COL G. MILLER 1843 / MAJ. GEN. SIR A. CAMERON 1850 / LT. H. TRYON 1854 / LT. GEN. SIR A. F. BARNARD / 1855 MAJ. G. SIMMONS 1858 / V.C. RFN. D. HAWKES 1858 / V.C. CPL. S. SHAW 1859 / LT GEN. SIR HARRY G. W. SMITH 1860 / CAPT. SIR J. KINCAID 1862 / V.C. RFN. F. WHEATLEY 1865 / BUGLER W. GREEN 1865 / SJT. E. COSTELLO 1869 / SJT. J. HIMBURY 1872 / V.C. CPL. W. WALSH 1875 / LT. GEN. SIR R. WALPOLE 1876

Memorial plaque: Ciudad Rodrigo, Spain. (On walls above breach). (Photograph)

MAJOR GENERAL ROBERT CRAUFURD / TO THE MEMORY OF MAJOR GENERAL ROBERT CRAUFURD AND THOSE OF THE 43RD AND 52ND LIGHT INFANTRY AND THE 95TH RIFLES OF THE LIGHT DIVISION, WHICH HE COMMANDED WITH SUCH DISTINCTION, AND THEIR COMRADES OF THE 60TH, ALL OF WHOM FELL IN THE STORMING OF THE BREACHES, THROUGH WHICH CIUDAD RODRIGO WAS LIBERATED ON 19TH JANUARY 1812. / THIS PLAQUE IS ERECTED BY THEIR HEIRS, THE ROYAL GREEN JACKETS, MINDFUL OF THE HISTORIC EFFORTS OF THE SPANISH AND BRITISH TO FREE THE PENINSULA 1808–1813.

REFERENCE: Verner, Willoughby, History and Campaigns of the Rifle Brigade, 2 vols, Part 1 1800–1809, Part 2 1809–1813, 1912.

Portuguese Army

1st and 3rd Caçadores and 17th Portuguese Regiment
Memorial window: Sir John Moore Library, Shorncliffe, Kent. (Photograph)

1ST & 3RD CAÇADORES / 17TH PORTUGUESE REGIMENT
Monument to Portuguese soldiers serving in the Peninsular War and other campaigns, Mafra, Portugal. (Photograph)

Left side of monument:

NA LUSA HISTORIA MEMORADOS ALTOS / FEITOS A FAMA CONSAGRADES

Right side of monument:

NAO HA NA EUROPA / INFANTARIA / COMO E PORTUGUSA / BERESFORD BATALHA DE VITTORIA 1813

British Officers, NCOs and Soldiers who fell at Waterloo

Memorial tablet: St Joseph's Church, Waterloo. (Photograph)

IN HONORED MEMORY OF / ALL BRITISH OFFICERS / NON COMMISSIONED OFFICERS AND SOLDIERS / WHO FELL IN BATTLE, / UPON THE 16TH 17TH AND 18TH OF JUNE 1815. / THIS TABLET WAS ERECTED / BY A FEW BROTHERS IN ARMS AND COUNTRYMEN / A.D. MDCC-CLVIII / GLORY ENCIRCLES WITH THE SAME NOBLE DIADEM / THE HUMBLE AS WELL AS THE EXALTED

Chelsea Pensioners

Obelisk: Brompton Cemetery, London. (Photograph)
Monument to 265 Chelsea Pensioners buried at this site between 1855–1893.

MYSORE / EGYPT / INDIA / PENINSULA / CORUNNA / SALAMANCA / FLANDERS / WATERLOO / NEPAUL / BURMAH / SOUTH AMERICA / AFGHANISTAN / CABUL / CANDAHAR / CHINA / NEW ZEALAND / PUNJAB / CRIMEA / ALMA / BALACLAVA / INKERMAN / SEBASTOPOL / PERSIA / INDIAN MUTINY / DELHI / LUCKNOW

Field Train Department of Ordnance

Regimental Memorial: British Cemetery, Lisbon, Portugal. (Grave number D 11). (M.I.)

"ERECTED BY THE OFFICERS OF THE FIELD TRAIN DEPARTMENT OF THE ORDNANCE IN MEMORY OF GEORGE BRADNOCK, ASST. COMMISSARY AND PAYMASTER OF THE FIELD TRAIN PARTMENT OF THE ORDNANCE, WHO DIED AT LISBON 9 JUNE 1808 AGE 39. / MR ROBERT WALSH, CLERK OF THE STORES, FIELD TRAIN ORDNANCE DEPT DIED AT LISBON 9 JUN 1809. MR ROBERT CLUBB CLERK OF STORES MR ROBERT BRANDON THORN, CLERK OF STORES, FIELD TRAIN DEPT OF ORDNANCE WHO WERE KILLED IN ACTION AT THE SIEGE OF ALMEIDA 27 AUGUST 1810. AS A MEMORIAL OF THE ESTEEM IN WHICH THE ABOVE GENTLEMEN WERE HELD BY THEIR BROTHER OFFICERS, THIS STONE WAS ERECTED BY THEM. ANNO DOMINI 1811."

Royal Artillery

Regimental Memorial: St Nicholas's Church, Plumstead, Kent. (M.I.) (Destroyed by a flying bomb in the Second World War).

TO THE GLORY OF GOD / AND / IN MEMORY OF CERTAIN OFFICERS OF THE / ROYAL REGI-MENT OF ARTILLERY / WHOSE BODIES WERE INTERRED IN THE / CHURCHYARD OF ST. NICHOLAS PLUMSTEAD / BETWEEN THE YEARS AD 1742 AND 1853. / THEY REPRESENTED A GENERATION WHOSE / FAITHFUL AND STRENUOUS LIVES HELPED TO LAY / THE FOUNDA-TIONS OF THE ROYAL ARTILLERY / OF TODAY.

LT $GEN^{L\ J}$. WALTON 1808 / CPT A. G. SPEARMAN 1808 / MAJOR GEN^{L} E. FAGE 1809 / MAJOR

GEN^{L} J. ROLLO 1809 / 2ND QM R. ROBINSON 1810 / M GEN^{L} D. GRANT 1812 / 2ND LIEUT G. CRAWFORD 1813 / LT GEN^{L} W. D. HUDDLESTONE 1814 / CAPT W. HALL 1814 / 2ND CAPT A. N. DAVIES / 1815 / LT GEN^{L} E. STEPHENS 1815 / LT COL J. W. UNETT 1815 / LIEUT D. N. MARTIN 1815 / LT GEN^{L} R. DAWSON 1816 / LT COL SIR JOHN DYER KCB 1816 / LT COL M. FOY 1817 / GENERAL V. LLOYD 1817 / 2ND LIEUT E. S. HALL 1817 / COL SIR WILLIAM ROBE KCB KCH KTS 1820 / 2ND CAPT J. WEST 1821 / LT COL C. A. QUICK 1821 / GENERAL SIR THOMAS BLOMFIELD BART 1822 / ASS^{T} SURGEON G. NAPPER 1823 / LT GEN^{L} B. WILLINGTON 1823 / LT GEN^{L} J. RAMSAY 1827 / LT GEN^{L} R. DOUGLAS 1827 / COL J. HAWKER CB 1827 / LT COL J. MACLASHLAN 1835 / COLONEL J. S. WILLIAMSON CB 1836 / MAJOR GEN^{L} SIR ALEXANDER DICKSON GCB KCH 1840 / MAJOR GEN^{L} D. DRUMMOND CB 1843 / MAJOR GEN^{L} A BREMNER 1845 / MAJOR GN^{L} SIR JOHN MAY KCB KCH 1847 / COL A. HUNT 1853

Memorial: St Mylor's Churchyard, Mylor, Falmouth, Cornwall. (Photograph)

TO THE / MEMORY OF THE WARRIORS, / WOMEN AND CHILDREN, / WHO ON THEIR RETURN TO ENGLAND / FROM THE COAST OF SPAIN; / UNHAPPILY PERISHED / IN THE WRECK OF THE / QUEEN TRANSPORT / ON TREFUSIS POINT, JAN^{Y} 14 1814. / THIS STONE IS ERECTED AS A TESTIMONY / OF REGRET FOR THEIR FATE BY THE / INHABITANTS OF THE PARISH.

The *Queen Transport* was wrecked in a storm on 14 Jan 1814 off Trefugis Point, Falmouth. The ship broke up in 45 minutes and of the 315 men, women and children aboard, only 124 reached the safety of the shore. She was bringing home mainly wounded Royal Artillery men from Lisbon. There were also 32 men from the 30th Foot. Among them was Robert Daniel, his wife and five children. They were all drowned except Lt Daniel who reached shore. He lies buried in Kensal Green Cemetery.
Reference: Saint George's Garrison Church Memorials. Royal Artillery (Manuscript record), 1919.

Named on the Battlefield memorial: Talavera, Spain. (Photograph)

Memorial stone showing position of Mercer's Troop at Waterloo, Waterloo, Belgium (Photograph)

THIS STONE MARKS THE LAST POSITION / OF G TROOP ROYAL HORSE ARTILLERY / COMMANDED BY CAPTAIN A. G. MERCER / DURING THE BATTLE OF WATERLOO / 18 JUNE 1815. FROM HERE THE TROOP / TOOK A CONSPICUOUS PART IN DEFEATING / THE ATTACKS OF THE FRENCH CAVALRY

Regimental memorial tablet: St Joseph's Church, Waterloo. (Photograph)

SACRED TO THE MEMORY / OF / MAJOR WILLIAM J LLOYD / MAJOR GEORGE BEAN / MAJOR W. NORMAN RAMSAY / MAJOR ROBERT M CAIRNES / CAPTAIN SAMUEL BOLTON / LIEUT WILLIAM L ROBE / LIEUT MICHAEL T CROMIE / LIEUT ROBERT MANNERS / LIEUT CHARLES SPEARMAN / ROYAL BRITISH ARTILLERY / LIEUT DETLEF DE SCHULZEN / KING'S GERMAN ARTILLERY / AND III SERGEANTS AND LXX RANK AND FILE / WHO FELL IN THE BATTLE OF / WATERLOO / JUNE XVIII MDCCCXV / THIS STONE WAS ERECTED BY / THE OFFICERS OF THOSE TWO CORPS / WHO WERE IN THE ACTION

Memorial to Royal Artillery.
Penryn Churchyard, Cornwall. (M.I.)

"BENEATH THIS STONE, (PLACED BY THE INHABITANTS OF PENRYN AS A MEMORIAL OF THE AWFUL DISPENSATION) WERE INTERRED IN ONE GRAVE THE BODIES OF TWENTY

SHIPWRECKED STRANGERS! THESE UNFORTUNATE PERSONS, INVALIDS AND FOLLOWERS OF THE BRITISH ARMY IN SPAIN, HAD RECENTLY ARRIVED AT FALMOUTH FROM LISBON, IN THE QUEEN TRANSPORT. EARLY IN MORNING OF JANUARY 14TH, 1814, DURING A VIOLENT SNOW STORM THE SHIP PARTED FROM HER ANCHOR, WAS DASHED IN PIECES ON TREFUSIS POINT".

REFERENCE: Duncan, Francis, History of the Royal Artillery, 3 vols, 1872–1879. Naval and Military Press reprint.

Royal Engineers

Memorial stained glass window: Rochester Cathedral, Rochester, Kent. (Photograph)

THE UPPER TIER OF THE ABOVE LIGHTS WAS FILLED WITH / STAINED GLASS IN 1888 BY THE CORPS OF ROYAL ENGINEERS / TO THE GLORY OF GOD AND IN MEMORY OF / THE OFFICERS OF THE CORPS OF ROYAL ENGINEERS WHO SERVED / IN THE PENINSULA AND WATERLOO CAMPAIGNS 1808 T0 1815. / THEIR NAMES ARE INSCRIBED IN THE MOSAIC PANELS OF / THE LOWER TIER OF WALL – ARCADING ON EITHER SIDE / OF THE GREAT WEST DOOR.

Regimental Memorial: Rochester Cathedral, Rochester, Kent. (Photograph)

PENINSULA AND WATERLOO CAMPAIGNS 1808–15 / ROYAL ENGINEERS / KILLED / LIEUTENANT COLONELS / SIR R. FLETCHER BART / CAPTAINS / C. LEFEBVRE BT. MAJOR J. SQUIRE BT. LT. COL. P. PATTON G. ROSS C. S. RHODES / W. NICHOLAS BT MAJOR G. HAMILTON J. A. WILLIAMS E. PARKER E. MULCASTER / S. DICKINSON G. COLLYER T. J. H. PITTS / LIEUTENANTS / T. LASCELLES W. FORSTER H. DAVY S. TRENCH J. LONGLEY R. HUNT T. SKELTON / R. G. POWER D. MELVILLE E. A. DE SALABERRY L. MACHELL / WOUNDED / LIEUTENANT COLONELS / SIR HOWARD ELPHINSTONE BART J. F. BIRCH / CAPTAINS / J. F. BURGOYNE BT LT COL J. T. JONES BT. MAJOR G. MACLEOD BT MAJOR G. G. LEWIS BT MAJOR T. M. DICKENS C. BOOTHBY W. C. E. HOLLOWAY R. BOTELER W. MACCULLOCH F. STANWAY A. EMMETT A. THOMSON H. D. JONES / LIEUTENANTS / A. MARSHALL G. GIPPS H. BARRY H. A. TAPP W. REID S. C. MELHUISH P. WRIGHT J. W. PRINGLE T. H. ELLIOT F. Y. GILBERT / MADRAS ENGINEERS – CAPTAIN / JOHN BLAKISTON / SERVED WITHOUT CASUALTY – LIEUTENANT COLONELS / A. BRYCE BRIG. GEN W. H. FORD F. R. THACKERAY S. R. CHAPMAN G. CARMICHAEL SMYTH G. LANDMANN C. W. PASLEY H. GOLDFINCH / CAPTAINS / J. BY BT. MAJOR G. H. HENDERSON BT MAJOR T. FYERS C. G. ELLICOMBE BT. LT. COL. E. FANSHAWE SIR C. FELIX SMITH KT. BT. LT. COL. G. JUDD HARDING SIR G. C. HOSTE KT. BT MAJOR H. W. VAVASOUR C. S. MERCER R. THOMSON T. ROBERTS F. A. YORKE RICE JONES R. S. HUSTLER J. OLDFIELD A. CHEYNE J. B. HARRIS W. B. TYLDEN BT. MAJOR / J. N. WELLS W. F. D. DAWSON R. E. JUDGE JAMES VETCH . W. D. SMITH F. ENGLISH Y. BLANSHARD BT MAJOR T. K. HUTCHINSON STAVELEY LOYALTY PEAKE A. THOMPSON E. FYERS W. C. WARD G. BARNEY D. M. DONALD R. S. PIPER W. R. ORD / LIEUTENANTS / J. L. HULME J. BIRCH J. S. MACAULAY H. J. SAVAGE M. A. WATERS P. COLE H N. SMITH / E. MATSON J. G. VICTOR G. GRIERSON R. J. BAROU L. A. HALL P. E. SCOTT F. BOND HEAD I. M. ELTON T. F. LANCEY J. SPERLING D. BOLTON A. W. ROBE G. J. WEST C. RIVERS H. Y. WORTHAM C. V. TINLING A. D. WHITE J. W. EYRE A. HENDERSON R. H. S. COOPER J. KER E. COVEY A. KAY H. SANDHAM C. MACKENZIE C. K. SANDERS T. C. LUXMOORE H. M. BUCKERIDGE C. H. MINCHIN W. FARIS W. S. SALKELD E. B. PATTEN F. H. BADDELEY W. ROGERS G. DALTON

Regimental Memorial tablet: Rochester Cathedral, Rochester, Kent. (Photograph)

THE CORPS OF / ROYAL ENGINEERS / REMEMBERING / SERVICE / AND / SACRIFICE. (Photograph)

Memorial tablet: King's Chapel, Gibraltar. (Photograph)

TO THE GLORY OF GOD AND / TO COMMEMORATE THE CONTINUOUS SERVICE GIVEN BY / THE CORPS OF ROYAL ENGINEERS / ON THE ROCK OF GIBRALTAR FROM 1704, / AND THE FORMATION HERE IN 1772 OF THE FIRST / BODY OF SOLDIERS OF THE CORPS / THEN KNOWN AS THE COMPANY OF SOLDIER ARTIFICERS / 27TH MARCH 1994

Statue on Stone block: Main Street, Gibraltar. (Photograph)

PRESENTED TO THE PEOPLE OF GIBRALTAR / BY THE CORPS OF ROYAL ENGINEERS / TO COMMEMORATE THE CONTINUOUS / SERVICE GIVEN BY THE CORPS FROM 1704, / AND THE FORMATION HERE IN 1772 / OF THE FIRST BODY OF SOLDIERS / OF THE CORPS, THEN KNOWN AS THE / COMPANY OF SOLDIER ARTIFICERS. / 26TH MARCH 1994

Note: Variation in date on two memorials.
Reference: Connolly, T. W. J., History of the Corps of Royal Sappers and Miners, 2nd edn, 1857.

Royal Waggon Train
Regimental memorial tablet: Hougoumont, Waterloo. (Photograph)

ROYAL WAGGON TRAIN / IN MEMORY OF / THE OFFICERS AND MEN / OF THE ROYAL WAGGON TRAIN / WHO TOOK PART IN THE / DEFENCE OF HOUGOUMONT / 18TH JUNE 1815. / THIS TABLET WAS ERECTED IN 1979 / BY THE ROYAL CORPS OF TRANSPORT / THE SUCCESSORS OF / THE ROYAL WAGGON TRAIN

Memorial: National Army Museum London. (Outside main door). (Photograph)

RCT / 1794–1993 / THE ROYAL WAGGONERS WERE RAISED BY ROYAL WARRANT / ON 7 MARCH 1794 TO SERVE IN FLANDERS UNDER / HRH THE DUKE OF YORK. THIS MEMORIAL WAS GIVEN BY / THE ROYAL CORPS OF TRANSPORT TO COMMEMORATE / TWO CENTURIES OF LOYAL SUPPORT TO THE BRITISH / ARMED FORCES BY THE ROYAL WAGGONERS, / THE COMMISSARIAT AND THEIR SUCCESSORS: / ROYAL WAGGON TRAIN 1799–1833 / LAND TRANSPORT CORPS 1855–1856 / MILITARY TRAIN 1856–1859 / COMMISSARIAT AND ASC 1869–1888 / ARMY SERVICE CORPS 1888–1918 / ROYAL ARMY SERVICE CORPS 1918–1965 / ROYAL CORPS OF TRANSPORT 1965–1993

IRELAND
Dublin

WITHIN THE PRECINCTS OF THIS CEMETERY HAVE BEEN LAID / TO REST THE REMAINS OF 334 IN PENSIONERS WHO HAVE DIED / IN THE ROYAL HOSPITAL KILMAINHAM THEIR NAMES REGIMENTS / AND DATES OF DECEASE WILL BE FOUND INSCRIBED ON BRASS / TABLETS IN THE RESPECTIVE CHAPELS OF THE INSTITUTION

King's German Legion
Regimental Monument: La Haye Sainte, Waterloo. (Photograph)

TO THE MEMORY / OF THEIR COMPANIONS IN ARMS / WHO GLORIOUSLY FELL ON THE

MEMORABLE / 18TH DAY OF JUNE 1815 / THIS MONUMENT / IS ERECTED BY THE OFFICERS OF THE KING'S / GERMAN LEGION

Belgian and Dutch Regiments

Monument to Belgian soldiers: Waterloo crossroads, Belgium. (Photograph)

AUX BELGES MORT LE XVIII JUIN / EN COMBATTANT POUR LA / DEFENSE DU DRAPEAU / ET L'HONNEUR DES ARMES

Memorial: Belgian Regiments, Quatre Bras, Waterloo, Belgium. (Photograph)

1815 / 16 JUIN / A LA MEMOIRE / DES / BELGES TUES / A LA BATAILLE / DE QUATRE BRAS / POUR LA DEFENSE , DU DRAPEAU / ET L'HONNEUR / DES ARMES

Dutch Regiments

Memorial tablet to Dutch Officers killed at Quatre Bras: Chapel Royal, Waterloo. (Photograph)

NEDERLANDSCHE OFFICIEREN / GESNEUVELD IN DEN SLAG BIJ QUATRE-BRAS / 16 JUNI 1815. / BAT^{ON} JAGERS N^{O} 27: KAPITEIN B. D. J. DE NAVE. / BAT^{ON} NA^{T} MILITIE N^{O} 5: 1^{e} LUIT^{T} J. DE HAAN. / BAT^{ON} NA^{T} MILITIE N^{O} 5: 1^{e} LUIT^{T} K. BOELTJES. / BAT^{ON} NA^{T} MILITIE N^{O} 5: 1^{e} LUIT^{T} A. WYNOLDY. / BAT^{ON} NA^{T} MILITIE N^{O} 2: 2^{e} LUIT^{T} P. R. KLEIJN / 1^{e} BAT^{ON} ORANJE-NASSAU N^{O} 28: 1^{e}LUIT^{T} ENGEL. / REG^{T} HUZAREN N^{O} 6; / 2^{e}LUIT^{T} W. WOLF. / ARTELLERIE: / KAP^{N} E. J. STEVENART.

Memorial tablet to Dutch Officers killed at Waterloo: St Joseph's Church, Waterloo. (Photograph)

NEDERLANDSCHE OFFICIEREN / GESNEUVELD IN DEN SLAG BIJ WATERLOO / 18 JUNI 1815 / STAF 1^{e} LUIT C. F. S. BARON VAN HAREN. / BAT^{ON} JAGER No 35 2^{e} LUIT ROBERTI / BAT^{ON}. INFANTERIE N° 7 1^{e} LUIT J. C. CARONDEL. / BAT^{ON}. INFANTERIE 1^{e} LUIT A. J. L. PONTHIEURE DE BERLAERE / BAT^{ON}. NAT. MIL No 6 LUIT KOL. A VAN THIELEN / BAT^{ON}. NAT. MIL No 7 2e LUIT J. W .E. JONQUIERE. / BAT^{ON}. NAT. MIL No 7 2e LUIT P. HEIL. / BAT^{ON} NAT. MIL No 8 1e LUIT G. J. WERNER. / 1^{e} 2^{e} R^{EG} NASSAU / 1e LUIT A. HARDT. / 1^{e} 9^{e} R^{EG} NASSAU 2e LUIT F .K. STAMMEL. / 2^{e} R^{EG} NASSAU 2e LUIT F. VON TRODT. / 3^{e} R^{EG} NASSAU MAJ. G. HECHMANN.

CAVELERIE / STAF LUIT-GEN. J. A. BARON DE COLLAERT. / STAF GEN-MAJ. J. B. VAN MERLEN. / R^{EG} KARABINIERS No 1 LUIT-KOL. L. P. COENEGRACHT / R^{EG} KARABINIERS No 1 MAJ. D. R. BISDOM. / R^{EG} KARABINIERS No 1 1^{e} LUIT. J. C. NORBERT / R^{EG} KARABINIERS No 2: 2^{e} J. J. HENRY. / R^{EG} KARABINIERS No 3: LT KOL C. M. LECHLEITNER. / R^{EG} DRAGONDERS No 4: RITM^{R} C. S. KREIJSIG. / R^{EG} DRAGONDERS No 4 RITM^{R} C. MASCHECK. / R^{EG} DRAGONDERS No 4 2^{e} LUIT H. A. DAEY. / R^{EG} DRAGONDERS No 4 2^{e} RT^{r} W. A. BARON VAN PALLANDT. / R^{EG} DRAGONDERS No 4 2^{e} L^{T} A. STRATENUS. / R^{EG} DRAGONDERS No 4 KAP. TISSOT VAN PATOT. / R^{EG} HUZAREN N° 8: RT^{r} C. GRAAF DUCHASTEL DE LA HOWARDERIE. / R^{EG} HUZAREN N° 8: MAJ. C. N. J. F. M. DE VILLERS. / R^{EG} HUZAREN N° 6: RITM^{R} W. L. VAN WIJNBERGEN. / R^{EG} HUZAREN N° 6: F. M. VON HEIDEN. / R^{EG} HUZAREN N° 6: 1^{e} L^{T} W. A. VERHELLOW.

Memorial tablet: St Joseph's Church, Waterloo. (Photograph)

DEN 18DE JUNY 1815, / SNEUVELDE INDE SLAG VAN WATERLOO / C^{L}F^{C}S^{D} BARON VAN HAREN / KAMER JONKER Z: M: / DEN KONING DER NEDERLANDEN / L^{TE} LEUT: BY DE GEN^{LE} STAF & / ADJ^{T} VAN DEN GENERAAL MAJOR / GRAVE W: VAN BYLANDT. / GEBOOREN DEN 21 JUNY

1793. / ZYN VADER / C[L] W[M] BARON VAN HAREN / LEUT: COL: EN CAP[T] INDE GARDES / DRAGONDERS DER NEDERLANDEN, / HAD INSGELYKS ZYN LEVEN / OOR ZYN VADERLAND GELATEN / DEN 18[DE] SEPT: 1793. / BY WERWICK. / OPGERIGT DOOR ZYN GENERALL.

6th Regiment of Dutch Hussars.
Memorial tablet: St Joseph's Church, Waterloo. (Photograph)

DE HEEREN OFFICIEREN VAN HET REGEMENT HUSSAREN NO 6 / IN DIENSTE VAN / ZIJNE MAJESTEIT DEN KONING DER NEDERLANDEN! / AANGEVOERD DOOR DEN COLONEL BOREEL, RIDDER DER MILITAIRE WILLEMS-ORDE 3[E] CLASSE; / AAN HUNNE BRAVE WAPENBROEDENS, GESNEUVELD OP DEN 18 JUNIJ 1815 BIJ DE BATAILLE VAN WATERLOO. / GENERAAL MAJOOR VAN MERLEN / COMMANDEERENDE DE BRIGADE LIGTE CAVALLERIE. / IDEM MAURITZ VAN HEYDEN. / RITMEESTER WILLEM VAN WYNBERGEN. / LUITENANT WILLEM VERHELLOUW. / IDEM WILLEM WOLFF. / JONKER CORNELIS BREDA. / HUN DIE VOOR HET VADERLAND, IN 'T HARNAS ZIJN GESTORVEN / IS DOOR DIEN HELDENDAAD ONSTERFLIJKE EER VERWORVEN.

Memorial tablet on wall: Quatre Bras, Waterloo. (Photograph)

AAN DE NEDERLANDERS EN / HUN MEDESTRYDERS VERDEDISERS / VAN QUATRE BRAS / 15–16 – VI – 1815 / A LA MEMOIRE DES / NEERLANDAIS ET LEURS / ALLIES DEFENSEURS DE / QUATRE BRAS

Memorial: Quatre Bras, Waterloo (Photograph)

TER NAGEDACHTENIS EN HULDE / AAN DE GEVALLENEN VAN DE / NEDERLANDSE CAVALERIE – / REGIMENTEN / HUZAREN NO 6 EN NO 8 / KARABINIERS NO 1, NO 2 EN NO 3 / LIGHTE DRAGONDERS NO 4 EN NO 5 / IN DE VELDSLAGEN BIJ / QUATRE BRAS 16–6–1815 EN / WATERLOO / 18 – 6–1815 / OPGERICHT / 21–9–1990 / REG HUZEREN VAN BOREEL / REG HUZAREN VAN SYTZAMA / REG HUZAREN PRIME ALEXANDER

Inscription also in Dutch and French.

FRANCE

Biarritz
Memorial: Porch of St Andrew's Church, (now Musée Historique), Biarritz, France. (Photographs)

PRISTINAE VIRTUTIS MEMOR / THIS PORCH / DEDICATED TO THE MEMORY OF THE / OFFICERS, NON-COMMISSIONED OFFICERS AND MEN, OF / THE BRITISH ARMY / WHO FELL IN THE SOUTH OF FRANCE / FROM THE 7TH OCTOBER 1813 TO THE 14TH APRIL 1814 / WAS ERECTED BY THEIR FELLOW SOLDIERS AND COMPATRIOTS AD 1882. / "GIVE PEACE IN OUR TIME, O LORD".

Memorial tablets to soldiers who died in the Peninsular War and South of France. The memorial contains names of the officers killed or died of wounds in the various battles fought in the Pyrenees and South of France from November 1813 to April 1814. All are listed by name in Vol. I (A – L) and Vol. II (M – Z)

King's German Legion and Royal Hanoverian Army

ALBERT, Anton
Lieutenant: 1st Battalion Light Infantry, King's German Legion.
Named on the Regimental Memorial: La Haye Sainte, Waterloo. (Photograph)
Named on the Waterloo Column, Hanover, Germany. (Photograph)

Ensign 21 May 1809. Lt 27 Jan 1811.
Served in the Peninsula Mar 1811 – Apr 1814. Present at Albuera, second siege of Badajoz, siege of Salamanca Forts, Moriscos, Salamanca, Venta del Poza, Vittoria, Tolosa, Bidassoa, Nivelle, Nive, St Etienne and Bayonne. Present at Waterloo where he was killed. Also served at Walcheren 1809 and the Netherlands 1814.
Reference: Beamish, N. L., History of the King's German Legion, Vol. 2, reprint 1997. No. 1008.

ALLEN, Thomas
Lieutenant. 1st Line Battalion, King's German Legion.
Ledger stone: All Saints' Churchyard, Springfield, Chelmsford, Essex. (Photograph)

LIEUTENANT THOMAS ALLEN / SON OF THE LATE THOMAS ALLEN OF CRANE HALL / NEAR IPSWICH / HAVING SERVED / HIS COUNTRY IN THE KING'S GERMAN LEGION / IN THE PENINSULAR AND AT WATERLOO / DIED IN PEACE AT SPRINGFIELD / NOV 12TH 1833 AGED 46.

Ensign 1 Feb 1809. Lt 8 Sep 1809.
Served in the Peninsula Jun 1809 – Apr 1814. Present at Talavera (wounded), Busaco, Fuentes d'Onoro, Ciudad Rodrigo, Moriscos, Salamanca, Burgos, Vittoria, Tolosa, San Sebastian, Bidassoa, Nivelle, Nive, St Etienne and Bayonne. Present at Waterloo. Also served in the Netherlands 1814.
Reference: Beamish, N. L., History of the King's German Legion, Vol. 2, reprint 1997. No. 390.

ALTEN, Count Charles von
Colonel Commandant. 1st Battalion Light Infantry, King's German Legion.
Statue: Waterloo Place, Hanover, Germany. (Photograph)

Front:

GENERAL GRAF CARL VON ALTEN.

Reverse side:

ERRICHTED IM IAHRE MDCCCXXXXVIIII (1849)

Left side:

GESTORBEN DEN XX APRIL MDCCCXXXX (20 APRIL 1840)

Right side:

GEBOREN DEN XX OCTOBER MDCCLXIIII (20 OCT 1764)

Memorial tablet: Neustädter Hof und Stadtkirche Church, Hanover, Germany. (Photograph)

HIER RUHET / GRAF CARL VON ALTEN / KGL HANN GENERAL U. STAATSMINSTER / 1764

1840 HERE LIES / COUNT CHARLES VON ALTEN / KGL HANNOVER GENERAL AND MINISTER OF STATE / 1764–1840

Ensign Hanoverian Foot Guards 1781. Lt 1785. Capt 1790. Major 1795. Bt Lt Colonel 1800 (Hanoverian Corps disbanded in 1803). Lt Colonel 1st Battalion Lt Infantry King's German Legion Nov 1803. Colonel Commandant 22 Dec 1804. Major General 25 Jul 1810. Hanoverian Army: Lt General 1814. General 1816.

Served in the Peninsula Aug 1808 – Jan 1809, Feb 1811 – Apr 1812 (Commanded 1 Brigade 7th Division) and Apr 1812 – Apr 1814 (GOC Light Division after the death of Major General Robert Craufurd). Present in the Corunna campaign, Vigo, Albuera (Mentioned in Despatches), second siege of Badajoz, Salamanca, San Munos, Hormanza (Mentioned in Despatches), San Millan (Mentioned in Despatches), Vittoria (Mentioned in Despatches), Pyrenees, Bidassoa (Mentioned in Despatches), Nivelle (Mentioned in Despatches), Nive (Mentioned in Despatches), Orthes (Mentioned in Despatches), Tarbes and Toulouse. Gold Cross for Albuera, Salamanca, Vittoria, Nivelle, Nive, Orthes and Toulouse. KCB 2 Jan 1815. Present at Waterloo (severely wounded) where he commanded the 3rd Division which was made up of one British brigade, one from the King's German Legion and one from Hanoverian troops. At Quatre Bras and at Waterloo the 3rd Division were in the thick of the fighting. Served with the Army of Occupation in command of the Hanoverian troops with the rank of General in the Hanoverian Army.

Also served in Flanders 1793–1795 with Hanoverian Army (present at Famars, Valenciennes, Hondschotte where he was placed in command of a battalion of Light troops along the River Lys and showed his skill at organising Light companies), Baltic 1807–1808, Walcheren 1809 and Netherlands 1814. After Waterloo returned to Hanover and was appointed Inspector General of Infantry and later Minister of War 1831. Died 20 Apr 1844 at Botzen in the Tyrol where he had gone for his health. Awarded honours from Britain and many of the European nations including GCB, GCH, Grand Cross of the Imperial Austrian Order of St Stephen, Grand Cross of the Imperial Russian Order of St Alexander Newsky, Grand Cross of the Royal Prussian Order of the Red Eagle, Knight Commander of Tower and Sword of Portugal and Knight's Cross of the Royal Order of William of the Netherlands.

REFERENCE: Dictionary of National Biography. United Service Journal, Jun 1840, pp. 244–6. Royal Military Calendar, Vol. 3, pp. 103–12. Beamish, N. L., History of the King's German Legion, Vol. 2, reprint 1997. No. 292.

AVEMANN, Charles Christian Frederick von

Captain. 1st Line Battalion, King's German Legion.

Named on the Memorial tablet: St Marien's Church, Celle, Lower Saxony, Germany. (Photograph)

BRIG MAJ C. V. AVEMANN 1813 B. D. PYRENAEEN

Capt 24 Apr 1808.

Served in the Peninsula Dec 1808 – Jul 1813 (ADC to Major General J. Murray Apr – Jul 1809. Brigade Major 1 Brigade 4th Division Aug 1812 – Jul 1813). Present at Douro, Talavera, Busaco, Fuentes d'Onoro, Ciudad Rodrigo, Vittoria and Pyrenees where he was killed near Pamplona 28 Jul 1813 whilst serving as Brigade Major. Also served in Hanover 1805 and the Baltic 1807–1808.

REFERENCE: Ludlow, History of the King's German Legion, Vol. 2, 1832, reprint, 1997. No. 976.

BACMEISTER, Johann Wilhelm Lucas

Captain. 5th Line Battalion, King's German Legion.

Named on the Memorial tablet: St Marien's Church, Celle, Lower Saxony, Germany. (Photograph)

HAUPTM: W. L. BACMEISTER. 1812. B. BURGOS

Capt 7 Nov 1803.

Served in the Peninsula Sep 1809 – Nov 1812. (Brigade Major 4 Brigade 1st Division Sep – Oct 1809, Brigade Major 3 Brigade 1st Division Nov 1809 – Sep 1810). Present at Douro, Talavera, Busaco, Ciudad Rodrigo, Moriscos, Salamanca and Burgos where he was severely wounded 18 Oct 1812 and died of his wounds at Penaranda 2 Nov 1812. Also served in Hanover 1805 and the Baltic 1807–1808.

Reference: Beamish, N. L., History of the King's German Legion, Vol. 2, reprint 1997. No. 1023.

BARING, Baron Georg von

Major. 2nd Battalion Light Infantry, King's German Legion.
Memorial: Waterloo Place, Hanover, Germany. (Photograph)

GEORG FREIHERR VON BARING / GEBOREN ZU HANNOVER DEN 8TEN MÄRZ 1773 / SEIT 1786 IN DER HANNÖVERISCHEN ARMEE / SPÄTET IN DER KÖNIGL: DEUTSCHEN LEGION / VERTHEIDIGER VON LA HAYE SAINTE / IN DER SCHLACHT VON WATERLOO / GESTORBEN ZU WIESBADEN ALS KÖNIGL: HANNOVER: / GENERAL LIEUTENANT DEN 27TEN FEBRUAR 1848.

GEORG BARON VON BARING / BORN HANOVER 8TH MARCH 1773 / FROM 1786 IN THE HANOVERIAN ARMY / LATER IN THE KING'S GERMAN LEGION / DEFENDER OF LA HAYE SAINTE / IN THE BATTLE OF WATERLOO / DIED AT WIESBADEN AS ROYAL HANOVERIAN / LIEUTENANT-GENERAL 27TH FEBRUARY 1848

Memorial tablet: La Haye Saint, Waterloo. (On outer wall). (M.I.)

TO MAJ. BARING AND THE 2ND LIGHT / BTN KGL'S HEROIC DEFENCE OF / LA HAIE SAINTE 18 JUNE 1815 / ALSO TO COL. VON OMPTEDA WHO FELL / LEADING A BRAVE COUNTER-ATTACK / AFTER THE FALL OF THE FARM / DEDICATED BY BEXHILL-ON-SEA ENGLAND / A KING'S GERMAN LEGION / GARRISON 1804–14 / ....

Hanoverian Army from 1786. Capt 1st Battalion Lt Infantry King's German Legion 10 Nov 1803. Bt Major 21 Jun 1813. Major 2nd Battalion Lt Infantry 4 Apr 1814.

Served in the Peninsula Aug 1808 – Jan 1809 and Mar 1811 – Apr 1814 (ADC to Major General Charles Alten). Present at Vigo, Albuera (wounded), Ciudad Rodrigo, first siege of Badajoz, Salamanca, Vittoria, Pyrenees, Bidassoa, Nivelle, Nive, Orthes, Tarbes and Toulouse. Also served at Hanover 1805, the Baltic 1807–1808, Walcheren 1809 and the Netherlands 1814. Present at Waterloo (defender of La Haye Sainte Farm from 1.30pm until they ran out of ammunition around 6pm and had to abandon the farm. The battalion had nearly 50 per cent casualties). CB. KH. Military Order of William of the Netherlands, King William's Cross of Hanover. Hanoverian Army: Major General and Commandant at Hanover.

Note: The monument is the original tombstone from Wiesbaden and was transferred when the cemetery became a park.

Reference: Beamish, N. L., History of the King's German Legion, Vol. 2, reprint 1997. No. 335.

BEHNE, Ludewig

Lieutenant. 2nd Battalion Light Infantry, King's German Legion.
Named on the Waterloo Memorial: Fallersleben, Lower Saxony, Germany. (Photograph)

LOUIS BEHNE AUS FALLERSLEBEN CAP. 2 TEN LEICHT. BAT. E. D. LEGION

Ensign 5 Jan 1810. Lt 1 Jul 1811. Capt 1815.

Served in the Peninsula Mar 1811 – Apr 1814. Present at Albuera, siege of Salamanca Forts, Moriscos,

Salamanca, Venta del Poza, San Millan, Bidassoa, Nivelle (severely wounded), Bayonne (severely wounded in the Sortie from Bayonne 14 Apr 1814). Present in the Waterloo campaign. Also served in the Netherlands 1814–1815. Died 11 Sep 1850 at Fallersleben as Major in the Hanoverian Army.
Reference: Beamish, N. L., History of the King's German Legion, Vol. 2, reprint 1997. No. 345.

BESSE, Conrad
Dragoon. 2nd Dragoons, King's German Legion.
Named on the Memorial tablet: St Marien's Church, Celle, Lower Saxony, Germany. (Photograph)

DRAG: C. BESSE 1812 B. GARZIA HERNANDEZ

Served in the Peninsula where he was killed at Garcia Hernandez 23 Jul 1812.

BEST, Wilhelm
Lieutenant. 1st Line Battalion, King's German Legion.
Memorial tablet: Garrison Cemetery, Hamelin, Lower Saxony, Germany. (M.I.)

KÖNIGL. HANNOV. OBERST / UND REG. COMMANDEUR / WILHELM BEST / GEB. 16. NOV. 1799 / GEST. 23. FEBR. 1886

COLONEL AND REGIMENTAL COMMANDER / KING'S GERMAN LEGION / WILHELM BEST / BORN 16 NOVEMBER 1799 / DIED 23 FEBRUARY 1886

Ensign 24 Apr 1813. Lt 26 Nov 1813.
Present at Waterloo. Also served in North Germany 1813 and the Netherlands 1814–1815. Awarded King William's Cross. Hanoverian Army: Captain Grenadier Guards. Died in Hamelin 23 Feb 1886.
Reference: Beamish, N. L., History of the King's German Legion, Vol. 2, reprint 1997. No. 403.

BLUMENBACH, Carl Edward
Lieutenant. Artillery, King's German Legion.
Named on the Memorial: St Andrew's Church (now Musée Historique), Biarritz, France. (Photograph)

Lt 9 Nov 1807.
Served in the Peninsula 1808–1814. Present at Albuera (wounded) and Toulouse where he was killed 10 Apr 1814. Also served in the Baltic 1807–1808.
Reference: Beamish, N. L., History of the King's German Legion, Vol. 2, reprint 1997. No. 786.

BOBERS, Carl von
Captain and Brigade Major. Staff Corps, King's German Legion.
Named on the Regimental Memorial: La Haye Sainte, Waterloo. (Photograph)
Named on the Waterloo Column, Hanover, Germany. (Photograph)
Named on the Memorial tablet: St Marien's Church, Celle, Lower Saxony, Germany. (Photograph)

BRIG: MAJ : C. A. V. BOBERS 1815 B. WATERLOO

Cornet 1st Hussars 10 Sep 1808. Lt 12 Jul 1811. Capt 13 Sep 1814.
Served in the Peninsula Jun 1809 – Apr 1814. Present at Talavera, Coa, Busaco, Pombal, Sabugal, Fuentes d'Onoro, El Bodon, Moriscos, Castrejon, Salamanca, Vittoria, Pyrenees, Nivelle, Orthes and Toulouse. Present at Waterloo where he was killed. Also served in the Netherlands 1814.
Reference: Beamish, N. L., History of the King's German Legion, Vol. 2, reprint 1997. No. 777.

BÖSEWIEL, Adolph
Major. 2nd Battalion Light Infantry, King's German Legion.
Named on the Regimental Memorial: La Haye Sainte, Waterloo. (Photograph)
Named on the Waterloo Column, Hanover, Germany. (Photograph)

Capt 5 May 1804. Bt Major 4 Jun 1814.

Served in the Peninsula Aug 1808 – Jan 1809 and Mar 1811 – Apr 1814. Present at Vigo and the first siege of Badajoz (wounded and taken prisoner). Remained in prison from Apr 1811 – Apr 1814. Present at Waterloo where he was killed. Also served at Hanover 1805, Copenhagen 1807, Walcheren 1809 and the Netherlands 1814.

REFERENCE: Beamish, N. L., History of the King's German Legion, Vol. 2, reprint 1997. No. 975.

BOYD, George
Lieutenant. 1st Line Battalion, King's German Legion.
Named on the Memorial: St Andrew's Church (now Musée Historique), Biarritz, France. (Photograph)

Ensign 29 May 1809. Lt 18 Mar 1812.

Served in the Peninsula Nov 1809 – Nov 1813. Present at Busaco, Fuentes d'Onoro, Ciudad Rodrigo, Moriscos, Salamanca, Burgos, Vittoria, Tolosa (wounded), San Sebastian, Bidassoa and Nivelle where he was killed 10 Nov 1813.

REFERENCE: Beamish, N. L., History of the King's German Legion, Vol. 2, reprint 1997. No. 1010.

BRANDIS, Eberhard von
Captain. 5th Line Battalion, King's German Legion.
Memorial slab: Schloss Ricklingen Churchyard, Lower Saxony, Germany. (Near Church door). (Photograph)

HIER / RUHET / GENERAL EBERHARD / FREIHERR VON BRANDIS / GEB. / 1795 / GEST. / 1884

HERE LIES / GENERAL BARON EBERHARD, / OF BRANDIS / BORN / 1795 / DIED / 1884.

Ensign 29 Sep 1807. Lt 18 Oct 1809. Capt 1815.

Served in the Peninsula Sep 1809 – Apr 1814. Present at Douro, Talavera (wounded), Busaco, Fuentes d'Onoro, Ciudad Rodrigo, Moriscos, Salamanca (wounded), Burgos, Vittoria, Tolosa, San Sebastian, Bidassoa, Nivelle, Nive, St Etienne and Bayonne. Present at Waterloo. Also served in the Baltic 1807–1808 and the Netherlands 1814–1815. MGS medal for Talavera, Busaco, Fuentes d'Onoro, Ciudad Rodrigo, Salamanca, Vittoria, San Sebastian, Nivelle and Nive. KH. King William's Cross. Hanoverian Army: Major 1838. Lt Colonel 1843. Colonel 1849. Major General 1851. Lt General 1855. General 1860. Died 13 Jun 1884. He was the last Hanoverian Minister of War.

REFERENCE: Beamish, N. L., History of the King's German Legion, Vol. 2, reprint 1997. No. 570. Dehnel, H., Erinnerungen Deutscher Offiziere in Britischen Diensten 1864 the diary of Eberhard von Brandis.

BRINCKMANN, Julius Johann Albrecht
Captain. 8th Line Battalion, King's German Legion.
Monument: Old Cemetery, Nienburg Weser, Lower Saxony, Germany. (Near main gate). (Photograph)

"FÜR GOTT" – "FÜR VATERLAND" – "UND KÖNIG" / HIER RUHET / JULIUS JOHANN ALBRECHT / BRINCKMANN / OBERST LIEUTENANT / IM 9 TEN K: H: INFANT: REGIMENT / GEBOREN D: 16 TEN DECB^{R}. 1766 / GESTORBEN D: 2.TEN SEPTB^{R}. 1825 / .... / ER DIENTE SEINEM KÖNIGE / 44 JAHRE / WOVON ER FÜNF / MÜHE- UND GEFAHR-VOLLE / IN OSTINDIEN / VERLEBTE

"FOR GOD" – "FOR FATHERLAND" – "AND KING" / HERE LIES / JULIUS JOHANN ALBRECHT / BRINCKMANN / LIEUTENANT COLONEL / IN THE 9TH KGL INFANTRY REGIMENT / BORN ON: 16TH DECBR. 1766 / DIED ON: 2ND SEPTBR. 1825 .... / HE SERVED HIS KING / FOR 44 YEARS / OF WHICH FIVE / DIFFICULT AND PERILOUS / YEARS WERE SPENT IN EAST INDIES

Capt 30 Jun 1806.

Served in the Peninsula Aug 1812 – Apr 1813. Present at Castalla. Present at Waterloo. Also served in India, the Baltic 1807–1809, the Mediterranean 1808–1812 and the Netherlands 1814–1815. Died at Nienburg 2 Sep 1825 when he was Bt Lt Colonel 9th Infantry Regiment in the Hanoverian Army.
Reference: Beamish, N. L., History of the King's German Legion, Vol. 2, reprint 1997. No. 698.

BROWN, William
2nd Captain. Artillery, King's German Legion.
Named on the Memorial tablet to Portuguese Commanders at Albuera: Albuera Wall, British Cemetery, Elvas, Portugal. (Photograph)

2nd Lt 5 May 1804. 1st Lt 9 Jul 1808. 2nd Capt 11 Dec 1812.

Served in the Peninsula 1808–1812 (with Portuguese Artillery 1810–1812). Present at Fuentes d'Onoro, Albuera and Ciudad Rodrigo. Present at Waterloo (severely wounded). Also served at Hanover 1805, the Baltic 1807–1808 and North Germany 1813–1814. Gold Medal for Albuera. Portuguese Cross for distinguished services. KH. Spanish Cross for distinguished service. King William's Cross. Became Bt Lt Colonel Hanoverian Artillery.
Reference: Beamish, N. L., History of the King's German Legion, Vol. 2, reprint 1997. No 38.

BRÜCKMANN, Friedrich Heinrich
Major. Artillery, King's German Legion.
Headstone: Garrison Cemetery, Stade, Lower Saxony, Germany. (Photograph)

Front side:

DENKMAL / GEWEIHET / DEM GENERAL MAJOR D. ARTILLERIE / F. H. BRÜCKMANN / VON / DEN SEINEN

MEMORIAL / DEDICATED / TO THE MAJOR GENERAL OF THE ARTILLERY / F. H. BRÜCKMANN / FROM / HIS FAMILY

Reverse side:

ER WARD / GEBOREN DEN 26. NOVEMBER / 1767 / GESTORBEN DEN 27. OCTOBER / 1834

HE WAS / BORN ON 26 NOVEMBER / 1767 / DIED ON 27 OCTOBER / 1834

Ensign 9th Line Battalion 3 Nov 1803. Capt KGL Artillery 1804. Major 26 Nov 1808. Lt Colonel 4 Jun 1814.

Present in the Waterloo campaign. Also served in Hanover 1805, the Baltic 1807–1808, North Germany 1813–1814 (present at Göhrde 16 Sep 1813 and Sehestadt 10 Dec 1813) and the Netherlands 1814–1815. KH. Order of St Vladimir of Russia. Hanoverian Army: Major General 1831. Died at Stade 27 Oct 1834.
Reference: Beamish, N. L., History of the King's German Legion, Vol. 2, reprint 1997. No. 27

BRÜGGEMANN, Heinrich
Lieutenant and Adjutant. 3rd Regiment of Hussars, King's German Legion.
Named on the Regimental Memorial: La Haye Sainte, Waterloo. (Photograph)
Named on the Waterloo Column, Hanover, Germany. (Photograph)

Cornet 30 Nov 1807. Adjt 4 Jan 1810. Lt 15 Feb 1812.

Served in the Peninsula Aug 1808 – Jan 1809. Present at Benevente (wounded). Present at Waterloo where he was killed. Also served in the Baltic 1807–1808, North Germany 1813–1814 (present at Göhrde where he was wounded) and the Netherlands 1814–1815.
Reference: Beamish, N. L., History of the King's German Legion, Vol. 2, reprint 1997. No.808.

BÜLOW, Friedrich von
Captain. 2nd Regiment of Dragoons, King's German Legion.
Named on the Regimental Memorial: La Haye Sainte, Waterloo. (Photograph)
Named on the Waterloo Column, Hanover, Germany. (Photograph)

Lt 10 May 1810.

Served in the Peninsula Jan 1812 – Apr 1814. Present at Castrejon, Salamanca, Garcia Hernandez, Majalahonda, Venta del Poza, San Millan, Vittoria, Vic Bigorre and Toulouse. Present at Waterloo where he was killed. Also served in the Netherlands 1814.
Reference: Beamish, N. L., History of the King's German Legion, Vol. 2, reprint 1997. No. 805.

BURFEINDT, Johann
Private. Militia Battalion, Royal Hanoverian Army.
Named on the Militia Battalion Memorial: Hesedorf, near Bremervörde, Lower Saxony, Germany. (Photograph)

Served in the Peninsula. Present at Waterloo where he was killed.

BUSSCHE, Hans von dem
Major. 1st Battalion Light Infantry, King's German Legion.
Pedestal tomb: Garrison Cemetery, Hamelin, Lower Saxony, Germany. (Photograph)

HANS VON DEM BUSSCHE / GENERAL / DER INFANTERIE / GEB. DEN 27 STEN AUG. 1774 / GEST. DEN 30 STEN SEPT 1851.

Lt 1793. Capt 1800. Capt King's German Legion 20 Oct 1803. Major 20 Jan 1811. Lt Colonel 18 Jun 1815.

Served in the Peninsula Aug 1808 – Apr 1814. Present at Douro, Talavera, Busaco, Sobral, Albuera, second siege of Badajoz, siege of Salamanca Forts, Moriscos, Salamanca, Venta del Poza, Tolosa, Vittoria, San Sebastian, Bidassoa, Nivelle, Nive, Adour, St Etienne and Bayonne. Present at Waterloo where he was severely wounded and his arm amputated. Also served in Hanover 1805, the Baltic 1807–1808 and the Netherlands 1814–1815. Gold Medal for Busaco. MGS medal for Talavera, Albuera, Salamanca, Vittoria, San Sebastian, Nivelle and Nive. CB. KCH and King William's Cross. Hanoverian Army: Colonel 1828. Major General 1838. Lt General 1843. General 1848. Died 30 Sep 1851.
Reference: Beamish, N. L., History of the King's German Legion, Vol. 2, reprint 1997. No. 294.

CARMICHAEL, Alexander
Lieutenant. 1st Line Battalion, King's German Legion.
Gravestone: Old Protestant Cemetery, Naples, Italy. (M.I.)

"ALEXANDER CARMICHAEL DIED 6TH JANUARY 1854, AGED 68 YEARS. CAPTAIN .... "

Ensign 20 May 1813. Lt 6 May 1814. Lt 97th Foot 25 Mar 1824. Capt 30 Dec 1836

Served in the Peninsula Aug 1813 – Apr 1814. Present at Nive, St Etienne and Bayonne. Present at Waterloo. Also served in the Netherlands 1814–1815. MGS medal for Nive.

Reference: Beamish, N. L., History of the King's German Legion, Vol. 2, reprint 1997. No. 405.

CHÜDEN, Georg Wilhelm Cyriaeus

Major. 4th Line Battalion, King's German Legion.
Named on the Regimental Memorial: La Haye Sainte, Waterloo. (Photograph)
Named on the Waterloo Column, Hanover, Germany. (Photograph)

Lt 9 Feb 1805. Bt Major 4 Jun 1814. Major 8 Sep 1814.

Present at Waterloo where he was severely wounded and died of his wounds 19 June 1815. Also served at Hanover 1805, the Baltic 1807, North Germany 1813–1814 and the Netherlands 1814.

Reference: Beamish, N. L., History of the King's German Legion, Vol. 2, reprint 1997. No. 1019.

CHÜDEN, Paul Gottlieb

Major. 2nd Line Battalion, King's German Legion.
Named on the Memorial: St Andrew's Church (now Musée Historique), Biarritz, France. (Photograph)

Capt 5th Line King's German Legion 18 Oct 1803. Major 2nd Line 7 Dec 1808.

Served in the Peninsula 1808 – Jan 1809 and Mar 1809 – Apr 1814. Present at Douro, Talavera, Busaco, Fuentes d'Onoro, Ciudad Rodrigo, Moriscos, Salamanca, Vittoria, Tolosa, San Sebastian, Bidassoa, Nivelle, Nive, St Etienne (severely wounded) and Bayonne where he was killed at the Sortie from Bayonne 14 Apr 1814. Also served in the Baltic 1807–1808.

Reference: Beamish, N. L., History of the King's German Legion, Vol. 2, reprint 1997. No. 974.

CLEEVES, Andrew

2nd Captain. Artillery, King's German Legion.
Ledger stone: Selby Abbey Churchyard, Selby, Yorkshire. (Photograph)

SACRED / TO THE MEMORY OF / LIEUTENANT COLONEL / ANDREW CLEEVES KH

2nd Capt 5 Jun 1807. Major 18 Jun 1815.

Served in the Peninsula May 1809 – Apr 1814. Present at Douro, Talavera, Busaco, Albuera (taken prisoner but escaped), second siege of Badajoz, Madrid (severely wounded), Salamanca, Vittoria and San Sebastian. At the retreat from Madrid 31 Oct 1812, the arsenal at the Retiro Fort had to be blown up. The mines used were so carelessly laid that two Commissariat officers were killed and Capt Cleeves in charge was severely burnt and nearly died. Present at Waterloo. Gold Medal for Albuera. Also served at Hanover 1804–1805 and the Baltic 1807–1808. Hanoverian Army: Bt Lt Colonel of Artillery. Died in Selby 8 Jun 1830 on his way back to Hanover.

Reference: Beamish, N. L., History of the King's German Legion, Vol. 2, reprint 1997. No. 31.

CRONHELM, Theodor von

Ensign. 4th Line Battalion, King's German Legion.
Named on the Regimental Memorial: La Haye Sainte, Waterloo. (Photograph)
Named on the Waterloo Column, Hanover, Germany. (Photograph)

Ensign 9 Jul 1814.

Present at Waterloo where he was killed. Also served in the Netherlands 1814–1815.

DANNENBERG, C.
Bugler. Royal Hanoverian Army.
Named on the Memorial tablet: St Marien's Church, Celle, Lower Saxony, Germany. (Photograph)

HORNBLSR: C. DANNENBERG 1814 V. BAYONNE

Served in the Peninsula where he was killed at Bayonne.

DEICHMANN, Wilhelm
Cornet. 3rd Regiment of Hussars, King's German Legion.
Named on the Regimental Memorial: La Haye Sainte, Waterloo. (Photograph)
Named on the Waterloo Column, Hanover, Germany. (Photograph)

Present at Waterloo where he was killed. Also served in North Germany 1813–1814 and the Netherlands 1814.
REFERENCE: Beamish, N. L., History of the King's German Legion, Vol. 2, reprint 1997. No. 815.

DENECKE, George
Physician. Medical Department.
Memorial tablet: St Thomas's Church, Newport, Isle of Wight. (Photograph)

SACRED / TO THE MEMORY OF / GEORGE DENECKE, ESQRE M.D. / WHO DEPARTED THIS LIFE / AUGUST 19TH 1838 / IN THE 63RD YEAR OF HIS AGE. / HIS AFFLICTED WIDOW, SUMS UP HIS CHARACTER / IN THE FOLLOWING COMPREHENSIVE SENTENCE, / HE LIVED AND DIED A CHRISTIAN.

Asst Surgeon King's German Legion 12 Jan 1805. Surgeon 2nd Line Battalion 25 May 1805. Staff Surgeon 6 Jul 1809. Physician 17 Jun 1813. Bt Deputy Inspector of Hospitals (on Continent) 22 Feb 1816. Deputy Inspector General 26 Oct 1826.

Served in the Peninsula Aug 1808 – Jan 1809 and Jun 1811 – Apr 1814 (Oct 1811 – Mar 1813 attached to 7th Division and Apr – Jun 1813 attached to 1st Division). Present at Vigo and the Corunna campaign. Present at Quatre Bras (wounded) and Waterloo. Also served at Hanover 1805, Copenhagen 1807, Walcheren 1809 and the Netherlands 1814–1815. MD 1801.
REFERENCE: Beamish, N. L., History of the King's German Legion, Vol. 2, reprint 1997. No. 1348.

DIEDEL, Friedrich
Captain. 3rd Line Battalion, King's German Legion.
Named on the Regimental Memorial: La Haye Sainte, Waterloo, Belgium. (Photograph)
Named on the Waterloo Column, Hanover, Germany. (Photograph)
Named on the Memorial tablet: St Marien's Church, Celle, Lower Saxony, Germany. (Photograph)

HAUPTMANN . F. DIEDEL 1815 B. WATERLOO

Lt 17 Dec 1804. Capt 28 Aug 1813.

Present at Waterloo where he was killed. Also served at Hanover 1805, the Baltic 1807, Mediterranean 1808–1814 and the Netherlands 1814.
REFERENCE: Beamish, N. L., History of the King's German Legion, Vol. 2, reprint 1997. No. 990.

DIEPENBROICK, Augustus Friedrich von
Captain. 5th Line Battalion, King's German Legion.
Headstone: All Saints' Churchyard, Freshwater, Isle of Wight. (Photograph)

IN MEMORY OF / CAPT AUGUSTUS VON DIEPENBROICK / OF THE 5TH LINE BATTALION / KING'S GERMAN LEGION / WHO WAS BORN AT HANOVER ON / ******* 1770 / AND DIED AT COLWELL BARRACKS / ON THE 21 SEPTEMBER / 1811.

Capt 5th Line 1 Jul 1806.

Served in the Peninsula Sep 1808 – Sep 1811. Present at Douro, Talavera and Busaco. Also served in the Baltic 1807–1808.

Reference: Beamish, N. L., History of the Kings German Legion. Vol. 2 reprint 1997. No. 1093.

DIERKS, David

Private. King's German Legion.

Named on the Militia Battalion Memorial: Hesedorf, near Bremervörde, Lower Saxony, Germany. (Photograph)

Served in the Peninsula and at Waterloo where he was killed.

DRANGMEISTER, Heinrich

Cornet. 2nd Regiment of Dragoons, King's German Legion.

Named on the Regimental Memorial: La Haye Sainte, Waterloo. (Photograph)

Named on the Waterloo Column, Hanover, Germany. (Photograph)

Cornet 2 Oct 1812.

Served in the Peninsula Nov 1812 – Apr 1814. Present at Vittoria, Vic Bigorre and Toulouse. Present at Waterloo where he was killed. Also served in the Netherlands 1814.

Reference: Beamish, N. L., History of the King's German Legion, Vol. 2, reprint 1997. No. 814.

DRECHSELL, Friedrich von

Captain and Brigade Major. Staff Corps, King's German Legion.

Named on the Memorial: St Andrew's Church (now Musée Historique), Biarritz, France. (Photograph)

Lt King's German Legion Artillery 20 Apr 1807. Lt 5th Line 1810. Capt and Brigade Major 18 Jul 1810.

Served in the Peninsula Oct 1810 – Apr 1814 (Brigade Major 3 Brigade 1st Division). Present at Fuentes d'Onoro, Ciudad Rodrigo, Salamanca, Burgos, Vittoria, Tolosa, Bidassoa, Nivelle, Nive, St Etienne, Bayonne (wounded) and the Sortie from Bayonne where he was killed 14 Apr 1814. Also served in the Baltic 1807.

Reference: Beamish, N. L., History of the King's German Legion, Vol. 2, reprint 1997. No. 776.

DRECHSEL, Friedrich Carl von

Colonel Commandant. 7th Line Battalion, King's German Legion.

Tombstone: Old Garden Cemetery, Hanover, Germany. (Photograph)

FRIEDRICH CARL VON DRECHSEL / KÖNIGL. GROSSBRIT. HANNOVERSCHER / GENERAL DER INFANTERIE / COMMANDANT / DER RESIDENTS / GR. KREUTZ DES KÖNIGLICHEN / GUELPHEN ORDENS / GEB. DEN 12. AUGUST 1740 / GEST. DEN 12. JANUAR 1827

FRIEDRICH CARL VON DRECHSEL / GENERAL KING'S GERMAN LEGION INFANTRY / RESIDENCY COMMANDANT / AWARDED THE GREAT CROSS OF THE ROYAL GUELPH ORDER / BORN 12 AUGUST 1740 / DIED 12 JANUARY 1827

Colonel Commandant 7th Line 21 Jan 1806. Lt General 4 Jun 1811.

Served in the Baltic (present at Isle of Rügen). KH. Hanoverian Army: General of Infantry 1815.

Commandant of Hanover 1816. Bt General 1827. Died in Hanover 12 Jan 1827.
Reference: Beamish, N. L., History of the King's German Legion, Vol. 2, reprint 1997. No. 645.

DU PLAT, Georg Carl August
Lieutenant Colonel. 4th Line Battalion, King's German Legion.
Named on the Regimental Memorial: La Haye Sainte, Waterloo. (Photograph)
Named on the Waterloo Column, Hanover, Germany. (Photograph)

Lt Colonel 30 Jun 1805. Bt Colonel 4 Jun 1813.

Served in the Peninsula Aug 1812 – Apr 1814 (Commanded Brigade from Oct 1813). Present in Eastern Spain, Castalla and Tarragona. Present at Waterloo where he was severely wounded and died of his wounds 21 June 1815. Also served in Hanover 1805, Copenhagen 1807, Mediterranean 1808–1812 and the Netherlands 1814.
Reference: Beamish, N. L., History of the King's German Legion, Vol. 2, reprint 1997. No. 1017.

DÜRING, Johann Christian von
Captain. Field Jaeger Corps.
Obelisk and grave in railed enclosure: Lent Barracks, Rotenburg / Wümme, Lower Saxony, Germany. (Photograph)

DEM / OBERFORSTMEISTER / VON DÜRING / GEBOREN ZU DANNENBERG AM 16. APRIL 1792 / GESTORBEN ZU HANNOVER AM 29. JANUAR 1862

THE / HEAD FORESTER / VON DÜRING / BORN AT DANNENBERG 16. APRIL 1792 / DIED AT HANOVER 29. JANUARY 1862

Present at Waterloo after having recruited men for the Jaeger Corps of Count von Kielmannsegge. He was the General Director of Forests at Lüneburg and the men he recruited were also foresters and known for their sharp shooting. They were deployed in the woods around Hougoumont to deter the French voltigeurs. Retired in 1820 and returned to his forestry work.

ENCKHAUSEN, Franz Heinrich
Private. Militia Battalion, Osnabrück, Germany.
Named on the Memorial tablet: St Marien's Church, Celle, Lower Saxony, Germany. (Photograph)

Served in the Peninsula. Present at Talavera where he was killed.

ERDMANN, Friedrich
Lieutenant. 5th Line Battalion, King's German Legion.
Memorial: Old Cemetery, Nienburg Weser, Lower Saxony, Germany. (M.I.)

FRIEDRICH ERDMANN / KÖNIGL. HANNOV. OBERST UND / COMMANDANT VON NIENBURG / GEB. ZU LEESE 17 SEPT 1779 / GEST. ZU NIENBURG 16 MAIN 1866

FRIERICH ERDMANN / ROYAL HANOVERIAN COLONEL AND / COMMANDANT OF NIENBURG / BORN AT LEESE 17TH SEPT. 1779. DIED AT NIENBURG 27TH MAY 1866

Ensign 21 Mar 1804. Lt 25 Jan 1806.

Served in the Peninsula Apr 1813–1814 attached to 1 Italian Levy. Present at Ordal. Also served in Hanover 1805, the Baltic 1807 and the Mediterranean 1808–1815.
Reference: Beamish, N. L., History of the King's German Legion, Vol. 2, reprint 1997. No 400.

FRANK, Georg
Ensign. 2nd Battalion Light Infantry, King's German Legion.
Named on the Waterloo Memorial: Fallersleben, Lower Saxony, Germany. (Photograph)

Ensign 5 Jan 1814.

Present at Waterloo where he was severely wounded at La Haye Sainte. Also served in the Netherlands 1814–1815. Hanoverian Army: Bt Captain. Died at Linden, Hanover 18 Aug 1857.
REFERENCE: Beamish, N. L., History of the King's German Legion, Vol. 2, reprint 1997. No. 361.

GERBER, Johann Georg Arnold
Major. 5th Line Battalion, King's German Legion.
Pedestal tomb: Garrison Cemetery, Hamelin, Lower Saxony, Germany. (Photograph)

HIER RUHET MIT BESONDERER TREUE / DER KÖNIGLICHE HAT ER DEM KÖNIG / GROSS-BRITTANNISCHE 42 JAHRE GEDIENT / OBERSTLIEUTNANT VORZÜGLICH ABER / JOHANN ARNOLD / GEORG GERBER IM 5. LINIEN BAT. DER K: DEUTSCH. LEGION / GEBOREN IN PORTUGAL / DEN 22. APRIL 1739 UND SPANIEN / GESTORBEN RUHM EINES BRAVEN / DEN 14. MERZ 1816 KRIEGERS / SICH ERWORBEN / ....

HERE RESTS ONE OF SPECIAL LOYALTY WHO SERVED ROYALLY THE KING OF GREAT BRITAIN FOR 42 YEARS, MOSTLY AS LT. COLONEL JOHANN ARNOLD GEORG GERBER OF THE 5TH LINE BATTALION OF THE KING'S GERMAN LEGION BORN IN PORTUGAL 22ND APRIL 1739 AND DIED IN SPAIN, 14TH MARCH 1816, HAVING ACHIEVED THE FAME OF A BRAVE SOLDIER.

Capt 8th Line 27 Oct 1803. Major 5th Line 10 Apr 1811. Bt Lt Colonel 21 Sep 1813.

Served in the Peninsula Oct 1811 – Apr 1814. Present at Ciudad Rodrigo, Moriscos, Salamanca, Burgos, Vittoria, Tolosa, San Sebastian, Bidassoa, Nivelle, Nive, St Etienne and Bayonne. Also served in the Baltic 1807, Mediterranean 1808–1810 and the Netherlands 1814–1815. Gold Medal for San Sebastian. Half pay 25 Jul 1815. Died in Hamelin 14 Mar 1816.
Note: Johann Arnold George Gerber on memorial inscription.
REFERENCE: Beamish, N. L., History of the King's German Legion, Vol. 2, reprint 1997. No. 1174.

GERSON, Georg Hartog
Assistant Surgeon. 5th Line, King's German Legion.
Obelisk: Jewish Cemetery, Hamburg, Germany. (Photograph)

DR GERSON / GEB. 25. AUGUST 1788 / GEST. 3. DECEMBER 1844

DR GERSON / BORN 25 AUGUST 1788 / DIED 3 DECEMBER 1844

Asst Surgeon 9 Aug 1811.

Served in the Peninsula Feb 1812 – Apr 1814. Present at Moriscos, Salamanca, Burgos, Vittoria, Tolosa, San Sebastian, Bidassoa, Nivelle, Nive, St Etienne and Bayonne. Present at Waterloo. Also served in the Netherlands 1814–1815. Died at Hamburg 3 Dec 1844.
REFERENCE: Beamish, N. L., History of the King's German Legion, Vol. 2, reprint 1997. No. 599.

GOEBEN, August Alexander von
Captain, 1st Battalion Light Infantry, King's German Legion.
Named on the Regimental Memorial: La Haye Sainte, Waterloo. (Photograph)
Named on the Waterloo Column, Hanover, Germany. (Photograph)

Ensign 25 Jan 1806. Lt 25 Nov 1809.

Served in the Peninsula Aug 1808 – Jan 1809 and Mar 1811 – Apr 1814. Present at Vigo, Albuera, second siege of Badajoz, siege of Salamanca Forts, Moriscos, Salamanca, Venta del Poza, San Millan, Vittoria, Tolosa, Bidassoa, Nivelle, Nive, Bayonne and St Etienne. Present at Waterloo where he was killed. Also served in the Baltic 1807–1808 and the Netherlands 1814.

REFERENCE: Beamish, N. L., History of the King's German Legion, Vol. 2, reprint 1997. No. 993.

GOTTSCHALK, Ernst

Sergeant. 1st Line Battalion, King's German Legion.
Named on the Waterloo Column, Hanover, Germany. (Photograph)
Named on the Memorial tablet: St Marien's Church, Celle, Lower Saxony, Germany. (Photograph)

SERGNT: E. GOTTSCHALK 1815 B. WATERLOO

Present at Waterloo where he was killed.

GROTE, Otto August Friedrich von

Major. 1st Regiment of Hussars, King's German Legion.
Pedestal tomb: Old Cemetery, Nienburg Weser, Lower Saxony, Germany. (Photograph)

OTTO AUGUST / FRIEDRICH / FREYHERR GROTE / OBERST UND / COMMANDANT / ZU / NIENBURG / GEBOREN ZU / NIENBURG / DEN 8TEN DECEMBER 1767 / GESTORBEN ZU / NIENBURG / DEN 27TEN JANUAR 1834

OTTO AUGUST FRIEDRICH BARON GROTE / COLONEL AND / COMMANDANT / AT NIENBURG / BORN AT NIENBURG / 8TH DECEMBER 1767 / DIED AT / NIENBURG / 27TH JANUARY 1834.

Major 17 May 1806.

Served in the Peninsula Jun 1809 – Jun 1810. Present at Talavera. Also served in the Baltic 1807. Resigned 30 Oct 1810. Colonel Commandant at Nienburg where he died 27 Jan 1834.

REFERENCE: Beamish, N. L., History of the King's German Legion, Vol. 2, reprint 1997. No. 889.

GÜNTHER, Johann Georg

Surgeon. 4th Line Battalion, King's German Legion.
Memorial: Old Cemetery, Nienburg Weser, Lower Saxony, Germany. (M. I.)

HIER RUHET / JOHANN GEORG GÜNTHER, / OBER-WUNDARZT / IN 4 TEN BATAILLON / KING'S GERMAN LEGION / GEBOREN DEN 29. MÄRZ 1774 / GESTORBEN DEN 10 TEN JANUARY 1830

HERE RESTS / JOHANN GEORG GÜNTHER / SURGEON / OF THE 4TH BATTALION / KING'S GERMAN LEGION / BORN 29 MARCH 1774 / DIED 10 JANUARY 1830

Surgeon 24 Dec 1805.

Served in the Peninsula Aug 1812 – Apr 1814. Present at Castalla and Tarragona. Present at Waterloo. Also served at Hanover 1805, the Baltic 1807, Mediterranean 1808–1812 and the Netherlands 1814–1815. Died at Nienburg 10 Jan 1830.

REFERENCE: Beamish, N. L., History of the King's German Legion, Vol. 2, reprint 1997. No. 555.

HALKETT, Sir Colin

Colonel. 2nd Battalion Light Infantry, King's German Legion.
Chest tomb: Royal Hospital Cemetery, Chelsea, London. (Photograph)

SACRED TO THE MEMORY OF / GENERAL SIR COLIN HALKETT GCB GCH / AND KNIGHT OF SEVERAL FOREIGN ORDERS / COLONEL OF THE 45TH NOTTINGHAMSHIRE REGIMENT OF FOOT / AND GOVERNOR OF CHELSEA HOSPITAL. / HE RAISED THE 2ND LIGHT BATTALION OF THE KINGS GERMAN LEGION. / IN THE CAMPAIGN OF 1813 HE COMMANDED A BRITISH BRIGADE / AND SERVED THROUGHOUT THE WHOLE OF THE PENINSULAR WAR WITH GREAT DISTINCTION / AND AT WATERLOO THE COMMAND OF THE 3RD DIVISION. / THEN AT WATERLOO HE / HIMSELF WAS SEVERELY WOUNDED. / HE DEPARTED THIS LIFE ON THE 24TH SEPTEMBER 1856 / IN THE 83RD YEAR OF HIS AGE. / BELOVED RESPECTED AND HONOURED BY ALL WHO HAD THE HAPPINESS OF KNOWING HIM.

Lt Colonel 2nd Lt Battalion King's German Legion 9 Feb1805. Bt Colonel 1 Jan 1812. Major General 4 Jun 1814. Lt General 22 Jul 1830. General 9 Nov 1846.

Served in the Peninsula Aug 1808 – Jan 1809 and Mar 1811 – Dec 1813. (Commanded 1 Brigade 7th Division Oct 1811 – Dec 1812 and 3 Brigade 1st Division Dec 1812 – Dec 1813). Raised the 2nd Battalion of the Light Infantry King's German Legion to serve in the Peninsula. Present at Vigo, first siege of Badajoz, Albuera, second siege of Badajoz, siege of Salamanca Forts, Moriscos, Salamanca, San Munos, Venta del Pozo (Mentioned in Despatches), Vittoria (Mentioned in Despatches), Tolosa, (Mentioned in Despatches), Bidassoa, Nivelle and Nive. Present at Waterloo where he commanded the 5th British Brigade (30th, 33rd, 69th and 73rd). Severely wounded and awarded pension of £350 per annum. Gold Cross for Albuera, Salamanca, Vittoria and Nive. GCB. GCH. KTS. Knight 3rd Class of Wilhelm of the Netherlands, Commander of Bavarian Order of Maximilian Joseph. Also served at Hanover 1805, Baltic 1808, Walcheren 1809 and Netherlands 1814. Lt Governor of Jersey 1830. Colonel 31st Foot 28 Mar 1838. Colonel 45th Foot 1847. Governor of Chelsea Hospital 1849 until his death in 1856. Brother of Sir Hugh Halkett Commander in Chief of Hanoverian Army who died in Hanover 1863.

REFERENCE: Gentleman's Magazine, Nov 1856, p. 649. Annual Register, 1856, Appx, p. 274. Royal Military Calendar, Vol. 3, pp. 380–2. Beamish, N. L., History of the King's German Legion, Vol. 2, reprint 1997. No. 333.

HALKETT, Hugh

Lieutenant Colonel. 7th Line Battalion, King's German Legion.
Ledger stone: Neuenhäuser Churchyard, Celle, Lower Saxony, Germany. (Photograph)

HUGH FREIHERR VON HALKETT . KÖNIGLICH HANNOVERSCHER / GENERAL DER INFANTERIE / GEB. 30. AUGUST 1783 / GEST. DEN 26. JULI 1863

BARON HUGH HALKETT / GENERAL OF THE KGL INFANTRY / BORN 30 AUGUST 1783 / DIED 26 JULY 1863.

Ledger stone: Old Cemetery, Neuenhäuser, Celle, Germany. (Photograph)

BEGRABNIS / DES / GENERAL HUGH HALKETT

Ensign 94th Foot 18 Apr 1794. Lt 15 Jul 1795. Capt Light Battalion 17 Oct 1803 (raised by his elder brother Colin Halkett in Hanover). Major 2nd Line Battalion, King's German Legion 1 Jul 1805. Bt Lt Colonel 1 Jun 1812. Lt Colonel 7th Line 22 Sep 1812.

Served in the Peninsula 19 Aug 1808 – Jan 1809, Mar – Aug 1811 and Mar – Nov 1812. Present at Vigo, Albuera, second siege of Badajoz, siege of Salamanca Forts, Moriscos, Salamanca, retreat from

Burgos and Venta del Poza. Present at Waterloo in command of 3rd and 4th Brigade of Hanoverian Militia in the woods near Hougoument. At the end of the day Halkett took General Cambronne prisoner. Also served in India 1798–1801 with 94th Foot, Hanover 1805, the Baltic 1807–1808 (present at Isle of Rügen), Walcheren (present at siege of Flushing), North Germany 1813–1814 (present at Göhrde and siege of Gluckstädt and siege of Harburg). Gold Medal for Albuera and Salamanca. CB. GCH. Received many awards including Prussian Black Eagle, St Anne of Russia, Prussian Order of Military Merit, Sword of Sweden and Spanish Gold Cross for Albuera. Hanoverian Army after KGL was disbanded: Colonel 1817. Major General 1818. Colonel 4th Infantry Brigade (Celle) 1819. Lt General 1834. General and Inspector of Hanoverian Infantry 1845. Died in Hanover 26 Jul 1863. Younger brother of Colonel Sir Colin Halkett 2nd Battalion Light Infantry, King's German Legion.
Reference: Dictionary of National Biography. Gentleman's Magazine, Sep 1863, pp. 376–7. Beamish, N. L., History of the King's German Legion, Vol. 2, reprint 1997. No. 646.

HALPIN, William
Paymaster. 1st Regiment of Dragoons, King's German Legion.
Low monument: Kensal Green Cemetery, London. (17459/125/8). (Photograph)
Half buried uninscribed stone. The photograph shows the stone of his son General George Halpin which lies next to his own, because it records the name of William Halpin and his regiment.

COLONEL GEORGE HALPIN, MADRAS ARMY, / SECOND SON OF CAPTN WILLIAM HALPIN, 1ST HEAVY DRAGOONS, K. G. L.

Paymaster 6 Jan 1807.

Served in the Peninsula Jan 1812 – Apr 1814. Present at Salamanca, Garcia Hernandez, Majalahonda, Venta del Pozo, Vittoria, Orthes, Tarbes and Toulouse. Present in the Waterloo campaign. Half pay 25 Jun 1816. MGS medal for Salamanca, Vittoria, Orthes and Toulouse. Also served in the Netherlands 1814. Died 1862.
Reference: Beamish, N. L., History of the King's German Legion, Vol. 2, reprint 1997. No. 120.

HAMELBERG, Ernst von
Captain 5th Line Battalion, King's German Legion.
Named on the Memorial tablet: St Marien's Church, Celle, Lower Saxony, Germany. (Photograph)

HAUPTM: I. E. V. HAMELBERG 1809 B. TALAVERA

Capt 19 Oct 1803.

Served in the Peninsula Sep 1808 – Aug 1809. Present at Douro and Talavera where he was severely wounded 28 Jul 1809 and died of his wounds 11 Aug 1809. Also served in the Baltic 1807–1808.
Reference: Beamish, N. L., History of the King's German Legion, Vol. 2, reprint 1997. No 1020.

HARTLEP, H.
Private. Royal Hanoverian Army.
Named on the Memorial tablet: St Marien's Church, Celle, Lower Saxony, Germany. (Photograph)

SOLDAT H. HARTLEP 1809 TALAVERA

Served in the Peninsula. Present at Talavera where he was killed.

HARTMANN, Sir Georg Julius von
Major. Artillery, King's German Legion.
Pedestal tomb: Engesohde Cemetery, Hanover, Germany. (Grave No. 36a–36b). (Photograph)

GENERAL SIR JULIUS / VON HARTMANN / GEBOREN DEN 6. MAI / 1774 / GESTORBEN DEN 7. JUNI 1856 / ....

GENERAL SIR JULIUS / VON HARTMANN / BORN 6 MAY 1774 / DIED 7 JUNE 1856 . ...

Capt KGL Artillery Jan 1804. Major 12 Apr 1806. Bt Lt Colonel 17 Aug 1812.

Served in the Peninsula 1809 – Apr 1814. With Portuguese Army Jan 1811 – Apr 1814 (in 1811 in temporary command of Portuguese Artillery during the absence of Colonel Dickson). Present at Douro, Talavera (wounded 28 Jul), Busaco, Campo Mayor, Olivencia, Albuera (senior artillery officer of Anglo Portuguese Artillery), Arroyo dos Molinos, first and second sieges of Badajoz, Badajoz, siege of Salamanca Forts, Salamanca (awarded Bt Lt Colonelcy), Madrid (destroyed the Retiro), Vittoria (commanded reserve artillery of Anglo-Portuguese Army), San Sebastian, Bidassoa, Nivelle, Nive, Adour, Bayonne (wounded at the Sortie from Bayonne 14 Apr 1814). Present at Waterloo in command of KGL Artillery and the newly raised Hanoverian Artillery. Present at the Capture of Paris. Also served in Flanders 1793–1795 (present at Famars, Valenciennes where he was taken prisoner until 1795), Hanover 1805, the Baltic 1807–1808 and the Netherlands 1814–1815. KCB 1814. Gold Cross for Talavera, Albuera, Salamanca, Vittoria, San Sebastian, and Nive. MGS medal for Busaco, Badajoz and Nivelle. The KGL was disbanded in Feb 1816 and Hartmann joined the Hanoverian Army: Colonel 1816. Major General 1818. Chief of Artillery Brigade 1833. Lt General 1836 taking command of the Engineers as well as Artillery. His responsibilities included superintendence of arsenals in 1848. Resigned in 1850 after 62 years service but was recalled in 1853 and became General of Artillery 1854. GCH. King William's Cross. Knight of 1st Class of Red Eagle of Prussia. 2nd Class of Lion of the Netherlands. Died 7 Jun 1856 aged 82 years.

Reference: Beamish, N. L., History of the King's German Legion, Vol. 2, reprint 1997. No. 26. United Service Journal, Aug 1856, pp. 639–40.

HARTWIG, Gottlieb von

Lieutenant. 7th Line, King's German Legion.

Memorial: Old Cemetery, Nienburg Weser, Lower Saxony, Germany. (Photograph)

HIER RUHET DER MAJOR / GOTTLIEB VON HARTWIG / VOM 7 TEN INFANTERIE REGIMENTE / RITTER DED KÖNIGL. GUELFEN-ORDENS / GEBOREN AM 12 NOVEMBER 1791 / GESTORBEN AM 31 JULY 1840 / DER VEREWIGTE DIENTE 34 JAHRE / UND WAR TEILNEHMER DER RUHM- /VOLLEN FELDZÜGE DER ENGLISCH-DEUTSCHEN / LEGION / .... / UNERSCHÜTTERLICHE TREUE GEGEN SEINEN / KÖNIG, STRENGE ERFÜLLUNG SEINER DIENST- / PFLICHTEN UND WARME ANHÄGLICHKEIT / AN SEINE KAMERADEN SICHERN IHM / EIT EHRENVOLLES ANDENKEN

HERE RESTS THE MAJOR / GOTTLIEB VON HARTWIG / FROM THE 7TH INFANTRY REGIMENT / KNIGHT OF THE ROYAL GUELPHIC ORDER / BORN 12TH NOVEMBER 1791 / DIED 31ST JULY 1840 / THE DECEASED SERVED 34 YEARS / AND TOOK PART IN THE GLORIOUS CAMPAIGNS OF THE ENGLISH-GERMAN / LEGION. / .... / UNSHAKABLE LOYALTY TO HIS / KING, STRONG PERFORMANCE OF / HIS DUTY AND A WARM DEVOTION / TO HIS COMRADES ENSURED HIM AN HONOURABLE REMEMBRANCE

Ensign 23 Jun 1806. Lt 17 Jan 1808. Adjutant 17 Jan 1810.

Served in the Peninsula Sep 1809 – Jul 1811. Present at Douro, Talavera, Busaco and Fuentes d'Onoro. Also served in the Baltic 1807–1808 and the Mediterranean 1812–1816. Hanoverian Army: Captain 10th Line Battalion.

Reference: Beamish, N. L., History of the King's German Legion, Vol. 2, reprint 1997. No. 657.

HEINE, Friedrich

Captain. 1st Line Battalion, King's German Legion.
Named on the Memorial tablet: St Marien's Church, Celle, Lower Saxony, Germany. (Photograph)

HAUPTM: F HEINE 1813 V. ST. SEBASTIAN

Ensign 6 Feb 1804. Lt 25 Jun 1806. Capt 30 Oct 1812.

Served in the Peninsula Dec 1808 – Sep 1813. Present at Douro, Talavera, Busaco, Fuentes d'Onoro, Ciudad Rodrigo, Moriscos, Salamanca, Burgos, Vittoria, Tolosa and San Sebastian where he was severely wounded 31 Aug 1813 and died of his wounds 3 Sep 1813. Also served at Hanover 1805, Mediterranean 1806–1807 and the Baltic 1807–1808.

REFERENCE: Beamish, N. L., History of the King's German Legion, Vol. 2, reprint 1997. No. 1030.

HEISE, Gabriel Wilhelm

Captain. 3rd Regiment of Hussars, King's German Legion.
Gravestone: St Mathew's Churchyard, Ipswich, Suffolk. (No longer extant). (M.I.)

"IN / MEMORY OF / .... GABRIEL HEISE / LATE CAPTAIN IN THE 3RD REGIMENT / KING'S GERMAN HUSSARS / WHO DIED JANUARY 2, 1810 IN THE / 46TH YEAR OF HIS AGE / OF WHICH HE SPENT 26 YEARS / IN THE HANOVERIAN AND 5 YEARS / IN THE ENGLISH SERVICE. / THIS STONE / IS ERECTED BY HIS BROTHER OFFICERS / AS A MARK OF THEIR ESTEEM / FOR HIS HIGH CHARACTER / AS AN OFFICER / AND A MAN."

Capt 7 Nov 1803.

Served in the Peninsula Aug 1808 – Jan 1809. Present at Benevente. Also served at Hanover 1805 and the Baltic 1807–1808.

REFERENCE: Beamish, N. L., History of the King's German Legion, Vol. 2, reprint 1997. No. 835.

HEISE, Georg

Captain. 4th Line Battalion, King's German Legion.
Named on the Waterloo Column, Hanover, Germany. (Photograph)
Named on the Regimental Memorial: La Haye Sainte, Waterloo. (Photograph)

Lt 18 Dec 1804. Capt 10 Mar 1812.

Served in the Peninsula Aug 1812 – Apr 1814. Present at Castalla and Tarragona. Present at Waterloo where he was severely wounded and died of his wounds 27 Jun 1815. Also served in Hanover 1805, the Baltic 1807, Mediterranean 1808–1812 and the Netherlands 1814.

Note: Named as Friedrich on memorial.

REFERENCE: Beamish, N. L., History of the King's German Legion, Vol. 2, reprint 1997. No. 1029.

HODENBERG, Friedrich von

Lieutenant. 1st Line Battalion, King's German Legion.
Family Memorial tablet: St George's Church, Grabow, Mecklenburg, Germany. (Photograph)

AM 3. DECEMBER 1813 STARB IM / PFARHAUSE ZU GRABOW / DER KURFFÜRSTL. HANNOVERSCHE FÄHNRICH / ADOLF FRIEDRICH GEORG V. HODENBERG / GEB. ZU HAMELN DEN 7. JANUAR 1795 / AN DEN IM GEFECHT BEI BÜCHEN AM / 6. OCTOBER 1813 ERHALTENEN WUNDEN. / ER FOLGTE SEINEN ÄLTEREN BRÜDERN / FRIEDRICH UND HEINRICH, DIE IN DES / KÖNIGS DEUTSCHER LEGION AUF SPANISCHEM / BODEN AM 28TEN JULI 1809BEI TALAVERA / DEN HELDENTOD FÜR DAS VATERLAND STARBEN.

ON THE 3RD OF DECEMBER 1813 DIED IN THE / RECTORY OF GRABOW / THE ELECTORAL HANOVERIAN ENSIGN / ADOLF FRIEDRICH GEORG VON HODENBERG, / BORN AT HAMELN ON THE 7TH OF JANUARY 1795, / AND DIED AS A RESULT OF WOUNDS / RECEIVED IN THE SKIRMISHES OF BÜCHEN / ON THE 6TH OF OCTOBER 1813. / HE FOLLOWS HIS ELDER BROTHERS / FRIEDRICH AND HEINRICH, WHO IN THE / KING'S GERMAN LEGION ON SPANISH / SOIL ON 28TH JULY 1809 DIED THE / DEATH OF HEROES / FOR THEIR FATHERLAND.

Named on the Memorial tablet: St Marien's Church, Celle, Lower Saxony, Germany. (Photograph)

LEIUT: F. A. A. V. HODENBERG 1809 B. TALAVERA

Ensign 25 Jan 1806. Lt 24 Apr 1808.

Served in the Peninsula Dec 1808 – Jul 1809. Present at Douro and Talavera where he was severely wounded 28 Jul 1809 and died of his wounds 30 Jul 1809. Also served in the Mediterranean 1806–1807 and the Baltic 1807–1808. Brother of Lt Georg Heinrich von Hodenberg 1st Line KGL, killed at Talavera and Ensign Adolf von Hodenberg died of wounds at Büchen 1813.
Reference: Beamish, N. L., History of the King's German Legion, Vol. 2, reprint 1997. No. 1034.

HODENBERG, Georg Heinrich von
Lieutenant. 1st Line Battalion, King's German Legion.
Family Memorial tablet: St George's Church, Grabow, Mecklenburg, Germany. (Photograph)

AM 3. DECEMBER 1813 STARB IM / PFARHAUSE ZU GRABOW / DER KURFFÜRSTL. HANNOVERSCHE FÄHNRICH / ADOLF FRIEDRICG GEORG V. HODENBERG / GEB. ZU HAMELN DEN 7. JANUAR 1795 / AN DEN IM GEFECHT BEI BÜCHEN AM / 6. OCTOBER 1813 ERHALTENEN WUNDEN. / ER FOLGTE SEINEN ÄLTEREN BRÜDERN / FRIEDRICH UND HEINRICH, DIE IN DES / KÖNIGS DEUTSCHER LEGION AUF SPANISCHEM / BODEN AM 28 TEN JULI 1809 BEI TALAVERA / DEN HELDENTOD FÜR DAS VATERLAND STARBEN.

ON THE 3RD OF DECEMBER 1813 DIED IN THE / RECTORY OF GRABOW / THE ELECTORAL HANOVERIAN ENSIGN / ADOLF FRIEDRICH GEORG VON HODENBERG, / BORN AT HAMELN ON THE 7TH OF JANUARY 1795, / AND DIED AS A RESULT OF WOUNDS / RECEIVED IN THE SKIRMISHES OF BÜCHEN / ON THE 6TH OF OCTOBER 1813. / HE FOLLOWS HIS ELDER BROTHERS / FRIEDRICH AND HEINRICH, WHO IN THE / KING'S GERMAN LEGION ON SPANISH / SOIL ON 28TH JULY 1809 DIED THE / DEATH OF HEROES / FOR THEIR FATHERLAND.

Named on the Memorial tablet: St Marien's Church, Celle, Lower Saxony, Germany. (Photograph)

LIEUT: G. A. V. HODENBERG 1809 B. TALAVERA

Ensign 27 Jan 1806. Lt 17 Feb 1809.

Served in the Peninsula Dec 1808 – Jul 1809. Present at Douro and Talavera where he was killed 28 Jul 1809. Also served in the Mediterranean 1806–1807 and the Baltic 1807–1809. Brother of Lt Friedrich von Hodenberg 1st Line KGL who died of wounds at Talavera and of Ensign Adolf von Hodenberg died of wounds at Büchen 1813.
Reference: Beamish, N. L., History of the King's German Legion, Vol. 2, reprint 1997. No. 1000.

HOFFMEISTER, I.
Sergeant. Royal Hanoverian Army.
Named on the Memorial tablet: St Marien's Church, Celle, Lower Saxony, Germany. (Photograph)

SERGNT: C. HOFFMEISTER 1810 B. BUZACO

Served in the Peninsula. Present at Busaco where he was killed 27 Sep 1810.

HOLLE, Carl von

Captain. 1st Line Battalion, King's German Legion.
Named on the Regimental Memorial: La Haye Sainte, Waterloo. (Photograph)
Named on the Waterloo Column, Hanover, Germany. (Photograph)
Pedestal tomb: Gehrdener Berg, Gehrden, Lower Saxony, Germany. (Photograph)

CARL LUDWIG / VON HOLLE / CAPIT. DES 1. LINI. BAT. / K. D. L. / GEBOREN D. 18 MAI 1783 / GEBLIEBEN BEY WATERLOO / D. 18. JUNI 1815

CARL LUDWIG / VON HOLLE / CAPTAIN OF THE 1ST LINE BATTALION / KGL BORN 18 MAY 1783 / DIED AND BURIED AT WATERLOO / 18 JUNE 1815

Lt 27 Jan 1806. Capt 19 Feb 1813.

Served in the Peninsula Dec 1808 – Apr 1814. Present at Douro, Talavera (severely wounded), Busaco, Fuentes d'Onoro, Ciudad Rodrigo, Moriscos, Salamanca, Burgos, Vittoria, Tolosa, San Sebastian, Bidassoa, Nivelle, Nive, St Etienne and Bayonne. Present at Waterloo where he was killed. Also served in Hanover 1805, Sicily 1806–1807, the Baltic 1807–1808 and the Netherlands 1814.
Reference: Beamish, N. L., History of the King's German Legion, Vol. 2, reprint 1997. No. 989.

HOLZERMAN, Philipp

Captain. 1st Line Battalion, King's German Legion.
Named on the Regimental Memorial: La Haye Sainte, Waterloo. (Photograph)
Named on the Waterloo Column, Hanover, Germany. (Photograph)

Ensign 23 Jan 1804. Lt 25 Jun 1806. Capt 20 Mar 1812.

Served in the Peninsula Aug 1808 – Jan 1809. Present at Vigo. Present at Waterloo where he was killed. Also served at Hanover 1805, the Baltic 1807–1808, Walcheren 1809 and North Germany 1813–1814.
Reference: Beamish, N. L., History of the King's German Legion, Vol. 2, reprint 1997. No. 987.

JANSSEN, Georg

Captain. 3rd Regiment of Hussars, King's German Legion.
Named on the Regimental Memorial: La Haye Sainte, Waterloo. (Photograph)
Named on the Waterloo Column, Hanover, Germany. (Photograph)

Lt 23 Dec 1805. Capt 25 Oct 1810.

Served in the Peninsula Aug 1808 – Jan 1809. Present at Benevente. Present at Waterloo where he was killed. Also served in the Baltic 1807–1808 (wounded at Kiöge), North Germany 1813–1814 and the Netherlands 1814.
Reference: Beamish, N. L., History of the King's German Legion, Vol. 2, reprint 1997. No. 802.

JASPER, Georg Ludwig

2nd Captain. Artillery, King's German Legion.
Pedestal tomb: Old Garden Cemetery, Hanover, Lower Saxony, Germany. (Photograph)

GEORG LUDWIG / JASPER / OBERSTLIEUTENANT / GEBOREN DEN 4. JUNI 1777 / GESTORBEN DEN 4. JANUAR / 1854

LIEUTENANT COLONEL / GEORG LUDWIG / JASPER / BORN 4 JUNE 1772 / DIED 4 JANUARY 1854

2nd Lt 7 Feb 1805. 1st Lt 8 May 1806. 2nd Capt 25 Nov 1813.

Served in the Netherlands 1814–1815. Also served in Hanover 1805, the Baltic 1807 and North Germany 1813–1814. Awarded King William's Cross. Hanoverian Army: Major. Died in Hanover 4 Jan 1854.

Reference: Beamish, N. L., History of the King's German Legion, Vol. 2, reprint 1997. No. 40.

JEINSEN, Friedrich Christoph von

Lieutenant. 3rd Line Battalion, King's German Legion.
Named on the Regimental Memorial: La Haye Sainte, Waterloo. (Photograph)
Named on the Waterloo Column, Hanover, Germany. (Photograph)
Named on the Memorial tablet: St Dionysius's Church, Adensen, Lower Saxony, Germany. (Photograph)

UNSEREN / BEY WATERLOO AM 18TEN JUNIUS 1815 / GEFALLENEN BRÜDERN / DEM BRIGADE-MAJOR HEINRICH WIEGMANN / DEM LIEUTENANT CHRISTOPH VAN JEINSEN / DEM SOLDATEN FRIEDRICH MATTHIES / ZU DANKBARER ERINNERUNG / VON / DER GEMEINE ADENSEN UND HALLERBURG

FOR OUR BROTHERS / KILLED AT WATERLOO ON 18TH JUNE 1815 / THE BRIGADE MAJOR HEINRICH WIEGMANN / THE LIEUTENANT CHRISTOPHER VON JEINSEN / THE SOLDIER FRIEDRICH MATTHIES / IN THANKFUL REMBERANCE / FROM / THE COMMUNITY OF ADENSEN AND HALLERBURG

Commissioned from the ranks. Ensign 27 Oct 1807. Lt 19 Mar 1812.

Served in the Peninsula 1812–1813. Present at Castalla and Tarragona. Present at Waterloo where he was severely wounded and died of his wounds 28 June at Brussels. Also served in Hanover 1805, the Baltic 1807, Mediterranean 1808–1812 and the Netherlands 1814.

Reference: Beamish, N. L., History of the King's German Legion, Vol. 2, reprint 1997. No. 1037.

KERSSENBRUCH. Agatz von

Captain. 3rd Regiment of Hussars, King's German Legion.
Named on the Regimental Memorial: La Haye Sainte, Waterloo. (Photograph)
Named on the Waterloo Column, Hanover, Germany. (Photograph)

Capt 9 Jun 1807.

Served in the Peninsula Aug 1808 – Jan 1809. Present at Benevente. Present at Waterloo where he was killed. Also present in Hanover 1805, the Baltic 1807–1808, North Germany 1813–1814 and the Netherlands 1814.

Reference: Beamish, N. L., History of the King's German Legion, Vol. 2, reprint 1997. No. 801.

KIELMANNSEGGE, Friedrich Otto Gothard Graf von

Colonel Commander. 1st Hanoverian Brigade
Chest tomb: Gartenfriedhof, Marienstrasse, Hanover, Germany. (Photograph)

CHARLOTTE WILHELMINE HEDWIG GRAF VON KIELMANSEGGE / GEB. VON SPORKEN / GEB. 28 APRIL 1744. GEST 27 DECEMB. 1830 / FRIEDRICH OTTO GOTHARD GRAF VON KIELMANSEGGE / KÖNIGL. HANNOV: GENERAL DER INFANTERIE / GEB. 15 DECEMB 1768. GEST 18 JULI 1851.

Present at Waterloo in command of the 1st Hanoverian Brigade in Alten's 3rd Division. Present at Quatre Bras where they reinforced the 95th Foot and re-took the Farm of Piraumont but suffered heavy losses. In 1813 he had raised the Kielmannseggeschen Jaeger Corps. These were men who were known for their sharp shooting and were included in his 1st Hanoverian Brigade. On 18 Jun Kielmannsegge deployed these men in the woods around Hougoumont. His Luneburg battalion was sent to help Major Baring and the King's German Legion at La Haye Sainte but they were heavily defeated by French cuirassiers. Later in the day when Alten and Halkett were wounded and Ompteda was killed, Kielmannsegge was in charge of the division but he too was wounded. Appointed Major General in the Hanoverian Army in 1815 and Lt General in 1816. Died in Hanover 18 Jul 1851.
REFERENCE: Allgemeine Deutsche Biographie.

KLENCK, Friedrich von
Lieutenant. 1st Battalion Light Infantry, King's German Legion.
Named on the Memorial: St Andrew's Church (now Musée Historique), Biarritz, France. (Photograph)

Ensign 1 Mar 1806. Lt 18 Jan 1811.
Served in the Peninsula Aug 1808 – Jan 1809 and Mar 1811 – Oct 1813. Present at Vigo, Albuera, second siege of Badajoz, siege of Salamanca Forts, Moriscos, Salamanca, Venta del Poza, San Munos, Vittoria, Tolosa and Bidassoa where he was killed at the crossing of the Bidassoa Oct 1813. Also served in the Baltic 1807–1808 and Walcheren 1809.
Note: Named as Klanck on memorial.
REFERENCE: Beamish, N. L., History of the King's German Legion, Vol. 2, reprint 1997. No. 1007.

KNUST, I.
Rifleman. Royal Hanoverian Army.
Named on the Memorial tablet: St Marien's Church, Celle, Lower Saxony, Germany. (Photograph)

SCHÜTZE I. KNUST 1812 B. SIMANCAS

Served in the Peninsula. Present at Salamanca where he was killed 1812.

KÖHLER, Carl
Lieutenant. 5th Line Battalion, King's German Legion.
Named on the Memorial: St Andrew's Church (now Musée Historique), Biarritz, France. (Photograph)

Ensign 15 Feb 1809. Lt 21 Sep 1810.
Served in the Peninsula Apr 1809 – Apr 1814. Present at Douro, Talavera (severely wounded), Busaco, Fuentes d'Onoro, Ciudad Rodrigo, Moriscos, Salamanca, Burgos, Vittoria, Tolosa, San Sebastian, Bidassoa, Nivelle, Nive, St Etienne and Bayonne where he was killed at the Sortie from Bayonne 14 Apr 1814. Also served in Hanover 1805 and the Baltic 1807–1808.
REFERENCE: Beamish, N. L., History of the King's German Legion, Vol. 2, reprint 1997. No. 1004.

KRAUCHENBERG, Louis
Captain. 1st Regiment of Hussars, King's German Legion.
Ledger stone: Neuenhäuser Churchyard, Celle, Lower Saxony, Germany. (Photograph)

HIER RUHET IN GOTT / DER KÖNIGLICH HANNOVERSCHE OBERST / LOUIS KRAUCHENBERG / GEB. AM 29. FEBRUAR 1788 / GEST. AM 5. APRIL 1852 / GEWIDMET VON SEINER TRAUERNDEN GATTIN / DU SAHEST OFT DES TODES HAND / EH' ER DICH KÄMPFER ÜBERWAND / NUN IST ER ALS DEIN FREUND GEKOMMEN / HAT DICH DEM LEBENSKAMPF ENTNOMMEN

HERE RESTS IN GOD'S HANDS / THE ROYAL HANOVERIAN COLONEL / LOUIS KRAUCHENBERG / BORN 29 FEBRUARY 1788 / DIED 5 APRIL 1852 / DEDICATED BY HIS MOURNING WIFE / YOU HAVE SEEN OFTEN THE HAND OF DEATH / BEFORE HE OVERCAME YOU, THE FIGHTER / NOW HE CAME AS A FRIEND / AND HAS TAKEN YOU FROM LIFE'S BATTLE

Ensign 1st Lt Battalion 15 Jan 1804. Cornet 1st Hussars 15 Nov 1804. Lt 13 Apr 1808. Capt 13 Jan 1813.

Served in the Peninsula Jun 1809 – Feb 1812. Present at Talavera, Coa, Busaco, Pombal, Sabugal, Fuentes d'Onoro (severely wounded). Present at Waterloo. Also served in Hanover 1805 and the Baltic 1807. MGS medal for Talavera, Busaco and Fuentes d'Onoro. KH. Order of St Vladimir. Hanoverian Army: Bt Lt Colonel 3rd Dragoons. Died at Celle 5 Apr 1852.
REFERENCE: Beamish, N. L., History of the King's German Legion, Vol. 2, reprint 1997. No. 175.

KUHLMANN, Heinrich Jacob
1st Captain. Artillery, King's German Legion.
Tombstone: Garrison Cemetery, Stade, Lower Saxony, Germany. (Photograph)

HIER RUHEN / JACOB KUHLMANN / OBERSTLT. K. H. ART. REGT. / GEB, 6. OCTOBER 1764 / GEST. 19. MÄRZ 1830 / ....

HERE LIES / LT COL. JACOB KUHLMANN / K. H. ART. REGT. / BORN 6. OCTOBER 1764 / DIED 19. MARCH 1830 / ....

Capt 11 Aug 1804. Bt Major 4 Jun 1814.

Present at Waterloo. Also served at Hanover 1805 and North Germany 1813–1814 (present at Göhrde) and the Netherlands 1814–1815. CB. KH. Hanoverian Army: Bt Lt Colonel. Died at Stade 19 Mar 1830.
REFERENCE: Beamish, N. L., History of the King's German Legion, Vol. 2, reprint 1997. No. 28.

KUHLMANN, Otto
Lieutenant. 1st Regiment of Dragoons, King's German Legion.
Named on the Regimental Memorial: La Haye Sainte, Waterloo. (Photograph)
Named on the Waterloo Column, Hanover, Germany. (Photograph)

Cornet 11 Apr 1812. Lt 15 Jun 1813.

Served in the Peninsula Apr 1814. Present at Waterloo where he was killed. Also served in the Netherlands 1814–1815.
REFERENCE: Beamish, N. L., History of the King's German Legion, Vol. 2, reprint 1997. No. 812.

LANGREHR, Friedrich Ernst Philipp
Captain. 5th Line Battalion, King's German Legion.
Named on the Memorial tablet: St Marien's Church, Celle, Lower Saxony, Germany. (Photograph)

HAUPTM: E. LANGREHR 1812 B. SALAMANCA

Capt 3 Nov 1803.

Served in the Peninsula Sep 1808 – Sep 1812. Present at Douro, Talavera (where he carried the colours), Busaco, Sobral, Fuentes d'Onoro, Ciudad Rodrigo, Moriscos and Salamanca where he was severely wounded 22 Jul 1812 and died of his wounds 12 Sep 1812. Also served at Hanover 1805 and the Baltic 1807–1808.
REFERENCE: Beamish, N. L., History of the King's German Legion, Vol. 2, reprint 1997. No. 1021.

LANGWERTH, Ernest Eberhard Kuno von
Colonel Commandant. 4th Line Battalion, King's German Legion.
Memorial tablet: St Paul's Cathedral, London. (North transept). (Joint memorial with Major General Mackenzie). (Photograph)

NATIONAL MONUMENT / TO MAJOR GENERAL / J. R. MACKENZIE / AND BRIGADIER GENERAL / E. LANGWERTH / WHO FELL AT / TALAVERA. / JULY 28TH / MDCCCIX

Colonel Commandant 4th Line KGL 1804.

Served in the Peninsula Sep 1808 – Jul 1809. (Commanded 3 Brigade 1st Division Jun – Jul 1809). Present at Douro and Talavera where he was killed 28 Jul 1809. Gold Medal for Talavera. Also served at Hanover 1805 and Copenhagen 1807.
REFERENCE: Beamish, N. L., History of the King's German Legion, Vol. 2, reprint 1997. No. 971.

LESCHEN, Friedrich
Lieutenant. 3rd Line Battalion, King's German Legion.
Named on the Regimental Memorial: La Haye Sainte, Waterloo. (Photograph)
Named on the Waterloo Column, Hanover, Germany. (Photograph)

Lt 29 Aug 1812.

Present at Waterloo where he was severely wounded and died at Brussels 28 Jun 1815. Also served in the Mediterranean 1808–1814 and the Netherlands 1814.
REFERENCE: Beamish, N. L., History of the King's German Legion, Vol. 2, reprint 1997. No. 1042.

LEUE, Georg Ludwig
Captain. 4th Line Battalion, King's German Legion.
Named on the Regimental Memorial: La Haye Sainte, Waterloo. (Photograph)
Named on the Waterloo Column, Hanover, Germany. (Photograph)

Capt 15 Nov 1804. Bt Major 4 Jun 1814.

Served in the Peninsula Aug 1812 – Apr 1814. Present at Castalla and Tarragona. Present at Waterloo where he was severely wounded and died of his wounds 23 Jun 1815. Also served in Hanover 1805, Baltic 1807, Mediterranean 1808–1812 and Netherlands 1814.
REFERENCE: Beamish, N. L., History of the King's German Legion, Vol. 2, reprint 1997. No. 1025.

LEVETZOW, Friedrich Carl Ludwig von
Lieutenant. 1st Regiment of Dragoons, King's German Legion.
Named on the Regimental Memorial: La Haye Sainte, Waterloo. (Photograph)
Named on the Waterloo Column, Hanover, Germany. (Photograph)

Cornet 22 Sep 1811. Lt 13 Mar 1812.

Present in the Peninsula Jan 1812 – Apr 1814. Present at Salamanca, Garcia Hernandez, Majalahonda, Vittoria, Tarbes and Toulouse. Present at Waterloo where he was killed. Also served in the Netherlands 1814–1815.
REFERENCE: Beamish, N. L., History of the King's German Legion, Vol. 2, reprint 1997. No. 810.

LINSINGEN, Carl Christian von
Colonel Commandant. 1st Regiment of Hussars, King's German Legion.
Pedestal tomb: Old Neustädter Cemetery, Hanover, Germany. (Photograph)

CARL CHRISTIAN DREIUNDSIEBENZIG JAHRE / GRAF VON LINSINGEN DIENTE ER TREU /

GENERAL DER CAVALLERIE SEINEN KÖNIGEN / GEB. 6. JAN[R]. 1742 DURCH DEREN HULD BEGLÜCHT / GEST. 5. SEP[T]. 1830

FOR SEVENTY THREE YEARS CARL CHRISTIAN / COUNT VON LINSINGEN SERVED FAITHFULLY / AS GENERAL OF THE KING'S CAVALRY / FAVOURED BY HIS GRACE / BORN 6 JAN[R]. 1742 / DIED 5 SEP[T] 1830.

Major General 8 Aug 1804. Colonel Commandant 1805. Lt General 4 Jun 1811.

Commanded the KGL Hussars who were part of the 5th British Cavalry Brigade, but they were not present at Waterloo as they were deployed on frontier duty near Courtrai. Also served at Hanover 1805 and the Baltic 1807–1808. KH. CB. Order of the Red Eagle. Hanoverian Army: General 1815. Inspector of Hanoverian Cavalry 1816. Died 5 Sep 1830.

Reference: Beamish, N. L., History of the King's German Legion, Vol. 2, reprint 1997. No. 167.

LÖSECKE, Friedrich William Von

Captain. 7th Line Battalion, King's German Legion.

Cast-iron Cross on Cemetery wall: St Michaelis's Cemetery, Lüneburg, Lower Saxony, Germany. (Near main gate). (Photograph)

MAJOR / WILLIAM CONRAD FRIEDRICH VON LÖSECKE, / GEBOREN DEN 22ND JANUAR 1774, / GESTORBEN DEN 23RD JULI 1832.

Lt 4 Jan 1806. Capt 9 Oct 1810.

Served in the Peninsula Sep 1808 – Jul 1811. Present at Douro, Busaco and Fuentes d'Onoro. Also served in the Baltic 1807–1808 and the Mediterranean 1812–1813. Half pay 25 Jul 1815. Hanoverian Army: Bt Major retired list. Died at Lüneburg 23 Jul 1832.

Reference: Beamish, N. L., History of the King's German Legion, Vol. 2, reprint 1997. No. 1185.

LÜCKEN, Hartwig von

Ensign. 1st Line Battalion, King's German Legion.

Named on the Regimental Memorial: La Haye Sainte, Waterloo. (Photograph)

Named on the Waterloo Column, Hanover, Germany. (Photograph)

Ensign 1 Feb 1814.

Present at Waterloo where he was killed. Also served in the Netherlands 1814.

Reference: Beamish, N. L., History of the King's German Legion, Vol 2, reprint 1997. No. 1014.

LUDOWIG, William von

Captain. Field Jäger Corps.

Cast-iron Cross on Cemetery Wall: St Michaelis's Cemetery, Lüneburg, Lower Saxony, Germany. (Near main gate). (Photograph)

GENERAL LIEUTENANT / WILLIAM VON LUDOWIG / GEB. DEN 28 OCTOBER 1787, / GEST DEN 11 JUNI 1870.

LIEUTENANT GENERAL / WILLIAM VON LUDOWIG / BORN 28 OCTOBER 1787, / DIED 11 JUNE 1870.

Ensign 1st Battalion Lt Infantry KGL. 7 Jul 1804. Lt 28 Jun 1806. Capt Field Jäger Corps 1811.

Served in the Peninsula Aug 1808 – Jan 1809. Present at Vigo. Also served in Hanover 1805, the Baltic 1807–1808 and Walcheren 1809. Joined Count Kielmannsegge's Field Jäger Corps as Captain in 1811.

Present at Waterloo in defence of the woods at Hougoumont. KH. King William's Cross. Hanoverian Army: Major 1826. Major and Commander 1836. Colonel 2nd Infantry Brigade 1848. Major General 1849. Bt Lt General 1855. Died 21 Jun 1870 at Lüneburg.
Reference: Beamish, N. L., History of the King's German Legion, Vol. 2, reprint 1997. No. 1241.

LUEDER, Eberhard Magnus Ludewig
Captain. 3rd Line Battalion, King's German Legion.
Pedestal tomb: Garrison Cemetery, Hamelin, Lower Saxony, Germany. (Photograph)

EBERHARD MAGNUS / LUDEWIG LUEDER / MAIOR / IN KÖNIGLICH / HANNOVERSCHEN / DIENSTEN / UND VORHIN CAPTAIN / IN DER ENGLISCH / DEUTSCHEN LEGION. / GEBOREN ZU LENTHE / DEN 13 TEN NOVEMBER: 1773 / GESTORBEN ZU HAMELN / DEN 19 TEN MÄRZ 1816 / ………………

EBERHARD MAGNUS / LUDEWIG LUEDER, / MAJOR / IN THE KING'S / HANOVERIAN SERVICE / AND FORMERLY CAPTAIN / IN THE ENGLISH / KING'S GERMAN LEGION. / BORN IN LENTHE / 13 NOVEMBER 1773, / DIED IN HAMELN, / 19 MARCH 1816 / ………………

Ensign 15 Jun 1804. Capt 3rd Line 14 Sep 1810.

Served in the Peninsula Aug 1812 – Apr 1813. Present at Castalla (Mentioned in Despatches). Present at Waterloo. Also served at Hanover 1805, the Baltic 1807, Mediterranean 1808–1814 and the Netherlands 1814–1815. Died in Hamelin 19 Mar 1816. Bt Major Hanoverian Militia Battalion of Veterans.
Reference: Beamish, N. L., History of the King's German Legion, Vol. 2, reprint 1997. No. 476.

MACBEAN, Alexander
Lieutenant. 2nd Battalion Light Infantry, King's German Legion.
Pedestal tomb: Rothiemurchus Churchyard, Speyside, Invernesshire, Scotland. (Photograph)

IN / LOVING MEMORY OF ALEXANDER McBEAN / LIEUT 2ND BATTALION LIGHT INFANTRY / K. G. L. / DIED AT AUCHTERBLAIR / 24TH AUGT 1850, AGED 64 YEARS"

Ensign 23 Apr 1813. Lt 27 Nov 1813.

Served in the Peninsula Nov 1813 – Apr 1814. Present at Nivelle, Nive (wounded 9 Dec 1813), St Etienne and Bayonne. Also served in the Netherlands 1814–1815.
Reference: Beamish, N. L., History of the King's German Legion, Vol. 2, reprint 1997. No. 387.

MACDONALD, Stephen
Lieutenant. 1st Battalion Light Infantry, King's German Legion.
Grave: Cheriton Churchyard, Sandgate, Kent. (No longer extant). (M.I.)

"STEPHEN MACDONALD / LIEUTENANT OF THE LATE 1st LT BN KING'S GERMAN LEGION SUBSEQUENTLY ADJUTANT OF THE HANOVERIAN JAGER GARDE / DIED AT SANDGATE NOV 13 1871 AGED 78"

Lt Pembroke Militia 1810. Ensign 1st Lt Battalion King's German Legion 22 Dec 1812. Lt 5 Apr 1814.

Present at Waterloo and with the Army of Occupation. Also served in North Germany 1813–1814 (wounded at Sehestadt 10 Dec 1813) and the Netherlands 1814–1815. After Waterloo the regiment was disbanded and he joined the Hanoverian Jaeger Garde as Adjutant until 1820, when he returned to England. Became Relieving Officer for Eltham district.
Reference: Jones, J., Stephen MacDonald: service in the KGL. Waterloo Journal, Aug 1981, pp. 12–14. Beamish, N. L., History of the King's German Legion, Vol. 2, reprint 1997. No. 314.

McGLASHAN, James Edwin
Lieutenant. 2nd Battalion Light Infantry, King's German Legion.
Ledger stone: British Garrison Cemetery, Kandy, Sri Lanka, Ceylon. (Photograph)

HERE LIES THE BODY / OF / CAPT JAMES McGLASHAN / OF HM'S XIXTH REGT / WHO DIED ON 2ND OF DEC, 1817 / AGED 26 YEARS. / HE DISTINGUISHED HIMSELF AT THE BATTLES / OF BUZACO AND ALBUERA. / HE SERVED IN GERMANY, WHERE HE WAS APPOINTED / A COMPANION OF THE GUELPHIC ORDER OF KNIGHTHOOD. / AND HE OBTAINED THE MEDAL / BESTOWED BY THIS GRATEFUL COUNTRY / ON ALL WHO FOUGHT AT WATERLOO. / IN HIS LAST ILLNESS HE RECEIVED THE HOLY SACRAMENT / WITH EXEMPLARY DEVOTION / AND UNDER THE LINGERING APPROACH OF A PAINFUL DEATH / HE WAS SUSTAINED BY MANLY FORTITUDE / AND CHRISTIAN HOPE.

Ensign 7 Nov 1809. Lt 24 Apr 1811. Capt 22 Aug 1815.

Served in the Peninsula Sep 1810 and Mar 1811 – Sep 1812. Present at Busaco, Albuera, second siege of Badajoz, siege of Salamanca Forts and Moriscos (severely wounded). Present at Waterloo (ADC to Major General Sir James Lyon). Also served in North Germany 1813–1814. After the war he was promoted Captain and served in Germany for a time. KH. Exchanged into the 1st Ceylon Regt 16 Sep 1817, but shortly afterwards succumbed to an attack of fever on his arrival in Ceylon and died 2 Dec 1817.
Reference: Lewis, J. Penry, List of inscriptions on tombstones and monuments in Ceylon, 1913, reprint 1994, pp. 296–7. Beamish, N. L., History of the King's German Legion, Vol 2, reprint 1997. No. 1330.

MARENHOLTZ, Wilhelm von
Lieutenant 8th Line Battalion, King's German Legion.
Named on the Waterloo Column, Hanover, Germany. (Photograph)
Named on the KGL Regimental Memorial, La Haye Sainte, Waterloo, (Photograph)
Named on the Memorial tablet: St Marien's Church, Celle, Lower Saxony, Germany. (Photograph)

LIEUT: W. V. MARENHOLZ 1815 B. WATERLOO

Ensign 17 Jun 1806. Lt 15 Jan 1808.

Served in the Peninsula Aug 1812 – Apr 1813. Present at Castalla. Present at Waterloo where he was killed. Also served in the Baltic 1807, Mediterranean 1808–1814 and the Netherlands 1814–1815.
Reference: Beamish, N. L., History of the King's German Legion, Vol. 2, reprint 1997. No. 998.

MARSCHALCK, Heinrich von
Captain. 1st Battalion Light Infantry, King's German Legion.
Named on the Regimental Memorial: La Haye Sainte, Waterloo. (Photograph)
Named on the Waterloo Column, Hanover, Germany. (Photograph)

Ensign 23 Mar 1805. Lt 17 Jul 1809. Capt 4 Apr 1814.

Served in the Peninsula Aug 1808 – Jan 1809 and Mar 1811 – Apr 1814. Present at Vigo, Albuera, siege of Salamanca Forts, Moriscos, Salamanca, Venta del Poza, San Millan, Vittoria, Tolosa, Bidassoa, Nivelle, Nive, Bayonne and St Etienne. Present at Waterloo where he was killed. Also served at Hanover 1805, the Baltic 1807–1808, Walcheren 1809 and the Netherlands 1814.
Reference: Beamish, N. L., History of the King's German Legion, Vol. 2, reprint 1997. No. 991.

MATTHIES, Friedrich
Driver. Artillery, King's German Legion.
Named on the Waterloo Column, Hanover, Germany. (Photograph)
Named on the Memorial tablet: St Dionysius's Church, Adensen, Lower Saxony, Germany. (Photograph)

UNSEREN / BEY WATERLOO AM 18TEN JUNIUS 1815 / GEFALLENEN BRÜDERN / DEM BRIGADE-MAJOR HEINRICH WIEGMANN / DEM LIEUTENANT CHRISTOPH VAN JEINSEN / DEM SOLDATEN FRIEDRICH MATTHIES / ZU DANKBARER ERINNERUNG / VON / DER GEMEINE ADENSEN UND HALLERBURG

FOR OUR BROTHERS / KILLED AT WATERLOO ON 18TH JUNE 1815 / THE BRIGADE MAJOR HEINRICH WIEGMANN / THE LIEUTENANT CHRISTOPHER VON JEINSEN / THE SOLDIER FRIEDRICH MATTHIES / IN THANKFUL REMBERANCE / FROM / THE COMMUNITY OF ADENSEN AND HALLERBURG

Present at Waterloo where he was killed.

MELDAU, I. H.
Sergeant. 1st Hussars. King's German Legion.
Named on the Memorial tablet: St Marien's Church, Celle, Lower Saxony, Germany. (Photograph)

WACHTM: I. H. MELDAU 1807 B. COPENHAGEN

Present in the Baltic where he was killed at Copenhagen 1807.

MEYER, August
Lieutenant. 5th Line Battalion, King's German Legion.
Named on the Memorial tablet: Town Church, Ludwigslust, Mecklenburg, Germany. (Photograph)

AUGUST MEYER LIEUT. IN DER ENGL. – DEUTSCHEN – LEGION

Ensign 1 Aug 1809. Lt 1 Dec 1810.

Served in the Peninsula Nov 1809 – Apr 1814. Present at Busaco, Moriscos, Salamanca, Burgos, San Sebastian, Bidassoa, Nivelle, Nive, St Etienne and Bayonne where he was severely wounded 27 Feb 1814. Present at Waterloo. Also served in the Netherlands 1814–1815. Died at Tournay in the Netherlands 28 Sep 1826.

Reference: Beamish, N. L., History of the King's German Legion, Vol. 2, reprint 1997. No. 757.

MEYER, Friedrich Ludwig
Lieutenant Colonel. 3rd Regiment of Hussars, King's German Legion.
Named on the Regimental Memorial: La Haye Sainte, Waterloo. (Photograph)
Named on the Waterloo Column, Hanover, Germany. (Photograph)

Capt 10 Oct 1803. Major 1st Hussars 25 Oct 1810. Lt Col 3rd Hussars 10 Oct 1813.

Served in the Peninsula Aug 1808 – Jan 1809 and Feb 1811 – Jun 1812. Present at Pombal, Sabugal, Fuentes d'Onoro (wounded) and El Bodon. Present at Waterloo where he was severely wounded and died of his wounds 6 Jul 1815. Also served in the Baltic 1807–1808 and Netherlands 1814.

Reference: Beamish, N. L., History of the King's German Legion, Vol. 2, reprint 1997. No. 816.

MEYER, Johann
Lieutenant. 5th Line Battalion, King's German Legion.
Named on the Memorial: St Andrew's Church (now Musée Historique), Biarritz, France. (Photograph)

Ensign 10 Jul 1806. Lt 6 Sep 1809.

Served in the Peninsula Sep 1808 – Apr 1814. Present at Douro, Talavera, Busaco, Fuentes d'Onoro, Ciudad Rodrigo, Moriscos, Salamanca, Burgos, Vittoria, Tolosa, San Sebastian, Bidassoa, Nivelle, Nive,

St Etienne and Bayonne where he was killed in the Sortie from Bayonne 14 Apr 1814. Also served at Hanover 1805 and the Baltic 1807–1808.
Reference: Beamish, N. L., History of the King's German Legion, Vol. 2, reprint 1997. No. 1012.

MICHAELIS, H.
Dragoon. Royal Hanoverian Army.
Named on the Memorial tablet: St Marien's Church, Celle, Lower Saxony, Germany. (Photograph)

DRAG: H. MICHAELIS 1812 B. SALAMANCA

Served in the Peninsula where he was killed at Salamanca.

MITCHELL, William
Paymaster. 2nd Regiment of Hussars, King's German Legion.
Headstone: Nunhead Cemetery, London. (Inscription not recorded). (Grave number 1115 Square 81)

Asst Paymaster 20th Lt Dragoons 27 Jun 1805. Paymaster 2nd Hussars King's German Legion 13 Aug 1812. Paymaster 1st Foot 3 Jul 1828.

Served in the Peninsula with 20th Lt Dragoons Feb – Sep 1809 and 2nd Hussars King's German Legion Sep 1810 – Jun 1813. Present at Cadiz and Barossa. Also served in the Cape of Good Hope 1806, South America 1807 (present at Montevideo and Buenos Ayres) and the Netherlands 1814–1815. Died 10 Apr 1848.
Reference: Beamish, N. L., History of the King's German Legion, Vol. 2, reprint 1997. No. 241.

MÜHLMANN, Johann
Private. Militia Battalion, Royal Hanoverian Army.
Named on the Militia Battalion Memorial: Hesedorf, near Bremervörde, Lower Saxony, Germany. (Photograph)

Present at Waterloo where he was killed.

MÜLLER, Heinrich
Captain. 2nd Line Battalion, King's German Legion.
Named on the Memorial: St Andrew's Church (now Musée Historique), Biarritz, France. (Photograph)

Lt 20 Aug 1805. Capt 12 Mar 1812.

Served in the Peninsula Sep 1808 – May 1812 and Nov 1813 – Apr 1814. Present at Douro, Busaco, Fuentes d'Onoro, Ciudad Rodrigo, Nivelle, Nive, St Etienne and Bayonne where he was killed in the Sortie from Bayonne 14 Apr 1814. Also served at Hanover 1805, Mediterranean 1806–1807 and the Baltic 1807–1808.
Reference: Beamish, N. L., History of the King's German Legion, Vol. 2, reprint 1997. No. 986.

OFFENEY, William
Lieutenant Colonel. 7th Line Battalion, King's German Legion.
Pedestal tomb: St George's Cemetery, Lisbon. (Grave number E11). (Photograph)

Inscription on four sides of memorial.

UNDERNEATH LIE THE REMAINS / OF / LIEU. COLONEL WILLIAM OFFENEY / OF THE / KING'S GERMAN LEGION. / ASSISTANT QUARTER MASTER GENERAL / TO THE CORPS OF THE BRITISH ARMY / UNDER / LT. GENERAL SIR R. HILL K.B. / WHO DIED AT BELEM / ON THE 12TH

OF AUGUST 1812 / AT THE AGE OF 45 / THIS TOMB IS ERECTED TO HIS MEMORY / BY ONE WHO HAD THE GOOD FORTUNE / TO SERVE EARLY UNDER HIS AUSPICES / AND TO WHOM HE WAS NEARLY RELATED / AND PARTICULARLY DEAR. / HIS DISTINGUISHED CHARACTER AS AN OFFICER / STANDS ESTABLISHED IN THE DISPATCHES OF / THE DIFFERENT GENERALS UNDER WHOM HE / SERVED AND IN PRIVATE SOCIETY HIS AMIABLE / QUALITIES WERE NO LESS CONSPICUOUS. / THIRTY THREE YEARS OF HIS SHORT LIFE / WERE DEVOTED TO HIS PROFESSION / ALMOST ENTIRELY SPENT ON ACTIVE SERVICE / IN THE EAST INDIES, HOLLAND, FLANDERS, / HANOVER, DENMARK, WALCHEREN / AND THE PENINSULA.

Lt Colonel 2nd Line King's German Legion 9 Feb 1805. Lt Colonel 7th Line King's German Legion 29 Nov 1810.

Served in the Peninsula Aug 1808 – Jan 1809 (AQMG) and Apr 1811 – Aug 1812 (AQMG 2nd Division). Present at Vigo, Fuentes d'Onoro, Arroyo dos Molinos (wounded and Mentioned in Hill's Despatches) and Almarez. Gold Medal for Fuentes d'Onoro. Also served in India, Hanover 1805, Copenhagen 1807 and Walcheren 1809. Died in the military hospital at Belem 17 Aug 1812.

OMPTEDA, Christian von

Colonel. 5th Line Battalion, King's German Legion.
Named on the Regimental Memorial: La Haye Sainte, Waterloo. (Photograph)
Named on the Waterloo Column, Hanover, Germany. (Photograph)

Memorial tablet: La Haye Saint, Waterloo. (On outer wall). (M.I.)

TO MAJ. BARING AND THE 2ND LIGHT / BTN KGL'S HEROIC DEFENCE OF / LA HAIE SAINTE 18 JUNE 1815 / ALSO TO COL. VON OMPTEDA WHO FELL / LEADING A BRAVE COUNTER-ATTACK / AFTER THE FALL OF THE FARM / DEDICATED BY BEXHILL-ON-SEA ENGLAND / A KING'S GERMAN LEGION / GARRISON 1804–14 / ....

Lt Colonel 1st Line 12 Jan 1805. Lt Colonel 1st Lt Infantry 29 Oct 1812. Bt Colonel 4 Jun 1813. Colonel 5th Line 17 Aug 1813.

Served in the Peninsula Dec 1808 – Jan 1809 and Feb 1813 – Apr 1814. Present at Vittoria, Tolosa, Bidassoa, Nivelle, Nive, St Etienne and Bayonne. Gold Medal for Vittoria, Nivelle and Nive. Also served at Hanover 1805, Mediterranean 1806–1807, the Baltic 1807–1808 and the Netherlands 1814. Present at Waterloo in command of 5th Line Battalion KGL where he was killed in an attempt to recapture La Haye Sainte. The Prince of Orange insisted that the 5th Light Battalion should attack even though Ompteda knew that the French cavalry was near. He had his infantry safe in a square because of this. Ompteda rode ahead of his two battalions knowing that he would be surrounded at any moment, but having been given the order he obeyed. The French cavalry swept around the south-west of the farrn and the KGL were caught in line. Ompteda was killed and the 5th Battalion nearly all destroyed. A very brave and professional soldier. Ompteda died needlessly due to the Prince of Orange's inexperience.
Reference: Ompteda, Ludwig Friedrich Christian Carl von., A Hanoverian-English officer a hundred years ago: Memoirs of Baron Ompteda, 1892. Republished as In the King's German Legion: the memoirs of Baron Ompteda, Colonel, in the King's German Legion during the Napoleonic Wars, 1987. Beamish, N. L., History of the King's German Legion, Vol. 2, reprint 1997. No. 972.

OMPTEDA, Ferdinand von

Captain. 1st Line Battalion, King's German Legion.
Ledger stone: St John the Baptist's Churchyard, Egham, Surrey. (Photograph)

SACRED / TO THE MEMORY OF / BARON FERDINAND OMPTEDA, / CAPTAIN & BRIGADE MAJOR / IN / THE KING'S GERMAN LEGION / WHO DIED OCTOBER 31ST 1809.

Lt and Adjutant 23 Apr 1805. Capt 24 Apr 1808.

Served in the Peninsula Sep 1808 – Jun 1809. Brigade Major to Colonel Langwerth Sep – Oct 1808 and Brigade Major to Colonel Dreiberg Nov 1808 – Jun 1809. Also served at Hanover 1805, Copenhagen 1807 and Sweden 1808. Died at Egham aged 28.

REFERENCE: *Beamish, N. L., History of the King's German Legion, Vol. 2, reprint 1997. No. 780.*

PASCHAL, George Frederick

Lieutenant. 2nd Line Battalion, King's German Legion.
Headstone: Brompton Cemetery, London. (Grave number BR 81798). (Photograph)

IN AFFECTIONATE REMEMBRANCE OF / LIEUT. COLONEL GEORGE FREDERICK PASCHAL / LATE 70TH REGT. / WHO DIED OCTOBER 23RD 1875, AGED 78 YEARS.

Ensign 17 Mar 1812. Lt 19 Oct 1812. Capt 70th Foot 23 Mar 1826. Lt Colonel Depot Battalion.

Served in the Peninsula Oct 1813 – Apr 1814. Present at Nivelle, Nive, St Etienne and Bayonne. Present at Quatre Bras and Waterloo. MGS medal for Nivelle and Nive. Also served in the Netherlands 1814. Half pay 19 Dec 1834. Retired 11 Nov 1851.

PETERS, Friedrich

Captain. 1st Regiment of Dragoons, King's German Legion.
Named on the Waterloo Column, Hanover, Germany. (Photograph)
Named on the Regimental Memorial: La Haye Sainte, Waterloo. (Photograph)
Named on the Memorial tablet: St Marien's Church, Celle, Lower Saxony, Germany. (Photograph)

HAUPTMANN F. PETERS 1815. WATERLOO

Capt 21 Mar 1804.

Present at Waterloo where he was killed. Also served in Ireland 1806 (present at Tullamore where he was wounded) and the Netherlands 1814–1815.

REFERENCE: *Beamish, N. L., History of the King's German Legion, Vol. 2, reprint 1997. No. 803.*

POPPE, Jürgen

Private. Militia Regiment Lüneburg, Royal Hanoverian Army.
Named on the Waterloo Column, Hanover, Germany. (Photograph)
Named on the Memorial tablet: St Jacobi's Church, Bleckede, Lower Saxony, Germany. (Photograph)

Present at Waterloo where he was killed.

POTEN, August Gottlieb

Captain. 2nd Regiment of Dragoons, King's German Legion.
Pedestal tomb: Engesohder Cemetery, Hanover, Germany. (Photograph)

AUGUST GOTTLIEB POTEN / GENERAL LIEUT / 1.10.1797 – 4.3.1867 / TOULOUSE VITTORIA SALAMACA WATERLOO

AUGUST GOTTLIEB POTEN / LT-GENERAL / 1.10.1797 – 4.3.1867 / TOULOUSE VITTORIA SALAMANCA WATERLOO

Cornet 16 May 1806. Lt 15 Feb 1812. Capt 1815.

Served in the Peninsula Jan 1812 – Apr 1814. Present at Castrejon, Salamanca, Garcia Hernandez, Majalahonda (wounded), Venta Del Poza, San Munos, Vittoria, Vic Bigorre and Toulouse. Present at

Waterloo where he was wounded and with the Army of Occupation. Also served in Hanover 1805 and the Netherlands 1814–1815. MGS medal for Salamanca, Vittoria and Toulouse. KH. King William's Cross. Hanoverian Army: Capt Guard Cuirassier Regt 1816. Major 1839. Lt Colonel 2nd Dragoon Regt 1845. Colonel 1851. Major General 1854. Lt General 1858. Died 4 Mar 1867.
Reference: Beamish, N. L., History of the King's German Legion, Vol. 2, reprint 1997. No. 138.

ROBERTSON, Friedrich von
Ensign. 2nd Battalion Light Infantry, King's German Legion.
Named on the Regimental Memorial: La Haye Sainte, Waterloo. (Photograph)
Named on the Waterloo Column, Hanover, Germany. (Photograph)

Ensign 7 Dec 1813.
Present at Waterloo where he was killed. Also served in the Netherlands 1814.
Reference: Beamish, N. L., History of the King's German Legion, Vol. 2, reprint 1997. No. 1013.

RÖMERMANN, Heinrich
Private. 2nd Battalion Light Infantry, King's German Legion.
Named on the Waterloo Column, Hanover, Germany. (Photograph)
Named on the Memorial tablet: St Marien's Church, Celle, Lower Saxony, Germany. (Photograph)

SOLDAT H. RÖMERMANN 1815 B. WATERLOO

Present at Waterloo where he was killed.

RÖSSING, Ferdinand Christoph Ludwig Friedrich von
Captain. 1st Line Battalion, King's German Legion.
Memorial tablet: On Family estate, Rössing, Nordstemmen, Lower Saxony, Germany. (Photograph)

HIER RUHET / DER LANDRATH UND / OBERSTLIEUTENANT / FERDINAND / CHRISTOPH / LUDWIG FRIEDRICH / FREIHERR VON RÖSSING / GEB. ZU OVELGÖNNE / DEN 20. NOVEMBER 1790 / GEST. ZU RÖSSING / DEN 22. FEBRUAR 1856

HERE LIES / DISTRICT COUNCILLOR AND LIEUTENANT COLONEL / FERDINAND / CHRISTOPH / LUDWIG FRIEDRICH / BARON VON RÖSSING / BORN AT OVELGÖNNE / ON 20 NOVEMBER 1790 / DIED AT RÖSSING / ON 22 FEBRUARY 1856

Lt 27 May 1809. Capt 1815.
Served in the Peninsula Dec 1808 – Apr 1814. Present at Douro, Talavera, Busaco, Fuentes d'Onoro, Ciudad Rodrigo, Moriscos, Salamanca, Burgos (severely wounded 22 Sep 1812), Vittoria, Tolosa, San Sebastian (wounded 31 Aug 1813), Bidassoa, Nivelle, Nive, St Etienne (severely wounded) and Bayonne. Present at Waterloo. Also served in the Mediterranean 1806–1807, the Baltic 1807–1808 and the Netherlands 1814–1815. KH. MGS medal for Talavera, Busaco, Fuentes d'Onoro, Ciudad Rodrigo, Salamanca, Vittoria, San Sebastian, Nivelle and Nive. Hanoverian Army: Bt Lt Colonel. Died at Rössing near Calenburg, Hanover, 22 Feb 1856.
Reference: Beamish, N. L., History of the King's German Legion, Vol. 2, reprint 1997. No. 387.

RÖTTIGER, August
Lieutenant Colonel. Artillery, King's German Legion.
Pedestal tomb: Old Nikolai Cemetery, Hanover, Germany. (Near Chapel ruins). (Photograph)

Inscription on three sides of the tomb:

DENKMAL / DES / GENERAL / RÖTTIGER / UND DESSEN / GATTIN HOCH BEGLUECKET / VEREINT IM LEBEN / NACH BEIDER WUNSCH / AUCH HIER VEREINT AUGUST THEODOR / RÕTTIGER / GENERAL / GEB. 11. DEZ. 1766 / GEST. 27. OKT. 1851

MEMORIAL TO GENERAL RÖTTIGER AND HIS WIFE, HAPPILY BLESSED AND UNITED IN LIFE AND ALSO HERE, ACCORDING TO THEIR WISHES. AUGUST THEODOR RÖTTIGER, GENERAL, BORN 11TH DECEMBER 1766, DIED 27TH OCTOBER 1851

Capt KGL Artillery 8 Nov 1803. Major 1805. Lt Colonel 25 Nov 1808. Bt Colonel 4 Jun 1814.

Served at Copenhagen 1807. Also served in Hanover 1805 and North Germany 1813–1814. Hanoverian Army: Major General 1831. Lt General 1833 and Director of the Ordnance Department. General 1848. KH. King William's Cross. Died 27 Oct 1851.

REFERENCE: Beamish, N. L., History of the King's German Legion, Vol. 2, reprint 1997. No. 25.

SAFFE, August von
Captain. 1st Line Battalion, King's German Legion.
Named on the Regimental Memorial: La Haye Sainte, Waterloo. (Photograph)
Named on the Waterloo Column, Hanover, Germany. (Photograph)

Lt 19 Aug 1805. Capt 11 Mar 1812.

Served in the Peninsula Dec 1808 – May 1812. Present at Douro, Talavera (wounded), Busaco, Fuentes d'Onoro, Ciudad Rodrigo, Moriscos and Salamanca. Present at Waterloo where he was killed. Promoted to Major during the battle, but the promotion did not reach him until after his death. Also served at Hanover 1805, Sicily 1806–1807, the Baltic 1807–1808, North Germany 1813–1814 and the Netherlands 1814.

REFERENCE: Beamish, N. L., History of the King's German Legion, Vol. 2, reprint 1997. No. 985.

SCHAUMANN, Friedrich Melchior Wilhelm
Captain. 2nd Battalion Light Infantry, King's German Legion.
Named on the Regimental Memorial: La Haye Sainte, Waterloo. (Photograph)
Named on the Waterloo Column, Hanover, Germany. (Photograph)

Lt 11 Sep 1807. Capt 25 May 1812.

Served in the Peninsula Aug 1808 – Jan 1809. Present at Vigo. Present at Waterloo where he was killed. Also served at Hanover 1805, Baltic 1807–1808, Walcheren 1809, North Germany 1813–1814 and the Netherlands 1814.
Note: Named as Schumann on Waterloo Column.

REFERENCE: Beamish, N. L., History of the King's German Legion, Vol. 2, reprint 1997. No. 988.

SCHRÖDER, Johann Christian von
Lieutenant Colonel. 2nd Line Battalion, King's German Legion.
Named on the Regimental Memorial: La Haye Sainte, Waterloo. (Photograph)
Named on the Waterloo Column, Hanover, Germany. (Photograph)

Lt Colonel 4 Jun 1813.

Present at Waterloo where he was severely wounded, and died of his wounds 22 Jun 1815. Also served in the Baltic 1807, Mediterranean 1808–1814 and the Netherlands 1814.

REFERENCE: Beamish, N. L., History of the King's German Legion, Vol. 2, reprint 1997. No. 1018.

SCHUCK, Johann Ludwig
Lieutenant and Adjutant. 5th Line Battalion, King's German Legion.
Named on the Regimental Memorial: La Haye Sainte, Waterloo. (Photograph)
Named on the Waterloo Column, Hanover, Germany. (Photograph)

Ensign and Adjutant 15 Oct 1812. Lt 25 Apr 1814.

Served in the Peninsula Dec 1812 – Apr 1814. Present at Vittoria, Tolosa, San Sebastian, Bidassoa, Nivelle, Nive, St Etienne and Bayonne. Present at Waterloo where he was killed. Also served in the Netherlands 1814.
Reference: Beamish, N. L., History of the King's German Legion, Vol. 2, reprint 1997. No. 1012

SCHULTZE, Johann Friedrich
Private. Militia Regiment Lüneburg, Royal Hanoverian Army.
Named on the Waterloo Column, Hanover, Germany. (Photograph)
Named on the Memorial tablet: St Jacobi's Church, Bleckede, Lower Saxony, Germany. (Photograph)

Present at Waterloo where he was killed.

SCHULZEN, Carl Detlef von
Lieutenant. Artillery, King's German Legion.
Named on the Regimental Memorial: La Haye Sainte, Waterloo. (Photograph)
Named on the Waterloo Column, Hanover, Germany. (Photograph)
Named on the Regimental Memorial to Royal Artillery and KGL Artillery, St Joseph's Church, Waterloo. (Photograph)

2nd Lt 22 Apr 1807. 1st Lt 11 Dec 1812.

Served in the Peninsula 1810 – Apr 1814. Present at Fuentes d'Onoro, Albuera, second siege of Badajoz, Ciudad Rodrigo, Badajoz, Salamanca, San Millan, Vittoria, San Sebastian, Pyrenees, Bidassoa, Nivelle, Nive, Orthes and Toulouse. Present at Waterloo where he was killed. Also served in the Baltic 1807–1808 and the Netherlands 1814.
Reference: Beamish, N. L., History of the King's German Legion, Vol. 2, reprint 1997. No. 787.

SOETEBEER, Heinrich Christoph
Private. Militia Regiment Lüneburg, Royal Hanoverian Army.
Named on the Waterloo Column, Hanover, Germany. (Photograph)
Named on the Memorial tablet: St Jacobi's Church, Bleckede, Lower Saxony, Germany. (Photograph)

Present at Waterloo where he was killed.

SPIEL, August Albrecht Hieronymus
Ensign. 8th Line Battalion, King's German Legion.
Pedestal tomb: Neuenhäuser Churchyard, Celle, Lower Saxony, Germany. (Photograph)

DEM ANDENKEN / DES LIEUTENANTS / AUGUST ALBRECHT / HIERONYMUS SPIEL / GEB. ZU CELLE AM 8. JAN. 1780 / GEST. ZU CELLE 27. JAN.1845

IN MEMORY OF / LIEUTENANT / AUGUST ALBRECHT / HIERONYMUS SPIEL / BORN IN CELLE ON 8 JANUARY 1780 / DIED IN CELLE 27 JANUARY 1845

Ensign 23 Mar 1814.

Present at Waterloo. Also served in the Netherlands 1814–1815. Died at Celle 27 Jan 1845.
Reference: Beamish, N. L., History of the King's German Legion, Vol. 2, reprint 1997. No. 726.

STIEGLITZ, Adolph Wilhelm
Ensign. 6th Line Battalion, King's German Legion.
Low monument: Neustädter Cemetery, Hanover, Germany. (Photograph)

HIER RUHET / ADOLPH WILHELM STIEGLITZ, KÖNIGL. HANNOVERSCHER CAPTAIN.

HERE LIES / CAPTAIN ADOLPH WILHELM STIEGLITZ KING'S GERMAN LEGION.

Ensign 22 Mar 1814.

Present at Waterloo. Also served in the Netherlands. Hanoverian Army: Bt Captain. Died at Hanover 22 Feb 1844.
Reference: Beamish, N. L., History of the King's German Legion, Vol. 2, reprint 1997. No. 632.

STIES, Conrad
Private. Royal Hanoverian Infantry Regiment.
Named on the Waterloo Column, Hanover, Germany. (Photograph)
Named on the Memorial tablet: St Marien's Church, Celle, Lower Saxony, Germany. (Photograph)

SOLDAT C. STIES 1815 B. WATERLOO

Present at Waterloo where he was severely wounded and died of his wounds in Brussels.

STRUBE, Julius Wilhelm von
Major. Miltia Battalion, Royal Hanoverian Army.
Monument: Garrison Cemetery, Hamelin, Lower Saxony, Germany. (Photograph)

JULIUS WILHELM VON STRUBE / KÖNIGL. HANNOVERSCHER OBERST / RITTER DES GUELPHEN ORDENS / INHABER DER WATERLOO MEDAILLE / GEBOREN DEN 17 NOVEMBER1774 / GESTORBEN 17 NOVEMBER 1834 / IM 60 LEBENS UND 44 DIENSTJAHRE /

JULIUS WILHELM STRUBE / ROYAL HANOVERIAN COLONEL / KNIGHT OF THE GUELPHIC ORDER / AWARDED THE WATERLOO MEDAL / BORN 17TH NOVEMBER 1774 / DIED 17TH NOVEMBER 1834 / IN THE 60TH OF HIS LIFE AFTER 44TH YEAR OF SERVICE / ………………..

Cornet 1 Jan 1806. Capt Militia Battalion of Hamelin 15 Feb 1806. Major 1815.

Present at Waterloo where he was wounded in command of the Militia Battalion of the 5th Hanoverian Brigade which was part of Picton's 5th Infantry Division. KH. Hanoverian Army: Major 1816. Lt Colonel 4th Infantry Regt. Bt Colonel. Died at Behrensen near Hamelin 17 Nov 1831.
Reference: Beamish, N. L., History of the King's German Legion, Vol. 2, reprint 1997. No. 942.

SUCHOW, Arthur
Ensign. 1st Line Battalion, King's German Legion.
Named on the Regimental Memorial: La Haye Sainte, Waterloo. (Photograph)

Present at Waterloo where he was killed.

SYMPHER, Frederick
Major. Artillery, King's German Legion.
Named on the Memorial: St Andrew's Church (now Musée Historique), Biarritz, France. (Photograph)

Capt 14 Feb 1804. Major 17 Aug 1812.

Served in the Peninsula 1810–1814. Present at Salamanca, Vittoria, San Sebastian, Pyrenees, Nivelle, Orthes where he was killed 27 Feb 1814. Gold Cross for Salamanca, Vittoria, San Sebastian, Pyrenees, Nivelle and Orthes.

REFERENCE: *Beamish, N. L., History of the King's German Legion, Vol. 2, reprint 1997. No. 785.*

THALMANN, Carl August

Major. 7th Line Battalion, King's German Legion.
Pedestal tomb: Garrison Cemetery, Hamelin, Lower Saxony, Germany. (Photograph)

Inscription on three sides:

DEM IN DER / ENGLISCHEN LEGION / GESTANDENEN MAJOR / CARL AUGUST / THALMANN, / GEB, ZU GÖTTINGEN / D. 17 TEN DECEMBER / 1753 / GEST. ZU HAMELN / D. 27 TEN APR. 1826

CARL AUGUST THALMANN, / MAJOR / IN THE ENGLISH KING'S GERMAN LEGION / BORN IN GÖTTINGEN / 17 DECEMBER 1753 / DIED IN HAMELN / 27 APRIL 1826

Capt 9 Oct 1803. Major 18 Jan 1808.

Served in the Peninsula Sep 1808 – Jul 1811. Present at Douro, Talavera and Fuentes d'Onoro. Gold Medal for Talavera. Also served at Hanover 1805, the Baltic 1807–1808, the Mediterranean 1812 and the Netherlands 1814–1815. Later Major in Foreign Veteran Battalion. Died at Hamelin 30 Apr 1826.

REFERENCE: *Beamish, N. L., History of the King's German Legion, Vol. 2, reprint 1997. No. 740.*

THILEE, Georg

Captain. 2nd Line Battalion, King's German Legion.
Named on the Regimental Memorial: La Haye Sainte, Waterloo. (Photograph)
Named on the Waterloo Column, Hanover, Germany. (Photograph)

Lt 16 Jun 1804. Adjutant 19 Nov 1807. Capt 5 Mar 1812.

Served in the Peninsula Sep 1808 – Apr 1812. Present at Douro, Talavera, Busaco, Fuentes d'Onoro and Ciudad Rodrigo. Present at Waterloo where he was killed. Also served at Hanover 1805, the Baltic 1807–1808, North Germany 1813–1814 and the Netherlands 1814–1815.
Note: Also named as Tilee.

USLAR, Ferdinand von

Ensign. 4th Line Battalion, King's German Legion.
Pedestal tomb: Engesohder Cemetery, Hanover, Germany. (Photograph)

FERDINAND / VON / USLAR / GLEICHEN / OBERSTLEUTN / GEB, 8. MAI / 1801 / GEST 18 NOVBR. / 1878

FERDINAND / VON / USLAR / GLEICHEN / LIEUTENANT COLONEL / BORN 8. MAI / 1801 / DIED 18 NOVBR. / 1878

Ensign 30 May 1814.

Present at Waterloo. Also served in the Netherlands 1814–1815. Hanoverian Army: Lt Grenadier Guard Regt 1816. 2nd Capt 1836. Capt 1841. Retired 1848 as Bt Major and Lt Colonel. KH. Knight of the Order of the Saxon Ernestine House. Died at Hanover 16 Nov 1878. Family named changed to Uslar-Gleichen in 1828.

REFERENCE: *Beamish, N. L., History of the King's German Legion, Vol. 2, reprint 1997. No. 547.*

USLAR, Otto
Private. Hussar Regiment Prinz Regent, Royal Hanoverian Army.
Named on the Memorial tablet: St Jacobi's Church, Bleckede, Lower Saxony, Germany. (Photograph)

Present at Waterloo where he was wounded and died of his wounds in Paris 13 Oct 1815.

USLAR, Otto Wilhelm Thilo von
Ensign. 2nd Line Battalion, King's German Legion.
Iron Cross: Old Cemetery, Flensburg, Schleswig-Holstein, Germany. (Around the Lion memorial). (Photograph)

HIER / RUHET / DER / CAPITAIN FREI HERR OTTO WILH. THILO / V. USLAR GLEICHEN / 1 BAT. 2 KONIGL. HANNÖV. INFY REGIMENTI / GEFALLEN / BEI / ULDERUP / 2O APR / 1848

HERE / LIES / CAPTAIN BARON OTTO WILH. THILO / VON USLAR GLEICHEN / 1ST BATTALION 2ND KGL INFANTRY REGIMENT / DIED / AT / ULDERUP / 20TH APRIL 1848

Ensign 29 May 1814.

Present at Waterloo. Also served in the Netherlands 1814–1815. Hanoverian Army: Lt 1816. Capt 1st Battalion 2nd Royal Hanoverian Infantry Regt. Killed in uprising in Schleswig-Holstein 1848. Family name changed to Uslar – Gleichen in 1828. Became Baron 1829.
Reference: Beamish, N. L., History of the King's German Legion, Vol. 2, reprint 1997. No. 460.

VOIGT, August Wilhelm von
Captain. 8th Line Battalion, King's German Legion.
Named on the Regimental Memorial: La Haye Sainte, Waterloo. (Photograph)
Named on the Waterloo Column, Hanover, Germany. (Photograph)

Lt 13 May 1806. Capt 10 Apr 1811.

Present at Waterloo where he was killed. Also served in the Baltic 1807, Mediterranean 1808–1814 and the Netherlands 1814.
Reference: Beamish, N. L., History of the King's German Legion, Vol 2, reprint 1997. No. 982.

VOLGER, Christoph Arnold
Lieutenant. 6th Line Battalion, King's German Legion.
Memorial: Old Cemetery, Nienburg Weser, Lower Saxony, Germany. (M.I.)

HIER RUHET / DER KÖNIGLICH / HANNOVERSCHE MAJOR / A. D. / CHRISTOPH ARNOLD / VOLGER / GEBOREN ZU KIRCHRODE / DEN 14 TEN MAY 1791 / GESTORBEN ZU NIENBURG / DEN 6 TEN FEBRUARY 1855

HERE RESTS / THE ROYAL / HANOVERIAN MAJOR / RTD. / CHRISTOPH ARNOLD / VOLGER / BORN AT KIRCHRODE / BY HANOVER / 14TH MAY 1791 / DIED AT NIENBURG / 6TH FEBRUARY 1855

Ensign 12 Nov 1806. Lt 27 Jan 1811.

Served in the Peninsula Aug 1812 - Apr 1813. Present at Castalla. Also served in the Baltic 1807 and the Mediterranean 1808-1815. Hanoverian Army: Captain 9th Line Battalion. Brother of Capt Heinrich Wilhelm Volger 7th Line Battalion.
Reference: Beamish, N. L., History of the King's German Legion, Vol. 2, reprint 1997. No. 619.

VOLGER, Heinrich Wilhelm
Captain. 7th Line Battalion, King's German Legion.
Pedestal tomb: Old Cemetery, Nienburg Weser, Lower Saxony, Germany. (Photograph)

English translation of inscription:

HERE RESTS / THE REMAINS OF THE / ROYAL HANOVERIAN MAJOR / HEINRICH WILHELM VOLGER / HE ENDED HIS LIFE ON EARTH ON THE 29TH APRIL 1841 IN HIS 70TH YEAR / REST IN PEACE YOU LAST OF MY / BROTHERS. / THE DECEASED ENROLLED IN HIS 16TH YEAR / IN THE HANOVERIAN MILITARY SERVICE IN / THE 7TH, LATER AN ENSIGN IN THE 14TH / INFANTRY-REGIMENT, AND THEN WENT IN / THE TIME OF HISTORICAL MISFORTUNE OF THE FRENCH / OCCUPATION, LOYAL TO HIS KING, TO / ENGLAND TO THE GERMAN LEGION, / IN WHICH HE REMAINED UNTIL THE RECONSTITUTION / OF HIS FATHERLAND, ENLISTED IN HANOVERIAN DUTIES / AS A MAJOR IN THE 10TH INFANTRY / REGIMENT. / DEATH, WHICH HE AVOIDED DURING / HIS LONG AND PERILOUS CAREER CAME SUDDENLY / WHEN HE WAS / 47 YEARS OLD / THE GLORIOUS SORTIE FROM / MENIN WHICH HIS NOBLE FRIENDS LIKED TO CELEBRATE / WITH HIM WAS IN VAIN. / HARD TESTED BUT UNDAUNTED, / LOYALTY TO KING AND COUNTRY / LOVE AND AFFECTION FOR / HIS CHOSEN CAREER, TO / HIS COMRADES AND FRIENDS, / TRUE PHILANTHROPY / AND CHARITY AGAINST PEOPLE / IN NEED FOR CARE FOLLOWED / HIM AS WITNESS / TO ETERNITY.

Lt 10 Jan 1806. Capt 12 Mar 1811.
##Served in the Peninsula Sep 1808 - Jul 1811. Present at Douro, Talavera (wounded) and Busaco. Also served in the Baltic 1807-1808 and the Mediterranean 1812-1816. Brother of Lt Christoph Arnold Volger, 4th Line Battalion.
Reference: Beamish, N. L., History of the King's German Legion, Vol. 2, reprint 1997. No. 651.

WAGNER, I. F. C.
Private. Royal Hanoverian Infantry Regiment.
Named on the Waterloo Column, Hanover, Germany. (Photograph)
Named on the Memorial tablet: St Marien's Church, Celle, Lower Saxony, Germany. (Photograph)

SOLDAT I. F. C. WAGNER 1811. BADAJOZ

Served in the Peninsula where he was killed at Badajoz 1811.

WALTHAUSEN, Charles Frederick William von
Captain. 8th Line, King's German Legion.
Obelisk: St Crucis's Cemetery, Einbeck, Lower Saxony, Germany.

CARL FRIEDRICH WILHELM / FREYHERR / VON WALTHAUSEN / HAUPTMANN / IM 8 TEN LINIEN BATTALION / DER KÖNIGLICH / DEUTSCHEN LEGION / WAR GEBOREN DEN 21 TEN DECEMBER / 1775 / UND FAND DEN 2 TEN APRIL / 1813 / AUF SICILIEN .... DURCH MEUCHELMÖRDER SEINEN TOD

CARL FIREDRICH WILHELM / BARON / VON WALTHAUSEN / CAPTAIN / IN THE 8 LINE BATTALION / OF THE KING'S / GERMAN LEGION / BORN 21 DECEMBER / 1775 / AND ASSASSINATED ON 2 APRIL / 1813 / IN SICILY

Capt 10 May 1806.

Served in the Baltic 1807. Also served in the Mediterranean 1807–1813. Murdered by brigands in Sicily 2 Apr 1813.
Reference: Beamish, N. L., History of the King's German Legion, Vol. 2, reprint 1997. No. 1096.

WESTERNHAGEN, Thilo von
Captain. 8th Line Battalion, King's German Legion.
Named on the Regimental Memorial: La Haye Sainte, Waterloo. (Photograph)
Named on the Waterloo Column, Hanover, Germany. (Photograph)

Lt 29 Jun 1806. Capt 10 Sep 1814.
Present at Waterloo where he was killed. Also served in the Baltic 1807, Mediterranean 1808–1814 and the Netherlands 1814.
Reference: Beamish, N. L., History of the King's German Legion, Vol. 2, reprint 1997. No. 992.

WEYHE, Wilhelm Georg Ferdinand von
Lieutenant. 3rd Line Battalion, King's German Legion.
Ledger stone: St Marien's Church, Eimke, near Ebsdorf, Germany. (Photograph)

WILHELM LUDWIG / JOHANN FERDINAND / VON WEYHE / CAPITAIN / DER ENGLISCH DEUTSCHEN LEGION / ERBHERR AUF EIMKE / PATRON DER KIRCHE / GEBOREN DEN 6. 8. 1787 / GESTORBEN DEN 22. 2. 1869 / ZU EIMKE

WILHELM LUDWIG / JOHANN FERDINAND / VON WEYHE / CAPTAIN / OF THE ENGLISH KING'S GERMAN LEGION / LORD OF THE MANOR AT EIMKE / PATRON OF THE CHURCH / BORN 6 AUGUST 1787 / AND DIED 22 FEBRUARY 1869 / AT EIMKE

Memorial tablet: St Marien's Church, Eimke, Lower Saxony, Germany. (Panel 9 of Family Memorial). (Photograph)

PATRONE / DIESER KIRCHE / AUS DEM HAUSE / WEYHE EIMKE / SEIT DEM JAHRE / 1600 / WILHELM / CAPITAIN DER DEUTSCH – / ENGLISCHEN LEGION / 1850–1869

PATRON / OF THIS CHURCH / FROM THE HOUSE / OF WEYHE EIMKE / SINCE THE YEAR 1600 / WILHELM, CAPTAIN OF / THE ENGLISH KING'S GERMAN LEGION / 1850–1869

Lt 23 Apr 1805.
Served in the Baltic 1807. Also served in the Mediterranean 1808–1814 and the Netherlands 1814–1815. Retired as Bt Captain in the Hanoverian Army. Died 22 Feb 1869.
Reference: Beamish, N. L., History of the King's German Legion, Vol. 2, reprint 1997. No. 484.

WIEGMANN, Heinrich
Captain. 2nd Battalion Light Infantry, King's German Legion.
Named on the Regimental Memorial: La Haye Sainte, Waterloo. (Photograph)
Named on the Waterloo Column, Hanover, Germany. (Photograph)
Named on the Memorial tablet: St Dionysius's Church, Adensen, Lower Saxony, Germany. (Photograph)

UNSEREN / BEY WATERLOO AM 18TEN JUNIUS 1815 / GEFALLENEN BRÜDERN / DEM BRIGADE-MAJOR HEINRICH WIEGMANN / DEM LIEUTENANT CHRISTOPH VAN JEINSEN / DEM SOLDATEN FRIEDRICH MATTHIES / ZU DANKBARER ERINNERUNG / VON / DER GEMEINE ADENSEN UND HALLERBURG

FOR OUR BROTHERS / KILLED AT WATERLOO ON 18TH JUNE 1815 / THE BRIGADE MAJOR HEINRICH WIEGMANN / THE LIEUTENANT CHRISTOPHER VON JEINSEN / THE SOLDIER FRIEDRICH MATTHIES / IN THANKFUL REMBERANCE / FROM / THE COMMUNITY OF ADENSEN AND HALLERBURG

Lt 7 Jan 1806. Capt and Brigade Major 24 Oct 1811.

Served in the Peninsula Aug 1808 – Jan 1809 and Mar 1811 – Apr 1814 (Dec 1811 – Nov 1812 – Brigade Major, 1 Brigade 7th Division and Dec 1812 – Apr 1814 – Brigade Major 3 Brigade 1st Division). Present at Vigo, Albuera, second siege of Badajoz, siege of Salamanca Forts, Moriscos, Salamanca, Burgos, Vittoria, Tolosa, St Sebastian, Bidassoa, Nivelle, Nive, St Etienne and Bayonne. Present at Waterloo where he was killed. Also served in the Baltic 1807–1808, Walcheren 1809 and the Netherlands 1814.
Reference: Beamish, N. L., History of the King's German Legion, Vol. 2, reprint 1997. No. 983.

WILDING, Georg
Lieutenant. 8th Line Battalion, King's German Legion.
Chest tomb: Old Garden Cemetery, Hanover, Lower Saxony, Germany. (Photograph)

HIER RUHET DIE STERBLICHE HÜLLE / DES H. GEORG WILDING, FÜRSTEN VON BUTERA RADALI / KÖNIGLICH NEAPOLITANISCHEM KAMMERHERRN UND / GESANDTEN AM KAISERLICH RUSSISCHEN HOFE / GEBOREN ZU UELZEN DEN 24. JUNI 1790 / GESTORBEN ZU WIESBADEN DEN 6. SEPTEMBER 1841 / DIESES DENKMAL SETZTE IHM / SEINE TIEF BETRÜBTE WITWE / BARBARA, GEBORENE FÜRSTIN SCHAKOWSKOI

HERE LIE THE MORTAL REMAINS / OF GEORG WILDING, PRINCE OF BUTERA RADALI / ROYAL NEAPOLITAN CHAMBERLAIN AND / AMBASSADOR AT THE IMPERIAL RUSSIAN COURT / BORN AT UELZEN 24. JUNE 1790 / DIED AT WIESBADEN 6. SEPTEMBER 1841 / THIS MEMORIAL ERECTED TO HIM / BY HIS DEEPLY SAD WIDOW / BARBARA, BORN PRINCESS SCHAKOWSKOI

Ensign 28 Jun 1806. Lt 24 Oct 1810.

Served in the Baltic 1807. Also served in the Mediterranean 1808–1814. Resigned 12 Apr 1814 and became Neapolitan Ambassador to the Court of St Petersburg. KH. Order of the Iron Cross of Austria. Order of St January of Sicily. Died at Wiesbaden 6 Sep 1841.
Reference: Beamish, N. L., History of the King's German Legion, Vol. 2, reprint 1997. No. 1256.

WINKELMANN, Heinrich
Private. Field Battalion Lüneburg, Royal Hanoverian Army.
Named on the Waterloo Column, Hanover.
Named on the Memorial tablet: St Marien's Church, Celle, Lower Saxony, Germany. (Photograph)

SOLDAT H. WINKELMANN 1815 B. WATERLOO

Present at Waterloo where he was killed.

WÜLPERN, Johann
Private. Militia Battalion, Royal Hanoverian Army.
Named on the Militia Battalion Memorial: Hesedorf, near Bremervörde, Lower Saxony, Germany. (Photograph)

Present at Waterloo where he was killed.

WURMB, Ernst Christian Carl von
Captain. 5th Line Battalion, King's German Legion.
Named on the Regimental Memorial: La Haye Sainte, Waterloo. (Photograph)
Named on the Waterloo Column, Hanover, Germany. (Photograph)

Lt 25 May 1805. Adjutant 21 Jan 1806. Capt 7 Dec 1809.

Served in the Peninsula Aug 1808 – Apr 1814. (ADC to Major General Murray Aug – Oct 1808, ADC to Col Dreiberg Nov 1808 – Jun 1809 and ADC to Major General Low Jul 1809 – Jun 1811). Present at Douro, Talavera, Busaco, Fuentes d'Onoro, Ciudad Rodrigo, Moriscos, Salamanca, Burgos, Vittoria, Tolosa, San Sebastian, Bidassoa, Nivelle, Nive, St Etienne and Bayonne. Present at Waterloo where he was killed. Also served at Hanover 1805, the Baltic 1807–1808 and the Netherlands 1814.
Reference: Beamish, N. L., History of the King's German Legion, Vol. 2, reprint 1997. No. 981.

Regimental Index
King's German Legion and Royal Hanoverian Army

4th Line Battalion

Chüden, Georg W. C.	Major
Cronhelm, Theodor von	Ensign
Du Plat, Georg Carl A.	Lt Colonel
Günther, Johann G.	Surgeon
Heise, Georg	Capt
Langwerth, Ernest E. K.	Col Commandant
Leue, Georg Ludwig	Capt
Uslar, Ferdinand von	Ensign

5th Line Battalion

Bacmeister, Johann W. L.	Capt
Brandis, Eberhard von	Capt
Diepenbroick, A. F. von	Capt
Erdmann, Friedrich	Lt
Gerber, Johann G. A.	Major
Gerson, George H.	Asst Surgeon
Hamelberg, Ernst von	Capt
Köhler, Carl	Lt
Langrehr, Friedrich E. P.	Capt
Meyer, August	Lt
Meyer, Johann	Lt
Ompteda, Christian von	Colonel
Schuck, Johann Ludwig	Lt and Adjt
Wurmb, Ernst C. C. von	Capt

6th Line Battalion

Stieglitz, Adolph W.	Ensign
Volger, Christoph Arnold	Lt

7th Line Battalion

Drechsel, Friedrich Carl	Col Commandant
Halkett, Hugh	Lt Colonel
Hartwig, Gottlieb von	Lt
Lösecke, Friedrich W.	Capt
Offeney, William	Lt Colonel
Thalmann, Carl August	Major
Volger, Heinrich Wilheld	Capt

8th Line Battalion

Brinckman, Julius J. A.	Capt
Marenholtz, Wilhelm von	Lt
Spiel, August Albrecht H.	Ensign
Voigt, August Wilhelm	Capt
Walthausen, Charles F.	Capt
Westernhagen, Thilo von	Capt
Wilding, Georg	Lt

KGL Artillery

Blumenbach, Carl E.	Lt
Brown, William	2nd Capt
Brückmann, Friedrich H.	Major
Cleeves, Andrew	2nd Capt
Hartmann, Sir George J.	Major
Jasper, Georg L.	2nd Capt
Kuhlmann, Heinrich	1st Capt
Matthies, Friedrich	Driver
Röttiger, August	Lt Colonel
Schulzen, Carl Detlef	Lt
Sympher, Frederick	Major

Royal Hanoverian Army

Dannenberg, Wilhelm	Bugler
Hartlep, H.	Pte
Hoffmeister, I.	Sgt
Kielmannsegge, Friedrich	Colonel Commandant
Knust, I.	Rifleman
Michaelis, H.	Dragoon
Sties, Conrad	Pte
Uslar, Otto	Pte
Wagner, I. F. C.	Pte

Militia Battalion Royal Hanoverian Army

Burfeindt, Johann	Pte
Dierks, David	Pte
Enckhausen, Friedrich	Pte
Mühlmann, Johann	Pte
Poppe, Jürgen	Pte
Schultze, Johann F.	Pte
Soetebeer, Heinrich C.	Pte
Strube, Julius Wilhelm	Major
Winkelmann Heinrich	Pte
Wülpern, Johann	Pte

Field Jaeger Corps

Düring, Johann Christian	Capt
Ludowig, William von	Ensign

Medical Department

Denecke, George	Physician

Place Index
King's German Legion and Royal Hanoverian Army

CEYLON
McGlashan, James Edward

FRANCE
Biarritz: Blumenbach, Carl E.
Biarritz: Boyd, George
Biarritz: Chüden, Paul Gottlieb
Biarritz: Drechsell, Friedrich von
Biarritz: Klenck, Friedrich von
Biarritz: Köhler, Carl
Biarritz: Meyer, Johann
Biarritz: Müller, Heinrich
Biarritz: Sympher, Frederick

GERMANY
Adensen: Matties, Frederick
Adensen: Wiegmann, Heinrich
Bleckede: Popper, Jürgen
Bleckede: Schultzew, Johann F.
Bleckede: Soetebeer, Heinrich C.
Bleckede: Uslar, Otto
Celle: Avemann, Charles C. F. von
Celle: Bacmeister, Johann W. L.
Celle: Besse, Conrad
Celle: Bobers, Carl von
Celle: Dannenberg, C.
Celle: Diedel, Friedrich
Celle: Gottschalk, Ernst
Celle: Halkett, Hugh
Celle: Hamelberg, Ernst von
Celle: Hartlep, H.
Celle: Heine, Friedrich
Celle: Hodenburg, Friedrich von
Celle: Hodenburg, Georg H. Von
Celle: Hoffmeister, C.
Celle: Knust, I.
Celle: Krauchenberg, Louis
Celle: Langrehr, Friedrich P.
Celle: Marenholz, Wilhelm von
Celle: Meldau, I. H.
Celle: Michaelis, H.
Celle: Peters, Friedrich
Celle: Römermann, Heinrich
Celle: Spiel, August A. H.
Celle: Sties, Conrad
Celle: Wagner, I. F. C.
Celle: Winkelmann, Heinrich
Eimke: Weyhe, Willhelm W. G. von
Einbeck: Walthausen, Charles F. W. Von
Fallersleben: Behne, Ludwig
Fallersladen: Franck, Georg
Flensburg: Uslar, Otto Willhelm T. Von
Gehrden: Holle, Carl von
Grabow: Hodenburg, Friedrich G. von
Grabow: Hodenburg, George H. von
Hamburg: Gerson, Georg H.
Hamelin: Best, Willhelm
Hamelin: Bussche, Hans von
Hamelin: Gerber, Johann G. A.
Hamelin: Lueder, Eberhard Magnus L.
Hamelin: Strube, Julius W. von
Hamelin: Thalmann, Carl Augustus
Hanover: Alten, Count Charles von
Hanover: Baring, Baron Georg von
Hanover: Bobers, Carl von
Hanover: Bösewiel, Adolph
Hanover: Brüggemann, Heinrich
Hanover: Bülow, Friedrich von

Hanover: Chüden, Georg W. C.
Hanover: Cronhelm, Theodor
Hanover: Deichmann, Willhelm
Hanover: Diedel, Friedrich
Hanover: Drangmeister, Heinrich
Hanover: Drechsell, Friedrich Carl von
Hanover: Du Plat, Georg C. A.
Hanover: Goeben, August A. von
Hanover: Gottschalk, Ernst
Hanover: Hartmann, Sir Georg J. von
Hanover: Heisse, Georg
Hanover: Holle, Carl von
Hanover: Holzermann, Philip
Hanover: Janssen, Georg
Hanover: Jasper, Georg L.
Hanover: Jeinsen, Friedrich C. Von
Hanover: Kerssenbruch, Agatz von
Hanover: Kielmannsegge, Friedrich
Hanover: Kuhlmann, Otto
Hanover: Leschen, Friedrich
Hanover: Leue, Georg L.
Hanover: Levetzow, Friedrich C. L. von
Hanover: Linsingen, Carl Christian von
Hanover: Lücken, Hartwig von
Hanover: Marenholz, Willhelm von
Hanover: Marschalk, Heinrich von
Hanover: Matthies, Friedrich
Hanover: Meyer, Friedrich L.
Hanover: Meyer, Johann
Hanover: Ompteda, Christian von
Hanover: Peters, Frederick
Hanover: Poppe, Jürgen
Hanover: Poten, August G.

Hanover: Robertson, Friedrich von
Hanover: Römermann, Heinrich
Hanover: Röttiger, August
Hanover: Saffe, August von
Hanover: Schaumann, Friedrich M. W.
Hanover: Schuck, Johann L.
Hanover: Schultze, Johann F.
Hanover: Schulzen, Carl Detlef von
Hanover: Soetebeer, Heinrich C.
Hanover: Stieglitz, Adolph W.
Hanover: Sties, Conrad
Hanover: Thilee, Georg
Hanover: Uslar, Ferdinand von
Hanover: Voigt, August W. von
Hanover: Wagner, I. F. C.
Hanover: Westernhagen, Thilo von
Hanover: Wiegmann, Heinrich
Hanover: Wilding, George
Hanover: Winkelmann, Heinrich
Hanover: Wurmb, Ernst Christian C. von
Hesedorf: Burfeindt, Johann
Hesedorf: Dierks, David
Hesedorf: Mühlmann, Johann
Hesedorf: Wülpern, Johann
Ludwigslust: Meyer, August
Lüneburg: Lösecke, Friedrich von
Lüneburg: Ludowig, Wilhelm von
Nienburg: Brinckmann, Julius J. A.
Nienburg: Erdmann, Friedrich
Nienburg: Grote, Otto August F. von
Nienburg: Günther, Johann G.
Nienburg: Hartwig, Gottlieb von
Nienburg: Volger, Christoph A.
Nienburg: Volger, Heinrich W.
Osnabrück: Enckhausen, Franz Heinich
Rössing: Rössing, Ferdinand C. L. F. von
Rotenburg: Düring, Johann C. Von
Schloss Ricklingen: Brandis, Eberhard von
Stade: Brückmann, Friedrich H.
Stade: Kuhlmann, Heinrich J.

ITALY

Naples: Carmichael, Alexander

PORTUGAL

Elvas: Brown, William
Lisbon: Offeney, William

MEMORIALS TO KING'S GERMAN LEGION

BELGIUM

Waterloo

Regimental Monument: La Haye Sainte, Waterloo. (Photograph)]

Side 1:

TO THE MEMORY / OF THEIR COMPANIONS IN ARMS / WHO GLORIOUSLY FELL ON THE MEMORABLE / 18TH DAY OF JUNE 1815 / THIS MONUMENT / IS ERECTED BY THE OFFICERS OF THE KING'S / GERMAN LEGION

Side 2:

OBRIST UND BRIGADIER CHRISTIAN VON OMPTEDA / OBRIST UND BRIGADIER CARL DU PLAT / 1ST LIGHT DRAGOON REGT / RITTMEISTER FRIEDRICH PETERS / LIEUTENANT FRIEDRICH VON LEVETZOW / LIEUTENANT OTTO KUHLMANN / 2ND LIGHT DRAGOONS REGT / RITTMEISTER FRIEDRICH VON BULOW / CORNET HEINRICH DRANKMEISTER / 1ST HUSSARS REGT / RITTMEISTER-BRIGADE MAJOR CARL BOBERS / 3RD HUSSARS REGT / OBRISTLIEUTENANT LUDWIG MEYER / RITTMEISTER AGATZ VON KERSENBRUCH / RITTMEISTER GEORGE JANSSEN / LIEUTENANT ADJUTANT HEINRICH BRÜGGEMANN / CORNET WILHELM DEICHMANN / 1ST LIGHT INFANTRY BATTALION / HAUPTMAN PHILIPP HOLZERMANN / HAUPTMAN HEINRICH MARSCHALK / HAUPTMAN ALEXANDER GOEBEN / LIEUTENANT ANTON ALBERT / 2ND LIGHT INFANTRY BATTALION / MAJOR ADOLF BÖSEWIEL / HAUPTMAN WILHELM SCHAUMANN / HAUPTMAN UND BRIGADE MAJOR HEINRICH WIEGMANN / FAMNDRICH FRIEDRICH ROBERTSON

Side 3:

1ST LINE BATTALION / HAUPTMAN BRIGADE MAJOR AUGUST SAFFE / HAUPTMAN CARL VON HOLLE / LIEUTENANT HARTWIG VON LUCKEN / 2ND LINE BATTALION / OBRIST LIEUTENANT JOHANN VON SCHRODER / HAUPTMAN GEORG THILEE / 3RD LINE BATTALION / HAUPTMAN FRIEDRICK DIEDEL / LIEUTENANT FRIEDRICH VON JEINSEN / LIEUTENANT FRIEDRICH LESCHEN / 4TH LINE BATTALION / MAJOR GEORGE CHUDEN / MAJOR GEORGE LEUE / HAUPTMAN FRIEDRICH HEISE / FAHNDRICH THEODORE CRONHELM / 5TH LINE BATTALION / HAUPTMAN CHRISTIAN VON WURMB / LIEUTENANT UND ADJUTANT LUDWIG SCHUCK / 8TH LINE BATTALION / HAUPTMAN AUGUST VOIGT / HAUPTMAN TE VON WESTERNHAGEN / LIEUTENANT WILHELM VON MARENHOLZ / ARTILLERY / LIEUTENANT CARL VON SCHULZEN / GEWIDMET / VON DEN OFFICEREN DER KÖNIGLICHE GROSS BRITTANNISCH / DEUTSCHEN LEGION

Side 4

TO THE MEMORY / OF / COLONEL CHRISTIAN BARON OMPTEDA, OF THE 5TH LINE BATTALION, R.G.H., / COLONEL CHARLES DU PLAT, OF THE 4TH LINE BATTALION, R.G.H. / CAPTAIN PHILIP HOLZERMANN, 1ST LINE BATTALION, / CAPTAIN HENRY BARON MARSCHALK, CAPTAIN ALEXANDER BARON GOEBEN, / LIEUTENANT ANTHONY ALBERT,

/ MAJOR ADOLPHUS BOSEWIEL, 2ND LINE BATTALION, / CAPTAIN WILLIAM SCHAUMAN, CAPTAIN HENRY WIEGMANN, / ENSIGN FREDERICK ROBERTSON, / CAPTAIN AUGUSTUS SAFFE, 1ST BATTALION, / CAPTAIN CHARLES BARON HOLLE, / ENSIGN ARTHUR SUCHOW, / LIEUTENANT-COLONEL JOHN SCHRODER, 2ND LINE BATTALION, / CAPTAIN GEORGE THILEE, / CAPTAIN FREDERICK DE JEINSEN, / LIEUTENANT FREDERICK LESCHEN, / MAJOR GEORGE CHUDEN, 4TH LINE BATTALION, / CAPTAIN GEORGE LEUE, CAPTAIN FREDERICK HEISE, / ENSIGN THEODORE CRONHELM, / CAPTAIN CHRISTIAN BARON WURMB, 5TH LINE BATTALION, / LIEUTENANT BARON MAHRENHOLZ, / WHO FELL / ON THE MEMORABLE 18TH DAY OF JUNE, 1815. / THIS MONUMENT / IS ERECTED / BY / THE OFFICERS OF THE INFANTRY / OF THE / KING'S GERMAN LEGION.

Memorial tablet: 2nd Light Battalion. La Haye Sainte, Outer Wall, Waterloo. (Photograph)

IHREN / IN DER VERTHEIDIGUNG DIESER MEYEREY / AN 18 TEN JUNI 1815 GEFALLENEN / WAFFENBRÜDERN: MAJOR H. BÖSEWIEL / CAPTAIN W. SCHAUMANN / FAHNDRICH F. VON ROBERTSON / UND 46 UNTEROFFICIERE UND JÄGER VOM 2TEN LEICHTEN BATAILLON. WIEDERHERGESTELLT / DURCH SEINE KÖNIGLICHE HOHET / DEN KRONPRINZEN GEORG VON HANNOVER AM 18TEN JUNII 1847 / UND ZUGLEICH GEWIDMET DEN EBENDASELBST BEI / DIESER GEDEGENHEIT GEFALLENEN: / CAPTAIN H. VON MARSCHALCK / VOM 1TEN LEICHTEN BATAILLON, / CAPTAIN C. VON WURMB / VOM 5TEN LINIEN BATAILLON / IN ANERKENNUNG DES VOM / IHNEN BEWIESENEN / HANNOVERSCHEN / HELDENMUTHS.

THE / OFFICERS / OF THE 2ND / LIGHT BATTALION / KING'S GERMAN LEGION /TO THEIR COMRADES-IN-ARMS WHO FELL IN THE DEFENCE OF / THIS FARMHOUSE / ON THE 18TH JUNE 1815 : MAJOR H. BÖSEWIEL / CAPTAIN W. SCHAUMANN / ENSIGN F. VON ROBERTSON / AND 46 NCOS AND RIFLEMEN OF THE 2ND LIGHT BATTALION / RESTORED BY HIS ROYAL HIGHNESS / CROWN PRINCE GEORGE OF HANOVER ON 18TH JUNE 1847 / DEDICATED AT THE SAME TIME / TO THOSE WHO ALSO FELL: CAPTAIN H. VON MARSCHALK / FROM THE 1ST LIGHT BATTALION / CAPTAIN VON WURMB / FROM THE 5TH LINE BATTALION / IN RECOGNITION OF THE HANOVERIAN HEROISM THEY SHOWED.

Erected in 1847 on the high pointed gable along the road, on the outside of the wall of La Haye Sainte.

Royal Artillery and King's German Legion
Regimental memorial tablet: St Joseph's Church, Waterloo (Photograph).

SACRED TO THE MEMORY / OF / MAJOR WILLIAM J LLOYD / MAJOR GEORGE BEAN / MAJOR W. NORMAN RAMSAY / MAJOR ROBERT M CAIRNES / CAPTAIN SAMUEL BOLTON / LIEUT WILLIAM L ROBE / LIEUT MICHAEL T CROMIE / LIEUT ROBERT MANNERS / LIEUT CHARLES SPEARMAN / ROYAL BRITISH ARTILLERY / LIEUT DETLEF DE SCHULZEN / KING'S GERMAN ARTILLERY / AND III SERGEANTS AND LXX RANK AND FILE / WHO FELL IN THE BATTLE OF / WATERLOO / JUNE XVIII MDCCCXV / THIS STONE WAS ERECTED BY / THE OFFICERS OF THOSE TWO CORPS / WHO WERE IN THE ACTION

ENGLAND
Memorial: All Saints' Churchyard, Dovercourt, Harwich, Essex. (Photograph)

AT OR NEAR THIS PLACE / THE BRITISH AND GERMAN SOLDIERS / WHO DIED IN THIS PARISH FROM DISEASE / CONTRACTED DURING THE WALCHEREN EXPEDITION 1809–1810

Stained Glass Window: All Saints' Church, Dovercourt, Harwich, Essex. (M.I.)

PRESENTED BY THE GERMAN EMPEROR IN MEMORY OF THE BRITISH AND GERMAN SOLDIERS WHO DIED OF DISEASE AS A RESULT OF THE WALCHEREN EXPEDITION

GERMANY

Adensen

Memorial tablet: St Dionysius's Church, Adensen, Lower Saxony, Germany. (No longer extant)

UNSEREN / BEY WATERLOO AM 18[TEN] JUNIUS 1815 / GEFALLENEN BRÜDERN / DEM BRIGADE-MAJOR HEINRICH WIEGMANN / DEM LIEUTENANT CHRISTOPH VAN JEINSEN / DEM SOLDATEN FRIEDRICH MATTHIES / ZU DANKBARER ERINNERUNG / VON / DER GEMEINE ADENSEN UND HALLERBURG

FOR OUR BROTHERS / KILLED AT WATERLOO ON 18TH JUNE 1815 / THE BRIGADE MAJOR HEINRICH WIEGMANN / THE LIEUTENANT CHRISTOPHER VON JEINSEN / THE SOLDIER FRIEDRICH MATTHIES / IN THANKFUL REMBERANCE / FROM / THE COMMUNITY OF ADENSEN AND HALLERBURG

Memorial tablet: St Dionysius's Church, Adensen, Lower Saxony, Germany. (No longer extant). (Photograph)

ZURN UNVERGESSLICHEN ANDENKEN AN DEN ZU / PARIS AM 30 TEN MAY 1814 ABGESCHLOSSENEN FRIE / DEN ZUR DANKBAREN ERINNERUNG AN / GEORG III, ALAXANDER I, FRANZ II / FRIEDRICH WILNHELM III UND MAX JOSEPH, / AN WELLINGTON, SCHWARZENBERG, BLUCHER, WREDE, / BARCLAY DE TOLLI UND IHR HEER, DURCH DEREN / WEISHEIT, EINTRACHT, TAFEL HIER AUF: / AM TAGE DER FRIEDENSFEIER W. BENEKEN . DEN 24[TEN] JULIUS 1814 PREDIGER HIE SELBST.

IN MEMORY OF THE PEACE TREATY SIGNED AT / PARIS ON 30TH MAY 1814 AND IN THANKFUL REMEMBRANCE TO GEORGE III, ALEXANDER I, FRANZ II / FREDERICK WILLIAM III AND MAX JOSEPH, / TO WELLINGTON, SCHWARZENBERG, BLUCHER, WREDE, / BARCLAY DE TOLLI AND THEIR ARMIES, / THEIR WISDOM AND CONCORD COMMEMORATED HERE ON THIS MEMORIAL: / ON THE DAY OF THE ANNIVERSARY OF PEACE / W. BENEKEN, 24TH JULY 1814, PREACHER AT THIS CHURCH

Bleckede

Memorial tablet: St Jacobi's Church, Bleckede, Lower Saxony, Germany. (Photograph)

ZUM DANKBAREN ANDENKEN / DER TAPFEREN LANDWEHRMÄNNER DES / AMTS BLECKEDE / WELCHE IN DER SCHLACHT BEI WATERLOO D: 18 / JUNI 1815 DEN TOD FÜRS VATERLAND STARBEN / JÜRGEN POPPE AUS BRACKEDE / HEINR: CHRIST: SOETEBEER AUS WINDISCHTHUN / JOH: FRIE: SCHULTZE AUSREESELN / OTTO USLAR AUS RADEGAST / VOM HUSAREN – REGIMENT – PRINZ – REG.

TO THE THANKFUL REMEMBRANCE / OF THE BRAVE MILITIA MEN / WHO DIED IN THE BATTLE OF WATERLOO 18TH JUNE 1815 / FOR THEIR COUNTRY / JÜRGEN POPPE FROM BRACKEDE / HEINRICH CHRIST SOETEBEER FROM WINDISCHTHUN / JOSEPH FRIDERICH SCHULTZE FROM REESELN / OTTO URSLAR FROM RADEGAST / OF THE HUSSARS REGIMENT

Celle

Memorial tablet: St Marien's Church, Celle, Hanover, Germany. (Photograph)

IM GLORREICHEN KAMPFE FÜR DES THEUREN VATERLANDES BEFREIUNG / FANDET AUCH IHR HOCHHER ZIGE KRIEGER DEN TOD DER HELDEN

IN THE GLORIOUS STRUGGLE FOR THE FREEDOM OF OUR DEAR FATHERLAND VALIANT WARRIORS DIED THE DEATH OF HEROES.

BRIG MAJ: G. V. AVEMANN 1812 B.D. PYRENAEEN / SERGNT: C. HOFFMEISTER 1810 B. BUZACCO / DRAG: C. BESSE 1812 B. GARZIA HERNANDEZ / SCHÜTZE I. KNUST 1812 B. SIMANCAS / BRIG MAJ: C. A. V. BOBERS 1815 B. WATERLOO / HAUPTM: E. LANGREHR 1812 B. SALAMANCA / HORNBLSR: C. DANNENBERG 1814 V. BAYONNE / LIEUT: E. V. MARENHOLTZ 1815 B. PARIS / HAUPTMANN: F. DIEDEL 1815 B. WATERLOO / LEIUT: W. V. MARENHOLZ 1815 B. WATERLOO / SOLDAT: F. ENCKHAUSEN 1809. B. TALAVERA / WACHTM: I. H. MELDAU 1807 B. COPENHAGEN / SERGNT: E. GOTTSCHALK 1815 B. WATERLOO / DRAG: H. MICHAELIS 1812 B. SALAMANCA / HAUPTM: I. E V. HAMELBERG 1809 B. TALAVERA / HAUPTMANN: F. PETERS 1815 B. WATERLOO / ADJ: P. T. GRF: V. HARDENBERG 1813 B. GADEBUSCH / LIEUTENANT A. F. REINBOLD 1813 B. BÜCHEN / SOLDAT: H. HARTLEP 1809 B. TALAVERA / SOLDAT: H. RÔMERMANN 1815 B. WATERLOO / HAUPTM: F. HEINE 1813 V. ST. SEBASIAN / SOLDAT: C. STIES 1815 B. WATERLOO / LEIUT: F. A. A. V. HODENBERG 1809 B. TALAVERA / SOLDAT: I. F. C. WAGNER 1811 B. BADAJOZ / LIEUT: G. A. V. HODENBERG 1809 B. TALAVERA / SOLDAT: H. WINKELMANN 1815 B. WATERLOO / FÄHND: G. F. A. V. HODENBERG 1813 BÜCHEN / HAUPTM: W. L. BACHMEISTER 1812 B. BURGOS

UNIVERGÄNGLICH LEBT EUER RUHM WIE IM DANKE DER ZEITGENOSSEN SO IN DER SPÄTESTEN NACHWELT BEWUNDERUNG

EVERLASTING IS YOUR FAME, THE THANKS OF THOSE STILL LIVING AND THE ADMIRATION FOR YOU IN THE WORLD TO COME

REFERENCE: Beamish, N. L., History of the King's German Legion, Vol. 2, reprint 1997. Buckland and Brown (issued in English and German language) Bernhard Schwertfeger Geschichte der Königlich Deutschen Legion Officer list Vol. II 1907 Hahn'sche Buchhandlung, Hanover.

Fallersleben

Pedestal tomb: Palace Park, Wolfsburg, Fallersleben, Lower Saxony, Germany. (Photograph)

Side 1:

DEN AM 18 TEN JUNI 1815 BEI WATERLOO / UND VORHER IN SPANIEN GEBLIEBENEN / UND VERWUNDETEN BRAVEN KRIEGER / FELDJÄGER. / F. HABEKOST AUS FALLESLEBEN / LANDWEHRMÄNNER / FR. FÜLLKRUG AUS FALLERSLEBEN / E. OEHLMANN = EHMEN / H. F. STEFFENS = OCHSENDORF / J. DÖSSELMANN = NEINDORF / C. MOHRMANN = RENNAU

TO THE BRAVE SOLDIERS WHO DIED AND WERE WOUNDED IN THE BATTLE OF WATERLOO ON 18TH JUNE 1815 AND PREVIOUSLY IN SPAIN FELDJÄGER. / F. HABEKOST AUS FALLESLEBEN / LANDWEHRMÄNNER / FR. FÜLLKRUG AUS FALLERSLEBEN / E. OEHLMANN = EHMEN / H. F. STEFFENS = OCHSENDORF / J. DÖSSELMANN = NEINDORF / C. MOHRMANN = RENNAU

Side 2:

DENKMAL FÜR DIE IN SPANIEN / VON DER E. D. LEGION GEBLIEBENEN / BRAVEN KRIEGER. / HUSAREN / DREY GEBRÜDER JÜRGES AUS HATTORF / J. F. SCHARENBERG AUS UHRY / VERWUNDET WURDEN. / LOUIS BEHNE AUS FALLERSLEBEN / CAP. 2 TEN LEICHT. BAT. E. D. LEGION / H. TIEDGE AUS SÜLFELD, HUSAR / A. FRICKE = UHRY = / F. KÖRTJE = ALMKE = / G. SPELLY = OCHSENDORF, MOUSQ.

MEMORIAL FOR THOSE BRAVE SOLDIERS FROM THE KGL WHO LOST THEIR LIVES IN SPAIN. HUSSARS: THE THREE JÜRGES BROTHERS FROM HATTORF, J. F. SCHARENBERG FROM UHRY WERE WOUNDED. LOUIS BEHNE FROM FALLERSLEBEN, CAPTAIN 2ND LIGHT BATTALION, H. TIEDGE FROM SÜLDFLED, HUSSAR, A. FRICKE FROM UHRY, F. KÖRTJE FROM ALKMKE AND G. SPELLY FROM OCHSENDORF, MOUSQ.

Side 3:

DIE BEI WATERLOO GEFALLENEN HELDEN / EHRT DANKBAR KÖNIG UND VATERLAND / SIE RUHEN IN FRIEDEN BEY GOTT / AUS / DEM AMTE FALLERSLEBEN / GEWIDMET / VON DEM AMTMANN J. H. FRANK / AM 18. JUNI 1817

KING AND FATHERLAND FOREVER THANKS THE HEROES WHO FELL AT WATERLOO. MAY THEY REST IN PEACE WITH GOD DEDICATED FROM THE FALLERSLEBEN OFFICE AND ITS BAILIFF J. H. FRANK ON 18TH JUNE 1817

Side 4:

BEI WATERLOO WURDEN VERWUNDET / GEORG FRANK AUS FALLERSLEBEN LIEUT / 2 TEN LEICHT. BAT. E. D. LEGION / FR. DUCKSTEIN AUS ROTHEHOF, FELDJ. / LANDWEHRMÄNNER / AND. KÖNIGSDORF AUS ROTTORF / FR, FRICKE = OCHSENDORF / J. F. STEFFENS = DAHER / FR. GEFFERS = AUS RENNAU

AT WATERLOO GEORG FRANK FROM FALLERSLEBEN, LIEUT, 2ND LIGHT BATTALION E.D. LEGION, FRIEDRICH DUCKSTEIN FROM ROTHEHOF, FELDJÄGER, INFANTRYMEN ANDREAS KONGISDORF FROM ROTTORF, FRIEDRICH FRICKE FROM OCHSENDORF, J. F. STEFFENS FROM DAHER AND FRIEDRICH GEFFERS FROM RENNAU WERE WOUNDED

Reference: Beamish, N. L., History of the King's German Legion, Vol. 2, reprint 1997.

Goslarer
Memorial tablet: Goslar, Lower Saxony, Germany, (Photograph)

DENKMAL DER GOSLARER JÄGER / DEN TOTEN DER WELTKRIEGE / 1914 – 1918 ——— 1939–1945 / DEN LEBENDEN ZUR MAHNUNG / DIE OPFEREICHE GESCHICHTE DER GOSLARER JÄGERIST VERBUNDEN / MIT DEM KURFURSTLICH-HANNOVERSCHEN EN JÄGERKORPS / SIEBENJÄHRIGER KREIG 1756–1763 / GIBRALTAR 1779–1873 / MIT DER ENGLISHEN, DES KÖNIGS DEUTSCHE LEGION 1803–1815 / DÄNEMARK – PORTUGAL – HOLLAND – SPANIEN – SUDFRANKREICH / WATERLOO 1815 / DER KONGLICH HANNOVER-SCHEN ARMEE DES DEUTSCHEN BUNDES / DANEMARK 1848 – LANGENSALZA 1866 / DER KONIGLICH HANNOVERSCHEN ARMEE DES DEUTSCHEN BUNDES / FRANKREICH 1870–1871 / DENMALSENTWURF: ARCHITEIKT KURT ELSTER, DESSAU / BILD HAUER: HANS LEHMANN-

BORGES, NEURUPPIN, WALTER VOLLAND, GOSLAR / ERBAUT 1926 – ERGANZT 1953 VON DER KAMERADSCHAFT GOSLARER JAGER

MEMORIAL OF THE GOSLARER JÄGER (LIGHT INFANTRY) / TO THE FALLEN OF THE WORLD WARS / 1914–1918 ———— 1939–1945 / A WARNING TO THE LIVING / THE HISTORY FULL OF SACRIFICE OF THE GOSLAR LIGHT INFANTRY / UNITS AND THE ELECTORAL HANOVERIAN LIGHT INFANTRY. / SEVEN YEARS WAR 1756–1763 / DEFENCE OF GIBRALTAR 1778–1783 / THE HISTORY OF THE KING'S ENGLISH-GERMAN LEGION / 1803–1815 / DENMARK – PORTUGAL – HOLLAND – SPAIN – SOUTH OF FRANCE / WATERLOO 1815 / THE ROYAL HANOVERIAN ARMY OF THE GERMAN CONFEDERATION / DENMARK 1848 / LANGENSALZA 1866 / WITH THE ROYAL PERMISSION KING OF THE NORTH GERMAN CONFEDERATION

Hamelin
Memorial tablet: Gable wall in a walk-way on edge of town of Hamelin, Brunswick, Germany. (Photograph)

HEIL / DEN VATERLANDISCHEN / KREIGERN! / MITT GOTT HABEN SIE / THATEN GETHAN / DEN TAPFEREN WELCHD / DEN GLORREICHEN SIEG / BEY WATERLOO / AM 18 TEN JUNII 1815 / UNS UND DEUTSCHLAND / RUHE UND FRIEDEN / ERKAMPFEN HALFEN, / DIE DANKBAREN BEHOWNER / HAMELNS / BEYM EINMARSCHE DES VOM / FELDE DER EHRE / HEIMKEHRENDEN HAEMELSCHEN / LANDWEHR BATAILLONS / DEN 25 TEN JANUAR 1816.

English translation:

HAIL / OUR PATRIOTIC / WARRIORS! / WITH GOD'S HELP / THOSE BRAVE MEN ACHIEVED GLORIOUS VICTORY / AT WATERLOO / ON 18TH JUNE 1815 / GERMANY NOW RESTS / PEACEFULLY AFTER THE / GREAT FIGHT AND / RECEIVED THE THANKS OF / THE PEOPLE OF HAMELIN / THE MILITIA BATTALIONS / MARCHED FROM / THE FIELD OF GLORY / ARRIVING HOME IN HAMELIN / ON 25TH JANUARY 1816.

Hanover
Waterloo Tower: Waterloo Square, Hanover, Germany. (Photograph)

DEN SIEGERN VON WATERLOO / DAS DANKBARE VATERLAND

TO THE VICTORS OF WATERLOO FROM THE GRATEFUL FATHERLAND

The memorial contains about 860 names to the men of the King's German Legion and Hanoverian Army who fought at Waterloo.

Reference: Carz Hummel Waterloo, Die Hannoverschen Gefallenen names from the Waterloo column Hanover, Welfenschriften No. 24.

Hesedorf
Militia Battalion Memorial: Hesedorf, Near Bremervörde, Lower Saxony, Germany. (Photograph)

ALS OPFER DER FREMDHESCHAFT / KÄMPFTEN U. FIELDEN IN RUSSLAND 1812 / JOHANN SCHOMAKER / CHRISTOPH VIEBROCK / FÜR DIE BEFREIUNG DES VATERLANDES / FOCHTEN IN DES KÖNIGS DEUTSCHER LEGION / AUF DER PENINSULA UND BEI WATERLOO / DAVID

DIERKS / JOHANN BURFEINDT / JOHANN MÜHLMANN / JOHANN WÜLPERN / EHRE IHREM ANDENKEN / ERRICHTET VON DER GEMEINDE HESEDORF / AUS FREIILLIGEN / GABEN 1911

AS VICTIM OF A FOREIGN RULE / JOHANN SCHOMAKER / CHRISTIAN VIEBROCK FOUGHT AND DIED IN RUSSIA 1812 / FOR THE LIBERATION OF THE FATHERLAND / FOUGHT IN THE KING'S GERMAN LEGION / IN THE PENINSULA AND BY WATERLOO / DAVID DIERKS / JOHANN BURFEINDT / JOHANN MÜHLMANN / JOHANN WÜLPERN / HONOUR THEIR MEMORY / ERECTED BY THE COMMUNITY OF HESEDORF / FROM SUBSCRIPTIONS DONATED IN 1911

Minden

Memorial Obelisk for the Engineers and Pioneers/Sappers, King's German Legion: Pionierstraße, Duke of Brunswick Barracks, Minden, County Nordrhein, Westfalen, Germany. (Photograph)

Side 1:

DEN / PENINSULA WATERLOO TALAVERA. TORRES VEDRAS. / FÜR DAS VATERLAND INGENIEUR-CORPS WATERLOO. MARS-LA-TOUR. / GEFALLENEN KAMERADEN / DER KÖNGL. DEUTSCHEN LEGION STRASSBURG. SCHLETTSTADT. / GEWIDMET VON EHEM. ANGEHÖRIGEN / UND DER 1813 NEU GEBILDETEN METZ. BEAUNE – LA-ROLANDE. / DES HANOV. INGENIEUR-CORPS HANOVERSCHEN TRUPPEN LE MANS. BELFORT. / UND DES / ES STARB DEN HELDENTOD HANOV. PIONIER-BATL. NO. 10 / KAPITÄN SCHAEFER 21. 4. 1904

TO THE COMRADES OF THE ENGINEERS AND SAPPERS OF THE KING'S GERMAN LEGION WHO DIED FOR THE FATHERLAND FROM PENINSULA – WATERLOO. TALAVERA. TORRES VEDRAS. MARS LA TOUR. STRASSBURG. SCHLETTSTADT. METZ. BEAUNE LA ROLANDE. LE MANS. BELFORT. DEDICATED BY THEIR FORMER MEMBERS AND THE NEWLY FORMED HANOVERIAN CORPS IN 1813. THEY DIED THE DEATHS OF HEROES. ENGINEER BATTALION NO. 10. CAPTAIN SCHAEFER 21. 4. 1904.

Side 2:

PENINSULA – WATERLOO / INGENIEUR-CORPS / DER KÖNGL. DEUTSCHEN LEGION / UND DER 1813 NEU GEBILDETEN / HANNOVERSCHEN TRUPPEN / ES STARB DEN HELDENTOD / KAPITÄN SCHAEFER / BEI DANNENBERG AM 14. 8. 1813

PENINSULA – WATERLOO / TO THE ENGINEER CORPS OF THE KING'S GERMAN LEGION AND THE NEWLY FORMED HANOVERIAN TROOPS OF 1813. CAPTAIN SCHAEFER FROM DANNENBERG DIED THE DEATH OF A HERO ON 14.8.1813

Side 3:

DEN / FÜR DAS VATERLAND / GEFALLENEN KAMERADEN / GEWIDMET VON EHEM. ANGEHÖRIGEN / DES HANNOV. INGENIEUR-CORPS / UND DES / HANNOV. PIONIER-BATL. NO. 10 / 21. 4. 1904

FOR THOSE FALLEN COMRADES WHO DIED FOR THE FATHERLAND, DEDICATED BY THE FORMER MEMBERS OF THE HANOVERIAN ENGINEER CORPS AND THE HANOVERIAN PIONEER BATTALION NO. 10 / 21.4.1904

Side 4:

TALAVERA. TORRES VEDRAS. / WATERLOO. MARS-LA-TOUR. / STRASSBURG. SCHLETTSTADT. / METZ. BEAUNE- LA-ROLANDE. / LE MANS. BELFORT.

Osnabruck
Waterloo Gate.
Monument: Place am Häger-Tor, Osnabrück, Lower Saxony, Germany. (Photograph)

DEN OSNABRÜCKISCHEN KRIEGERN DIE BEI WATERLOO / DEN 18. JUNI 1815 DEUTSCHEN MUTH BEWIESEN / WIDMET DIESES DENKMAL G. F. V.. GÜLICH D. R. D.

TO THE OSNABRÜCKIAN WARRIORS WHO DIED AT WATERLOO / ON 18, JUNE 1815 GERMAN BRAVERY WAS PROVED. / THIS MEMORIAL DONATED G.F. V. GÜLICH D. R. D.

In 1817 a new gate was built in the Osnabrück town wall dedicated to the men of the King's German Legion and the Militia Field-Battalion Osnabrück who fought in the battle of Waterloo.

Wiesbaden
Obelisk: Wiesbaden, Hessen, Gemany, (Photograph)

18 / JUNI / 1815

Records 342 names of the Nassau Regiment who fell at Waterloo.

SPAIN
Talavera
Named on the Battlefield memorial: 'Pyramid', Talavera, Spain. (Photograph)